Jancis Robinson's
Concise Wine Companion

Jancis Robinson's

CONCISE Wine COMPANION

OXFORD

UNIVERSITY PRESS

OXFORD

UNIVERSITY PRESS

Great Clarendon Street, Oxford OX2 6DP

Oxford University Press is a department of the University of Oxford.
It furthers the University's objective of excellence in research, scholarship,
and education by publishing worldwide in

Oxford New York

Athens Auckland Bangkok Bogotá Buenos Aires Calcutta
Cape Town Chennai Dar es Salaam Delhi Florence Hong Kong Istanbul
Karachi Kuala Lumpur Madrid Melbourne Mexico City Mumbai
Nairobi Paris São Paulo Shanghai Singapore Taipei Tokyo Toronto Warsaw

with associated companies in Berlin Ibadan

Oxford is a registered trade mark of Oxford University Press
in the UK and in certain other countries

Published in the United States
by Oxford University Press Inc., New York

British Library Cataloguing in Publication Data
Data available

Library of Congress Cataloging in Publication Data
Data available

ISBN 0-19-866274-2

1 3 5 7 9 10 8 6 4 2

Typeset by Selwood Systems, Midsomer Norton
Printed in Spain
by Book Print S. L.

Contents

Preface

As a wine book, *The Oxford Companion to Wine*, now in its second edition, seems to have fulfilled a need, to judge from its worldwide sales and the awards it has garnered. As its editor, I am aware of only one serious complaint about it—that it is too heavy and unwieldy.

This concise version answers that criticism. It is just over a third as long, not weighed down by hard covers, and easy to flick through.

By dint of some extremely hard work and agonizing decision-making, mainly by my assistant Julia Harding, we have somehow managed to squeeze a world of wine knowledge into these pages, without sacrificing the sort of thoroughness and comprehensiveness for which Oxford reference books are famous. The only two subjects which we have had respectively to omit or cut dramatically, simply for reasons of space, are distilled wine (brandy) and fortified wine (port, sherry, madeira, and so on).

I can think of no other wine book that offers this much information about the wonderful world of wine at this sort of price. And the beauty of this alphabetical listing of over 2,350 essential entries is that they are cross-referenced. Even I find that I start to read one entry and am led unwittingly, by a reference looking like THIS, to another entry, and another, and, sometimes, far more entries than I ever intended to read.

I hope that you, like me, will find this book an invaluable and informative companion to your wine-drinking pleasure.

JANCIS ROBINSON

London,
October 2000

Contributors

Listed in alphabetical order of surname. MW stands for Master of Wine.
Unsigned entries are written by the Editor.

J.A. Professor Jean Aitchison
T.A. Tony Aspler
S.A. Susy Atkins
N.J.B. Nicolas Belfrage MW
E.J.R.B. Elizabeth Berry MW
W.B. William Bolter
S.B. Stephen Brook
L.B. Larry Brooks
R.F.C. Bob Campbell MW
B.C.C. Bruce Cass
S.C. Sham Chougule
B.G.C. Dr Bryan Coombe
G.L.C. Dr Glen Creasy
M.J.E. Margaret Emery
N.F. Nicholas Faith
L.F. Lucy Faulkner
M.F. Michael Fridjhon
Mo.F. Monty Friendship
D.G. Denis Gastin
R.G. Rosemary George MW
D.J.G. David Gill MW
J.G. Dr John Gladstones
H.G. Howard Goldberg
L.S.H. Lisa Hall
P.A.H. Dr Peter Hallgarten
J.H. James Halliday
J.M.H. Professor Jake Hancock

J.H.H. Dr Judith Harvey
P.H. Dr Paul Henschke
L.H.-S. Dr Leofranc Holford-
   Strevens
I.J. Ian Jamieson
T.J. Tony Jordan
J.K. Jane Kay MW
M.K. Mel Knox
M.P.L. Martin Lam
R.S.L. Richard Lander
G.J.L. Gareth Lawrence
T.H.L. Professor Terry Lee
H.L. Harriet Lembeck
P.L. Peter Leske
D.V.L. Dennis Lindley
S.P.D.L. Simon Loftus
Z.L. Zelma Long
N.McG. Nico McGough
M.McN. Maggie McNie MW
R.J.M. Richard Mayson
M.M.-F. Mark Miceli-Farrugia
J.T.C.M. Jasper Morris MW
A.H.M. Angela Muir MW
R.M.B. Rose Murray Brown MW
J.J.P. Jeremy Paterson
E.P.-R. Edmund Penning-Rowsell
J.P. John Platter

J.V.P. Dr John Possingham
H.L.R. Helen Robinson
J.Ro. Jancis Robinson MW
A.H.L.R. Anthony Rose
V.R. Viàcheslav Rybinstev
M.S. Mark Savage MW
M.W.E.S. Michael Schuster
T.S. Dr Tom Scott
V. de la S. Victor de la Serna
R.E.S. Dr Richard Smart
D.F.S. David Stevens MW
K.B.S. Kerry Brady Stewart

K.S. Keith Sutton
G.T. Gabriel Tam
D.E.T. Diane E. Teitelbaum
D.T. Daniel Thomases
P.T.H.U. Dr Tim Unwin
B.M.W. Dr Bernard Watney
A.D.W. Professor A. Dinsmoor
    Webb
A.G.W. Andrew Williams
P.J.W. Dr Pat Williams
H.M.W. Dr Hanneke Wilson
V.Z. Vangjel Zigori

abboccato, Italian for medium sweet (less sweet than AMABILE). See also SWEETNESS.

ABC, acronym for the weary sentiment 'Anything But Chardonnay (or Cabernet)', which has encouraged interest in grapes other than the (two most famous) INTERNATIONAL VARIETIES on the part of both producers and consumers.

abocado, Spanish for medium sweet. See also SWEETNESS.

Abona, denominated Spanish wine region covering the semi-desert south of Tenerife in the vinously revitalized CANARY ISLANDS. Inland, at Vilaflor, it boasts Europe's highest vineyard, reaching 1,600 m/5,200 ft above sea level. It produces white wines of little distinction from the LISTÁN Blanco grape.   V. de la S.

Abouriou, minor south-western dark-berried vine variety that is slowly disappearing from France's vineyards. It is still theoretically allowed into Côtes du MARMANDAIS and is also found in some red VINS DE PAYS of the south west.

Abruzzi, mountainous region in central Italy with a significant coastline on the Adriatic sea to the south of the Marches and an important producer of wine. The Abruzzi is fifth among Italy's regions in terms of production.

Despite the presence of two qualitatively important vine varieties (MONTEPULCIANO d'Abruzzo and TREBBIANO d'Abruzzo), despite the warm climate, and despite favourable vineyard sites, most of the region's production is undistinguished. The region's DOCS are not particularly well conceived, with excessively generous production limits and little attempt to define suitable subzones for the varieties.

In spite of this rickety legislative framework, some good wine is produced in the Abruzzi. The Montepulciano grape, at its best, gives wines of deep colour and substantial EXTRACT, firm tannins, and low acidity. It was once much prized as a blending wine in the north of Italy, particularly in Tuscany and Piedmont. The wine frequently has a detectable animal quality to it, which can range from the attractively 'sweaty saddle' to the intolerably gamey. Cask ageing was virtually universal before the Second World War but has been less practised recently as some producers, particularly the CO-OPERATIVES, have aimed at a simple quaffing style, which hardly demonstrates the innate character of the variety, or at wines that could be sold quickly for blending.

Trebbiano d'Abruzzo is not made from Trebbiano at all but rather from the BOMBINO, a variety widely employed in Apulia. Better Trebbiano d'Abruzzo is a pleasurable, if not memorable, wine, but in the hands of Edoardo Valentini it is one of Italy's outstanding, and certainly its longest-lived, dry white wines. Valentini's Trebbiano d'Abruzzo is so startlingly different from that of his peers that it is difficult to decide whether it is a quirk of fate or the hand of genius that has revealed the potential of an otherwise quite obscure grape variety.   D.T.

AC, sometimes AOC, common abbreviation for APPELLATION CONTRÔLÉE, the French quality-wine category.

Acadie, sometimes known as L'Acadie, winter-hardy grape variety speciality of CANADA.

acid. See TASTING TERMS.

acid adjustment, euphemism for DE-ACIDIFICATION or more usually ACIDIFICATION.

acidification is the wine-making process of increasing the ACIDITY in a grape must or wine. This is a common practice in warm wine regions (as common as CHAPTALIZATION in cool wine regions), and is often the only course open to a wine-maker wanting to make a balanced wine. A good level of ACIDS not only increases the apparent freshness and fruitiness of many wines, it also protects the wine against attack from bacteria and improves COLOUR (as explained under ACIDITY).

Acidification is usually sanctioned by local wine regulations within carefully delineated limits in order to prevent stretching of wine by adding sugar and water along with the permitted acid. In temperate zones such as Bordeaux and Burgundy, acidification is allowed, but with the understandable proviso that no wine may be both acidified and chaptalized.

A.D.W.

acidity is a general term for the fresh, tart, or sour taste produced by the natural organic ACIDS present in a liquid. Wines, together with most other refreshing or appetizing drinks, owe their attractive qualities to a proper balance between this acidic character and the sweet and bitter sensations of other components. All refreshing drinks contain some acidity, which is typically sensed on the human palate by a prickling sensation on the sides of the tongue (see TASTING).

The acidity of the original grape juice has an important influence on wine quality because of its direct influence on COLOUR (see below), its effect on the growth of YEASTS and bacteria (harmful and beneficial), and its inherent effects on flavour qualities.

Acidity helps to preserve the colour of red wines. Red wines from warmer regions and made without ACIDIFICATION can have colours that are less red (and often with a brownish tinge) than those from colder regions which produce wines with higher acidity.

Excessive acidity makes wines sharp, tart, and sometimes unpleasant to drink. Too little acidity, on the other hand, results in wines that are flat, uninteresting, and described typically by wine tasters as 'flabby'.

A.D.W., B.G.C., & P.J.W.

acids, members of a group of chemical compounds which are responsible for the sharp or sour taste of all drinks and foods, including wine. The most important acids contained in grapes are TARTARIC ACID and, in slightly lower concentrations, MALIC ACID. Malic acid occurs in many different plants and fruits, but vines are among the very few plants with large concentrations of tartaric acid in their fruit.

Acids are important in wine not just because, in moderation, they make it taste refreshing, but also because they prevent the growth of harmful bacteria.

A.D.W. & P.J.W.

adega, Portuguese word for cellar or winery.

Adelaide is the name of a Super Zone, SOUTH AUSTRALIA's unique addition to official Australian wine geography, comprising Adelaide Hills, Clare Valley, McLaren Vale, Langhorne Creek, Barossa Valley, and Eden Valley.

Adelaide Hills, fashionable, relatively high, cool wine region in SOUTH AUSTRALIA and one of Australia's very few areas capable of growing fine Sauvignon Blanc.

adulteration and fraud have dogged the wine trade throughout its history. The variability and value of wine have traditionally made it a target for unscrupulous operators. The long human chain stretching from grower to consumer affords many opportunities for illegal practices. It is important to remember, however, that at various times the law has viewed the same practices differently, sometimes condoning, sometimes condemning them. What we know as adulteration, our ancestors may have classed as a legitimate part of the wine-making process.

The simplest and most obvious form of adulterating wine is to add water. This is not necessarily fraudulent—wine made from extremely ripe grapes may achieve better BALANCE if slightly diluted. The practice becomes illegal when done surreptitiously to cheat the consumer or defraud the taxman.

Another means of stretching wine is to 'cut', or blend, it with spirits or other (usually poorer-quality) wines. BORDEAUX merchants in the 18th century cut fine clarets with rough, stronger wine imported from Spain, the Rhône, or the Midi to increase profits, but also because it was genuinely believed that the resulting fuller-bodied concoction was more to the English taste.

One particular method of altering the

nature of wine remains controversial; the addition of sugar during fermentation to increase the eventual ALCOHOLIC STRENGTH, known as CHAPTALIZATION. Producers in wine regions warm enough to need no such assistance tend to be scornful of the practice (although they may well indulge in ACIDIFICATION to increase the ACIDITY of their wines).

One of the most common forms of fraud does not involve any doctoring or fabricating of the wine, but merely the LABEL.

The adulteration or fraudulent sale of wine can be dangerous and the consumer may even be put medically at risk. Illegal practices frequently hurt the grower and merchant as well. Once the reputation of a wine has been jeopardized, economic hardship may result.

Consumers, growers, and merchants are not alone in trying to prevent adulteration and fraud. Local authorities and (in this century) governments have fought it. Regulations and legislation have been passed for many reasons: to protect the consumer; to preserve the good name of the local wine; or to facilitate TAXATION.

The legal apparatus existing to combat fraud and adulteration today is the culmination of many battles waged by both consumers and trade. The French government produced a legal definition of wine in 1889, the Germans framed the first GERMAN WINE LAW in 1892 (superseded by the more thorough 1909 version), and the Italians in 1904. The French APPELLATION CONTRÔLÉE system, defining wines by geography rather than simply composition, did not become nationally viable until the 1930s.

Although once rife, adulteration and fraud have been considerably rarer in the wine trade since the adoption of CONTROLLED APPELLATION systems and methods by which to enforce them. There have been examples of CONTAMINANTS in wine, both deliberate and accidental, but passing off has become increasingly difficult and, just possibly, less rewarding as wine consumers become ever more sophisticated and more concerned with inherent wine quality than the hierarchy of famous names. Consumers may with justification feel that the wine trade has attracted more than its fair share of charlatans because fraud in any field in which expertise is difficult to acquire and viewed with suspicion (such as wine and fine art) attracts more media attention than most other types of commercial fraud.

See also CONTAMINANTS.   H.B. & J.Ro.

age in a wine is not necessarily a virtue. See AGEING. See also VINE AGE.

ageing of wine, an important aspect of wine connoisseurship, and one which distinguishes wine from almost every other drink—even if the FINE WINE market of the late 1990s seemed to value young wines more highly than old ones. When a fine wine is allowed to age, spectacular changes can occur which increase both its complexity and monetary value.

Which wines to age

The ageing of wine is an important element in getting the most from it but, contrary to popular opinion, only a small subgroup of wines benefit from extended BOTTLE AGEING. The great bulk of wine sold today, red as well as white and pink, is designed to be drunk within a year, or at most two, of bottling. Before bottling, most wines are usually aged for several months in tanks or wooden casks but they are not expected to undergo the subtle evolution involved in bottle ageing.

Wines which generally do not improve with time spent in bottle, and which are usually best consumed as soon as possible after bottling (although after a few weeks in bottle has eliminated any BOTTLE SICKNESS) include the following—although the following is only the most approximate generalization: wines packaged in any containers other than bottles—BOXES, for example; wines designated TABLE WINES in the European Union, JUG WINES in the USA, and their everyday, commercial equivalents elsewhere; almost all branded wines, with the possible exception of some red bordeaux; most FIGHTING VARIETALS, with the possible exception of the best made from Cabernet Sauvignon grapes; most German QBA wines; almost all French VINS DE PAYS, Italian IGT, and Spanish VINO DE LA TIERRA; almost all wine coloured pink; all wines released within less than six months of the vintage such as those labelled NOUVEAU and the like; fino and manzanilla and similar light, dry SHERRIES; most wines labelled MOSCATO and all ASTI.

Even among finer wines, different wines mature at different rates, according to individual VINTAGE characteristics, their exact provenance, and how they were made. Such factors as BARREL FERMENTATION for whites and BARREL MATURATION for wines of any colour play a part in the likely life cycle of the wine. In general, the lower a wine's PH, the longer it is capable of evolving. Among reds, generally speaking the higher the level of FLAVOUR COMPOUNDS and PHENOLICS, particularly TANNINS, the longer it is capable of being aged. Wines made from the Cabernet Sauvignon and Nebbiolo grapes, for example, and many of those made from Syrah/Shiraz, should be aged longer than those based on Merlot or Pinot Noir—and certainly much longer than the average wine made from Gamay or Grenache. Among white wines, partly because of their higher acidity, the finest Riesling and Loire Chenin Blanc evolve more slowly than wines based on Chardonnay.

In general terms, better-quality wines made from the following grape varieties should benefit from some bottle age, with a *very* approximate number of years in bottle in brackets:

Red wines
Aglianico of Taurasi (4–15)
Baga of Bairrada (4–8)
Cabernet Sauvignon (4–20)
Melnik of Bulgaria (3–7)
Merlot (2–12)
Nebbiolo (4–20)
Pinot Noir (2–8)
Raboso of Piave (4–8)
Sangiovese (2–8)
Saperavi (3–10)
Syrah/Shiraz (4–16)
Tannat of Madiran (4–12)
Tempranillo (2–10)
Xynomavro of Greece (4–10)
Zinfandel (2–6)

White wines
Chardonnay (1–6)
Chenin Blanc of the Loire (4–30)
Furmint of Hungary (3–25)
Petit Manseng of Jurançon (3–10)
Pinot Gris (1–6)
Riesling (2–30)
Semillon (dry wines) (2–7)
and all botrytized wines (5–25)

Most fortified wines and their like, such as VINS DOUX NATURELS, are bottled when their producers think they are ready to drink. Exceptions to this are the extremely rare bottle-aged sherries, vintage PORT (which is expressly designed for many years' bottle ageing), single quinta ports, and crusted port.

Producers of SPARKLING WINES usually claim that their wines are ready to drink on release, but experience has shown that release dates have in some instances relied more on commercial considerations than on a wine's matur-

ity. Better-quality young sparkling wines with their high levels of acidity can often improve considerably with an additional year or so in bottle. And top-quality champagne has been known to withstand several decades in bottle, even if it can be appreciated only by those who share the GOÛT *anglais*.

Factors affecting ageing

STORING WINE in particular conditions can affect the rate at which wine ages; the lower the TEMPERATURE, the slower the maturation. Conversely, ageing can be hastened by stripping a young wine of its solids (by very heavy FILTRATION or FINING, for example), and by storing wine in warmer conditions. Thus, a wine stored in a centrally heated Manhattan apartment will mature very much faster than one stored in an unheated warehouse in Scandinavia. In general, the more slowly a wine matures, the greater the complexity of the flavour compounds that go to make up its BOUQUET (see below).

Also, in general, the smaller the BOTTLE SIZE, the faster its contents mature, presumably because of the greater proportion of OXYGEN in the bottle, both as a consequence of the bottling process and any possible oxygen ingress via the cork seal during ageing. This is part of the reason LARGE FORMATS carry a premium.

See also STORING WINE.

How wine ages

The descriptions below concern only those wines designed specifically to be aged.

Red wines To the untutored taster, older red wines seem to be softer and gentler than harsh, inky young ones. Those who notice such things will also observe a change in colour, typically from deep purple to light brick red. There should also be more SEDIMENT in an old wine than a young one. All these phenomena are related, and are related in particular to the behaviour of PHENOLICS, the compounds of the grape, particularly the skins, including the blue/red ANTHOCYANINS which together with the astringent but colourless FLAVONOIDS form further compounds that are responsible for a red wine's COLOUR and MOUTHFEEL.

Most phenolics are leeched out of the grape skins and seeds during RED-WINE-MAKING. They react with each other in young wine, initially under the influence of the wine's ACIDS and later, during barrel maturation and bottle ageing, under the influence of the small amounts of oxygen dissolved in the wine during such processes as RACKING, TOPPING UP, and, later, bottling. Under these influences, the phenolic molecules agglomerate to form much more complex, larger molecules. This process continues in bottle. When these polymers reach a certain size, they are too heavy to be held in solution and precipitate as dark reddish-brown sediment, leaving wine that is progressively less astringent, some of the red/blue anthocyanins having been precipitated and the tannins having been oxidized. Thus, to a certain extent, holding a bottle of wine up to the light to determine how much sediment it has precipitated can give some indication of its maturity (although the amount of sediment deposited is a function not just of time, but of storage conditions and the initial composition of the wine).

At the same time as these visible changes occur, the impact of the wine on the nose and palate also evolves. Other flavour compounds responsible for the initial primary AROMAS of the grape and those of fermentation (sometimes called secondary aroma, or secondary bouquet) are also interacting, with each other and with other phenolics, so that gradually the smell of the wine is said to be transformed into a bouquet of tertiary aromas, a very much more subtle array and arrangement of flavours which can be sensed by the nose (see TASTING).

The rate at which all these things happen is influenced by a host of factors: storage conditions (particularly temperature), the state of the cork, the ULLAGE when the wine was bottled, its pH level, and SULPHUR DIOXIDE concentration, both of which can inhibit or slow the all-important influence of oxygen.

OENOLOGISTS understand this much about the maturation of age-worthy red wine, but are unable to predict with any degree of certainty when such a wine is likely to reach that complex stage called full MATURITY, when it has dispensed with its uncomfortably harsh tannins and acquired maximum complexity of flavour without starting to decay. This may be of minority interest since relatively few wine consumers are interested in storing wine and maintaining their own cellar (which is why so much recent research has been focused on making young red wines taste lower in tannins). Part of the joy of wine has long been said to be the monitoring of the progress of a case of wine, bottle by bottle, but this is strictly a rich person's sport.

White wines If our understanding of red wine maturation is incomplete, even less is known about the ageing process in white wines. White wines become browner with age, presumably because of the slow oxidation of their phenolic content. They may also throw a sediment, although very, very much less than a red wine of similar quality.

Ageing potential is clearly not directly related to a white wine's obvious concentration of phenolics since fine Rieslings, which are relatively low in phenolics, can in general age much longer than comparable Chardonnays, which contain more phenolics.

Experienced tasters, however, often note that wines affected by NOBLE ROT have a much greater ability to last than their non-botrytized counterparts. Experience also seems to suggest that white wines which undergo barrel fermentation also seem capable of lasting longer than those fermented in inert containers and then transferred to barrel for barrel maturation.

Most white wines which can mature over several decades rather than years are notably high in acidity, and few of them undergo MALOLACTIC FERMENTATION. Many of those venerable wines which demonstrate exceptional ageing ability today may well have been bottled with higher levels of sulphur dioxide than are acceptable to the modern consumer.

Stages of ageing
Maturing fine wines go through a number of perceptibly different stages. Very young wines are usually delicious, full of fruit and vivacity, but slightly simple. At some (unpredictable) time after bottling, anything between a few months and a few years, fine wines can seem to close up, to become surly, to lose their aroma without having gained a bouquet. Their dimensions can be sensed but little else (see TASTING). A variable number of years afterwards, they begin to smell like wine again and to have considerably more palate LENGTH. After this they enter into their most satisfying stage at which the bouquet seems fully developed and astringency has receded making the mouthfeel attractive, so that the wine is delightful in terms of flavour, texture, length, and all-important BALANCE. If, however, wine is aged for too long (and no one, alas, can predict when this will be), it enters a stage of decrepitude during which the acidity starts to predominate. This unpredictable journey may

help to explain apparently contradictory judgements of the same wine, from WINE WRITERS, wine professionals, and wine consumers alike.

J.Ro, A.D.W., & P.J.W.

Aghiorghitiko, also known as **Agiorgitiko** and St George, red grape variety native to Nemea in the Peloponnese in GREECE, whose wines may be made from no other variety. It blends well with other varieties (notably with Cabernet Sauvignon grown many miles north in Metsovo to make the popular table wine Katoi) and can also produce good-quality rosé. The wine produced by Aghiorghitiko is fruity but can lack acidity. Grapes grown on the higher vineyards of Nemea can yield long-lived reds, however, and the grape is Greece's second most planted red, after XYNOMAVRO.

Aglianico, a dark-skinned Italian grape variety of Greek origin (the name itself is a corruption of the word Ellenico, the Italian word for Hellenic), is cultivated in the mountainous centre of Italy's south. The grape seems to prefer soils of volcanic origin and achieves its finest results in the two DOCS of TAURASI in CAMPANIA and AGLIANICO DEL VULTURE in BASILICATA. These two wines share the deep ruby colour, the full aromas, and the powerful, intense flavours which make the variety, at least potentially, one of Italy's finest. D.T.

Aglianico del Vulture is BASILICATA'S only DOC wine but is also one of the most important wines of Italy's south, showing the potential, in its finest bottles, to offer worthy competition to a fine Sangiovese of Tuscany or Nebbiolo of Piedmont.

The expansion of the DOC zone has not resulted in higher production of wine, and much of the wine is sold either in bulk or for blending. Marketing of the wine is controlled by NÉGOCIANTS in the zone, most of whom have demonstrated an admirable commitment to Aglianico during the 1980s. They have largely replaced chestnut casks with OAK casks, experimented with small BARREL MATURATION, and generally improved the quality of their product. The zone is handicapped by an ageing work-force, by its distance from major markets, and by the general obscurity of its grape and its wine, but there are signs that the potential of Aglianico del Vulture is gradually being recognized by informed and discriminating consumers. D.T.

Ahr, small but expanding wine region in Germany specializing in red wine and named after the river which flows east from the hills of the Eifel to join the Rhine near Remagen. The most westerly vineyards are in dramatic, rocky, wooded scenery near Altenahr, where the steep slopes on either side of the river sometimes narrow to the dimensions of a gorge. Many are covered in slate and greywacke clay of volcanic origin, well suited to Spätburgunder (PINOT NOIR).

Spätburgunder has been gaining ground steadily and was planted on 55 per cent of the area under vine by the late 1990s, while POR-TUGIESER, RIESLING, and MÜLLER-THURGAU vine varieties are on the decline. Many producers still offer soft, late-picked, medium-sweet Spätburgunder.

Leading estates, however, produce fully fermented, dry, BARRIQUE-aged, tannic Spätburgunder of good colour from low-yielding vineyards. Some 10 per cent of the region's Spätburgunder wines are of this style and they sell with ease at high prices to Germany's many red-wine lovers. Almost 75 per cent of the region's grape harvest is processed by five CO-OPERATIVE cellars, and the state of Rheinland-Pfalz owns the largest estate. These, and the few private estate bottlers, sell most of their wine directly to the consumer and, in particular, to the hordes of visiting tourists from the Ruhr district and the Benelux countries.

I.J. & K.B.S.

Airén, Spain's most planted vine variety, and one that is planted at such a low VINE DENSITY that its vineyards cover more area than any other vine variety in the world, despite vigorous VINE PULL SCHEMES in La MANCHA, where, as in VALDEPEÑAS, it is by far the most planted variety. The resultant wine is the major ingredient in the important Spanish brandy business. In central Spain it has traditionally been blended with dark-skinned Cencibel (TEMPRANILLO) grapes, which are steadily replacing Airén, to produce light red wines. It is increasingly vinified as a white wine, however, nowadays using TEMPERATURE CONTROL to yield crisp, slightly neutral dry white wines for early consumption. In several ways, therefore, Airén is the Spanish equivalent of France's UGNI BLANC. The variety is also grown around MADRID and in ANDALUCÍA, where it is known as Lairén.

Aix-en-Provence, Coteaux d'. Mainly dry rosé and some red wines are made, often in spectacularly situated vineyards among the lavender and *garrigue* of PROVENCE, many of them quite distant from this famous university town. The extensive area entitled to this appellation stretches from the frontier with the Les BAUX DE PROVENCE subappellation created in 1995 in the west as far as the Coteaux VAROIS, but also includes land all round the Étang de Berres, the lagoon dominated by Marseilles's airport. The wines produced are serviceable if generally unsophisticated reds and pale-pink wines for early, often local, consumption. CO-OPERATIVES are relatively important here, but a number of individual estates are trying to establish a distinctive style from blends of Grenache, Cinsaut, Mourvèdre, the local Counoise, Syrah, Carignan, and Cabernet Sauvignon grapes. Neither of the last two may make up more than 30 per cent of a blend. A little white is made from a wide range of southern, and SOUTH WEST FRANCE, grape varieties. Ch Vignelaure in the far west of the appellation was one of the first properties to achieve some degree of fame outside the region (by grafting Bordeaux techniques and some grape varieties on to the Provençal terrain).

ORGANIC VITICULTURE has established a significant hold in this arid, MEDITERRANEAN CLIMATE. This is an appellation ready for an upgrade.

Alba, town which provides a focus for the famous wines of the LANGHE hills in Piedmont in north-west Italy. Regarded as the region's red-wine, and white-truffle, capital. See also ROERO and NEBBIOLO D'ALBA.

Albana di Romagna, dry white wine made in ROMAGNA in central Italy from the Albana grape which was, amid much incredulity, awarded DOCG status in 1986. The best Albana comes almost entirely from the red clay soils of the hills between Faenza and the river Ronco to the east of Forlì. DOCG rules permit YIELDS of 100 hl/ha (5.7 tons/acre), hardly compatible with the supposed purpose of the DOCG, to distinguish Italy's finest wines.

Albana di Romagna comes in four different styles: secco (dry), amabile (medium dry), dolce (sweet), and PASSITO. Dry Albana is a rather neutral, characterless wine, and although modern cellar techniques have partially solved the chronic problems of OXIDATION which existed in the past, they have not succeeded in giving the wines significant flavour. Medium-dry Albana normally seems neither fish nor fowl. The future of the grape seems to lie in the dessert version, achieved either with raisined grapes or, in more recent experiments, with NOBLE ROT and small BARREL MATURATION. These can be wines of surprisingly good quality, although they represent a minuscule portion of the total annual production of the DOCG vineyards. D.T.

Albani, Colli, white wines from the hills south east of Rome. See CASTELLI ROMANI.

Albania, small European country on the Adriatic Sea with KOSOVO and MONTENEGRO to the north and GREECE to the south. It was under hard-line communist control for much of the 20th century but has been since 1996 in a state of some anarchy.

Albania is divided into four wine regions. The coastal plain rises to 300 m/990 ft and encompasses the towns of Tirana, Durrësi, Shkodra, Lezha, Lushnja, Fier, Vlora, and Delvina. The hilly region varies between 300 and 600 m/1,980 ft altitude and includes Elbasan, Krujë, Gramsh, Berat, Prmet, Librazhd, and Mirdita. The submountainous region lies between 600 and 800 m and surrounds the towns of Pogradec, Korça, Leskovic, and Peshkopi. Some vines are also grown in the mountains as high as 1,000 m/3,300 ft.

The main indigenous vine varieties for winemaking are Shesh i bardhë, Debin e bardhë, and Pulés for white wines and Shesh i zi, Kallmet, Vlosh, Serinë, and Debin e zezë for red wines. Shesh i bardhë and Shesh i zi are the two most important vines, accounting for about 35 per cent of the crop. At low yields the former has an attractive floral aroma while the latter is capable of producing wines worthy of ageing. Kallmet is the country's noblest red grape, known in Hungary as KADARKA. Vlosh, a speciality of the village of Narta, makes full-bodied, quite astringent wines that may have some RANCIO character. V.Z.

Albariño, Spanish name of the distinctive, aromatic, peachy, almost VIOGNIER-like high-quality vine grown in Galicia (and as Alvarinho in the north of Portugal's Vinho Verde region). The grapes' thick skins help them withstand the particularly damp climate, and can result in white wines notably high in alcohol, acidity, and flavour. Albariño is one of the few Spanish white grape varieties produced as a varietal and encountered on labels. Most common in Spain in the RÍAS BAIXAS zone, it has become so popular (and expensive) that it accounts for about 90 per cent of all plantings. Sometimes oak-matured, it can age well however it is made. Occasionally blended with Loureiro, Treixadura, Caiño.

alcohol, the common name for ethanol or ethyl alcohol, an important, intoxicating constituent of wine and all other alcoholic drinks. Alcohol is the most potent component of wine (and the most obvious of those that distinguish it from GRAPE JUICE), but it is probably the least discussed by wine consumers (unless in the context of HANGOVERS). For although alcohol does not have a taste, it has an effect, not just on the human nervous system, but on how a wine tastes. Wines relatively high in alcohol—over 13 per cent for example—can taste sweet even if they contain practically no RESIDUAL SUGAR. The alcohol content in a perfectly balanced wine should be unfathomable, but wines that are slightly too high in alcohol can have a hot aftertaste. As a general rule, wines described as 'full bodied' (see BODY) are high in alcohol, while those described as 'light' are low in alcohol.

See ALCOHOLIC STRENGTH for the varied concentrations of alcohol to be found in different wines, HEALTH AND WINE for the effects of alcohol consumption in the form of wine, and REDUCED-ALCOHOL WINES.

alcoholic, usually pejorative tasting term for a wine which tastes 'hot' and seems to contain excess alcohol.

alcoholic strength, an important measurement of any wine, is its concentration of the intoxicant ethyl alcohol, or alcohol.

The alcoholic strength of wine that has not had alcohol added by FORTIFICATION is usually between 9 and 15 per cent, with the great majority of wines being between 11.5 and 13.5 per cent alcohol (slightly higher than a decade ago, thanks to current FASHION and a tendency to later picking). In Europe, fermented grape juice must usually reach at least 8.5 per cent alcohol before it legally constitutes wine, although exceptions are made for better-quality wines that have traditionally been low in alcohol such as German QMP wines and Italian MOSCATO. The technical European legal maximum alcoholic strength for wines that have had no alcohol added is 15 per cent, but derogations are frequently made at this upper limit too, notably for Italy's strongest wines such as AMARONE. In the United States, grape-based table wine must legally be between 7

and 14 per cent, while DESSERT WINES must be between 14 and 24 per cent.

Since alcohol is the product by FERMENTATION of grape sugar, itself the product of PHOTOSYNTHESIS driven by sunlight, the alcoholic strength of a wine is, very generally, proportional to the proximity of its provenance to the equator, although many other factors play a part. High vineyard ALTITUDE, poor WEATHER in a particular year, high YIELD, and any RESIDUAL SUGAR, are just some of the factors which may decrease alcoholic strength. Severe PRUNING in the vineyard and cellar techniques such as CHAPTALIZATION, CONCENTRATION, and fortification allow alcoholic strength to be manipulated upwards.

See also REDUCED-ALCOHOL WINES.

Aleatico, bizarre Italian red grape variety with a strong MUSCAT aroma.

Alella, town near Barcelona in CATALONIA which gives its name to a small Spanish denominated wine zone making mainly white wines in increasingly urbanized countryside. The chief grape variety is the Pansá Blanca, the local name for XAREL-LO, which is now grown along with some Chenin Blanc and Chardonnay to make both CAVA sparkling wines and dry, still white wine. The reputation of Alella was salvaged by Parxet/Marqués de Alella, which pioneered these new styles of wine. The local co-operative and a newer private producer, Roura, joined the drive to better quality in the late 1990s.   R.J.M. & V. de la S.

Alenquer, a DOC in western Portugal. See ESTREMADURA.

Alentejo, DOC in southern PORTUGAL corresponding with a province of the same name. As well as being a DOC, the entire province is entitled to the VINHO REGIONAL designation of Alentejano.

The undulating Alentejo plains south and east of Lisbon cover a third of mainland Portugal and most of the country south of the river Tagus (Tejo in Portuguese)—although see also RIBATEJO. In complete contrast to the north, this is a sparsely populated region where cereal farms stretch as far as the eye can see.

For centuries, the Alentejo's main link with wine was CORK. Over half the world's supply of cork is grown in Portugal and almost all of it is stripped from the cork oaks that fleck the vast Alentejo wheat fields.

At the beginning of the 1980s, the Alentejo was in complete disarray, but over the next decade or so five vineyard enclaves emerged from the confusion. Until quite recently, the CO-OPERATIVE wineries in the towns of Portalegre, Borba, Redondo, Reguengos de Monsaraz, Granja, and Vidigueira produced wines for the undemanding local market but, with financial assistance from the European Union, they have begun to tap Alentejo's wine-making potential and export their wines. Likewise, single estates are emerging with new wines, and the Alentejo is currently one of the most fashionable regions in Portugal.

The climate in the Alentejo is hardly conducive to the production of fine wine, but modern technology can now compensate for natural deficiencies. IRRIGATION supplements an annual rainfall total which rarely reaches 600 mm/23 in. Temperatures in the summer months frequently exceed 35 or even 40 °C (104 °F), so for white grapes which ripen as early as mid-August, sophisticated TEMPERATURE CONTROL is essential. The production of red wine, principally from ARAGONÊZ, TRINCADEIRA, MORETO, and CASTELÃO FRANCÊS grapes, exceeds white, although some growers see potential in white varieties such as ROUPEIRO and Perrum.

Individual DOCs are Borba, Evora, Granja-Amareleja, Moura, Portalegre, Redondo, Reguengos and Vidigueira.   R.J.M.

Alexander Valley. California wine region and AVA in northern Sonoma County east of Healdsburg and south of Cloverdale. See SONOMA.

Alfrocheiro Preto, Portuguese grape variety which can add useful colour to red-wine blends. It is grown in the Alentejo, Terras do Sado, and Dão.

Algarve, the southernmost province of Portugal, now better known for tourism than for wine, which is predominantly red, high in alcohol, undistinguished, and made by the region's four co-operatives. The Algarve was demarcated in 1980 (perhaps for political motives) and has since been split into four DOC districts—Lagos, Portimão, Lagoa, and Tavira.
                                              R.J.M.

Algeria has known world renown in its turbulent recent history as a wine producer but has more recently been grappling with the economic and cultural problems posed by having almost as great an area under vine as Germany or South Africa, for example, but in an Islamic environment. A colonial legacy became a problem of economic dependency. New initiatives, including a 10,000 ha/24,700 acre replanting programme, were begun in 1994.

Viticultural regions within the littoral Mediterranean climate zone of Algeria with its mild winters and hot, dry, and sunny summers produce mostly relatively concentrated red wines from old vines of those varieties planted, typically, in the 1950s. In 1962, at the time of independence, Algeria's plantings of CARIGNAN, ALICANTE BOUSCHET, CINSAUT, and GRENACHE were producing fiery stuff that almost certainly contributed substantially to a high proportion of the wine then sold as burgundy as well as to everyday table wine. If Algerian wine has a fault today, it may be a lack of acidity or an overdose of alcohol but in no other country could the term VIEILLES VIGNES be so widely and literally applied, with 80 per cent of vines estimated at more than 40 years old.

Most wine is still vinified on a semi-industrial scale in the country's 70-plus wineries that demands fast fermentations and early bottling. The country saw practically zero investment in technology in the second half of the 20th century.

The centralized Office National de Commercialisation des Produits Vinicoles (ONCV), which exercises a near monopoly on both the production and sale of wine, markets several standard labels, liberally adorned with such expressions as 'grand cru', but their prestige brand, Cuvée du Président, reveals nothing about the origin of the wine other than its region, if that. In 1997, ONCV embarked on a joint venture with a British importer to harness all this potential and make wines specifically for export. Some Cabernet Sauvignon, Merlot, Syrah, Mourvèdre, and, perhaps inevitably, Chardonnay are being planted, although among light-skinned grapes UGNI BLANC and CLAIRETTE predominate. The introduction of TEMPERATURE CONTROL and keeping different vine varieties separate were two of the most pressing problems in the late 1990s.

Algeria is also a substantial producer of CORKS, which are mainly processed in Portugal and Spain.   K.S. & J.Ro.

Alicante, city on Spain's Mediterranean coast long associated with strong, rustic wines which now gives its name to a denominated wine zone. This DO in the LEVANTE extends from the city towards YECLA on the foothills of Spain's central plateau. The climate becomes progressively hotter and the landscape more arid away from the coast and YIELDS rarely exceed 20 hl/ha (1.1 ton/acre). The principal grape variety, the red MONASTRELL, frequently ripens to produce wines with 16 to 18 per cent natural alcohol. Other red varieties well suited to the MEDITERRANEAN CLIMATE include GARNACHA and BOBAL. Ninety per cent of the region's wine is produced in poorly equipped CO-OPERATIVES but the Bocopa co-op at Petrer and such private firms as Gutiérrez de la Vega and Enrique Mendoza have made noticeable strides in quality.

Alicante is also a synonym for Garnacha Tintorera, or ALICANTE BOUSCHET, in Spain and is even sometimes used as a synonym for GRENACHE.   R.J.M. & V. de la S.

Alicante Bouschet, often known simply as **Alicante**, the most widely planted of France's red-fleshed grape varieties. This useful but somewhat spurious variety was still being planted in the late 1980s. It is usually the first variety to be harvested in the south of France, in late August, and is blended with other varieties for colour or sometimes used for GRAPE JUICE.

Outside France it is perhaps most widely cultivated in Spain, where it is also known as Garnacha Tintorera. It is particularly common in Almansa.

Alicante is also grown in Portugal, Corsica, Tuscany, Calabria in southern Italy, Yugoslavia, Israel, and North Africa; and there were still 2,000 acres/800 ha of it in California in 1992, mainly in the hot Central Valley.

Aligoté, Burgundy's 'other' white grape variety, may be very much Chardonnay's underdog but in a fine year, when ripeness can compensate for its characteristic ACIDITY, Aligoté is not short of champions. If grown on Burgundy's best slopes on the poorest soils in warmer years, Aligoté could produce fine dry whites with more nerve than most Chardonnays, but it would not be nearly as profitable. Aligoté is, typically, an angular wine short on obvious flavour and usually too spindly to subject to oak ageing.

In the CÔTE D'OR it is being replaced by the two obviously nobler grape varieties Chardonnay and Pinot Noir. It is now largely rele-

gated to the highest and lowest vineyards, where it produces light, early maturing wines allowed only the Bourgogne Aligoté appellation and drunk either with simple meals or, traditionally, mixed with blackcurrant liqueur as a KIR. Only the village of Bouzeron, where some of the finest examples are produced, has its own appellation for Aligoté, Bourgogne Aligoté-Bouzeron, in which the maximum yield is only 45 hl/ha (2.5 ton/acre) as opposed to the 60 hl/ha allowed for Bourgogne Aligoté.

Aligoté is extraordinarily popular in eastern Europe. Bulgaria, for example, had far more of it than France in the 1980s and presumably prized it for its high natural acidity. In Romania, it is productively cultivated, mainly for varietal wines on its fertile plains, while it is also grown in RUSSIA, UKRAINE, MOLDOVA, GEORGIA, AZERBAIJAN, and KAZAKHSTAN. It is Russia's second most planted white wine grape and is prized as an ingredient in sparkling wine. Aligoté is also grown in Chile and to a very limited extent in California.

allergies to wines of various sorts are by no means unknown. The most common **allergens**, chemicals capable of causing an allergic reaction in humans, are proteinaceous compounds. Among possible allergens in wines are traces of the natural proteins not precipitated and removed with the dead yeast cells after FERMENTATION, and traces of proteins from a FINING agent used to clarify and stabilize the wine. One amine, HISTAMINE, was once thought to be a cause of allergic reactions to red wines.

The most common wine allergies are a sensitivity to either white wine or red wine. Since red wine contains a much wider range of constituents than white wine, having been fermented with the grape SKINS and other grape solids, an allergic reaction to all red wines and no whites seems more easily comprehensible than vice versa. SULPHUR DIOXIDE, used at higher concentrations in making white wines than red, has been suggested as a cause of so-called white-wine allergies, and a small proportion of the population, notably asthmatics, is sensitive to SULPHITES. Controlled experiments have yet to add any scientific weight to either red- or white-wine allergy as a phenomenon and some scientists suspect psychosomatic causes, at least in part.

Some people, particularly members of some ethnic groups, experience some form of allergic reaction such as face flushing and high pulse rate to even quite moderate amounts of ALCOHOL.

This field is under-researched, perhaps because wine researchers are almost by definition unlikely to be allergic to wine themselves. See also HEALTH AND WINE.

Almansa, small denominated wine zone in the eastern corner of CASTILLA-LA MANCHA in central Spain. The Almansa DO borders the LEVANTE regions JUMILLA and YECLA, which produce similarly strong, sturdy red wines, traditionally used for blending, principally from MONASTRELL and GARNACHA Tintorera grapes. The climate is extreme. Temperatures rise to 40 °C (104 °F) in summer but can dip below 0 °C (32 °F) in winter. Since the late 1980s, Bodegas Piqueras has been making consistently good wine using Cencibel (TEMPRANILLO) to lighten the load of Almansa's traditionally overripe grapes.   R.J.M.

Almeirim, DOC in central, southern Portugal dominated by a huge co-operative winery. See RIBATEJO.

Aloxe-Corton, a small village of charm at the northern end of the Côte de Beaune in Burgundy. Aloxe is dominated by the hill of Corton, planted on three sides with vineyards including the GRANDS CRUS Corton (almost all red) and Corton-Charlemagne (white).

Corton is the sole grand-cru appellation for red wine in the Côte de BEAUNE and covers several vineyards which may be described simply as Corton or as Corton hyphenated with their names. While all Corton tends to be a dense, closed wine when young, Bressandes is noted for its comparative suppleness and charm; Renardes for its rustic, gamey character; Perrières for extra finesse; and Clos du Roi for the optimum balance between weight and elegance. It is often regarded as superior to Le Corton itself. Other Corton vineyards are Le Charlemagne, Les Pougets, and Les Languettes, all of which more often produce white Corton-Charlemagne, and Les Chaumes, Les Grèves, Les Fiètres, Les Meix, Clos de la Vigne au Saint, and part of Les Paulands and Les Marechaudes. Further Corton vineyards extend into LADOIX-Serrigny. Although Corton is planted almost entirely with Pinot Noir vines, a tiny amount of white Corton is made, including the HOSPICES DE BEAUNE cuvée Paul Chanson from Chardonnay.

The great white wines, however, are those made within the **Corton-Charlemagne** appellation, which stretches in a narrow band around the top of the hill from Ladoix-Serrigny, through Aloxe-Corton to PERNAND-VERGELESSES, where it descends down the western edge of the hillside.

There remains some Pinot Blanc in the otherwise Chardonnay-dominated Corton-Charlemagne vineyards, which formerly were widely planted with Pinot Beurot (see PINOT GRIS) and Aligoté.

A great Corton may seem ungainly in its sturdiness when young but should have the power to develop into a rich wine with complex, gamey flavours at 8 to 10 years old. Cortons should, with POMMARD, be the most intense and longest-lived wines of the Côte de Beaune. A great Corton-Charlemagne also needs time to develop its exceptional character of breed, backbone, and racy power. Needing a minimum of five years, a good example will be better for a full decade in bottle and can last substantially thereafter.

Although more than half the vineyard area is given over to the grands crus, Aloxe-Corton also has its share of PREMIER CRU and village vineyards producing mainly red wines which can be supple and well coloured but mostly do not justify their significant premium over the wines of SAVIGNY-LÈS-BEAUNE. Apart from Les Guérets and Les Vercots, which are adjacent to Les Fichots in the commune of Pernand-Vergelesses, the premier crus of Aloxe-Corton form a band just below the swathe of grand-cru vineyards, extending into Ladoix-Serrigny.

See also CÔTE D'OR.   J.T.C.M.

Alsace, historically much-disputed region now on the eastern border of France, producing a unique style of largely VARIETAL wine, over 90 per cent of which is white. For much of its existence it has been the western German region Elsass. Because of its location it has been the subject of many a territorial dispute between France and Germany. Now separated from Germany by the river RHINE, and from France by the Vosges mountains, the language and culture of Alsace owe much to both origins, but are at the same time unique. Many families speak Alsacien, a dialect peculiar to the region, quite different from either French or German.

Of all the regions of France this is the one in which it is still easiest to find villages outwardly much as they were in the Middle Ages, with traditional half-timbered houses and extant fortifications. The hilltops of the lower Vosges are dotted with ruined castles and fortresses, witnesses to past invasions.

Up to 2,000 growers bottle and sell their own wines, although over 80 per cent of the total volume is produced by just 175 companies. Even the large companies are usually family owned, however. One of the unique aspects of Alsace is that even the smallest growers regularly produce at least six to eight different wines each year, whilst the larger producers may extend to a range of 20 to 30 different bottlings.

All Alsace wines are, by law, bottled in the region of production in tall BOTTLES called *flûtes*.

Geography and climate

The narrow vineyard strip runs from north to south, along the lower contours of the Vosges mountains, and spans the two French *départements* of Haut-Rhin and Bas-Rhin. The majority of large producers are based in the more southerly Haut-Rhin *département*, which is generally associated with better quality, especially for Gewürztraminer (often spelt Gewurztraminer in Alsace) and Pinot Gris, producing fatter, more powerful wines towards the south of the region. In the Bas-Rhin, individual vineyard sites become even more important to ensure full RIPENESS.

Winters can be very cold, spring is generally mild, and the summer is warm and sometimes very dry, with heavy hail and thunderstorms possible in summer and autumn. In some vintages summer DROUGHT can be a problem, and younger vines planted in the drier, sandy soils can suffer, whereas vineyards on the water-retentive clay soils have an advantage.

As a general rule, the heavier clay and marl soils give a wine with broader flavours, more body and weight, whilst a lighter limestone or sand soil gives more elegance and finesse. Flint, schist, shale, and slate soils tend to give wines with a characteristic oily, minerally aroma reminiscent of petrol and sometimes described as 'gunflint', especially those made from the Riesling grape.

Vine varieties

At the beginning of the 20th century the many varieties planted in Alsace were divided into 'noble' and others. The number has been rationalized over the years, and now the region produces eight major varietal wines: RIESLING, GEWÜRZTRAMINER, PINOT GRIS, PINOT NOIR, PINOT BLANC, MUSCAT, CHASSELAS, and SYLVANER. Chasselas is generally used for blending, and only a handful of producers still bottle it as a varietal. AUXERROIS is also planted, and is usually blended with Pinot Blanc, although it increasingly features on a label. There is also an increasing interest in planting the ubiquitous CHARDONNAY, forbidden by law, but tolerated when labelled as Pinot Blanc, or used in the sparkling wine CRÉMANT d'Alsace.

Most growers, wherever in the region they are based, plant all of the above varieties. As some varieties fetch higher prices, and some are much more fussy about vineyard site, each grower must make an economic as well as a practical decision when deciding what to plant where.

Riesling is one of the most widely planted varieties, accounting for over 20 per cent of the area under vine. Plantings are steadily increasing, mainly in place of Sylvaner, which has been losing ground, and now accounts for only about 15 per cent of the area planted, with higher proportions in the Bas-Rhin than the Haut-Rhin. Pinot Blanc and Auxerrois are also on the increase, accounting for another 20 per cent between them. Gewürztraminer represents a similar acreage of plantation, but usually a smaller percentage of the production, which can fluctuate alarmingly. Its average yield is the smallest of all the varieties. The largest plantations of Gewürztraminer are in the Haut-Rhin. Pinot Gris is increasingly popular and now accounts for almost 10 per cent of the total area under vine, but is registering a slow increase. Pinot Noir is also increasing its share, rather more rapidly, as the only red varietal of Alsace. It represented nearly nine per cent of the total vineyard area in the late 1990s. The remaining vineyard area is planted with MUSCAT D'ALSACE, MUSCAT OTTONEL, Chasselas, Chardonnay, and small amounts of old plantings, of varieties no longer permitted but not yet replaced.

Wine-making

Most Alsace wines are CHAPTALIZED, with the notable exception of Vendange Tardive wines (see below), which must rely totally on natural sugars present in the grape. ACIDIFICATION is not practised.

Most wine-makers deliberately prevent MALOLACTIC FERMENTATION in white wines by keeping them cool and lightly sulphured, preferring to keep the fresh grape aromas—although some CUVÉES in some 1990s vintages managed to complete malolactic fermentation, often by accident. Although initially making such wines softer, more vinous, and less floral, it does not seem to have altered the quality or keeping ability of the wines, so an increasing number of reputable cellars are allowing malolactic fermentation to take place.

Because over 95 per cent of the wine is white, and because wine-makers are emphasizing the primary grape flavours, most wine is vinified and stored in inert containers, and new wood is very seldom used. Traditional cellars have large oval wood *cuves*, many over 100 years of age, literally built into the cellar. Traditionally the same cask will be used each year for the same varietal. The build-up of TARTRATES forms a glass-like lining to the cask, and there is no likelihood of wood flavours masking the wine's character. If a cask has to be replaced, the new cask will be well washed out to remove as much as possible of the wood flavour, and will be used for Edelzwicker (see below) until all wood flavours have disappeared. A few growers are experimenting with BARREL MATURATION, most widely for Pinot Noir, but also occasionally with Pinot Blanc, Pinot Gris, Auxerrois, and even Sylvaner.

Alsace wines are generally fermented dry, and the only wines with significant RESIDUAL SUGAR are Vendange Tardive. A few growers, however, like to leave 3 to 4 g/l of residual sugar in their wines to give a softer flavour.

Most wines are bottled within a year of the vintage, to retain freshness.

A few growers have experimented with late-picked, BOTRYTIZED wines, not merely for the four permitted varietals (see Vendange Tardive below), but also with such diverse varieties as Auxerrois and Sylvaner, which can make outstanding wines. One or two growers produce a small quantity of VIN DE PAILLE, from healthy, ripe grapes picked in October, and dried on straw over the winter months. There have also been experiments with EISWEIN, from healthy grapes picked in December, and even in early January.

Some specific wines

Alsace was awarded AC status in 1962, with the one appellation Alsace, or Vin d'Alsace. The appellation Crémant d'Alsace was added in 1976, and Grand Cru in 1983. In addition, laws

for Vendange Tardive wines were drawn up in 1983. For the still wines, the appellation Alsace can stand on its own, but is usually accompanied by one of the following names.

Riesling Considered by growers to be the most noble variety, Alsace Riesling is almost invariably bone dry. Young Riesling can display floral aromas, although it is sometimes fairly neutral. With age it takes on complex, gunflint, mineral aromas, with crisp steely acidity and very pure fruit flavours. It is one of the most difficult varieties for beginners, but one of the most rewarding wines for connoisseurs.

Gewürztraminer Usually dry to off-dry, but its low ACIDITY, combined with high alcohol and GLYCEROL, give an impression of sweetness. Gewürztraminer has a distinctive spicy aroma and flavour, with hints of lychees and grapefruit. The naturally high sugar levels of Gewürztraminer make it ideal for late-harvest sweet wines, and this is the most frequent varietal found as Vendange Tardive. The high sugar can, however, put some wines out of BALANCE, and poorly made examples can be blowsy, flat, and over-alcoholic. Gewürztraminer from the southern end of Alsace, around Eguisheim southwards, tends to have quite a different character, and is generally more aromatic as well as richer in weight.

Pinot Gris Traditionally known as Tokay-Pinot Gris or Tokay d'Alsace, Pinot Gris is the only accepted name according to a 1993 agreement between Hungary and the European Union (although many growers still use the term Tokay for everything but labels). Pinot Gris has been underrated in Alsace. It combines some of the spicy flavours of Gewürztraminer with the firm backbone of acidity found in Riesling, giving a wine which ages particularly well. Young Pinot Gris is reminiscent of peaches and apricot, with a hint of smoke, developing biscuity, buttery flavours with age. It is very successful in a Vendange Tardive style.

Muscat Two varieties of Muscat are found in the Alsace region: MUSCAT BLANC À PETITS GRAINS, known as Muscat d'Alsace, and Muscat Ottonel. Most wines are a blend of the two. Alsace Muscat is always dry, and has a fresh grapey aroma and flavour. The taste should be reminiscent of biting into a fresh grape, with young, crisp fruitiness. Muscat is low in alcohol, and quite low in acidity. Because of its sensitivity to poor weather at flowering, Muscat only produces well in favourable vintages, and may only produce top-quality wine in five or six vintages out of 10.

Sylvaner Sylvaner suffers from bad press in Alsace. It is difficult to grow, needs a good site, yet fetches comparatively little money. Good Sylvaner has a slightly bitter, slightly perfumed aroma and flavour, with very firm acidity. It has moderate alcohol, and is at its best when it is young and fresh. Sylvaner is at its best in hot vintages.

Pinot Blanc Also labelled Clevner or Klevner, Pinot Blanc is the workhorse of Alsace. As well as forming the base wine for Crémant d'Alsace, Pinot Blanc can produce very good, clean, dry white that is not particularly aromatic but has good acidity, with moderate alcohol. It is often blended with Auxerrois, giving a fuller flavoured, broader, more spicy wine.

Pinot Noir The only red varietal of Alsace seldom achieves a particularly deep colour in this northerly climate. Many a Rouge d'Alsace has a light-strawberry-pink colour, whilst some Rosé d'Alsace can be deeper. Alsace Pinot Noir was always light, fresh quaffing wine, with raspberry fruit flavours, but increasingly it has suffered an identity crisis, with many growers experimenting with OAK AGEING. Although some very good oak-matured wines have resulted, many growers have produced over-oaked, dried-out thin wines.

Edelzwicker Literally, this is German for 'noble mixture'. A blend of more than one variety can be labelled as Edelzwicker or, more occasionally, as Gentil. It can also be given a general name, such as 'Fruits de Mer'. Usually Edelzwicker is one of the cheapest wines in the range. Most are pleasant and bland, some may have attractive richness and spiciness. Some growers are reverting to the practice of naming an individual vineyard site, or using a fantasy name, and blending the wine from more than one noble variety, in which case the wine may not be cheap. Some of these wines can be extremely good.

Auxerrois This variety is rarely mentioned on the label, although it may form the total or the majority of some wines labelled as Pinot Blanc, Klevner, or Clevner. A wine from pure Auxerrois is spicy, soft, and quite broad, with low acidity and good alcohol. It is occasionally vinified in oak, quite successfully.

Chasselas This variety's name is also seldom seen on the label. It is usually used for Edelzwicker, although the few growers who bottle

Chasselas as a varietal can produce a very pretty, quite lightweight wine, dry with soft grapey fruit, low acidity, and light alcohol.

Klevener de Heiligenstein The village of Heiligenstein in the Bas-Rhin has always been known for its 'Klevener', a local name for a variety long forgotten in the rest of Alsace, similar if not identical to the SAVAGNIN Rosé of the Jura, and also probably related to Gewürztraminer. Klevener has a lightly spicy, sometimes slightly buttery flavour. It is dry, less scented than Gewürztraminer, with less alcohol and a little more acidity. In good vintages it can age well.

Crémant d'Alsace An increasing amount of sparkling wine is produced in Alsace, under this appellation Crémant. Any variety may in theory be used, with the exception of Gewürztraminer, which would give too overpowering a flavour. In practice, most Crémant is from a base of Pinot Blanc, although some particularly good (white) Crémants are produced from Pinot Noir. See also CRÉMANT.

Vendange Tardive Late-picked wines have always been produced in small quantities in outstanding vintages. They were formerly sold as 'Spätlese', 'Auslese', and 'Beerenauslese', and growers were free to decide which category they would choose. It was only in 1983, however, that legislation was passed to give a legal definition to Alsace's late-picked, sweet wines. To be labelled as Vendange Tardive, a wine must come from a single vintage, from one of the four permitted varieties Riesling, Muscat, Gewürztraminer, or Pinot Gris. The wine must not be CHAPTALIZED, and the minimum sugar concentration at harvest must be 220 g/l (95° Oechsle) for Riesling or Muscat, and 243 g/l (105° Oechsle) for Gewürztraminer or Pinot Gris. Picking must take place after a certain date, determined annually by the authorities, who must be informed beforehand of the grower's intention to pick a Vendange Tardive wine, and will inspect the vineyard at the time of picking to check the sugar concentration and quantity produced. The wine must also undergo an analysis and tasting after bottling, before the label is granted. Vendange Tardive wines do not have to be BOTRYTIS affected. The most commonly found varietal for Vendange Tardive wines is Gewürztraminer, which can easily attain very high sugar levels. Pinot Gris is the next varietal for ease of production, although as less is grown, it is only made in small quantities. Riesling, too, is only made in limited amounts, as producers must usually wait until November to attain the must weights needed. Muscat is the rarest of all, and is only possible in occasional vintages. Vendange Tardive wine is not necessarily sweet, and may vary from bone dry to medium sweet, and labels signify what style of wine to expect only very rarely. Although few producers made Vendange Tardive wines prior to 1983, many more are now attempting this style.

Sélection des Grains Nobles SGN is a further refinement of Vendange Tardive, where the grapes have reached even higher sugar levels. Wines labelled as Sélection des Grains Nobles, however, nearly always contain a proportion of grapes affected by botrytis, or NOBLE ROT. The same four varieties are permitted, with minimum sugar levels of 256 g/l (110° Oechsle) for Riesling and Muscat, and 279 g/l (120° Oechsle) for Gewürztraminer and Pinot Gris. The same legislation as for Vendange Tardive governs production (see above). Sélection des Grains Nobles wine is sweet, although there is a variation in richness, depending on the grape and the grower.

In the mid and late 1990s, there were probably too many late-picked wines produced in Alsace, as producers tried to cash in on a lucrative market. It takes skill to vinify a wine with high sugar and from botrytis-affected grapes, and many producers do not have this skill. Prices and quality vary considerably, some wines scraping in with the minimum sugar levels, whilst others far surpass these minima, and are wines of extraordinary richness and complexity.

Alsace Grand Cru The Alsace Grand Cru appellation, created in 1983, signifies a wine from a single named vineyard site, a single vintage, from one of four permitted varieties, Riesling, Muscat, Gewürztraminer, or Pinot Gris. The site, vintage, and variety must be stated. Maximum permitted yields are lower than for the basic appellation Alsace. Wines must undergo technical analysis and tasting for typicality. Minimum sugar levels are higher than for basic Alsace.

Certain vineyards have always had a high reputation for the style and quality of their wines, due to the unique TERROIR. A list of the best sites was drawn up with the help of growers, and historical documents were

unearthed to prove the reputation of the nominated sites.

The appellation is the subject of much controversy. Out of 94 sites originally considered, 25 were initially chosen in 1983, and by the mid 1990s there were more than 50 provisional Grand Cru vineyard sites in Alsace (listed overleaf), and some of the boundaries were still under discussion. This caused much confusion as it was possible to find a wine labelled for example Riesling Grand Cru Kaefferkopf and one labelled simply Riesling Kaefferkopf. Some of the nominated sites are of only moderate quality (Kaefferkopf is in fact the one site which decided not to pursue its application for Grand Cru status). Some named vineyards cover an unreasonably large area, often extending over a number of hillsides, including a number of soils and aspects, some greatly superior to others. Some growers do not want to reduce their yield for the sake of the Grand Cru appellation.

Whilst single-vineyard wines are an excellent way forward for quality-wine production, much depends on the attitude of the grower, as well as on the quality of the vineyard site. The best sites and growers have undoubtedly benefited from the Grand Cru appellation, but many growers and co-operatives are producing wines of average quality, cashing in on the Grand Cru name. Some of the top négociants have Grand Cru vineyard sites, but prefer to use the names by which they have historically sold such wines: Trimbach's famous Clos Ste-Hune Riesling comes from the Grand Cru Rosacker, while Beyer's Riesling Cuvée Particulière is from the Grand Cru Pfersigberg. Some Grand Cru sites are only outstanding when planted with one or two of the four permitted varietals. On Kastelberg, for example, only Riesling is permitted. Many more should be further delimited in this way. Some of the sites more recently admitted into the classification already had a reputation for a variety other than the four permitted for Grand Cru, and we have already lost wines as fine and characterful as Zotzenberg Sylvaner, for example, a fine, vibrant wine, often from old vines. Sylvaner is now being removed in favour of Riesling and Gewürztraminer, both producing adequate wines on the Zotzenberg, but replacing a very individual wine.

There were further moves afoot in the late 1990s to delimit about half the Alsace vineyards as Premier Cru. With such a large percentage of growers currently unwilling to declare their existing Grand Cru sites, this seems a pointless exercise.

Altenberg de Bergbieten, Bergbieten
Altenberg de Bergheim, Bergheim
Altenberg de Wolxheim, Wolxheim
Brand, Turckheim
Bruderthal, Molsheim Eichberg, Eguisheim
Engelberg, Dahlenheim
Florimont, Ingersheim
Frankstein, Dambach-la-Ville
Froehn, Zellenberg
Furstentum, Kientzheim/Sigolsheim
Geisberg, Ribeauvillé
Gloeckelberg (or Kloeckelberg), Rodern, St-Hippolyte
Goldert, Gueberschwihr
Hatschbourg, Hattstatt, Voegtlinshoffen
Hengst, Wintzenheim
Kanzlerberg, Bergheim
Kastelberg, Andlau
Kessler, Guebwiller
Kirchberg de Barr, Barr
Kirchberg de Ribeauvillé
Kitterlé, Guebwiller
Mambourg, Sigolsheim
Mandelberg, Mittelwihr
Marckrain, Bennwihr/Sigolsheim
Moenchberg, Andlau/Eichhoffen
Muenchberg, Nothalten
Ollwiller, Wuenheim
Osterberg, Ribeauvillé
Pfersigberg, Eguisheim
Pfingstberg, Orschwihr
Praelatenberg, Orschwiller, Kintzheim
Rangen, Thann/Vieux Thann
Rosacker, Hunawihr
Saering, Guebwiller
Schlossberg, Kayserberg/Kientzheim
Schoenenbourg, Riquewihr
Sommerberg, Niedermorschwihr/Katzenthal
Sonnenglanz, Beblenheim
Spiegel, Bergholtz, Guebwiller
Sporen, Riquewihr
Steinert, Pfaffenheim
Steingrubler, Wettolsheim
Steinklotz, Marlenheim
Vorbourg, Rouffach, Westhalten
Wiebelsberg, Andlau
Wineck-Schlossberg,
Katzenthal/Ammerschwihr
Winzenberg, Blienschwiller
Zinnkoepflé, Westhalten, Soultzmatt
Zotzenberg, Mittelbergheim   E.J.R.B.

altitude, the height above sea level of a vineyard, can have important effects on its climate and therefore on its viticultural potential. Other things being equal, temperature falls by about 0.6 °C (1.1 °F) per 100 m (330 ft) greater altitude.

Alto Adige, the northern, predominantly German-speaking part of the TRENTINO-ALTO ADIGE region, bordering on the Austrian Tyrol. It was ceded to Italy only after the First World War and most of its inhabitants, who enjoy a certain amount of autonomy, call it the Südtirol, or South Tyrol. (Throughout this article, German names appear in brackets after Italian names.) The region owes its Italian name to the river Adige (Etsch), which flows through it on its way to the Adriatic.

SCHIAVA (Vernatsch) is the dominant grape in the Alto Adige, accounting for close to 60 per cent of the total wine produced and giving a light- to medium-bodied red wine with a hint of violets in the nose and almonds on the finish. It is the base of the Caldaro (Kalterer), Colli di Bolzano (Bozner Leiten), Meranese (Meraner), and SANTA MADDALENA (Sankt Magdalener) DOCS, and is the most important varietal DOC within the overall Alto Adige appellation. The DOC structure of the Alto Adige has a variety of geographically specific DOC zones together with a general DOC which embraces the entire zone, whose wines are further identified by VARIETAL, 18 in all. There are two other specific and delimited DOC zones in addition to these Schiava-dominated zones: Valle Isarco (Eisacktaler), where production is dominated by SILVANER and MÜLLER-THURGAU in addition to small amounts of GEWÜRZTRAMINER (itself supposedly a native of this region); and Terlano (Terlaner), a white DOC based on PINOT BIANCO, and with limited but high-quality production of Sauvignon Blanc.

Schiava accounts for a third of the overall production in the general Alto Adige DOC; other varieties of some significance are Pinot Grigio, Chardonnay, and Pinot Bianco amongst the whites plus LAGREIN, Pinot Noir, and—to a lesser extent—Cabernet and Merlot amongst the reds. Lagrein is frequently added to both Schiava and Pinot Noir to deepen the colour and supply extra tannins and structure, giving a characteristic bitter finish.

Apart from the almost ubiquitous Schiava, the Alto Adige is best known for clean, crisp, fruity white wines made in a modern style with

TEMPERATURE CONTROL, and solid, if somewhat rustic, reds. The whites compare quite favourably, particularly in terms of value, with the more famous produce of FRIULI.

Styles began to change in the 1980s, with producers seeking a richer and fuller style in the whites and a more polished character in the reds. BARRIQUES are increasingly used to add dimension. A substantial part of the improvement in the overall quality level has been the result of better matching of varieties to subzones, a matching which in many cases merely confirms the historic tradition of certain terroirs for certain grapes: Magré (Margreid) and Cortaccia (Kurtatsch) in the south west and Settequerce (Siebeneich) to the west of Bolzano for Cabernet and Merlot; Mazzon and Montagna (Montan) in the valley's south east and Cornaiano (Girlan) to the south west of Bolzano for Pinot Noir; Terlano (Terlan) for Sauvignon; Appiano (Eppan) and Monte (Berg) for Pinot Bianco; Ora (Auer) and the sandy and gravelly soils adjacent to Bolzano for Lagrein; Termeno (Tramin), Caldaro (Kaltern), and Cortaccia in addition to Santa Maddalena for Schiava; Cortaccia, Magré, and Salorno for Pinot Grigio.

The dominance of Schiava as the basis for the local viticulture, however, seems destined gradually to end. As vineyards are replaced, INTERNATIONAL VARIETIES are increasingly planted as a response to consumers' enthusiasm for these wines in the 1990s.

See also SANTA MADDALENA, and compare with TRENTINO.   D.T.

Alvarinho, the Portuguese name of a distinctive white grape variety grown around the town of Moncão in the extreme north west of Portugal's VINHO VERDE country (and, as ALBARIÑO, in GALICIA). The grapes' thick skins help them withstand the particularly damp climate, and can result in wines notably high in alcohol, acidity, and flavour. Alvarinho was one of the first Portuguese grape varieties to appear on the labels of VARIETAL wines and is therefore one of the best known.

amabile, Italian for sweet (sweeter than ABBOCCATO) or, literally, 'lovable'. See also SWEETNESS.

Amador, California county. See SIERRA FOOTHILLS.

Amarone. The most famous of Italy's dry DRIED-GRAPE WINES has recently been revitalized. It is produced from identical grape varieties and in the same production zone as VALPOLICELLA, with the same distinction between the classical zone, where Amarone Classico is produced, and an enlarged zone, where simple Amarone is produced. No longer obliged to call itself RECIOTO Amarone, it has become one of Italy's DOC wines in its own right.

The wine is made from selected superior whole bunches which are dried or raisined in special drying lodges or chambers. Here the grapes are spread out on mats or wickerwork shelving, or are strung up from the ceiling or rafters. It is increasingly common to dry the grapes in the slatted packing cases in which they were harvested. The length of the drying period varies from producer to producer. It was often prolonged until late February or March with ample development of BOTRYTIS, which became increasingly common during the 1970s and 1980s as the vineyards and production facilities of Valpolicella descended from the drier hills to the more humid valley floor. There has been a tendency to shorten the raisining period in recent years, however, in order to produce a wine less obviously affected by botrytis. Ventilating systems, to prevent botrytis development during the initial phase of the drying process, are also now quite common. Some producers now eliminate botrytis-affected grapes completely in order to produce a fresher, fruitier wine without the OXIDIZED flavours which once characterized the wine. After the drying process is finished, the grapes are pressed and fermented dry, and the wine aged in wooden casks. Smaller casks of new OAK are being experimented with. The finished wine easily reaches 15 per cent of alcohol and is rarely released until five years after the vintage, even though this is not a legal requirement.

Current production is approximately 15,000 hl/396,000 gal a year, although successful recent vintages such as 1995 and 1997 are likely to have produced more in response to current market enthusiasm for today's fruitier style of Amarone.   D.T.

Amigne, Swiss white grape variety and a speciality of Vetroz in the Valais, site of 16 ha/40 acres of the world's 18 ha/45 acres. The wine produced is usually quite sweet and may smell of brown bread. Arguably the least refreshing of the Valais white specialities.

Ampurdán-Costa Brava, Castilian name for the denominated Catalan wine zone EMPORDÀ-COSTA BRAVA.

Anbaugebiet, wine region in GERMANY, of which there are 13. The A in QBA stands for Anbaugebiet and these regions are fundamental to Germany's wine labelling and GERMAN WINE LAW.

Ancenis, Coteaux d', small VDQS zone in the Loire around the historic town of Ancenis between Nantes and Angers. It is used for a limited number of VARIETAL wines, and the name of the variety must be stated on the label: Pineau de la Loire or Chenin Blanc; Malvoisie or Pinot Beurot (Pinot Gris); Gamay; or Cabernet. In fact, the great majority of wine produced here is light red or pink made from Gamay, and some Cabernet, but some serious medium-sweet white wine is also produced. See also LOIRE.

Andalucía, or Andalusia, the southernmost of Spain's autonomous regions, encompassing eight provinces and the DO regions of JEREZ, MÁLAGA, MONTILLA-MORILES, and CONDADO DE HUELVA. Andalucía is the hottest part of Spain and has traditionally been associated with strong, alcoholic wines. They bear a marked resemblance to each other, and particularly to SHERRY. Most are FORTIFIED, although grapes from the arid plateau around Córdoba and Jaén are often so rich in natural sugar that they do not require the addition of spirit to reach an ALCOHOLIC STRENGTH of between 14 and 18 per cent. Until laws were tightened up following the foundation of the Jerez Consejo Regulador in 1934, wines from other parts of Andalucía would frequently find their way into sherry blends. Prince Alfonso de Hohenlohe's ground-breaking venture up in the Ronda hills, with an estate devoted to producing red and rosé table wines that first won acclaim in the late 1990s, opened up new perspectives for Andalusian wine.   R.J.M. & V. de la S.

Anderson Valley, cool California wine region and AVA on the western slope of the coastal mountain range 80 miles north of San Francisco. See MENDOCINO.

Anjou, important, revitalized, and varied wine region in the western Loire centred on the town of Angers, whose influence once extended all over north-west France. White wine represents hardly 15 per cent of Anjou's total wine production, rosé may be its commercial mainstay, but reds are increasingly fine and important.

The region is relatively mild, being influenced by the Atlantic and protected by the woods of the Vendée to the south west (rather as the MÉDOC is protected by the Landes). Rainfall is particularly low here, with annual totals of just 500 mm/19 in.

The GROLLEAU vine, and the sickly Rosé d'Anjou it all too often produced, are in retreat. Much more refined, and incredibly long-lasting, is rosé Cabernet d'Anjou, which must be made from Cabernet Sauvignon or, much more likely, Cabernet Franc grapes. It can be quite sweet but usually has very high acidity which can preserve it for decades and makes it an interesting partner for a wide range of savoury dishes.

Cabernet Franc represents about one vine in three in Anjou and is increasingly favoured by growers there, encouraged by the creation in 1987 of the serious red-wine appellation Anjou-Villages, which can provide luscious, and often better priced, alternatives to the more famous Cabernet Franc-dominated red Loires of SAUMUR-CHAMPIGNY to the east. Best areas for such reds are immediately south of Angers in the Coteaux de l'Aubance. There is increasing experimentation with CANOPY MANAGEMENT and use of PUMPING OVER and BARREL MATURATION. Lighter reds are produced as Anjou-Gamay, from the Gamay grape of Beaujolais, and Anjou Rouge is the catch-all appellation for lighter, often quite crisp, red wines.

Of dry white wines, Anjou Blanc is the most common, and is most successful when produced on the schist close to the river. The wine must contain at least 80 per cent Chenin Blanc, but increasing proportions of Chardonnay, and Sauvignon, are included in the blend. Tiny amounts of sweet white Anjou-Coteaux de la Loire, made exclusively from Chenin Blanc, are also made.

Superior producers of Anjou appellations include Domaine de Bablut, Philippe Delesvaux, Domaine de Haute Perche, Ogereau, Ch Pierre-Bise, and Richou. Within the Anjou region are certain areas which have produced white wines of such quality that they have earned their own appellations: Coteaux de l'AUBANCE; BONNEZEAUX; Coteaux du LAYON; QUARTS DE CHAUME for sweet wines and SAVENNIÈRES for dry wines.

See also LOIRE.

Antão Vaz, white, hot-climate grape grown mainly in southern Portugal, especially in the south of the Alentejo around Reguengos and Vidiguera and in parts of Estremadura and Terras do Sado.

anthocyanins, members of a complex group of natural PHENOLICS responsible for the colour of black and red grapes and red wines. Anthocyanins are common in the plant world and are responsible for the red to blue colours of leaves, fruits, and flowers.

Anthocyanins have another important characteristic. They are capable of changing form slightly, depending upon the PH, or degree of ACIDITY, of the medium in which they are dissolved, the different forms having slightly different colours. In general, the more acid the grape juice or wine, the brighter red the colour. Less acid wines tend to shade through dull purple to almost bluish. (Gardeners will recognize similar behaviour in the colour of hydrangea flowers after adjustment of soil acidity.)

One important operation during the FERMENTATION of most red wines, therefore, is to transfer the anthocyanin pigments from the skin cells to the wine. This occurs as fermentation proceeds because alcohol makes the skin cell walls more permeable to the diffusion of pigment molecules. Colour transfer is thus achieved by keeping the skins adequately mixed with the fermenting wine during and after fermentation (see MACERATION).

One might reasonably expect that the pigments in the new wine would be identical to those found in the grape skin. This may be the case for a few hours, but once the anthocyanins are mixed with the ACIDS of the wine and other phenolics as well as the many products of fermentation, they begin a series of interactions leading to much larger and more complicated molecules. Within a few years only traces of the relatively simple monomeric anthocyanins remain. With wine ageing, the anthocyanin molecules are included in polymers which may become larger and heavier so that some of them exceed their solubility in the wine and are precipitated as SEDIMENT. See AGEING.

A.D.W., B.G.C., & P.J.W.

Antinori, the most important NÉGOCIANT firm in TUSCANY, and probably in the whole of ITALY. The modern wine firm was founded by brothers Lodovico and Piero Antinori in 1895, although the Antinori family can trace their history in the wine trade back to 1385.

The work of the 19th-century brothers was continued by Piero's son Niccolò, who extended the house's commercial network both in Italy and into foreign markets and purchased the Castello della Sala estate near ORVIETO in Umbria. The house made a certain reputation for its white wines, sold under the Villa Antinori label, and for its Chianti, made in a soft and fruity style, by focusing its purchases of wine on various areas of the province of Florence, a style in contrast to the more austere wines of Ricasoli, the dominant Chianti house of the period. A vineyard was also planted with the Bordeaux grape variety CABERNET SAUVIGNON and cultivated during the 1930s. Although the family fortunes flourished, Antinori was only a medium-sized operation, with an annual production of approximately 1 million bottles, in 1966 when Piero Antinori, the son of Niccolò Antinori, assumed the direction of the firm's activities.

By the early 1990s, he had increased the annual production 15-fold, giving the house a commanding position in Tuscany, a position based both on the excellent quality of all the firm's wines at various price levels and, above all, on the innovative work of Antinori and house OENOLOGIST Giacomo Tachis in creating a new category of outstanding wines at the top of the range: Tignanello, the prototype SUPERTUSCAN, which eliminated white grapes from the basic blend of Tuscan reds and introduced small BARREL MATURATION for wines made from the local SANGIOVESE grape; Solaia, which, together with SASSICAIA (initially marketed by Antinori and whose development was assisted by Tachis), showed the potential for outstanding Cabernet in Tuscany; Cervaro, a white wine produced at the Castello della Sala based on CHARDONNAY grapes and, then unusual for Italy, BARREL FERMENTED. While firmly anchored in central Italy, Antinori is, at the same time, becoming more international in its overall perspective, with JOINT VENTURES under way in Hungary, Malta, and Washington state and ownership of Atlas Peak in the Napa Valley.

Piero's brother Lodovico Antinori independently produces such internationally famous Supertuscans as Ornellaia and the all-Merlot Masseto at his own estate near BOLGHERI.

D.T.

Aosta, or the Valle d'Aosta (Vallée d'Aoste to the region's many French speakers), is Italy's smallest region. The long, narrow valley formed by the river Dora Baltea as it courses through the mountains of Italy's extreme north west is Italy's connecting link to France and Switzerland and to the north of Europe beyond.

This rugged Alpine terrain is more suited to the grazing of animals than to the cultivation of the vine, and the vineyards are frequently terraced into dizzyingly steep slopes. No more than 30,000 hl/790,000 gal of wine is produced in an average year, of which only about 4,000 hl/105,200 gal qualifies as DOC. A good deal of it is sold privately either to the thriving tourist trade or to the intense flow of motorists which passes through the region.

At the crossroads between northern and southern Europe, the Valle d'Aosta has found itself with an extremely rich diversity of vine varieties. Native regional and other Italian varieties include NEBBIOLO, DOLCETTO, Petit and Gros Rouge, Fumin, Vien de Nus, Prëmetta, Moscato di Chambave, and Blanc de Morgex. French varieties include Pinot Noir, Gamay, Syrah, Grenache, Pinot Gris (known as Malvoisie), Pinot Blanc, and Chardonnay. There is also the Petite Arvine of Switzerland and the MÜLLER-THURGAU of Germany.

The most interesting wines being made in the early 1990s were the Nebbiolo-based Donnas or Donnaz, produced close to CAREMA across the border in Piedmont and more interesting than the neighbouring Nebbiolo-based Arnad-Monjovet; the family of fruity reds with Petit Rouge as their base which encompass Enfer d'Arvier, Torrette, and Chambave Rosso; the Nus Rosso, made from Vien de Nus and with Petit Rouge (spicier and more herbaceous than the Petit Rouge-based reds); the Moscato of Chambave, particularly in the PASSITO or dessert version; Gamay, fruity and soft but with some bitterness on the aftertaste which is not present in BEAUJOLAIS; Müller-Thurgau; the floral Blanc de Morgex et La Salle, produced in some of the highest vineyards in Europe, up to 1,300 m/4,260 ft, in whose aromas its devotees profess to find the aromas of Alpine meadows. The dessert version of Pinot Gris, a passito, was a legendary wine of the past, but has virtually gone out of production. Local producers are showing a new interest in the Fumin, the grape which supplies structure and intensity in many of the Petit Rouge-based blends, and interesting experiments with small BARREL MATURATION of VARIETAL Fumin wines have begun.

The overall viticultural production of the valley is almost entirely consumed within the regional confines and export trade seems highly unlikely to develop in view of the small quantities and high prices. D.T.

aperitifs, drinks served before a meal to 'open' (from the Latin *aperire*) the digestive system and stimulate the appetite, of which VERMOUTH and similar drinks are archetypal. Wines commonly served as aperitifs are dry, white, and not too alcoholic: CHAMPAGNE or any brut SPARKLING WINE; fino and manzanilla SHERRY; MOSEL wines up to SPÄTLESE level of sweetness; less rich ALSACE whites; MUSCADET, CHABLIS, and virtually any light, dry, still white wine. Customs vary nationally, however, and the French have customarily served spirits, FORTIFIED WINES, VINS DOUX NATURELS, VINS DE LIQUEUR, and strong, sweet wines such as SAUTERNES before meals (and dry champagne with the sweet course). A common all-purpose aperitif, apparently acceptable to French and non-French alike, is the KIR, or *vin blanc cassis*, as well as a blend of white wine and sparkling water sometimes known as a spritzer. The port trade serves white port as an aperitif, sherry producers a dry oloroso or fino, too many amateurs a full-bodied Chardonnay.

AP number, or Amtliche Prüfungsnummer, adorns the label of every bottle of German quality wine, whether QBA or QMP. This 10- to 12-digit number is an outward sign that the wine has passed Germany's much-vaunted official testing procedure, for which the pass rate is well above 90 per cent. The final two digits signify the year in which the wine was tested and the number immediately before this one is the number of the particular bottling in that year.

appellation. See CONTROLLED APPELLATION.

appellation contrôlée, short for appellation d'origine contrôlée, is France's prototype CONTROLLED APPELLATION, her much-imitated system of designating and controlling her all-important geographically based names, not just of wines, but also of spirits such as cognac, armagnac, and calvados, as well as of certain foodstuffs. This inherently protectionist and highly successful system is administered by the Institut National des Appellations d'Origine (INAO), a powerful Paris-based body which controls an increasing proportion of French wine production (more than 43 per cent in the late 1990s).

The French system of categorizing wine, including its main plank appellation contrôlée, has been taken as a model for European Union wine legislation, and AC is France's equivalent of what the European authorities consider a QUALITY WINE. The legal powers of the INAO, both within France and in its dealings with the EU and beyond, were strengthened substantially in 1990, when it took the conscious decision to build the future of French wine on the concept of geographical appellations (eschewing even the mention of vine varieties on the main label) and adopted the specific aim of preserving agricultural activity in certain zones. It wages unceasing war on all misused GENERIC wine and spirit names and such products as Turkey's 'St-Émilion', Yugoslavia's 'Calvados', and Davidoff's 'Château Margaux' cigars.

The regulations' scope

The INAO's complete list of wine and spirit appellation regulations is an unwieldy, annually revised tome, divided regionally with up to four tightly written pages of specification for each appellation and VDQS, covering the following aspects.

Production area All those communes allowed to produce the wine or spirit in question are listed, but within each of these communes only certain plots of land are deemed worthy, details of which are lodged with each commune's all-important *mairie* or administrative centre. Vines grown elsewhere within the commune are normally entitled only to be sold as a less specific appellation, a VIN DE PAYS or VIN DE TABLE.

Vine varieties The permitted grapes are specified in great detail, along with permitted maximum and minimum proportions. Many appellation regulations include long lists of half-forgotten local varieties. White grape varieties are permitted to a certain extent in a number of red-wine appellations.

Ripeness and alcoholic strength Specific MUST WEIGHTS are generally cited for freshly picked grapes before any CHAPTALIZATION, generally given in g/l of sugar. A maximum ALCOHOLIC STRENGTH after any chaptalization, if allowed, is also usually specified.

Yields Control of YIELDS is a fundamental tenet of the appellation contrôlée system, however sceptical some New World viticulturists are of the concept. The maximum yields cited in the regulations were almost routinely increased, however, by about 20 per cent throughout the 1970s and 1980s. In 1993, the INAO announced its intention of curbing yields (as the EU has done) but this has yet to be implemented in many regions.

This section usually includes information on a minimum VINE AGE allowed for appellation contrôlée production (which explains some of the more famous names on labels of vin de table in, particularly, the recently expanded appellations of the northern Rhône).

Viticulture This usually specifies a minimum VINE DENSITY, the approved PRUNING regime down to the number of buds, and the permitted vine-training system. In some southern appellations, the (limited) extent to which IRRIGATION is allowed may be outlined.

Wine-making and distillation This long section may well specify such aspects as compulsory DESTEMMING, method of ROSÉ-WINE-MAKING (usually by SAIGNÉE), although there is generous use of the vague phrase '*usages locaux*'. Precise distillation techniques are usually specified for spirits.

Pros and cons

France's appellation contrôlée designation is in general a very much more reliable guide to the country's best wines than, for example, the QBA category of 'quality wines' in Germany, the liberally applied DOC designation in Italy and Portugal, and its DO counterpart in Spain (all of the last three modelled on the AC system). The French system is by no means perfect, however, and policing remains a problem. Contraventions of the regulations, particularly over-chaptalization, or chaptalization and ACIDIFICATION of the same wine, are difficult to detect (although a complex bureaucracy controls over-production). Misdemeanours are only very rarely publicized, and then usually only as a result of local politics.

A more serious disadvantage of the appellation contrôlée system is the extent to which it stifles experimentation. In dramatic contrast to the New World, vine-growers may plant only certain vine varieties. Those wishing to experiment may be restricted to selling the wine not-merely as a vin de pays, but as an anonymous, undated vin de table.

The appellation contrôlée regulations have been drawn up not with a clean slate and a pencil devoted to the best possible options, but to legitimize the best current practices. In the various GRANDS CRUS and PREMIERS CRUS of the CÔTE D'OR, few would argue with the restriction that Pinot Noir and Chardonnay grapes should be cultivated; Burgundians have had at least seven centuries to test this hypothesis. In southern France, however, particularly in the LANGUEDOC-ROUSSILLON (far from INAO headquarters), there is widespread dissatisfaction with regulations which are based on declining but dominant proportions of the controversial CARIGNAN vine, planted in great quantity earlier this century for reasons of expediency rather than quality. Even within France itself, there is increasing respect for vins de pays from this southern part of France, and market recognition that AC wines are not necessarily superior.

It is also fanciful to suggest that every wine produced within an appellation betrays its uniquely geographical provenance. Few blind tasters would unhesitatingly identify a Côtes du MARMANDAIS, for example. And then there are the catch-all appellations such as BORDEAUX AC and CHAMPAGNE whose quality variation is simply frustrating.

See also FRANCE, LABELLING, and VDQS.

Apulia, or Puglia in Italian, long (350 km/210 miles) and fertile region along the Adriatic coast in Italy's extreme south east which has long been of major importance for the production of wine and TABLE GRAPES. A MEDITERRANEAN CLIMATE and a predominance of soils well suited to grape-growing have created an ideal viticultural environment. Close to 190,000 ha/470,000 acres of land is dedicated to the vine, and annual wine production in the 1980s occasionally reached almost 13 million hl/343 million gal (more than three times as much as the entire production of Chile, for example). Only Sicily rivals Apulia as Italy's most productive wine region, and yet the region has the grand total of only 54 bottlers, of whom only 10 are responsible for half of all bottled production.

Quantity has been in inverse proportion to quality in Apulia, however, and a large part of the region's viticultural production is utilized, now as in the past, for anonymous ingredients

in BLENDING that are usefully high in alcohol, as a base for VERMOUTH, or are either compulsorily distilled or transformed into GRAPE CONCENTRATE as part of efforts to drain the European wine lake. Production of DOC wines in Apulia rarely exceeds two per cent of the regional total, and less than a quarter of the regional production is ever sold in bottle. Although Apulia is fortunate in its topography, with a virtual absence of the hard-to-cultivate rocky, arid hills and mountains which dominate neighbouring CAMPANIA, MOLISE, and BASILICATA, over 70 per cent of vineyards are in the plains, where evenings and nights offer little relief from the torrid daytime TEMPERATURES. High YIELDS are the rule, and a significant number of DOCs have lost credibility with excessively tolerant production limits.

Apulia's finest wines are produced in the Salento peninsula, the heel of the boot, where distinctively full but not unappetizingly alcoholic wines are made. Negroamaro is the principal and most interesting variety grown, with some supplementary MALVASIA Nera of Brindisi or Lecce. When yields are limited, the resulting wines are not unlike a savoury CHÂTEAUNEUF-DU-PAPE. Eight DOCs share this soil and these varieties: Alezio, Brindisi, Copertino, Leverano, Matino, Nardò, Salice Salento, and Squinzano.

The PRIMITIVO grape, identical to California's ZINFANDEL, suffers from a poorly conceived DOC in its home territory of Manduria: a minimum alcohol level of 14 per cent for the regular production and higher alcohol for the *liquoroso* versions (both sweet and dry), which reach a leg-wobbling 17.5 to 18 per cent. The UVA DI TROIA grape, used in several DOCs (the large one of Castel del Monte and the small ones of Rosso Barletta, Rosso Canosa, Rosso di Cerignola, Cacc'e Mmitte di Lucera) is considered by many a variety with real potential, so far ignored by producers deterred by its relatively low productivity.

MONTEPULCIANO and BOMBINO BIANCO are both cultivated in the northern part of the region, in the province of Foggia, but bear little resemblance to the better ABRUZZI wines from these grapes. Sporadic attempts at cultivating INTERNATIONAL VARIETIES are being made both in the province of Foggia and in Minervino Murge, a high-altitude area of the province of Bari, which have enjoyed some export success. Even Chardonnay grown in the Salento area, now sold as IGT, can provide successful warm-climate wines such as those pioneered by Apulia's most successful OENOLOGIST Severino Garofano. Apulia has six IGTs: Salento, Tarantino, Valle d'Itria, Daunia, Le Murge, and Puglia. This has resulted in an increase in VARIETAL wines such as Negroamaro del Salento and Uva di Troia di Puglia, many of them made by FLYING WINEMAKERS, sometimes using OAK.

CO-OPERATIVES are responsible for 60 per cent of Apulia's production. Some of them have experienced serious financial difficulties, but others have benefited from flying-winemaker input. Meanwhile, many small growers have been persuaded to accept EU-funded VINE PULL SCHEMES and plant alternative crops.

Thanks to the decline of per capita CONSUMPTION in Italy, Apulia's wine production dropped below 7 million hl/185 million gal in 1990, but, partly in response to new demand from northern Europe, averaged over 10 million from 1992 to 1996. D.T.

Aquileia, or Aquileia del Friuli, one of the more variable and less exported DOCs of the FRIULI region in north-east Italy.

Aragon, known as Aragón in Spanish, is one of Spain's 17 autonomous regions. In the north east of the country, it spans the broad valley of the river Ebro, which is flanked by mountains on either side. The north is dominated by the Pyrenees, which feed water on to the arid Ebro plain. To the south and east, the climate becomes progressively extreme as the land rises towards the central Spanish plateau.

The wines of Aragon have traditionally been strapping potions with natural alcohol reaching levels as high as 17 or 18 per cent. Red wines, made predominantly from the GARNACHA grape, were mostly sold in bulk for blending. However, four DO regions designated between 1980 and 1990 are helping to raise the profile of Aragon wines. SOMONTANO in the lush Pyrenean foothills east of the city of Huesca certainly has the most potential, but south of the Ebro, wines from the DOs of CAMPO DE BORJA, CARIÑENA, and CALATAYUD are starting to benefit from investment in modern winemaking technology. Throughout much of Aragon, large CO-OPERATIVES continue to dominate production, buying in grapes from smallholders. R.J.M.

Aragonêz, Portuguese name for the Spanish red grape variety TEMPRANILLO used particularly in the ALENTEJO region. In the Alentejo, it makes concentrated, deep-coloured reds, rather like those which go under the name Tinta Roriz in the Douro.

Aramon is now, happily, a remnant of French viticultural history, a vine variety that burgeoned throughout the LANGUEDOC in the second half of the 19th century and was displaced as France's most popular only in the 1960s by CARIGNAN.

Arbois, the most important appellation in the JURA region in eastern France including about 800 ha/1,976 acres of vineyard and named after the region's main wine town. Until recently, Arbois was the name most commonly given to Jura wines. Arbois has been famous as the location of the Jura's most famous wine producer, the energetic Henri Maire, whose BRAND Vin Fou has been much advertised all over France. So important is this NÉGOCIANT that it grows or buys, blends, sometimes induces bubbles by the TRANSFER METHOD, and then sells about half of the entire Jura wine production.

Arbois may be any colour, particularly *corail* or *rubis*, intermediate hues between pink and red which result from applying normal REDWINE-MAKING techniques to the light-coloured POULSARD grape, which, often known as Ploussard, is a speciality here (although Pinot Noir and the local Trousseau are also grown). Production of white wine has been increasing so that it represented about half of the appellation's output by the early 1990s. White wines are often VARIETAL Chardonnay, and those in which some of the local SAVAGNIN, or Naturé, is included can taste distinctly nutty. A significant proportion of wine is made bubbly by the traditional method of SPARKLING-WINEMAKING and sold as **Arbois Mousseux**. Wines made from grapes grown within the commune of Pupillin have the right to the appellation **Arbois Pupillin**.

See also VIN JAUNE and VIN DE PAILLE, both of which rarities are made within this appellation.

Arbois is also the name of a white grape variety grown in the Loire to produce such wines as VALENÇAY and CHEVERNY. Although Arbois is declining, it is also a permitted ingredient in white wines labelled TOURAINE (and, in theory, Vouvray). Often called Menu Pineau or Petit Pineau, it is a vigorous vine whose wines are softer than those of the Chenin Blanc that is more common in the middle Loire valley.

Ardèche, region of France on the right bank of the Rhône between the main concentrations of vineyards which constitute the northern and southern Rhône valley in south-east France. Its steadily improving wines are sold as VIN DE PAYS des Coteaux de l'Ardèche, from the southern VIVARAIS area, or Vin de Pays des Collines Rhodaniennes from the much larger surrounding region. VARIETAL Chardonnay and Viognier have been particularly successful here. Louis LATOUR of Burgundy was a pioneer, notably with Grand Ardèche Chardonnay, and the Vignerons Ardéchois is a co-operative with high standards.

Argentina, the most important wine-producing country in South America and, at long last, one of the most dynamic wine producers in the world. Eight countries had more land planted with vines than Argentina in 1996, the most recent year for which Argentina has meaningful statistics, but only four countries produced more wine.

Of the 250,000 ha/617,750 acres of vineyard in 1996, almost 50 per cent was planted with pink-skinned varieties, 30 per cent with white-skinned varieties, and just 20 per cent with red-skinned varieties. But the new wave of optimism is fast changing these proportions in favour of premium varieties and styles, particularly reds, that are now allowing Argentine wine producers to compete successfully internationally. Considerable investments in new vineyard areas and improved wine-making technology were made in the 1990s and the Argentine desire to export is now one of the most manifest in the world of wine.

Regions

Mendoza In the far west of the country, only a (substantial) mountain range from Santiago in Chile, this is by far the biggest and most important wine-growing province in Argentina, accounting for over 70 per cent of all Argentina's wine production. The Andes dominate the western skyline, with Mount Aconcagua, at over 7,000 m/23,000 ft, the highest mountain in the Americas, rising above the rest. Average vineyard altitudes are about 600 to 1,100 m (1,970–3,610 ft) above sea level. The climate is CONTINENTAL, with the four seasons clearly defined but without any extremes of temperature. Rainfall occurs mostly in the summer months, which encourages growth, but it seldom exceeds 300 mm/12 in a year, with 200 mm/8 in being the average. Early summer hail is the main risk to the vines and frost is rare.

The most important wine-producing areas in and around Mendoza are:

Maipú department: Cruz de Piedra, Barrancas, Russell, Coquimbito, Lunlunta, and Maipú districts.

Luján department: Carrodilla, Chacras de Coria, Mayor Drummond, Luján, Vistalba, Las Compuertas, Pedriel, Agrelo, Ugarteche, Carrizal, Tres Esquinas, Anchoris.

San Martín to the east and San Raphael to the south of the region are also major centres of production, although less important than formerly following the swing to classic varieties.

Luján de Cuyo (which created Argentina's first CONTROLLED APPELLATION in 1993) is in the upper Mendoza valley at altitudes between 800 and 1,100 m (2,640 and 3,630 ft). Average rainfall is about 190 mm/7.2 in a year and the mean annual temperature is 15 °C/37.5 °F. The Malbec vine does particularly well here.

Pink-skinned grapes, notably CRIOLLA GRANDE and CEREZA, account for about a half of all Mendoza plantings and are used for inexpensive wine and for grape concentrate. Red wine grapes account for another quarter, with the Malbec predominating, but Italian varieties and Tempranillo are also important. Cabernet Sauvignon is catching up. White wine varieties such as Chardonnay are increasingly common, especially in high-altitude vineyards, such as those of Tupungato in the Valle de Uco south west of the city of Mendoza, which can be as high as 1,200 m/3,960 ft and are already regarded as some of Argentina's most valuable vineyards.

San Juan This is Argentina's second biggest wine-producing region. The climate is much hotter than that of Mendoza, with summer temperatures of 42 °C/107 °F not uncommon and with rainfall averaging only 150 mm/6 in per annum.

For long the home of high-yielding pink varieties, especially Cereza, whose high sugar content made them ideal for wine blending, concentrating, or for selling as fresh TABLE GRAPES or raisins, San Juan was being developed as a producer of quality wine in the late 1990s. The best areas are in the Ullun, Zonda, and Tulum valleys.

La Rioja Historically the oldest of the wine-producing provinces, and home of the Torrontés

Riojano, La Rioja had only 7,000 ha/17,290 acres of vineyard in 1996. By world standards the area is unimportant, although aromatic white wines from the TORRONTÉS grape can be good, and wines made from the Moscatel de Alejandría (MUSCAT OF ALEXANDRIA) have a following in Argentina itself. The lack of water for IRRIGATION purposes makes wine-making a marginal activity.

Salta, Jujuy, and Catamarca These three far-northern provinces cover 500,000 square km/193,000 square miles and it is in the province of Salta (1,500 ha/3,700 acres) that the best wine is produced (and one of the world's highest vineyards is situated; see ALTITUDE). Here the Torrontés Riojano is very much at home. Around Cafayate in the Calchaquies valley it is producing an outstandingly aromatic, full, dryish white wine. Of the other grape varieties grown in Salta, Cabernet Sauvignon is the most successful.

Río Negro and Neuquén This southern area of Patagonia is much cooler than the higher-yielding areas to the north but has yet to reach its full potential. Historically the Río Negro has been the fruit-growing centre of Argentina, but the cooler climate and chalky soil combined with a long warm ripening season under clear skies make it ideal for the production of good-quality white wine (notably Torrontés Riojano and Semillon) and for sparkling-wine base material.

Vine varieties
Although in the late 1990s the high-yielding Criollas and Cereza (see Pinks below) still account for almost half the total crop, they are slowly decreasing as vineyard owners were slowly increasing their production of the classic varieties originating in Europe. While these pink-skinned varieties are typically planted in flat vineyards in the deep, fertile, heavily irrigated soils of the warmer wine regions, Argentina's signature variety, Malbec, is more likely to be planted in the less fertile Andean foothills.

White The swing to white-wine consumption in the late 1980s generated a need for relatively inexpensive neutral styles of wine. UGNI BLANC often serves, and CHENIN BLANC, oddly called Pinot de la Loire here, is also grown successfully, albeit demonstrating the somewhat anodyne characteristics of a California rather than Loire example. It provides much of the

base wine for the sparkling wine popular with Argentines.

The Pedro Giménez (not identical to Spain's PEDRO XIMÉNEZ) is the most planted white grape variety, grown particularly in Mendoza and the province of San Juan, where it yields alcoholic, full-bodied wine suitable for blending.

The second most planted light-skinned variety in 1990 was Moscatel de Alejandría, or Muscat of Alexandria, but perhaps the most interesting, and certainly the most distinctive, white wine grape variety is the third most important, Torrontés, of which, of the three different strains, Torrontés Riojano, from La Rioja province, is by far the most common. Others are Torrontés Mendocino and Torrontés Sanjuanino. There is no evidence that Argentina's Torrontés is the same as that grown in GALICIA, north-west Spain, but it is the nearest thing to an indigenous white variety in Argentina and produces a light wine with a strong MUSCAT aroma. Originally it was planted almost exclusively in the northern province of Salta, particularly in the Calchaquies valley and around Cafayate. It can now be found in the province of Mendoza, where it is often used for blending. Its flowery, strongly aromatic character makes it ideal for this purpose.

Chardonnay is the wine that everyone wants to produce and the Argentines are no exception, particularly with their eye on the US and British markets. Of the classic white grape varieties, Chardonnay has proved to be the most adaptable in Argentina. The country has its own Chardonnay clone developed at the University of California at Davis, the so-called Mendoza clone, which is widely used in Australia and elsewhere. The variety has been particularly successfully grown at higher altitudes such as the Tupungato area at 1,200 m/3,940 ft.

True Sauvignon Blanc, which the more enlightened producers believe they must try to produce if they are to carve out a niche in the world market, is as yet unproven and relatively rare. Other varieties include Riesling, Sémillon, Pinot Gris, and even Viognier.

Red Paradoxically the predominant red wine grape variety in Argentina is one that has never achieved greatness in its original birthplace in the south west of France. The Malbec, often spelt Malbeck, of Bordeaux, BOURG, BLAYE, and CAHORS seems to have discovered its true home in upper Mendoza. There it produces a deep-coloured, robust, and fruity red wine with enough alcohol, weight, and structure to benefit from OAK ageing. Cabernet Sauvignon is as popular with Argentine wine-growers as any others, but there is no doubt that the Malbec produces by far the best and most balanced red wine and, with careful nurturing and strict temperature control during fermentation, has become Argentina's vinous trademark.

So enthusiastically was Malbec pulled out in the 1970s and 1980s, however, that by 1990 there was slightly more vineyard planted with a variety called BONARDA, whose exact identity is still the subject of some debate. This variety, along with many other Italian varieties (most notably SANGIOVESE and BARBERA but also FREISA, NEBBIOLO, RABOSO, DOLCETTO, and LAMBRUSCO), was brought to the country by the substantial numbers of Italian immigrants. Also important is the Spanish variety Tempranillo, known here as Tempranilla, often used to make light, fruity wines by CARBONIC MACERATION.

There were nearly 2,500 ha/6,200 acres of productive Cabernet Sauvignon vines in 1990 and by 1998 Argentina was already exporting considerable quantities of fine varietal Cabernet and Cabernet/Merlot blends, the Catena Alta 1994 breaking new, distinctly modern, ground while Weinert still nurtured stocks of concentrated wines in the slightly more syrupy traditional mould. Other red wine varieties apart from Merlot included Pinot Noir, which in the late 1990s had yet to find a suitable home in Argentina, and Syrah, which clearly had and which is expected to be more widely planted.

Pinks The grapes of this, Argentina's most quantitatively important category of vine varieties, can hardly be described as either white skinned or dark skinned since at full ripeness their skins are distinctly pink. The CRIOLLA GRANDE, CRIOLLA CHICA, and CEREZA are some of Argentina's oldest varieties. The wine produced from these varieties is usually very deeply coloured white, occasionally pink, often quite sweet, and sold at the bottom end of the market, either in bulk or in litre bottles or cardboard cartons, as everyday wine within Argentina, or blended with basic Malbec to produce a light red.

Wine-making

The overwhelming demands of the domestic market in the late 1960s and early 1970s meant that wine-making techniques were geared to processing the vast yields of Criolla Grande, Criolla Chica, and Cereza grapes. Changes are well under way, however. The export-led drive for improved quality has forced even the biggest producers of cheap wine into a reappraisal of their wine-making techniques in order to supply international demand for sound VARIETAL wines.

Wine trade organization

The majority of Argentina's vineyards are in the hands of specialist grape-growers, of which many are relatively large commercial concerns. Wine producers exert increasing control on the grapes they buy in, however, and almost all of them own at least some vineyards.

The single greatest factor in making Argentina's wine suitable for export has arguably been the widespread use of foreign consultants and in some cases FLYING WINE-MAKERS.

The great majority of Argentina's wineries, like the country's vineyards, are in Mendoza province, often on the outskirts of the city of Mendoza itself. The largest companies have traditionally had sales offices in the distant capital Buenos Aires, but the largest producer by far, Peñaflor, now masterminds its export campaign from Mendoza. Its main winery is at Coquimbito just outside Mendoza.

Valentin Bianchi, situated in San Rafael in the south of Mendoza province, is another producer to have exported successfully, particularly to the USA, as have Finca Flichman (now owned by SOGRAPE of Portugal) and Pascual Toso and substantial vineyard owners Bodegas Lopez. Other successful exporters include Weinert, La Agricola, Santa Ana, Michel Torino, Norton, and Balbi. Bodegas Esmeralda, Bodega La Rural, and Bodegas Escorihuela are part of the wine empire built up by Dr Nicolas Catena, who, with help from California wine-maker Paul Hobbs and itinerant Jacques LURTON, has set a new standard for Argentina. Regional specialists with some degree of success outside Argentina include Etchart of Salta, for whom Michel ROLLAND has acted as consultant, and Canale in the Río Negro.

Bodega Norton of Luján de Cuyo was acquired by Austrian interests in 1989. In the 1990s Argentina attracted a substantial wave of foreign investors, notably Santa Rita, Concha y Toro, and San Pedro from Chile, attracted by

Argentina's lower land costs. Italian vermouth producers Martini & Rossi have long had Argentine investments, as have MOËT Hennessy, whose wholly owned subsidiary Chandon has been the biggest producer of sparkling 'Champaña' in Argentina for three decades. Other foreign investors include the champagne houses of Mumm, Deutz, and Piper-Heidsieck.

D.F.S. & J.Ro.

Arinto, Portuguese white grape variety most commonly encountered in BUCELAS in which it must constitute at least 75 per cent of the blend. It is also grown in many other parts of Portugal, notably the RIBATEJO and TERRAS DO SADO. Arinto is respected for its high acidity and can yield wines which gain interest and, sometimes, a citrus quality with age. Arinto Miudo and Arinto Cachudo are subvarieties. As an ingredient in VINHO VERDE it is known as Pederná.

Arinto do Dão is a different, less distinguished variety.

Armenia, relatively small mountainous, inland CIS republic on TURKEY's north-east border. One of the oldest viticultural regions, its altitude compensates for its LATITUDE, which is five to seven degrees more southerly than the famous vineyards of France. It specializes in high-strength white wines and brandies, but is not today one of the more important CIS wine producers. Small quantities of table wines are produced, mostly for local consumption. Wineries are mainly in the Ararat valley and in the hills just above it. V.R.

Arneis, white grape variety and dry, scented VARIETAL wine of PIEDMONT in north-west Italy. Originally from ROERO, where it may be used to soften the intense NEBBIOLO in red wines, it is also sometimes called BAROLO Bianco, or white Barolo, by some of its more fervent admirers. In the 1980s, thanks to growing demand for white wine in Piedmont, there was an explosion of interest in Arneis, and plantings now total 400 ha/990 acres. The wine received DOC status in 1989 and production has risen as consumers have come to appreciate its aromas of pears and herbs and the almond flavours on the palate and aftertaste. If Arneis, at its best, can undoubtedly be a pleasing wine, it suffers from a lack of acidity when the grapes ripen properly and an inability, in the vast majority of cases, to age well. After a dip in demand in the early 1990s, the wine now seems to have found a solid and loyal customer base,

undoubtedly aided by the general popularity of Piedmontese wines. Experiments with a PASSITO version have given interesting initial results. D.T.

aroma, imprecise tasting term for a relatively simple smell such as that of a grape, fermenting MUST, or young wine. Wine-tasting professionals tend to use the word aroma to distinguish the smells associated with young wines from the more complex aromatic compounds which result from extended BOTTLE AGE for which the term BOUQUET is used. In Australia the word aroma is often used to refer specifically to VARIETAL characteristics rather than those associated with wine-making. See also AROMA WHEEL and FLAVOUR COMPOUNDS.

A.D.W.

aroma compounds. See FLAVOUR COMPOUNDS.

aromatized wines. See FLAVOURED WINES.

aroma wheel, graphical representation of TASTING terms used for AROMA, devised at the University of California at Davis by Ann C. Noble and others in the early 1980s. Her research into sensory evaluation of wine had indicated that there was no general agreement either on terminology or on its application. The aroma wheel was developed to provide a standardized lexicon which can be used widely to describe wine aroma in non-judgemental terms, grouping specific terms which can be defined to provide a basis for communication. It may be used by professionals for the purposes of clarification and categorization and provides a good basis on which tasting terms for aroma can be taught to novices. In practice, however, most individuals tend to develop their own terms, which may be just as precise and descriptive. The aroma wheel does not include terms which describe the physical dimensions of a wine (such as 'full bodied' or 'tart').

Arrábida, former IPR in southern Portugal named after the Serra da Arrábida and now part of the PALMELA DOC. See TERRAS DO SADO.

Arroyo Grande. California wine region and AVA. See SAN LUIS OBISPO.

Arroyo Seco. California wine region and AVA. See MONTEREY.

Arruda, a DOC in western Portugal. See ESTREMADURA.

Arrufiac, also known as **Arrufiat** and RUFFIAC, is a light-skinned grape variety enjoying a modest renaissance in Gascony in SOUTH WEST FRANCE. An ingredient in PACHERENC DU VIC-BILH and Côtes de ST-MONT, it is typically blended with the MANSENGS and COURBU.

Artisans & Estates. See KENDALL-JACKSON.

artists' labels, wine LABELS illustrated by works of art, often a different one for each vintage. Baron Philippe de Rothschild commissioned the Cubist Jean Carlu to design a mould-breaking label for the 1924 vintage of Ch MOUTON-ROTHSCHILD, the first to be CHÂTEAU BOTTLED. He instituted this as an annual custom from the 1945 vintage, with the result that COLLECTORS may seek particular missing labels, thereby adding value even to Mouton Rothschild in earlier maturing vintages (of which most bottles tend to have been opened). Since then, vintages of Mouton have enjoyed particular réclame in countries (Japan, Denmark, Holland, Spain) associated with the artist responsible for that year's label. Wine producers all over the world have since emulated this phenomenon, although none to such clever effect.

Asia. Until the 1990s it was assumed that this most populous of continents would never play an important role in the world of wine. There was something in the physical make-up of most Asians, it was thought by those in the continent which produces the lion's share of all wine, that made them prefer either non-alcoholic or grain-based drinks. This assumption was rapidly disproved in the mid to late 1990s when the world's AUCTION prices were inflated at an unprecedented rate thanks largely to sudden interest from the Far East. Thanks to a (short-lived) boom in the so-called tiger economies, and the much-vaunted HEALTH benefits claimed for red wine, wine-drinking changed from bizarre foreign practice to status symbol in a remarkably short time in countries as varied as Thailand, Taiwan, India, Korea, and—the country with the greatest potential as both consumer and producer—China. Wine-drinking further infiltrated Japan meanwhile, while several Asian countries embarked on their own domestic wine industries in the 1990s. See CHINA, KOREA, INDIA, INDONESIA, JAPAN, NEPAL, TAIWAN, and VIETNAM. See also the ex-Soviet Central Asian republics of KAZAKHSTAN, KYRGYZSTAN, TAJIKISTAN, TURKMENISTAN, and UZBEKISTAN. Countries such as Afghanistan, Iraq, Iran, JORDAN, PAKISTAN, SYRIA, and Yemen devote most of their vineyards to the production of DRYING GRAPES but ISRAEL and LEBANON both have flourishing wine industries.

Aspiran, very old dark-skinned grape variety of the LANGUEDOC which once represented about a quarter of all vines planted in the Hérault *département*, but was not replanted on any great scale after PHYLLOXERA because it is not particularly productive. It yields limited quantities of light but perfumed red wine and is a permitted grape variety in MINERVOIS.

Asprinio, light grape speciality of CAMPANIA in southern Italy, where it often makes slightly sparkling wines.

Assario Branco, Portuguese white grape encountered particularly in the Dão region which may be PALOMINO.

assemblage, French word for the important operation in the production of fine wines of deciding which lots will be assembled to make up the final blend. It plays a crucial role in SPARKLING-WINE-MAKING, when some CUVÉES may be assembled from several hundred different components. Here the complementary nature of each component is of great importance, as is, for NON-VINTAGE wines, adherence to a house style.

Assemblage is of almost ritual significance in BORDEAUX, where many CHÂTEAUX make their so-called GRAND VIN carrying the château name by selecting and BLENDING only the best lots. The rejected lots may either be blended together to make a SECOND WINE (and occasionally even a third wine) or be sold off in bulk to a NÉGOCIANT carrying only the local APPELLATION (Margaux or St-Julien, for example).

The normal procedure is to taste samples from each lot and then simply decide whether it is of sufficiently high quality for the *grand vin*. It is assumed that any blend of wines from the same property is likely to be harmonious. In most other Old World wine regions, especially BURGUNDY, holdings are too small to allow this selectivity, although Chave of HERMITAGE in the Rhône, for example, is notable for keeping lots from different parcels of vineyard separate until a final assembly just before bottling.

In the New World, such a process is likely to involve the assembly of blends of various different quality levels and character. In this case, the wine-maker is concerned not just with each lot's inherent quality but also with its affinity with other components in the blend.

Assyrtico, or Assyrtiko, top-quality white grape variety grown increasingly widely in GREECE. Its origins lie on the island of SANTORINI but its ability to retain acidity in a hot climate has encouraged successful experimentation with it elsewhere, notably on the north-eastern mainland around Halkidiki. It may also help to compensate for the relatively low acidity of the SAVATIANO grape grown widely in Attica.

Asti, town and province in PIEDMONT in north-west Italy whose name appears in those of fruity local VARIETAL wines made from the likes of BARBERA, DOLCETTO, FREISA, GRIGNOLINO, MALVASIA, and MOSCATO grapes. MOSCATO D'ASTI is the superior version of the well-known sparkling wine that was until recently known as **Asti Spumante**.

In 1993, along with Moscato d'Asti, Asti Spumante was elevated to DOCG status and renamed **Asti**, largely in an effort to distinguish it from the host of FRIZZANTE or sparkling wines produced in Italy from a host of grape varieties of very varying quality.

Producers of Asti are modelling themselves on their counterparts in FRANCIACORTA (and, more indirectly, Champagne). The light, sweet SPUMANTE of Asti is, like the superior Moscato d'Asti, produced from the MOSCATO Bianco grape in the provinces of Asti, Cuneo, and Alessandria.

As a blended wine produced in extremely large quantities (nearly 650,000 hl/17 million gal per year, by far the largest single Italian DOC, more than half as much again as SOAVE, Italy's second most important DOC), Asti is dominated by the large commercial houses of Piedmont, most if not all clustered around the town of Canelli. The combination of large-volume production and small-scale viticulture has necessarily made Asti a blended wine from many sources, a fact which has tended to mask the significant quality differences from zone to zone and the different characteristics of the Moscato Bianco grape in a variety of TERROIRS.

Asti differs significantly from its cousin, Moscato d'Asti: its ALCOHOLIC STRENGTH is higher (between 7 and 9.5 per cent against the maximum 5.5 per cent of Moscato d'Asti), as is

its FIZZINESS (3.5–4 atmospheres of pressure in the bottle against a maximum of one atmosphere in Moscato d'Asti). As a more alcoholic wine with a smaller quantity of RESIDUAL SUGAR, Asti should, in theory, taste drier than Moscato d'Asti; in practice, the sweetness is even more marked due to the less pronounced aromas and flavours that are the inevitable result of blending, and to a significant use of base material from zones that have been planted more to supply the needs of the négociant houses than for any verifiable aptitude for producing fine Moscato.

One encouraging sign, however, is the recent decision on the part of important small estates, in many cases prestigious producers of Moscato d'Asti, to produce an Asti from their own grapes, a development which, in terms of image, can only be helpful to the wine.   D.T.

astringency, a property of wine that causes a complex of sensations resulting from the shrinking, drawing, or puckering of the tissues of the mouth. Earlier, it was thought that astringency provoked one of the primary TASTE sensations, like sweetness, sourness, and particularly BITTERNESS, with which it has often been confused. However, the response to astringency is now recognized as tactile and not dependent on the taste receptors. The most important astringent materials are TANNINS, and it is these components of a wine that are responsible for the puckery, tactile sensation that is most noticeable in young red wines. However, an appropriate degree of astringency contributes very positively to the palatability of a red wine, and astringency is central to the MOUTHFEEL of a wine. Some of the terms used by tasters to describe the astringency of a wine—hard, soft, green, resinous, leathery, gripping, aggressive, supple, for example—are the same as those used to describe the tannins of the wine.   P.J.W.

Athiri, widely grown white Greek vine variety whose lemony produce is often used for blending, notably with the nobler ASSYRTICO.

Aubance, Coteaux de l', small but excellent sweet-white-wine appellation in Anjou on the left bank of the river Loire just south of the town of Angers. It takes its name from the Aubance, a tributary of the Loire. Total production is hardly more than that of SAVENNIÈRES across the river to the west, but the best results come from Chenin planted on outcrops of heat-retaining slate. The standard of wine-making is high, and a high proportion of the racy, sweet white Chenin Blanc wines made here are snapped up locally or in Paris. Red and dry white ANJOU make up the bulk of production in this zone, but Coteaux de l'Aubance can be just as noble, if not always as long-lived, as the Loire's more famous sweet whites. According to the vintage, the wines may be BOTRYTIZED, as in 1990, or partly raisined on the vine. The wines must have a RESIDUAL SUGAR level of at least 17 g/l; any lower and they must be declassified to Anjou Blanc. Domaines de Montgilet and Richou are star performers. See also LOIRE.

Aubun, rather ordinary black-berried vine variety of the southern Rhône, now in decline. It produces wine not unlike a softer version of CARIGNAN. Officially approved as an ingredient in many appellations of the southern Rhône, eastern LANGUEDOC, and PROVENCE (including CHÂTEAUNEUF-DU-PAPE), it is found in the southern Rhône, Gard, and the Aude, but is being systematically pulled up as a vine with no useful future for quality-wine production.

auctions of wine are the sale of wine by lots by an auctioneer acting as agent for the seller or, in certain instances, as the seller in his or her own right.

Today's commercial auction scene is dominated by regular sales conducted by the professional auction houses, Christie's and Sotheby's, whose headquarters are in London. An infrastructure of wine auction facilities from FINE WINE TRADERS and BROKERS to warehousing has grown up around the two companies' London headquarters. The fact that customers can buy wines at market prices as well as store and ship them with the minimum of difficulty helped draw a dominant proportion of wine-auction business through the London salerooms.

Both houses hold regular wine auctions elsewhere, however, particularly in the United States, which presented an increasingly serious challenge to London's hegemony in the late 1990s.

Commercial auctions are also held to a certain extent in other countries, notably France, Belgium, Holland, Switzerland, Italy, and Australia, with occasional sales in Japan.

How to buy and sell at auction
The public forum of the auction room and the intrinsically competitive aspect of bidding for lots often creates an atmosphere of tension and excitement in the saleroom in which it is easy for inexperienced participants to get carried away. All the information required about a particular auction is contained in the auction catalogue, an increasingly glossy publication thanks to the rivalry between Christie's and Sotheby's.

The wines to be sold are contained in numbered lots. Apart from a number and an estimated price band from lowest to highest, the description of each lot identifies the wine by name, bottle size, and vintage where applicable. The more reputable the auction house, the more it takes steps to guarantee the provenance of the wine to protect both the buyer and its own reputation. Given the importance of the condition of the wine, especially older wines, and since wines are not generally available for inspection, the catalogue specifies exact fill, or ULLAGE levels, the condition of the LABEL, whether the wine comes in its own wooden CASE (sometimes abbreviated to 'o.w.c.'), and will generally mention if a cellar is of exceptional pedigree or in previously undisturbed condition.

Auction-house policy may vary on the condition of the wine to be sold. Sotheby's do not open original wooden cases, while Christie's do unless the wines are young. Pre-sale tastings are not the lavish affairs they once were, but limited pre-sale tastings are still the practice. Lots which are of special interest may be supplemented by the auctioneer's tasting notes. Bidding may be by hand or, more often today, by waving a numbered paddle to attract the auctioneer's attention. Bidding is, unless otherwise stated, per dozen bottles.

Advance commission bids form a substantial proportion of bids received. Whereas on average nearly two-thirds of lots used to go under the hammer in the saleroom itself, that proportion dropped to only about a third in the intensely international fine-wine market of the late 1990s. Commission bids are treated in exactly the same way as bids in the room. Successful bidders obtain their lot at one increment above the underbidder. In the event of two commission bids of the same amount, it is the one received first that takes precedence.

A.H.L.R.

Aurore, otherwise known as Seibel 5279, a French HYBRID once widely planted in the United States. Adaptable and productive, it ripens early but its wines are of no great distinction.

Ausbruch, famous wine style of AUSTRIA, a speciality of the town of RUST on the Neusiedlersee in Burgenland. Ausbruch is a close etymological relative of Aszú, a term commonly used in TOKAJI, where Hungary's most famous sweet wine is made. Ausbruch was traditionally made by adding the juice of freshly picked grapes to that of, mainly FURMINT, grapes concentrated by NOBLE ROT, whose incidence is encouraged by the proximity of the shallow lake and the warm climate of the Pannonian plain. Modern Austrian wine law requires Ausbruch to be made entirely from overripe, naturally shrivelled, or BOTRYTIZED grapes which reach a MUST WEIGHT of 138 OECHSLE, but Furmint, subject to a current revival in Austria, is so far only rarely grown.

Auslese, one of the riper Prädikats in the QMP quality wine category defined by the GERMAN WINE LAW. Auslese means literally 'selected harvest' and, from the 1994 vintage, the grapes should have been picked at least a week after a preliminary picking of less ripe grapes. Specific minimum MUST WEIGHTS are laid down for each combination of vine variety and region and the tendency is to increase them. At their best, these are sweet, often BOTRYTIZED, wines which can be sold at lower prices than the even riper and considerably rarer BEERENAUSLESE and TROCKENBEERENAUSLESE Prädikats. (Auslese is usually better dedicated to SWEET WINES than TROCKEN as the resulting alcohol can be so high as to be out of BALANCE, and in any case NOBLE ROT character sits uneasily with dry wines.) Auslesen made from most of the new GERMAN CROSSINGS should be treated with suspicion as they rarely have the ACIDITY to balance the sweetness, but Riesling Auslesen can be some of Germany's finest and most characteristic wines, best savoured without food. They can last for decades.

See also AUSTRIA.

Ausone, Château, minuscule but exceptionally fine estate on the edge of the town of ST-ÉMILION. Edouard Dubois-Challon raised the reputation of the château to the leading position in St-Émilion up to the 1920s, when it was challenged by Ch CHEVAL-BLANC, the only other château to be ranked 'A' in the official CLASSIFICATION of St-Émilion in 1955.

In the late 1990s, Alain Vauthier took control of, and completely renovated, the extraordinary cellars in limestone caves originally excavated to provide stone for building the town. The wine itself is also being dramatically modernized, not least because Michel ROLLAND is consultant.

The vineyard consists of a mere 7 ha/18 acres—50 per cent MERLOT vines and 50 per cent CABERNET FRANC—on the steep slopes of the Côtes (see ST-ÉMILION) that run along the right bank of the DORDOGNE just below the town. Production of Ausone averages 2,000 cases.

E.P.-R. & J.Ro.

Australia has moved into the top 10 wine producers in the world, averaging 7 million hl/185 million gal a year (an increase of more than 50 per cent in the last five years). It makes every one of the major wine styles from aromatic, dry white table wine through to wines fashioned in the image of vintage port. Some of its wines—the unwooded Semillons of the Hunter Valley, the fortified Muscats and Tokays of north-east Victoria—have no direct equivalent elsewhere, but overall the wines manage to be at once distinctively Australian yet fit easily into the world scene.

Over 1,000 wineries are spread through every state and territory; there is even a vineyard at Alice Springs in the hot, arid Northern Territory. Most of the wineries are small; 80 per cent of the annual crush comes from the four largest companies, headed by the vast SOUTHCORP with a market share of 40 per cent.

As in California, over 700 of those small wineries have come into existence since the late 1960s, offering weekend or retirement occupations for people from all walks of life, notably doctors and lawyers. In typical Australian style, however, the owners have frequently appointed themselves as wine-makers. Nevertheless, perhaps due to the trickle-down effect of the renowned Australian Wine Research Institute, standards are extremely high.

The Australian wine-show system (see COMPETITIONS) has also played a major role in promoting technical excellence and in shaping style. Each state has a series of regional shows, but the most important are the capital-city shows, typically attracting around 2,000 entries. The trophies and medals awarded to the more successful exhibitors are used extensively in marketing and promotion, and are accepted as reliable indicators of quality by retailers and consumers alike. But the greater long-term benefit has been for the wine-maker judges, drawn from the leading wineries and schooled by chairmen such as Len Evans.

The lessons of the show ring have been reinforced by the well-known penchant Australians have for travel. Indeed, Australia spawned the so-called FLYING WINE-MAKERS, a group of oenological guns for hire who follow the vintage around the world. On a less formal basis, many Australian wine-makers have made a point of travelling and working overseas, principally in Europe. See AUSTRALIAN INFLUENCE.

Add this experience to the technological base, take in the effect of the sunny Australian climate, and allow for the surge in plantings of such popular grape varieties as Chardonnay and Cabernet Sauvignon, and it is not hard to see why Australian exports increased twentyfold between 1984 and 1998, and at least a further 50 per cent by the year 2000. It is not too fanciful to suggest that the wines have an openness, a confident, user-friendly style which reflects the national character (and climate). Australian wine-makers have opted to preserve as much as possible of the flavour of the grape, yet to do so with a delicacy of touch, producing intensely fruity white wines and soft, mouth-filling red wines which appeal to the heart as much as to the mind. In so doing they have (willingly) sacrificed structural complexity at the altar of simple fruit flavour.

Fifty per cent of all Australian wine sold locally is packaged in the ubiquitous wine 'cask' (see BOXES), usually in a 4.5-l (1.2-gal) configuration. It should come as no surprise to find that Australia has the highest annual per capita wine consumption in the English-speaking world, peaking at 21.6 l in 1986 before declining to a low of 17.6 l in 1991. It has since risen to between 18 and 19 l, reflecting offsetting trends in 750-ml quality-wine consumption (rising) and cask-quality consumption (falling).

Climate

With a land mass similar to that of the United States of America, winter snowfields larger than those of Switzerland, and with viticulture in every state, one-line descriptions of the Australian climate are hazardous. For all that, there are two basic weather patterns, one affecting Western Australia, South Australia, Victoria, and Tasmania (the southern states), the other governing Queensland and New South Wales.

The southern states experience a winter–spring rainfall pattern, with a dry summer and early autumn. Daytime temperatures typically range between 25 °C/77 °F and 35 °C/95 °F.

There is a less profound maritime influence than in California; the sea temperature is warmer, and the diurnal temperature ranges are less. The resultant even accumulation of heat in the premium wine regions is seen by Australian researchers to be a major factor in promoting wine quality (and, more controversially, style).

Because of the lack of summer rainfall, IRRIGATION is considered as important for quality as for quantity. In the much hotter and drier Riverland of South Australia, Victoria, and New South Wales, it becomes as essential as it is in California's San Joaquin Valley, and is unashamedly used to boost production.

The other, more northerly weather system derives from the tropics. It provides a more even rainfall pattern, higher temperatures, and higher humidity. The Hunter Valley is prone to receive rather too much of its annual rainfall during HARVEST, only to suffer the subsequent dual burden of winter and spring drought. Its redeeming feature is the humidity and after-noon cloud cover.

Geography

Vine-growing in Australia is concentrated in the south-eastern corner of this vast country. For more detail, see under the state or territory names, which are, in declining order of importance as grape growers, SOUTH AUSTRALIA, NEW SOUTH WALES, VICTORIA, WESTERN AUSTRALIA, TASMANIA, and QUEENSLAND. Considerable quantities of grapes and wine are trucked over state boundaries, however, for blending and bottling. European Union laws demand that VARIETAL wines, labelled with a grape variety, be labelled with an officially recognized region. **South Eastern Australia** was created for this purpose and is a vast area encompassing all three of the most important wine states, including the important irrigated regions RIVERLAND and Murrumbidgee Irrigation Area, or RIVERINA. This somewhat vague description is one of the most common on Australian wine labels in export markets.

Wine-making

The typical medium-sized modern Australian winery is comprehensively equipped, especially in comparison with its counterpart in Europe. The winery will routinely work 24 hours a day through the six to eight weeks of harvest using two shifts. It is this efficient use of equipment, and the underlying technology, which differentiates Australian wine-makers (and their wines) from wine-makers (and wines) in most other parts of the world.

The basic aims are the maximum preservation of varietal fruit flavour, and an essentially soft and supple structure for wood-matured wines, both white and red. The majority of white wines are made without MALOLACTIC FERMENTATION, and are bottled within six to nine months after the harvest. ACIDIFICATION is routine.

Extended MACERATION after FERMENTATION is less commonly practised than in Europe or the United States, and is bypassed altogether with classic wines such as Penfolds Grange, which, like a significant proportion of fine Australian red wines, is pressed and put into barrel while still actively fermenting. The Australian belief is that post-fermentation maceration initially extracts more TANNINS, which entails extending the maceration to soften those tannins, and that this process dulls the fruit aroma and flavour.

French OAK is preferred for top-quality white wines, for Pinot Noir, and much of the Cabernet Sauvignon produced. American oak is widely used for SHIRAZ, Cabernet-Shiraz blends, and for some Cabernet Sauvignon. For lesser-quality wines, the use of OAK CHIPS (in conjunction with older barrels) is becoming increasingly widespread.

Vine varieties

The following are the country's most widely planted varieties, red wine varieties first, in descending order of volume of wine produced.

Shiraz For long Australia's premier red wine grape in terms of area planted, Shiraz is at long last respectable too. It is grown in virtually every wine region, responding generously to the varying imperatives of TERROIR and climate. The variety is identical to the SYRAH of France and has a long Australian history. During the period in which Cabernet Sauvignon came into vogue, the familiarity of Shiraz led to its being treated with a thoroughly undeserved degree of contempt. However, the old non-irrigated plantings of the Barossa Valley (producing spicy Rhône-like wines) and the traditional Hunter Valley wines (which become silky with age) led to a surge of popularity in both domestic and export markets in the late 1980s.

Cabernet Sauvignon Although Cabernet is second to Shiraz in terms of plantings, it leads it in terms of both reputation and geographical spread. The thick-skinned small berries stand up to rain, and impart distinctive varietal flavour in almost all growing conditions. Partly due to the excess demand of the 1960s and 1970s, the blending of Cabernet and Shiraz—or, more probably, Shiraz with a little Cabernet—became widespread, but with a few notable exceptions the trend for premium wines is towards the traditional Bordeaux blend with MERLOT and CABERNET FRANC. The rate of increase in the planting of these latter two varieties exceeds all others, and varietal Merlots, uncommon at the start of the 1990s, are proliferating.

Grenache Until the mid 1960s, 90 per cent of Australia's red wine was fashioned from the three Rhône varieties: Shiraz, Grenache, and Mourvèdre. Then Cabernet Sauvignon and its Bordeaux handmaidens started to make inroads, followed in due course—though initially less convincingly—by Pinot Noir. Shiraz became less fashionable, Grenache and Mourvèdre even less so. Just when it seemed these varieties would cease to be at all significant, the worldwide interest in the Rhône varieties and wine styles reversed the trend. Century-old, dry-farmed, BUSH-vine Grenache in McLaren Vale (especially) and the Barossa Valley is now in great demand for table wine (previously most went into fortified wines). But, as ever, that portion of the crop produced from high-yielding, irrigated Riverland vineyards will make bland, lollyish wines.

Mourvèdre (often called Mataro) is used in precisely the same fashion as Grenache, and has enjoyed the same recovery.

Pinot Noir Much is used in making sparkling wine; only in a few cool regions around Melbourne, Victoria, the Adelaide Hills, Albany in Western Australia, and Tasmania does it produce table wine of genuine, at times exhilarating, distinction.

Sultana It depends on the exigencies of the vintage as to how much of the Sultana crop of relatively flavourless white grapes is made into wine, how much is sold fresh, and how much is dried. However, not infrequently more Sultana is vinified than any other white grape variety. It is grown entirely in the Riverlands and is destined for the cheapest table and FOR-TIFIED wine. See both SULTANA and THOMPSON SEEDLESS.

Muscat Gordo Blanco Australia's MUSCAT OF ALEXANDRIA is the white-grape equivalent of Grenache. It provides a more positively fla-voured wine than does Sultana.

Chardonnay In Australia as elsewhere in the world, Chardonnay is seen as the grape of today and of tomorrow. Plantings have soared from a negligible level in 1970. It is grown in every wine region, bending as much to the wills of the viticulturists and wine-makers as to the influence of climate and terroir. The style varies from simple to complex and quality from mediocre to excellent, parameters increasingly recognized by a widening range of prices. Market demand engendered blends with Semillon, Colombard, and almost any other white grape variety in the 1980s.

Riesling The great grape of GERMANY, trad-itionally known as Rhine Riesling in Australia, finally yielded pride of place to Chardonnay among premium white grapes in 1992. Its chief home is South Australia; its qualitative home-away-from-home the Lower Great Southern region of Western Australia. Most is made dry or near dry (less than 7.5 g/l of RESIDUAL SUGAR), producing a very distinctive Australian style which is better understood (and appreciated) within the country than outside it. Small quan-tities of delicious BOTRYTIZED Riesling are made which are of world quality but (as with those of Germany and California) have a minuscule, if devoted, following.

Semillon Semillon (rarely written Sémillon in the New World) is Australia's traditional coun-terpart to Shiraz. As with Shiraz and Cabernet, Semillon is emerging from the shadow of Char-donnay, and production is increasing. Classic Hunter Semillon is made without the use of new OAK, relying on extended BOTTLE AGEING to weave its magic. Latter-day variations incorp-orate BARREL FERMENTATION and BARREL MAT-URATION, or blending with Sauvignon Blanc.

Sauvignon Blanc is another recent arrival on the scene, essentially since 1980, and pro-duction is rapidly increasing, spurred on by competition from NEW ZEALAND.

Colombard The ability of this variety to retain ACIDITY has the same attractions in the warmer regions of Australia as in California. It is used chiefly as a blend component for cheap GENERIC table wines.

Other Australian vine variety specialities include the red crossing TARRANGO and a richly historic legacy of Iberian varieties (including, notably, VERDELHO) that is rapidly being replaced with more fashionable or productive varieties.

Labelling laws

A common geographical designation found on lower-priced wines is the barely helpful South Eastern Australia, which takes in part of Queensland, all of New South Wales, all of Vic-toria, and that part of South Australia in which it is possible to grow grapes. In practice, it often signifies a wine made from fruit grown in areas as unglamorous as RIVERLAND and/or RIVERINA.

Australia has had the major components of an APPELLATION system since 1963, initially through the framework of state legislation, but since 1987 effectively embodied in federal law, and since 1990 actively enforced by the official Wine and Brandy Corporation through the Label Integrity Programme (LIP).

This is designed to ensure that where a variety or a region is specified, at least 85 per cent of the wine is of that variety and/or of that region; that 85 per cent is of the stated vintage; and, if more than one variety or region are specified, that they are listed in descending order. Thus Cabernet-Shiraz means the wine has more Cabernet Sauvignon grapes than Shiraz; Shiraz-Cabernet the reverse.

By 1996 each state had divided itself into viticultural zones: for example, New South Wales has eight, Victoria six, South Australia eight, and Western Australia five. The division into regions has taken far longer, and has been fraught with far more argument, than the authorities' worst dreams could have envis-aged. By mid 1998, 19 regions had been finally determined; there were three interim deter-minations; some work had been carried out on a further 25 regions; while another 11 or so had still to take any steps towards registration under the legislation.

Wine trade organization

The Australian wine market is dominated by the SOUTHCORP group and a few other large companies. The majority of the largest wineries in the country are in South Australia. In the Barossa Valley are Penfolds, Orlando, Seppelt (also part of Southcorp) in the first rank; Wolf Blass, Yalumba, Saltram, Peter Lehmann, and Krondorf in the second rank. BRL HARDY is the amalgamated Thomas Hardy/Berri Renmano group spanning the South Australian River-land and the Southern Vales. The notable absentee is Lindemans, another Southcorp company, which is based at Karadoc in the Riverlands of Victoria not far from the South Australian border.

The sale of wine within Australia is relatively simple, and notably free of the restraints which apply in the UNITED STATES. Movement between the states is unhindered, and wine producers can sell to whomever they wish (distributors, retailers, or the public), wherever they wish.

J.H.

Australian influence on wine production in the 1990s is difficult to overestimate. When the chips are finally counted, Australia will be credited with having had an enormous influence on the wine world of the late 20th century. Its VITICULTURISTS have pioneered sophisticated CANOPY MANAGEMENT. Its wine-makers now travel the world—especially the northern hemisphere, where the HARVEST conveniently takes place during their quiet time—quietly infiltrating all manner of wineries with Australian technology, obsession with HYGIENE, and record WATER usage (see FLYING WINE-MAKERS).

Austria, increasingly important wine-producing country in central Europe with an annual production of about 3 million hl/79 million gal, often more than a third as much as GERMANY to the north, with which it shares many grape varieties, wine styles, and labelling customs. The wines themselves are more varied and full bodied than the German norm, however, often enlivened by characteristics shared with vineyards just across Austria's borders with, respectively, the CZECH REPUBLIC, SLOVAKIA, HUNGARY, and SLOVENIA. The majority of wines are white, dry, and VARIETAL, but there is also a keen appreciation of geographical variation, particularly among Austria's many fine-wine enthusiasts. Widespread adulteration on the part of certain merchants, resulting in a major wine scandal in 1985, led to major reforms in wine law and a determination to emphasize quality at the expense of quantity.

Wine-making

Dry wines with both EXTRACT and pronounced ACIDITY are fashionable with connoisseurs even more markedly in Austria than Germany so that the most sought-after wines are those labelled TROCKEN (dry). All but the great sweet wines of Burgenland are fermented to almost

complete dryness, with a RESIDUAL SUGAR level under 4 g/l (increased to a maximum level of 9 g/l in 1994 to bring it into line with EU labelling requirements).

Most wineries are well equipped and use stainless-steel or large old wooden vats for fermentation and ageing. Bottling usually takes place in the spring following the vintage.

The most obvious wine-making development of the 1980s was the introduction of MALOLACTIC FERMENTATION for red wines. Producers in Burgenland and Styria of a wide range of red wines, and many of those who produce Chardonnay, or Morillon, routinely use BARREL MATURATION and, for some fuller-bodied white wines, BARREL FERMENTATION.

Austrian specialities include HEURIGER wine, G'spritzer (Heuriger wine mixed with an equal quantity of sparkling soda water), Schilcher (see Weststeiermark below), and Sturm, still-fermenting grape must, a popular, sweet, cloudy drink in Austria at harvest time.

Despite the fashion for dry wines, MUST WEIGHT measurement is the key to wine labelling (see below) and wine quality in Austria, as it is in Germany.

Vine varieties

Austria's varietal mix reflects the country's geographical position between Germany on the one hand and Hungary and Slovenia on the other. Austria's most planted variety is a national speciality, however, GRÜNER VELT-LINER, which by 1995 was planted in more than 36 per cent of Austria's total vineyard area. It is particularly important in lower Austria, Vienna, and, to a lesser extent, Burgenland. Second most important variety WELSCHRIESLING can produce sweet wines of great quality in Burgenland, and many perfectly respectable dry wines too, notably in Styria. MÜLLER-THURGAU is fast declining in importance but was still the country's fourth most planted vine variety in the mid 1990s, even if rarely producing wines of real excitement. The indigenous red wine grape ZWEIGELT is now the country's third most planted variety and is found in all districts. Almost as much land is planted with the central European red grape varieties Blauer PORTUGIESER and BLAU-FRÄNKISCH, however, with the former predominating in lower Austria and the latter in Burgenland. Weissburgunder (PINOT BLANC) is another widely planted white wine variety. CHARDONNAY has established itself as more than a fashionable novelty in most districts, and has been grown and known as Morillon (an old CHABLIS synonym) in Styria for more than a century. The specifically Austrian NEUBURGER was a speciality of Neusiedlersee, Thermenregion, and the Wachau, where RIESLING reigns, as it does in Kamptal, Kremstal, and Vienna. MUSCAT OTTONEL is Austria's most commonly planted Muscat variety (although the superior (Gelber) Muskateller, planted in Styria, enjoys more respect). Both TRAMINER and GEWÜRZTRAMINER are widely planted, if often underestimated, while PINOT GRIS (known, as in Germany, both as Grauer Burgunder and Ruländer) is grown mainly in the southern wine districts, as is Sauvignon Blanc (sometimes still called Muskat-Sylvaner). ZIERFANDLER (or Spätrot) and ROTGIPFLER are the curious white wine grape specialities of Gumpoldskirchen in Thermenregion, while Blauer WILDBACHER is a light-red grape grown almost exclusively in western Styria. CABERNET SAUVIGNON is a relatively new arrival, concentrated in Burgenland, but Blauer Burgunder (PINOT NOIR) is relatively well established, if on a limited scale, in lower Austria and Burgenland. ST-LAURENT is a useful variant of it particularly well adapted to conditions in lower Austria and Burgenland. Other less common vine varieties include FRÜHROTER VELTLINER and Roter Veltliner (see GRÜNER VELTLINER), BOUVIER, GOLDBURGER, SYLVANER, Sämling 88 (see SCHEUREBE), and FURMINT.

Wine regions

Almost all of Austria's vineyards are, like most of the country's agriculture, in the east of the country, far from the mountains—although Styria's vineyards are in the Southern Alps, on inclines up to 60 per cent and at altitudes of up to 650 m/2,130 ft. The boundaries and names of the country's wine regions have been reorganized twice since 1985, most recently in 1995.

Nearly 6 in every 10 bottles produced come from Niederösterreich, or lower Austria, on the fertile Danube plain in the north-eastern corner of the country. Lower Austria includes, in declining order of the amount of wine produced, the districts of Weinviertel, Kamptal, Donauland, Thermenregion, Kremstal, the highly respected Wachau, Carnuntum, and Traisental.

Burgenland, on the Hungarian border in the far east, makes more than a third of all Austrian wine, and a far higher proportion of Austria's best reds and sweet whites. Neusiedlersee on the eastern shores of the eponymous lake (or 'See') is by far the most important district, followed by Neusiedlersee-Hügelland on the western shores. Some wine is also produced in Mittelburgenland, Austria's red-wine corner, and Südburgenland in the middle and south of the region respectively.

Styria is a mountainous viticultural district with more in common with SLOVENIA over the border than with the rest of Austria. It is officially divided into south, south-east, and west (Süd-, Süd-Ost-, and West- respectively) districts, which combine to produce less than five per cent of an average Austrian vintage.

The city of Vienna, or Wien, is given its own status as a wine region, climatically a particularly favoured enclave within lower Austria.

Weinviertel Austria's largest wine district, the so-called 'wine quarter', is also the least distinguished. Much of the land is flat, fertile, and very dry. The region typically produces relatively light, dry, white wines from Austria's signature Grüner Veltliner grape produced at yields higher than the national average. The Müller-Thurgau and Welschriesling vines common here also help to bolster the volume produced. Some fine Weissburgunder (PINOT BLANC) is produced here, however, around villages such as Retz, Röschitz, and Hollabrunn in the west and Falkenstein, Poysdorf, Wolkersdorf, Matzen, and Mannersdorf in the east. Mailberg, almost due north of Vienna, has earned itself a particular reputation for its confident red wines, notably from the Malteser estate managed by LENZ MOSER, arguably the wine company best known outside Austria. Much of Austria's sparkling wine, or SEKT, is produced in the north-east part along the Brünner Strasse, the road north from Vienna to Brno in Moravia.

Kamptal This district, named after the river Kamp and centred on the important wine town of Langenlois, produces some of Austria's most concentrated Grüner Veltliner. Some fine Rieslings are also made here. The most famous Riesling site is probably the Zöbinger Heiligenstein. The district is also associated with a number of Austria's most innovative wine-makers (Jurtschitsch, Retzl, Schloss Gobelsburg, and Bründlmayer, for example), keen to join the international wine market by playing by the same rules.

Donauland This district stretches east along the Danube from just east of Krems to KLOSTERNEUBURG, which is both Austria's leading viticultural and horticultural school, and the country's largest vineyard owner. The soils of Wagram favour Grüner Veltliner. Other better-known villages in this western part are Kirchberg and Fels. Vine varieties planted are as in Vienna.

Thermenregion This is the relatively new name for the district centred on the once world-famous village of Gumpoldskirchen. This is the warmest part of lower Austria and is also one of the most distinctive wine regions in the world, dependent for its best wines on two specially adapted grape varieties found nowhere else (and here only in very limited quantity), ZIERFANDLER (or Spätrot) and ROTGIPFLER. Wines made from Spätrot-Rotgipfler grown in Gumpoldskirchen and ripened to AUSLESE level are rich, spicy, and potentially long-lived whites in quite a different style from the lean raciness evinced by the famous Rieslings of the Wachau, or even the BOTRYTIZED sweet wines of Burgenland. Neuburger is also planted here as well as the full range of Austria's red wine varieties. Other wine villages in the region include Traiskirchen, Baden, Tattendorf, Sooss, and Bad Vöslau.

Kremstal district is centred on the beautiful twin towns of Krems and Stein. Clay and limestone in the area east of Krems seem to imbue the finest Veltliners with a density all of their own. The headquarters of Lenz Moser is in Rohrendorf. Leading producers include Malat, Nigl, and Undhof-Salomon.

Wachau Austria's westernmost wine district is one of lower Austria's smallest. It is also the one of which many Austrian connoisseurs are most proud, however, on account of the elegance and refinement of its dry Rieslings and Grüner Veltliners, made from terraces sculpted from the steep banks of the river Danube as it flows through some of this beautiful country's most beautiful scenery. The region produces fine white wines with high levels of both EXTRACT and ACIDITY—Austria's (more consistent) answer to German RHEINGAU perhaps. As in the Rheingau, most of the vineyards are on the steeper northern bank of the broad river, and presumably benefit from some reflected sunlight. More than any other Austrian wine region, the Wachau is marked by wide variations between day and night temperatures, which helps to preserve aroma and acidity. Vineyards in the heartland of this region, which styles itself Vinea Wachau Nobilis Districtus, range hardly more than 20 km/12 miles as the crow flies from Schwallenbach in the west, downstream through Spitz, Weissenkirchen, Dürnstein (where the admirable and important co-operative Freie Weingärtner Wachau is based), and Loiben to Mautern. Some of these grapes are vinified by producers in the town of Krems just over the border in Kremstal, but respected family estates such as Alzinger, F. X. Pichler, Prager, Knoll, Jamek, and Hirtzberger which did much to create the Vinea Wachau association and affirm the district's commitment to quality in 1983 are all based in the medieval wine villages of the Wachau itself. The association has established three quality levels of its own for its distinctively racy dry white wines. Steinfeder is the lightest, while Federspiel wines have higher must weights and alcoholic strength. Smaragd wines are the most concentrated and alcoholic. In very ripe years, sweet wines may also be made, and some producers are beginning to make BOTRYTIZED wines.

Carnuntum This recently created district stretches east along the north bank of the Danube from the eastern outskirts of Vienna towards the Slovakian border. The viticultural centre is the tiny village of Göttlesbrunn. The region benefits from a MESOCLIMATE influenced by the Neusiedlersee and river Danube nearby. Red grape varieties are increasingly planted with fruity Zweigelt predominating. Leading producers include Glatzer and Pittnauer.

Traisental The vineyards of lower Austria's smallest wine district are situated on both sides of the river Traisen, north of lower Austria's capital St Pölten. The right bank generally produces softer, broader whites than the left bank, which produces racy wines comparable with those of the famous Wachau. Neumayer is the leading producer.

Neusiedlersee The shallow lake of Neusiedlersee, surrounded by sandy marshes, is the natural focus for Austria's Burgenland. Mainly sandy, rich soils produce some very fine, full-bodied Weissburgunder (Pinot Blanc) together with Traminer and, especially, Welschriesling of all levels of sweetness, from dry and fiery to late-harvest TROCKENBEERENAUSLESE, often superior to that produced anywhere else in the world. The lake and its surrounding marshes encourage the formation of NOBLE ROT so that very sweet wines are a speciality of the lakeshore vineyards and, in the best vintages, have a balance and structure that can rival the world's finest sweet wines. Strohwein (straw wines) and EISWEIN are local sweet-wine specialities. Some of Austria's more ambitious red wines come, in small quantities, from Neusiedlersee. ZWEIGELT is the most common red wine vine variety but Cabernet Sauvignon is encroaching. Apetlon, Neusiedl, Podersdorf, Frauenkirchen, Halbturn, Illmitz, and Gols are some of the more important wine villages. Some of the more dynamic producers include Kracher (world famous for his botrytized wines), Stiegelmar, Umathum, Heinrich, Nittnaus, and hypercreative Willi Opitz, whose inventions include special Italianate bottles and Schilfwein, or reed wine, from grapes dried on reeds from the lake (see DRIED-GRAPE WINES). The Pannonischer Reigen is one of the most successful wine-producer associations in Austria.

Neusiedlersee-Hügelland This is the name given to the wine region on the western shore of the lake. The range of wines produced, from full-bodied dry and very sweet whites to increasingly 'international' reds, is very similar to that of the Neusiedlersee region on the opposite shore, with the addition of the famous sweet white AUSBRUCH wines from the town of Rust almost directly on the lake. Specialists in this historic wine style include Feiler, Landauer, Schandl, and Wenzel. There are many family wine holdings here dedicated to both quality and innovation and it is not unusual for the likes of the Triebaumer brothers and Anton Kollwentz at the Römerhof estate to make wines as varied as a Sauvignon Blanc, Chardonnay, Welschriesling Eiswein, Cabernet Sauvignon, and perhaps an oak-aged Blaufränkisch. Welschriesling, Pinot Blanc, and Neuburger are also common in this district.

Mittelburgenland The central Burgenland district, immediately south of the Neusiedlersee-Hügelland, extends to the Hungarian border, sheltered by hills. With its warm climate, it has long been associated with red grapes, which constitute about 70 per cent of those grown. Mittelburgenland has its own association, the Verband Blaufränkischland, dedicated to

extracting maximum quality from this lively eastern European red grape variety. But the district has more recently become a hotbed of experimentation and increasing sophistication. Deep-coloured, intensely flavoured and often oak-aged wines are made in quantity from Blaufränkisch grapes as well as from various combinations of Blaufränkisch and Zweigelt with St Laurent, Pinot Noir, and, particularly, Cabernet Sauvignon by producers such as Gesellmann and Igler based in Deutschkreutz. Neckenmarkt and Horitschon are the other important areas where several successful co-operatives are based.

Südburgenland Southern Burgenland sprawls along the Hungarian border between Styria and Mittelburgenland and producers have remained largely unaffected by fashions in wine-making and consumer taste. Best-known wines are Blaufränkisch made in the Eisenberg area and dry Welschrieslings from around Rechnitz. Uhudler is a curious speciality of the far south, well removed from the bureaucrats of Vienna, made from a wide range of American HYBRID vines. Krutzler is probably the best producer of the region, specializing in red wines in which Blaufränkisch plays an important part.

Südsteiermark The wines of Styria, representing hardly five per cent of Austria's total production, became particularly fashionable after the 1985 scandal; since Styrian wines are quintessentially dry and fragrant, no one had been tempted to adulterate them with diethylene glycol. The smallest of the Styrian districts, southern Styria around Leibnitz and some of it within sight of Slovenia, is the most important in terms of wine production. The region has long cultivated two of the most popular 'international' vine varieties, Sauvignon Blanc (occasionally still called Muskat-Silvaner) and Chardonnay (here usually called Morillon). Welschriesling, Pinot Blanc (called Klevner here), and Gelber Muskateller (MUSCAT BLANC À PETITS GRAINS) are also grown and all of these varieties can produce distinctively crisp yet full and aromatic white wines, an Austrian answer to Alsace but with more obvious acidity. Sattlerhof, Erich and Walter Polz, Alois Gross, Lackner Tinnacher, and Tement are some of the best-known producers.

Süd-Oststeiermark South-east Styria is a vast area of widely dispersed vineyards, notably on the volcanic soils of Klöch, where Traminer is a speciality. Welschriesling, Pinot Blanc, Ruländer, Chardonnay, and Sauvignon Blanc are also cultivated in this relatively warm area.

Weststeiermark Western Styria has its own extremely local speciality, Schilcher rosé made from lightly pressed Blauer Wildbacher grapes, known only here and, to a much more limited extent, in the VENETO.

Vienna Vienna boasts of being the only capital city with a serious wine industry within its boundaries (although PARIS could at one time have made the same claim). Strict laws protect the city's 600 ha of vines. Attractively youthful, relatively simple wines, typically made from Grüner Veltliner, are served to locals and tourists alike in HEURIGER (traditional wine taverns) in outlying suburbs. Vienna also produces wines of real quality and ageing potential, however, notably those made from Riesling and various Pinot grapes grown on vineyards on the slopes of the Nussberg and the Kahlenberg at Döbling, and those of Bisamberg on the left bank. Red grapes are increasingly important. Traditional customs are maintained in many less ambitious vineyards still cultivated with a mixture of grape varieties which are vinified together and called Gemischter Satz. Franz Mayer and Wieninger are two of Vienna's best producers.

Wine labelling

Wine laws drawn up since 1985 are some of the strictest in the world. They share much of the nomenclature of the GERMAN WINE LAW but standards in general and minimum MUST WEIGHTS in particular are higher. Qualitätswein is a genuinely exclusive category, for example, and Kabinett is regarded as a subcategory of Qualitätswein rather than a fully fledged Prädikatswein, as only Spätlese, Auslese, Strohwein, Eiswein, Beerenauslese, Ausbruch and Trockenbeerenauslese are in Austria. All Austrian wines should have a red-and-white-striped 'Banderole' around the neck or on top of the cork, which must be purchased by the producer to ensure that official quotas are not breached and to provide some sort of tracking system.

Wines are also labelled according to sugar content, the permitted limits having been increased. A trocken wine must have a residual sugar level of no more than 9 g/l, a halbtrocken wine 9 to 12 g/l, a medium-sweet, halbsüss or lieblich wine 12 to 45 g/l, and a sweet or süss wine more than 45 g/l. (The term extra trocken may be used for a wine with less than 4 g/l, the former standard for trocken.) Wines carrying the name of a grape variety or a vintage date must be composed of at least 85 per cent of that grape variety and 85 per cent of wine from that vintage.

Tafelwein The bottom rung, and the great majority of all wine produced, is represented by TAFELWEIN, for which grapes must achieve a must weight of 51° Oechsle. No Tafelwein other than BERGWEIN, wine produced on steeper slopes, may be sold in regular bottles. This is by far the most common wine category.

Landwein One step up from Tafelwein, LANDWEIN must be made from certain specified grape varieties, must reach 68° Oechsle, and be sold either in 25-cl (9-fl oz), 1-l, or 2-l bottles. ALCOHOLIC STRENGTH must be less than 11.5 per cent and residual sugar cannot exceed 6 g/l. Only about five per cent of all Austrian wine qualifies as Landwein.

Qualitätswein This is the name both of a category which includes the subcategory Kabinett (below) and of a subcategory itself. To qualify as Qualitätswein, the wine must come from a single district specified on the label and must demonstrate the characteristics of the recognized grape variety from which it is made. The must weight must reach 73° Oechsle and the wine must have nine per cent alcohol. As in Germany, wines are tasted, analysed, and awarded a code that is the Austrian equivalent of Germany's AP NUMBER.

Kabinett Regarded as merely a Qualitätswein in Austria, Kabinett wines, like Prädikatswein below, may nevertheless not be chaptalized. Oechsle levels must reach 84° and residual sugar cannot exceed 9 g/l.

Spätlese All Prädikatswein must be from one wine district, must be vintage dated, and must have its must weight officially certified. As in Germany, no Prädikatswein may be chaptalized. No Austrian Spätlese may be sweetened by added SÜSSRESERVE; all alcohol and residual sugar must be the result of natural grape sugars. A Spätlese must be made from fully-ripe grapes picked at a minimum must weight of 94° Oechsle.

Auslese Must weight must be at least 105° Oechsle and any unripe or unhealthy grapes must be excluded.

Strohwein 'Straw wine' made from overripe grapes with a must weight of at least 127°

Oechsle which are dried on straw or reeds for at least three months (see DRIED-GRAPE WINES).

Eiswein 'Ice wine' should be made from grapes with a must weight of 127° Oechsle, picked and pressed while still frozen (see ICE WINE).

Beerenauslese Sweet wine made from grapes that are affected by noble rot, or simply overripe, with a must weight of at least 127° Oechsle.

Ausbruch A speciality of Rust in Neusiedlersee-Hügelland, made from grapes with a must weight of at least 139° Oechsle that are naturally shrivelled, overripe, and affected by noble rot. See also AUSBRUCH.

Trockenbeerenauslese Very sweet wine made from grapes with a must weight of at least 156° Oechsle that are naturally shrivelled, overripe and affected by noble rot.

Auvergne, Côtes d', VDQS which is administratively considered part of the greater LOIRE region but these Massif Central vineyards, around Clermont-Ferrand, are in fact closer to the vineyards of the northern RHÔNE than they are to the river Loire itself. From mainly Gamay and some Chardonnay vines, light reds, pinks, and whites are made in quantity, with considerable skill, from some of the many small enterprises here. The names of the communes Boudes, Chanturgue, Châteaugay, Corent, and Madargues may be appended to Côtes d'Auvergne on wine labels. Most wines are consumed locally; none is expensive.

Auxerre, Côtes d' produce light-red and white wines made in the mould of light BURGUNDY and CHABLIS respectively. The zone includes Chitry, Coulanges-la-Vineuse, Épineuil, and Irancy. They may all append their names to the BOURGOGNE appellation.

Auxerrois is both the name used for the black-berried MALBEC in CAHORS, where it is the dominant vine variety, and the name of a relatively important white-berried variety in Alsace. And as if that were not confusing enough, Auxerrois Gris is a synonym for PINOT GRIS in Alsace, while Chardonnay, before it became so famous, was once known as Auxerrois Blanc in the Moselle—as distinct from Auxerrois Blanc de Laquenexy which is the variety today called Auxerrois in north-east France (including Alsace) and LUXEMBOURG.

There are still minuscule plantings of Auxerrois in the Loire but today it is most important in Alsace, the French Moselle (including Côtes de TOUL) and Luxembourg, where it is most valued, particularly for its low acidity. If yields are suppressed, which they rarely are, the variety can produce excitingly rich wines in both Moselle regions that are worth ageing until they achieve a bouquet with a honeyed note like that of mature Chablis, the wine which today could be described as 'from Auxerre' or, in French, Auxerrois.

Auxerrois is Alsace's *éminence grise*, covering considerably more Alsace vineyard than any one of the three true PINOTS planted there. Rarely seen on a label, it produces slightly flabby, broad wines which are blended into many a PINOT BLANC. Auxerrois can add substance if not subtlety to over-produced or under-ripened Pinot Blanc. Many Alsace wine enthusiasts have never heard of Auxerrois but Alsace wine labelled 'Pinot Blanc' could contain nothing but Auxerrois, which is also a major ingredient in EDELZWICKER.

Auxey-Duresses, a village in Burgundy producing medium-priced red and white wines not dissimilar to neighbouring VOLNAY and MEURSAULT respectively, although more austere in style. The vineyards, which include those of the hamlets of Petit Auxey and Melin, are located on either side of a valley subject to cooler winds than the main Côte de BEAUNE. PINOT NOIR vineyards, including such PREMIERS CRUS as Les Duresses and Le Climat de Val, are grown on the south-east slope of the Montagne du Bourdon. White wines, made from CHARDONNAY, account for just above a quarter of the production, covering the slopes adjacent to Meursault.

In the past, wines from Auxey-Duresses were likely to have been sold under the names of grander neighbours. Many are now labelled as Côte de Beaune-Villages, although the village appellation is becoming more popular.

See CÔTE D'OR and BURGUNDY. J.T.C.M.

AVA, the acronym for **American Viticultural Area** and the UNITED STATES' so far rudimentary answer to France's APPELLATION CONTRÔLÉE system of permitted geographical designations. Under existing regulations, AVAs are theoretically defined by geographic and climatic boundaries, rather than pre-existing political ones, although this is not invariably true and there is some overlap of boundaries. The system requires no limitations on varieties planted, YIELDS, or other specifics familiar to those who know France's AC or Italy's DOC laws.

The only requirement for their use is that 85 per cent of the grapes in a wine labelled with an AVA come from that region; if the wine is a VARIETAL, the legal minimum of 75 per cent of the named variety must come from the named AVA. (Unlike the AC, or DOC system, however, neither the expression 'AVA' nor 'American Viticultural Area' appears on wine labels.)

Avesso, Iberian white grape variety used for VINHO VERDE. It produces scented, relatively full-bodied wine and is most common in the south of the Vinho Verde region. See also JAÉN.

AXR1, variety of rootstock widely used in northern California until, in the late 1980s, it became fatally obvious that it was not resistant to PHYLLOXERA. See ROOTSTOCK.

Azerbaijan, eastern, wine-producing republic in the CIS situated between ARMENIA and the Caspian Sea.

The climate varies between moderately warm with dry winters, to cold with abundant rainfall. Modern viticulture is concentrated in the Kirovabad-Kazakh and Shirvan regions, in the Republics of Nagorno-Karabakh and Nakhichevan.

Seventeen vine varieties are officially recognized for wine production, and the most common ones are RKATSITELI and PINOT NOIR. New vineyards are planted to PINOT BLANC, ALIGOTÉ, Podarok Magaratcha, Pervenets Magaratcha, Doina, Viorica, Ranni Magaracha, and Kishmish Moldavski.

Commerce in this oil-rich republic can best be described as entrepreneurial. In the 1990s, the leading wine enterprises, which produce more than 90 different brands of wine and brandy, were the two Baku wineries, the Baku sparkling-wines enterprise, and the Khanlar winery. V.R.

azienda, Italian for a business. An azienda agricola is a farm, the equivalent of a French DOMAINE, and the phrase should appear on a wine label only if the grapes were grown and the wine produced on that estate; an azienda vinicola, on the other hand, may buy in grapes from elsewhere.

BA, common abbreviation, used particularly by English-speakers, for the sweet-wine designation BEERENAUSLESE, the second-sweetest Prädikat in GERMAN WINE LAW.

Băbească Neagră, Romanian variety whose name, meaning 'grandmother's grape', compares directly with the much more popular FETEASCA or 'young girl's grape'. The wines produced are mostly light, fruity reds, considerably less 'serious' than Fetească Neagră.

Bacchus is one of the most important GERMAN CROSSINGS. It was bred from a Silvaner × Riesling crossing and the lacklustre MÜLLER-THURGAU and in good years can provide growers with musts notching up the all-important numbers on the OECHSLE scale as well as powerful flavours and character, and is therefore useful for blending with Müller-Thurgau. Unlike the more aristocratic and more popular crossing KERNER, however, the wine produced lacks acidity and is not even useful for blending with high-acid musts in poor years since it too needs to be fully ripe before it can express its own exuberant flavours.

Bacchus's great allure for growers, however, is that it can be planted on sites on which Riesling is an unreliable ripener and will ripen as early and as productively as Müller-Thurgau.

Bacchus is also the fourth most planted grape variety in ENGLAND, where it can produce relatively full, currant-flavoured wines.

Baco Blanc, sometimes called Baco 22A, was, for much of the 20th century until the late 1970s, the prime ingredient in armagnac (a role now occupied by UGNI BLANC but previously occupied by FOLLE BLANCHE). Once planted quite widely in western France, Baco Blanc is now being fast pulled up, however, as the French authorities seek to purge hybrids from their vineyards. New Zealand grew Baco Blanc in some quantity at one time but here too evidence of a hybrid past is being rapidly eradicated.

Baco Noir, or **Baco 1,** a crossing of Folle Blanche with a variety of *Vitis riparia*, was at one time cultivated in such disparate French wine regions as Burgundy, Anjou, and the Landes. It has also been widely planted in the eastern United States (see NEW YORK and CANADA), where its relatively fruity wines are not marked by the foxy flavours associated with *Vitis* LABRUSCA and are sometimes harnessed to make NOUVEAU reds.

Baden, GERMANY'S longest wine region, stretching over 400 km/250 miles from the border with FRANKEN in the north to Lake Constance (the Bodensee) and German-speaking SWITZERLAND in the south. The general and local climate, the varying soils, and the height above sea level have a marked effect on the wines of Baden's nine districts, or BEREICHE. Baden is Germany's stronghold of the PINOT family of vine varieties, with fashionable SPÄT-BURGUNDER and GRAUBURGUNDER particular specialities.

Baden is the southernmost region of Germany, with some of its vineyards at lower LATITUDES than those in ALSACE across the river RHINE in France. As a result, Baden wines are typically higher in ALCOHOLIC STRENGTH than most other German wines.

Bereich **Tauberfranken** intermittently follows the river Tauber until the confluence with the Main at Wertheim. Vines (primarily MÜLLER-THURGAU and Spätburgunder) are grown mainly on slopes above the cool valley floor (see HILLSIDE VINEYARDS). The wine is similar to that of FRANKEN and for historical reasons the QUALITÄTSWEIN is sold in its neighbour's flagon-shaped BOCKSBEUTEL.

East across the Odenwald, the vineyards of Bereich **Badische Bergstrasse** and Bereich **Kraichgau** run north and south of Heidelberg. The first district is simply a continuation of the HESSISCHE BERGSTRASSE. In this southern stretch of the Bergstrasse, RIESLING is less widely grown and Müller-Thurgau is the leading vine. The northern Baden wines have good acidity, with Riesling on the granite soil showing charm and delicacy. Most of the harvest is handled by co-operative cellars and there are fewer private estates of note than in Bereich Ortenau, south of Baden-Baden.

There are two Bereiche in Baden whose wines are especially well known amongst wine lovers in Germany. In **Kaiserstuhl** and in **Ortenau**, the names of some communities carry the same weight in the German wine world as the better-known villages of the MOSEL-SAAR-RUWER. This may be because almost the entire grape harvest of some villages is vinified by one good co-operative cellar. Such establishments are regarded as the equals of the large, private estates of the northern German regions.

South of Baden-Baden, there are a few villages which, like those in Tauberfranken, sell their wines in the Bocksbeutel. Riesling predominates and certainly cheaper versions can be found further south in the Bereich Ortenau, away from the inflationary effect of Baden-Baden. The steep vineyards of Neuweier and Varnhalt are impressive and lie on the spurs of the Black Forest which run west, towards the Rhine. At nearby Bühl, Sasbachwalden, Kappelrodeck, and Waldulm, good Spätburgunder is produced at prices which reflect its quality. If wines are aged in new BARRIQUES, or come from vines older than 20 years, a premium is liable to be asked, whether or not it is justified.

Durbach near Offenburg is one of the best and most versatile Ortenau wine villages. There is a large area planted in Spätburgunder, and the Riesling (known locally as Klingelberger) has that vital ingredient in Germany of good ACIDITY. Durbach also claims more Traminer (see GEWÜRZTRAMINER), or Clevner as it is called in the Ortenau, than any other village in the country. Besides a good co-operative cellar there are at least 11 successful private estates, with vineyards on extremely steep and high slopes directly above the village.

Low YIELDS contribute to the quality of better Baden wine today. Village co-operatives encourage the production of a crop far smaller than the maximum legal amount, through the way in which they pay their members. Nevertheless, yields from the white wine varieties are often greater in Baden than they are in Alsace, and the wines are usually less concentrated as a result. Less sugar is added to them to increase the alcohol content (see CHAPTALIZATION) and many Baden wines are lighter in style. With the red wines, the situation is different and the better Baden Spätburgunder is impressive, a dark-coloured wine with a wealth of flavour.

Between Offenburg and Freiburg, the capital of the Baden wine trade, Bereich **Breisgau** rolls across the rural foothills of the Black Forest. Private-estate bottlers are rare and much of the wine is made by the vast central co-operative cellars in Kaiserstuhl, the Badischer Winzerkeller. Its members include 90 local CO-OPERATIVES and one wine estate. The co-operatives are responsible for some 85 per cent of Baden's wine production. The range it offers is understandably enormous, and each year 500 or so wines are individually vinified. Half of the turnover, however, is concentrated on 20 wines only.

The wines of Bereich **Tuniberg** are lighter than those of Kaiserstuhl and virtually all are produced by the Badischer Winzerkeller. South of Freiburg, the pleasant landscape of Bereich **Markgräflerland** is known for its easy-to-drink wine from Gutedel (CHASSELAS), and near Lake Constance the wines of Bereich **Bodensee** have more acidity and elegance. Baden-Württemberg has a fine DOMÄNE overlooking the lake at Meersburg.   I.J. & K.B.S.

Baga, the most common grape variety planted in the BAIRRADA region of Portugal, also grown in the Dão and Ribatejo regions and sometimes called Tinta Bairrada or Poeirinha. Baga means 'berry' in Portuguese, and its berries are notable for their thick skins and the high levels of TANNINS and ACIDITY in the wines they produce (particularly when, as was traditionally the case, there is no DESTEMMING). In the MARITIME CLIMATE of Bairrada, Baga is very susceptible to rot, which means that grapes are often harvested before they are fully ripe, a factor which accentuates the natural astringency of Baga-based wines. However, well-made wines from a ripe year can age well and vinification techniques are in the process of modification in an effort to produce softer, more commercially acceptable wines. An increase in blending with other varieties is expected. A substantial proportion of the Baga crop is bought in bulk for MATEUS ROSÉ.

bag-in-box. See BOXES.

Bairrada, an evolving wine region and DOC in northern PORTUGAL.

Like much of northern Portugal, Bairrada is an area of agricultural smallholdings. Most growers send their grapes to one of six CO-OPERATIVES but more than 20 merchants also have cellars in the region where wines from Bairrada and neighbouring DÃO are bought in for AGEING and BLENDING. A number of larger individual estates have started to produce their own wines.

Bairrada is unusual in Portugal in that it is almost a one-grape region. Over 70 per cent of the wines are red, made principally from the BAGA vine. This small, dark, thick-skinned grape produces solid wines that often suffer from an excess of TANNINS. Baga is also very susceptible to rot and Bairrada's perennial threat of early autumn rain means that grapes from high-yielding vineyards are frequently harvested before they are fully ripe. But wine styles are changing and firms such as Aliança and SOGRAPE (who produce MATEUS ROSÉ in Bairrada) are gradually adapting their vinification methods to make their wines softer and more approachable. Some TOURIGA NACIONAL is also being planted to add roundness to Baga. White grapes, mostly Maria Gomes (or FERNÃO PIRES) and BICAL, are grown to produce traditional-method sparkling wines (see SPARKLING-WINE-MAKING), although these are not entitled to the denomination.

On the edge of the region, the Palace Hotel at Buçaco blends its own red and white wines from grapes bought from growers in Dão and Bairrada. These are widely regarded as some of the best table wines in Portugal but are available only to guests dining at the hotel or one of its few associated establishments.   R.J.M.

balance is essential for quality wine. Wine tasters say that a wine has balance, or is well balanced, if its ALCOHOLIC STRENGTH, ACIDITY, RESIDUAL SUGAR, and TANNINS complement each other so that no single one of them is obtrusive on the PALATE. It is a wine characteristic quite unrelated to FLAVOUR.

Banat Riesling or Banat Rizling, white grape variety grown in ROMANIA and just across the border with what was Yugoslavia in VOJVODINA. Its produce tends to be somewhat heavy, a sort of LASKI RIZLING without the lift.

Bandol, the most serious wine of PROVENCE, typically a deep-flavoured, lush red blend dominated by the Mourvèdre grape. Like CHÂTEAUNEUF-DU-PAPE, Bandol produces quintessentially Mediterranean red wines which are easy to appreciate despite their longevity.

The appellation is named after the port from which they were once shipped all over the world. Bandol is now a Mediterranean resort town with little to offer the wine tourist, and the vineyards are on south-facing terraces well above the coast. As in the smaller appellation of CASSIS just along the coast, the vines are protected from the cold north winds, but have to fight property developers for their right to continued existence. A total of about 1,300 ha · were cultivated in the late 1990s.

This particularly well-favoured southern corner is one of the few parts of France in which MOURVÈDRE, the characteristic grape of Bandol, can be relied upon to ripen. Other dark-berried varieties grown include Grenache and Cinsaut, much used for the local herby rosés which account for about one bottle of Bandol in three, together with strictly limited additions of Syrah and Carignan. A small quantity of white Bandol is made from Bourboulenc, Clairette, and Ugni Blanc with a maximum of 40 per cent Sauvignon Blanc, but little of it escapes the region's fish restaurants.

Wine-making techniques are traditional but evolving. All reds must have at least 18 months in cask. Mechanical harvesting is banned. Domaine Tempier is one of the few domaines to have a well-established market outside France but the likes of Domaine de Frégate, La Rouvière, Domaine de l'Olivette, Moulin des Costes, and Chx Pibarnon and Pradeaux have all made fine wines.

Banyuls and **Banyuls Grand Cru** are the appellations for France's finest and certainly most complex VINS DOUX NATURELS, made from vertiginous terraced vineyards above the Mediterranean at the southern limit of ROUSSILLON, and indeed mainland France. The dry but powerful red wine produced in the same vineyards is entitled to the appellation COLLIOURE, Banyuls-sur-Mer and Collioure being two of the four dramatic seaside communes included in these two appellations.

Banyuls differs from RIVESALTES, Roussillon's catch-all vin doux naturel, not only in terms of quality but also in style. Grenache Noir must dominate the blend, constituting at least 50 per cent of a Banyuls and 75 per cent of a Banyuls Grand Cru (which latter appellation is ignored by individual producers of the calibre of Dr Parcé of Domaine du Mas Blanc).

Some Banyuls is made to preserve the heady aromas of macerated red fruits; others to display the characteristics of a particularly successful and long-past year (sometimes labelled *rimage*); while other Banyuls demonstrate the extraordinary levels of concentration that can be achieved by Grenache, heat, and time. Such wines are some of the few that go well with chocolate, although many a French chef has created savoury dishes, often with a hint of sweetness, to be served expressly with a particular Banyuls. This is the only French wine region able to offer 20- and 30-year-old wines as a serious proportion of its total production. See also MAURY.

Barbaresco, powerful red wine based on the NEBBIOLO grape grown around the village of Barbaresco in the PIEDMONT region in north-west Italy. For long considered very much the junior of BAROLO in terms of its size and the power and prestige of its wines, Barbaresco emerged from Barolo's shadow in the 1960s to win recognition of its own striking qualities of elegance and aromatic intensity.

The production zone of the Barbaresco DOCG is to the north east and east of the city of Alba and is considerably smaller than that of Barolo. The wine is produced in the townships of Barbaresco, Treiso, Neive, and a fragment of ALBA.

The wines, in their relative softness and fruitiness and their perfumed aromas, bear a certain resemblance to Barolo produced around the villages of La Morra and Barolo, although it is rare to find a Barbaresco with the body and concentration of a fine Cannubi or Brunate. A few positions in Neive, however—notably Santo Stefano and Bricco di Neive—give wines which resemble a Barolo.

Nebbiolo ripens earlier in Barbaresco than in Barolo, a factor which frequently saves at least a part of the Barbaresco harvest in the rainy Octobers which dilute Barolo; there are therefore in theory likely to be more successful VINTAGES in a given decade in Barbaresco than in Barolo.

Wine-making techniques evolved in the 1970s and 1980s, much as in Barolo, towards considerably shorter periods in cask in an effort to respond to modern tastes for rounder, fruitier wines. If Barbaresco is generally a lighter-bodied wine than Barolo (although these are wines which must have a minimum ALCOHOLIC STRENGTH of 12.5° and easily reach 13.5°), it is not lacking in the TANNINS and ACIDITY that mark the Nebbiolo grape; young Barbaresco is by no means an inevitably pleasurable glass of wine. It does mature more rapidly than Barolo, however, and rarely ages as well. Barbaresco is normally at its best between 5 and 10 years of age, with the exception of the above-mentioned vineyards in Neive. The general level of wine-making skills is lower in Barbaresco than in Barolo. However, in partial compensation, the zone does benefit from the presence of an important CO-OPERATIVE winery in Barbaresco itself. Produttori del Barbaresco is Italy's finest co-operative, which has established admirable quality levels in both its blended Barbaresco and its designated-vineyard selections; its example has been followed by the co-operative of Treiso.

Single-vineyard bottlings are a relatively recent phenomenon, in Barbaresco as in the rest of Italy, and there is a less firmly established written record of CRU designation here than in Barolo. NÉGOCIANTS' willingness to pay higher prices for grapes from certain vineyards, however, does establish the existence of a certain consensus existing in the zone, a tradition which gave an undeniable prestige to Asili, Montefico, Montestefano, and Rabajà in Barbaresco; Albesani, and Gallina in Neive; and Pajorè in Treiso. A certain number of the most famous vineyards—San Lorenzo, Tildin, and Martinenga in Barbaresco, Santo Stefano in Neive—are, in effect, 'man-made' crus which have gained their current prestige from the dedicated work and exacting standards of producers such as GAJA, Giacosa, and Alberto di Gresy, and have no precise historical tradition behind them.

Ultra-short FERMENTATIONS and BARRIQUE ageing of the wines were introduced to Barbaresco in the mid 1980s, although the former phenomenon has found fewer converts than in Barolo; the softer quality of Nebbiolo in Barbaresco—conserved by a shorter, one-year minimum ageing period in wood—makes radical innovations in wine-making techniques less of a necessity. The use of new OAK spread rapidly, however, due to the powerful influence of Angelo Gaja, headquartered in Barbaresco itself, and its spicy and aromatic qualities seem to blend well with the character of the wine, although by far the majority of Barbaresco continues to be aged in the zone's traditional large oval casks.   D.T.

Barbera, productive and versatile red grape variety which is challenged only by SANGIOVESE in its many forms as Italy's most planted darkberried vine. There were nearly 50,000 ha/123,500 acres of Barbera planted in Italy in 1990, but it has travelled widely, most notably to the Americas.

Barbera ripens relatively late, as much as two weeks after the other 'lesser' black grape variety of Piedmont DOLCETTO, although still in advance of the stately NEBBIOLO. Its chief characteristic is its high level of natural acidity even when fully ripe, which has helped its popularity in hot climates. Such a widely planted variety (see below) has understandably developed various strains in its various spheres of Italian influence, PIEDMONT, the OLTREPÒ PAVESE, EMILIA-ROMAGNA, and the Mezzogiorno.

A white-berried **Barbera Bianca** is also known.

Piedmont

Barbera has been called 'the people's wine' of Piedmont for its versatility and its abundant production; it usually accounts for well over 40 per cent of all the wine produced in the region in a given year. The wine comes in a bewildering range of styles, from the young and spritzy to powerful and intense wines that need extended cellaring, reflecting the extreme heterogeneousness of the soils and MESOCLIMATES of the zones where it is planted.

Certain characteristics are constant none the less: a deep ruby colour (the wine was frequently used in the past to 'correct' the colour of Nebbiolo grapes grown in BAROLO and BARBARESCO); a full body with notably low levels of TANNINS; pronounced ACIDITY which is aggravated by over-production, Barbera being a

variety of exemplary VIGOUR and productivity. The use of southern Italian blending wine to compensate for the thinness and sharpness of overcropped Barbera, a common practice in the past, seems to be coming to an end as YIELDS drop. The DOC regulations, which regrettably permit generous yields (70 hl/ha), relatively low ALCOHOLIC STRENGTH (12° in Alba and Asti, 11.5° in the Monferrato), and high minimum acidity in relation to the alcohol and body of the wines, do little to restrain yields or exalt quality.

ALBA, ASTI, and the Monferrato give their names to the three DOC zones of Piedmont, although the zones tend to sprawl across rather vast extensions of territory. A number of leading producers in Asti and Monferrato have, in fact, refused DOC status for their wines, preferring to label them VINO DA TAVOLA on the grounds that the net has been far too widely cast. Given the enormous acreage devoted to Barbera, it is no surprise that little mapping of the most suitable subzones has occurred, but, at the level of folk knowledge, the hills immediately to the north and south of Alba and Monforte d'Alba in the Alba DOC and, in the province of Asti, the area from Nizza Monferrato north west towards Vinchio, Castelnuovo Calcea, Agliano, Belveglio, and Rocchetta Tanaro are considered classic zones for Barbera. Much remains to be done, obviously, in matching variety and TERROIR.

A small number of Barberas underwent a significant metamorphosis during the 1980s and 1990s as producers, in a parallel development to the Sangiovese-based SUPER-TUSCANS, undertook BARREL MATURATION. The prototype was Giacomo Bologna's Bricco dell'Uccellone. There can be no question that new oak substantially modifies the character of Barbera, adding a real spiciness to its rather neutral aromas and a certain quantity of ligneous tannins which firm up its structure and soften the impact of its acidity. It should be remembered, however, that these avant-garde Barberas, being invariably the product of low yields and careful vinification, already have more body and flavour than traditional Barbera, even of a better sort, and that small barrels are unlikely to become a panacea for this grape. The new wave Barberas which rather self-consciously strive for greatness have also doubtless created some confusion for consumers used to regarding Barbera merely as a hearty and warming glass to accompany the traditionally robust fare of the Piedmontese kitchen. D.T.

Elsewhere in Italy

Barbera dominates much of Lombardy, in particular the vineyards of Oltrepò Pavese, where it makes VARIETAL wines of varying quality and degrees of fizziness, some fine and lively, as well as being blended with the softer local Croatina or BONARDA grape. It is a minor, and decreasing, ingredient in Terre di FRANCIACORTA and is found, as elsewhere in Italy, in oceans of basic VINO DA TAVOLA.

Barbera is also much planted immediately south east of Piedmont in the Colli Piacentini, the hills above Piacenza, of EMILIA-ROMAGNA. Here too it is often blended with Bonarda, particularly in the Val Tidone for the DOC red Gutturnio. It is also planted in the Bologna and Parma hills, the Colli Bolognesi and Colli di Parma, where it may also produce a VARIETAL wine which rarely has the concentration of Piedmont's best and is regularly fizzy. Most of central Italy's Barbera plays a minor role in blends with more locally indigenous varieties, adding (not always) useful acidity, although that is its real purpose in the deep south.

A Barbera Sarda is grown in SARDINIA, where some argue that the local Perricone, or Pignatello, is also Barbera. D.T.

Outside Italy

Only just outside Italy, Barbera is also grown over the border with what was Yugoslavia in SLOVENIA, chiefly in the Primorski coastal zone. Elsewhere in Europe it is barely known, but Italian immigrants took Barbera with them to both North and, particularly, South America. It is planted in Argentina, where there are several thousand hectares, mainly in Mendoza and San Juan provinces. The variety is planted to a much more limited extent in the rest of South America. In California, however, there are now well over 10,000 acres/4,050 ha, by no means all in the hot CENTRAL VALLEY, thanks to the fashion for all things Italian and epicurean. Among grape varieties hopefully brought to California from Piedmont, Barbera has consistently outperformed the nobler Nebbiolo, as it has in Australia, where it has made some creditable wine in both the Mornington Peninsula in VICTORIA and Mudgee in NEW SOUTH WALES.

Bardolino, cheerful and uncomplicated light-red wine from the south-eastern shores of Lake Garda in the VENETO region of north-east Italy. It is produced from CORVINA, Rondinella, and Molinara grapes. As in the other two important Veneto DOCS SOAVE and VALPOLICELLA, the original production zone is that now known as CLASSICO (Bardolino, Garda, Lazise, Affa, Costermano, and Cavaion). This has been extended to a considerably larger zone whose wines are simply called Bardolino. Exact TERROIR seems to have rather less effect on the quality of this relatively simple wine than it does on Soave and Valpolicella, and good Bardolino is regularly produced outside the Classico zone, notably in Sommacampagna.

Although the DOC blend differs little from Valpolicella, Bardolino producers tend to use less Corvina (the variety which gives body and structure) and more of the somewhat neutral Rondinella than their neighbours in Valpolicella.

The rosé version of the wine is called Bardolino Chiaretto. Bardolino Superiore, a slightly headier wine with an extra one per cent of alcohol, must be aged a year before being released. Bardolino NOVELLO, an attempt to ape Beaujolais NOUVEAU, was born in the late 1980s, but the competition of similar novello wines from every grape and corner of Italy considerably lessened the marketing impact of the move. D.T.

Barolo, the most powerful and dramatic expression of the NEBBIOLO grape, takes its name from the village of the same name 15 km/9 miles to the south of the town of ALBA in the region of PIEDMONT in north-west Italy.

The core of Barolo has always been the townships of Barolo, La Morra, Castiglione Falletto, Serralunga d'Alba, and the northern half of Monforte d'Alba, supplemented by outlying areas in a variety of other townships which have changed over the course of time. These five core townships contain 87 per cent of the total Barolo area. This sensible demarcation of the zone, disciplined YIELDS (56 hl/ha (3.2 tons/acre) maximum), and reasonable requirements for CASK AGEING (originally three years, subsequently lowered to two years with a pending proposal to lower it to one year) make this DOC (promoted to DOCG in 1980) one of Italy's most intelligent. These sensible restraints have also curbed the multiplicity of superior wines labelled VINO DA TAVOLA characteristic of other areas of Italy (see SUPER-TUSCAN, for example).

Although Barolo is always a rich, concentrated, and heady wine, with pronounced TANNINS and ACIDITY, significant stylistic differences among the various wines of the zone do exist and tend to reflect the two major soil types which are conveniently separated by the Alba–Barolo road, which runs along the valley floor, separating La Morra and Barolo to the west from Castiglione Falletto, Monforte d'Alba, and Serralunga d'Alba to the east. The vineyards of the townships of La Morra and Barolo produce softer, fruitier, aromatic wines which age relatively rapidly for a Barolo. The townships of Castiglione Falletto, Monforte d'Alba, and Serralunga d'Alba yield more intense, structured wines that mature more slowly.

All fine Barolo, however, shares certain common traits: a garnet hue, tending toward ruby in La Morra and Barolo and towards brick in Castiglione Falletto, Monforte d'Alba, and Serralunga d'Alba; complex and expansive aromas of plums, dried roses, tar, liquorice, and—according to a few fortunate connoisseurs—the local white truffles. Full flavours are backed by substantial tannins, a dense texture, and real alcoholic warmth (often surpassing 14°, and over 15° in superior vintages). Excessive EXTRACTION and/or cask ageing can easily lead to overly tannic and bitter wines, and obtaining the proper richness while maintaining a certain drinkability is the fundamental, and not easy, task of the individual producer, a balancing act which is not rendered easier by the late ripening character of the Nebbiolo grape.

Two developments have marked contemporary, post-DOC Barolo: the move towards estate bottling and single-vineyard bottling (principally by small producers), and an attempt to find a fruitier, less austere style of Barolo more in tune with modern palates. NÉGOCIANT houses, dealing in large quantities, necessarily blended the wines of different provenances into a house Barolo (just like their counterparts in BURGUNDY). When skilfully done, this did—and still does—accomplish the creation of balanced and harmonious wines which exemplify the general characteristics of Barolo. It is none the less true that certain privileged positions have long enjoyed a greater prestige and given more distinctive wines. While there is no absolute unanimity, most short lists of the finest CRUS include Rocche and Cerequio in La Morra; Cannubi,

Sarmazza, and Brunate in Barolo (this latter vineyard shared with La Morra); Rocche, Villero, and Monprivato in Castiglione Falletto; Bussia, Ginestra, and Santo Stefano di Perno in Monforte d'Alba; Lazzarito and Vigna Rionda in Serralunga d'Alba.

Like many of the world's powerful and age-worthy red wines, Barolo has had to come to terms in the 1970s and 1980s with market demands for fruitier, less tannic wines that can more easily be drunk while young—not an easy transition for a zone where FERMENTATION and MACERATION have regularly lasted as long as two months. The leaders of the movement towards a softer style of Barolo were Renato Ratti, Paolo Cordero di Montezemolo, and the house of Ceretto. Their methods consisted of shorter fermentations (generally 10 to 14 days) and an abbreviated ageing period in wood followed by extended BOTTLE AGEING prior to commercial release.

'Modernists' and 'traditionalists' continue to coexist in the zone, at times uneasily and polemically, although results thus far tend to confirm that Barolo, always rich in tannins and acidity, best benefits from abbreviated fermentation and cask ageing when producers accept the discipline of smaller yields to give adequate flavour concentration. That 'modern' Barolo ages less well and oxidizes more easily (see OXIDATION) than 'traditional' Barolo is, however, beyond discussion. The use of new small oak barrels is as yet unproven, although the preliminary results—hamfisted in many cases, imperceptible in others—suggest that Barolo and new oak may not be made for one another. New oak is none the less quite popular with younger producers in the zone, who identify it both with 'modernity' and a new commercial acceptance of Barolo in international markets and seem presently less concerned with the potential loss of specific identity for the wine.

See also BARBARESCO.

Barolo Bianco is an occasional name for the ARNEIS grape. D.T.

Baroque, sometimes spelt **Barroque**, is the intensely local grape variety of which white TURSAN must be made. Recent investment in the Tursan appellation by the proprietor of the famously epicurean establishment at Eugénie-les-Bains may help save this characterful variety from extinction.

The wine produced, sold as Baron de Bachen,

displays the unusual combination of high alcohol and fine aroma, something akin to ripe pears.

Barossa Valley, the heart of the Australian wine industry, the most famous wine region in AUSTRALIA, and the one in which most wine is produced, even if a high proportion of it is shipped in from vineyards outside the valley itself. There is an increasing trend towards planting off the valley floor and on higher ground in the Barossa Ranges. According to Australia's official wine geography, the **Barossa** zone includes the Barossa Valley and Eden Valley wine regions. See SOUTH AUSTRALIA.

barrel, fashionable cylindrical container traditionally made from WOOD and used almost exclusively in the production of fine wines and spirits. The bulge, or bilge, of barrels means that they can be rolled and spun easily, and that, when they are kept horizontal, any sediment naturally collects in one place, from which the wine can easily be separated by RACKING.

Barrels come in many sizes and qualities. The word barrel is conventionally used for a wooden container small enough to be moved, while VATS are larger, permanent containers, sometimes with an open top, and the word CASK is used for wooden containers of all sizes. Some Britons use the word cask deliberately in place of the more American word barrel.

BARREL MATURATION is the term used in this book for ageing a wine in a barrel, while CASK AGEING has been used as a general term for keeping a wine in a larger wooden container. BARREL FERMENTATION is the technique of fermenting wine in barrel.

See also OAK and TOAST.   J.J.P.

barrel fermentation, wine-making technique of fermenting grape juice or must in small BARRELS. The technique is used principally for white wines because of the difficulty of extracting through a barrel's small bung-hole the mass of skins and seeds which necessarily remains after red-wine fermentation. In Burgundy, California, and especially Australia, however, some wine-makers deliberately put pressed red wines which still retain some unfermented sugars into barrel, thus allowing completion of red wine FERMENTATION in barrel in an attempt to make softer, more approachable wines.

The technique seems particularly well adapted to wine made from CHARDONNAY grapes and some of the finest SWEET WINES. Its advantages are that it offers the possibility of extracting a controlled amount of wood flavour into the wine and, since barrels have a large surface to volume ratio, artificial TEMPERATURE CONTROL may not be needed. It also provides a natural prelude to BARREL MATURATION and LEES STIRRING since the lees and the wine are already in the same container.

White wine which is fermented and stored in oak with its yeast solids, or LEES, has a softened, less obvious, and more integrated oak flavour than wine that has been fermented in a larger container before being matured in barrels. Fermentation in barrel also adds richness and apparent LENGTH of flavour on the palate.

White wines matured for a few months on their lees in barrel usually have a much lighter colour than those put into barrel after fermentation to mature.

Stirring up the lees in the barrel also affects wood flavour. If the lees are stirred, they act as an even more effective buffer between the wine and the wood, limiting the extent to which wood TANNINS, and colouring matter, are extracted into the wine. Wines subjected to lees stirring therefore tend to be much paler and less tannic than those whose lees are not stirred.

Fermentation in barrel can also have secondary flavour effects due to temperature, lot size, and precise level of TOAST. The often higher temperature of fermentation in barrel rather than vat causes a loss of floral flavours and a reduction of the most obvious white-wine AROMAS reminiscent of tropical fruit. There are fewer fatty acid esters and fatty acids, which are described as perfumed or soapy, and more higher alcohols, which makes the wine taste fuller bodied. And because each fermentation even of identical juice has a slightly different flavour outcome, the larger number of small volume lots that are common in barrel fermentation create more complexity. A 10,000-l/2,642-gal lot would create one fermentation flavour if it were fermented in one tank, for example, but the same lot fermented in 70 barrels would produce a much more complex array of flavours.

The disadvantages of barrel fermentation are the relatively small size of the barrel and the time and effort required to clean, fill, and empty it, although the extra degree of complexity gained by the wine is usually worth any extra production costs. The cost of new barrels themselves is such, however, that the technique is restricted to higher-priced wines. With so many fermentations in a non-sterile material, it is always possible that some barrels may be infected with bacteria or undesirable yeasts, so extra vigilance is required to eliminate any defective wines. A.D.W. & L.B.

barrel inserts, imprecise and expanding group of wood, usually OAK, additions to a barrel too old to impart much wood flavour. They may take the form of small planks, called inner staves, inserted in the barrel through the bunghole, or hung from a hook on the underside of the bung, or small cubes of oak in a perforated bag.

barrel maturation is the wine-making operation of storing a fermented wine in wooden BARRELS to create ideal conditions for the components of the wine to evolve and so that the wood imparts some wood flavour. This is an increasingly common practice for superior-quality still wines of all colours and styles, providing them, as it does, with the ideal preparation for BOTTLE AGEING.

The better properties in BORDEAUX provide the paradigm for the barrel maturation of wines based on Cabernet Sauvignon and Merlot grapes. Here top-quality wines are put into barrels with a light to medium TOAST immediately after MALOLACTIC FERMENTATION and left to mature for up to two years. RACKING every three or four months helps CLARIFICATION, softens the wood flavour, and inevitably involves some oxygenation. FINING takes place at the beginning of the second year, further encouraging stabilization. The timing of bottling is the final crucial human input of barrel maturation.

Whereas in Bordeaux, red wine has traditionally been racked into barrel only after malolactic fermentation, a significant proportion of New World Cabernet, Syrah, Zinfandel, and Merlot is now racked straight into barrel after primary alcoholic fermentation with the result that wine and wood flavours are better integrated. Even in Bordeaux, particularly on smaller properties where the necessary barrel-by-barrel surveillance is easier, there is a FASHION for encouraging malolactic fermentation in barrel in an attempt to make wines that are more flattering to taste young—particularly useful when selling EN PRIMEUR.

All over the world, many top-quality white wines are subjected to BARREL FERMENTATION prior to barrel maturation, another practice which tends to result in much better integration of wood and wine than putting white wine into barrel only after fermentation.

An alternative to barrel maturation for wines of all hues is CASK AGEING, whereby wine is stored in large, old wooden containers which impart no wood flavour but exert some of the favourable aspects of wood influence, provided they are kept clean. Other alternatives, and possible supplements, to barrel maturation are ageing in inert containers; BOTTLE AGEING; and bottling almost immediately after fermentation as in NOUVEAU wines. M.K. & L.B.

barrica, Spanish term for a barrel or BARRIQUE. A *barrica bordelesa* is the specific term for a Bordeaux barrique, the most common barrel type used in Spain.

barrique, the most famous of the barrel types, Bordeaux's relatively tall 225-l/59-gal wooden cask with thinner staves than the Burgundian pièce and most other barrels. The word barrique is often used, particularly outside France, for all manner of wooden BARRELS.

Barsac, important sweet-white-wine appellation in BORDEAUX on the left bank of the river GARONNE just over the climatologically important cool river Ciron from the even bigger and more famous Sauternes appellation. All wines produced within Barsac are also entitled to use the appellation Sauternes (although the reverse is not the case). It is traditionally said that the wines of Barsac are slightly lighter than those of Sauternes, perhaps because of the soil and because the land is flatter, but much depends on individual properties and wine-making policies too. For more detail of viticultural and wine-making practices, see SAUTERNES. Some of the finest current achievers within the Barsac appellation are Chx Climens, Rabaud-Promis, and Doisy-Daëne. See also the Barsac properties included in the Sauternes CLASSIFICATION.

Basilicata, mountainous, sparsely populated, and virtually land-locked area of southern Italy. Its name has become synonymous with the extreme poverty in, and abandonment of, much of Italy's deep south. Little exists in the way of viticulture, and less than two per cent of the region's total wine production is of DOC status. The Basilicata has only one DOC wine, AGLIANICO del Vulture, although the Aglianico grape also gives interesting, if not superior, results in other areas of the region. The most significant viticultural zone is undoubtedly that of the Vulture, an extinct volcano 56 km/35 miles to the north of Potenza, where, in addition to Aglianico, limited quantities of MALVASIA (dry, sweet, or sparkling) and MOSCATO (usually both sweet and lightly sparkling) are also produced.   D.T.

Basque country produces wines in Spain and France on either side of the western Pyrenees.

Spain

The Basque country (País Vasco in Castilian, Euskadi in Basque) is the most ferociously independent of all Spain's 17 autonomous regions. This densely populated, heavily industrialized strip of country facing the Bay of Biscay is not normally associated with wine, even though the important RIOJA region stretches north of the river Ebro into the Basque province of Alava. Wine is also made in the hills of the Alto Ebro. The two wholly Basque DOs are the tiny region of CHACOLÍ DE GUETARIA on the coast 25 km/15 miles west of San Sebastián and the smaller CHACOLÍ DE VIZCAYA around Bilbao.

France

See BÉARN and IROULÉGUY.

Bastardo, Portuguese name for a much-travelled, dark-skinned grape variety known as TROUSSEAU in the JURA, south-east France. In the Douro it is regarded as usefully productive but one of the less exciting ingredients in PORT; it ripens to high sugar levels but cannot contribute any great complexity of flavour. It is also grown in the DÃO and BAIRRADA regions of Portugal, and a variety called Bastardo continues to be cultivated in tiny quantities on the island of MADEIRA. It has also been planted, under a variety of aliases, in Australia and California.

Bâtard-Montrachet, great white GRAND CRU in Burgundy's CÔTE D'OR. See MONTRACHET.

bâtonnage, French term for the wine-making operation of LEES STIRRING.

Baumé, scale of measuring total dissolved compounds in grape juice, and therefore its approximate concentration of grape sugars (see MUST WEIGHT). It is used in much of Europe, including France, and Australia. The Baumé scale is particularly useful in wine-making since the number of degrees Baumé indicates the POTENTIAL ALCOHOL in percentage by volume. (Grape juice of 12° Baumé, for example, would produce a wine of about 12 per cent alcohol if fermented out to dryness.)
B.G.C.

Baux de Provence, Les. A spectacular and famous small hilltop settlement in the far west of PROVENCE gives its name to a local APPELLATION CONTRÔLÉE created in 1995. Red wines are made, from Grenache, Syrah, and Mourvèdre grapes, which must together make up at least 60 per cent of the blend, together with Cinsaut, Counoise, Carignan, and Cabernet Sauvignon (which last must represent no more than 20 per cent of the total, thus excluding the area's best estate, Domaine de Trévallon, from the appellation). Cinsaut takes the place of Mourvèdre in the rosés, which make up about a fifth of the appellation (there is no white). Domaine des Terres Blanches was one of France's earliest converts to ORGANIC VITICULTURE.

Béarn, wine made in SOUTH WEST FRANCE either in the MADIRAN or JURANÇON zones, or in a third zone of 13 communes around Salies-de-Béarn and Bellocq dedicated exclusively to the production of **Béarn-Bellocq.** Characterful reds (often very similar to Madiran) and some firm rosés are made with up to 60 per cent Tannat grapes blended with Cabernet Franc, Cabernet Sauvignon, Fer, Manseng Noir, and Courbu Noir, while the very rare, tangy white wines may be made from such classic south-west white grape varieties as Manseng, Courbu, Lauzet, Camaralet (as in Jurançon), which, together with Raffiat de Moncade (as well as Sauvignon), are conserved in the letter of the appellation law if not in the reality of the vineyard. Fewer than 200 ha/494 acres of vineyards are dedicated to the wines of Béarn (most of which are quite concentrated enough to go with a steak and Béarn's famous sauce), and the great majority of the wine is made by the CO-OPERATIVE at Bellocq.

Beaujolais, quantitatively extremely important wine region in east-central France producing a single, unique style of fruity and often relatively light wine. For administrative purposes, Beaujolais is often included as part of greater BURGUNDY, but in terms of climate, topography, soil types, and even distribution of grape varieties, it is quite different. In a typical vintage, Beaujolais produces more than the whole of the rest of greater Burgundy to the north put together, well over a million hl of wine, almost all of which is produced from a single red grape variety, GAMAY Noir à Jus Blanc, and most of it by a single, distinctive wine-making method. Beaujolais at its best provides the yardstick for all the world's attempts to put red refreshment into a bottle, being a wine that is essentially flirtatious, with a juicy aroma which, combined with its promise of appetizing acidity, is sufficient to release the gastric juices before even a mouthful of the wine has been drunk. In this sense, Beaujolais is the very antithesis of the intense, BARREL MATURED reds currently considered the height of FASHION. In the French market-place, Beaujolais has become almost a commodity, with attendant pressures on prices, so that generic blended Beaujolais can simply be a thin, inky liquid that is in all senses lacklustre—or an ultra-commercial blend all too dependent on CHAPTALIZATION. A DOMAINE-BOTTLED wine may well be the most direct route to quality (although see also Georges DUBŒUF, whose importance is that of a major NÉGOCIANT, but whose philosophy was based on an attempt to be true to TERROIR).

Geography and climate

The total vineyard area of the Beaujolais region is well over 20,000 ha/49,420 acres and includes nearly 100 communes with the MÂCONNAIS on its northern boundary (indeed some vineyards may be classified either as Beaujolais Blanc or ST-VÉRAN). Snow may fall in the foothills of the Massif Central to the immediate west by the time Beaujolais Nouveau is launched, but summers are sufficiently hot for the local houses to have the shutters and gentle, tiled roofs of the south of France.

In the northern, narrower part of the region, the landscape is made up of gentle, rolling hills, based on granite and schist with some limestone, while the flatter, southern, more recently developed sector south of Villefranche has much richer soils, often with some clay, making much lighter wines, typically for earlier consumption, on the plains which stretch down towards Lyons.

The appellations

About half of all Beaujolais is sold under the basic appellation **Beaujolais**, which comes from the Bas Beaujolais and the flatter land to the immediate west of the main north–south *autoroute* around Belleville. A small amount may be sold as **Beaujolais Supérieur**, for which the minimum POTENTIAL ALCOHOL of the grapes

when picked must be 10.5 rather than 10 per cent.

The second most important Beaujolais appellation is **Beaujolais-Villages**, which accounts for about a quarter of total production. Beaujolais-Villages must come from the hillier, northern part of the Beaujolais region, its vineyards pushing up into the foothills of the Massif Central. If a Beaujolais-Villages is the produce of just one village or commune, it can append the name of that commune. In the finest sectors of this superior, northern part are the so-called **Beaujolais crus**, 10 named communes or CRUS whose wines are considered so distinctive, and so good, that they have earned their own appellations. Some of these have the most evocative names in the wine lexicon, but their existence as separate entities can be confusing for newcomers to wine since there is rarely mention of the word Beaujolais on their labels. For more details of individual crus, see, approximately from north to south, ST-AMOUR, JULIÉNAS, CHÉNAS, MOULIN-À-VENT, FLEURIE, CHIROUBLES, MORGON, REGNIÉ, BROUILLY, and Côte de Brouilly.

A small amount of **Beaujolais Blanc** and **Beaujolais-Villages Blanc** is made each year, mainly from Chardonnay grapes, although Aligoté is also allowed. White grapes do best on patches of limestone and are planted mainly on these outcrops in the north of the region so that they are effectively southern neighbours of MÂCON Blanc and taste exactly like it. Growers are supposed to devote no more than 10 per cent of their vineyard to white grape varieties. Even smaller amounts of refreshing **Beaujolais Rosé** are made.

Another extremely important sort of Beaujolais is that sold as NOUVEAU, which may carry the appellation Beaujolais, Beaujolais Supérieur, or Beaujolais-Villages. When demand for **Beaujolais Nouveau** reached its peak, in 1992, nearly half of all Beaujolais AC was sold in this youthful state, for immediate consumption and, from the point of view of the producer, as an immediate generator of cash flow.

Vine varieties

Gamay Noir à Jus Blanc (so called to distinguish it from the relatively widely planted red-fleshed Gamays) accounts for about 98 per cent of the Beaujolais vineyard. Virtually all the rest is Chardonnay. According to the official regulations, up to 15 per cent of white varieties may be included in most Beaujolais appellations.

Wine-making

Beaujolais is distinguished not just by the Gamay grape, but by its characteristic wine-making method, CARBONIC MACERATION. Only in Beaujolais is this technique used so widely, and, thanks to the commercial success of Nouveau, with such speed. It produces aromas reminiscent of pear drops and bananas.

Some Beaujolais, particularly in the crus, is made at a much more leisurely pace, given some CASK AGEING, and possibly even bottled by hand from individual barrels.

Serving Beaujolais

Beaujolais has traditionally been served in a special 46-cl/1.2-gal bottle known as a *pot*. Most Beaujolais is designed to be *drunk* rather than discussed or collected. This is the archetypal lubrication wine, and can be particularly *gouleyant*, or gulpable, if served cellar cool. Most Beaujolais is best drunk within a year of harvest, most Beaujolais-Villages within two, most crus within three, although traditionally vinified wines, particularly Morgon, Moulin-à-Vent, Chénas, and Juliénas, from a good vintage, can improve in bottle for up to 10 years. The tendency with time, however, is for a serious old Beaujolais cru to taste increasingly like a red burgundy.

Beaumes-de-Venise is a pretty village in the Vaucluse that produces serviceable southern red Côtes du Rhône-Villages (see RHÔNE) but is most famous for its unusually fragrant, sweet, pale gold VIN DOUX NATUREL.

Like the Muscats of the Languedoc (see FRONTIGNAN, LUNEL, MIREVAL, and, particularly, ST-JEAN-DE-MINERVOIS), this southern Rhône Muscat is made exclusively from the best Muscat variety, MUSCAT BLANC À PETITS GRAINS, and occasionally its darker-berried mutation. Beaumes-de-Venise is usually more delicate and refreshing than the Languedoc Muscats. Like all Muscats, this wine should be drunk as young as possible and is best served chilled. The French prefer it as an aperitif, while most anglophones prefer it with or after dessert.

Beaune, vinous capital of BURGUNDY giving its name to the Côte de Beaune section of the CÔTE D'OR vineyards, and home to such leading NÉGOCIANTS as Louis JADOT, Joseph DROUHIN, Louis LATOUR, and BOUCHARD Père et Fils.

Beaune wines are mostly red, made from Pinot Noir grapes, although recently plantings of Chardonnay have increased. There is more sand in the soil here than in most Côte d'Or

villages so the red wines tend to be no more than medium bodied, best drunk between 5 and 10 years old. While neither as powerful as POMMARD nor as elegant as VOLNAY, Beaune wines are more supple than Corton (see ALOXE-CORTON) and can be a charming introduction to good burgundy.

The town has a good rather than great reputation for its wines, perhaps because there are few outstanding DOMAINES in an appellation dominated by merchants. However, Beaune is blessed with an unusually high proportion, nearly three-quarters, of PREMIER CRU vineyards, which form a broad swathe from the border with SAVIGNY-LÈS-BEAUNE to Pommard.

The finest vineyards are regarded as those situated almost directly between the town and the hill of Les Mondes Rondes: Les Grèves, Les Bressandes, Les Teurons, Les Avaux, and Les Champs Pimont. Beaune-Grèves includes Bouchard's noted Vigne de l'Enfant Jésus vineyard while Beaune-Boucherottes includes Louis Jadot's Clos des Ursules.

Other noted premier-cru vineyards are Les Marconnets and Clos du Roi near the border with Savigny, and Clos des Mouches abutting Pommard. Although the red wines from this vineyard are not always memorable, Joseph Drouhin makes a rich, complex, and age-worthy white Clos des Mouches, which is highly sought after.

Leading producers include Louis Jadot, Bouchard Père et Fils (from the 1996 vintage), and Albert Morot, although see also those of CHOREY-LÈS-BEAUNE.

See also HOSPICES DE BEAUNE and CÔTE D'OR.

J.T.C.M.

Beaune, Côte de. The Côte de Beaune is the southern half of the escarpment of the CÔTE D'OR, named after the important town and wine centre of Beaune. The greatest white wines of Burgundy and some very fine reds are grown on this stretch. The principal appellations, from north to south, are Corton and Corton-Charlemagne (see ALOXE-CORTON), BEAUNE, POMMARD, VOLNAY, MEURSAULT, PULIGNY-MONTRACHET, and CHASSAGNE-MONTRACHET. See also the separate entry under MONTRACHET.

Red wines from the lesser villages of the Côte may be sold under their own names or as **Côte de Beaune-Villages**. This appellation is available for the wines of AUXEY-DURESSES, Chassagne-Montrachet, CHOREY-LÈS-BEAUNE, LADOIX-

SERRIGNY, Meursault, MONTHELIE, PERNAND-VERGELESSES, Puligny-Montrachet, ST-AUBIN, ST-ROMAIN, SANTENAY, and SAVIGNY-LÈS-BEAUNE. See also MARANGES.

Whereas wines labelled Beaune come from the appellation adjoining the town, there is a small group of vineyards on the hill above whose wines are sold under the confusing appellation Côte de Beaune. Of these the best known are Clos des Monsnières and Les Topes Bizot. Both red and white wines are produced.

See also NUITS, CÔTE DE.   J.T.C.M.

Beerenauslese, sometimes known as BA, one of the two rare and very ripe Prädikats in the QMP quality-wine category defined by the GERMAN WINE LAW. In many VINTAGES, hardly any Beerenauslese wine is produced anywhere in Germany. This rich, usually deep-golden wine should be made from individually selected overripe grapes (*Beeren* means 'berries' in German), usually affected by NOBLE ROT. Specific minimum MUST WEIGHTS are laid down for each combination of vine variety and region. These rarities command extremely high prices but taste like honey-soaked raisins, essences of the relevant grape variety. Riesling in general produces the most refined and long-lasting examples, although Huxelrebe can also reach the necessary ripeness. Beerenauslesen from such vintages as 1975 and 1976 were high in sugar and very low in alcohol (often lower than the technical minimum ALCOHOLIC STRENGTH) but Beerenauslesen from, say, the 1989 and 1990 vintages are more likely to be slightly drier and more alcoholic, reflecting changes in FASHION. Some TROCKEN, or dry, Beerenauslesen have also been produced, but there is a certain element of perversion in their production.

See also AUSTRIA.

Beiras, VINHO REGIONAL in central Portugal including the DÃO and BAIRRADA zones as well as a number of smaller IPR regions.

Belgium, north European country which has traditionally been one of Bordeaux's best customers but is also evincing an increasing interest in NEW WORLD wines. It also produces a minuscule amount of wine of its own.

Most vineyards are hardly more than 1 ha, produce wine merely for local sale, sometimes simply for HOME WINE-MAKING, and were, typically, planted in the 1960s and 1970s.

Belgian wine is made with varying degrees of competence but is, typically, light, dry, white similar to that made just over the border in the southern NETHERLANDS.

Bellet, historic, distinctive but minute and shrinking appellation in the far south east of PROVENCE in the hills above Nice. Almost equal quantities of all three colours are produced. The scented, full-bodied whites made from the local Rolle grapes with some Chardonnay are the appellation's most distinctive wines. Rosés may be made from Braquet (the BRACHETTO of Piedmont across the Italian border), while the intriguing Folle Noire (Fuella) is traditional for red wines, although it is often supplemented by Grenache and Cinsaut. Ch de Crémat and Ch de Bellet are the principal producers.

Bendigo, small, isolated but historic wine region in Australia's Central VICTORIA zone.

Bereich, German for a district, bigger than a GROSSLAGE but smaller than a region or ANBAUGEBIET. The boundaries of these wine-making units in GERMANY are often drawn more for political than geographical reasons. A wine labelled Bereich Something (Bernkastel, for example) is unlikely to be very exciting.

Bergerac, extensive and renascent wine appellation in SOUTH WEST FRANCE producing red, dry white, and sweet white wines in the image of BORDEAUX to the immediate west of the region, often at more appealing prices. The greater Bergerac region, named after the principal town at its centre on the river DORDOGNE, is the principal appellation of the Dordogne *département*, and can boast more beautiful and varied countryside than its vinously more glamorous neighbour. Lacking distinctions other than touristic (and gastronomic; Périgord is the home of the truffle), it has long been difficult for the wines of Bergerac to escape from the shadow of Bordeaux's more serious wine reputation, but thanks to much more sophisticated use of OAK, pioneering producers such as Luc de Conti, and a new dynamism in wine production, some truly fine wine is being made.

Within the region are smaller districts, generally on higher sites with more obvious potential, which have their own appellations for specific wine types. MONBAZILLAC on the left bank of the river is potentially the greatest of these, and is making more and more good-quality BOTRYTIZED wine. MONTRAVEL on the right bank makes lightish dry and sweet white wines in the west of the region.

Vines grown are the classic Bordeaux varieties: Cabernets and Merlot for red wines and Sauvignon, Sémillon, and Muscadelle for whites. Sémillon is still the most planted variety, accounting for one vine in every three, although Merlot is pressing for second place.

The most common form of Bergerac is a still red wine generally very similar to red BORDEAUX AC. An increasing proportion of red wine is sold as longer-lasting, more usually barrel-aged Côtes de Bergerac, however, for which yields are generally lower.

Some **Bergerac Rosé** is made, generally of Cabernet, but the second most common form of Bergerac is the dry white **Bergerac Sec**, increasingly well made thanks to the application of some of the techniques employed for better dry white bordeaux. About a quarter of all white wine is sweet, made mainly from Sémillon, and sold as **Côtes de Bergerac Mœlleux**.

Particularly reliable names include Ch La Brie, Ch de la Colline, Domaine Moulin des Dames, Ch Theulet, and Ch Tour des Gendres.

See also PÉCHARMANT, ROSETTE, and SAUSSIGNAC.

Bergeron, local name for ROUSSANNE in the Savoie appellation of Chignin.

Bergwein, term in AUSTRIA for wine made on slopes steeper than 26 per cent, most common in the Wachau and Styria. Unlike wine made from flatter land, it may be sold in a regular 75-cl/27-fl oz bottle even without satisfying Qualitätswein requirements.

berry size is considered by many to be a factor in wine quality, in that smaller berries contribute to better wine quality, especially for red wines, since the ANTHOCYANINS, PHENOLICS, and FLAVOUR COMPOUNDS are mostly contained in the skins. Smaller berries' higher surface-to-volume ratio results in a higher concentration of these skin compounds in the juice and hence in the wine. Good-quality wine grape varieties typically have small berries, at least compared with both lower-quality varieties and TABLE GRAPES. R.E.S.

bianco means 'white' in Italian and the names of many Italian white wines therefore are Bianco d'/da/di/del Place-name. For more details, see under the place-name.

Note, however, that Bianco is also the name of a small town in CALABRIA and that GRECO di Bianco can be an exceptional sweet white wine.

Bical, Portuguese white grape variety grown mainly in BAIRRADA, and DÃO, where it is called Borrado das Moscas, or fly droppings. The wines have good acidity and can be persuaded to display some aroma in a few still VARIETAL versions, although the grapes are often used in blends for sparkling wines. Some capacity for AGEING has been demonstrated, Bical developing an almost RIESLING-like bouquet after a decade in bottle.

Bienvenues-Bâtard-Montrachet, a great white GRAND CRU in Burgundy's CÔTE D'OR. See MONTRACHET.

Bierzo, or El Bierzo, small DO region in northwest Spain which administratively forms part of CASTILE-LEÓN. The river Sil, which bisects it, however, is a tributary of the Miño (Minho in Portugal) and the wines have more in common with those of GALICIA than those of the DOURO 140 km/88 miles to the south. Sheltered from the climatic excesses of the Atlantic and the central plateau, Bierzo shows promise as a wine region. The MENCÍA grape is capable of producing balanced, fruity red wines in well-drained soils on the slate and granite of this part of Spain. Some modernization of production methods and winery equipment may still be needed for Bierzo to fulfil its potential, however. R.J.M.

Biferno, effectively the only DOC in the Italian MOLISE region.

bin, traditional term for a collection of wine bottles, normally stacked horizontally on top of each other, or the process of so storing, or **binning,** them. Thus a **bin end** has come to signify a small quantity of wine bottles left over from a larger lot.

Binissalem, sometimes spelt **Benissalem.** Wines from Spain's first offshore DO on the Mediterranean island of MAJORCA are mostly destined for the Balearic holiday resorts. Binissalem's dominant grape, the Manto Negro, is certainly capable of making well-balanced reds, but most suffer from a heavy-handed approach to wine-making. The most common white variety is the Moll, also called Prensal Blanc, which produces bland, neutral wines. R.J.M.

biodynamic viticulture, sometimes called *biodynamie* in France, is the most extreme, ideological, even spiritual of all alternative approaches to viticulture, and is heavily influenced by the theories of Rudolf Steiner. Biodynamism emphasizes the health and balance of the soil, as do many other ORGANIC VITICULTURE philosophies, but crucially views the soil as an integral part of the symbiosis between planet, air, and cosmos. Its most controversial aspect is its belief in the influence of the cosmos and constellations on different aspects of the plant's growth so that biodynamic farmers plan their activities according to the positions of the moon and stars, the time of year, and even the time of day, favouring the growth of either leaves, roots, flowers, or fruit. They claim that by following these rhythms of nature, healthier plants are produced and ultimately better wines will result (and certainly the presence of weeds will increase WATER STRESS, which may contribute to eventual wine quality). Conventional agrochemicals and fertilizers are absolutely forbidden. Biodynamism's three main viticultural preparations are dung compost for the soil, horn dung for the roots, and horn silica, finely ground silicum buried in cow horns over the summer, to aid PHOTOSYNTHESIS. All are 'dynamized' before use: mixed with water and stirred first one way and then the other for a specific time. Other preparations include yarrow, camomile, nettle, oak, dandelion, and valerian, and alternatives to pesticides are homeopathic dilutions of dead bodies of the relevant pest. New recruits tend to begin by experimenting with biodynamism on selected plots and generally claim to observe much more upright growth, leaves with a healthier sheen, less shading, stronger wood, thicker grape skins, and earlier ripening. Biodynamism is being adopted by increasing numbers of top-quality producers including Domaine Huet of VOUVRAY, Nicolas Joly in SAVENNIÈRES, Domaine Leflaive of PULIGNY-MONTRACHET, Domaine LEROY in Vosne-Romanée, Comtes Lafon in MEURSAULT, CHAPOUTIER in Hermitage, Kreydenweiss and Ostertag in ALSACE and the Millton Vineyard in NEW ZEALAND. See also ORGANIC VITICULTURE, SUSTAINABLE VITICULTURE.   L.F.

biological viticulture, a loose term since all viticulture involves biology, but for more details of the general philosophy implied, see ORGANIC VITICULTURE. In France, many ORGANIC WINES are sold as *vins biologiques*.

Biondi-Santi, family popularly credited with establishing the repute of BRUNELLO DI MONTALCINO in Tuscany, central Italy.

biotechnology. See GENETIC ENGINEERING for some examples of viticultural biotechnology.

bitterness, tasting attribute to which the flat part of the back of the tongue is generally most sensitive. It is not as common in wine as SWEETNESS and ACIDITY, and is often confused with the quite different tactile sensation caused by ASTRINGENCY, which chiefly affects the insides of the cheeks. Some Italian red wines are relatively bitter, as are some less successful examples of particularly aromatic grape varieties such as Gewürztraminer. Both poorly seasoned OAK and an excess of OAK CHIPS can make a wine taste bitter. Many flavoured VERMOUTHS, notably Punt e Mes, are deliberately very bitter. Sweetness can help to mask bitterness.

black goo, a condition associated with poor health of young vineyards in California and elsewhere in the 1980s. The name arises from the black staining and exudate that oozes from vessels of cut trunks of unhealthy plants.
                                    R.E.S.

Black Muscat, synonym for MUSCAT HAMBURG.

Blackwood Valley, wine region in the South West Australia zone of WESTERN AUSTRALIA.

black xylem decline, a more formal name for the condition BLACK GOO.

Blagny, small village in Burgundy's CÔTE D'OR. See both MEURSAULT and PULIGNY-MONTRACHET.

blanc, blanche, masculine and feminine French adjectives meaning 'white' and therefore a common suffix for light-berried grape variety names.

blanc de blancs, French for 'white of whites', may justifiably be used to describe white wines made from pale-skinned grapes, as the great majority of them are. The term has real significance, however, only when used for white SPARKLING WINES, in the production of which dark-skinned grapes often predominate. A blanc de blancs CHAMPAGNE, for example, is, unusually, made exclusively from CHARDONNAY grapes.

Blanc de Morgex, Alpine white grape, a speciality of the Valle d'AOSTA.

blanc de noirs, French for 'white of blacks', describes a white wine made from dark-skinned grapes by pressing them very gently and running the pale juice off the skins as early as possible. Many such still wines have a slightly pink tinge (see WHITE ZINFANDEL and DÔLE Blanche, for example). The term has a specific meaning in the Champagne region, where it is used to describe a CHAMPAGNE made exclusively from PINOT NOIR and PINOT MEUNIER grapes. It is a speciality of the Aube in Champagne. See also VIN GRIS and BLUSH.

Blanc Fumé is a French synonym for SAUVIGNON BLANC, notably in Pouilly-sur-Loire, centre of the POUILLY-FUMÉ, or Blanc Fumé de Pouilly, appellation, many of whose aromatic dry whites do indeed have a smoky, if not exactly smoked, perfume. Thanks to one imaginative American, FUMÉ BLANC is today a much more widely known term (see MONDAVI).

blanco, Spanish term for white as in *vino blanco*, or white wine.

Blanquette, occasionally used as a synonym for a wide range of white wine grapes in SOUTH WEST FRANCE including Bourboulenc, Clairette, Mauzac, and Ondenc. It has also been used for Clairette in Australia.

Blanquette de Limoux. See LIMOUX.

Blau or **Blauer** is the adjective meaning 'blue' in German, often used for darker-berried vine varieties. Blauer Burgunder is PINOT NOIR, for example.

Blauburger, Austrian red wine grape variety, a crossing of Portugieser and Blaufränkisch. In the 1990s, there were about 500 ha/1,200 acres of it, the majority planted in lower Austria, where it produces relatively undistinguished light reds.

Blauburgunder, sometimes Blauer Burgunder, common name for PINOT NOIR in Austria and Switzerland. In Germany, SPÄTBURGUNDER (occasionally Blauer Spätburgunder) is more common.

Blaufränkisch is the Austrian name for the middle European black grape variety the Germans call LIMBERGER, and growers in Washington state call Lemberger. It is one of Austria's most widely planted dark-berried varieties, producing wines of real character, if notably high acidity, when carefully grown. Its good colour, tannin, and raciness encourage the most ambitious Austrian producers to lavish new oak on it and treat it like SYRAH.

Outsiders, however, can find its build reminiscent of, say, the MONDEUSE of Savoie or one of the denser crus of BEAUJOLAIS and for many years it was thought to be the Beaujolais grape GAMAY. Bulgarians still call it Gamé, while Hungarians translate its Austrian name more directly as KÉKFRANKOS.

Its Austrian home is Burgenland, where it is grown particularly on the warm shores of the Neusiedlersee, on the Hungarian side of which it also grows, as Kékfrankos, in Sopron. It is increasingly recognized by Austrian winemakers as worthy of attention, ageing, and, often, BARREL MATURATION. While Austrian plantings of INTERNATIONAL VARIETIES are limited, Blaufränkisch is being used to add fruit to blends of Cabernet Sauvignon and Pinot Noir. The variety called Frankovka in the CZECH REPUBLIC and VOJVODINA is one and the same here and can produce lively, fruity, vigorous wines for early consumption. In FRIULI in the far north-eastern corner of Italy, the variety is called Franconia and can yield wines with zip and fruit.

Blaye, fortified town on the north bank of the Gironde estuary just opposite Margaux in the BORDEAUX region which has been exporting wine much longer than the famous MÉDOC across the water. It lends its name to several of the so-called BORDEAUX CÔTES appellations. By far the most important wine produced here is robust red **Premières Côtes de Blaye**, made mainly from Merlot grapes supplemented by Cabernet Sauvignon. Such wines vary in quality but the region is rich in conscientious PETITS CHÂTEAUX such as Chx Anglade-Bellevue, Bertinerie, Haut-Grelot, Les Jonqueyres, des Tourtes, which can provide increasingly good value for early drinking. White wine may be called **Blaye, Blayais,** or **Côtes de Blaye,** the latter limited to a higher minimum ALCOHOLIC STRENGTH and lower maximum YIELD. Although plantings of Sauvignon Blanc are increasing, the much more neutral Ugni Blanc predominates here and, curiously, is supposed to make up 90 per cent of any white Blaye.

blend, any product of BLENDING but specifically a wine deliberately made from more than one grape variety.

blending different batches of wine is a practice more distrusted than understood. Almost all of the world's finest wines are made by blending the contents of different vats and different barrels (see ASSEMBLAGE); CHAMPAGNE and SHERRY are examples of wines which are quintessentially blends. It is often the case, as has been proved by the most rigorous of experiments, that a wine blend is superior to any one of its component parts.

Blending earned its dubious reputation before the mid 20th century when wine laws were either non-existent or under-enforced, and 'stretching' a superior wine by blending it with inferior wines was commonplace (see ADULTERATION). Blending of different lots of the same wine as it is commonly practised today to ensure that quality is maximal and consistent was not possible before the days of large blending vats; before then wine was bottled from individual casks or vats, which is one explanation of the much higher degree of BOTTLE VARIATION in older vintages.

Modern blending, important in the production of both fine and everyday wines, may combine wines with different but complementary characteristics: heavily oak-influenced lots aged in new barrels may be muted by blending with less oaky lots of the same wine; wines that have undergone MALOLACTIC FERMENTATION may be blended with crisper ones that have not. In the case of ordinary table wines, blending is an important ingredient in smoothing out the difference between one VINTAGE and its successor. Such practices are by no means unknown in the realm of fine-wine production, whether legally sanctioned or not. The wine regulations in many regions permit the addition of a certain proportion of another vintage to a vintage-dated wine, as they frequently do a certain proportion, generally less than 15 per cent, of wine from a region or even grape variety other than that specified on the label.

In today's competitive and quality-conscious wine market, motivation for blending is more often improvement than deception.

Perhaps the most enthusiastic blenders are the AUSTRALIANS, who regularly blend the produce of two or even three different wine regions, possibly many hundreds of miles apart.

For details of **fractional blending**, see SOLERA. See also ASSEMBLAGE.

blind tasting, form of wine TASTING in which the taster attempts to evaluate and/or identify wines without knowing their identity. Only by blind tasting can a true assessment of a wine's

style and quality be made, so SUBJECTIVE is the wine-tasting process. Most professional tastings, those designed to make significant judgements about quality and possibly value, are therefore conducted blind. A comparative tasting, for example, comprises a group of wines of the same approximate age and provenance served blind together in order to evaluate them without prejudicial knowledge of their identity.

Blind tasting with the sole purpose of identification is a particularly masochistic but potentially rewarding exercise, conducted sometimes round the dining table, sometimes in the examination room (as part of a MASTER OF WINE exam, for example). The blind taster generally attempts to identify VINE VARIETY, geographical provenance, and VINTAGE. The first of these should be the easiest but, while wines from different varieties are generally considered to be distinctive, trained tasters have been found unable correctly to identify varieties in University of California blind-tasting tests. The percentage of correct identification was high for characteristic varieties such as Muscat at 59 per cent; the success rate with Cabernet Sauvignon was 39 per cent, while some minor varieties could not be identified at all. Some well-known varieties with non-distinctive flavours were recognized only infrequently, such as Chenin Blanc's 15 per cent and Merlot's 14 per cent. Vintage variation was also considerable; Gewürztraminer was identified correctly from one vintage on 50 per cent of occasions, but on only 6 per cent from the following year.

In some cases, a wine's geographical provenance can be easier to detect than specific grape variety or blend of varieties. Red bordeaux and white Alsace, for example, tend to express place before grape.

In identifying vintage and general maturity, a wine's COLOUR can be particularly helpful.

The OPTIONS GAME is a way of combining the arcane process of blind tasting with general entertainment. Beginners often make the best blind tasters; experience can confuse.

Blue Nun, the most successful German wine BRAND, and for most of the 20th century a LIEBFRAUMILCH owned by H. SICHEL Söhne of Mainz. It was launched with the 1921 vintage in 1927 as a more accessible product than the host of German bottles adorned with Gothic script and long, complicated names. Long before

MATEUS ROSÉ, Blue Nun became a substantial commercial success as a result of heavy investment in advertising which preyed on the fears of what was then an unsophisticated wine-drinking public. Blue Nun was advertised as the wine you could drink 'right through the meal', thereby solving the awkward problem of FOOD AND WINE MATCHING. It began to grow rapidly, mainly in Britain and America, in the 1950s when German wines enjoyed greater prestige than they do today and Blue Nun commanded about the same price as a SECOND GROWTH red bordeaux. At its zenith, in 1984/5, annual sales in the USA alone were 1.25 million cases, with a further 750,000 cases sold elsewhere. Quality was reliably high, despite the quantities needed to satisfy world sales, and blending at the Mainz headquarters was conscientiously undertaken (at this stage by Rainer Lingenfelder among others, who went on to establish a reputation for himself in Germany's PFALZ region). A static wine market, economic recession, and increasing sophistication on the part of wine consumers saw worldwide sales fall to well under a million cases in the 1990s, although there were attempts to widen the range of Blue Nun products, even into French red wine. In 1997, Blue Nun underwent a face-lift, being transformed from a Liebfraumilch to a slightly drier QBA from the RHEINHESSEN.

blush wine is a very-pale-pink popular American speciality made, rather like France's VIN GRIS, by using black-skinned grapes as if to make white wine. A marketing triumph emanating from California in the late 1980s (the name was originally coined by Mill Creek winery), it differs from ROSÉ mainly in ethos rather than substance, having become fashionable just when and where rosé was losing its market appeal (although a blush wine is likely to be perceptibly paler than a rosé). WHITE ZINFANDEL was initially the dominant type in this class, but it spawned many other pinks-from-reds such as VARIETALS labelled White Grenache, Cabernet Blanc, Merlot Blanc, Blanc de Pinot Noir, as well as GENERICS called Blanc de Noirs. Most are sweet, vaguely aromatic and faintly fizzy. CALIFORNIA produces a few dry, oaked blush wines, most of them labelled 'vin gris'. In 1997, 28 per cent of all wines shipped from California were either rosé or, more likely, blush wines. See also SAIGNÉE.   J.Ro. & B.C.C.

Boal, name of several Portuguese white grape varieties, grown on the mainland but also, most famously, on the island of MADEIRA, where its name was Anglicized to BUAL. Nowadays total plantings of any form of Boal are still quite small, and are almost exclusively **Boal Cachudo** clustered around Camara de Lobos on the south coast of Madeira.

Bobal, important Spanish dark-skinned grape variety which produces deep-coloured red wines and even GRAPE CONCENTRATE in ALICANTE, UTIEL-REQUENA, and other regions for bulk-wine production in south-east Spain. It is widely planted, even though not associated with fine wine. It retains its acidity better than MONASTRELL, with which it is often grown, and is notably lower in alcohol. The only DO wine it is allowed into is Utiel-Requena.

Boca, rare but historically important red-wine DOC in the Novara hills in the sub-Alpine north of the PIEDMONT region of north-west Italy. GHEMME, SIZZANO, and FARA, also in Novara, are similar, as are GATTINARA, LESSONA, and BRAMATERRA in the Vercelli hills across the river Sesia. See also SPANNA.

Bocksbeutel, special bottle in the shape of a flattened flask used in the German wine region of FRANKEN and four communes in the northern Ortenau area of BADEN.

bodega, Spanish term for a wine CELLAR, a WINERY, or a tavern or grocery store selling wine.

body, tasting term for the perceived 'weight'—the sensation of fullness, resulting from density or VISCOSITY—of a wine on the palate. Wines at either end of the scale are described as **full bodied** and **light bodied**.

Next to water, ALCOHOL is the major constituent of wines. It has a much higher viscosity than water and is the major component responsible for the sensation of fullness, or body, as a wine is rinsed around the mouth. ALCOHOLIC STRENGTH is therefore clearly an important factor: the more potent a wine the more full bodied it is usually said to be.

The dissolved solids in a wine, its EXTRACT, can also contribute significantly to body, although sweet wines are not necessarily full bodied (ASTI, for example, being sweet but very light bodied, thanks to its low alcohol content).

Contrary to popular conception, GLYCEROL makes only a very minor contribution to density, viscosity and therefore to body (although it does have a slight effect on apparent sweetness).

Body is not related to wine quality, BALANCE being more important in a wine than whether it is full or light bodied. One of the less desirable effects of the increase in comparative TASTING, however, is that full-bodied wines make a more obvious impression and therefore tend to be glorified.

Bohemia, western part of the CZECH REPUBLIC that is better known for the production of beer and GLASSES than wine. There are some small vineyard areas around the town of Melnik, and the Lobkowicz estate in particular has made some good-quality red wine. A substantial business making sparkling wines from base wine imported into the region is based here.

Bolgheri, small town in the Tuscan MAREMMA which gives its name to a DOC for relatively ordinary white and rosé wines, but provides a geographical reference point for at least two of the most famous SUPERTUSCANS, SASSICAIA and Ornellaia, made by cousins and members of the extended Antinori family. Red wines from Bolgheri—principally from Cabernet and Merlot although Sangiovese is also permitted—were granted DOC status in the mid 1990s, with Sassicaia given its own DOC as a subzone of Bolgheri. Both Bolgheri and the neighbouring township of Castagneto Carducci have become magnets for investors from outside the zone, including Angelo GAJA of Piedmont, as the wines have attained wide international recognition and popularity.   D.T.

Bolivia in SOUTH AMERICA has a long history of vine-growing but its modern wine industry is as yet undeveloped. Some creditable Cabernet/Merlot blends are produced, and examples of varietal Torrontés, Riesling, and Chenin Blanc. There are experimental plantings of most INTERNATIONAL VARIETIES for the production of VARIETAL wines with the Vinos de Altura appellation.

The wine produced for domestic consumption by foot treading and vinification in clay jars is called *patero*.

Bollinger, independent Champagne house based in Ay near Rheims producing a range of top-quality wines based on Pinot Noir grapes. The traditional Bollinger style is achieved with a backbone of Pinot Noir from the Ay vineyards, a certain proportion of BARREL FERMENTATION (unusual for sparkling wine), and TIRAGE in bottles stoppered, unusually, with corks rather than crown caps, often for a decade or more.

Bollinger RD ('recently disgorged') is the vintage-dated Grande Année with extra age. Rarest of all the Bollinger range of champagnes is the Vieilles Vignes Françaises, a BLANC DE NOIRS produced exclusively from ungrafted Pinot Noir vines that grow in a vineyard behind Bollinger's headquarters which was never affected by PHYLLOXERA.

Bollinger also owns a majority stake in the SAUMUR house Langlois Chateau. In 1985, Bollinger daringly took a 40 per cent share (reduced to just over 10 per cent when the company went public) of Petaluma in SOUTH AUSTRALIA, with particular involvement in the development of the associated sparkling-wine operation at Bridgewater Mill in the Adelaide Hills.

See also CHAMPAGNE.   S.A. & J.Ro.

Bolognesi, Colli, small DOC zone in the hills of Bologna in north-central Italy. See EMILIA-ROMAGNA.

Bolzano, or Bozen in German, the main town of the ALTO ADIGE in northern Italy. Local light-red wines may carry the name **Colli di Bolzano** or **Bozner Leiten.**

Bombino Bianco, important white grape variety, especially in APULIA in southern Italy, although its vineyard area is only a tenth of that of the southern red varieties Montepulciano and Negroamaro. Bombino Bianco is probably the most planted white grape variety in the productive and heavily milked vineyards of Apulia but is also planted in EMILIA-ROMAGNA, LATIUM, the MARCHES, and the ABRUZZI, where it is thought to be the true identity of the variety that is so common that it is, confusingly, called Trebbiano d'Abruzzo, even though it is distinctly less acidic than true TREBBIANO.

The vine yields extremely high quantities of relatively neutral wine, much of which has been shipped north, particularly to the energetic blenders of Germany. Many an ordinary SEKT or EU blend of TABLE WINE is made up substantially of Bombino Bianco, perhaps scented with a particularly aromatic German variety such as MORIO-MUSKAT. There is also a much less common dark-berried **Bombino Nero** in Apulia.

Bonarda, Italian red grape variety, or more accurately the name of three distinct varieties: (1) the Bonarda of the OLTREPÒ PAVESE and COLLI PIACENTINI, which is, in fact, not Bonarda at all but rather the CROATINA grape; (2) the Bonarda Novarese, used to soften SPANNA in its range of DOC reds in the Novara and Vercelli hills, which again is not Bonarda, but UVA RARA, a variety more widely employed in the Oltrepò Pavese; and (3) the so-called Bonarda Piemontese, an aromatic variety which has been virtually abandoned because of its small bunches and low productivity. In the mid 1990s, desultory attempts were being made to revive this last variety, in the belief that it will add aromatic interest when blended with the BARBERA grape. The only DOC wines in production which bear the name Bonarda are from the Oltrepò Pavese and are made from Croatina.   D.T.

Bonarda is also the name of the most widely grown red wine grape variety in ARGENTINA.

bonded warehouse or bonded winery, one in which no DUTY has been paid on the goods inside it. Prices for wines and, especially, spirits held in bond (IB) are therefore considerably lower than those quoted duty paid, or duty paid and delivered (DPD).

Bonnes Mares, great red GRAND CRU in Burgundy's CÔTE D'OR. See CHAMBOLLE-MUSIGNY and MOREY-ST-DENIS.

Bonnezeaux, particularly well-favoured enclave for sweet-white-wine production within the Coteaux du LAYON appellation in the Anjou district of the Loire. In this respect Bonnezeaux resembles QUARTS DE CHAUME to the north west but, despite its greater extent, it has not enjoyed such fame. A Bonnezeaux from a producer as reliable as Ch de Fesles can be a deep green-gold nectar at 10 to 20 years old. The wines are made exclusively from Chenin Blanc grapes grown on steep slopes near Thouarcé. These grapes should ideally be attacked by NOBLE ROT, or at the very least have been picked only after several TRIS through the vineyard. POTENTIAL ALCOHOL should be at least 13.5 per cent, half a per cent more than Quarts de Chaume, and yields are usually very low. See also LOIRE.

Borba, DOC in southern Portugal. See ALENTEJO. It is also the name of a productive Spanish white grape grown in EXTREMADURA.

Bordeaux, important French port on the GARONNE river leading to the GIRONDE estuary on the west coast. Bordeaux gives its name to the wine region which produces more top-quality wine than any other, from a total vineyard area of about 100,000 ha/247,000 acres

divided among 13,000 producers. Bordeaux has a higher proportion of large estates than any other French wine region, and produces more of the world's most expensive and sought-after wines than anywhere else. Red bordeaux is known in Britain as CLARET. The most famous examples, which represent less than five per cent of the region's total production, are characterized by their ability to evolve after years, sometimes decades, of BOTTLE AGEING. About a quarter of all bordeaux is white, however, some sweet as well as dry. Small quantities of rosé, light-red CLAIRET, and sparkling CRÉMANT are also made. The total quantity of wine produced each year is about 660 million bottles, which represents more than a quarter of France's total APPELLATION CONTRÔLÉE wine production, but the total can vary quite considerably owing to the vagaries of the climate. See BORDEAUX AC for bordeaux wine at its most basic and BORDEAUX TRADE for an account of the workings of the wine trade in Bordeaux.

Geography
The wine districts of Bordeaux hug the Gironde estuary and the rivers DORDOGNE and GARONNE which flow into it. The largest and most important appellation is BORDEAUX AC, but there are more than 50 appellations in all, although many of them are rarely seen outside the region. The notably flat Bordeaux vineyards are rarely at altitudes of more than a few metres above sea level.

Conventionally, in terms of the all-important fine red wines at least, the whole region is split into 'left bank' and 'right bank', or MÉDOC and GRAVES on one side of the Gironde, and ST-ÉMILION and POMEROL on the other, leaving the vast ENTRE-DEUX-MERS ('between two seas') district in the middle. Within the Haut Médoc, the superior land closer to Bordeaux, are the world-famous communes MARGAUX, ST-JULIEN, PAUILLAC, and ST-ESTÈPHE, together with the slightly less illustrious and, significantly, more inland appellations of LISTRAC and MOULIS. Most of the finest wines of the Graves, on the other hand, have come from an enclave awarded its own appellation in 1987, PESSAC-LÉOGNAN. Pomerol and St-Émilion have their 'satellite' appellations: LALANDE-DE-POMEROL; and Montagne-St-Émilion, Lussac-St-Émilion, St-Georges-St-Émilion, and Puisseguin-St-Émilion (see ST-ÉMILION). And just west of Pomerol are the increasingly respected appellations of FRONSAC and Canon-Fronsac.

Although a certain amount of white wine is made between the two rivers, most of Bordeaux's best white wines are made south of the river Garonne: dry wines from Graves and Pessac-Léognan, and sweet white wines which include some of the finest in the world from SAUTERNES and BARSAC. (See Climate below for a more detailed explanation.)

Also important quantitatively, however, are the so-called BORDEAUX CÔTES: the PREMIÈRES CÔTES DE BORDEAUX along the right bank of the Garonne; the GRAVES DE VAYRES enclave near Libourne on the left bank of the Dordogne; Côtes de BOURG across the wide Gironde estuary from Margaux; BLAYE, Côtes de Blaye, and Premières Côtes de Blaye in Côtes de Bourg's green, hilly hinterland; and the appellations which lie between Bordeaux and Bergerac to the east: Côtes de CASTILLON, Bordeaux Côtes de FRANCS, and STE-FOY-Bordeaux (not technically part of the Bordeaux Côtes).

The most famous vineyards are on particularly well-drained soils, notably gravels in the Médoc and Graves, and more calcareous terrain in parts of St-Émilion and Ste-Croix-du-Mont. For more details, see under these appellation names.

Climate

The mild climate of Bordeaux is tailor-made to produce mild wines, wines that are marked more by subtlety than power. (It is the vine varieties, described below, which endow the wines with longevity.) Unlike the much more CONTINENTAL CLIMATE of inland France, or the more arid Mediterranean influence in the south of the country, the vineyards of Bordeaux are moderated and heavily influenced by their proximity to the Atlantic, here warmed by the Gulf Stream, and this gentle oceanic regulation of the climate extends well inland, thanks to the wide Gironde estuary. Most years the MARITIME CLIMATE protects the vines from winter freeze (although February 1956 was so cold that many vines were killed) and spring frost (although April 1991 was so cold that much of that year's growth was frozen to extinction and the crop much reduced).

Spring is generally mild and damp, providing ample supplies of water for the growing season. Bordeaux's climate is hardly marginal, in that most grapes are usually ripened, but the region's weather is sufficiently unpredictable that the period of the FLOWERING in June is critical, with unsettled weather, especially cold

rain and strong winds, seriously prejudicing the quantity of the forthcoming crop.

Summers are usually hot, with occasional storms but rarely prolonged rainfall. The forests of the Landes to the south help to moderate temperatures (and to protect the wine districts from strong winds off the Atlantic), which reach an average maximum of 26 °C/79 °F in August, the hottest month. July is usually the driest and sunniest month. Annual average sunshine is well over 2,000 hours. Occasionally, as in 1989 and 1990, some periods in August can be so hot and dry that the vines suffer WATER STRESS and the ripening process may stop altogether, but generally Bordeaux's grapes ripen steadily, swollen by occasional rainfall, until a harvest between mid September and mid October. Rainfall can vary considerably from vintage to vintage and within the Bordeaux region itself, with the Médoc being wetter overall.

Excessive rain is the chief hazard at harvest, especially in a year during which full ripeness has yet to be achieved. In the sweet-wine areas, on the other hand, humidity is sought in autumn, particularly morning mists which evaporate during the day to encourage the spread of NOBLE ROT. It is no coincidence that Bordeaux's sweet-white-wine districts are clustered together on either side of the Garonne, about 20 miles upstream of the city, where the river Ciron flows into the Garonne. The waters of the Ciron, shaded for most of its length by the forests of the Landes, are invariably cooler than those of the Garonne and encourage the autumn morning mists which promote the BOTRYTIS fungus. In years when these are followed by warm, dry afternoons, the benevolent form of botrytis, noble rot, forms and great sweet white wine may be made. In damp years the malevolent form, grey rot, simply rots the fruit.

Vine varieties

Bordeaux's most famous, and best-travelled, grape variety is that on which the Médoc and Graves depend for their red wines, Cabernet Sauvignon. Bordeaux's most planted variety by far, however, is Merlot. It predominates not just in the famous right-bank appellations of St-Émilion and Pomerol but more importantly in the Entre-Deux-Mers and throughout the Bordeaux Côtes, in whose damper, cooler soils Cabernet Sauvignon can be difficult to ripen. CABERNET FRANC, also important on the right bank, where it is often called Bouchet, is the third most planted grape variety. PETIT VERDOT is the only other red grape variety of any importance, playing a minor, but in ripe vintages useful, role in the Médoc. Cot, Pressac, or MALBEC is an ingredient in some right-bank wines on the other hand, although it is declining in importance. CARMENÈRE is a red grape variety of historical importance.

In the early 1970s, Bordeaux's single most planted grape variety of either colour was Sémillon but it has become progressively less important since then, especially in the Entre-Deux-Mers. Sauvignon Blanc is Sémillon's traditional minor blending partner in sweet white bordeaux but is used increasingly for dry white wines, often unblended. The only other white grape variety fully sanctioned by the appellation laws is the Bordeaux speciality MUSCADELLE, but small quantities of UGNI BLANC, COLOMBARD, and Merlot Blanc are also planted and used in white BORDEAUX AC.

In stark contrast to France's other famous fine wine, BURGUNDY, red bordeaux is quintessentially a wine made from a blend of different vine varieties. This is only partly because Merlot and Cabernet are complementary, the flesh of the former filling in the frame of the latter. It is also an insurance policy on the part of growers in an unpredictable climate. Merlot grapes bud, flower, and ripen earlier than Cabernet Sauvignon, and are much more susceptible to COULURE, which can seriously affect quantity. Cabernet Sauvignon, on the other hand, ripens so late that a cool, cloudy late summer can seriously affect its quality. Having several grape varieties mitigates the climatological disasters which struck Merlot in 1984 and 1991, for example, and Cabernet Sauvignon in 1992. Although the ENCÉPAGEMENT, the exact proportions of different vine varieties, varies from château to château, a typical Médoc recipe is 70 per cent Cabernet Sauvignon, 15 per cent Cabernet Franc, 15 per cent Merlot, while a typical St-Émilion recipe might be 60 per cent Merlot, 30 per cent Cabernet Franc, and 10 per cent Cabernet Sauvignon.

Among dry white wines, the recipe is less predictable, although some all-Sauvignon wines are produced. The classic recipe for sweet white wines is 80 per cent Sémillon to 20 per cent Sauvignon Blanc. Bordeaux produces some of the world's finest dry Sémillon-dominated wines.

Wine-making

Wine-making techniques in Bordeaux's top estates are regarded as the paradigm by producers of Cabernet and Merlot wines, and fine sweet white wines, throughout the world. These techniques underwent considerable modernization in the 1970s and are continually being refined, with a trend towards much more approachable, more concentrated red wines. And the way in which dry white bordeaux is made was revolutionized in the 1980s.

Red wines Classic vinification of red bordeaux involves time and, because of the size of most top estates, considerable space in which to house the wine as it slowly makes itself (see RED-WINE-MAKING). The process begins in the vat hall or cuvier, then moves to a first-year CHAI, in which a year's production is stored in barrel, continues in the second-year *chai*, and may well necessitate an area for bottle storage.

Grapes are fermented in large fermentation vessels, known as CUVES in Bordeaux, which may be made of cement, stainless steel, or even wood, for between five and 10 or more days. Some form of TEMPERATURE CONTROL was installed at most properties in the 1970s or early 1980s, but is needed for only the hotter vintages; indeed it is increasingly common practice to heat the *cuves* at the beginning of FERMENTATION. Fermentation TEMPERATURES are generally slightly higher in Bordeaux than in the NEW WORLD. The concentration of PHENOLICS in ripe Bordeaux Cabernet Sauvignon grapes is such that EXTRACTION is an extremely important aspect of vinification. The post-fermentation MACERATION is therefore seen as crucial by most wine-makers, who allow the newly made wine at least a week 'on the skins'.

Some degree of CHAPTALIZATION is commonplace, and generally well judged, in Bordeaux, although CONCENTRATION techniques have been increasingly practised alternatives since the early 1990s. Natural YEASTS are the norm and vines have been such an important crop in Bordeaux for so long that the indigenous yeast population is reliable and well adapted.

After, and increasingly before, MALOLACTIC FERMENTATION, the wine is racked into French OAK BARRIQUES. The luxury of new barrels was introduced only in the 1980s, and the proportion of new barrels used even at top estates tends to be lower than in the most lavish New

World wineries: rarely more than 60 per cent, and even lower in less ripe vintages. During the first year, the wine is racked off its LEES into a fresh barrel every three months or so, as well as being clarified by egg-white FINING. The wine is traditionally moved to a separate second-year *chai*, where it remains until the wine is blended immediately prior to bottling, usually in early summer. The wine then undergoes the all-important period of BOTTLE AGEING, although this is likely, depending on the state of the market, to take place in the cellars of the BORDEAUX TRADE, the wine merchant, and, most typically, the consumer.

The ASSEMBLAGE is a crucial operation of selection, undertaken in the first few months after fermentation, during which it is decided which lots of wine will be blended together to form the principal *grand vin* for that year, which lots will form the SECOND WINE, and which may be sold off at an even lower level, either in bulk or in bottle. In less successful years, less than half of the wine produced on an estate might be selected for the *grand vin*.

The procedure above is that followed by the CLASSED GROWTHS and those who aspire to that quality level. Most wine which qualifies merely as BORDEAUX AC is more likely to be fairly ruthlessly filtered than fined, and is not given any BARREL MATURATION, but is bottled after a few months in tank. Some PETITS CHÂTEAUX may treat their wines to a stint in barrique, but such barrels are likely to be hand-me-downs from properties whose wines sell at a higher price.

For Bordeaux's exclusively red-wine appellations, see MÉDOC, HAUT-MÉDOC, ST-ESTÈPHE, PAUILLAC, ST-JULIEN, MARGAUX, LISTRAC, MOULIS, ST-ÉMILION, POMEROL, FRONSAC, and CASTILLON.

Dry whites WHITE-WINE-MAKING is relatively unremarkable in Bordeaux, except that the region was one of the last in France to cling to high doses of SULPHUR in finished dry wines, and in the upper echelons of white Graves and Pessac-Léognan BARREL MATURATION has one of the longest histories in the world. Additional flavour may be imbued by prefermentation SKIN CONTACT at low temperatures, known here as *macération pelliculaire*.

For Bordeaux's principal dry-white-wine appellations, see PESSAC-LÉOGNAN, GRAVES, ENTRE-DEUX-MERS, BLAYE, and GRAVES DE VAYRES.

Sweet whites Bordeaux's sweet-white-wine appellations are, in very approximate descending order of quality, SAUTERNES, BARSAC, STE-CROIX-DU-MONT, LOUPIAC, CÉRONS, CADILLAC, PREMIÈRES CÔTES DE BORDEAUX, GRAVES Supérieures, STE-FOY-Bordeaux, and Bordeaux ST-MACAIRE and Bordeaux Supérieur (for which see BORDEAUX AC).

Basic sweet white bordeaux, often described as *moelleux*, is a simple, sugary wine, typically made either by fermenting the grapes out to produce a regular dry wine which is then sweetened by adding concentrated grape must, or by enthusiastic CHAPTALIZATION followed by stopping the alcoholic FERMENTATION by chilling or with high doses of sulphur. Winemakers in Sauternes and Barsac, however, and their more ambitious counterparts elsewhere, aim to make very rich BOTRYTIZED wines from grapes at the full limit of ripeness, which may be described as LIQUOREUX. This involves a considerably more painstaking wine-making regime, even more dependent than any other on events in the vineyard, which is described in SAUTERNES.

CONCENTRATION of all sorts is becoming more common for all types of bordeaux.

Bordeaux AC. The most important sort of wine produced in Bordeaux, quantitatively if not qualitatively, is that which qualifies for the simple appellation Bordeaux. Approximately 40 per cent of all red APPELLATION CONTRÔLÉE wine produced in the region, and almost 70 per cent of all white, is straightforward Bordeaux AC. This wine is typically produced outside the more specific commune or regional appellations, although a great deal of red Bordeaux AC comes from the ENTRE-DEUX-MERS region, whose eponymous appellation applies only to white wine. (A counterpoint to this is the fact that the appellations of the Médoc apply only to red wines, so that even the Médoc's smartest white wines, such as Pavillon Blanc du Ch MARGAUX, are not allowed any appellation grander than Bordeaux AC. Similarly, dry white wines made from grapes usually grown for SAUTERNES qualify only for Bordeaux AC.) The other area with the greatest concentration of vineyard dedicated to the production of Bordeaux and Bordeaux Supérieur is that north of Libourne, where Merlot grapes predominate.

The great majority of Bordeaux AC produced is made, often by CO-OPERATIVES, to be sold for blending anonymously into humble GENERIC wines, of very varying quality, but there are also individual properties, so-called PETITS CHÂ-

TEAUX, which lie outside any grander appellation but which express their own TERROIR and practise CHÂTEAU BOTTLING. About two-thirds of all Bordeaux AC produced is red, and the white, which may be called **Bordeaux Sec**, is invariably dry. Bordeaux is relatively low in alcohol, the minimum ALCOHOLIC STRENGTH after FERMENTATION being 10 per cent (although most wines are between 11 and 12.5).

More specific appellations which incorporate the word Bordeaux include **Bordeaux Supérieur**, whose minimum permitted alcoholic strength is half a per cent higher than Bordeaux AC and which is mainly red, but is occasionally sweet and white; **Bordeaux CLAIRET**, which is a light red recalling the precursors of CLARET; the bottle-fermented sparkling wine **Bordeaux Mousseux**, which is being replaced by CRÉMANT de Bordeaux; and a very minor dry white oddity, **Bordeaux Haut-Benauge** from the south of the Entre-Deux-Mers.

Most of these wines are designed to be drunk within a year of bottling if white, rosé, or clairet and within two or three years if red. The better examples are unmistakably lighter versions of Bordeaux's grander wines, while the worst can taste like homeless TABLE WINE. Few producers can afford to age wines at this level in OAK, and even fewer of the wines have the concentration to benefit from it, although exceptions are becoming more numerous. Most of the Bordeaux BRANDS are Bordeaux AC, most notably MOUTON CADET, which started off life with the much grander and more specific appellation of PAUILLAC.

The Bordeaux authorities call the above appellations the 'Bordeaux regional appellations' (all of which may much more simply be labelled Bordeaux), and include with them the Entre-Deux-Mers, STE-FOY-Bordeaux, and Côtes de Bordeaux-ST-MACAIRE appellation, which applies to the everyday sweet white wines made in a small district immediately south west of Haut-Benauge.

Other appellations which incorporate or have at one time incorporated the word Bordeaux are Bordeaux Côtes de CASTILLON, Bordeaux Côtes de FRANCS, and PREMIÈRES CÔTES DE BORDEAUX, all of which belong to the sub-group of Bordeaux appellations known as the BORDEAUX CÔTES.

Bordeaux Côtes, local name in BORDEAUX for appellations on the, often historic, outer fringes of the region: BLAYE, Côtes de Blaye, Premières Côtes de Blaye; Côtes de BOURG; PREMIÈRES CÔTES DE BORDEAUX; Côtes de CASTILLON; Bordeaux Côtes de FRANCS; and GRAVES DE VAYRES. These wines tend to have considerably more personality than regular BORDEAUX AC, the result perhaps of local pride, and can provide some of Bordeaux's best wine value.

Bordeaux trade. The sheer quantity of wine produced in Bordeaux, the fact that so much requires AGEING, and the historical importance of Bordeaux as a port, mean that its wine trade is more stratified than most—even if wine is no longer the city's economically most important commodity.

Bordeaux wines have always been produced by one category of people and sold by another. The wine producers of the region range from world-famous estates with 200 ha/500 acres under vine, to owners of 2.5 ha or less, whose wines nowadays may also be world-famous (see MICROCHÂTEAUX) or whose grapes are delivered to one of the region's wine CO-OPERATIVES, or vinified in conditions of precarious HYGIENE for personal consumption.

The wine merchants, or NÉGOCIANTS, sometimes called *négociants-éleveurs* for their role in wine ÉLEVAGE, traditionally brought most of the wines they bought into their CHAIS in or around Bordeaux (notably its Quai des Chartrons) to be matured and shipped out to export customers, particularly in Britain and Scandinavia, either in barrels, or after bottling. They were joined in the early 20th century by merchants in LIBOURNE, who concentrated on markets in northern France and northern Europe.

So great was the quantity of wine to be traded that numbers of middlemen were needed between producers and the merchants, of whom professional brokers, or *courtiers*, such as Tastet & Lawton have become an essential part of Bordeaux's vinous commercial structure. What the merchant supplied in addition to the mere buying and selling of wine was technical ability (his cellarmaster and team were likely to be considerably better technicians than the producers'), and financing for the grower.

This way of doing business changed considerably after 1945, when even some of the FIRST GROWTHS were still made available to the merchants in bulk, and most of the CLASSED

GROWTHS have since 1959 been sold to the merchants on the condition that they are CHÂTEAU BOTTLED.

Since 1945, improvements in wine-making at all levels and, since the 1980s, PRICE increases and inflation levels which have made it impossible for even the biggest merchants to finance large quantities of wine, have tended to transform the role of the merchant from principal to broker. Some of the merchants have been more aggressive than most in adapting wine-making techniques at the bottom end of the market, particularly for BORDEAUX AC, to international changes in taste.

For examples of specific Bordeaux merchants, see SICHEL and MOUEIX.   W.B.

bore, wine. For some reason, wine bores exist in public consciousness and, it has to be said, reality in a more vividly pestilential way than art bores, music bores, or even sport bores. Perhaps this is because for most people wine is associated with sensual pleasure rather than analysis and verbal communication and so their wine-related boredom threshold is low. So far, wine bores are usually men, although women wine bores may be an eventual consequence of female financial emancipation. One woman's wine bore can be another person's wine expert, however.

Borraçal, synonym for Galicia's CAIÑO TINTO in Portugal's Vinho Verde region.

Borrado das Moscas, the DÃO region's name for the Portuguese variety BICAL.

Bosco, ordinary white grape of LIGURIA.

Bosnia Hercegovina, central part of what was YUGOSLAVIA before civil war erupted. The vineyards are in Hercegovina, sometimes spelt Hertzegovina or Herzegovina, in the south, down towards the coast around Mostar, inland, and to the north of Dubrovnik.

The region has its own grape types: the white ZILAVKA, famed for its generous alcohol levels combined with unusually refreshing ACIDITY; and the much less impressive red Blatina. Zilavka has begun to be planted in neighbouring territories.   A.H.M.

botrytis, without the capital B it botanically deserves, is commonly used as an abbreviation for the fungus *Botrytis cinerea*, and also for the benevolent NOBLE ROT and occasionally for the malevolent grey rot that this fungus causes. Grapes affected by noble rot and the wines produced from them are often called BOTRYTIZED, or **botrytis affected**.

botrytized, or **botrytis-affected, wines** are those made from white grapes affected by NOBLE ROT. Distinctively scented in youth, and with considerably more EXTRACT than most wines, they are the most complex and longest lived of all the sweet, white table wines. The noble rot smell is often described as honeyed, but it can also have an (attractive) overtone of boiled cabbage.

The risks and costs involved in making naturally botrytized wine make it necessarily expensive. It has therefore been an economical proposition only when sweet wines are highly valued. Germany's botrytized wines have always been regarded as precious rarities for which a ready market can be found within Germany. France's output of botrytized wines is potentially much greater, but when sweet wines were out of FASHION in the 1960s and 1970s, enthusiasm for producing them inevitably waned, only to be rekindled in the 1980s.

Geography and climate

Many conditions have to be met before botrytized wines can be produced. Not only is a MESOCLIMATE which favours misty mornings and warm afternoons in autumn needed, but producers must have the knowledge and the will to sacrifice quantity for nothing more certain than possible quality. Botrytized wines are very much a product of psyche as well as nature.

The district with the potential to produce the greatest quantity of top-quality botrytized wine is SAUTERNES (although it all depends, as everywhere, on the precise WEATHER of the year). The confluence of the rivers Ciron and GARONNE provide an ideal mesoclimate for the satisfactory development of noble rot. Nearby sweet-white-wine districts CÉRONS, LOUPIAC, CADILLAC, and STE-CROIX-DU-MONT may also produce small quantities of botrytized wines, although the price fetched by these appellations rarely justifies the additional production costs.

In extremely good vintages such as 1988–90 and 1997–9, botrytized wine is also made in MONBAZILLAC, and occasionally even in BERGERAC on the river Dordogne from Sémillon, Sauvignon, and Muscadelle grapes. One or two fine examples of this style have also emerged from Gaillac.

On the river Loire, appellations such as

Coteaux de l'AUBANCE, Coteaux du LAYON, QUARTS DE CHAUME, BONNEZEAUX, MONTLOUIS, and VOUVRAY can produce botrytized wines in good years, and they are given even greater ageing potential for being made from the acidic CHENIN BLANC grape.

Botrytized wines may also be made from such varied grapes as Mâconnais Chardonnays and Alsace Rieslings in exceptional years.

Germany is the other famous source of botrytized wines, usually labelled BEERENAUSLESE or TROCKENBEERENAUSLESE, although the quantities made vary enormously according to vintage. Riesling is the classic grape, although some of the GERMAN CROSSINGS can be persuaded to rot nobly in an exceptionally suitable year. Noble-rot infections are much more reliable in the Burgenland district of AUSTRIA, where, thanks to the influence of the Neusiedlersee, considerable quantities of botrytized Beerenauslesen and Trockenbeerenauslesen are made most years. Over the border in Hungary, Tokaj is still closely associated with botrytized-wine-making, as are various parts of ROMANIA, notably COTNARI.

Botrytized-wine-making is an embryonic art in Italy, Spain, and most of Portugal, where producers and consumers tend to favour either DRIED-GRAPE WINES or FORTIFIED wines.

In the New World, botrytized wines are made with increasing frequency. Edelkeur was a South African prototype which enjoyed international acclaim in the 1970s. Griffith in NEW SOUTH WALES's Riverland was producing Australian botrytized PEDRO XIMÉNEZ as early as the late 1950s, and is now a centre for the production of relatively early maturing botrytized Semillon. In Australia, New Zealand, and in California particularly, a host of botrytized Rieslings have emerged.

California has also seen attempts to simulate noble rot, by growing spores of the botrytis fungus in a laboratory and spraying them on picked, healthy, ripe grapes before subjecting them to alternately humid and warm conditions for a couple of weeks. A series of such wines has been made at Beringer in the Napa Valley.

As awareness of noble rot and botrytized wines grows, the number of wine-makers anxious to experiment also increases, even if the market is not always rapturous, and they are usually at the mercy of the weather. Even ENGLAND has succeeded in producing botrytized wine.

Vine varieties

Any white grape variety may be infected benevolently by the botrytis fungus; red varieties simply lose their colour. Certain varieties seem particularly sensitive to the fungus and well adapted to the production of botrytized wines, however: Sémillon, Sauvignon Blanc, Chenin Blanc, Riesling, Gewürztraminer, and Furmint are traditional.

Viticulture and wine-making

The chief viticultural aspect of making botrytized wines is the number of passages or TRIS through the vineyard which may have to be made in order to pick grapes only at the optimum point of botrytis infection, because noble rot is so crucial to quality. See SAUTERNES for a description of the likely routine there.

If picking botrytized grapes is painstaking, obtaining their juice and persuading it to ferment is at least as difficult because of its composition. Botrytized wines are capable of extremely long BOTTLE AGEING, for many decades in some cases.

botte, Italian word for a large wooden cask. The plural is **botti**.

bottle ageing, the process of deliberately maturing a wine after bottling, whether for a few weeks as a conscious effort on the part of the bottler to allow the wine to recover from BOTTLE SICKNESS or, in the case of very fine wines, for many years in order to allow the wine to mature. See AGEING.

bottle deposit in red wines is a lacquer-like pigmented deposit adhering to the inner bottle surface and is different from SEDIMENT. This deposition, which may begin in the first few months after bottling, may cover only a small area of the bottle shoulder or may eventually cover the entire glass surface with which the wine is in contact. Wine quality is not affected by bottle deposit and experience has shown that premium reds (particularly those made from RHÔNE varieties) tend to exhibit this deposit more than lower-quality wines.   P.J.W.

bottle fermented, description of some SPARKLING WINES made either by the traditional method, or by the transfer method. See SPARKLING-WINE-MAKING.

bottles, by far the most common CONTAINERS for finished wine. Being made of glass, bottles are inconveniently fragile and relatively heavy, but, importantly for long-term AGEING, they are inert. A standard bottle contains 75 cl/27 fl oz although see also BOTTLE SIZES.

Bottle shapes There are certain standard bottle shapes associated most commonly with certain regions or, increasingly, styles of wine associated with those regions. Ambitiously made Chardonnays the world over, for example, tend to be put into burgundy bottles. Since the geographical provenance of most wines should be clear from the label, understanding bottle shapes is most useful for the clues they provide as to the intended style of the wine inside them. Some RIOJA producers, for example, put their Garnacha-dominated, richer blends into burgundy bottles, while their Tempranillo wines designed for longer ageing are put into bordeaux bottles. The red bordeaux bottle itself, incidentally, has been the subject of much research and revision to increase the durability of the wine stored inside it (see also Bottle colour below).

Many German wine producers in particular have employed bottle shapes as their most eloquent marketing tool in distancing drier, non-aromatic styles of wine from traditional German wines sold in the elongated bottle shape which has come to be associated with aromatic wines, though this shape has been retained by some of the most quality-conscious German producers as a defiant statement of their reverence for tradition.

Most champagne and sparkling wines are sold in much the same shape of bottle, moulded to be thick and strong enough to withstand the pressure of up to six atmospheres inside each bottle. Considerable energy and money is expended, however, on designing special bottles for PRESTIGE CUVÉES, the Dom Pérignon bottle of MOËT & CHANDON having set a formidable standard. The precise shape of the lip of a champagne bottle indicates whether the second fermentation took place under a crown cap or under a cork, as it does in some very rare cases.

Bottles vary in the extent to which they have a punt, or inverse indentation in their base. Most champagne and sparkling-wine bottles have a particularly deep indentation because of the need to stack inverted bottles one on top of the other during the traditional method of SPARKLING-WINE-MAKING. Punts are less obviously useful for still wines—although they can make 75-cl capacity bottles look bigger and more impressive—and deep punts can provide

useful purchase for the thumb when SERVING wine from a bottle.

The exact shape and design of the neck and lip of the bottle is determined by what is used to STOPPER it. Most stoppers other than cork require some modification of the lip. In the 1990s, furthermore, many producers tried to distinguish their packaging by adopting bottles with a flange but no CAPSULE around the top. These can make difficulties for some CORKSCREWS and denote nothing more substantial than a FASHION in bottle design.

In some regions, one specific bottle has been adopted by all but the most anarchic producers, and indeed adoption of a special local, regional, or appellational bottle became particularly fashionable in the 1980s. Examples of special bottles are the heavy, embossed CHATEAUNEUF-DU-PAPE bottle; the BOCKSBEUTEL of FRANKEN; the CH GRILLET bottle peculiar to a single property; and the long-necked green bottle particular to MUSCADET.

In general, Italians, with their firm belief in the importance of design, offer the most dazzling range of wine bottles. Weight and darkness of glass seem to be highly valued by the Italians in particular, although it is a general rule throughout the wine world that the heavier a bottle, the greater the aspirations of the producer of the wine for its longevity. Bottling wine in the lightest, cheapest glass is one way of paring production costs to a minimum.

Bottle colour Wine keeps best in dark glass—as the Champenois, the most energetic researchers into the effects of bottle choice on wine, have found (ROEDERER Cristal, which has traditionally been sold in clear glass, is always swathed in an orange wrap designed to filter out ultraviolet light). On the other hand, dark glass prevents the consumer from being impressed by the colour of a wine. For this reason, most ROSÉS, not designed for BOTTLE AGEING in any case, are sold in clear glass. It is less clear why SAUTERNES and other sweet white bordeaux is sold in clear glass; TRADITION is the explanation. Most wine bottles are, for reasons of both tradition and the orientation of glass furnaces, some shade of green, from pale blueish green to a colour that to all intents and purposes is black. For traditional reasons again, brown glass is used for some Italian wines, for FORTIFIED wines, and was the traditional way of telling a HOCK or Rhine wine from a MOSELLE in green glass. However, German producers are increasingly using powerfully blue-green glass. One of the most distinctive glass colours for wine bottles is the yellow-green used for white burgundy, called *feuille morte* in France and therefore 'dead leaf' in much of the New World.

More clues from the bottle

Most wine bottles are moulded with the mark of their manufacturers, sometimes with their capacity, and all wine sold within Europe from the 1990s should have a lot marking, a small code stamped on the label, foil, or bottle, so that each bottle can be traced back to its precise bottling and dispatch.

bottle sickness, also known less politely as **bottle stink,** unpleasant and increasingly rare smell apparent in a wine immediately on opening which dissipates after a few minutes.

Off-odour compounds may occasionally be formed by moulds embedded in poor CORKS, or by a small amount of wine which has escaped through the cork or capsule and is then acetified or otherwise subjected to bacterial spoilage. This is the principal reason why some people advocate allowing a bottle of wine to BREATHE before serving (and one of the reasons why it is wise to wipe the top of an opened bottle). DECANTING can achieve the same end.

A similar phenomenon should perhaps more properly be called 'bottling sickness' as it is usually an unpleasant smell that results directly from the addition of SULPHUR DIOXIDE during the bottling process. If the wine is tasted in the first few weeks after bottling, the smell of sulphur dioxide may be obtrusive and it is wise to wait until the sulphur dioxide has reacted with the oxygen and the wine once more tastes as it did prior to bottling.

bottle sizes are standardized in most countries. A bottle containing 75 cl (27 fl oz) is now accepted almost universally as the standard wine bottle, with the magnum being 1.5 l, exactly twice the capacity.

Half-bottles usually contain 37.5 cl and tend to hasten wine AGEING, partly because they contain more OXYGEN per centilitre of wine since the bottle neck and ULLAGE are the same as for a full bottle. Most wine bottlers have viewed halves and other bottles smaller than the standard bottle as an unwelcome inconvenience, but there continues to be strong demand for half-bottles, particularly in res-

taurants. There have been various attempts to launch a 50-cl bottle.

The bottle capacities permitted within Europe for still wines are 10 cl, 25 cl, 37.5 cl, 50 cl, 75 cl, and 1, 1.5, 2, 3, 4, 5, 6, 8, 9, and 10 litres (and wine may be served in 18.7-cl bottles aboard trains, planes, and the like). Sparkling-wine bottles come in 12.5-, 20-, 37.5- and 75-cl and 1.5-, 3-, 4.5-, 6- and 9-litre capacities. The larger-sized bottles, some of them no longer in production, have different names in different regions.

Capacity (l)	Bordeaux	Champagne/Burgundy
1.5 (2 bottles)	magnum	magnum
2.25 (3 bottles)	Marie-Jeanne	not found
3 (4 bottles)	double magnum	Jéroboam
4.5 (6 bottles)	Jéroboam	Rehoboam
6 (8 bottles)	Impériale	Methuselah
9 (12 bottles)	not found	Salmanazar
16 bottles	not found	Balthazar
20 bottles	not found	Nebuchadnezzar

Larger bottles (often known as 'large formats' or *grands formats*) up to Impériale size favour slow but subtle wine AGEING. Giant champagne bottles, on the other hand, tend to favour publicity rather than wine quality (sizes larger than a magnum tend to be filled with wine made in smaller bottles).

bottle variation is one of the more tantalizing aspects of wine appreciation. It is only to be expected with a product as sensitive to STORAGE conditions as wine that bottles of the same wine will differ—perhaps because one has been exposed to higher temperatures or greater humidity. There can easily be a perceptible difference in quality and character between bottles from the very same CASE. SUBJECTIVISM may play a part, as well as a difference in FILL LEVELS. It was not until the 1970s, for example, that it became commonplace for Bordeaux châteaux to ensure that a uniform blend was made before bottling; some of the world's more artisanal producers still bottle by hand from cask to cask. Similarly, wines bottled on two different occasions may find themselves packed in the same case (although modern lot marking provides more clues in this respect). CORKS can also contribute to bottle variation with individual bottles exhibiting odours from TCA originating from the cork, and the ability of the cork seal to allow varying degrees of oxygen into bottles.

bottling information. Most wine labels should divulge where the wine was bottled. Wines bottled in the same place as they were vinified are described under CHÂTEAU BOTTLED, DOMAINE BOTTLED, ESTATE BOTTLED, ERZEUGER-ABFÜLLUNG, or GUTSABFÜLLUNG.

Common phrases for 'bottled' are *mis en bouteille* in French, *imbottigliato* in Italian, *embotellado* in Spanish, and *engarrafado* in Portuguese.

Many of the wines bottled by an enterprise other than the one which made the wine are labelled relatively obliquely. Within the European Union, a bottler's address may not be specified on the label of a basic TABLE WINE if it incorporates the name of a QUALITY WINE; the bottler's postal code is usually employed instead.

Bouchard, Père et Fils, one of Beaune's large merchant houses and the most important vineyard owner on Burgundy's Côte de BEAUNE, owned by Joseph Henriot of the eponymous champagne house who once ran VEUVE CLICQUOT. Bouchard have holdings in 25 different Beaune vineyards, including their exclusivities Beaune-Grèves, Vigne de l'Enfant Jésus and Beaune, Clos de la Mousse. They are also particularly proud of their holding in Le MONTRACHET, their particularly significant share of Chevalier-Montrachet, and their exclusive distribution rights to the VOSNE-ROMANÉE La Romanée GRAND CRU. In all, 71 of their 92 ha are in grands crus or PREMIERS CRUS.

Wines from their own vineyards are undoubtedly Bouchard's best, although they are rarely Burgundy's most concentrated. For the much larger NÉGOCIANT business, the firm buys in considerable quantities of grapes (including all of those grown in the Clos-St-Marc premier cru in Nuits-St-Georges), must (notably in Chablis), and young wines for ÉLEVAGE in the medieval cellars below the Ch de Beaune. Under Henriot, even relatively inexpensive red wines have become noticeably deeper, more concentrated and more aggressively modern.

Bouchet, the name for CABERNET FRANC used in ST-ÉMILION and elsewhere on the right bank of the GIRONDE.

Bouchy, the local name for the CABERNET FRANC grape when grown in MADIRAN.

bouquet, oft-ridiculed tasting term for the smell of a wine, particularly that of a mature or maturing wine. It is used loosely by many wine tasters to describe any pleasant wine smell or smells but, just as a bouquet of flowers suggests a composition of several varied elements, many wine professionals distinguish between the simple AROMA of the grape and the bouquet of the more complex compounds which evolve as a result of FERMENTATION, ÉLEVAGE, and BOTTLE AGEING. See also AGEING, FLAVOUR COMPOUNDS, and FLAVOUR PRECURSORS.

Bourboulenc is an ancient white grape variety that may well have originated in Greece, as the now rarely seen Asprokondoura, and has been grown throughout southern France for centuries. Ripening late but keeping its acidity well, it is allowed into a wide variety of Provençal and southern Rhône appellations (including Châteauneuf-du-Pape) but is rarely encountered as a dominant variety other than in the distinctive whites of La CLAPE in the Languedoc. France's total area planted with Bourboulenc halved in the 1970s and then doubled again in the 1980s thanks in part to a re-evaluation in the Languedoc, where it is also, confusingly, known as Malvoisie. Together with Maccabéo, it should constitute more than 50 per cent of the blend for any white MINERVOIS, and the two, with Grenache Blanc, should dominate CORBIÈRES Blanc. Wine produced can be fine, with a hint of smoke.

Bourg, small town in the BORDEAUX region on the right bank of the river DORDOGNE, just up river of its confluence with the Garonne, which is surrounded by the **Côtes de Bourg** appellation. In most years, 210,000 hl/5.5 million gal of Côtes de Bourg red is produced, more than any other BORDEAUX CÔTES appellation. Grape varieties and organization are very similar to the larger BLAYE area to the immediate north. Almost all wine produced is red, based on Merlot grapes, and designed to last slightly longer than Premières Côtes de Blaye, to be consumed at four to six or even more years old. The average quality of Bourg's PETITS CHÂTEAUX (some of them not that small) has been improving. A little dry white wine is also made, chiefly from the eminently distillable UGNI BLANC and COLOMBARD grapes which still predominate here. The star of the appellation is Roc des Combes, produced by the owner of St-Émilion's Ch Tertre-Roteboeuf on a particularly well-favoured site on the Gironde itself, but top cuvées of Ch Tayac and Ch Terrefort-Bellegrave are also notable. This is an appellation worth watching. See BORDEAUX.

Bourgogne, the French name for both the region of BURGUNDY (La Bourgogne) and burgundy, the wines thereof (*le bourgogne*), which are red, white, and very occasionally rosé. In particular, Bourgogne refers to the most basic, generic category of APPELLATIONS in Burgundy.

For white wines, the generic appellations are BOURGOGNE ALIGOTÉ, **Bourgogne Blanc** (made from Chardonnay grapes, although Pinot Blanc and Pinot Gris are tolerated), and **Bourgogne Grand Ordinaire**, which may contain Chardonnay, Aligoté, Melon de Bourgogne, and (in the Yonne, the Chablis *département*) Sacy.

For red wines, the generic appellations are BOURGOGNE PASSETOUTGRAINS, **Bourgogne Grand Ordinaire**, and **Bourgogne Rouge**. The last is usually pure Pinot Noir, although it may technically include the César and Tressot once grown in the Yonne, and may be made from Gamay grapes if grown in one of the BEAUJOLAIS crus. Bourgogne Passetoutgrains is a blend of Gamay and Pinot Noir, requiring a minimum of one-third of the latter. Bourgogne Grand Ordinaire may include Pinot, Gamay, César, and Tressot.

A small amount of pink wine is sold as **Bourgogne Rosé** or **Bourgogne Clairet**.

Bourgogne of whatever colour may be followed by a geographical suffix, either denoting a region (Hautes Côtes de Nuits, Hautes Côtes de Beaune, Côte Chalonnaise, Côtes d'Auxerre); a village (Chitry, Coulanges-la-Vineuse, Epineuil, Irancy, Vézelay); or in certain cases a vineyard (Côte St-Jacques at Joigny; La Chapelle Notre Dame, Le Chapitre, and Montrecul in the Côte d'Or).

Thus it is evident that the scope of 'Bourgogne', be it white or red, encompasses wide variations in provenance, quality, and style of wine, which may not be clear from the label. A Bourgogne Rouge or Bourgogne Blanc made by a grower in one of the major villages of the Côte d'Or (such as MEURSAULT for whites and VOLNAY or CHAMBOLLE-MUSIGNY for reds) is likely to be reliably fashioned in the image of classic CÔTE D'OR burgundy, however, and may well represent excellent value. There is every chance that the wine will be made from vines only just outside the village appellation yet be sold at half the price.

CRÉMANT de Bourgogne is the generic appellation for sparkling Burgundy, either white or rosé, while the now rare red version is classified as **Bourgogne Mousseux**.

See also BOURGOGNE ALIGOTÉ and BOURGOGNE PASSETOUTGRAINS. J.T.C.M.

Bourgogne Aligoté, a generic appellation in Burgundy for white wines made from the ALIGOTÉ grape. These wines vary between refreshingly crisp and disagreeably tart, although the latter characteristic suits their role as the basis for *vin blanc cassis*, known as 'KIR' after the canon of Dijon who perfected this aperitif. Aligoté is primarily for early consumption although wines from the best locations such as Chitry in the Yonne, PERNAND-VERGELESSES in the Côte de Beaune, and Bouzeron in the Côte CHALONNAISE can age well. Since 1979, Bouzeron has enjoyed a specific appellation, Bourgogne Aligoté de Bouzeron, promoted to the simple appellation Bouzeron in 1997. J.T.C.M.

Bourgogne Passetoutgrains, red thirst-quencher from Burgundy made from Pinot Noir (minimum one-third) and Gamay grapes. Often deep in colour and rather savagely animal when young, Passetoutgrains with age can attain greater refinement as the Pinot Noir flavours start to dominate. The best examples come from vineyards in the CÔTE D'OR. Almost two-thirds as much of this appellation is made each year as Bourgogne Rouge but relatively little leaves the region. J.T.C.M.

Bourgueil, potentially captivating red wines made on the north bank of the Loire in the west of the TOURAINE district. The climate here is particularly gentle and rainfall is low, as in much of ANJOU to the immediate west.

The CABERNET FRANC grape is mainly responsible for these medium-bodied wines, which are typically marked by a more powerful aroma (reminding some of raspberries, others of pencil shavings) and slightly more noticeable tannins than the wines of CHINON to the south. As in Chinon, up to 25 per cent Cabernet Sauvignon is allowed in the blend. Bourgueil can be aged for five or many more years in really successful, fully ripe VINTAGES such as 1989, 1990, 1995, and 1996, while **St-Nicolas-de-Bourgueil**, produced on lighter soils in the west of the region, is generally a lighter, earlier-maturing wine. These fragrant wines are extremely popular in Paris and northern France but have yet to be discovered by most non-French wine lovers.

A little dry rosé Bourgueil is also made, but

the appellation does not, unlike Chinon, encompass white wines. Reliable producers include Yannick Amirault, Druet, and Joel Taluau. See LOIRE.

Bouvier, minor white grape variety now grown mainly in the Burgenland region of AUSTRIA, where it is particularly used for Sturm, the cloudy, part-fermented sweet grape juice that is a local speciality at harvest time. It is also grown in the Mátra Foothills of HUNGARY.

Bouzeron, village in the Côte Chalonnaise with its own appellation for its justly famous BOURGOGNE ALIGOTÉ.

boxes, wine. In the 1970s, an entirely new way of packaging wine was developed, expressly to provide a significant volume of wine in a package that is not as breakable or heavy as a bottle, and is better able to preserve any wine left in the container. It comprises a collapsible laminated bag inside a strong carton with a handle, and wine is drawn out of a tap specially designed to minimize the ingress of potentially harmful OXYGEN. Filling and packaging costs for **bag-in-box** wines, together with the difficulty of making the wine container completely airtight, have been the main brakes on what was initially a remarkably rapid sales success. The package, commonly holding four litres of wine, is particularly popular in Australia and New Zealand, where it is known flatteringly as the 'cask' or, more prosaically, 'bladder pack'. Wine boxes have also enjoyed success in northern Europe, notably 3-l boxes. Boxes are generally filled with less expensive wines designed for early drinking and are bought either in bulk for parties or catering purposes, or by those who want to enjoy a simple wine one glass at a time over several weeks and who do not object to or notice the deterioration in quality towards the end of that period. The wine inside a bag, even one whose tap has remained sealed, is best immediately after filling, and has usually deteriorated quite markedly 12 months after filling, which is why most wine boxes are dated. (See LEFTOVER WINE for details of devices for preserving wine in partially empty bottles.)

Brachetto, distinctively aromatic light-red grape variety found principally round Asti, Roero, and Alessandria, where it is particularly successful, in the PIEDMONT region of Italy. It produces wines, notably **Brachetto d'Acqui** promoted to DOCG status in 1996, that are fizzy,

relatively alcoholic, and have both the colour and flavour of strawberries.

Bramaterra, a lighter variation on the NEBBIOLO theme of LESSONA in the PIEDMONT region of north-west Italy. See SPANNA, the local name for Nebbiolo, for more details. See also the nearby BOCA, GATTINARA, GHEMME, SIZZANO, and FARA in Novara.

branco, Portuguese word meaning 'white'. *Vinho branco* is therefore white wine.

brands, interpreted strictly as individual products marketed on the basis of their name and image rather than on their inherent qualities, have a less secure place in the early-21st-century wine market than branded goods do in many others. Most sectors of the wine market are extremely fragmented (although the FORTIFIED WINE business is not and has been built on brands), so that brand promotion is difficult to make cost effective, and can leave **branded wines** looking extremely poor value. Wine brands offer a familiar lifeline to new wine consumers baffled by a multiplicity of unfamiliar, often foreign, proper names. But as wine drinkers become more sophisticated, they learn to decode what initially seems the arcane language of wine names, usually by identifying the major VARIETALS and some of the more important place-names. Thus, brands are most in demand in embryonic and fast-growing markets, such as northern Europe and the rest of the English-speaking world between the 1950s and the 1980s, and in Africa, South America, and some Asian countries in the 1990s.

It may be difficult to market branded wines in a competitive market, but it can be even more difficult to maintain consistency of a product as variable as wine. Supplies are strictly limited to an annual batch-production process. Wine cannot be manufactured to suit demand, and different vintages impose their own characteristics on the product regardless of consumer taste. A high proportion of all wine drinkers were introduced to wine through brands, and it is to the credit of those brand owners most dedicated to maintaining quality standards whenever the introduction was a happy one.

Notably successful international individual wine brands are relatively few, and they have perforce to be based on wine of which there is no shortage of supply. BLUE NUN, LANCERS, MATEUS ROSÉ, MOUTON CADET are all examples of such brands which have in their time achieved annual sales measured in millions of cases.

Many of the world's bigger wine companies are attempting to market themselves to the consumer as a brand: GALLO, HARDYS, and PENFOLDS come immediately to mind. The definition of a wine brand is certainly a loose one. In some respects, French CLARETS named after the estate which produced them were the first wine brands. And any definition which incorporates the notion of relatively elastic supply and some studied promotion would allow that the most successful wine brands of all are the so-called *grande marque* (which translates directly as 'big brand') CHAMPAGNES.

Braquet, historic light-red grape variety of PROVENCE which is a valued ingredient in the distinctive red and pink wines of BELLET near Nice.

Brazil, vast country and third most important wine producer in SOUTH AMERICA, after Argentina and Chile.

Wines with serious claims to quality were not developed until the 1970s, when several important multinational corporations, including MOËT & CHANDON, SEAGRAM, Bacardi, Heublein, Domecq, and MARTINI & ROSSI, established wine companies in Brazil and invested in modern wine-making equipment and imported BARRIQUES. Vine varieties such as Chardonnay, Welschriesling (Riesling Italico), Sémillon, Gewürztraminer, Cabernet Franc, Merlot, and Cabernet Sauvignon were also imported, and a programme of viticultural improvements embarked upon.

Modern Brazilian viticulture is concentrated in the extreme south of the country in the state of Rio Grande do Sul, principally on the high, hilly Serra Gaucha region, north and inland of the state capital Pôrto Alegre, and also in the much smaller, newer Frontera wine region on the border with URUGUAY and Argentina.

The grapes are often picked before full ripeness is reached and CHAPTALIZATION is almost always necessary. The white wines of Serra Gaucha are usually high in MALIC ACID without being unpleasantly tart. Different wineries have different policies on the desirability of MALOLACTIC FERMENTATION for white wines. Red wines are, inevitably in this climate, relatively light and acid, although there has been some experimentation with new OAK.

Within Serra Gaucha, Garibaldi, where the Moët subsidiary Provifin (an important producer of still and sparkling wine) is based, is the centre for sparkling-wine production, many of these wines being made in the image of SPUMANTE, for Italian influence is strong in the region. Farroupilha can produce good-quality grapes for red wine (and substantial quantities for local VERMOUTH), while Flores de Cunha is the source of much everyday wine. Bento Gonçalves is a sort of tourist centre for the wine industry.

Between 1975 and the early 1990s, about 800 ha of vines were planted in the new Frontera wine region on the border with Uruguay, chiefly in the communes of Santana do Livramento and Pinheiro Machado. It is too early to pass judgement on this new wine region.

Small amounts of wine are also made from the vines grown in the San Francisco Valley region in the arid north of the country near Recife in Pernambuco state. TROPICAL VITICULTURE is the rule at this LATITUDE of just nine degrees, and up to five crops can be produced in a two-year period. The grapes here, mainly Piróvano, are chiefly sold as TABLE GRAPES but some particularly alcoholic wine, both red and white, is made.

Local wine is a relatively recent addition to Brazilian culture, and average consumption is still extremely low, well below 2 l per head per year, except in the predominantly European communities of the south, although interest in Brazilian wine both domestically and on export markets is growing and the country has played host to the odd FLYING WINE-MAKER.

breathing, an operation, believed beneficial by some consumers, involving pulling the cork and letting the open bottle stand for a few hours before it is poured. In fact, in such circumstances the wine can take only the most minimal of 'breaths', and any change is bound to be imperceptible (except possibly in the case of BOTTLE SICKNESS). The surface area of wine exposed to the air is so small that the effects of any aeration are negligible. See DECANTING.

Breganze, DOC zone for a range of red and white often VARIETAL wines in the VENETO region of north-east Italy. Although some of the vineyards are in the foothills of the Alps to the north of the city of Vicenza, a large percentage of them are in the gravel soils of the plain. Some rather anonymous wines based on TOCAI, PINOT BLANC, VESPAIOLA, Cabernet, Merlot, and Pinot Noir are made, none of which is widely known outside the zone itself. Such international fame as the zone has is due to the efforts of a single producer, Fausto Maculan, who has travelled widely in France and California, planted Cabernet Sauvignon, Chardonnay, and Sauvignon Blanc, invested heavily in small oak barrels, and experimented with densely planted vineyards on French models, as well as producing important dessert wines from grapes with NOBLE ROT (the rare Acininobili, and the Torcolato mentioned under DRIED-GRAPE WINES). D.T.

Brettanomyces, sometimes called Brett, one of the YEAST genera found occasionally on grapes and in wines. It is usually considered a spoilage yeast since it can produce off-flavours in wines variously described as 'mousy' and 'metallic' (see FAULTS for an explanation of how this fault is not immediately apparent). Nearly all of the Brettanomyces species are very sensitive to SULPHUR DIOXIDE so their presence in a winery may indicate less than perfect HYGIENE, or a low-sulphur wine-making regime. A.D.W.

bricco, or *bric* in the dialect of the north-west Italian region of PIEDMONT, indicates the highest part of an elevation in the landscape or, in particular, a vineyard with a steep gradient at the top of a hill. The term was first used on a wine label by Luciano de Giacomi in 1969 for his Bricco del Drago, a blend of DOLCETTO and NEBBIOLO grapes from Alba, and has been extensively used for the other wines of Piedmont ever since. D.T.

Brindisi, Adriatic port and DOC for robust red wine made mainly from NEGROAMARO grapes in south-east Italy. See APULIA.

Britain, or Great Britain, has long been one of the most important international markets for wine. It regularly imports more wine than any country other than Germany. Its long wine-merchant tradition has made it one of the most fastidious, yet open-minded, wine-consuming nations. Domestic vine-growing in England and Wales is on too small a scale to affect consumers who expect to find the wines of the world on the shelves of their specialist merchants and, increasingly, supermarkets. A certain amount of wine is also made from imported grape concentrate (see BRITISH WINE). Historically, Britain's commercial influence helped shape the very existence of such wines as claret, madeira, Marsala, port, and sherry.

In the 1980s and 1990s, Great Britain was targeted by many of the world's wine producers as one of the few substantial wine markets in which per capita wine consumption is not falling.

The presence of the principal wine auctioneers (see AUCTIONS) and the resultant BROKERS have made London the focus of the fine-wine market, just as it is of wine-trade education by virtue of the Institute of MASTERS OF WINE.

See also ENGLAND, SCOTLAND, and WALES.

British wine, a curious alcoholic drink made in the image of WINE from GRAPE CONCENTRATE imported into Great Britain. It is known as MADE WINE, and a decidedly manufactured product it is. Concentrated grape must, the consistency of thin honey, is imported in bulk throughout the year from wherever happens to be able to supply the best value. The must is eventually reconstituted by adding water and is fermented using selected YEAST strains, under the most rigorous technical controls, according to the wine style required. Until the 1980s, almost all British wine produced was FORTIFIED, and made to resemble sherry or port, or flavoured with ginger or other spices or fruits. Since then, British wines of normal TABLE WINE strength have also been made, much to the dismay of the producers of English wine (see ENGLAND), with whose products made from freshly picked grapes there is considerable confusion.

Brix, scale used in the United States to measure total dissolved compounds in grape juice at a specified temperature, and therefore its approximate concentration of grape sugars (see MUST WEIGHT). The **Balling** scale is similar.

BRL Hardy. See HARDYS.

brokers, important members of any trade, and increasingly important in the wine trade. Known charmingly as *courtiers* in French, brokers can play a vital role as middlemen between vine-growers and merchants, or NÉGOCIANTS, collecting and exhibiting hundreds of samples, taking a small percentage of any eventual sale. Another class of brokers, further along the distribution chain, guide those who sell wine through the maze of those who produce it, some of them nursing 'stables' of producers rather in the manner of a literary agent representing a rollcall of authors. And then, just one or two links away from those who actually pull the cork, there are the fine-wine brokers, those who sell from a list of glamorous properties and vintages which may, but often do not, belong to them.

This last group, most of whom are based in Britain clustered round the two major AUCTION houses like bees round a honeypot, represents one of the very few sectors of the wine trade that has been highly profitable. Farr Vintners sold more wine than Sotheby's and Christie's combined in 1997. The sort of wine of interest to this new breed of wine merchant typically sits in an unbroken CASE in a BONDED WARE-HOUSE in Britain while being traded so profitably around the world.

Brouilly, largest of the BEAUJOLAIS CRUS, produces some of the most robust, most textured of these red wines from vineyards that flank the volcanic Mont Brouilly. **Côte de Brouilly** is an entirely separate appellation higher up the hillside. The wine produced tends to be more concentrated and longer lived than that of Brouilly. Ch de Thivin is a landmark producer.

Brulhois, Côtes du, red-wine VDQS in SOUTH WEST FRANCE. Bordeaux vine varieties plus the Gascon TANNAT are grown in the rolling farmland down river of Moissac on both sides of the river Garonne. The wines are usually well coloured and the best can offer a good meeting-point between Gascon and Bordelais influences. Most are made by one of the two CO-OPERATIVES and consumed locally.

Brunello, conventionally the name for a strain of SANGIOVESE particularly well adapted to the vineyards of Montalcino in TUSCANY in central Italy producing most notably, therefore, BRUNELLO DI MONTALCINO.

Brunello di Montalcino, youngest of Italy's prestigious red wines, having been invented as a wine in its own right by Ferruccio Biondi-Santi, the first to bottle it and give it a distinctive name, in 1888.

Climate is perhaps a more significant factor than the specific BRUNELLO CLONES of SAN-GIOVESE in creating the characteristics of the wine: the town of Montalcino, 112 km/70 miles south of Florence, enjoys a warmer, drier climate than the various zones of CHIANTI, and the open countryside around it ensures both excellent ventilation and cool evenings and nights. Sangiovese reaches its maximum ripeness here, giving fuller, richer wines than any-where else in Tuscany, with high levels of dry EXTRACT and an ALCOHOLIC STRENGTH frequently over 14°. Brunello di Montalcino is the only important Tuscan red wine whose Sangiovese has never been blended with other varieties.

Prolonged FERMENTATION and five to six years' CASK AGEING for the superior RISERVA established a model of Brunello as a full, intense, and long-lasting wine. Only four vintages—1888, 1891, 1925, 1945—were declared in the first 57 years of production, contributing an aura of rarity to the wine that translated into high prices and, in Italy at least, incomparable prestige. The Biondi-Santi were the only commercial producers until after the Second World War, and even in 1960 there were only 11 bottlers, rising to 87 in 1990. Substantial amounts of outside capital entered Montalcino in the 1970s and 1980s, restoring vineyards and wine-making facilities; a considerable number of small peasant proprietors also began to bottle their own Brunello. Although the better wines have been widely in demand at high prices, quality levels have undeniably been irregular. The dubious condition of many of the casks and the lengthy obligatory ageing periods regardless of the characteristics of the vintage have unquestionably not helped the wine, although revisions in the late 1990s promise to remedy the worst aspects of the situation.

The DOC minimum period of cask ageing was lowered to two years in 1998. Total ageing before release, however, remains 48 months. The lower minimum ageing period is likely to lead to an increase in the use of BARRIQUES, not an unqualified blessing in this zone; their recent use, which in the past was limited by the very lengthy ageing requirements, has tended to give a standardized 'barrique-aged Sangiovese' character to a wine which had previously been notably different from those produced in other parts of Tuscany.

The financial burden imposed by this lengthy period has led to a corresponding increase in the production of Rosso di Montalcino, a red DOC wine that can be marketed after one year. The availability of a second DOC into which lesser wines can be declassified has had a positive impact on the quality of Brunello, in addition to its obvious advantages for the cash flow of producers.

See also VINO NOBILE DI MONTEPULCIANO.

D.T.

brut, French word meaning 'crude' or 'raw', adapted by the CHAMPAGNE industry for wines made without (much) added sweetening or DOSAGE. It has come to be used widely for any SPARKLING WINE to indicate one that tastes bone dry. Technically a brut champagne should contain fewer than 15 g/l RESIDUAL SUGAR, a maximum level which, in less naturally acidic still wines, would seem medium dry (see SWEETNESS). A wine labelled **extra brut** should contain less than 6 g/l residual sugar and may incorporate no dosage at all. Particularly dry wines may also be labelled **brut natur(e)**. The word **bruto** may be used in Portugal.

Bual, Anglicized form of BOAL. See also MADEIRA.

Buçaco, range of forested hills between DÃO and BAIRRADA in central Portugal where the Palace Hotel bottles some of the country's most sought-after wines. See BAIRRADA.

Bucelas, historic white wine, formerly spelt Bucellas, enjoying a revival of interest in its native Portugal. Both ARINTO, the main variety in Bucelas, and its aptly named partner ESGANA CÃO, meaning 'dog strangler', share the ability to make acidic, dry white wine in the sub-mediterranean climate of this tiny white-wine denomination just north of Lisbon.   R.J.M.

Budai Zöld, Transylvanian white grape grown in Hungary around Lake Balaton making deep-coloured, full-bodied wine for local consumption.

budbreak, or budburst, a stage of annual vine development during which small shoots emerge from vine BUDS in the spring. This process begins the new growing season and signals the end of dormancy, their period of winter sleep.

For the vine-grower, budbreak represents the beginning of about eight months' work before HARVEST, during which the vine must be protected from pests, vine diseases, and trained as necessary. The biggest problem for many vineyards at this time of the year is spring frost, to which the young shoot growth is particularly sensitive.   R.E.S.

Bugey, Vins du, collective name for the VDQS wines of the Ain *département* just west of SAVOIE in eastern France. Many of the same grape varieties are grown here, although some from nearby JURA are also grown. Almost all of its varied wines are consumed locally. About half of all wines are white, but there are rosés as well as light reds, fully sparkling **Vin du Bugey Mousseux** and lightly sparkling **Vin du Bugey Pétillant**, varietal wines as in ROUSSETTE du Bugey, and wines to which the name of a CRU may be suffixed, as, for example, **Vin du Bugey Cerdon** (which comes in still, pétillant, and mousseux versions!). The vines are widely dispersed and, among reds, may be the POULSARD (Mescle) of Jura, the MONDEUSE of Savoie, the Gamay of Beaujolais, or the Pinot Noir of Burgundy. White grapes grown are Burgundy's Chardonnay, Pinot Gris, and Aligoté; Savoie's ROUSSETTE (Altesse), MOLETTE, JACQUÈRE, and even a Mondeuse Blanche (Dongine). Wines sold as VARIETALS are made exclusively from that variety. Most of these wines are drunk locally, notably with the local cuisine of Bresse. A particular speciality among this disparate collection of grape varieties, wine styles, and TERROIRS is Rosé de Cerdon, which is usually lightly sparkling.

Bukettraube, white grape variety used mainly in South Africa for sweet and occasionally BOTRYTIZED dessert wines, with a slightly grapey aroma.

Bulgaria, eastern European wine producer whose western export success in the 1980s was built on inexpensive VARIETAL wines, especially Cabernet Sauvignon.

Geography and climate

Bulgaria is a small country just 400 km/250 miles from the western border to the Black Sea and 300 km/200 miles from Romania to the north and Greece and Turkey to the south. With the exception of the Balkan mountain range, which runs east to west, vines are planted all over the country, although the modern wine industry has been based on rolling fertile flatlands.

Summers tend to be hot, with temperatures up to 40 °C/104 °F, while the temperature can fall to −25 °C in winter. The Black Sea has a moderating effect on the eastern side of the country. The most common climatological hazards are fungal diseases caused by humidity. Irrigation is not generally necessary and nor, thanks to hot summers, is CHAPTALIZATION.

Recent developments

Between the mid 1960s and mid 1980s, the Bulgarian wine industry was making significant progress, in terms of both quality and exports of inexpensive but competently made varietals to the west, especially to Britain. Gorbachev's arrival as Soviet premier, however, had dire consequences for Bulgarian wine. His campaign to curb alcohol consumption in the USSR involved uprooting huge tracts of Bulgarian vineyard, some but not all of inferior quality. Grape prices were then fixed every year, irrespective of quality, which encouraged the CO-OPERATIVES to turn their attention away from vines to other crops. Dead, dying, or diseased vines were not replaced. Many vineyards were simply abandoned, and few were systematically trained or pruned.

In 1985, Bulgaria produced 4.5 million hl of wine, but in 1990, probably the best vintage in 45 years, the total crop was just 1.8 million hl/40 million gal, and this at a time when exports to the west were at record levels. Yields did not recover during the 1990s.

In 1990, the wine sector was suddenly liberalized as part of the free-market reforms introduced in the wake of the fall of communism in 1989. Throughout the early 1990s, the Bulgarian wine industry was in disarray. Small-scale land restitution to those who could prove they owned it before 1947 has been maladroitly handled. Rampant inflation took its toll on the domestic market and the export market was in the throes of substantial reorganization in response to the realities of the new free-market economy. In the late 1990s, the wine industry did at least move slowly forward with the process of privatization—although by 1997 the state still owned at least part of most wineries, and all of the four biggest: Russe, Sliven, Varna, and Preslav. Those wineries that were privatized usually involved management buy-outs. Foreign investment in the privatization process has been much more limited than in HUNGARY, for example.

The biggest threat to the Bulgarian wine industry is the continued neglect of vineyards, resulting in a shortage of grapes for quality-wine production. In 1997, Bulgaria had twice the crushing capacity it needed and competition for grapes was often fierce.

On a positive note, many of the privatization contracts include plans to acquire vines and restructure vineyards. Suhindol, privatized in 1991, owned 1,500 ha by the mid 1990s and was developing CLONAL SELECTION.

Grape varieties

Unusually, Bulgaria's vineyards are dominated by such popular INTERNATIONAL VARIETIES as Cabernet Sauvignon, Merlot, and, to a lesser extent, Pinot Noir—although taking into account low-quality wines produced for local markets, there are more white grapes planted than reds. In many cases, they are regarded as everyday grapes and vinified as such, although some CONTROLIRAN wines achieve distinction. Some wineries have made a speciality of combinations that in France would be unthinkable, such as Sliven's blend of Merlot and Pinot Noir. Gamza, the KADARKA of Hungary, is widely planted in the north of the country, where it has a tendency to over-produce but can produce interestingly spicy wines if the growing season is long enough. More interesting to many palates are the indigenous red grape varieties MAVRUD and MELNIK, which may also be called Shiroka Melnishka Losa. The most widely planted indigenous red grape variety, however, is the undistinguished PAMID. There is also some SAPERAVI and a little of the variety known as Senzo, or Senso (CINSAUT).

Bulgaria grows a curious mix of white grape varieties, showing evidence of Serbian influence in its everyday DIMIAT, Georgian influence in its plantings of RKATSITELI, Romanian influence in its FETEASCA (often written Fetiaska), and general central European influence in its WELSCHRIESLING and MUSCAT OTTONEL. MISKET is a peculiarly Bulgarian crossing of Dimiat and Riesling and a red Misket is also a common ingredient in grapey white wines, most notably in the eastern region. Chardonnay, Riesling, Sauvignon, and Gewürztraminer are also planted, as well as Aligoté and Ugni Blanc, which may be blended together as at Varna. Bulgaria's white wines have betrayed the shortfall in winery investment more obviously than its reds.

The regions

Although vines are grown all over Bulgaria, there are five distinct wine regions with about 45 winery complexes. The only region that has no real wine production is the area round the capital Sofia, which does, however, have a large winery for processing and finishing. The winery, and its level of equipment, expertise, and commitment, is the most important quality determinant for Bulgarian wine.

Northern region This important area runs from Vidin in the north west across to Russe and south to the Balkan foothills. The region's wineries, of which some are very important, take their grapes from the rolling Transdanubian Plain, the Danube to the north providing water and moderation of summer temperatures. Key wineries include:

Russe: A well-equipped winery at Bulgaria's fourth city, on the Danube and the Romanian border. One of the few wineries to draw grapes from HILLSIDE sites, this winery produces sound commercial whites as well as reds, most notably Cabernet Sauvignon from the Yantra valley.

Suhindol: Bulgaria's showcase winery, the rock upon which western markets were built, specializing in red wines, particularly Gamza but also Cabernet and Merlot in vast quantities. Real control is exercised over vineyards thanks to the formation of a larger co-operative with local growers.

Svishtov: Right on the Danube, specializes in Cabernet Sauvignon.

Eastern region The heart of white-wine country, where the climate is moderated by the Black Sea. Key wineries include:

Preslav, Khan Krum, Novi Pazar, Schumen: These inland wineries produce a high proportion of Bulgaria's higher-priced white wine, especially Chardonnay, some of which is oak aged and some barrel fermented. Some of these wineries are also producing Sauvignon Blanc, Gewürztraminer, and Riesling.

Varna: Bulgaria's major port also has a winery which specializes in more aromatic whites. Ch Euxinograd produces small quantities of promising Chardonnay.

Burgas, Pomorie: Neighbours on the Black Sea producing considerable quantities of white and increasing quantities of red wine, from Muscat Ottonel, Aligoté, Ugni Blanc, a little Chardonnay, Cabernet Sauvignon, and Merlot. Burgas rosé a speciality.

Sub-Balkan region The most mountainous region. Key wineries include:

Slaviantzi: Most noted for its Sungurlare wines made from Chardonnay and Misket.

Sliven: On the south-eastern foothills of the Balkans and therefore bordering on the diverse southern region (see below), Bulgaria's largest wine producer making spirits as well as Cabernet, Merlot, Chardonnay, Misket, and some Pinot Noir in huge quantities.

Southern region Vast area on the flat upper Thracian Plain from the Pirin mountains to the Black Sea producing a wide range of crops other than grapes. Main wineries include:

Haskovo, Stambolovo, Sakar, Liubimetz: In the deep south of the country specializing in Merlot, with those of Sakar being richer than those of Stambolovo.

Peruschitza, Assenovgrad: Neighbouring wineries near Plovdiv, Bulgaria's second city, best known for reds, with robust Mavrud an Assenovgrad speciality.

Stara Zagora: Most famous for its Cabernet and Merlot from the Oriachovitza region.

South-western region This hot region by the Greek border is most notable for the picturesque town of Melnik, which gives its name to the indigenous distinctive vine, grown on nearby rugged hillsides and capable of much more concentration and longevity than is the current Bulgarian norm. Wineries which may eventually capitalize on this are at Harsovo, Petrich, and Damianitza.

Quality categories

A scheme drawn up in 1978 delineated four main categories of Bulgarian quality wine. Country wines are the equivalent of France's VIN DE PAYS. Varietal wines of denominated geographical origin are the equivalent of France's VDQS, while Reserve and Special Reserve wines are superior VARIETAL wines aged for at least two years in the case of whites and three in the case of reds. Controliran is Bulgaria's answer to France's APPELLATION CONTRÔLÉE, wines from named varieties in specific vineyard sites. About 28 Controlirans had been registered by the mid 1990s, by submitting three consecutive vintages to the state authority and conforming to this standard in subsequent vintages.

D.J.G. & H.L.R.

Bullas, DO zone in Spain's LEVANTE. It shares many features with neighbouring JUMILLA and YECLA, including the predominance of the MONASTRELL grape.

Bull's Blood, historic and robust style of red wine made in HUNGARY, known as Bikavér in Hungarian. The town of EGER was most famously associated with it, producing a wine named Egri Bikavér within Hungary. As the export BRAND Bull's Blood, it enjoyed notable success in the 1970s, then produced exclusively by the state-owned Egervin winery, which shrouded the product in possibly convenient mystery. The principal grape variety used to be KADARKA supplemented by an aromatic, deep-coloured grape known locally as Médoc Noir. They have been replaced by increasing proportions of KÉKFRANKOS, CABERNET SAUVIGNON, and KÉKOPORTO. The wines were the product of longer MACERATION than was perhaps common at the time, and the blend was certainly given some age before bottling. Today, Bikavér is also made in Szekszárd, based on Kadarka, and a fine, traditional Egri Bikavér is made by the Hungarian wine-maker from the SUPERTUSCAN Ornellaia winery in BOLGHERI.

bunch, or cluster, the viticultural term for that part of the grapevine to which berries are attached.

Burgenland, the second most important wine region in AUSTRIA, in the far east of the country on the Hungarian border, most famous for sweet white and red wines.

Burger, white grape variety that was once very important in CALIFORNIA. It produces sizeable quantities of neutral wine. In the late 1990s, it was planted on just 1,800 acres/730 ha, mainly in the hot SAN JOAQUIN VALLEY.

Burgunder, common suffix in German, meaning literally 'of BURGUNDY', for such members of the PINOT family as Spätburgunder, Blauer Spätburgunder, Blauburgunder, or Blauer Burgunder (PINOT NOIR); Weissburgunder or Weisser Burgunder (PINOT BLANC); and Grauburgunder (drier styles of PINOT GRIS).

Burgund Mare means 'big Burgundian' in ROMANIA and is the name of a PINOT-like red grape variety grown there which may be Pinot MEUNIER.

Burgundy, known as BOURGOGNE in French, province of eastern France famous for its great red and white wines produced mostly from Pinot Noir and Chardonnay grapes respectively. The province includes the viticultural regions of the Côte de Nuits and Côte de Beaune in the *département* of the CÔTE D'OR, and the Côte CHALONNAISE and MÂCONNAIS in the Saône-et-Loire. BEAUJOLAIS in the Rhône *département* and CHABLIS and the AUXERROIS in the Yonne *département* are distinct regions viticulturally, if not administratively, and are treated separately.

Geography and climate
The vineyards of Burgundy are based on limestone originating in the Jurassic period. This takes the form of undulating chalk hills in Chablis; a long narrow escarpment running south and a touch west from Dijon to Chagny, the CÔTE D'OR; more isolated limestone outcrops in the Côte Chalonnaise and Mâconnais;

with the vineyards of POUILLY-FUISSÉ beneath the imposing crags of Solutré and Vergisson in the extreme south.

In contrast to BORDEAUX, Burgundy is noticeably colder in the winter months, similar in temperature in the spring, but a little cooler during the summer. Although usually dry in winter, Burgundy tends to suffer from particularly heavy rainfall in May and June and again in October, which may or may not fall after the HARVEST. Spring frost can be a problem (especially in Chablis), while hail causes local damage almost every year.

Overall, there is a shorter and more variable summer than in Bordeaux (which is why only early-ripening grape varieties can be grown there). And whereas the hardy Chardonnay vine can thrive under these conditions, producing what are widely considered the finest full-bodied dry white wines in the world, the temperamental Pinot Noir vine is less regularly successful.

Burgundy is at the limit of successful ripening, the red wines of Auxerrois rarely achieving much depth or body. The great red wines of Burgundy are produced on the escarpment of the Côte d'Or, especially in the Côte de Nuits sector. Even here several vintages in a decade may lack sufficient sun to ripen properly.

Among the white wines of Burgundy, the wines of Chablis, reflecting their northern origin, are green tinted in colour and comparatively austere to taste. The most revered white wines are those of the Côte de Beaune, there being practically none in the Côte de Nuits, while the whites of the Côte Chalonnaise are lighter and attractive to drink young. Further south the white wines of the Mâconnais enjoy enough sun to make fat and ripe wines, although many of them lack finesse.

J.T.C.M.

Viticulture and wine-making
For details, see CÔTE D'OR; CHALONNAISE; and MÂCONNAIS.

Vine varieties
Burgundy has one of the world's least varied ranges of vine varieties. Almost all of the region's best red and white wines are made from Pinot Noir and Chardonnay respectively. On the Côte d'Or, more than 7 in every 10 vines planted were Pinot Noir in the late 1980s, while Chardonnay plantings were increasing so that even at the most recent vineyard census of 1988

they represented nearly 2 in every 10 vines. Gamay and ALIGOTÉ, the 'lesser' red and white wine vines respectively, were in hasty retreat, although BOURGOGNE ALIGOTÉ has its followers.

In the Côte Chalonnaise and Mâconnais, Chardonnay plantings increased notably during the 1970s and 1980s and became an important source of wine labelled Bourgogne Blanc.

Organization of Burgundian vineyards

The vineyards of Burgundy, especially those of the Côte d'Or, are the most minutely parcellated in the world. This is mainly because the land has been continuously managed and owned by individual smallholders—there was no influx of outside capital with which to establish great estates as in BORDEAUX. But the combination of the Napoleonic Code, with its insistence on equal inheritance for every family member, and the fact that the land has proved so valuable, has meant that small family holdings have been divided and subdivided over generations. One vineyard, or *climat*, as it is known in this, the cradle of TERROIR, may therefore be owned by scores of different individual owners, each of them cultivating sometimes just a row or two of vines (see CLOS DE VOUGEOT, for example).

Organization of trade

Unlike the BORDEAUX TRADE with its large volume of single appellations, and many stratifications of those who sell it, the Burgundian wine trade is polarized between growers and NÉGOCIANTS, or merchants. Because the laws of equal inheritance have been strictly applied in a region of such valuable vineyards, individual growers may for example produce just one barrel, enough to fill just 25 cases, of a particular appellation. The market for burgundy was built by the merchants, who would buy grapes and wine from many different growers before blending and selling the results. Behind a merchant's Aloxe-Corton label, for example, may well be the produce of many different plots and cellars. Although in some cases these blends may be better than any individual ingredient, and in most cases today the merchants have better equipment and wine-making skills than the average Burgundian vine-grower, such blends have met increasing consumer resistance. Wine merchants such as Frank Schoonmaker and Alexis Lichine introduced particularly the American public to the notion of DOMAINE BOTTLED burgundy in the 1950s and 1960s, creating a demand which resulted in a widespread improvement in the quality and authenticity of the merchants' produce. The merchants increasingly own their own vineyards, and are able to label the wines they produce 'mise en bouteille au domaine'.

See also HOSPICES DE BEAUNE and see BOURGOGNE for details of Burgundy's generic appellations. For the names of individual appellations, see BEAUNE; NUITS; CHALONNAISE; and MÂCONNAIS.

CHABLIS and BEAUJOLAIS are treated separately.

bush vines, a term used to describe vines trained to a short trunk, normally free-standing, and pruned to a few spurs commonly arranged in a ring on short arms from the trunk. There was a FASHION for using it on labels in the late 1990s, although most of these old, and typically low-vigour, vineyards are being replaced by vines with a trellis system.

R.E.S.

Buzet, known until 1988 as Côtes de Buzet, archetypically Gascon red-wine appellation in SOUTH WEST FRANCE up the Garonne river from BORDEAUX energetically producing notably bordeaux-like wines. The recent history of the appellation, created in 1973, is inextricably intertwined with the dynamism of the local CO-OPERATIVE, Les Vignerons Réunis de Buzet, which makes all but a tiny proportion of Buzet. Thanks to their use of BARRIQUES, the average Buzet is given much more sophisticated ÉLEVAGE than the average BORDEAUX AC, without an enormous price differential.

These inland hills are planted with classic red Bordeaux vine varieties Cabernet Sauvignon, Cabernet Franc, and, especially, Merlot. The co-operative has invested heavily in the most modern wine-making equipment, and its policy is to make strict selections according to TERROIR and quality each VINTAGE so that, although all Buzet should receive at least a year's BARREL MATURATION, the finest wines are blended to produce their top bottling Cuvée Napoléon. The co-operative also vinifies the produce of a number of individual parcels of land and bottles them separately as CHÂTEAU wines, such as Chx Balesté, de Gueyze, and du Bouchet.

BYO stands for 'Bring Your Own' (Wine) and is a type of restaurant most common in Australia and New Zealand, where the term was coined.

Cabardès, promising appellation to the north of Carcassonne in south-western France which produces red and some rosé wines that testify to its location on the cusp of Atlantic and Mediterranean influences. The grape varieties planted also represent a Bordeaux/Languedoc cocktail of Cabernet Sauvignon, Cabernet Franc, Merlot, Cot (Malbec), and some Fer Servadou (of MARCILLAC fame), spiced and fleshed out with the more meridional Syrah, Grenache, Cinsaut (mainly for rosé) and a limited, and declining, proportion of Carignan. In contrast to the somewhat similar Côtes de la MALEPÈRE to the south of Carcassonne, production here is mainly in the hands of a small but committed band of individuals constrained by low financial returns. Winemaking equipment and methods are far from sophisticated, but the wines boast an originality and potential for longevity that is unusual for this part of France.

Cabernet is loosely used as an abbreviation for either or both of the black grape varieties CABERNET FRANC and CABERNET SAUVIGNON.

Cabernet Franc, fine French black grape variety, much blended with and overshadowed by the more widely planted Cabernet Sauvignon. Only in Anjou-Touraine in the Loire valley and on the right bank of the Gironde in Bordeaux is it quantitatively more important than Cabernet Sauvignon.

The two varieties share so many characteristics that they have for long been thought to be related. In 1997, thanks to DNA 'FIN-GERPRINTING' techniques, it was established that Cabernet Franc was, with the Bordeaux white vine variety Sauvignon Blanc, a parent of the noble Cabernet Sauvignon (see CABERNET SAUVIGNON).

Cabernet Franc is particularly well suited to cool, inland climates such as the middle Loire and the Libournais. It buds and matures more than a week earlier than Cabernet Sauvignon, which makes it more susceptible to COULURE, but it is easier to ripen fully and is much less susceptible to poor weather during harvest. In the Médoc and Graves districts of Bordeaux, where Cabernet Franc constitutes about 15 per cent of a typical vineyard and is always blended with other varieties, it is regarded as a form of insurance against the weather's predations on Cabernet Sauvignon and Merlot grapes. Most Libournais bet on Cabernet Franc in preference to the later, and therefore riskier, Cabernet Sauvignon to provide a framework for Merlot, Bordeaux's most planted variety.

As a wine, Cabernet Franc tends to be rather lighter in colour and tannins, and therefore earlier maturing, than Cabernet Sauvignon, although CHEVAL BLANC, the world's grandest Cabernet Franc-dominated wine, proves that majestic durability is also possible. Cabernet Franc is, typically, light to medium bodied with more immediate fruit than Cabernet Sauvignon and marked fragrance, including sometimes some of the herbaceous aromas evident in unripe Cabernet Sauvignon.

Cabernet Franc is still planted all over south-western France, although, in appellations such as Bergerac and Madiran (where Cabernet

Franc is known as Bouchy), Cabernet Sauvignon is gaining ground.

If Cabernet Franc was France's eighth most planted black grape variety at the end of the 1980s, this was largely thanks to its ascendancy in the LOIRE. Steadily increasing appreciation of relatively light, early-maturing reds such as Saumur-Champigny, Bourgueil, Chinon, and Anjou-Villages fuelled demand for Cabernet Franc in the Loire at the expense of Rosé d'Anjou and Chenin Blanc whites.

Cabernet Franc is also well established in Italy, particularly in the north east (see FRIULI in particular), where it has typically been encouraged to yield such a quantity that over-herbaceous aromas scent wines that can be decidedly short on fruit. A certain quantity of what has long been considered Cabernet Franc in Friuli, however, is now thought to be another historic Bordeaux variety CARMENÈRE. Tuscan and central Italian producers of Cabernet, many with decidedly lesser experience with Cabernet, are now showing a new interest in Cabernet Franc as a supplement to their Cabernet Sauvignon, in an effort to add more varietal aroma and complexity to their wines. It is occasionally called Cabernet Frank or even Bordo, but more usually labelled simply Cabernet once in the bottle. Italian vine-growers tend to be as insouciant about the distinction between the two Cabernets as their counterparts over the border in SLOVENIA and further east.

Elsewhere, Cabernet Franc tends to be grown for the express purpose of blending with Cabernet Sauvignon, following the Bordeaux recipe whether or not the climate suggests that such insurance would be wise. Cabernet Franc plantings have slowly increased in New World wine regions as wine-makers embrace the sophistication of Bordeaux blends as opposed to single VARIETALS. In Australia, for example, Cabernet Franc plays a very minor part. The variety has so far done best in cooler regions such as the far south of WESTERN AUSTRALIA. NEW ZEALAND also shows promise (although Cabernet Sauvignon grown in this relatively cool climate can often taste like Cabernet Franc).

Californians have been rearing Cabernet Franc since the late 1960s, and with zeal since the 1980s, mainly in Napa and Sonoma counties. This was originally a ploy to add complexity to Cabernet Sauvignons accused by some of simplicity. A handful of varietal Cabernet Francs are bottled in California today but the majority of the state's crop is used in MERITAGE-like blends. Its relative scarcity make the grapes some of California's most expensive.

In the cooler northern and eastern wine regions of North America (especially the Niagara Peninsula of CANADA, Pennsylvania, Virginia, and Long Island in NEW YORK state), Cabernet Franc is planted more widely than Cabernet Sauvignon since it ripens much more reliably and provides much more EXTRACT than most HYBRIDS. The variety is also responsible for some well-balanced, fruity wines in the Pacific north-western state of WASHINGTON, and the winter-hardy Cabernet Franc has been re-evaluated by many growers there after winter freeze killed off many Merlot vines in 1996.

The vine is increasingly planted in South America. ARGENTINA now grows Cabernet Franc, most of it in Mendoza.

Cabernet Sauvignon, the world's most renowned, but relatively recent, grape variety for the production of fine red wine. From its power base in Bordeaux, where it is almost invariably blended with other grapes, it has been taken up in other French wine regions and in much of the Old and New Worlds, where it has been blended with traditional native varieties and often used to produce pure VARIETAL wine.

Perhaps the most extraordinary aspect of Cabernet Sauvignon is its ability to produce a wine that is so recognizably Cabernet. And what makes Cabernet Sauvignon remarkable to taste is not primarily its exact fruit flavour—although that is often likened to blackcurrants, its aroma sometimes to green bell peppers—but its structure and its ability to provide the perfect vehicle for individual vintage characteristics, wine-making and ÉLEVAGE techniques, and, especially, local physical attributes, or TERROIR. Late-ripening Cabernet Sauvignon must be grown somewhere relatively warm, and can in some years fail to reach full RIPENESS even somewhere as mild as the Médoc.

It is Cabernet Sauvignon's remarkable concentration of PHENOLICS that really sets it aside from most other widely grown vine varieties. It is therefore capable of producing deeply coloured wines worthy of long MACERATION and AGEING for the long term. Over the centuries it has demonstrated a special but by no means exclusive affinity for densely textured French

OAK. The particular appeal of Cabernet Sauvignon lies much less in primary fruit aromas (with which other varieties such as Gamay and Pinot Noir are more obviously associated) than in the much more subtle flavour compounds that evolve over years of BOTTLE AGEING from complex interaction between compounds derived from fruit, fermentation, alcohol, and oak. It is also true, however, that so distinctive is Cabernet Sauvignon's imprint on the palate memory that part of the reason why it is so widely planted is that even when irrigated to greedily high yields and hastily vinified without even a glimpse of wood, it can produce a wine with some recognizable relationship to the great Bordeaux growths of the Médoc and Graves on which its reputation has been built.

The mystery of Cabernet Sauvignon's origins was solved in 1997, thanks to the relatively new technique DNA 'FINGERPRINTING', which showed beyond all reasonable doubt that Cabernet Sauvignon's parents are none other than Cabernet Franc and the Bordeaux white-wine grape Sauvignon Blanc, a crossing that is thought to have happened spontaneously in one of the many vineyards planted with a mixture of different vines in the old days. This neatly explains why Cabernet Sauvignon can smell like either or both of its parents.

The distinguishing marks of the Cabernet Sauvignon berry are its small size, its high ratio of pip to pulp, and the thickness of its distinctively blue skins. The pips are a major factor in high TANNIN level while the thickness of its skins accounts for the depth of colour that is the tell-tale sign of a Cabernet Sauvignon in so many BLIND TASTINGS.

The vine both buds and ripens late, one to two weeks after Merlot and Cabernet Franc, the two varieties with which it is typically blended in Bordeaux. Cabernet Sauvignon ripens slowly, which has the advantage that picking dates are less crucial than with other varieties (such as Syrah, for example); but this has the disadvantage that Cabernet Sauvignon simply cannot be relied upon to ripen in the coolest wine regions. Cabernet Sauvignon that fails to reach full ripeness can taste eerily like Cabernet Franc (just as unripe Sémillon, coincidentally, resembles Sauvignon Blanc).

Even in the temperate climate of Bordeaux, the flowering of the vine can be dogged by cold weather and the ripening by rain, so that Bordeaux's vine-growers have traditionally hedged their bets by planting a mix of early and late local varieties, typically in the Médoc and Graves districts 75 per cent of Cabernet Sauvignon plus a mixture of Merlot, Cabernet Franc, and sometimes a little Petit Verdot. (See CABERNET FRANC for reasons why the Cabernet in St-Émilion and Pomerol is much less likely to be Cabernet Sauvignon.)

A practice that had its origins in canny fruit farming has proved itself in the blending vat. The plump, fruity, earlier-maturing Merlot is a natural blending partner for the more rigorous Cabernet Sauvignon, while Petit Verdot can add extra spice (if only in the sunniest years) and Cabernet Franc can perfume the blend to a certain extent. Wines made solely from Cabernet Sauvignon can lack charm and stuffing; the framework is sensational but tannin and colour alone make poor nourishment. As demonstrated by the increasing popularity of Merlot and Cabernet Franc and even Petit Verdot cuttings, newer wine regions have begun to follow the Bordeaux example of blending their Cabernet Sauvignon with other varieties, although the Médoc recipe is by no means the only one. In Tuscany, it is commonly blended with Sangiovese. In Australia and, increasingly but with very different results, in Provence it is blended with Syrah (Shiraz).

Cabernet Sauvignon is by quite a margin the most planted top-quality vine variety in the world (if one excludes Grenache, which, in its most common form Garnacha, rarely performs at the peak of its potential). In fact, as the world's wine regions have been introduced to the demands of the modern international market-place, one of the first signs of 'modernization' of a wine region has been its importation of and experimentation with Cabernet Sauvignon cuttings. Only those regions, such as England, Germany, and Luxembourg, disbarred for reasons of climate, have resisted joining this particular club on any significant scale. Cabernet production has become almost a rite of passage for modern wine-makers wishing to make their mark.

France

French plantings of Cabernet Sauvignon increased enormously in the 1980s. The vine's stronghold is the left bank of the Gironde estuary and the river Garonne, most notably the famously well-drained gravels of the Médoc and Graves CRUS classés, whose selling price can well justify the efficacious luxury of ageing their wine in small, often new, oak casks. Chx

Latour and Mouton-Rothschild, two of the most famous wine farms in the world and both of them FIRST GROWTHS in Pauillac, are famous for their high proportion of Cabernet Sauvignon: approximately four vines in every five, although nowadays planted in parcels of individual varieties rather than ready-blended in the vineyard. The wines of both, although differing in character, are known for their solidity and longevity.

Cabernet Sauvignon, although little planted north of the river Dordogne, is now much more common in the ENTRE-DEUX-MERS between the Garonne and Dordogne rivers as less profitable white varieties have been uprooted. Such is the size of the Entre-Deux-Mers district that there is more Cabernet Sauvignon planted there than in any other Bordeaux district, including the Médoc (although there is considerably more Merlot in Entre-Deux-Mers than Cabernet Sauvignon).

The vine is also planted over much of SOUTH WEST FRANCE, often as an optional ingredient in its red, and occasionally rosé, wines. Only in BERGERAC and BUZET does it play a substantial part. In more internationally styled wines, however, it may add structure to the Négrette of GAILLAC and Côtes du FRONTONNAIS, and the Tannat of BÉARN, IROULÉGUY, and MADIRAN. It is also increasingly used to add substance to the red Côtes de ST-MONT.

Plantings in the Languedoc-Roussillon increased substantially in the 1980s, but Cabernet Sauvignon has not been nearly so successful here as Syrah. Cabernet Sauvignon does not tolerate very dry conditions without more substantial IRRIGATION than is condoned by the French authorities. Varietal Cabernet Sauvignon wines made in the Languedoc-Roussillon have tended towards herbaceousness and suffered lack of substance.

The most obviously successful southern French Cabernet Sauvignons are those used as ingredients in low-yield blends with Syrah and other Rhône varieties, such as Mas de Daumas Gassac in the Hérault or, further east in Provence, Domaine de Trévallon and Ch Vignelaure.

Provence and the southern Rhône are no more impervious to the winds of FASHION than they are to the famous local mistral. The variety has also been gaining ground and reputation in CORSICA.

Cabernet Sauvignon's only other French territory is the Loire, but, despite the freedom allowed by most appellation regulations to choose either Cabernet Franc or Cabernet Sauvignon or both for local reds, and Cabernet Sauvignon is de rigueur for the swelling ranks of truly ambitious wine producers in the Loire, most vine-growers prefer the regularity of the former to the risks involved with growing the latter in relatively cool conditions. Only ANJOU-SAUMUR has any substantial area of Cabernet Sauvignon—far less than of Cabernet Franc, or even than of Grolleau or Gamay.

Outside France

According to the most accurate estimates available, there were approximately 30,000 ha/75,000 acres of Cabernet Sauvignon in the Soviet Union before it was broken up, with some of the most impressive bottle-aged examples coming from MOLDOVA. The variety is widely planted in RUSSIA and the UKRAINE, although in Russia's cooler wine regions the cold-hardy hybrid CABERNET SEVERNY is becoming increasingly popular. Cabernet Sauvignon is also grown in GEORGIA, AZERBAIJAN, KAZAKHSTAN, TAJIKISTAN, and KYRGYZSTAN.

Another country with an important area planted with the world's noblest black grape variety is Chile, where it is now the country's most important vine variety. Here the fruit is exceptionally healthy and the wine, if made carefully in one of the more modern wineries, almost rudely exuberant. See CHILE for more on Chilean Cabernet Sauvignon.

Not surprisingly, Cabernet Sauvignon also flourishes in the rest of South America's vineyards: in ARGENTINA, where in terms of quantity it is dwarfed by Malbec; in BRAZIL, URUGUAY, MEXICO, PERU, and BOLIVIA.

Cabernet Sauvignon, even less surprisingly, has been the bedrock of that construct called California collectable (see CALIFORNIA CULT wines), and such has been the quality of some of these wines that northern California could fairly be said to have proved itself Cabernet Sauvignon's second home.

Although Cabernet Sauvignon was no stranger to California, it was during the wine boom of the 1970s and early 1980s that plantings multiplied rapidly, especially in the premium North Coast sites of Sonoma and, especially, Napa. During this period, little expense was spared in replicating what were commonly thought to be the wine-making methods of a top Bordeaux château, although it was only from the mid 1980s that tannin, fruit, and alcohol levels were brought into harmony on a wide scale, and blending with Merlot and Cabernet Franc became at all common. For more detail on the golden state's Cabernet achievements, see CALIFORNIA.

Cabernet Sauvignon is also one of WASHINGTON state's two major black grape varieties, even if it fell firmly into second place during the 1990s mania for Merlot. Cabernet Sauvignon's vigour and late ripening make it unattractive to growers in damp, cool Oregon but it has been most successful in other American states including Arizona and TEXAS. Even the wine industry in CANADA, with its natural climatic disadvantages, persists with the variety.

If Californians decided early on that the Napa Valley was their Cabernet Sauvignon hotspot, Australians did the same about Coonawarra. They, however, have for decades employed a much less reverential policy towards blending their Cabernet. Cabernet–Shiraz blends have been popular items in the Australian market-place since the 1960s. The richness and softness of Australian Shiraz is such that it fills in the gaps left by Cabernet Sauvignon. The classic Bordeaux blend is still very much rarer, on the other hand, as one might expect from wine producers more determined than the Californians to go their own way independently of Europe. See AUSTRALIA for more detail on Australian Cabernet Sauvignon.

Cabernet Sauvignon has long played a quantitatively important part in the NEW ZEALAND wine industry; it was the country's fourth most planted vine variety in the 1990s. It took mastery of CANOPY MANAGEMENT techniques in the early 1990s to imbue New Zealand Cabernets with any real colour and substance, however, and even today New Zealand's Pinot Noir is a more obvious candidate for export than its Cabernet Sauvignon, which in most sites has to struggle to reach full ripeness.

Cabernet Sauvignon is equally revered within SOUTH AFRICA and it is increasingly being blended with other Bordeaux varieties such as Merlot and Cabernet Franc—although here, as in Australia and New Zealand, there is a domestic tendency to view Cabernet–Merlot blends as inherently inferior to wines made chiefly or wholly of Cabernet Sauvignon, with concomitant effects on choosing wines for blends and on pricing.

Cabernet Sauvignon has been an increasingly popular choice for internationally minded wine producers in Spain, where it was planted by the Marqués de Riscal at his Rioja estate in the mid 19th century, and could also be found in the vineyards of VEGA SICILIA. It was otherwise virtually unknown on the Iberian peninsula until the 1960s, when it was imported into Penedès by both Miguel TORRES, Jr, and Jean León. It is fast broadening its base in Spain, not just for wines dominated by it but for blending, notably with Tempranillo. In Portugal, it is rare but could already be found by the mid 1980s, blended with indigenous grape varieties in a handful of lush red wines made in the Lisbon area.

Italy, where Cabernet Sauvignon was introduced, via Piedmont, in the early 19th century, now has a very substantial area of Cabernet vineyard, although Italians have been somewhat cavalier about distinguishing between the two very different sorts of Cabernet, either on the label or, sometimes, in the vineyard. Remarkably few of the denominations which begin with the word Cabernet specify which should be used and in what proportions. Cabernet Sauvignon is much more difficult to ripen than the sometimes grassy Cabernet Franc in Friuli, but the variety, which continues to spread southwards through Italy and even as far as the islands, features in many of Italy's more cosmopolitan producers' most cherished wines. Cabernet Sauvignon has played a considerable role in the emergence of SUPERTUSCANS, and can be found as a seasoning in an increasing proportion of CHIANTI. It is officially sanctioned, and individually specified, in such DOCS as CARMIGNANO in Tuscany; Colli BOLOGNESI in Emilia-Romagna; in TRENTINO; in LISON-PRAMAGGIORE in the Veneto; and in COLLI ORIENTALI, COLLIO, GRAVE DEL FRIULI, ISONZO, and Latisana in Friuli. Cabernet Sauvignon is a major ingredient in such Tuscan wines as Solaia, Sassicaia, Venegazzù, and Castello di Rampolla's Sammarco, and is increasingly common (occasionally blended with BARBERA grapes) in the NEBBIOLO territory of Piedmont in such bottlings as Darmagi from GAJA and Alberto Bertelli's I Fossaretti.

East of Italy there are many thousands of hectares of Cabernet Sauvignon, which plays an important part in the wine industries of BULGARIA in particular, ROMANIA, and what was YUGOSLAVIA. Even when expected to produce relatively high yields, eastern European Cabernet Sauvignon is unmistakably Cabernet, and the best Romanian and Bulgarian wines have real depth of flavour as well as colour. There are smaller amounts of Cabernet Sauvignon grown in HUNGARY, AUSTRIA, and GREECE, where it was first planted, in modern times at least, at the Carras domaine.

Perhaps the most tenacious Cabernet Sauvignon grower has been Serge Hochar of Ch Musar in the LEBANON, and there are other, rather less war-torn, pockets of Cabernet Sauvignon vines all over the eastern Mediterranean in TURKEY, ISRAEL, and CYPRUS, as well as a little in MOROCCO. In ASIA, there have also been experiments with the vine, notably in CHINA and JAPAN, where its strong links with the famous châteaux of Bordeaux are particularly prized.

Wherever there are vine-growers with any grounding in the wines of the world, and late-ripening grapes are economically viable, they are almost certain to try Cabernet Sauvignon—unless they inhabit one of Bordeaux's great rival regions Burgundy and the Rhône.

Cabernet Severny, red-wine grape variety specially bred for cold climates at the All-Russia Potapenko Institute in the Rostov region of RUSSIA.

Cabrières, village and named TERROIR within the Coteaux du LANGUEDOC in southern France, just east of FAUGÈRES and within the CLAIRETTE DU LANGUEDOC zone. The CO-OPERATIVE dominates production, which has historically favoured rosé, which must contain at least 45 per cent CINSAUT grapes.

Cadarcă, Romanian name for Hungary's KADARKA.

Cadillac, small, sweet-white appellation just north of LOUPIAC in the BORDEAUX region, once particularly popular with the Dutch, named after the walled town built by the English in the 12th century. Until 1973, it was part of the surrounding PREMIÈRES CÔTES DE BORDEAUX appellation but its special combination of chalk and gravel theoretically justifies a distinction which is still too rarely found in the wines. Low selling prices make high-quality production methods such as those practised in SAUTERNES difficult to justify, and few producers are brave enough to try to make BOTRYTIZED WINES. The area's reds qualify as Premières Côtes de Bordeaux.

Cagnina, synonym for REFOSCO in Italy's Romagna region.

Cahors, significant wine region in the Quercy district in SOUTH WEST FRANCE, producing exclusively red wine, uniquely dependent on the MALBEC or Cot grape. In the 1980s and 1990s, it benefited from considerable inward investment.

Cahors is influenced by the Mediterranean as well as by the Atlantic, and, although winters are rather colder than in Bordeaux, the wines tend to be more concentrated. They were appreciated as suitable blending material with the lighter wines of Bordeaux, and in the early 19th century were famed as the 'black wines of Cahors'.

Cahors was awarded full APPELLATION CONTRÔLÉE status in 1971. Within South West France, only BERGERAC makes more wine. Vines planted on the *causses*, the notably thin topsoil of the arid, limestone plateau, produce wine for long ageing, a more traditional style of Cahors, while the wine made on the *coteaux*, the sand and gravel terraces between the plateau and the river, can be drunk much younger.

The notorious winter freeze of 1956 had a marked effect on the Cahors *vignoble* and provided a clean slate at an appropriate moment in the appellation's evolution. By far the largest number of growers planted an overwhelming majority of Malbec, called here for obscure reasons Auxerrois, a traditional Cahors variety which is nowhere else associated with particularly long-living wines. The appellation rules stipulate at least 70 per cent Auxerrois, supplemented by the tannic TANNAT and/or the supple Merlot. A strictly local variety known as Jurançon Noir is being phased out. Again, debate rages over the most suitable mix of grape varieties. Cahors is exceptional among the important appellations of South West France in that neither Cabernet vine is allowed.

Cahors was still in flux in the late 1990s, attempting to find a style that would suit the impatient modern consumer, while remaining faithful to the region's long viticultural history. Prominent domaines include Ch du Cèdre, Clos de Gamot, Ch Lagrezette, and Clos Triguedina.

The local VIN DE PAYS, a speciality of the Caves d'Olt CO-OPERATIVE, is Vin de Pays des Coteaux de Quercy.

Caiño Tinto, strongly perfumed, delicate red-wine vine in Galicia found in tart reds in RÍAS BAIXAS and RIBEIRO. Known as BORRAÇAL in Portugal's Vinho Verde region. A light-berried **Caiño Blanco** is also found, particularly in Rías Baixas.

Cairanne, probably the best of the Côtes du Rhône villages led by Domaines l'Oratoire St-Martin, Rabasse-Charavin, and Richaud. See RHÔNE.

Calabrese, meaning 'of Calabria', is a common synonym for the NERO D'AVOLA Sicilian red grape variety.

Calabria, the rugged toe of the boot of Italy, is closer to SICILY than to Rome in every way. It has lagged behind the rest of Italy in its agricultural and industrial development with a per capita income barely half the national average. It is not surprising, therefore, that its wines have made little impact and have little significance in national and international markets.

Only five per cent of the total surface area of the region's agricultural land is planted with vines, most of them close to the northern, Tyrrhenian coast or the southern, Ionian coast. The average size of the properties is hardly more than half a hectare, most of them yielding a particularly low annual income. The total DOC production of the region is only three per cent of the region's annual wine crop and almost 90 per cent of the wine produced is red.

The most important DOC by far is Cirò (on the sole of Italy's boot), yet even Cirò produces only a quarter of its potential. Its wines are warm and alcoholic.

GAGLIOPPO, the principal red grape of the region, is the base of Cirò, and seems to have real potential; interesting experiments with small oak BARREL MATURATION have begun in the zone in an effort to give the wine a more international character. It may be blended with red and white GRECO, TREBBIANO, and NERELLO grapes to produce Calabria's hefty reds and rosés. The white Greco grape, partially dried, produces a strong, coppery dessert wine of real interest and personality in its DOC zone around the town of Bianco almost at the tip of the boot, making the confusingly named Greco di Bianco Calabria's most distinguished wine. Cabernet Sauvignon and Cabernet Franc, Chardonnay, and Sauvignon Blanc are being experimented with in a desultory fashion, although real conviction and truly convincing results, with the exception of Librandi's Gravello, are rare. D.T.

Calatayud, denominated wine zone in ARAGON in north-east Spain, in arid country on either side of the river Jalon, a tributary of the Ebro. As in much of central Spain, YIELDS rarely rise above 20 hl/ha (1 ton/acre). The DO regulations limit growers to indigenous grape varieties, which are mostly sold to one of nine local CO-OPERATIVES. The GARNACHA grape, which accounts for around two-thirds of the Calatayud's production, makes heady, potent red wine, although TEMPRANILLO is slowly gaining in popularity among the more quality-conscious producers. Investment in new technology is increasing the proportion of Garnacha-based rosés and crisp white wines made from VIURA. The Maluenda co-operative has taken the lead in producing wines of an international standard, including some Syrah from its new vineyards. R.J.M. & V. de la S.

Caldaro, or Kaltern in German, township in the ALTO ADIGE of northern Italy. It gives its name to **Lago di Caldaro** or **Kalterersee,** a large DOC zone for lightish red wines which extends into neighbouring TRENTINO.

California, highly successful 'wine state' of the UNITED STATES and the largest source of American wine by far, producing 90 per cent of all US-grown wine well into the 1990s, and three out of every four bottles sold in the USA. California wine, like most things Californian, has arrived at its current position by a series of bold investments, natural disasters, scientific achievements, external pressures, and political calamities. That the USA is not a nation of wine drinkers has tended to exaggerate the cycle of giant strides and general retreats.

Climate

Those unfamiliar with California assign it a two-season MEDITERRANEAN CLIMATE. This is but a partial truth. Offshore ocean currents cause an intermittent fog-bank along California's coast, creating long stretches with insufficient sunshine to ripen most grapes. These fogs do not penetrate far inland, because of the coastal range, leaving the SAN JOAQUIN VALLEY too warm and sunny to grow fine table wines. However, in the sharply convoluted in-between of the Coast Ranges, jumbled terrain and variable fog produce more and less perfect growing season echoes of Castellina-in-CHIANTI, ST-ESTÈPHE, BEAUNE, and even Hattenheim in the RHEINGAU. There is no linear pattern. NAPA, 20 miles north across the bay from San Francisco, is one of the warmer, drier regions on the coast. Westerly parts of SANTA BARBARA County, 300 miles/500 km to the south, are cooler and foggier than any part of Napa, while much of MENDOCINO, nearly 80 miles north of Napa, has hotter summers. Openings to the Pacific Ocean in the Coast Ranges indicate the cool spots, while mountain barriers locate the warmer ones.

The rainy season follows a more orderly pattern. Total annual rainfall north of San Francisco is between 24 and 45 in (615–1,150 mm), while from San Francisco southwards totals range from 20 in to the low teens. DROUGHT occurs regularly but since the phase of the cycle is 10 to 20 years, the last severe drought striking between 1987 to 1992, it can take new entrants on California's agricultural scene by surprise. Winters in California's grape-growing regions are mild to outright balmy. Damaging winter freezes are virtually unheard of.

Spring frosts vex growers more than any other fact of climate. Although late cold snaps occur infrequently, growers in the NORTH COAST are geared to mitigate the effects. Spring rains sometimes interfere with flowering and fruit set, but never in disastrous proportion.

Geography

California's wine regions extend over more than 600 miles/960 km of the state's 900-mile length from north to south. The clear demarcation of regions and the establishment of regional specialities is an important task which gained increased public awareness in 1983 when the Bureau of Alcohol, Tobacco, and Firearms (BATF) began holding hearings to approve American Viticultural Area (AVA) names for use on labels. Before then, California's geographical appellations, by and large, were its counties. Those county names much used in practice on wine labels have been, in very approximate descending order of popularity, NAPA, SONOMA, SANTA BARBARA, MONTEREY, SAN LUIS OBISPO, MENDOCINO, AMADOR, EL DORADO, and LAKE. Other, usually larger and often vaguer, geographical descriptions in use are NORTH COAST, CENTRAL COAST, SOUTH COAST, SAN JOAQUIN VALLEY, SANTA CRUZ MOUNTAINS, and SIERRA FOOTHILLS.

AVAs are rudimentary, imposing no restrictions on varieties planted or vineyard practices. By 1990, California had more than 60 (out of a national total of 115), many such complete unknowns that Napa, Sonoma, Mendocino,

Santa Barbara, and a few other county names remain more effective at communicating vineyard location.

Individual AVAs are detailed under the name of the county or larger geographical unit in which they fall, except for the following AVAs, of varying sizes, which have their own individual entries: CARNEROS, LIVERMORE VALLEY, SANTA CLARA VALLEY, and TEMECULA.

Wine-making

Without tradition as either guide or limitation, most California wine-makers have consistently looked to achieve the kind of reproducible results their university training exalts. Understanding a process and then controlling it are, thus, the first two goals of the state's typical OENOLOGIST. Of all the steps in wine-making, FERMENTATION has received the most vigorous attention. YEASTS, the very engine of fermentation, are also much studied and carefully monitored. Both pure strains of specially cultured yeast and natural yeast are used in order to achieve greater aromatic complexity.

Until the early 1980s, ACIDIFICATION was the norm throughout the state, but it has become less commonplace as grapes are increasingly sourced from the more marginal climates of the coastal regions, where grapes often have higher natural ACIDITY than their counterparts in Bordeaux or Burgundy.

A broad panoply of maceration techniques is employed for reds in a quest called 'TANNIN management'. The goal is soft MOUTHFEEL achieved through a high degree of EXTRACT and seeking ripe tannins.

Ageing in oak, for whites and reds, became a whole art form in itself, with wine-makers diligently matching COOPERS, TOAST levels, and new versus used BARRELS to wine types and regions. Length of time in oak also became a subject of much debate and experimentation.

Wine types

The most important California wine type is the VARIETAL, the principal sorts of which are outlined below (see Vine varieties).

The production of inexpensive wines, largely from the Central or San Joaquin Valley, is in the hands of a relatively few very large wineries. Most of the state's wineries concentrate on more expensive wines, many of limited production and available only in a few markets. By 1997, 31 per cent of all California table wines were red with 41 per cent white and 28 per cent blush or rosé.

American wine diction tends to be based more on tax rates than wine characteristics. Table wine is anything with an ALCOHOLIC STRENGTH of up to 13.9 per cent. Even the finest late-harvest imitations of TBAs (see TROCKEN-BEERENAUSLESE), the ones with 40 per cent RESIDUAL SUGAR, are table wines to the taxman. Quality, or lack of it, is not implied by nomenclature as it is in Europe. Dessert wine, meanwhile, is anything with more than 16 per cent of alcohol, even the driest of SHERRY types. Sparkling wine, sensibly, is the stuff with bubbles.

That mastered, California offers few other terms not found elsewhere, or else mutated too little to require explanation, although see also FIGHTING VARIETAL, GENERIC, JUG WINE, and MERITAGE. In addition, there are the proprietary blends, which were originally only tarted-up generics. A Rhine would become Rhine Castle, a Chablis would become Golden Chablis, or somesuch. Some of those continue to exist. However, the advent of fighting varietals in the late 1980s called the supremacy of varietals into question and spawned a new breed of high-priced proprietaries based on blends of classic grape varieties that were traditional in Europe. Meritages, for example, imitate BORDEAUX and there are also equivalent counterparts to RHÔNE blends.

There is also a long and complex history of producing sparkling wine in California, which has had few inhibitions about calling it champagne. In the years since 1970, European- and especially French-owned firms have come to dominate production of California TRADITIONAL METHOD wines made using traditional grape varieties. Domaine Chandon was the forerunner. Piper-Sonoma, Mumm-Napa Valley, Roederer Estate, Maison Deutz, Domaine Carneros (Taittinger), and Scharffenberger (Pommery) followed from France, Gloria Ferrer (Freixenet) and Codorníu Napa from Spain. There remains a strong domestic element led by Schramsberg, Iron Horse, and, more recently, Jordan. During the 1990s competition among foreign producers of sparkling wine in California produced a situation of immense benefit to consumers: quality rose dramatically while prices were ever more deeply discounted. In 1997, Deutz and Piper-Heidsieck sold their California properties and went back home to Champagne.

These are the sources of complex sparkling wines. Producers of inexpensive mass-market bubblies make less complicated wines yet complicate the story. American law permits wines made from a wide range of non-traditional grape varieties and methods to be called Champagne so long as that word is accompanied by a clear appellation of origin (almost always 'California') and indication of the method used. Such wines are the sparkling equivalents of generic table wines.

Vine varieties

California's mix of vine varieties is one of the world's most fluid. The most planted varieties, in declining order, are Chardonnay, Zinfandel, French Colombard, Cabernet Sauvignon, Merlot, and Chenin Blanc. Of these, Chardonnay, Cabernet Sauvignon, Merlot, and Zinfandel dominate labels, while French Colombard and Chenin Blanc are more often non-trumpeted ingredients in less expensive blends, the great majority of them either white or blush. There are also substantial total acreages of Sauvignon Blanc, Grenache, Barbera, the red-fleshed Rubired, Pinot Noir, Carignane (as CARIGNAN is spelt in California), and Ruby Cabernet. Italian influence is again likely to increase in California's vineyards, most particularly with Sangiovese. Other varieties enjoying modish popularity in the late 1990s were Pinot Noir, Cabernet Franc, and some which have origins in the Rhône—Syrah and Viognier are foremost.

Apart from Zinfandel, varieties that constitute a California speciality, many of them specifically bred in and for the state, are CARNELIAN, CHARBONO, EMERALD RIESLING, FLORA, Green Hungarian, PETITE SIRAH, RUBIRED, RUBY CABERNET, and SYMPHONY.

The following are the most important varieties found on California wine labels, listed alphabetically. For details of other California vine varieties, see under the variety name.

Cabernet Sauvignon Of all the transplants of European varieties to California, it is Cabernet Sauvignon that seems most at home, particularly in the Napa Valley. Napa Cabernet has much of the alcohol-induced weight of BURGUNDY. Plantings alongside rainy forests and in deserts, on mountain slopes and old river beds, and in scores of sites less extreme, have stretched Cabernet's varietal character to wide limits. Some of the fattest, most alcoholic models from California's hottest districts (see

SAN JOAQUIN VALLEY) come perilously close to port. Some thin, sharp-featured examples from notably chilly districts taste not merely herbaceous, but downright vegetal.

The best ones offer rich textures and an entrancing tennis match of opposing flavours, berries on one side, herbs on the other. Napa produces a majority of the memorably distinctive, age-worthy examples from California. Some show off particular subzones such as the Rutherford-Oakville west side (of which two of the first to establish their credentials were Beaulieu Vineyard's Georges de Latour bottling and Heitz Cellars' Martha's Vineyard), Howell Mountain, or the Stags Leap District (from which a Stag's Leap Wine Cellars offering famously 'beat' some of the great names of France at a much-reported tasting in Paris in 1976). A long list of others come from less-defined regions or are blended from vineyards in differing parts of the valley.

Sonoma does not lag far behind with its finest examples, but they are fewer and more scattered in provenance. Its superior districts appear to be Alexander Valley and Sonoma Valley. The other coastal wine-growing northern county Mendocino shows a kinship in growing conditions with similar wines. The Central Coast is a different kettle of fish. While flavours of fruit and herb play against each other in North Coast Cabernet Sauvignons, their Central Coast counterparts often pitted herb against vegetable in their first 20-odd vintages before being resurrected in the early 1970s. More recently, growers have introduced CANOPY MANAGEMENT and IRRIGATION in order to rein in the flavours. Greatest success has been achieved in the warmer districts inland of the coastal mountains such as Paso Robles and the southernmost sections of the Salinas Valley.

Chardonnay The great white grape variety of Burgundy came late to California but, once arrived, it swiftly came to play vanilla to Cabernet Sauvignon's chocolate. It has become so ubiquitous that many consumers use the name almost synonymously with white wine. However, grown in appropriate vineyards and made with care, it can be glorious and is still the premier white varietal wine of the state. By the late 1980s, California wineries were producing more than 700 different Chardonnays in each vintage.

During the 1970s, the majority of California Chardonnays were fermented in stainless steel,

racked off their lees and presented untroubled by oak. As such, and given the warmer climate (Napa Valley is 37 rather than Burgundy's 47 degrees north of the equator), California did much to introduce the notion of FRUIT DRIVEN Chardonnays to the world. Some more independent individuals began to experiment with what were then considered the much riskier techniques of BARREL FERMENTATION and LEES CONTACT.

Today, as in Burgundy, indeed because of Burgundy, California Chardonnay is often made as much or more in the cellar as in the vineyard. Barrel fermentation and OAK ageing, MALOLACTIC FERMENTATION, and all the other tricks in the wine-maker's bag go into a wide range of styles from outright butterscotchy to straightforwardly fruity, with every stage in between. Most are dry, but a considerable number offer a softening dollop of sweetness.

The grape variety has proven remarkably adaptable, growing well throughout the coastal counties, and not badly in the SIERRA FOOTHILLS. Chardonnay is most widely planted in Napa, Monterey, Santa Barbara, and Sonoma counties, in almost equal measure.

Gewürztraminer This distinctive ALSACE variety, most often spelt without the umlaut here, did not come into its own as a varietal wine until the 1950s, and remains limited in acreage. The variety takes on a particular flavour in California: floral, almost sweet pea, in most of Napa and the warmer parts of Sonoma; very close to lychee in the cooler climates of the Russian River district, the western portion of Santa Ynez Valley in Santa Barbara, Edna Valley in San Luis Obispo, the northern half of Salinas Valley in Monterey, and, above all, Mendocino County's Anderson Valley. A substantial majority of California's larger producers opt for off-dry styles, but a solid core make the wine fairly dry. By and large, the dry wines are the ones to age in order to bring Gewürztraminer's perfumes to their most concentrated.

Merlot In the mid 1990s, Merlot suddenly took off, becoming the faddish red varietal of choice, a less tannic alternative to Cabernet Sauvignon, particularly when offered in restaurants by the glass. Of all the districts in which it has been tried to date, the most promising appear to be Napa's Stags Leap District, the Russian River Valley, and the Santa Ynez Valley. Many fine examples still go into blends with Cabernet Sauvignon, usually in the amount of 10 to 15 per cent, or into MERITAGE-like blends in larger proportions.

Pinot Blanc Grapes and wines that go by this name in California may be either true PINOT BLANC or Melon de Bourgogne, the Muscadet grape. Only a few patches of the sparse acreage of California Pinot Blanc have ever produced wines of real interest but these have had sufficient depth and longevity to maintain the variety's status. The most singular examples came long ago from Spring Mountain in the Napa Valley, more recently from the Santa Cruz Mountains, and Redwood Valley in Mendocino County. Today, Laetitia winery (formerly Maison Deutz) on the coast in San Luis Obispo County has the most authoritatively true vineyard planting. Sonoma County, Livermore Valley, and Monterey County are other sources.

Pinot Gris The faddishness of the American market-place has wine-makers constantly on the look-out for a new trend (see ABC). By 1998, Pinot Gris had begun to be discussed as a potential candidate, although plantings remain minuscule. Among the handful of examples available, no consensus style had yet emerged, but it was clear the variety would be given a significant trial in the near future.

Pinot Noir The secrets of Pinot Noir in California turned out to be two: fog in the vineyards and less time in wood in the cellars than it was given in the early 1980s. Pinot Noir perplexed California wine-makers for decades by producing truly outstanding wine once in a great while, but dull stuff most of the time. The harder people tried to make something grand, the more often they fell short. In the 1970s the search for more suitable vineyards began to move ever closer to tidal shores. By the end of the 1980s, three districts had emerged, if not triumphant then at least much closer to triumph. Unified only by the persistence of their fogs, they are Carneros, the Russian River Valley of Sonoma, and Santa Barbara County, especially its Santa Maria Valley. On a slightly later curve, more and more wineries were trimming the time they left their Pinot Noirs in French oak barrels from two years or more to one year or less. With rare exceptions, long wood ageing diminishes California-grown Pinot Noirs to extinction. They emerge browning, raisiny, and dried out. The shorter span confers complexity of bouquet, yet leaves the wines richer in texture and readier to age well

in bottle. Pinot Noir enthusiasts tend to have their own favourites but Au Bon Climat, Gary Farrell, Rochioli, and Williams Selyem have been some of the most consistently successful producers.

Riesling California Riesling cannot be mistaken for its German counterparts, being riper in flavour and weightier with higher alcohol. It certainly is no competitor as an aperitif, but dry versions can outstrip most German Rieslings with meals because of a balance closer to traditional dry white wines from Italy or France. Its finest homes in California include Mendocino's Anderson Valley, the higher reaches of El Dorado County, Monterey's Arroyo Seco district, Santa Barbara County, Sonoma's Russian River Valley, and selected parts of the Napa Valley. Although winemakers' fascination with BOTRYTIS-affected sweet wines may have helped cause its downfall as a drier wine, examples of the former have been memorable from the likes of Newlan, Madroña, Hidden Cellars, Freemark Abbey, Chateau St Jean, and Joseph Phelps.

Sangiovese The classic Tuscan variety has received vigorous attention in California since the end of the 1980s, partly as a result of the ABC phenomenon and partly because of the success of Italianate restaurants throughout the USA. Artistic success has lagged well behind marketing interest, with many initial offerings appearing distinctly thin and often strawberry flavoured. Quality should improve with acquaintance and VINE AGE.

Sauvignon Blanc has been called California's greatest white grape. However, the variety's forceful flavours probably need tempering to appeal to the American public. There, in a nutshell, is its career, whether under its own name or under the California-coined synonym FUMÉ BLANC. It makes outstanding wines that many find too specific to enjoy, especially against the milder charms of Chardonnay. Some age their Sauvignons in new oak, disguising it as a sort of poor man's Chardonnay. Some blend in proportions of Semillon to temper the flavour and fill out a characteristically light body. Some do both.

Certainly no other white-wine variety is so widely adapted in the state. In a reverse of the situation in so many of the world's wine regions, California has much more Sauvignon Blanc than Semillon. Memorable Sauvignon Blanc examples have come from Livermore

Valley, Sonoma Valley, Napa Valley, and Santa Barbara. Scores of producers compete well; nearly every region in the state produces at least agreeably balanced wines from the variety. Generally speaking, straightforwardly styled Central Coast Sauvignon Blancs (Santa Ynez Valley, Monterey) smack sharply of the herbaceous or grassy flavours for which the Sauvignon is so widely noted. Their North Coast counterparts are more subtly herbaceous from the cooler zones (Russian River Valley, lower Napa Valley), almost melony from warmer areas (upper Napa Valley, upper Alexander Valley). Temecula gives a curiously floral twist to the flavours, and Amador County in the Sierra Foothills yields a slightly brackish quality.

In recent years, an ever-increasing number of growers have been allowing grapes to become botrytis affected for sweet wines styled after SAUTERNES. Early results have charmed in youth, but tended to fade quickly.

Syrah California's RHÔNE RANGERS have generated growing interest in this French import. Fleshy and plum-scented, perhaps more reminiscent of Australian HUNTER VALLEY Shiraz than the more rustic examples of France, these California Syrahs have achieved remarkable success in only a few years. Already the Sierra Foothills, the warmer canyons of eastern Santa Barbara County, the Hopland area of Mendocino, and Sonoma's Dry Creek Valley have distinguished themselves.

Viognier The 1980s explosion of interest in red Rhône varieties was echoed in the 1990s with their white counterparts. Although a handful of California producers have dabbled with Marsanne and Roussanne, the majority of entrants have cast their lot with Viognier. Pioneers included Ritchie Creek, La Jota, and Calera but the first major commitment was made by John Alban, who planted 30 acres in San Luis Obispo's Edna Valley district in 1989. Quality and style have been about as variable as the prices, with many expensive offerings being mediocre at best, prejudicing the variety's prospects, although there have been some successes.

Zinfandel The 'native' variety for long suffered from an image problem. Lacking a famous European forebear (see ZINFANDEL), it must be taken on its own terms. Few critics have had the independence of mind to do so, and so it has struggled to find a style.

Although sometimes deliberately vinified to minimize this characteristic, Zinfandel can easily be chewier than a Cabernet. Beyond its robust textures, Zinfandel at the height of its powers tastes of a berry not unlike but more wonderful than the wild blackberries found only in burned-over foothills in the Pacific Northwest and, maybe, the strain of raspberry Americans call boysenberry. Although it often has the structure and balance to age well, time does not replace its glorious flavours of berry with anything as pleasing. Flavours from oak barrels can also be difficult to work into harmony with the taste of berries. All the foregoing means that Zinfandel must come from a superior vineyard or be ordinary. Since it must compete for territory with Cabernet Sauvignon, the broad commercial success of red Zinfandel has been modest, limited primarily to a fervent cult of worshippers who have lived for some time in California.

The variety finds its most congenial home on dry-farmed hillsides. A centrepiece of this cultural community is Sonoma's Dry Creek Valley, the Russian River district, Mendocino County, Sonoma Valley and, though the fact is little recognized, the Napa Valley. San Luis Obispo County's Paso Robles AVA has a long, strong history with Zinfandel, as does Amador County in the Sierra Foothills AVA and Lodi and the Delta region of the Central Valley. All of these tend to make headier, riper wines than Sonoma. See also WHITE ZINFANDEL. B.C.C.

California cult wines, a phrase coined in the late 1990s to encompass wines made in the state of California, typically but not exclusively Napa Valley Cabernets, for which COLLECTORS, and possibly a few INVESTORS, will pay PRICES higher than those of Bordeaux's FIRST GROWTHS. They include such names as Araujo, Bryant Family, Caymus Special Select, Colgin, Dalla Valle Maya, Diamond Creek, Dominus, Dunn Howell Mountain, Grace Family, Harlan, Screaming Eagle, Vineyard 29. The most sought-after California Chardonnays are Marcassin and Kistler. What many of these names have in common is that they are made in extremely limited quantity, by talented winemaker CONSULTANTS currently favoured by FASHION.

Caluso, town in northern PIEDMONT most famous for its sweet white ERBALUCE.

Campania, region of south-west Italy of which Naples is the capital. Only about two per cent of the region's vineyards are in DOC zones, and the regional production of DOC wines is still just over 3.5 per cent of the region's total production, one of the lowest proportions of any of Italy's 20 regions.

Campania's natural beauty does not reflect the grinding poverty of the depopulated interior, which has also been severely damaged in recent earthquakes, and Naples, Italy's third largest city, offers little in terms of an interesting market. The possibility of good-quality viticulture none the less exists: abundant sunshine and HILLSIDE sites, volcanic soil quite suitable for vine-growing, and, most important of all, local vine varieties of real interest. AGLIANICO produces red wine of unquestionable character in the TAURASI DOC near Avellino, and non-DOC Aglianico wines of some potential can also be found in the province of Avellino and in the province of Benevento, where the so-called Aglianico del Sannio is produced.

The Solopaca DOC in the province of Benevento produces an interesting, if rustic, red wine with occasional notes of tobacco, from a blend of SANGIOVESE grapes, AGLIANICO, PIEDIROSSO, and other red varieties. Attempts to revive the glory of FALERNIAN are under way, with the new Falerno del Massico DOC on the slopes of Monte Massico near Mondragone stipulating a blend of Aglianico, Piedirosso, plus PRIMITIVO or BARBERA. White and all-Primitivo versions are also made.

White wines are less significant in Campania, although FIANO d'Avellino and Greco di Tufo, both from the province of Avellino, have their devotees. Fiano d'Avellino is said to be redolent of pears and hazelnuts. Greco di Tufo, made from a clone of the GRECO BIANCO vine grown around the village of Tufo, is said to recall peaches and almonds. Both of these descriptions correspond to the epoch in which the wines underwent some ageing in wood. Now made in a lighter, fresher style, they have become more technically correct, if less pronounced in flavour (although they can still display considerably more character than the average Italian white).

While the once-renowned viticulture of the island of Capri has virtually disappeared before the Gadarene onrush of modern tourism, ISCHIA produces small quantities of white and minuscule quantities of red wine.   D.T.

Campo de Borja, promising Spanish wine zone in the undulating plains around the town of Borja in the ARAGON region in the north east, producing mainly alcoholic red wines. This is one of the most arid parts of the country and low-yielding vineyards planted predominantly with GARNACHA vines produce intensely sweet, dark grapes which are made into heady red wines. Tempranillo and Cabernet Sauvignon are now accepted varieties. The Borsao Borja CO-OPERATIVE has revolutionized the region with its young, intensely fruity reds that have won a large following on export markets and shown the way to the future for the DO.

R.J.M. & V. de la S.

Canada has a thriving wine industry with almost as much acreage under vine as New Zealand. The growing areas are concentrated in four provinces, Ontario, British Columbia, and to a lesser extent Quebec and Nova Scotia. Given the exigencies of the Canadian climate, grapes are invariably grown near large bodies of water to moderate the effects of Canada's severe winters and decrease the risk of damaging winter freeze and spring frosts (see LAKE EFFECT). Until the late 1970s, the majority of Canadian vines were the winter-hardy North American LABRUSCA varieties such as CONCORD and Niagara. Next to follow were early-ripening, winter-resistant French HYBRIDS such as VIDAL BLANC, SEYVAL BLANC, BACO NOIR, and MARÉCHAL FOCH, usually spelt Marechal Foch and often called simply Foch in Canada. Since the late 1980s, however, growers have put greater emphasis on VINIFERA vine varieties, whose wines enjoy increasing success both at home and abroad. Riesling and Chardonnay are particularly important in Ontario, while Pinot Blanc and Merlot are specialities of British Columbia. In warm pockets, Viognier, Syrah, and Petite Sirah can be found and some success has been recorded with Cabernets and Pinot Noir in warmer years.

Perhaps the most notable accomplishment has been the consistently high quality of sweet wines produced in Canada, especially ICE WINE (spelt Icewine here) and late-harvest Riesling, Vidal, Ehrenfelser, and Optima. Canada is the world's largest producer of Icewine, which is not surprising since sustained temperatures of $-8\ °C$ can be relied upon each winter. See also EISWEIN.

Climate

Geographically, the major concentration of Canadian vineyards is on the same latitude as the LANGUEDOC and CHIANTI, but polar temperatures in winter, the freeze–thaw–freeze cycle of early spring, and unpredictable weather at HARVEST rank Canada as a COOL CLIMATE wine region, with all the vintage variation and wine-making problems that entails.

While some of Canada's vineyards may enjoy hotter summers than either Bordeaux or Burgundy, the growing season tends to be shorter. As in Burgundy, a high proportion of grapes require CHAPTALIZATION. DROUGHT is rarely a problem.

Wine laws

The production and sale of beverage alcohol is a provincial jurisdiction, which means that wine regulations vary from province to province. Most wine is retailed by provincial monopolies such as the Liquor Control Board of Ontario.

For wine production, the national Vintners Quality Alliance (VQA) regulations delimit viticultural areas and set minimum standards of production, including that water may not be added! Minimum MUST WEIGHTS and limits to chaptalization are specified but not maximum YIELDS. Special minimum must weights are set for specified grape varieties and the classifications Late Harvest, Select Late Harvest, Special Select Late Harvest, and Icewine. To receive the VQA seal, the wines must be subjected to ANALYSIS and assessed by a tasting panel.

Canadian wineries may also bottle wines which contain imported produce and which are not entitled to the VQA designation. A wine labelled Product of Canada may—indeed typically does—contain or even comprise grapes or grape-based material produced outside Canada (Chile became a popular source in the 1980s). Even (non-VQA) wines exported from Canada may contain non-Canadian grapes.

Ontario

Canada's most important wine province, with 60 wineries, has a climate similar to that of the Finger Lakes region in NEW YORK state, ameliorated by two bodies of water, Lakes Ontario and Erie. The major concentration of vineyards around the Niagara Peninsula is further protected by an escarpment which encourages onshore air drainage and thereby dissipates fog and minimizes frost damage.

Climatically similar to Burgundy, the region regularly produces fine Riesling, which in Germany would vary from KABINETT to BEERENAUSLESE degrees of ripeness, increasingly opulent Chardonnay, and, in warmer years, fully ripe Cabernet Franc and Merlot. Some Pinot Noir has been vinified, including wines made at Inniskillin in co-operation with the house of Jaffelin in Burgundy. The rich ethnic mix of grape-growers in Ontario is reflected in an unusually broad range of grape varieties, including GRÜNER VELTLINER and PINOT GRIGIO. Hybrids still play a significant role, however, with BACO making some of the most successful reds and VIDAL especially treasured for Icewine and other sweet wines.

No VQA wine labelled 'Ontario' may contain grapes grown outside Canada, or a hybrid blend. A wine labelled 'Ontario varietal' must contain at least 85 per cent of that varietal, hybrid or *vinifera*. Only those wines carrying one of the province's three geographical designations—Niagara Peninsula, Lake Erie North Shore and, the most southerly in Canada, Pelee Island—are obliged to contain 100 per cent Ontario-grown grapes (with at least 85 per cent of them coming from the designated region). Wines carrying a geographical designation must be made exclusively from *vinifera* grapes.

British Columbia

The BC wine industry, comprising 55 wineries, is thousands of miles west of Ontario, much nearer the vineyards of WASHINGTON state in the United States than any other Canadian wine region. It is centred on the arid Okanagan valley in the south east of British Columbia, where the deep Okanagan lake warms the vineyards in winter. The southern part of the valley, technically a desert, which borders on Washington state, alternates between summer daytime temperatures which can reach 35 °C and very cool nights. IRRIGATION is a necessity in this region characterized by small wineries and mainly *vinifera* production. Wines are typically fragrant and, often, made without recourse to oak. Varieties grown include Ehrenfelser, Riesling, Gewürztraminer, Auxerrois, Chardonnay, Pinot Blanc, Pinot Gris, and the usual range of French red varieties.

The number of vineyards and wineries has grown consistently since 1988 (when free trade with the USA was established). British Columbia's viticultural areas other than the Okanagan Valley (which produces more than 95 per cent of the province's wine) are Similkameen Valley, Fraser Valley, and Vancouver Island. VQA wines must be produced from 100 per cent British Columbia grapes, while those carrying the name of a designated viticultural area must contain at least 85 per cent of grapes grown there. Varietally labelled wines must contain at least 85 per cent of that variety.

Quebec

Quebec is the least likely of all Canadian wine regions. The centre of the province's small but enthusiastic wine-growing zone is the old town of Dunham. The 30 wineries, for the most part strung out along the American border, have to battle the elements to produce wine for the tourist trade. The vines need time-consuming winter protection. Average sunshine hours during the growing season in Dunham are approximately 1,150 (in Burgundy they are 1,315; Niagara has 1,426 and the Okanagan Valley 1,423). Despite relatively low temperatures, topographical features create highly localized warm spots that allow the hardiest vines to survive, if not flourish. Quebec's cottage wineries produce mainly white wines, mostly very fresh Seyval Blanc, Vidal, Chardonnay, and Riesling. Aurore, Cayuga, Ortega, Bacchus, and the Geisenheim 318 clone are also grown. Red wine is made from a wide range of cool-climate varieties, both *vinifera* and hybrids.

Nova Scotia

Midway between the equator and the North Pole, Nova Scotia boasts four farm wineries and vineyards which concentrate mainly on hybrids as well as Russian red varieties such as Michurinetz and SEVERNY. The short growing season restricts the number of varieties that can be planted in the Annapolis Valley and Northumberland Strait. Plantings include local speciality L'ACADIE, Vidal, Seyval Blanc, Marechal Foch, and De Chaunac, and effort is being put into finding new, earlier-ripening clones. Like Quebec, Nova Scotia has yet to join the Vintners Quality Alliance.   T.A. & J.Ro.

Canaiolo, or Canaiolo Nero, red grape variety grown all over central Italy and, perhaps most famously, a permitted ingredient in the controversial recipe for CHIANTI, in which it played a more important part than SANGIOVESE in the 18th century. It has declined considerably but good-quality Canaiolo does still exist in scattered spots in Chianti Classico—at Castello di Brolio and Castello di Cacchiano in Gaiole in Chianti, in Panzano (where the Castello di Paneretta produces a VINO DA TAVOLA made up of equal parts of Canaiolo and Sangiovese), and in the VINO NOBILE DI MONTEPULCIANO pro-

duction zone. Efforts to salvage the variety are under way in Tuscany, but there are few illusions that this will be accomplished either easily or fast. Canaiolo is also grown, to an even more limited extent, in LATIUM, SARDINIA, and the MARCHES. Italy's total plantings of Canaiolo Nero declined considerably in the 1980s, although the variety is specified in the regulations for 17 DOC wines.   D.T.

Canandaigua, based in Canandaigua in the Finger Lake region of NEW YORK state, is the second largest wine company in the UNITED STATES, after E & J GALLO. Its image is mass market. It owns three wineries in New York and eight in CALIFORNIA, including the relatively upmarket Simi. The wine BRANDS include Almadén, Dunnewood, Gold Seal, Great Western, Inglenook, Manischewitz (America's best-selling KOSHER wine), Marcus James (made in Argentina), Paul Masson, Taylor California Cellars, and Widmer. The company deliberately owns relatively few vineyards.   H.G.

Canary Islands, Spanish islands in the Atlantic ocean off the coast of Morocco. The mediocre wines for the tourist trade are slowly being replaced by more interesting products, much subsidized by the regional government, including young reds from the LISTÁN NEGRO and NEGRAMOLL grapes and whites from LISTÁN Blanco, as well as the sweet MALVASÍAS from La Palma and Lanzarote islands. The number of denominated zones has ballooned, and by the late 1990s included one for each of the islands of La Palma, El Hierro, and Lanzarote and no fewer than five for the island of Tenerife (Abona, Tacoronte-Acentejo, Valle de Güimar, Valle de la Orotava, and Ycoden-Daute-Isora).
V. de la S.

Canberra, the capital of AUSTRALIA, is ringed by wineries which together constitute a wine region called the Canberra District even if, because freeholds are not granted in the Australian Capital Territory itself, they are all over the border in NEW SOUTH WALES.

cane, the stem of a mature grapevine shoot after the bark becomes tan-coloured at VERAISON and starts its overwintering form.

Cannonau, sometimes spelt **Cannonao**, the SARDINIAN name for the widely planted red grape variety known in Spain as Garnacha and in France as GRENACHE. A high proportion of the grapes are grown on the east of the island to produce a varietal **Cannonau di Sardegna,**

which comes in several forms, but most commonly as a full-throttle dryish red. Although the variety is being pulled out by some Sardinian growers, the admirable Cannonau-based Turriga made by the Argiolas winery near Cagliari indicates that there is significant potential, yet to be exploited, for high-quality wine from the island's old Cannonau vines.

D.T.

Cañocazo. See FALSE PEDRO.

Canon-Fronsac, underrated Bordeaux wine appellation, the heartland of Fronsac. See FRONSAC.

canopy, that part of the vine above the ground, which includes stems, leaves, and fruit. See CANOPY MANAGEMENT.

canopy management, a portfolio of vineyard management techniques used to improve vineyard YIELD, wine quality, and the control of vine diseases, especially where vines are of high VIGOUR. These techniques essentially improve the exposure of leaves and fruit to the sun. The phrase became popular in many parts of the NEW WORLD in the 1980s and early 1990s as part of a growing awareness of the way in which CANOPY MICROCLIMATE affects vineyards. This awareness was not restricted to the New World. Considerable experimental work was also conducted in Europe, and the effects of canopy microclimate are now recognized as an explanation for the ability of distinguished vineyards to produce great wines (see TERROIR).

canopy microclimate, the climate within and immediately around the grapevine CANOPY.

cans. Ordinary wine is occasionally packaged in cans, which have no harmful effect on wine destined for early consumption. The advantages are that cans are lighter and less fragile than BOTTLES, but the material from which they are made is not, unlike glass, inert.

cantina, Italian for a cellar, a wine shop (although the word ENOTECA is more promising), and a winery. A **cantina sociale** is a CO-OPERATIVE winery.

Cape Riesling, South African name for the French white grape variety CROUCHEN Blanc that is virtually extinct in its native France but is grown in Australia as Clare Riesling. Also known as Paarl Riesling and South African Riesling, but much less distinguished than true RIESLING, which is also known as Weisser Riesling in South Africa, Cape Riesling produces an unexceptional dry white, its popularity due to a combination of the name, its undemanding blandness, and reasonable price.

J.P.

Capitolare, name given in 1993 by a group of producers in TUSCANY to a special group of wines previously described as Predicato. It means 'chapter' or 'classification', and refers to wines made from INTERNATIONAL VARIETIES using BARREL MATURATION.

capsule, French and occasional English name for the sheath over the top of a cork and bottleneck, otherwise known as a FOIL, just as the **capsule cutter** is more widely known as a FOIL CUTTER. French wine released for sale within France, as opposed to export, must have its capsules embossed with a customs seal, known as a **capsule congé.** Traditionally LEAD or lead alloys were used to manufacture capsules, but in Europe these were found to be a major source of soil contamination in disposal sites, and lead contamination of wine was traced to this source, so the use of lead capsules has been phased out. Older bottles with lead capsules should be wiped carefully around the bottleneck between pulling the cork and serving.

Caramany is a commune constituting a special, named enclave in the area designated for Côtes du ROUSSILLON-Villages. At least 60 per cent of the total blend, including any Carignan used, must be vinified by CARBONIC MACERATION, which technique was pioneered in the area by the Caramany CO-OPERATIVE.

carbon dioxide, or CO_2, a naturally occurring atmospheric gas, commonly encountered as the sparkle in soft drinks, beers, and SPARKLING WINES. Its content in the atmosphere is only about 0.03 per cent; yet upon that small amount depends the growth of all living systems. Not least, it is the ultimate raw material of wine and, via a series of biochemical reactions involving the grapevine, YEAST cells and the consumer, carbon dioxide is both assimilated and produced.

The cycle begins with the combination of carbon dioxide and water into sugars in the vine leaves by PHOTOSYNTHESIS; conversion in the leaves and berries of some of that sugar into a variety of compounds, including those directly or indirectly responsible for ACIDS, COLOUR, and FLAVOUR in the grapes and wine; and, as the final step, transformation of the grape juice into wine by FERMENTATION. Carbon dioxide is released in substantial amounts during fermentation. It returns whence it came with the metabolism of the alcohol and other wine constituents back to carbon dioxide and water, primarily in the liver of the wine drinker.   J.G. & R.E.S.

In wine-making

Carbon dioxide is used throughout the wine-making process to displace oxygen from contact with crushed grapes or wine. At some wineries, carbon dioxide is deliberately pumped over white grapes as they are received at the winery and pass through the destemmer in order to minimize OXIDATION.

In most still wines, this carbon dioxide is encouraged to dissipate leaving only very small amounts in the finished wine—although the more PROTECTIVE the wine-making, the more substantial these traces may be, as in, for example, many German and other light, aromatic, white wines. (Wine-makers may, however, choose to remove carbon dioxide from such wines just before bottling.)

In sparkling wines, however, substantial quantities of dissolved carbon dioxide, between two and six atmospheres, are encouraged to remain in the bottle by one of the methods outlined in SPARKLING-WINE-MAKING. Lesser quantities of carbon dioxide, between one and two atmospheres, may be encouraged in wines such as those labelled PERLANT, PÉTILLANT, or FRIZZANTE by inducing a second but less violent fermentation and preserving the carbon dioxide produced.

Since the 1960s, however, a number of wine-makers in hotter, particularly New World, regions have pursued a deliberate policy of bottling wine, particularly white wine, with up to one atmosphere of carbon dioxide dissolved in it. The warmer the wine is served, the more obvious is the carbon dioxide to the taster.

While most tasters would be surprised and probably shocked to notice any carbon dioxide in a mature red bordeaux (in which case it could even be taken to be an unwelcome sign of FERMENTATION IN BOTTLE), it is not necessarily a fault in most types of white and rosé wines. Portugal's VINHO VERDE provides many examples of this deliberate wine style, as do many young whites from the MOSEL, and some Italian red wines contain a perceptible level of carbon dioxide.

Carbon dioxide also plays an essential role in CARBONIC MACERATION.   A.D.W.

carbonic maceration, red-wine-making process which transforms a small amount of sugar in grapes to alcohol without the intervention of yeasts, and without even crushing the grapes. It is used typically to produce light-bodied, brightly coloured, fruity red wines for early consumption, most famously but by no means exclusively in the Beaujolais region of France.

Whole bunches or clusters of grapes are deliberately placed, with care to ensure that the berries are not broken, in an anaerobic atmosphere, generally obtained by using CARBON DIOXIDE to exclude OXYGEN. An intracellular fermentation takes place within the intact berry and a small amount of alcohol is formed, along with traces of many flavourful aromatic compounds. All of these contribute to the distinctive flavour and aroma of the resultant wines.

In practical terms, it is almost impossible to produce a wine that depends wholly on carbonic maceration. Whole clusters are poured into a vat which is then filled with carbon dioxide and sealed. The weight of the upper grapes breaks open the bottom layer of grapes, which begin to ferment in the normal way with oxygen excluded. In the middle layer are whole grapes surrounded by juice, and only on the top layer are whole grapes surrounded by carbon dioxide which undergo full carbonic maceration. The grapes in the middle layer undergo similar intracellular transformations, but at a much slower rate.

In traditional wine-making, it was common for uncrushed grapes at the top of a closed fermentation vessel to undergo carbonic maceration since the fermenting crushed grapes at the bottom would give off carbon dioxide which would exclude oxygen from the top of the vat. Thus, alcoholic fermentation and carbonic maceration would proceed simultaneously. This also applies to some red burgundy made today using whole-grape fermentations.

Although Beaujolais is the most famous wine region where carbonic maceration is the most common wine-making technique, it is also widely used for the Beaujolais grape Gamay in other parts of France, for more commercial reds in the southern Rhône, and has been a major factor in persuading the tough CARIGNAN grape to yield red wines for early drinking in the Languedoc-Roussillon in southern France (although there is an increasing tendency to blend these with traditionally made wines). Its use in the New World has been limited to some novel products such as the 'CabMac' designed as Australia's answer to Beaujolais. The wines produced by carbonic maceration tend to have a very particular aroma which some find reminiscent of bananas, others of kirsch or bubble-gum.

A.D.W. & P.L.

carbonization, the cheapest and least effective method of SPARKLING-WINE-MAKING, involving the simple pumping of CARBON DIOXIDE into a tank of wine.

Carcavelos, historic Portuguese DOC region just west of Lisbon.

Cardinal, red TABLE GRAPE variety, a CROSSING made in California in 1939. It has been grown quite widely in the south of France, Spain, Italy, Romania, and Bulgaria, and has more recently underpinned the wine industries of VIETNAM and THAILAND.

Cardinal is also a, usually Burgundian, name for a red wine mixed with CASSIS.

Carema, almost Alpine red-wine zone of PIEDMONT in north-west Italy, bordering on the Valle d'AOSTA, is the northernmost zone of Piedmont in which the great NEBBIOLO is cultivated (although see also VALTELLINA). Viticulture is not an easy task in this mountainous region, and the vineyards have been wrested from steep gradients by means of TERRACES.

The wine itself has a recognizably Nebbiolo character, with higher ACIDITY and less BODY than the better wines of the LANGHE or of GATTINARA, but interesting, perfumed, and pleasurable wines are regularly made in hot years. The 40 ha producing DOC wines are divided among over 120 growers, for most of whom viticulture is of course only a part-time activity at best. The resulting wines have been of variable quality in the past, although mastery of MALOLACTIC FERMENTATION has resulted in better and more consistent wines from the local co-operative winery. The lengthy ageing periods imposed by the DOC rules have clearly been a commercial handicap. Producer Luigi Ferrando works hard at maintaining the wine's reputation.

D.T.

Carignan, known as **Carignane** in the USA, **Carignano** in Italy, and **Cariñena** in Spain, late-ripening black grape variety which could fairly be called the bane of the European wine industry. Carignan, distinguished only by its dis-

advantages, has dug its roots into so much of the southern French *vignoble* that even the most generous of European Union bribes are having their work cut out to eradicate it. It is better than the ARAMON it replaced, however, and the produce of old vines on very poor soils such as at Domaine d'Aupilhac in MONTPEYROUX and Château de Lastours in CORBIÈRES is exceptional.

It has been France's most planted black grape variety ever since the mid 1960s and, although declining rapidly (almost half of all Carignan vines are well over 30 years old), is still almost twice as popular as its nearest rival GRENACHE Noir.

From the perspective of the 21st century, Carignan seems a very odd choice indeed. Its wine is high in everything— ACIDITY, TANNINS, COLOUR, BITTERNESS—but finesse and charm. This gives it the double inconvenience of being unsuitable for early consumption yet unworthy of maturation. There must have been some attribute to have Carignan disseminated so exclusively throughout the Midi in the 1950s and 1960s, and there was—yield—making it ideal for a thirsty but not discriminating market.

The regulations for the Languedoc-Roussillon's appellations have been forced to embrace the ubiquitous Carignan, which still accounts for a third of all vines planted there. But it is hard to argue that, for example, Minervois or Corbières are improved by their (continually reduced) Carignan component. Those wines that depend most heavily on 'improving' varieties such as Syrah and Mourvèdre and least on Carignan are almost invariably the most successful.

Only the most carefully farmed old vines on well-placed, low-yielding sites such as Fernand Vaquer's in ROUSSILLON can produce Carignan with real character. Elsewhere, the widespread introduction of CARBONIC MACERATION has helped disguise, if not exactly compensate for, Carignan's lack of youthful charm. The ASTRINGENCY of basic VIN DE TABLE has owed much to this vine, although blending with Cinsaut or Grenache helps considerably.

The white mutation **Carignan Blanc** can still be found in some vineyards of the Languedoc and, in particular, Roussillon.

Although the vine (like Grenache) originated in Spain in the province of Aragon, it is not widely planted there today. Carignan is not even the principal grape variety in the wine that carries its Spanish synonym CARIÑENA. It is grown chiefly in Catalonia today although it was historically a not particularly distinguished ingredient in Rioja, known there as Mazuelo. It also plays a major part in the wines of COSTERS DEL SEGRE, PENEDÈS, TARRAGONA, and TERRA ALTA.

The vine, gaining a vowel as Carignane, has been important in the Americas. Although it is rarely seen as a varietal, the vine's productivity and VIGOUR are valued by growers in California's hotter regions, if not by consumers. Carignan is also grown in Mexico and (to a much lesser extent) in Argentina, Chile, and Uruguay.

Because of its late-ripening habits, Carignan can thrive only in relatively hot climates. At one time it underpinned Israel's wine industry and it is by no means unknown in Italy. As Carignano is grown in Latium and most commonly in Sardinia, where it makes strong and sometimes pleasing reds and rosés, notably some toothsome Carignano del Sulcis.

Let some interesting old Carignan vines be treasured but let it not be planted.

Cariñena, town in north-east Spain which lends its name to both a denominated wine zone and a vine variety, widely grown in southern France as CARIGNAN. Although it is known to originate in the area, the vine (also called Mazuelo) has been widely abandoned in its native region in favour of GARNACHA, which seems better suited to the arid growing conditions in this, the largest of the four DO zones of the ARAGON region. Until the 1980s, most of Cariñena's hefty red wines were sold in bulk for blending with lighter wines from other parts of Spain. Natural alcohol levels of 18 and sometimes 19 per cent were not uncommon. But Cariñena, like so many other regions of Spain, is trying to break with the past. The minimum ALCOHOLIC STRENGTH permitted by DO regulations for red Cariñena was reduced from 14 to 12 per cent in 1990, while some Garnacha vines are gradually being uprooted and replaced by Tempranillo and Cabernet Sauvignon. Among the white vine varieties that cover a fifth of Cariñena's total vineyard area, Macabeo and Garnacha Blanca have been joined by Parellada from Penedès. The CO-OPERATIVES, which produce over three-quarters of all Cariñena's wines, are playing their part in this modernization process. Another positive development has been the creation of progressive private bodegas such as Solar de Urbezo.   R.J.M. & V. de la S.

Carmel Valley, California wine region and AVA where vines have recently joined golf courses and tennis ranches. See MONTEREY.

Carmenère is rarely encountered in the vineyards of Bordeaux today but was widely cultivated in the Médoc in the early 18th century and, with Cabernet Franc, established the reputations of its best properties. It yields small quantities of exceptionally deep-coloured, full-bodied wines and may even be, like PETIT VERDOT, the subject of a revival. Its new power base may turn out to be CHILE, where, it was discovered in 1991, a substantial proportion of the vines believed to be Merlot are in fact this historic variety, presumably imported directly from Bordeaux in the late 19th century. It ripens between Merlot and Cabernet Sauvignon and, grafted on to low-vigour ROOTSTOCKS, has the potential to make very fine wines, combining some of the charm of Merlot with the structure of Cabernet Sauvignon. It is frequently sold under the synonym Grand Vidure. Some vines previously thought to be Cabernet Franc in Friuli, northern Italy, are also thought to be Carmenère.

Carmignano, historic central Italian red wine made 16 km/10 miles north west of Florence in a zone noted as one of TUSCANY's finest for red wine production since the Middle Ages. The vineyards are located on a series of low hills between 50 and 200 m (160–650 ft) above sea level, unusually low for the SANGIOVESE grape, which forms the base of the blend and gives wines with lower ACIDITY and firmer TANNINS than the wines of CHIANTI CLASSICO. The relatively low altitudes allow Sangiovese to ripen fully here in one of the few places in Tuscany where Sangiovese can be successfully cultivated on the north bank of the Arno.

Carmignano, awarded DOCG status in 1990, is the only Tuscan DOC to require the inclusion of Cabernet Sauvignon (years before its use became common in Chianti). The vineyards of Ugo Contini-Bonacossi, the zone's major producer, were grafted with cuttings from Château LAFITE in the 1970s, and not with locally available Cabernet.

A few producers have begun to experiment with oak barrels, BARRIQUES and bigger casks, although the phenomenon has not become generalized as it has in Chianti Classico.   D.T.

Carnelian, black grape variety developed in and specifically for California. It is the result of crossing a 1936 crossing of Carignan and Cabernet Sauvignon with Grenache and was released in 1972. It was supposed to be a hot-climate Cabernet but too many of the Grenache characteristics predominate to make it easy to pick. Its California influence is limited, and restricted to the SAN JOAQUIN VALLEY, where its liberal produce goes into blends. Curiously, one of its loftiest expressions has come from a Texas vineyard, Fall Creek.

Carneros, also known as **Los Carneros**, a moderately cool, windy CALIFORNIA wine region, an AVA that spans the extreme south of both NAPA and SONOMA counties. Carneros sprang to public notice in and outside California in the mid 1980s, partly on the strength of some impressive Pinot Noirs and as much or more because of traditionally made SPARKLING WINES blended from Chardonnay and Pinot Noir grown in Carneros. Acacia, Buena Vista, Carneros Creek, and Saintsbury were important producers of still wines throughout the 1980s; Gloria Ferrer, Domaine Carneros, and Codorníu Napa were the pioneer sparkling-wine producers following the lead of Domaine Chandon of Yountville (see MOËT & CHANDON), which first sourced grapes here.

Carneros sprawls across the last, low hills of the Mayacamas range before it slips beneath San Francisco Bay. The larger part of the AVA lies within Sonoma County; grapes from that portion can also use the Sonoma Valley AVA. The smaller segment, in Napa County, is equally entitled to use Napa Valley as an AVA. In addition to Chardonnay and Pinot Noir, Carneros is gaining a reputation for Merlot. Many wineries further north in Napa Valley either own vineyards or buy grapes, particularly Chardonnay, in the Carneros district in order to have a cooler-climate blending component.

Growers and wineries within the AVA have banded together in a promotional body called the Carneros Quality Alliance, the seal of which appears on many of its wines.

Carso, zone in FRIULI in north-east Italy very close to Trieste and the border with SLOVENIA producing mainly red wines from the Terrano/Teran (REFOSCO) grape, and some whites from MALVASIA, which are not often exported. Like their colleagues in COLLIO, some producers have been experimenting with barrel-fermented Chardonnay and Sauvignon Blanc, often with positive results.

Cartagène is the largely domestically produced strong, sweet aperitif of the Languedoc, made by adding grape spirit to barely fermenting grape juice.

Cartaxo, DOC in central southern Portugal. See RIBATEJO.

cartons, wine packaging, sometimes known as tetrapacks, that has been particularly popular for everyday wines in Latin American countries such as CHILE.

casa vinicola on the label of an Italian wine indicates a producer who buys in grapes or wine, like a French NÉGOCIANT.

case. Beer and milk may be sold in crates but, contrary to popular usage, wine is sold in cases. A case holds a dozen bottles, the basic trading unit in the fine-wine trade and much of the wholesale wine trade. Most cases are made of cardboard outers, with cardboard vertical or papier mâché horizontal dividers. Most (but not all) fine wines designed for prolonged BOTTLE AGEING are dispatched from their producers in thick wooden cases, usually made of rough pine, branded with the name, and often logo, of the producer on the **case ends** (which can be attractive enough for future use). These cases are usually nailed down and can only be opened with a chisel or screwdriver and hammer, often breaking the wooden lid. Wine sold in unopened cases is presumed, in the fine-wine market, to be worth sufficient premium that they are usually designated 'o.w.c.', or 'original wooden cases'.

The German wine trade has long sold wine in six-bottle cartons. A **split case** may be one that is torn, but may be one that contains six bottles of each of two different wines, or four bottles of each of three different wines. One bottle of each of 12 different wines becomes a **mixed case.**

cask, wooden container for wine, often used interchangeably with BARREL (particularly by the British), a cylindrical container small enough to be rolled. The term is also used less precisely, however, for wooden containers of any size (which may or may not be open topped), including large, immobile, storage containers such as the ovals common in Germany and Alsace, or the *botte* of Italy.

The Australian wine industry coined the

term **cask wine** for wine packaged in a bag packed inside a cardboard BOX, a wine type highly unlikely to have been either made or aged in wood of any sort (although OAK CHIPS could have played a part in some).

cask ageing, wine-making practice of ageing a wine after fermentation (see ÉLEVAGE) in a large wooden container usually too old to impart any wood flavour. It may well, however, exert some wood influence and help considerably to achieve natural CLARIFICATION and STABILIZATION. White wines subjected to cask ageing for several months include some of the great white wines of the LOIRE, GERMANY, and ALSACE. Red wines subjected to cask ageing, sometimes for several years, include many of the traditional wines of the RHÔNE, ITALY, SPAIN, PORTUGAL, and GREECE.

The alternatives, and possible supplements, to cask ageing are BARREL MATURATION, AGEING in inert containers such as stainless-steel tanks, BOTTLE AGEING, and bottling almost immediately after FERMENTATION as in NOUVEAU wines.

cassis is French for blackcurrant and is used often as a tasting note for red wines, particularly red wines based on Cabernet Sauvignon grapes.

Dry white wine mixed with some blackcurrant liqueur is known as both a **vin blanc cassis** and KIR (while red wine mixed with blackcurrant liqueur is sometimes called a *cardinal*).

Cassis, small, mainly white-wine appellation in PROVENCE. Three-quarters of the wine is full, dry, herby white, made from increasing proportions of Clairette and Marsanne, together with some Ugni Blanc and Sauvignon Blanc. The best producers such as La Ferme Blanche and Ch de Fontcreuse can make wines that age gracefully. A little red and rosé is also made, mainly from Mourvèdre (which ripens easily here), Grenache, and Cinsaut. Little Cassis is allowed to escape by the annual influx of summer visitors, however.

Castelão Francês, dark-skinned grape variety planted all over southern Portugal and known variously as PERIQUITA in Terras do Sado and Ribatejo; as João de Santarém or Santarém in parts of Ribatejo; Mortágua in Estremadura; and even TRINCADEIRA PRETA in parts of the country. This versatile vine can produce fruity, relatively fleshy, even gamey red wines which can be drunk young or aged.

Castel del Monte, DOC in the far south east of Italy. See APULIA.

Castelli Romani, general term for the white wines of the volcanic hills south east of Rome in the region of LATIUM which stretch from just outside the city gates into the province of Latina. The DOC vineyards are divided into six different appellations: Colli Albani, Colli Lanuvini, FRASCATI, Marino, Montecompatri, and Velletri. The wines are made principally from MALVASIA grapes with usually at least 25 per cent TREBBIANO. BOMBINO (here also called Bonvino) and Bellone are also permitted in the blend, up to a maximum of 10 per cent, and can add a welcome note of complexity, but these vines are gradually being abandoned by growers. Malvasia di Candia is more widely utilized than Malvasia di Lazio, principally for its high productivity, although better producers prefer the quality of the latter. A wide variety of different strains of Trebbiano are employed. High YIELDS make many of the discussions of blends and subvarieties purely nugatory; interesting wines from Malvasia and Trebbiano cannot be made in these quantities. The wines of the separate DOCs tend to resemble one another closely, in fact, although Marino can be somewhat fuller than its neighbours.

Over three-quarters of the total production is in the hands of CO-OPERATIVES, the rest principally in the hands of large commercial wineries. Both have followed a marketing strategy based on high volume and low prices, counting on the advantages of the proximity of the large Roman market and on the more extended recognition that has come from the millions of visitors who flock to the city each year and encounter the wines in the city's taverns and *trattorie*.

If the Castelli Romani wines are principally intended for the guzzling needs of their public, the character of the wines themselves has changed rather drastically. Once fermented on their skins, these wines were golden in colour, full in flavour and aroma. The colour deepened as the Malvasia, a variety whose wines oxidize quite rapidly, began to age, and the aromas and flavours followed suit. The results were not always wines of great finesse, but they provided an excellent accompaniment to the flavoursome cuisine of Rome. Modern Castelli Romani wines, cold fermented off the skins, filtered, and stabilized, are a product without the defects of old but without the character of the past, a character which made them an integral part of the life and culture of Rome.

Several avant-garde estates in Marino and Frascati are now producing interesting wines from Cabernet and Merlot, Chardonnay, and Sauvignon Blanc, and even more exotic varieties such as Viognier and Syrah.　　D.T.

Castile and León, known as Castilla y León in Spanish, is the largest of the 17 autonomous regions of SPAIN. This northern part of Spain's central plateau, rising to between 880 and 1,000 m (2,900–3,300 ft) above sea level, takes up about a fifth of the entire country. Centred on its capital, the university city of Valladolid, most of Castile-León is thinly populated table land almost encircled by mountains.

The climate here is harsh. Short, hot summers are followed by long, cold winters when temperatures can drop to −10 °C/14 °F. Under often clear skies, temperatures drop quickly after sunset and, even in summer, nights are cool. Frost continues to be a threat until mid May. Rain falls mainly in winter. Much of the land is poor and unable to support anything other than nomadic flocks of sheep. However, the river Duero (known as DOURO in Portugal) provides a natural water source.

A regional variant of the red TEMPRANILLO vine, variously called Tinta del País, Tinto Fino, and Tinta de Toro, is the chief good-quality grape variety in three of the five DO wine regions in Castile-León. The largest of these is RIBERA DEL DUERO, which is internationally known for its red wines. Downstream of Ribera del Duero, RUEDA made enormous progress in its white-wine production in the 1980s, while TORO, straddling the Duero near the Portuguese border, is slowly improving its once heavy reds. CIGALES, north of Valladolid, specializes in rosé wine. BIERZO, abutting GALICIA in the north west, shows promise with its light fragrant reds from the Mencía grape. Another wine zone awaiting official recognition is León.　　R.J.M. & V. de la S.

Castile-La Mancha, known as Castilla-La Mancha (historically, Castilla la Nueva) in Spanish and New Castile in English, the lower, southern half of the plateau that makes up central SPAIN. At altitudes between 500 and 700 m (1,650–2,300 ft) above sea level, this is Spain at her most extreme. Winters are long and cold. In summer, the heat is gruelling. The thermometer regularly rises above 35 °C, even 40 °C (104 °F), and little if any rain falls between May

and September. Despite these fierce conditions, Castile-La Mancha produces half of all the wine made in Spain, with average yields of just over 25 hl/ha (1.4 tons/acre).

One of Castile-La Mancha's four DO regions, LA MANCHA itself, is planted mainly with the robust white-wine vine AIRÉN, the world's most widely planted vine variety. Cencibel (alias TEMPRANILLO) comes a poor second in this region behind the drought-resistant Airén, but dominates in the Valdepeñas DO, while north west of Toledo, MÉNTRIDA produces rough-and-ready reds from overripe Garnacha (GRENACHE). Although the fourth DO, ALMANSA, belongs administratively to Castile-La Mancha, the style of wine-making there is closer to that of the LEVANTE. MONASTRELL, Cencibel, and the red-fleshed Garnacha Tintorera produce big, alcoholic red wines.

Until the 1970s, the wines from Castile-La Mancha were mainly sold in bulk to be drunk by undiscerning palates in bars all over Spain. But in the 1970s and 1980s, parts of the region were quietly revolutionized and a new generation of cleanly made and often inexpensive red and white wine from Castile-La Mancha is finding favour with buyers both at home and abroad.　　R.J.M. & V. de la S.

Castillon, Côtes de, once Bordeaux Côtes de Castillon, is a good-value red-wine appellation in the BORDEAUX region immediately east of ST-ÉMILION. It produces sturdy red wines based on Merlot grapes with generally better structure than regular red BORDEAUX AC. The 400 vine-growers here elected in 1989 to establish their own identity rather than depend on the name of Bordeaux. Those vineyards closest to the river DORDOGNE tend to produce more supple wine than those at higher altitudes such as Ch de Belcier, one of the more important producers.

Catalonia, a proud and industrious region on the Mediterranean coast which encompasses a part of southern France and a part of northeast Spain, some of whose inhabitants consider themselves neither French nor Spanish, and even those who do, think of themselves as Catalan first. Self-government was achieved in 1977, when Catalonia became one of Spain's 17 autonomous regions. Barcelona, the second largest city in Spain and the busiest port on the Mediterranean, became the Catalan capital. Centuries of political infighting have left Catalonia with a strong sense of independence. The Catalan language, akin to the French *langue d'oc* (see LANGUEDOC), often suppressed in the past in favour of Castilian Spanish, has now been restored as the official language and Catalonia (Cataluña in Castilian, Catalunya in Catalan) is now officially bilingual (which leads to some confusion and anomalies in proper names). For details of French Catalonia, see ROUSSILLON.

Catalonia was at the vanguard of Spain's 20th-century wine-making revolution. The region began to stir in the early 1870s when José Raventos began making sparkling wine by the TRADITIONAL METHOD in the small town of San Sadurní de Noya (Sant Sadurni d'Anoia in Catalan). He founded the giant CODORNÍU firm, and his foresight generated the CAVA industry, which earned its own Denominación de Origen (see DO) in 1986.

In addition to most of Spain's Cava, Catalonia produces an eclectic range of wines from traditional, powerful reds to cool-fermented dry whites.

Much of the credit for the transformation of Catalonia's wine industry in recent years must go to the late Don Miguel Torres Carbó and his son Miguel A. TORRES, who imported INTERNATIONAL VINE VARIETIES to plant alongside indigenous varieties such as GARNACHA, MONASTRELL, and TEMPRANILLO (called Ull de Llebre in Catalan) and the Cava grapes, PARELLADA, MACABEO, and XAREL-LO.

The climate in Catalonia is strongly influenced by the Mediterranean. The coastal belt is warm and equable with moderate rainfall but conditions become progressively more arid and extreme further inland. There are eight DO regions: ALELLA, EMPORDÀ-COSTA BRAVA, CONCA DE BARBERÀ, COSTERS DEL SEGRE, PENEDÈS, PLA DE BAGES, PRIORAT, TARRAGONA, and TERRA ALTA. Of these, Penedès is the most important in terms of quantity, although most others, especially Priorat, have made great progress in quality.

Catalonia has long been an important centre of CORK production and is a particularly important source of corks for sparkling wines.

R.J.M.

Catarratto, Sicilian white grape variety with potential which was identified as the second most planted single variety in all of Italy in the 1990 agricultural census.

The variety is planted almost exclusively in the far western province of Trapani and has in the past been much used for the production of MARSALA. Despite its profusion, this variety is specified in the regulations of just three DOC zones; familiarity seems to have bred the usual contempt from locals. Visiting FLYING WINEMAKERS have learnt more respect for this grape and some fine, crisp but characterful table wines have been produced from it. See SICILY.

Catawba, deep-pink-skinned grape variety grown to a great extent in NEW YORK state. It is a cross between LABRUSCA and VINIFERA, producing wines of all shades of pink. It can even yield light reds.

Cava, Spanish SPARKLING WINES made using the traditional method of SPARKLING-WINE-MAKING.

Unlike any other Spanish DO, the Cava denominación is not restricted to a single delimited area. However, since Spain joined the European Union in 1986, the EU authorities have insisted that Cava should be made from grapes grown in prescribed regions. As a result, the use of the term Cava is restricted to sparkling wines from a list of municipalities in CATALONIA, VALENCIA, ARAGON, NAVARRA, RIOJA, and the BASQUE country. Ninety-five per cent of all Cava is made in Catalonia, however, mostly in and around the town of San Sadurní de Noya. Total production amounts to about a third that of Champagne.

The somewhat neutral MACABEO (the Viura of Rioja) comprises about half of the blend for a typical Cava. The productive and indigenous XAREL-LO vine is the second most important, and its earthy aroma has been one of Cava's distinguishing features, although it thrives only at relatively low altitudes. PARELLADA performs better above 300 m/900 ft, where it produces finer wines relatively low in BODY. Plantings of the French vine CHARDONNAY, officially authorized for Cava in 1986, are increasing rapidly.

To qualify for the DO, Cava must be made according to the local, and in some respects less rigorous, adaptation of the traditional method. The wine must spend at least nine months on its lees before DISGORGEMENT, achieve at least four atmospheres of pressure, and attain an ALCOHOLIC STRENGTH of between 10.8 and 12.8 per cent by volume. YIELDS are higher than those allowed in Champagne.

(The bitter competition between the two giants of Cava, CODORNÍU and FREIXENET, produced a series of ugly court battles in the late

1990s, with Codorníu charging that its competitor's less expensive wines did not spend the minimum time on lees, and Freixenet counterattacking with charges that its rival was using still illegal Pinot Noir grapes.)

The best Cavas tend to be produced by the larger firms who control their own vinification rather than those producers who buy in readymade base wine from one of the large but often outdated CO-OPERATIVES that continue to flourish all over Catalonia.   R.J.M. & V. de la S.

cave, French for a CELLAR or wine-making establishment and as close as the French language comes to an equivalent of a WINERY. A caviste is a specialist wine retailer, of which there are surprisingly few in France, presumably since so many consumers buy direct from the producer.

cave co-opérative, French for one of France's more than 1,000 wine CO-OPERATIVES.

Cayetana, high-yielding Spanish white grape variety which produces neutral-flavoured wine. It is particularly popular in the EXTREMADURA region. In Rioja it may be known as Cazagal.

Cebreros, wine zone in north-west Spain. See CASTILE AND LEÓN.

cellar, widely used word that is roughly the English counterpart to CAVE, CANTINA, and BODEGA in French, Italian, and Spanish respectively. It can therefore be applied to wine shops and wine-making premises, but is here considered only in its domestic sense, as a collection of wine and the place in which it is stored.

Location

Traditional underground cellars have the great advantages of being secure, dark, at a constant low temperature, slightly damp, and rarely disturbed. As outlined in STORING WINE, these constitute ideal conditions. It is also possible to buy special cabinets which look like refrigerators and can be programmed to maintain certain temperature and humidity levels, but they are expensive relative to their capacity. Less expensive options include insulating a small room or large cupboard, insulating a space under some stairs, using a dark corner of a distant spare room or a closet against an outside wall, or a secure outhouse (although care must be taken that the temperature never falls so low as to freeze the wine and push the corks out). It is important that any makeshift

cellar is far from any heat source, even a hot water pipe and, especially, a boiler, but a constant medium temperature is less harmful than a place in which there are violent temperature swings. Those living on ground level can even excavate, and depend on a trapdoor.

Paying for professional storage may be the only realistic option for some, but in this case cellar records (see below) are essential.

Design

Wine can be stored in the CASES in which it is bought, but this is practical only for wines years away from being ready to drink. Some form of wine rack is usually most user-friendly, allowing the bottles to be kept horizontal and withdrawn easily. Racks with slots for individual bottles are best for very mixed cellars but larger compartments, or BINS, can be used for larger quantities of bottles of the same wine.

It of course makes sense to keep the wines nearest MATURITY in the most accessible positions. There will be a slight temperature variation between the top and bottom of the cellar. Light levels are also likely to be higher at the top than the bottom, so there are at least two reasons why the fullest, least fragile, slowest maturing wines such as vintage port should be stored at the top and bottles as sensitive as, say, those containing sparkling wines should be stored close to floor level.

Contents

There is little point in devoting space and capital to storing wine unless it is difficult or expensive to replace, or will positively improve as a result of BOTTLE AGEING. In general, it is wise to be ruthless about cellar space, and accord it only to wines which are available only for a brief period (such as EN PRIMEUR rarities) or the wines recommended as worth AGEING.

Records

The ideal cellar record has a good-sized page for each case of wine acquired, stating price, supplier, and date of purchase. Below this a dated tasting note for each bottle tasted can be inserted, together perhaps with details of the circumstances in which it was opened. The pages can be grouped by wine type (red bordeaux, for example) and individual bottles can be grouped appropriately together on pages. (Those using professional wine storage need, for obvious reasons, to keep full details of where and since when the wine has been stored.)

Personal computers offer other, often more sophisticated and flexible, possibilities for cellar record-keeping but it is worth remembering that cellars are usually kept for many years longer than a pc.

See also STORING WINE.

cellar work, general term for all the processing steps requiring human intervention or monitoring in WINE-MAKING. Cellars in which small barrels are used for both fermentation and maturation involve the most physical work. See also ÉLEVAGE.

Cencibel, synonym for the Spanish black grape variety TEMPRANILLO, especially in central and southern Spain, notably in LA MANCHA and VALDEPEÑAS, where it is the principal dark-skinned variety.

Central Coast, one of CALIFORNIA'S umbrella AVAS, this large wine region encompasses all of the major vineyards in eight thoroughly disparate counties from Contra Costa in the north to Santa Barbara in the south. The counties (and their AVAs) are Alameda (LIVERMORE VALLEY); Contra Costa; MONTEREY (Arroyo Seco, Carmel Valley, Chalone, San Lucas); SAN BENITO (Cienega Valley, Lime Kiln Valley, Mount Harlan, Paicines); SAN LUIS OBISPO (Arroyo Grande, Edna Valley, Paso Robles, York Mountain); SANTA CLARA (most of Santa Cruz Mountains, San Ysidro); and SANTA BARBARA (Santa Maria Valley, Santa Ynez Valley).

Central Valley. In CALIFORNIA, this great expanse is divided into the SACRAMENTO VALLEY in the north, which produces small quantities of wine, and the vast SAN JOAQUIN VALLEY in the south, which supplies the majority of the state's bulk. Plumbed by an extensive system of rivers out of the Sierra Nevada and IRRIGATION canals built since the 1920s, this large, fertile, sunny region is arguably the most productive farmland in the world with more agricultural output than the whole of China until 1990.

The Sacramento river from the north and the San Joaquin river from the south drain into the **Central Valley Delta,** which includes such AVAS as CLARKSBURG and, on slightly higher ground, LODI.

CHILE also has a Central Valley, although in this case it is the source of a high proportion of Chile's best wine.

Central Victoria is a wine zone within the Australian state of VICTORIA comprising Goul-

burn Valley, Bendigo, and the **Central Victorian High Country**.

Centurian, CALIFORNIA vine crossing with the same parentage as CARNELIAN grown in the central SAN JOAQUIN VALLEY. It has viticultural advantages over Carnelian but no organoleptic distinction.

cépage, French for VINE VARIETY. A VARIETAL wine, one that is sold by the name of the principal grape variety from which it is made, is known as a **vin de cépage** within France, a term which has had some pejorative sense in comparison with a geographically named wine which qualifies as APPELLATION CONTRÔLÉE. With very few exceptions, AC wines should not specify the name of a vine variety on the main label.

Cerceal, name of several white Portuguese grape varieties, whose Anglicized form is SERCIAL, a variety most commonly associated with the island of MADEIRA. Forms of Cerceal are planted in many mainland wine regions, where, because of the grapes' high acidity, they are often called Esgana Cão, or 'dog strangler'. **Cerceal do Dão** is a quite distinct ingredient in white DÃO.

Cereza, pink-skinned grape variety of considerable though declining importance in ARGENTINA, most notably in San Juan province. It produces mainly white and some rosé wine of extremely mediocre quality for early consumption within Argentina.

Cérons, the least important sweet-white-wine appellation in the BORDEAUX region, on the left bank of the river GARONNE. Just north of BARSAC and SAUTERNES, it produces wines which rarely demonstrate either the finesse of the first or the concentration of the second of these two more famous appellations, possibly partly because higher YIELDS are allowed. In effect, Cérons is a buffer zone between Barsac and the GRAVES, and indeed it produces dry wines entitled to the Graves appellation as well as its own sweet wine. The best bottlings from the likes of Ch de Cérons can demonstrate real vivacity, but apathy and depressed prices have discouraged many producers from making the investments of faith and equipment needed to make great sweet wine. The generally flatter land may also play a part in reducing the likelihood of BOTRYTIZED WINES.

certified planting material, budwood, cuttings, or grafted plants which have normally been through a form of quality assurance to ensure trueness to type, freedom from known virus diseases, and typically designated clonal origin. Various bodies, often government controlled, offer such certification programmes around the world. See CLONE and CLONAL SELECTION. R.E.S.

Cesanese, the red grape variety apparently indigenous to LATIUM. The superior **Cesanese d'Affile** is more common but is losing ground. **Cesanese Comune** has larger berries and is also known as Bonvino Nero.

César, vine speciality of the far north of Burgundy, where it can contribute to such light, soft reds as IRANCY.

Chablis is the steely, dry, ageworthy white wine of the most northern vineyards of BURGUNDY in north-east France, made, like all fine white Burgundy, from Chardonnay grapes. Paradoxically, however, in the New World, particularly in North America and Australia in whose vineyards a wine as austere as Chablis is virtually impossible to produce, the name Chablis has been borrowed as a GENERIC name and abused so that it is more often used to describe a dry white wine of uncertain provenance and no specific grape variety bearing no resemblance other than its colour to true Chablis.

The appellation covers almost 3,000 ha/7,500 acres around the small town of Chablis and 19 other villages and hamlets in the *département* of the Yonne, near the city of AUXERRE. The appellation comprises four ranks, of which the top is grand cru Chablis, with seven named vineyards. Then come the premiers crus, including 40 vineyard names, then Chablis, by far the most common appellation, and finally Petit Chablis, the lowliest. The best vineyard sites are on the south-west facing slopes of the valley of the Serein, the small river that flows through the town of Chablis to join the Yonne.

Chablis is quite separate from the rest of Burgundy, divided from the CÔTE D'OR by the hills of the Morvan, so that BEAUNE, for example, is over 100 km to the south. In fact, the vineyards of Chablis are much closer to CHAMPAGNE and its southernmost vineyards in the Aube *département*, than to the rest of Burgundy.

Climate

Climate has always played an important role in determining the success and quality of Chablis.

Winters are long and hard and summers often, but not always, fairly hot. There is all the climatic uncertainty, and therefore vintage variation, both in quality and quantity, of a vineyard far from the equator.

One of the key factors in determining how much wine will be produced is the possibility of spring frosts, which can cause enormous damage to the young vine shoots.

Vineyard expansion

The development of effective frost protection in the early 1960s was followed by a tremendous increase in the vineyard area of Chablis, which has not been without controversy, with those who believe that the vineyards should be restricted in area arguing their cause as fervently as those who favour the expansion of the appellation. The seven grands crus total just 100 ha and are all on one slope facing south west just outside the town. They are Les Clos, Blanchots, Bougros, Vaudésir, Valmur, Preuses, and Grenouilles. There is also, in true Burgundian fashion, an anomaly. The tiny vineyard of La Moutonne is partly in Vaudésir and partly in Preuses, but for some illogical and doubtless bureaucratic reason does not have the status of a grand cru in its own right, even though its wines certainly demonstrate that it qualifies.

Much of the dispute over the vineyard expansion has centred on the premiers crus. By the mid 1990s, there were 40 named premier-cru vineyards. Some of the lesser-known vineyards may use the umbrella name of a better-known premier cru, as listed below (lesser-known names in italics). For example, *L'Homme Mort* may be sold as Fourchaume.

Mont de Milieu
Montée de Tonnerre: *Chapelot, Pied d'Aloue, Côte de Bréchain*
Fourchaume: *Vaupulent, Côte de Fontenay, L'Homme Mort, Vaulorent*
Vaillons: *Châtains, Séchet, Beugnons, Les Lys, Mélinots, Roncières, Les Epinottes*
Montmains: *Forêt, Butteaux*
Côte de Léchet
Beauroy: *Troesme, Côte de Savant*
Vauligneau
Vaudevey: *Vaux Ragons*
Vaucoupin
Vosgros: *Vaugiraut*
Les Fourneaux: *Morein, Côte de Prés Girots*
Côte de Vaubarousse
Berdiot

Chaume de Talvat
Côte de Jouan
Les Beauregards: *Côte de Cuissy*

It is in the village appellation that there has been the greatest growth, with the planting of vines on much of the arable land.

Soil is another significant factor in determining not only the unique flavour of Chablis, but also the vineyard area. The grand-cru vineyards are all on Kimmeridge, a mixture of limestone and clay, containing a multitude of tiny fossilized oyster shells, while Portlandien, which is very similar in structure to Kimmeridge but is generally deemed not to give as much finesse to the wine, constitutes most of the outlying vineyards of Petit Chablis.

Viticultural practices in Chablis are very similar to those in the rest of Burgundy, apart from the overriding need to protect the vines from frost.

The use of oak

The most interesting and controversial aspect of vinification in Chablis is the use of OAK. This is a most significant factor in influencing the taste of a Chablis, for it is where the winemaker can make the most impact. Chablis is the one fine-wine area where Chardonnay is not automatically given some contact with oak.

In the 1960s, oak barrels were used simply for storage. Concrete vats, then steel, and more recently stainless steel have all provided more inert materials for containers. Some producers abandoned their oak barrels in favour of stainless steel, which, although expensive, is very much easier to use, allowing for impeccable HYGIENE and a meticulous control of TEMPERATURE. Inert vats have no effect on the taste of Chablis and allow the wine to express the TERROIR of a particular cru, without any external influence. Those who favour stainless steel want the purest flavour of Chablis, with the firm streak of acidity and the mineral quality that the French describe as *goût de pierre à fusil*, or gunflint. Louis Michel's is generally considered to be the epitome of this style, although others who employ it successfully include Jean Durup, Jean-Marc Brocard, A. Régnard, and Long-Depaquit.

Other producers, such as René and Vincent Dauvissat, and François and Jean-Marie Raveneau, have never completely abandoned their barrels. They may ferment their wine in vats and then, once the alcoholic fermentation is finished, the wine goes into oak for a few months' BARREL MATURATION. Those who favour the use of oak barrels believe that the gentle process of oxygenation adds an extra dimension of complexity to the flavour of their wine. However, oak barrels are much more demanding in terms of labour and if you replace your barrels on a regular three-yearly rotation, they are expensive. The proportion of new barrels in a cellar in Chablis can vary. Some producers buy very few each year, wishing to avoid the marked vanilla flavours that new wood can impart. Others such as William Fèvre regularly replace a third of their barrels.

Experimentation with oak reached almost fever pitch in the early 1990s. Some who had abandoned it have returned to it, or their children have. Some, such as Gilles Collet, Jean-Paul Droin, and Domaine Laroche for some crus, ferment in barrel; others just age their wine in oak, with annual variations according to the quality of the wine. Few wines other than the grands crus and premiers crus are matured in wood, however, for it is generally recognized that a wine needs a certain structure and extract to avoid being overwhelmed by the taste of oak, as is the case with some Chablis *cuvée bois*, the product of barrel maturation. LEES STIRRING, degrees of barrel TOAST, origins of oak and coopers are all topics of consideration, and there are of course no conclusive answers. Paradoxically it is not unknown for a Chablis that has seen no wood to take on, as it matures, a certain firm nuttiness that suggests some ageing in oak. Ultimately, as with all Burgundy, where vineyards and crus are split amongst several families, the choice of a bottle depends on the name of the grower and the estate on the label.

The Chablis market

Nearly a third of all Chablis is vinified by the local co-operative, La Chablisienne, which works well for its appellation. There are also five NÉGOCIANTS based in the town, some with vineyards and some without. However, the trend of the last decade or two has been for an increasing number of producers who originally sold their wine in bulk to négociants, to bottle and sell their wine themselves. Consequently, the négociants have tended to decline in importance and the choice of Chablis producers has grown significantly.

Chablis has always been affected by significant variations in the size of the vintage and prices fluctuate accordingly. However, some of the commercial instability has disappeared with the growth in the vineyard area, so that there is more Chablis available to satisfy world demand.

Chablis remains one of the great white wines of the world. It is sometimes overshadowed by the greater opulence of a fine Meursault or Corton-Charlemagne, but it has an individuality of its own that sets it apart from the great white burgundies of the CÔTE D'OR. There is a unique streak of steely acidity, a firm flintiness and a mineral quality that is not found elsewhere in Burgundy. Like all great white burgundy, it benefits from but all too rarely receives BOTTLE AGEING. A premier cru will be at its best at 10 years, while a grand cru could easily benefit from 15 or more years of maturation. A 1947 Côte de Léchet, not one of the best premiers crus, but from a great vintage, was still showing a remarkable depth of flavour with the characteristic *goût de pierre à fusil* when it was 40 years old. Perhaps the 1996 vintage, with its excellent balance of concentration and acidity, will eventually prove to have the same potential. R.G.

Chacolí de Guetaria, or Getariako Txakolina in the Basque language, one of Spain's smallest DO regions and a matter of considerable pride to those few BASQUE farmers who stubbornly refuse to give in to the elements and have even increased their vineyards on the rocky Biscay coast west of San Sebastian. With cool summers, and an annual rainfall of 1,500 mm/58 in, this is hardly ideal grape-growing country. The high-trained Hondarribi Zuri white grape variety, which accounts for 85 per cent of Chacolí, traditionally produces thin wines, but the quality was noticeably lifted during the 1990s to a level similar to decent MUSCADET. Hondarribi Beltz makes light reds for local consumption. R.J.M. & V. de la S.

Chacolí de Vizcaya, or Bizkaiko Txakolina in the Basque language, an even smaller DO region than its neighbour at Guetaria (see above). Its vineyards are dispersed in Vizcaya province around the main city of Bilbao. The predominance of FOLLE BLANCHE grapes makes for more acidic and herbaceous wines than in Guetaria. V. de la S.

chai, French, and particularly Bordelais, term for a place where wine is stored, typically in BARREL.

Chalk Hill, California wine region and AVA north of Santa Rosa and south east of Healdsburg. See SONOMA.

Chalone, small California wine region and AVA in the mountains east of the Salinas Valley. See MONTEREY.

Chalonnaise, Côte, red- and white-wine-producing region in the Saône-et-Loire *département* of BURGUNDY between the CÔTE D'OR and the Mâconnais. As well as generic BOURGOGNE Côte Chalonnaise, mostly red from the Pinot Noir grape, there are five village appellations: MERCUREY, which stands apart in both quality and price, produces mostly Pinot Noir with small quantities of white wine; GIVRY the same; MONTAGNY is exclusively a white-wine appellation growing the Chardonnay grape; RULLY offers both red and white wines and is a centre for the sparkling-wine industry in a small way; while BOUZERON has its own appellation exclusively for the Aligoté grape.

Although the soils in the Côte Chalonnaise are similar to those of the Côte d'Or, the vineyards are more scattered since there is no regular escarpment to provide continuity of suitable slopes.

Viticultural practices are broadly similar to those in the Côte d'Or. Vinification is sometimes carried out in barrels, although only the best producers use any new OAK. Bottling normally takes place in the summer before the new vintage.

Maximum yields for Mercurey are the same as those for VILLAGE WINES in the Côte d'Or, whereas those for the other appellations of Côte Chalonnaise are slightly higher. Although cheerfully fruity while young, few wines from this region have enough BODY to age well. The Côte Chalonnaise is best served by such NÉGOCIANTS as Antonin Rodet and Faiveley, although growers such as Michel Juillot occasionally stand out. J.T.C.M.

Chambertin, Chambertin-Clos de Bèze, Chapelle-Chambertin, Charmes-Chambertin, Griottes-Chambertin, Latricières-Chambertin, Mazis-Chambertin, and Ruchottes-Chambertin, great red GRANDS CRUS in Burgundy's CÔTE D'OR. See GEVREY-CHAMBERTIN.

Chambéry, not a wine at all but a delicate, aromatic VERMOUTH made in the French Alps.

Chambolle-Musigny, village and appellation of particular charm in the Côte de Nuits district of Burgundy producing red wines from Pinot Noir grapes. A fine Chambolle-Musigny has a rich, velvety elegance which rivals the finesse of Vosne-Romanée or the power of Gevrey-Chambertin. There are two GRAND CRU vineyards, Le Musigny and Bonnes Mares (in part), and some exceptional PREMIERS CRUS worthy of promotion.

Le **Musigny** ranks with Romanée-Conti, La Tâche, Richebourg, Chambertin, and Chambertin-Clos de Bèze as one of the pinnacles of great burgundy (see DOMAINE DE LA ROMANÉE-CONTI, VOSNE-ROMANÉE, and GEVREY-CHAMBERTIN for details of these). The vineyard lies between the scrubland at the top of the slope and the upper part of CLOS DE VOUGEOT, on a slope which drains particularly well through the limestone. The soil is more chalk than clay, covered by a fine silt, a combination which leads to the exceptional grace and power of Le Musigny, an iron fist in a velvet glove.

Of the 10.7 ha/26 acres of Le Musigny which is split between Musigny, Petits Musigny, and La Combe d'Orveau, 7 are owned by Domaine Comte de Vogüé. Other significant producers are the Château de Chambolle Musigny, Joseph Drouhin, and Domaine Jacques Prieur.

Adjacent to Le Musigny lies the premier cru Les Amoureuses, whose reputation and price suggest that this vineyard is worthy of elevation to grand cru. If a little less powerful than Le Musigny itself, the wines of Les Amoureuses demonstrate a very similar style. The next most sought-after premier cru, and the largest, is Les Charmes.

The other grand cru of Chambolle Musigny is **Bonnes Mares**, situated to the north of the village and overflowing into MOREY-ST-DENIS. The wines show more sturdiness than silkiness, are less graceful than Le Musigny but have evident power and structure. Bonnes Mares is noted for its ageing capacity. Ownership is spread over more than 30 proprietors, the largest being again Domaine Comte de Vogüé, a producer who also makes a very small quantity of white Musigny. Other notable producers based in Chambolle-Musigny include Groffier, Roumier, and Mugnier.

See also CÔTE D'OR.   J.T.C.M.

Chambourcin is a relatively recent dark-berried French HYBRID which was popular in the 1970s, particularly in the MUSCADET area.

This extremely vigorous, productive vine produces better-quality wine than most hybrids, being deep coloured and full of relatively aromatic flavour, although it is not officially allowed even into the local VINS DE PAYS. It has also been grown with some success by Cassegrain in the warm, damp climate of NEW SOUTH WALES in Australia, a culture unfettered by anti-hybrid prejudice, and looks promising in VIETNAM.

chambré, French word also used in English to describe a wine that has been deliberately warmed to room TEMPERATURE before serving (from *chambre*, 'room'). Most rooms nowadays are rather warmer than the ideal serving temperatures for most wines.

Champagne, area in north-east France now divided into the so-called 'Champagne pouilleuse', the once-barren but now cereal-growing chalky plains east of Rheims, and the 'Champagne viticole' (capital letters indicate the geographical descriptions, while lower case is used for the wine).

Champagne, with its three champagne towns Rheims, Épernay, and Ay, was the first region to make SPARKLING WINE in any quantity and historically the name champagne became synonymous with the finest, although Champagne is now responsible for less than one bottle in 12 of total world production of all sparkling wine.

Geography and climate

The region permitted to call its wines champagne is strictly defined. It sprawls from Charly a mere 30 miles east of Paris in the Marne valley to Rheims and south from Épernay along the Côte des Blancs and its southern extension, the Côtes de Sézanne. A separate region is the Aube, 112 km south east of Épernay. Only a tenth of the vines are owned by merchants, who can now add to their holdings only under very strict conditions. The remainder is owned by nearly 20,000 growers, many of whom own less than a hectare of vines.

Much of the appellation (and Champagne is now the only major French region to have just one appellation), and all the better CRUS, are on the slopes of the hills typical of Champagne region. The vines' roots dig deep into chalky depths, providing ideal conditions of DRAINAGE and humidity. Exposure to the cold northern winter inevitably makes grape-growing a precarious operation, with the quality of the wines varying from year to year. As a result, champagne is traditionally a wine blended, not only from a number of different villages, but also from several vintages.

Vine varieties

In the past, a number of grape varieties were planted in Champagne. But today the whole vineyard is planted with three: Pinot Noir, Pinot Meunier, and Chardonnay. The Pinot Noir, planted on about a third of the total acreage, is no longer as dominant as it was, but still provides the basic structure and depth of fruit in the blend. In Champagne, the Chardonnay, planted in a quarter of the vineyard, grows vigorously and buds early, thus making it susceptible to spring frosts. It imparts a certain austerity and elegance to young champagnes, but is long lived and matures to a fine fruitiness. The remaining third is planted with Pinot MEUNIER, a variety widely grown only in Champagne, particularly in the Valley of the Marne. It provides many champagnes with an early-maturing richness and fruitiness.

The grapes are picked in late September, on dates now fixed village by village. They cannot be harvested unless they contain that year's fixed minimum level of POTENTIAL ALCOHOL. But since the level can be as low as 8 per cent, sugar can be added to provide another degree and a half (see CHAPTALIZATION), and the second fermentation supplements the final ALCOHOLIC STRENGTH by up to another 2 per cent. Most champagne is about 12.5 per cent alcohol.

Wine-making

The pressing of the grapes is difficult, since the juice of what is to be a white wine must not be tainted by the skin of the mainly black grapes used. The juice is allowed to settle for between 12 and 48 hours, at a low temperature. A few firms ferment some or all of their grapes in oak, but the overwhelming majority of the grapes are fermented in stainless-steel vats.

Immediately after the first fermentation, most, but by no means all, champagnes now undergo MALOLACTIC FERMENTATION. Traditionally champagne has been made from wines from a number of different vineyards within the appellation although large numbers of growers (and a few firms) make wines from a single commune or vineyard. Major firms use wines from between 50 and 200 communes for their blend. They also use between 10 and 50 per cent of *vins de réserve* from earlier vintages, generally stored in stainless steel or cement vats. Before the wine is

bottled, a measured dose of bottling liquor (*liqueur de tirage*), a mixture of wine, sugar, and specially developed yeasts, is added to the wine. The bottles are then capped, usually with a crown cap lined with plastic. Following TIRAGE, LEES CONTACT, RIDDLING, and DISGORGEMENT, a sweetening DOSAGE is usually added before final corking. A few champagnes are sold without any added sugar at all; most are BRUT.

For more information, see SPARKLING-WINE-MAKING, traditional method.

Styles of champagne

In addition to their basic wine, their non-vintage brut, major firms also make single vintage champagnes typically three or four times in every decade. BLANC DE BLANCS is made exclusively from the Chardonnay grape while BLANC DE NOIRS is made exclusively from black grapes. Pink or rosé champagne is made either by adding a small proportion of red wine to the blend or, less usually, by letting the juice remain in contact with the skin of the grapes for a short time during fermentation. All the major firms have now followed the example of Roederer with their Cristal bottling and Moët & Chandon with Dom Pérignon and produce 'luxury', 'de luxe', or PRESTIGE CUVÉES to show their house styles at their best.

The small proportion of still wines made in the region are sold under the appellations Coteaux CHAMPENOIS and the rare pink ROSÉ DES RICEYS. N.F.

champagne method. See SPARKLING-WINE-MAKING, traditional method.

Champenois, Coteaux. Appellation used for the unusual still wines of CHAMPAGNE in northern France. For every one bottle of still white Coteaux Champenois produced, perhaps 20 of still red Coteaux Champenois are produced (in a good vintage), and 16,000 bottles of sparkling champagne. The wines of this cool region with their naturally high acidity and light body are much improved by dissolved CARBON DIOXIDE. The village of Bouzy on the MONTAGNE DE REIMS has a particular reputation for its red Coteaux Champenois, partly perhaps because of the appeal of the name Bouzy Rouge, as do Ay, Cumières, and Ambonnay. These red wines are of interest to outsiders only in the ripest vintages, while the whites and rosés serve only to compliment the Champenois on their wise decision to concentrate on sparkling wines.

See also ROSÉ DES RICEYS.

Chancellor, productive red French HYBRID. See SEIBEL.

Chapoutier, family-owned merchant-grower based at Tain-l'HERMITAGE in France's northern RHÔNE. One of the Rhône valley's great names, established in 1808 and owning some 160 ha/390 acres of vineyard, principally in the northern Rhône and notably 34 ha of Hermitage. More recent purchases have been made in Coteaux d'Aix-en-Provence, Banyuls, and South Australia. Viticulture is BIODYNAMIC, YIELDS are low, the wines are aged in OAK (new as appropriate), and the top reds are subjected to neither FINING nor FILTRATION. As a result, the wines have more concentration, polish, and distinction, and Chapoutier's Hermitage, CÔTE RÔTIE, and CHÂTEAUNEUF-DU-PAPE can compete with the very best from the region.

M.W.E.S.

chaptalization, common wine-making practice whereby the final ALCOHOLIC STRENGTH of a wine is increased by the addition of sugar to the grape juice or must, before and/or during FERMENTATION.

Charbono, CALIFORNIA's obscure black grape variety may well be the DOLCETTO of Italy. It clings to existence on a handful of acres on the NORTH COAST, especially in the NAPA Valley. As varietal wine (made chiefly by Inglenook), it can be difficult to distinguish from BARBERA grown under similar circumstances. See also the Bonarda of ARGENTINA.

Chardonel, recently named vine CROSSING of Seyval Blanc and Chardonnay. The wine is similar to Chardonnay and this appealingly named variety may be useful in warm to hot climates, like its famous parent. R.E.S.

Chardonnay, a name so familiar to modern wine lovers around the world that many do not realize that it is the name of a white grape variety. In its Burgundian homeland, Chardonnay has for long been the sole vine responsible for all of the finest white burgundy. As such, in a region devoted to geographical labelling, its name was known only to vine-growers. All this changed with the advent of VARIETAL labelling in the late 20th century, when Chardonnay virtually became a brand name.

The wine's relatively high level of alcohol, which can often taste slightly sweet, has probably played a part in this popularity, as has the obvious appeal of the OAK so often used in making Chardonnay. But it is not just wine drinkers who appreciate the broad, easy-to-appreciate if difficult-to-describe charms of golden Chardonnay.

Vine-growers appreciate the ease with which, in a wide range of climates, they can coax relatively high yields from this vine. Wine quality is severely prejudiced, however, if yields are high, and low yields are needed for seriously fine wine. Growers' only major reservation is that it buds quite early, just after Pinot Noir, which regularly puts the coolest vineyards of Chablis and Champagne at risk from spring frosts. It can thrive in climates as diverse as those of Chablis in northern France and Australia's hot Riverland. Picking time is vital for, unlike Cabernet Sauvignon, Chardonnay can lose its crucial acidity fast in the latter stages of ripening.

Wine-makers love Chardonnay for its reliably high ripeness levels and its malleability. It will happily respond to a far wider range of wine-making techniques than most white varieties. The Mosel or Vouvray wine-making recipe of a long, cool fermentation followed by early bottling can be applied to Chardonnay. Or it can be treated to BARREL FERMENTATION and/or BARREL MATURATION, some of the highest-quality fruit being able to stand up to new oak. It accommodates each individual wine-maker's policy on the second, softening MALOLACTIC FERMENTATION and LEES STIRRING without demur. Chardonnay is also a crucial ingredient in most of the world's best SPARKLING WINE, not just in Champagne, demonstrating its ability to age in bottle even when picked early. And, picked late, it has even been known to produce some creditable BOTRYTIZED wines, notably in the Mâconnais, Romania, and New Zealand. Chardonnay also manages to retain a remarkable amount of its own character even when blended with other less fashionable varieties such as Chenin Blanc, Sémillon, or Colombard to meet demand at the lower end of the market. But perhaps this is because its own character is, unlike that of the other ultra-fashionable white, Sauvignon Blanc, not too pronounced. Chardonnay from young or over-productive vines can taste almost aqueous. Basic Chardonnay may be vaguely fruity (apples or melons) but at its best, Chardonnay, like Pinot Noir, is merely a vehicle for the character of the vineyard in which it is grown (see TERROIR). In many other ambitious wines fashioned in the image of top white burgundy, its 'flavour' is actually that of the oak in which it was matured, or the relics of the wine-making techniques used (see above). When the vineyard site is right, yields are not too high, acid not too low, and wine-making skilled, Chardonnay can produce wines that will continue to improve in bottle for one, two, or, exceptionally, more decades but—unlike RIESLING and the best, nobly rotten CHENIN BLANC and SÉMILLON—it is not a variety capable of making whites for the very long term.

There is a rare but distinct pink-berried mutation, **Chardonnay Rose**, as well as a headily perfumed **Chardonnay Blanc Musqué** version, sometimes used in blends. The arguably over-enthusiastic application of CLONAL SELECTION techniques in Burgundy means that growers can now choose from a wide range of Chardonnay clones specially selected for their productivity or quality. Many New World wine regions began their love affair with Chardonnay on blowsy or inferior clones such as the Mendoza clone, only to find it rekindled by the introduction of better clones from Burgundy, sometimes known as Dijon clones.

Chardonnay's popularity in the late 1980s was sufficient to propel it to first or second place in terms of area planted in each of France, California, Washington state, Australia, and New Zealand in the early 1990s. A remarkable feat for a vine credited with such nobility.

France

In the Burgundian heartland, the CÔTE D'OR, Chardonnay plantings increased by one-quarter in the 1980s to a grand total of 1,400 ha—just half as much Chardonnay as was actually planted in a single year, 1988, in California! Although Chardonnay has gradually been replacing GAMAY and ALIGOTÉ, Pinot Noir vines still outnumber Chardonnay vines more than four to one on the Côte d'Or. Notably more Chardonnay is grown on the southern Côte de Beaune than on the Côte de Nuits. Famous white-wine appellations (with typical characteristics in brackets) include, from north to south, Corton-Charlemagne (marzipan), Meursault (buttery), Puligny-Montrachet (fine and steely), Chassagne-Montrachet (hazelnuts), and any name that includes the word Montrachet (enormous concentration, and alcohol levels of 13 per cent and above).

In the Côte Chalonnaise and Mâconnais to the south, plantings overtook those of Gamay

in the 1980s. From the Côte Chalonnaise, the whites of Rully, Mercurey, and Montagny can offer economical, if slightly rustic, versions of the grander names of the Côte d'Or. The Mâconnais, where Chardonnay can take on a broad, appley character, produces not just white Mâcon with a range of geographical suffixes but also various Pouillys, most famously the full-bodied Pouilly-Fuissé. From further south still come the very similar St-Véran and Beaujolais Blanc. Although the regulations allow Aligoté into Beaujolais Blanc and PINOT BLANC into white wines labelled Bourgogne and Mâcon, most of these less expensive white burgundies are in practice made predominantly from Chardonnay. There is an increasing trend towards slipping the word Chardonnay on to white burgundy labels to increase their appeal to non-French consumers.

Although nearly three-quarters of France's Chardonnay is still in either Champagne or Greater Burgundy, the variety has been sweeping south and west from this base. It is embraced by an ever wider variety of appellations, and plantings can be found in Alsace, Ardèche, Jura, Savoie, Loire, and, especially, the Languedoc, where it was first planted to add international appeal to the lemony wines of Limoux. Much of it is now used in varietal VINS DE PAYS d'Oc of extremely varying quality.

America

Few would have believed in 1980 that California's total plantings of Chardonnay would overtake France's (rapidly increasing) total. The rate of new plantings reached a peak in 1988, however, and the early 1990s brought a new red-wine fashion for California grape-growers to grapple with. Nearly half of all California Chardonnay is concentrated in Sonoma, Napa, and Monterey counties but there are also sizeable plantings further south in Santa Barbara and San Luis Obispo. See CALIFORNIA.

Chardonnay, now North American for 'white wine', has been embraced with equal fervour throughout the rest of North America, from British Columbia in CANADA to Long Island in NEW YORK. In 1990, it overtook Riesling to become the most planted variety of any hue in WASHINGTON state. Chardonnay is also popular, if not always desperately successful, in Oregon, Virginia, and Texas.

Various South American countries have been seeking out cooler spots to imbue their Chardonnay with real concentration. Chile's Casablanca region and Argentina's Tupungato are the most obvious examples, whose best wines combine those New World virtues of accessibility and value.

Australia and New Zealand

The Australian wine industry's all-important export trade has been centred on its peculiarly exuberant style of Chardonnay. Rich fruit flavours, often disciplined by added acid and flavoured by OAK CHIPS, are available at carefully judged prices. Such was the strength of demand for Australian Chardonnay in the late 1980s that the area of Chardonnay vines increased more than fivefold during the decade so that in 1990 Chardonnay became Australia's most planted white wine grape variety. Plantings continued even more bullishly throughout the 1990s. Meanwhile, wine-making has become increasingly sophisticated. Wines vary from limey essences grown in cooler spots in Victoria and Tasmania to almost syrupy, smokey blends concocted from the hot irrigated vineyards of the interior. The average life expectancy of an Australian (and most other New World) Chardonnay is short.

Nor has NEW ZEALAND escaped Chardonnay-mania. New Zealand's Chardonnays, the country's most common if not necessarily most famous wine, have perceptibly more natural acid than their trans-Tasman neighbours.

Rest of the world

Chardonnay has had a chequered history in South Africa, with some of the first cuttings so named being eventually identified as the very much less fashionably exciting AUXERROIS. The quality of the clones planted has since improved steadily.

Although Chardonnay can thrive in relatively hot climates (such as Australia's irrigation zones), it has to be picked before acids plummet (often before the grapes have developed much real character) and it does require relatively sophisticated techniques, including TEMPERATURE CONTROL, in the cellar. This is why it is not well suited to the less-developed Mediterranean wine regions. Even in the Lebanon, where local strains of Chardonnay are well entrenched, the wine tends to betray its torrid origins. With human skill and investment in technology, however, more well-balanced Chardonnays with the real interest of isolated examples from Israel may emerge, as they have done from Greece, for example.

The variety continues to be planted in an ever wider range of locations, but Italy has a long history of Chardonnay cultivation, especially on its sub-Alpine slopes in the north. For decades Italians were casual about distinguishing between their Pinot Bianco (PINOT BLANC, also known as Weissburgunder in the Italian Tyrol) and their Chardonnay (traditionally called Gelber, or Golden, Weissburgunder in the Italian Tyrol). Alto Adige Chardonnay was the first accorded DOC status, in 1984, although the vine has since been working its magic on producers all over Italy from Apulia to Piedmont and, of course, Aosta towards the French border.

Nowadays much of Italy's Chardonnay is produced, often without much distinction, in Friuli, Trentino, and, to a more limited extent, the Veneto, where much of it is used as ballast for GARGANEGA. Some fine examples are produced in favoured sites in both Friuli and Trentino but a considerable proportion is siphoned off to become SPUMANTE, as it is in Lombardy. Most of Italy's most ambitious still Chardonnays, exhibiting every possible wine-making technique, are white versions of SUPER-TUSCANS (typically a BARRIQUE-aged VINO DA TAVOLA from Tuscany) with some counterparts in Umbria too. Chardonnay is gaining ground rapidly in Italy, being planted in Tuscan spots where Sangiovese is difficult to ripen and in Piedmont replacing Dolcetto, which can be difficult to sell. Piedmont, cooler than Tuscany, has, not surprisingly, had more overall success with the variety and by the mid 1990s many Tuscan and central Italian producers were looking more to Merlot than to Chardonnay as an alternative to native red varieties in vineyards with difficult, cool positions. See under these geographical names for more details of Italian Chardonnays.

Much less dramatic Chardonnay is also produced in Switzerland, particularly in Geneva and the Valais. In Austria, a foreign vine known as Morillon in Styria and Feinburgunder in Vienna and Burgenland was not identified as the modish Chardonnay until the late 1980s. Austria's Chardonnays include relatively rich, oak-matured versions; lean, aromatic styles modelled on their finest Rieslings; and even sweet AUSBRUCH wines.

BULGARIA has a vast area of Chardonnay vineyard but, perhaps because of over-production or for wine-making reasons, has only rarely been able to demonstrate real Chardonnay character in the bottle. There are limited plantings in Slovenia, Hungary, and Romania (whence Late Harvest Chardonnays have been exported) but it seems that the Soviet Union's political turbulence during the late 1980s may have saved it from the major Chardonnay invasion that took place almost everywhere else at that time.

Germany was one of the last wine-producing countries to admit Chardonnay to the ranks of accepted vine varieties, in 1991, to a very limited extent.

Such is Chardonnay's fame and popularity that it is grown to a certain extent in climates as dissimilar as those of England, India, and Uruguay. In Spanish Catalonia, Chardonnay has added class and an internationally recognizable flavour to CAVA sparkling wines as well as producing some increasingly sophisticated still wines both here and in Costers del Segre, Navarra, and Somontano. Portugal, almost alone, seems to have withstood Chardonnay-mania.

Charta (pronounced 'karta'), important organization of 30 RHEINGAU wine producers in Germany dedicated to making a traditional style of dry to off-dry RIESLING according to much stricter rules than those imposed by the GERMAN WINE LAW. Founded in 1983 by a small group of far-sighted producers, most notably Bernhard Breuer, who still heads the organization, Charta distinguishes individual wines that meet its standards, unlike the VDP association, whose quality standards apply to an estate's overall performance. Charta wines must be made entirely of Rheingau Riesling grapes with minimum MUST WEIGHTS higher than prescribed by law. The RESIDUAL SUGAR cannot exceed TOTAL ACIDITY by more than 3 g/l. The goal is to produce concentrated, harmonious wines that go well with food and are suitable for ageing. Only after passing three blind tasting tests and 12 months' BOTTLE AGEING are the wines released. Charta wines are sold in a tall brown bottle embossed with a double romanesque arch.

Charta labels bordered in black and depicting the same romanesque arch are reserved for wines classified Erstes Gewächs or FIRST GROWTH. These wines are made from hand-picked, non-BOTRYTIZED grapes from a (Charta-defined) classified top vineyard. YIELDS may not exceed 50 hl/ha (3 tons/acre). Such wines are offered EN PRIMEUR 12 months after the harvest

but none is released until after 18 months in bottle. K.B.S.

Chasan, CROSSING of Palomino (known in France as LISTÁN) and Chardonnay vines. The resulting wine bears a lightweight imprint of Chardonnay while the vine buds early. It is planted on a limited scale in the Midi, particularly in the Aude *département*.

Chassagne-Montrachet, village in the Côte de Beaune district of Burgundy's CÔTE D'OR more famed for its white wines from the Chardonnay grape than for its equally plentiful red wines from Pinot Noir. Until the mid 1980s, the village produced more red wine than white, but the significant premium for white Chassagne led to considerable planting of Chardonnay, even on relatively unsuitable soils.

The better soil for Pinot Noir lies mainly on the south side of the village towards Santenay and incorporates most of the village appellation, although La Boudriotte and Morgeot, among the PREMIERS CRUS, make excellent red wines, as can Clos St-Jean to the north of the village. Red Chassagne-Montrachet tends to be somewhat hard and earthy when young, mellowing with age but rarely achieving the delicacy of truly fine red burgundy.

The fame of Chassagne rests with the white wines at village, premier cru, and especially GRAND CRU level. Chassagne shares the Le Montrachet and Bâtard-Montrachet vineyards with neighbouring Puligny and enjoys sole possession of a third grand cru, Criots-Bâtard-Montrachet (see MONTRACHET for more details). Among the premiers crus, the best known are Les Chenevottes, Clos de la Maltroie, En Cailleret, and Les Ruchottes.

The white wines of Chassagne are noted for their steely power, less flattering than MEURSAULT when young, sometimes too similar to PULIGNY-MONTRACHET to tell apart. Good vintages from good producers such as Ramonet and the extended Gagnard family should age from 5 to 10 years. J.T.C.M.

Chasselas, even if by no means the most revered white grape variety, is widely planted around the world.

The principal synonym of the Chasselas grown in France for wine production is **Chasselas de Moissac**. It is rapidly disappearing from Alsace, where it is regarded as the lowest of the low and is generally sold as Edelzwicker or under some proprietary name that excludes mention of any grape variety. Planted in the area responsible for Pouilly-Fumé, it makes the distinctly inferior white labelled Pouilly-sur-Loire and, as might be expected, approaches respectability only as it nears Switzerland, in SAVOIE. Here it is at its most noble in CRÉPY, where it has a long, sometimes noble, history.

On the shores of Lake Geneva, skilfully grown Chasselas can yield good quantities of fairly neutral, soft white which achieves a peak of concentration in isolated sites such as the grand cru of Dézaley in the canton of Vaud. Chasselas, known as FENDANT in the Valais, is by far Switzerland's most planted variety.

In Germany, it is known as Weisser GUTEDEL. In Austria, it is known as Moster and Wälscher but not widely grown. It is reputedly grown widely in Romania, in Hungary, to a limited extent in Moldova and Ukraine, in both the north and far south of Italy (where it is sometimes called Marzemina Bianca), around the Mediterranean including North Africa, in Chile, and was at one time curiously important in New Zealand.

Chassellas de Courtillier is a similar but distinct variety.

château may be French for castle but in wine parlance it usually means a vine-growing, wine-making estate, to include the vineyards, the cellars, often the wine itself, and any building or buildings on the property, which can range from the non-existent (as in the case of Ch Léoville-BARTON, for example), through the most rudimentary shack, to the sumptuous classical edifice called Ch MARGAUX. The term is most commonly used in BORDEAUX, where there are around 7,000 châteaux. The word château is by no means uncommon outside Bordeaux, however, mainly within but sometimes outside FRANCE (where it tends to lose its circumflex). According to current French law, the word château may be used only of a specified plot of land, which means that it is perfectly possible for CO-OPERATIVES, for example, to produce a wine labelled as Château Quelque-chose (see CHÂTEAU BOTTLING). Some producers make a range of wines carrying the name of the property, but reserve the word château for their top bottlings.

château bottling, the relatively recent practice of bottling the produce of a CHÂTEAU on that property. Such a wine is said to be **château bottled,** or *mis(e) en bouteille au château* in French, an expression used throughout France

but particularly in BORDEAUX. (Its counterpart in BURGUNDY is DOMAINE BOTTLING, while in the NEW WORLD the term ESTATE BOTTLED is often used.)

Initially all wine was sold in bulk, and subsequently it was up to the merchants, whether in the region of consumption or production, to put the wine into bottle. It was the young Baron Philippe de Rothschild who did most to promote château bottling when he took over Ch MOUTON-ROTHSCHILD in the early 1920s. He succeeded in persuading all the first growths (and Ch Mouton-Rothschild of course) of the wisdom of bottling all of their principal output, the so-called *grand vin*, on their own territory.

Today, a producer of château-bottled wine, described on the label as *mis(e) en bouteille au château*, is likely to care about quality. It is worth noting in addition that wines made from specific plots of land but vinified and bottled by CO-OPERATIVES may also be described as château bottled.

See also DOMAINE BOTTLING and ESTATE BOTTLED.

Château-Chalon, extraordinary wine made in the JURA region of eastern France with its own small appellation named after the hilltop village where it is produced. Unlike other Jura appellations, Ch-Chalon must be a VIN JAUNE and must be made exclusively from SAVAGNIN grapes. The resulting wine, exceptionally nutty, deep golden brown, and long lasting, is allowed to use a special 62-cl *clavelin* bottle. The result is a wine that shares many taste characteristics with SHERRY but is more actively promoted as a gastronomic partner and as a candidate for BOTTLE AGEING. In some years, in this quality-conscious appellation the producers (known as *castel-Chalonnais*) nobly decide that the quality does not merit the production of any wine from the appellation.

Château-Grillet, one of France's smallest wine appellations and one of the few with a single owner (although see also DOMAINE DE LA ROMANÉE-CONTI). Ch-Grillet's few hectares of vineyard represent an enclave within the CONDRIEU zone in the north of the northern Rhône. A virtual amphitheatre carved out of the granite shelters the narrow terraces of VIOGNIER vines from the north winds which can so seriously prejudice both quantity and quality in Condrieu.

Since the 1970s, the wine has maintained its

high price more by its rarity than because it is one of France's finest wines. The grapes have traditionally been picked rather earlier than in Condrieu so that the wine is usually more austere and less headily perfumed than the best Condrieu. The wine is kept in cask and is not usually bottled until well after the next harvest, considerably later than most Condrieu is bottled. The result is a restrained, taut, longer-living wine which, unlike Condrieu, may improve in its distinctive brown bottle for a decade or even two. The potential of the vineyard is undoubted.

Châteaumeillant, small, isolated red and rosé wine VDQS zone in central France around the town of Châteaumeillant between ST POUR-ÇAIN-sur-Sioule and TOURAINE. The wines are mainly the produce of Gamay vines (although Pinot Noir and Pinot Gris are allowed) grown on volcanic soils. VIN GRIS is a local speciality, and one CO-OPERATIVE dominates production.

Châteauneuf-du-Pape, the most important, and variable, appellation in the southern RHÔNE in terms of quality, producing mainly rich, spicy, full-bodied red wines which can be some of the most alluring expressions of warm-climate viticulture, but can be either impossibly tannic or disappointingly jammy. About one in every 16 distinctively heavy and embossed Châteauneuf-du-Pape bottles contains white wine. The wine takes its name, which means 'Pope's new castle', from the relocation of the papal court to Avignon in the 14th century.

Reconstruction of the vineyards after PHYL-LOXERA was financially devastating, and the Châteauneuf-du-Pape vignerons were just some of those affected by the ADULTERATION AND FRAUD that were rife in the early 20th century. By 1923, the most energetic and well connected of their number, Baron Le Roy of Ch Fortia, had successfully drawn up a set of rules for the production of Châteauneuf-du-Pape, with the co-operation of his peers, which was the prototype for the entire APPELLATION CON-TRÔLÉE system. One notable feature was the minimum specified ALCOHOLIC STRENGTH, at 12.5 per cent still the highest in France, and in the southern Rhône this must be achieved without the aid of CHAPTALIZATION. TRIAGE of picked grapes was mandatory and ROSÉ was outlawed.

Perhaps it is because of the antiquity of Châteauneuf-du-Pape's wine regulations that quite so many VINE VARIETIES are theoretically permitted by the Châteauneuf-du-Pape appellation. In 1936, three more varieties were added to the original 10. The Châteauneuf-du-Pape grape *par excellence* is GRENACHE and, conversely, Châteauneuf-du-Pape is its finest expression. Grenache dominates plantings in the Châteauneuf-du-Pape vineyards and on their impoverished soils, with yields officially restricted to a base rate of just 35 hl/ha (2 tons/acre), it can produce wines which combine concentration with the usual sweet fruit of Grenache.

MOURVÈDRE also plays a part at many properties, although it needs the warmest MESO-CLIMATES to ripen fully, while SYRAH from the northern Rhône has also been planted by a number of producers who admire its TANNINS and structure, although, unlike Grenache and Mourvèdre, it needs care to avoid overripeness. CINSAUT is also grown, but to a declining extent. Of the other permitted red-wine varieties, Muscardin, Vaccarèse, PICPOUL, TERRET Noir, and COUNOISE, only the last is grown to any significant extent, and has its admirers, particularly at Ch de Beaucastel, one of the most rigorous producers of Châteauneuf-du-Pape, and one of the few to cultivate all 13 permitted varieties. For white Châteauneuf-du-Pape, there is considerable variation in the proportions of Grenache Blanc, CLAIRETTE, BOUR-BOULENC, and ROUSSANNE planted, although Ch de Beaucastel have demonstrated that a VAR-IETAL Roussanne can be a worthy candidate for BARREL MATURATION. Picardan, which is not widely planted, produces light, relatively neutral wine.

The Châteauneuf-du-Pape appellation extends over more than 3,000 ha/7,500 acres of relatively flat vineyards at varying altitudes and expositions above the river in Châteauneuf-du-Pape and the neighbouring communes of Bédarrides, Courthézon, Orange, and Sorgues. The terrain is traditionally characterized by the large pebbles, or *galets*, some of them several inches across, which cover many of the more photographed vineyards, supposedly retaining heat and speeding the ripening process of the traditionally low-trained vines, but the soils in Châteauneuf-du-Pape are more varied than this.

Indeed, the key with red Châteauneuf-du-Pape in general is to balance the accumulation of sugar in the grapes, and therefore alcohol content, with the PHENOLICS, and tannins in particular. Since the 1970s, a number of producers have used CARBONIC MACERATION or semi-carbonic maceration to produce lighter, fruitier wines which can be drunk from about three years rather than from five or six. This is by no means a high-tech wine region, however. Some notable domaines include Ch de Beaucastel, Henri Bonneau, Chapoutier's Barbe Rac, Domaine de la Janasse, Domaine de Pegaü, Ch Rayas, and Domaine du Vieux Télégraphe.

White Châteauneuf-du-Pape is a relative rarity, and may be made according to a wide range of formulas. Only the very best are worth their price premium, although the overall quality is steadily increasing. The wines are always full bodied and the less successful lack acidity and BOUQUET. They should usually be drunk young, although the all-Roussanne Vieilles Vignes bottling from Ch de Beaucastel can withstand several years in bottle.

See also RHÔNE.

Châtillon-en-Diois, small appellation for still wines in the DIOIS area round Die in the far east of the greater RHÔNE region in the cooler reaches of the Drôme: light, Gamay-based reds and light whites made from Aligoté and Chardonnay.

Chénas, the smallest of the 10 Beaujolais crus in the far north of the region. Its vines are divided between the villages of Chénas and La Chapelle de Guinchay. Hubert Lapierre is a reliable producer. See BEAUJOLAIS.

Chenin or Chenin Blanc, in its native region often called Pineau or Pineau de la Loire, is probably the world's most versatile grape variety, capable of producing some of the finest, longest-living sweet whites although more usually harnessed to the yoke of basic New World table-wine production. In between these two extremes, it is responsible for a considerable volume of sparkling wine and, in SOUTH AFRICA, where it is by far the most planted vine, it is even used as the base for a wide range of fortified wines and spirits. Although, in its high-yield, New World form, its distinctive flavour reminiscent of honey and damp straw is usually lost, it retains the naturally high acidity that dogs it in some of the Loire's less ripe vintages but can be so useful in hot climates.

South Africa now has more than three times as much Chenin planted as France and the Cape's strain of the variety, often called STEEN, constitutes nearly 30 per cent of the country's entire vineyard. In the late 1960s and early 1970s, it provided ideal material for new low-temperature, high-tech wine-making techniques so that a flood of off-dry, refreshingly crisp, but otherwise rather bland white washed over the South African wine market.

CALIFORNIA also has more Chenin planted than France, and uses it for much the same purposes as South Africa, as the often anonymous base for everyday commercial blends of reasonably crisp white of varying degrees of sweetness, often blended with the even more widely planted French COLOMBARD. Both of these workhorse varieties are planted primarily in the hot Central Valley, a setting that might be described as the antithesis of Chenin's Loire homeland. Only a handful of producers take Chenin seriously enough to try to make wines worth ageing. In the Clarksburg AVA at the north end of the SAN JOAQUIN VALLEY, it can take on a distinctive melony, musky flavour.

One or two try to make a wine in the image of the great sweet Loire Chenins, as do one or two producers in NEW ZEALAND, mainly in the North Island. AUSTRALIA treats it largely with disdain as suitably acid blending material, usually extending Chardonnay, or even spiking a blend of Chardonnay and Semillon.

Chenin is widely planted throughout the Americas because it will obligingly produce a decent yield of relatively crisp wine. Argentina's heavily irrigated vineyards yield an even more blurred expression of the variety's character, and there are substantial plantings in Chile. In Mexico, Brazil, and Uruguay, it is still more usually called Pinot Blanco, as it still is by some Argentine growers. It is also common though not particularly popular in many North American states outside California—Washington, for example.

If Chenin appears to lead a double life—biddable workhorse in the New World, superstar in Anjou-Touraine—it seems clear that the explanation lies in a combination of climate, soil, and yield. In California's Central Valley, the vine is often expected to yield 10 tons per acre (175 hl/ha), while even the most basic Anjou Blanc should not be produced from vines that yield more than 45 hl/ha. It is hardly surprising that Chenin's character seems diluted outside the Loire.

The vine is vigorous and has a tendency to bud early and ripen late, both of which are highly inconvenient attributes in the cool Loire valley (though hardly noticeable characteristics in the hotter vineyards of the New World).

Chenin is the second most planted variety in the heart of Anjou-Touraine, as well it might be to judge from the superlative quality of the best wines of such appellations as ANJOU, BONNEZEAUX, Coteaux de l'AUBANCE, Coteaux du LAYON, JASNIÈRES, MONTLOUIS, QUARTS DE CHAUME, SAUMUR, SAVENNIÈRES, VOUVRAY, and CRÉMANT de Loire.

In most of the best wines, and certainly all of the great sweet wines, Chenin is unblended, but up to 20 per cent of Chardonnay or Sauvignon is allowed into an Anjou or a Saumur and even more catholic blends are allowed into whites labelled Touraine—although even here Chardonnay's pervasive influence is officially limited to 20 per cent of the total blend.

While basic Loire Chenin exhibits simply vaguely floral aromas and refreshingly high acidity, the best have a physically thrilling concentration of honeyed flavour, whether the wine is made sweet (MOELLEUX), dry or demisec, together with Chenin's characteristically vibrant acidity level.

It is undoubtedly this acid, emphasized by a conscious distaste for MALOLACTIC FERMENTATION and concentrated in some years by BOTRYTIS, that helps preserve the finest Chenins for decades after their relatively early bottling. (In all of these respects, together with lateness of ripening and a wide range of sweetness levels that are customary, Chenin is France's answer to Germany's RIESLING.)

Chenin with its high acidity is a useful base for a wide range of sparkling wines, most importantly Saumur Mousseux but also Crémant de Loire and even some rich sparkling Vouvrays, which, like their still counterparts, can age beautifully. Treasured for its reliably high acidity, and useful perfume, it is also an ingredient, with Mauzac and, increasingly, Chardonnay, in the sparkling wines of LIMOUX.

The twin great vintages for middle Loire sweet whites of 1989 and 1990 did something to raise the profile, and price, of great Chenin, but a variety whose best wines demand time to be fully appreciated inevitably suffers in the 21st century.

Chenin Noir is a rarely used synonym for PINEAU D'AUNIS, a dark-berried grape variety.

Cheval Blanc, Château, very fine BORDEAUX property in ST-ÉMILION, owned by Bernard Arnault, chairman of LVMH, and Belgian businessman Albert Frère.

The vineyard is 66 per cent Cabernet Franc vines, 33 per cent Merlot, and 1 per cent Malbec. The average production is about 11,500 cases. The unusual ENCÉPAGEMENT is a result of the special soil and the fact that it adjoins Pomerol's leading vineyards, La Conseillante and L'Évangile, giving it a deep colour and a rich, concentrated blackcurrant bouquet and flavour. The property's international reputation was made with the 1921, which had enormous concentration and sweetness. Other very successful wines were made in the 1920s, and even in 1934 and 1937, but its modern fame was achieved with the rich, porty 1947. Consistently good wines have been made with few exceptions ever since, although, like other St-Émilions and Pomerols, they usually do not last as long as the top red wines from MÉDOC and GRAVES.   E.P.-R.

Chevalier, Domaine de, important CHÂTEAU in Bordeaux producing top-quality red and white wines. See PESSAC-LÉOGNAN.

Chevalier-Montrachet, great white GRAND CRU in Burgundy's CÔTE D'OR. See MONTRACHET.

Cheverny. The most important of the VDQS zones of the middle Loire was promoted to full APPELLATION CONTRÔLÉE status in 1993 and produces a wide range of wines in an enclave in the north-east corner of TOURAINE near Blois. Light reds may be made from Cabernet Franc, Gamay, or Pinot Noir, while Pineau d'Aunis and Grolleau are allowed for the small quantity of rosé produced. Whites are as common as red Cheverny, and are usually keen, lean Sauvignons which can offer good value northern ripostes to Sancerre and Pouilly-Fumé. Both Chenin Blanc and Chardonnay are also allowed in the appellation of Cheverny, and wines made from the local ROMORANTIN grape have their own appellation **Cour Cheverny**. See also LOIRE.

Chianti, the name of a specific geographical area between Florence and Siena in the central Italian region of Tuscany, associated with tangy, dry red wines of very varied quality. Oenological Chianti covers a much wider area than this historic zone. Seven zones of Tuscany can call their wines Chianti: CHIANTI CLASSICO; Chianti Montalbano; the Florentine hills (Chianti Colli Fiorentini); CHIANTI RUFINA; the hills of Siena (Colli Senesi); the Pisan hills

(Colline Pisane); and the hills of Arezzo (Colli Aretini). There are also peripheral zones which can call their wines simply Chianti without an additional appellative.

The philosophy behind the enlargement of the production zone may have aimed at transferring some of the prestige and historical reputation of the Classico zone to secondary or generic Chianti, but in practice the results have been precisely the opposite; mere 'Chianti' has sunk, in terms of consumer image and producer remuneration, to the level of a quaffing wine without notable characteristics of quality and with little ability to be cellared and aged.

Most non-Classico Chianti was sold in bulk until the mid 1990s, when the rapid rise in prices of Chianti Classico, largely as a result of the overall quality improvement, led to an increase in demand for a simpler, less expensive alternative. Chianti Classico costs at least twice as much as these other versions, with the exception of Chianti Rufina. D.T.

Chianti Classico, the heartland of the CHIANTI zone, was given its fundamental geographical DELIMITATION by the Medici Grand Duke Cosimo III in 1716, one of the first examples of such legislation.

Modern Chianti can be said to have been invented in a certain sense by Baron Bettino Ricasoli, who, in a letter of 1872, synthesized decades of experimentation and recommended that the wine be based on SANGIOVESE ('for bouquet and vigour') with the addition of CANAIOLO to soften the wine. The DOC regulations of 1967 canonized a mythical 'Ricasoli formula' which included between 10 and 30 per cent of the white grapes TREBBIANO and Malvasia.

Replanting of the vineyards in the 1960s and 1970s resulted in a general lowering of the quality of the wine, difficult economic conditions for producers, and a tendency for many houses to forgo DOC status for their better products and label them VINO DA TAVOLA.

The DOCG regulations of 1984, in addition to lowering the minimum requirement of white grapes to a cosmetic two per cent, lowered yield limits, established a higher minimum extract level, and forced producers to declassify the entire crop when yields exceeded legal limits by 20 per cent. A general improvement in the quality level has resulted from this stricter legal framework, as well as from greater willingness to experiment.

Appellation regulations now permit Chianti Classico to be a 100 per cent Sangiovese wine, an obvious attempt to lure some of the more famous vini da tavola back into the DOC fold which is meeting some success. The use of small BARREL MATURATION for Chianti Classico and for Chianti Classico Riserva in particular is increasing, although in the case of the former this often represents a mere recycling of BARRIQUES previously used for vini da tavola. The standard casks for ageing remain the large ovals of Slovenian oak, BOTTI.

The 1990s saw a return to using the Chianti Classico name for Riserva, single-vineyard wines and superior selections, perhaps inevitably given the dizzying plethora of fantasy names with no geographical precision used for SUPERTUSCANS. Price differentials between an expensive vino da tavola and a Riserva from the same house were reduced if not entirely eliminated. Meanwhile the wines themselves, often marked with new oak, became increasingly 'international' in style, an uneasy balance between tradition and innovation. D.T.

Chianti Rufina, north-eastern DOCG zone of CHIANTI, was first identified as an area of superior production in 1716.

Although the Chianti produced here has always enjoyed an excellent reputation, especially for longevity, the wines experienced the generalized obscurity attendant on all Chianti with the exception of Chianti Classico until the 1990s. Prices remained modest, even for producers with international markets and recognition, although they began to rise to more remunerative levels as a result of the high quality of the 1988 and 1990 vintages. This enabled much-needed investment in fermentation equipment and casks for ageing. New, good-quality wines were launched in the 1990s, indicating that Chianti Rufina was at last recognized in its own right. D.T.

Chiavennasca, synonym for the noble NEBBIOLO vine and grape in VALTELLINA.

Chile, long, exceptionally narrow country down the south-west coast of SOUTH AMERICA that has become one of the world's prime resources of keenly priced VARIETAL wine, although it produces only about a quarter as much wine as the vineyards of Argentina just over the Andes. Chile's dry summers tend to yield exceptionally healthy fruit. The wines exported from Chile have been almost exclusively varietal, with a preponderance of fruitily uncomplicated Cabernet Sauvignon.

Geography and climate

With its 5,000 km/3,000 miles of coastline to the west, the Andes at heights of up to 7,000 m/23,000 ft to the east, extensive desert to the north, and Antarctic region in the south, Chile is unusually isolated, and this has played a major part in keeping PHYLLOXERA at bay, thus saving vine-growers from the cost of grafting.

The great majority of Chilean wine is produced between the latitudes of 32 and 38 degrees. A northern hemisphere counterpart of these latitudes might be North Africa and southern Spain, but in Chile temperatures are considerably mitigated by the influence of the Pacific and its cold Humboldt current. Chilean wine producers describe their climate as somewhere between those of California's NAPA Valley and Bordeaux.

Although the coastal area of Casablanca is being energetically developed, most of Chile's wine has traditionally come from the Central Valley, a 1,000-km-long plateau. The Central Valley is separated from the Pacific Ocean to the west by a relatively low coastal range, and from the Argentine Mendoza wine region to the east by the Andes. The valley is dissected by rivers which, during the growing season, carry torrents of melted snow from the Andes to the Pacific: IRRIGATION made easy.

Although there are distinct variations between individual regions and even subregions (see below), the Central Valley generally has warm, dry summers, and rainfall is restricted to the winter.

Regions

The great bulk of Chile's wine is grown in the southern wine regions. In general, vineyards are planted on flat, fertile land where water is readily available either naturally or through irrigation. From north to south the main wine regions, with their subregions, are:

Aconcagua: Casablanca

Maipo: Santiago, Talagante, Pirque, Llano del Maipo, Buin

Rapel: Cachapoal, Colchagua, Santa Cruz, Peralillo

Maule: Curicó (including Lontué), Talca, Cauquenes, Linares, Parral

Bío-Bío: Ñuble (including Chillán).

Aconcagua The most northerly of Chile's wine regions, named after the river which bisects it, is made up of two very distinct zones. The interior of Aconcagua is Chile's hottest, driest wine region. In the summer, clouds are rarely seen, and temperatures are often above 30 °C/86 °F. Errázuriz is one of the few important wine exporters to have its base in this region, at Panquehue in the much gentler intermediate region, cooled by coastal breezes.

Casablanca One of the coolest and newest wine regions in Chile, on the coast close to Valparaiso. Officially part of the Aconcagua region, it is quite different from the vineyards of the hot interior. Casablanca's vineyards are cooled by morning fogs, the result of the Pacific's icy Humboldt current (which has a similar effect thousands of miles up the coast in CARNEROS in California), and frequent cloud slows ripening. There have been extensive plantings, mainly of Chardonnay vines, by both wine producers (notably Concha y Toro and Franciscan of California) and specialist grapegrowers. Spring frosts are a real hazard here.

Maipo The most famous wine region in Chile, just south of the capital Santiago, is not one of the largest. It has a clear predominance of red over white grapes, Cabernet Sauvignon and Chardonnay being the most widely planted varieties according to official 1997 statistics, although Merlot and Sauvignon are also important. Irrigation is common, although the water can be quite high in salt around the Maipo river from which the region takes its name. Official subregions are Santiago, Talagante, Pirque, Llano del Maipo, and Buin. Although this is quantitatively not one of the most important wine regions in Chile, it is one often named on export labels, perhaps because, being closest to Santiago, it houses the headquarters of so many of the major companies.

Rapel Wine region in Chile with a majority of red grapes. The region is officially divided into the subregions Cachapoal and Colchagua. Cabernet Sauvignon and Sauvignon are the most planted grape varieties, and the region has a particularly good reputation for full-flavoured red wines. Los Vascos winery, in which Ch LAFITE-Rothschild has an important stake, is at Peralillo. The region overall is hotter than Maule to the immediate south. Large wineries such as Santa Emiliana, Santa Rita, Undurraga, and the smaller Discover Wine (Montes) operation made considerable vineyard investments in the Colchagua subregion in the early 1990s.

Maule Important wine region in Chile which includes the subregions of Curicó, Talca, Cauquenes, Linares, Lontué, and Parral. Well to the south of Santiago, this region is one of Chile's cooler and cloudier, thanks to the Pacific influence, although it is hotter and drier than Bío-Bío to the south. The rustic PAÍS vine variety dominates plantings, especially in the rain-fed areas, although Cabernet Sauvignon, Sauvignon, and Merlot are also important. Spanish wine-maker Miguel TORRES' purchase of vineyards in the Curicó area, in 1979, was interpreted as an unusual act of faith in the region, although San Pedro also have their headquarters here.

Bío-Bío The most southerly wine region is split quite evenly between red and white grapes. At the south of the Central Valley, Bío-Bío is more open than Maipo and Rapel to the north, lacking the protection of a high coastal range, so that rainfall is higher and average temperature and sunshine hours are lower. Official subregions are Ñuble in the north, around Chillán and Quillón, and Bío-Bío around Yumbel and Mulchén. By far the most planted vine variety is the humble PAÍS, although Moscatel Alejandria (MUSCAT OF ALEXANDRIA) is also widely grown for basic wine to be consumed within Chile. Research in the early 1990s in the Chillán area, however, suggested that some good-quality wine from the best-known INTERNATIONAL VARIETIES could be made here.

Vine varieties

Vine identification is an underdeveloped science in Chile. The majority of the vines called Sauvignon by the Chileans, for example, are almost certainly Sauvignon Vert, Sauvignonasse (or TOCAI Friulano) and occasionally Sauvignon Gris, rather than the more familiar Sauvignon Blanc. Only a small but increasing proportion of Sauvignon Blanc had been planted by the early 1990s.

Similarly, vines called Merlot are in fact a mixture, and sometimes a FIELD BLEND, of Merlot and the old Bordeaux variety CARMENÈRE. Since the mid 1990s, some varietal Carmenère has been produced, and is often sold under the synonym Grand Vidure. Until the 1990s, the most commonly planted grape variety was the dark-skinned PAÍS, found only in Chile. However, Cabernet Sauvignon is now the most important variety by quite a margin, followed by 'Sauvignon', Moscatel Alejandria

(MUSCAT OF ALEXANDRIA), Chardonnay, 'Merlot', and Carmenère. Other varieties include SÉMILLON (spelt Semillón) and Torontél (the local form of Argentina's TORRONTÉS), Cot (MALBEC), and Pinot Noir. Some Syrah has also been planted, with success.

Wine-making

Chile is undergoing possibly the most dramatic technological revolution in the wine world. Wineries were for decades underfunded as the domestic market could be satisfied with often oxidized white wines and faded reds. In the late 1980s, however, the wine industry made a commitment to the long-term future of Chile as a wine exporter and began to invest in the equipment necessary for that goal.

Industry organization

Most of the big wine-exporting companies, many of them run by descendants of the wine dynasties of the mid 19th century, have their headquarters in Santiago or nearby in the Maipo region. Some of the biggest are Concha y Toro, Santa Rita, and Santa Carolina. Many own several wineries and many different vineyards, although it is also the norm to buy grapes from a wide range of growers. The estate wineries such as the historic Cousiño Macul, Los Vascos, Montes, Portal del Alto, Santa Monica, and Santa Inés, for which practically all grapes used are grown by the owner/winemaker, are relatively rare. Foreign investment has come from California (MONDAVI), France (Chx Mouton- and Lafite-ROTHSCHILD *et al.*), Spain (TORRES), and the Far East.

Wine styles

Wines exported from Chile are, typically, extremely fruity and clean but did not until the early 1990s display the structure which can only be imposed by low yields and/or BARREL MATURATION. Yields are still relatively high, although there are some plots of very old vines which produce concentrated wine. Cabernet Sauvignon, Merlot, and Cabernet blends dominate Chile's red-wine exports and can provide extremely good-value wines for drinking within two or three years, although an increasing proportion of wine capable of BOTTLE AGEING is likely to be made.

The new generation of white wines has been clean and well made rather than strongly characteristic of any particular grape variety, although this was evolving dramatically with each vintage in the early 1990s. Pink and sweet wines are certainly made (Concha y Toro make a late-harvest 'Sauterne'), and Alberto Valdivieso was the first to make sparkling wines using TRADITIONAL METHOD techniques, as early as 1879.

So far Chile has lacked a wine style to call its own. It is still to a certain extent the Bordeaux of the southern hemisphere; some specialist advisers are advocating the development of Carmenère as Chile's unique gift to the world of wine.

China, vast Asian country currently in the grip of a wine boom. China's vineyards are spread across provinces north of the Yangtze river, from Xinjiang in the extreme north west to the coastal regions of Hebei, Shandong, Tianjin, Liaoning, and Jilin in the north east. The largest vineyard area in China is on the same latitude as the south of France, but is as far away from western influence as possible. Production in all regions is still largely concentrated on TABLE GRAPES and DRYING GRAPES, with China's 200 state 'alcohol manufacturing factories' (the literal translation of the word for winery) vinifying only about one-sixth of the total grape harvest.

Lack of modern equipment, absence of western influence, and a desire for strong, sweet drinks made syrupy, MADERIZED wines the norm in state wineries in the past. However, modern equipment introduced into joint-venture wineries is now starting to revolutionize wine styles.

Since 1979, several moves have been made to allow foreign investors to install a modern wine industry in north-east China. In May 1980, Cognac giant Rémy Martin set up the first JOINT VENTURE winery, Sino-French Joint Venture Winery, with the Tianjin Agriculture Bureau. The Great Wall winery was also established in 1982 at Shacheng of Hebei by the monopolistic China National Cereals, Oils, Foodstuffs Import & Export Corporation with some technical assistance from the North American distiller Seagram. Both wineries applied modern wine-making techniques but produced relatively simple table wines from Dragon's Eye table grapes. The Huadong (East China) winery, China's first 'château-style' wine estate to plant and produce VARIETAL and vintage-dated wines with an APPELLATION, Tsingtao, on the label, was established at Qingdao in 1985 by a British wine merchant from Hong Kong and from 1990 was acquired and run by the multinational

Allied Domecq. Another multinational, Pernod Ricard, set up the Beijing Friendship winery in 1987 and an Italian venture set up the Marco Polo winery at Yantai in 1990. Other joint-venture wineries include Summer Palace, in which Seagram is involved. All imported advanced vinification equipment, European *vinifera* vine cuttings, and foreign OENOLOGISTS to produce the first 'western style' grape wines in China, suitable for the domestic and export markets. State wineries are slowly following their lead. Amongst them, Chang Yu and Qingdao at Shandong are the most progressive.

In 1995 and 1996, the Chinese government repeatedly encouraged the replacement of cereal-based spirits with fruit-based wines, motivated both by HEALTH concerns and by an acute grain shortage. Official recommendation of red wine as reducing the risk of cardiovascular disease sparked a wine boom throughout China. Thousands of cases of red wine from Europe were shipped in and rushed on to the market. Millions of litres of wine were shipped in bulk for local bottling. Distillers for traditional baijiu (white spirits) adapted their plants to make or bottle wines. Small wineries and bottling plants mushroomed all over China. Many Chinese adults now drink wine, even if often mixed with soft drinks.

China's wine boom has prompted considerable developments in viticulture. In addition to the thousands of native grape varieties that exist in northern China, there are widespread plantings imported from the ex Soviet Union, of MUSCAT HAMBURG and RKATSITELI, here, where it has reasonable potential for quality, known as Baiyu. Alongside large acreages of Italian Riesling (see WELSCHRIESLING), these varieties have formed the backbone of China's modern wine industry. In the 1980s, classic European varieties such as Cabernet Sauvignon and Chardonnay were introduced by foreign investors.

Chinon, significant red-wine appellation in the TOURAINE district of the Loire which also produces a small amount of rosé, and an even smaller amount of white wine from Chenin Blanc grapes. The vineyards extend south of the Loire on the banks of the Vienne, not far east of the fashionable red Saumur-Champigny, another product of mainly CABERNET FRANC grapes, here often called Breton. From 2000, up to 25 per cent of Cabernet Sauvignon grapes was allowed.

Two distinct styles of Chinon are made. A fuller, long-term BOURGUEIL-like wine comes from sites on the limestone slopes and plateaux, most notably the south-facing slopes of Cravant-les-Coteaux, and the plateau above Beaumont. Lighter wines are made from sand and gravel vineyards near the river, with the most elegant examples coming from the gravel beds around Panzoult. These wines are closer to St Nicolas-de-Bourgueil in style.

Chinon is quintessentially a wine of refreshment, being light to medium bodied, often extravagantly scented (lead pencils is one common tasting note), and with an appetizing combination of fruit and acidity. The best wines can benefit from BOTTLE AGEING, but that is not the point of the wine. Chinon is essentially a Frenchman's wine, and it takes some local knowledge to seek out the best, often artisanal, bottlings from the likes of Charles Joguet and Olga Raffault. A high proportion of the wine is sold to merchants, whose blends vary considerably in quality.

See also LOIRE.

Chiroubles, highest of the Beaujolais crus, producing some of the lightest but most genuinely refreshing wines, best drunk young. Perhaps the most archetypically Beaujolais of all the crus. Domaines Cheysson and de la Rocassière are reliable. See BEAUJOLAIS.

Chorey-lès-Beaune, village near Beaune in Burgundy producing red wines from Pinot Noir grapes. There are no vineyards of PREMIER CRU status, and much of the wine is sold as Côte de BEAUNE-Villages. Exceptional producers based here are Domaines Tollot Beaut and Jacques Germain, which make some of the finest wines of the Beaune appellation. A good Chorey is similar to a village SAVIGNY-LÈS-BEAUNE or a lesser ALOXE-CORTON. A tiny quantity of white Chorey-lès-Beaune is made from Chardonnay. See also CÔTE D'OR.   J.T.C.M.

Chusclan, the most famous of the Côtes-du-RHÔNE villages on the right bank of the river. As in nearby Tavel, its rosé is particularly appreciated.

Cigales, wine zone in northern Spain, north of Valladolid in CASTILE AND LEÓN. This DO has traditionally produced dry rosé wines made from Tinto del Pais (TEMPRANILLO) and GARNACHA grapes, but some dry reds showed real potential in the late 1990s.   R.J.M. & V. de la S.

cigars and wine, controversial combination fostered by Marvin Shanken, publisher of the leading periodicals in both. *Cigar Aficionado* was launched in the USA in 1992, just in time to ride a wave of anti-puritan self-indulgence that swept across the country in the mid 1990s. FINE WINE has inevitably played a part in this, featuring heavily in high-profile dinners (some of them involving FIRST GROWTH proprietors) and in the smoking clubs that have been generated by renewed interest in cigars. Combining cigar smoking with wine TASTING is certainly exclusive.

Ciliegiolo, central Italian red grape variety of Tuscan origin named after its supposed cherry-like flavour and colour. It is declining in popularity, although it can make some excellent wines, and could be a usefully soft blending partner for SANGIOVESE. Some good VARIETAL Ciliegiolo from Umbria, Tuscany, and an outstanding one from the Rascioni and Cecconello estate in the MAREMMA raised interest in the variety in the 1990s.

Cinsaut, sometimes written **Cinsault**, is a red grape variety known for centuries in the Languedoc region of southern France that has much in common with GRENACHE. The wines it produces tend to be lighter, softer, and, in extreme youth, more aromatic than most reds. It is particularly well adapted for rosé production and is widely planted throughout southern France, and Corsica, where it is the dominant vine variety.

Cinsaut is used almost exclusively to add suppleness, perfume, and immediate fruit to blends (typically of the ubiquitous but curmudgeonly Carignan), although all-Cinsaut rosés are increasingly common.

It is an approved but hardly venerated ingredient in the CHÂTEAUNEUF-DU-PAPE cocktail and is often found further east in Provence, as well as in the north of Corsica, where it has been widely pulled up in favour of more profitable crops. The variety is still cultivated quite extensively in MOROCCO (and has long played an important part in the wine industry of the LEBANON).

Cinsaut has in its time played a major part in South as well as North Africa (which makes it all the stranger that South Africa has virtually no ROSÉ culture). It was South Africa's most important vine until the mid 1960s and was overtaken by Cabernet Sauvignon as the Cape's most planted red grape variety only in

1993. Cinsaut was known carelessly as Hermitage in South Africa (although there is no Cinsaut in the northern Rhône). Thus South Africa's own grape variety speciality, a crossing of Pinot Noir with Cinsaut, was named PINOTAGE, now a much more respected South African vine variety than Cinsaut.

Cirò, the only DOC of any quantitative significance in the southern Italian region of CALABRIA.

CIS, or Commonwealth of Independent States, approximates to what was once the Russian empire and was known for much of the 20th century as the Soviet Union, or USSR, the world's largest country. With the fall of communism at the end of the 1980s, the Union fragmented into its separate republics, which acquired, or regained, administrative and economic independence. Overall wine production fell considerably.

In 1996, the republics with the most land planted with vines (many of them, especially in the five central Asian republics, for TABLE GRAPES, raisins, or other non-wine grape products) were, in descending order, MOLDOVA, UKRAINE, UZBEKISTAN, RUSSIA, GEORGIA, and AZERBAIJAN. Vine-growing makes an important financial and social contribution in many regions.

Moldova has the most suitable climate, and range of vine varieties planted, for regular production of European VARIETALS, while the central Asian republics are more likely to be planted with indigenous vine varieties producing heavier, sweeter wines.

The wine grape varieties regarded as specialities of the CIS are the white RKATSITELI and the red SAPERAVI. Of varieties imported from classic European wine regions, Riesling is surprisingly widely planted, even in some relatively hot regions, as are ALIGOTÉ and, perhaps more usefully on the international marketplace, Cabernet Sauvignon. Some particularly cold-hardy crossings of classic varieties have been developed especially for Russia's cold winters and are usually described as *Severny*, or Northern.

The break-up of the Soviet Union affected the international wine market to a certain extent and the eastern European wine market enormously. Eastern bloc countries such as BULGARIA, ROMANIA, and HUNGARY suddenly had to find new customers for an important proportion of their annual wine production,

customers who would certainly be more demanding than their Soviet predecessors. Wine produced within the CIS, on the other hand, was viewed by some republics as a potential earner of hard currency, by others as useful barter. As individuals struggled for economic survival in the new free-market economies, the markets were flooded with alcohol substitutes, cheap vodkas, brandies and wines from central and western Europe.

The first example of outside wine investment was the Australian company PENFOLDS' joint venture in Moldova, announced in 1993 and quietly abandoned only two vintages later. Wente of LIVERMORE in California persisted rather longer with their Russian adventure.

For more detail, see under the names of individual republics. V.R.

clairet, dark-pink wine style that is a speciality of the BORDEAUX region and which originally inspired the English word CLARET. Dark-skinned grapes are fermented in contact with the skins for about 24 hours before fermentation of this lightly coloured wine continues to dryness. Small quantities of potentially refreshing wine are bottled to be sold under the appellation Bordeaux Clairet, and should be drunk as young as possible.

Clairette is a much-used name for southern French white grape varieties. Clairette Ronde, for example, is the Languedoc name for the ubiquitous UGNI BLANC, and various Clairettes serve as synonyms for the much finer BOURBOULENC.

True Clairette Blanc, however, is a decidedly old-fashioned variety, producing slightly flabby, alcoholic whites that MADERIZE easily, but it is allowed into a wide range of southern Rhône, Provençal, and Languedoc appellations, even lending its name to three (see below). It is still one of the principal ingredients in the Languedoc's white VINS DE PAYS—usually enlivened by Ugni Blanc and Terret.

Its presence in many southern white appellations such as LIRAC, Côtes-du-RHÔNE, COSTIÈRES DE NÎMES, and PALETTE explains why Ugni Blanc is also needed in these blends, to add counterbalancing acid. Its other common partner in the blending vat, and often vineyard, GRENACHE Blanc, certainly does nothing to compensate for Clairette's weight and premature senility, although low-temperature fermentation and minimal exposure to oxygen can do something to offset these tendencies.

Clairette is widely distributed throughout the eastern Midi, especially in the Gard, where it produces CLAIRETTE DE BELLEGARDE, and in the Hérault for CLAIRETTE DU LANGUEDOC, two of the Languedoc's earliest controlled appellations, presumably because these white wines were so unlike, rather than superior to, the typical produce of the Midi. Clairette's noblest incarnation is undoubtedly the usually sparkling CLAIRETTE DE DIE of the mid Rhône, although it must be admitted that the most interesting examples are those which rely more on Muscat than Clairette.

The variety is known as Clairette Blanche in South Africa, where it is almost as widely planted as in France. It can still be found in Australia's Hunter Valley, where it is known as Blanquette but is declining fast. It is also planted in Romania, Israel, Tuscany, and Sardinia, where it is a permitted ingredient in NURAGUS di Cagliari.

A Clairette is grown in RUSSIA in some quantity.

Clairette de Bellegarde is a small enclave of exclusively white-wine production in the south of the COSTIÈRES DE NÎMES appellation in the eastern Languedoc. Like CLAIRETTE DU LANGUEDOC, it is made entirely of the somewhat flabby CLAIRETTE grape and needs all the streamlining that modern vinification can impart to make this old-fashioned wine appeal to wine drinkers outside the region. Total production is low, declining, and dominated by the Bellegarde co-operative. This wine demands to be drunk as young as possible.

Clairette de Die is a sparkling-white appellation centred on the town of DIE on the Drôme tributary east of the Rhône between Valence and Montélimar. Die's gently fizzing wines may pre-date those of Champagne. Clairette de Die is a drink much more likely to refresh than either of the Languedoc's Clairettes (see above and below), but often despite rather than because of the CLAIRETTE grape. As well as a small quantity of still Clairette, a bit like CLAIRETTE DE BELLEGARDE but with the benefit of a slightly cooler climate, two very different sorts of sparkling Clairette de Die have been made, from Clairette and MUSCAT BLANC À PETITS GRAINS grapes.

The more distinctive and more important is Clairette de Die Tradition, a refreshingly grapey fizz with Muscat flavours (Clairette may account for no more than 30 per cent of the blend) and an ALCOHOLIC STRENGTH of between 7 and 8 per cent, made by the *méthode dioise*, which should be signalled on the label. After pressing, the juice is filtered and kept at a sub-zero temperature until it has fermented to about three per cent alcohol. It is then bottled and a second fermentation (see SPARKLING-WINE-MAKING) is activated, unusually, by the inherent grape sugar rather than added sugar and yeast. After at least four months on the grapey lees of this process, the wine is decanted off and rebottled under pressure, leaving varying degrees of residual sweetness. No last-minute adjustments with DOSAGE are allowed.

CRÉMANT de Die is the more ordinary but usually well-made brut version made by the TRADITIONAL METHOD, mainly exclusively from Clairette grapes and until 1999 called Clairette de Die Brut.

The local co-operative, geographically justified in calling itself the Cellier Hannibal, has been responsible for dynamizing the appellation and makes three in every four bottles carrying it. Perhaps it is significant that their top cuvée, and that of some smaller producers, contains no Clairette at all.

Other local still reds and whites may qualify as CHÂTILLON-EN-DIOIS.

Clairette du Languedoc is a slightly more important appellation than CLAIRETTE DE BELLEGARDE, again exclusively from the overweight Clairette grape. It is one of the named subappellations of the southern French Coteaux du LANGUEDOC appellation. The wine can be anything from an ultra-modern, early-picked, yellowish green, dry wine for drinking almost before the end of the year in which it was harvested, to a deep-brown RANCIO sweet, alcoholic VIN DE LIQUEUR to suit French taste in aperitifs. Although CO-OPERATIVES dominate production quantitatively, the Condamine-Bertrand domaine makes a flavourful dry white for early drinking. There has been an impressive sweet version from Adissan. PICPOUL DE PINET, made just to the south, shares many of these characteristics.

Clape, La, named TERROIR within the Coteaux du LANGUEDOC in southern France which is probably unfairly penalized for its name in Anglophone markets. La Clape is a quintessentially Mediterranean coastal mountain just south of Narbonne which has one of France's highest average annual totals of sunshine. On the southern slopes of the mountain, the climate is heavily influenced by the sea. La Clape is particularly well suited to growing BOURBOULENC, which must represent at least 60 per cent of the grapes used in the production of La Clape's sea-scented white wines such as those produced by Rouquette-sur-Mer, although these represent a distinct minority of the wine produced within the appellation and most La Clape is full-blooded red, virtually indistinguishable from maritime CORBIÈRES. Some sweet wines are now made on the extensive l'Hospitalet domaine.

Clare Riesling. See CROUCHEN.

claret, English (not American) term generally used to describe red wines from the BORDEAUX region, or red bordeaux. Claret has also been used as a GENERIC term for a vaguely identified class of red table wines supposedly drier, and possibly higher in TANNINS, than those wines sold as generic burgundy (although, in the history of Australian wine SHOWS, it has been known for the same wine to win both claret and burgundy classes). The name derives from the medieval French term CLAIRET.

clarete is a Spanish term for a particularly Spanish hue of wine somewhere between a rosé (which the Spaniards would call rosado) and a light red. It derives from *claro*, the Spanish word meaning 'clear'. The term is now prohibited on labels but is still sometimes used in Spanish as a descriptive term.

claret jugs. See DECANTERS.

Clare Valley, fine wine region in SOUTH AUSTRALIA.

clarification, wine-making operation which removes suspended and insoluble material from grape juice, or new wine, in which these solids are known as LEES. See also STABILIZATION.

Clarksburg, California wine region and AVA. Much of the AVA is composed of islands in the CENTRAL VALLEY Delta west of Sacramento. Although a spectrum of varieties grows within the zone, only Chenin Blanc truly distinguishes itself. Indeed, only here in all of California does Chenin Blanc become regionally identifiable.

classed growth is a vineyard, estate, or château included in a wine CLASSIFICATION. The term is used almost exclusively in BORDEAUX for those châteaux included in the 1855 clas-

sification of the Médoc and Sauternes, the 1955 classification of Graves, and sometimes for those properties included in the regularly revised St-Émilion classification. The term is a direct translation of the French term CRU classé.

Classico, Italian term appended to the names of various DOC or DOCG wines to indicate that they have been produced in the historic zone which gave the wine its name, the zone which, at least in theory, offers the ideal conditions of soil and climate.

classification of various wine estates and vineyards is in general a relatively recent phenomenon, dictated by the increasingly sophisticated wine market of the late 19th and 20th centuries. It has to a certain extent been superseded by the even more recent phenomenon of SCORING individual wines.

Bordeaux

BORDEAUX, with its plethora of fine, long-lasting wine from well-established estates and its well-organized market, is the wine region which has been most subject to classification of individual châteaux. The most famous wine classification in the world is that drawn up in 1855 of what became known as the CLASSED GROWTHS of the MÉDOC, and one GRAVES (see following pages). In response to a request from Napoleon III's 1855 Exposition Universelle in Paris (possibly so that dignitaries there should effectively know what to be impressed by), the Bordeaux BROKERS formalized their own and the market's ranking with a five-class classification of 61 of the leading Médoc châteaux and the particularly famous and historic Graves, HAUT-BRION; and a two-class classification of SAUTERNES and BARSAC. This classification merely codified the market's view of relative quality as expressed by the prices fetched by individual estates' wines.

The 1855 classification has endured remarkably well considering the many and various changes to the management and precise extent of individual properties since it was compiled, with only Chx MOUTON-ROTHSCHILD and Léoville-Barton in the same hands. The only official revision of this much-discussed list took place in 1973, when, after much lobbying on the part of Baron Philippe de Rothschild, Ch Mouton-Rothschild made the all-important leap from top of the second growths to become a first growth (although see also SUPER SECOND).

The 1855 classification of Sauternes and

Bordeaux

The Official Classification of Médoc and Graves of 1855

First Growths (Premiers Crus)

	Commune	Appellation
Ch Lafite-Rothschild	Pauillac	Pauillac
Ch Margaux	Margaux	Margaux
Ch Latour	Pauillac	Pauillac
Ch Haut-Brion*	Pessac	Graves, now Pessac-Léognan
Ch Mouton-Rothschild**	Pauillac	Pauillac

Second Growths (Deuxièmes Crus)

	Commune	Appellation
Ch Rauzan-Segla	Margaux	Margaux
Ch Rauzan-Gassies	Margaux	Margaux
Ch Léoville Las Cases	St-Julien	St-Julien
Ch Léoville-Poyferré	St-Julien	St-Julien
Ch Léoville-Barton	St-Julien	St-Julien
Ch Durfort-Vivens	Margaux	Margaux
Ch Gruaud-Larose	St-Julien	St-Julien
Ch Lascombes	Margaux	Margaux
Ch Brane-Cantenac	Cantenac	Margaux
Ch Pichon-Longueville (Baron)	Pauillac	Pauillac
Ch Pichon-Longueville, Comtesse de Lalande	Pauillac	Pauillac
Ch Ducru-Beaucaillou	St-Julien	St-Julien
Ch Cos d'Estournel (Cos)	St-Estèphe	St-Estèphe
Ch Montrose	St-Estèphe	St-Estèphe

Third Growths (Troisièmes Crus)

	Commune	Appellation
Ch Kirwan	Cantenac	Margaux
Ch d'Issan	Cantenac	Margaux
Ch Lagrange	St-Julien	St-Julien
Ch Langoa-Barton	St-Julien	St-Julien
Ch Giscours	Labarde	Margaux
Ch Malescot St-Exupéry	Margaux	Margaux
Ch Boyd-Cantenac	Cantenac	Margaux
Ch Cantenac-Brown	Cantenac	Margaux
Ch Palmer	Cantenac	Margaux
Ch La Lagune	Ludon	Haut-Médoc
Ch Desmirail	Margaux	Margaux
Ch Calon-Ségur	St-Estèphe	St-Estèphe
Ch Ferrière	Margaux	Margaux
Ch Marquis d'Alesme Becker	Margaux	Margaux

* This wine, although a Graves, was universally recognized and classified as one of the original four first growths.
** This wine was decreed a first growth in 1973.

Fourth Growths (Quatrièmes Crus)

	Commune	Appellation
Ch St-Pierre	St-Julien	St-Julien
Ch Talbot	St-Julien	St-Julien
Ch Branaire-Ducru	St-Julien	St-Julien
Ch Duhart-Milon	Pauillac	Pauillac
Ch Pouget	Cantenac	Margaux
Ch La Tour-Carnet	St-Laurent	Haut-Médoc
Ch Lafon-Rochet	St-Estèphe	St-Estèphe
Ch Beychevelle	St-Julien	St-Julien
Ch Prieuré-Lichine	Cantenac	Margaux
Ch Marquis-de-Terme	Margaux	Margaux

Fifth Growths (Cinquièmes Crus)

	Commune	Appellation
Ch Pontet-Canet	Pauillac	Pauillac
Ch Batailley	Pauillac	Pauillac
Ch Haut-Batailley	Pauillac	Pauillac
Ch Grand-Puy-Lacoste	Pauillac	Pauillac
Ch Grand-Puy-Ducasse	Pauillac	Pauillac
Ch Lynch-Bages	Pauillac	Pauillac
Ch Lynch-Moussas	Pauillac	Pauillac
Ch Dauzac	Labarde	Margaux
Ch d'Armailhac***	Pauillac	Pauillac
Ch du Tertre	Arsac	Margaux
Ch Haut-Bages-Liberal	Pauillac	Pauillac
Ch Pédesclaux	Pauillac	Pauillac
Ch Belgrave	St-Laurent	Haut-Médoc
Ch de Camensac	St-Laurent	Haut-Médoc
Ch Cos-Labory	St-Estèphe	St-Estèphe
Ch Clerc-Milon	Pauillac	Pauillac
Ch Croizet-Bages	Pauillac	Pauillac
Ch Cantemerle	Macau	Haut-Médoc

*** Previously Ch d'Armailhaq, Ch Mouton-Baron-Philippe, and Ch Mouton-Baronne-Philippe.

The Official Classification of St-Émilion of 1955
(Most Recently Reclassified 1996)

Premiers Grands Crus Classés

A

Ch Ausone   Ch Cheval Blanc

B

Ch Angélus	Ch Canon	Ch Magdelaine
Ch Beau-Séjour Bécot	Clos Fourtet	Ch Pavie
Ch Beauséjour-Duffaux la Garrosse	Ch Figeac	Ch Trottevieille
Ch Belair	Ch la Gaffelière	

Grands Crus Classés

Ch l'Arrosée
Ch Balestard-La-Tonnelle
Ch Bellevue
Ch Bergat
Ch Berliquet
Ch Cadet-Bon
Ch Cadet-Piola
Ch Canon-La Gaffelière
Ch Cap de Mourlin
Ch Chauvin
Ch Clos des Jacobins
Clos de l'Oratoire
Clos St-Martin
Ch la Clotte
Ch la Clusière
Ch Corbin
Ch Corbin-Michotte
Ch la Couspaude
Couvent des Jacobins

Ch Curé-Bon
Ch Dassault
Ch la Dominique
Ch Faurie-de-Souchard
Ch Fonplégade
Ch Fonroque
Ch Franc-Mayne
Ch Grand-Mayne
Ch Grand-Pontet
Ch les Grandes Murailles
Ch Guadet St-Julien
Ch Haut-Corbin
Ch Haute-Sarpe
Ch Lamarzelle
Ch Laniote
Ch Larcis-Ducasse
Ch Larmande
Ch Laroque
Ch Laroze

Ch Matras
Ch Moulin du Cadet
Ch Pavie-Decesse
Ch Pavie-Macquin
Ch Petit Faurie de Soutard
Ch le Prieuré
Ch Ripeau
Ch St-Georges-Côte-Pavie
Ch la Serre
Ch Soutard
Ch Tertre-Daugay
Ch La Tour-Figeac
Ch la Tour du Pin Figeac
   (Giraud-Bélivier)
Ch la Tour du Pin Figeac
   (Moueix)
Ch Troplong-Mondot
Ch Villemaurine
Ch Yon-Figeac

The Official Classification of Sauternes-Barsac of 1855

First Great Growth (Grand Premier Cru)

	Commune
Ch d'Yquem	Sauternes

First Growths (Premiers Crus)

	Commune		Commune
Ch La Tour-Blanche	Bommes	Ch Climens	Barsac
Ch Lafaurie-Peyraguey	Bommes	Ch Guiraud	Sauternes
Ch Clos Haut-Peyraguey	Bommes	Ch Rieussec	Fargues
Ch de Rayne-Vigneau	Bommes	Ch Rabaud-Promis	Bommes
Ch Suduiraut	Preignac	Ch Sigalas-Rabaud	Bommes
Ch Coutet	Barsac		

Second Growths (Deuxièmes Crus)

	Commune		Commune
Ch de Myrat	Barsac	Ch Nairac	Barsac
Ch Doisy-Daëne	Barsac	Ch Caillou	Barsac
Ch Doisy-Dubroca	Barsac	Ch Suau	Barsac
Ch Doisy-Vedrines	Barsac	Ch de Malle	Preignac
Ch d'Arche	Sauternes	Ch Romer-du-Hayot	Fargues
Ch Filhot	Sauternes	Ch Lamothe-Despujols	Sauternes
Ch Broustet	Barsac	Ch Lamothe-Guignard	Sauternes

The Official Classification of Graves of 1959

Classified Red Wines of Graves

	Commune		Commune
Ch Bouscaut	Cadaujac	Ch La Tour-Martillac	Martillac
Ch Haut-Bailly	Léognan	Ch Smith-Haut-Lafitte	Martillac
Ch Carbonnieux	Léognan	Ch Haut-Brion	Pessac
Domaine de Chevalier	Léognan	Ch La Mission-Haut-Brion	Talence
Ch de Fieuzal	Léognan	Ch Pape-Clément	Pessac
Ch Olivier	Léognan	Ch La Tour-Haut-Brion	Talence
Ch Malartic-Lagravière	Léognan		

Classified White Wines of Graves

	Commune		Commune
Ch Bouscaut	Cadaujac	Ch La Tour-Martillac	Martillac
Ch Carbonnieux	Léognan	Ch Laville-Haut-Brion	Talence
Domaine de Chevalier	Léognan	Ch Couhins	Villenave d'Ornon
Ch d'Olivier	Léognan	Ch Haut-Brion*	Pessac
Ch Malartic-Lagravière	Léognan		

*Added to the list in 1960

Barsac is printed on p. 129. Reflecting price and the *réclame* then attached to sweet wines, it elevated Ch d'YQUEM to grand PREMIER CRU, a rank higher even than any of the red-wine FIRST GROWTHS, and listed 11 châteaux as first growths and 14 as seconds.

Other than Haut-Brion's inclusion in the 1855 Médoc classification, the red wines of the GRAVES district were not officially classified until 1953. This one-class list, together with an official classification of the white wines, made in 1959, appears above. It avoided some possible controversy by employing a democratically alphabetical order. It should be said, however, that there is a wide differential between the prices commanded by Ch Haut-Brion and its close rival Ch La Mission-Haut-Brion, and those fetched by Chx Bouscaut and de Fieuzal, for example. The Graves district was subsequently divided into Graves and PESSAC-LÉOGNAN.

The classification of ST-ÉMILION, formally drawn up in 1955, is most frequently amended. There were modifications in 1969, 1985, and 1996 and these are likely to continue on the basis of monitoring of wine quality, vineyard boundaries, prices, and the like (vineyards cannot be extended between reclassifications). The top two properties Chx CHEVAL BLANC and AUSONE are ranked, somewhat inelegantly,

premiers grands crus classés A, while 11 properties qualify as premiers grands crus classés B. Below this are 55 grands crus classés, whose quality can vary considerably, and then in each vintage, on the basis of tastings, the deceptively grandiose rank of GRAND CRU (minus the classé) is awarded to scores of individual wines from properties below grand cru classé status. The 1996 classification is reproduced on pp. 128–9; a revision based on tastings of wines made between 1994 and 2004 is expected to be published in 2006.

POMEROL is the only important fine-wine district of Bordeaux never to have been classified, although its star Ch PÉTRUS is conventionally included with Chx LAFITE, LATOUR, MARGAUX, Haut-Brion, Mouton-Rothschild, Cheval Blanc, and Ausone as a first growth.

There have been regular attempts to revise and assimilate the various classifications of Bordeaux. Most serious writers on bordeaux make their own revisions, more or less confirmed by the market.

See also CRU BOURGEOIS for those MÉDOC properties classified as just below the status of a fifth growth.

Burgundy

Burgundians were also well aware of the considerable variation in quality of the wines produced by different plots of land, or *climats*, as they are known in Burgundy. An informal classification of the best vineyards in 1855 was formalized in 1861 by the Beaune Committee of Agriculture, which devised three classes. Most *climats* included in the first class eventually became grands crus when the APPELLATION CONTRÔLÉE system was introduced in the 1930s. See under CÔTE D'OR for a full list of Burgundian grands crus, and see under individual village names for details of their premiers crus.

Elsewhere

Few other regions of France have anything approaching an official classification, although see ALSACE for a list of those vineyards accorded grand-cru status, CHABLIS for details of crus in this northern outpost of Burgundy, and CHAMPAGNE for some details of the classification of individual villages there.

There have been attempts, typically by WINE WRITERS and/or wine waiters, to produce classifications of the best vineyards, or best wines, of many countries, notably Germany and Italy (see VERONELLI), but these have so far been too controversial to be generally adopted. With the exception of the DOURO, where individual vineyards have been classified for the quality of port they produce, the wine regions of Portugal and Spain are in too great a state of flux to submit satisfactorily to classification, like those of eastern Europe and the rest of the Mediterranean.

In the New World, Australia prefers to classify not vineyards but individual wines, often much blended between areas, by awarding them medals and trophies in their famous SHOWS, while classification may never appeal to the democratic California wine industry.

Clevner, grape variety, usually part of the PINOT family. In SWITZERLAND, the name is often applied to PINOT NOIR or Blauburgunder grown in the canton of Zurich. In ALSACE, Clevner or Klevner are usually synonyms for PINOT BLANC but see also KLEVENER DE HEILIGENSTEIN.

climat, French, particularly Burgundian, term for a specific vineyard site defined by, as the name suggests, all of its climatological as well as geographical characteristics, otherwise known as TERROIR. Thus the Burgundian grower uses the word *climat* interchangeably with 'vineyard'. A *climat* is generally smaller than a specific appellation, and most appellations have over the centuries been subdivided into small parcels of a few hectares.

climate, long-term WEATHER pattern of an area, and an extremely important variable in the wine-making equation. For more details, see MACROCLIMATE, MESOCLIMATE, and MICROCLIMATE.

climate and wine quality. Climate influences both the quality and styles of wine that an area can produce best. At the extremes, a climate can be so unsuitable for grape-growing that to produce good wines regularly is impossible or, at best, uneconomic. Cooler climates are best suited to producing light, delicate wines, while hotter climates are most suitable for FORTIFIED WINE production.

Two climatic types appear to offer the best compromises for both viticulture and wine quality. The first is that with cool to mild growing-season temperatures and uniform to predominantly summer rainfall, such as is found in western and central Europe. Within that context, the best vineyard sites have specialized MESOCLIMATES with more than usual sunshine, warmth, and length of frost-free period.

The second broad climatic type, extending more or less contiguously from the first, comprises the cooler and more humid of the summer-dry Mediterranean climates, whenever summer heat is regularly moderated by afternoon sea breezes, and irrigation can be supplied in late summer if needed and permitted. Advantages over the uniform and summer-rainfall climates include more reliable summer sunshine and less risk of excessive rain and humidity during the ripening period.

The world's greatest table wines have traditionally come from the cool to mild temperate climates with uniform to summer-dominant rainfall.   J.G. & R.E.S.

climate change. The lifetimes of individual vines are usually measured in decades, and those of vineyards or vineyard areas often in centuries. The prospects of long-term climatic change are therefore crucial to viticultural planning.

Past changes in the growing-season temperatures have almost certainly played a role in shaping central and western European viticulture, from Roman times onwards.

The future course of TEMPERATURES, locally and worldwide, cannot fail to have a profound influence on viticulture. One lesson to be learned from history is that growing-season temperatures can drop suddenly, and remain low for years or decades. The effects on viticulture towards its cool limit can be drastic.

What, then, of the immediate future? A study of recent medium-term temperature fluctuations, and their possible causes, suggests that the warm 1980s probably represented a temperature peak. If so, a moderate cyclic fall could follow. Students of longer-term fluctuations have further predicted the possibility of a full return to Little Ice Age conditions, for at least a period, sometime early in the 21st century.

Against this must be balanced the forecasts of global warming due to a 'greenhouse effect', caused by increasing atmospheric concentrations of CARBON DIOXIDE and various other gases produced by fossil-fuel burning and industry. The most recent consensus forecast by viridomologists (proponents of the greenhouse effect) has been for a temperature rise of some 2 °C/3.6 °F by the mid 21st century, which, if fulfilled, will override even the largest natural fluctuations. The expected result would then be a poleward migration of viticulture. Regions such as England, northern France and Germany, Oregon, Washington, and British Columbia, southern Argentina and Chile, and Tasmania and southern New Zealand would become the main table-wine producers of the mid to late 21st century under such conditions. Existing warm to hot viticultural regions will presumably become less tenable, especially for table wines. Warm, summer-rainfall climates, such as the east coast of Australia, could suffer doubly, with an increase in rainfall during the ripening period and therefore in the risk of vine disease.

The Australian agronomist Gladstones argues a contrary case. He finds no sign in recent viticultural history of the 0.5 °C global warming claimed to have occurred already, and sides with those who believe the apparent warming has been due to a disproportionate placing of thermometers in growing towns and cities, which create their own local warming. He maintains that, if anything, the record of European vintages suggests a slight average cooling since 1850 in the open countryside. He further argues that any future temperature increases due to rising atmospheric carbon dioxide concentrations are likely to be small; that the main effect of more carbon dioxide will be to improve both vine YIELD and wine quality; and that the greatest benefits will be

in warm and sunny climates. Typical, of the regions expected to benefit most in these circumstances are southern France, Portugal, California, Chile, mainland Australia, and South Africa. Indeed, they may already have done so.   J.G.

Clinton, dark-skinned American HYBRID planted in Brazil. Its wine has a pronounced FOXY flavour. It has also been known in Italian SWITZERLAND.

clonal selection, one of the two principal means of improving a vine variety (the other being the elimination of virus diseases). Clonal selection is the practice of selecting a single superior plant in the vineyard and then taking cuttings from this vine for propagation. The selection is generally made with a particular attribute such as YIELD or fruit RIPENESS in mind. Clonal selection contrasts with MASS SELECTION.

New grapevines, in common with many other perennial crops, are produced by vegetative propagation, that is by using cuttings which are genetically identical. Each bud from a so-called 'mother vine' essentially gives rise to a plant of the same CLONE.

The process of clonal selection is necessarily long and requires considerable investment of resources. To make reliable field selections requires several years of records followed by comparative trials of many different clones of the one variety for evaluation. After waiting 3 years for the first harvest, 5 to 10 more years are necessary to monitor yields and fruit ripeness. These trials are often conducted in several locations and with several rootstocks. Clonal selection should also involve making trial wine to assure trueness to VARIETAL type. Selected clones may not therefore be released until 15 or more years after the initial selection in the field.

There is no doubt that clonal selection has played an important part in improving both yield and wine quality from modern vineyards. When grafting became popular in the 1880s to overcome PHYLLOXERA, virus diseases were inadvertently spread. Many vineyards of both the Old World and the New World planted as late as the 1960s contained off-types, rogue vines, and virus diseases. As more healthy and true-to-type planting material becomes available as a result of clonal selection, then these problems disappear.

It is difficult to understand the effect of

clonal selection on commercial wine quality since so many vineyards are planted with mixed clones. While most Old World countries have a wide range of clones available, sometimes, because of limited importations, a New World country might have only a few for any one variety. An extreme example is Sauvignon Blanc in New Zealand, where all commercial plantings up until the early 1990s can be traced to a single clone imported from the United States. Some producers are critical of the limited availability of only improved clones from nurserymen. They argue that either mass selection or a range of clones produces better, more characterful wine than a single virus-free, high-yielding clone. R.E.S.

clone in a viticultural context is a population of vines all derived by vegetative propagation from cuttings or buds from a single 'mother vine' by deliberate CLONAL SELECTION.

By the late 1980s, many quality-conscious wine producers were wary of being dependent on a single clone of a particular variety—particularly Pinot Noir—deliberately seeking instead a mixture of clones or, less likely, vines from MASS SELECTION, for both viticultural and wine-quality reasons. R.E.S. & B.G.C.

clos is French for enclosed, and any vineyard described as a Clos should be enclosed, generally by a wall. This is a particularly common term in Burgundy, but is also used elsewhere. Similarly, the term *cuve close* refers to the need to use a sealed tank for this bulk method of SPARKLING-WINE-MAKING. The new producers of PRIORAT have adopted this term for their single-vineyard wines.

Clos de la Roche, great red GRAND CRU in Burgundy's CÔTE D'OR. See MOREY-ST-DENIS.

Clos de Tart, Clos des Lambrays, and Clos St-Denis, red GRANDS CRUS in Burgundy's CÔTE D'OR. See MOREY-ST-DENIS.

Clos de Vougeot, also frequently known as Clos Vougeot, famous walled vineyard in BURGUNDY. Ownership is highly fragmented, with over 80 proprietors.

Ch du Clos de Vougeot is a major tourist attraction. It is also home to the CONFRÉRIE des Chevaliers du Tastevin, a brotherhood which organizes copious feasts and the tastings for the Tastevinage. For this, producers submit wines to a jury; those selected are entitled to use the 'tasteviné' label, which should enable the wine to be sold more easily or at a higher price.

The vineyard and wines of Clos de Vougeot are described under VOUGEOT. J.T.C.M.

cloudy wine. See FAULTS and STABILIZATION.

Cloudy Bay, seminal winery in the Marlborough region of NEW ZEALAND, the brainchild of David Hohnen of Cape Mentelle in WESTERN AUSTRALIA. Its debut release of a moodily labelled varietal Sauvignon Blanc in 1986 on export markets created a reputation for Marlborough Sauvignon and a cult following for Cloudy Bay almost overnight, even though initially the grapes were bought in and the wine made under contract at another winery. The enterprise, based in its own premises, became a distant offshoot of the VEUVE CLICQUOT, and hence LVMH, empire in 1990.

Coal River, wine region in TASMANIA.

Cococciola, one of the few Italian vine varieties to have expanded its total area between 1982 and 1990. It is an ingredient in Trebbiano d'ABRUZZO.

Códega, Douro name for ROUPEIRO.

Codorníu, the world's largest producer of bottle-fermented SPARKLING WINES made by the TRADITIONAL METHOD. The Codorníu group, which incorporates the Spanish CAVA brands Codorníu and Rondel, the still wine Masia Bach, and also Raimat, which makes both Cava and still wine (see COSTERS DEL SEGRE), sells over 45 million bottles of wine in its domestic market and over 60 million worldwide, with an annual turnover of more than 30 billion pesetas. The group's Cava is made from Parellada, Macabeo, and Xarel-lo grapes (no still wine is bought in) and 10 per cent of the blend is usually older reserve wine. A vintage premium Cava made substantially from Chardonnay and named Anna de Codorníu was launched in 1992. In the same year, the group opened Codorníu Napa, a new winery in the CARNEROS district of California. More than $50 million have been invested in a winery at Raimat. In 1997, Codorníu acquired the traditional Bodegas Bilbaínas firm in the Rioja Alta, a major investment outside its Catalan base. S.A. & V. de la S.

Colares, exceptional but minuscule DOC wine region on the west coast of PORTUGAL just north of the capital Lisbon buffeted by relentless winds from the Atlantic. These vineyards were spared from the PHYLLOXERA pest in the 19th century (thanks to their sandy composition) but look unlikely to survive the more recent commercial pressures. RAMISCO, the Colares vine, is probably the only VINIFERA grape variety never to have been grafted. It is to be found planted only in a narrow strip of sand dunes on the clifftops above the Atlantic, its roots anchored in the clay below. It is ironic that the soils that saved Colares are making them today less and less viable.

Three different styles of wine are permitted to use the name Colares: two red and one white. The most highly prized comes from the sandiest soils and the Ramisco grape must make up 80 per cent of the blend. A second red comes from the firmer ground away from the coast, although this is usually sold in bulk for blending. A small amount of white Colares is also made, principally from MALVASIA grapes.

R.J.M.

collecting wine became a popular hobby in the 1980s. Americans in particular tend to call anyone who buys fine wine a **collector** rather than a wine enthusiast, connoisseur, or *amateur* (the French term), suggesting that the thrill lies in acquisition rather than in consumption. The rapid economic growth of the late 1970s and 1980s, together with a succession of good vintages to be bought EN PRIMEUR and the emergence of a truly international consumer wine press (see Robert PARKER, for example), resulted in the emergence of a significant group of serious wine collectors around the globe (notably in the United States, Germany, and the Far East). They communicate and trade with each other through the AUCTION houses and the specialist BROKERS, and for many of them the purpose of collecting is to enable occasional but usually sumptuous marathon TASTING events.

colli, also written **colline** and **collio**, is the Italian word for hills. Its use in a wine name indicates that the wine is produced on slopes of a certain altitude (it is an almost direct equivalent of France's CÔTE, Côtes, and Coteaux). Accordingly, articles about Colli Somewhere are listed not under Colli, but under S for Somewhere.

Colli and its variations can be found not only as the title of various DOCs but also as a part of their descriptive apparatus: CHIANTI, for example, is produced in the Colli Senesi and the Colline Pisane (Chianti dei Colli Senesi,

Chianti delle Colline Pisane). The absence of the word does not imply that a given wine is produced in the flatlands; much of Italy's finest wine—BARBARESCO, BAROLO, BRUNELLO DI MONTALCINO, VINO NOBILE DI MONTEPULCIANO—is produced from HILLSIDE VINEYARDS without that fact being indicated in the wine's name.

D.T.

Collio, more properly **Collio Goriziano**, is a qualitatively important, predominantly white-wine DOC zone on the north-eastern border of Italy with Slovenia. Collio did much to increase Italians' confidence in their ability to make fine white wine.

Collio, a corruption of the Italian word for hills (see COLLI), is in the province of Gorizia (hence Colli Goriziano) and was only reunified with Italy after the First World War. Within the region of FRIULI, it is the third biggest DOC in terms of area planted and volume of production after GRAVE DEL FRIULI and COLLI ORIENTALI del Friuli, but its fragrant and lively white wines, which account for 85 per cent of total production, have created an image of quality for Friuli throughout the world. Collio's red wines, overwhelmingly from Merlot and Cabernets, tend to resemble LOIRE reds, at times with an identical vegetal quality underlined by a certain lightness of body and texture.

The cellars of Collio and of the Colli Orientali tend to be extremely well equipped. When pushed to extremes, this technological approach, together with relatively high yields, has created a certain blandness and monotony in the wines, with primary fermentation AROMAS and flavours dominating varietal character. A certain readjustment has taken place since the mid 1980s, as producers have begun to search for more character; a small minority has begun to strive for a more international style using BARRIQUES.

The grape variety mix is very similar to that in the Colli Orientali to the immediate west. TOCAI is the dominant variety of the DOC; Pinot Grigio, Sauvignon Blanc, Pinot Bianco, and Chardonnay are also significantly represented. Merlot accounts for over half of red grapes planted, with Cabernets accounting for more than half of the rest. Cabernet Franc, whose herbaceousness is much appreciated in the zone, is 10 times as common as Cabernet Sauvignon. Merlot has gradually proven itself to be more suited to the local climate and, as it has begun to predominate in the bordeaux-styled blends, the wines have become fuller, fleshier, and more convincing.

See also SLOVENIA, which is capable of producing some extremely similar wines.   D.T.

Colli Orientali del Friuli, literally the eastern hills of the FRIULI region in north-east Italy, is the region's second largest DOC. It is a versatile area, however, producing interesting white wines, high-quality dessert wines, and what are indisputably the finest, longest-lived red wines of Friuli. In a region known principally for its white wines, the Colli Orientali has 35 per cent of its vineyards planted to red varieties such as Cabernet and Merlot as well as the renascent native varieties REFOSCO, SCHIOP-PETTINO, and PIGNOLO.

Significant development of red wines came in the 1980s as producers began to move away from lighter, fruitier styles towards a fuller, more structured style more worthy of ageing, a move that was frequently accompanied by the use of small oak barrels. A certain number of these more ambitious reds were released as expensive VINI DA TAVOLA, because individual producers wanted either to distance the wines from their more facile antecedents, to make an unorthodox blend of varieties, or to emphasize their own name or that of Friuli. White wine, particularly from CHARDONNAY or PINOT BIANCO, was either fermented or aged in BAR-RIQUES; these wines were also marketed as vini da tavola to distinguish them from the fresher style of whites, which remained the backbone of production.

Current production is dominated by TOCAI among the white-wine grapes, followed by SAU-VIGNON BLANC, VERDUZZO, PINOT GRIGIO, and Pinot Bianco. Small quantities of the sweet white PICOLIT are also made. Merlot is by far the most significant red variety, representing more than half of all red-grape plantings, with Cabernet, Refosco, and minor quantities of Pinot Noir, Schioppettino, and Pignolo making up the rest. If the potential for fine wine is at least as high as in Collio, the wines themselves have been less consistent.   D.T.

Collioure to tourists is one of the prettiest seaside villages on the Mediterranean coast just north of the Franco-Spanish border. To wine lovers it is a rare, particularly heady, deep-red table wine whose aromas of overripe fruits and spice reflect the fact that Collioure comes from exactly the same area as BANYULS, France's most concentrated VIN DOUX NATUREL: steep,

terraced vineyards in the communes of, Spain-wards down the coast, Collioure, Port-Vendres, Banyuls-sur-Mer, and Cerbère. The characteristics of the vintage determine what proportion of grapes become Collioure rather than Banyuls, but the grapes for Collioure are certainly picked before those destined to become vin doux naturel, and generally represent a fraction of those destined to become France's answer to port.

The region's MOURVÈDRE is grown expressly for Collioure, however, as it, Syrah, and Grenache Noir must make up at least 60 per cent of the blend for the table wine. Cinsaut and Carignan are tolerated components. As in Banyuls, yields are some of the lowest in France. There is, unusually, an official maximum alcohol level, 15 per cent, as well as a maximum RESIDUAL SUGAR level of 5 gm/l—although many of these wines taste so ripe that they do give the impression of sweetness. Fine producers include Domaine du Mas Blanc, Les Clos de Paulilles, and Domaine de la Rectorie.

Colombard, which may be the offspring of GOUAIS BLANC and CHENIN BLANC, was originally a Charentais white grape variety used with Ugni Blanc (TREBBIANO) and FOLLE BLANCHE, but considered inferior to both, as an ingredient in cognac. As Colombard's star waned in France, it waxed quite spectacularly in California's CENTRAL VALLEY, where, as FRENCH COLOMBARD, it became the state's most planted variety of all, providing generous quantities of reasonably neutral but reliably crisp base wine for commercial, often quite sweet, white blends.

It would take some sorcery to transform Colombard into an exciting wine, but pleasantly lively innocuousness is well within reach for well-equipped modern wineries. In a nice example of transatlantic switchback, the producers of the Armagnac region set about duplicating California's modern wine-making transformation of the dull Colombard grape on their own varieties surplus to brandy production, thus creating the hugely successful VIN DE PAYS des Côtes de Gascogne. Colombard, still third most important variety in the region after Ugni Blanc and BACO Blanc, which are particularly well-suited to distillation, has been a prime ingredient in this much exported wine. The Charentais later tried to work the same magic to produce their own version Vin de Pays Charentais, often from Colombard.

More than half of the Colombard still cultivated in France by the end of the 1980s was in either cognac or, particularly, armagnac country, but there were still 1,700 ha in the Bordeaux region, particularly in the north west around BOURG and BLAYE, where much of it acts as a subordinate ingredient in dull, blended BORDEAUX Blanc. It is still planted to a limited extent in much of SOUTH WEST FRANCE.

The variety also reached a peak of popularity for cheap, commercial off-dry white in SOUTH AFRICA. Colombar, as it is known there, was still the country's second most important wine grape in the late 1990s, and, as in Australia, it provides usefully crisp blending material with Chenin Blanc and the much more fashionable Chardonnay.

Colombia, South American country with a TROPICAL climate and a relatively short history of viticulture. The main wine-grape zone is in the south east of the country in the upper Cauca valley. ISABELLA and Italia TABLE GRAPES are grown in the main but there are experimental plantings of Cabernet Sauvignon, Chardonnay, and other INTERNATIONAL VARIETIES. The bulk of production is wine-based aperitifs and fortified wines and brandies, but a subsidiary of Pedro Domecq is at the forefront of experimentation with dry table wines.

Colorino, rare, deep-coloured dark grape variety used traditionally in Tuscany. The late 1980s and early 1990s saw an upsurge in interest in Colorino as a sort of Tuscan version of PETIT VERDOT, capable of adding tannins and colour to firm up the structure of Sangiovese. Interesting early results are already being seen in both the CHIANTI and the VINO NOBILE DI MONTEPULCIANO zones.   D.T.

colour of wines. Wines are classified as red, white, or rosé but can vary widely in colour within these broad categories, sometimes with little obvious distinction between a light red and a dark rosé.

Red wines

Red wines, currently much favoured by FASHION, derive their colour from the natural organic red/blue ANTHOCYANIN pigments, of which there are varying concentrations in the skins of darker-skinned grapes. These concentrations depend on the VINE VARIETY, the RIPENESS of the grape, and the weather conditions of the VINTAGE year. The amount of anthocyanins leached into the resulting wine depends on many factors including BERRY SIZE,

homogeneity of berry ripeness, length and temperature of the MACERATION of skins and new wine, together with the extent to which techniques to encourage EXTRACTION are used. All these factors influence the intensity of colour in a young red wine.

The actual hue of a young red wine is influenced partly by the grape variety (Cabernet Sauvignon grape skins, for example, are blue-black, while those of Grenache are much more crimson), although much less than one might expect (see ANTHOCYANINS). A more important influence is the acidity of the grape juice. In general, the more acid the grape juice, the brighter the colour—although very high acid grapes may be unripe and deficient in available anthocyanins.

The anthocyanins as they occur in the grape are responsible for the colour of a red wine only in its very early life. In a red wine more than a few weeks old, the colour is due to a combination of pigments and tannins which have stable colours tending to brick red.

Red wines which undergo BARREL MATURATION also tend to have more stable colour than those which do not. During AGEING, the tannins and anthocyanins interact, fall out as sediment and deplete the wine of pigment.

The colour of a young red wine can vary from blackish purple (as in a vintage PORT, for example) through many hues of crimson to ruby. With age, red wines take on brick and then amber hues, lightening with time. The colour at the rim of a glassful of wine can give the most telling indication of the hue and therefore age of a wine, while looking straight down through a glassful of wine from above can clearly indicate the intensity of colour (see TASTING).

During the 1990s, wine-makers tended to make ever-deeper-coloured red wines. This trend was encouraged by the increasing importance of large comparative tastings in JUDGING wine. Because many (though by no means all) of the world's best red wines are deeply coloured (particularly those based on Cabernet Sauvignon and Syrah grapes, for example), and because EXTRACTION may be associated with depth of FLAVOUR, there was a tendency among wine judges to favour deeply coloured wines. This led to a considerable increase in the number of red wines which owe their deep colour to over-extraction and/or added colour.

See also RED-WINE-MAKING and RED WINES for

more information, including names for red wines in languages other than English.

White wines

Although red wines are red, white wines are not white. Very occasionally they are colourless, but they usually range from pale green, through straw, pale copper, and deep gold to amber.

The stems, skins, and pulp of the light-skinned grapes used for making white wines contain a large and complex mixture of phenolics similar to the red/blue-coloured anthocyanins except that they are not capable of the multiplicity of forms which result in pigment expression.

Different 'white' grape varieties contain a slightly different array of phenolics, which results in differently coloured wines. Palomino and Pinot Blanc, for example, are particularly prone to oxidation and browning, while Riesling has traces of non-phenolic compounds which can cause a greenish tinge to the basic yellow. Some white grape varieties contain leucoanthocyanidins, which under some circumstances can produce a pink tinge to the basic yellow. Some varieties used for white wines such as Gewürztraminer and Pinot Gris have greyish pink to purple skins and tend to result in deeply coloured wines with a strong pinkish yellow hue. (White wines may also be made from dark-skinned grape varieties using minimum skin contact.)

With age, small amounts of oxygen act on these phenolic compounds to brown them and apparently deepen a white wine's colour. With extreme BOTTLE AGEING of many decades, a very old white wine can be the same medium-intensity amber colour as a red wine of the same age.

Wines made from grapes affected by NOBLE ROT tend to have a particularly deep golden colour. Those which have been given extended SKIN CONTACT tend to brown relatively early, while young white wines subjected to BARREL FERMENTATION and LEES CONTACT tend to be markedly paler than those fermented in STAINLESS STEEL and then transferred to cask for barrel maturation because darker pigments are absorbed by the lees.

During the 1990s, white wines have in general become paler, as unintended oxidation becomes rarer, barrel fermentation has become more common, and barrel maturation has become more skilfully handled. See also WHITE-WINE-MAKING and WHITE WINES.

Rosé wines

These wines, which vary enormously in hue and intensity, owe their combination of pink colour and white-wine characteristics either to a very short skin contact with dark-skinned grapes, or, for some everyday wines and pink sparkling wines, to the BLENDING of red and white wines.

Wines that are pale bluish pink are likely to be the results of PROTECTIVE techniques, while those with an orange tinge may well have been exposed to some, possibly deliberate, oxidation. While a blindfold taster can in some circumstances find it difficult to distinguish between low-tannin red wines and fuller-bodied white wines, it can be almost impossible on the basis of taste alone to distinguish a rosé wine from a white one.

See also ROSÉ-WINE-MAKING, ROSÉ WINES, and AGEING.

Columbard is how the white variety COLOMBARD is occasionally spelt on labels.

Comité Interprofessionnel, body representing all interests concerned with the production of a certain wine and the French counterpart to the CONSORZIO of Italy and Spain's CONSEJO REGULADOR.

Commandaria, a dark, FORTIFIED dessert-wine speciality of the island of CYPRUS with a honeyed, raisiny flavour and alcohol content usually around 15 per cent, produced from partially raisined MAVRO and XYNISTERI grapes.

Though of limited commercial importance, even within Cyprus, Commandaria is one of the world's classic wines, and may well have the longest continuous history of any wine still in production.

Commonwealth of Independent States. See CIS.

commune, French for village or parish.

competitions, wine. Well-run reputable wine competitions can play an important part in the sales success of a wine producer, which is why some wine labels are adorned with MEDALS and the like, and some wine merchants' lists are dotted with lists of awards. Care should be taken when studying these claims that the competition was a recent and respected one, and that the successful wine was exactly the same bottling as the one being offered. One of the most ambitious and successful international wine competitions is the International Wine Challenge held every May in London and now in several other cities. It attracts many thousands of entries from around the world and most of its gold-medal-winning wines are of genuinely superior quality. It should be remembered, however, that few of the world's most revered producers enter such competitions, and certainly none of those who produce very limited quantities. It is difficult to imagine there will ever be a wine competition which will identify the best, rather than the best of those who have something to gain by entering.

For more details of how competitions work, see JUDGING WINE.

computers. See INFORMATION TECHNOLOGY.

Conca de Barberá, small but promising wine zone in Spanish CATALONIA, sandwiched in between PENEDÈS, COSTERS DEL SEGRE, and TARRAGONA. At around 500 m/1,600 ft above sea level, this DO experiences cold winters, and hot summer days are tempered by cool winds from the sea. Miguel TORRES of Penedès recognized the grape-growing potential of the LIMESTONE country around the Castillo de Milmanda and some of his best CABERNET, PINOT NOIR, and CHARDONNAY grapes are sourced in the zone. Some interesting rosé wines are also made from the local TREPAT vine.

Most of Conca de Barberá's grapes are used to produce CAVA, however, and consequently few wines carry the name of the DO on the label.   R.J.M. & V. de la S.

concentrated grape must. See GRAPE CONCENTRATE.

concentration, umbrella term for any wine-making operation which serves to remove volatile substances, mainly water, from grape juice or wine. Its most common application has been in the production of GRAPE CONCENTRATE but a range of more sophisticated concentration techniques is increasingly used on grapes and musts, often only on a certain portion of the total must, in order to produce more concentrated wines, notably in some of BORDEAUX's grandest cellars.

Freeze concentration, using differences in freezing points, is used to make a range of sweet wines of varying qualities. The EISWEIN of Germany and Austria and the ICE WINE of Canada and elsewhere is made by picking frozen grapes from the vine, crushing them, and filtering the juice without allowing the

mixture to thaw so that water is removed in the form of ice. The result is grape juice with a lower concentration of water, but a higher concentration of sugars, acids, and other soluble solids.

Natural freezing on the vine is replicated by producers in such different regions as SAUTERNES and NEW ZEALAND. Freshly picked grapes may be frozen in special chillers prior to crushing and filtering. This technique is often practised selectively, not just for sweet white wines, but also on grapes destined to make dry white wines, not all of which are fully ripe.

Differences in molecular size have long been used to purify substances other than wine. The development of physically strong plastic membrane filters with very small pores of nearly uniform size means that the technique known as reverse osmosis can be applied to concentrating wine.

One final method of concentrating grape must is also the oldest: desiccation. See DRIED-GRAPE WINES.

Because in general these methods remove only water from the grapes or must, all other components are concentrated. An increased concentration of fermentable sugars results in a wine with a higher ALCOHOLIC STRENGTH. Increased concentrations of PHENOLICS in many cases result in wines with more BODY, potential for AGEING, and possibly more flavour. Increased ACIDITY, however, can result in wines that are aggressively tart, especially in less ripe years or in cooler wine regions. In some cases, particularly in cooler areas, musts which have been concentrated may have to be further subjected to DEACIDIFICATION.

Concord, the most important vine variety grown in the eastern United States, notably in NEW YORK state. The majority of its genes clearly belong to the American vine species *Vitis* LABRUSCA. The pronounced FOXY flavour of its juice makes its wine an acquired taste for those raised on the produce of VINIFERA vines. It is particularly important for the production of GRAPE JUICE and grape jelly, but it produces a wide range of wines, often with some considerable RESIDUAL SUGAR. Viticulturally, the vine is extremely well adapted to the low temperatures of New York and is both productive and vigorous. Some Concord has also been grown in Brazil.

Condado de Huelva, Spanish denominated wine zone in ANDALUCÍA, close to the city of

Huelva between the JEREZ region and the Portuguese border. Nowadays few of its wines, which have typically been FORTIFIED and made in the image of its neighbour SHERRY, are exported. The principal grape is the rather neutral ZALEMA along with a little PALOMINO. Three styles of wine are made. Condado Pálido is a pale, dry fortified wine matured in a SOLERA and resembling a coarse fino sherry. Condado Viejo is a RANCIO style of wine aged in a solera and resembling a somewhat rustic oloroso sherry. Vino Joven, on the other hand, is an unfortified dry table wine which now accounts for about half the regional production, and which is often somewhat fruitier than similar white wines produced in the Jerez area.

R.J.M. & V. de la S.

Condrieu, distinctive and fashionable white wine made in minuscule quantities in the northern RHÔNE. It is made exclusively from the VIOGNIER grape, whose successful wines manage the unusual combination of a pronounced yet elusive perfume with substantial BODY. There was a wave of Viognier planting all over southern France and California in the 1980s and early 1990s, often on the strength of the grower's enthusiasm for Condrieu.

This small appellation encompasses seven right-bank communes just south of the red-wine appellation CÔTE-RÔTIE where the river turns a bend and the best vineyards are exposed to the south.

Since the 1970s, Condrieu's fame and price have risen steadily, and an increasing number of growers have been prepared to reconstruct small patches of vineyard on the steep, often granitic slopes. Average yields here are notoriously low (and very much lower than for Viognier planted further south), which is one reason why Condrieu is relatively expensive for a wine that is best drunk young, at between two and four years in general.

At one time Condrieu was a sweet or medium-sweet wine but almost all is made dry today. Vinification standards are extremely variable, particularly since some vignerons are relative newcomers (even if their grandfathers were experienced in making Condrieu). Three of the most experienced wine-makers are Multier at Ch du Rozay, Georges Vernay, and GUIGAL, who now has a single-vineyard bottling La Doriane, but they have been definitively challenged by the likes of Cuilleron, Perret, and Villard. Policies on such fundamentals as the desirability of MALOLACTIC FERMENTATION and use of OAK vary considerably in Condrieu.

In 1990, there were 40 ha/100 acres of vineyard old enough to produce AC wine, but the total area under vine grew so rapidly in the early 1990s that bottlings from Viognier vines too young for full appellation status were almost as common as Condrieu itself. By 1996, more than 100 ha qualified for the Condrieu AC. CH-GRILLET, France's other all-Viognier appellation, is an enclave within the Condrieu zone.

confréries, French 'brotherhoods' or associations, dedicated in particular to advancing the cause of various foods and drinks throughout France. More than 150 of them, most of them founded in the second half of the 20th century, are devoted to such various products as macaroons, jams, olives, and local shellfish. A high proportion of them, almost half, are based on specific wines and other alcoholic drinks. One of the most famous is the Confrérie des Chevaliers de Tastevin in Burgundy (see CLOS DE VOUGEOT). The Commanderie du Bontemps du MÉDOC et des Graves in Bordeaux is also well known and even markets its own Cuvée de la Commanderie du Bontemps Médoc. These confréries are devoted to an annual programme of pageantry, feasting, and the *intronisation* (enthronement) of honorary converts to the cause. The *intronisation* process of the Commanderie du Bontemps du Médoc et des Graves involves public, but assisted, BLIND TASTING.

connoisseurship of wine is an art in search of a less emotive name. The word **connoisseur** in English, and its counterpart *connaisseur* in French, conjures up a frightening vision of an elderly male so steeped in wine, wine knowledge, and wine prejudices as to be completely unapproachable. Much more attractive and widely acceptable terms are those which convey not just knowledge but an element of relish such as wine lover, wine enthusiast, or the common and attractive French term *amateur du vin*. None of these terms, incidentally, has any connotation of gender.

Whatever the drawbacks of the term, connoisseurship or wine expertise is an art that can give pleasure, and involves less an arid grasp of the precise ENCÉPAGEMENT of each vineyard and fermentation regimes for each vintage than an intelligent appreciation of how wines are likely to taste in a given environment, at a certain stage in their evolution, before or after other wines, and, importantly, with different foods. This is what consumers rather than producers are for. Experience can contribute to connoisseurship, but only if the consumer tastes with attention and an open mind. Some newcomers to wine have an instinctive grasp of connoisseurship.

See wine TASTING, AGEING, SERVING, and FOOD AND WINE MATCHING. A connoisseur is not necessarily a wine BORE.

Consejo Regulador, Spanish term meaning 'regulating council'. Spanish wine law is administered through a network of Consejos Reguladores representing each and every DO. They comprise vine-growers, wine producers, and merchants who between them decide on the ground rules for their region.

Consorzio, Italian word for a consortium or association, notably of wine-growers dedicated to regulation. The most famous in Italian wine is the **Consorzio Chianti Classico**, which has been instrumental in promoting and defending the wines of CHIANTI CLASSICO. Its counterpart in France is the COMITÉ INTER-PROFESSIONNEL; in Spain the CONSEJO REGU-LADOR.

Constantia, legendary, aromatic, concentrated 18th-century dessert wines from the Cape, SOUTH AFRICA, then a Dutch colony. Their fame was never matched by any other New World wines and at their height they commanded more prestige, more fabulous prices, and enjoyed more crowned patronage than the most celebrated wines of Europe (with the possible exception of Hungarian TOKAJI). Constantia was even ordered by Napoleon from his exile on St Helena.

The sweet wines of Constantia, both red and white, the latter the more expensive, were made principally from MUSCAT BLANC À PETITS GRAINS and its dark-berried mutation, probably including the lesser MUSCAT OF ALEX-ANDRIA together with the dark red PONTAC. Analyses of recently opened bottles (still perfumed with a tang of citrus and smoky richness) show they were unfortified although high in alcohol, apparently confirming records that the grapes were left on the vines long after ripeness to achieve shrivelled, but not BOTRYTIZED, concentration (see DRIED-GRAPE WINES for more details of the technique). Other stories suggest the wines may have been fortified by shippers for protection on the long,

rough, and hot journey across the equator to Europe.

Groot Constantia has been a government wine estate since 1885. In 1975, management of its activities passed into the hands of a control board and in 1993 into a trust. In recent times, Constantia has made sound, unexciting conventional wines. A neighbouring privately owned estate, Klein (Little) Constantia, a subdivision of the original farm, has been first to take up the challenge to re-enact the legend. It replanted vineyards of Muscat of Frontignan in 1980 and now produces naturally high-alcohol white dessert wines known as Vin de Constance (also without botrytis—in the manner of the old Constantia) to local and international acclaim.   J.P. & M.F.

consultants are used with increasing frequency in wine production, selling, and occasionally consumption. Consultant VITI-CULTURISTS are particularly useful since they can work for much of the year and those who operate on an international scale can impart knowledge gleaned from a wide variety of different vine-growing environments. They are commonly used to introduce new CANOPY MANAGEMENT techniques to established vineyards, or to advise, for example, on suitable ROOTSTOCKS for new vineyards. Like viticulturists, the more energetic consultant OEN-OLOGISTS can use their expertise in both hemispheres, although their work is necessarily limited by the timing of HARVEST. One of the first internationally famous consultant oenologists was Professor Émile Peynaud. Today his best-known successor from Bordeaux is Michel ROLLAND, although there are now scores and probably hundreds of wine-makers who travel the globe and offer, if not consultancy, then hard graft (see FLYING WINE-MAKERS). Many restaurateurs and hoteliers, most airlines, and even some wine retailers employ consultants in their wine selection. Some well-heeled COLLECTORS also take advice from consultants.

consumption of wine throughout the world has fallen from a peak of around 285 million hl/7,500 million gal a year in the years 1976–80 to just over 220 million hl/5,800 million gal a year in the late 1990s, having increased very slightly each year since 1994. Total world PRO-DUCTION is considerably more than this, resulting in a serious global wine surplus that is most acute in Europe, the most important producer and consumer of wine. The main reason for the drop in global consumption has been sharp falls in average wine consumption by the world's two most important producers and consumers, France and Italy. The generation of Frenchmen and Italians who routinely consumed a litre of wine a day has been dying off.

The countries with the highest per capita wine consumption in the late 1990s were still mainly the most important wine producers: France, Italy, Portugal, Luxembourg, Argentina, Switzerland, Spain, Austria, Romania, Greece, Hungary, and, the non-producing country with the highest wine consumption, Denmark. Of these, the only countries in which per capita wine consumption rose during the 1990s were Portugal, Romania, and Denmark. Of anglophone countries, the most enthusiastic wine consumers are Australia (more than 18 l, or 24 bottles per capita a year), followed by New Zealand, Ireland, United Kingdom, South Africa, Canada, and then the USA (7.25 l, or nearly 10 bottles).

National annual per capita wine consumption figures in litres are to be found in Appendix 2. See HEALTH for official medical advice on safe personal consumption levels of alcoholic drinks.

containers for wine are used at four main stages in a wine's life: during the FERMENTATION that creates it, during its MATURATION, for its TRANSPORT, and for SERVING it. Moreover, while wine containers have changed throughout history, they have also varied through space, with each wine-making region becoming characterized by vessels of different dimensions.

Fermentation vessels may be either open topped or closed, and may have a capacity as big as 300 hl. Wines are matured prior to bottling in closed containers (to avoid OXIDATION), either in tanks made from materials such as stainless steel or concrete, or in some form of wooden container, from small, new oak barrels to large, old casks, or even in some cases in ceramic tinajas or glass bonbonnes. Wine may be blended in even larger tanks holding up to 15,000 hl. Wine is transported either in bulk, usually in food-grade 250-hl stainless-steel tankers, or, increasingly, in bottle, its final container before the wine GLASS, possibly after spending a short time in a DECANTER. Newer containers used in packaging wine include BOXES, CARTONS, and CANS.

When transport containers are used for shipping wine in bottle, care is taken by some fine-wine merchants and some fine-wine producers that the wine is shipped only in temperature-controlled containers, and sometimes only during cooler times of year. This is particularly important for wines which have undergone a minimum of FILTRATION. See TRANSPORT.

contaminants, potentially harmful substances found in wine, either as a result of air or water pollution, vineyard treatment RESIDUES, poor winery HYGIENE, ignorance, or ADULTERATION AND FRAUD.

Of these, ignorance is possibly the most forgivable reason for contamination since the scope of what is regarded as, and can be measured as, a contaminant grows wider with the rapid progress of science and measuring techniques. LEAD, for example, which was deliberately added to wines by the Romans, is now known to be a serious neural toxin. Carbamates, on the other hand, have been regarded as contaminants only since the late 1980s. And it was only in the 1990s that the contaminating effect of some apparently innocuous treatments of wooden beams in some wine-making establishments became apparent.

Nowadays, contamination as a result of poor winery hygiene is extremely rare. Pollution is difficult to guard against. Wine producers are increasingly wary of some agrochemicals, however. Orthene, a fungicide used widely in the early 1980s, with no ill effects apparent during wine-making, produced a range of wines with an extremely unpleasant smell after several years' BOTTLE AGE. And American authorities, in particular, have regularly applied stringent tests for traces of recently suspected contaminants to imported wines.

The wine trade, like every other commercial activity, has its villains, but they are increasingly rare. Fortunately, very few of the substances which the least scrupulous producers are tempted to add illegally to wine are harmful—with the notable and horrifying exception of lethal doses of methanol added to one Italian producer's wines in 1987.

See also ADULTERATION, which sometimes involves the deliberate addition of contaminants.

continental climate is one with a high degree of **continentality**, defined for any place as the difference between the average mean temperature of its hottest month and that of its coldest month. Climates with a wide annual range are called continental; those with a narrow range, MARITIME.

Controliran, Bulgarian answer to France's APPELLATION CONTRÔLÉE category of superior wines. See BULGARIA.

controlled appellations, a method of LABELLING wine and designating quality that is modelled on France's APPELLATION CONTRÔLÉE system. It embraces geographical DELIMITATION and is the principle on which QUALITY WINE schemes such as the DOC of Italy and Portugal, the DO of Spain, and the AVA system of the United States are based. France has more than 400, Italy more than 200, Greece about 60, and Spain and Portugal an ever-lengthening list. Countries such as BULGARIA and HUNGARY have devised similar schemes, as have the UNITED KINGDOM and, most recently, BELGIUM. Modern Greece has even adopted the French phrases used by the appellation contrôlée system in France for designating its better-quality wines. See Appendix 1 for a complete list of controlled appellations for which particular grape varieties are specified, with their permitted grapes.

cooking with wine. Good wine used in the kitchen adds depth and dimension to a dish that no other ingredient can.

Wine is an essential ingredient in many dishes and can be used in every stage of cooking from the preparation and tenderizing of meat to providing the final, often sweet, finish to a dessert. It is all the more curious, therefore, that so little research has been done into exactly what happens to wine during cooking, particularly as a result of the application of heat. Since the boiling point of alcohol is 78 °C/172 °F, considerably lower than that of water, however, it is reasonable to suppose that any wine used in cooking becomes progressively less alcoholic if heated to above 78 °C for any length of time. As a sauce is 'reduced' with wine, the other components in the wine such as any RESIDUAL SUGAR and, especially, its ACIDITY become even more marked. This is presumably why over-reduced sauces can taste so acid, and why they can have an almost caramelized appearance and taste. Other uses for wine in cooking do not involve changing the wine's composition by heating.

There is much debate about the necessary quality of **cooking wine**, some regarding the saucepan as the ideal repository for any wine considered too nasty to drink, others insisting that only the finest wine will do. Wine with an unpleasant flavour will not lose that flavour in the kitchen (although some connoisseurs believe that a good-quality wine that is CORKED will lose that taint if heated sufficiently). On the other hand, the complex BALANCE and full range of volatile FLAVOUR COMPOUNDS of a great wine will not survive the application of any fierce heat.

The following are some of the most common ways in which wine is used in the kitchen.

Deglazing: pouring wine (or another liquid such as stock) into a pan in which something has been roasted or sautéed in order to dissolve the remnants of that operation in the liquid to make a sauce. Wine adds body and depth to the sauce.

Marinade: a method of imparting extra flavour, principally to meat and game, via a mixture based on carrots, shallots, onions, pepper, salt, vinegar, garlic, and red or white wine which takes the form of cooked and uncooked marinades. Instant marinades, using brandy or MADEIRA, are used for the ingredients of pâtés and terrines. After the meat has been removed, the marinade may be used for deglazing or for a more complicated sauce.

Stocks: wine is often used instead of, or as well as, water, to provide the essential base for soups and sauces. Red wine is used in game stock, white wine in chicken and fish stocks. (Wine features in many risotto recipes.)

Court-bouillon: a method of cooking fish, shellfish, or white meat in which herbs and spices are infused in white wine and water in which the food is subsequently poached.

Sauces: of the many which form the basis of classic French cuisine, bordelaise comprises red wine and shallots; périgueux uses madeira, veal stock, and truffles; sauce Robert is white wine, onion, and mustard; and ravigote is made with white wine and vinegar.

Stews and casseroles: wine, preferably from the same area as the dish, is an integral part of *coq au vin*, daube of beef, fish stew, beef bourguignonne, and many more classics of *la cuisine bourgeoise*. Acidic wine will detract rather than enhance.

Desserts: wine has a surprisingly wide range of applications for sweet foods and patisserie. Red wine is used for poaching pears and macerating strawberries (a speciality of Bordeaux) while dessert wines such as MARSALA and

SHERRY are used in, respectively, zabaglione and English trifle. In Italy, strong, usually sweet wines, typically VIN SANTO, are served with dry biscuits which are moistened in them.

J.Ro. & M.P.L.

coolers. There are two very different types of **wine cooler**. One is a blend of usually rather ordinary wine with fruit juice, water, carbon dioxide, and/or flavourings to produce a LOW-ALCOHOL drink designed to cool the drinker, and introduce him or her gently to the taste of wine. These products, only distantly related to wine itself, enjoyed a vogue in the mid 1980s, particularly in the United States.

The other sort of wine cooler was designed to cool the wine in the days before domestic refrigeration.

Coonawarra, historic, if much-disputed, wine region in South Australia's Limestone Coast zone and the most popularly revered wine region in AUSTRALIA for Cabernet Sauvignon, grown on its famous strip of TERRA ROSSA soil. See SOUTH AUSTRALIA.

co-operatives, ventures owned jointly by a number of different members, are extremely important as wine producers and have the advantage for their members of pooling wine-making and marketing costs. Collectively, they usually have access to a broad range of financial advantages, including subsidies in the European Union, over individual producers. In most countries, they also enjoy the commercial advantage of being able to describe their wines as bottled by the producer, using such reassuring phrases as MIS EN BOUTEILLE *à la propriété* and ERZEUGERABFÜLLUNG more usually associated with much smaller, individually managed wine enterprises. The better co-operatives are becoming increasingly skilled not just at wine-making but also at marketing specific bottlings designed to look and taste every bit as distinctive as the individually produced competition. The worst co-operatives play almost exclusively with subsidies and politics. Co-operatives are at their strongest in areas where wine's selling price is relatively low and where the average size of individual holdings is low, although co-operatives are quite significant in CHAMPAGNE and there are several in the MÉDOC, for example.

France

Since 1975, more than half of the wine produced in France has been produced by co-operatives, or *caves coopératives*, and the total area of

vineyard owned by their members is also more than half the French total. The total number of French co-operatives is declining but they are a particularly strong force in the LANGUEDOC-ROUSSILLON, the greater RHÔNE valley, PROVENCE, and CORSICA, where *la cave* can dominate local economic life.

The co-operatives produce an impressive quantity of APPELLATION CONTRÔLÉE wine, nearly half of the country's total, and those which have established a reputation for particularly sound AC wines outside their own region include La Chablisienne of CHABLIS, the co-operative at Tain l'HERMITAGE, and a number of ALSACE co-operatives, notably that of Turckheim. The co-operatives' speciality, however, is VINS DE PAYS. Their combined output of these intensely local wines represents three-quarters of the national total, and scores of co-operatives in the Languedoc-Roussillon have established a reputation abroad for their vins de pays, as has the Plaimont co-operative organization in GASCONY and the Haut POITOU co-operative in west central France.

Germany

In GERMANY, the co-operative (which may be called a *Winzergenossenschaft*, *Winzerverein*, *Winzervereinigung*, and in Württemberg *Weingärtnergenossenschaft*) has played an increasingly significant role since 1869, when the first German wine co-operative was formally established in the AHR.

Two in every three German vine-growers today belong to the local co-operative, although their vineyards are often a small, part-time activity. Many of the 13 wine regions of Germany have a central co-operative cellar, or ZENTRALKELLEREI, which is fed grapes, wine, or must by more localized co-operatives. In 1997, there were more than 280 co-operatives in Germany, of which 165 made wine on the premises.

The co-operative movement is particularly strong, and particularly successful, in the most southerly region of BADEN, where about 85 per cent of all wine produced is sold under the auspices of the giant central Badischer Winzerkeller at Breisach. Co-operatives are also extremely important in the WÜRTTEMBERG region, and in Germany's four smallest regions, SAALE-UNSTRUT, AHR, HESSISCHE BERGSTRASSE, and SACHSEN.

Italy

In Italy, the *cantina sociale* is no less important,

particularly in the south, where EU policies can be interpreted most profitably and co-operatives dominate production. One of the most respected Italian co-operatives is in the far north west, however, the Produttori del BAR-BARESCO, which has a direct counterpart in the Terre del BAROLO. The influence of the *cantina sociale*, or *Kellereigenossenschaft* in German, is particularly strong in TRENTINO-ALTO ADIGE, where Cavit is perhaps the most exported name.

The co-operative best known outside Italy is Riunite of EMILIA-ROMAGNA, famous in the early 1980s for engulfing the United States, and other markets, in a tidal wave of LAMBRUSCO. Tollo co-operative is the star of ABRUZZO and TUSCANY's co-operatives tend to be well focused on quality, with the largest being that at Pitigliano in the MAREMMA. The Copertino co-operative in APULIA makes a good job of its eponymous red. The islands SARDINIA and SICILY are dominated by co-operatives, of which Settesoli in Sicily and several ambitious Sardinian co-operatives export with zeal.

Spain and Portugal

As in Italy, co-operatives are extremely important in Iberia, where grapes are so often grown alongside other crops. It has been estimated that more than 60 per cent of each vintage is delivered to one of Spain's 1,000 wine co-operatives or Portugal's 300. One of the earliest wine co-operatives was in Olite in NAVARRE, where the movement is particularly powerful and where it can absorb as much as 90 per cent of grape production, although here, as elsewhere, links are being forged with individual producers to increase overall quality and technical expertise.

Co-operatives are important in most Spanish wine regions (although in famed RIOJA they process only about 40 per cent of the region's grapes). In the vineyard vastness of La MANCHA, there are about 100 co-operatives of very varied quality, while YECLA and JUMILLA have export-minded co-operatives whose level of modern equipment and expertise is considerably above average. In the fortified wine regions of JEREZ, much of the rest of ANDALUCÍA, and the DOURO, co-operatives are less important than the long-standing links between vine-growers and individual wine producers. The 20th-century Portuguese table-wine industry was revolutionized by the government's formation of co-operatives, however not always for the better (see DÃO).

Rest of the world

Practically wherever wine is made, co-operatives thrive, although the movement is not particularly strong in the UNITED STATES and has had its own variants in eastern Europe. Co-operatives have played a particularly important role in the development of the wine industry in SOUTH AFRICA (see also KWV).

Copertino, DOC for robust red wine made mainly from NEGROAMARO grapes in south-east Italy. See APULIA. The co-operative winery of Copertino, directed by Severino Garofano, southern Italy's leading consulting OEN-OLOGIST, has attracted attention for its well-made wines at extremely reasonable prices.

copita, special glass in which SHERRY is customarily served in Spain. It is designed to maximize the AROMA and larger sizes can be used as a glass for general wine TASTING.

Corbières, the most important appellation in the LANGUEDOC region of southern France producing some excitingly dense, herby red wines, a small amount of rosé, and a little increasingly well-made white wine. The terrain here in the Pyrenean foothills is extremely varied. In recognition of this, the appellation has been subdivided into 11 so-called TERROIRS, although not without a certain amount of local dissent. The basic distinctions in this southernmost corner of the Aude *département* are between coastal zones influenced by the Mediterranean, the northern strip on the Montagne d'Alaric (some of which has more in common with MINERVOIS), the westernmost vineyards, which are cooled both by Atlantic influence and by ALTITUDE, and the rugged, mountainous terrain in the south and centre in which the FITOU appellation forms two enclaves. One of the most admired terroirs is that of Boutenac, which has particularly poor soils on a limestone base.

Carignan is still the dominant variety, representing well over half of all vines planted. The appellation regulations specified local maxima of between 50 and 70 per cent depending on location and proportion of Syrah grown, and these proportions were expected to decrease further, to the dismay of those who value the spice and concentration of wine from old vines. Warmer parts of Corbières offer good possibilities to ripen Mourvèdre on a regular basis. Plantings of Cinsaut, useful along with Syrah for rosé, are more limited here than in neighbouring Minervois. Grenache, its relative

Lladoner Pelut, Picpoul Noir, Terret, and the local white grape varieties are also allowed in red and rosé Corbières.

White Corbières, a rare but often refreshing dry wine, is made principally from Bourboulenc, Maccabéo, and Grenache Blanc but Clairette, Muscat (sometimes vinified alone to make a dry wine), Picpoul, Terret, Marsanne, Roussanne, and Rolle or Vermentino are all also allowed, providing an interesting aromatic palette for the increasing number of producers prepared to experiment with superior white-wine-making.

CO-OPERATIVES, some of them particularly quality conscious, dominate the region, but there are many seriously ambitious individual estates too, including Domaine du Grand Crès, Ch Haut-Gléon, Ch de Lastours, Ch Mansenoble, Domaine du Roque-Sestière, Ch Rouqette-sur-Mer, and Ch Voulte-Gasparets.

Cordier, a major owner of estates and one of the largest NÉGOCIANTS in BORDEAUX. In 1985, the entire company was sold to a large French merchant bank, and in 1997, the Val d'Orbieu-Listel group acquired a majority shareholding in the négociant side of the business. Cordier's principal Bordeaux properties are now Ch Lafaurie-Peyraguey in SAUTERNES, Ch Meyney in the MÉDOC, and Clos des Jacobins in ST-ÉMILION. Over half of Établissement Cordier's business is export. Cordier make two exceptional first-growth Sauternes: Lafaurie-Peyraguey has been an outstanding wine since the early 1980s, as has Sigalas-Rabaud since 1995, when Cordier took over its management and wine-making.   M.W.E.S.

corkage, charge customarily levied in a restaurant for each bottle of wine brought in and consumed on the premises rather than bought from the restaurant's own selection (see also BYO). There is considerable variation in the amount charged, and the grace with which the practice is accepted.

corked, pejorative tasting term for a wine spoiled by a cork stopper contaminated with CORK TAINT. This is one of the most serious wine FAULTS as in most cases it irrevocably imbues the wine with such a powerfully offputting smell that it cannot be drunk with any enjoyment (although it can be used for the more vigorous methods of COOKING WITH WINE). The unpleasantly, almost mould-like, chemical smell is occasionally present in smaller doses that may initially be noticed only by noses par-

ticularly sensitive to it, but the odour usually intensifies with aeration. A wine spoiled by cork taint may also be described as **corky** and the condition is known as **corkiness**.

At the end of the 1980s, estimates of the proportion of corked wine bottles varied from less than 2 to more than 5 per cent of the total. This soured relations between the wine industry and the cork industry and led to a marked increase in the use of alternative STOPPERS, particularly cylinders known commonly, if inaccurately, as 'plastic corks'.

It is commonly, but erroneously, believed that a wine with small fragments of cork floating in it is 'corked'. This may be a SERVING fault but is certainly not a wine fault.

corks, wine bottle stoppers, without which the appreciation of fine wine, and in particular BOTTLE AGEING, might never have evolved. Cork's unique combination of qualities have made it by far the most popular stopper for wine, but in the late 20th century the science of wine production bounded ahead of the science of cork production, to the detriment of relations between the two industries (see CORKED wine).

Clues from the cork

In general, the narrower and more misshapen a cork extracted from a bottle, the longer it has been there. This is a particularly useful clue to the likely age of a non-vintage sparkling wine, or at least to the time that has elapsed since DISGORGEMENT. It can also provide a clue to the likely age of any other non-vintage wine, or fine wine which has lost its label or, perhaps in the case of vintage PORT, never had one (although see also RECORKING).

Most corks are branded with the code of the cork producer. Most fine-wine corks are emblazoned with the name of the wine producer (if not the wine itself) and, often, the vintage. Different countries adopt different conventions. Italian corks, which fit particularly tightly into their narrow bottle-necks, are often marked with a two-letter regional code (UD for Udine on many FRIULI wine corks, for example). Most British wine bottlers brand their corks with a W followed by their own numerical code. The regular French message is simply MIS EN BOUTEILLE à la propriété.

A short agglomerate cork suggests that the bottler had little regard for the ageing ability of this wine, while a particularly long cork is indicative at least of ambition or optimism.

New World bottlers seem to favour smoother corks with more obvious cork coatings than their Old World counterparts.

If a cork has crystals on the end that has been in contact with the wine (white in the case of a white wine and dyed dark red by a red wine), these are harmless TARTRATES. If a cork seems damp or mouldy at either end, this is not necessarily a sign of any wine fault. Some wine waiters are taught to smell the cork and present it to the customer as an essential part of wine SERVICE, but the state of a cork is no sure guide to the state of the wine it stoppered.

For alternatives to corks, including so-called plastic corks, see STOPPERS.

corkscrews, wide range of devices for extracting CORKS from the necks of wine BOTTLES. Despite the many hundreds of inventions since the middle of the 18th century, no corkscrew has been accepted as the perfect instrument. In particular, no corkscrew has yet been shown to be infallible with old PORT corks so PORT TONGS are sometimes employed instead.

The variety of corkscrews available on the market today may easily confuse the wine drinker who just needs to open bottles with speed and efficiency. Corkscrews with poorly finished or blunt worms should be rejected and the two-armed Italian examples are best avoided as they usually have a solid core to the worm which tends to destroy the cork of an aged bordeaux or port rather than extract it; not surprisingly, such corkscrews are better adapted to the tightly compressed, almost wooden, corks found in bottles of Italian wine. The so-called waiter's friend, the folding lever, can have a well-formed helix but there is a danger of breaking the bottle rim during extraction unless the knack of applying the correct leverage has been acquired.

The most reliable worm is an open, smooth helix or spiral at least 5.7 cm/2.2 in long. This may be fitted with a simple wooden T-piece handle or given useful mechanical advantage by being, for example, coated with teflon and built into a modern high-tensile plastic frame. The American 'Screwpull' was the first of these efficient mechanisms to be marketed and was followed by modifications of the same theme from Holland and elsewhere.   B.M.W.

cork taint. CORKS are normally bleached in a strong chlorine solution prior to washing and drying. Research work in the 1980s demonstrated that this chlorine treatment could inadvertently produce trichloroanisole or TCA, which can be smelt at concentrations of just a few parts per trillion. TCA appears to be at least part of the explanation for CORKED wines. The cork industry is therefore replacing chlorine bleaching with other processes.

This may not provide a complete solution to the problem, however, as moulds growing on unbleached corks can still generate a corked aroma and taste and corks can be recontaminated with mould spores at any point during the preparation process. Corks can furthermore pick up off-flavours that migrate from other surfaces, even the floorboards in shipping containers, or as a result of poor storage conditions at the winery.

A new method of disinfecting corks with ozone seems to avoid cork taint.   T.H.L.

Cornas, red-wine appellation in the northern RHÔNE with the potential to provide dense, long-lived serious challengers to HERMITAGE on the opposite bank to the north. The appellation experienced a revival of interest in the late 1980s with the arrival of ambitious newcomers prepared to re-establish the TERRACES needed for high-quality vineyards.

Many of the best slopes such as Les Renards in the south are well sheltered from the cold north winds and enjoy some of the best positions in the northern Rhône. It is not surprising therefore that Cornas, which is made exclusively from SYRAH, can be one of the valley's finest wines. What is surprising is that so many of the wines are still made for mandatory extended BOTTLE AGEING. For those who can afford the time, Cornas can provide some of the most satisfying red-wine drinking, and offers a much more uniform and dependable quality level than the elastic ST-JOSEPH appellation to the immediate north.

Corse is the French, and therefore Corsican, name for CORSICA.

Corsica, mountainous Mediterranean island under French jurisdiction—although much closer to Italy than to France—whose wines are improving in quality. Corsica produces many different types and styles of wine: red, white, rosé; still, sparkling; dry, sweet; APPELLATION CONTRÔLÉE, VIN DE PAYS, and VIN DE TABLE. The great majority of these are of relatively ordinary quality and are sold only on the island. Its most exported product is its single vin de pays, Vin de Pays de l'île de Beauté.

Almost 70 per cent of all Corsican wine is made by CO-OPERATIVES, which, like some of the smaller wineries, have taken advantage of European Union grants available for the installation of modern equipment to make cool-fermented and clean-tasting whites and rosés. Red-wine-making is relatively traditional. The use of OAK was still extremely limited in the mid 1990s.

Vine varieties

While CINSAUT, CARIGNAN, GRENACHE, and the particularly undistinguished ALICANTE BOUSCHET had declined to only 27 per cent of the total by 1995, indigenous varieties such as NIELLUCCIO and VERMENTINO had increased their respective shares of the island's vineyard to 22 and 10 per cent. INTERNATIONAL VARIETIES increased to 20 per cent in 1996. A host of more traditional Corsican varieties exist but few are planted in any significant quantity.

Nielluccio is the most widely planted (even if its origins are probably Italian rather than Corsican), particularly in the north of the island, where it thrives on the chalky clay soils of Patrimonio. Nielluccio may be vinified as either a rosé or, if well vinified, an intensely coloured red with good, structured tannins and a balanced acidity. There is only about a third as much SCIACARELLO, which is unique to Corsica, where it is most successful on the granitic south-west coast between Ajaccio and Sartène, producing relatively crisp, peppery reds and rosés, light in colour but high in alcohol. It is often blended with Nielluccio or Grenache. The only significant white native grape variety is also the best travelled. Vermentino, also known as Malvoisie on Corsica, and as Rolle by the host of growers planting it all over the south of France, is grown all over the island but performs best in the far north. It produces wines ranging from a pale, crisp version to a full-bodied golden wine with a ripe fruit flavour, depending on when it is picked. Although many of the wines are dry, sweet Vermentino wines are also produced. Codivarta, a white grape grown on the Cap Corse, is the only other uniquely Corsican variety.

The wines produced

Rosé is as important in Corsica as it is in its nearest mainland wine region PROVENCE, representing about 30 per cent of total production. White wine accounts for an increasing proportion of all wine produced but it is still only about 10 per cent.

There has been a dramatic drop in the amount of basic TABLE WINE produced, while the proportion of wine which qualified as VIN DE PAYS de l'île de Beauté had reached 43 per cent by 1996 and the proportion of AC wines had doubled to 24 per cent.

Nine different appellations exist: Patrimonio, Ajaccio, Muscat de Cap Corse, Vin de Corse (Corsican wine), and Vin de Corse followed by either Coteaux du Cap Corse, Calvi, Sartène, Figari, or Porto Vecchio.

Patrimonio Patrimonio was the first region in Corsica to gain AC status, in 1968. Red, rosé, and white wines are produced and YIELDS are restricted to 50 hl/ha (2.8 tons/acre). In the past, the wines of Patrimonio often included a mix of different imported grape varieties, notably Grenache, but from the year 2000, Nielluccio must account for 95 per cent of the blend in red wines and Vermentino for 100 per cent in the white. This has caused considerable controversy amongst the growers. Clos de Bernardi, one of the oldest estates reputed for its red, is situated in Patrimonio. Other growers such as Orenga de Gaffory, Gentile, Leccia, and Arena have also invested much time and money to make dramatic improvements in quality.

Ajaccio Ajaccio was given AC status in 1984. Some of Corsica's highest vineyards are in this area, which produces mainly red and rosé wines with a little white. Sciacarello is the grape variety typical of the appellation. Domaine Peraldi, which overlooks the bay of Ajaccio, is one of the best producers.

Vin de Corse—Coteaux du Cap Corse The most northerly tip of the island, the Cap Corse, is renowned for its sweet Muscat and Rappu (a sweet MUSCAT-style red wine made from the ALEATICO vine variety). Some of Corsica's best dry white wines, such as Clos Nicrosi, are produced here.

Muscat du Cap Corse This relatively elegant VIN DOUX NATUREL, made from MUSCAT BLANC À PETITS GRAINS was elevated to full AC status in 1993.

Vin de Corse This generic AC represented 45 per cent of all Corsican AC wine in the late 1990s. These tend to be Corsica's least distinguished AC wines, although Nielluccio, Sciacarello, and Grenache must represent at least 50 per cent of any red or rosé, while whites must be at least 75 per cent Vermentino.   J.K.

Cortese, Italian white grape variety most closely associated with south-east PIEDMONT. Its most highly regarded wine is GAVI, produced initially to serve the fish restaurants of Genoa and the Ligurian coast not far to the south.

Cortese is also grown in the OLTREPÒ PAVESE in Lombardy and may be part of the blend in the Veneto's Bianco di CUSTOZA. The wine produced is rarely complex but sustains a good level of acidity through to full ripeness.   D.T.

Corton and Corton-Charlemagne, respectively the great red and white GRANDS CRUS in ALOXE-CORTON in Burgundy's CÔTE D'OR.

Corvina, or Corvina Veronese, the dominant and best grape variety of VALPOLICELLA and BARDOLINO in north-east Italy, producing fruity, red wines with a certain almond quality. Wines from the better Valpolicella producers who have reduced yields demonstrate that lack of BODY is not an inherent characteristic of Corvina. Valpolicella DOC regulations, which stipulate that the relatively bland Rondinella, and some of the tart Molinara, must constitute a combined total of at least 30 per cent of the blend are criticized for diluting the most characterful of the permitted grape varieties. Corvina, sometimes called Cruina, is the variety most prized in the making of such DRIED-GRAPE WINES as RECIOTO and AMARONE.

cosecha is Spanish for VINTAGE year.

Costers del Segre, small wine zone in north-east Spain in semi-desert near the Catalan city of Lerida. The climate is severe. The thermometer often dips below freezing point in winter and exceeds 35 °C in high summer. Rainfall barely reaches 400 mm/15 in in a year. The river Segre, a tributary of the Ebro after which this fragmented DO is named, is little more than a seasonal stream.

The history of Costers del Segre is really the history of one estate: Raimat, whose vineyard now amounts to a third of the Costers del Segre DO. A labyrinthine irrigation system starts automatically whenever the temperature rises above 35 °C/95 °F, and provides frost protection when the thermometer falls below 1 °C. As a result, imported vine varieties such as Cabernet Sauvignon, Merlot, Pinot Noir, and Chardonnay flourish alongside indigenous vines such as Tempranillo, Parellada, and Macabeo. Elsewhere in the region, which splits into four separate subzones, other quality-conscious producers include Castell del Remei and L'Olivera.   R.J.M. & V. de la S.

Costières de Nîmes, the generally reliable easternmost appellation of the LANGUEDOC in southern France, elevated from VDQS to AC status in 1986. It is effectively part of the RHÔNE since the climate, soil, and topography are so similar to those just over the river in the southern Côtes du Rhône vineyards.

This is an important zone for the production of VIN DE PAYS. As in the nearby southern Rhône, Grenache is an important vine variety here, and must represent at least 25 per cent of any red; while Carignan is slowly being removed, it may still make up 40 per cent. Syrah is becoming increasingly important in many of the best wines. This is an appellation in transition, not just geographically between the Languedoc and the Rhône, but temporally between a bulk-wine producer and a source of genuinely characterful, well-made wines. CO-OPERATIVES are less important here than in most of the Languedoc and most of the development and experimentation is taking place on dynamic, smaller estates such as Ch l'Amarine, Ch Paul Blanc/Mas Carlot, Ch de Campuget, Mas de Bressades, and Ch Mourgues du Grès.

Cot or Côt is an important synonym for the black grape variety of French origin also known as MALBEC and, in Cahors, Auxerrois.

Côte means literally 'slope' or 'hill' in French, Côtes is the plural, while Coteau (of which Coteaux is the plural) means much the same thing but possibly on a smaller scale. Since French vine-growers are great believers in the viticultural merits of HILLSIDES, all of these make suitable wine names. Thus, any index of French wine names contains long lists of Côte, Côtes, and Coteaux de, du, de la, and des various place-names, suggesting, often with reason, that the wine comes from the slopes above these places. Some of these prefixes are eventually dropped, however. Côtes de Buzet, for example, was renamed plain BUZET in the late 1980s.

For this reason, and to save readers having to remember whether a wine is, for example, a Coteaux de or a Coteaux du Somewhere, such an entry would be listed under S for Somewhere, rather than under Coteaux. Their Côte and Côtes counterparts are listed similarly. The only exceptions to this are names in which the Côte, Côtes, or Coteaux are integral. They follow.

Côte des Blancs, area of CHAMPAGNE on east-facing slopes south of Épernay noted for the quality of its Chardonnay grapes.

Côte d'Or, the heart of the BURGUNDY wine region in eastern France. Although the name Côte d'Or apparently translates directly as 'golden slope', evoking its autumnal aspect, it may be an abbreviation of Côte d'Orient, a reference to the fact that the escarpment on which the vines flourish faces east. Viticulturally it is divided into two sectors, the Côte de NUITS, in which great red wines are made from the Pinot Noir vine, and the Côte de BEAUNE, where the reds are joined by the finest white wines made from Chardonnay.

A cross-section of the Côte reveals topsoil too sparse on the hilltop and too fertile in the plain to produce wine of any quality. The vineyard area begins to the west of the Dijon-Lyons railway line but only the most basic wines made from Aligoté and Gamay are produced here. Approaching the main Dijon–Chagny road, the RN74, the vineyards are still on flat, fertile land but Pinot Noir and Chardonnay are planted to produce BOURGOGNE Rouge and Bourgogne Blanc. These in turn give way to VILLAGE appellation vineyards; as the ground starts to slope upwards, drainage improves, and the soil is less fertile.

Where the slope becomes more pronounced and clay gives way to stonier topsoil, the vineyards are designated PREMIERS CRUS, reflecting the potential quality of the wines from land which drains well and enjoys greater exposure to the sun. The finest of these vineyards, in certain villages only, are classified as GRANDS CRUS. (See right for a list of Burgundy's grands crus.) The premier- and grand-cru vineyards are mainly at elevations between 250 and 300 m (800–1,000 ft) above sea level. Near the top of the slope, where the soil is almost too poor, there is usually a narrow band of village appellation vineyards providing fine but light wines.

VINE DENSITY is notably high and harvesting is still mostly manual, especially for Pinot Noir. Maximum yields are officially set at 40 hl/ha (2.3 tons/acre) for red wines at village and premier-cru level, 45 hl/ha for whites. Maximum permitted yields for grands crus are mostly at 35 hl/ha for reds and 40 hl/ha for whites. In most vintages a supplementary allowance of 20 per cent is allowed.

There are no set rules for the production

Grands Crus of the Côte d'Or
(listed from north to south)

Commune	Grand Cru
Côte de Nuits (all for red wine unless otherwise stated)	
Gevrey-Chambertin	Mazis-Chambertin
	Ruchottes-Chambertin
	Chambertin-Clos de Bèze
	Chapelle-Chambertin
	Griotte-Chambertin
	Charmes-Chambertin (and Mazoyères-Chambertin)
	Le Chambertin
	Latricières-Chambertin
Morey-St-Denis	Clos de la Roche
	Clos St-Denis
	Clos des Lambrays
	Clos de Tart
	Bonnes Mares (some)
Chambolle-Musigny	Bonnes Mares (most)
	Le Musigny (some white wine too)
Vougeot	Clos de Vougeot
Flagey-Échezeaux	Grands Échezeaux
	Échezeaux
Vosne-Romanée	Richebourg
	Romanée-St-Vivant
	Romanée-Conti
	La Romanée
	La Grande Rue
	La Tâche
Côte de Beaune (all for white wine unless otherwise stated)	
Aloxe-Corton	Le Corton (almost all red)
Ladoix-Serrigny	Corton-Charlemagne
Puligny-Montrachet	Chevalier-Montrachet
	Bienvenues-Bâtard-Montrachet
with Chassagne-Montrachet	Le Montrachet
	Bâtard-Montrachet
Chassagne-Montrachet	Criots-Bâtard-Montrachet

of great red burgundy, and every domaine or NÉGOCIANT house revels in its own idiosyncrasies. The better wines of the Côte d'Or are all matured for at least a year, more often 18 months, in 228-l (59-gal) oak BARRELS, a proportion of which are usually new. Before bottling, some producers fine the wine and filter it; others prefer one treatment to the other; a few use neither in the belief that the wine thereby has more depth of flavour and capacity to evolve, even though it is less stable.

The qualities of great red burgundy are not easy to judge young, especially since the wine tends to be less deeply coloured than equivalent wines from Bordeaux or the Rhône. When young, a fine burgundy should show a bouquet of soft red fruit, ranging from cherries to plums depending on the vineyard and vigneron; complexity comes with maturity, the fresh fruit components giving way to more vegetal aromas, often redolent of truffles or undergrowth (*sous-bois*, according to French palates).

Some wines are weighty, others intensely elegant, but all should have concentration. Style depends in part on the character of the village: GEVREY-CHAMBERTIN, VOUGEOT, NUITS-ST-GEORGES, CORTON, and POMMARD tend to produce robust, long-lived wines; CHAMBOLLE-MUSIGNY, VOSNE-ROMANÉE, and VOLNAY epitomize finesse and elegance. Even within each village, different vineyards display their individual characteristics.

Differences in annual WEATHER patterns are crucial in determining quality in the region. There is probably greater vintage variation in Burgundy than in any other wine region. In some VINTAGES—1972, 1980, 1984, 1987, for instance—most Pinot Noir grapes do not fully ripen, although growers who conscientiously restrict yields often produce excellent wines. The 1996 vintage, which produced fine wines for ageing, was unusual in that September sunshine ripened the grapes fully, judging by the sugar levels, yet cool nights maintained the acidity at levels normally associated with an unripe year. In other years, excessive rainfall can either swell the crop to produce dilute wines (as in 1982 and 1992) or encourage ROT (as in 1986 and 1994). Most difficult to judge are the hot vintages in which the fruit in the wine is either supported, or sometimes overwhelmed, by TANNINS (as in 1976 and 1983). Certain vintages, such as 1985, 1989, and 1997, produce fully ripe grapes and many wines which are attractive to taste throughout their lives.

Great white burgundy is produced in the Côte de Beaune, notably in the villages of MEURSAULT, PULIGNY-MONTRACHET, and CHASSAGNE-MONTRACHET, along with a small enclave further north yielding the grand cru Corton-Charlemagne (see ALOXE-CORTON). The Chardonnay vine is hardier than the Pinot, the grapes ripen more easily, and the wines require less delicate handling. It is easier to make good white burgundy than red but very little great white burgundy is made.

Fine white burgundy, when young, is more likely to show the character of the oak in which it has been vinified than the grapes from which it came. Hallmarks of quality are fullness of BODY, balance of ACIDITY, and persistence of flavour. Only after two or more years of bottle age will a fine Meursault or Puligny-Montrachet start to show the quality of the fruit. This will deepen with age and, while vegetal tones will appear, they should not overwhelm the natural elegance of the wine. A village appellation wine should be at its best between three and five years old, a premier cru from 5 to 10 years, while a grand cru worthy of its status needs a full decade of BOTTLE AGEING.

For more detail, see under names of individual villages or appellations. See BEAUNE, CÔTE DE and NUITS, CÔTE DE for a full list of the villages in each. To most of the villages and towns in the Côte d'Or was appended the name of their most famous vineyard, typically in the late 19th century. Thus, for example, Vosne became Vosne-Romanée and Puligny became Puligny-Montrachet. J.T.C.M.

Côte Rôtie, one of the most exciting red-wine appellations in France, in the far north of the northern RHÔNE. In the 1970s, the area and its wines were somewhat moribund. One man, Marcel GUIGAL, is chiefly responsible for the recent renaissance of this zone (helped by the adulation of another, the American wine critic Robert PARKER). Guigal's single-vineyard bottlings of La Mouline, La Landonne, and, later, La Turque reminded the wine-buying world of the potential majesty of wines hewn from the Côte Rôtie, or 'roasted slope'. Even today, however, many of the meticulous small-scale producers such as Champet and Jasmin depend more on farming other fruits such as apricots than on their wines for income.

Because of the turn of the river here, the terraced vineyards banked up the schist behind the unremarkable town of Ampuis face directly south east, and are angled so as to maximize the ripening effect of any SUNLIGHT, while being sheltered from the cold winds. The slopes have traditionally been distinguished, with associated legend, either as Côte Blonde, supposedly producing alluring wines for relatively early consumption (often as a result of blending up to the permitted maximum of 20 per cent scented white VIOGNIER in with the mandatory SYRAH grape), or Côte Brune, associated with firmer, more durable, all-Syrah wines. The finest Côte Rôtie, local lore had it, was a blend of the two. More recently, the fame, and record prices, of wines flaunting specific vineyard sites has rather put paid to this theory, and the appellation is a hotbed of activity and ambition.

The theoretical minimum potential alcohol of these wines is 10 per cent, but most growers manage to achieve considerably more ripeness than this, and wines are made, with more or less new OAK (more *chez* Guigal), with considerable EXTRACTION and ambition, producing deep-coloured, relatively tannic, savoury wines which take 10 years or more to develop one of the more rewarding BOUQUETS of the wine world, all undergrowth and ripe black fruits. Clusel-Roch and René Rostaing also produce very fine wines.

Cotnari, once-famous sweet white wine produced in wild, hilly countryside in the north Romanian Moldavia (see ROMANIA). NOBLE ROT has played an important role here for several centuries, and continues to do so every three or four years today.

The wine is made from a blend of white grape varieties of which GRASĂ (whose very name means 'fat') provides the body and sugar, TĂMÎIOASĂ Românească provides its 'frank-incense' nerve (and sugar without losing acidity in the Cotnari MESOCLIMATE), Frîncuşă the acidity (it must make up at least 30 per cent of the blend), and Fetească Albă the aroma. Cotnari usually has at least 60 g/l RESIDUAL SUGAR and an alcoholic strength of at least 12 per cent. Unlike Tokaji, it is aged in WOOD for no more than a year, and is carefully protected from oxygen. Although golden, it retains a greenish tinge after many years in bottle.

Coulanges-la-Vineuse, commune just west of Chablis. See Côtes d'AUXERRE.

coulure, French term, commonly used by English speakers too, for one form of poor FRUIT SET in grapes in which, soon after FLOWERING, the small berries fall off. GRENACHE vines are particularly susceptible to coulure, as are MALBEC, MUSCAT OTTONEL, and certain clones of MERLOT.

Cowra, well-established Australian wine region in NEW SOUTH WALES.

Crémant, term used as France's shorthand for the country's finest dry sparkling wines · made outside Champagne using the traditional method of SPARKLING-WINE-MAKING. The principal provenances of modern Crémants, in declining order of importance, are Alsace, Die, Bourgogne (Burgundy), Loire, Limoux, and Bordeaux, although others, such as Gaillac, are anticipated. The best sparkling wines of LUXEMBOURG are also called Crémant. Although grape varieties and TERROIRS vary from region to region, certain strict sparkling-wine-making rules are imposed, as well as a compulsory tasting control.

Crémant d'Alsace

Sparkling-wine-making using the traditional method became an important commercial activity in the 1980s, representing about 10 per cent of the region's output. Only the grape varieties Pinots Blanc, Noir, and Gris, together with the related Auxerrois, and Riesling and such Chardonnay as is planted in Alsace, may be used (i.e. no Gewürztraminer or Chasselas). The wines are well made, tend to have a particularly fine mousse, high acidity, and to be relatively light in BODY. Only if substantial proportions of Riesling are used do they acquire strong flavour. Production is in the hands of nearly 500 different small-scale producers whose blending capability is usually limited.

Crémant de Bordeaux

A small and declining amount of sparkling wine has been made in the BORDEAUX region since the end of the 19th century. Today production is controlled by several companies who produce Crémant de Bordeaux—either Blanc de Blancs from Sémillon, Sauvignon, and Muscadelle grapes, Rosé from Bordeaux's red grape varieties, or Blanc from any combination of red or white grapes. The wines have yet to establish a clear style or identity.

Crémant de Bourgogne

This appellation, created in 1975, has replaced that of Bourgogne Mousseux. In the mid 1990s, there were just over 100 producers of Crémant de Bourgogne. All grape varieties grown in BURGUNDY are allowed into Crémant, although Gamay may not constitute more than a fifth of the blend. RULLY in the Côte Chalonnaise and AUXERROIS in the far north of Burgundy are the principal sources of Crémant de Bourgogne (CÔTE D'OR grapes being in general worth considerably more when sold as still wine), and there can be considerable stylistic differences between their produce. Crémant from southern Burgundy can be full and soft, a good-value alternative to bigger styles of champagne, while Crémant made in the north is usually much lighter and crisper.

Crémant de Die

A dry wine made exclusively from CLAIRETTE grapes, while Clairette de Die Tradition is the arguably more distinctive sweet sparkling wine made principally from MUSCAT BLANC. See CLAIRETTE DE DIE.

Crémant de Limoux

This appellation represents the increasing champenization of the ancient sparkling wines of LIMOUX in a particularly cool, high corner of the southern Languedoc. In 1990, Blanquette de Limoux became an appellation reserved for sparkling wines made principally from the MAUZAC grape grown traditionally in the region, while Crémant de Limoux contains a decreasing proportion of Mauzac, together with Chenin Blanc and Chardonnay. The result is refined, racy wines which exhibit some of Mauzac's apple-skin flavour and acidity. A very high proportion is made by the CO-OPERATIVE.

Crémant de Loire

Crémant de Loire was created in 1975 and encompasses the Anjou, Saumur, and Touraine regions. Most of the Loire's wide palette of grape varieties may be used to produce Crémant, with the notable and sensible exception of Sauvignon Blanc, whose aroma has yet to prove itself an attractive sparkling-wine ingredient. GROLLEAU grapes may not represent more than 30 per cent of any blend, and in practice Chenin Blanc is the most common dominant component, clearly distinguishing the flavour of most Crémant de Loire from Crémants made from Pinots and Chardonnay to the east. Levels of wine-making are generally high among the nearly 200 producers (including four co-operatives and several important NÉGOCIANTS) and an increasing level of complexity in the bottle is evident. Some producers are Loire offshoots of Champagne houses, notably Langlois Chateau of BOLLINGER, Gratien & Meyer of Alfred Gratien, and the ambitious Bouvet-Ladubay of Taittinger.

Crémant de Luxembourg

Luxembourg has a long tradition of sparkling-wine-making, and its particularly acid wines were at one time valued as base wines for SEKT. The Crémant de Luxembourg appellation was created in 1991. Permitted grape varieties are Elbling, Pinot Blanc, and Riesling for white wines, Pinot Noir for rosé.

crème de tête, French phrase occasionally found on wine labels, notably white BORDEAUX, denoting special, superior bottlings.

Crépy, wine appellation within the eastern French region of SAVOIE on the south-eastern shore of Lake Geneva producing light, dry white wines from the CHASSELAS grape which would be difficult to distinguish from their Swiss neighbours in a BLIND TASTING.

Crete. See GREECE.

crianza, Spanish term used both to describe the process of AGEING a wine and also for the youngest officially recognized category of a wood-matured wine. A crianza wine may not be sold until its third year, and must have spent a minimum of six months in 225-l/59-gal oak *barricas* (BARRIQUES). In RIOJA and other regions such as RIBERA DEL DUERO, where the term is most commonly used, the wine must have spent at least 12 months in oak casks. An increasingly frequent, albeit unofficial, category now is **semi-crianza**, for wine aged in cask for less time than the crianza minimum.

Crimea, peninsula off southern UKRAINE surrounded by the Black Sea. Modern wine production on the south coast is chiefly under the control of the MASSANDRA central winery on the outskirts of Yalta. Average July temperatures of 24 °C/75 °F and annual sunshine of 2,250 hours at Yalta result in extremely ripe grapes best suited to the production of strong, sweet wines, most of them made like VINS DOUX NATURELS.

Criolla Chica is the Argentine name for the PAIS of Chile, the MISSION of California, and the Negra Corriente of PERU. It is much less common in Argentina than the other pink-skinned grape varieties CRIOLLA GRANDE and CEREZA. Its wine is generally paler but slightly better quality.

Criolla Grande, the most important vine variety in ARGENTINA in quantitative, if not qualitative, terms. Most Criolla Grande is in Mendoza province, where it is the most planted vine variety by far. It is a low-quality, coarse, pink-skinned VINIFERA variety that was probably one of the first vines cultivated in the Americas, and is much deeper skinned than CRIOLLA CHICA. The two Criollas, along with CEREZA and Moscatel Rosada, form the basis of Argentina's declining trade in basic deep-coloured white wine sold very cheaply in litre bottles or cardboard cartons. Pink wine can also be made from Criolla Grande.

Criots-Bâtard-Montrachet, great white GRAND CRU in Burgundy's CÔTE D'OR. See MONTRACHET.

Croatia, northern state in what was YUGO-SLAVIA, is like its north-western neighbour SLO-VENIA in having two very different regions split by the ranges of hills which follow the coast. The area of Kontinentalna Hrvatska (inland Croatia) runs south and east from the eastern tip of Austria along the Drava tributary of the Danube, which marks the Hungarian border, down to the ill-fated town of Vukovar. Like northern Slovenia, the area produces mostly whites (67 per cent of the country's production and 93 per cent of inland Croatia's is white). The dominant variety is Laski Rizling or WELSCHRIESLING (here known by the more graceful name of Graševina). Other varieties planted include GEWÜRZTRAMINER, PINOT BLANC, RIESLING, SAUVIGNON BLANC, and some SÉMILLON. The wines are generally riper and more earthy in style than their Slovenian counterparts.

The four subregions of Istria and the spectacular Dalmatian coast which stretches south past Split to Dubrovnik and the offshore islands make up Primorska Hrvatska (coastal Croatia). Istria has its fair share of Bordeaux red grapes such as Cabernet Sauvignon and Merlot and Italian varieties such as Teran (REFOSCO) as well as MALVASIA, GAMAY, and PINOT NOIR, but most of the rest of the coast boasts a whole selection of grapes which appear to be native to this region. The PLAVAC MALI grape (see ZINFANDEL) is responsible for two potentially excellent red wines, Dingač and Postup, both of which tend to be heavy and very ripe, with a natural ALCOHOLIC STRENGTH of 15 per cent being perfectly possible for a Dingač. Babić is another good-quality red grape. White grapes include Pošip, Grk, Vugava, and Marastina. The last named can produce wines that are fresh, quite light, and herbal. The other three, which all come from separate islands, are heavier, deeper coloured, often rather MADERIZED, and too old-fashioned to travel well. This coastal region produces 70 per cent red wine.

Croatia has adopted wine laws which, like those of Slovenia, allow for the quality grading of wine through a tasting system known as the Buxbaum method operated by the Republic export vice-commission for wine grading.

A.H.M.

Croatina, declining red grape variety from the borders of the PIEDMONT and LOMBARDY regions of northern Italy. The vine yields good quantities of fruity wine with a certain bite, designed to be drunk relatively young. Its common synonym is Bonarda, under which name it has a VARIETAL appetizing red DOC in the OLTREPÒ PAVESE zone of south-west Lombardy. The variety is quite distinct from BONARDA Piemontese.

crop thinning, viticultural practice which, it is claimed, improves wine quality by encouraging fruit RIPENING. It is known as *éclaircissage* or *vendange verte* (green harvest) in French. Simply, some bunches are removed from the vine and those remaining should in theory ripen more quickly with the benefit of improved LEAF TO FRUIT RATIO. Crop thinning is usually carried out by hand, and is therefore expensive. MECHANICAL HARVESTERS are occasionally used to thin crops, but here individual berries or parts of bunches are removed.

The theory of crop thinning is that the remaining fruit ripens earlier, and so has better levels of sugars and ANTHOCYANINS for red varieties. However, many studies have shown that these benefits are small in magnitude, and that crop levels need to be greatly reduced for a small change in GRAPE COMPOSITION. R.E.S.

Crouchen or Cruchen, white grape variety producing neutral wines in both South Africa and Australia. It is increasingly popular with grape-growers in South Africa, where it is known as Cape Riesling and occasionally South African Riesling or Paarl Riesling, but may be sold simply as Riesling (true Riesling is known as White or Weisser Riesling). It shares with that much greater German grape variety the ability to benefit from BOTTLE AGEING.

Crozes-Hermitage, the northern RHÔNE'S biggest appellation, regularly producing about eight times as much wine as the much more distinguished vineyards of HERMITAGE which it surrounds, and still considerably more than the similarly priced, and similarly extended, appellation of ST-JOSEPH across the river. Like both these appellations, Crozes-Hermitage is usually red and made exclusively of the SYRAH grape, although a certain proportion, just over a tenth, of full-bodied dry white wine is made from the MARSANNE grape supplemented by ROUSSANNE. Up to 15 per cent of white grapes may be added to red Crozes at the time of FER-

MENTATION, although rarely to much effect. Although some bottlers have treated the appellation with little respect for quality, a nucleus of excitingly ambitious producers such as Belle, Combier, Graillot, Pochon, Tardieu-Laurent, and Tardy et Ange emerged from the late 1980s to provide thoughtfully made Crozes-Hermitage of real distinction and mass. The best reds are rather softer and fruitier than Hermitage, but they tend to share more of Hermitage's solidity than average St-Joseph. A more typical red Crozes, however, exhibits the burnt-rubber smell and sinewy build of overstretched Syrah, although the CO-OPERATIVE in the town of Tain l'Hermitage, two-thirds of whose production is Crozes-Hermitage, should not be underestimated. JABOULET's Domaine de Thalabert was for long the appellation's principal standard-bearer. The soils of Crozes-Hermitage seem generally less well suited to white-wine production, although there are some successful vineyards around Mercurol. The best reds can be kept for five years or more (and in good years can happily survive for 10) but the average Crozes, red or white, is probably at its best drunk young.

cru, French specialist term for a vineyard, usually reserved for those officially recognized as of superior quality.

In English, the word is often translated as 'growth'. For example, PREMIERS CRUS, an official category in one of Bordeaux's CLASSIFICATIONS, are known as FIRST GROWTHS. A cru that has been 'classified' is a cru classé, or CLASSED GROWTH. GRANDS CRUS can also have a very specific meaning, notably in BURGUNDY and ALSACE.

The top-ranked communes in BEAUJOLAIS are called crus, and their produce is Cru Beaujolais.

In SWITZERLAND, the first two vineyards to be officially awarded cru status were the neighbouring Dézaley and Calamin in the Vaud.

In Italy, there have been some attempts to define various superior vineyards as crus. The local dialect for such a site in PIEDMONT is SORI.

cru artisan, a category of Médoc wine estate in Bordeaux more humble, and generally smaller, than the CRU BOURGEOIS. It includes much of the produce of the CO-OPERATIVES there and some excellent value.

cru bourgeois, a typical invention for the MÉDOC district of Bordeaux, a category of red-wine properties, or CRUS, designated bourgeois, or a social stratum below the supposedly aristocratic crus classés. While the crus classés represent about 25 per cent of the Médoc's total wine production from about 60 estates, the crus bourgeois represent a further 40 per cent, mainly from much smaller properties. These can vary, however, from simple smallholdings to properties such as Ch Larose-Trintaudon, the largest estate in the Médoc with its own vast château buildings, or Ch Clarke of Listrac, on which Baron Edmond de Rothschild lavished a large fortune.

In terms of wine quality, there is wide variation between the best and worst of the crus bourgeois. The best are producing wine that is seriously better, and occasionally more expensive, than that of the under-performing crus classés, while the worst make wine that is just slightly more exciting than red BORDEAUX AC. In general, however, this category can offer some of Bordeaux's best value. They are made mainly from Cabernet Sauvignon grapes but often contain quite a high proportion of Merlot, usually supplemented by some Cabernet Franc. Some BARREL MATURATION is usually involved in the making of the most highly priced crus bourgeois, even if only a small proportion of new OAK is lavished on this wine category. The wines are generally ready to drink at between four and eight years old.

The Syndicate of Crus Bourgeois has grouped the properties into **Crus Bourgeois Exceptionnels**, **Crus Grands Bourgeois**, and **Crus Bourgeois**, but European Union authorities would grant use only of the term Cru Bourgeois.

The crus bourgeois are particularly important in MOULIS and LISTRAC, where they represent 85 and 66 per cent of these appellations' total production. In PAUILLAC and ST-JULIEN, on the other hand, the crus classés are much more important and the crus bourgeois represent just 10 and 15 per cent of total production.

crush, mainly American term for the whole HARVEST season, named after one of the first processes in the winery (CRUSHING) rather than what happens in the vineyard.

crushing, wine-making operation of breaking open the grape berry so that the juice is more readily available to the YEAST for FERMENTATION.

crystals in a bottle of white wine, on the underside of a cork, or on the inside of a vat, are harmless deposits. See TARTRATES.

Cuba. The ubiquitous Chardonnay is now grown on this Caribbean island in the tobacco-growing region of Pinar del Rio.

cultivar, term developed by professional botanists to mean a cultivated variety.

custom crush facility, American term for a winery specializing in vinifying grapes on behalf of many different vine-growers, typically those without their own wine-making equipment. The various wines are kept separate and marketed by the growers under their own labels. Such operations have played an important part in establishing ambitious new wine producers, as in CALIFORNIA, and indeed new wine regions such as Marlborough in NEW ZEALAND.

Custoza, Bianco di, straightforward dry white wine produced in the VENETO region of north-east Italy. The substantial presence of TREBBIANO Toscano, along with GARGANEGA, TOCAI Friulano, and a variety of other grapes tends to yield a rather colourless, neutral wine.

D.T.

cut cane, Australian name for the viticultural technique designed to increase the sugar concentration in almost-ripe grapes to produce sweet wines. By cutting the CANES almost at the time of HARVEST, water supply to the fruit is halted, and so the berries start to shrivel (as in the production of DRIED-GRAPE WINES). Sugar concentration is elevated as water is lost through the berry skin and ACIDITY may also be increased.

R.E.S.

cuve is French for a vat or tank. Thus, a **cuverie** is the vat hall, typically where fermentation takes place. *Cuves* may be made of any material: wood, concrete, or, most likely, stainless steel.

cuve close, French for sealed tank, and a name for a bulk sparkling-wine-making process (sometimes called Charmat) which involves provoking a second fermentation in wine stored in a pressure tank. See SPARKLING-WINE-MAKING.

cuvée, French wine term derived from CUVE, with many different meanings in different contexts. In general terms, it can be used to mean any container-ful, or lot, of wine and therefore wine labels often carry relatively meaningless

descriptions incorporating the word cuvée. Tête de cuvée, on the other hand, is occasionally used for the top bottling of a French wine producer, particularly in Sauternes.

In CHAMPAGNE and other environments in which traditional-method sparkling wines are made, cuvée is a name for the first and best juice to flow from the press (see SPARKLING-WINE-MAKING). The blend of base wines assembled for second fermentation in bottle is also known as the cuvée. Thus the term is often used in many champagne and sparkling-wine names.

Elsewhere, particularly in German-speaking wine regions oddly enough, cuvée may be used to describe any ambitious blend, particularly of different vine varieties.

Cyprus, eastern Mediterranean island less than 100 km/60 miles from Syria to the east and Turkey to the north. For most of the 20th century, Cyprus wine languished in terms of quality. The 1990s saw substantial investment leading to an improvement in production techniques and resulting wines, however. Today, wine continues to play an important role in the agricultural economy of the Greek Cypriot, southern Republic of Cyprus.

Climate and geography

Commercial wine-growing is confined to the southern foothills and slopes of the Troodos mountain range. The vineyard area is divided into six regions: Pitsilia (the highest), Marathasa, Commandaria, Troodhos South, Troodhos East, and Troodhos North.

The climate is typically MEDITERRANEAN: mild winters and hot summers with precipitation confined to the winter months. Rainfall is low and IRRIGATION is not permitted. The great variation in temperatures between low- and high-ALTITUDE vineyards results in one of the most extended vintage periods in the world. Picking usually starts in mid July and continues until early November. Climatic hazards are restricted to hail and, at higher-altitude vineyards, spring and autumn frost. Since PHYLLOXERA has never reached Cyprus, vines are ungrafted.

Vine varieties

The vast majority, almost three-quarters, of the Cyprus vineyard area is planted with the indigenous Mavro (black) grape variety. Only when cultivated at altitudes above 1,000 m/3,300 ft, where yields can be as low as 25 hl/ha (1.4 tons/acre) is Mavro capable of producing wine of quality and character. Elsewhere it gives high yields of very large grapes. With its high skin to juice ratio, Mavro has a tendency to give pale, unattractive colours when vinified as a red wine. To counteract this problem, wine-makers often remove up to 40 per cent of the juice prior to fermentation. The juice removed has commonly been used for 'Cyprus fortified wine'. At its best, Mavro gives wine with a cherry or blackcurrant candy character when young, developing vegetal characteristics with three to five years' age. The wine rarely loses its faint iodine background flavour and is often high in alcohol.

The second most planted wine grape is the indigenous white grape Xynisteri, which, if picked before overripe and carefully vinified, has the ability to produce aromatic wines with a good balance between sugar, alcohol, and acids, and a tendency towards earthiness of flavour. In the better-quality wines, Xynisteri may be supplemented by PALOMINO, a variety imported with a view to improving Cyprus fortified wine, and MALVASIA Grossa.

Fear of phylloxera has made the island's authorities particularly cautious about the introduction of non-indigenous grape varieties. Of imported varieties, CARIGNAN and GRENACHE have been most widely planted, with some CABERNET SAUVIGNON as well as some surprisingly successful RIESLING, some WELSCH-RIESLING, and a small amount of CHARDONNAY also grown.

There has been a renewed interest in the island's less planted indigenous varieties and commercial wineries are divided in their opinions on the value of new INTERNATIONAL VARIETIES as opposed to native grape varieties.

With the exception of a very few estates owned by the commercial wineries or the Ministry of Agriculture, Cyprus vineyards are divided into thousands of smallholdings. Typically, the land is worked by the older generation. Children and grandchildren may be employed in the local tourist industry but are more likely to have moved to the towns to work in Cyprus's service and manufacturing industries.

Wine-making

Until the late 1980s, almost all Cypriot wine was made in large wineries near the docks of Limassol or Paphos, but at considerable distance from the vineyards. Equipment was basic. In the 1990s, however, there was a marked change in the island's wineries. The large wineries have invested in much-improved equipment while some small, very well-equipped regional wineries have been built in the vineyard areas. The industry has also started to employ foreign consultant wine-makers, notably Australians who have experience in making fresh, fruity wines in hot climates (see FLYING WINE-MAKERS).

Organization of trade

Almost all Cypriot wine is made by four large firms—SODAP, KEO, ETKO, and Loel. These firms not only own the large wineries of Limassol and Paphos but have also built a number of the regional wineries. SODAP is a CO-OPERATIVE while the others are public companies, with a substantial proportion of their shareholding owned by vine-growers.

The four large firms rely on exports for the majority of their sales since per capita wine consumption in Cyprus is extremely small.

Some of the drier examples of Cyprus fortified wine can stand comparison with the products of JEREZ, but the majority of Cyprus fortified wine is sweet, less distinguished wine. The principal market for Cyprus fortified wine is the United Kingdom.

The early 1990s brought grave problems to the Cypriot wine industry and the cost of supporting it became an increasingly embarrassing problem for the Cypriot government. In 1992, a fine four-point plan to improve vine varieties and wine-making practices and to pull up vineyards in least favoured sites was issued by the government, and, despite the scheme's cost, and the opposition of certain vine-growers, the area under vine has been reduced, and the proportion of better-quality vine varieties, although still small, is increasing. The ambitious plan also incorporated the establishment of 'designation of origin' legislation, with Commandaria the first wine to be granted full legal protection in 1993. By the late 1990s, the changes to the Cypriot wine industry were becoming evident. Although exports of basic wines remained important, and sales of better-quality wines tended to be limited to the domestic market and expatriate communities, some top wines were beginning to achieve success in international COMPETITIONS, demonstrating some of the island's potential. See also COMMANDARIA. G.J.L.

Czech Republic. The republic and its vineyards divide into two distinct regions: the tiny, touristy vineyards of BOHEMIA on the banks of the river Labe (Germany's Elbe) in the north; and, quantitatively much more important, MORAVIA to the south along the Austrian and Slovakian borders. The following comments apply both to the Czech Republic and to Slovakia.

About two-fifths of the vineyards lie on gentle slopes, usually topped by woodland, while the rest are on undulating plains which fall away to the flatter Danube basin. The major influences on these vineyards are the relatively low ALTITUDE and the CONTINENTAL CLIMATE. Rainfall here is relatively low, on average between a half and two-thirds of the annual rainfall in French vineyards on an equivalent latitude (Burgundy and Alsace). Because of their position north of the Danube, most of the slopes face between south west and south east and are very protected by higher land in the north.

Under the old, state-run system, the vintage was graded first by grape variety. Only Cabernet Sauvignon, Pinot Noir, Sauvignon, Gewürztraminer (often known as Traminer or Tramin), (Rhine) Riesling, and, sometimes, Pinots Blanc and Gris could qualify in the top grade. Most of these varieties are not widely planted as they did not reward Czechoslovakia's rather careless viticultural practices with generous yields. Apart from Riesling and Pinot Blanc, Rizling Vlassky (WELSCHRIESLING), MÜLLER-THURGAU, Veltlin Zelene (GRÜNER VELTLINER), and SILVANER are the major white wine varieties, together with the Muscat-scented IRSAY OLIVER. Frankovka (BLAUFRÄNKISCH) and Vavrinecke, or Svatovavrinecke (ST LAURENT) are the principal red-wine varieties.

Privatization broke up the state winery system first through ill-fated management/worker buyouts and then through state auctions of the assets. Since virtually all the wines are sold with ease on the undemanding local market, there has been little or no incentive to modernize or re-equip the wineries.

The wines show very good intrinsic fruit character, although this may be masked by sloppy wine-making practices. Identification of the best individual sites and MESOCLIMATES is so far in its infancy, and an injection of technical knowledge and capital investment to realize the potential of both Moravia and Slovakia was still to materialize in the late 1990s. A.H.M.

Dão, DOC in north central PORTUGAL with the reputation of producing some of the country's best red wines. There is no doubt that the region has great potential. Locked in on three sides by high, granite mountains and sheltered from the Atlantic, Dão benefits from long, warm summers and abundant winter rainfall. The sandy soils are well drained and the vineyards are stocked with a wealth of indigenous grape varieties. In most of the late 20th century, when production was tightly controlled by government CO-OPERATIVES, the wines rarely lived up to expectations but things are changing.

Over two-thirds of Dão wines are red and made from anything up to nine different authorized grapes. TOURIGA NACIONAL, one of the main PORT grapes, is accepted as the best in the region and must now account for at least 20 per cent of any one wine. The other grapes permitted to make up the remainder are BASTARDO, JAEN, TINTA PINHEIRA, ALFROCHEIRO PRETO, and another port grape, Tinta Roriz, alias Spain's TEMPRANILLO. Red Dão tends to be firm and tannic and, in the past, many wines suffered from excessively prolonged MACERATION with the stalks and protracted ageing in old casks or cement tanks. The new generation of producers is more meticulous and some have invested in new French and Portuguese OAK.

White wines have also suffered from being aged for too long, often tasting flat and OXIDIZED. By the late 1990s, younger, fresher wines were being produced by modern, private wineries. ENCRUZADO, the best grape for white Dão,

produces some crisp, fragrant wines but all too often it is blended with other less successful varieties such as Assario Branco and Borrado das Moscas ('fly droppings'), the obscure local name for the BICAL of Bairrada.   R.J.M.

deacidification, wine-making process of decreasing the excessive ACIDITY of grape juice or wine made in cold wine regions or, in particularly cool years, in temperate wine regions. A number of techniques for making excessively acid wines more palatable have been developed and are usually strictly governed by local regulations.

Deacidification is not the commonplace procedure that ACIDIFICATION is in warmer regions. It is practised in northern Germany, Luxembourg, the United Kingdom, Canada, New York state, Tasmania, and New Zealand's South Island in certain years.   A.D.W.

dealcoholized wine became popular as wine drinkers searched for a drink that tastes like wine but has none of the negative implications for HEALTH or subsequent activity such as driving. Such wines also have fewer calories than regular wine, fewer than 150 calories per bottle in many cases. They may broadly be divided into 'no-alcohol wines', with an ALCOHOLIC STRENGTH of less than 1 or at the most 2 per cent, and 'low-alcohol wines' with between 2 and 5.5 per cent alcohol.

Wine may be dealcoholized in several ways, all of which involve removing ALCOHOL from normally fermented wine, using either thermal or membrane techniques, yet retaining all other components. All methods of removing alcohol to produce no-alcohol or low-alcohol wines are expensive, however, relative to the methods used to make REDUCED-ALCOHOL WINES, which are low-alcohol wines made by either dilution or partial fermentation.

By the mid 1990s, more than a dozen companies in France, Germany, Australia, and the United States were producing dealcoholized wine.

Debina, the sprightly white grape variety that is responsible for the lightly sparkling white wines of Zitsa in Epirus, high in north-west GREECE near the Albanian border. It seems likely that the variety is also cultivated in Albania. At these altitudes, acidity levels remain high, and a tendency to OXIDATION has largely been checked by improved vinification methods.

decanters, vessels, usually glass and stoppered, into which wine is poured during DECANTING. The decanter as we know it today has changed form very little in the last 250 years, in that it is a handleless clear glass bottle with a capacity of about 1 l and, normally, a stopper. Since the capacity is noticeably more than that of a standard 75-cl/27-fl oz bottle, it allows the wine to 'breathe' and develop.

Any container can be used as a vessel for wine, so long as it is made of an inert material and can hold at least the contents of a bottle while, ideally, leaving a considerable surface area in contact with air. Some decanters are designed specifically for magnums, or double-sized bottles. Others have handles, all manner of different shapes, engravings, shadings, and designs, including one to ensure circulation with a semi-spherical base that cannot be laid to rest other than in a special cradle by the host's elbow (see PASSING THE PORT). Wine need not be served from clear glass, or even glass at all, but most wine's COLOUR (whites as much as reds) can give great aesthetic and anticipatory pleasure.

See LEAD for details of the limited extent to which this toxic element may be leached from different sorts of decanters.

decanting, optional and controversial step in SERVING wine, involving pouring wine out of its bottle into another container called a DECANTER.

Reasons for decanting
The most obvious reason for decanting a wine is to separate it from any SEDIMENT that has formed in the bottle which not only looks unappetizing in the glass, but usually tastes bitter and/or astringent. Before wine-makers mastered the art of CLARIFICATION, this was necessary for all wines. Today such a justification of the decanting process effectively limits it to those wines outlined in AGEING as capable of development in bottle, in most of which some solids are precipitated as part of the maturation process. Vintage and crusted PORTS in particular always throw a heavy deposit (since they are bottled so early in their evolution), as do red wines made with no or minimal FILTRATION. It is rare for inexpensive, everyday TABLE WINES to throw a deposit, and most large retailers insist on such heavy filtration that a deposit is unlikely (although not unknown in older, higher-quality reds). To check whether a wine bottle contains any sediment, it should be stood upright for at least 24 hours and then carefully held up to the light for inspection at the base (although some BOTTLES are too dark for this exercise to be effective).

Another, traditional but disputed, reason for decanting is to promote aeration and therefore encourage the development of the wine's BOUQUET. Authorities as scientifically respectable as Bordeaux's Professor Émile Peynaud argue that this is OENOLOGICALLY indefensible: that the action of OXYGEN dissolved in a sound wine is usually detrimental and that the longer it is prolonged—i.e. the longer before serving a wine is decanted—the more diffuse its aroma and the less marked its sensory attributes. His advice is to decant only wines with a sediment, and then only just before serving. If they need aeration because of some wine FAULT such as REDUCTION or MERCAPTANS, then the taster can simply aerate the wine by agitating it in the glass. His argument is that from the moment the wine is fully exposed to air (which happens when it is poured, but not to any significant extent during so-called 'BREATHING') some of its sensory impressions may be lost, and that decanting immediately before serving gives the taster maximum control.

It is certainly wise advice to decant fully mature wines only just before serving, since some are so fragile that they can withstand oxygen for only a few minutes before succumbing to OXIDATION. And it is also true that the aeration process of an individual glass of wine can be controlled by the person drinking out of it. However, there are certain types of wines, BAROLO most obviously, which may not have been included in Professor Peynaud's experiments with decanting regimes, which can be so concentrated and tannic in youth that to lose some of their initial sensory impressions is a positive benefit.

There is also the very practical fact that many hosts find it more convenient to decant before a meal is served rather than in the middle of it. There are also people who enjoy the sight of (perhaps both red and white) wine in a decanter so much that they are prepared to sacrifice the potential reduction in gustatory impact.

How to decant

The ideal method is to stand the bottle upright for at least 24 hours before opening, preferably longer with wines which have a great deal of sediment. Ensure that the decanter looks and smells absolutely clean, and find a strong light source against which the bottle can be held (a candle, flashlight, desk light, or unshaded table lamp will do). After opening the bottle, as gently as possible, and wiping the lip of the bottle clean, steadily pour the contents of the bottle into the decanter watching the lower shoulder of the bottle with the light source behind it. The sediment should eventually collect in the shoulder and the pouring action can be halted as soon as any sediment starts to spill into the bottleneck.

To extract maximum volume of liquid from a bottle with sediment, or if there is no time to let all the sediment fall to the bottom of the bottle, or if a cork collapses into fragments in the bottle during extraction, the wine can be filtered into the decanter through clean fabric such as muslin, or a paper coffee filter, with no perceptible harmful effects.

Conclusion and guidelines

In sum, of course, decanting is a personal choice, but the following are suggested guiding principles:

- decant, or pour extremely carefully, wines with a sediment;
- decant old wines, say more than 20 to 30 years old depending on their concentration, only immediately before serving.

decanting cradles, bottle carriers, usually made of wicker or metal, which keep the bottle at a perpetually inclined angle so that, in theory anyway, any SEDIMENT remains in the base while wine is poured off, either into a glass or decanter.

Special **decanting machines** have also been constructed, designed to invert a bottle mechanically and smoothly as its contents are poured into a DECANTER.

Delaware, dark-pink-skinned *Vitis labruscana* vine variety that is quite popular in NEW YORK and, for reasons that are now obscure, is the most widely planted in JAPAN. The wine is not as markedly FOXY as that of its great New York rival CONCORD.

delimitation, geographical. The central purpose of geographical delimitation of a wine area, typically into a CONTROLLED APPELLATION, is to establish a distinctive identity for the wines produced within it, and provide a means whereby the provenance of those wines can be guaranteed. It is based primarily upon the assumption that different environments give rise to wines of different character (see TERROIR).

The precise practical methods of geographical demarcation vary from country to country, but are usually based on the compilation of a detailed vineyard register and include varying degrees of political intrigue. Producers wishing to gain a certain status must satisfy regional and national committees of both the quality, origin, and distinction of their wines. One of the most rigorous systems of geographical delimitation is that adopted in France. This requires that commissions of inquiry examine the relationships between such factors as geology, soils, topography, drainage, slope, exposure, and wine quality. In BURGUNDY, for example, the geological origin of the soils is a determining factor in differentiating the GRANDS CRUS.

The central feature of geographical delimitation as it applies to wine is not just that it usually leads to an improvement in wine quality, thus enabling the wines to be sold at a higher PRICE, but also that it is a legislative procedure whereby a privileged monopolistic position is created for producers within a demarcated area. Whether a given vineyard falls within or outside the legal boundary of a delimited wine region can have important commercial consequences, which is why the much more recent demarcation of America's AVAS can be such a contentious process.

The creation of geographically delimited areas remains highly controversial, and many New World wine-makers argue that, in its historical form involving prescribed vine varieties and techniques, it limits innovation and tends to maintain traditional practices and TRADITION.   P.T.H.U.

demi-sec, French term meaning 'medium dry'. See SWEETNESS. In practice, the term is used particularly for Chenin Blanc wines in the ANJOU, SAUMUR, and TOURAINE as well as for some SPARKLING WINES.

Denominação de Origem Controlada, the name of a controlled appellation in PORTUGAL. See DOC.

Denominación de Origen, Spanish controlled appellation. See DO.

Denominación de Origen Calificada, Spain's superior controlled appellation. RIOJA was the first DO to be promoted to this status. See DOCA.

deposit. See BOTTLE DEPOSIT and SEDIMENT.

desert, an arid, treeless region. True deserts are not conducive to growing grapes for wine, even where IRRIGATION water is available. See CLIMATE AND WINE QUALITY.

Some near-desert regions used extensively for viticulture include the SAN JOAQUIN VALLEY of California; the Bekaa valley of LEBANON; parts of ISRAEL; AZERBAIJAN on the west coast of the Caspian Sea; the north west of CHINA; the lower Murray Valley of SOUTH AUSTRALIA and VICTORIA; and the Little Karoo of SOUTH AFRICA.
                                                                J.G.

designations. Within the European Union, wine is broadly designated either a QUALITY WINE or a TABLE WINE. Within these broad categories, there are more precise designations, usually CONTROLLED APPELLATIONS or categories such as VIN DE PAYS, IGT, LANDWEIN, or VINO DE LA TIERRA.

dessert wines usually mean SWEET WINES but according to American regulations they mean FORTIFIED WINES both sweet and dry.

destalking. See DESTEMMING.

destemming, the wine-making process of removing the stems, or stalks, from clusters of grape berries. Most white and the majority of black grapes are destemmed. The exceptions are those white grapes subjected to WHOLE-BUNCH PRESSING and black grapes used for CARBONIC MACERATION and those few employed in WHOLE-BUNCH FERMENTATION. Some producers, notably in BURGUNDY and parts of the RHÔNE,

believe in retaining a certain proportion of the stems to add structure, colour, and to ease the drainage of the juice during MACERATION of red wines and during PRESSING of white wines. See WINE-MAKING.

Deutsche means literally 'German', thus the **Deutsche Weinstrasse** is a particularly famous route through the vineyards of the PFALZ region in Germany; **Deutscher Sekt** is that relative rarity, a SEKT or sparkling wine made in Germany that is actually made of German wine; and **Deutscher Tafelwein**, or DTW, means literally 'German table wine' and is distinct from European Union TABLE WINE in that it is made exclusively from German grapes.

The **Deutsches Weinsiegel**, or German Wine Seal, is a significant award made to superior bottlings assessed by BLIND TASTING panels whose standards are more exacting than those which award the official AP NUMBER. Award-winning bottles can be identified by a large, round paper seal on the bottle-neck: a yellow seal for dry wines, green for medium dry, and red for other styles.

Die, town between the RHÔNE valley and the Alps whose name features in the Clairette de Die and Crémant de Die appellations. Most wines are sparkling and many of them are sweet and grapey. See CLAIRETTE DE DIE, CRÉMANT, and CHÂTILLON-EN-DIOIS.

diet, wine as part of. Medical research increasingly indicates that wine may be drunk for dietary reasons. Wine contains various vitamins and minerals but in such small concentrations that, for them to make any sufficient contribution to the human diet, excessive amounts of ALCOHOL would also have to be ingested. 'Moderate' wine consumption can have a beneficial effect for some medical conditions, however, and wine consumption clearly plays a part in the much-vaunted Mediterranean diet (see HEALTH AND WINE).

No wine is 'slimming', but dry **dealcoholized wine** is usually lower in calories than most.

Dimiat, Bulgaria's most planted indigenous white grape variety, although it may not cover as much ground as RKATSITELI. It is grown mainly in the east and south of Bulgaria, where it is regarded as a producer of perfumed everyday whites of varying levels of sweetness but usefully dependable quality. The wines should be consumed young and cool.

Dinka, very ordinary but widely planted white grape variety in HUNGARY and VOJVODINA. It is also known as Kövidinka and Kevedinka.

Diois, Coteaux. Appellation created in 1993 for the still wines produced around DIE on the Drôme tributary of the RHÔNE. For more details of likely grape varieties, see CLAIRETTE DE DIE and CRÉMANT.

disgorgement, or *dégorgement* in French, an integral stage in the traditional method of SPARKLING-WINE-MAKING. It entails the removal of a pellet of frozen sediment from the neck of each bottle and does nothing to improve the quality of the wine.

DNA 'fingerprinting', more formally DNA typing, a development of modern technology allowing the potential and unequivocal identification of all living material from small samples of tissue. First suggested for human identification in 1985, the technique has been applied to the identification of different VINE VARIETIES and, possibly, CLONES and strains of YEAST.

One of the first significant results in the early 1990s was to establish that ZINFANDEL and PRIMITIVO have identical DNA patterns and can therefore, after years of speculation, be regarded as identical. One of the more surprising discoveries was that Cabernet Sauvignon is a crossing of Cabernet Franc and Sauvignon Blanc.

DO stands for Denominación de Origen, a Spanish CONTROLLED APPELLATION and the mainstay of SPAIN'S wine-quality control system. Each region awarded DO status is governed by a Consejo Regulador made up of representatives of the Ministry of Agriculture and vine-growers, wine-makers, and merchants who earn their livelihoods in the region. The regulations include the boundaries of the region, permitted VINE VARIETIES, maximum YIELDS, limits of ALCOHOLIC STRENGTH, and any other limitations pertaining to the zone. Back labels or neck seals are granted by the Consejo to certify that a wine meets the standards laid out in the DO regulations. A Denominación de Origen Provisional (DOP) may be awarded to regions on their way to becoming full DOs. A superior category, Denominación de Origen Calificada (see DOCA), was created in 1991.

Spanish wine law has been subject to some criticism as the list of regions promoted to DO status continues to lengthen (see also

PORTUGAL). The system has most often helped the newer, lesser known DOs improve quality levels to no small degree, but some older, well-known Consejos Reguladores continue to uphold certain local quirks which may sometimes stifle enterprise and initiative among growers and wine-makers.

See also VINO DE MESA and VINO DE LA TIERRA.

doble pasta, dark, full-bodied Spanish wine produced by running off a proportion of fermenting must after two days and adding more crushed grapes to refill the vat. The ratio of skin to pulp is effectively doubled, producing wines with a deep, black colour and very high levels of TANNIN. Doble pasta wines have traditionally been made in JUMILLA, YECLA, UTIEL-REQUENA, and ALÍCANTE, where they are used for blending, but they are being superseded by GRAPE CONCENTRATE.   R.J.M.

DOC, initials which stand for Denominação de Origem Controlada in PORTUGAL and Denominazione di Origine Controllata in ITALY, those countries' much more embryonic counterparts of the French Appellation Contrôlée system of CONTROLLED APPELLATIONS. In both countries, DOC wines represent those regarded as QUALITY WINES by European Union wine law. A DOC system is also evolving in ARGENTINA.

Denominação de Origem Controlada
In Portugal, the DOC system equates roughly with the French APPELLATION CONTRÔLÉE and sets out permitted grape varieties, maximum yields, periods of ageing in bulk and bottle, and analytical standards for specified types of wine. Samples must be submitted to the Instituto da Vinha e do Vinho (IVV), the national authority controlling Portugal's wine industry, who grant numbered seals of origin to producers whose wines have satisfied the regulations.

Many of Portugal's best wines have traditionally been blends from more than one region (see GARRAFEIRA) and therefore excluded from the DOC legislation. A second tier of delimited regions, Indicação de Proveniencia Regulamentada (see IPR), was also introduced following Portugal's entry into the EU, along with a third catch-all category named VINHO REGIONAL roughly equivalent to France's VIN DE PAYS.   R.J.M.

Denominazione di Origine Controllata
Italy's DOC and DOCG classification system of strict and precise regulations established in

1963 did not generally work well since it failed to delimit quality. It was therefore reformed in 1992 in an attempt to give it the credibility it had previously lacked.

Larger DOC zones may now be broken down into subzones, townships, hamlets, microzones, individual estates, and vineyards, giving the entire structure a vertical and hierarchical basis: the new and smaller units more specific than DOC or DOCG zones will be required to have stricter production limits and criteria.

Various DOCs or DOCGs may now cover the same geographical limits, and producers have the option of declassifying their wines from a more restricted to a more extended DOC. Quality is thereby given a geographical basis by anchoring it in smaller, homogeneous areas with a real and proven aptitude for producing fine wines, instead of attaching to definitions such as SUPERIORE or RISERVA, which attempted, and failed, to link better quality with higher levels of alcohol and/or longer periods of ageing. All DOCG and DOC wines are now required to undergo and pass analysis and tasting panels.

A new category of wines called IGT (Indicazione Geografica Tipica), intended as the approximate equivalent of the French VIN DE PAYS, has been created in an attempt to bring all the renowned and high-quality wines selling as vino da tavola into the overall DOC system. See also SUPERTUSCANS. D.T.

DOCa, Denominación de Origen Calificada, is the highest category in Spanish wine law, reserved for regions complying with certain conditions including above-average grape prices, and particularly stringent quality controls. R.J.M.

doce, Portuguese for 'sweet'. See SWEETNESS.

DOCG (Denominazione di Origine Controllata e Garantita) is a legal category intended to identify and reward the finest Italian wines, which were to be 'guaranteed' (the G), and not merely 'controlled' (C). The first five DOCGs to be conferred—BAROLO, BARBARESCO, CHIANTI, BRUNELLO DI MONTALCINO, and VINO NOBILE DI MONTEPULCIANO—are likely to be on everyone's shortlist of Italy's most important wines. The awarding of DOCG status to the undistinguished ALBANA DI ROMAGNA in 1986, however, widely regarded as political in inspiration, met such criticism that it may well have prevented repetition of such an episode.

Fourteen further DOCGs have been approved since 1986, in this chronological order: TORGIANO Riserva, CARMIGNANO, GATTINARA, SAGRANTINO di Montefalco, TAURASI, VERNACCIA DI SAN GIMIGNANO, ASTI and MOSCATO D'ASTI, FRANCIACORTA, BRACHETTO d'Acqui, VERMENTINO di Gallura, GHEMME, GAVI, and VALTELLINA.

The greatest single success of the DOCG, however, was unquestionably the revision of the regulations for CHIANTI when it was promoted from DOC to DOCG in 1984. D.T.

dolce, Italian for 'sweet'. See SWEETNESS.

Dolceacqua, or Rossese di Dolceacqua, wine from the north-western coast of Italy. See LIGURIA.

Dolcetto, an early-ripening, low-acid red grape variety cultivated almost exclusively in the provinces of Cuneo and Alessandria in the north-west Italian region of PIEDMONT. The wines produced are soft, round, fruity, and fragrant with flavours of liquorice and almonds. Most are designed to be drunk in their first two or three years, although well-made bottles of Dolcetto d'Alba and Dolcetto d'Ovada can easily last at least five years.

While low in ACIDITY, relative to BARBERA at least, and therefore 'dolce' (sweet) to the Piedmontese palate, Dolcetto (little sweet one) does have significant TANNINS, which producers have learned to soften with shorter fermentations. So rich are the skins of Dolcetto in ANTHOCYANINS that even the shortest fermentation rarely compromises the deep ruby and purple tones of the wine.

There are seven Dolcetto DOCs in Piedmont: Acqui, ALBA, ASTI, Diano d'Alba, Dogliani, Langhe Monregalesi, and Ovada. Alba, Ovada, and Dogliani are quantitatively the most significant, while Alba is generally considered to produce the finest quality.

Ormeasco is LIGURIA's version of Dolcetto and is therefore the southernmost extent of Dolcetto territory in Italy. It grows just on the Ligurian side of the mountains that separate Piedmont from Liguria. D.T. & J.Ro.

Dôle, red wine made from mainly Pinot Noir with Gamay grapes grown in the Valais of SWITZERLAND. A high proportion of Dôle lacks real interest and concentration but exceptions exist. **Dôle Blanche** is a lightly pressed, pale-pink version. See also BOURGOGNE PASSETOUTGRAINS.

domaine, French word for an estate, typically a vine-growing and wine-making estate in BUR-GUNDY.

domaine bottling, the relatively recent practice of bottling the produce of a DOMAINE on the property which produced it. Such wines are described as **domaine bottled**, or *mis(e) en bouteille au domaine* in French. The term is the BURGUNDY equivalent of Bordeaux's CHÂTEAU BOTTLING, whose history is mirrored by the practice of domaine bottling. Domaine bottling was even later and less common, however, since burgundy is generally produced in very much smaller quantities than bordeaux. Even today, a high proportion of all burgundy is still sold in bulk to be blended for the NÉGOCIANTS' own labels. Poor standards of HYGIENE, and even faults in basic WINE-MAKING, can still dog some domaines and it is by no means the case that all domaine-bottled burgundy is necessarily superior to one bottled by a négociant. A domaine-bottled wine should, however, lack bland anonymity, and any Burgundians prepared to bottle their own wine show signs of ambition.

See also ESTATE BOTTLED.

Domaine de la Romanée-Conti, the most prestigious wine estate in Burgundy, based in Vosne-Romanée. 'The Domaine', as it is frequently called, is co-owned by the de Villaine and Leroy families and produces only GRAND CRU wines: one white, Le MONTRACHET, and six reds: Romanée-Conti and La Tâche, both monopolies (see MONOPOLE) of the domaine, Richebourg, Romanée-St-Vivant, Échezeaux, and Grands Échezeaux. For more details of individual wines, see VOSNE-ROMANÉE and ÉCHEZEAUX. The Domaine is the exception to the law by which no estate in Burgundy may be named after a specific vineyard. Its wines are notable for their richness and longevity. The 1990 Romanée-Conti was released at a record $US900 or £550 a bottle.

Domäne is the German word for 'domaine' but has the additional significance among the wine estates of GERMANY of distinguishing those in the hands of aristocratic families, which may be described as a Domänenweingut, or those in the hands of the state, which may be described as a Weinbaudomäne. If the word Domäne appears on a wine label, the wine should have been produced entirely on the estate.

Domina is a modern red vine CROSSING that has had a certain success in Germany's cooler sites such as the Ahr and Franken. Its parents are Portugieser × Spätburgunder (Pinot Noir) and it combines the productivity of the first with the ripeness, tannins, and colour of the second but not its finesse and fruit.

Dom Pérignon. See PÉRIGNON, DOM.

Doña Ḷlanca, also known as Doña Branco and Moza Fresca, GALICIAN variety grown in north-west Spain, particularly in Monterrei, Bierzo, and to a much lesser extent Valdeorras, where it is known as Valenciana. The slightly bitter white wines of Monterrei suggest there may be potential.

Donnaz, red wine based on NEBBIOLO grapes made in Italy's Valle d'AOSTA.

Doradillo, white grape variety, possibly of Spanish origin, but known today only in AUSTRALIA. It produces handsome quantities of entirely unremarkable wine more suitable for distillation or basic FORTIFIED wines than for bottling as a table wine.

Dordogne, river in SOUTH WEST FRANCE which rises on the Massif Central south west of Clermont-Ferrand, flows through the Corrèze *département*, flows through BERGERAC and related appellations, and in to the GIRONDE estuary, with ST-ÉMILION, POMEROL, FRONSAC, and finally BOURG on its right bank. It is the more northerly of the two 'seas' referred to in the name of ENTRE-DEUX-MERS. VIN DE PAYS de la Dordogne, typically a dry white wine made from Bordeaux grape varieties, may come from anywhere within the *département* named Dordogne, of which Périgueux is the principal town.

Dorin, traditional name of the CHASSELAS grape in the canton of Vaud in SWITZERLAND.

Dornfelder, a HELFENSTEINER × Heroldrebe cross, is increasingly appreciated as the most successful red GERMAN CROSSING. The wine is notable for its depth of colour, its good acidity but attractively aromatic fruit, and, in some cases, its ability to benefit from BARRIQUE ageing and even to develop in bottle. Velvety textured, slightly floral, and sometimes with just a hint of sweetness, Dornfelder can often provide more drinking pleasure than a Spätburgunder (Pinot Noir), perhaps because its producer's ambitions are more limited. It is hardly surprising that it continues to gain ground in most German wine regions, especially Rheinhessen and the Pfalz, where results are particularly appetizing.

dosage, the final addition to a SPARKLING WINE. It may top up a bottle in the case of traditional-method wines, and also determines the sweetness of the finished wine. Some champagnes are made with no, or zero, dosage. See SPARKLING-WINE-MAKING.

Douro, river which rises, as the **Duero,** in the hills far upstream of RIBERA DEL DUERO and flows for more than half its course in Spain until it turns south to form the frontier with PORTUGAL before turning west towards the Atlantic coast to cut a cleft through the hard, granite mountains of northern Portugal. The Douro valley is most famous as the source of the famous fortified wine PORT, although the Douro DOC is increasingly well known for the production of unfortified table wine. Of the Douro's 39,000 ha/96,300 acres of vines, 29,000 ha are authorized for the production of port.

Depending on the year, around half the Douro's total wine production is not FORTIFIED but fermented out to make table wine, the proportion of the crop used to make port being increased only in years when grapes are in short supply. In the past, the best grapes were always used for producing port, but a number of individual properties are now giving Douro red table wines greater priority.

The grape varieties used in making Douro table wines are similar to those used to produce port, more than 90 different grapes being permitted, of which TOURIGA NACIONAL and Tinta Roriz (TEMPRANILLO) are widely accepted as the best for red wines, many of which share the ripe, spicy, tannic character of a young ruby port. Gouveio (thought to be VERDELHO), Malvasia Fina, and Viosinho are the favoured white grapes, although in the late 1990s most Douro white table wines still suffered from poor handling. Wines made from grape varieties (including Cabernet Sauvignon) which are not authorized under the DOC may be designated under the local VINHO REGIONAL Terras Durienses. R.J.M.

Douro bake, traditional expression for the character imparted to wines, especially PORT, matured in the hot, dry climate of the DOURO valley (rather than the much cooler, damper atmosphere of Vila Nova de Gaia, where port has traditionally been matured by the shippers). Some wines matured in the Douro

seem to develop faster, losing colour, browning, and sometimes acquiring a slightly sweet, caramelized flavour—although poor and often unhygienic storage conditions often have a greater impact on wine quality than the climate, and many reputable shippers successfully age large stocks of port in the Douro. R.J.M.

doux, French for sweet, may be applied to still wines with a RESIDUAL SUGAR of 20–30 g/l (and therefore less sweet than MOELLEUX and LIQUOREUX). See SWEETNESS.

drainage, free movement of water through the soil profile or across the land surface; alternatively, the removal of surplus water by artificial means. The importance of good soil drainage for viticulture and wine quality cannot be overstated. See also TERROIR and SOIL AND WINE QUALITY.

DRC, famous initials in the world of fine wine, standing for the DOMAINE DE LA ROMANÉE-CONTI.

dried-grape wines, varied category of generally intense, complex wines made from partially raisined grapes. Grapes with maximum EXTRACT and sugars are required, which normally entails restricting YIELDS. Only the ripest, healthiest grapes are generally picked, which today means a pre-selection by experienced pickers (although see RECIOTO).

Sun drying is still practised in places such as the Sicilian island of PANTELLERIA off Tunisia, and the Greek island of Santorini, but most grape drying for commercial purposes happens in a winery loft, where windows may be opened to let in plenty of air (essential against the development of rot and mould). The duration of the drying process is dictated by the grape variety, the type of wine required, and microclimatic conditions during drying. Sugar-rich Greek grape varieties such as Muscat, Aleatico, and Malvasia require less time than more northern varieties. The main effect of drying grapes is loss of water and the consequent concentration of sugars.

NOBLE ROT may develop on the grapes during dehydration but it is not desired by most practitioners, particularly those making the drier styles of dried-grape wines such as AMARONE.

Dried-grape wines may be divided into two categories: those in which the fresh primary AROMAS are retained and those in which primary aromas are sacrificed to the development of a more complex BOUQUET. The former include most wines based on aromatic varieties such as Muscat, Brachetto, Aleatico, and Riesling, as well as sweet whites where the emphasis is on fruit, such as Recioto di Soave. These are subjected as far as possible to PROTECTIVE wine-making techniques. Vin de paille, Vin Santo, Amarone, and Recioto della Valpolicella of the traditional type are treated oxidatively, the aim being to incorporate in the final tasting experience an evolution of aromas due in some measure to exposure to OXYGEN. See AMARONE and RECIOTO.   S.P.D.L. & N.J.B.

drip irrigation, a form of IRRIGATION in which water is applied literally as drops to each vine from a dripper attached to a plastic pipe. Drip irrigation has transformed viticulture since it allows irrigation of vineyards on undulating land, and uses a limited water supply to maximum advantage.

drought, a severe and prolonged deficit of rainfall, compared with that normally received. Its implications for viticulture depend on the region and its normal climate. In cool and wet viticultural regions, drought years often produce the best vintages, especially of red wines. Such effects are well known in Europe and New Zealand.

Most dry viticultural climates are regularly warm and sunny enough, and drought is nearly always detrimental. Drought in such climates drastically reduces growth and yield, and if very severe can disrupt the RIPENING process more or less completely. Drought in Australia as a consequence of EL NIÑO has had substantial effects on production.

See also CLIMATE AND WINE QUALITY.
                                                    J.G. & R.E.S.

Drouhin, Joseph, one of the most respected NÉGOCIANTS and wine-makers in Burgundy, founded in 1880. Robert Drouhin, who took over control of the firm in 1957, was the first Burgundian to make a significant investment in a wine region outside France. **Domaine Drouhin,** established in 1988, owns significant land in OREGON and 1989 was its first commercial vintage of Pinot Noir, made from bought-in fruit. In 1994, the firm was acquired by its Japanese distributor Snobrand.

Drumborg, particularly cool wine region in the state of Victoria in AUSTRALIA much used as a source of grapes for sparkling wines. See VICTORIA.

Drupeggio, name for the light-berried CANAIOLO Bianco that adds interest, with Trebbiano grapes, to Grechetto, Malvasia, and Verdello, in the ORVIETO wine of central Italy.

dry, adjective often applied to wines, usually to describe those in which there is no perceptible SWEETNESS. Such wines may have as many as 10 g/l RESIDUAL SUGAR, or even more in wines with particularly high ACIDITY (which tends to counterbalance sweetness). In this sense, virtually all red wines are dry, while white, rosé, sparkling, and fortified wines can vary considerably between **bone dry, dry, medium dry,** medium sweet, and sweet. Some wines, particularly reds, are said to have a 'dry finish' if they are especially ASTRINGENT.

Dry Creek Valley, California wine region and AVA north west of Healdsburg. See SONOMA.

drying grapes, which become **dried grapes,** second most common commercial use for viticulture, less important than wine but more important than TABLE GRAPES.

dryland viticulture, viticulture relying entirely on natural rainfall, and a term used, sometimes as a sales pitch, only in regions where IRRIGATION is common.

DTW, DEUTSCHER Tafelwein.

Dubœuf, Georges (1933–), important producer and indefatigable promoter of BEAUJOLAIS, controlling more than 10 per cent of the wine produced in the region, with considerable interests outside it. His company has an annual production of 24 million bottles, and although the famous floral Dubœuf label goes on bottles containing many styles of wine, it is Beaujolais, and white Mâconnais, for which he is best known. More than 4.5 million bottles of his production each year are Beaujolais Nouveau alone. Indeed, the Dubœuf name appears on the label of more than 15 per cent of all the Beaujolais sold anywhere. In the 1980s, Dubœuf expanded outside the Beaujolais region to sell wines from the ARDÈCHE, RHÔNE, and LANGUEDOC.   S.A.

dulce, Spanish for 'sweet'. See SWEETNESS.

Dunkelfelder, dark-skinned GERMAN CROSSING notable mainly for the depth of its colour, a useful commodity in Germany's blending vats.

Duras is perhaps the oldest vine variety still used in the once-famous red wines of GAILLAC. Its presence distinguishes them from the complex mosaic of other blending permutations that comprise the reds of SOUTH WEST FRANCE. It is not grown in the Côtes de Duras, nor anywhere else in any significant amount outside the Tarn *département*, where Gaillac is the chief appellation. In the Tarn, however, it has steadily gained ground, thanks to Gaillac's powerful internal lobby against incoming INTERNATIONAL VARIETIES. Duras, FER, and Syrah are regarded as the principal red wine varieties and Gaillac growers are preparing to increase the proportion of Fer and Duras in their reds as the parvenu Gamay is gradually sent packing. The wine is deeply coloured, full bodied, and lively with good structure and acidity. Varietal Duras produced in Gaillac eloquently demonstrates a marriage of cépage to TERROIR well worth defending.

Duras, Côtes de, red- and white-wine appellation on the north-eastern fringe of BORDEAUX which is regarded as one of the wine districts of SOUTH WEST FRANCE. It is bounded by Côtes du MARMANDAIS to the south, BERGERAC to the north, and ENTRE-DEUX-MERS and Ste-Foy-Bordeaux to the west. The vine varieties are essentially those of Bordeaux, and a specifically Duras character in the red wines is certainly difficult to discern. White Côtes de Duras can display originality, however, especially in the sweet or MOELLEUX wines sometimes produced from the Bordeaux grape varieties Sémillon, Sauvignon Blanc, and Muscadelle together with the south-western specialities ONDENC and MAUZAC. Some Chenin Blanc has also been imported from the Loire. Red-wine production was slightly greater than white-wine production in the early 1990s, and some imported talent (see FLYING WINE-MAKERS) had demonstrated that the appellation was capable of producing good quality at sensible prices.

Durif is a well-travelled black grape variety, a selection of another variety, PELOURSIN. It has all but disappeared from France but was for long erroneously thought to be one and the same as the variety known in both North and South America as PETITE SIRAH. DNA 'FINGERPRINTING' techniques suggested in 1997 that Durif is a crossing of Peloursin with the noble Syrah.

Durif, and Peloursin, are also grown in north-east VICTORIA and the Riverina district of NEW SOUTH WALES in Australia, where De Bortoli make an earthy VARIETAL version.

duty is levied on wine importation and movement into circulation from bond in many countries at an extremely variable level. In general, countries in which viticulture is an economically (and therefore politically) important activity, such as France and Italy, tend to have extremely low duties on wine, while almost non-producing countries, such as Great Britain, and/or those with restrictive policies on the sale of alcoholic drinks, such as Norway, tend to have high duties.

Early Muscat, bred in California as a TABLE GRAPE but successful on a small scale as a wine grape in Oregon.

Échezeaux, GRAND CRU of the village of Flagey-Échezeaux in Burgundy's Côte de Nuits, producing red wines from Pinot Noir grapes. While wines of VILLAGE or PREMIER CRU status in Flagey-Échezeaux are sold under the name of neighbouring VOSNE-ROMANÉE, the majority of the commune's vineyard land is shared between the two grands crus Échezeaux and Grands Échezeaux.

Échezeaux is perhaps fortunate to be rated grand cru as many of its wines are disturbingly light. There are 21 owners of Grands Échezeaux and over 80 of Échezeaux. Proprietors of both include DOMAINE DE LA ROMANÉE-CONTI, Domaine René Engel, and Domaine Mongeard-Mugneret.

See also CÔTE D'OR.   J.T.C.M.

ecological viticulture. See ORGANIC VITI-CULTURE.

Ecuador bottles a considerable quantity of wine (including a SCHEUREBE), but the extent of its vineyards is considerably more limited.

edel means 'noble' in German and thus Edel-fäule is German for NOBLE ROT, Edelkeur is the brand name of one of the most successful sweet wines of SOUTH AFRICA, and EDELZWICKER is the name chosen to add lustre to a not particularly noble blend in ALSACE. Similarly, Gutedel is the German synonym for the not particularly noble CHASSELAS grape.

Edelzwicker, Alsace term, originally German, for what is usually a relatively basic blend. See ALSACE.

Eden Valley, wine region near the important Barossa Valley with a particularly fine reputation for Riesling. See SOUTH AUSTRALIA.

Edna Valley, California wine region and AVA on the ocean side of the coastal mountains. See SAN LUIS OBISPO.

education, wine. Education plays an important part in the production, sale, and enjoyment of a product as complex and, in many countries, as foreign as wine. Detailed knowledge of wine involves an appreciation of history, geography (inevitably including a host of foreign names), science, and technology, quite apart from the development of practical tasting skills.

Education for wine-producing professionals is, naturally, concentrated in the world's wine regions. Some universities, such as Bordeaux, offer courses, especially in tasting, that are open to wine merchants and the general public. There is even more overlap between wine-trade education, courses designed specifically for the wholesale and retail trade, and consumer education; the most enthusiastic wine consumers may well want to know more about wine than the less academically inclined wine traders. The Institute of MASTERS OF WINE, for example, the leading international wine-trade educational body which opened its notoriously stiff series of trade examinations to those unconnected with the wine trade in the early 1990s, admitted its first non-trade 'MW', a Hollywood lawyer, in 1993.

While trade education is usually undertaken by this sort of professional body (the United States has its Society of Wine Educators), consumer education may be undertaken by professional lecturers and wine merchants. This can take the form of TASTINGS so informal as to constitute a party, tutored tastings, BLIND TASTINGS, or some form of wine TOURISM.

Other forms of wine education include wine articles (see WINE WRITERS), books, and various forms of audio-visual instruction such as television programmes, and computer software (see INFORMATION TECHNOLOGY). Interactive wine tasting is a way of combining the practical with the theoretical.

Eger, much-disputed town in north-east HUNGARY whose wines have been exported with success since the 13th century, although various Turkish incursions interrupted this trade. Eger's most famous siege was during the Ottoman occupation of the 16th century, when, according to legend, the defenders of Eger were so dramatically fortified by a red liquid which stained their beards and armour that the Turks retreated, believing their opponents to have drunk Bikavér, or BULL'S BLOOD.

The town gives its name to a wine region on the foothills of the volcanic Bükk mountains. As well as producing Egri Bikavér, currently being revived and rehabilitated, the region produces white wines, notably from LEÁNYKA grapes.

Egypt, North African country which continues to make small quantities of wine (slightly more than ENGLAND produces). The centre of production is in the Gianaclis area about 75 km from Alexandria. Varieties planted include THOMPSON SEEDLESS, CHASSE-LAS, Ezazi, Muscat Samos, Kleopatra, and Talioni for white wines, and the late-ripening Rumi Red, Cabernet Sauvignon, and CARIGNAN for rosés and reds, which are sometimes made sweet. Harvest lasts from mid July to mid September and wines are sold, mainly to tourists, and drunk young.

Ehrenfelser is one of the better GERMAN CROSSINGS, a Riesling × Silvaner. In this case the aim of producing a super-Riesling that will ripen in a wider range of sites was achieved and the crossing's only inherent disadvantages are that the wine is slightly too low in acidity for long-term ageing and that it cannot be called Riesling. It is not nearly as versatile in terms of site as the more recently developed KERNER, which became a more obvious choice as a flexible Riesling substitute.The largest areas of Ehrenfelser are in the Pfalz and Rheinhessen.

Einzellage, literally 'individual site' in the wine regions of GERMANY. Almost all of Germany's vineyards are officially registered as one of these approximately 2,600 **Einzellagen**, which can vary in size from a fraction of 1 ha to more than 200 ha/494 acres. The average size of an Einzellage is about 38 ha, about the same size as a typical BORDEAUX estate. As in BURGUNDY, for example, the vines may be divided among many different owners, who are allowed to put the name of the Einzellage only on QBA and QMP wines. Such names must usually be preceded by the name of the village in which they were produced; thus a wine from the Mandelring vineyard in the village of Haardt is called Haardter Mandelring. In the case of estates such as SCHLOSS JOHANNISBERG and Schloss Vollrads in the RHEINGAU, the name of the property itself suffices as provenance, and Scharzhofberger in the SAAR is considered so important that it dispenses with the prefix Wiltinger, but these cases are rare.

Producers whose output includes a range of bottlings of varying quality have tended to reserve their finest grapes for wines labelled thus, although this, as so much in German wine marketing, is currently in flux. A wine labelled with the name of an Einzellage is likely to be superior to, and certainly more characterful than, one labelled with the name of a GROSSLAGE, a collection of individual Einzellagen for long used as a difficult-to-distinguish commercial entity for labelling purposes.

See also the Austrian term RIED.

Eire. See IRELAND.

Eisacktaler, German for Valle Isarco, pure, dry white wines from the ALTO ADIGE.

Eisenberg, famous wine town in the Burgenland region of AUSTRIA, now part of the Südburgenland district.

Eiswein, German for ICE WINE and a special Prädikat within the QMP quality-wine category defined by the GERMAN WINE LAW. Eisweine are very high in sugar and very high in acidity (like BOTRYTIZED wines), except that in this case the concentration is a direct result of the grapes freezing on the vine. They are then picked and pressed immediately so that water crystals are left in the press and only the sweetest juice, which has a lower freezing point than water, runs from the press. Temperatures of −8 °C/18 °F in the vineyard or cooler are required, so picking of Eisweine usually takes place very early in the morning. The grapes have to be left on the vine at least until November and often until the following calendar year. The resulting wines lack NOBLE ROT, or *Edelfäule*, character, which makes them easier to drink when young, and their high acidity makes them extremely refreshing. The 1962 vintage was the first famous Eiswein vintage in Germany and it is still too early to say how their evolution compares with that of a BEERENAUSLESE (which must reach the same MUST WEIGHT) since very old examples are rare.

The cost of harvesting an Eiswein is less than that of picking individual bunches of grapes for AUSLESE wine; the must weight of an Eiswein is increased by the elimination of some of the water in the grape by freezing; and the market price of Eiswein is much greater than that of an Auslese.

See also AUSTRIA.

Elba, Mediterranean island off TUSCANY. Emigration from the island and the increasing attractions of the booming tourist industry have drastically reduced the role of wine in the overall economic picture. The wines, three-quarters of which are white, are standard Tuscan products: SANGIOVESE with CANAIOLO and/or white grapes for the reds; TREBBIANO (known locally as Procanico) for the whites. Elba's wines are correct but hardly inspiring, and rarely seen outside Tuscany.   D.T.

Elbling is an ancient, and some would say outdated, vine variety. Though still planted in LUXEMBOURG, it is far less important there than Rivaner (MÜLLER-THURGAU). In Germany, it retains a fairly constant 1,100 ha/2,720 acres of vineyard, most of it in the upper reaches of the MOSEL-SAAR-RUWER above Trier, where Riesling has difficulty ripening. Much of the Elbling grown here is used for SEKT. Elbling's wines are distinguished by their often searing acidity and their relatively low alcohol, making them an even tarter, lighter version of SILVANER. Only the most dedicated wine-maker can extract any suggestion of Elbling's evanescent flavour of just-ripe apricots.

El Dorado, California county. See SIERRA FOOTHILLS.

élevage, French word that describes an important aspect of wine-making but has no direct equivalent in English (other than the Anglicization 'elevage'). *Élevage* means literally 'rearing', 'breeding', or 'raising'. When applied to wines, it means the series of cellar operations that take place between FERMENTATION and bottling, suggesting that the wine-maker's role is rather like that of a loving parent who guides, disciplines, and civilizes the raw young wine that emerges from the fermentation vessel. The word *élevage* implies that all this effort is worth it, and is therefore normally applied only above a certain level of wine quality.   A.D.W.

Elgin, cool, promising wine region in SOUTH AFRICA.

El Hierro, denominated Spanish wine region covering the whole of the eponymous island in the CANARY ISLANDS, with 500 ha/1,200 acres of vineyards dominated by the white Vijariego grape, and producing undistinguished table wines.

El Niño, anomalous seasonal ocean current along the coast of Peru, and part of a much larger atmospheric phenomenon called the 'southern oscillation', which can have a substantial impact on vineyard production in several countries where climate is affected by the Pacific Ocean. The phenomenon recurs every 2 to 10 years, and is associated with atmospheric pressure changes in the South Pacific and can be predicted well in advance.

Typical effects were felt in 1998, which started with serious flooding in California and continued there throughout spring and early summer to retard the likely harvest dates. The Australian 1997–8 growing season on the other hand was generally affected by drought, decreasing quantity but greatly improving quality. There was a similar weather pattern in New Zealand. Chile's wine regions experienced a generally cooler, wetter growing season, and in Argentina, around Mendoza, summer storms before vintage created problems. These effects were all predictable with El Niño-induced weather patterns; when combined with long-range weather forecasting, there exist opportunities for speculative wine purchasing.   R.E.S.

embotellado is Spanish for bottled.

Emerald Riesling, one of the earliest of vine varieties developed at the University of California to emerge in VARIETAL (white) wine. It is a Muscadelle × Riesling cross and had its heyday in the late 1960s and early 1970s before slumping towards oblivion. Most of what remains is in the very south of the SAN JOAQUIN VALLEY. It has also been tried with a certain degree of success in SOUTH AFRICA.

Emilia. Western part of EMILIA-ROMAGNA.

Emilia-Romagna, Italian wine region which stretches across north central Italy from the eastern Adriatic coast to include vast tracts of inland Emilia in the west, which is quite distinct from coastal Romagna in the east. The region contains some of Italy's most fertile agricultural land, so it is no surprise that the region's viticulture also produces abundantly.

Quantity, however, is in inverse proportion to quality in the case of Emilia-Romagna: only 15 per cent of the region's total output is DOC wine, and many of the DOC wines—TREBBIANO DI ROMAGNA and Emilia's LAMBRUSCO in particular—fall more into the quaffing than the quality category.

The potential for good wine does exist, none the less, in the sub-Apennine strip on the region's southern border. SANGIOVESE has a long history in Romagna and certain areas to the south of Faenza and Forlì have demonstrated over the past decades that reasonable yields and careful vinification can give SANGIOVESE DI ROMAGNA wines that can compete with good, if not yet the best, Tuscan Sangiovese.

The hills to the south west of Bologna, a DOC zone known as Colli Bolognesi or Monte San Pietro, have given good results with the Bordeaux grapes Sauvignon Blanc, Merlot, and Cabernet Sauvignon, although the quantities made are small.

The Colli Piacentini at the western edge of Emilia-Romagna are geologically and climatically similar to the contiguous OLTREPÒ PAVESE of Lombardy. Its best-known wine, Gutturnio, made from Barbera and CROATINA grapes, can reach the level of a good Oltrepò Rosso and has shown a certain affinity for wood ageing, including small BARREL MATURATION. In addition, the zone produces varietal Barbera, Bonarda (made from the Croatina grape), and refreshing white wines from Malvasia and Sauvignon Blanc grapes. The area's most interesting recent developments, however, have come from the subzone of Riverargo-Vigolzone, where important, age-worthy wines from Chardonnay, Pinot Noir, and, especially, Cabernet Sauvignon indicate that the real potential of the Colli Piacentini is yet to be discovered. These superior wines, just as in the case of the best Sangiovese of Romagna, have generally been marketed as VINO DA TAVOLA, indicating that the DOC label in Emilia-Romagna carries few, if any, connotations of quality or character.   D.T.

Emperor, red table grape that has occasionally been pressed into wine-making duty in times of serious shortage in Australia.

Empordà-Costa Brava, denominated wine region in the extreme north-east corner of Spanish CATALONIA separated from ROUSSILLON only by the French border. The zone, now a DO, used to produce heavy RANCIOS, sometimes called Garnatxa, the Catalan name for the GRENACHE grape. This vine variety and Cariñena (CARIGNAN) still account for 80 per cent of production, although they are mostly turned into bulk rosé for the local market. Exports amount to no more than three per cent of the region's production.   R.J.M. & V. de la S.

Enantio, vine grown in TRENTINO to produce deep-red wine.

encépagement, widely used French term for the mix of *cépages*, or VINE VARIETIES, planted on a particular property. These proportions (typically for a MÉDOC estate, for example, Cabernet Sauvignon 60 per cent, Cabernet Franc 20 per cent, and Merlot 20 per cent) do not necessarily correspond to the proportions of each grape in a given wine.

Encostas d'Aire, an IPR in western Portugal. See ESTREMADURA.

Encruzado, Portuguese white grape variety most commonly planted in DÃO. It can yield quite respectable wine.

engarrafado, Portuguese for bottled.

England, the largest and warmest country in Great BRITAIN and the only one which produces wine in any quantity, albeit minuscule relative to most European wine-producing countries. English wine is an increasingly respectable drink, despite being produced at relatively high LATITUDES. Almost as much as the weather, nomenclature has dogged the fortunes of English wine. Too few consumers realize that English wine is quite distinct from BRITISH WINE: that it is the produce of freshly picked grapes grown in England and Wales, rather than of reconstituted, imported, GRAPE CONCENTRATE. The British government did little to encourage 20th-century English viticulture, for many years charging a lower excise duty on British wine than on the indigenous product.

Vineyards are concentrated in the warmest southern counties of Kent and Sussex, although there are about 400 vineyards all over southern England, and nearly 20 on the southern coast of Wales. Vineyards are planted in all but six counties of England, and the most northerly vineyard in the world is planted in Durham, near latitude 55°. Wine is made in about 115 wineries, some of which make wine for dozens of vineyards.

The maritime influence and the Gulf Stream help to moderate the climate, but grape RIPENING so far from the equator is still hazardous, and grapes may remain on the vine until late October or even November. Vineyard site selection is critical in such a climate.

The most planted varieties are MÜLLER-THURGAU, REICHENSTEINER, and SEYVAL BLANC, whose HYBRID status presented a major stumbling block to introducing a QUALITY WINE scheme that meets with European Union approval (see below). On the remaining 60 per cent of English vineyard is grown a patchwork of dozens of other varieties, typically white GERMAN CROSSINGS, representing the frustrations of a nascent industry trying to coax RIPENESS from the English climate. BACCHUS, SCHÖNBURGER, MADELEINE ANGEVINE, and PINOT NOIR have their devotees and there has been considerable recent interest in red-wine-making in general, often relying on red-fleshed varieties or occasionally plastic tunnels.

Total wine production can vary considerably, according to VINTAGE. Average yields are about 35 hl/ha (2 tons/acre) in a good year. English wine's hallmark, high acidity, is useful for traditional-method SPARKLING WINE, which may turn out to be England's finest vinous product. Increasingly sophisticated wine-making techniques are being introduced for still wines, however, such as MALOLACTIC FERMENTATION, BARREL MATURATION (or added OAK CHIPS), and even some BOTRYTIZED WINE.

In the 1980s, a high proportion of English wine was sweetened using (often imported)

SWEET RESERVE, but a more typical current style is dry, aromatic, its acidity balanced by a certain amount of BODY, even if considerably assisted by CHAPTALIZATION.

The average vineyard is just over 2 ha in size, and often lacks marketing skills, relying heavily on tourist traffic (not unlike the other far-northern wine industries of CANADA and upstate NEW YORK, with which England shares many features, although not their extremely low winter temperatures).

To fit into the EU's requirements for nomenclature, wine may be labelled either as United Kingdom TABLE WINE, occasionally English (or Welsh) Vineyards QUALITY WINE or, if it contains a HYBRID such as Seyval Blanc, Regional Counties wine.

enologist is the American and South African spelling of OENOLOGIST, just as **enology** is the alternative spelling of OENOLOGY, the study of wine and, especially, wine-making.

enoteca, term used frequently in Italy for a wine shop with a significant range of high-quality wines, as opposed to a *bottiglieria*, a shop with a more pedestrian selection, and a *vineria*, more of a tavern, in which wine is sold by the glass as well as by the bottle. Various **enoteche** in Italy offer tasting facilities and some serve food to accompany the wines.   D.T.

en primeur, wine-trade term, French in origin, for wine sold as FUTURES before being bottled. It comes from the word PRIMEUR. En primeur sales are a relatively recent speciality, but not exclusivity, of CLASSED GROWTHS by the BORDEAUX TRADE. Cask samples of wines have customarily been shown in the spring following the vintage and sales solicited, through BROKERS and NÉGOCIANTS, almost immediately. A particular property often releases only a certain proportion of its total production, depending on its need for cash and reading of the market.

The consumer pays the opening price as soon as the offer is made and then, up to two years later, having paid the additional shipping costs and DUTY, takes delivery of the wine after it has been bottled and shipped. The theory is that by buying wine early, the consumer not only secures sought-after wines, he or she also pays less. This is by no means invariably the case, however, as outlined in INVESTMENT in wine.

En primeur purchases have many disadvantages in periods of economic recession. Not only do prices stagnate or even fall, but there is a much higher risk that one of the many commercial concerns in the chain between wine producer and wine consumer will fail, leaving the consumer with the possibility of having paid for the wine without any prospect of receiving it. There is also the important fact that en primeur purchases inevitably mean investing in an embryonic product. A third-party's assessment of a single cask sample taken at six months is a poor justification for financial outlay on a liquid that is bottled only a year later (and is particularly hazardous for a wine as notoriously transient as red BURGUNDY), unless the wine market is extremely buoyant.

Buying en primeur may make financial sense only for the most authoritatively lauded vintages and the most sought-after wines, although it can of course give a great deal of pleasure to those with a strong wine-COLLECTING instinct.

Entraygues, or Entraygues et du Fel, Vins d', miniature VDQS around Entraygues on the river Lot in SOUTH WEST FRANCE. Reds can be made from a wide range of south-western vine varieties while the even rarer whites are made from Chenin Blanc and Mauzac.

Entre-Deux-Mers, large area of the BORDEAUX wine region between the rivers DORDOGNE and GARONNE; hence a name which means 'between two seas'. A high proportion of the vineyard land in this pretty, green region produces light-red, often slightly austere wine from Merlot and Cabernet grapes which is sold as BORDEAUX AC. Indeed, since vine-growers converted their white-wine vineyards to red varieties in the 1960s and 1970s, the Entre-Deux-Mers district has become the chief source of red Bordeaux AC. The Entre-Deux-Mers region contains a number of other appellations, some of them enclaves such as GRAVES DE VAYRES, STE-FOY, Bordeaux-Haut-Benauge (dry white wines which may also be sold as Entre-Deux-Mers-Haut-Benauge). The PREMIÈRES CÔTES DE BORDEAUX and its sweet-white-wine-making enclave lie between the Entre-Deux-Mers appellation and the river Garonne. Wines sold as Entre-Deux-Mers are dry whites made, with degrees of wine-making skill which vary from minimal to dazzling, mainly from Sauvignon together with Sémillon, Muscadelle, and Ugni Blanc grapes. After Bordeaux AC, this is the biggest dry-white-wine appellation in the Bordeaux region, producing a declining total that was almost 150,000 hl/3.96 million gal in 1996. Most Entre-Deux-Mers should be drunk as young as possible. Chx Haut-Rian, Moulin de Launay, and Ninon make better wine than most.

Épineuil, commune just west of Chablis. See Côtes d'AUXERRE.

Erbaluce, white grape variety, speciality of Caluso in the north of the PIEDMONT region of north-west Italy. Most dry Erbaluce is relatively light bodied and acidic, although there are some fine examples. In the 1990s, significantly improved versions from the NÉGOCIANT houses of Orsolani and Bava indicated the wine is potentially as interesting as ARNEIS and fuller and richer than GAVI, Piedmont's two best-known white wines. Erbaluce's most famous, if rare, manifestation is the golden sweet Caluso PASSITO.

Ermitage, alternative and historic name for HERMITAGE in the northern Rhône.

Erzeugerabfüllung, German word meaning literally 'producer bottled'. In theory this word should indicate quality, and certainly all the finest wines of Germany qualify as Erzeugerabfüllung, but, as in France (see MIS EN BOUTEILLE), the term may be used by CO-OPERATIVES to describe blends of wines from many different member-producers over whose viticultural techniques the bottler exercises no control. One useful aspect of the term, however, in a country where wine-label obfuscation is rife, is that it cannot be used by the giant mass-market bottlers (see GERMANY and, particularly, MOSEL-SAAR-RUWER), except for those vineyards they themselves own. GUT-SABFÜLLUNG is a more exclusive term.

Esgana Cão, synonym for the Portuguese white grape variety known on the island of Madeira as SERCIAL. Its name on the mainland means 'dog strangler', presumably a reference to its notably high ACIDITY. It can be found as an ingredient in VINHO VERDE, BUCELAS, and white PORT.

Espadeiro, red grape variety known, although not widely grown, in both the RÍAS BAIXAS zone of Galicia and Portugal's VINHO VERDE country. It can produce quite heavily and rarely reaches high sugar levels. A vine called Espadeiro grown near Lisbon may in fact be TINTA AMARELA.

Esquitxagos, common grape with an uncommon name found around Tarragona in eastern Spain. It may be identical to MER-SEGUERA.

Estaing, Vins d', miniature VDQS around Estaing up the river Lot from ENTRAYGUES in SOUTH WEST FRANCE. Reds can be made from a wide range of south-western vine varieties. A very small quantity of white wine is made from Chenin Blanc and Mauzac. The climate here makes MARCILLAC look positively balmy.

estate bottled, term used on labels which has a very specific meaning in the United States, where an estate-bottled wine must come from the winery's own vineyards or those on which the winery has a long lease; both vineyards and winery must be in the geographical area specified on the label. This is the American counterpart of CHÂTEAU BOTTLED or DOMAINE BOTTLED.

Estremadura, VINHO REGIONAL in western Portugal. It covers a group of six wine regions north of Lisbon on the west coast of PORTUGAL: the three IPRS Encostas d'Aire, Alcobaça, Óbidos, and the three DOCS Alenquer, Torres Vedras, and Arruda. Few consumers have heard of them and there are still few wines of any real quality, yet Estremadura produces more wine than any other part of Portugal. Some wine continues to be sold for the manufacture of Portugal's national brands of VERMOUTH. Most of the wine from Estremadura's productive, maritime vineyards is sold in returnable 5-l/1.3-gal flagons known as *garrafoes* that are to be found in taverns and restaurants all over the Portuguese-speaking world.

The region is dominated by 15 large CO-OPERATIVES. Most growers have so far put quantity before quality in order to maximize returns from their tiny plots of land and so vine varieties have been chosen for their yield and resistance to disease in the warm, humid Atlantic climate. As many as 30 different varieties are officially permitted and, because of a tradition of making wine for DISTILLATION, white grapes outnumber red. Wine-making in Estremadura has begun to improve, however. With financial help from the European Union, co-operatives are installing more modern equipment. A number of single estates in the Alenquer district are producing more individual wines.   R.J.M.

Étoile, L'. See L'ÉTOILE.

EU stands for European Union.

Euskadi. See BASQUE.

EU table wine is wine at its most basically European, a blend of TABLE WINES from more than one country in the European Union. The constituents of an EU table wine tend to vary with the vagaries of the bottom layer of the European wine market. One of the most common blends, however, has been neutralized cheap white VINO DA TAVOLA from Italy 'Germanized' by the addition of some German TAFELWEIN made from a heavily aromatic variety such as MORIO-MUSKAT, and sold as EWG TAFELWEIN. In France, EU table-wine blends have included blends of French red VIN DE TABLE and much deeper coloured vino da tavola from southern Italy, and blends of French white vin de table with the much cheaper Spanish white VINO DE MESA. The market for such concoctions is, thankfully, shrinking.

evaporation, the conversion of water (or other liquids) from the liquid to the gaseous or vapour state, brought about by the input and absorption of heat energy, has important implications for maturing wines.

Evaporation causes a loss of liquid stored in tight wooden containers, such as wine undergoing BARREL MATURATION. WATER, the principal component in wines, diffuses through small pores of OAK, eventually reaching the outer surface of the stave, where it evaporates into the atmosphere. ALCOHOL also diffuses through the stave, but at a rate considerably slower than that of water. Wine subjected to barrel maturation in a high-humidity storage cellar will decrease in ALCOHOLIC STRENGTH whereas that stored in a dry cellar will increase.

Evaporation makes regular TOPPING UP of a barrel necessary. The space left by evaporation is called the ULLAGE.

EWG Tafelwein, German term for EU TABLE WINE.

ex cellar(s), way of buying direct from wine producers and the price they quote.

extract, or dry extract, the sum of the non-volatile solids of a wine: the sugars, non-volatile ACIDS, minerals, PHENOLICS, GLYCEROL, glycols, and traces of other substances such as proteins, pectins, and gums. A wine's extract can vary considerably depending on the wine's SWEETNESS, COLOUR (red wines usually having a higher extract than whites, thanks to their greater phenolic content), and age, since some extract is precipitated as SEDIMENT over the years.

To be high in extract, a wine does not necessarily have to be high in alcohol or BODY. Many fine German wines are high in extract, and yet are low in alcohol and are light bodied, especially low-yield Rieslings after dry summers. A.D.W.

extraction in a wine context usually refers to the extraction of desirable PHENOLICS from grape solids during and after FERMENTATION, although **over-extraction** is an increasingly common fault in an era when colour is associated with quality. Such wines lack FRUIT and BALANCE. See MACERATION.

Extremadura, one of the 17 autonomous regions in SPAIN and, perhaps surprisingly, the country's fourth most important wine region. Spain's wild west is hardly ideal for growing grapes. Sheep are reputed to outnumber people in this semi-arid upland area between CASTILE-LA MANCHA and PORTUGAL. Most of the wine is sold in bulk for distillation and ends up as brandy de Jerez. Local names were beginning to appear on wine labels with increasing frequency in the late 1990s, however, following the trail blazed by Bodegas Inviosa in the Tierra de Barros ('land of mud') zone near the Portuguese border, which shares climate and soil features with neighbouring ALENTEJO.

The regional administration settled in the late 1990s for a single DO for the wine areas in Extremadura—Ribera del Guadiana. CENCIBEL, GARNACHA, GRACIANO, and, increasingly, CABERNET SAUVIGNON dominate amongst red grape varieties, and CAYETANA and PARDINA amongst white ones. With European Union financing, a rapid overhaul of production methods has been taking place. CORK is an important crop here. R.J.M. & V. de la S.

Ezerjó, white grape variety widely planted in HUNGARY but scarcely known outside it. Most of the wine produced is relatively anodyne, but Móri Ezerjó produced from the vineyards near the town of Mór enjoys a certain following as a light, crisp, refreshing drink, and the Ezerjó grown, in quantity, in the far north west of Hungary can also yield lively dry whites for early consumption. Ezerjó means 'a thousand boons'.

Faber, or Faberrebe, a German vine crossing of Weissburgunder (Pinot Blanc) and Müller-Thurgau. It will ripen easily in sites unsuitable for Riesling and is planted mainly in Rheinhessen. Germans see Faber as a 'traditional' variety in that it shows some of the raciness of Riesling and has markedly more acidity than Müller-Thurgau. Acidity levels are even higher than those of Silvaner, which adds considerably to its appeal, although the wines are not intensely flavoured, are not designed to age, and are generally more useful for blending than for VARIETAL wines. A little is also grown in England.

Falanghina, or Falanghina Greco, very characterful ancient white grape which may have provided a basis for the classical FALERNIAN and is still grown on the coast of Campania north of Naples. It is enjoying a small revival in southern Italy.

Falernian or Falernum was the most famous and most highly prized wine of Italy in the Roman period. It was produced on the southern slopes of Monte Massico, the range of hills which runs down to the west coast of Italy in northern CAMPANIA.

The contemporary revival is Falerno del Massico, produced in white, blended red, and all-PRIMITIVO-grape versions in modern CAMPANIA.   J.J.P.

Fara, small red-wine DOC in the Novara hills of eastern PIEDMONT in north-west Italy. The wines are made from the NEBBIOLO grape. See SPANNA, the local name for Nebbiolo.

Far South West, strange new name for the Australian wine region formerly known as Drumborg in the Western VICTORIA zone.

fashion has played a part in wine consumption, and therefore eventually wine production, for at least two millennia. What was most remarkable about fashions in wine consumption in the late 20th century, however, was how rapidly wine production reacted to them, and in some cases created them (see wine BRANDS, LOW-ALCOHOL WINE, and wine BOXES among others). The speed of producer reaction is doubtless related to the development of wine criticism, and its publication in the more immediate media of newspapers, newsletters, magazines, radio, and television, rather than books (see WINE WRITERS).

Perhaps the most significant fashion of the 1970s and 1980s was for VARIETAL wines, especially but by no means exclusively in the NEW WORLD. This led to a dramatic increase in the area planted with INTERNATIONAL VARIETIES—Chardonnay, Cabernet Sauvignon, and more recently Merlot, in particular. During a single decade, the 1980s, the world's total area planted with Chardonnay vines quadrupled, to nearly 100,000 ha/247,000 acres. There is hardly a country in which wine is produced that does not at least try to produce commercially acceptable Chardonnay in marketable quantities.

On a much more limited scale, the development of a cult following for the distinctive wines of CONDRIEU in the northern Rhône meant that VIOGNIER, the vine variety from which it is made, was introduced to wine regions as far afield as ROUSSILLON, South Australia, and several parts of California in the late 1980s and early 1990s. The RHÔNE RANGERS have had the effect of imbuing all varieties with a Rhône connection with glamour—both increasing new plantings of them and enforcing a re-evaluation of such previously unfashionable varieties as MOURVÈDRE/Mataro and GRENACHE.

The 1990s saw an even more significant development, however, a dramatic shift in consumer taste away from white wines to red. Just as a high proportion of northern CALIFORNIA's post-PHYLLOXERA replantings and AUSTRALIA's ambitious new plantings were assigned to the then fashionable Chardonnay, it became clear that the wine drinker of the 1990s would in fact prefer red—partly for heavily touted, perceived HEALTH benefits. A Chardonnay glut was forecast, and Merlot became the most fashionable wine in the United States by quite a margin. This led to imaginative sourcing of Merlot, any Merlot, imported in bulk from CHILE (where much of it may in fact have been CARMENÈRE) and the LANGUEDOC by North American bottlers.

There have inevitably been casualties among unfashionable vine varieties. Many workhorse varieties have lost ground, which is no great shame, but so has an often rich diversity of indigenous varieties, which is surely regrettable. Outside Germany and Austria, the Riesling vine was one of the most significant varieties to have suffered an unwarranted contraction of influence during the 1980s. Riesling grape prices in many regions seem unreasonably low considering the intrinsic quality of the wine.

In the vineyard, there has been a fashion for seeking not just RIPENESS, but PHYSIOLOGICAL RIPENESS, and in the mouth, the all-important, satisfying MOUTHFEEL. Indeed, American winemakers of the 1990s were primarily concerned with texture rather than flavour.

Another viticultural fashion in evidence around the world has been the long overdue acceptance of the now much-vaunted maxim that 'wine is made in the vineyard not the winery'. But if WINE-MAKERS were so much more fashionable than VITICULTURISTS in the 1980s, some of what they did seemed heavily influenced by fashion. Just as the flavour of new OAK, particularly French oak, became extremely fashionable in the 1980s, as to a lesser extent did the overt flavours of MAL-OLACTIC FERMENTATION in some quarters, there

was a strong, anti-oak backlash in the 1990s. In Australia in particular, there has been a fashion for wines deliberately sold as 'unoaked'.

Of course, fashions change rapidly and can be at least national if not parochial. What is fashionable in southern England, for example, may not be fashionable in Sydney or San Francisco. But for certain periods there are wine types and whole wine regions which can be said to be generally out of fashion outside their region or country of production. Obvious examples in the late 1990s included most German wines, sherry, and Beaujolais, although there were signs of a revival in the fortunes of at least the first two.

The problem with Beaujolais is that it is almost exactly the opposite of the ultra-fashionable wine archetype of the late 1990s: deeply red, smoothly textured, intensely flavoured, low in acidity, high in alcohol. Perhaps by the year 2010 it will be considered the height of fashion.

fattoria, Italian for a farm, also used for a wine estate. A *fattoria* is generally bigger than a PODERE, which is often a small farm carved out of a larger property and designed to be just large enough to support a sharecropper/tenant and his family.

Faugères, promising red-wine appellation in the LANGUEDOC in southern France. The vineyards are mainly at relatively high altitudes (often well above 250 m/820 ft) in the foothills of the Cévennes, looking down on the plains around Béziers, where vines are dedicated to VIN DE PAYS and VIN DE TABLE. The Faugères appellation vineyards are planted with quintessentially Mediterranean grape varieties to produce big, southern reds that taste like a cross between the spice of the southern RHÔNE and wild, rustic CORBIÈRES to the south west. The ubiquitous Carignan is gradually being replaced by Syrah, Grenache, and Mourvèdre (each of them mandatory in Faugères), and Cinsaut is still grown for fruit and rosés. As Carignan declines in importance, so CARBONIC MACERATION is expected to be replaced by more traditional vinification techniques. From 1997, Carignan may represent no more than 40 per cent of the blend. Top-quality producers such as Alquier, Léon Barral, Estanilles, and La Liquière have been experimenting with BARREL MATURATION since the mid 1980s. In the late 1990s, there were plans afoot to approve a white version made from Marsanne, Roussanne,

Grenache Blanc, Rolle, and possibly Viognier (rather than selling their whites as Coteaux du Languedoc).

faults in wines vary, of course, according to the taste of the consumer. Some diners will quite wrongly 'send back' a wine (see SERVING WINE and SOMMELIER) simply because they find it is not to their taste. Taste varies not only according to individuals but also according to nationality. Italians are generally more tolerant of BITTERNESS, Americans of SWEETNESS, Germans of SULPHUR DIOXIDE, the French of TANNINS, and the British of decrepitude (see MATURITY) in their wines, while Australians tend to be particularly sensitive to MERCAPTANS and most Americans view HERBACEOUSNESS as a fault rather than a characteristic. To winemakers, however, wine faults are specific departures from an acceptable norm, the least quantifiable of which may be a lack of TYPICALITY.

Visible faults

Faults in a wine's appearance are generally either hazes, clouds, or precipitates in the bottle, all of which hazards STABILIZATION is designed to avoid. Haze and cloud in bottled wines can have a variety of causes, of which the most common today is the growth of the micro-organisms YEAST or bacteria. Mycoderma is a yeast-related fault which forms a film on the wine's surface (and so may be visible to wine-makers, if not wine consumers).

Precipitates, especially crystalline ones, are found from time to time and are usually the harmless result of excess potassium or calcium TARTRATES finally coming out of solution. (Tartrate stabilization usually prevents this.) From white wines, these may form as needle-like colourless or white crystals on the end of the cork in contact with the wine or in the bottom of the bottle, where they look misleadingly like shards of glass. From red wine, tartrate crystals are usually dyed red or brown from the adsorbed PHENOLICS. See SEDIMENT.

Visible bubbles in a supposedly still wine are frequently viewed as a fault. Some wines, particularly off-dry whites, are deliberately bottled with a trace of CARBON DIOXIDE gas to make them taste more refreshing. Bubbles in a bottle of older wine, particularly a red wine, usually indicate unintentional FERMENTATION IN BOTTLE, however, and are definitely a fault.

While most consumers would agree that cloudy wines are faulty, there is much less

agreement about COLOUR. Some wine judges in COMPETITIONS automatically disqualify rosé wines with a hint of amber, even though it is almost impossible to make a blueish-pink wine out of the GRENACHE grape variety, for example—and wines of all sorts and hues turn amber with age.

OXIDATION, which can brown wines prematurely, is a fault in young table wines but is best confirmed by the nose.

Smellable faults

Some wines smell so stale and unpleasant that the taster is unwilling even to taste them. The most likely explanation for this is a mouldy cork causing CORK TAINT. Such a wine is said to be CORKED, but a wine served with small pieces of cork floating in it indicates a fault in the SERVICE of the wine rather than a fault in the wine. Contact with fragments of sound cork does not harm wine.

Other off-odours can vary considerably. OXIDIZED wines smell flat and aldehydic. Vinegary wines indicate the presence of acetic acid due to microbiological activity by bacteria and yeast. Ethyl acetate, hydrogen sulphide, mercaptans, excess sulphur dioxide, and the smellable compounds generated by some bacteria all can be reasons for judging a wine faulty. The picture is complicated, however, by the fact that we all vary in our sensitivities to most of these compounds (see TASTING), and some of them may be more acceptable in some sorts of wine than others. Acetaldehyde, for example, is the principal odorant of fino SHERRIES, but definitely indicates over-oxidation in white wines, and makes red wines taste vapid and flat. Although the average palate should not detect acetic acid on a fault-free wine, there are some much-admired, full-bodied red wines (such as some PORT, PENFOLDS Grange, and VEGA SICILIA) whose VOLATILITY is much higher than the norm. Many fine German wine-makers at one time deliberately used relatively high concentrations of sulphur dioxide to preserve some of their best wines for a long life in bottle.

A wine may not smell clean because of the influence of one or several CONTAMINANTS such as agrochemical residues. If it smells of geranium leaves, there has probably been some bacterial degradation of sorbic acid, although this can easily be controlled by adding sulphur dioxide at the same time.

A wine may smell MOULDY either because of bacterial spoilage, or because it has taken on the smell of a less-than-clean container. A wine tainted by waterlogged casks may be described as stagnant.

Another much-discussed microbiological fault, which can cause a wine to smell mousy, may be caused by yeasts of the BRETTANOMYCES genus. It can be a symptom of other bacterial and yeast activity and cannot normally be smelled in wine unless it is alkalinized or rubbed in the palm of the hand (an action which neutralizes wine acidity). This mousy flavour is not immediately apparent but builds up in the back of the mouth once a wine has been swallowed or expectorated.

Tastable faults

Most faults are already obvious to the nose and need only confirmation on the palate (which is why in a restaurant it is, strictly speaking, necessary only to smell a sample of wine offered by the waiter). Some contaminations, notably from metal, are easier to taste than smell, however, and a wine that is excessively tannic or bitter (see BALANCE) will not display this fault to the eye or nose. See also CONTAMINANTS. A.D.W.

Favorita, white grape of PIEDMONT in north-west Italy, cultivated near ALBA, both on the left bank of the Tanaro in the ROERO zone, and on the right bank in the LANGHE hills. The wine has a pleasant citric tang, and its higher ACIDITY seems to permit longer AGEING, but it has no very marked personality. Experiments with small BARREL MATURATION have added more aromatic qualities, as have blends with more characterful grape varieties, Chardonnay in particular. Favorita may have more of a future as the base wine of a blend than as a VARIETAL wine. D.T.

Fendant, Valais name for the most planted grape variety in SWITZERLAND, the productive CHASSELAS. Fendant is therefore one of the most common Swiss VARIETAL wines, although the finest examples of Valais wines made from this grape variety tend to have some geographical designation on the label.

Fer, alias Fer Servadou (and many other aliases), is a black grape variety traditionally encouraged in a wide variety of the sturdy red wines of SOUTH WEST FRANCE. In MADIRAN, where it is often called Pinenc, it is a distinctly minor ingredient, alongside Tannat and the two Cabernets. In GAILLAC, where it is known as Brocol or Braucol, it has also lost ground. It

is technically allowed into wines as far north as BERGERAC, but today it is most important to the red wines of ENTRAYGUES, ESTAING, and the defiantly smoky, rustic MARCILLAC. The iron-hardness of the name refers to the vine's wood rather than the resulting wine, although it is well coloured, concentrated, and interestingly scented. Fer has also been invited to join the already crowded party of varieties permitted in CABARDÈS.

The variety called Fer in Argentina is apparently a clone of MALBEC.

fermentation, as it applies to wine, is the process of converting sugar to ethyl alcohol and CARBON DIOXIDE effected by the anaerobic (oxygen-free) metabolism of YEAST.

The time required for complete fermentation of white grape juice or crushed red grapes varies greatly. The TEMPERATURE maintained in the fermenting mass is the principal factor affecting duration of fermentation (as well as resultant character of the wine). In general, red-wine fermentations are complete within four to seven days but white wines, which are frequently fermented at much lower temperatures, may require several weeks, occasionally months, and sometimes years in the case of extremely sweet musts (see DRIED-GRAPE WINES, for instance).

Styles of wines in the making of which the fermentation may be arrested deliberately include PORT, VIN DOUX NATUREL, and other VINS DE LIQUEUR in which yeast is overpowered by the addition of alcohol, usually GRAPE SPIRIT.

Variants in the fermentation process include BARREL FERMENTATION, CARBONIC MACERATION, ROSÉ-WINE-MAKING, and, quite distinct from the primary or alcoholic fermentation, FERMENTATION IN BOTTLE, MALOLACTIC FERMENTATION, and SECONDARY FERMENTATION.

See also MACERATION, the process that inevitably accompanies red-wine fermentation, and also RED-WINE-MAKING, WHITE-WINE-MAKING, and SPARKLING-WINE-MAKING. A.D.W.

fermentation in bottle plays an important part in SPARKLING-WINE-MAKING. In most still wines, however, it is one of the wine FAULTS most feared by wine-makers.

The implications of a fermentation in bottle for the wine consumer can range from an inconsequential level of CARBON DIOXIDE in the wine to the generation of such large quantities of the gas that it explodes. This latter, potentially dangerous, occurrence is most likely if the wine contains significant amounts of fermentable sugar and is kept at warm room temperatures. If the fermentation is bacterial rather than by yeast, gas is usually produced, together with off-flavours, cloud, or haze.

A low level of gas in a wine, particularly a young white wine, is by no means necessarily a sign of unwanted fermentation in bottle. Many wine-makers deliberately incorporate a low level of carbon dioxide to enliven some wines.

A.D.W.

fermented in bottle, legitimate description of a SPARKLING WINE made by the traditional, transversage, or transfer methods described in SPARKLING-WINE-MAKING. Only traditional-method wines could claim to be **fermented in this bottle,** however.

Fernão Pires, versatile white Portuguese variety that is the country's most planted. Its distinctive aroma can be somewhat reminiscent of boiled cabbage. Useful in blends, it is planted all over Portugal, notably in the RIBATEJO (where some oak-aged and botrytized sweet wines have been produced) and, as Maria Gomes, is the most common white grape variety in BAIRRADA, where it is often used for sparkling wines.

Ferreira, one of the leading Portuguese port shippers, established in 1715, and now part of SOGRAPE. Ferreira own four properties in the Douro: Quinta do Seixo and Quinta do Porto near Pinhão and Quinta da Leda high up in the Douro and Quinta do Caêdo near Pinhão. Ferreira is the leading brand of port in Portugal and pioneered the production of high-quality dry red wines of the DOURO of which their famous Barca Velha was the prototype.

Feteasca, Fetiaska, or Feteaska, scented white grape variety grown widely in eastern Europe. ROMANIA, where the variety is the most widely grown vine by far, has two subvarieties, respectively white and royal: Fetească Albă and the exclusively Romanian Fetească Regală. There is also a dark-skinned variant, Fetească Neagră, whose red wines show potential when well vinified. Feteasca is made into peachy, aromatic, almost MUSCAT-like wines with definite if varying degrees of RESIDUAL SUGAR and, often, slightly too little ACIDITY. Fetească Regală was Romania's most planted grape variety in the early 1990s.

The vine is also important in HUNGARY, where it is known as LEÁNYKA, in Bulgaria, Moldova, and the Ukraine.

Fiano, strongly flavoured classical vine responsible for CAMPANIA's Fiano di Avellino in southern Italy. Wines made from this variety are sturdy, are capable of developing for many years in bottle, and can mature from honeyed through spicy to nutty flavours (although old-fashioned wine-making has in some cases added its own notes of heaviness and premature OXIDATION).

Fiddletown, California wine region and higher of the two AVAS in the SIERRA FOOTHILLS.

Fié, occasionally written Fiét, old Loire white grape variety that is thought to be an ancestor of SAUVIGNON BLANC. The variety has largely been abandoned because of its remarkably low yield, but producers such as Jacky Preys of Touraine pride themselves on their richer versions of Sauvignon made from particularly old Fié vines.

Fiefs Vendéens, small, oceanic VDQS zone south of the Muscadet zone near the mouth of the Loire. Most wines are red, from Gamay and Cabernet, but there are rosés, and some whites made from varying combinations of Loire grapes, including Chenin Blanc, Sauvignon Blanc, and Grolleau Gris.

field blend, a mixture of different vine varieties planted in the same vineyard, as was once common. It is rare today but some of California's oldest vineyards are thus planted.

fifth growth. See the CLASSIFICATION of Bordeaux.

fighting varietal, term coined in CALIFORNIA in the mid 1980s for relatively inexpensive, cork-finished (as opposed to JUG) VARIETAL wines. As varietal names gained currency in the US market, producers of low-priced wines began bottling Cabernet Sauvignon, Chardonnay, and other sought-after varieties from areas capable of producing large crops at low prices, and thus was born a replacement class of wines for old-fashioned GENERIC jug wines. Fighting varietals, though far from grand, improve upon what went before.

fill level, an aspect of individual bottles of wine which can be closely related to the condition of the wine. The lower the fill level when a wine is bottled, the greater the space between the top of the wine and the bottom of the cork (the so-called ULLAGE) in which OXYGEN may be trapped in the bottle and may hasten the AGEING process. Most bottlers try to ensure that there is minimal ullage space in the bottle immediately after bottling, perhaps a depth of 1 mm/0.04 in. Subsequent reductions in temperature cause a reduction in the wine's volume, thereby apparently lowering the fill level. For wines designed for early consumption, this is unlikely to make much difference, but fill levels are important indicators of the condition of a fine and, especially, mature wine, so that fill levels should always be specified by the AUCTION houses and other FINE-WINE TRADERS. The lower the fill level, the more likely a harmful level of OXIDATION and therefore the lower should be the selling price. Despite this perception, experience shows many wines which age in bottle with substantial ullage exhibit no signs of oxidation. Some sorts of wine seem more resilient to low fill levels than others—vintage port and Sauternes are examples—and a low fill level can apparently, sometimes usefully, hasten the ageing process of an extremely TANNIC wine.

During long-term BOTTLE AGEING, some wine is likely to be absorbed by the CORK, resulting in a drop in fill level of perhaps 7 mm after 10 years. (To reduce this absorption effect, Ch MOUTON-ROTHSCHILD adopted a policy of using shorter corks from the 1991 vintage.) Some wine may also evaporate from the top of the bottle during this time, especially if some was trapped between the cork and the inside of the bottle-neck during bottling. Other reasons for a low fill level include poor control during bottling, wine being bottled at too high a temperature, and a faulty cork. In any event, it is always wise policy to pick bottles with the highest fill levels off the shelf, and to drink bottles of wine from the same case from lowest to highest fill level since the wine in bottles with the lowest fill level is likely to be the most evolved.

Note that the fill level in wine GLASSES should ideally be less than half the height of the glass and never more than two-thirds, in order to provide somewhere for the AROMA to collect.

filtration, controversial wine-making process whereby solid particles are strained out of the wine with various sorts of filter. Filtration is a physical alternative to natural SETTLING and requires more expensive equipment but much less patience. Basically, filtration speeds the wine-making process and allows

better control, thereby lowering production costs.

Filtration of fine wines is a controversial issue. While it may be a necessity for ordinary commercial wines, too heavy a filtration can indeed rob a fine wine of some of its complexity and capacity to age, not to mention some loss of colour, particularly a red wine as subtle as some fine red BURGUNDY. Carefully made fine red wine which has benefited from extended BARREL MATURATION should not need filtration. Some commentators and wine-makers claim that filtration of any sort is harmful, and some labels trumpet 'unfiltered' as an attribute. Even though examples of unstable wines spoilt by less than perfect storage or transport conditions are not rare, some producers and consumers feel this is a risk worth taking, and are prepared for the added inconvenience and cost involved in shipping such wines in temperature-controlled conditions. An unfiltered wine throws a much heavier crust, or SEDIMENT, than one that has been filtered.

See also FINING.   A.D.W.

fine wine is a nebulous term, used by the AUCTION houses to describe the sort of wines they sell, which roughly coincide with those described in INVESTMENT. For example, within Bordeaux, a wine would have to be of CLASSED GROWTH level to qualify as 'fine'.

The extent to which this category of wine coincides with the best wine the world produces has declined slowly but steadily since the 1970s. Buying from, selling to, and in many cases in direct competition with, the auction houses are the **fine-wine traders**, a small group of wine merchants who specialize in servicing the needs of COLLECTORS and the like. See BROKERS.

fining, wine-making process with the aim of CLARIFICATION and STABILIZATION of a wine. Most young wines, if left long enough under good conditions, would eventually reach the same state of clarity as fining can achieve within months, but fining saves money for the producer and therefore eventually the consumer. Everyday wines, both white and red, are normally fined earlier and to a greater extent than fine wines. In general, white wines need fining to preserve their lighter colour and to prevent heat-unstable proteins forming a cloud, while red wines need it for a reduction of astringent and bitter tannins. See also FILTRATION.   A.D.W.

first growth is a direct translation of the French PREMIER CRU but its meaning tends to be limited to those BORDEAUX wine properties judged in the top rank according to the various CLASSIFICATIONS: Chx LAFITE, LATOUR, MARGAUX, HAUT-BRION, MOUTON-ROTHSCHILD, CHEVAL BLANC, AUSONE, together often with the unclassified but generally acknowledged star of POMEROL, Ch PÉTRUS. Just below these red bordeaux in terms of status are the so-called SUPER SECONDS.

Fitou, large red-wine appellation in the LANGUEDOC in two enclaves in the CORBIÈRES where it meets ROUSSILLON. The clay-limestone soils of coastal Fitou, Fitou Maritime, are quite different from the mountainous schists of the other Fitou, Fitou Montagneux, 20 minutes' drive inland. The low-yielding vines on the poor soils in these Pyrenean foothills should be capable of great expression, but the appellation underperformed in the 1970s and 1980s. The region is even more in the grip of CO-OPERATIVES than its northern neighbour, with the Mont Tauch co-operative in Tuchan, the oldest in the Languedoc, responsible for half of all production. It and the Cave Pilote at Villeneuve-lès-Corbières, also in Fitou Montagneux, raised their game and introduced OAK AGEING in the early 1990s. The dominant vine variety is still Carignan, which had to constitute 40 per cent of the blend in 1997, but it is supplemented by increasing amounts of Grenache, its relative Lladoner Pelut, Mourvèdre (in Fitou Maritime), and Syrah (in Fitou Montagneux). By 2007, Syrah must make up between 10 and 30 per cent of any Fitou. The territory demarcated for Fitou may also produce RIVESALTES.

Fixin, appellation abutting Gevrey-Chambertin in the Côte de Nuits district of Burgundy, producing red wines of a similar style to its neighbour, though currently of lesser fame. Fixin wines have a similar sturdiness to Gevrey but have less powerful fruit and fragrance.

There are five PREMIER CRU vineyards: Les Arvelets and Les Hervelets (seemingly interchangeable; certainly wine grown in the former may be labelled the latter), Clos de la Perrière, Clos Napoléon, and Clos du Chapître. See also CÔTE D'OR. J.T.C.M.

fizziness, the property of a SPARKLING WINE to bubble, which may be measured as the pressure inside the stoppered bottle. A wine bubbles when the bottle is opened because the dissolved CARBON DIOXIDE in the wine moves from a stable to a meta-stable state once the pressure is reduced on opening.

Most fully sparkling wines such as CHAMPAGNE are sold with a pressure of between five and six atmospheres, about three times that inside a tyre, which is the pressure which a normal champagne cork and bottle can withstand without undue risk. Such wines may be described as mousseux or CRÉMANT in French, espumoso in Spanish, SPUMANTE in Italian, and SEKT in German.

Many wines are somewhere between still and this level of fizziness, however. Wines with a gentle but definite sparkle may be described as PÉTILLANT in French, FRIZZANTE in Italian, and SPRITZIG in German, although many variations in nomenclature exist. European wine law defines a sparkling wine as any wine with an excess pressure of more than three atmospheres, while a semi-sparkling wine has a pressure of between 1 and 2.5 atmospheres.

Some wines sold as still wines may fizz very gently, however. This could be a sign of a FAULT but is more likely to be a deliberate winemaking feature. See CARBON DIOXIDE.

J.Ro. & T.J.

flavescence dorée, a vine disease which has the potential to threaten many of the world's vineyards and which belongs to a group now known generically as GRAPEVINE YELLOWS. A similar disease has been described in Germany, Switzerland, Romania, Israel, Chile, Italy, and Australia, and more recently in the eastern United States, Slovenia, Croatia, Hungary, and Spain.

flavonoids, a large group of PHENOLIC compounds that includes ANTHOCYANINS, catechins, and the **flavenols**. In wine, they contribute to COLOUR, ASTRINGENCY, BITTERNESS, and MOUTHFEEL. Up to 90 per cent of the phenolic content in red wine is made up of flavonoids; in white wines the proportion may be lower because of less EXTRACTION from the skins, stems, and seeds. The antioxidant and cancer chemopreventive capacity of many flavonoids may contribute to the HEALTH benefits of moderate wine consumption. G.L.C.

flavour, arguably a wine's most important distinguishing mark. As outlined in TASTING, most of what is commonly described as wine's flavour is in fact its AROMA (or alternatively, in the case of older wines, its BOUQUET). This, the 'smell' of a wine, may be its greatest sensory characteristic, but is also the most difficult of its attributes to measure and describe. A wine's flavour could, in its widest sense, be said to be the overall sensory impression of both aroma (as sensed both by the nose and from the mouth), and the taste components, and may therefore incorporate the other, more measurable, aspects of ACIDITY, SWEETNESS, BITTERNESS, ALCOHOLIC STRENGTH, FIZZINESS, and ASTRINGENCY. It has, further, been proposed that the definition of flavour be enlarged to include not just how a wine smells, tastes, and feels (including, for example, the burning sensation associated with particularly alcoholic wines), but also SUBJECTIVISM, including individual tasters' personal preferences, expectations, and tolerances determined by their cultural, regional, and psychological influences. In this book, however, the word flavour is used interchangeably with aroma.

flavour compounds, imprecise and inclusive term for substances in wines that can be smelled or tasted (see TASTING), sometimes called aroma compounds. The term flavour compounds is used more particularly for the volatile compounds which are sensed olfactorily, by the nose, and which contribute to both AROMA and, later, BOUQUET, the flavour changing rapidly and markedly during the first few months of a wine's life and then more and more slowly as it matures. Certain compounds are associated with particular VINE VARIETIES although the exact chemical nature of compounds associated with varietal flavours is still the subject of study.

There is no doubt that increasing knowledge about flavour compounds, and their manipulation in the vineyard and winery (as, for example, by the addition of selected enzymes), represent the most important likely technological advances in the wine industry today. Flavour chemistry is likely to have an enormous effect on our understanding and manipulation of wine quality, although it also raises the more sinister possibility of 'manufacturing' wines by the addition of traces of flavour compounds to neutral, low-quality wines.

See PHENOLICS, AGEING, and BOTTLE AGEING.

R.E.S. & B.G.C.

flavoured wines, somewhat amorphous category of wines whose basic wine-grape flavour is modified by the addition of other flavouring materials. VERMOUTH is a flavoured FORTIFIED wine, while the Greek RETSINA is

perhaps the most strikingly flavoured unfortified wine.

The category has been much expanded in recent years, however, by the emergence of flavoured, often low-alcohol wines such as those marketed as COOLERS, an attempt to persuade those who do not see themselves as wine drinkers to buy wine diluted and disguised as something else. They come in all degrees of alcoholic strength, sweetness, and fizziness and are popularly flavoured with such fruits as strawberry, peach, mango, and so on. Such products should be distinguished from FRUIT WINES, whose alcohol derives from the sugars of the (non-grape) fruit itself. A.D.W.

flavourings are available to wine producers, and are used, illegally, to an unknown extent. Of the three sorts of flavourings available to the beverage industry—natural, nature-identical, and artificial—the latter can be discounted because they are easily detectable, and natural and nature-identical flavourings are readily available, no more expensive, and extremely difficult to detect. Natural and nature-identical flavourings which impose the characteristics of a range of noble grape varieties such as Cabernet Sauvignon and Sauvignon Blanc are marketed. Because they are natural or nature-identical, their use is extremely difficult to detect. As with one of the most obvious wine flavourings, OAK ESSENCE, however, the apparent benefits of these flavourings are relatively short lived and they should be of interest to only the most cynical wine producer. G.T.

flavour precursors are sugar derivatives of compounds that would otherwise be flavour active. These flavourless compounds occur naturally in grapes (and many other fruits) as products of the normal metabolic activity of the fruit, and they are both numerous and more abundant than the free FLAVOUR COMPOUNDS. Their importance to wine comes from their ability to undergo hydrolysis, so releasing, and augmenting the level of, flavour compounds. This may be a prolonged process during AGEING, for example, or one accelerated through the use of enzymes in the winemaking process. Flavour precursors are important in development of VARIETAL flavours and BOUQUET in wines.

Fleurie, one of the 10 BEAUJOLAIS crus, and surely the appellation with the prettiest name in France. Fleurie has a particularly efficacious

CO-OPERATIVE, and produces wines which, it is easy to believe, have a particularly floral perfume. Partly because of its name perhaps, Fleurie is one of the most expensive Beaujolais. Reliable producers include Georges DUBŒUF and Domaine de la Roilette.

Fleurieu, up-and-coming wine region in SOUTH AUSTRALIA.

Floc de Gascogne. This strong, sweet VIN DE LIQUEUR is the Armagnac region's answer to the PINEAU DES CHARENTES of Cognac. It is usually drunk as an aperitif.

flood irrigation. See IRRIGATION.

flor, or flor yeasts, are benevolent yeasts which form a film of yeast cells which floats on the surface of a wine. Flor yeasts are typified by those native to the JEREZ region of southern Spain, which produce fino and manzanilla SHERRY.

Flor wines are made in MONTILLA, RUEDA, and Huelva (see CONDADO DE HUELVA) in Spain, and the ALGARVE in southern Portugal, where flor is also used to make a rather crude aperitif wine. See also JURA, whose VIN JAUNE is very similar to sherry, and TOKAJI in Hungary. Similar wines are also made in ROMANIA and, by Plageoles, in GAILLAC.   A.D.W.

Flora, CALIFORNIA aromatic white vine crossing which deserves a rather better fate than it had endured by the early 1990s, when acreage was too small for official statistics and Flora rarely appeared as varietal wine. The easiest place to find it has been in Schramsberg Crémant sparkling wine. A result of Gewürztraminer × Sémillon, it appears to take after Gewürztraminer in cooler climates, Sémillon in warmer ones.

flowering, important event in the annual growth cycle of vines, the process preceding the fertilization of vine flowers and their subsequent development into berries. This process is particularly important in the chain of events that leads up to HARVEST, and, with some varieties and some weather conditions, a poor flowering can mean financial disaster for the vineyard owner.

flying wine-makers, term coined by English wine merchant Tony Laithwaite for a team of young Australian wine-makers he hired to work the 1987 vintage in French CO-OPERATIVE wineries. The idea was to apply Australian hard work and technological expertise

to inexpensive grapes, thereby producing a unique range of wines for his mail-order wine business. The concept was such a success that it has since been much imitated and developed into a phenomenon with a long-term impact on wine-making techniques and wine styles all over the world.

The scheme originally depended on the fact that AUSTRALIA has a substantial number of highly trained wine-makers who are relatively idle during HARVEST time in the northern hemisphere, where most of the world's wine is made. By the late 1980s, an increasing number of antipodeans were to be found using record amounts of WATER and working record hours in various European wineries. AUSTRALIAN INFLUENCE almost invariably played a part in the background of these flying wine-makers.

The scheme has since been developed into the creation of the flying wine-maker, or rather 'international wine-maker', since Laithwaite has registered his original name, as a long-term vocation. By the early 1990s, Australian-trained individuals such as Jacques LURTON and Hugh Ryman, son of an English Monbazillac producer, were running teams of wine-makers around the globe, from MOLDOVA to Mendoza, often creating special wines or wine styles specifically to order from potential customers in northern Europe, typically quite different from the sort of wine traditionally made in that region.

This sort of bought-in OENOLOGY initially worked best in areas with a considerable quantity of relatively inexpensive grapes but whose technical potential was yet to be realized, thus excluding the classic wine regions and much of the NEW WORLD but decisively including southern France, much of Italy (especially Apulia and Sicily) and Iberia, eastern Europe, some of the more open-minded South African wineries, and South America. Southern French CO-OPERATIVE wineries were some of the first to admit, if not exactly welcome, this new breed of specialized expertise. More recently, flying wine-makers have invaded some larger wineries in Germany, California, the eastern Mediterranean, and North Africa.

By the late 1990s, several teams of flying wine-makers had developed from permanent bases in both France and Britain. INFORMATION TECHNOLOGY has enabled virtual wine-making from a distance of several time zones and many thousands of miles. And the commercial success of many of the products of flying wine-maker activity has had a real effect on wine styles made and sold locally too.

Foch, common North American name for the MARÉCHAL FOCH vine.

foil, alternative name for the CAPSULE which covers the cork and neck of a wine bottle. The term is most commonly used for bottles of sparkling wine because in this case it is almost invariably made of metal foil, whereas the 'foil' covering tops of bottles of still wine may be made from a wide range of materials. LEAD was once common but was prohibited in the USA and the EU in 1993 because of both health and ecological concerns. Various plastics and tin are used, as is, increasingly, paper. The foil is there largely for aesthetic reasons since the CORK should provide an airtight seal and only a faulty one will allow any seepage of wine. The length and design of a foil is another purely aesthetic matter, although some clear identification on the top of the foil can be very useful in a CELLAR full of bottles on wine racks.

foil cutter, gadget for SERVING wine which helps cut the FOIL neatly just below the lip of the bottle with the advantages that this avoids unsightly and possibly dangerous torn metal edges, and that there is no likelihood of the wine's being poured over a foil which might taint it. Some foil cutters are blades incorporated into CORKSCREWS; others are separate prongs with small circular blades which cut the foil when rotated. Life without a foil cutter is quite feasible; living without one after being introduced to it is not.

Folle Blanche, white grape variety once grown in profusion along the Atlantic seaboard of western France, providing very acidic but otherwise neutral base wine for distillation. It never regained its position after PHYLLOXERA ravaged the vineyards of Europe in the late 19th century, and France's total plantings of Folle Blanche, now mainly for GROS PLANT production, continue to decline. It has also been grown to a very limited extent in California.

Folle Noire, occasional synonym for various French dark-berried grape varieties including JURANÇON and NÉGRETTE.

Fondillón, strong RANCID wine from ALICANTE matured like an oloroso SHERRY.

Fonseca, common Portuguese surname associated with two important but unrelated wine producers in PORTUGAL.

Fonseca, or **Fonseca Guimaräens,** are PORT shippers established in 1822.

José Maria da Fonseca Successores, on the other hand, is based in the south of the country at Azeitão in ARRÁBIDA on the Setúbal peninsula. Originally a producer of rich, fortified SETÚBAL, it is now more important as a producer of a wide range of unfortified Portuguese wines, notably Periquita, designed for the international market from grapes from their own vineyards in the vicinity and beyond. See TERRAS DO SADO.

food, wine as. See DIET.

food and wine matching is either an extremely complex, detailed subject, a set of rules embedded in one's national culture, or an activity only for gastro-BORES, according to one's point of view.

To the French, not surprisingly, wine is simply part of *gastronomie* in general, and few French people would dream of describing a wine without suggesting which dish or dishes it should be served with. France has traditionally looked to its chefs for expertise in tasting and selecting wine, and it was only in the late 1980s that wine began to be viewed as a distinct subject in its own right.

In the United States, food and wine matching became a subject of intense scrutiny in the 1980s as wine producers, under pressure from so-called neo-Prohibitionists, sought to distance wine from drinks consumed principally for their alcohol content by putting it firmly on the dining table.

For some of the most fanatical wine enthusiasts, food is an obstacle between palate and wine glass, whose flavours can get in the way of a decent wine-TASTING session.

It is certainly true that it is perfectly physically possible to drink any sort of wine with any sort of food. It is also true that 'white wine with fish and red wine with meat' is an absurd generalization built on a couple of sound maxims. There are also certain foods which have very specific effects on wine, and others which distort the PALATE to such an extent that wine tastes very odd or downright nasty in their wake.

But wine and food matching is an ongoing process of sensory adaptation. If a sensory message to the brain is constantly repeated (such as the taste of sourness in food), then it will suppress our sensitivity to the source of stimulation, making the wine that follows taste less sour.

The following should be read in conjunction with the article on TASTING.

Some specific reactions

The wine-merchant's maxim 'buy on an apple and sell on cheese' has a sound basis in gustatory fact. Fresh, uncooked apples, like most fruits high in both SWEETNESS and ACIDITY, make many wines taste thin and metallic; any wine that impressed when tasted with an apple must have been seriously good. Hard cheese such as cheddar, on the other hand, tends to make wines taste softer and fuller. Strongly acidic foods such as dishes containing lemon juice and VINEGAR were for long cast as villains in terms of serving with wine, but thanks to sensory adaptation can make a slightly too acid wine taste fuller and more agreeable (while reacting badly with top-quality wines). Raw garlic can react with water to produce a burning sensation in many palates, while an acidic drink such as wine (Provençal rosé with aïoli) neutralizes the garlic and refreshes the palate. To the majority of palates, freshly ground pepper is a sensitizing element that may ruin the nuances of a fine, old wine, but can flatter a young, light-bodied wine by making it taste stronger, fuller, and more complex.

Some wine-unfriendly foods

Globe artichokes and asparagus: A significant proportion of the population are sensitive to a substance in artichokes which has been dubbed 'cynarin' and which has the effect on them of making water taste sweet, and making wine taste metallic. A similar effect has been observed with fresh asparagus.

Some forms of chocolate are not only so sweet that it is difficult to find a wine sweeter than they are, they also coat the inside of the mouth. In this case a very strong, very sweet wine will overcome these disadvantages: lively young port, Australian Liqueur Muscat or Tokay, and Málaga, seem to manage.

Some general rules

White wines generally (although not universally) taste more acid than red wines, so it makes sense to serve them with simple fish dishes which would normally call for the sort of acidity in lemon juice or vinegar.

Sweetness in food (which can be from as unexpected a source as tomatoes or balsamic vinegar) increases the perception of sourness, BITTERNESS, and ASTRINGENCY in wine, while making the wine appear less sweet, stronger, and less fruity.

Very acid foods (such as those dressed with vinegar or citrus juice) decrease our perception of sourness in wine, making the wine taste richer and more mellow. If the wine is at all sweet, it will taste sweeter.

Bitter, sweet, and umami (see TASTING) flavours in food make the wine seem more bitter.

Sourness and salt in food suppress apparent bitterness in wine.

Red wines high in TANNINS taste less tannic if served with heavily textured foods, so it can make sense to partner a rare steak with a young wine based on Cabernet Sauvignon, Syrah, Nebbiolo, or Sangiovese.

Bitterness and astringency in wines can be muted by judicious use of salt in the food served with them.

Astringency in wine is suppressed by foods that are acid, salty, or fatty and accentuated by food that is sweet or spicy.

Salty foods may make sweet wines taste sweeter.

Many cheeses are too pungent or greasy textured for very fine or mature red wine. Sweet wines, whether fortified or not, can be more flattered by the savoury, salty nature of cheese, and are less overwhelmed by it than, say, a mature red bordeaux.

All dry wines taste horrible with sweet foods, which seem to emphasize their acidity. Even quite sweet wines can taste very thin and nasty if served with dishes that are sweeter than they are themselves. It is therefore advisable to choose only relatively sweet, full-bodied wines with the sweet course. Germany's delicious sweet AUSLESEN are best sipped without food.

Clever use of lemon juice, vinegar, fresh pepper, and chewy meats can compensate for the shortcomings of ordinary wines. With very fine wine, however, it is probably safest to serve relatively neutral foods.

Some particularly successful combinations

Riesling and smoked salmon or other smoked fish.

Riesling (even medium-sweet Riesling) with onion tart.

Chablis with oysters.

Cru Beaujolais with charcuterie, particularly *rosette de Lyon*.

Red bordeaux and lamb.

Red burgundy with feathered game.
Sauternes and Roquefort or other blue cheese.
See also ORDER OF WINES.

foot treading, traditional method of CRUSH-ING only rarely found but enjoying a revival in Portugal's DOURO valley for the production of the finest ports. CHAPOUTIER of Hermitage also use foot treading in the production of their top red table wines.

Forastera, common light-berried grape on the CANARY ISLANDS.

Forez, Côtes du. A range of hills between the upper reaches of the Loire and Lyons in eastern France give their name to light, vigorous red and rosé wines made, like BEAU-JOLAIS, from the GAMAY grape. The wines, designed for early drinking, may taste reminiscent of those of the Côtes ROANNAISES to the north. Both regions have known greater glory. Both were awarded VDQS status in the mid 1950s. The more southerly of the pair is higher, has a slightly less dependable climate, and has taken an almost exclusively CO-OPERA-TIVE route. The Vignerons Foréziens co-operative is based in Boën-sur-Lignon and has won acclaim for its policy of developing quality through a series of different cuvées.

Fortana, tart dark grape, speciality of EMILIA, known as Uva d'Oro in neighbouring ROMAGNA.

fortification, the practice of adding spirits, usually GRAPE SPIRIT, to wine to ensure microbiological stability, thereby adding ALCOHOLIC STRENGTH and precluding any further FER-MENTATION.

The principle behind this addition of alcohol is that most bacteria and strains of YEAST are rendered impotent, unable to react with sugar or other wine constituents, in solutions containing more than 16 to 18 per cent alcohol, depending on the strain of yeast.

The stage at which spirit is added has enormous implications for the style of fortified wine produced. The earlier it is added in the fermentation process, the sweeter the resulting wine will be. See FORTIFIED WINES. A.D.W.

fortified wines are those which have been subject to FORTIFICATION and therefore include SHERRY, PORT, MADEIRA, VERMOUTH, MÁLAGA, MONTILLA, MARSALA, LIQUEUR MUSCAT, Liqueur Tokay, and several strictly local specialities (although liquids made by adding spirit to grape juice rather than wine such as VIN DOUX NATUREL are not, strictly, fortified wines). Prac-tically all warm wine regions make some sort of fortified wine, often in the image of port and sherry even if they are not allowed to use those protected names, within Europe anyway. It is an almost invariable rule that anywhere hot enough to produce good fortified wine is too hot to provide the ideal climate for its consumption.

fourth growth. See the CLASSIFICATION of Bordeaux.

foxy, usually deeply pejorative TASTING TERM for the peculiar flavour of many wines, particularly red wines, made from American HYBRIDS, vine varieties developed from both American and European species of the VITIS genus, particularly Vitis LABRUSCA. (Wines made from many other hybrids—SEYVAL, for example—are completely free of foxiness.) The CONCORD grape, widely planted in NEW YORK state, is one of the most heavily scented, reeking of something closer to animal fur than fruit, flowers, or any other aroma associated with fine wine, although the 'candy'-like aroma is, incidentally, quite close to that of the tiny wild strawberry or fraise des bois.

It has been discovered that earlier harvesting or long CASK AGEING reduces some of Concord's foxy characteristics. Aged New York sherry-style wines are a good example of wines that contain Concord that is virtually undetectable in their blends.   H.L. & B.G.C.

France, the country that produces more fine wine than any other, and in which wine is firmly embedded in the culture to the extent that such French people as are interested in it have a quasi-spiritual relationship with wine. Although wine consumption, and to a lesser extent production, fell in the late 20th century, the total quantity of wine produced in most French vintages in the 1990s was over 55 million hl/1,400 million gal.

There are few wine producers anywhere who would not freely admit that they have been influenced by the great wines of BORDEAUX, BURGUNDY, CHAMPAGNE, or possibly the RHÔNE. Other qualitatively significant wine regions, perhaps better appreciated within France than abroad, include ALSACE, BEAUJOLAIS, CHABLIS, JURA, LOIRE, PROVENCE, SAVOIE, and SOUTH WEST FRANCE. France's most important wine region by far in terms of quantity, however, is the LANGUEDOC, and ROUSSILLON to the immediate south, whose output of VIN DE TABLE still makes a contribution to the European wine lake, but whose better-quality wines provide some of the world's best wine value. The Mediterranean island of CORSICA is also under French jurisdiction, although it shares many characteristics with the Italian island of SARDINIA.

Although the first instance of geographical DELIMITATION was in Portugal's DOURO valley, France is the birthplace of the widespread application of the notion that geography, or TERROIR, is fundamental in shaping the character and quality of a wine. This resulted in the early 20th century in the much-copied APPELLATION CONTRÔLÉE, or AC, system. AC wines are the wines of which France has traditionally been most proud, sold under the geographical name of the appellation rather than by vine variety, as the substantially VARIETAL wines of the NEW WORLD have been. AC wines represent an increasing proportion of all wine produced in France, more than 40 per cent since the late 1980s, and an increasing proportion of French vineyards is dedicated to their production each year. (See below, Wine quality categories.)

Curiously, and perhaps because wine is so deeply entrenched in French history and culture, wine CONNOISSEURSHIP and to a certain extent the wine TRADE are not as evolved in France as, for example, in Australia, Belgium, Great Britain, Switzerland, and the United States. Although things are slowly changing, the average French citizen has bought and drunk little other than the wine produced closest to him or her, whether geographically or by virtue of family or friendship. This has tended to stifle the development of wine retailing, although the number of specialist wine merchants, known here as *cavistes*, has increased significantly since the early 1980s. As might be expected in a country associated with so many forms of gastronomic excellence, wine appreciation in France is closely tethered to the table. Wine is rarely drunk without food, and France's chefs and SOMMELIERS have been regarded as the rightful repositories of wine knowledge.

Although France is rivalled only by Italy as the world's principal wine exporter, it is also an important importer of wine. The development of the Languedoc as a virtual factory for particularly light red wines at the end of the 19th century and the beginning of the 20th meant that vast quantities of strong, deep-coloured red wines had to be imported for BLENDING, from North African colonies initially and subsequently from southern Italy and, to an increasing extent, Spain. In 1995/6, France imported more than 7 million hl/185 million gal of wine and exported 20 million hl. (By contrast, Italy, its major source of imported wine, imported about 0.3 million hl and exported 15 million hl.)

France is so important as a role model to the world of wine that many terms used internationally are French in origin (BLANC DE BLANCS and VERAISON are just two examples). France is recognized the world over as a centre of wine research and academe. The OENOLOGICAL and viticultural faculties of the universities of Bordeaux and Montpellier have long enjoyed international prestige, and considerable viticultural research emanates from stations of l'Institut National de Recherche Agronomique (INRA).

One of France's great commercial strengths in recent years has been that it is the world's prime source of oak for top-quality wine casks. France is an important exporter of barrels, notably but by no means exclusively to the United States.

Geography and climate

France does not have the monopoly on fine-wine production, but its geographical position is exceptionally favoured for growing a wide range of different styles of grapes with a good balance of sugar and acidity. With wine regions lying between LATITUDES 42 degrees and 49.5 degrees, France can provide the two most suitable environments identified in CLIMATE AND WINE QUALITY for growing grapes. In the south, the MEDITERRANEAN CLIMATE can be depended upon to ripen grapes fully, but not so fast that they do not have time to develop an interesting array of FLAVOUR COMPOUNDS and PHENOLICS. In the west, relatively high latitudes are tempered by the influence of the Atlantic's Gulf Stream. In the east, centuries of viticultural tradition have established what seem to be potentially perfect marriages between grape variety and particularly favoured terroir in the more CONTINENTAL CLIMATE of Burgundy, Alsace, and Champagne, France's most northerly wine region where, over the centuries, the ideal wine style has evolved to take advantage of the area's climate and special geology. France also has a wide variety of soil types, much charted and revered.

Vine-growing in modern France is concentrated in the south but there are vineyards in all regions other than the most mountainous and the most cloudy.

Vine varieties

CARIGNAN has been France's most planted vine variety for many decades, thanks to its ubiquity in France's largest wine region, the Languedoc-Roussillon. For the same reasons, ARAMON was important in the mid 20th century but was by 1988 France's seventh most planted variety. Second most planted variety was UGNI BLANC, the white grape which provides so much base wine for cognac. Other important red wine grape varieties were, in decreasing order of total area planted, Grenache, Merlot, Cinsaut, and Cabernet Sauvignon, Merlot and Cabernet having increased considerably in popularity. No light-skinned grape variety other than Ugni Blanc was planted to anything like the extent of these red wine grapes, but Chardonnay has become increasingly popular, as elsewhere, in Burgundy, Champagne, and throughout France, so that it was already the second most planted white grape variety in France, overtaking Sémillon, by the late 1980s.

One of France's strengths is her treasury of traditional local varieties, either imported as a result of shifting political power (most of France's most planted red varieties were originally Spanish), or the apparently indigenous likes of those still to be found in limited quantity in SOUTH WEST FRANCE. More than 100 different varieties are still planted to a significant extent, even though the trend has been towards increasing reliance on what are now known as INTERNATIONAL VARIETIES (most of them apparently French in origin).

Wine-making

In many wine regions, TRADITION is as important as science in determining wine-making techniques, which vary enormously in France's hundreds of thousands of *caves*. However, in general, and in sharp contrast to the New World, PROTECTIVE JUICE HANDLING and an obsession with winery HYGIENE are relatively rare. Mastery of MALOLACTIC FERMENTATION and OAK AGEING, on the other hand, are taken for granted.

Part of French wine-makers' easy relationship with BARREL MATURATION comes from the fact that France is the centre of the world's cooperage industry, or at least that part of it of interest to wine-makers. French OAK is revered the world over, and one of the major investments of many a non-French wine producer is in shipping quantities of new BARRELS from France.

France is also the birthplace of CHAPTALIZATION, and a high proportion of her wines depend on it to some degree.

Wine in France is red. Less than a quarter of all wine consumed in France is white, and in the hot summers of the south of France, rosé is more likely to be consumed than white, as a sort of red for high temperatures. Wine consumption, which used to be one of the highest in the world, has been falling rapidly in France. In 1980, the average per capita wine consumption was 91 l/24 gal a year but this had fallen to 60 l by 1996. The average quality of wine drunk in France has been increasing substantially, however.

Wine quality categories

Of the average French harvest, wines from the most revered quality wine category APPELLATION CONTRÔLÉE now represent the most significant proportion, while the most basic wine for direct consumption, that classified as VIN DE TABLE, is made in ever-decreasing quantities and, in 1998, for example, represented less than 11 per cent. The VIN DE PAYS category, distinctly superior to table wine, represented 25 per cent, while the VDQS wines waiting in the wings for promotion to full AC status represented about 1 per cent. The remaining up to 20 per cent of an average year's French wine production is designed for distillation into brandy. France dominates the production not just of fine wine but also of fine brandy.

For individual regions, see also ALSACE, BEAUJOLAIS, BORDEAUX, BUGEY, BURGUNDY, CHABLIS, CHAMPAGNE, CORSICA, JURA, LANGUEDOC-ROUSSILLON, LOIRE, PROVENCE, SAVOIE, RHÔNE, and SOUTH WEST FRANCE. See also VIN and immediately following entries, as well as CRÉMANT for some of France's better-quality sparkling wines.

Franciacorta, one of ITALY's newest areas for the production of high-quality red, white, and sparkling wines, extends across the hills of a series of townships to the south of Lake Iseo in the province of Brescia in LOMBARDY. Since 1995, the name Franciacorta has applied solely to the DOCG sparkling wines made by the TRADITIONAL METHOD, while the zone's superior table wines may qualify for the DOC **Terre di Franciacorta**.

Although the zone presents a certain number of indisputable natural advantages, the wine had only a local reputation until the 1960s, when the SPUMANTE house of Berlucchi launched the first Franciacorta sparkling wines. The ensuing demand for the wines of this house gave national prominence to Franciacorta.

Traditional-method sparkling wine, made from Chardonnay, Pinot Blanc, Pinot Noir, and Pinot Gris grapes, still represents nearly half of the zone's production, but there was a significant development of French-style still wines in the 1980s, made at least partially from the classic red grapes of BORDEAUX and the red and white grapes of BURGUNDY, frequently given a full-blown international treatment including lavish amounts of new OAK ageing.

Although Franciacorta made great progress in the 1970s and 1980s, the zone still suffers from an excessive variation in quality between the excellent products of such vanguard estates as Cà del Bosco, Bellavista, and Cavalleri and the more pedestrian efforts of younger houses, many of whose owners have invested more capital and enthusiasm than technical competence.

A revision of the DOC rules, approved in 1995, divided the zone's production into two categories: a DOCG, reserved for sparkling wines and called simply Franciacorta with the clear intention of identifying zone and a specific product as in CHAMPAGNE, and a DOC named Terre di Franciacorta for the still wines. The latter category consists of two types: a Burgundy-style Bianco based on Chardonnay and/or Pinot Bianco and a Bordeaux-style Rosso based on Cabernet (either Franc or Sauvignon, or both) and Merlot. Pinot Noir is permitted only in the zone's sparkling wines.   D.T.

Franconia, alternative English name for the German wine region FRANKEN, and a local name for the BLAUFRÄNKISCH in FRIULI in northern Italy.

Francs, Côtes de, or Bordeaux Côtes de Francs, small BORDEAUX CÔTES appellation just north of CÔTES de CASTILLON between ST-ÉMILION and BERGERAC. The Côtes de Francs wine region has considerably more personality than regular BORDEAUX AC and its revival in the 1980s owed much to the Belgian Thienpont family (also associated with Ch Le PIN, Vieux-Ch-Certan, and Ch Labegorce-Zédé). Vines are planted on high clay-limestone slopes, many of which enjoy a favourable west-south-west exposure. Almost all of the wine produced is well-structured red from Cabernet and Merlot grapes, but a little sweet white is made in memory of a style once traditional for this area. Chx de Francs and Puygueraud are generally reliable. See BORDEAUX.

Franken, known in English as **Franconia**, distinctive wine region in central GERMANY. The sometimes severe winters and the risks of autumn and spring frosts have largely decided where vines should now be grown. Since the 1960s, the area under vine has nearly tripled, and old vineyards have been rebuilt and modernized.

Hard frosts are all too frequent in some villages, including Hammelburg on the river Saale, 51 km/32 miles north of Würzburg. When weather permits, Hammelburger Silvaner is a lively wine with high acidity, and elegance. During the first half of this century, SILVANER was the most widely grown vine in Franken. It does well in the famous Würzburger Stein vineyard and on the slopes of the Steigerwald near Castell in the east of the region. MÜLLER-THURGAU grows in just over 40 per cent of the region's vineyards. Other plantings include BACCHUS, KERNER, RIESLING, SCHEUREBE. Those producers who sell their wine in bottle directly to the consumer often like to have a range based on different vine varieties, particularly if their vineyard holding is in only one site. The range of VINE VARIETIES planted is great and probably larger than necessary.

Although red and rosé wine represents only eight per cent of the region's production, interest is growing in red wines for drinking with food. The retail price of a bottle of QBA Spätburgunder (Pinot Noir) may be 30 per cent more than that of a Riesling of equivalent quality, but buyers are not deterred.

The best QUALITÄTSWEIN of Franken are sold in the flagon-shaped BOCKSBEUTEL, as are those of a few villages in neighbouring north BADEN. Its use within Germany is protected by law. Most Franken wines come from a single vine variety. Because of their rather different structure, sweetness suits the cheaper versions less well than it does those from the northern Rhine regions. In fact, 32 per cent or so of the volume of Franken quality wine is TROCKEN (dry). A further 24 per cent falls below the upper limit of the official European Union definition of what qualifies as dry. Müller-Thurgau from a restricted yield with adequate acidity can produce solid, concentrated wine which improves with age.

Riesling does not play a leading role in Franken but the quality of its best wine from good estates is excellent and the style unique to the region. The Rieslings of the Stein and Innere Leiste vineyards at Würzburg, of Randersackerer Pfülben, Escherndorfer Lump, Iphöfer Julius-Echter-Berg, and of the Homburger Kallmuth, can be quite splendid. Much cheap Franken wine is overpriced compared with wines from the PFALZ, but the best, although expensive, is good value.

The crossing BACCHUS produces surprisingly elegant wine from the Steigerwald, when the yield is restricted, reminding some of Sauvignon Blanc. The RIESLANER grape produces wines with high acidity, but not the quality of Riesling. They can, nevertheless, be very impressive at AUSLESE level or above.

The CO-OPERATIVE movement in Franken achieves on average some of the highest wine prices per litre of any co-operative cellars in Germany. The large cellar at Kitzingen receives the crop from nearly a quarter of the region's vines, and smaller co-operatives account for another 15 per cent. Most of the regional co-operative's customers are in south Germany and the quantities exported are small.

I.J. & K.B.S.

Franken Riesling, occasional German name for SYLVANER.

Frankland, relatively cool, promising vineyard area in the Lower Great Southern region of the state of WESTERN AUSTRALIA.

Frankovka, synonym for the red BLAUFRÄNKISCH grape used in SLOVAKIA and VOJVODINA.

Fransdruif, or just **Frans,** traditional Afrikaans name for the PALOMINO grape in South Africa.

Frappato, lesser Sicilian red grape variety, which can add fruit and freshness to the more powerful NERO D'AVOLA in the Cerasuolo di Vittoria DOC.

Frascati is both the most famous and quantitatively the most important of the CASTELLI ROMANI wines. Its fame is less by virtue of its intrinsic quality—it differs little from the wines of its neighbouring DOC zones—than by virtue of its constant citation in the literature of Italy and in the accounts of the countless foreign visitors to Rome, a mere 24 km/15 miles away. The wine itself, the standard blend of Malvasia

with Trebbiano of the Castelli Romani, is a sound, if rarely exciting, commercial product. A lightly sweet or AMABILE version also exists, as does a sweet DOLCE or *cannellino* version. Declining demand for white wine in general, and the central Italian Malvasia-Trebbiano blend in particular, put notable commercial pressures on the zone in the 1990s, inspiring much talk of a new commitment to quality.

D.T.

fraud, wine. See ADULTERATION AND FRAUD.

free-run is the name used by wine-makers for the juice or wine that will drain without pressing from a mass of freshly crushed grapes or from a fermentation vessel. It constitutes between 60 and 70 per cent of the total juice available and is generally superior to, and much lower in TANNINS than, juice or wine whose extraction depends on pressing. Many wine-makers boast of using only free-run juice in the production of fine white wines, but PRESS WINE, the wine produced by pressing what is left, may be useful as a BLENDING element.

A.D.W.

freeze concentration. See CONCENTRATION.

Freisa, or Freisa Piccolo, is a light-red grape variety indigenous to the PIEDMONT region of north-west Italy.

Freisa musts can be quite high in both ACIDITY and TANNINS even if relatively light coloured for the region.

The wine exists as a VARIETAL in a range of styles, but the predominant one is slightly frothy from a SECONDARY FERMENTATION, which retains some unfermented RESIDUAL SUGAR to balance the slight bitterness from the LEES. Freisa's decisively purple colour and aromas of raspberries and violets tend to find favour much more readily than its bitter-sweet flavours.

Three DOCS exist for Freisa, in both dry and sweet (amabile) form: the larger Freisa d'Asti and the minuscule Freisa di Chieri, plus the brand-new Monferrato Freisa. These are dwarfed, however, by the 3 million bottles produced each year of the regional VINO DA TAVOLA Freisa del Piedmonte, which encompasses some of the best Freisa from the zones of BAROLO and BARBARESCO.

Modern technology now allows producers better control of both the residual-sugar level and the amount of CARBON DIOXIDE in the wine, and this type of Freisa, which does not undergo a secondary fermentation in the bottle, tends to be distinctively drier and almost imperceptibly fizzy. Producers such as Aldo Vajra, Coppo, and Ascheri are experimenting with a more age-worthy, completely dry, and completely still type of Freisa aged in BARRIQUE.

A larger-berried, quite distinct red grape variety called **Freisa Grossa** or Freisa di Nizza is also grown on flatter vineyards but produces much less distinguished wine. A vine variety called Freisa is quite widely grown in Argentina.   D.T.

Freisamer is a 20th-century German vine crossing (SILVANER × Ruländer or PINOT GRIS). It reached a peak of popularity in the German wine region of Baden in the early 1970s but is declining in popularity. It is still grown today in a number of north and central cantons in SWITZERLAND, and sweeter versions are a speciality of the Herrschaft in Graubünden.

Freixenet, the largest exporter of CAVA in the world, although not as strong on the Spanish domestic market as CODORNÍU. The brand was born at the beginning of the 20th century and named after an estate in Mediona, PENEDÈS, known as La Freixeneda, meaning 'plantation of ash trees'. The company was initially keen to establish export markets, a policy which paid off in the latter half of the 20th century. It now has six production centres in San Sadurní de Noya producing a total of almost 100 million bottles per year. Best-known brands are the medium-dry Carta Nevada, and Cordon Negro, a brut Cava in a distinctive black bottle. Freixenet's overseas interests are the Freixenet Sonoma Caves in the CARNEROS district of California, which produce the sparkling wine Gloria Ferrer; an estate in Mexico where the sparkling brand is called Sala Vivé; and ownership of the Champagne house Henri Abelé.

S.A. & V. de la S.

French Colombard, common California name for one of the state's most planted grape varieties, the French white COLOMBARD, now much more widely planted in California than in France. Originally brought from Cognac and throughout the 1980s California's most planted wine grape variety, Colombard is no longer often seen as a VARIETAL wine. Most of it grows in the SAN JOAQUIN VALLEY for JUG whites and sparklers produced by the tank method (see SPARKLING-WINE-MAKING). A small and shrinking acreage remains in the coastal counties where—especially along the Russian river

from Healdsburg (Sonoma County) north to Ukiah (Mendocino County)—it makes an off-dry white of greater interest and better balance than most Chenin Blanc, if harvested while still crisply acidic and before its perfumes coarsen.

During the 1970s, it became the state's most planted wine grape variety, a position it retained until 1991 when it was usurped by the market's apparently insatiable demand for something richer, more expensive, and called Chardonnay.

French paradox, term coined in the United States in 1991 to express the infuriating fact that the French apparently eat and drink themselves silly with no apparent ill effects on their coronary health. Immediately after this thesis was aired on prime-time television in the United States, and red-wine consumption cited as a possible factor in reducing the risk of heart disease, sales of red wine quadrupled and GALLO had to put their leading branded GENERIC Hearty Burgundy on allocation. See HEALTH. A similar association between redwine consumption and health benefits played an important part in the 1990s wine boom in ASIA.

Frescobaldi, one of Florence's most prominent noble families since the 13th century, are the largest private owners of vineyards in TUSCANY. The Frescobaldi holdings can be divided into three distinct blocks: the first, to the south west of Florence, produces light and refreshing white and red wines; the second, to the east of Florence, produces classic CHIANTI RUFINA from the Nipozzano estate and the distinctive red and white wines of Pomino, a highaltitude property with vineyards that rise to 700 m/2,300 ft above sea level; the third block is Castelgiocondo in MONTALCINO, its acquisition in the late 1980s having made the Frescobaldi the largest potential producer of Brunello.

The Frescobaldi were the first Italian producers of a BARRIQUE-aged white wine, beginning in the mid 1970s with the grapes from their Benefizio vineyard at Pomino. Their single-vineyard Chianti Rufina, Montesodi, was also among the first superior all-Sangiovese wines aged in small barrels. The house currently produces approximately 5.5 million bottles of wine each year.

In the mid-1990s, the Frescobaldi entered into a JOINT VENTURE with MONDAVI of California, producing two wines, Luce and Lucente, from the Sangiovese and Merlot grapes of the Castelgiocondo estate in Montalcino. D.T.

Friuli, or Friuli-Venezia Giulia, the north-easternmost region of ITALY, borders on Austria to the north and on SLOVENIA to the east and has long been a confluence of three distinct peoples and cultures: Italian, Germanic, and Slavic. Friuli had little commercial history of distinctive wines until the late 1960s, when the introduction both of German wine-making philosophy and TEMPERATURE CONTROL gave Italy's first truly clean, fresh, fruity white wines. This created a FASHION which has lasted to this day.

Friuli's geographical position ensured that a large number of varieties would be available for planting. TOCAI Friulano, RIBOLLA, MALVASIA di Istria, VERDUZZO, PICOLIT, REFOSCO, SCHIOPETTINO, PIGNOLO, and the acidic red wine grape Tazzelenghe are considered indigenous (although see ROBOLA, for example). RIESLING, WELSCHRIESLING (here called Riesling Italico), TRAMINER, MÜLLER-THURGAU, and BLAUFRÄNKISCH (locally called Franconia) are imports from Austria. The French varieties PINOT BIANCO, PINOT GRIGIO, CHARDONNAY, SAUVIGNON, CABERNET, MERLOT, PINOT NERO were introduced during the 19th-century Habsburg domination (and greatly expanded during the replanting of Friuli's vineyards after the ravages of PHYLLOXERA), a domination which lasted until 1918 in the case of the province of Gorizia. The result has been the multiplicity of single VARIETAL wines in each DOC.

To the south of Udine exist two distinct bands of territory for the growing of grapes: the two hillside DOCs of COLLI ORIENTALI and COLLIO and the five DOCs on the flatlands: LISON-PRAMAGGIORE, LATISANA, GRAVE DEL FRIULI, AQUILEIA, and ISONZO. The HILLSIDE VINEYARDS give wines of much the greater personality, with Collio generally offering more delicacy and bouquet, Colli Orientali much body and length. The white, and red, wines of this latter zone have shown a real suitability for small BARREL MATURATION, a phenomenon much less widespread in Collio. Isonzo, which borders on Collio, stands out among the DOCs of the plain and, in the 1990s, began to produce wines which, from the best producers, challenge those of the hillsides.

The region's overall production is modest by Italian standards, but the percentage of DOC production, now over 50 per cent, is one of Italy's highest.

Although Friuli enjoyed almost uninterrupted commercial success and expansion throughout the 1970s and 1980s, the formula of crisp and refreshing technologically sound wines is not difficult to copy, and the early 1990s saw increased competition and price pressure from other areas of Italy, particularly from the Trentino-Alto Adige.

For more details of notable specific wines, see also AQUILEIA, CARSO, COLLI ORIENTALI, COLLIO, GRAVE DEL FRIULI, ISONZO, LATISANA, LISON-PRAMAGGIORE, and see specific grape varieties mentioned above. D.T.

frizzante, Italian wine term for semi-sparkling wine (as opposed to SPUMANTE, which is used for fully sparkling wines). Frizzante wines generally owe their bubbles to a partial second fermentation in tank.

Fromenteau, name for several grape varieties, most importantly the medieval name for a Burgundian variety which had pale red berries and white juice, and is probably the ancestor of PINOT GRIS. It is also used as a synonym for both the ROUSSANNE of the Rhône and SAVAGNIN of the Jura.

Fronsac, small but once-famed red-wine appellation in the Bordeaux region just west of the town of Libourne on the RIGHT BANK of the river DORDOGNE. The wooded low hills of Fronsac, and **Canon-Fronsac,** the even smaller and more famous appellation to the immediate south, constitute Bordeaux's prettiest countryside.

The low-lying land beside the river and any alluvial soils further inland from the Dordogne and its tributary the Isle are entitled to only the BORDEAUX AC, while the Fronsac and Canon-Fronsac appellations are concentrated on the higher land where limestone predominates and sandstone is also characteristic. Merlot and Cabernet Franc (Bouchet) are the dominant grape varieties, supplemented by Malbec and, where it will ripen, Cabernet Sauvignon, densely planted on the land entitled to the Fronsac appellation and the more restricted area, mainly around the villages of St-Michel-de-Fronsac and Fronsac itself, which is entitled to the supposedly superior Canon-Fronsac appellation.

Wines made in the 1960s and 1970s were often concentrated but also austere and slightly rustic. The 1980s saw considerable refinement of techniques, and investment in wine-making equipment, notably some new barrels, so that Fronsac is now both supple and dense. It does not have the lush character of Pomerol but can offer a keenly priced alternative to more famous red bordeaux, with the juicy fruit of a St-Émilion and the ageing potential of a Médoc. The interest shown in the region by the likes of the MOUEIX family, who since the 1980s have owned Chx Canon-Moueix, La Dauphine, and Canon de Brem, as well as distributing several others, has indubitably injected confidence into the region. Other properties making superior wine include Chx Moulin Pey-Labrie and La Vieille Cure and Michel ROLLAND's Ch Fontenil. The largest and most picturesque property on the entire right bank is Ch de la Rivière.

Frontignac is used as a name for grapey, sweet wines, particularly in South Africa. It derives from the Languedoc town of FRONT-IGNAN, once famous for its Muscat. Frontignac is also a common Australian synonym for MUSCAT BLANC À PETITS GRAINS, the finest Muscat grape variety of all.

Frontignan is the name of the wine for long called Muscat de Frontignan, the most important of the Languedoc's four VINS DOUX NAT-URELS made from MUSCAT BLANC À PETITS GRAINS. Co-operatives dominate output, but Ch de la Peyrade can take much of the credit for revitalizing wine-making in Frontignan.

Frontonnais, Côtes du, growing and dynamic appellation just north of Toulouse in SOUTH WEST FRANCE distinguished by its local red grape variety the NÉGRETTE, which must constitute 50 to 70 per cent of the appellation's reds, plus some rosés. Complementary grape varieties are usually Fer, Syrah, and the Cabernets, and the character of the wines can vary considerably according to the exact TERROIR and ENCÉPAGEMENT. Soils on the gravelly terraces of the Tarn are particularly poor. The CO-OPERATIVE is an important producer (of table wine too) but there is considerable experimentation on the part of some relative newcomers to the region, although a high proportion of the wine is drunk without ceremony in Toulouse. The local VIN DE PAYS, used for white wines, is Vin de Pays du Comté Tolosan. Fine wines are made by Chx Bellevue La Forêt and Le Roc.

früh is German for 'early'. Thus, for example, Früher Roter Malvasier is early red MALVASIA.

Frühburgunder, Blauer, is an early-ripening strain of Spätburgunder (Pinot Noir) grown to a very limited extent in WÜRT-TEMBERG. It tastes like a paler, leaner version of the lightest red burgundy.

Frühroter Veltliner, or Früher Roter Veltliner, early-ripening red-skinned VELTLINER, is a white wine grape variety most commonly encountered in the Weinviertel district of lower Austria. The wine produced is often less distinguished than that made from Austria's most common grape variety GRÜNER VELTLINER, being notably lower in acidity in many cases. Yields are also lower.

fruit. To a VITICULTURIST, fruit is a synonym for GRAPE. To an OENOLOGIST or wine taster, fruit is a perceptible element essential to a young wine. Young wines should taste fruity, although not necessarily of grapes, or any particular grape variety. During BOTTLE AGEING, the fruity FLAVOUR COMPOUNDS in a good wine evolve into more complex elements which are described as BOUQUET; in a less good wine, the fruit simply dissipates to leave a non-fruity wine sometimes described as 'hollow'. The word **fruity** is sometimes used in wine descriptions concocted for marketing purposes as a euphemism for 'sweet'.

fruit driven, a TASTING TERM used to convey the fact that a wine has a dominance of grape-derived fruit flavour. For a wine to merit this description, the dominance of fruit overrides flavours in the wine that originate from other processes or treatments which the wine has undergone such as BARREL MATURATION. Wines described as fruit driven are, typically, NEW WORLD reds which contrast with classic European wines with complex oxidative flavours, together with prominent aromas of both primary and secondary FERMENTATION, but with little fruit evident.   P.J.W.

fruit set, an important stage of the vine's development which marks the transition from flower to grape berry.

fruit wines, made by the FERMENTATION of fruits other than grapes, include cider and perry. They are particularly common in cool climates such as in the northern UNITED STATES and in Scandinavia. A wine-like beverage can be made from almost any fruit, berry, or other plant material containing sugar. Most of these sources contain so little fermentable sugar, however, that it is usually necessary to add sugar from another source to obtain sufficient ALCOHOL for stability. Very few fruit wines improve with BOTTLE AGE. Characteristic fruit flavours fade very rapidly and most are best consumed well within a year of bottling.

A.D.W.

full. A wine is described as full, or **full bodied**, if it is high, but not excessively high, in ALCOHOL and VISCOSITY. See BODY.

Fumé Blanc is the curious descendant of the Loire synonym BLANC FUMÉ for the white grape variety Sauvignon Blanc. In the early 1970s, California's famous ideas man Robert MONDAVI had one of his most famous inspirations, that of renaming his unfashionable Sauvignon Blanc, Fumé Blanc, thereby imbuing it with some of the glamour of imported French Pouilly-Fumé. He also gave it some OAK ageing and a dark-green bordeaux-shaped BOTTLE (both entirely alien to Pouilly-Fumé). This less-than-authentic formula proved a runaway success and Fumé Blanc became the highly successful name of a wine type in America, New Zealand, and elsewhere, even if there is little agreement about what exactly that wine type is. Most, but not all, producers who release both a Sauvignon Blanc and a Fumé Blanc tend to give the Fumé Blanc some oak ageing and, possibly, some added Sémillon so that, ironically, the Sauvignon Blanc is more Loire-like and the Fumé Blanc in fact more Bordelais.

Fumin, dark-berried vine speciality of the Valle d'AOSTA whose produce is usually used for blending.

Furmint, fine, fiery white grape variety which is the principal ingredient in TOKAJI, one of the world's most famous dessert wines. It is therefore grown not only in Hungary but also just over the border with SLOVAKIA. The grapes are particularly sensitive to NOBLE ROT, yet the wine is characterized by very high acidity, which endows the wine with long ageing potential, high sugar levels, and rich, fiery flavours. In Tokaji, it is usually blended with up to half as much of the more aromatic grape variety HÁRSLEVELÜ, and some Muscat (Blanc à Petits Grains) is also sometimes included in the blend.

Furmint can easily produce wines with an ALCOHOLIC STRENGTH as high as 14 per cent, and sturdy, characterful dry Furmint can be a delicious wine, even when drunk very young. Furmint is planted quite widely in Hungary but is most common in the Tokaj-Hegyalja region. The botrytized (*aszú*) grapes may not be picked until well into November in some years.

Furmint's traditional stronghold was in Austria's Burgenland just over the border from Hungary's Sopron. It was habitually used here for AUSBRUCH wines until more commercially reliable varieties such as WELSCHRIESLING were introduced in the late 19th and early 20th centuries. Furmint is currently being revived in Austria. The variety is still grown to a limited extent in South Africa.

futures in wine, wine bought before it is bottled and therefore long before it can be delivered. See EN PRIMEUR and INVESTMENT.

Gaglioppo, predominant red grape variety in CALABRIA in the far south of Italy. It thrives in dry conditions and reaches high sugar levels, which result in robust, if rarely subtle, wines. It is also grown in the ABRUZZI, the MARCHES, and UMBRIA.

Gaillac, dynamic, variegated wine district in SOUTH WEST FRANCE where the area devoted to AC wine production grew from about 1,600 ha/3,900 acres of vines to around 2,500 ha in the 1990s. The district is distinguished by its rich heritage of local VINE VARIETIES, and by its unusual diversity of wine styles.

The most distinctive local white grape variety is MAUZAC (which is also characteristic of Limoux), whose wines have a strong apple-peel aroma and sometimes a certain astringency. LEN DE L'EL is another strictly local variety whose wine can lack acidity; appellation regulations insist on at least 15 per cent of Len de l'El and/or Sauvignon Blanc (although iconoclasts such as Robert Plageoles happily ignore these and produce a range of VARIETAL Gaillacs in an extraordinary range of styles). Some well-made Sauvignon is produced among dry whites, and the quality of still Mauzac has improved greatly. The other two white Bordeaux varieties Sémillon and Muscadelle are also grown but the indigenous ONDENC is also being revived, notably for sweet wines.

Some of Gaillac's finest wine is BARREL MATURED sweet white made from Mauzac, Muscadelle, and recently resurrected Ondenc, distinguished either as **Gaillac doux** or, if grown on certain demarcated limestone slopes, as

Gaillac Premières Côtes (which may also produce whites that are dry, or sec). Yields for these last two appellations are lower than for regular Gaillac.

Red wine, which can be an exciting southwestern ambassador, with the structure of a good bordeaux but more spicy flavours, is Gaillac's most common product, however, with DURAS as the intriguing local vine speciality. Its combination of colour, fruit, and BODY suggests that it may well have been largely responsible for Gaillac red wines' past reputation. FER Servadou, called locally Braucol, may also have added structure in the form of TANNINS, and the mandatory proportion of these two varieties in red Gaillac is being increased. Gamay, a relatively recent arrival imported to provide Gaillac vignerons with income from PRIMEUR wines, is being written out of the regulations and Gaillac's history. Syrah, however, is encouraged to add its concentration to that of the local varieties, while the Cabernets and Merlot of Bordeaux are tolerated minor ingredients.

About a third of all white grapes, and much of the Mauzac, is vinified as a slightly sparkling wine sold as Gaillac Perlé, most notably by one of the two important CO-OPERATIVES in the region. More interesting and artisanal, however, are the medium-sweet, lightly sparkling wines made by the *méthode gaillacoise*, a close relation of the *méthode ancestrale* (see SPARKLING-WINE-MAKING), sold by some with the sediment still in bottle.

Plageoles also makes a VIN JAUNE style of wine sold as Vin de Voile.

Gaja, the most renowned producer of high-quality, estate-bottled wines in PIEDMONT, traces its origins to 1856. The firm became an important force after the Second World War under the direction of Giovanni Gaja, who began an important series of vineyard purchases in what is now the BARBARESCO DOC zone.

Gaja wines have gained worldwide recognition under Giovanni's son Angelo Gaja, who has given a new international perspective and a new elegance to the traditionally robust and powerful Piedmontese red wines, pioneering small BARREL MATURATION of both Barbaresco and BARBERA, and introducing INTERNATIONAL GRAPE VARIETIES—Cabernet Sauvignon, Chardonnay, and Sauvignon Blanc—to the vineyards of Piedmont (his Cabernet Sauvignon is called Darmagi, Piedmontese for 'what a shame', supposedly his father's reaction). He also acquired land in nearby BAROLO.

In the 1990s, Gaja expanded his horizons even further, purchasing the Pieve di Santa Restituta estate in Montalcino, where the first BRUNELLO DI MONTALCINO produced under his supervision was made in 1993, and, more recently, taking a long-term lease on vineyards in BOLGHERI on the Tuscan coast.   D.T.

Galego Dourado, white grape grown on the Atlantic coast of Portugal and known for its high-alcohol wines.

Galestro, the Italian name for the friable rock of the marl-like soil that characterizes many of the best vineyard sites in CHIANTI CLASSICO, and also the name with which a Tuscan white wine based on TREBBIANO grapes was baptized when it was born at the end of the 1970s. The wine must contain from 60 to 85 per cent Trebbiano Toscano from central Tuscany, together with a number of other varieties, both local and international: MALVASIA, VERNACCIA di San Gimignano, Chardonnay, Pinot Blanc, and Riesling. Like any Italian VINO DA TAVOLA with a specific geographical indication, Galestro can contain up to 15 per cent of wine from outside its specific production zone. Galestro is regulated and heavily promoted by a consortium founded in the late 1970s by the dominant NÉGOCIANT houses of Tuscany—ANTINORI, FRESCOBALDI, RICASOLI, Ruffino, and others. The wine was produced to specifications aimed at creating a light and fresh thirst-quencher and was an immediate commercial success in Italy,

followed by Germany. Market difficulties with this type of wine and the probability that much Trebbiano and Malvasia will not be replanted when current vineyards reach the end of their production cycle have raised some doubts, even among the producers themselves, about the long-range future of this wine.   D.T.

Galicia, Spain's wet, Atlantic north west and one of the country's 17 autonomous regions encompassing the DO wine regions of RÍAS BAIXAS, RIBEIRO, RIBEIRA SACRA, Monterrei, and VALDEORRAS. Separated by mountains from CASTILE AND LEÓN, Galicia has developed in isolation from the rest of Spain, the region being geographically and culturally closer to northern Portugal than to Madrid. The wines used to share an affinity with the light, acidic VINHO VERDE produced south of the Miño (Minho in Portuguese), the river that divides this part of Spain from Portugal, but they have become fuller and more substantial with the recovery of old native grape varieties and the use of modern wine-making techniques. Since Spain joined the European Union in 1986, Galicia has benefited from a massive injection of funds which has transformed its wine industry.

Galicia is one of the wettest parts of Iberia but an annual average of over 2,000 hours of sunshine compensates for the rainfall. Vines flourish in these humid conditions and YIELDS in excess of 100 hl/ha (5.7 tons/acre) are unequalled anywhere else in Spain. Most of the vineyards are to be found towards the south in the provinces of Orense, Pontevedra, and also in Lugo to the east. Rías Baixas, with its prized ALBARIÑO grape, revered in Spain but largely unknown abroad, is the fulcrum of the Galician rebirth and its peachy, dense wines can command high prices. But success has also meant, in the case of some producers, excessive yields. On the Minho river, wines are often blends of Albariño, Loureiro, and Caiño. Inland, the Ribeiro DO is making slow progress, almost all of it through the efforts of small producers such as Arsenio Paz, Emilio Rojo, and Viña Mein.

Local whites are based on complex blends, dominated by Treixadura and Torrontés, while reds from native varieties are making a timid comeback. In the inland Valdeorras and Ribeira Sacra DOs, light reds from the Mencía grape are prevalent, but the appley, white Godello grape is its main asset.   R.J.M. & V. de la S.

Gallo winery of Modesto, CALIFORNIA, the largest single wine-making establishment in the world, was developed by the brothers Ernest (1909–) and Julio (1910–93) from the vineyards of their father, who shipped grapes for HOME WINE-MAKING during Prohibition.

By 1950, Gallo had the largest wine-production capacity in the United States. By 1967, it held first position in sales, and has continued to do so. In the process of its growth, Gallo has encouraged the planting of superior vine varieties, the use of modern crop-management methods, and the best available wine-making technology. It has thus been involved in improving the basic standards of the California wine industry.

Moreover, Gallo's sales and marketing operation was long considered the academy for such functions in America. At one time almost all the top wine sales executives in the USA had at least a short stint with Gallo on their resumés.

Known from the beginning for sound, inexpensive wines of every kind, including FLAVOURED WINES, wine COOLERS and FRUIT WINES, brandy, and bulk-process SPARKLING WINES, Gallo inevitably became synonymous with 'pop' wine and JUG WINE, i.e. PLONK, generally recognized in the US by their screwcap bottles. Since 1977, however, Gallo has made a determined effort to associate its name with premium wines, in the USA understood to be VARIETAL wines sold in bottles stoppered with a CORK. In the 1970s and early 1980s, Gallo was already the largest purchaser of grapes in the Napa Valley. But by the end of the 1980s, Gallo was the largest vineyard owner in Sonoma County. Two of Julio's grandchildren, Matt and Gina, run a 3-million-gallon winery in Dry Creek Valley with 3,000 acres of vineyard spread all over the county, which still only accounts for about one per cent of the company's volume. Their estate wines are sold under the name Gallo Sonoma while names such as Anapuma, Zabaco, and Indigo Hills are used for wines made from grapes purchased from Monterey, Sonoma, and Mendocino respectively. Less expensive wines sold under other Gallo brands such as Carlo Rossi and Livingston Cellars are made in Modesto. The firm is wholly owned by the family and discloses little information about its operations.

Gamay, French red grape variety solely responsible for the distinctive, and unjus-tifiably unfashionable, wines of BEAUJOLAIS. There are scores of different Gamays, many quite unrelated to the Beaujolais archetype, many of them particular CLONAL SELECTIONS of it, and many more of them red-fleshed grapes once widely used to add colour to vapid blends. The red-fleshed version can still be found in the Mâconnais and in Touraine. The 'real' Gamay is officially known as Gamay Noir à Jus Blanc to draw attention to its noble pale flesh, and is probably related to PINOT.

Gamay juice also tends to be vinified in a hurry, not least because of market pressure for Beaujolais NOUVEAU, and if Gamay-based wines are cellared for more than two or three years, it is usually by mistake. As a wine, Gamay tends to be paler and bluer than most other reds, with relatively high acidity and a simple but vivacious aroma of freshly picked red fruits, often overlaid by the less subtle smells associated with rapid, anaerated fermentation such as bananas, boiled sweets, and acetone. In France and Switzerland, it is often blended with Pinot Noir, endowing the nobler grape with some precocity, but often blurring the very distinct attributes of each. Gamay fruit is naturally low in potential alcohol, and for many Gamay's charm lies in its refreshing lightness, but prevailing perceptions equating weight with worth have encouraged many wine-makers towards over-CHAPTALIZATION. Beaujolais regulations stipulated a maximum ALCOHOLIC STRENGTH of 13 per cent from 1985, as well they might.

Gamay and Beaujolais are entirely interdependent. In 1988, well over half of the world's total Gamay plantings were in this single region. Vinification techniques vary but most common is a local variant on CARBONIC MACERATION. Similar, often lighter and arguably truer, wines are made from the Gamay grown in the small wine regions of central France, particularly those around Lyons and in the upper reaches of the Loire such as CHÂTEAUMEILLANT, Coteaux du LYONNAIS, Coteaux du GIENNOIS, Côtes d'AUVERGNE, Côtes du FOREZ, Côtes ROANNAISES, and ST-POURÇAIN.

Outside Beaujolais, and perhaps because its wines have been seen as too different from the intense, fashionable norm, the Gamay vine has been losing ground. In the Côte Chalonnaise and the Mâconnais between Beaujolais and the CÔTE D'OR, the Gamay was displaced as principal grape variety by Chardonnay during the 1980s. In the Côte d'Or, it is fast being supplanted by more rewarding Pinot Noir and Chardonnay.

Gamay is grown all over the Loire but is not glorified by any of the Loire's greatest appellations. Gamay de Touraine can provide a light, sometimes acid, but usually cheaper alternative to Beaujolais, but it is most widely grown west of Touraine, alongside Sauvignon, for such light, lesser-known names as CHEVERNY and Coteaux du VENDÔMOIS. Gamay also provides about 40 per cent of all of the Loire's important generic Vin de Pays du Jardin de la France.

Outside France there is even less incentive to develop this under-appreciated variety, although a few California growers have bothered to import and vinify true Gamay as opposed to the less distinguished vine known there at one time as Napa Gamay (see VALDIGUIÉ) or the variety called Gamay Beaujolais, which is probably a lesser clone of Pinot Noir. It is also grown in minute quantities in Canada and is confused on a grand scale with BLAUFRÄNKISCH throughout eastern Europe. It is grown to a certain extent in Italy, and plays a relatively important role in the vineyards of what was YUGOSLAVIA, notably in CROATIA, SERBIA, KOSOVO, and, to least effect, in MACEDONIA. Outside Beaujolais, it is chiefly valued by the Swiss, who grow it widely and, often blending with Pinot Noir, take it seriously—although they too are apt to chaptalize the life out of it (see SWITZERLAND).

Gambellara, dry white wine from the VENETO region of north-east Italy. Based on GARGANEGA grapes (a minimum of 80 per cent, with 20 per cent of TREBBIANO di Soave or Trebbiano Toscano permitted in the blend), it is produced in the townships of Gambellara, Montebello Vicentino, Montorso, and Zermeghedo, only a short distance from SOAVE but in the neighbouring province of Vicenza rather than that of Verona. The wines share the blandness of the vast majority of Soave, without sharing the reputation or the instant consumer recognition that Soave enjoys.   D.T.

Gamé, Bulgarian name for BLAUFRÄNKISCH.

Gamza, Bulgarian name for KADARKA.

Gancia, large Italian wine-merchant house headquartered in Canelli in the heart of the production zone of MOSCATO D'ASTI which has played a leading role in the development of SPARKLING WINE in Italy since the 1850s. The

house's fortunes were built on its pioneering 'Moscato Champagne' (*sic*), whose production began in the early 1870s. Asti producers agreed to rename the wine ASTI Spumante around 1910. Gancia purchased an important estate in APULIA in 1983, the Tenuta Torrebianco in Minervino Murge, with the express purpose of developing a line of still wines; Chardonnay and Sauvignon Blanc have dominated the first plantings. Current production of Gancia is approximately 1.5 million cases.   D.T.

Garganega, vigorous, productive, often over-productive white grape variety of the VENETO region in north-east Italy. Its most famous incarnation is SOAVE, in which it may constitute anything from 70 to 100 per cent of the blend, often sharpened up by the addition of TREBBIANO di Soave, but increasingly plumped up by CHARDONNAY and other imports. In the Soave CLASSICO zone, with yields kept well in check, it can produce the fine, delicate whites redolent of lemon and almonds which give Soave a good name. The vine is also responsible for GAMBELLARA and plays a major part in Bianco di CUSTOZA, Colli Berici, Colli Euganei. It is also grown to a more limited extent in both FRIULI and UMBRIA.

Garnacha is the Spanish, and therefore original, name for the grape known in France and elsewhere as Grenache. Its most common and noblest form is the dark-berried and light-fleshed **Garnacha Tinta,** sometimes known as **Garnacho Tinto. Garnacha Blanca** is the light-berried GRENACHE BLANC. VARIETAL versions are becoming more common, as are blends with the firmer TEMPRANILLO, and the word Garnacha is increasingly seen on wine labels.

In Spain, Garnacha Tinta is grown particularly in the north and east, being an important variety in such wine regions as Rioja, Navarre, Empordà-Costa-Brava, Campo de Borja, Cariñena, Costers del Segre, Madrid, La Mancha, Méntrida, Penedès, Priorat, Somontano, Tarragona, Terra Alta, Utiel-Requena, and Valdeorras. In Rioja, it provides stuffing and immediate charm when blended with the more austere Tempranillo. The cooler, higher vineyards of Rioja Alta are reserved for Tempranillo, while Garnacha is the most common grape variety of the warm eastern Rioja Baja region, where the vines can enjoy a long ripening season. The juiciness apparent in these early-maturing Riojas can be tasted in a host of other Spanish reds and, especially, rosados.

Grenache has been adopted with particular enthusiasm in Navarre, where it has been the dominant grape variety and dictates a lighter, more obviously fruity style of red and rosado than in Rioja. The authorities, anxious to modernize Navarre's image, have been positively discouraging new plantings of Garnacha, however.

Perhaps the most distinctive, and certainly the most expensive, Spanish wine based on Garnacha Tinta (often incorporating some **Garnacha Peluda**, or 'downy Garnacha', known as LLADONER PELUT in Languedoc-Roussillon), is Priorat, the concentrated Catalonian cult wine in which the produce of old Garnacha vines may be modernized by blending it with young Merlot, Cabernet, or even Syrah fruit.

Garnacha Tintorera, synonym for the red-fleshed ALICANTE BOUSCHET.

Garonne, river that rises south of Toulouse in SOUTH WEST FRANCE and flows north west towards the Atlantic and on which the city of BORDEAUX is situated. The confluence of the Garonne and the DORDOGNE, between MARGAUX and BOURG, marks the southern end of the GIRONDE estuary.

garrafeira, word used by wine-makers, wine bottlers, and wine collectors in PORTUGAL meaning 'private wine cellar' or 'reserve'. The term is used on wine labels to denote a red wine from an exceptional year that has aged in bulk for at least two years prior to bottling and then aged a further year in bottle before sale. White garrafeira wines must be aged for at least six months in bulk followed by six months in bottle to qualify. The law states that both red and white DOC wines must have an ALCOHOLIC STRENGTH at least 0.5 per cent above the legal minimum for the DOC region. Traditionally most garrafeiras were blends of wines from different parts of the country, labelled with the name of the merchant who bottled them. Under legislation introduced in the early 1990s, all garrafeiras must display their region of origin.   R.J.M.

Garrut is a CATALONIAN black grape variety producing aromatic wines reminiscent of liquorice that are high in tannins.

Gascony, proud region in SOUTH WEST FRANCE which today comprises armagnac country and such wines as MADIRAN and JURANÇON. Its name appears on labels of the highly successful VIN DE PAYS des Côtes de Gascogne.

Gattinara, sometimes intense red wine based on NEBBIOLO grapes, here known as Spanna, grown in the cluster of hills which span Vercelli and Novara provinces in the PIEDMONT region of north-west Italy. It was awarded DOCG status in 1990. These HILLSIDE VINEYARDS are capable of producing some of the most serious rivals to the great BAROLO and BARBARESCO. It is traditional here to add a small softening portion of local BONARDA and/or VESPOLINA grapes, a ploy needed particularly in less ripe vintages when Nebbiolo grown well to the north of the Langhe can seem austere rather than majestic. Of the seven SPANNA zones, Gattinara should produce the most long-lived wines, and the most substantial are given extended ageing in cask.

D.T.

Gavi, fashionable Italian dry white and the most interesting expression of the CORTESE grape in PIEDMONT. It is produced around the town of Gavi in the south east of the province of Alessandria (thus some bottles may be labelled Cortese di Gavi and others, made close to the town, Gavi di Gavi).

At its best, Gavi is fruity and aromatic, occasionally with mineral notes and a tangy, citric finish; comparisons with white burgundy on the part of its more fervent admirers seem far-fetched. Total production more than tripled in the 20 years since approval of DOC status in 1974.

Increasing competition in its category from TRENTINO and the ALTO ADIGE, as well as from FRIULI, has subsequently put Gavi under a certain commercial pressure, and estates in the zone seem uncertain as to where to position their production: as a medium-quality, medium-priced wine or as a wine with higher quality and price aspirations. The production of a certain amount of bland Gavi has not helped the wine's image, although good bottles of Gavi are by no means difficult to find. In 1998, Gavi was awarded DOCG status.   D.T.

Geelong, relatively small, relatively isolated wine region in the Port Phillip zone of the Australian state of VICTORIA.

generic wine, one named after a wine type (and usually borrowed European place-name) as opposed to a VARIETAL wine named after the grape variety from which the wine was made. The term has been used particularly in AUSTRALIA and the UNITED STATES. Under American law, wines labelled as generics may be made from any grape variety or blend of varieties, and called either after their colour (red, white, rosé) or after places. With nothing else to call their results, early CALIFORNIA wineries borrowed European place-names shamelessly. Chablis could and can be just as sickly sweet as Rhine, and both can be made from THOMPSON SEEDLESS or any other white grape. Burgundy, Chianti, and Claret could all come from the same tank, and admittedly have done. Towards the end of the 1980s, Red Table Wine, White Table Wine, and Rosé began to replace place-names on many of the more reputable labels. However, Chablis, Burgundy, and other borrowed names remain in widespread use by a number of large-volume producers, giants GALLO foremost among them.

Generic names can still be found on many wine labels, particularly in non-exporting or developing wine regions. No third-country wine entering the European Union may carry a geographical name recognized by European wine officials. Thus, for example, the Australian company PENFOLDS had to change the name of their most famous wine from Penfolds Grange Hermitage to Penfolds Grange and, more fatuously, EU officials have objected to established New World place-names incorporating the word Port.

Outside Europe, CHAMPAGNE is still widely used as a generic name for SPARKLING WINE, although not usually for the best-quality products.

generoso is a Spanish and Portuguese term for a FORTIFIED wine.

genetic engineering, sometimes called **genetic manipulation**, modern approach to breeding which involves transfer of genes between organisms. This new technology has applications in both VITICULTURE and OENOLOGY. A proposed benefit of genetic engineering is to insert foreign genes, carrying a particular desirable characteristic, into the genetic material of traditional VINE VARIETIES such as Cabernet Sauvignon, without altering the genes concerned with their other characteristics. Although governments have introduced strict testing procedures for any genetically modified organisms, consumer resistance in parts of Europe has been considerable. R.E.S.

Geographe, subregion in the South West Australia wine zone of WESTERN AUSTRALIA.

geographical delimitation and geographical designation. See DELIMITATION, GEOGRAPHICAL.

Georgia, independent ex-member of the Soviet Union (see CIS) immediately north east of Turkey between the Black Sea and the High Caucasus. Within the CIS, only Russia produces more wine. A JOINT VENTURE with Pernod Ricard of France has ambitious export plans.

Viticultural zones

Georgia has five viticultural zones: Kakheti, Kartli, Imereti, Racha-Lechkhumi, and the humid subtropical zone.

Kakheti, which grows 70 per cent of Georgia's wine and brandy grapes, is in the south east of the country in the Alazani and Iori valleys. The distinctive Kakhetian wines are made peculiarly tannic by FERMENTATION in special earthenware jars followed by an extended MACERATION of three or four months.

Kartli occupies a vast territory in the Kura valley, the Gori and Mukhran lowlands included. These wines are the most European and the region produces materials for sparkling wines (especially) and brandy. The capital, Tbilisi, where wineries producing sparkling wines and brandy are located, is in this zone.

Imereti is in the eastern part of west Georgia, in the basins and in the gullies of Rioni, Kvirila, and other rivers. Imereti also uses an original wine-production method, similar to Kakheti's except that grape skins are *added* to the clay jars during fermentation, and this is followed by a maceration of six to eight weeks. The vine variety particular to this region is Tzitzka.

Racha-Lechkhumi is north of Imereti, on the banks of the Rioni and Tskhenistskali rivers.

The Khvanchkara microregion is famous for its semi-sweet Ehvanchkara wine, often made from Alexandrouli and Mujuretuli vine varieties. The **humid subtropical zone** is also noted for its sweet wines.

Vine varieties

Thirty-eight grape varieties are officially allowed for commercial viticulture in Georgia. Wine varieties include RKATSITELI, Tsolikouri, Tsitska, Chinuri, SAPERAVI, Goruli Mtsvane, Mtsvane Kakhetinski, Ojaleshi, Aladasturi, Khikhvi, Chkhaveri, Dzvelshvari Obchuri, ALIGOTÉ, PINOT NOIR, CHARDONNAY, and CABERNET SAUVIGNON. V.R.

German crossings, an important group of VINE VARIETIES that are the result of vine breeding, an activity that was particularly vigorous in the first half of the 20th century but which continues to this day, most notably at Geisenheim and Geilweilerhof.

The most successful white wine varieties, in descending order of area planted in Germany in the late 1990s, are KERNER, SCHEUREBE, BACCHUS, FABER(REBE), MORIO-MUSKAT, HUXELREBE, ORTEGA, EHRENFELSER, OPTIMA, REICHENSTEINER, PERLE, SIEGERREBE, REGNER, Nobling, Würzer, Kanzler, SCHÖNBURGER, FREISAMER, Findling, RIESLANER, Juwel, Albalonga, and, more popular in England than Germany, GUTENBORNER. Few of these crossings make distinctive, attractive, and characterful wines, although Kerner, Ehrenfelser and, particularly, Scheurebe and Rieslaner can make fine wines if sufficiently ripe. More typically, the vines have been planted to yield good quantities of high-must-weight wines.

Successful German crossings for red wine include DORNFELDER, HEROLDREBE, and HELFENSTEINER.

German Wine Law was until recently a source of pride for German wine producers. In its fifth generation, however, it was an animal bred with particular care in 1971 but which grew fairly rapidly into a monster which many of the best wine producers in GERMANY have since done their best to amend or ignore.

Each vineyard is delineated and registered (see EINZELLAGE) and its produce can be used to make wine at any quality level, depending not on YIELDS but on the ripeness, or MUST WEIGHT, of the grapes. The least ripe grapes qualify as Deutscher TAFELWEIN, or table wine, which represents less than five per cent of all wine produced in a typical German vintage. All the rest is graded as QUALITY WINE according to the generous terms of the German Wine Law.

The bottom layer of Germany's quality wine is made from grapes whose ripeness qualifies for QBA status, a 'quality wine from a specified region'. This is the category under which most German wine is usually sold. Wines made from riper grapes, however, are qualified as QMP, 'quality wine with distinction': the riper the grapes, the higher the official Prädikat or distinction (and selling price), rising from KABINETT through SPÄTLESE, AUSLESE, BEERENAUSLESE, TROCKENBEERENAUSLESE, to EISWEIN.

Germany, the most distinctive major wine producer in Europe with both wines and problems quite unlike those of anywhere else. Grape growing in Germany is a small but prestigious part of the whole country's farming industry. Whilst a small part of the grape harvest results in wines of exquisite finesse, unique in style to Germany, over half the crop is sold on price, and not on quality. There are individual vineyard sites, EINZELLAGEN, in part or all of which superior grapes can be harvested nearly every year, but the trail that leads to the best German wines is discovered most easily through the name of the producer. Producing fine wines in Germany requires not only technical ability, but imagination and a dedication to excellence. It is upon the lustre and prestige of names associated with the best wines, both geographical and qualitative, that many cheaper versions have been allowed to draw since the 1970s, devaluing Germany's official quality system in the process.

Geography

Many of Germany's best vineyards are on the steepest slopes, quite unsuited to anything other than the vine. Overlooking the rivers RHINE, Neckar, Main, Nahe, Ahr, MOSEL and its tributaries, their high cost of cultivation is justified only by the quality of the wine they can produce. In the steep vineyards, three times as many man-hours are spent tending the vine as is the case on flat or rolling terrain, where the natural position of the vine-grower is on the seat of a tractor.

Several other factors limit MECHANIZATION in the vineyards, amongst which are the smallness of the holdings and the principle of grape selection. Vine-growing in Germany has become a mainly female, mainly part-time occupation, based on an average holding of 1.5 ha (3.7 acres). The majority of vineyard owners do not make wine but supply grapes to merchants or, more likely, to the CO-OPERATIVE cellars which receive the crop from 30 per cent of the total German vineyard.

See also entries under the names of individual wine regions, which are, in declining area of total vineyard, RHEINHESSEN, PFALZ, BADEN, MOSEL-SAAR-RUWER, WÜRTTEMBERG, FRANKEN, NAHE, RHEINGAU, MITTELRHEIN, SAALEUNSTRUT, AHR, HESSISCHE BERGSTRASSE, and SACHSEN. Most German wine labels carry the name of the region in which the wine was produced.

Wine-making

The aim of good, modern German WINE-

MAKING is wine that is true to its region and vine variety. It must be clean and fruity, the result of physics rather than chemistry.

The use of SÜSSRESERVE or unfermented grape juice to sweeten wine is no longer so common in the cellars of private estates. Great sweetness and finesse combine in AUSLESE and TROCKENBEERENAUSLESE wines produced from grapes that have been attacked by *Botrytis cinerea* that has developed into NOBLE ROT. A similar sweetness, but without the flavour or complexity of noble rot, is achieved by gathering grapes when they are frozen on the vine, to produce EISWEIN.

CHAPTALIZATION, or the adding of sugar to increase ALCOHOLIC STRENGTH, is permitted for TAFELWEIN and QBA but is specifically prohibited for QMP wines. DEACIDIFICATION is allowed but only in exceptionally poor vintages. The somewhat experimental BARREL MATURATION of white and red wine, from vine varieties which do not have the firm structure of Riesling, is common, especially for the PINOT family. Liveliness, some CARBON DIOXIDE in white wine, is widely admired.

As a general statement it is true that difficult trading conditions since 1985, helped by a series of outstanding vintages from 1988 to 1997, have improved the quality of producer-bottled wines (labelled ERZEUGERABFÜLLUNG, or GUTSABFÜLLUNG if estate bottled). Without a veil of sweetness, the flavour of a wine is more clearly exposed, and the new preference for drier wines labelled TROCKEN and HALBTROCKEN, especially marketed within Germany, has meant a readjustment of the way in which German white wine is popularly assessed. By 1997, half of all German wine submitted for quality control testing was either dry or medium dry. Sweeter wines are less fashionable and producers in the northern regions of the Rhine and Nahe are more likely to be judged by their drier SPÄTLESE trocken, for example, which are destined to be drunk with food, than by their declining output of sweet or medium-sweet wines. This change in taste has also completely revitalized the German red-wine market.

Vine varieties

As most vine varieties approach the outer edge of their climatically possible growing area, there is a steep decline in the qualities that make their wine worthwhile. With RIESLING, the classic German wine, matters run differently. Near the northern edge of the vineyards in the Mosel-Saar-Ruwer, Rheingau, and Nahe, Riesling sheds all unnecessary fat. What remains is style, and structure—the analogy to an elegant, slim fashion model may be banal but it is accurate.

Just under 80 per cent of Germany's vineyard was planted in white vine varieties in the late 1990s with Riesling and its offspring MÜLLER-THURGAU together occupying 43 per cent of the total area under vine. Red vine varieties, particularly Spätburgunder (Pinot Noir), PORTUGIESER, and DORNFELDER, are spreading at the expense of some of the white wine varieties, including the less fashionable GERMAN CROSSINGS and the sadly declining SILVANER.

After the name of the producer, that of the vine variety is probably the next most important fact about a German wine. No one region has a monopoly of fine wine but there are more top producers of Germany's best-known Riesling wine in the Rheingau and the Mosel-Saar-Ruwer than anywhere else.

Wine labelling

The official European Union-recognized category of table wine is TAFELWEIN, and quality wine is QUALITÄTSWEIN. The latter is subdivided into simple quality wine QBA, and quality wine with distinction QMP, which embraces Kabinett, Spätlese, Auslese, Beerenauslese, and Trockenbeerenauslese wines, as well as Eiswein. Each of these 'predicates' represents very approximate differences in style and total alcohol content, rather than in true quality. Within the range offered by one producer, a Spätlese wine would normally be superior to a Kabinett wine, and be priced accordingly. However, a QbA from a top estate will be a far better wine than a Spätlese bottled for a supermarket and sold at less than half the price.

All German quality wines (some 97 per cent of the annual harvest from 1988 to 1997!) are analysed by officially approved laboratories and tasted without having the name of their bottler revealed. Any serious technical faults, or deviation from the regional style, obvious at the time of examination will prevent a wine from receiving a control number (see AP NUMBER) and being sold as quality wine. The system is certainly open to criticism for being too lenient in its judgements, but there is no other member of the EU which has anything much better to offer on a national scale.

The range of German wine on offer is particularly complicated in the 1990s, as it includes the notions of nomenclature and quality categories of the past as well as the latest innovations based on different standards. A CLASSIFICATION of German estates similar to that of the Médoc has been suggested by commentators and those who believe it would be to their advantage. Whereas the Bordelais in their 1855 classification were concerned with one wine only per château per year, the huge number of German estate bottlings (an estate of 10 ha/25 acres may well have a list of 30 or more different wines), with their many varieties, makes a true and correct estate classification seem almost impossible. Were such a classification to be attempted, it might be an aid to sales in Germany, but beyond that its value would be questionable. Equally controversial, other than in a few instances, would be a classification of the present individual vineyards. The variations in quality within any one site are considerable.

The German wine producers are faced with the fact that, if a special characteristic of a wine is individuality, by definition, the quantity available is strictly limited. Marketing efforts therefore have to be concentrated not on specific wines but on the name of the producer. German wine is better today than it has ever been before, even if finding the ideal name under which it can be sold sometimes causes difficulties. Well-known and ancient estates are expected to produce top-quality wine, but many are now willing to experiment in a limited way, while still making their classic Rieslings. Wine lovers will also be pleased by the rise of a number of relatively unknown private estates, particularly in the Pfalz. Here, and in Baden, the new drier wines sold under a vine variety name by co-operative cellars at a fair, but not ultra-cheap, price are a good starting-point for understanding serious German wine. For most producers, marketing and not wine-making is the problem.

I.J. & K.B.S.

Gevrey-Chambertin, small town in the Côte de Nuits producing some of Burgundy's most famous red wines from Pinot Noir grapes. The area allowed the appellation was sharply reduced in the late 1990s to exclude some less favoured land towards the plain, but it is still the largest viticultural source in the CÔTE D'OR.

Gevrey-Chambertin wines are typically deeper in colour and firmer than their rivals from Vosne-Romanée and Chambolle-Musigny. Good examples may take time to develop into perhaps the richest and most complete wines of the Côte d'Or. Sadly, owing to the ease with which a famous name sells, there are too many underachievers, both at VILLAGE WINE level and amongst the GRANDS CRUS. Among traditionalists, Rousseau is an exception, however, while Denis Mortet dazzles in a more modern way.

In all, Gevrey boasts eight grands crus, the pick of which are Chambertin and Chambertin-Clos de Bèze. The latter may equally be sold as Le Chambertin. It is hard to differentiate between the two qualitatively although Clos de Bèze wines tend to be fractionally less powerful but full of sensual charm.

Le Chambertin is the flagship. Theoretically the most powerful vineyard of them all, Chambertin has tended to suffer from over-production since the appellation commands such a high price. None the less, Chambertin has always been regarded as the most complete vineyard of the Côte d'Or: if not quite as sumptuous as Musigny or Richebourg, or as divinely elegant as La Tâche or Romanée-St-Vivant, Chambertin is matched only by Romanée-Conti (see VOSNE-ROMANÉE) for its completeness and its intensity.

Mazis-Chambertin, also written Mazy-, is usually regarded as being next in quality to Chambertin and Clos de Bèze. The flavours are just as intense, the structure perhaps just a little less firm. Latricières-Chambertin is less powerful, although the wines are explosively fruity when young, with an entrancingly silky texture. Ruchottes-Chambertin is lighter in colour, angular in style, but again impressively intense. The wines are finer than those of Chapelle-Chambertin, which also tends to lightness of colour.

Griotte-Chambertin produces wines which are better than those of neighbouring Chapelle- or Charmes-Chambertin. The latter, at 31.6 ha, is the largest grand cru in the village and, as with Clos de Vougeot and Échezeaux, its size precludes homogeneous quality. Some of the vineyard should perhaps not be classified as grand cru, although a good Charmes is one of Gevrey-Chambertin's most seductive, fragrant wines when young.

Some of the grand crus are matched, if not surpassed, by the best of the premier-cru vineyards, especially those with an ideal south-eastern exposition such as Les Cazetiers and Clos St-Jacques. Indeed, Domaine Armand Rousseau charges significantly more for Clos St-Jacques than for several grand crus in an impressive range of wines.   J.T.C.M.

Gewürztraminer, often written Gewurz-traminer, and quite often abbreviated to Tra-miner, pink-skinned grape variety responsible for particularly pungent, full-bodied white wines. Gewürztraminer may not be easy to spell, even for wine merchants, but is blissfully easy to recognize—indeed many wine drinkers find it is the first, possibly only, grape variety they are able to recognize from the wine's heady perfume alone. Deeply coloured, opulently aromatic, and fuller bodied than almost any other white wine, Gewürztraminer's faults are only in having too much of everything. It is easy to tire of its weight and its exotic flavour of lychees and heavily scented roses, although ALSACE's finest Gewürztraminers are extremely serious wines, capable of at least medium-term ageing.

This by now internationally famous vine variety's genealogy is both ramified and fascinating. The variety which truly deserves the name TRAMINER, like Gewürztraminer but with pale-green berries and much less scent, is the original variety, first noted in the village of Tramin or Termeno in what is now the Italian Tyrol (see ALTO ADIGE). Gewürztraminer is the name adopted in the late 19th century for the dark-pink-berried MUSQUÉ mutation of Tra-miner.

Gewürztraminer has become by far the most planted variant of Traminer. The grapes are certainly notable at harvest for their variegated but incontrovertibly pink colour, which is translated into very deep golden wines, sometimes with a slight coppery tinge. Gewürz-traminers also attain higher alcohol levels than most white wines, with over 13 per cent being by no means uncommon, and acidities can correspondingly be precariously low. MAL-OLACTIC FERMENTATION is almost invariably suppressed for Gewürztraminer and steps must be taken to avoid OXIDATION.

If all goes well, the result is deep-golden, full-bodied wines with a substantial spine and concentrated heady aromas whose acidity level will preserve them while those aromas unfurl. In a lesser year or too hot a climate the result is either an early-picked, neutral wine or an oppressively oily, flabby one that can easily taste bitter to boot.

Few wine-makers outside Alsace have expended real energy on making great Gewurz. By the early 1990s, the finest examples still came almost exclusively from this region in eastern France, where Gewürztraminer was the second most planted in Alsace as a whole. It is particularly successful on the richer clay soils of the Haut-Rhin and it inspired a raft of late-harvest examples labelled VENDANGE TARDIVE or even SÉLECTION DE GRAINS NOBLES in the sunnier harvests of the 1980s and 1990s. Such late-harvest Gewürztraminers may not last as long as their Riesling counterparts but many last longer than their first decade. The trick for wine-makers is to achieve BALANCE in these potentially heavyweight wines.

Earlier-picked Alsace Gewürztraminer should be intriguingly aromatic yet dry and sturdy enough to accompany savoury food but too many examples are simply scented fly-by-nights, lightweight wines produced from heavily cropped vines that taste as though they have been aromatized by a drop of MUSCAT OTTONEL. Producers with a particularly fine reputation for their Gewürztraminer include Léon Beyer of the bigger houses and Zind-Humbrecht and Cattin among the grower/bottlers.

Germany relegates its (Roter) Traminer to a very minor rank, well behind Riesling. Almost two thirds of Germany's Traminer is planted in Baden and the Pfalz, where it can produce wines of discernible character but is too often associated with somewhat oily sickliness.

There is almost as much Traminer planted in AUSTRIA as in Germany but here too it has been consigned to the non-modish wilderness, even though some examples, particularly later-picked sweet wines from Styria, can exhibit an exciting blend of race and aroma and can develop for a few years in bottle.

The variety is grown, in no great quantity but usually distinctively, throughout eastern Europe, called Tramini in Hungary; Traminac in Slovenia; Drumin, Pinat Cervena, or Liwora in what was Czechoslovakia; occasionally just Rusa in Romania; and Mala Dinka in Bulgaria. Most of the vines are the aromatic mutation and demonstrate some of Gewürztraminer's distinctive perfume but often in extremely dilute, and often sullied, form, typically over-laying a relatively sweet, lightish white. Hungarians are particularly proud of their Tramini grown on the rich shores of Lake Balaton.

It is grown in small quantities, sometimes called Haiden or Heida, in Switzerland and in ever smaller quantity in Luxembourg. In Iberia, Torres grow it in the High PENEDÈS for their Viña Esmeralda and it is essentially a mountain grape even in Italy, where Traminer Aromatico is grown almost exclusively, and decreasingly, in its seat, the ALTO ADIGE. The less scented and less interesting Traminer is also grown to a limited extent.

In the New World, Gewürztraminer presents a challenge. Many wine regions are simply too warm to produce wine with sufficient acidity, unless the grapes are picked so early that they have developed little Gewürztraminer character.

The variety has been more obviously successful in the cooler climate of NEW ZEALAND, although even here total plantings have been falling quite dramatically, despite some lively examples from Gisborne on the east coast of the North Island.

Another happy home for Gewürztraminer is in the Pacific Northwest of America, particularly in Washington and Oregon, although even here the variety has been losing ground to the inevitable Chardonnay.

Gewürztraminer remains a relatively minor variety in California, found mainly in Monterey, where the wines too often bring forth oil rather than aroma (see CALIFORNIA). There are a few hectares of Traminer in Argentina, and one or two quite convincing bottlings from Chile, but generally South America relies on TORRONTÉS and MOSCATEL to provide aromatic whites. Limited plantings in South Africa have so far yielded sweet wines but some of the right aromas.

It seems likely that serious Gewürztraminer will remain an Alsace speciality for some years yet.

Ghemme, red-wine DOCG, promoted in 1997, high up in the sub-Alpine Novara hills in the north of the PIEDMONT region of north-west Italy. Like GATTINARA across the river Seisa in the Vercelli hills, Ghemme is made from the NEBBIOLO grape leavened with BONARDA and VESPOLINA. For more details, see SPANNA, the local name for Nebbiolo.

Giennois, Coteaux du, once known as Côtes de Gien, zone which extends on both banks of the Loire to the north of POUILLY-FUMÉ in the upper Loire to the town of Gien. Most of the wines produced are light reds made from

Gamay, and occasionally Pinot Noir grapes, while crisp, pale whites are made exclusively from Sauvignon Blanc. Joseph Balland Chapuis is one of the most dedicated producers in this region. The wine was promoted from VDQS to AC in the late 1990s.

See also LOIRE.

Gigondas, potentially excellent-value red- and rosé-wine appellation in the southern RHÔNE. From about a third of the total area, the best wines are remarkably similar to good red CHÂTEAUNEUF-DU-PAPE, and overall wine standards are high, even if Gigondas wine-making is more rustic than high-tech. Gigondas can taste delightfully untamed (even if inappropriate in the heat of a typical Gigondas summer's day). Gigondas shares Châteauneuf's low maximum YIELD, 35 hl/ha (2 tons/acre); high minimum natural ALCOHOLIC STRENGTH, 12.5 per cent; and a compulsory TRIAGE to eliminate imperfect grapes.

The total *vignoble* is about 1,200 ha/3,000 acres of rugged, herb-scented vineyard just below the much-painted rocks, the Dentelles de Montmirail. For red wines, Grenache grapes must account for no more than 80 per cent of the total blend, while Syrah and/or Mourvèdre make up at least 15 per cent. The varieties permitted for Côtes-du-RHÔNE, except Carignan, may be used for the rest. Neither Syrah nor Mourvèdre are mandatory in the rosés, however.

In the 20th century, it laboured under the commercial disadvantage of qualifying merely for the Côtes du Rhône appellation for several decades. In 1966, it was elevated to Côtes du Rhône-Villages, and in 1971, finally won its own appellation. The best wines can repay BOTTLE AGEING for a decade or more. Over-achieving producers include Domaines de Cayron, Les Goubert, St-Gayan, and Santa Duc.

Gippsland, vast wine zone in the Australian state of VICTORIA.

Gironde, the estuary which separates the MÉDOC from BLAYE and the south-western extreme of Cognac country gives its name to the *département* in which the city of Bordeaux and the BORDEAUX wine region are to be found. The rivers DORDOGNE and GARONNE flow into the Gironde.

Givry produces mostly red wine in the Côte CHALONNAISE district of Burgundy. The rare white wines, a tenth of the total production, are often particularly interesting, with a soft bouquet reminiscent of liquorice. The reds have more structure and ability to age than those of neighbouring RULLY, but less depth than Mercurey. About one-sixth of the vineyard area is designated PREMIER CRU, including Clos Marceaux, Clos Salomon, and Clos Jus. J.T.C.M.

glass, wine by the. In many of the world's restaurants and bars, particularly in the United States, wine is served by the glass. This is especially useful for those who want to drink less than a half or full bottle, or want to taste as many different wines as possible, or want to practise focused FOOD AND WINE MATCHING in a group that has ordered a wide range of different dishes. When carefully administered, with due attention to LEFTOVERS in opened bottles, possibly using special storage systems involving INERT GAS, this is an admirable service to the consumer (and occasionally producer; part of the mythology of Opus One, the luxury Napa Valley Cabernet that resulted from the Mondavi-Mouton JOINT VENTURE, is that it was both launched and commercially saved by extensive by-the-glass serving programmes). The practice is still in its infancy in many countries, however, notably in Britain, where wine by the glass is still typically the dregs from a badly kept bottle of very ordinary wine served in a pub. This despite, or perhaps because of, the fact that there is strict UK legislation ordaining that wine must be served in measures of 125 ml, 175 ml, or occasionally 250 ml.

glasses, not just the final CONTAINER for wine but an important instrument for communicating it to the human senses (see TASTING). Wine can be drunk from any drinking vessel but clean (and only clean) glass has the advantage of being completely inert and, if it is clear, of allowing the taster the pleasure (or in the case of BLIND TASTING the clues) afforded by the wine's appearance: colour, clarity, and so on.

For this reason, wine professionals and keen amateurs prefer completely plain, uncoloured, unengraved, uncut glass, preferably as thin as is practicable to allow the palate to commune as closely as possible with the liquid. Thin-rimmed glasses are particularly highly valued.

The ideal wine glass also has a stem—indeed Americans call wine glasses 'stemware'—so that the wine taster can hold the glass without necessarily affecting the wine's TEMPERATURE (a critical element in wine tasting). The stem also enables a glass to be rotated easily in order to maximize AROMA or BOUQUET. This rotation process also means that the ideal wine glass narrows towards the rim, to minimize the chance of spillage during rotation, and to encourage the volatile FLAVOUR COMPOUNDS to collect in the space between the surface of the wine and the rim of the glass.

Individuals will have their own aesthetic preferences, but any glass which fits the above criteria will serve as a wine glass, including some relatively inexpensive examples. There is a sensual thrill to be had, however, in really thin crystal. This is usually expensive, although central Europe, and BOHEMIA in particular, has a long tradition of producing fine glasses at good prices.

For many households, a single wine glass model will do, perhaps supplemented by smaller glasses for FORTIFIED wines and an elongated one for SPARKLING WINES (see below). Purists, however, use slightly different glasses for different sorts of wine, conventionally (although not particularly logically) a smaller glass for white wines, and traditionally Germanic shapes for German and Alsace wines.

In this respect, there is no greater purist than Georg Riedel, an Austrian glass-maker who is unusual for his wine CONNOISSEURSHIP. He has designed a series of different glasses not just for young red bordeaux and mature red bordeaux, but also, for example, different glasses for vintage port and tawny port, and for Brunello di Montalcino and for Chianti. These designs are all based purely on analysing how different taste characteristics are optimized on the nose and palate by minute variations in glass design.

Special glass types

Over the centuries, various specific glasses have come to be associated with different wine types.

CHAMPAGNE and other sparkling wines were for long drunk in a flat, saucer-like glass called a **coupe**, but this has been abandoned in favour of the tall **flûte**, which preserves the wine's MOUSSE. This has evolved into a slightly more bulbous **tulipe**, which combines height with narrowing towards the rim.

In Spain, SHERRY has traditionally been served in the **copita**, and tastes infinitely better in a part-filled glass in this elongated tulip shape than it does brimming over a cut-glass thimble.

The ideal PORT glass is not so very different from the copita, although it is usually rather bigger in order to allow maximum appreciation of the complex bouquet of a vintage port. Glasses like this are ideal for almost all fortified wines, which, for obvious reasons, are served in smaller quantities than table wines.

BURGUNDY, particularly red burgundy, has come to be served in glass balloons, sometimes so large they resemble fish-bowls. The idea, apart from lusty exhibitionism, is that a good burgundy can offer such a rich panoply of aromas that they should be given every chance to escape the wine and titillate the taster. Most wine connoisseurs use the shape on a reduced scale.

The wines of ALSACE and GERMANY are sometimes served in particular forms of glass such as the **Rohmer**, often with green or brown glass stems, mainly for traditional reasons.

See also SERVING WINE.

Glenrowan, historic wine region in VICTORIA, Australia. See LIQUEUR MUSCAT.

Glühwein, German for 'glow wine', seems a particularly apt name for the MULLED WINE that has cheered many an Alpine skier. Pre-mixed wine, sugar, and spices are also available under this name.

glycerol, or glycerine, a minor product of alcoholic fermentation. The name derives from the Greek word for sweet and glycerol does indeed taste slightly sweet, as well as oily and heavy. It is present in most wines and at higher concentrations in BOTRYTIZED wines.

Glycerol does have a slight effect on the apparent sweetness of a wine but, contrary to popular conception, glycerol makes only a very minor contribution to the apparent VISCOSITY of a wine, and bears no relation to the TEARS observed on the inside of many a wine glass.

A.D.W. & T.H.L.

Godello, fine white grape variety native to north-west Spain and northern Portugal. As Godello it is most successful in VALDEORRAS, where plantings are increasing once more, although it is also known as Verdello in other parts of northern Galicia. It is almost certainly identical to VERDELHO, also known as Gouveio, in northern Portugal.

Goldburger, Austrian gold-skinned grape variety, a crossing of WELSCHRIESLING and Orangetraube. It is grown mainly in BUR-GENLAND, where it reaches high MUST WEIGHTS but rarely produces exciting wines.

Goldkapsel. Some producers in GERMANY deliberately give their finest bottlings a gold CAPSULE over the cork, rather as some SAUTERNES producers in France make a wine labelled CRÈME DE TÊTE or TÊTE DE CUVÉE in particularly successful vintages. Goldkapsel bottlings are usually available in very small quantity and invariably command a considerable premium, although there are no legal controls over the use of Goldkapsels. The VDP group of top estates reserve Goldkapsel for particularly good SPÄTLESE or AUSLESE wines (presumably on the basis that wines richer than this have no difficulty in fetching high prices). The position is further complicated (or enriched, depending on your budget) by the fact that some producers use gold capsules of two different lengths, thus their very finest bottlings qualify as **lange Goldkapsel**.

Goldmuskateller, German name for the golden-berried MOSCATO Giallo grape speciality in the ALTO ADIGE.

Gordo or Gordo Blanco, originally Spanish synonyms for MUSCAT OF ALEXANDRIA, adopted by Australia.

Gouais Blanc, light-skinned grape variety commonly planted in central and north-eastern France in the Middle Ages which produced very ordinary, acid wine, while the more highly valued Pinots were planted on more favoured sites. See PINOT for more details of its possible significance in the world of wine.

Goulburn Valley, relatively sprawling wine region in Australia's Central VICTORIA zone.

goût, French noun for TASTE in all its senses. Some wines, particularly old CHAMPAGNES, are described as suiting the goût anglais, or English taste (supposedly for wine necrophilia). A wine made from fruit adversely affected by hail, for example, might be described in French as having a goût de grêle. Another much-discussed and loosely applied TASTING TERM is goût de terroir, sometimes used about those aspects of flavour deemed to derive from the TERROIR rather than the grape variety but sometimes erroneously used synonymously with the term 'earthy'.

Gouveio, synonym for the white grape variety VERDELHO in the DOURO in northern Portugal. See also GODELLO.

Graciano, sometimes called **Graciana,** is a richly coloured, perfumed black grape variety once widely grown in Rioja in northern Spain. It has fallen from favour because of its inconveniently low yields, thereby depriving modern Rioja of an important flavour ingredient. It is still planted in a handful of Rioja vineyards (Bodegas Ijalba have even bottled a VARIETAL Graciano) and is being encouraged in Navarre. The vine can produce wine of great character and extract, albeit quite tannic in youth. Known as Morrastel in France, it is still grown in southern France in minute quantities.

There is ample possibility for confusion since the Spaniards use the name Morrastel as a synonym for their very different, and widely planted, variety Monastrell (MOURVÈDRE). Even today in North Africa the name Morrastel is used for both Graciano and Mourvèdre.

The variety known as Xeres in California, which has also been planted on a similarly limited scale in Australia, is probably Graciano, as is Mendoza's Graciana. Argentina has the distinction of being home to the world's largest plantation of this interesting grape variety.

See also the TINTA MIÚDA of Portugal.

grafting, the connection of two pieces of living plant tissue so that they unite and grow as one plant, has been a particularly important element in growing vines since the end of the 19th century, when it was discovered that grafting on to resistant ROOTSTOCKS was the only effective weapon against the PHYLLOXERA louse.

Vines are grafted to take advantage of the desirable properties of the rootstock variety. Foremost is resistance or tolerance to soil-borne pests and diseases, especially phylloxera and nematodes. Other properties are tolerance to soil salinity, to high lime levels, to soil waterlogging or DROUGHT, and an ability to modify VIGOUR or to hasten or delay RIPENING. If conducted in the vineyard, the practice offers a method of changing a VINE VARIETY.   B.G.C.

Grampians, Australian wine region formerly known as Great Western in the Western VICTORIA zone.

Granaccia or **Granacha,** Italian names for GRENACHE.

grand cru means literally 'great growth' in French. In Burgundy's CÔTE D'OR, a grand cru is one of 34 particularly favoured vineyards (see CÔTE D'OR for list), a decided notch above

PREMIER CRU. In Alsace, Grand Cru is a recent, elevated appellation accorded several dozen specific vineyards (see list under ALSACE). In Bordeaux, the words grand cru usually apply to a specific property or château and depend on the region in which it is located (see CLASSIFICATION).

Grande Rue, La, red burgundy GRAND CRU vineyard in VOSNE-ROMANÉE.

grandes marques, obsolete, self-imposed term for some of the major firms or BRANDS of CHAMPAGNE meaning literally 'big brands' in French.

grand format, bottle size larger than the standard 75-cl size and of particular interest to COLLECTORS and INVESTORS (provided it is filled with FINE WINE).

Grand Roussillon, little-used ROUSSILLON VIN DOUX NATUREL appellation used effectively for declassified RIVESALTES. It also comes in RANCIO form.

Grands Échezeaux, red GRAND CRU in Burgundy's CÔTE D'OR. See ÉCHEZEAUX.

Grand Vidure, old Bordeaux synonym for the CARMENÈRE vine variety, now being used by some exporters in CHILE.

grand vin, name current in BORDEAUX for the main wine produced by a CHÂTEAU (as opposed to a SECOND WINE).

Granite Belt, the only established wine region in QUEENSLAND, Australia.

Granja-Amareleja, DOC region in southern Portugal. See ALENTEJO.

Gran Reserva, Spanish term for a wine supposedly from an outstanding VINTAGE which has been subject to lengthy AGEING before release. Red wines must spend a minimum of two years in cask, and another three years in tank or bottle. The wine may not leave the BODEGA until the sixth year after the vintage. White wines must spend a total of at least four years in cask and bottle, including at least six months' CASK AGEING. See also RESERVA.   R.J.M.

grape, the berry or fruit of the grapevine, or VINE, whose juice is the essential ingredient in WINE. A grape is *raisin* in French, *uva* in Italian and Spanish, and *Rebe* in German. Wine production accounts for some 80 per cent of the world's grape production.

The form and appearance of grape berries

varies hugely between VINE VARIETIES. Their shape varies from flattened, through spherical and oval, to elongated and finger-like; colour from green to yellow, pink, crimson, dark blue, and black; and size from as small as a pea to the huge, egg-like berries of some recently bred TABLE GRAPE varieties. The majority of wine grapes, however, are spherical to short oval, 1–2 g in weight, and are coloured yellow (called 'white' by vine-growers) or very dark purple (called 'black' or 'red').

Flesh or pulp

The flesh or pulp and the juice are the most important parts of the grape to the wine-maker, and the wine drinker, for they contain the main components of the finished wine. Because the juice of all grapes (apart from the specialist red-fleshed varieties) is a pale grey, whatever the colour of the grape's skin, white wine can be made from grapes of all colours, so long as the juice is not left in contact with dark skins. Red wines can be made only by leaching colour from such skins, while pink wines can be made either from short contact with dark skins or more prolonged contact with pink or red skins.

Skin

The grape's skin contains most of the berry PIGMENTS and the red and blue ANTHOCYANINS important in the making of red wine. As well as some TANNINS, a significant amount of a grape's FLAVOUR COMPOUNDS are also associated with the skin.

Seeds

Seeds are only of minor importance in wine-making, although if they are crushed, as those who eat seeded grapes know, the bitter tannins they contain are released. In WHITE-WINE-MAKING, the contact time between juice and seeds and absorption of tannins from the seeds is minimal. In RED-WINE-MAKING, on the other hand, the prolonged contact between the seeds and an increasingly alcoholic solution means that tannins are very likely to be dissolved.

B.G.C. & A.D.W.

grape composition and wine quality.

Grape composition is the essential basis of wine quality, and knowledge of grape composition is critical for those wine-makers interested in making the appropriate wine style. The concentrations of all component chemical groups play a part. Grape sugars, for example (see MUST WEIGHT), determine the possible potential ALCOHOLIC STRENGTH of the wine.

ACIDS and nitrogenous compounds affect the course of FERMENTATION and exert their own effects on flavour. PHENOLICS contribute to levels of COLOUR and TANNINS. A multitude of volatile compounds alter AROMA. Quality epitomizes the integration of these and other chemical groups in such a way that there is a balance between individual components, coupled with an intensity of VARIETAL character. B.G.C. & P.J.W.

grape concentrate is what is left when the volatile elements are removed from fresh grape juice. It is the main ingredient, for example, in so-called MADE WINES produced without the benefit of freshly picked grapes (see BRITISH WINES and HOME WINE-MAKING). Grape concentrate can also be used in BLENDING to soften and sweeten dry wines of everyday commercial standard made in cooler regions. It is widely used in Germany, for example, where it is called *Süssreserve* (see SWEET RESERVE). Grape concentrate is also used in some circumstances to increase the eventual alcohol content of a wine. It is also used to sweeten some other fruit juices and foodstuffs. A.D.W.

grape juice is a sweet, clear, non-alcoholic liquid. Wine-makers generally use the term to refer to MUST that has undergone CLARIFICATION and STABILIZATION. A certain amount of grape juice is bottled and sold as a drink, although grape juice is a minor beverage compared with juices of other fruits such as citrus and apple. Wine drinkers generally find grape juice bears disappointingly little relation to wine.

grape sorting. See TRIAGE.

grape varieties. This term is often used interchangeably with vine varieties since different varieties of vine have predictably different grapes or berries. The effect of grape varieties on wine quality is discussed under VINE VARIETIES. Different varieties of vine produce grapes with very different and distinct characteristics (many of them outlined under the names of individual varieties). Wines made predominantly from a single grape variety, usually specified on the label, are called VARIETAL wines. The wine consumer is thus familiar with the names of many popular varieties such as Chardonnay, Cabernet Sauvignon, Merlot, Pinot Noir, Riesling, and Sauvignon Blanc.

See VINE VARIETIES and under the names of individual varieties.

grapevine, an alternative name for the plant on which most of the world's wine trade depends. It is known by most wine producers and consumers as the VINE.

grapevine yellows, generic term for a group of related diseases of grapevines which pose a serious threat to vineyards in many wine regions of the world because there is no known control. The best known of these diseases is FLAVESCENCE DORÉE. It is spread by infected plants from the nursery and further spread by insects called leaf hoppers. The disease occurs sporadically in epidemics, and varieties vary in their sensitivity to it.

Flavescence dorée has recently spread rapidly throughout France. In 1982, only isolated vineyards in Armagnac were affected, as well as a very restricted area in Languedoc. By 1987, this disease had spread to Cognac, throughout Languedoc, and to the northern and southern Rhône, and by 1992 to the Loire Valley, Bordeaux, and the Côtes du Rhône. Several variants have also been noted, including Bois Noir in north-eastern France and Switzerland, Vergilbungskrankeit in Germany, leaf curl and berry shrivel in New York state, and a form known as Australian grapevine yellows.

The disease can kill young vines, and old vines do not recover completely from infection. Symptoms seem to vary from year to year, and crop levels fluctuate. During epidemics, as for example in northern Italy in 1995, yields of some vineyards dropped to one-tenth of a normal crop. The Australian experience is that vineyards with well-established infections yield at about half the rate of healthy vineyards.

Chardonnay and Riesling are among the most susceptible VINIFERA varieties, followed by Grenache, Tannat, Pinot Noir, and Pinot Gris. Some American vine species are tolerant. Grapevine yellows diseases may eventually be more destructive to the world's viticulture than was PHYLLOXERA, because they are widespread, are spreading even further, and cannot be controlled with resistant ROOTSTOCKS. Wine quality does not appear to be affected, but the supply of grapes, especially of Chardonnay, can be.   R.E.S.

Grasă, the 'fat' white grape of COTNARI in ROMANIA, where it is grown exclusively. It can reach extremely high MUST WEIGHTS but needs the balancing acidity of grapes such as TĂMÎIOASĂ Românească in a blend. The vine is usefully sensitive to NOBLE ROT. A few authorities believe that this is the same variety as the FURMINT of Tokay.

Graševina, Croatian name for the republic's most planted vine variety, WELSCHRIESLING. The name **Grassica** may also be used.

grassy. See TASTING TERMS.

grau, German for grey or *gris*.

Grauburgunder, German synonym for PINOT GRIS used by many, particularly in BADEN and the PFALZ, to designate a crisp, dry style of wine as opposed to sweeter wines normally labelled with the variety's more common German synonym RULÄNDER, under which more details can be found.

Grave del Friuli, vast DOC zone in the FRIULI region of north-east Italy which sprawls across the southern portion of the provinces of Pordenone and Udine. This is flatland with GRAVEL- and sand-based soil. It owes its name to the same root as the gravelly GRAVES region of Bordeaux in France.

The zone produces light, fruity reds and fresh, aromatic whites. Merlot is the dominant vine variety here, as in the neighbouring LISON-PRAMAGGIORE DOC to the west. Various CABERNETS and REFOSCO dal Peduncolo Rosso, plus minuscule quantities of PINOT NERO, bring the total area of red varieties to virtually 3,500 ha, more than half the total, making this, the largest DOC, something of an anomaly in Friuli.

As elsewhere in the region, TOCAI Friulano dominates among the white varieties, although there are significant plantings of PINOT BIANCO, PINOT GRIGIO, Sauvignon Blanc, and VERDUZZO. Sauvignons of marked character are produced here, with an aromatic intensity that appeals to lovers of the powerfully herbaceous. The Merlots and Cabernets of Grave del Friuli seem intrinsically lighter than the better reds from the COLLI ORIENTALI, Friuli's second most important DOC.   D.T.

gravel, a soil or unconsolidated rock in which pebbles are the most obvious component, known in French as *graves*, from which the two appellations below, and the DOC above, take their names. Gravel is the most distinctive soil type of Bordeaux's so-called LEFT BANK wine regions. The vineyards of the GRAVES are, not surprisingly, characterized by their gravelly surface and gravel is nowhere so prevalent as at Ch HAUT-BRION, where in places it is 16–20 m/50–65 ft deep. Such soils offer excellent DRAINAGE, imposing on the vine the slight WATER STRESS favoured for wine quality. See SOIL AND WINE QUALITY.

Gravel soils are also highly prized for quality-wine production on the plateau of ST-ÉMILION, in CHÂTEAUNEUF-DU-PAPE, GRAVE DEL FRIULI, and in the Gimblett Road region of Hawkes Bay in NEW ZEALAND. However, many gravel areas may well be used for viticulture simply because they are too difficult to work and too infertile for any other form of agriculture.

M.J.E., R.E.S., & J.M.H.

Graves, French for gravelly terrain, and the name of the large region extending 50 km/30 miles south east of Bordeaux along the left bank of the river GARONNE. Graves is Bordeaux's only region famous for both its red and white wines, although its aristocratic, mineral-scented, Cabernet-dominated red wines are made in much greater quantity than its dry whites. The Graves, and in particular the outskirts of Bordeaux, the Grabas de Burdeus, is the birthplace of CLARET. **Graves Supérieur** is another growing appellation, this time reserved for sweet wines, producing wines very similar to, but often coarser than, those from the enclave entitled to the CÉRONS appellation.

In 1987, the separate appellation of Pessac-Léognan was formed, a slice of the original Graves appellation which includes all of its most famous properties, and the southern suburbs of Bordeaux itself. For more details of the wines produced there, see PESSAC-LÉOGNAN.

The creation of this new premium appellation has had the effect of somewhat declassifying the historic name Graves, although some excellent wines are conscientiously made within the modern Graves appellation on the varied GRAVEL terraces. The reds, which can truly taste like country cousins of their more urbane neighbours in Pessac-Léognan, can often be good value, and mature earlier than their Médoc counterparts. It is in this area that some serious barrel-fermented, or at least oak-aged, dry whites are made, from Sauvignon and Sémillon grapes in varying proportions, at properties such as Clos Floridène and Chx Chantegrive, La Grave, St-Robert, du Seuil, and Vieux Ch Gaubert (although better value can sometimes be found on the opposite bank of

the Garonne; see PREMIÈRES CÔTES DE BORDEAUX and ENTRE-DEUX-MERS).

Graves de Vayres, a small BORDEAUX district, named after the historic town of Vayres, which has nothing to do with GRAVES but is just across the river DORDOGNE from the town of Libourne. The appellation produces mainly light red wines made substantially from Merlot grapes, although many of them are sold under the simple BORDEAUX AC. White wines, both sweet and dry, were once more important. Today the white is usually dry, occasionally given BARREL MATURATION, and constitutes the minority of wine sold as Graves de Vayres.

Great Southern, wine region in the extreme south west of WESTERN AUSTRALIA, including subregions Mount Barker and Porongurup.

Great Western, small, isolated but historic wine region in the state of VICTORIA in Australia renamed Grampians.

Grecanico Dorato, Sicilian white grape variety whose name suggests Greek origins. The wines currently made may not be maximizing its full aromatic, rather Sauvignon-like potential.

Grechetto, sometimes **Greghetto**, characterful central Italian white grape variety most closely associated with UMBRIA. It is an ingredient in ORVIETO and in the whites of TORGIANO and the Colli Martani DOC. The vine is sufficiently sturdy to make good VIN SANTO. It is typically blended with TREBBIANO, VERDELLO, and MALVASIA. In ANTINORI's most admired white wine Cervaro, it has played a supporting role to CHARDONNAY, and this type of wine is now being copied by other ambitious producers in Umbria. Grechetto di Todi is probably even more widely planted than Grechetto Spoletino. Intrinsically more interesting than either TREBBIANO or DRUPEGGIO, it is expected to have a much larger role in Umbrian white wines, particularly Orvieto, in the future. Occasionally called **Greco Spoletino** or **Greco Bianco di Perugia**, it is by no means identical to GRECO BIANCO, although it is presumed to share its Greek origins.

Greco Bianco, name of one or perhaps several, usually noble, white grape varieties of Greek origin currently grown in southern Italy. In CAMPANIA, it produces the respected full-bodied dry white **Greco di Tufo** around the village of Tufo, while, blended with FAL-

ANGHINA and BIANCOLELLA grapes, it makes a contribution to the inconsequential dry whites of the island of Capri. It is also used in the blend of Gravina DOC of Apulia, where the high altitude of the vineyards, bordering on Basilicata, brings out the variety's aromatic character.

Perhaps the finest Greco-based wine is the sweet **Greco di Bianco** made from semi-dried grapes grown around the town of Bianco on the south coast of CALABRIA.

Greco Nero, the most widely planted Greco vine variety in Italy, mainly in CALABRIA, where it is often blended with GAGLIOPPO.

Greece, renascent Mediterranean wine producer with a particularly rich history of winemaking. About 60 per cent of the annual wine production of between 4.5 and 5.0 million hl (132 million gal) is of white, often sweet, wine.

Since the 1960s, there has been considerable investment in modern technology, and its results have been evident since the early 1980s with the emergence of Greece's first generation of trained OENOLOGISTS. Such is their enthusiasm that, although in strict commercial terms the big companies Achaia Clauss, Boutari, Kourtakis, and Tsantalis still dominate the market, an increasing number of small, quality-minded estates is emerging. Most modern Greek wine finds a ready market within Greece, where the appreciation of good wine has increased considerably. Some fine wines have been exported from the likes of Antonopoulos, Domaine Carras, Ktima Gerovassiliou, Gaia, Oenoforos, and the Samos co-operative, however.

Geography and climate

There are vineyards in all parts of Greece. At latitudes of between 33 and 41 degrees north, they constitute some of the world's hotter wine regions, although some vines are deliberately planted at relatively high ALTITUDES.

The climate is generally predictably MEDITERRANEAN, with short winters and very hot summers in which DROUGHT can be a serious threat in some years, particularly in the south. There can be considerable variation between the CONTINENTAL-influenced cooler vineyards in the mountains, whether on the plateau of Mantinia in the Peloponnese or in Epirus and Macedonia, where grapes may not even reach full RIPENESS, and the intense heat of Pátras or islands such as Crete and Rhodes on which some grapes may be picked in July. Most of the vineyards are sufficiently close to the sea for maritime breezes to moderate temperatures, but lack of water, particularly on the islands and in the south, is a major problem. IRRIGATION is not generally permitted but may be used to establish new vineyards.

Most of Greece is extremely mountainous. Vines can be found growing on flat land near sea level, such as at Ankhialos; on foothills as at Rapsani on the lower slopes of Mount Olympus; and at altitudes as high as 800 m/2,600 ft on the highest slopes in Neméa. Vines are often planted on north-facing slopes in the hottest areas in order to slow ripening. There are many soil types in Greece but the soil is generally of low fertility.

Vine varieties

Greece is a still underdeveloped source of indigenous, ancient grape varieties, of which more than 300 have been identified. The most important Greek white grape varieties are ASSYRTIKO, RHODITIS, ROBOLA, SAVATIANO, MOSCOPHILERO, VILANA, DEBINA, and both MUSCAT BLANC À PETITS GRAINS and the slightly less important MUSCAT OF ALEXANDRIA. The Greek port of Monemvasia also gave its name to the MALVASIA grape. Among Greek red grape varieties, the most important to the modern Greek wine industry have been AGHIORGHITIKO, LIMNIO, MANDELARIA, and XYNOMAVRO. See regional details below for more local grape varieties.

In addition to these native varieties, a number have been imported, particularly from France. These include Chardonnay, Sauvignon Blanc, and Ugni Blanc among whites and both Cabernet Sauvignon and Cabernet Franc, a little Merlot, Grenache, Cinsaut, and Syrah among red grape varieties. Some wines, particularly from the newer, small estates, may be made exclusively from one of these imported varieties, but it is far more usual to find these foreign varieties playing a minor role in blends with Greek varieties.

Wine-making

Since the mid 1980s, almost all Greek wineries have had some sort of refrigeration and the sort of HYGIENE afforded by the use of stainless-steel vats. As in other Mediterranean areas, early picking and cool fermentations enabled by temperature control resulted in clean but characterless white wines of about 11.5 per cent alcohol. Such techniques as SKIN CONTACT, slightly later picking, and deliberate OXIDATION of the must prior to fermentation were used by some of the more daring producers from the early 1990s to develop more interesting wines.

Better-quality red wines have traditionally been matured in large, old casks, but imported French BARRIQUES are increasingly used for the BARREL MATURATION of reds and even some whites.

Wine laws

Greek wine laws were drawn up in the early 1970s and refined in the early 1980s as Greece prepared to join the European Union. It is hardly surprising, therefore, that the laws conform strictly to EU guidelines, often even employing the use on the label of the French terms Appellation d'Origine Contrôlée and VIN DE PAYS.

Wines which qualify as QUALITY WINES according to EU law are either sweet wines, from Mavrodaphne or Muscat grapes, described as Controlled Appellation of Origin (OPE), with a blue seal over the cork, or dry wines described as Appellation of Superior Quality (OPAP), with a pink seal. The words Réserve or Grande Réserve indicate superior wines with extended AGEING.

Vins de pays may be made in a wide variety of specified areas, nearly always from a range of vine varieties which includes both Greek and foreign grape varieties. Commercially the most important vin de pays areas are Attica, Drama, Epanomi, and Thívai (or Thebes).

The large TABLE WINE category includes wine BRANDS that were Greece's most successful wines, as well as some more interesting wines made outside the appellation regulations. The Greeks have also used the term CAVA to indicate high-quality table wine which is made only in small quantities and which has been subject to prolonged ageing.

The official list of Greek wine appellations was drawn up in the 1950s, although some more recent wine areas, such as the Côtes de Meliton on the Khalkhidhikhi peninsula, were subsequently grafted on to the official list. Of the 28 appellations in Greece's widely differing regions, some are produced only in tiny quantities and some are in danger of extinction. Many are seen rarely outside their area of origin while some are well known and thriving.

Wine regions

Wine is made all over Greece, often on a very small, traditional scale. The following includes those quality wine regions which have established their own identity within Greece and sometimes abroad.

Northern Greece The regions of Macedonia and Thrace are noted mainly for their red wines, although wines of all hues are made there today. Náoussa, home of red wine from Xynomavro grapes, is on the south-eastern slopes of Mount Vermio. Náoussa must be aged for at least a year in OAK, traditionally in old wooden casks, but there has been considerable experimentation with new, small barriques.

Xynomavro is also grown in this area to produce Goumenissa, where it is blended with Negoska grapes, and to make Amyndeo, which lies on the opposite, north-western slopes of Mount Vermio from Náoussa but at higher altitudes. Sparkling rosé is made here as well as red wine.

Perhaps the most famous appellation in northern Greece is its most recent, the Côtes de Meliton on the slopes of Mount Meliton in Sithoniá. This is the appellation specially created by Domaine Carras. Here both white and red wines are made with a mixture of Greek and French vine varieties, notably Cabernet Sauvignon. It is significant, however, that, as the domaine extends its vineyards, many of the new vines planted are Greek varieties, including the recently rediscovered and elegant indigenous white Malagousia.

Also in Thrace is an area around Drama where some good-quality vins de pays are made from a mixture of Greek and French grape varieties.

Central Greece Not far from the town of Ioánnina and near the border with ALBANIA lies Zitsa, which produces a dry or medium lightly sparkling white wine from the local Debina grape variety. To the immediate south west, in the mountains round Ioánnina, are Greece's highest vineyards at Métsovon, which yield the popular vin de pays Katoi from locally grown Cabernet Sauvignon grapes blended with Aghiorghitiko grapes grown in Neméa.

On the east coast in Thessaly, Rapsani is produced on the foothills of Mount Olympus from Xynomavro blended with Krassato and Stavroto grapes and given extended CASK AGEING. This appellation is undergoing much-needed revival but old vintages suggest that the potential for long-lived, concentrated reds is there. Thessaly's other appellation is Ankhíalos, a dry white wine made from Rhoditis with some Savatiano grapes grown near Vólos at sea level.

Peloponnese This dramatically formed, large southern peninsula has the greatest number of Greek wine appellations, as well as some interesting vins de pays and table wines. On the plateau of Mantinia in Arcadia, the Moscophilero grape produces a fresh, dry, aromatic, slightly spicy white appellation wine, while the same grape can be vinified, with extended MACERATION, to yield a simple, fruity rosé.

At Neméa, not far from the Corinth canal, which separates the Peloponnese from mainland Greece, the Aghiorghitiko grape is grown on deep red soil and, if yields are not too high, can produce intense red wine. Grapes from the lowest vineyards frequently lack acidity and can be used to make a sweet wine. As in Náoussa (see above), barriques are increasingly used for the maturation, and semi-CARBONIC MACERATION has even been used to make a sort of Neméa NOUVEAU.

The vineyards around Pátras on the north coast are responsible for four different appellations. Pátras itself is a dry white wine made from Rhoditis grapes grown on the slopes around the town. Muscat of Pátras is a dessert wine made strong and sweet like a VIN DOUX NATUREL from Muscat Blanc à Petits Grains grapes. Mavrodaphne of Pátras is a very popular sweet fortified wine, consisting of a blend in which Mavrodaphne makes up the majority but may be supplemented by the locally grown Korinthiaki. Examples aged for 10 to 12 years in cask can be delicious.

The islands Among the Ionian islands off the west coast, Cephalonia is best known for its wine, particularly the powerful dry white Robola, made from grapes of the same name, which is almost certainly the same variety as the RIBOLLA of north-east Italy. Vines here were individually trained on high, stony land, and mainly ungrafted (although PHYLLOXERA's arrival in the late 1980s presumably signals an end to this). Mavrodaphne and Muscat dessert wines, similar to those of Pátras, are also produced on the island.

From the Cyclades come the wines of Páros and SANTORINI. Páros is a powerful, quite tannic red made from a curious blend of grapes in which the deep colour of the Mandelaria is lightened by the addition of half as much of the white grape called Monemvasia (see MALVASIA). The Santorini appellation is for a dry white made from Assyrtiko grapes blended with a little Athiri and Aedani, but a sweet DRIED-GRAPE WINE, Vissanto, is also made.

The island of Rhodes has three appellations: one for a sweet Muscat made in very limited quantities, one for a dry white from Athiri grapes, and another for a red from the Mandelaria, here known as Amorgiano. The Rhodes co-operative, the CAIR, also makes a considerable quantity of improving sparkling wine.

Two of Greece's most famous wines are made among the Aegean islands. Lemnos was the original home of the Limnio grape, which is still grown there, but the appellation wines are both Muscats. The dry version is rarely seen off the island, but the VIN DE LIQUEUR Muscat of Lemnos is widely admired, being surprisingly delicate.

Muscat of Sámos, made from Muscat Blanc à Petits Grains, can claim to be Greece's most famous wine (after retsina). Muscat of Sámos comes in several forms: Sámos Doux is a vin de liqueur, while Sámos Vin Doux Naturel is made by stopping the fermentation even earlier. Potentially finest of all, however, is Sámos Nectar, a dried-grape wine made from grapes dried in the sun so that they are capable of being fermented into a wine of 14 per cent alcohol, which is then given three years in cask.

The last of the appellation wines of any commercial importance comes from Crete from a variety of grape varieties unique to the island, together with Mandelaria. The pale-red Liatiko reaches high alcohol levels and ripens very early, while the powerful, deep-coloured Kotsifali produces particularly robust red wines. The most important local white grape is Vilana. Local red-wine appellations for dry and sometimes sweet wines are Archanes, Daphnes, and Siteaia, while Peza, the most common wine appellation on the island, may be either dry red or white.

See also RETSINA.   M.McN.

green. See TASTING TERMS.

greenhouse effect and viticulture. See CLIMATE CHANGE.

Grenache, increasingly fashionable vine variety that is the world's second most widely planted, sprawling, in several hues, all over Spain and southern France.

Grenache covers more vine-dedicated ground than any grape variety other than AIRÉN, most commonly encountered in its darkest-berried form as GARNACHA TINTA. It is Spain's most planted black grape variety and the French census of 1988 demonstrated Grenache Noir's influence in the Languedoc-Roussillon. For a variety that covers so much terrain, it has until recently been a name rarely encountered by name by the wine drinker, much of it being blended with other varieties with more colour and tannin.

The wine produced is, typically, paler than most reds (although low yields tend to concentrate the pigments in Spain), with a tendency to oxidize early, a certain rusticity, and more than a hint of sweetness. If the vine is irrigated, as it has tended to be in the New World, it may lose even these taste characteristics. If, however, as by the most punctilious Châteauneuf-du-Pape producers, it is pruned severely on the poorest of soils and allowed to reach full maturity of both vine and grape, it can produce excitingly dense reds that demand several decades' cellaring. The rediscovery of Rhône reds in the late 1980s (see RHÔNE RANGERS for example) encouraged some New World producers to invest more effort in their own Grenache.

In Spain, Garnacha Tinta is grown extensively, particularly in the north and east, being an important variety in such wine regions as Rioja, Navarre, Empurdá-Costa Brava, Campo de Borja, Cariñena, Costers del Segre, Madrid, La Mancha, Méntrida, Penedès, Priorat, Somontano, Tarragona, Terra Alta, Utiel-Requena, and Valdeorras. In Rioja, it provides stuffing and immediate charm when blended with the more austere TEMPRANILLO. The juiciness apparent in these early-maturing Riojas can be tasted in a host of other Spanish reds and, especially, rosados. Grenache has been adopted with particular enthusiasm in Navarre, where it is by far the dominant grape variety and dictates a lighter, more obviously fruity style of red and *rosado* in Rioja.

Perhaps the most distinctive wine based on Garnacha Tinta (often incorporating some Garnacha Peluda, otherwise known as LLADONER PELUT, and Cariñena) is Spain's PRIORAT, along with exceptional Grenache-based age-worthy VINS DOUX NATURELS such as BANYULS, RIVES-ALTES, and MAURY from France. Such wines are further proof that Grenache is capable of producing great wine, albeit a very particular sort of wine.

In France, the great majority of Grenache's extensive vineyards are in the windswept southern Rhône, where seas of Côtes du Rhône of varying degrees of distinction are produced alongside smaller quantities of Châteauneuf-du-Pape (and the isolated vin doux naturel RASTEAU). It is undoubtedly the Grenache ingredient that determined Châteauneuf-du-Pape's unusual official requirement of a minimum alcoholic strength (of 12.5°). Although blending has been the watchword here, notably with the more structured Syrah, such monoliths as the famously concentrated Châteauneuf-du-Pape Ch Rayas show what can be done by Grenache and determination alone. Grenache is also responsible for much of southern France's rosé, most obviously and traditionally in Tavel and in neighbouring Lirac, but also much further eastwards into Provence proper. In the Languedoc-Roussillon, Grenache plays an unsung supporting role, together with its close relative Lladoner Pelut, which is also habitually cited in the APPELLATION CONTRÔLÉE regulations for red wines. The exception is Roussillon, where it is the vital ingredient in such distinctive vins doux naturels as BANYULS.

Grenache Noir is being uprooted in Corsica but in Sardinia, as CANNONAU, it plays a dominant role in the island's reds, which can achieve daunting levels of natural ripeness, whether in deep, dark dry reds, which may have as many as 15° of natural alcohol, or dessert wines. The vine is also grown in Calabria and Sicily.

Grenache's ability to withstand drought and heat made it a popular choice with New World growers when FASHION had little effect on market forces. Thanks to extensive historic acreage in the central San Joaquin Valley, and some in Mendocino, there were still 11,500 acres/4,600 ha of it planted in California in 1996 but it was declining fast. Not even California's Rhône Rangers were expected to reverse this downward trend, although fruit from dry-farmed, short-pruned old vines has been sought out by some wine producers. Grenache has consistently been difficult to ripen in coastal counties and so its primary contributions have been in the form of sweetish rosés and tawny-port-style wines made from Central Valley fruit. Its fortunes suffered a brief reprise in the late 1980s when White Grenache (made to BLUSH from black grapes) was developed as the natural alternative to WHITE ZINFANDEL when cheap Zinfandel grapes were in short supply.

Grenache was Australia's most planted black grape variety until the mid 1960s. Shiraz (Syrah) overtook it in the late 1970s but it was not until the early 1990s that Australia's Cabernet Sauvignon output overtook that of Grenache. The variety has been shamelessly degraded and milked in the heavily irrigated, undistinguished vineyards in which it has been expected to produce large quantities of wine for basic blends. Only a handful of producers, mainly in the Barossa Valley, take it seriously enough to emulate Châteauneuf-du-Pape, but total plantings are growing once more.

Grenache Noir is also grown in Israel, to a very limited degree in South Africa, and still, to a much greater extent, in North Africa, where it was once an important element in the usefully soupy reds of Algeria and in some fine Moroccan rosés.

Grenache Rosé and **Grenache Gris** are also commonly encountered in southern French whites and some pale rosés.

Grenache Blanc, the white-berried form of GRENACHE Noir, is discreetly important in France. Although in decline, the variety is by far the most important light-berried vine in Roussillon, where it produces fat, soft white wines and can be an important ingredient in the paler Rivesaltes.

Grenache Blanc is also often encountered—with the likes of Marsanne, Roussanne, Viognier, and Rolle—in the blended white wines of the Languedoc-Roussillon, to which it can add supple fruit if not longevity. It need not necessarily be consigned to the blending vat, however. If carefully pruned and vinified, it can produce richly flavoured, full-bodied varietals that share some characteristics with Marsanne and can even be worthy of ageing in small oak barrels. It is also the most important white grape in Châteauneuf-du-Pape and is widely planted in the southern Rhône valley.

As Garnacha Blanca, it plays a role in north-eastern Spanish whites such as those of Alella, Priorato, Tarragona, Rioja, and Navarre.

Grignolino, very localized grape variety of the PIEDMONT region in north-west Italy sold almost invariably as a pale-red VARIETAL wine with an almost Alpine scent and a tangy ACIDITY. Grignolino provides a wine that can be drunk young with pleasure while the brawnier wines of the zone are shedding their youthful asperity. The light colour and relatively low alcohol (11 to 12°) can be deceptive; the wine draws significant TANNINS from the abundant pips of the Grignolino grape and takes its name from *grignole*, the dialect name for pips in the province of Asti.

Although Piedmont's producers have been regularly predicting a breakthrough for Grignolino that would transform it into Italy's answer to BEAUJOLAIS, the wine remains an unquestionably local taste, with its rather odd combination of pale colour, perceptible acidity, and tannins. The two DOC areas, Asti and Monferrato Casalese, are rather large, but they produce only 2 million bottles a year between them; Grignolino del Monferrato Casale is much the better and more characterful of the two. Grignolino del Piemonte, a blander VINO DA TAVOLA version, accounts for another 6 million bottles. The substantial variation from producer to producer, a variation which is as much in character as in quality, can be accounted for both by substantial variation in CLONES between different vineyards and by the variety's sensitivity to particular soils.

The future of the vine appears uncertain, partly because of its extreme susceptibility to disease and, perhaps even more importantly, because of its tendency to ripen late and unevenly. This means that it requires the best sites and exposures, which, in its home base of the Monferrato, are increasingly being reserved for BARBERA or, in the case of the highest vineyards, for international white varieties such as CHARDONNAY.

Grignolino has also been grown in California, thanks to the high proportion of Italians among early grape-growers. Wine-maker Joe Heitz is a particular fan.   D.T.

Grillet, Château-. See CHÂTEAU-GRILLET.

Grillo, Sicilian white grape variety which may have potential but of which plantings halved in the 1980s. The wines tend to be citrus-flavoured, full bodied, can demonstrate an earthiness, even astringency, and can respond well to BARREL MATURATION. See SICILY.

Gringet, synonym for SAVAGNIN.

Grolleau or Groslot, is the Loire's everyday red grape variety. It produces extremely high yields of relatively thin, acid wine and it is to the benefit of wine drinkers that it is so systematically being replaced with Gamay and, more recently, Cabernet Franc. Total French plantings are falling steadily. The status of the variety is such that it is allowed into the rosé but not red versions of APPELLATION CONTRÔLÉE wines such as ANJOU, SAUMUR, and TOURAINE. It has played a major part only in Rosé d'Anjou, in which it is commonly blended with Gamay.

Grolleau Gris produces innocuous white wines which may form part of the blend for the Loire's hugely successful VIN DE PAYS du Jardin de la France, although if yields are restricted (which can be difficult), it can produce wines of real character.

Groslot is a common synonym for the Loire's rather commonplace red vine variety GROL-LEAU. Both names are of course identical in pronunciation.

Gros Manseng, Basque white grape grown in SOUTH WEST FRANCE to produce mainly drier versions of Jurançon and various Béarn wines. It is also now allowed into Gascony's PACH-ERENC DU VIC-BIHL. The vine looks similar to but is distinct from PETIT MANSENG. It yields more generously and produces discernibly less elegant, less rich, but still powerful wine. Gros Manseng, unlike Petit Manseng, is rarely used for sweet wines.

Gros Plant, or, to give it a name that is more of a mouthful than the wine usually is, **Gros Plant du Pays Nantais**, is the country cousin of MUSCADET. Made from FOLLE BLANCHE vines, called Gros Plant here, grown in a wide arc east but mainly south of the city of Nantes on the Loire, Gros Plant is one of the most acidic-tasting wines made anywhere, and Gros Plant's aggressively dry style serves only to accentuate its inherent tartness. Gros Plant qualifies as a VDQS and about a third as much Gros Plant is made as Muscadet, although a much smaller proportion ever leaves the region. A small amount of sparkling Gros Plant is also made.

Gros Rhin, Swiss synonym for SILVANER, to distinguish it from Petit Rhin, or Riesling.

Grosslage, literally a 'large site' in GERMANY, is in wine terms a collection of individual sites (EINZELLAGEN) and a decidedly opportunistic geographical device which has enabled some very ordinary wines to be labelled as though they were from a single vineyard. About 150 Grosslagen were created by the GERMAN WINE LAW of 1971, each of them given a popular name. The average size of a Grosslage is about 600 ha/1,500 acres, while the average size of an Einzellage is just 38 ha. Wines produced anywhere within the Grosslage, all of which fall within individual wine regions, may use the Grosslage name. Thus in RHEINHESSEN, for example, the Krötenbrunnen Grosslage covers 1,800 ha of flat land which includes 27 individual vineyards, or Einzellagen, in 13 different villages. Since the name of one of these villages, Oppenheim, is the most famous, wine from anywhere in the Grosslage area may be sold as Oppenheimer Krötenbrunnen. Lawmakers may know that there is at the very least a quantitative difference between an Oppenheimer Krötenbrunnen and, for example, an Oppenheimer Kreuz from a single vineyard on the elevated RHEINTERRASSE, capable of producing really concentrated wines of distinction, but the average consumer does not.

Some of the most commonly exported combinations of village name and Grosslage name (a village name must always be prefixed) are, in the MOSEL-SAAR-RUWER, Zeller Schwarze Katz, Kröver Nacktarsch, Bernkasteler Badstube, Bernkasteler Kurfürstlay, Piesporter Michelsberg, Klüsserather St Michael, Wiltinger Scharzberg; in the NAHE, Binger Schlosskapelle, Rüdesheimer Rosengarten; in Rheinhessen, Niersteiner Gutes Domtal, Oppenheimer Krötenbrunnen; and in the PFALZ, Forster Mariengarten.

In 1993, there were moves to abandon Grosslagen altogether and replace them with more rigorously defined URSPRUNGSLAGEN. This has so far been fiercely resisted by those merchants who find Grosslagen so commercially convenient, although members of the VDP abandoned the use of Grosslagen from the 1998 vintage.

The wine regions of AUSTRIA have also been divided into Grosslagen, or collective sites. Some of them, such as Retzer Weinberge in the Weinviertel, encompass a vast vineyard area, but none of them has any reputation outside Austria.

grower, the all-important producer of the raw material for wine-making. This individual may be called a grape-grower, more precisely a vine-grower, possibly even a wine-grower if he or she also vinifies. Terms in other languages include *vigneron* and *viticulteur* in French, and *vignaiolo* in Italian. Wine producers who grow their own grapes and vinify them into wine but on a limited scale are often referred to somewhat carelessly and often inaccurately as **small growers**. A significant proportion of all vine-growers produce only grapes, however, which they sell to CO-OPERATIVES, merchant-bottlers, or larger wineries.

Grumello, subzone of VALTELLINA in the far north of Italy.

Grüner Veltliner, the most commonly planted vine variety in AUSTRIA and grown elsewhere in eastern Europe. In 1997, this well-adapted variety was planted on more than a third of Austria's 52,000 ha/128,000 acres of vineyard, particularly in lower Austria, where it represents more than half of total white-grape production, and in the Vienna region, where it comprises about a third and plays an important part in HEURIGER wine.

At its best, arguably in the Wachau and in the hands of some of the most ambitious growers in Vienna, Grüner Veltliner can produce wines which combine both perfume and substance, in style not unlike some from ALSACE. The wine is typically dry, peppery, or spicy, and with time in bottle can start to taste positively burgundian.

The variety is also grown just over lower Austria's northern border in the CZECH REPUBLIC, where it is known as Veltlin Zelene or Veltlinske Zelené and in the Sopron vineyards of HUNGARY as Zöldveltelini.

Roter Veltliner (once planted in California) and, less importantly, **Brauner Veltliner** are grown to a much more limited extent in lower Austria. The combined plantings of both of these dark-skinned mutations of Grüner Veltliner totalled not much more than one per cent of the area planted with Grüner Veltliner, in the 1990s. See also FRÜHROTER VELTLINER, however.

Guarnaccia, a strain of GRENACHE local to the island of Ischia off Naples.

Guenoc Valley, CALIFORNIA inland wine region and AVA promoted by Orville Magoon's Guenoc winery. North of Napa Valley and east of Alexander Valley, it is in LAKE County.

Guigal, family-owned merchant-grower based at Ampuis, CÔTE RÔTIE, in the northern RHÔNE. Although established as recently as 1946 by Étienne Guigal, Établissements Guigal is the most famous of any of the Rhône valley's merchants or growers with COLLECTORS and INVESTORS. This is very largely due to the efforts of its manager since 1971, Étienne's only son Marcel, a man of exceptional modesty and a gifted, meticulous wine-maker. Guigal owns 20 ha/50 acres of prime vineyard in Côte Rôtie, and it was the wines made from three of its best parcels, extravagantly praised by influential American wine writer Robert PARKER in the early to mid 1980s, that first drew international attention to Marcel Guigal. It would be fair to say that the quality of Guigal's top wines, along with Parker's persistent enthusiasm for them among many other Rhône wines, spearheaded a resurgence of interest in the whole region.

Guigal's so-called CRU wines (La Mouline, La Landonne, and La Turque) are dark, dramatic, mouth-fillingly rich and oaky expressions of the SYRAH grape (supplemented by up to 11 per cent of VIOGNIER in the case of La Mouline); made from low yields of very ripe, late-picked fruit aged for three and a half years in 100 per cent new oak, and bottled without FINING or FILTRATION. They are particularly impressive when young and their quality is beyond question, but opinions are divided about their style; purists in particular feel that their character is masked by excessive oak. Reputation and rarity combined (only 400 to 700 cases of each are made each year) have also made them extremely expensive and therefore game for criticism, fair or not. More recent offerings include the more plentiful Côte Rôtie Château d'Ampuis, and La Doriane, a special CONDRIEU. Because of the ballyhoo over his top wines, it is easy to overlook the fact that Guigal's NÉGO-CIANT wines, made substantially from bought-in grapes, are also very good and deservedly popular.

In 1984, Guigal bought and revitalized the firm of Vidal Fleury, the company where Étienne Guigal worked for 15 years before founding his own. Vidal Fleury is run quite independently of Guigal although Marcel makes its Côte Rôtie wines.   M.W.E.S.

Gumpoldskirchen, wine centre in lower AUSTRIA famous for its fiery, full-bodied whites made from ZIERFANDLER (or Spätrot) and ROT-GIPFLER grapes. Now part of the district known as Thermenregion.

Gutedel, meaning 'good and noble' in German, is not the most obvious synonym for CHASSELAS today but Germany still grows more than 1,200 ha/3,000 acres of Weisser Gutedel, almost all of them in the Markgräflerland region of BADEN, where it continues to be popular with growers. A dark-berried form, Roter Gutedel, is also known here.

Gutenborner is a very minor white-berried German vine crossing bred from Müller-Thurgau × Chasselas Napoleon which has had some success in sheltered sites in ENGLAND and, unusually for a modern crossing, the Rheingau and Mosel-Saar-Ruwer in Germany. Its main attribute is its ability to ripen in cool climates.

Gutsabfüllung, term found on wine labels in GERMANY meaning 'estate bottled'. The wine must be bottled by the cellar which harvested the grapes and made the wine. The bottler must have cultivated the vineyard for at least three years and must have kept detailed records. The wine-maker must have had some professional training in OENOLOGY. This is therefore a much more exclusive term than ERZEUGERABFÜLLUNG.

Gutturnio, red wine from EMILIA-ROMAGNA in Italy.

gyropalette or girasol, special metal crate holding many dozen inverted bottles of traditional-method sparkling wine in a remote-controlled, movable frame. This is the mechanized form of RIDDLING and was developed in Catalonia in the 1970s. See SPARKLING-WINE-MAKING.

halbsüss, literally 'half sweet' in German. Used on labels in AUSTRIA to designate wines whose RESIDUAL SUGAR is between 9 and 18 g/l.

halbtrocken, German for 'half dry' and an intermediate wine style between the sweet wines so popular in GERMANY throughout the 1970s and early 1980s and the dry TROCKEN wines so popular with Germans from the early 1980s. The RESIDUAL SUGAR should be less than 18 g/l and not more than 10 g/l greater than the total acidity. By the late 1990s, over 22 per cent of German wine was officially described as halbtrocken. However, dryness and sweetness do not of themselves determine quality. Under European Union law, the use of the term halbtrocken is optional and, with the general move to a lower sugar content in all German wines, many bottlings are halbtrocken or indeed trocken without this being indicated on the label.

A sparkling wine produced within the EU can be described as halbtrocken if it contains between 33 and 50 g/l residual sugar and, therefore, tastes perceptibly sweet.

See also SWEETNESS.

Hanepoot, traditional Afrikaans name meaning literally 'honey pot', for SOUTH AFRICA'S most planted Muscat vine variety, MUSCAT OF ALEXANDRIA. A few commercial, low-priced wines are sold under this name.

hangover, one of wine's least welcome effects, normally following excessive consumption. Drinking wine with or after food and drinking at least as much water as wine can lessen the likelihood of a hangover. Homeo-pathic prophylactics include milk thistle extract (silymarin) and nux vomica. There is no evidence that wine hangovers are different from those caused by any other form of ALCOHOL, although inexpensive wine, non-organic wine, wine consumed with grain-based alcholic drinks, and bottle-aged PORT have all been accused of increasing the risk of hangover. The only effective control is moderation.

hang time, American expression for the growing season, or total period between FLOWERING and HARVEST. It is much used by those who deliberately extend it, hoping to achieve the holy grail of full PHYSIOLOGICAL RIPENESS without SURMATURITÉ.

hard. See TASTING TERMS.

Hardys, or BRL Hardy, second most important wine company in AUSTRALIA, the result of a 1992 merger between the family-owned Thomas Hardy & Son and the RIVERLAND Berri-Renmano CO-OPERATIVE group. In 1990, Hardys broke new, if cripplingly expensive, ground for an Australian company, by buying La Baume, then a decrepit winery in the LANGUEDOC, and the much more substantial Chianti estate of RICASOLI, which was not included in the 1992 merger. A renovated La Baume continues to produce fine-value French VARIETALS and international expansion has continued in the form of JOINT VENTURES in both Chile (Mopocho) and Sicily (D'istinto). In Australia, Hardys bought Yarra Burn winery in the YARRA VALLEY in 1995, a half share in Brookland Valley winery in MARGARET RIVER in 1997, and have invested substantially in vineyards in the new, cooler wine regions of South Australia and in developing vineyards, and a new tourism/winery project, in CANBERRA.

Harriague, name for TANNAT in Uruguay.

Hárslevelü, white grape variety most widely grown in HUNGARY, where it produces characteristically spicy, aromatic white wines. This is the variety which brings perfume to the FURMINT grapes which make up the majority of the blend for the famous dessert wine TOKAJI, although it is widely planted elsewhere in Hungary and produces a range of VARIETAL wines which vary considerably in quality. Good Hárslevelü is typically deep green-gold, very viscous, full, and powerfully flavoured. The variety makes particularly full-bodied wines in Villány in the far south of Hungary and is popularly associated with the village of Debrö in the Mátra Foothills (although much of the wine sold as Debröi Hárslevelü has been a much less specific and less distinguished off-dry blend).

The variety is also grown over the border from Hungary's Tokaji region in SLOVAKIA and in South Africa is even more widely grown than Furmint.

harvest, both the process of picking ripe grapes from the vine and transferring them to the winery (or field pressing station), and its occasionally festive, if frenetic, duration.

This transition period in the wine-making cycle from vineyard to cellar is also known as VINTAGE (crush in much of the New World), and RÉCOLTE or *vendange* in France, *vendemmia* in Italy, *Ernte* in Germany, *cosecha* in Spain, and *vindima* in the DOURO and *colheita* in the rest of Portugal.

The single most critical aspect of harvest is its timing, choosing that point during the grape-RIPENING process when the grape is physiologically mature and the balance between its natural accumulation of sugars and its decreasing tally of natural plant ACIDS is optimal. Timing of the harvest is additionally complicated by the fact that the fruit in different parts of a single vineyard may vary in ripeness, and the picking of a single plot may take several days.

Although the timing of harvest depends on fruit RIPENESS, it also depends on the region, the grape variety, and the type of wine required (Pinot Noir grapes destined for sparkling white wine are invariably picked much earlier than they would be for a still, red wine, for example).

Harvest typically takes place in autumn: September and October in the northern hemisphere and March and April in the southern hemisphere.

The traditional method of harvesting, by hand, consists of cutting the stem of individual bunches and putting the bunches into a suitable container. This method, as opposed to MECHANICAL HARVESTING, can be employed regardless of terrain, row spacing, and precise vine-training system. It also allows pickers to select individual bunches according to their ripeness and to eliminate unhealthy fruit affected by ROT or DISEASE.

Occasionally, individual berries are harvested, in the case of bunches affected by BOTRYTIS, an operation that is possible only with a high labour input. This is most famously practised at Ch d'YQUEM and in other vineyards specializing in botrytized sweet wines in SOUTH WEST FRANCE, Austria, and Germany (see AUSLESE, BEERENAUSLESE, and TROCKENBEERENAUSLESE) but the technique may also be employed in the production of (necessarily expensive) dry wines when the vineyard has been attacked by less noble rot.

The cost of manual harvesting increases dramatically when yields are low, for particularly widely spaced vines, or on particularly steep vineyards as in the MOSEL.

See also MECHANICAL HARVESTING.

R.E.S. & A.D.W.

Haut-Brion, Château, the most famous property in the GRAVES district in BORDEAUX producing both red and white wines.

Partly, no doubt, owing to its historic reputation, Haut-Brion was the only non-MÉDOC to be included in the famous 1855 CLASSIFICATION of the wines of Bordeaux. Enclosed in the Bordeaux suburb of Pessac, the château building dates from the 16th century, and the 53 ha/130 acres of vineyards are composed of 55 per cent Cabernet Sauvignon vines, 22 per cent Cabernet Franc, and 23 per cent Merlot. Average production is 13,000 cases, including a SECOND WINE, Ch Bahans-Haut-Brion, since 1976 sold with a vintage date. About 10 TONNEAUX a year of the property's rare dry white wine, **Haut-Brion Blanc**, is made from almost equal parts of Sémillon and Sauvignon.

For many years, Haut-Brion was in fierce competition with its neighbour **Ch La Mission-Haut-Brion**, where a second red wine **Ch La Tour-Haut-Brion** and a full, waxy white wine

Ch Laville-Haut-Brion are also made. La Mission itself usually contains considerably more Merlot than Haut-Brion, and very much more than La Tour-Haut-Brion. In 1983, however, La Mission was sold to the Dillons, owners of Haut-Brion, so that both these famous estates, the flagships of the newer PESSAC-LÉOGNAN appellation, are run, retaining their quite distinct premises and characters, by the same team.

Hautes Côtes de Beaune and Hautes Côtes de Nuits, sometimes known collectively as the Hautes Côtes, vineyards dispersed in the hills above the escarpment of the CÔTE D'OR in Burgundy. Most of the production is red wine from Pinot Noir, with some white wine made from Chardonnay or occasionally Pinot Blanc or Pinot Gris. This is also suitable ground for BOURGOGNE ALIGOTÉ, especially as the blackcurrant bushes needed for the production of CASSIS can often be seen growing alongside.

Forty-seven communes are included in the Hautes Côtes appellations. The most prolific villages include Meloisey, Nantoux, and Échevronne above the Côte de Beaune and Villars-Fontaine, Magny-lès-Villars, and Marey-lès-Fussey above the Côte de Nuits. There is a good CO-OPERATIVE for the Hautes Côtes wines located just outside Beaune. Jayer-Gilles' Hautes-Côtes red burgundy is more ambitious than most.   J.T.C.M.

Haut-Médoc, the higher, southern part of the Médoc district of Bordeaux which includes the world-famous communes of MARGAUX, PAUILLAC, ST-ESTÈPHE, and ST-JULIEN, as well as the less glamorous ones of LISTRAC and MOULIS. Red wines made here outside one of these appellations usually qualify for the appellation of Haut-Médoc. See MÉDOC.

Haut-Poitou. See POITOU.

Hawaii, chain of islands in the Pacific Ocean, outside continental USA, but one of the 50 UNITED STATES. It produces mainly FRUIT WINES, notably a sparkling pineapple wine, as well as some grape wines, on the island of Maui.

health, effects of wine consumption on. In the 1970s and early 1980s, wine drinking, like all forms of alcohol consumption, was targeted by some health campaigners, and warning labels proliferated on wine bottles (see LABELLING). Wine contains alcohol, and alcohol is toxic. Its contribution to liver damage, brain damage, and accidents is well known. Less well

known is that the incidence of many cancers, nerve and muscle wasting, blood disorders, raised blood pressure, strokes, skin infections, psoriasis, and infertility increases with high intake, and the babies of mothers who drink excessively during pregnancy may have abnormal facial features and low intelligence (so-called fetal alcohol syndrome). While it was recognized that wine drinking in moderation—one to three standard glasses per day—could have social benefits, few believed that its physical effects could be other than potentially harmful. Yet at the same time, research was showing that modest drinkers had lower mortality than heavy drinkers or non-drinkers. Sceptics assumed that the abstainers had given up drinking because of poor health, or that the relationship could be explained by a confounding factor, but the evidence that prudent drinking can be beneficial to health is now overwhelming.

Coronary heart disease
The western world's major killer, coronary heart disease is the deposition of plaques of cholesterol in the arteries supplying the heart muscle. These furred-up arteries cannot supply the heart muscle with enough oxygen, resulting in the pain of angina. Heart attacks happen when blood clots block these narrowed arteries completely, cutting off the oxygen supply. Heavy drinkers develop increased cholesterol levels as well as raised blood pressure, weakened heart muscle, and a susceptibility to potentially fatal abnormal heart rhythms. Yet there is now a mass of evidence that those who drink moderately are less likely to develop coronary heart disease and to die from it than either those who drink heavily or those who have never drunk alcohol. Furthermore, wine stands out as the most beneficial alcoholic drink.

Alcohol, it seems, moderates the level of inflammatory blood chemicals called cytokines which adversely affect blood cholesterol and blood-clotting proteins. Blood carries LDL (low-density lipoprotein) cholesterol, which forms the plaques which block arteries, and HDL (high-density lipoprotein) cholesterol, which mops them up. Moderate alcohol consumption improves the balance between the harmful and beneficial forms of cholesterol. Alcohol has two anticoagulant effects which make blood less likely to clot in the wrong place.

Part of the specific benefit of wine, it seems, comes from how it is drunk. Its anticoagulant effect lasts less than 24 hours. This may explain why the risk of a heart attack is reduced in the day following a couple of drinks. The wine drinker's glass or two with the evening meal provides a steady, safe level of alcohol. In contrast, the beer drinker's Saturday night binge leaves him temporarily over-anticoagulated (and at increased risk of a stroke due to bleeding) until he has metabolized the alcohol, then at increased risk of heart attack until the next night out. The pattern of heavier, episodic intake common to spirit drinkers also deprives them of the benefits of modest regular imbibing.

Alcohol is not the only compound of cardiovascular significance in wine. Red wine, much more than white, is rich in PHENOLICS which have antioxidant properties. Attention has focused on RESVERATROL. In the laboratory, it inhibits not only the oxidation reaction by which LDL-cholesterol is formed, but also inhibits reactions which make platelets more sticky and the lining of blood vessels liable to promote a blood clot. Red wine or red grape juice, although not white wine, increases the level of resveratrol in the blood and its antioxidant activity. It is likely, although as yet unproven, that resveratrol makes a significant contribution to the cardioprotective effects of wine and, as a particular characteristic of red wine, may help to explain the FRENCH PARADOX.

Most of wine's health benefit lies in its effects on the heart. For every 24 men who drink moderately for six years, one will be saved a major cardiovascular problem—a better ratio than many medications can offer.

Respiratory problems

Very heavy drinkers are prone to pneumonia, but three to four drinks a day appear to protect non-smokers from the effects of the common cold virus.

Some asthmatics experience an adverse reaction to wine. A variety of constituents may be responsible. SULPHITES can irritate the airways, triggering wheeze in sensitive people. Sulphur levels in wine are being reduced and some countries insist that the presence of sulphites is indicated on wine labels. TANNINS have also been implicated as red wine is more often problematic than white, and an allergic reaction due to the HISTAMINE in some red wines is the culprit for a few.

Headaches

Some migraine sufferers identify red wine as a trigger. Their downfall is likely to be the phenolics which in the test tube liberate from cells the chemical messenger 5-hydroxytryptamine (serotonin) which plays a part in the initiation of migraine. Red wines may also contain histamine, which can induce headache in susceptible subjects. As antihistamines can interact with alcohol, choosing a wine low in histamine may be the best strategy for avoiding the problem.

Dementia

The intoxified brain does not function well (whatever its owner may temporarily believe), and the deleterious effect on intellectual function of long-term assault with heavy alcohol is well known. It comes as a pleasant bonus to find that moderate wine drinkers are less likely to develop dementia than their non-drinking or heavy-drinking compatriots.

Vision

A common cause of declining vision in old age is macular degeneration—wearing out of the light-sensitive cells at the back of the eye. An American study published in 1998 showed that the visual cells of moderate wine drinkers are 20 per cent better preserved than those of non-drinkers and drinkers of beer and spirits. As with heart disease, wine's anticoagulant and antioxidant properties may be responsible.

Bones

Very heavy drinkers are prone to fracture their bones; a consequence of the effects of too much alcohol on their bone structure and on their lifestyle. Laboratory work shows that alcohol has a damaging effect on the cellular bone-forming mechanism. However, some population studies show an association between moderate drinking and improvement in bone density. Those such as post-menopausal women at risk of osteoporosis may find a glass of wine a day beneficial rather than harmful.

Cancer

Awareness of the influence of lifestyle on cancer risks has stimulated research into the relationship between drinking and cancers. As antioxidants are thought to be part of the body's defence against cancer, the phenolics in red wine could plausibly bolster that defence. Indeed, in the laboratory, resveratrol protects cells from cancerous change. Resveratrol in wine is absorbed from the digestive tract into the body, but so is alcohol, which causes damage, so wine's rich mixture of chemicals has potential for harm as well as benefit.

Sadly, the news so far from studies on wine and cancer is largely bad. Alcohol consumption is a risk factor, albeit minor, for cancer of the digestive tract. The association is strongest for cancer of the oesophagus (gullet) and becomes progressively weaker for stomach cancer and cancer of the colon. Cancer of the pancreas does not seem to be related to alcohol consumption except at very high levels. Studies in several countries of the incidence of breast cancer show that wine drinking is associated with a modest increase in risk, especially for younger women.

Diabetes mellitus

Although diabetics are obliged to watch carefully what they eat and drink, alcohol taken with a meal does not substantially alter their blood sugar. Non-insulin diabetes mellitus, the form of diabetes which usually develops in middle age, is due not so much to lack of insulin but to decreased response to it. This is another effect of cytokines, so may explain Italian research showing that moderate drinkers are more sensitive to insulin than non-drinkers, and an American study which found that moderate drinking is associated with a significantly lower risk of developing non-insulin-dependent diabetes. Men drinking 30–50 gm of alcohol per day appear to benefit the most.

Peptic ulcers and stomach upsets

Ulcer sufferers have traditionally been advised to avoid alcohol lest it irritate the lining of the stomach. This advice is now less often needed. Gastritis, peptic ulcers, and stomach cancer are now known to be strongly associated with infection by the bacterium *Helicobacter pylori* and a short course of treatment designed to eradicate *H. pylori* is saving many former sufferers a lifetime of treatment. Furthermore, a study in Germany in 1997 showed that moderate wine and beer drinkers were significantly less likely to be infected with *H. pylori* than non-drinkers, possibly due to the antimicrobial effects of alcohol.

Gallstones are another cause of upper abdominal misery. There is some evidence that moderate drinking reduces gallstone formation. The major component of most gallstones is cholesterol, so the benefit is probably due to wine's effect on cholesterol metabolism.

Wine is more active against the bacteria which cause travellers' diarrhoea than bismuth, another traditional and distinctly less palatable prophylactic. Wines appear to become more effective as they age although their antibacterial potential declines after about 10 years.

Sensible drinking

Health authorities in many countries have disseminated 'sensible drinking levels', suggested maxima for personal consumption of alcohol usually expressed in 'units', or STANDARD DRINKS, of alcohol. There is wide variation between what constitutes a unit and how many of them may safely be consumed. An intake of as much as 60 g alcohol a day is safe for men according to French health authorities, whereas their counterparts in the UK counsel limiting daily consumption to less than half this level.

These limits are at best only a rough guide as some people are at greater risk of harm than others. Sex, age, build, genetic make-up, state of health, and drug intake all affect the way alcohol is metabolized. For instance, glass for glass, women are at greater risk than men. Whatever their weight or size, they absorb relatively more alcohol because of differences in levels of stomach enzymes, their lower body water content meaning that alcohol is more concentrated in their tissues and, if also taking the contraceptive pill, more slowly eliminated.

Now we must add the health benefits into the equation. The fact that moderate drinking reduces deaths from cardiovascular disease by about 30 per cent is much better news for someone whose risk is high, such as a middle-aged man, than for a young woman who has a low risk of heart disease but is vulnerable to breast cancer. Nevertheless, healthy and prudent drinkers can expect that two to three glasses of wine a day will make them feel better and live longer. Seldom can medication have been made available in so palatable a form.

J.H.H.

hectare, common agricultural measurement of area equivalent to 10,000 sq m, or 2.47 acres.

Heida, or occasionally **Heiden,** Swiss synonym for TRAMINER and a speciality of Vispertermin.

Helfensteiner is famous principally as a parent of the successful German crossing DORNFELDER. It is itself a crossing of FRÜHBURGUNDER × TROLLINGER.

herbaceous, TASTING TERM for the leafy or grassy aroma of crushed green leaves or freshly cut grass. **Herbaceousness** is generally considered a defect only when present in excess (although American tasters are much less tolerant of it than, for example, the British). Wines made from the produce of Sauvignon Blanc, Sémillon, Cabernet Sauvignon, Cabernet Franc, or Merlot vines which failed to ripen fully are often excessively herbaceous. Another reason why a wine may taste herbaceous is from vine leaves inadvertently picked with the grapes. Early MECHANICAL HARVESTERS were particularly prone to do this, and the grapes were often so mangled that it was impossible to separate the wet leaves from them.   A.D.W. & P.J.W.

Hercegovina. See BOSNIA HERCEGOVINA.

Hermitage, the most famous northern RHÔNE appellation of all, producing extremely limited quantities of seriously long-lived reds and about a third as much full-bodied dry white wine.

The wine comes from an almost unenlargeable 132 ha/326 acres of particularly well-favoured vines on the extraordinary hill of Hermitage, a south-facing bank of granite, thinly covered with extremely varied and well-charted soil types, which almost pushes the town of Tain l'Hermitage into the river Rhône just as it turns sharp left.

The combination of heat-retaining granite and a reasonably steep southern exposition do much to encourage grape RIPENING here. It is not surprising that such a celebrated vineyard has for long been divided into various CLIMATS, all with their own soil types and reputations for wine types. The most famous *climats* are at the western end of the hill, which benefits from the highest temperatures. Les Bessards produces some of the sturdiest wines; Le Méal produces more aromatic wines. Other famous *climats* include Les Gréffieux, Les Diognières, Beaume(s), Maison Blanche, Péléat, Les Murets, Rocoule, La Croix, and Les Signeaux in the extreme east. Although white and red grapes are planted all over the hill, some of the finest white Hermitage comes from the higher vineyards, and clay-limestone soils are considered the best suited.

Producers such as Gérard Chave, the modest master of Hermitage, delight in blending the produce of holdings all over the hill to produce a complex, well-balanced expression of each vintage. Producers with less diversified holdings may produce less complex wines, some of them labelled with a single *climat*.

Unlike CÔTE RÔTIE upriver, red Hermitage is made from the SYRAH vine alone, indeed Hermitage has laid claim to be the cradle of Syrah, while white Hermitage may be made from the robust MARSANNE or the nervier, and less common, ROUSSANNE.

The appellation regulations limit yields to a basic 40 hl/ha (2.3 tons/acre) but CHAPTALIZATION may be allowed in some vintages, so long as the ALCOHOLIC STRENGTH of the resultant wine is no more than 13.5 per cent for reds and 14 per cent for whites.

Wine-making philosophies vary here, but are essentially traditional. Red wines are the result of relatively hot FERMENTATIONS matured in often quite old casks of varied capacity, according to vintage characteristics. Red Hermitage should be very deeply coloured and headily perfumed. They can evolve for two or three decades, after which they may be mistaken for great red bordeaux. Some of the finest red wines of Hermitage come from Chave, Le Pavillon from CHAPOUTIER, La Chapelle from JABOULET, and Le Gréal from Sorrel.

White wines are possibly even more varied, according to the blend of grape varieties used, RIPENESS, whether MALOLACTIC FERMENTATION has taken place, and whether WOOD is used for fermentation and/or AGEING. Almost all white Hermitage is notably full in BODY, and some of the more serious examples such as Chave's and Chapoutier's Chante Alouette are among the longest-living dry white wines of France.

In very ripe years, some of Hermitage's white grapes may be transformed into VIN DE PAILLE so long as the must is not chaptalized and the yield is no more than 15 hl/ha. This sweet white Hermitage is delicious but all too rare.

Hermitage has also been used as a synonym for SHIRAZ in Australia, where, for example, PENFOLDS Grange was originally called Penfolds Grange Hermitage. Hermitage was also the historic South African synonym for CINSAUT and is sometimes used in Switzerland for MARSANNE.

Heroldrebe is the marginal dark-berried GERMAN CROSSING of PORTUGIESER and LIMBERGER. Its most useful function was that it spawned the promising DORNFELDER.

Hessische Bergstrasse, one of the smallest wine regions in GERMANY. The northern vineyards on the western slopes of Germany's Odenwald have formed a separate region since 1971. They comprise just 454 ha/1,122 acres, of which a large and growing proportion, 56 per cent in 1997, is planted in RIESLING. The best produces distinguished wine, comparable with that of the RHEINGAU. The area devoted to red grapes, particularly SPÄTBURGUNDER, was eight per cent in 1997 and continues to grow. Of the 850 or so growers, approximately 620 deliver their grapes to a large regional CO-OPERATIVE cellar at Heppenheim, which sells 70 per cent of its stock in litre bottles within the region. Only a small and decreasing amount of the co-operative's wine is sold by supermarkets, and sales directly to the consumer and to the wine trade are increasing (although Hessische Bergstrasse wines are rarely seen outside Germany). More than 80 per cent of Hessische Bergstrasse wines are dry: TROCKEN, or HALBTROCKEN.   I.J. & K.B.S.

Heuriger is an Austrian wine speciality. *Heurig* literally means 'this season's' but Heuriger has come to mean both wine from the most recent vintage and the place where the wine is offered for consumption by its producer. These small, often family-run, wine taverns can be found throughout Austria's wine regions but are a particularly popular tourist attraction in the suburbs of VIENNA. Food is usually served alongside the owner's wine, usually crackling new Heuriger wine but sometimes supplemented by old, or *alte*, wines. The wine of the new vintage officially becomes Heurige on St Martin's Day, 11 November. Before that it may have been sold at the unfermented MUST (*Most*) stage, as partially fermented Sturm, or as still-cloudy new wine (*Staubiger*). Local by-laws determine when a Heurige may sell its new wine, which period it signals by hanging out a bush of pine twigs above the entrance. See also PRIMEUR, the French counterpart, minus the hospitality.

hillside vineyards. Even in Ancient Rome it was said *Bacchus amat colles*, or Bacchus loves the hills, suggesting that hillside vineyards have long been regarded as a source of high-quality wine.

This is partly because hillside soils are typically shallow, so that vineyard VIGOUR is relatively low, a factor commonly associated with high wine quality. Vines may also be planted on hillsides for reasons of MESOCLIMATE, as hillsides are less prone to frost because cold air can drain freely away at night. If the slopes face the equator, they receive more sunshine during the day and can reradiate the heat absorbed during the day at night or during cloudy weather. In warmer regions, some vineyards may be planted on hillsides to take advantage of cooler temperatures at higher ALTITUDES and therefore extend the growing season. Since the early 1980s, there has been an increasing tendency to plant elevated sites in Australia, Argentina, South Africa, and California, for example, in order to produce a more cool-climate style of table wine.

Hillside vineyard sites have their drawbacks, such as soil erosion. Working on steep slopes is particularly tiring, productivity is affected, and the costs are higher. In most vineyards of the world, rows run up and down the slopes. Where the slopes are too steep for tractors, as in CÔTE RÔTIE, parts of the MOSEL valley, and SWITZERLAND, everything must be done by hand, or by machines winched down into the vineyards. Where rows run across the slopes, the vineyard is normally laid out in TERRACES, as in Portugal's DOURO valley or France's hill of HERMITAGE.   R.E.S.

Hilltops, new wine region in NEW SOUTH WALES, Australia, also known as Young.

histamine, the amine involved in a range of allergic reactions in humans, was once thought the cause of some people's allergy to red wine. Improved methods of wine analysis have demonstrated that the amounts of histamine in wine are at least an order of magnitude below that required to cause an allergic reaction in the great majority of people. However, a few people have low levels of the enzyme which breaks down histamine, so histamine levels in their blood rise high enough to cause allergic reactions after drinking wine with even low levels of histamine.

A.D.W. & J.H.H.

Hochgewächs, one of a number of label clues to one of GERMANY'S better wines launched to supplement those provided by the GERMAN WINE LAW. A wine labelled Riesling-Hochgewächs is a QBA which has reached much higher MUST WEIGHT and overall quality than the legal minimum. The term applies exclusively to Riesling.

hock, generic term in use since the 17th century for (white) Rhenish wines, from the RHINE regions of GERMANY, sometimes for the wines of Germany in general. A contraction of hockamore, an English rendering of the adjective Hochheimer, denoting wines from Hochheim on the river Main just west of Frankfurt (see RHEINGAU).

In modern commerce, a wine labelled 'Hock' is likely to be a simple QBA wine from a German Rhine wine region such as RHEINHESSEN or possibly the PFALZ. It has been by no means uncommon for the same wine to be offered as Hock to a gentlemen's club and LIEBFRAUMILCH to a supermarket buyer. Hock has also occasionally been used as a name for non-German sweetish white wine.

Holland, the heartland of the small north European country now called the Netherlands, has had considerable influence on the wine and, particularly, spirit industry, thanks to Dutch naval power in the late Middle Ages. See NETHERLANDS.

home wine-making, popular hobby for individuals who make wine in their own homes, either for fun, to save money, or both. Because such wine attracts no DUTY, it has great appeal in countries such as Great Britain, where wine duties are relatively high. It also enjoyed enormous popularity in the United States during Prohibition, when vinifying an annual allowance of 200 gal/7.5 hl of fruit juice (a limit that still applies in the USA) was the only legal way the average American household could procure alcoholic drink. In 1992, it was estimated that a total of 400,000 Americans make the equivalent of a total of 2.5 million cases of wine a year from grapes (and another 500,000 cases of non-grape FRUIT WINES). Most of them buy fresh, American-grown grapes, mainly from California, which has a long tradition of shipping grapes by rail to Midwest and East Coast cities. Others buy juice or GRAPE CONCENTRATE. British home wine-makers determined to make wine based on grapes rather than other fruits, flowers, or vegetables (parsnip has its devotees) tend to use grape concentrate as their raw material, so that their produce is technically MADE WINE and lacks the fresh fruitiness of wine made from the juice of freshly picked grapes.

Hondarrabi, family of Spanish BASQUE vine varieties. **Hondarrabi Zuri** is light berried and more common in CHACOLÍ DE GUETARIA than the dark-berried **Hondarrabi Beltza**, which is more common in Chacolí de Vizcaya around Bilbao.

Hospices de Beaune, charity auction which has taken place in BEAUNE annually since 1851 on the third Sunday in November, a key feature of the Burgundian calendar. The produce of vineyard holdings donated by benefactors over the centuries is auctioned at prices usually well in excess of current commercial values. Nevertheless, the results serve as some indication of the trend in bulk-wine prices for the new vintage.

The Hospices de Nuits also holds a charity wine auction; see NUITS-ST-GEORGES.

See also AUCTIONS.   J.T.C.M.

Howell Mountain, California wine region and AVA east of St Helena, defined by elevation of about 1,400 ft/425 m. See NAPA Valley.

Hugel, one of the best-known and oldest wine producers in ALSACE, having been established in 1639. The family business is run today by the 12th and 13th generations. The Hugels, based in Riquewihr, make fine wines from their own 26 ha/65 acres of vineyard around the village planted mainly with Riesling and Gewürztraminer, together with a little Pinot Gris and Pinot Noir. Their Tradition range can be excitingly full and the Jubilee range masterful. The Hugel family also pioneered the resurrection of Alsace's late-harvest wines and were instrumental in drawing up the rigorous requirements for these VENDANGE TARDIVE and SÉLECTION DE GRAINS NOBLES wines. They are arch exponents of these styles themselves, and produce them, and the Jubilee range, exclusively from their own ALSACE GRAND CRU vineyards. The Hugel family have long been champions of maximizing quality in Alsace's finest wines, and are vociferous opponents of the Alsace Grand Cru appellation, which they feel is no guarantee of quality. The Hugels buy in grapes, never wine, for their basic generic range of wines.

Humagne Blanche, Swiss Valais white grape which has no apparent relation to HUMAGNE ROUGE, however similar the vines look. The wine produced is fairly neutral relative to Petite Arvine.

Humagne Rouge, relatively rare red wine grape of the Swiss Valais region whose wines are wild, rustic, and relatively high in TANNINS. They are particularly recommended with venison. The variety is probably more closely related to the Opriou vine of the Valle d'AOSTA than to Humagne Blanche.

Hungary, important eastern European wine-producing country with its own particularly distinctive range of vine varieties and wines. Hungary usually produces less wine than its eastern neighbour Romania, but considerably more than, for example, Austria and Bulgaria. About 130,000 ha/321,000 acres were devoted to vines in the late 1990s, and about 70 per cent of them produced white wines. Total Hungarian wine production has been decreasing and now varies between 3.2 and 4.1 million hl (108 million gal) a year, of which about a third is exported.

Geography

Hungary is land-locked but includes Europe's largest lake, Balaton. The river Danube (called Duna in Hungary) flows through it from north to south, dividing the country in almost equal halves. To the west lies Transdanubia, while to the immediate east of the river is the Great Plain. North east of the capital Budapest are the volcanic hills which constitute the Northern Massif, whose south-facing slopes are particularly well suited to vine-growing. In the extreme north east of the country is the Tokaj-Hegyalja region, which borders SLOVAKIA. See TOKAJI for more details. See below for details of individual wine regions.

Climate

Hungary's climate is essentially CONTINENTAL and central European, involving fairly predictably cold winters and hot summers. The relatively northerly latitude (on a par with Burgundy) makes it ideally situated to produce aromatic and semi-aromatic varieties such as Sauvignon Blanc and Gewürztraminer, while its continentality allows full ripening of such red varieties as Cabernet Sauvignon, especially in the south. Prolonged, sunny autumns which favour the development of noble rot are by no means rare.

Vine varieties

Wine labelling in Hungary is largely VARIETAL so that wine producers and consumers have a keen appreciation of specific vine varieties. A potentially exciting selection of localized white grape varieties can still be found, although some such as KÉKNYELÜ, found almost exclusively in Badacsony on the north shore of Lake Balaton, and JUHFARK, known mainly in Somló, are dangerously close to extinction.

Indigenous varieties which are relatively widely planted include the EZERJÓ, a light speciality of the Mór region west of Budapest; FURMINT, which is widely grown but is the most characteristic ingredient of Tokaji; HÁRSLE-VELÜ, which is usually a lesser Tokaji ingredient and is also widely grown throughout Hungary; and MEZESFEHÉR is widely planted and used for sweet wine, particularly in Eger and Gyöngyös. Kövidinka, or DINKA, produces ordinary wines in quantity on the Great Plain, as it does across the southern border with VOJVODINA. New crossings such as the Muscatlike IRSAI OLIVER and the spicy Cserszegi Füszeres (a crossing of Irsai Oliver and Gewürztraminer) are now being more widely planted for their own intrinsic character and quality. Hungary's most characteristic red grape variety is KADARKA, although KÉKOPORTO (Portugieser) can also make some appetizing wines here.

The usual range of central European vine varieties is grown: Olaszrizling (the Hungarian name for WELSCHRIESLING), Leányka (the FETE-ASCA of Romania), Zöldveltelini (Austria's GRÜNER VELTLINER), Cirfandli (Austria's ZIER-FANDLER, a speciality of Pécs); and, for red-wine production, KÉKFRANKOS (along with Nagyburgundi the Hungarian name for BLAU-FRÄNKISCH), and Austria's ZWEIGELT.

A wide range of vine varieties have been imported into Hungary from western Europe, however, including Chardonnay, Sauvignon, Sémillon, Riesling (sometimes called Rajnai Rizling or Rheinriesling), Gewürztraminer (Tramini), Muscat Ottonel and Gold Muscat, the deeper-hued Muscat Blanc à Petits Grains (both of which are sometimes called Muskotály), Silvaner (Zöldszilváni), Müller-Thurgau (Riesling Silvaner or Rizlingszilváni), and Pinot Gris, whose distinctively Hungarian synonym is SZÜRKEBARÁT. Red wine varieties imported from the west include Merlot and, to a much lesser extent, Cabernet Sauvignon and Cabernet Franc and a small amount of Pinot Noir. The term Medoc Noir has been used loosely for any superior red wine but this practice is waning.

The 1997 wine law permitted a wider range of grape varieties in each region.

Wine regions

According to Hungarian law, there are 20 official Hungarian wine regions but the following may be considered pre-eminent today: Ászár-Neszmély, Badacsony, Balaton, EGER, the Mátra Foothills, Mór, SOPRON, Szekszárd, Villány-Siklós, and Tokaj-Hegyalja (for details of which see TOKAJI). Names such as Gyöngyös may also be familiar from export labels. The wine regions fall into three major geographical groups, as outlined below.

Transdanubia This western part of Hungary, between the Austrian border and the Danube, contains 13 of the designated wine regions which are increasingly bringing their own marked characteristics to the wines. The area is heavily influenced by the waters of Lake Balaton, the Neusiedlersee in AUSTRIA, and the Danube itself.

Traditionally, the northern side of Lake Balaton was the vine-growing area, with the famous Badacsony area on the volcanic slopes at the south-west end. The surface area of water in the lake has a considerable ameliorating effect on the MESOCLIMATE and the wines tend to be full and powerful. This is home to the ancient Kéknyelü, but also makes fine Pinot Gris (Szürkebarát), as well as Olaszrizling. Balatonfüred-Csopak also lies on the northern shore, on slate, and produces a range of western varieties and Olaszrizling.

On the slopes of an extinct volcano north west of Lake Balaton is the once historic wine region of Somló, whose oxidized, wood-aged, blended wines once enjoyed a similar reputation to those of Tokay. Juhfark was once prized here, along with Furmint, but today Riesling, Olaszrizling, and Traminer are in the ascendant.

On the south shore of the lake is a relatively new area, southern Balaton or Balatonboglár. Important grapes grown here are Merlot, Pinot Noir, Chardonnay, Muscat, and Sémillon.

Sopron, the most westerly wine region of northern Transdanubia, is mainly a red-wine region and the principal vine varieties are Cabernet Sauvignon, Cabernet Franc, Merlot, and Pinot Noir. Its Sauvignon Blanc is also gaining a good reputation, however.

In the north are two increasingly important white wine areas. Ászár-Neszmély is now as well known for its exceptionally modern Hilltop winery at Neszmély as for its Sauvignon Blanc, Pinot Gris, Irsai Oliver, and Olaszrizling. Mór, between Sopron and Budapest, is better known for the more aromatic Ezerjó, Leanyka, and Gewürztraminer.

Southern Transdanubia has three important wine regions close together in the far south of the country just west of the Danube. Villány-Siklós produces highly prized reds even in difficult years. Cabernet is most successful here, although Kékfrankos, Merlot, Zweigelt are also good. Some good Pinot Noir is also produced.

Szekszárd has traditionally been associated with Kadarka, which it has managed to ripen more healthily than most regions, owing to its long, warm summers. A BOTRYTIZED sweet version was even sold, as Nemes Kadar. This native red variety has been supplanted, however, by vigorous Kékfrankos, Merlot, and Cabernet. The area around Bátaszék, 15 km/9 miles to the south, is also producing some particularly good Sauvignon Blanc.

The Mecsek Hills is a wine region better known by the name of its principal town Pécs. A wide range of vine varieties is cultivated here, often on very small estates. They include Olaszrizling, Chardonnay, Kadarka, Cabernet, Merlot, and Pinot Noir.

The Northern Massif This range of hills running north east from Budapest along the border with Slovakia contains three wine regions, the Mátra Foothills (or Mátraalja), Eger, and Tokaj-Hegyalja (for details of which, see TOKAJI).

In the foothills of the Mátra mountains, most of the wine produced is white. Muscat, Olaszrizling, and Kadarka predominate, and within Hungary the area is associated with Debröi Hárslevelü, once a noted cask-aged sweet wine but now usually made as a modern, inexpensive dry white. In western Europe at least, the area is well known for the German-owned Gyöngyös Estate on which modern Chardonnay, Sauvignon Blanc, and Sémillon have been made for export.

Just to the east of the Mátra Foothills, in the foothills of the Bükk mountains, is the wine region named after the historic town of EGER. Some white wines are made, principally from Leányka, but the region is best known for age-worthy red wine, notably Egri Bikavér or, on export markets, BULL'S BLOOD.

In the past, only Tokaji, made even further east, has rivalled Bull's Blood for recognition outside Hungary, although the situation has been changing rapidly as wine-making and exporting skills have passed into private, and often non-Hungarian, hands.

The Great Plain This vast, flat expanse south of Budapest and between the Danube and Hungary's second river the Tisza accounts for nearly half the country's vineyards. Most of the wide variety of vines planted here are the western, INTERNATIONAL VARIETIES or Olaszrizling, although some Kadarka and a little Ezerjó are planted. The three official wine regions of the Great Plain are Csongrád, Hajós-

Vaskút, and Kiskun but wine quality is generally indifferent.

Structure of the trade

Prior to the reintroduction of a capitalist system in the early 1990s, the Hungarian wine industry was under the control of the state. In the early 1980s, Hungary was the principal eastern European wine exporter, shipping out more than 3 million hl/79 million gal, or 60 per cent of production, notably very ordinary quality wine in bulk to the USSR and East Germany. These markets shrank abruptly at the end of the 1980s, leading to sudden over-supply.

In 1989, the national association of these vine growers and wine-makers re-formed, as the Federation of Hungarian Grape and Wine Producers, with the aim of rebuilding the image of Hungarian wine. The Association of Hungarian Wine Merchants acts primarily on export control. Per capita wine consumption within Hungary rose markedly in the early 1990s, when the official target was to export about one-third of all wine production.

The state of flux of the early 1990s was followed by a far more stable economic and political environment. The influx of western European capital enabled much-needed investment in modern winery equipment, resulting in a marked improvement in quality for all wines but particularly for flavoursome dry whites.

The legislators seem to have welcomed these advances and the 1997 Hungarian wine law takes account of many of them, particularly with reference to the varieties permitted in each region. With a new lease of life for Tokaji, Chardonnay and Sauvignon Blanc increasingly rivalling those of New Zealand, and Pinot Gris and Gewürztraminer challenging those of Alsace, Hungary is poised to become one of the finest, and certainly best-value, producers of characterful white wines in the world.

M.McN. & D.J.G.

Hunter Valley, historic Australian wine region within striking distance of Sydney. It is now the name of a zone in which **Hunter** is a region made up of two very distinct subregions, the Lower Hunter, including Broke Fordwich, Pokolbin, and Rothbury, and the more recently developed Upper Hunter. See NEW SOUTH WALES.

Huxelrebe, an early-20th-century German vine crossing of GUTEDEL (Chasselas) and Court-illier Musqué, has enjoyed some popularity both in Germany and, on a much smaller scale, in ENGLAND. It is capable of producing enormous quantities of rather ordinary wine—so enormous in fact that the vines can collapse under the strain. If pruned carefully, however, and planted on an average to good site, it can easily reach Auslese MUST WEIGHTS even in an ordinary year and produce a fulsome if not exactly subtle wine for reasonably early consumption. Huxelrebe's flavours are more reminiscent of Muscat than Riesling and in England its ripeness is a useful counterbalance to naturally high acidity. In Germany, it is grown almost exclusively in the Pfalz and Rheinhessen.

hybrids, in common viticultural terms, the offspring of two varieties of different species, as distinct from a CROSS between two varieties of the same species. European Union authorities prefer the somewhat cumbersome term 'interspecific cross' to the word hybrid, which has pejorative connotations within Europe.

Hybrids can occur naturally by cross-pollination. More commonly, however, hybrids have been deliberately produced by man to combine in the progeny some of the desirable characteristics of the parents. This viticultural activity was particularly important in the late 19th century, when European, and especially French, breeders tried to combine the desirable wine quality of European VINIFERA varieties with American vine species' resistance to introduced American pests and diseases, especially the PHYLLOXERA louse, which was devastating European vineyards. Grafting European vines on to American ROOTSTOCKS proved the eventual solution, and many of today's commercially important rootstocks are hybrids.

Hybrids can yield good wine with no recognizably non-*vinifera* characteristics; see SEYVAL BLANC, CHAMBOURCIN, and specialities of NEW YORK and CANADA.   R.E.S.

hydrogen sulphide, or H_2S, is the foul-smelling gas, reminiscent of rotten eggs, which can form during FERMENTATION, either in the active phase or towards the end.

Even traces of hydrogen sulphide can spoil a wine's aroma. Fortunately, however, hydrogen sulphide is very volatile and can usually be removed by the stripping action of CARBON DIOXIDE produced during fermentation. However, H_2S formed towards the end of fermentation or, worse still, after fermentation is completed is of greater concern to the wine-maker. If allowed to remain in the wine, it is thought to react with other wine components to form MERCAPTANS, thiols, and disulphides (see SULPHIDES), which have pungent garlic/onion/rubber aromas. The smell of rotten eggs is always a FAULT in a finished wine but acceptance of the presence of trace amounts of mercaptans and disulphides is more controversial. A.D.W. & P.H.

hygiene, an essential discipline in modern cellar management, involving cleanliness of wine-making premises and equipment, and a great deal of WATER.

Hygiene is regarded as vital by modern wine-makers (although it is still ignored by some traditional or peasant wine-makers, several of whom somehow manage to produce top-quality wine). Old cellars, while usually more picturesque, are almost impossible to keep clean and free of bacteria and wild YEASTS. Most modern wineries, on the other hand, are designed with sanitation and hygiene in mind. Stainless-steel tanks can be easily cleaned and sanitized; hard floors are designed to drain dry; and all equipment is sited and mounted so that it can be cleaned thoroughly. In many wineries, all places where finished wine is exposed to the atmosphere are in separate, essentially sterile rooms, and care is taken particularly during bottling.

Some local wine-making traditions supposedly rely on cellar moulds (see TOKAJI in Hungary, for example).

Hygiene, or sanitation, is also important where the grapes are received, as overripe and damaged fruit can easily attract insects.

A.D.W.

ice wine, direct Anglicization of the German EISWEIN, sweet wine made from ripe grapes picked when frozen on the vine and pressed so that water crystals remain in the press and the sugar content of the resulting wine is increased. This sort of true ice wine is a speciality of CANADA, where it is written **Icewine** and where more is produced each year than in any other country (50,000 cases in a good year by the late 1990s). It is also increasingly made in Luxembourg, Oregon, and in Michigan in the United States. The term has also been used in other English-speaking, wine-producing countries for wines made by artificial freeze CONCENTRATION.

Idaho, state in the PACIFIC NORTHWEST of the UNITED STATES which, as a wine region, has more in common with its neighbour eastern WASHINGTON than with western Oregon. With vineyards at an altitude of around 2,500 ft/762 m, however, it is close to if not beyond the normal viticultural fringe. Riesling vines produce very successful sweet white wines in which the sugar is well balanced by natural acidity. Both Chardonnay and Pinot Noir are grown with some success, although the growing season is usually too short for Cabernet Sauvignon.

The industry has been dominated by Ste Chapelle Winery, one of the Northwest's largest and more successful wineries, situated in the Snake River valley to the west of Boise, in an area renowned for its cherries, apples, and peaches, always an indication of winegrape potential. Their cool growing season does not always produce fruit ripe enough for quality still wines; a sparkling-wine operation provides an outlet for the less ripe Pinot Noir and Chardonnay grapes, using both traditional-method and bulk-process SPARKLING-WINE-MAKING. M.S. & L.S.H.

IGT stands for Indicazione Geografica Tipica, a category of wines created in ITALY in 1992 as an approximate equivalent of the French VIN DE PAYS. It was also designed to include Italy's myriad esteemed, and often extremely expensive, wines selling as a VINO DA TAVOLA outside the much-criticized DOC system. From the 1995 vintage on, most of Italy's better-known and better-quality vini da tavola have been marketed as IGT. D.T.

Île de Beauté is VIN DE PAYS language for CORSICA and, along with the Loire's similar denomination as 'Jardin de la France', one of the most alluring vin de pays names.

imbottigliato is Italian for bottled.

impériale. See BOTTLE SIZES.

INAO, the Institut National des Appellations d'Origine, is the organization in charge of administering, regulating, granting, and protecting the French APPELLATIONS CONTRÔLÉES.

India, large Asian country where some wine ventures are breaking new ground, despite the general unsuitability of most of the country for conventional wine-growing.

Until the 1990s, the small Indian wine industry went virtually unnoticed outside the country, partly because of the quality of the wine, which was typically sweet, alcoholic, and MADERIZED and made by rudimentary village operations, with the exception of a large winery and distillery established in Hyderābād in 1966 by the Shaw Wallace group. Even within India, the prevailing religious and official attitude towards alcohol hardly encouraged a wine industry.

The current renaissance of Indian viticulture began in the early 1980s with the establishment of Chateau Indage in the traditional area of Maharashira and Grover Vineyards north of Bangalore, both of which set themselves the highest standards and the goal of exporting. Chateau Indage planted Chardonnay, Ugni Blanc, Pinot Blanc, Pinot Noir, Cabernet Sauvignon, Merlot, and Syrah and imported French equipment and expertise from Champagne to establish India's most sophisticated winery, producing a surprisingly elegant sparkling wine sold under the names Omar Khayyam and Marquise de Pompadour. Of the other eight serious wine producers, Grover Vineyards in the state of Kamataka trialled 35 vine varieties initially and settled principally on Cabernet Sauvignon and Clairette. The first wine was released in 1992 and in 1996 the champagne house Veuve Clicquot took a minority stake in the company.

Thanks to the more liberal government policy and improved economic conditions, a prosperous, wine-drinking middle class has emerged in India; demand for wine exceeded supply in the late 1990s, when the market was growing 40 per cent a year, from a base annual per capita wine consumption of 7 ml! Market estimates suggest that this will rise to 1 l by 2005, creating a total local demand of one billion bottles. Several major French, German, and Australian companies have been exploring JOINT VENTURE possibilities. R.M.B., S.C., & D.G.

Indicação de Proveniencia Regulamentada, the second tier of designated wine regions in PORTUGAL. See IPR.

Indonesia has one solitary wine-making enterprise, Hatten Wines, founded in 1992 and operating on the southern tip of the exotic resort island of Bali. The grapes, however, are grown at the northern extreme of the island, where the ELEVATION provides some modest respite from the relentless TROPICAL heat and humidity but climatic conditions are such that the vines crop almost continuously. The winery

has made both still and traditional-method SPARKLING WINES. D.G.

Inferno, subzone of VALTELLINA in the far north of Italy.

information technology has revolutionized the world of wine as much as any other. Computers are now used throughout the production process. In the vineyard, they can schedule and control IRRIGATION, for example, or measure weather and predict and even control SPRAYING regimes. They can assist vineyard site selection by analysing and mapping data on climate, soil, and topography. In the winery, they can weigh and sample grapes, control crushing and pressing operations, ensure the most vigilant TEMPERATURE CONTROL, and oversee bottling. They cannot, yet, oversee the progress of wine in individual barrels.

Thanks to information technology, wine analysis is today much more sophisticated than could have been imagined even a decade ago, and there have even been attempts to mechanize the process of TASTING. Information technology has greatly assisted such techniques as DNA 'FINGERPRINTING' in vine-variety identification, and the possible new technique of fingerprinting a vineyard by analysis of its minerals.

Those who sell wine can use information technology to administer all aspects of transport, storage, stock control, and retailing, as well as being able to present their wares to potential customers via the Internet—which can be an advantage when selling a commodity as tightly regulated as an alcoholic beverage.

As well as offering wine consumers a new market-place, for both buying and selling, and a new medium for wine information and EDUCATION, the Internet has provided them with an unprecedented forum for discussion.

Those who keep detailed cellar records and TASTING NOTES have reason to be grateful for the flexibility and sorting ability of personal computers.

As Internet technologies develop, the international wine market will be revolutionized. For example, we will be able to dispatch 'personal agents', smart pieces of software programmed with our tastes in wine, across the Internet in search of the precise wines we want according to parameters such as price, vintage, producer, variety, and APPELLATION.

It is also likely that wine AUCTIONS will be

transformed as Internet auctions are held in cyberspace, cutting out the auctioneer middlemen.

Eventually, the price of computing microchips is likely to fall to such an extent that every BOTTLE and CASE of wine will be networked with a chip costing a fraction of a penny. It is no fantasy to believe that by 2020, the uncorking of the last bottle in a case will automatically send an order to a local retailer for a refill. J.Ro. & R.S.L.

inner staves, or inserts. See BARREL INSERTS.

integrated pest management, or IPM, relatively new, environmentally friendly approach to the control of vineyard pests, diseases, and weeds. It has the potential result of increasing economic returns for the grower and improving environmental and human safety. Philosophically it is not dissimilar to ORGANIC VITICULTURE, although the judicious use of agrochemicals is allowed under IPM.

There is no doubt that pest and disease control in the vineyards of the future will rely less on calendar-based sprays of agrochemicals and more on timely application of remedies which are based on more thorough knowledge of the biology of the pest to be controlled.

R.E.S.

integrated production, or IP, European system of viticulture aimed at reducing environmental degradation in vineyards yet at the same time maintaining economic viability of viticulture. It is similar in philosophy to SUSTAINABLE VITICULTURE as practised in the USA. As the name suggests, it has its roots in INTEGRATED PEST MANAGEMENT, or IPM, which dates back to the mid 1970s in Europe. Initially developed for insect pests, IPM now encompasses diseases, weeds, and physiological vine disorders. R.E.S.

international varieties, loose term for those VINE VARIETIES with an international reputation for their VARIETAL wines. They are planted in almost every major wine region in which they stand a chance of ripening. Foremost among them are the red wine variety Cabernet Sauvignon and the white wine variety Chardonnay (which many consumers take to be either a place or, more usually, a BRAND). Other strong candidates as international varieties are Merlot, Pinot Noir, and Syrah/Shiraz among reds and Sauvignon Blanc, Riesling, Muscat, Gewürztraminer, Viognier,

Sémillon, and possibly Pinot Blanc and Pinot Gris among whites. As wine-makers and wine consumers constantly search for new excitement, the list of possibilities grows longer. Mourvèdre, Tempranillo, Sangiovese, and Nebbiolo could already be said to have joined this elite.

Internet. See INFORMATION TECHNOLOGY.

invecchiato, Italian for aged.

investment in wine is the acquisition of wine for gain, whether as a means of making money or financing consumption or a combination of the two.

'This crisis is perfectly rational. It was even foreseeable. The day I saw in *Time* magazine a photograph of a bank vault with a bottle of Lafite in it, I assembled my staff and told them: "the crisis has started". Indeed from the moment when you start to think of wine as an investment and not as something to be drunk, that's the end' (Baron Elie de Rothschild of Ch LAFITE-Rothschild, quoted in *The Winemasters* by Nicholas Faith).

The principal object of wine investment is to make a profit on wine which has increased in value as it matures. The essential premise on which wine investment is based is that demand for the wine in question exceeds supply, a premise that is often hard to gauge accurately.

Speculation and buying for consumption need not be mutually exclusive. Indeed, spreading the risk by buying mixed portfolios of wine with both disposal and consumption in mind makes sound sense and is normally advised by companies dealing in wine investment. The benefits can make wine investment an attractive proposition. As a wasting asset with a life expectancy for tax purposes of less than 50 years, wine does not generally attract Capital Gains Tax in Great Britain. There may, however, be circumstances in which tax officials would regard wine investment as a business and tax it accordingly. Vintage PORT, in particular, with a life expectancy of 50 years or more, is liable not to be regarded as a wasting asset for tax purposes.

But wine investment is inevitably a gamble, especially for anyone under the mistaken impression that making money from it is simply a question of holding on long enough to one's stock. Speculation in wine tends to be especially risky because wine is subject to both the vagaries of the weather and the unpredictable fluctuations of market forces. Buyers' and sellers' markets come and go and wine PRICES are as liable to go down as up. BORDEAUX is the principal medium of wine investment.

How to minimize the risks

In order to fulfil the promise of any investment, timing, knowledge, and skill (not to mention a measure of luck) are all essential preconditions for would-be investors, whether individuals or companies. Timing requires knowledge both of market conditions and of the potential of a wine for maturing. The finer the wine, generally speaking, the longer it takes to reach its peak, and the longer it remains on a plateau of maturity. It takes knowledge and skill to be aware of and interpret the likely future trends of individual properties and vintages, taking into account their real and perceived qualities. (One of the best ways to acquire such knowledge is to keep abreast of the pronouncements of the most influential wine critics, notably Robert PARKER. It is not easy to gauge precisely to what extent their opinions affect FASHION and therefore price, but there is undoubtedly a relationship.)

At the same time, investors need to be aware of less immediately obvious features of wine investment such as the importance of optimum STORAGE conditions, the costs involved, and the disposal options.

Investors need also to take full account of the buying options. If the conditions are right, the simplest and most attractive method of purchasing is buying EN PRIMEUR, as buying futures is known in the French wine trade.

Wine may also be bought at AUCTION, in which case care should be taken to ensure that the wine has been properly stored and that the initial outlay is not prohibitive. For both reasons, any such purchase should be made at a commercial auction house holding regular, professionally run sales, such as Christie's or Sotheby's. And wine should ideally be bought in complete, original CASES offered in BOND, to avoid the additional expenses of paying duty and any value added tax.

Suitable wines for investment

The factors that make wine a worthwhile investment are numerous and complex. For one thing, political and economic auguries, specific market conditions, and likely future trends all need to be taken into account. Purchasing is always best made in a buyer's market when conditions allow investors to take advantage of low prices such as occurred in the mid

1970s following the Bordeaux crisis, or during a glut as occurred at the end of the 1980s. A period of relatively high inflation too, in contributing towards the creation of demand and putting pressure on supplies, such as occurred at the end of the 1960s and early 1980s, may also help bring about the desired preconditions for investing in wine.

The type and format of wine chosen must be intrinsically capable of increasing sufficiently in value over a period of time. Generally speaking, investment wines should be capable of ageing for a good 20 years or longer so that investors are able to hold on to the wines and sell when the market is right (although the fine-wine market today seems to prefer young wines to old). Investment wines must either have an established reputation or, where the investor is in a position to evaluate likely trends, be lesser-known wines with the potential to gain in value. And, where appropriate, wines should come from a good, preferably great, vintage and should be capable of being easily traded. Account should be taken of the fact that magnums and LARGE FORMAT bottles are popular with COLLECTORS.

Only a handful of wines fulfil these limited but strict criteria. Beyond wines with established reputations, the market for investment becomes too highly specialized for any but the best-informed insiders to dabble in with any degree of confidence or measure of success.

A.H.L.R.

Inzolia, sometimes spelt **Insolia**, white grape variety grown mainly in Sicily and to a much more limited extent in Tuscany. Known also as Ansonica or Anzonica, it is grown mainly in western Sicily, where it is valued as a relatively aromatic ingredient, often with the much more common CATARRATTO, in dry white table wines. The best examples show a certain nuttiness, the worst could do with more acid and more flavour. It may be related to the Ghirghentina of MALTA.

IPR stands for Indicação de Proveniencia Regulamentada, a second-tier designated wine region in PORTUGAL. In theory, all are candidates for promotion to full DOC status but few of the 31 regions delimited in the late 1980s and early 1990s are likely to make the grade. Portugal's IPRs are an approximate, if proportionately more significant, counterpart to the VDQS wines of FRANCE, with specified grape varieties, minimum alcohol content, and maximum yields. Several years after the legislation, however, the laws remained confused, and many of Portugal's wine producers were either ignoring them or labelling their wines VQPRD, standing for Vinho de Qualidade Produzido em Região Determinada but also the standard European Union abbreviation for quality wine produced in a specific region.

R.J.M.

Irancy, town near Chablis country whose light-red Pinot Noir has a certain reputation. See Côtes d'AUXERRE.

Ireland, or Irish Republic, country with several small vineyards (not dissimilar to those of ENGLAND).

Irouléguy, unique and isolated French wine appellation in BASQUE country in the extreme south west of the country fuelled almost entirely by national pride. The language and lettering used on labels here are distinctively Basque, with a heavy sprinkling of Xs. These vineyards of lower NAVARRE and the Spanish CHACOLÍ DE GUETARIA are the last officially recognized vestiges of what was once a thriving wine industry. An APPELLATION CONTRÔLÉE was granted in 1970, and by the early 1990s the vineyard area was once again expanding. About 100 ha of vineyards are now cultivated by about 60 vine-growers (one of them the winemaker at Ch PÉTRUS, no less), many of them on TERRACES cut painstakingly from steep, south-facing slopes in the Pyrenees. The vines are protected from north winds and enjoy more sunshine than most French wine regions. The local TANNAT grape must be blended with at least as much Cabernet Sauvignon or Cabernet Franc and much of the wine produced is a fragrant, relatively substantial rosé, although an increasing amount of red wine is made and Domaine Brana, one of the few wine producers outside the CO-OPERATIVE, also makes a little distinctive white wine from COURBU, GROS MANSENG, and PETIT MANSENG.

irrigation, the application of water to growing plants such as vines, effectively a man-made simulation of rainfall, which can be useful in drier regions. Few vineyard practices are more maligned than irrigation.

In its commonly visualized form, irrigation is carried out in hot, arid regions, and employs heavy furrow or sprinkler irrigation to maximize yield for bulk wines. That is the background for the widely held view, especially in France, that only DRYLAND VITICULTURE can produce outstanding wines, and that irrigation inevitably reduces quality.

Widespread adoption of trickle irrigation since the 1960s has now greatly blurred the distinction. The technique has found its major viticultural use for supplementary watering. That is, the vineyards rely mainly on natural rainfall, and irrigation is used to make up deficits.

While a modicum of WATER STRESS is desirable to encourage fruit RIPENING and enhance wine quality, excessive water stress has serious implications. In these circumstances, irrigation applied in a restricted fashion can actually improve quality.

Irrigation is widely practised in the New World but less frequently in the Old. In principle, it is banned in much of the European Union other than for young vines, but this is a restriction which is easy, if initially quite expensive, to flout. While some still believe that irrigation is intrinsically inimical to wine quality, and there are many examples of deliberate over-irrigation, some of those who deliberately install irrigation systems in southern Europe are motivated by the desire to make better wine (see COSTERS DEL SEGRE, for example).

Methods of irrigation vary considerably. The ancient method is **flood irrigation**. For this to work, the vineyard floor must be flat and the rows not too long. More recent developments have been **sprinkler** and **drip** (or **trickle**) **irrigation**. Both are capable of delivering exact amounts of water fairly uniformly over a vineyard.

R.E.S.

Irsay Oliver, aromatic, relatively recent white vine crossing (Pozsony × Pearl of Csaba) grown in SLOVAKIA and also known in HUNGARY as **Irsai Olivér**. It produces relatively heavy, but intensely aromatic, wines strongly reminiscent of MUSCAT.

Isabella, sometimes Isabelle, widely distributed and widely planted *labrusca × vinifera* American HYBRID of unknown origin. It has been planted all over Portugal, the Ukraine, Japan, and occasionally crops up in the southern hemisphere, notably in Brazil, where it is by a substantial margin the leading vine. In New York state, it has largely been replaced by CONCORD. New plantings were banned in France in 1934. The vine is high yielding but the wines are very obviously FOXY.

Ischia, island and tourist destination in the bay of Naples in the Italian region of CAMPANIA which has managed to preserve a small part of the vineyards which once covered a significant part of the island. The DOC Ischia wine exists in both red and white versions: the former from GUARNACCIA grapes plus some PIEDIROSSO and a little BARBERA, the latter from Forastera with Biancolella and others. A Bianco Superiore, with at least 50 per cent Biancolella, is also produced with both lower yields and more alcohol. D'Ambra, the island's principal producer, also makes 100 per cent VARIETAL wines from Forastera, Biancolella, and Piedirosso (the last of which is called by its local name Per'e Palummo); originally marketed as VINO DA TAVOLA but now DOC wines, they showed marked improvement in the 1980s and indicate that Biancolella and Piedirosso have an interesting future.   D.T.

Isonzo, small DOC in the extreme north east of Italy in the FRIULI region. The zone produces, with the aid of cold technology, the fruity reds and the aromatic whites which typify the wines of Friuli. TOCAI Friulano, PINOT GRIGIO, Sauvignon Blanc, and PINOT BIANCO are the significant white varieties; Merlot and Cabernet (with a dominance of Cabernet Franc) are the important red grapes planted.

The wines have been slower to emerge and find their place in the market than those of COLLIO and the COLLI ORIENTALI. This lesser reputation, coupled with higher yields, has resulted in lower prices and some spotty quality, although the better producers of the Isonzo have demonstrated that the wines can compete with the better products of their neighbours to the north.   D.T.

Israel lays claim to being the cradle of the world's wine industry, yet has leapt to international prominence only since new, cooler vineyards were planted in the Golan Heights in the early 1980s.

Climate

The vine thrives in Israel's conditions. The seasons divide in two: the winter with rain from October to March, and the summer almost totally dry from April to October. IRRIGATION is essential to nourish the vines, which are pruned to provide maximum shade for the grapes from the harsh sunlight. Much harvesting is mechanical, the white varieties being picked mainly at night to minimize temperatures.

Geography

By the mid 1990s, the area dedicated to vines for wine production had increased rapidly to 3,000 ha/7,500 acres. Israel's viticulture is divided into five regions: Galilee (Galil in Hebrew) in northern Israel, including the Golan Heights; Samaria (Shomron), upper central Israel, south of Haifa and including Mount Carmel; Samson (Shimshon), lower coastal Israel between the Judean lowlands and the coastal plain; the Judean Hills (Harey Yehuda), including the hill vineyards around Jerusalem and the West Bank; and the Negev, southern, desert Israel.

Vine varieties

Descendants of the original cuttings imported from France—Carignan, Grenache, Alicante Bouschet, Sémillon, Chenin Blanc, and Muscat of Alexandria—are still widely planted. In the more recently planted vineyards, however, particularly those in the cooler areas of Galilee, varieties such as Cabernet Sauvignon, Merlot, Sauvignon Blanc, Riesling, and Chardonnay (the latter used for sparkling as well as still wines) have been planted with considerable success. The high-altitude vineyards tend to produce much more elegant wines than those made in the coastal areas, where acid levels tend to be low.

Modern wine production

In the mid 1990s, Israel's total annual production of a wide range of wine types was 30 million bottles, of which 15 to 20 per cent was exported. Most vineyards are owned either by Kibbutz or Moshavim (collective and co-operative farms) although there are some private owners.

The dominant, and oldest, producer is the co-operative based at Rishon Le Zion and Zichron Jaacov, which accounts for as much as 60 per cent of the domestic market and exports rather sweet, heady sacramental wines and table wines as well as spirits and liqueurs under the brand name Carmel. Modern wine-making techniques are most apparent at the newer wineries Tishbi Estate and Golan Heights, where picking at optimum RIPENESS, TEMPERATURE CONTROL, and the use of new OAK barrels resulted in dramatic improvement in wine quality. Golan Heights sells under the names Yarden, Gamla, and Golan, in declining order of price.

Most Israeli wines exported are produced by either Carmel or Golan Heights but other, smaller exporters include Tishbi, Barkan and, to a lesser extent, Binyamina, Segal, and Efrat.

In all there are more than 20 wineries in Israel, including estate wineries at Kibbutz-Tsora, Moshav-Dalton and the Latroun Monastery. The 1990s saw the establishment of several BOUTIQUE wineries, the best of which are Margalit, Castel, and Meron.

See also KOSHER (although not all Israel's wine is kosher).   P.A.H.

Italian Riesling, or Italian Rizling; sometimes **Italianski Rizling**, white grape variety. See RIESLING ITALICO and WELSCHRIESLING.

Italy, with FRANCE one of the world's two mammoth wine producers, producing annual volumes of wine which sometimes reach 60 million hl/1,584 million gal. Italy has more land under vine than any other country with the exception of SPAIN, although thanks to the European VINE PULL SCHEME, the total has been reduced from close to 1.4 million ha/3.4 million acres in the early 1990s to 922,000 ha/2.3 million acres by 1996. Italy routinely exports more wine than any other country, including France—much of it inexpensive wine for BLENDING in and possible re-export from France and Germany.

Unlike either France or Spain, however, the vine is cultivated virtually everywhere in the Italian peninsula, from the Alps in the north to islands that are closer to the coast of North Africa than to the Italian mainland. Viticulture impinges on the national consciousness, on the national imagination, and on daily life in a way that is hardly conceivable to those not accustomed to the Mediterranean way of life and its dietary trinity of bread, olive oil, and wine; until the late 1980s, it was unthinkable for Italians to sit down and eat without wine on the table.

The Italian's relationship to wine is not necessarily a hedonistic one. The average Italian is far from a connoisseur of fine bottles, but is rather the heir of thousands of years of vineyard cultivation and wine-making. The result is what might be called the Italian paradox: a country with a plurimillennial tradition of wine, a country where wine is omnipresent in the nation's life and customs, is also a country where wine is, for the most part, taken for granted in the national consciousness. While France and Germany played a major role from the beginning of the age of modern wine—an era in which wine circulates

in bottles with labels which identify both its provenance and its maker—wine in most of Italy was sold in bulk until well after the Second World War and little of the country's better wine was exported until the 1970s. Knowledge of non-Italian viticulture and OENOLOGY was virtually non-existent in Italy, and circulation of foreign wines was confined to a tiny élite in the country's major cities. Even in the early 1990s, wine appreciation was an activity of very little significance to Italians.

D.T.

Geography and climate

Generalizations about a peninsula 1,200 km/750 miles long extending through about 10 degrees of LATITUDE are not easy. The dominant geographical feature of the 'boot' is the Apennines, which begin close to the border with France and then form the central ridge, the national spinal column, down the peninsula to the 'toe' in Calabria. In the far north are the Alps; in Sicily, the Madonie form yet another chain of central mountains. Good-quality viticulture is almost entirely a HILLSIDE phenomenon in Italy, and the Grave del Friuli and other flat viticultural areas of Friuli do not produce wine at the same quality level as the higher nearby districts of COLLIO and COLLI ORIENTALI.

Climate is inevitably affected by ALTITUDE. Latitude is not a sure guide to temperature and further south is not always synonymous with hotter temperatures. Altitude, exposure, wind currents, topography, soil composition, and proximity to the sea are other relevant factors. Umbria is generally cooler than Tuscany albeit further to the south; a wide span of central Italy—Umbria, the Marches, Latium—is more renowned for its white wines than for its reds, while Piedmont, in the far north on the French and Swiss border, is principally a producer of powerful, dense red wines. Even Sicily produces considerably more white wine than red.

Poor VINTAGES are by no means a strange or inexplicable phenomenon in Italy, and in a typical decade there are usually at least two vintages of unacceptable quality.

Wine-making

Substantial investments in cellar equipment have made Italian wine-making facilities some of the most modern in Europe, and Italians make equipment such as bottling lines that is some of the best, and most exported, in the world.

Wooden fermentation vessels have, for better or for worse, been eliminated and, although cement vats and tanks are still widely in use both for fermentation and for storage, stainless-steel tanks are very much more common. TEMPERATURE CONTROL is widely accepted. The lengthy fermentations and MACERATIONS of the past have been shortened.

WHITE-WINE-MAKING techniques changed drastically in the 1970s and 1980s, with the introduction of cool fermentations, filters, and centrifuges. The most fundamental change of all, however, has been the end of the practice of fermenting white wines on their skins, which was once widespread in Friuli and throughout central Italy. Gains in lightness and freshness have been obvious, even if at the price of a certain standardization. Producing white wines of more character without sacrificing the newly achieved crispness and cleanliness is the current challenge for Italian white-wine-making.

Fermentation may have evolved considerably in the second half of the 20th century, but ÉLEVAGE has undergone more profound modifications during the same period. Large casks have always been the preferred containers for AGEING red wine in Italian cellars; long ageing periods, particularly for what were considered the grandest wines, was an almost unvarying rule; wood of a certain age was generally preferred to new wood (although this may often have been for financial rather than qualitative reasons). Current practice favours smaller casks; ageing periods have been diminished, but many of Italy's most renowned red wines have tannins which need a considerable time in cask to soften and round, and periods of two years in cask (for Chianti Classico Riserva, Barolo, and Vino Nobile di Montepulciano), or even three years in cask (for Brunello di Montalcino and Barolo Riserva), are by no means uncommon. Regular replacement of excessively old wood has been accepted as an integral part of correct cellar techniques.

OAK has generally been the preferred wood for casks, much of it from Slovenia or elsewhere in central Europe. In the south of Italy, in areas such as the Basilicata and Sicily, where chestnut forests abound and there are no local sources of oak, the traditional chestnut casks are gradually being replaced by oak casks to achieve a more international style and to avoid the bitterness which old chestnut casks can impart. French oak became increasingly popular, if controversial, in the 1980s, initially in the form of BARRIQUES to be supplemented by larger casks. Sangiovese and Barbera were the first varieties to be widely aged in new small oak barrels, and the generally positive results have led to widespread use of BARREL MATURATION in many zones of Italy, albeit only by the most ambitious producers. Their use for such international varieties as Cabernet, Merlot, Pinot Noir, Chardonnay, and Sauvignon Blanc is also a recent phenomenon which has yielded both excellent results and some heavily over-oaked wines.

General inexperience in modern wine-making techniques is a chronic problem in Italy, where fine wine is such a recent phenomenon. This led to a major boom, particularly in the 1980s and 1990s, in the employment of consulting OENOLOGISTS in Tuscany, Piedmont, and Friuli, the three most important fine-wine regions, a practice which was to spread to Umbria and the Marches.

Vine varieties

Despite the recent appearance of widely acclaimed wines from INTERNATIONAL VARIETIES, Italian viticulture as a whole remains firmly wedded to traditional, indigenous varieties, whose number has been estimated as over 2,000. Of the country's 20 most widely planted grapes, only Merlot is an obvious import. According to an agricultural census conducted in 1990, Sangiovese was by far the most planted variety in Italy, followed by the Sicilian white grape Catarratto, the central Italian white Trebbiano Toscano, Piedmont's Barbera, Merlot, Apulia's Negroamaro, the central and southern red Montepulciano, Trebbiano Romagnolo, Primitivo of the south, and white Malvasia. See articles on individual regions and zones for the names of other Italian vine varieties.

Large-scale plantings of international varieties—principally French, although there is also some Riesling and Gewürztraminer—are on the whole confined to the country's north east and have tended to follow international FASHION: various members of the Pinot family in the 1970s; Chardonnay, Sauvignon Blanc, and Cabernet in the 1980s; Syrah and Viognier in the 1990s. Central Italy, with only the late-ripening Sangiovese an important red grape and with the relatively uninteresting Trebbiano as its major white grape, is likely to see expanded plantings of international varieties in the coming decades. The high costs of viti-culture in its important hillside zones make it imperative to obtain a higher return from the vineyards, an objective which may be real-izable only with non-native varieties and which may lead to neglect of the less well-known native varieties with a significant potential such as MONTEPULCIANO D'ABRUZZO, COLORINO, and GRECHETTO.

Organization of trade

Italy's wine trade resembles those of its Euro-pean neighbours in terms of a division of labour between individual properties, com-mercial and NÉGOCIANT houses, and CO-OPERA-TIVE wineries. What distinguishes Italy is the overwhelming importance of the latter two cat-egories, a dominance which is the direct result of the extreme fractioning of vineyard prop-erty. Close to 40 per cent of the country's agri-cultural properties grow grapes and the average size of their 'vineyards' is 0.8 ha. Private estates of a certain size are an import-ant reality only in Tuscany and, to a lesser extent, in Friuli, while the recent development of a significant number of prestigious small 'domaines' in the finest zones of Piedmont might be considered a miniature, but embry-onic, version of Burgundy. It is no coincidence that these are the three regions producing Italy's best wines.

Large commercial houses were a relatively late development in Italy, virtually all of them having been founded after the unification of the country in 1861, and even today négociant houses are a major presence only in Tuscany,

the Veneto, and Sicily, while co-operative win-eries play a more significant role in other Italian regions. They became the dominant force in the production and distribution of Italian wine in the late 20th century. Quality has not always been the strong point of the resulting wines, although individual co-opera-tives, particularly in the north, have always been responsive to the market.

As European Union and national subsidies are reduced, Italian wines will have to respond more readily to free-market economics. Rapidly falling wine consumption (in Italy alone, per capita consumption fell more than 50 per cent between 1960 and 1990) signals that a fundamental modification of Italy's pro-duction philosophy is only a matter of time.

There can be few doubts that Italy's new pros-perity and the worldwide popularity of the 'Mediterranean diet' (a shorthand, in most cases, for Italian cooking) have changed pro-spects and possibilities for Italian wine and created a new viewpoint amongst the country's producers. And there can be even fewer doubts that admirers and enthusiasts of Italian wine have never had such an embarrassment of riches.

For details of individual regions, see ABRUZZI, ALTO ADIGE, APULIA, BASILICATA, CALABRIA, CAM-PANIA, EMILIA ROMAGNA, FRIULI, LATIUM, LIGURIA, LOMBARDY, MARCHES, MOLISE, PIED-MONT, SARDINIA, SICILY, TRENTINO, TUSCANY, UMBRIA, Valle d'AOSTA, and VENETO.

For details of terms to be found on Italian wine labels, see CLASSICO, DOC, DOCG, IGT, RISERVA, and VINO DA TAVOLA.   D.T.

Jaboulet Aîné, Paul, important RHÔNE-valley merchant and wine producer, whose most famous wine is Hermitage la Chapelle. The house was founded in the early 19th century by Antoine Jaboulet and takes its name from the older of his twin sons. Jaboulet's own vineyard holdings, which provide between a quarter and a third of the firm's needs, totalled more than 90 ha/220 acres, in every northern Rhône appellation but Côte Rôtie in the late 1990s. Of the raw materials bought in, from 150 growers the length of the Rhône valley, two-thirds is wine rather than grapes. Jaboulet sell a range of more than 20 different wines, most of them in the firm's own deep-PUNTED bottle, and the best are their own special cuvées. Their CROZES-HERMITAGE, Domaine de Thalabert, was some of the earliest proof offered to wine drinkers outside France that this appellation could produce serious, age-worthy wine. Some vintages of their CHÂT-EAUNEUF-DU-PAPE, Les Cèdres, and CÔTE RÔTIE, Les Jumelles, have been exemplars of those appellations. Other blends can be less distinctive, but Jaboulet's red and white HER-MITAGE, La Chapelle and Chevalier de Stérimberg respectively, are extremely fine wines. La Chapelle 1961 is an acknowledged classic, and Chevalier de Stérimberg demonstrates the late Gérard Jaboulet's admiration for the ROUSSANNE grape.

Jacquère is the common white grape variety in SAVOIE, where it produces high yields of lightly scented, essentially Alpine dry white. It is also successfully grown in some CONDRIEU vineyards even though it is not permitted by the APPELLATION CONTRÔLÉE regulations.

Jadot, Louis, merchant-grower based in BEAUNE, dealing exclusively in Burgundy and owners of some 50 ha/122 acres of vineyards in the CÔTE D'OR and 35 ha/86 acres in BEAUJOLAIS. Founded in 1859 by the eponymous Louis Jadot, it has been owned since 1985 by its American importer Kobrand.

Both red and white NÉGOCIANT wines, made from bought-in fruit, are thoroughly reliable, but the firm's reputation is based on the high quality of its domain wines. Jadot's holdings increased during the 1980s with the acquisition of the cream of the Clair Daü and Maison Champy vineyards, followed by substantial purchases in Beaujolais in the 1990s. The company also manages and vinifies the Côte d'Or vineyards of Domaine Gagey and Domaine Duc de Magenta. A large, beautiful, and flexible new winery was accordingly built on the Jadot premises in 1997. Among the reds, the Côte de Beaune wines stand out, with the MONOPOLE Beaune, Clos des Ursules, being especially fine. The domain whites are wines of concentration, class, and distinction. Never over-oaked, they are a clear expression of their TERROIR and wines such as their Puligny-Montrachet, Les Folatières; Corton-Charlemagne; and Chevalier-Montrachet, Les Demoiselles, are regularly among the best bottles of white burgundy to be had.   M.W.E.S.

Jaen, widely planted red grape in Portugal's DÃO region, where it ripens early to produce alcoholic wines that are notable for their lack of acidity and normally stiffened with TOURIGA NACIONAL and ALFROCHEIRO PRETO. The vine is thought to be identical to Galicia's MENCÍA.

Jaén Blanco Spanish white grape that is said by some to be Portugal's AVESSO.

Jahrgang, German for VINTAGE (as in the year rather than the HARVEST process, for which the word is *Ernte*).

Jampal, southern Portuguese grape variety with possibly unrealized potential.

Japan. Grape-growing and, to a lesser extent, wine production have a long history in this Far Eastern country, even though wine drinking on any appreciable scale is a relatively recent phenomenon. Between 1993 and 1997, wine consumption doubled but was still relatively low. The typical wine made from Japanese grapes (as opposed to the typical Japanese wine) was sweetish, white, and noticeably light.

Geography and climate
Grapes are now grown in 46 of the 47 prefectures, the exception being tropical Okinawa. Three prefectures (Yamanashi, Yamagata, and Nagano) on the main island, Honshu, however, account for 40 per cent of the 26,000 ha/64,220 acres under vine throughout Japan. Only one-tenth of these grapes are used for wine-making.

Japan's climate is not naturally suited to viticulture and successful grape-growing has always been a struggle. In Yamanashi Prefecture, where 27 per cent of Japan's grapes are grown and around two-thirds of the wine is made, a monsoonal climate presents a serious problem of excess water and humidity. Grapes from the district of Katsunuma, with about 15 per cent of the Prefecture's vines, are those generally preferred by wine-makers. Katsunuma fares considerably better climatically than districts lower down in the Kōfu basin, with better ripening conditions for wine grapes generally. Yamagata and Nagano prefectures do better again but conditions are still far from ideal.

In the 1960s, a second frontier of the modern Japanese industry was opened up in an even more unlikely location, in central Hokkaidō, Japan's northernmost island. This is an extremely cold environment for grape-growing.

Vine varieties
History, the dominant demand for TABLE GRAPES, and the climatic vagaries with which growers have had to contend over the years, have combined to result in the rather exotic range of grape varieties which form the basis of viticulture in Japan.

Strictly speaking, there are no vines native to Japan. There are several introduced vines which have evolved here uniquely, however, and these are now regarded justifiably as Japanese varieties.

The most significant of these is the *Vitis* VINIFERA Koshu, which is most suitable as a table grape, but is also used to make a wine which is almost colourless and, as might be expected, without a great deal of body.

Neo-Muscat, a variety developed from a crossing of Koshu Sanjaku with MUSCAT OF ALEXANDRIA, is also *vinifera* and is now, in fact, more widely planted than Koshu, but is less well known. Another Koshu cousin, Ryugan (also known as Senkoji, and probably the same as the Longyan of CHINA), is grown only in tiny quantities, chiefly in Nagano Prefecture in central Honshu. As with Koshu, Neo-Muscat and Ryugan produce grapes which are best suited to the table, but which are also made into light and generally sweetish wine.

In Hokkaidō, a vine growing wild in the region for centuries and known locally as *yamabudo* (literally, mountain grape) has been the subject of a great deal of research and genetic development since the 1960s. The variety has been identified as belonging to the oriental, cold-resistant *amurensis* species of *Vitis* originating along the Amur river which forms the border between China and Siberia. The only wine of this variety is produced in small quantities by the large Tokachi winery at Ikeda, in central Hokkaidō, from grapes picked in the wild by local townsfolk. The small black berries make an interesting, although unconventional, red wine with a distinctive gamey bouquet and an austere, earthy palate. It is labelled, simply, Amurensis.

However, the vines which are by far the most widely planted throughout Japan, accounting for almost 80 per cent of the total area under vine, are HYBRIDS based on *Vitis* LABRUSCA, most of which were introduced directly from the United States. DELAWARE is most popular, comprising around a third of the total vineyard area.

Industry organization
Japan's first (and much-vaunted in Europe) 'wine boom' saw per capita consumption

double during the 1980s, albeit from a low base. Consumption levelled off towards the end of the decade but a second wine boom quickly gathered momentum around 1993, when a strong yen encouraged a surge in imports. Annual per capita consumption was almost two litres by 1997, encouraging local wine producers to improve the quality of their wines to better profit from this growth in demand.

Initially they had focused on investment in modern wine-making equipment and on training their wine-makers in the methods used in the major wine-producing nations (Suntory even went so far as to buy the ST-JULIEN classed growth Ch Lagrange, and the 1980s saw several substantial Japanese investments in the California and Australian wine industries). They had hoped that this, along with various practices in the winery aimed at extracting more flavour and body from the flimsy local fruit base, would be sufficient to match the competition from the foreign producers.

The domestic industry has also tried to hold its ground by using imported bulk wine, GRAPE CONCENTRATE, MUST, and even imported grapes to extend the quantity and improve the quality of its own base material. Labelling laws have allowed considerable leeway for producers in this regard and some wines sold as domestic BRANDS are known to contain the barest minimum of genuine domestic material.

But the increasing sophistication of the Japanese consumer and the persistence of the European and New World producers has seen, nevertheless, major inroads into the domestic industry's hold on the market. Furthermore, the extent to which even this reduced market share depends on imported product is now more readily evident because of a voluntary labelling code, adopted by the Japan Wineries Association. Wine bottled under domestic labels must now be declared either as *kokunai san* (domestic wine) or *yunyu san* (imported bulk wine). If they are blended, the larger portion must be specified first.

Genuine domestic wine can command a significant premium. Increasingly, serious producers make a feature of this on their labels when they can. To be called *kokunai san* the wine has to have been wholly fermented in Japan, although some imported grapes or must is still allowed. The wine-makers of Katsunuma have taken this one stage further with a certificate of origin seal for the district's top wines. Belatedly, therefore, wine-makers have come to accept that if they are to retain their relevance in the domestic wine market they will have to do it with inherent quality. In turn, this will require major alterations to vineyard practices.

The large domestic wine producers rely overwhelmingly on bought-in grapes. Most of them do also have vineyards, but these are small and primarily for experimental purposes.

The small number of growers who also make and sell their own wine, therefore, may represent some of the most interesting possibilities for Japanese wine quality, at least in the short term. Some have been responsible for serious attempts to improve the quality of wine and, as small-scale operations, their outcomes are more readily discernible.

Both large and small producers have accelerated their efforts recently to expand the small area of land planted to superior European *vinifera* varieties. However, such varieties comprised little more than five per cent of the total area under vine in the late 1990s.

In contrast to the fragmentation of the grape-growing industry, wine-making is extraordinarily concentrated. Five giant, diversified beverage conglomerates account for three-quarters of the total production of wine. Suntory (with Chateau Lion, Delica, and Wine Café as its main labels) and Sanraku (using the Mercian label) vie for top position accounting for almost half the industry's total production. They are followed by brewer Sapporo (Polaire label) and Manns Wine (subsidiary of soy sauce maker Kikkoman), who together account for another 15 per cent of the market. Kyowa Hakko Kogyo (Ste Neige label) has just over three per cent. The largest of the remainder is Tokachi winery in Hokkaidō

Some of the best wines in Japan are to be found amongst the much smaller family-owned or city-owned wineries. In Yamanishi, benchmark Koshu is produced by Marufuji (Rubaiyat label), Kizan, Katsunuma Jō zō, and Grace wineries. Some of the better examples of Cabernet Sauvignon and Chardonnay are found among this group too. Other small wineries with a reputation for quality include Alps (Merlot from Nagano), Takeda (Cabernet, Merlot, and Chardonnay from Yamagata), Okuizumo (Chardonnay from Shimane), and Kobe Wine in Hyogo prefecture. D.G.

Jardin de la France is the cleverly evocative name devised for the Loire, 'garden of France', as a vast VIN DE PAYS regional entity. It has been one of the most successful vins de pays, typically a red made from Gamay and Grolleau, although one bottle in every three is a white, which may be made from Sauvignon Blanc, Chardonnay, and/or Chenin Blanc. Gamays and even Sauvignons are sometimes sold as PRIMEUR wines.

Jasnières, small but revived white-wine appellation in an enclave within the Coteaux du LOIR district in the northern Loire. The appellation all but expired in the 1950s but Joël Gigou at Domaine de la Charrière and others such as Domaine Renard-Potaire have injected new passion into the making of these traditionally dry wines from the Chenin Blanc grape. Locals see Jasnières as 'the SAVENNIÈRES of Touraine', so dry and steely are these traditional wines in their youth, and so well do they respond to BOTTLE AGEING. In particularly ripe vintages since the late 1980s, however, extraordinarily rich, appley, BOTRYTIZED wines have been fashioned, either dry or sweet according to the extent of NOBLE ROT infection.

The local VDQS is Coteaux du VENDÔMOIS. See also LOIRE.

Jerez, or Jerez de la Frontera, see SHERRY.

jeroboam. See BOTTLE SIZES.

João de Santarém, name used for the widely planted CASTELÃO FRANCÊS in parts of the Ribatejo region of Portugal.

Johannisberg, Valais name for fuller-than-average dry white wine made from SILVANER grapes in SWITZERLAND.

Johannisberg Riesling, sometimes abbreviated simply to JR, common synonym for the great white RIESLING grape variety of Germany, notably in California.

joint venture, increasingly common phenomenon in the world's wine business whereby two enterprises with very different strengths combine to produce a wine or wines. The modern prototype was that announced in 1979 between Baron Philippe de Rothschild of Bordeaux and Robert MONDAVI of California to produce Opus One, the luxuriously priced Napa Valley Cabernet Sauvignon, combining Mondavi's knowledge of and holdings in the Napa Valley with the prestige and wine-making expertise associated with Baron Philippe's first growth Pauillac Ch MOUTON-ROTHSCHILD. Most joint ventures are designed to justify a premium over the other wines made *in situ* by

virtue of a much-heralded connection with a glamorous outsider. Joint ventures are particularly well suited to new wine regions such as those in CHINA and INDIA, for example, where the wine-making expertise of an established wine producer blends well with an enterprise which can offer local knowledge and contacts.

Jordan, Middle Eastern country which produces a small amount of wine each year from a total vineyard area of just 2,000 ha/5,000 acres, which is mainly dedicated to TABLE GRAPES.

joven, Spanish for young. Some wines destined for early consumption are sometimes sold as a Vino Joven.

Juan Garcia, crisp, lively, local speciality of the Fermoselle-Arribes zone west of TORO in north-west central Spain, where it is usually mixed in the vineyard with other, lesser vines. On rocky hillside sites, the vine can produce highly perfumed if relatively light reds.

Juan Ibañez, dark-berried vine grown to a limited extent and mainly in mixed vineyards in Cariñena in north-east central Spain. Known as Miguel del Arco in Calatayud.

judging wine, an activity that most wine drinkers undertake every time they open a new bottle, but also a serious business on which the commercial future of some wine producers may to a certain extent depend. For details of domestic, amateur wine judging, see TASTING.

The judging process at a more professional level can vary from a gathering of a few friends, a few bottles, and much hot air to an event in which wines have been carefully categorized by wine type, style, and possibly price and are tasted BLIND, in ideal conditions, without any consultation until a possible final discussion of controversial wines. SCORING systems vary but typically involve awarding a specific allocation of points for various different aspects such as appearance, nose, palate, perhaps TYPICITY, and overall quality. MEDALS and trophies are often awarded as a result. Wine shows, often part of much broader annual agricultural shows, are particularly important in Australia, where to be invited to act as a judge, or even associate judge, is a great honour. Wine judges usually wear white coats, work in silence, and may be expected to evaluate as many as 200 wines a day.

See also COMPETITIONS.

jugs for serving wine. See DECANTERS.

jug wine, term used in CALIFORNIA for the most basic sort of wine, an American counterpart to VIN ordinaire or PLONK. See also FIGHTING VARIETALS.

Juhfark, distinctive but almost extinct white grape variety once widely grown in HUNGARY but today found almost exclusively in the Somló region, where it can produce wine usefully high in acidity which ages well. It is usually blended with the more widely planted FURMINT and RIESLING.

Juliénas, one of the 10 BEAUJOLAIS crus in the far north of the region, producing wines with real backbone, although most should be drunk within two or three years of the vintage. Reliable producers include Jean-François Perraud and Michel Tête.

Jumilla, arid, denominated wine region in the LEVANTE north of Murcia in central, southern Spain producing mainly strong, often coarse, red wines. The principal grape variety in this DO is the red Monastrell (MOURVÈDRE), which produces wines that can reach a natural ALCOHOLIC STRENGTH of 18 per cent. Average YIELDS have been uneconomically low, but more recent planting of GRAFTED vines has improved prospects.

Much of the wine from Jumilla was traditionally produced by the DOBLE PASTA method and used for blending with lighter wines from other parts of Spain. The vast San Isidro CO-OPERATIVE dominates the region's production, although since the mid 1980s a number of smaller, private producers such as Agapito Rico and Casa Castillo have been striving, with some success, to tame Monastrell, often by blending it with Tempranillo or Merlot. The Merseguera grape produces rather fat, bland, hot-country white wine.   R.J.M. & V. de la S.

Jura, far eastern French wine region, between Burgundy and Switzerland, that is sufficiently isolated to have retained TRADITION, some unique grape varieties, and such unusual wine types as VIN JAUNE and the occasional VIN DE PAILLE, as well as the local VIN DE LIQUEUR, Macvin du Jura. Henri Maire is the dominant wine company.

Although this was once an important wine region, there are only about 1,500 ha of vineyards today, on slopes mainly at ALTITUDES of between 250 and 400 m/820–1,310 ft on the first upland between the Bresse plain and the Jura mountains. The chief town is Lons-le-Saunier, although Arbois, L'Étoile, and Ch-Chalon are more famous for their wines. The climate here is even more CONTINENTAL than in Burgundy and winters can be very cold.

Five grape varieties are of importance in modern Jura. PINOT NOIR and CHARDONNAY, the latter often known here proprietorially as Melon d'Arbois, have been borrowed from Burgundy, although they have been grown in the Jura vineyards since the Middle Ages. Chardonnay has been increasing in importance here as elsewhere, and had reached 45 per cent of total plantings by the late 1980s. Pinot Noir is valued because it can add useful colour and sometimes structure to the local POULSARD, often called Plousard, which is grown chiefly in the north of the region and makes deep-coloured rosés, often with an orange tint, sometimes described as *corail*. Poulsard may account for as much as 20 per cent of total vine plantings in the Jura. Another local red wine grape variety is TROUSSEAU, now extremely rare. It needs the additional warmth of gravelly soils to ripen and Pinot Noir has largely replaced it, but some producers are capable of fashioning it into a deep-flavoured VARIETAL wine.

The Jura's really distinctive grape variety, however, is the white SAVAGNIN, also called Naturé here, which is probably an antecedent of TRAMINER and hence GEWÜRZTRAMINER. Grown to a limited extent all over the region, it is a permitted ingredient in all of its white wines but in practice is chiefly used to produce the extraordinary, nutty, long-lived vin jaune, sold in the distinctive *clavelin* squat bottle. (Other Jura wines are mainly sold in another specially shaped bottle with the word Jura stamped on the shoulder.) See CHÂTEAU-CHALON and L'ÉTOILE, which specialize in this unusual drink, France's answer to top-quality dry SHERRY.

See also the more varied appellation ARBOIS. Most Jura appellations produced both sparkling and still wines, and vin de paille may be produced anywhere.

Wine-making techniques are generally traditional, and CHAPTALIZATION is as common as one would expect of a region sited between Burgundy and Switzerland. All grapes must have a POTENTIAL ALCOHOL of 10 per cent (much more for vin jaune and vin de paille), and may be chaptalized up to a final ALCOHOLIC STRENGTH of 13.5 per cent.

The wines are distinctive, particularly those which contain the local grape varieties, but remain a mainly local treat. At their worst they taste like thin burgundy; at their best they are particularly good candidates for FOOD AND WINE MATCHING. **Côtes du Jura** is the region's second most important appellation, after Arbois, and wines may be red, white, or dark pink; still or sparkling; vinified normally or matured slowly into vin jaune. About a fifth of the wine produced is still red or pink. Ch d'Arlay is one of the appellation's most notable producers. An increasing proportion of varietal wines are made, whether Chardonnay, Poulsard, Pinot Noir, or even Trousseau. **Côtes du Jura Mousseux** is generally dry white and must be made by the traditional method (see SPARKLING-WINE-MAKING).

Jurançon is a name closely associated with SOUTH WEST FRANCE, of a distinguished white wine both dry and sweet, of a relatively important, if undistinguished, dark-berried vine variety, and of an entirely unimportant light-berried vine.

The wine

This fashionable, tangy, distinctive white wine was one of France's earliest APPELLATION CONTRÔLÉES. PETIT MANSENG, GROS MANSENG, the local COURBU, and some local Camaralet and Lauzet vines are grown in this hilly, relatively cool corner of southern France near Pau at the relatively high average ALTITUDE of 300 m/984 ft. GROS MANSENG is chiefly responsible for Jurançon Sec, the more common dry but strongly flavoured version of this wine. Petit Manseng, with its small, thick-skinned berries, is ideal for the production of Jurançon's real speciality, sweet Jurançon made from grapes partially dried on the vine which in some years may not be harvested until December. If several TRIS are made through the vineyard (two are mandatory), the results may be bottled separately. These wines, whose green tinge seems to deepen with age, serve well as aperitifs and with a wide range of foods. One of France's best-value SWEET WINES is made particularly successfully by the likes of Bru-Baché, Cauhapé, and Clos Uroulat.

The vine varieties

Vines called Jurançon have in their time been cultivated in practically every region of South West France, other than Jurançon itself. The black- or red-berried Jurançon Noir was once the high-yielding ARAMON-like workhorse of this part of France. Some south-western appellations still sanction Jurançon Noir in their red wines, but its inclusion is today usually theoretical. **Jurançon Blanc** was once quite widely planted in Gascony but is nearly extinct.

Kabinett, typically delicate wines, the most basic Prädikat in the QMP quality-wine category defined by the GERMAN WINE LAW. Specific minimum MUST WEIGHTS are laid down for each combination of vine variety and region and are being increased. Because CHAPTALIZATION of QmP wines is not allowed, Kabinett wines are usually the lightest German wines and can make excellent APERITIFS. Their lack of BODY makes them generally less appropriate candidates for TROCKEN wine-making than SPÄT-LESE, the next ripest Prädikat.

Kadarka is the most famous red wine grape of HUNGARY, largely because of the important role it once played in BULL'S BLOOD. The variety is in marked decline and has been substantially replaced by the viticulturally sturdier KÉK-FRANKOS, and KÉKOPORTO in Villány, but it is still cultivated on the Great Plain and in the Szekszárd wine region just across the Danube to the west. Fully ripened Szekszárdi Kadarka can be a fine, tannic, full-bodied wine worthy of ageing but is produced in minuscule quantities. Kadarka is too often overproduced and picked when still low in colour and flavour and is no longer the backbone of Hungary's red-wine production.

Today the variety is cultivated on a very limited scale over the eastern border in Burgenland in Austria, over the southern border in Vojvodina in what was Yugoslavia, in Romania, where it is called Cadarca, and, most importantly, in Bulgaria, where it is called Gamza and is widely planted in the north, where it can produce wines of interest. See also IZSÁKI.

Kalterer or Kalterersee, German for the TREN-TINO and ALTO ADIGE zone known as Caldaro or Lago di Caldaro in Italian.

Kazakhstan, independent central Asian republic, member of the CIS. This large area south of Russia and bordering China is subject to great extremes of climate. Less than four per cent of Kazakhstan offers favourable soil and climatic conditions for commercial grape culture.

At present, 43 grape varieties are allowed, of which 24 are for TABLE GRAPES, an important crop here. Wine varieties include RKATSITELI, Riesling, Pinot Noir, SAPERAVI, ALIGOTÉ, ALE-ATICO, Bayan Shirey, Kuljinski, Maiski Cherny, Cabernet Franc, Cabernet Sauvignon, Rubinovy Magaratcha, Hungarian Muscat (probably MUSCAT OTTONEL), and Muscat Rosé.

The areas best suited for the production of high-quality table wines and sparkling wines are the foothills of the Dzhambul, the Alma-Ata, and the Chimkent regions. Lower and more southern vineyards specialize in dessert wines.

Kazakhstan has the potential to become one of the main suppliers of wines and especially grapes to eastern portions of Russia.   V.R.

kék means 'blue' in Hungarian and, as such, can be a direct equivalent of BLAU in German or even Noir in French.

Kékfrankos, Hungarian name for the red grape variety known in Austria as BLAU-FRÄNKISCH (of which it is a direct translation).

This useful variety, which produces lively, juicy, peppery, well-coloured reds for relatively early consumption, is grown widely in HUNGARY. It is most successful in Sopron near the Austrian border although it can also produce full-bodied wines in Villány. On the Great Plain, its wines can be relatively heavy.

Kéknyelü, revered but rare white grape variety grown in HUNGARY. Once widely planted, it was becoming rare even in its last stronghold Badacsony on the north shore of Lake Balaton in the mid 1990s. True, well-made Kéknyelü can be aromatic and exciting, but some very ordinary blends have been labelled Badacsony Kéknyelü.

Kékoporto, sometimes written **Kékoportó,** useful red grape variety in HUNGARY identified as Blauer PORTUGIESER. It produces well-coloured lively red wine not unlike that of KÉK-FRANKOS but with a little more body and possibly a better aptitude for cask ageing. It is grown in the red-wine region of Villány, where it can yield wines of real concentration, is an ingredient in BULL'S BLOOD, and is also grown, with slightly less success, on the Great Plain. It is often called simply Oporto (kék means 'blue') and is also grown in ROMANIA.

Keller is German for a cellar, even a small domestic cellar, while **Kellerei** is used in much the same way as the word CAVE in French, for any sort of wine-producing premises whether above or below ground. A German wine specifying a Keller rather than a WEINGUT on the label is usually the produce of a merchant rather than an estate. In the ALTO ADIGE, the Italian Tyrol, **Kellereigenossenschaft** is a common name for one of the many wine CO-OPERATIVES. **Kellermeister** is German for cellarmaster, a position very similar to MAÎTRE DE CHAI in France.

Kendall–Jackson, original brand name of the winery and vineyard empire begun by Jess Jackson (Kendall was his former wife's maiden name) in Lake County, California, during the mid 1970s. By the early 1990s, expansion and acquisition had resulted in such a proliferation of brand names that the formal title of the umbrella company was changed to Artisans & Estates, but in US trade jargon 'K-J' is still used for the whole collection, as well as for the Kendall–Jackson labels specifically.

In many ways, Jess Jackson exemplifies the entrepreneurial nature of the CALIFORNIA wine industry as well as the go-go climate of the 1980s. Artisans & Estates is not just the biggest fish in a small, remote, underdeveloped California pond called LAKE COUNTY. It is the fastest growing wine entity in the world's biggest economy, and its success in the domestic US wine market helped to prompt acquisition fever among alcohol beverage companies worldwide during the 1990s.

Artisans & Estates own 10,000 acres of vineyards in Santa Barbara, Monterey, Sonoma, Napa, and Mendocino counties as well as in Lake. They also own Villa Archeno wine estate in Tuscany, Viña Calina in Chile, Mariposa in Argentina, and a cooperage in France.

In the 1980s, Kendall–Jackson happily disregarded the California industry's movement toward vineyard designations, concentrating instead on blending from various regions to achieve certain taste characteristics. The hallmarks of K-J's blended Chardonnays were refreshingly strong ACIDITY, creamy oak vanillins, exotic pineapple fruit flavour, and softness and immediate drinkability from just-perceptible RESIDUAL SUGAR. Classically inclined show JUDGES put up token resistance to the residual sugar, but consumers had no such reservations.

In 1987, Jackson acquired 1,000 acres in Santa Barbara County and opened the first of his additional winery labels, Cambria Winery and Vineyard. Since that time, acquisitions have been so frequent that any book is obsolete on the subject long before publication. Particularly notable was the 1993 purchase of Vinwood Cellars, a 500,000-case former CUSTOM CRUSH FACILITY in Alexander Valley; the 1994 purchase of Robert Pepi Winery in Napa Valley; and the 1995 purchase of the 1,800-acre Gauer Estate vineyards in Alexander Valley. Other important A & E brands as of mid-1998 included: Hartford Court (Russian River Pinot Noir and Zinfandel), Edmeades (Mendocino old-vine Zinfandel), La Crema, Kristone (Central Coast sparkling wines), and Cardinale. Several of these portfolio brands represent a marked departure from the Kendall–Jackson brand philosophy in that they are sold with a marketing story which attempts to capitalize to some extent on REGIONALITY.   B.C.C.

Kenya, African country virtually on the equator, with a very limited production of wines. Since the mid 1980s, VINIFERA vines have been cultivated and have been harvested every eight months, providing three vintages every two years, chiefly from vineyards around Lake Naivasha. The best white wines have been made from Sauvignon Blanc grapes together with some experimental Chardonnay, Colombard, and Chenin Blanc, while some decent red wine has been made from Ruby Cabernet with some Carnelian. The pioneer growers were John and Guy d'Olier of Lake Naivasha Vineyards.   J.P.

Kerner is the great success story of modern German vine breeding. Bred only in 1969, this reliable ripener became Germany's third most planted light-berried vine in the 1990s. The bulk of Germany's Kerner is planted in Rheinhessen and the Pfalz, but it is still popular in Württemberg, where it was bred from a red parent TROLLINGER (Schiava Grossa) × Riesling. The large white berries produce wines commendably close to Riesling in flavour except with their own leafy aroma and very slightly coarser texture. It can well produce fine VARIETAL wines, up to quite high PRÄDIKAT levels, on its own account, and it has the ability to age thanks to its high acidity.

Kerner has also been planted in South Africa but it seems unlikely that there is a long future for it there. The variety is planted to a limited extent in ENGLAND.

Kevedinka, ordinary white eastern European grape variety. See DINKA.

King Valley, increasingly important wine region in the Australian state of VICTORIA.

kir, alternative name for a *vin blanc cassis*, dry white wine and blackcurrant liqueur, named after a hero of the Burgundian resistance movement during the Second World War, Canon Kir, who was also mayor of Dijon. The CÔTE D'OR is an important grower of blackcurrants and most of the best-quality blackcurrant liqueurs, or *eaux-de-vie de cassis*, are made here. The typical base wine is the relatively acid Bourgogne ALIGOTÉ and to most palates a dash of full-strength liqueur is all that is needed. In a French bar, however, the *cassis* may make up to a fifth of the mix.

Királyleányka, Hungarian name for Romania's grapey FETEASCĂ Regală, a crossing of Fetească Albă and GRASĂ, or LEÁNYKA. It is sometimes known as Dánosi Leányka after its geographical origins in Transylvania. Balaton Boglar is its chief home in modern Hungary.

K–J. See KENDALL–JACKSON.

Klein Karoo, inland wine region in SOUTH AFRICA also known as Little Karoo.

Klevener de Heiligenstein is an Alsace oddity, a vine speciality of the village of Heiligenstein. It is a locally adapted TRAMINER, occasionally known as Clevner de Heiligenstein, which is increasingly popular. See also ALSACE.   T.S. & J.Ro.

Klevner, like CLEVNER, is, and more particularly was, used fairly indiscriminately in Alsace and other German-speaking wine regions for various vine varieties, notably but not exclusively for CHARDONNAY and various members of the PINOT family.

Kloster Eberbach, monastery in the RHEINGAU region of Germany with a tradition of viticulture; now seen as the cultural wine centre of the Rheingau. It is the home of the educational organization the German Wine Academy and the Rheingau Wine Society. It also provides a regional centre for wine auctions, trade fairs, and seminars. The Steinberg vineyard, planted by monks 700 years ago next to the monastery, is still producing highly rated wines.   S.A.

Knights Valley, inland California wine region and AVA between the northern end of Napa Valley and the southern end of Alexander Valley. See SONOMA.

Koppamurra, name for Naracoorte Ranges, in the Limestone Coast zone of SOUTH AUSTRALIA, superseded by Wrattonbully.

Korea, rugged, mountainous peninsula on the Asian mainland, between China and Japan, for long a producer of TABLE GRAPES but of wine only since 1977, when the large beverages group, DooSan Baekwha, launched its Majuang label. DooSan's chief rival is the world's largest *soju* (white grain spirit) maker, Jinro. By 1997, these two had been joined by Shinwoo, Cheil, Haitai, Kambokjoo, and the tiny SooSeok Farm but DooSan's Majuang label claims 80 per cent of sales.

Vineyards attached to wine-making operations are in the south west of the peninsula in the provinces of North and South Kyongsang. The main varieties grown for wine are Riesling, Seibel, and Muscat Bailey A. However, the Korean domestic wine industry is heavily dependent on wine imported in bulk, mostly from Europe. Premium labels, such as DooSan's Majuang Special and SooSeok's

Wehayeux, are generally a 50 : 50 blend of domestic and imported wine. Anything below this level will generally consist entirely of imported bulk wine. D.G.

kosher wine satisfies the strict rabbinical production criteria that make it suitable for consumption by religious Jews. These 'kosher' (meaning literally 'right' or 'correct') wines are produced under strict supervision of the rabbinate, and only sabbath-observing, strictly orthodox Jews are allowed involvement with the production and bottling processes. Some rabbis insist on the wine's being 'boiled' (subjected to PASTEURIZATION) so that non-Jews, heathens, would no longer recognize it as wine and there would be no danger of their using it for their religious rites. The treated wine, *meshuval*, regrettably loses most of its qualities, even if modern flash-pasteurization techniques are used.

Wines described as 'kosher for Passover' have not come into contact with bread, dough, or leavened dough.

Kosher wine produced in ISRAEL must conform to the following strict dietary laws:

1. No wine may be produced from a vine until its fourth year.
2. The vineyard, if within the biblical lands, must be left fallow every seven years.
3. Only vines may be grown in vineyards.
4. From arrival at the winery, the grapes and resulting wine may be handled only by strictly sabbath-observing Jews, and only 100 per cent kosher materials may be used in the wine-making, maturation, and bottling processes.

In practice, kosher winery employees include many non-sabbath-observing Jews, who may be allowed to handle freshly picked grapes but not must or wine. Wine technologists or OENOLOGISTS who are not themselves sabbath-observing may instruct observant Jews to carry out the necessary operations in the winery.

Any winery outside Israel can make kosher wine provided that the fourth law is strictly observed. Good kosher wines are made each year in various parts of France, Italy, South Africa, Morocco, Australia, and the United States, and some kosher wine for local consumption is made in most wine-producing countries. P.A.H. & H.G.

Kosovo, small, autonomous region within SERBIA in the south of what was YUGOSLAVIA between MACEDONIA, Serbia, and ALBANIA. Until the onset of civil war, its vineyards were largely devoted to the production of Amselfelder branded wine for sale in Germany. Trainloads of light red were sent in bulk to Belgrade for STABILIZATION, sweetening, and shipment. The light aromatic fruit of the Pinot Noir was certainly the inspiration behind this brand. Cabernet Franc, Merlot, PROKUPAC, and GAMAY are also part of the region's production. A.H.M.

Kotsifali. Generous, spicy, if soft wines are produced from this red grape speciality of the Greek island of Crete. They are best blended with something more tannic such as MANDELARI.

Kövidinka, ordinary white eastern European grape variety. See DINKA.

Kratosija, relatively important grape in Macedonia and Montenegro.

Krems, important wine town in lower AUSTRIA, now part of the Kamptal-Donauland district.

Krug, small but important Champagne house founded in Rheims in 1843 by Johann-Joseph Krug, who was born in Mainz, Germany, in 1830. Krug does not make an ordinary NONVINTAGE champagne but specializes exclusively in PRESTIGE CUVÉES, of which the multi-vintage Grande Cuvée is the flagship. Consistently producing champagne that is among the most admired in its region of origin, Krug is the only house to persist in BARREL FERMENTATION of its entire production of base wine, in old 205-l/54-gal casks. Wines from at least six and sometimes nine different vintages make up the blend for Grande Cuvée, one of the most distinctive and long lived of champagnes. Grande Cuvée, with new packaging and a special bottle, succeeded the rather fuller-bodied Private Cuvée as Krug's most important product in 1979. In 1971, Krug acquired and replanted the Clos du Mesnil, a walled vineyard of less than 2 ha/5 acres. Its Chardonnay grapes provide one of Champagne's very few single-vineyard, or CRU, wines of which the 1979 vintage was the first. Although the firm is run by members of the fifth and sixth generation of champagne-making Krugs, the majority of the shares were held by Rémy-Cointreau, which also owns Rémy Martin cognac, and were acquired by LVMH in 1999.

Kuč. See TRBLJAN.

KWV, the South African Co-operative Wine-growers Association, or Ko-operatiewe Wijn-bowers Vereniging van Zuid Afrika, is the mainly export wine producer which emerged from the transformation in 1997 of South Africa's grape-grower body from co-operative to company. Until its conversion, it combined the functions of producer, marketing body, and statutory government control board, only gradually releasing its tight grip on the country's wine industry in the early 1990s.

The newly structured KWV has been relieved of all the statutory functions previously performed by the 4,600-strong growers' co-operative. Nevertheless, the organization still exerts considerable influence. As a shareholder in the major national wholesalers, as the most important supplier of bulk brandy to the country's spirit producers, as the proprietor of grape-juice concentrating facilities, through domination of many of the industry organizations and as a major supplier of goods, plant material, and services to the country's grape farmers and wine producers, the KWV's position remains largely unassailed.

The KWV exports a wide range of table wines, including blends such as Roodeberg (made up of Cabernet Sauvignon, Shiraz, Pinotage, and Tinta Barroca), and has a wide range of FORTIFIED WINES made in the image of port and sherry.

Most top-quality South African table wine, however, comes from private producers, a few wholesaler-producers, and individual estates which make wine as well as grow their own grapes (fewer than 80 in the early 1990s). The biggest wholesalers, Stellenbosch Farmers' Winery (SFW) and Distillers Corporation (selling under the name Bergkelder, or 'mountain cellar'), together with the KWV, have controlled the great majority of South Africa's vine-related alcohol products since 1979.

The KWV's functions include research, vine propagation, advisory services, administrating the WINE OF ORIGIN system, wine education, and marketing campaigns. These activities are co-ordinated from the KWV's depot at Paarl, 60 km/37 miles north of Cape Town.   J.P. & M.F.

Kyrgyzstan, mountainous central Asian republic of the CIS on the border between KAZAKHSTAN and China of only minor wine-producing importance.

The south of Kyrgyzstan (the Dzhalal-Abad and Osh regions) produces central Asian varieties destined for drying or the production of sweet, heavy wine. The Issyk-Kul depression, especially the central part of this region, on the south and north banks of Lake Issyk-Kul, is particularly favourable for viticulture and the production of dessert wines and base materials for sparkling wines.

Forty-five grape varieties are recognized, including 23 wine varieties such as RKATSITELI, Pinot Noir, Bayan Shirey, Kuljinski, Cabernet Sauvignon, Riesling, SAPERAVI, Budeshiru Tetri, Mairam, Mourvèdre Kirghizski, Hungarian Muscat, and Black Muscat. Table varieties include CINSAUT and MADELEINE ANGEVINE.

V.R.

label, the principal means by which a wine producer or bottler can communicate with a potential customer and consumer (although see also BOTTLES, CASE, FOIL).

Every wine in commercial circulation has to have a main label, as its passport quite apart from its function as a sales aid. Many wines also have a **neck label**, typically carrying the VINTAGE year. See LABELLING INFORMATION for details of the information available on a main label. As wine consumers have become ever more sophisticated and curious, however, an increasing proportion of bottles carry a **back label** giving additional background information. This can vary from a genuinely useful outline of grape varieties used, vintage conditions, approximate SWEETNESS level, and serving advice, to a collection of fine-sounding words involving the 'finest' grape varieties picked at 'perfect ripeness' in 'optimum conditions' and vinified according to the 'highest standards', but which contain no genuine information whatsoever. Now that the amount of mandatory information required on wine labels is so considerable, some design-conscious bottlers try to beat the system by conveying all of this detail on what is obviously meant to be the back label, while applying a dramatic design statement without all the clutter of the mandatory information which the retailer, but not the labelling inspector, is meant to treat as the main label.

Labels matter to lawyers and officials, and they matter enormously to the retail wine trade, in which they communicate far more effectively with many consumers than any rec-ommendation or award, but they are relatively unimportant to wine sales from a list, such as by mail or in the hotel and restaurant industry. The Italians have been as innovative in label design as in that of bottles, and some NEW WORLD designs can be arresting, effective, innovative, and sometimes all three. ARTISTS' LABELS have a certain following. Producers of established wines have usually inherited a label and rarely do anything more than slightly modify it (although even most of the established Bordeaux CLASSED GROWTHS have incorporated some design modification into their labels in the last 10 years). The fact that the label of Ch PÉTRUS would win no design award seems to do little to hinder sales. The label design of wine BRANDS, however, is an extremely important factor in their success. One of the most evocative labels is that used for MATEUS Rosé depicting a beautiful palace in northern Portugal, which has nothing whatever to do with the wine.

Wine labels have such a fascination of their own, and can help recollection of the circumstances of their consumption, that wine **label collecting** is a recognized activity. Some of those who practise it call themselves vintitulists.

labelling information. The amount of information required on wine LABELS seems to increase dramatically each year. The following are the main categories of usually mandatory information, with national or international minimum criteria (which may be stricter on a local or regional basis).

Wine designation: wines made within the European Union have to be identified as to whether they qualify as TABLE WINE, QUALITY WINE, or one of several specific intermediate categories such as France's VIN DE PAYS or Germany's LANDWEIN. They will accordingly carry one of the descriptions listed under these headings (Appellation Contrôlée, or Vino de Mesa, for example). Labels on wines made outside the European Union have to carry the tell-tale word 'wine' when travelling within Europe. In the United States, wines are usually identified as 'table wine'. See DESIGNATIONS.

Geographical reference: this may take the form of the name of a country (as in Greek table wine, for example), or the name of an AVA or any other state or smaller region in the United States, or could be the name of a tiny controlled appellation (such as BOCA in north-west Italy, for example). In France, this is often written Appellation X Contrôlée, where X is the name of the geographical reference, or even Appellation d'Origine X Contrôlée. Within Europe, if a geographical zone is cited on the label, all the wine should usually come from this zone. In the United States, if an AVA is stated on the label, then 85 per cent should come from that area. Eighty-five per cent of an Australian wine must also come from the region specified. Exported wine has to carry the name of the country of origin.

Volume of wine: this is most likely to be 75 cl/27 fl oz but must, quite rightly, be stated on all labels. See BOTTLE SIZES and BOXES.

Alcoholic strength: this is usually stated as a percentage of the volume but may be expressed in degrees (°) or, in Italy in particular, as *gradi*. See ALCOHOLIC STRENGTH.

Vintage year: within Europe, a vintage may not be stated for a TABLE WINE, and, wherever it is stated, at least 85 per cent of the wine should be the produce of that year. See VINTAGE and NON-VINTAGE.

Name and address of producer or bottler: this is usually provided in a fairly straightforward fashion, although, within Europe, an address which happens to incorporate the name of a controlled appellation cannot be used on the label of a table wine, or even a vin de pays, so some sort of postal code is usually substituted.

Bottling information: the relationship between the source of the grapes and the producer or bottler is indicated by exactly how this is expressed. See BOTTLING INFORMATION.

On a CHAMPAGNE label, the following codes printed next to the registered number of the bottler are useful:

NM: *négociant-manipulant*, one of the big houses/firms/négociants;

RM: *récoltant-manipulant*, a grower who makes his or her own wine;

CM: *coopérative de manipulation*, one of the co-operatives;

RC: *récoltant-coopérateur*, grower selling wine made by a co-op;

MA: *marque d'acheteur*, buyer's own brand;

SR: *société de récoltant*, a small family company (rare);

R: *récoltant*, very small-scale growers (very rare).

Varietal information: this is entirely optional, but, if a variety is specified on a label of wine in Europe, then it must comprise at least 85 per cent of the wine. In the United States, it must comprise at least 75 per cent (or 51 per cent in the case of some particularly FOXY native varieties: see NEW YORK). In Australia, it must comprise at least 85 per cent of the stated variety.

gratuitous government interference: in some countries, wine labels have to carry 'warnings', usually as a result of some scientifically vague but much-publicized connection between wine and ill HEALTH. In the United States, labels on all wine have to warn that pregnant women and those in charge of heavy machinery are ill advised to consume any or much of it. In several countries, including the UNITED STATES, all wine labels must warn 'contains sulfites'. In Australia, all additives must be mentioned, so a label may say 'contains antioxidant (300) and preservative (220)', 300 and 220 being the respective numerical codes for erythorbic acid and SULPHUR DIOXIDE. Sulphur dioxide is used to a certain extent in the making of virtually all wine, therefore virtually all wine contains sulfites, or SULPHITES. Wine labels all over the world have had to be redesigned because, unfortunately, severe asthmatics can suffer if they consume excessive amounts of sulphites (which are present, in much higher concentrations, in a wide range of other products such as fruit juices).

Sweetness: see SWEETNESS.

Fizziness: see FIZZINESS.

Colour: see COLOUR.

labrusca, species of the *Vitis* genus native to North America. The juice of its grapes, and wine made from them, usually have a pronounced flavour described as FOXY.

La Clape. See CLAPE.

Lacrima di Morro, fast-maturing, strangely scented red grape speciality of the MARCHES.

Lacrima Nera is sometimes used as a synonym for GAGLIOPPO.

lactic acid, one of the milder ACIDS in wine, present in much lower concentrations than either MALIC ACID or TARTARIC ACID. In wine, lactic acid can be produced by bacteria both from traces of sugar and from malic acid. The function of the second MALOLACTIC FERMENTATION which a high proportion of red wines and some white wines undergo is to transform harsh malic acid into the much milder lactic acid.   A.D.W.

Lado, native white grape variety that is an important component of blends in the Arnoia valley in RIBEIRO, north-west Spain.

Ladoix, the appellation from the village of Ladoix-Serrigny in the Côte de Beaune district of Burgundy's Côte d'Or producing mostly red wines from Pinot Noir grapes. They are more frequently sold as Côte de Beaune-Villages (see BEAUNE, CÔTE DE). Although there are 14 ha/34 acres of Ladoix PREMIERS CRUS, a further 8 ha of the best-placed vineyards are sold as Aloxe-Corton premier cru. Furthermore, 6 ha of Corton-Charlemagne and 22 ha (out of 160) of Le Corton, including part of Le Rognet and Les Vergennes, are actually sited in Ladoix (see ALOXE-CORTON for more details).

As well as the Corton-Charlemagne, a tiny amount of white Ladoix-Serrigny is made from Chardonnay or Pinot Blanc.

See also CÔTE D'OR.   J.T.C.M.

Lafite, Château, subsequently Ch Lafite-Rothschild, FIRST GROWTH in the MÉDOC region of BORDEAUX. The vineyard, to the north of the small town of PAUILLAC and adjoining Ch MOUTON-ROTHSCHILD, was probably planted in the last third of the 17th century. It has been owned by the Rothschild family since 1868, when it was bought by Baron James de Rothschild of the Paris bank, for 4.4 million francs, including part of the Carruades vineyard. Baron Eric de Rothschild took over direction of the property from his uncle Baron Élie in 1977. In the famous 1855 CLASSIFICATION, Lafite was placed first of the premiers crus, although there is controversy as to whether the order was alphabetical or by rank.

The château itself is a 16th-century manor. The vineyard, one of the largest in the Haut-Médoc, was 90 ha/222 acres in 1993 with an ENCÉPAGEMENT of 70 per cent Cabernet Sauvignon, 13 per cent Cabernet Franc, 15 per cent Merlot, and 2 per cent Petit Verdot. Annual production is about 35,000 cases, of which about a third may be the SECOND WINE, called Carruades de Lafite but not restricted to wine produced on the plateau in the vineyard known as Les Carruades.   E.P.-R.

lagar, term used in PORTUGAL for a low-sided stone trough where grapes are trodden and fermented. Most have now been replaced by conventional fermentation vats except in the DOURO valley, where some of the best PORTS continue to be foot-trodden in *lagares*.

Lagorthi, rare Greek white grape whose aromatic produce may save it from extinction.

Lagrein, red grape variety grown in TRENTINO-ALTO ADIGE. Although often over-produced, it can produce **Lagrein Scuro** or **Lagrein Dunkel,** somewhat tannic reds of real character, as well as fragrant yet sturdy rosé called **Lagrein Rosato** or **Lagrein Kretzer.** Lagrein can be slightly bitter on the finish and its presence, valued both for TANNINS and for colour, can at times be detected as an element in other wines of the zone, particularly Pinot Nero and Schiava. Wine-making techniques have changed in recent years, as younger producers have shortened maceration times and used barriques to achieve rounder, less aggressive flavours.

Lairén, southern Spanish name for the white grape variety AIRÉN.

Lake County, smallest viticultural district among CALIFORNIA'S NORTH COAST counties and also the least understood. The county's vines and its small population of wineries are concentrated in the Clear Lake AVA. A much smaller AVA is further south in the Guenoc Valley.

Clear Lake AVA

Nearly all of the AVA's vineyards nestle between steep hills to the west and the lake, California's largest, to the east. By the early 1990s, this warm inland district, north of NAPA and east of MENDOCINO, had grown some excellent Sauvignon Blanc and pleasant, early-maturing Cabernet Sauvignon. Zinfandel may be well adapted, although evidence remains scant.

Although several wineries (especially Konocti and KENDALL-JACKSON) are located near the town of Lakeport, a fair proportion of the region's grapes go to wineries in Mendocino and SONOMA counties.

Guenoc Valley AVA
See GUENOC VALLEY.

lake effect, the year-round climate-moderating influence on vineyards from nearby large lakes which permits vine-growing in areas such as the north-east UNITED STATES and Ontario in CANADA despite their high LATITUDE.

Lalande-de-Pomerol, appellation to the immediate north of Pomerol that is very much in the shadow of this great red-wine district of Bordeaux. It includes the communes of Lalande-de-Pomerol and Néac and produces lush, Merlot-dominated wines which can offer a suggestion, sometimes a decidedly rustic suggestion, of the concentration available in a bottle of fine Pomerol but at a fraction of the price. The Lalande-de-Pomerol appellation is much bigger than that of Pomerol, and its soils are composed of well-drained gravels, particularly in the south, where it is divided from the Pomerol appellation only by the Barbanne river. Ch Grand Ormeau makes wines better than most. See also POMEROL.

La Mancha. See MANCHA.

Lambrusco, central Italian VARIETAL wine based on the eponymous red grape variety, enormously popular with the mass market in the USA and northern Europe in the early 1980s.

The several different vines called Lambrusco are grown principally in the three central provinces of EMILIA-Modena, Parma, and Reggio nell'Emilia.

Modern Lambrusco, a frothing, fruity, typically red wine meant to be drunk young, is produced principally by the CO-OPERATIVES of Emilia in four separate DOCs: **Lambrusco di Sorbara** (from the varieties Lambrusco di Sorbara and, the most planted, Lambrusco Salamino); **Lambrusco Grasparossa di Castelvetro** (85 per cent of which must come from the variety of the same name); **Lambrusco Reggiano** (produced principally from Lambrusco Marani and Lambrusco Salamino); and **Lambrusco Salamino di Santa Croce** (which should include 90 per cent of the synonymous

variety). The Lambrusco Grasparossa, Sorbara, and Salamino tend to be dry or off-dry wines with a pronounced ACIDITY, which, together with its bubbles, are reputed to assist the digestion of Emilia's hearty cuisine.

Lambrusco Reggiano, on the other hand, tends to be AMABILE or slightly sweet, the sweetness generally being supplied by the partially fermented must of the Ancellotta grape, which DOC rules permit (up to a maximum of 15 per cent) in the blend. This is the wine that took America by storm in the late 1970s and early 1980s when the Cantine Riunite of Reggio nell'Emilia, a consortium of co-operatives, succeeded in exporting up to 3 million cases per year to the United States. So successful has Lambrusco been on export markets that special white, pink, and light (LOW-ALCOHOL) versions have perversely been created, the colour and alcohol often being deliberately removed.

Most Lambrusco made today is a fairly anonymous, standardized product made in industrial quantities by co-operatives or large commercial wineries using the tank method (see SPARKLING-WINE-MAKING). 'Proper' Lambrusco, whose SECONDARY FERMENTATION takes place in the bottle, has become something of a relic of the past, although occasional artisan Lambruscos of this type can be found in the production zones themselves. The distinctive qualities of the different clones and different zones have tended to disappear but, in theory, Lambrusco Grasparossa is the fullest and most alcoholic and Lambrusco di Sorbara, in its combination of balanced fruit and acidity, is precisely that classic accompaniment to Emilian egg pasta and charcuterie which made the name of the wine. Lambrusco Reggiano is the most common, followed by Lambrusco di Sorbara, Lambrusco Grasparossa, and Lambrusco Salamino.

There are also several hundred hectares of a red grape variety known as **Lambrusco Maesini** in Argentina.   D.T.

Lancers, BRAND of medium-sweet, lightly sparkling wine made by the firm of J. M. da FONSECA at Azeitão, near SETÚBAL in PORTUGAL. The brand was created in 1944, when Vintage Wines of New York saw that American veterans of the Second World War were returning home from Europe with a taste for wine. Lancers, initially sold in a stone crock, continues to be moderately successful in the United States, whereas MATEUS Rosé, created two years earlier, tends to be better known in Europe. A fully sparkling Lancers, made by the continuous method (see SPARKLING-WINE-MAKING), was introduced in the late 1980s.   R.J.M.

Landwein, superior category of dry or medium-dry table wine, or TAFELWEIN, in German-speaking countries. In GERMANY, Landwein must have an ALCOHOLIC STRENGTH of at least half a per cent more than the minimum level for German table wine. Although all the German wine regions contain Landwein areas, their names are not widely used. Since an average of 95 per cent of each German vintage has been classified as QUALITÄTSWEIN, or quality wine, much of it sold at a very low price, the scope for Landwein is small. It does not enjoy the reputation of its French equivalent VIN DE PAYS, which is so successful on the German market.   I.J.

In AUSTRIA, Landwein is slightly more common but must be sold either in bottles of 25 cl/9 fl oz or less, or in 1-l or 2-l ('Doppler') bottles. It must be dry, with no more than 6 g/l RESIDUAL SUGAR, and reach at least 68° OECHSLE (considerably riper than the German minimum, reflecting the warmer climate).

Langenlois, important wine town in lower AUSTRIA, now part of the Kamptal-Donauland district.

Langhe, plural of Langa, name given to the hills to the north and south of the city of Alba in the province of Cuneo in PIEDMONT. The soils are the classic ones for the NEBBIOLO grape, and produce the Langhe's most famous wines BAROLO and BARBARESCO, although they can also yield BARBERA and DOLCETTO of excellent quality. Langhe is also the name of a regional DOC for Piedmont, used for non-traditional grape varieties (Langhe Chardonnay or, for Sauvignon Blanc, Langhe Bianco) or as a lower DOC category into which more geographically limited DOC wines can be declassified, Dolcetto d'Alba becoming Langhe Dolcetto, for example, and Barbera d'Alba becoming Langhe Rosso.   D.T.

Langhorne Creek, wine region in SOUTH AUSTRALIA.

language of wine. Wine-talk is a problem: 'When trying to talk about wine in depth, one rapidly comes up against the limitations of our means of expression . . . We need to be able to describe the indescribable. We tasters feel to some extent betrayed by language', comments Bordeaux OENOLOGIST Émile Peynaud.

Wine-talk is triply disadvantaged: first, people TASTE and smell wine differently from each other; second, a partially obscure conventional vocabulary has arisen: the wine flavour described as gooseberry, for example, does not taste very much like gooseberries; third, the need to impress customers in a cutthroat market has led to ear-catching and sometimes bizarre descriptions: 'a fascinating old, old smell of unswept floorboards', 'old tarpaulin fringed with lace', 'Wham bam thankyou mam red, all rich, gooey, almost treacly fruit-dark plums and prunes awash with liquorice and chocolate and cream'.

Descriptive terms should be distinguished from expressive or evaluative ones, it is sometimes argued. Yet even this proves to be difficult for wine: even the most straightforward descriptions are bizarre by the standards of 'normal' usage. An English speaker asked to describe the colours red and white is likely to mention blood versus snow, yet a red wine is typically reddish-purple and a white one pale straw, each with a range that goes beyond the usual boundaries for red and white. Other wine colour terms are equally odd: black, as in Greek Mavrodaphne 'black-daphne' or the old 'black wine' of Cahors, refers simply to a hue darker than is usual for wines.

Yet colours illustrate one useful way in which wine terms can be partially analysed, by looking at the internal structure of the wine vocabulary. Red and white are opposites on a scale with rosé in the middle. Such antonyms are an anchor-point in descriptions. Possibly for this reason, the terms sweet versus dry are the first technical terms to be widely understood, and are now regularly found in supermarket classifications, even though, outside a wine context, the average person would oppose sweet to sour, and dry to wet.

Technically, antonyms such as sweet versus dry are gradable, in that sweet means 'sweet in relation to a norm', even though the norm is far from clear. Further opposites/scales have not generally caught on, though some recur in descriptions, as young vs. mature, light vs. heavy, crisp (nicely acidic) vs. flabby—though a basic problem is that a word such as flabby tends to be used as a general derogatory term, so is also found in opposition to terms such as hearty, sturdy, meaty, which indicate a wine with body.

Synonyms are also useful in understanding vocabulary structure, and words for wines with 'body' abound: beefy, big, broad, chunky, powerful, robust—though none has yet won out over others.

Readers of wine columns sometimes get the misleading impression that 'anything goes'. Yet the majority of wine flavour descriptions cover a fairly narrow range, mostly of other food words, as appley, gamey, grapefruity, minty, peachy, plummy, raspberry—though these are often 'code' terms, in that a wine described as grapefruity or minty does not (to the uninitiated) taste very much like either. Terms that move outside these food flavours relate easily only to a small portion of wine qualities, as with the power terms listed above for wines with body. A further set relate perceived smoothness to fabrics, so wines may be velvety, silky, satiny—though even here, the range of fabrics is limited: a wine may be soft, though is not normally woolly. Shape and texture terms tend to be applied to wines with a high degree of acidity, as angular, austere, flinty, steely. The AROMA (nose) is perhaps the aspect of wine that has caused the greatest controversy in recent years, and seems to be hardest to convey: cat's pee, pencil shavings, sweaty saddles, tobacco had relatively little attention paid to them, yet fury erupted when a serious critic referred to a wine as smelling of hamster cages. Any successful metaphor must fit in with existing traditions and preconceptions or risk being rejected.

Yet in many cases, wine descriptions are unclear only out of context or when single words are used. Increasingly, wines are acquiring shorthand labels for these bundles of characteristics: some Chardonnays, such as those produced in Meursault, are labelled buttery for a fairly rich white wine—a description accepted even by those that love Meursault wines, but dislike butter. A Rioja is recognized and labelled oaky, even by those who have no idea why this tag is used.

All of this suggests that wine knowledge is becoming increasingly sophisticated. A future hope is that a more sophisticated classification system of the vocabulary of wine can match the knowledge of its drinkers.

See AROMA WHEEL, TASTING, TASTING TERMS.

J.A.

Languedoc, France's best-value, most fluid wine region and certainly its most important in terms of volume of wine produced, and in terms of the importance of viticulture to the region's economy. Its relative freedom from vinous regulation has led to its being called France's New World.

The Languedoc is the land of the proud peasant farmer. The size of the average holding is small, and usually much divided between parcels inherited from various different branches of the family. The area comprises the three central southern *départements* of the Aude, Hérault, and Gard, a sea of little other than vines just inland from the beaches of the Mediterranean. Between them they had a total of nearly 300,000 ha/741,000 acres of vineyard in the early 1990s—about a third of all French vines, or just under the total area of the United States under vine. This was despite 10 years' strenuous European Union-inspired VINE PULL SCHEMES aimed at reducing Europe's wine surplus. By the late 1990s, the total area planted with vines was still well over 250,000 ha, three times as much as the whole of Australia.

The Languedoc is often bracketed with the region to its immediate south, as in LANGUE-DOC-ROUSSILLON, although the ROUSSILLON has a perceptibly different character, and is better equipped to replace vines with the other fruit crops it has for long cultivated.

Despite its quantitative importance, the Languedoc produces only just over 10 per cent of France's AC wines. For many years its only appellation was Fitou, but in 1985 Corbières, Minervois, and the catch-all appellation Coteaux du Languedoc were elevated from VDQS to AC status. A high proportion of the vast area technically included in these AC zones is dedicated to non-appellation wine, however, either because the ENCÉPAGEMENT is outside the appellation specifications, or because the vigneron is more interested in quantity than quality. The Languedoc is still by far the principal producer of VIN DE TABLE, as well as producing more than 80 per cent of France's intermediate category VIN DE PAYS, much of it labelled regionally as Vin de Pays d'Oc. A much wider range of VINE VARIETIES is usually allowed for vin de pays than for appellation wines. In a very real sense, the Languedoc is France's most anarchic wine region. Not only is it the only one in which vignerons still take direct and often violent action in protest at the organization of their sector of the wine business, it is also the one in which wine producers are most obviously dissatisfied with the detail of the, admittedly relatively recent, appellation laws. Some important producers ignore the AC system completely and put most of their effort into making high-quality vins de pays.

Only about 10 per cent of the region's wine output was white in the late 1990s, but the best whites, after a decidedly OAKY phase, have become increasingly fine and interesting. The small proportion of dry rosé is mainly for local consumption. A substantial quantity of VIN DOUX NATUREL is made (see MUSCAT), and LIMOUX is the Languedoc's centre of SPARKLING-WINE-MAKING. The Languedoc is still principally a source of red wine, however, a typical representative being no longer a thin, pale remnant of the region's past as a bulk-wine supplier but a dense, exciting, increasingly supple ambassador of some of France's wildest countryside.

Geography and climate

The great majority of the Languedoc's vines are planted on flat, low-lying alluvial plain, particularly in the southern Hérault and Gard. In the northern Hérault and western Aude, vines may be planted several hundred metres above sea level however, in the foothills of the Cévennes and the Corbières Pyrenean foothills respectively, sometimes at quite an angle and on very varied soils which can include gravels and limestone.

The climate in all but the far western limits of the Languedoc (where some definite Atlantic influence is apparent) is definitively MED-ITERRANEAN and one of the major viticultural hazards is DROUGHT.

Vine varieties

The dominant vine variety is CARIGNAN, which is declining but still accounted for nearly a third of all vines in 1997, despite considerable incentives to plant better-quality varieties such as GRENACHE, CINSAUT (useful for rosés), and especially SYRAH and MOURVÈDRE. Other varieties have made substantial inroads in the region since the mid 1980s, many of them outlawed for the production of APPELLATION CON-TRÔLÉE wines but used to produce VIN DE PAYS, about 70 per cent of which are sold as VARIETAL wines. These include such obvious candidates as Merlot and, rather less successful, Cabernet Sauvignon, but also Sauvignon Blanc, Viognier, and of course the LIMOUX speciality Chardonnay, the Languedoc's most important white

grape. Since the late 1980s, there have also been considerable plantings of Rolle, Roussanne, and Marsanne for blending with Viognier and/or the traditional full-bodied Grenache Blanc, of which only Viognier had not been fully embraced by AC regulations by the late 1990s. The light-red Aramon that dominated plantings until Carignan took hold in the 1970s has been reduced to under 8,000 ha, about the same area as the red-fleshed Alicante Bouschet, which was so often blended with it. Other 'traditional' Languedoc vine varieties included Aspiran, Bourboulenc, Clairette, Mac-cabéo, and Œillade, Picpoul, Ribarenc, and Terret. Petit Manseng is being tried.

Wine-making

Winery equipment and techniques are still relatively unsophisticated in the Languedoc, where selling prices have rarely been high enough to justify major investment. New oak BARRELS, for example, are beyond the means of most producers. (In any case, the fruit is so intense in many red wines that they do not necessarily benefit from oak.) The great majority of Languedoc wine is made in one of the CO-OPERATIVE CELLARS whose will to make good-quality wine varies considerably. Fermentation and ÉLEVAGE typically take place in large concrete cuves, although stainless steel is slowly invading the region. Partly in an effort to tame the natural astringency of Carignan, full or partial CARBONIC MACERATION is the most common red-wine-making technique. Bottling usually takes place at a merchant's cellar rather than on the premises where the wine was made. The wine container most frequently seen by the consumer in the region is probably the road tanker (a high proportion of the locals buy their wine in bulk rather than bottle). There is increasing experimentation with SWEET-WINE-MAKING of various sorts.

For more specific information, see the individual appellations CABARDÈS, CLAIRETTE DE BELLEGARDE, CLAIRETTE DU LANGUEDOC, COR-BIÈRES, COSTIÈRES DE NÎMES, FAUGÈRES, FITOU, LIMOUX, MINERVOIS, ST-CHINIAN, and Coteaux du LANGUEDOC. See also Côtes de la MALEPÈRE, the vin de liqueur CARTAGÈNE, and various MUSCAT vins doux naturels, plus FRONTIGNAN.

Languedoc, Coteaux du, varied and probably too extensive appellation whose zone includes some of France's best-value vineyards and most of the land suitable for growing vines above the coastal plain in a swathe through the Hérault *département* from Narbonne towards Nîmes. As elsewhere in the Languedoc, much of the land technically included within the appellation is used for other purposes (other crops or VIN DE PAYS, for example). The total vineyard area dedicated to producing Coteaux du Languedoc by 1996 was more than 7,700 ha/19,000 acres, a considerable increase on the early 1990s.

Although much of the zone qualifies for the basic Coteaux du Languedoc appellation, a number of subappellations, CRUS, or specific TERROIRS have been identified and are allowed to append their own name to that of the appellation on labels. Of these, CLAIRETTE DU LANGUE-DOC, FAUGÈRES, and ST-CHINIAN were long ago allowed to break free and establish their own independent identity. Others waiting with particular impatience in the wings are La CLAPE, PICPOUL DE PINET, PIC-ST-LOUP, MONTPEYROUX, and ST-SATURNIN. Others, some of which produce relatively little wine of distinction, are CABRIÈRES, Coteaux de la MÉJANELLE, QUA-TOURZE, Coteaux de ST-CHRISTOL, ST-DRÉZÉRY, the historically celebrated St-Georges-d'Orques, and Coteaux de VÉRARGUES. With the exception of Picpoul de Pinet and Clairette de Languedoc, which are white wines, most of the wine produced under these names is a full-bodied blend of southern red wine grape varieties, supplemented by some crisp, light rosé, often made from Cinsaut.

On the schists of the highest sites such as St-Saturnin and Montpeyroux, yields are particularly low but the wines can be powerful, concentrated, long-lived essences of the Languedoc. Well-drained gravelly limestone can yield more forward, fruity wines. La Clape, on the other hand, produces wines from vineyards heavily influenced by the Mediterranean.

The appellation regulations have been concerned to diminish the proportion of Carignan and Cinsaut permitted for red wines. Grenache, its relative Lladoner Pelut, Syrah, and Mourvèdre are the principal varieties encouraged for the appellation's red wines. Grenache Blanc, Clairette, Picpoul, and Bourboulenc are the principal white grape varieties and white Coteaux du Languedoc must contain at least two of them. The late 1990s saw a significant increase in the number of seriously interesting white wines, typically made from blends including at least two of Grenache Blanc, Bourboulenc, Roussanne, Rolle, and Viognier,

although this last is not officially sanctioned by the appellation regulations.

Some fine producers making wines with the simple Coteaux du Languedoc appellation are Abbaye de Valmagne, Mas Cal Demoura, Mas Jullien, Ch la Sauvageonne, Domaine Peyre Rose, Prieuré de St-Jean de Bébian, and Ch St-Martin de la Garrigue.

For more information, see under individual subappellation names.

Languedoc-Roussillon, common name for the wide sweep of varied vineyards from Marseilles around the Mediterranean coast of the south of France to the Spanish border, incorporating both LANGUEDOC and the contiguous ROUSSILLON region.

Lanuvini, Colli, white wines from the hills south east of Rome. See CASTELLI ROMANI.

Lanzarote, Spanish DO including the whole of this black-soiled, volcanic, but relatively flat island in the CANARY ISLANDS. Vineyards are dominated by the white Malvasía grape, as on LA PALMA. The technically up-to-date El Grifo winery has been a pioneer in the development of modern dry Malvasía of some originality.

V. de la S.

La Palma, Spanish DO including the entire eponymous volcanic island in the CANARY ISLANDS. A large variety of grape varieties are cultivated, but La Palma's most distinguished wine is traditional sweet Malvasías. V. de la S.

large format, bottle size larger than the standard 75-cl size and of particular interest to COLLECTORS and INVESTORS (provided it is filled with FINE WINE).

Laski Rizling, the name current in SLOVENIA, VOJVODINA, and some other parts of what was Yugoslavia for the white grape variety known in Austria as WELSCHRIESLING (under which name more details appear). The vine is cultivated widely in Yugoslavia, but most successfully in the higher vineyards of Slovenia (just over the border from the spirited Welschrieslings of STYRIA), and Fruška Gora in Vojvodina, where it can produce equally crisp and delicately aromatic wines. Few of these have been exported, however, and most of the large bottling enterprises have been hampered by poor equipment and importers who have been more concerned with quantity than quality. For decades, a Slovenian BRAND, Lutomer Riesling (eventually renamed

Lutomer Laski Rizling after German lobbying), was the best-selling white wine in the UK, its heavily sweetened style conveying little of the intrinsic character of the variety. The Rizling Vlassky is the variant known in the CZECH REPUBLIC.

Latin America. See SOUTH AMERICA and MEXICO.

latitude, angular distance north or south of the equator, measured in degrees and minutes. The main northern-hemisphere viticultural regions extend between 32 and 51 degrees north, and most of those in the southern hemisphere between 28 and 42 degrees south. Extreme poleward limits are at about 52 degrees north in ENGLAND (and Ireland), and just over 46 degrees south in Otago, NEW ZEALAND. Some vines are also cultivated for wine production in tropical highlands close to the equator in MEXICO, BOLIVIA, PERU, BRAZIL, and KENYA. See also TROPICAL VITICULTURE.

Comparisons between hemispheres based purely on latitude are misleading. The northern hemisphere is on average warmer than the southern hemisphere at similar latitudes, partly because of the greater land mass and its disposition around the North Pole, and partly (in the case of western Europe) because of warming by the Gulf Stream.   J.G.

Latium, known as Lazio in Italy itself, is the seat of Italy's government and administration in the capital, Rome. The region also has a significant viticultural production, making it sixth among Italy's regions. Some 15 per cent of the total Latium vineyard is dedicated to the production of DOC wine. White wines, almost exclusively from MALVASIA and TREBBIANO grapes, represent over 85 per cent of the total DOC production, with the wines of the CASTELLI ROMANI representing by far the majority. Malvasia and Trebbiano blends are also produced in some quantities in the DOC zones of Cerveteri, Est!Est!!Est!!!, and in that small portion of the ORVIETO zone which spills over the Umbrian border into Latium. Lazio has no significant red DOCs although an occasional Cabernet/Merlot blend of significant quality—from the Boncompagni Ludovisi estate near Rome, the Di Mauro estate in Marino, and the newer Castel De Paolis estate in Grottaferrata, for example—suggests that the soil and climate are well suited to red-wine production, even if no real tradition exists in the region. The CESANESE grape has its proponents in its home

province of Frosinone, but most Cesanese is neither well made nor interesting. A number of fine red wines made in the mid 1990s suggests a new consciousness of the region's potential, possibly partly inspired by neighbouring UMBRIA's success.   D.T.

Latour, Château, famously long-lived FIRST GROWTH in the MÉDOC region of BORDEAUX, where vines were already planted in the late 14th century.

In 1989, the estate was bought by multinational corporation Allied-Lyons, already owners of Harveys, for the equivalent of £110 million. In 1993, Allied-Lyons sold their 94 per cent share of the property to French businessman François Pinault (who acquired the London AUCTION house of Christie's in 1998), when Latour was valued at £86 million.

The estate of 65 ha/160 acres of vineyard consists of 75 per cent Cabernet Sauvignon vines, 20 per cent Merlot, 3.5 per cent Cabernet Franc, and 1.5 per cent Petit Verdot, with an average annual production of 30,000 cases of the three wines made there. In 1966 was first produced a SECOND WINE, Les Forts de Latour, made from the young vines and from three small plots on the other side of the St-Julien–Pauillac road. A third wine is also bottled and sold as Pauillac. Latour's wines generally require much longer to develop than those of the other first growths, and they often have greater longevity. Latour is also known for its ability to produce good wines in lesser vintages.   E.P.-R.

Latour, Louis, one of Burgundy's most commercially astute, and oldest, merchants. Jean Latour first planted vines in Aloxe-Corton, then called simply Aloxe, in 1768. Jean's son was the first in a long line of Louis Latours and enlarged the domaine considerably and it was not until the late 19th century that the family added wine brokering to their vine-growing activities.

With an eye to the developing export markets, the third Louis Latour bought the Lamarosse family's NÉGOCIANT business in 1867, and was so successful that in 1891 he was able to buy Ch Corton-Grancey in Aloxe-Corton. With this acquisition came extensive winemaking premises, and some notable vineyards around the hill of Corton to add to the Latour family holdings, which already included some Chambertin; Romanée-St-Vivant, Les Quatre Journaux; and Chevalier-Montrachet, Les Demoiselles.

It was the third Louis Latour who is reputed to have realized the hill of Corton's potential for great white wine when he replanted some of the hill now designated Corton-Charlemagne with Chardonnay vines after PHYLLOXERA had laid waste vineyards originally planted with Pinot Noir and Aligoté.

Innovations of succeeding Louis Latours include a succession of 'new' and increasingly daring white wines, including Grand Pouilly (subsequently known as Pouilly-Fuissé), MÂCON-LUGNY, a respectable alternative to CÔTE D'OR white wines produced in close co-operation with the Lugny CO-OPERATIVE. Louis Latour also pioneered the planting of Chardonnay vines in the relatively unknown ARDÈCHE in the early 1980s. In the late 1980s, Louis Latour bought land in the Var *département* in PROVENCE with the aim of planting the Beurot selection of Pinot Noir to produce gentle red wines sold as Pinot Noir, Domaine de Valmoissine.

The house enjoys a solid reputation for its white wines, but has incited controversy over its endorsement of PASTEURIZATION of even its finest red wines. In 1997, they celebrated the bicentenary of the négociant business and the firm is currently run by the sixth Louis Latour and his son Louis Fabrice.

Latour-de-France, like CARAMANY, is a small village singled out for special mention as a suffix to the appellation Côtes du Roussillon-Villages. It may have been accorded this distinction less because of the superior quality of the wine than because the name had been successfully promoted to the French wine consumer by wine merchants Nicolas, who once bought the majority of production. See ROUSSILLON.

Lavilledieu, Vins de, almost extinct VDQS in SOUTH WEST FRANCE on terraces between the GARONNE and Tarn rivers north of the Côtes du FRONTONNAIS. In 1990, just 842 hl/22,230 gal of red and rosé wine was produced, all by the local CO-OPERATIVE. A wide variety of south-western vine varieties are allowed, notably the NÉGRETTE of the Côtes du FRONTONNAIS.

laying down wine is an English expression for holding wine as it undergoes BOTTLE AGEING. Thus most people lay down wine in their (however notional) CELLARS. Considerable quantities of red bordeaux of vintages in the 1980s have been **laid down** by COLLECTORS all over the globe, for example.

Layon, Coteaux du, large appellation, for generally medium-sweet white wine made from the Chenin Blanc grape, in the ANJOU district of the Loire. Two small areas within the area produce wines of such quality that they have earned their own appellations, BONNEZEAUX and QUARTS DE CHAUME. They, and most of the best vineyards of the Coteaux du Layon, are on the steep slopes on the right bank of the Layon tributary of the Loire. TERROIR is all here, for Coteaux du Layon should be an intense wine made ideally from several TRIS through the vineyard, selecting BOTRYTIZED grapes, or those that have begun to raisin on the vine. Producers such as Claude Papin of Ch Pierre Bise vinify grapes picked on slate, schist, clay, and sandstone separately to demonstrate the variation in style and potential longevity. Other fine producers include Vincent Ogereau and Philippe Delesvaux, but this variable appellation is also a hotbed of ambition. Yields vary enormously according to the conditions of the vintage, but are officially limited to 30 hl/ha (1.7 tons/acre), and 25 hl/ha for wines produced in the clay soils around Chaume and sold as **Coteaux du Layon-Chaume**. The villages Beaulieu-sur-Layon, Faye d'Anjou, Rablay-sur-Layon, Rochefort-sur-Loire, St-Aubin-de-Luigné, and St-Lambert-du-Lattay can append their name to that of Coteaux du Layon, or sell it as **Coteaux du Layon-Villages**, provided the wines have a POTENTIAL ALCOHOL of 13 per cent, and an actual ALCOHOLIC STRENGTH of 12 per cent rather than the 11 per cent minimum demanded of the rest of Coteaux du Layon. In favourable vintages, some great wine is produced in this appellation, but producers are dogged by the depressing effect on selling prices of a substantial quantity of extremely ordinary just-sweet wine sold under the name Coteaux du Layon. Wines may be sold as DEMI-SEC, MOELLEUX, and, sweetest of all, LIQUOREUX.

See also LOIRE.

Lazio, Italian for the region of LATIUM.

Le. For anything prefixed Le, see under the next letter of the name.

lead, one of the familiar and widely dispersed heavy metals which occurs naturally in trace amounts in all plants, therefore in grapes, and therefore, usually in microgram-per-litre quantities only, in wines.

Most of the traces of lead from grapes are precipitated out with the LEES during winemaking. However, as analytical methods continue to improve, microgram quantities per litre are likely to be found in most wines.

The equipment used in modern wineries should not result in any lead contamination. The few wines which contain lead in milligram-per-litre concentrations derive it principally from capsules or FOILS which contain lead, or from lead-crystal DECANTERS. To protect those who do not clean obvious lead salts from a bottle lip before pouring, however, the use of lead capsules or foils is now declining or prohibited in many regions.

Lengthy storage of wines in lead-crystal decanters provides time for the wine acids to leach some lead from the glass, but keeping a wine in a lead-crystal glass or decanter for the usual period of no more than a few hours is too short for dangerous amounts of lead contamination.

Analyses of thousands of representative samples of wine suggest that the lead content of wines is decreasing in general but in the early 1990s ranged from 0 to 1.26 mg/l, with the average lead content being 0.13 mg/l, values well below any legal maximum.

An Australian study found that there was minimal uptake of lead from wine when it was consumed with food.   A.D.W. & J.Ro.

leaf (*feuille* in French). Vine leaves range in size up to that of a dinner plate but are normally the area of a human hand (100 to 200 cm^2). Their individual area correlates with shoot VIGOUR and also varies with vine variety (Merlot has large leaves, for example, while Gewürztraminer has small leaves). The total leaf and shoot system of a vine is known as the CANOPY.

leaf removal, vineyard practice aimed at helping to control fungal diseases, and at improving GRAPE COMPOSITION and therefore wine quality. Typically the leaves are removed around the bunches to increase exposure to the sun and wind. The bunches dry out more quickly after dew and rain so that moulds are less likely to develop. Increased exposure to sunlight helps the berries produce more of the PHENOLICS important in wine quality. Grape sugars are also increased and MALIC ACID reduced, both of which contribute to improved wine quality.

Traditionally leaf removal has been done by hand, but machines which remove leaves by suction and/or cutting have been developed.
                                                      R.E.S.

leaf to fruit ratio, viticultural measurement which indicates the capacity of a vine to ripen grapes. The ratio of vine leaf area to fruit (grape) weight determines just how well a vine can mature grapes and how suitable they will be for wine-making. It can have an even more important effect on wine quality than YIELD.

leafy. See TASTING TERMS.

Leányka, Hungarian name for the white grape variety called FETEASCA in Romania. Varietal Leányka has long been produced in EGER. It can produce good-quality wine if yields are restricted, and a particularly aromatic strain is grown on the south shore of Lake Balaton. See HUNGARY. See also KIRÁLEÁNKA.

Leatico, synonym for ALEATICO.

Lebanon, one of the oldest sites of wine production.

Apart from some vineyards in the Lebanese mountains, most vines are grown in the wide Bekaa valley, where an altitude of around 1,000 m/3,280 ft and mountain ranges on either side provide cool nights and rainfall respectively so that the grapes rarely ripen before the middle of September (considerably later than some southern French vineyards, for example).

French influence on the country is still apparent in the grape varieties most commonly planted—Cinsaut, Carignan, Cabernet Sauvignon, Merlot, Mourvèdre, Grenache, and Syrah. Chateau Musar, the country's innovative producer of good-quality wines, has a long track record of intense red wine made from 50 to 80 per cent Cabernet Sauvignon fleshed out with Cinsaut and Carignan. Following lessons learned in Bordeaux in the 1950s, Chateau Musar introduced DESTEMMING and BARREL MATURATION in new French OAK. The result, sold only after the second of three years has been spent in NEVERS oak, and perhaps as many as four years in bottle, is a heady, rich, often gamey red that has a Mediterranean character that is entirely its own. Ch Musar also produces small quantities of an equally full-bodied, oak-aged white, primarily from the indigenous white grape variety Obaideh, thought by some to be identical to Chardonnay, as well as some relatively hard indigenous Meroué, or Merweh (Sémillon). Ch Musar exports 95 per cent of production to markets including the UK, US, Sweden, and, more recently, France and southeast Asia. Lebanon's other important wineries, Kefraya and Ksara (already benefiting from

lees

foreign CONSULTANTS), are close to the vineyards of the Bekaa valley, while Chateau Musar's grapes have to be trucked over the mountains to the winery in Ghazir just north of Beirut. No wine was made in 1976, and the 1984 vintage was the only one, miraculously, to fall prey to the effects of the conflict of the 1980s.

lees, old English word for the dregs or sediment that settles at the bottom of a container such as a fermentation vessel. Wine lees are made up of dead YEAST cells, grape seeds, pulp, stem and skin fragments, and insoluble TARTRATES that are deposited during the making and ageing of wine.

In the production of everyday wines, clear wine is separated from the lees as soon as possible after FERMENTATION, to begin CLARIFICATION and STABILIZATION. Some wines, both red and, especially, white, may be deliberately left on some of their lees, the so-called **fine lees** (as opposed to the coarser **gross lees**, off which most wines are racked early in their life if greater complexity and reduction of MALIC ACID is desired), for some months in order to gain greater complexity of flavour. This is called LEES CONTACT.

Fine wines left on lees for a considerable time usually require much less drastic processing than more ordinary wines that were separated early from the lees, because the PHENOLICS and tartrates gradually precipitate during this AGEING period.

Once the maximum amount of good wine has been recovered, usually by RACKING after prolonged settling, or by the harsher process of FILTRATION, the lees are valuable only for their potassium acid tartrate (cream of tartar) and small amounts of alcohol.   A.D.W.

lees contact, increasingly popular and currently fashionable wine-making practice known to the Ancient Romans whereby newly fermented wine is deliberately left in contact with the LEES. This period of lees contact may take place in any container, from a bottle (as in the making of any BOTTLE-FERMENTED sparkling wine to produce desirable flavour compounds) to a large tank or vat—although a small oak BARREL is the most common location for lees contact. It may take place for anything between a few weeks and, in the special case of some sparkling wines, several years (see SPARKLING-WINE-MAKING). Most commonly, however, lees

contact is prolonged for less than a year after the completion of FERMENTATION.

Lees contact encourages the second, softening MALOLACTIC FERMENTATION because the lactic bacteria necessary for malolactic fermentation feed on micro-nutrients in the lees. This has the effect of adding complexity to the resultant wine's flavour. Many producers, particularly those of white BURGUNDY and other wines based on CHARDONNAY grapes, try to increase the influence of the lees on flavour by LEES STIRRING.

White wines made with deliberate lees contact are sometimes described as SUR LIE, a description commonly used to differentiate one type of MUSCADET from another, although in this case small barrels rarely play a part in the process. Lees contact even in bulk storage is increasingly used as a way of increasing flavour in everyday white wines—South Africa's Chenin Blanc, for example.

Red wines, with their more robust flavours, gain less from lees contact, but, for many red wines, the added complexity of the malolactic fermentation, which is encouraged by lees contact, is very valuable.

Wines left in contact with a layer of lees more than 10 cm/4 in thick for more than a week or so, however, are very likely to develop HYDROGEN SULPHIDE, disulphide, or MERCAPTAN odours. This is why it is important to rack new wine from its gross lees (see LEES) so that the lees level does not become too thick.

lees stirring is the wine-making operation of mixing up the LEES in a barrel, cask, tank, or vat with the wine resting on them. It is an optional addition to the process of LEES CONTACT and is often employed, particularly for whites which have undergone BARREL FERMENTATION.

Lees stirring is done partly to avoid the development of malodorous HYDROGEN SULPHIDE. Stirring up the lees in the barrel also affects wood flavour, however. If the lees are stirred, they act as an even more effective buffer between the wine and the wood, limiting the extent to which wood TANNINS and PIGMENTS are extracted into the wine. Wines subjected to lees stirring therefore tend to be much paler and less tannic than those whose lees are not stirred.

left bank, an expression for that part of the BORDEAUX wine region that is on the left bank of the river GARONNE. It includes, travelling down river, GRAVES, SAUTERNES, BARSAC, PESSAC-LÉOGNAN, MÉDOC, and all the appellations of the Médoc. The most obvious characteristic shared by the red wines of these appellations, as distinct from RIGHT BANK appellations, is that the dominant grape variety is Cabernet Sauvignon rather than Merlot and Cabernet Franc, although there are many other distinctions.

leftover wine in an opened container such as a half-empty bottle is prey to OXIDATION and steps must be taken in order to prevent it turning to VINEGAR—which could happen within hours or even minutes for a very old wine, within two or three days for most young table wines, fino and manzanilla SHERRY, and most bottle-matured PORT, within a few weeks for a robust wood-matured port such as common or garden Ruby or Tawny or oloroso sherry, or within months for most MADEIRA.

Because OXYGEN is the villain in this piece, the easiest way to avoid spoilage of leftover wine is to decant it into a smaller container, perhaps a half-bottle, which approximates as closely as possible to the volume of wine left. There are also patent devices for filling the ULLAGE in a bottle or decanter with inert gas, by pumping or spraying, or an attempt can be made to create a vacuum with a pump device.

The most satisfactory way of disposing of wine leftovers is surely to drink them, and the leftovers of some wines, particularly concentrated young red wines, can taste better, and certainly softer, after a day or even two on ullage (see DECANTING).

Leftover wine can also be used quite satisfactorily as COOKING wine and can also be used deliberately to make vinegar. See also RECORKING.

legs, tasting term and alternative name for the TEARS left on the inside of a glass by some wines.

Lemberger, name for the LIMBERGER vine in WASHINGTON state, where it is relatively important. Its lowish acidity is no disadvantage in this climate and Lemberger has an increasing number of fans among wine-makers, even if consumers tend to think it is a cheese.

Len de l'El and Len de l'Elh has, like MANSENG, been a beneficiary of proud regionalism in SOUTH WEST FRANCE. It was once a major and

is now a compulsory minor ingredient in the white wines of GAILLAC. The wine is powerful, characterful, but can be flabby. Its name is local dialect for *loin de l'œil*, or 'far from sight'.

length or persistence of flavour is an important indicator of wine quality. See also TASTING TERMS.

Lenz Moser, important wine producer in AUSTRIA which can trace its history back to the 12th century. In the 1920s, Dr Lenz Moser III experimented with a new way of training vines which revolutionized Austrian viticulture, making it feasible despite high labour costs. The company was taken over in 1986 by a large Austrian drinks company and Lenz Moser V has channelled considerable investments into renewing vineyards and into the winery at Rohrendorf in Kamptal-Donauland, concentrating increasingly on ORGANIC VITICULTURE and innovations such as paper (as opposed to lead) CAPSULES. The company has managed the Malteser (Knights of Malta) wine estate at Mailberg near the Czech border since 1969 and has here pioneered both BARRIQUE maturation for red wines and the Cabernet Sauvignon grape in lower Austria. In 1988, Lenz Moser acquired the Klosterkeller Siegendorf in Burgenland and is developing Pinot Blanc there.

León, wine zone in north-west Spain. See CASTILE AND LEÓN.

Léoville Las Cases, Château, the flagship wine of ST-JULIEN and one run as though it were a FIRST GROWTH (down to the pricing policy) by the owners Michel and his son Jean-Hubert Delon. It is perhaps the most obvious candidate as a SUPER SECOND.

The Delon policy is admirably strict in terms of viticulture, wine quality, and longevity. These firm, deep-coloured, Cabernet-based wines are supported by a strict selection process which can make Clos du Marquis one of Bordeaux's finest SECOND WINES, more like Les Forts de LATOUR in that certain plots of land are always designated for this fine wine, than a dump bin for less satisfactory *cuves*.

Ch Léoville Las Cases currently includes 97 ha/240 acres of vineyard planted to 65 per cent Cabernet Sauvignon, 19 per cent Merlot, 13 per cent Cabernet Franc, and 3 per cent Petit Verdot. The Delons' policy is to release EN PRIMEUR prices very late, typically after the first growths and at a level far closer to them than those of their fellow second growths. In the early 1990s, the Delons also acquired the POMEROL property Ch Nenin.

Leroy, famous name in French wine, not just because **Baron le Roy** of CHÂTEAUNEUF-DU-PAPE was instrumental in the development of the APPELLATION CONTRÔLÉE system, but also in the CÔTE D'OR.

The NÉGOCIANT house **Maison Leroy** was founded in the small village of Auxey-Duresses in 1868 and its extensive warehouses there still house substantial stocks of fine, mature burgundy. Henri Leroy bought a half share in the world-famous DOMAINE DE LA ROMANÉE-CONTI, a share inherited equally by his two daughters Pauline Roch-Leroy and **Lalou Bize-Leroy** on his death in 1980.

Lalou, a prodigious taster, rock climber, and glamorous dresser, had been co-director of the Domaine since 1974 and contributed considerably to its wine-making policy of quality above all. She also ran Maison Leroy, but Burgundy's steady move towards DOMAINE BOTTLING made her job of buying the finest raw materials for her négociant skills of ÉLEVAGE increasingly difficult. In 1988, helped by an £8 million investment from her Japanese importers Takashimaya, she succeeded in buying the Domaine Noëllat of VOSNE-ROMANÉE, an already fine canvas on which to paint her vision of the perfect domaine, soon renamed **Domaine Leroy**. This domaine now comprises more than 22 ha/54 acres of some of the Côte d'Or's finest vineyards, including a total of more than 6 ha in nine different GRANDS CRUS.

This effectively entailed setting up in competition with DRC, since the Domaine Leroy is based in the same village and, like DRC, has holdings in the grand cru RICHEBOURG and Romanée St Vivant. Unfettered by the commercial considerations of the dozen or so shareholders in DRC, Lalou was able to institute fully BIODYNAMIC VITICULTURE, almost uneconomically low YIELDS, and to invest in every possible wine-making luxury. The wines, which come from a much broader range of (mainly red-wine) appellations than those of DRC, are extremely concentrated, expressing as definitively as possible their exact geographical provenance, as well as considerable oak sometimes.

Independently of her sister Pauline but with her husband Marcel, Lalou owns the Domaine

d'Auvenay, another biodynamically farmed enterprise founded in 1988, with total holdings of around 4 ha, including small plots in four different grands crus.

Les Baux. See BAUX.

Lessona, small but historically important red-wine district in the Vercelli hills in the sub-Alpine north of the PIEDMONT region of northwest Italy. Nebbiolo grapes, here called Spanna, make up the majority of the wine although some Bonarda or Vespolina may be added to produce a slightly less austere wine. Sella is the only producer of note. See SPANNA.

See also BRAMATERRA, GATTINARA, BOCA, GHEMME, SIZZANO, and FARA.

L'Étoile, small, rarely exported appellation in the JURA region of eastern France, dominated by the CO-OPERATIVE, which specializes in the production of the extraordinarily nutty VIN JAUNE which is sold in the 62-cl/22-fl oz *clavelin* bottle like the more famous CH-CHALON made nearby. L'Étoile also produces sweet white VIN DE PAILLE in some years, and regular light, dry whites from Chardonnay and the region's SAVAGNIN grape.

L'Étoile Mousseux is also made, using the traditional method of SPARKLING-WINE-MAKING.

Levante, the collective name for four Mediterranean provinces of SPAIN forming two autonomous regions officially known as Comunidad Valenciana and Murcia. The Levante encompasses five DO wine zones: ALICANTE, UTIEL-REQUENA, VALENCIA in the Valencian autonomy; and Bullas, JUMILLA, and YECLA in Murcia. The climate becomes progressively extreme away from the coast with summer TEMPERATURES reaching 45 °C/113 °F in places and annual rainfall amounting to less than 300 mm/12 in. Most of the wines are correspondingly coarse but progress has been made in Jumilla, Yecla, and Alicante. The port of Valencia itself is one of the largest wine entrepôts in the world with five huge firms handling millions of litres of bulk wine from all over south and central Spain, although this trade has been declining since the early 1990s.

R.J.M.

Leverano, DOC for robust red wine made mainly from NEGROAMARO grapes in south-east Italy. See APULIA.

Liatiko, ancient Cretan vine producing relatively soft wine, usually blended with the stronger MANDELARIA and KOTSIFALI to make sweet reds.

Libourne, small port on the RIGHT BANK of the Dordogne in the Bordeaux region. It is the commercial centre for the right-bank appellations. Of merchants based here, J. P. MOUEIX is the most important. See POMEROL, the wine region on the eastern outskirts of the town.

The wines ST-ÉMILION, Pomerol, and FRONSAC are sometimes referred to collectively as Libournais.

lie or lies, French for LEES.

Liebfraumilch, quintessentially mild white wine from GERMANY known almost exclusively in export markets. It accounts for an extraordinary 60 per cent of all German wine exported. As defined by law, it is a QBA from any one of the following regions: RHEINHESSEN, PFALZ, NAHE, and RHEINGAU, of which the first two account for some 64 and 27 per cent of the total production respectively. Liebfraumilch must contain not less than 18 g/l RESIDUAL SUGAR and at least 70 per cent of RIESLING, SILVANER, MÜLLER-THURGAU, or KERNER grapes, although in practice Müller-Thurgau usually dominates the blend. Consumed within 18 months of the vintage, most Liebfraumilch is fresh, low in alcohol, flatteringly sweet, and deliberately designed to wean newcomers to wine off soft drinks. Well-known BRANDS include BLUE NUN and Black Tower. I.J. & K.B.S.

Liechtenstein. The principality's 15 ha/37 acres of vineyard are concentrated on the capital Vaduz, above and at some distance from the river RHINE, where the climate is strongly influenced by the warming föhn effect of the wind from the south. The largest vineyard owners, the domain of the Fürst von und zu Liechtenstein, produces good-quality wine in the style of eastern SWITZERLAND, from Blauburgunder (PINOT NOIR) and from a small plantation of CHARDONNAY. Seventy per cent is sold directly to local consumers.   I.J.

lieu-dit, French, usually Burgundian, term for a specific, named plot of land which is in practice used on labels for vineyards below PREMIER CRU in rank.

lifestyle winery, term coined in NEW ZEALAND for a small winery established and run, typically by an educated young to middle-aged couple who have access to funds generated by another career, more for its bucolic appeal than as a strictly commercial proposition.

lifted. See TASTING TERMS.

light. A wine is described by wine tasters as light, or **light bodied**, if it is low in ALCOHOL and VISCOSITY. See BODY for more details.

Liguria, the crescent-shaped strip that runs along Italy's Mediterranean coast from the French border to the edge of Tuscany, is Italy's third smallest region after the Valle d'Aosta and Molise. The extremely rugged terrain—the Apennines descend virtually all the way to the sea—combined with the microscopic size of individual properties make agriculture in general and viticulture in particular a marginal activity. Total Ligurian wine production is less than 300,000 hl/7.9 million gal, and DOC wines represent just seven per cent of this figure.

A crossroads of trade and traffic between Italy, France, and Spain, Liguria has long cultivated a multitude of different vine varieties. Although the undistinguished Albarola is the region's most planted variety, the region is concentrating its efforts on three white varieties (VERMENTINO, PIGATO, and the less characterful Bosco) and three red varieties (ROSSESE, SANGIOVESE, and DOLCETTO, the last of these called Ormeasco in Liguria). Ormeasco, Pigato, Rossese, and Vermentino each have their own DOC within the Riviera di Ponente zone, a wide stretch of territory between Genoa and the French border.

Liguria's most renowned wine, the white Cinqueterre, is perhaps most famous for its vertigo-inducing vineyards perched on TERRACES sculpted into cliffsides high above the Tyrrhenian sea. The wine itself, made from Bosco plus Albarola and/or Vermentino, rarely rises above the thirst-quenching level. The once-renowned Sciacchetrà, a sweet Cinqueterre made from raisined grapes, has virtually disappeared.

Production of Vermentino is concentrated in Castelnuovo Magra, to the south of La Spezia (where the wine is not a DOC), and in Diano Castello and Imperia in the province of Imperia. Good bottles of Vermentino can be delicate and floral, although they cannot be compared with a fine BELLET made across the French border from the same grape variety or with a fuller Vermentino from Sardinia. Pigato, a fleshier wine with more intense flavours, is potentially more interesting than Vermentino, although well-made bottles are more difficult to find; production of the wine is concentrated in Ranzo and Pieve di Teco, to the north of the city of Imperia. Ormeasco (Dolcetto) is produced almost exclusively in Pornassio and Pieve di Teco. The Rossese grape, of minor significance in the Riviera di Ponente DOC, has its own DOC near Ventimiglia, Rossese di Dolceacqua or simply Dolceacqua. The wine has its fanatical admirers, who have found in it blackcurrants and roses, power and delicacy.   D.T.

Limberger, also known as **Blauer Limberger** or **Lemberger**, is the German name for the black grape variety much more widely grown in Austria as BLAUFRÄNKISCH. Germany has very much less of the variety planted, almost exclusively in WÜRTTEMBERG, where both climate and consumers are tolerant of pale reds made from late-ripening vines (see TROLLINGER). The wine, often blended with Trollinger to produce a light red suitable for early drinking, has a better colour than that of most Germanic red wine varieties and has a good bite, notably of acidity. It is known as LEMBERGER in Washington state.

Limestone Coast, wine zone in SOUTH AUSTRALIA encompassing five regions of rapidly growing importance: Mount Benson, Robe, Naracoorte Ranges (Wrattonbully), Coonawarra, and Padthaway.

Limnio, dark grape variety native to the island of Lemnos in GREECE, where it can still be found. It has also transferred successfully to Khalkhidhikhi in north-east Greece, however, where it produces a full-bodied wine with a good level of acidity.

Limousin, old French province centred on the town of Limoges, and a term encountered most frequently in the wine world in reference to the region's OAK.

Limoux, small town and appellation in the eastern Pyrenean foothills in southern France. For centuries it has been devoted to the production of white wines that would sparkle naturally after a second fermentation during the spring. They became known as Blanquette de Limoux, Blanquette meaning 'white' in Occitan. Locals claim that fermentation in bottle was developed here long before it was consciously practised in CHAMPAGNE.

The region's vineyards are so much higher, cooler, and further from Mediterranean influence than any other Languedoc appellation (even Côtes de la MALEPÈRE to its immediate north) that it is classified as part of Atlantic-influenced SOUTH WEST FRANCE rather than as part of LANGUEDOC-ROUSSILLON even though it is just inland from the CORBIÈRES hills. Within the region, there are distinctly different zones, according to factors such as altitude, soil types, and the influence of the Atlantic or Mediterranean.

The grape used traditionally was the MAUZAC, called locally Blanquette, but increasing amounts of Chardonnay and, to a lesser extent, CHENIN BLANC have been planted so that in the 1980s the Limoux vineyards were much valued as one of southern France's very few sources of CHARDONNAY grapes from mature vines. Still wines made from them were therefore in great demand, especially for export markets. This international success was cleverly capitalized upon by Toques et Clochers, an annual charity AUCTION of different Chardonnay barrel samples, inspired by the famous HOSPICES DE BEAUNE auction but embellished by the involvement of some of France's most famous chefs. These often lean, oak-aged Chardonnays regularly fetched prices far in excess of their then classification as VINS DE PAYS so the Limoux appellation was thoroughly overhauled in 1993. It now encompasses still whites made mainly from Chardonnay (although Chenin Blanc may be included and at least 15 per cent of Mauzac must be included), with, unusually, compulsory WHOLE-BUNCH PRESSING and BARREL FERMENTATION.

This activity, together with light Cabernet and Merlot reds sold as Vins de Pays de la Haute Vallée de l'Aude, supplements Limoux's sparkling-wine business, dominated by the dynamic local CO-OPERATIVE, which sells a range of bottlings under such names as Aimery and Sieur d'Arques. The most notable individual estate in the region is Domaine de l'Aigle.

Blanquette de Limoux is the region's most famous product, sparkling wine containing at least 90 per cent of Mauzac with perhaps a little Chardonnay and Chenin Blanc. The CRÉMANT de Limoux was devised in 1990 for less rustic, more internationally designed sparkling wines made from a maximum of 70 per cent Mauzac together with Chardonnay and/or Chenin.

Limoux's distinctly marginal speciality is

Blanquette Méthode Ancestrale (see SPARKLING-WINE-MAKING), a sweeter, often slightly cloudy, less fizzy sparkling wine made exclusively from Mauzac left to ferment a second time in bottle without subsequent disgorgement of the resultant sediment. Like the GAILLAC Mousseux made from Mauzac by the *méthode gaillacoise* with similar regard for tradition and disdain for technology, these hand-crafted wines are low in alcohol, high in Mauzac's old-apple-peel flavours, and can taste remarkably like a superior sweet cider.

Lindemans, Australia's largest vineyard owner and wine company for long a rival of PENFOLDS but since the late 1980s part of the same SOUTHCORP group. Lindemans' origins lie in the Hunter Valley in NEW SOUTH WALES and it still owns more than 300 ha there. It also owns Australia's biggest vineyard, 596 ha at Padthaway in SOUTH AUSTRALIA as well as over 200 ha in Coonawarra, also in South Australia, and holdings in Mildura, VICTORIA, which is home to the company's major winery, Karadoc, which routinely processes 1,500 tonnes of grapes a day. Lindemans was among the first to exploit Padthaway's potential, establishing a vineyard there in 1970. Lindemans Padthaway Chardonnay, BARREL FERMENTED in French oak, played a key role in establishing the region's reputation in the early 1980s, being the first Australian Chardonnay to win an international trophy. Lindemans Bin 65 Chardonnay, made in vast quantities at Karadoc, is Australia's biggest-selling single VARIETAL wine and has become one of the world's most successful, and consistent, wine BRANDS.

Liqueur Muscat and **Liqueur Tokay** are two of AUSTRALIA's great gifts to the world: sumptuously hedonistic dark, sweet, alcoholic liquids that taste something like a cross between Madeira and Málaga. They are made from, respectively, a very dark-skinned strain of MUSCAT BLANC À PETITS GRAINS, called here Brown Muscat, and MUSCADELLE, traditionally known as Tokay in Australia. The centre of production is a hot north-western corner of the state of Victoria around the towns of Rutherglen and Glenrowan. These FORTIFIED wines can be uncannily fine quality, are bottled when they are ready to drink, and do not generally improve with BOTTLE AGE. They are quite sweet enough to serve with virtually any dessert.

RUTHERGLEN Muscat is becoming a more common name than Liqueur Muscat.

liquoreux, French term meaning 'syrupy sweet', used for very rich, often BOTRYTIZED, wines that are markedly sweeter than MOELLEUX wines.

Lirac, large appellation on the right bank of the southern RHÔNE producing mainly full-bodied reds and rosés, and a small amount of sometimes heavy white wine. The rosés can offer good-value alternatives to nearby TAVEL, made in very similar conditions and from the same sort of grape varieties, while the reds resemble a particularly soft, earlier-maturing Côte-du-Rhône-Villages.

Modern red and rosé Lirac is quite different from that nearby appellation in that it may contain no more than 40 per cent Grenache, while white wines must contain at least a third of Clairette, supplemented by a range of other southern white grapes and Ugni Blanc. The official maximum yield is notably lower than Tavel. Ch St-Roch and Domaine Maby are more ambitious producers than most.

Lison-Pramaggiore, DOC mainly in the VENETO region of north-east Italy created in 1986 by the fusion of two previous DOCs, the CABERNET di Pramaggiore and TOCAI di Lison. Other grapes are grown in the zone, however, and each of Chardonnay, Pinot Grigio, Riesling Italico or WELSCHRIESLING, Sauvignon Blanc, VERDUZZO, Merlot, and REFOSCO is entitled to DOC status as a VARIETAL wine. Tocai is the workhorse grape amongst the white, but Merlot has surpassed Cabernet (predominantly Franc rather than Sauvignon) amongst the red wine varieties.

The wines are fresh and pleasurable, if not memorable, with Cabernet regularly giving the most interesting results, in warm years approaching the level of a medium-quality CHINON or BOURGUEIL from France's Loire valley. Cooler vintages, together with the high percentage of Cabernet Franc and high yields, tend to bring out an aggressive herbaceousness which is perhaps more appealing to local markets than to international ones.   D.T.

Listán, synonym for PALOMINO, the white grape variety that can produce superb SHERRY around JEREZ, but results in dull, flabby white table wines almost everywhere else. Listán is the name by which the variety is known in much of Spain and in France. There are still several hundred hectares of it in the western Languedoc and in armagnac country although it is being systematically grubbed up here and in large parts of north-western Spain. However, Listán has found one last refuge on the CANARY ISLANDS' volcanic soils, where it can produce table wines of much greater individuality and distinction than on the Spanish mainland.

V. de la S.

Listán Negro, recently appreciated grape which dominates wine production on the island of Tenerife in the CANARY ISLANDS. CARBONIC MACERATION has managed to coax exceptional aromas out of this medium-bodied wine. The grape may also be called Almuñeco.

Listrac, or Listrac-Médoc, one of the six communal appellations of the Haut-Médoc district of Bordeaux. In relation to the other five (MARGAUX, ST-JULIEN, PAUILLAC, ST-ESTÈPHE, and even MOULIS, with which it is often compared), Listrac seems the least well favoured. It is, just, the furthest of them all from the Gironde estuary and the vineyards are planted on mainly clay-limestone on a gentle rise which, at an altitude of about 40 m/131 ft, constitutes some of the highest land in the Médoc. Although the Merlot grape is increasingly widely planted, the wines can be relatively austere in youth and their chief characteristic is their reliable density even in lighter vintages. The most cosseted property is probably the late Baron Edmond de Rothschild's Ch Clarke, while the similarly renovated Ch Fourcas-Hosten has a reputation as solid as its wines. Yields of 45 hl/ha (2.6 tons/acre) are officially tolerated here, whereas the limit is 40 hl/ha in Moulis and other Haut-Médoc village appellations.

See MÉDOC and BORDEAUX.

Little Karoo, wine region in SOUTH AFRICA.

Livermore Valley, California wine region and AVA east of San Francisco bay. Livermore hides behind hills high enough to screen out nearly all of the sea fogs common on the bay itself. It is therefore warm and—a passage between the cool, marine air of the bay and the hot, rising air of the CENTRAL VALLEY—windy, as evinced by thousands of turbines blanketing the hills of Altamont Pass at the eastern edge of the valley.

If the gods had got it all right, Sauvignon Blanc and Semillon would dominate in Livermore Valley, for no other grape does half so well in this small bowl in Alameda County. Acreage is under severe pressure from urban-

ization but the Wente winery is holding out by developing two prime golf courses surrounded by vineyards and homes. B.C.C.

Livinière, La. Commune in the far north of MINERVOIS in the south of France which has its own appellation as Minervois La Livinière.

Lladoner Pelut, a black grape variety also known as GRENACHE Poilu or Velu in the south of France and GARNACHA Peluda in Spain. Both vine and wine closely resemble Grenache Noir. It is officially and widely sanctioned in the Languedoc-Roussillon, often being specified alongside Grenache, although in practice it is declining in popularity. There are some plantings in Spain around Tarragona.

Lledoner. See LLADONER.

Lodi, town in the CENTRAL VALLEY of California that also gives its name to an AVA. Cooler than either the northern or southern halves of the valley, this prolific farming region is inland from, less watery, and thus warmer than the CLARKSBURG AVA to the north west, but much less warm than MADERA, Fresno, and other districts further south in the San Joaquin Valley. Zinfandel and Ruby Cabernet have shown the greatest adaptability to Lodi's growing conditions. Ruby Cabernet yielded agreeable, well-balanced wines throughout the 1960s and early 1970s, but the variety has faded with expanded plantings of Cabernet Sauvignon. Zinfandels from here tend to cluster at the fleshy, plummy, ripe end of the spectrum. Since the mid 1980s, Chardonnay and Merlot plantings have increased substantially but high YIELDS tend to reduce their distinctiveness beyond recognition.

Lodi AVA also encompasses the town of Woodbridge, site and name of Robert MONDAVI'S vast FIGHTING VARIETAL operation. For the same market sector, Sebastiani of SONOMA also have wineries in Lodi, and Glen Ellen, J. Lohr, and others also reach into the area regularly. B.C.C.

Loir, Coteaux du, northerly wine outpost of the greater LOIRE region on the confusingly named but usefully warming Loir tributary about 40 km/25 miles north of Tours. Viticulture seriously declined here, but enthusiasts such as Joël Gigou at Domaine de la Charrière are investing in a bright future for the varied wines of this small area, of which JASNIÈRES is the most famous appellation.

Bright reds, occasionally the product of BARREL MATURATION, are being made from Gamay, which does well on the clay-limestone sectors of the appellation. In ripe years such as 1989, 1990, 1995, and 1996, Pineau d'Aunis can be good enough to shine in a VARIETAL wine. Cabernet Franc and Cot (Malbec) are also allowed for reds, and Grolleau may be used in its light, dry rosés. Dry white wines are made from Chenin Blanc, but red-wine production predominates.

The local VDQS is Coteaux du VENDÔMOIS. See also LOIRE.

Loire, France's most famous river and name of one of its most varied wine regions whose wines are greatly appreciated locally and in Paris, but—with the famous exceptions of Sancerre and Pouilly-Fumé—are widely underrated outside France. This may be partly because the Loire's best red wines are distinguished by their delicacy rather than by their weight and longevity, and because so many of its finest white wines are made solely from Chenin Blanc, a grape variety associated with very ordinary wine outside the middle Loire: Anjou, Saumur, and Touraine.

Geography and climate

So long is the extent of the viticultural Loire that generalizations are impossible. The Loire's vineyards vary from the CONTINENTAL climate which produces Sancerre and Pouilly-Fumé, to the Muscadet region warmed by the Gulf Stream. Loire wine regions represent today, however, the north-western limit of vine cultivation in Europe (with the exception of ENGLAND's vineyards). The character of Loire wines can vary considerably from VINTAGE to vintage, since in a cool summer the grapes may struggle to reach full RIPENESS, while a particularly hot year such as 1989, 1990, 1995, and 1996 may result in some exceptional sweet white wines, some of them BOTRYTIZED in the middle Loire, but can rob the Loire's dry white Sauvignons of their nerve, and leave Muscadet dangerously limp.

The region is sufficiently far from the equator, however, that few of its red wines can be accused of being TANNIC, and the naturally high acidity associated with these latitudes, and some of its grape varieties, make much of the Loire's produce ideal base wine for sparkling wines.

Wine-making

White-wine-makers of the Loire have traditionally followed very similar principles to their counterparts in Germany, assiduously avoiding MALOLACTIC FERMENTATION and any new OAK influence, preferring instead to ferment and store wines in inert containers, and to bottle wines early, possibly after some LEES CONTACT in the case of Muscadet. For years, Loire reds suffered from a lack of EXTRACTION.

The result of the particularly competitive wine market of the 1980s, however, was to stimulate a rash of experimentation in cellars along the length of the Loire. BARREL MATURATION and in some cases BARREL FERMENTATION were introduced for reds and whites. Some producers encouraged their white wines to go through malolactic fermentation, while red-wine-makers worked hard to extract greater colour and TANNINS from their red-wine musts. SKIN CONTACT prior to fermentation was also introduced for some white wines, especially Sauvignons.

CHAPTALIZATION is the norm in the Loire, for both reds and whites, and is usually done to a maximum of an additional 2.5 per cent ALCOHOLIC STRENGTH of the finished wine.

Vine varieties

At the mouth of the Loire, MELON de Bourgogne and FOLLE BLANCHE predominate. The upper Loire is the terrain of Sauvignon Blanc for white wines and Pinot Noir for reds and rosés. The majority of the most successful sites in the middle Loire have proved themselves suitable for either CABERNET FRANC or CHENIN BLANC, but in the thousands of hectares of vineyard planted around them, there is a greater diversity of vine varieties than anywhere else in France, including a mix of Cabernet Sauvignon, Malbec, Gamay, Meunier, Pinot Gris, Chardonnay, and of course seas of Sauvignon and Pinot Noir. The maximum proportion of 20 per cent Chardonnay written into the rules of so many Loire appellations shows that the authorities at least are aware of the danger of the Loire losing its own identity (although Cabernet Sauvignon plantings are increasing). Those varieties that are exclusive to the Loire such as PINEAU D'AUNIS, GROLLEAU, ARBOIS, ROMORANTIN, and Meslier-St-François are in retreat.

Wines produced

Of all French wine regions, the Loire produces the greatest diversity of wine styles: from still through all types of sparkling wine, including the generic CRÉMANT de Loire; from bone dry and searingly tart to unctuous LIQUOREUX (although still with a high degree of acidity); and all hues from water white to (quite) deep purple. Rosés are a speciality of the Loire, whether the various VINS GRIS made well upstream, the famous Rosé d'Anjou, various pink Cabernets, or the generic ROSÉ DE LOIRE.

Travelling upstream, the major districts, with each appellation for which there is a separate entry, are:

Pays Nantais: MUSCADET, GROS PLANT du Pays Nantais, Coteaux d'ANCENIS, FIEFS VENDÉENS.

ANJOU: SAVENNIÈRES, Coteaux du LAYON, QUARTS DE CHAUME, BONNEZEAUX, Coteaux de l'AUBANCE.

SAUMUR.

TOURAINE: CHINON, BOURGUEIL, VOUVRAY, MONT-LOUIS, CHEVERNY, VALENÇAY.

Upper Loire: REUILLY, QUINCY, MENETOU-SALON, SANCERRE, POUILLY-FUMÉ.

Northern outposts: Coteaux du LOIR, JASNIÈRES, Coteaux du VENDÔMOIS.

On the bend: Vins de l'ORLÉANAIS, Coteaux du GIENNOIS.

Southern outposts: Vins du THOUARSAIS, Haut-POITOU, CHÂTEAUMEILLANT, ST-POURÇAIN, Côtes d'AUVERGNE, Côtes ROANNAISES, Côtes du FOREZ (although some of these are very far from the Loire and its climatic influence).

Lombardy, or Lombardia in Italian, the largest and most populous region of ITALY, and the driving force behind the country's post-Second World War economic boom, the dynamo which has given Milan and its hinterland one of Europe's highest standards of living. The region is a viticultural centre of some importance: its annual production of over 1.6 million hl/42.2 million gal (with DOC wines accounting for more than a third of the total) is larger than that of such famous wine regions as FRIULI, TRENTINO-ALTO ADIGE, UMBRIA, or the MARCHES.

Lombardy's centres of viticulture are in the Valtellina, the Oltrepò Pavese, and Franciacorta. Each area cultivates different grapes and makes wine in a completely different style from the others: the region has neither a key grape nor a key wine to make it better known, and its sheer size and disparity are marketing handicaps.

Valtellina is the northernmost outpost of the NEBBIOLO vine and its wines—often labelled with the subzones INFERNO, GRUMELLO, SASSELLA, VALGELLA—are the most widely known in national and international markets. The Oltrepò Pavese, by far the largest DOC of Lombardy, supplies sturdy red wines from BARBERA, Croatina, and UVA RARA grapes (either singly or as blends), everyday dry SPUMANTE, and innocuous white from RIESLING ITALICO, and is largely dependent on the local market of Milan; price cutting and over-production have left the area performing well below its potential. Franciacorta is the youngest and most dynamic of the three major DOC zones, the new centre for high-quality spumante production in Italy, and an interesting source of ambitious Chardonnay, Bordeaux-style red Cabernet/Merlot blends, and Pinot Noir.

Other DOCs include Lugana, whose Trebbiano-based white wines are produced to the south of Lake Garda. Botticino and Cellatica are red blends (the former with a slight suggestion of sweetness) from SCHIAVA, BARBERA, and MARZEMINO grapes grown in the province of Brescia and served with the local versions of *pot-au-feu* or wine-laced stews. Riviera del Garda are light-red and rosé wines produced on the western shore of Lake Garda in the image of BARDOLINO across the lake, although the grapes (Groppello, Sangiovese, Barbera, and Marzemino) could not be more different.

For more detail on specific notable wines, see BONARDA, CROATINA, FRANCIACORTA, LUGANA, OLTREPÒ PAVESE, VALTELLINA, as well as Colli BOLOGNESI and Colli PIACENTINI.   D.T.

long. See TASTING and TASTING TERMS.   P.J.W.

Los Carneros. See CARNEROS, wine region and AVA of California.

Loupiac, sweet-white-wine appellation on the right bank of the GARONNE in the BORDEAUX region sandwiched between CADILLAC and STE-CROIX-DU-MONT. In much of the 20th century, the wines failed to fetch the prices necessary to justify truly meticulous wine-making. The best vineyards are on clay-limestone slopes overlooking the river and are well situated to benefit from NOBLE ROT, provided producers are prepared to take the necessary risks. Good Loupiac such as that produced at Domaine du Noble and Chx du Cros and Loupiac-Gaudiet is generally deeply coloured and noticeably full bodied; the use of new OAK became gradually more common from the late 1980s (see SAUTERNES for more details).

Loureiro, fine, 'laurel-scented', white grape variety grown in VINHO VERDE country in northern Portugal and also, increasingly, as Loureira in RÍAS BAIXAS in north-west Spain. It has often been blended with TRAJADURA (Treixadura in Spain) but can also be found as an aromatic VARIETAL wine. It produces its best quality, usually quite low in alcohol, around Braga and the coast.

low-alcohol wine is usually REDUCED-ALCOHOL WINE but may also be, like NO-ALCOHOL WINE, regular wine from which alcohol has been deliberately removed, usually but not necessarily with harmful effects on flavour and quality. Such wines are usually reduced to an ALCOHOLIC STRENGTH which excludes them from DUTY, reducing their price. See also WINE COOLERS and DEALCOHOLIZED WINE.

Lower Great Southern. See GREAT SOUTH-ERN.

low-input viticulture, an alternative to conventional viticulture with the aim of minimizing all inputs to the vineyard—agrochemicals and labour, for example.

Lubéron, Côtes du, wines made on the fashionable slopes of the Lubéron, where vineyards add colour and bucolic allure to one of the more sought-after corners of Provence. The appellation is a sort of buffer state between the RHÔNE and PROVENCE, or more precisely between the Côtes du VENTOUX appellation and that of Coteaux d'AIX-EN-PROVENCE (although French officialdom places it firmly in the Rhône).

The appellation was created only in 1988 and produces significant quantities of all three colours of wine, although single VARIETAL wines must be sold as VINS DE PAYS du Vaucluse. All reds contain some Syrah, augmented by Grenache, possibly Mourvèdre and Cinsaut, and no more than 20 per cent Carignan. Those who try hard, such as old-timers Chx de Mille and de l'Isolette and the more recent Domaine de Mayol and Chx Val Joanis and La Canorgue, can produce herb-scented reds with some concentration and ageing potential. Whites are made from Grenache, Clairette, Bourboulenc, possibly some Marsanne and Roussanne, and no more than 50 per cent Ugni Blanc. The region's rather cooler nights (and winters) than in most Côtes du Rhône vineyards help to produce some of the crisper, more interesting white wines of the southern Rhône. Rosés may incorporate up to 20 per cent of white grapes, and have particular allure when drunk locally to the sound of cicadas.

Lugana, dry white Italian wine based on the TREBBIANO grape (in this case the Trebbiano di Lugana or Trebbiano Veronese) produced to the south and south west of Lake Garda in the province of Brescia, straddling the provinces of Lombardy and Veneto. The wine, most of which is fairly anonymous, demonstrates the limits of its variety, and also of the DOC rules, which permit yields of 85 hl/ha (4.8 tons/acre), but an occasional Lugana with more developed aromas and the refreshing tang of Trebbiano's high ACIDITY can provide an enjoyable bottle for summer quaffing. Local *aficionados* insist that it is the perfect accompaniment for Garda fish, a claim that can be verified only on the spot. D.T.

Lunel is the centre of the Muscat de Lunel appellation for sweet golden VIN DOUX NATUREL made from MUSCAT BLANC À PETITS GRAINS grapes grown between Montpellier and Nîmes. Yields are low and vinification techniques improving although many local vine-growers have been more interested in developing lower alcohol, dry vins de CÉPAGE or wines that qualify as COTEAUX DU LANGUEDOC. A single CO-OPERATIVE is responsible for almost all the wine produced, which tastes like a cross between the Muscats of FRONTIGNAN and ST-JEAN-DE-MINER-VOIS.

Lunel is also the occasional Hungarian name for a yellow-berried form of Muscat Blanc à Petits Grains grown in the TOKAJI region.

Lungarotti, owners of an eponymous estate in the village of Torgiano Perugia in UMBRIA, central Italy. The estate is the leading vineyard property in the region, with an annual output of about 2 million bottles. Beginning with Torgiano Rosso 'Rubesco' (SANGIOVESE grapes with CANAIOLO) and Torgiano Bianco 'Torre di Giano' (TREBBIANO with GRECHETTO), Torgiano was awarded the DOC in 1968, and the exceptional Rubesco Riserva the DOCG in 1990. Fourteen other wines are produced, including large quantities of Chardonnay dell'Umbria, Pinot Grigio dell'Umbria, Cabernet Sauvignon di Miralduolo, as well as VIN SANTO and Metodo Classico Lungarotti Brut sparkling wine. Almost half of all wine is exported. E.P.-R.

Lurtons, ramified family of property owners and wine-makers in BORDEAUX, owning more wine estates in the Bordeaux region than any other single family, including Ch Bonnet in the ENTRE-DEUX-MERS, Chx La Louvière, Couhins, Rochemorin, Cruzeau in GRAVES, Chx Brane-

Cantenac, Durfort-Vivens, and Desmirail in Margaux, Ch Bouscaut in Pessac-Léognan, and Chx Doisy-Dubroca and Climens in Barsac. The younger generation of Lurtons seem likely to continue to be a significant presence in Bordeaux and beyond and the great majority of them work in the wine business. Jacques and François Lurton, for example, started a world-wide wine-making service in 1988, advising and installing FLYING WINE-MAKERS in France, Spain, Italy, South America, and at one time South Australia and Moldova.

Lussac-St-Émilion, satellite appellation of ST-ÉMILION in Bordeaux.

Lutomer, known as Ljutomer in SLOVENIA, small town in the far east of the country which lends its name to a popular British BRAND, most famously of LASKI RIZLING.

Luxembourg, or Luxemburg, was for long the European Union's smallest and coolest wine producer before being rivalled in both respects by ENGLAND. The rarely exported wines produced are relatively dry and, depending on grape variety, reminiscent of those of Alsace or England in style. With the exception of an increasing number of light reds and rosés made from Pinot Noir vines, the wines made on the western, Luxembourg bank of the river MOSELLE are white. Except in very ripe years such as 1990, CHAPTALIZATION is a necessity here and the wines are marked by relatively high acidity (although DEACIDIFICATION may be practised by some producers). A national law passed in 1996 was designed to encourage higher-alcohol wines.

Geography

Luxembourg's vineyards are in two of the grand duchy's eastern cantons, Remich and Grevenmacher. On the alluvial plain of Remich, the heavier soils tend to produce less aromatic, heavier, earlier-maturing wines from such villages as Remich, Wintrange, and Schengen. Parts of the narrower valley of Grevenmacher to the north have been reshaped by terracing, as in the Mosel across the German border, but yields are lower, calcareous soils predominate, and wines such as the village of Ahn's fine Rieslings are particularly slow maturing.

Vine varieties

Most Luxembourg still wines are varietal wines and are almost invariably labelled as such.

Rivaner Luxembourg's own strain of MÜLLER-

THURGAU. Its ability to yield obligingly high quantities was so abused by many growers that it became synonymous with mediocrity and is now in decline.

Elbling Consumers increasingly exposed to softer, fuller, and more aromatic wines are rejecting Elbling in favour of various members of the PINOT family.

Riesling Not the most sought-after wine in Luxembourg, it nevertheless accounts for about one-eighth of Luxembourg's vineyards. Here, as elsewhere, Riesling's slow development in bottle meant that it did not enjoy the public esteem enjoyed by those listed below.

Auxerrois This has higher status in Luxembourg than anywhere else in the world. Its low acidity is a positive attribute this far from the equator and when yields are curbed it can produce smoky, full-bodied wines worth ageing. See AUXERROIS.

Other varieties Pinot Gris is also highly regarded in Luxembourg, again for its low acidity and its weight, as are, for much the same reasons, Pinot Blanc and Gewürztraminer, which is still relatively rare. Pinot Gris in particular has won acclaim in international comparative tastings. Luxembourg growers have flirted with Chardonnay but the wines have so far been marked by a certain bitterness.

Appellations

Luxembourg's answer to the APPELLATION CONTRÔLÉE system of France is highly individual and would be difficult to apply to a bigger wine industry. There is just one appellation, Moselle Luxembourgeoise, which is allowed to practically all wines, both still and sparkling, although they are all submitted to analysis and a tasting. Superior wines may be ranked as Vins Classés, Premiers Crus, or even Grands Premiers Crus. This generous system, which ignores geographical differences and the influence of TERROIR, has attracted some criticism and a rival organization in the form of Domaine et Tradition, which encourages local variation and expression and imposes a maximum yield of 85 hl/ha (4.8 tons/acre). (The maximum yield allowed on the French MOSELLE is 60 hl/ha.)

Since 1995, there has been some limited experimentation with ICE WINES, although few growers have been prepared to make BOTRYTIZED wines in the image of the AUSLESE and BEERENAUSLESE wines made by the best producers in the neighbouring SAAR in Germany.

For details of Luxembourg's appellation for traditional-method sparkling wines, see CRÉMANT de Luxembourg.

Industry organization

As in the German Mosel, the average vine-holding is extremely small—just over 2 ha—although it has gradually increased as more and more of the smallest holdings are sold to larger landowners. The number of growers halved during the 20 years up to 1997. About 20 per cent of vines are grown by independent domaines which make wine themselves. Several wine CO-OPERATIVES together function as Vinsmoselle and represent about 60 per cent of the grand duchy's wine production.

LVMH, scrupulously even-handed acronym for Moët Hennessy-Louis Vuitton, the French luxury-goods conglomerate which has a dominant interest in the CHAMPAGNE industry, not least through its subsidiaries, which include MOËT & CHANDON, KRUG, and VEUVE CLICQUOT, and a substantial position in Cognac through Hennessy. Its distribution, and production, companies throughout the world play an important part in the international wine and spirits trade. In 1987, LVMH acquired a 12 per cent stake in the Guinness Group, which rose to a 24 per cent stake in 1990. In 1997, LVMH exchanged its shares in Guinness and Grand Metropolitan for 11 per cent in the newly created Diageo amalgamation of the two, thus becoming the largest shareholder in this dominant drinks group. In 1998, LVMH acquired a substantial stake in Ch d'YQUEM, while its chief executive Bernard Arnault became co-owner of Ch CHEVAL BLANC.

Lyonnais, Coteaux du. Light red wines made chiefly from Gamay grapes grown in the hills both north and south west of the city of Lyons, and drunk mainly by its inhabitants. The red wines can be every bit as good as nearby BEAUJOLAIS, although the appellation was granted only in 1984. A small amount of white wine is also made, from Chardonnay and Aligoté. The CO-OPERATIVE at Saint-Bel vinifies three-quarters of production.

Macabeo is northern Spain's most planted white grape variety and, as Maccabéo or Maccabeu, has become very popular in ROUSSILLON.

In early-picked form, in Côtes du Roussillon it is either a fairly characterless white, a useful ingredient in rosé, or, as in Spain, a common lightener of potent reds in which it is officially sanctioned up to 10 per cent of the total blend. Later picked, it may be an ingredient in, or even sole constituent of, one of Roussillon's distinctive VINS DOUX NATURELS. It is also common in the LANGUEDOC. In the white wines of Minervois and Corbières, it is regarded as a principal ingredient, often blended with BOURBOULENC, GRENACHE BLANC, and a host of other southern white varieties.

The wine produced tends to have a vaguely floral character and relatively low acidity unless the grapes are picked so early that the floral character is even more difficult to discern, but it has the advantage, unlike other, more traditional RIOJA varieties, of withstanding OXIDATION well. Perhaps this is one of the reasons why it was so enthusiastically embraced by the growers of Rioja, where, as Viura, it all but displaced Malvasía and Garnacha Blanca to represent more than 90 per cent of all white varieties planted. However, by the late 1990s, the CONSEJO REGULADOR was systematically refusing authorization for any new Viura plantings as it encouraged red varieties.

Macabeo is also grown widely in Penedès and, especially, Conca de Barberá, where, with Parellada and Xarel-lo, it makes up the triumvirate of CAVA varieties, as well as being found throughout north-eastern Spain as far south as Tarragona.

Macedonia is now split: half in what was Yugoslavia and half a province of modern GREECE.

Ex-Yugoslavian republic

Squeezed into an enclave surrounded by BULGARIA, SERBIA, KOSOVO, ALBANIA, and Greece, the republic is hot and the climate is extremely favourable to vine cultivation. It produces TABLE GRAPES, red wine in great quantity, and a little white.

Macedonia has some good modern vineyards, 80 per cent of which are planted with red wine grapes including Cabernet Sauvignon and Merlot as well as the indigenous grapes VRANAC and Kratosija, which together make up around 90 per cent of red-wine production. White grapes are mainly SMEDEREVKA and Laski Rizling (WELSCHRIESLING) with some Chardonnay, Sauvignon Blanc, and the more interesting local variety ZILAVKA.

The big CO-OPERATIVE bottling operation at Povardarie, confusingly in the Povardarje region near Skopje, was showing signs of both improvement and export potential in the late 1990s. The other two major regions are Pcinja-Osogovo on the Bulgarian border and Pelagonija-Polog around Lake Ohrid and the Albanian border.   A.H.M.

Macedon Ranges, top-quality wine region in the Port Phillip zone of the Australian state of VICTORIA.

maceration, ancient word for steeping a material in liquid with or without a kneading action to separate the softened parts of the material from the harder ones. This important process in RED-WINE-MAKING involves extraction of the PHENOLICS from the grape skins, seeds, and stem fragments into the juice or new wine. Time and temperature are critical factors. Although everyday red wines are made simply by a rapid fermentation lasting just two or three days, many wine-makers encourage an additional maceration period after fermentation has been completed, particularly for long-lived wines such as red BORDEAUX.

Wine-makers must use trial and error, often over many years, to decide which are the optimum maceration conditions for each grape variety and season. Rapid laboratory analyses can help to estimate colour and tannins, but the wine-maker's eye and palate often prove surer guides.

Some wine producers favour a pre-fermentation cold maceration of red grapes rather than maceration of skins in an alcoholic liquid. This optional wine-making operation involves the maceration of grape skins with juice while the mass is held at a low temperature.

See also BARREL FERMENTATION for an outline of a red-wine-making option which dispenses with post-fermentation maceration altogether.

In WHITE-WINE-MAKING, maceration is usually actively discouraged by separating the juice from the skins as soon as possible in order to avoid extraction of tannins, since no colouring matter is required and the resultant astringency is viewed as a fault in white wines. Some wine-makers deliberately allow a certain period of SKIN CONTACT for white grapes before they are crushed, however, and in the late 1980s this technique was encouraged in order to produce more flavourful dry white bordeaux.

A quite different red-wine-making technique is CARBONIC MACERATION, practised particularly in Beaujolais and for other red wines designed for early consumption.   A.D.W. & P.J.W.

McLaren Vale, historic SOUTH AUSTRALIAN wine region enjoying a renaissance.

Mâcon, important commercial centre on the river Saône and capital of the **Mâconnais** district of BURGUNDY which produces considerable quantities of white wine and some red.

Viticultural practices are broadly similar to those in the CÔTE D'OR, although yields may be a little higher. Vinification is sometimes carried out in barrels, although only the best producers use new OAK. Bottling normally takes place in the summer before the next vintage.

The appellations of the Mâconnais, in approximately ascending order of quality, are, for white wines made from Chardonnay: **Mâcon**; **Mâcon Supérieur**; **Mâcon-Villages** or **Mâcon** followed by a particular village name (see MÂCON-VILLAGES); ST-VÉRAN; Pouilly-Vinzelles, Pouilly-Loché, and Pouilly-Fuissé (see POUILLY-FUISSÉ). Red-wine appellations are **Mâcon**, **Mâcon Supérieur**, and **Mâcon** followed by a particular village name. Almost all these red wines are made from the Gamay grape since, although Pinot Noir is permitted, such wines may be sold as BOURGOGNE Rouge at a higher price than Mâcon fetches.

In 1998, the village of Viré and the adjacent hamlet of Clessé were given their own single appellation VIRÉ-CLESSÉ. This may promote a spate of individual appellations from other leading villages such as Lugny, which have habitually appeared on labels as a suffix to the name Mâcon (see MÂCON-VILLAGES).

Guffens Heynen, Merlin, Verget, Vincent, and Thévenet were among the most talented wine producers based in the Mâconnais region in the late 1990s.   J.T.C.M.

Mâcon-Villages, appellation covering the great majority of the white wines of MÂCON. The wines may be sold either as Mâcon-Villages or as Mâcon followed by the name of the particular village. Viré and Lugny have been the best known by virtue of their CO-OPERATIVES. The full list of 43 villages with the right to the appellation is: Azé, Berzé-la-Ville, Berzé-le-Châtel, Bissy-la-Mâconnaise, Burgy, Bussières, Chaintré, Chânes, La Chapelle-de-Guinchay, Chardonnay (whence the grape may have taken its name), Charnay-lès-Mâcon, Chasselas, Chevagny-lès-Chevrières, Clessé, Crèches-sur-Saône, Cruzilles, Davayé, Fuissé, Grévilly, Hurigny, Igé, Leynes, Loché, Lugny, Milly-Lamartine, Montbellet, Péronne, Pierreclos, Prissé, Pruzilly, La Roche-Vineuse, Romanèche-Thorins, St-Amour-Bellevue, St-Gengoux-de-Scissé, St-Symphorien-d'Ancelles, St-Vérand, Sologny, Solutré-Pouilly, Vergisson, Verzé, Vinzelles, Viré, and Uchizy.

Most Mâconnais wines are vinified in stainless-steel or glass-lined concrete vats for early bottling and consumption within a year or two of the vintage. A handful of growers are producing significantly finer wines through low yields followed by BARREL FERMENTATION and BARREL MATURATION. Jean Thévenet has also made a speciality of an extraordinary late-picked and sometimes BOTRYTIZED sweet white Mâcon.   J.T.C.M.

macroclimate, also called regional climate, means a climate broadly representing an area or region. Unlike the more precise terms MICROCLIMATE and MESOCLIMATE, macroclimate approximates to what is normally meant by the word 'climate'.

Macvin du Jura, powerful VIN DE LIQUEUR made in the JURA in eastern France. This sweet but curiously earthy drink should be served cool as an APERITIF or with sweet dishes. It was awarded its own APPELLATION CONTRÔLÉE in 1991.

Madagascar, large tropical island off the east African coast which produces about 88,000 hl/2.3 million gal of wine a year (about as much as LUXEMBOURG). About 700 vine-growers, with an average of 2 ha of vineyard, are centred on Fianarantsoa and Ambalavo. See TROPICAL VITICULTURE.

Madeira, volcanic island in the Atlantic belonging to Portugal, nearly 1,000 km/625 miles from the Portuguese mainland and 750 km off the coast of North Africa, a DOC producing madeira, a FORTIFIED wine that is probably the world's most resilient and longest living because of the way it is 'cooked' during production. The best will keep in cask and bottle for a century or more. Quality levels are determined by the method of production, the grape varieties (see below) and the length of ageing. The main styles of madeira are listed below.

Standard blends—made from TINTA NEGRA MOLE and labelled simply 'Dry', 'Medium Dry', 'Medium Sweet', and 'Rich' or 'Sweet'.

Sercial—made from the SERCIAL grape, the best wines develop high-toned, almond-like aromas with a nervy character and a searing dry finish.

Verdelho—a medium-dry wine made from the VERDELHO grape which, with age, develops an extraordinary smoky complexity while retaining its characteristic tang of acidity.

Bual—a dark, medium-rich, raisiny wine made from the BUAL grape which retains its acidic verve with age.

Malmsey—produced from the two varieties Malvasia Cândida (MALVASIA DI CANDIA) and Malvasia Babosa, this very sweet madeira is balanced by characteristically high levels of acidity and gains in richness and concentration with time in cask.

Decanting is recommended for older, vintage wines but is not always necessary. Drier Sercial and Verdelho styles benefit from being served 'cellar cool' rather than iced. Sweeter Buals and malmseys should be served at room temperature. Once opened, a bottle of madeira has the advantage of lasting almost indefinitely.
                                                          R.J.M.

Madeleine Angevine, early-ripening vine variety used for TABLE GRAPES and for wine production in ENGLAND and KYRGYZSTAN. Several different varieties go by this name. Some wines are attractively scented and crisp.

Madera, town and county at the very heart of California's vast SAN JOAQUIN VALLEY that is also the name of an AVA. Most of the AVA's acreage is in Madera County, but some lies across the line in Fresno County. The AVA's long-term reason for being may come to be dessert wines, especially port types and Muscats. Its table wines are for every day.

maderization, occasionally **madeirization,** is the process by which a wine is made to taste like MADEIRA, involving mild OXIDATION over a long period and, usually, heat. Such a wine is said to be **maderized.** Very few maderized wines are made today by simply ageing the wine at cellar temperature; the oxidation process is instead hastened by heating or 'baking' the wine as on the island of Madeira. Maderized wines are normally amber to brown in colour and have a distinctive cooked or mildly caramelized flavour. Wines processed at excessively high temperatures may taste burnt and harsh. Most such wines and especially those made from American vines or American HYBRIDS are fortified and sweetened before being marketed. See also RANCIO wines.
                                                          A.D.W.

made wine, somewhat inelegant name for wine made not from freshly picked grapes but from reconstituted GRAPE CONCENTRATE. The advantages for producers are that it can be made throughout the year, and that grapes can be sourced wherever they happen to be cheapest. CYPRUS has been an important source. BRITISH WINE is one of the most commercially successful made wines, but made wines have also been produced in JAPAN and eastern Europe.

Madiran, dynamic red-wine appellation in SOUTH WEST FRANCE which has remodelled its concentrated, traditionally tannic wines, GASCONY's signature red.

The traditional grape variety is TANNAT, its very name hinting at the naturally astringent character of its high TANNIN level. The proportion of Tannat allowed to add local flavour to Cabernet Sauvignon and Cabernet Franc is anything between 40 and 60 per cent of the blend. A little FER (Pinenc) is also grown. The wine traditionally needed long BOTTLE AGEING but some of Madiran's most dynamic winemakers have been experimenting with ways of softening the impact of Tannat to produce wines which have density, potential for ageing, but considerable charm in youth. Madiran can taste like a classed-growth claret given the sort of Gascon twist needed to cope with *magret de canard*. The leader of the appellation is Alain Brumont, who produces both Montus and Bouscassé. Other reliable producers include Ch d'Aydie, Domaine Capmartin, and Ch Laffitte-Teston.

From the same area comes white PACHERENC DU VIC-BILH.

Madrid, Vinos de. The name of the Spanish capital is much less well known as the name of a wine denomination. The DO Vinos de Madrid forms a semicircle around the southern suburbs. Of the three officially recognized subzones, the most important is round the town of Arganda del Rey to the east of Madrid. White wines are made from the Malvar and AIRÉN. Reds are produced from Tinto Fino (TEMPRANILLO), also known (in east central Spain, but not in Madrid) as Tinta Madrid, and Garnacha (GRENACHE). Few wines stray further than city bars and cafés.   R.J.M.

Magliocco Canino, dark-berried Italian vine variety and speciality of CALABRIA, where it is often blended with GAGLIOPPO.

magnum, large BOTTLE SIZE containing 1.5 l/54 fl oz, or the equivalent of two bottles. It is widely regarded as being the ideal size for BOTTLE AGEING fine wine, being large enough to slow the AGEING process, but not so big as to be unwieldy, or unthinkably expensive (unlike some other LARGE FORMATS).

maître de chai, term often used in France, particularly in Bordeaux, for the cellarmaster, as opposed to the RÉGISSEUR, who might manage the whole estate, or certainly the vineyards. It means literally 'master of the CHAI'. As science and academe invade wine-making, the wine-making decisions are increasingly made by an OENOLOGIST.

Majarcă Albă, Romanian white grape.

Majorca, known as **Mallorca** in Spanish and Catalan, Spanish Balearic island in the northwest Mediterranean. Of the 2,500 ha/6,175 acres of vines currently in production on the island, 400 belong to the BINISSALEM, Spain's first offshore DO wine region on the island's central plateau, with good, original reds from the local MANTO NEGRO grape made by J. L. Ferrer.

Mala Dinka, occasional Bulgarian name for GEWÜRZTRAMINER.

Málaga, city and Mediterranean port in ANDALUCÍA, southern Spain, which lends its name to a shrinking denominated wine zone producing rich, raisiny FORTIFIED wines. The principal grape variety is PEDRO XIMÉNEZ, although considerable amounts of the more productive AIRÉN vine were also planted in the 1980s. In the cooler mountain zone immediately north of the city, Moscatel de Alejandría (MUSCAT OF ALEXANDRIA) is the dominant vine. Most wines are deep brown, intensely sweet, and raisiny. Dry wines are paler with a rather undistinguished nutty character.

Malagousia or sometimes **Malagoussia,** elegant white grape variety rediscovered and identified only recently in modern GREECE. It may be related to Malvasia and yields similarly full-bodied, perfumed wines.

Malbec, black grape variety once popular in Bordeaux but now more readily associated with ARGENTINA and CAHORS, in both of which it is one of the most planted vines. It has many synonyms, for example Cot, as it is known in much of western France, including the Loire, where it is quite widely grown. In Argentina, it was often called Malbeck (until Argentina joined the rest of the wine world), in the Libournais Pressac, and in Cahors, suggesting origins in northern Burgundy, Auxerrois.

Malbec has been declining in popularity in France for it has many of the disadvantages of Merlot without as much obvious fruit quality. Indeed it can taste like a rather rustic, even shorter-lived version of Merlot, although when grown on the least fertile, high, rugged, limestone vineyards of Cahors it can occasionally remind us why the English used to refer to Cahors as 'the black wine'. Cahors APPELLATION CONTRÔLÉE regulations stipulate that Cot must constitute at least 70 per cent of the wine. Other appellations of SOUTH WEST FRANCE in which Malbec may play a (smaller) part are Bergerac, Buzet, Côtes de Duras, Côtes du Frontonnais, Côtes du Marmandais, Pécharmant, and Côtes du Brulhois. It is also theoretically allowed into the Midi-threshold appellations of Cabardès and Côtes de la Malepère but is rarely found this far from Atlantic influence.

At one time, Malbec was quite popular in Bordeaux and is still permitted by all major red bordeaux appellations. It persists most obviously in Bourg, Blaye, and the Entre-Deux-Mers region but is being systematically replaced with varieties whose wines are more durable.

It is in Argentina that Malbec really holds sway, planted in most of Argentina's wine regions. Varietal Argentine Malbecs have some perceptibly Bordelais characteristics, of flavour rather than structure. The wines can be ripe and lush and capable of extended AGEING here. Malbec, usually spelt without a k but sometimes called Cot, is Chile's third most important black grape variety after Pais and Cabernet Sauvignon. Chile's version tends to be more tannic than those raised across the Andes and is often blended with Merlot and (Petit) Verdot.

Australians have no great respect for their Malbec and had been uprooting it systematically until the early 1990s. Plantings totalled just over 300 ha in 1997. Californians had got their total down to about the same level, but who knows when this may be driven up by a desire to replicate, for example, the country wines of France? Most of today's California Malbec is dutifully added to MERITAGE-style bordeaux blends.

A small amount of Malbec, Malbech, or Malbeck is also planted in north-east Italy.

Malepère, Côtes de la, shares many of the wine characteristics of CABARDÈS, another small wine region where the Midi and Aquitaine meet near Carcassonne in the south west of France. The wines, mainly red, are made up of a blend of Bordeaux and Languedoc varieties but in the case of Malepère, with its wetter, more Atlantic climate, it is the Bordeaux varieties of Merlot and Cot (Malbec)—together

with Cinsaut in the east of the region—that predominate. Secondary varieties include Cabernet Franc, Cabernet Sauvignon, Grenache, and Syrah. In contrast to Cabardès, Carignan is not allowed. The region, awarded VDQS status in 1983, has been working actively towards full APPELLATION CONTRÔLÉE recognition. It belongs climatically to south-western France rather than to the LANGUEDOC, from which it is geographically protected by the Hautes Corbières peaks. The vineyards are immediately north of those responsible for Blanquette de LIMOUX. Wine production is dominated by several large CO-OPERATIVES, of which the determinedly *océanique* Cave du Razès alone is responsible for almost two-thirds of the region's entire production.

Mali Plavac. See PLAVAC MALI.

malic acid, one of the two principal organic acids of grapes and wines (see also TARTARIC ACID). Its name comes from *malum*, Latin for apple, the fruit in which it was first identified.

Malic acid is lost not just during grape ripening, but also in many cases as a result of MALOLACTIC FERMENTATION of wines either during or after alcoholic FERMENTATION. Just as high temperatures favour the loss of malic acid in grapes, they encourage the lactic organisms responsible for malolactic fermentation.

malmsey, English corruption of the word MALVASIA, derived from the port of Monemvasia which was important in Ancient GREECE. Malmsey, which originally denoted any strong, sweet wine, was eventually used specifically for the sweetest style of MADEIRA, particularly that made from Malvasia grapes.

See also MALVASIA.

malolactic fermentation, occasionally abbreviated to MLF, conversion of stronger MALIC ACID naturally present in new wine into LACTIC ACID (which has lower ACIDITY) and CARBON DIOXIDE. It is accomplished by lactic bacteria, which are naturally present in most established wineries but may have to be cultured and carefully introduced in newer establishments where malolactic fermentation is desired. This process is unrelated to and almost never precedes the main, alcoholic FERMENTATION, for which reason it is sometimes called a secondary fermentation.

Malolactic fermentation is desirable in wines which have excessive ACIDITY, particularly red wines produced in cooler climates. Malolactic fermentation can also add flavour and complexity to both red and white wines, as well as rendering the wine impervious to the danger of malolactic fermentation in bottle. Recognition and mastery of malolactic fermentation (which would traditionally happen as if by accident when temperatures rose in the spring) was one of the key developments in wine-making in France and elsewhere in the mid 20th century. By the early 1990s, most fine red wines, many sparkling wines, and a small but increasing proportion of the world's white wine involved full or partial malolactic fermentation. In hotter climates or warmer years in cooler areas, some wine-makers deliberately suppress malolactic fermentation in some or all batches of a wine in order to maintain the wine's acidity. Some grape varieties seem to have a greater affinity with malolactic fermentation than others. Among white grapes, Chardonnay is a generally successful candidate for the process, while most producers of Riesling and Chenin Blanc deliberately avoid it, despite the high natural acidity in these latter two.

Malolactic fermentation may well be regarded as undesirable in wines to be bottled and sold young, most white wines, massmarket bottlings of any hue, for example, together with light reds such as Beaujolais and Dolcetto. Such techniques as sterile FILTRATION, sterile bottling, and PASTEURIZATION can insure against the commercial embarrassment of malolactic fermentation's taking place in bottle. If a bottled still wine starts to fizz, this is the most likely cause.   A.D.W.

Malta, the central Mediterranean island, has a small wine industry. In the 1990s, just under 1,000 ha/2,500 acres of vineyard were mainly in the hands of relatively unskilled, part-time farmers. The majority of vines planted were TABLE GRAPE varieties which produced wines so low in sugar and acid that considerable adjustments were needed in wineries rarely equipped for high-quality wine production. Demand for wine on this tourist island is such that local grapes are supplemented by grapes imported from Italy. Until recently, it has been hard to distinguish on the label between local and imported wines.

The most common grape varieties are local specialities. Gellewza makes soft, fleshy reds and aromatic, fruity dry rosés, while Gennarua and the superior Ghirghentina (which may be

related to Sicily's INZOLIA) make weighty white wines. Emmanuel Delicata, with Marsovin one of two companies which currently control about 90 per cent of the island's wine market, has made wines of export quality.

A third company, Meridiana, backed by the Italian producer ANTINORI, is involved in an ambitious new wine estate near Mdina specializing in INTERNATIONAL VARIETIES.
                                    M.M.-F. & D.J.G.

Malvar, white grape commonly grown around MADRID producing slightly rustic wines but with more body and personality than the ubiquitous AIRÉN.

Malvasia, the Italian corruption of Monemvasia, the southern Greek port, is the name used widely, especially in Iberia and Italy, for a complex web of grape varieties, typically ancient and of Greek origin and producing characterful wines high in alcohol and, often, RESIDUAL SUGAR. Most are deeply coloured whites but some are, usually light, reds. Malvasia is widely disseminated, even if it is not grown in enormous quantity anywhere nowadays.

Most Malvasia, which, like the somewhat similar MUSCAT, exists in many guises and hues, is a subvariety of Malvasia Bianca, with the exception of MALVASIA DI CANDIA.

The French corruption of Malvasia has been used particularly loosely; see MALVOISIE. The word was also corrupted into MALMSEY in English, which continues to be an important style of MADEIRA, traditionally based on the Malvasia grape. The Germans call their various though rare forms of Malvasia **Malvasier** and occasionally early, or *früh*, VELTLINER in various colours of berry.

Malvasia, in its various forms—white and red, dry and sweet—is one of Italy's most widely planted grapes. White **Malvasia Bianca**, the larger part of the production, is widely used throughout Latium, Umbria, and Tuscany, frequently in combination with various types of Trebbiano, forming what might be called the standard central Italian white blend. This type of wine has lost considerable ground in Tuscany, and then Umbria, since the 1970s, however, as producers replaced both Malvasia and Trebbiano with more strongly characterized INTERNATIONAL VARIETIES. Monovarietal Malvasia wines are rare in central Italy, but pioneering efforts began to appear in the CASTELLI ROMANI zone in the early 1990s.

The finest dry white VARIETAL Malvasia is made in Friuli, where two DOCs—COLLIO and ISONZO—cultivate what is called locally **Malvasia Istriana**. Substantial quantities are also produced as a DOC wine in the Colli Piacentini, where a slight sparkle is quite common. Lightly sparkling dry to demi-sec Malvasia is frequently encountered in Emilia, where it is referred to as *champagnino* or 'little champagne'.

Sweet white Malvasia, normally a PASSITO and once considered one of Italy's finest dessert wines, has become extremely rare. However, **Malvasia delle Lipari** was revived in the 1980s and the survival of this distinctive sweet orange relic from the volcanic island of Lipari off SICILY seems assured, at least in the short run. The BASILICATA has its own version of sweet Malvasia, produced in the same zone as Aglianico del Vulture, and local producers, buoyed by the new interest in their red wine, are attempting to capture the market's favour with their Malvasia, which also exists in dry and spumante versions.

Red Malvasia, also known as **Malvasia Nera**, is most commonly used in conjunction with other grapes: as the minority partner of Negroamaro in the standard red blend of the provinces of Lecce and Brindisi in APULIA, and as a useful supplement to Sangiovese in Tuscany, where it adds both colour and perfume. The introduction of the even more aromatic and deeply coloured Cabernet Sauvignon to Sangiovese-based Tuscan blends in the 1970s and 1980s (see TUSCANY) has led to a distinct loss of favour for Malvasia Nera and uncertain long-term prospects.

Piedmont is the only significant producer of varietal Malvasia Nera wines, with two DOC zones: **Malvasia di Casorzo**, in both a dry and sweet version, and **Malvasia di Castelnuovo Don Bosco**.

On the French island of CORSICA, most growers believe that their Malvoisie is identical to VERMENTINO, which may be related to the greater Malvasia family.

Malvasia is planted to a declining extent in northern Spain, notably in RIOJA and NAVARRA, although the less interesting Viura (MACABEO) has been gaining ground. Malvasia is also planted on the CANARY ISLANDS.

Myriad Malvasias are also grown on the mainland in PORTUGAL. **Malvasia Fina**, known as Vital in Estremadura, is grown in higher vineyards in the Douro and can be a crisp contribution to the blend for a white PORT. **Malvasia Rei** is a less distinguished grape which tends to make rather flabby wines in the Douro, Beiras, and Estremadura. Another ingredient in white port, it may be the same as Palomino.

In California, there are more than 2,000 acres/800 ha of Malvasia Bianca, the most substantial plantings being in Tulare County at the very southern end of the SAN JOAQUIN VALLEY. The potential for California Malvasia Bianca has been demonstrated in appetizing white table wines made by Randall Grahm of Bonny Doon.   D.T. & J.Ro.

Malvasia di Candia, historic white grape variety distinct from the myriad subvarieties of MALVASIA Bianca. It is beginning to gain ground once more in the vineyards of MADEIRA, where it was traditionally the variety used to produce malmsey.

Malvoisie is one of France's most confusing vine names. There is no single variety whose principal name is Malvoisie, but it has been used as a synonym for a wide range of, usually white-berried, grape varieties producing full-bodied, aromatic whites. Malvoisie is today found on the labels of some Loire and Savoie wines made from such plantings of PINOT GRIS as remain, as Malvoisie du Valais is a common synonym for, usually sweet, Pinot Gris in Switzerland. It is also sometimes used for BOURBOULENC in the Languedoc, and occasionally for MACCABÉO in the Aude, for CLAIRETTE in Bordeaux, and for TORBATO in Roussillon. VERMENTINO is sometimes called Malvoisie in Iberia and is known as Malvoisie de Corse in Corsica.

Malvoisie Rose and **Malvoisie Rouge** are occasionally used as synonyms for FRÜHROTER VELTLINER in Savoie and northern Italy, while the **Malvoisie Noire** of the Lot in south-western France may be TROUSSEAU.

Mammolo, heavily perfumed red grape variety producing wines which supposedly smell of violets, or *mammole*, in central Italy. This, a permitted ingredient in CHIANTI, is relatively rare today, although a small amount is also grown in the VINO NOBILE DI MONTEPULCIANO zone.

Mancha, La. Europe's largest single demarcated wine region in the heart of Spain. The vineyards of the DO La Mancha cover 170,000 ha/419,900 acres of arid table land from the satellite towns south of Madrid to the hills beyond VALDEPEÑAS nearly 200 km/125 miles to the south. Vineyards not registered for the DO brought the total area of La Mancha devoted to the vine to 400,000 ha/990,000 acres in the late 1990s. Summers are hot with temperatures rising to over 40 °C/104 °F, while winters are bitterly cold with prolonged frosts.

The doughty AIRÉN vine seems to be well suited to these extreme conditions and is therefore popular among La Mancha's 18,000 smallholders. YIELDS of between 20 and 25 hl/ha (1.4 tons/acre) seem puny by international standards, and, despite limited MECHANIZATION, production costs remain low.

Traditionally, Manchegan wine was coarse and alcoholic. Much was distilled or sold in bulk, and most wines were brown and OXIDIZED by the time they reached consumers. During the 1980s, however, a sea change took place in La Mancha. In an effort to make the wines more appealing to the changing tastes of both domestic and international customers, producers began to pick their grapes up to a month earlier and vinify them at low temperatures in stainless steel.

Technological development has given La Mancha a new lease of life and opened new and more discerning markets for the region's fresh, inexpensive, if rather neutral dry white wines. Red wines, made increasingly from Cencibel (TEMPRANILLO) grapes, have also improved enormously and a number of enterprising growers are experimenting with other grape varieties, including Cabernet Sauvignon and Chardonnay, now admitted and even encouraged by DO regulations. Of the 2 million hl/53 million gal produced annually, a large part is still distilled into industrial alcohol or sent to JEREZ to make brandy.   R.J.M. & V. de la S.

Mandelaria, sometimes Mandelari, powerful speciality of various Greek islands, including Crete, where it is often blended with the much softer KOTSIFALI. It is probably Greece's third most planted red wine variety. The grapes have thick skins and therefore the wine produced is deep coloured and notably high in tannins. It can produce harmonious dry reds such as Peza, or even sweet reds.

Manseng in both GROS MANSENG and, even finer, PETIT MANSENG forms is the Basque vine variety responsible for the exceptional tangy rich white wines of JURANÇON in the western foothills of the French Pyrenees. It is also grown in nearby Gascony for the somewhat similar PACHERENC DU VIC-BILH and can be found in some of the rare white wines of BÉARN.

Manseng, usually Petit Manseng, can also be found in Uruguay.

Manto Negro, principal grape on MAJORCA, producing scented but light reds which tend to age and even OXIDIZE early. It may be best blended with a more structured grape.

Maranges, the southernmost VILLAGE WINE appellation in the Côte de Beaune district of Burgundy, produces medium-bodied red wines of some charm when young but of unproven distinction in the long term. The vineyard stretches across the three villages of Cheilly, Dezize, and Sampigny, each of which takes Les Maranges as a suffix. Formerly the wines were sold either under the village name or, much more frequently, as Côte de Beaune-Villages. Since 1988, such wines may be called Maranges or Maranges Côte de Beaune. White wines are permitted but are scarcely made.

See also CÔTE D'OR.   J.T.C.M.

Marches or, in Italian, **Marche**, the easternmost region in the central belt of Italy stretching from TUSCANY through UMBRIA to the Adriatic coast. It shares a variety of characteristics with these neighbours to the west, including a TEMPERATE climate marked by hot, dry summers; HILLSIDE VINEYARDS; and substantial plantings of SANGIOVESE and TREBBIANO vines. The Marches has been the last of the three regions to realize its potential for good-quality wines, however.

In the 1990s, about 17 per cent of total production qualified for one of 11 regional DOCs. VERDICCHIO in its two versions—from the Castelli di Jesi and from Matelica—dominates this DOC production. The better wines of these appellations are now demonstrating that Verdicchio is one of the few central Italian white varieties with character and personality. Bianchello del Metauro, Falerio dei Colli Ascolani, and Bianco dei Colli Maceratesi are bland and anonymous white wines, the first from the local Bianchello grape variety, the latter two based on Trebbiano.

The greatest potential in the region, however, is represented by its two outstanding red varieties, Sangiovese and MONTEPULCIANO, far superior to any of the local white varieties grown. Both of the major red DOCs, Rosso Conero and Rosso Piceno, employ these two red varieties. Rosso Conero is produced from Montepulciano along with a maximum 15 per

cent of Sangiovese, while Rosso Piceno is produced from a minimum of 60 per cent Sangiovese and a maximum of 40 per cent
Montepulciano in a large part of the region's
hill country outside the Rosso Conero zone.
Maximum permitted YIELDS in both DOCs are
excessively generous, wine-making is frequently slipshod and haphazard, and it is far
easier to find a poor bottle of Rosso Conero or
Rosso Piceno than a genuinely interesting one.
However, a general rise in the overall quality
level was observable in the 1990s, partly due
to renewed interest in distinctive wines from
local rather than INTERNATIONAL VARIETIES. The
new presence in the region of some of the most
famous—and expensive—names among Italy's
consulting OENOLOGISTS was a sign of both a
commitment to higher quality and an awareness that local technique needs help to satisfy
international consumers.

See also VERDICCHIO.   D.T.

Marcillac, isolated, small, but growing AC in
SOUTH WEST FRANCE whose vigorous red wines
can have real character. Marcillac, usually red
and sometimes rosé, must be made of at least
90 per cent FER, here often called Mansois, a
hard-wooded vine capable of making peppery,
aromatic mountain wines with good structure.
BARREL MATURATION has been introduced to
temper the high acidity of wines, which, unlike
many of the Bordeaux duplicates produced in
the south west, are highly distinctive. The local
CO-OPERATIVE at Valady is an important producer, as is Le Vieux Porche.

Maréchal Foch, red wine grape variety
named after a famous French First World War
general. This French HYBRID was once widely
cultivated in the Loire and is still popular in
CANADA and NEW YORK, where it is spelt **Marechal Foch**, is sometimes called simply Foch,
and may be vinified using CARBONIC MACER-
ATION. It produces fruity, non-FOXY wines with
a very loose and much promoted similarity to
Pinot Noir. Although it is sometimes given
BARREL MATURATION, it is not particularly
stable.

Maremma, long, loosely defined strip of
TUSCAN coastline south of Livorno (Leghorn)
extending southward through the province of
Grosseto. The Alta Maremma, or upper
Maremma includes the now-famous pro-
duction zone of BOLGHERI.

Like the MÉDOC in Bordeaux, the low-lying
parts of the Maremma were swampy or marshy
for much of their history with chronic problems of malaria. Poverty and banditry were generalized phenomena until the draining of the
swamps and the elimination of malaria in the
20th century.

Production of wine is consequently a recent
phenomenon and quality wine can be said to
date from the first bottles of SASSICAIA in the
1970s, although the zone of Morellino di Scansano enjoyed a certain reputation in the past.
Bolgheri continued to develop in the 1980s, but
the late 1980s and 1990s saw the emergence of
important wines in other parts of the
Maremma as well, and three specific zones can
now be said to exist in addition to a variety of
single, and at times isolated, estates. Suvereto,
a village in the Val di Cornia, 12 km/7 miles to
the south east of Bolgheri, has become a centre
of production not only of high-level Cabernet
and Merlot but also of Sangiovese and Montepulciano.

Sangiovese, Cabernet, and Syrah have shown
very good results further to the south near
the city of Massa Marittima in the province of
Grosseto. In what is the Maremma's classic
zone for Sangiovese, Morellino di Scansano has
improved considerably. The mid 1990s saw a
boom in investment in the zone, with many of
Tuscany's most prestigious high-quality wineries purchasing properties and vineyard land,
attracted both by the potential shown in the
better wines and the relatively low prices compared with other, better-known, central Tuscan
DOCs.

The wines of the Maremma, in most cases,
are still too young for definitive judgements to
be drawn, but the high quality and decisive
character already shown in many of them
made the zone the new frontier of Tuscan viticulture in the 1990s.   D.T.

Margaret River, successful and growing
wine region in the south west of WESTERN AUS-
TRALIA.

Margaux, potentially the most seductive
communal appellation of the Haut-MÉDOC district of Bordeaux but one in which dis-
appointments are currently easier to find than
successes. At their stereotypical best, the wines
of Margaux combine the deep ruby colour,
structure, and concentration of any top-quality
Médoc with a seductive perfume and a silkier
texture than is found to the north in ST-JULIEN,
PAUILLAC, and ST-ESTÈPHE.

Margaux is the most southerly, most isolated, and most extensive of the Médoc's communal appellations, taking in not just the substantial village of Margaux but also the neighbouring communities of Cantenac, Soussans, Labarde, and Arsac.

In total, more than 1,300 ha/3,210 acres qualified for the Margaux appellation in the late 1990s, and within its boundaries there are inevitably considerable variations in both topography and soil type, but most of the finest wines should come from gentle outcrops where gravel predominates and DRAINAGE is good—although properties here are particularly parcellated and intermingled with one estate often comprising very different, and often distant, plots of land. Ch Margaux, for example, has vineyards in both Cantenac and Soussans.

Margaux has in the past enjoyed enormous *réclame*, and more Margaux properties were included in the 1855 CLASSIFICATION of the Médoc and Graves (more than 20) than from any other appellation. The appellation clearly still has great potential, but in the 1970s, 1980s, and even 1990s a curious number of châteaux failed to keep pace with the substantial improvements in wine quality achieved in the other three major appellations of the Médoc.

Ch Margaux itself, the FIRST GROWTH standard-bearer for the appellation, was revived only in 1978 after more than a decade of disappointing vintages (see below for more details). Of the five second growths within the appellation, Chx Rauzan-Ségla, Rauzan-Gassies, Durfort-Vivens, Lascombes, and Brane-Cantenac, the first was seriously revived only when the owners of the couture house Chanel bought it in 1994, and the second and third are some of the most notable under-performers in the whole Médoc. Among the original 10 third growths, Desmirail, Ferrière, and Dubignon-Talbot were practically abandoned for years, the last apparently for ever. Only Ch Palmer, officially a third growth, could be said to have represented the appellation with any glory and consistency in the second half of the 20th century. Ch Palmer, part owned and managed by the late Peter A. SICHEL, produced a wine that could without hyperbole be described as legendary in 1961.

Ch Lascombes passed from Alexis Lichine to a British brewer in 1971 and, after considerable land acquisitions, took more than a decade to hit form, while the large Ch Brane-Cantenac estate, like Durfort-Vivens owned by a LURTON,

has been producing lighter wines than its status in the 1855 classification suggests.

Of Margaux's many third growths other than Palmer, Kirwan is improving; Issan is more famous for its romantic moated château than its modern wines; Giscours and Cantenac-Brown can please in a rich, rather obvious way; Malescot St-Exupéry, originally called St-Exupéry, is slowly taking on more flesh; Boyd-Cantenac is too often dull; while Marquis d'Alesme-Becker, originally called Becker, can be uncomfortably lean.

Thanks to the efforts of Alexis Lichine, more care has been lavished on Ch Prieuré-Lichine (one of the Médoc's first châteaux ever to welcome tourists) than on Margaux's other fourth growths Chx Pouget and Marquis de Terme, although the latter is much improved since the mid 1980s. Chx Dauzac and du Tertre are Margaux's somewhat dreary fifth growths, and such unclassified growths as Chx d'Angludet, Bel Air Marquis d'Aligre, La Gurgue, Labégorce-Zédé, Monbrison, and Siran can often provide more excitement and wine-making integrity, particularly in terms of value.

One of the Médoc's most famous white wines is made here, even though it qualifies only as BORDEAUX AC (see below).

See MÉDOC, BORDEAUX, and MARGAUX, CH.

Margaux, Château, exceptional building and the most important wine estate in the village of MARGAUX in the Bordeaux wine region, and a FIRST GROWTH in the 1855 CLASSIFICATION. There is much potential for confusion since both Ch Margaux and GENERIC wine from the commune of Margaux are colloquially referred to as 'Margaux', but the former is likely to cost several times the latter.

In 1977, the château was acquired by the French grocery and finance group Félix Potin, headed by the Greek André Mentzelopoulos, domiciled in France. A great deal of money was spent on restoring the neglected vineyard, *chais*, and mansion and Bordeaux OENOLOGIST Émile Peynaud was taken on as consultant. André Mentzelopoulos died suddenly in December 1980, and first his wife Laura and then his daughter Corinne took over control, assisted by Paul Pontallier, the young director who joined the estate in 1983 (coincidentally one of the property's most successful vintages). In 1992, in a complicated international deal involving Perrier mineral water, the Italian

Agnelli family of Fiat motor cars became involved in ownership of the estate, but Corinne Mentzelopoulos remained in charge and took a personal stake in the property.

The 78 ha/192 acres are planted with 75 per cent Cabernet Sauvignon grapes, 20 per cent Merlot, and 5 per cent of Cabernet Franc and Petit Verdot. Average output is about 30,000 cases, of which the resurrected Pavillon Rouge de Ch Margaux is the excellent SECOND WINE. A hitherto somewhat uninspiring white wine Pavillon Blanc was transformed into an ambitious dry wine. It is made in a new and separate temperature-controlled cellar, with BARREL FERMENTATION, exclusively from Sauvignon Blanc grapes planted on 12 ha of separate vineyard. Ch Margaux, unusually, still has its own cooperage.   E.P.-R.

Maria Gomes, Bairrada synonym for the Portuguese white grape variety FERNÃO PIRES.

Maria Ordoña. See MERENZAO.

Marino. See CASTELLI ROMANI.

maritime climate, the opposite of a CONTINENTAL climate, has a relatively narrow annual range of temperatures. Places with a maritime climate tend to be near oceans or other large bodies of water.

Marmandais, Côtes du, Bordeaux satellite wine district in SOUTH WEST FRANCE on either side of the river GARONNE, elevated from VDQS to full AC status in 1990. Bordeaux grape varieties Cabernet Sauvignon, Cabernet Franc, and Merlot predominate, and the cooler climate here upriver tends to result in light versions of red, and some rosé, bordeaux. But these varieties may not exceed three-quarters of production, and Côtes du Marmandais's distinction is in the local variety ABOURIOU, which, with FER, Gamay, and Syrah, must make up the rest. Total vineyard area increased sharply in the 1990s, although only a small proportion is planted with the white wine varieties Sémillon, UGNI BLANC, MUSCADELLE, and, increasingly, Sauvignon Blanc, which is the principal white variety.

Almost all of the increasingly sophisticated wine production is in the hands of CO-OPERATIVES.

Marqués, occasional name for LOUREIRO.

Marsala, town in western SICILY and the FORTIFIED wine produced around it. While GRILLO is considered the quality grape for Marsala Oro or Marsala Ambra (see below), the DOC regulations also permit the less suitable CATARRATTO and the quite unsuitable Damaschino.

Modern Marsala comes in three different colours—Oro (golden), Ambra (amber), and Rubino (ruby)—and each colour comes in dry, medium-dry, and sweet versions. Quality levels depend on how long the wine spends in wood: 1 year for Fine, 2 years for Superiore, 4 for Superiore Riserva, 5 for Vergine, 10 for the Stravecchio version of Vergine.

Production figures show a wine virtually on its death-bed.   D.T.

Marsana, Spanish name for the MARSANNE grape.

Marsannay, northernmost appellation of the Côte de Nuits district of the CÔTE D'OR. It is unique in Burgundy for having APPELLATION CONTRÔLÉE status for red, white, and pink wines. The vineyards of Couchey and Chenove are included with those of Marsannay. Bruno Clair is the outstanding Marsannay producer today.

The small white-wine production has yet to show particular character. The red wines are attractive and fruity, if lighter than those of neighbouring FIXIN. There are no PREMIER CRU vineyards.   J.T.C.M.

Marsanne has become an increasingly popular white grape variety in three continents. Probably originating in the northern RHÔNE, it has all but taken over here from its traditional blending partner ROUSSANNE in such appellations as ST-JOSEPH, ST-PÉRAY, CROZES-HERMITAGE, and, to a slightly lesser extent, HERMITAGE itself. It is increasingly planted in the south of France, where, as well as being embraced as an ingredient in most appellations, it is earning itself a reputation as a full-bodied, characterful varietal, or a blending partner for more aromatic, acid varieties such as Roussanne, VIOGNIER, and ROLLE. The wine is particularly deep coloured, full bodied with a heady, if often heavy, aroma of glue, sometimes honeysuckle, verging occasionally on almonds. It is not one of the chosen varieties for Châteauneuf-du-Pape, in which CLAIRETTE shares many of Marsanne's characteristics.

California's RHÔNE RANGERS are also generating interest in the variety. Australia has some of the world's oldest Marsanne vineyards, notably in the state of Victoria, and a fine tradition of valuing this Rhône import and the hefty wines it produces, which can brown relatively fast in bottle. In Switzerland, as Ermitage Blanc, it produces a lighter wine that is nevertheless one of the Valais's heaviest.

Marzemina Bianca, occasional southern Italian synonym for CHASSELAS.

Marzemino, interesting, late-ripening red grape variety grown to a strictly limited extent in northern Italy. Once much more famous than now, it can yield lively wines, some of them lightly sparkling. See TRENTINO and LOMBARDY.

mas, southern French term for a domaine.

The most famous wine-producing *mas* is **Mas de Daumas Gassac**, established by outsiders to the world of wine just south east of MONTPEYROUX in the Languedoc in the 1970s. Aimé Guibert was the first to prove that a French non-appellation wine, labelled merely VIN DE PAYS de l'Hérault, can be an extremely serious, long-living red which can fetch the same sort of prices as a Bordeaux CLASSED GROWTH. Mas de Daumas Gassac also makes some unusual rosé and some ambitious white, from a blend of unusual but trend-setting grape varieties including VIOGNIER, PETIT MANSENG, COURBU, Petite Arvine, AMIGNE, and NEHERLESCHOL.

Massandra, winery built to extremely high specifications on the outskirts of Yalta in the CRIMEA in the 1890s. The most successful wines are strong and sweet, many of them VINS DOUX NATURELS as well as FORTIFIED. The modern installation at Massandra is used not for winemaking, but for AGEING and bottling. Massandra staff oversee production in a number of satellite wineries from the vines under Massandra control. Grapes grown on the southern hillsides and in mountain valleys are responsible for such unique dessert wines as White Muscat of the Red Stone, White Muscat Livadia, Rosé Muscat Yuzhnoberezhny, Black Muscat Massandra, Tocay Yuzhnoberezhny, Pinot Ai-Danil, and Kokur Surozh.

mass selection, viticultural technique used to provide large quantities of buds for the propagation of vines. Field vine selection can be either by mass selection, when many vines are selected to provide budwood, or by CLONAL SELECTION, in which a single mother vine is selected to provide CLONES. In mass selection, the identity of individual vines is not maintained.

Since there is not the same detailed recording and selection of individual vines, the gains in yield or quality from mass selection are typically less than for clonal selection, but the resultant wine, made from vines with a mixture of different characteristics, may be more interesting than one made from a single clone.   R.E.S.

Masters of Wine, those who have passed the examinations held every year by the Institute of Masters of Wine, the wine trade's most famous and most demanding professional qualification. The Institute had its origins in the British wine trade in the early 1950s, when a counterpart to the qualifying examinations for other professions was devised by a group of wine merchants in conjunction with the Vintners' Company. The first examination was held in London in 1953 and six of the 21 candidates were deemed to have qualified as Masters of Wine. The Institute of Masters of Wine was formed in 1955. The examinations, which consist of four written papers and three 'practical' (i.e. wine-tasting) tests, are distinguished by the breadth of their scope. University courses offer more detailed instruction in the OENOLOGY or VITICULTURE of a particular country or region, while the MW examinations test knowledge of both subjects on a worldwide basis, as well as of such varied subjects as ÉLEVAGE, bottling, transport, quality control, marketing, commercial aspects of the wine trade, and general wine knowledge. Each tasting paper requires candidates to describe, assess, and, often, identify up to 12 wines served BLIND. These wines may come from anywhere in the world. From 1999, candidates have also been required to prepare an original dissertation.

Despite a notoriously low pass rate (although it has risen markedly in recent years and candidates have always been allowed to pass practical and theoretical parts in separate years), by 1978 the number of Masters of Wine had reached 100, including two women. In 1983, it relaxed its entry requirements and allowed candidates from the fringes of the wine trade, such as WINE WRITERS, to take the examinations. In 1987, the examinations were opened up to those outside the United Kingdom and the next year the first overseas candidate, an Australian, passed the examinations, at this stage still held in London. In 1990, two Americans qualified as Masters of Wine and since 1991 examinations have been held, on the same dates, in London, Sydney, and North America. By 1998, there were 224 Masters of Wine, including 46 women, 44 non-Britons, and several MWs with no professional connection with wine at all.

Mastroberardino, the most important producer of TAURASI in the southern Italian region of CAMPANIA.

Mataro is one of the many synonyms of MOUR-VÈDRE used primarily in Australia, sometimes in Roussillon, and, by those who do not realize how fashionable Mourvèdre has become, in California (see RHÔNE RANGERS). It is almost invariably the case that someone who refers to Mourvèdre as Mataro does not have a particularly high opinion of it.

Mateus. The Palace of Mateus near Vila Real just north of the DOURO valley in northern Portugal lent its name to **Mateus Rosé**, a medium-sweet, sparkling rosé that has become one of the world's most famous wine BRANDS. Production began at the end of the Second World War (at very much the same time as that of its rival LANCERS) in a winery built close to the Mateus Palace.

In the 1950s and 1960s, sales grew rapidly and by the late 1980s Mateus, by then supplemented by a white version, accounted for over 40 per cent of Portugal's total table wine exports with worldwide sales amounting to 3.25 million cases. A small quantity of Mateus Rosé is still made at Vila Real but most of the wine is produced at Anadia in BAIRRADA.

R.J.M.

Matino, DOC for robust red wine made mainly from NEGROAMARO grapes in south-east Italy. See APULIA.

Matrassa, dominant, dark-berried vine of AZERBAIJAN. It is found in other central ASIAN republics and may also be called Kara Shirei and Kara Shirai.

maturation of wine. See AGEING.

mature, tasting term for a fine wine that seems to have enjoyed sufficient AGEING for it to have reached the peak of its potential. In practice it is also used by the most polite, or determinedly optimistic, tasters to describe wines that are past that point. Any hint of orange at the rim of a red wine suggests MATURITY.

maturity, desirable state in a wine when it is consumed. In a sense, the most basic wine designed for early drinking is mature almost as soon as it is bottled, but mature when applied to a wine carries with it the implication that the maturity is the result of a certain amount of BOTTLE AGEING. Such a (red) wine is deemed fully mature when it has dispensed with its uncomfortably harsh TANNINS and acquired maximum complexity of flavour (sometimes described as BOUQUET) without starting to decay. The period of maturity varies considerably with wine type, but is probably longer than most wine consumers believe. A wine that has been followed since its youth and begins to taste mature may continue to delight, and possibly evolve for the better, for a decade or more. For more details of the process, and of the difference between individual wine types, see AGEING.

Maury is one of ROUSSILLON's famous VINS DOUX NATURELS, a cousin from the hilly, slatey hinterland of seaside BANYULS, which is actually produced in greater quantity even if it is less famous. Like Banyuls it is produced predominantly from Grenache Noir and is almost invariably strong, sweet, red, and possibly RANCIO.

Maury is at the northern limit of the Côtes du Roussillon-Villages area in the Agly valley. Table wines produced here qualify as Côtes du Roussillon-Villages (just as those produced in the Banyuls area belong to the COLLIOURE appellation). The wines are particularly tannic in youth and often have a deeper colour than Banyuls. The CO-OPERATIVE, Les Vignerons du Maury, dominates production but other producers manage to surface too, notably Mas Amiel. The wines serve much the same purpose as Banyuls but more insistently demand ageing.

Mauzac, or more properly **Mauzac Blanc,** is a declining but still surprisingly important white grape in SOUTH WEST FRANCE, especially in GAILLAC and LIMOUX, where it is the traditional and still principal vine variety. It produces relatively aromatic wines which are usually blended, with Len de l'El around Gaillac and with Chenin and Chardonnay in Limoux.

Thanks to energetic wine-makers such as Robert Plageoles, since the late 1980s there has been a revival of interest in Gaillac's Mauzac, which comes in several different hues, sweetness levels, and degrees of fizziness. During the 1970s and 1980s in Limoux, total plantings of

Mauzac rose, thanks to demand for the sparkling Blanquette de Limoux, in which it is the dominant ingredient, although the region is fast being invaded by Chardonnay.

Mauzac grapes were traditionally picked well into autumn so that musts fermented slowly and gently in the cool Limoux winters, ready to referment in bottle in the spring. Today Mauzac tends to be picked much earlier, preserving its naturally high acidity but sacrificing much of its particular flavour reminiscent of the skin of shrivelled apples, before being subjected to the usual SPARKLING-WINE-MAKING techniques. Some gently sparkling Gaillacs are still made by the traditional *méthode gaillacoise*, however, just as a small portion of Limoux's Blanquette is made by the *méthode ancestrale*.

Mavro means 'black' in Greek and is the common name of the dominant but undistinguished grape on the island of CYPRUS.

Mavrodaphne, dark-skinned grape variety grown particularly round Pátras in the Peloponnese in GREECE, where it is the foundation of a port-like dessert wine, **Mavrodaphne of Pátras,** which responds well to extended CASK AGEING. This aromatic, powerful variety, also grown to a much more limited extent on the island of Cephalonia, is occasionally vinified dry but only for use as a blending component. Mavrodaphne means 'black laurel'.

Mavro Nemeas, alternative name for the dominant Nemean dark-skinned vine AGHIORGHITIKO.

Mavrud, indigenous Balkan grape variety most closely associated with BULGARIA, capable of producing intense, tannic wine if allowed to ripen fully. It is grown in central southern Bulgaria and is a speciality of Assenovgrad near Plovdiv. The robust wine produced responds well to oak ageing, although it tends to age rather faster than Bulgaria's other noble indigenous vine MELNIK. Mavrud is also grown in Albania.

Mazuelo and Mazuela, RIOJA name for CARIGNAN.

mechanical harvesting, harvesting by machine in place of the traditional manual HARVEST. Undoubtedly one of the greatest changes from ancient to modern vineyards has been the adoption of machine harvesting, which was first introduced commercially in the 1960s.

The effect of machine harvesting on wine quality has been the subject of much scientific study and commercial experience. The majority of studies have shown that sophisticated mechanical harvesting has no negative effect on wine quality, and some have even argued that there is a positive effect. Despite much evidence in favour of machine harvesting, some producers will remain with hand harvesting. The gentler nature of hand harvesting (which can also involve some degree of selection) is preferable for many top-quality wines, especially sparkling wines, for which WHOLE BUNCHES may be pressed without first crushing.   R.E.S.

mechanical pruning involves using machines for pruning vines in winter. Viticulture is a very traditional form of agriculture and many who tend the vines regard the annual winter pruning as their prime opportunity to interact physically with each vine. Because of this, and because they feel that mechanical pruning cannot offer the precision of manual pruning, many vine-growers oppose mechanical pruning, even at the expense of hours of back-breaking labour in cold and sometimes wet weather.

Mechanical pruning is now widespread in Australia. Other parts of the world have been much slower to embrace mechanical pruning, however, especially those where labour is plentiful and relatively inexpensive.   R.E.S.

mechanization. Most WINE-MAKING operations other than tasting and overseeing individual barrels can be fully mechanized, but mechanization has been much slower to invade the vineyard. See MECHANICAL HARVESTING and MECHANICAL PRUNING.

medals from wine COMPETITIONS and other JUDGINGS are coveted by many wine producers. There is a certain hierarchy of medals, however. State and national wine shows are important to the wine trade in AUSTRALIA, but a Hobart gold medal may be reckoned less glamorous than a Canberra silver. In France, medals awarded by the fairs in Paris and Mâcon are usually indications of real quality, as are those awarded in Germany by the Deutscher Landwirtschaft Gesellschaft, or DLG.

medical aspects of wine consumption. See HEALTH.

Mediterranean climate, a climate type characterized by warm, dry, sunny summers and mostly mild, wet winters.

Médoc, the most famous red-wine district in BORDEAUX, and possibly the world. The Médoc stretches north west from the city of Bordeaux along the left bank of the Gironde estuary, a virtually monocultural strip of flat, unremarkable land sandwiched between the coastal marshes and the pine forests which extend for miles south into the Landes. The vineyard strip is about 5 to 12 km/3 to 8 miles wide, and runs northwards, with various intermissions for scrub, pasture, polder, and riverbank, more than 70 km/50 miles from the northern suburbs of Bordeaux to the marshes of the lower, more northerly part of the Médoc, the so-called Bas-Médoc. Wines produced in the Bas-Médoc may use the **Médoc** appellation, while those on the higher ground in the south-eastern section are entitled to the **Haut-Médoc** appellation, although many of them qualify for the smarter individual village, or communal, appellations. From south to north, these are MARGAUX, MOULIS, LISTRAC, ST-JULIEN, PAUILLAC, and ST-ESTÈPHE.

The climate on this peninsula is Bordeaux's mildest, moderated both by the estuary and by the Atlantic Ocean just over the pines. These forests protect the vineyard strip from strong winds off the ocean, and help to moderate summer temperatures, but it is only in the Médoc and the GRAVES district further south that Bordeaux vignerons are confident of ripening Cabernet Sauvignon grapes with any frequency. The Médoc is also Bordeaux's wettest region, which makes rot a constant threat and SPRAYING a habit.

A typical estate, or CHÂTEAU, in the greater Médoc district hedges its viticultural bets and grows at least three different grape varieties: a majority of Cabernet Sauvignon, supplemented principally by Merlot, together with some Cabernet Franc with, perhaps, a little late-ripening Petit Verdot and occasionally some Malbec. However, Merlot often predominates in the damper, cooler soils of the Bas-Médoc as it is easier to ripen in lesser vintages, and Cabernet Sauvignon comprises only about half of all the vines planted in the district.

While the Médoc possesses few distinctive geographical features, many man-hours have been spent charting the subterranean Médoc.

It has long been argued that its great distinction is its soil, in particular its GRAVEL. One of the most important soil attributes is good DRAINAGE (see SOIL AND WINE QUALITY). The gravels of the Médoc are ideal in this respect, and are particularly important in such a damp climate—although in hotter vintages mature vines can benefit from the extensive root systems encouraged by the gravel. The gravels of the Médoc are also good at storing valuable heat, thereby promoting RIPENING. It is traditionally said that the best vines of the Médoc are those which grow within sight of the Gironde, and certainly this is true of all the district's FIRST GROWTHS.

A total of about 1,500 vine-growers farm this land, about a quarter of which forms part of one of the classed growths ranked in the famous 1855 CLASSIFICATION of the Médoc (and Graves).

The Haut-Médoc appellation

The landscape of the Haut-Médoc may not be remarkable but it is peppered with grandiose château buildings erected and embellished with the money to be made from selling CLASSED GROWTH red bordeaux. Certainly the Haut-Médoc today is nothing if not stratified, thanks largely to the effects of the 1855 classification of its most famous estates, which recognized scores of them as first, second, third, fourth, and fifth growths, commercial and social positions from which none but Ch MOUTON-ROTHSCHILD has so far been able to escape.

Most of these classed growths are entitled to a village appellation such as Pauillac or Margaux, but five of them are in communes without their own appellations and qualify merely as Haut-Médoc. The most highly ranked of these is the third growth Ch La Lagune in Ludon just outside the city, a property which has retained its reputation for robust, concentrated wines. Just north of this well-run property is the fifth growth Ch Cantemerle, renovated in the 1980s. The commune of St-Laurent, inland from ST-JULIEN on the main road through the forests of the Médoc, boasts the under-performing fourth growth Ch La Tour-Carnet and two improving fifth growths, Chx Belgrave and Camensac.

The area classified as Haut-Médoc had grown to nearly 4,300 ha/10,600 acres by 1996. Many of these vineyards are CRUS BOURGEOIS offering some of the best value to be found in Bordeaux.

The best wines share the deep colour, concentration, tannins, and ageing potential of the classed growths, and are made in a very similar fashion except that the basic YIELD allowed is 43 hl/ha (2.4 tons/acre) rather than the 40 hl/ha permitted for the Médoc's four important village or communal appellations, and a leap of faith and selling price is needed to justify the use of new BARRELS. Some of the most ambitious properties include Chx Belgrave, Cantemerle, Citran, Coufran, Lamothe-Bergeron, Lanessan, Maucamps, Moulin Rouge, Sociando-Mallet, and Tour du Haut-Moulin.

The appellation Médoc
The total area qualifying for the basic Médoc appellation had reached 4,700 ha/11,600 acres by 1996, just more than that of the generally finer Haut-Médoc. The basic limit to yields was increased from 45 to 50 hl/ha in 1994, and a high proportion of the wines are dominated by Merlot. Much of the wine produced on these lower, less well-drained, heavier soils is solid if uninspiring claret sold in bulk to CO-OPERATIVES or to the BORDEAUX TRADE for blending into GENERIC Médoc. Estates on which an effort is made to produce something more distinctive than this, usually by restricting yields, include Chx Les Grands Chênes, Les Ormes Sorbet, Potensac (run particularly fastidiously by the owners of Ch LÉOVILLE LAS CASES of St-Julien), La Tour de By, Tour Haut-Caussan (one of Bordeaux's rare ORGANIC WINES), and Vieux Robin. See also CRU ARTISAN.

Méjanelle, Coteaux de la, sometimes called **Méjanelle**, named TERROIR within the Coteaux du LANGUEDOC in southern France, just outside the city of Montpellier. Unlike the rest of the Coteaux du Languedoc, this is a historic zone of individual estates, most notably Ch de Flaugergues. Syrah, Grenache, and Mourvèdre dominate in these particularly Mediterranean vineyards, at a much lower altitude than much of the rest of the Coteaux du Languedoc.

Melnik, powerful indigenous Bulgarian red grape variety that is grown exclusively around the ancient town of Melnik close to the Greek border in what was Thrace. Its wines certainly taste more Greek in their extract, tannin, and alcohol than typical of modern Bulgaria. Its full name is Shiroka Melnishka Losa, or 'broad-leaved vine of Melnik', and its berries are notably small with thick, blue skins. Some wines have the aroma of tobacco leaves, another local crop. Oak ageing and several years bring out a warmth and powerful subtlety not unlike a CHÂTEAUNEUF-DU-PAPE. This is probably the Bulgarian wine with the greatest longevity, but see also MAVRUD.

Melon, or Melon de Bourgogne, French white grape variety, famous in only one respect and one region, MUSCADET. As its full name suggests, its origins are Burgundian (see PINOT). Unlike its fellow white burgundian Chardonnay, several of whose synonyms include the word Melon, it is not a noble grape variety but it does resist cold well and produces quite regularly and generously.

Melon's increasing importance today rests solely on MUSCADET, whose main attribute could be said to be that it has so few distinguishing features.

Many of the older cuttings of the variety called PINOT BLANC in California are in fact Melon.

Mencía, red grape variety grown widely in north-west Spain, especially in such zones as BIERZO and RIBEIRA SACRA. True, indigenous Mencía produces light, pale, relatively fragrant red wines for early consumption, while a local strain of Cabernet Franc also, confusingly, goes by this name.

True Mencía is thought to be identical to Portugal's JAEN.

Mendocino, one of CALIFORNIA's largest and climatically most diverse counties. All of its vineyards are in the southern half. Even there, the meteorological range between the coastal Anderson Valley AVA and the interior McDowell Valley AVA beggars the imagination.

Most of the plantings flank the town of Ukiah, near the headwaters of the Russian River. Although the districts of Redwood Valley, Ukiah, and Hopland are fairly well defined, they were slow to seek individual AVA status, contenting themselves with a blanket Mendocino AVA because of its wider consumer recognition. Fetzer is based here.

Mendocino AVA
The coverall AVA in Mendocino County includes the more specific Anderson Valley, McDowell Valley, and Potter Valley AVAs, as well as the county's most substantial vineyard plantings along the Russian River course from Redwood Valley southward through Ukiah to

Hopland and on south into Sonoma County's Alexander Valley. Cabernet Sauvignon and Sauvignon Blanc have been reliable in the large zone along the Russian River. Zinfandel and Petite Sirah from third-generation Italian–American growers on the benchlands can reach great heights in the hands of an artisan wine-maker. Chardonnay from vineyards such as Lolonis has been surprisingly fine. Fetzer is the dominant winery by size; Jepson, Parducci, and Hidden Cellars are others of commercial importance.

Anderson Valley AVA

Scouts for Louis ROEDERER of Champagne say they hunted in California until they found somewhere with weather as bleak as Roederer's home in north-eastern France, and that Mendocino County's coast-hugging Anderson Valley fitted their requirement perfectly. Close framed by steep hills, the valley has only a couple of patches that might pass for floor and, unusually for California's valley vineyards, only one or two of the 20 or so are flat. Anderson Valley is hardly 10 miles end to end, but a steady rise in elevation from 80 to 1,300 feet combines with a rising wall of hills to make the inland end at Boonville warmer and sunnier than the oft-befogged area between Philo and Navarro, where most of the vines grow.

A couple of extraordinary Gewürztraminers have come from Anderson Valley. Some of its Rieslings and Chardonnays have been memorable. Ridgetops to the west have yielded a succession of wonderfully oak-ribbed Zinfandels from a scattering of tiny patches. Greenwood Ridge, Handley, Husch, Lazy Creek, and Navarro vineyards are the mainstay wineries for table-wine production. However, since 1984, first Roederer then Scharffenberger have thrown the region's weight behind traditional-method sparkling wines from Chardonnay and Pinot Noir which many critics think may be America's best so far.

McDowell Valley AVA

In practice this is a one-winery AVA located in a small, upland valley east of the town of Hopland in southern Mendocino County. It has been of interest primarily for Grenache, Syrah, and Zinfandel first planted before the turn of the century.

Potter Valley AVA

Without a winery of its own, the upland district in eastern Mendocino County is seldom identified on labels. Sauvignon Blanc has been its premier achievement to date. Planting began in the 1970s. Prior to the drought years of 1987–92, the district was particularly noted for BOTRYTIZED wines.   B.C.C.

Mendoza. See ARGENTINA.

Menetou-Salon is just west of, and very much smaller than, the much more famous SANCERRE, near the city of Bourges, producing a not dissimilar range of red, white, and rosé wines which can often offer better value. Sauvignon Blanc grown here is capable of making wines every bit as refreshingly aromatic as Sancerre. Soils in the appellation are mainly limestone and can be very similar to those in the more famous zone to the east, especially in its best zone around the village of Morogues, a name used on the labels of producers such as Henry Pellé. The village of Parassy also has a high concentration of vineyards. Sauvignon represents about 60 per cent of the appellation's total production, while Pinot Noir grapes are responsible for scented, light reds and pinks for early consumption.

See also LOIRE.

Méntrida, Spanish town and wine zone south west of Madrid in CASTILE-LA MANCHA producing robust red wines from GARNACHA grapes. It is by no means clear what the winemakers in the hills around the town have done to deserve DO status. Most of the wines are hefty reds made in old-fashioned, often unhygienic CO-OPERATIVES that travel no further than the bars in nearby Madrid. The one producer who is making high-quality wine in this part of Spain, Marqués de Griñon, has Cabernet Sauvignon, Chardonnay, Syrah, and PETIT VERDOT vines growing in his vineyard at Malpica de Tajo just outside the denomination. He spurned the opportunity to jump rank from VINO DE MESA de Toledo to DO by countenancing an extension of the boundary, thereby initiating a fashion for superior non-DO wines sometimes called super-Spanish, after Italy's SUPER-TUSCANS.   R.J.M. & V. de la S.

Menu Pineau, synonym for the ARBOIS vine.

Meranese, or **Meraner** in German, red wines from around the town of Merano in the ALTO ADIGE.

mercaptans, a group of foul-smelling chemical compounds in which one of the hydrogen atoms of HYDROGEN SULPHIDE has been replaced by an alkyl group, a chain of carbon atoms with hydrogen atoms attached at all vacant sites. Mercaptans, which smell uncomfortably skunk-like, are formed by YEAST after the primary alcoholic FERMENTATION reacting with SULPHUR in the LEES. If not removed from the new wine (which can usually be achieved by simple aeration, by prompt RACKING, for example), less volatile and even more unpleasant compounds tend to be formed.

Mercurey, most important village in the Côte CHALONNAISE district of Burgundy. While most of the production is in red wines made from Pinot Noir, a small quantity of unusually scented white wine from Chardonnay is also made. Mercurey produces almost as much wine as the other Côte Chalonnaise appellations Givry, Rully, and Montagny combined. The appellation, including the commune of St-Martin-sous-Montaigu, includes 29 PREMIER CRU vineyards making up 20 per cent of the total.

The red wines tend to be deeper in colour, fuller in body, more capable of ageing, and half as expensive again as those of the neighbouring villages.   J.T.C.M.

Merenzao, lesser red grape speciality of the VALDEORRAS region in north-west Spain, sometimes known as Maria Ordoña. Some recent experiments suggest it has real potential. It is sometimes known as Bastardo but there are no indications that it is the same as the Portuguese variety of the same name.

Meritage (rhymes with heritage), name coined in 1981, by the winner of a competition in the *Los Angeles Times*, for American wines made from a blend of grape varieties in the image of BORDEAUX, devised to distinguish these wines from VARIETAL Cabernet Sauvignon, Merlot, etc., most usefully on wine lists. This trade-marked name is legally available on labels only to American wineries that agree to join the Meritage Association and uphold the following requirements of the wine labelled Meritage: made exclusively from Cabernet Sauvignon, Cabernet Franc, Merlot, Malbec, Petit Verdot grapes for red wines and Sauvignon Blanc, Sémillon, and Muscadelle for whites; produced in quantities of no more than 25,000 cases a year; one of the two most expensive wines produced by the winery. Nearly but not all of the members are in CALIFORNIA.
                                                    B.C.C.

Merlot or Merlot Noir, extremely popular black grape variety associated with the great wines of St-Émilion and Pomerol by traditionalists and with FIGHTING VARIETALS by followers of FASHION. Merlot is Bordeaux's most planted black grape variety, and has been enjoying unaccustomed popularity elsewhere. It has no direct relationship to the much less distinguished white-berried MERLOT BLANC.

Although Merlot has become the red (and therefore fashionable) answer to Chardonnay, few of those who order it in such quantity—typically by the GLASS in the United States—would be able to describe its flavour with any precision. One thing they would be agreed on though is that it is 'smooth'. If any single wine promoted texture rather than flavour to the front rank of concerns for American winemakers it is Merlot, 'Cabernet without the pain' (cf. ASTRINGENCY). Indeed, one of its flavour characteristics in France, a fragrance bordering on HERBACEOUSNESS, is seen as a positive drawback by many American tasters.

France

Throughout SOUTH WEST FRANCE and, increasingly, much of the rest of the world, Merlot plays the role of constant companion to the more austere, aristocratic, long-living CABERNET SAUVIGNON. Its early-maturing, plump, lush fruitiness provides a more obvious complement to Cabernet Sauvignon's attributes than the CABERNET FRANC that often makes up the third ingredient in the common 'Bordelais' blend. Merlot responds much better than the late-ripening Cabernet Sauvignon to damp, cool soils, such as those of St-Émilion and Pomerol, that retain their moisture well and allow the grapes to reach full size.

For the vine-grower in anything cooler than a warm or hot climate, Merlot is much easier to ripen than Cabernet Sauvignon, and has the further advantage of yielding a little higher. It is not surprising therefore that, in France and northern Italy, total Merlot plantings have for long been greatly superior to those of Cabernet Sauvignon.

This is particularly marked in Bordeaux, where Cabernet Sauvignon dominates Merlot only in the well-drained soils of the Médoc and Graves. Elsewhere, not just in St-Émilion and Pomerol but also in Bourg, Blaye, Fronsac, and, importantly, those areas qualifying for basic Bordeaux or the rest of the so-called BORDEAUX CÔTES appellation, Merlot predominates.

Merlot

It is clearly in St-Émilion and, especially, the clay soils of Pomerol that the variety produces its more glorious wines (see under ST-ÉMILION and POMEROL for more detail). Even here, however, except for notable exceptions such as Ch PÉTRUS, Merlot produces wines perceptibly lower in colour, acid, and, especially, tannin than left-bank red bordeaux dominated by the thicker-skinned Cabernet Sauvignon. The relatively early maturing, easy-to-appreciate Merlot is a wine with distinct advantages over Cabernet Sauvignon in times of inflation.

Such was the increase in popularity of Merlot with the vine-growers of Bordeaux, Bergerac, and Languedoc-Roussillon in the 1980s that Merlot was France's third most planted black grape variety, after Carignan and Grenache, by 1988. Merlot is more widely planted than either sort of Cabernet, not just in Bordeaux but also in the rest of SOUTH WEST FRANCE. Wherever in this quarter of France the APPELLATION CONTRÔLÉE regulations sanction Cabernet Sauvignon (see CABERNET SAUVIGNON for details), they also sanction Merlot, although the latter is favoured in the Dordogne while the Cabernets are preferred in Gascony.

With Syrah, Merlot has been a major beneficiary of the Languedoc's replanting with 'improving' grape varieties. Total plantings in the Languedoc more than doubled between 1988 and 1998 to reach 18,500 ha. Most of this is destined for VINS DE PAYS for the only Languedoc appellations to sanction Merlot within their regulations are CABARDÈS and Côtes de la MALEPÈRE. Merlot has been a much more successful import here than Cabernet Sauvignon and can produce some good-value, fruity wines for drinking young, many of which were shipped to the United States in the mid 1990s to satisfy American demand for this most fashionable of wines.

Rest of Europe

The Merlot of northern Italy was pressed into similar duty, as California's new plantings were still too young to be productive. The variety is extremely important in Italy, particularly in the north east, often alongside Cabernet Franc, where output of the wine called there 'Merlott' can be easily 100,000 hl/2.6 million gal a year from the plains of both GRAVE DEL FRIULI and PIAVE, even if better, more concentrated wines come in smaller quantities from higher vineyards. In FRIULI, where Merlot performs perceptibly better than most CAB-ERNET, there is even a Strada del Merlot, a tourist route along the Isonzo river. Individual denominations for Merlot abound in FRIULI, the VENETO, and TRENTINO-ALTO ADIGE. Merlot is also planted on the Colli BOLOGNESI in Emilia-Romagna. The variety is planted in 14 of Italy's 20 regions. In general, little has been expected from or delivered by the sea of light, vaguely fruity Merlot from northern Italy, which makes it all the more remarkable that the variety is being taken seriously by a handful of producers in Tuscany and Umbria and, more recently, in Friuli itself.

Lodovico Antinori at Ornellaia in BOLGHERI and the Fattoria di Ama in CHIANTI CLASSICO were the first to show that Italy could provide something more in the mould of serious Pomerol. Significant quantities of Merlot are likely to be produced in Tuscany and central Italy in the near future, some vinified on its own but an even larger proportion used to supplement SANGIOVESE. Many producers have come to prefer the variety to Cabernet Sauvignon, both for ripening more easily and for being a less dominant blending component with native Italian varieties.

Merlot is vital to the wine industry of Italian SWITZERLAND and is made at a wide range of quality levels, including some very fine wines indeed incorporating top-quality BARREL MATURATION.

Merlot has also been popular over Italy's north-eastern border in SLOVENIA and all down the Dalmatian coast, where it can be attractively plummy when yields are restricted. It is also known in HUNGARY, notably around Eger in the north east and Villány in the south. It is also the most widely planted red wine variety in ROMANIA, and is the second most planted variety in BULGARIA after Cabernet Sauvignon, with which it is often blended. It is also planted in RUSSIA and, particularly, MOLDOVA.

Outside these traditional strongholds, Merlot was until the early 1990s taken up much more slowly than the world-famous Cabernet Sauvignon. The fact that it is slightly lower in acidity as well as international *réclame* may have hindered its progress in some warmer climates such as Iberia and most of the eastern Mediterranean, where it was still relatively rare in the early 1990s (although the mid-Portuguese Ma Partilha already showed promise).

Rest of the world

A lift in Merlot's reputation was already apparent, however, by 1990, most obviously in North America. Merlot was suddenly regarded as 'the hot varietal' in the Cabernet-soaked state of California, and demonstrated decisively that it had a particular affinity with the conditions of Washington state and possibly even of those of Long Island in the state of NEW YORK.

In 1985, California had a total of hardly 2,000 acres/800 ha of Merlot. By the end of 1996 there were 33,000 acres in the ground. Half of the red grapes planted to replace PHYLLOXERA-infected vines in Napa during 1996 were Merlot, but a similar area of Merlot was also planted in the less glamorous Central Valley counties of Merced, King, Madera, and San Joaquin. In 1997, the variety was in great demand both for blending with other Bordeaux varieties for MERITAGE and the like, and for varietal reds that were softer and milder than the state's Cabernet Sauvignons. With very few exceptions, however, Cabernet Sauvignon was left to command California's highest wine prices, Merlot to swell sales volumes. As elsewhere, there has been confusion between Merlot and Cabernet Franc cuttings. See CALIFORNIA for more detail of the wine style.

Merlot has had little success in Oregon's vineyards, but in Washington's sunny inland Columbia basin Merlot has produced consistently fine, fruity, well-structured reds (see WASHINGTON). Merlot is also grown increasingly in other North American states.

In South America, Merlot is quite important to the wine industry of ARGENTINA, although among Bordeaux red grapevines Cabernet Sauvignon and, especially, Malbec are much more commonly planted. Merlot is also planted to a more limited extent in URUGUAY, BRAZIL, and BOLIVIA but it is in CHILE that it has become extremely important to the country's prolific wine exports. Vines called Merlot do particularly well in the damper soils of the more southerly wine regions in Chile's Central Valley, although by no means all of the 3,500 ha/8,600 acres are true Merlot Noir. An increasing proportion is being identified as another old Bordeaux variety CARMENÈRE—and some is even sold as such.

California's relatively late but almost demented enthusiasm for Merlot is mirrored in Australia, where, of the 2,500 ha planted in 1997, less than half were old enough to bear fruit. There is great potential for Merlot in selected spots there but the prevailing tradition has been to soften Cabernet Sauvignon (inasmuch

as ultraripe Australian Cabernet needs softening) with Shiraz rather than Merlot.

Merlot clearly has great potential in New Zealand too and plantings had reached about two-thirds the Cabernet Sauvignon total by 1997. It has so far been used mainly for filling in the flavour holes of the more angular Cabernet Sauvignon. South Africa has produced some interesting varietal Merlots as well as using it to good effect in Bordeaux blends but the variety had yet to establish a distinct identity for itself on the Cape in the late 1990s.

Merlot Blanc, white wine grape variety which has been cultivated in Bordeaux, on a much smaller and decreasing scale than MERLOT Noir, to which it is not directly related.

Merseguera, lacklustre Spanish white grape variety (Ezquitxagos in Penedès) widely grown in ALICANTE, JUMILLA, and VALENCIA.

mesoclimate, a term of climatic scale, intermediate between regional climate or MACROCLIMATE, and the very small-scale MICROCLIMATE.

méthode ancestrale, sometimes called méthode artisanale or méthode rurale, very traditional SPARKLING-WINE-MAKING method used chiefly in Limoux, resulting in a lightly sparkling, medium-sweet wine, sometimes complete with sediment.

méthode champenoise, French term for the traditional method described in detail in SPARKLING-WINE-MAKING. This description was once a valuable aid to the consumer in distinguishing the most meticulously made sparkling wines from those made by less complicated methods. From 1994, this description was outlawed by European Union authorities, however, in favour of one of the following: 'fermentation en bouteille selon la méthode champenoise'; 'méthode traditionnelle'; 'méthode classique'; 'méthode traditionnelle classique'. English-language equivalents are 'fermented in this bottle' and TRADITIONAL METHOD.

méthode classique, term for the traditional method of SPARKLING-WINE-MAKING approved by the European Union.

méthode dioise, SPARKLING-WINE-MAKING process used for CLAIRETTE DE DIE.

méthode gaillacoise, GAILLAC's version of the MÉTHODE ANCESTRALE. See SPARKLING-WINE-MAKING.

méthode traditionnelle and méthode traditionnelle classique, alternative terms for the traditional method of SPARKLING-WINE-MAKING that are approved by the European Union. See MÉTHODE CHAMPENOISE.

metodo classico and metodo tradizionale, Italian terms for SPARKLING WINES made by the traditional method.

Meunier is one of France's dozen most planted black grape varieties but neither it nor its common synonym **Pinot Meunier** are often encountered on a wine label. In Germany, it is known as Müllerrebe (miller's grape) as well as Schwarzriesling.

Meunier is treasured in Champagne because it buds later and ripens earlier than Pinot Noir and is more dependably productive. Acid levels are slightly higher although alcohol levels are by no means necessarily lower than those of Pinot Noir. Meunier is therefore the popular choice for Champagne's growers, especially those in cooler north-facing vineyards, in the damp, frost-prone Vallée de la Marne, and in the cold valleys of the Aisne *département*. In fact, so commercially reliable is Meunier for Champagne's powerful vine-growers that it is Champagne's most popular variety by far, covering more than 40 per cent of the region's vineyards. Plantings of Pinot Noir and Chardonnay increased at a greater rate than those of Meunier in the 1980s, partly because of premiums paid for these 'nobler' varieties, but Meunier will remain the region's principal variety in terms of quantity for many years to come.

Common wisdom has it that, as an ingredient in the traditional three-variety champagne blend, Meunier contributes youthful fruitiness to complement Pinot Noir's weight and Chardonnay's finesse. Few producers boast of their Meunier, however (with the honourable exception of KRUG), and few preponderantly Meunier growers' champagnes have great weight or staying power. Meunier is generally lower in pigments than Pinot Noir, and one of its common French synonyms is Gris Meunier.

It has largely disappeared elsewhere in northern France although it is still technically allowed into the rosés and light reds of Côtes de TOUL, wines of MOSELLE, and, in the Loire, TOURAINE and wines of the ORLÉANAIS.

As Müllerrebe or Schwarzriesling, a selection of Meunier is relatively, and increasingly, popular in Germany, especially in the WÜRTTEMBERG region. It is also grown in German-speaking SWITZERLAND, and to a much lesser extent in Austria and Yugoslavia. See also BURGUND MARE in Romania.

Curiously, in Australia, Meunier has a longer documented history as a still red varietal wine (at one time called Miller's Burgundy) than Pinot Noir, notably at Great Western (now called Grampians) in VICTORIA. New-found enthusiasm for authentic replicas of champagne saved the variety from extinction in Australia and there have been some new plantings in cooler spots.

It was also with an eye to producing 'genuine' replicas of champagne that growers in California sought Meunier cuttings in the 1980s, which they planted almost exclusively in CARNEROS.

Meursault, large and prosperous village in the Côte de Beaune district of Burgundy's CÔTE D'OR producing mostly white wines from the Chardonnay grape. Although Meursault contains no GRAND CRU vineyards, the quality of white burgundy from Meursault's best PREMIERS CRUS is rarely surpassed.

The finest vineyards are Les Perrières, Les Genevrières, and Les Charmes. Between them and the village of Meursault are three more premiers crus, Le Poruzot, Les Bouchères, and La Goutte d'Or. Another group by the hamlet of BLAGNY are sold as Meursault-Blagny if white or Blagny premier cru if red, while, at the other end of the village, Les Santenots is sold as Meursault Santenots if white and Volnay Santenots if red, as it usually is. Apart from Les Santenots, and the lean but fine red wines of Blagny, the other red wines of Meursault tend to be grown low on the slope and do not feature among the best of the Côte de Beaune.

The character of Les Perrières derives from the quantity of stones, after which the vineyard is named, which reflect the sun back onto the vines. If Les Perrières is regularly the richest wine in Meursault, Les Genevrières comes close, producing particularly elegant wines. Les Charmes is the biggest of the three major vineyards and produces the most forward wines, seductive even in their youth.

Meursault also enjoys a wealth of good wines from other named vineyards such as Chevalières, Tessons, Clos de la Barre, Luchets, Narvaux, and Tillets. These are frequently more interesting than the village wines of PULIGNY-

MONTRACHET. Furthermore, because it is possible to dig cellars significantly deeper in Meursault, many growers are able to prolong BARREL MATURATION through a second winter, which improves the depth, stability, and ageing potential of the wines.

Comte Lafon is still one of the finest producers of Meursault, along with Coche Dury and Guy Roulot.   J.T.C.M.

Mexico, the Americas' oldest wine-producing country, had 47,000 ha/116,000 acres under vine in 1996, almost half as much as Chile, for example, although only a small fraction of this land is designed to produce wine, and an even smaller percentage of that is exported.

The main wine regions are Parras, Zacatecas, and Baja California between California and the Tropic of Cancer. Here IRRIGATION is practised wherever possible, and low rainfall is Mexico's greatest viticultural disadvantage. Vineyards planted (up to 2,100 m/7,000 ft) on the plateaux of Aguascalientes and in Querétaro have been dogged by the timing of the heavy rainy season, just before harvest.

Vine varieties planted include a wide range of European red wine varieties such as CABERNET SAUVIGNON, MERLOT, MALBEC, NEBBIOLO, GRENACHE, and CARIGNAN, supplemented by varieties more common in California such as ZINFANDEL, PETITE SIRAH, and RUBY CABERNET as well as American HYBRIDS Black Spanish and Lenoir. A wide range of European light-skinned grape varieties are also planted, including brandy grapes such as TREBBIANO, COLOMBARD, and PALOMINO as well as CHENIN BLANC. The historic MISSION grape, whose ancestors were planted by the early Spanish settlers, has all but disappeared.

Mexico is the fourth most important wine producer in Latin America after ARGENTINA, BRAZIL, and CHILE. Of all Latin American wine producers, Mexico is probably most strongly influenced by California.

Mexico's own influence on New World wine has also been considerable, if indirect. Without Mexicans as the prime labour source for vineyard work, California's late-20th-century wine industry might have developed quite differently.

Mezesfehér, white grape variety grown widely in HUNGARY, where its soft, usually sweet, white wines are much admired. Such wines are rarely exported to western markets, however. Its name means 'white honey' and it

is perhaps most successful around Eger and Gyöngyös.

MIA or **Murrumbidgee Irrigation Area**, one of the irrigated wine regions of AUSTRALIA associated mainly with inexpensive wine for blending. See NEW SOUTH WALES.

microchâteau, unofficial name for a new phenomenon on Bordeaux's RIGHT BANK, miniature wine estates producing ultra-modern wines, deep-coloured, early-maturing, flattering reds typically produced in quantities of a few hundred cases from low YIELDS, careful SELECTION, fairly warm and short FERMENTATIONS, short MACERATION, MALOLACTIC FERMENTATION in barrel, 15 to 18 months of 100 per cent new BARREL MATURATION, minimal FILTRATION, and, often, Michel ROLLAND as consultant oenologist. Le PIN in Pomerol was the archetype, and as its PRICES soared was born a host of microchâteaux in St-Émilion (where there is more available land). Ch Valandraud is an obvious example, and does not even consist of a single, contiguous plot of vines, nor even of exclusively respected TERROIRS. Others include Le Dôme, La Gomerie, L'Hermitage, La Mondotte (produced by the owner of Ch Canon-La-Gaffelière), and Rol Valentin, although the list will doubtless continue to lengthen. The wines are not reliably great but they are reliably expensive.

The prices, fuelled by rarity, hype, and FASHION, are sufficient to justify the production costs of these hand-crafted wines for which each individual barrel must be kept under constant surveillance. The size of a typical LEFT BANK estate would not support such an exclusive, in several senses, formula.

microclimate, widely misused term meaning strictly the climate within a defined and usually very restricted space or position. In viticulture, it might be at specified positions between rows of vines, or distances above the ground.

Common use of the term microclimate to describe the climate of a vineyard site, hillside, or valley is clearly wrong. The correct term for these is usually MESOCLIMATE, or possibly site climate or topoclimate.

CANOPY MICROCLIMATE is that within and immediately surrounding the vine canopy, or green parts of the vine.

Midi, common name for the south of France. Like Mezzogiorno in Italy it means literally 'midday' and refers to regions where midday is a time of extreme heat and inactivity, at least in summer. Midi is often used synonymously with LANGUEDOC-ROUSSILLON, although strictly speaking the Midi encompasses PROVENCE as well.

Milawa, significant Australian wine region in north-east VICTORIA. Brown Brothers is the best-known producer.

Millau, Côtes de, small zone in the Gorges du Tarn in the south of France promoted to VDQS status in 1994 making reds and some rosés mainly from a blend of Gamay and Syrah. The Aguessac CO-OPERATIVE dominates production.

millerandage, abnormal FRUIT SET in the vine which is shown by the joint presence of large and small berries in the same bunch. Millerandage can cause a major loss of YIELD, especially where the proportion of small berries is high. Wine-makers have, however, been known to welcome the condition, as there is a widely held view that small BERRY SIZE makes better-quality wine.   R.E.S.

Minervois, western LANGUEDOC appellation for characterful reds, generally suppler than those from CORBIÈRES to the south, together with some rosé and white, produced on nearly 4,000 ha/9,880 acres of varied inland terrain in the Aude and eastern Hérault *départements*.

Since 1985, when Minervois was granted APPELLATION CONTRÔLÉE status, strenuous efforts have been made to upgrade overall quality, and a number of CO-OPERATIVES and individual wine producers have made considerable investments both in winery equipment and in planting better vine varieties. Carignan must account for no more than 40 per cent of the blend, with Grenache, Lladoner Pelut, Syrah, and Mourvèdre accounting for at least 60 per cent (although other traditional Languedoc varieties are also allowed). Various combinations of Bourboulenc, Rolle (Vermentino), Maccabéo, Roussanne, Marsanne, and Grenache Blanc are responsible for the varied quality and character of white Minervois, which is increasingly aromatic and, after some heavy-handed experiments with BARREL MATURATION, sophisticated. Some producers have attempted to revive an ancient SHERRY-like style once called Vin Noble du Minervois.

For red wines, most Carignan is vinified using full or partial CARBONIC MACERATION for

5 to 12 days, while other red wine varieties are given longer in the fermentation vat, with frequent pumping over or punching down to encourage EXTRACTION of PHENOLICS. Red wines have traditionally been given at least a year in cement tanks or large old casks. Small-barrel maturation is slowly becoming more common, but there are constraints on investment in a region whose selling prices have been relatively low. Many other vine varieties are being planted in the varied soils of the region.

In the extreme north east of the region, some of France's rarest and most delicate VIN DOUX NATUREL is produced: MUSCAT DE ST-JEAN-DE-MINERVOIS.

Reliable Minervois producers include Borie de Maurel (Cuvée Sylla), Clos Centeilles, Ch Coupe Rose, Ch de Gourgazaud, Ch Laville-Bertrou, Ch d'Oupia, Domaine Piccinini, and Ch Villerambert Julien.

Minho, province in northern Portugal named after the river (called Miño in Spanish) which forms its boundary with Spain. See RIOS DO MINHO.

Mireval is the large village that gives its name to Muscat de Mireval, the sweet golden VIN DOUX NATUREL appellation that adjoins and is somewhat overshadowed by FRONTIGNAN to the west of it. Production has been almost exclusively in the hands of the CO-OPERATIVE La Cave de Rabelais.

mis(e) en bouteille is French for bottled. A wine that is **mis(e) en bouteille au château** is CHÂTEAU BOTTLED, while **mis(e) en bouteille au domaine** is DOMAINE BOTTLED. **Mis(e) en bouteille du château/domaine** is a term used by CO-OPERATIVES for their bottlings of wines they vinified from the grapes of individual properties.

Misket, Bulgarian grape-scented white grape variety that is a crossing of the native DIMIAT with Riesling and is a speciality of the sub-Balkan region (see BULGARIA). **Red Misket**, also used for perfumed white wines, is probably a pink-berried mutant of Misket and is relatively well established in Bulgaria with numerous local subvarieties such as **Sliven Misket** and **Varna Misket**. Misket is a speciality of the Sungurlare region.

Mission, the original black grape variety planted for sacramental purposes by Franciscan missionaries in Mexico, the south west of the UNITED STATES, and CALIFORNIA in the 17th and 18th centuries. It is identical to the PAIS of Chile, is a darker-skinned version of the CRIOLLA CHICA of Argentina, and is thought by some to be the same as the MONICA of Spain and Sardinia. In California, there were still almost 1,000 acres/405 ha grown in the early 1990s, mainly in the south of the state, and used for sweet wines. The wine made from Mission is not particularly distinguished but the variety has enormous historical significance.

Mission Haut-Brion, Château La Important wine estate in Bordeaux. See Ch HAUT-BRION.

Missouri, midwestern state in the USA which has played an important part in the country's wine history.

Today Missouri has 30 wineries and about 700 acres under vine, perhaps 480 (190 ha) of them French HYBRIDS and the rest native American vine varieties. The first AVA in the USA was Augusta, Missouri, approved in 1980. Two further AVAs are Hermann and Ozark Mountain Region. The state's most interesting wine, red and ageworthy, comes from NORTON and Cynthiana grapes; about 16 wineries produce it, in varying styles. Vignoles, SEYVAL Blanc, and VIDAL Blanc are the most popular white grapes. Missouri's most distinguished wineries are Stone Hill, Mount Pleasant, and St James. A few wineries, however, such as Mount Pleasant in Augusta, grow VINIFERA varieties successfully. And in Saints of the East (named because so many of its cities are named for saints), is Ste Genevieve, Missouri's oldest permanent settlement, with its winery of the same name. This area and its wines show a strong French influence from northern Louisiana. H.G. & H.L.

mistela is the Spanish term and **mistelle** the French for a mixture of grape juice and alcohol.

Mittelrhein, small and shrinking wine region in GERMANY of predominantly local interest. Most of the vines grow within sight of the river RHINE, often looking down upon it from a considerable height. The first commercial vineyards start about 8 km/5 miles south of Bonn and none is found on the west bank of the river until Koblenz is reached, 58 km/36 miles upstream. Thereafter, they climb both sides of the Rhine gorge, wherever site, the MESOCLIMATE, and much hard work make vine-growing a more or less viable exercise.

Riesling is planted on 74 per cent of the area under vine. At its best, the wine is characterized by ripe, firm ACIDITY, and about 65 per cent is dry (TROCKEN or HALBTROCKEN). The greatest amount of good wine comes from south of Koblenz, at Spay, Boppard, and at Bacharach. Riesling from the vineyards near Bacharach has a strong, attractive taste from the soil, and in its simplest form converts well into good sparkling wine. MÜLLER-THURGAU wine made from a low yield is often more concentrated in flavour than it is in RHEIN-HESSEN or in the south of the PFALZ.

The Mittelrhein vineyard is slowly shrinking, giving way in the north of the region to urban development and in the south to easier and more lucrative ways of earning a living. Little wine is exported, or even leaves the region, but there are a few private estates such as Toni Jost which are of sufficient standing to be members of the prestigious VDP association of German high-quality estates. About a quarter of the harvest is processed by CO-OPERATIVE cellars at Bacharach and six other towns, and grape-growing is very much a part-time occupation, or simply a weekend hobby. Costs are most likely to be covered if the producer sells directly to tourists. I.J. & K.B.S.

moelleux, French term meaning literally 'like (bone) marrow', or 'mellow'. Wines described as *moelleux* are usually medium sweet. Very rich BOTRYTIZED wines, however, may be described as LIQUOREUX.

Moët & Chandon, Champagne house founded in 1743, producing the single most important champagne BRAND in the world, and part of the vast LVMH group.

In 1962, Moët & Chandon's shares were quoted for the first time on the Paris Stock Exchange, leading to a period of considerable expansion. First, Moët bought shares in Ruinart Père et Fils, the oldest Champagne house, in 1963. Five years later, it acquired a 34 per cent stake in Parfums Christian Dior, increasing this to a 50 per cent stake shortly afterwards. In 1970, Moët took control of Champagne Mercier, a popular brand in France, and capped it all by buying out Dior and merging with Hennessy in 1971 to form the holding company Moët Hennessy. The acquisitions continued unabated, including, in 1981, a stake in the American importers Schieffelin. This American investment also involves the Simi winery in Sonoma, Moët having established Domaine Chandon, a seminal sparkling-wine-making establishment in the Napa Valley, in 1973.

This was by no means the company's first venture into the New World. Bodegas Chandon was established in Argentina in 1960, and Provifin followed in Brazil in 1974, both companies making considerable amounts of wine for the domestic market, much of it sparkling. In Germany too, a SEKT business had been established in the form of Chandon GmbH in 1968. In 1985, the group founded Domaine Chandon, Australia, to make a premium sparkling wine sold as Domaine Chandon in Australia and Green Point in the UK, and in 1987 established a company in Spain for the production of a CAVA called Cava Chandon (Torre del Gall outside Spain).

In 1987, Moët Hennessy merged with the Louis Vuitton Group, makers of luxury leather goods and owners of Champagne houses VEUVE CLICQUOT, Canard-Duchêne, and Henriot, and Givenchy perfumes. By 1999 the LVMH group owned eight Champagne houses: Moët & Chandon, Mercier, Ruinart, Veuve Clicquot, Canard-Duchêne, Henriot, Krug, and Pommery (having briefly bought Lanson and stripped it of its extensive vineyard holdings before selling it on).

Moët, the brand, continues to sell at over twice the rate of its nearest competitors and claims that one in four bottles of Champagne exported comes from the house. It is the leading brand of champagne in most world markets with a share of the champagne market in the United States that can be as high as 50 per cent. Non-vintage blends have been inconsistent, but at their best are fine, well-balanced champagnes. In 1994, an innovative and informative back label was introduced for non-vintage Brut Impérial. The house prestige cuvée is named after Dom PÉRIGNON, the legendary figure of the Abbey of Hautvillers, and broke new ground in terms of packaging, pricing, and qualitative ambitions when it was launched in 1936.   S.A.

Moldavia. Important wine-producing member of the CIS now known as MOLDOVA.

Moldova, one of the geographically smallest but viticulturally most important members of the CIS. Once its problems of infrastructure are solved, it has the greatest potential for wine quality and range, thanks to its extensive vineyards, temperate CONTINENTAL CLIMATE, and

gently undulating landscape sandwiched between eastern ROMANIA and the UKRAINE. Moldova is more 'European', and has more land planted to vines than any other CIS member.

More than 90 per cent of vineyards are in southern or central Moldova, more than half the total area belonging to the state farms. The remainder of the vineyards belong to individuals or collective farms, in the throes of sometimes painful and complex privatization.

Vine varieties

Moldova has a more European range of grape varieties than any other ex-Soviet republic. In the 1990s, it included ALIGOTÉ, FETEASCA, RKATSITELI, Sauvignon Blanc, MUSCAT OTTONEL, Chardonnay, Pinot Gris, Riesling, and Gewürztraminer among grape varieties for white wine and Cabernet Sauvignon, Gamay Fréaux, SAPERAVI, Merlot, Pinot Noir, and Black Sereksia for red wines. Indigenous varieties include PLAVAI.

Wines produced

Acid levels are good to high, CHAPTALIZATION rare, MALOLACTIC FERMENTATION haphazard, and winery hardware and HYGIENE lag many years behind what the West has come to regard as the norm. Potential is exciting, however, especially since commercially popular vine varieties are in place. Sparkling-wine production is important, particularly at Cricova, while sherry styles are a promising speciality of the Yaloveni winery. The Moldovan range also includes answers to Australia's LIQUEUR MUSCAT. Most saleable of Moldova's wines, however, are probably those based on Chardonnay, Sauvignon Blanc, and Cabernet Sauvignon. Reds made in the early 1960s such as Negru de Purkar and Roshu de Purkar were exported to and acclaimed in Britain as the Soviet Union was breaking up. Pucar in the east of the country is a source of fine, age-worthy red wines. Tarakliya in the south, almost on the border with Ukraine, is a source of fruity Cabernet Sauvignon from old vines.

Industry organization

Moldova has been less damaged than most eastern European wine producers by the disappearance of the centralized Soviet wine market. Its wines are highly prized within the CIS. Since independence, some Moldovan wineries have wooed outside expertise, notably with a Dutch JOINT VENTURE. FLYING WINEMAKERS have tried hard here but have been frustrated by such practical problems as poor transport and bottling facilities.   V.R. & J.Ro.

Molette is a common white grape variety used particularly for the sparkling wines of SEYSSEL in SAVOIE. The base wine produced is neutral and much improved by the addition of some ROUSSETTE.

Molinara, red grape variety grown in the Veneto region of north-east Italy, particularly for VALPOLICELLA. Its wines tend to be high in acidity.

Molise, after the Valle d'AOSTA, Italy's smallest and least populated region, is a poor and mountainous area situated south of the ABRUZZI in the south east of Italy. Production is almost entirely in the hands of CO-OPERATIVE wineries, which sell virtually all of the wine in bulk.

The proximity of the Abruzzi has left its mark on Molise's viticulture: the two predominant vine varieties are MONTEPULCIANO d'Abruzzo and TREBBIANO d'Abruzzo. There are attempts to diversify, however, with the planting of grape varieties from southern Italy such as FIANO and GRECO DI TUFO and of more international varieties such as Chardonnay, Riesling, Sylvaner, and Pinot Blanc. The region has a mere two DOCs, and the only one of any significance is Biferno, which may be red, rosé, or white, and is produced in the uplands of the regional capital of Campobasso. Reds and pinks are based on Montepulciano grapes with some red AGLIANICO and white TREBBIANO TOSCANO; Biferno Bianco is based on Trebbiano Toscano, with additions of BOMBINO and MALVASIA.

The best wines of the region, produced by the De Majo Norante winery, have chosen the VINO DA TAVOLA route in response to the world's lack of interest in Molise's DOCs, although the wines are strictly made from southern Italian varieties.   D.T.

Moll, robust but potentially interesting red grape grown on the Spanish island of MAJORCA, also known as Prensal.

Monastrell is the main Spanish name for the black grape variety known in France as MOURVÈDRE and also as Mataro.

Monbazillac, increasingly serious sweet-white-wine appellation within the BERGERAC district in SOUTH WEST FRANCE immediately south of the town of Bergerac.

Like SAUTERNES, it is made from Sémillon, Sauvignon, and, particularly successful here, Muscadelle grapes and the vineyards lie on the left bank of the GARONNE close to its confluence with a small tributary, the Gardonette. This environment favours autumn morning mists and the development of NOBLE ROT, and an increasing number of producers are willing to take the risks involved in trying to produce fully BOTRYTIZED wines. In a determined quest for quality, MECHANICAL HARVESTING was banned from 1993 and successive TRIS through the vineyard insisted upon. The exceptional VINTAGE of 1990 had already inspired some producers to make top-quality botrytized wines which offer exceptional value. Basic maximum permitted yields here are lower than in Sauternes, but in a good vintage such as 1996, the average yield in Monbazillac was 26 hl/ha. About 2,000 ha/5,000 acres of vineyard are dedicated to Monbazillac, considerably more than Sauternes.

The POTENTIAL ALCOHOL must be at least 14.5 per cent. The most conscientious producers have quite rightly relied on nature for the richness of their often markedly orange-tinged wines. In the past, too much Monbazillac has been simply a sweetened, heavy wine, sometimes redolent of SULPHUR DIOXIDE, blended and bottled by a NÉGOCIANT with little passion for the possibilities that exist within this region. From 1993, there has been a clear distinction between serious sweet Monbazillac and early-picked dry white wine, which may be sold as Bergerac Sec. The leading property by far is Ch Tirecul La Gravière, but fine wines are also made by the likes of Chx La Borderie and La Brie.

Mondavi, important family in the recent history of CALIFORNIA wine, with Robert Mondavi (1913–) in particular doing more than anyone to raise awareness of the civilizing influence of wine in general and of California as a source of top-quality wine in particular.

The opening of the Robert Mondavi winery on the Oakville highway in 1966, strikingly Californian, in the mission style, marked the beginning of a new chapter not just for the Mondavis but for California wine. The winery was at the forefront of developing VARIETAL wines based on Europe's most famous vine varieties; continual experimentation; special Reserve bottlings; comparative tastings with France's most famous wines; wine TOURISM;

and cultural events associated with the winery and its wines. In 1979, a JOINT VENTURE was announced between Robert Mondavi and Baron Philippe de Rothschild: Opus One is a Napa Valley Cabernet-based wine made jointly by Tim Mondavi and Mouton's wine-maker. Also in 1979, the company bought a co-operative in Lodi which, producing the high-volume, lower-priced range of Woodbridge FIGHTING VARIETALS, has been its single most profitable venture by far.

During the 1990s, Robert Mondavi extricated himself from day-to-day operations, which now also include: a Chilean venture with Eduardo Chadwick producing Caliterra varietal wines and the highly priced Seña; a joint venture in Italy with the FRESCOBALDI family producing wines called Luce; a venture in the Languedoc producing French wines sold under the name Vichon; and the Byron winery in the Santa Maria Valley. His children, Michael, Tim, and Marcia, divided up responsibilities and left him more time for an itinerary of tireless evangelism on behalf of California wine.

Although the Robert Mondavi winery had considerable assets, borrowings and the prospect of significant inheritance taxes forced this family-owned winery to make a public share issue in 1993.

Mondéjar, denominated wine zone in northern Castilla-La Mancha, Spain, near Guadalajara, created in 1996 and producing table wines of modest distinction. Tempranillo and Cabernet Sauvignon are the main varieties.

Mondeuse, one of the oldest and most distinctive red grape varieties of SAVOIE, bringing an Italianate depth of colour and bite to the region in contrast to the softer reds produced by Gamay. The juicy, peppery wines are powerfully flavoured and coloured and are some of Savoie's few to respond well to careful small oak ageing (although when grown prolifically on Savoie's more fertile, lower sites Mondeuse can easily be dull. Some authorities argue that Mondeuse is identical to the REFOSCO of FRIULI.

Total French plantings of Mondeuse Noire fell sharply in the 1970s but it is to be hoped that there will be a local renaissance in this characterful variety, much of whose produce is sold as a varietal Vin de Savoie unusually capable of ageing. See also BUGEY.

Mondeuse Blanche is a light-berried vine occasionally found in Savoie, and BUGEY, where it may be called Dongine and is capable of producing fine white wine which can be aged for up to 30 years.

Monferrato in PIEDMONT has assumed a new significance with the overall reorganization of Piedmont's DOC structure in the 1990s. Barbera del Monferrato is still a light and simple product, frequently fizzy and definitely intended to be drunk young. But important red wines from blends of native and INTERNATIONAL VARIETIES, as for example Barbera and Cabernet or Pinot Noir, can now be sold as a Monferrato Rosso DOC, as can varietal wines from these non-native grapes. Either Chardonnay or Sauvignon can be labelled Monferrato Bianco. D.T.

Monica, red grape variety grown in great quantity on SARDINIA, where some varietal Monica di Sardegna is thus labelled. Its wines are generally undistinguished and should be drunk young, although more recent wines from the Santadi co-operative suggest that with lower YIELDS, Monica could be a pleasurable, if not always memorable, wine.

monopole, Burgundian term for wholly owned vineyard or CLIMAT.

monoterpenes, members of the group of natural products called terpenoids, are major contributors to the characteristic flavour properties of MUSCAT grapes and wines, and responsible for the floral aromas of many non-Muscat wines such as RIESLING. See also FLAVOUR COMPOUNDS and FLAVOUR PRECURSORS. P.J.W.

Montagne de Reims, the 'mountain of Rheims', or the forested high ground between the CHAMPAGNE towns of Rheims and Épernay. Its lower slopes are famed for the quality of the PINOT NOIR base wine they produce.

Montagne-St-Émilion, the largest satellite appellation of ST-ÉMILION in Bordeaux. Chx Faizeau and Maison Blanche are two of the most admired properties.

Montagny, the appellation for white burgundy produced in the communes of Montagny-lès-Buxy, Jully-lès-Buxy, Buxy, and St-Vallerin in the Côte CHALONNAISE. The wines have a little more body and more acidity than other whites from this region. Uniquely, all vineyards may be designated as PREMIER CRU on condition that the wine has an ALCOHOLIC STRENGTH of at least 11.5 per cent. Much of the production passes through the excellent CO-OPERATIVE founded in 1929 at Buxy. J.T.C.M.

Montalcino. See BRUNELLO DI MONTALCINO.

Montecarlo, zone near Lucca in north-west TUSCANY which was one of the first to produce modern dry red and white wines, blending the ubiquitous TREBBIANO and SANGIOVESE with a host of more interesting grape varieties. Good Chardonnay, Pinot Blanc, Syrah, and Cabernet-Merlot blends began to appear with some regularity in the 1990s, indicating that this northerly part of Tuscany is capable of producing much better wines than it has in the past.

Montefalco. See SAGRANTINO.

Montenegro, comparatively small southern coastal region of what was YUGOSLAVIA, immediately north of ALBANIA. Montenegro has been most famous for VRANAC, a red grape which gives intense, deeply coloured VARIETAL wine capable of developing a velvety texture and intense flavours if aged for three or four years in bulk and then bottle. In the early 1990s, the main producer here began to use an element of young oak, which lent a fashionably soft, spicy edge to the wines. A.H.M.

Montepulciano, vigorous red grape variety planted over much of central Italy and recommended for 20 of Italy's 95 provinces. It is most widely planted in the ABRUZZI, where it is responsible for the often excellent value **Montepulciano d'Abruzzo,** and in the MARCHES, where it is a principal ingredient in such reds as Rosso Conero and Rosso Piceno. It is also grown in MOLISE and APULIA.

Montepulciano has recently shown it can yield dependable quantities of deep-coloured, well-ripened grapes with good levels of alcohol and extract in UMBRIA and the Tuscan MAREMMA. It is sometimes called Cordisco, Morellone, Primaticcio, and Uva Abruzzi.

See also VINO NOBILE DI MONTEPULCIANO.

Monterey, one of the major agricultural counties south of San Francisco in CALIFORNIA, with a reputation as 'America's salad bowl'. As a wine region, Monterey is not cut from the normal cloth. Rainfall is so low that grapes cannot be grown there without IRRIGATION. Water supply is ample, however, from the underground Salinas river, which defines the large valley so open to the Pacific Ocean that sea fogs cool and darken its northern end so that few or no grape varieties will ripen there.

Monterey AVA

The blanket AVA for Monterey County encompasses Arroyo Seco AVA, Carmel Valley AVA, San Lucas AVA, Hames Valley AVA, and all other vineyards not included in these more specific regions. The county contains the largest contiguous vineyard in the world, San Bernabe's 13,000 acres (of which 7,500 were planted in the late 1990s), owned by Delicato of the Central Valley.

Arroyo Seco AVA

The most coherent district within the vastness of Monterey County's Salinas valley has its anchor point at the town of Greenfield. Most of its vineyards lie to the west of that town, on either bank of the dry wash for which it is named in Spanish, but some range east and north to the precincts of Soledad. Chardonnay is the mainstay for most of the wineries who draw upon it, but some cleave resolutely, and less successfully, to Cabernet Sauvignon. Rieslings from the area, with their reliable aroma of nectarines, can be of great interest. Jekel is the largest winery inside the AVA boundaries and many of the grapes are sold to the likes of Wente in LIVERMORE.

Carmel Valley AVA

The only seaward-facing wine district in Monterey County, with a much more affluent, less agricultural population than Salinas valley. It has a handful of small wineries and vineyards draped across steep slopes in the drainage area of the Carmel river, 10 to 12 miles/19 km inland from Carmel Bay. Durney Vineyards is the oldest of its estates; Bernardus is up and coming.

Chalone AVA

Chalone's reputation was made by the winery of the same name set high in the Gavilan mountains, on the east side of Monterey's Salinas valley, notably with Chardonnay, Pinot Blanc, and Pinot Noir. B.C.C.

Monterrei, relatively new DO in southern Galicia, on Spain's border with Portugal. Most of the wine is still sold in bulk, and the recovery of local grape varieties is much less developed than elsewhere in Galicia. For the moment, this is more a project based on distant glories, than a current reality. V. de la S.

Monthelie, a village producing red and occasionally white wine in the Côte de Beaune district of Burgundy's CÔTE D'OR. The wines resemble those of VOLNAY but are neither quite as rich nor as elegant, although they age well and are more powerful than those of AUXEY-DURESSES, the neighbouring appellation to the south with which the PREMIER CRU vineyard Les Duresses is shared. The other premier cru vineyards of Monthelie such as Meix Bataille and Champs Fulliot lie adjacent to Volnay. Some Chardonnay was planted in the 1980s, for Monthelie also borders the white-wine village of MEURSAULT.   J.T.C.M.

Montilla-Moriles, southern Spanish denominated wine zone in ANDALUCÍA, 40 km/25 miles south of Cordoba, producing both FORTIFIED and unfortified wines in the style of SHERRY, usually known simply as **Montilla.** Since it became a region in its own right, Montilla has had to contend with a popular image as an inferior, cheap alternative to sherry.

The Pedro Ximénez vine, which accounts for over 70 per cent of production, seems to thrive in the hot conditions, yielding extremely sweet grapes. The wines therefore achieve ALCOHOLIC STRENGTHS between 14 and 16 per cent without FORTIFICATION. Other grape varieties include the Lairén (AIRÉN) and MUSCAT OF ALEXANDRIA, which tend to produce lighter wines for blending.

Wine-making practices in Montilla parallel those for sherry. Pale, dry fino- and amontillado-style wines are made from FREE-RUN juice, while heavier styles similar to oloroso are made from the subsequent pressings. (The terms Fino, Amontillado, and Oloroso are permitted on Montilla labels within Spain but may not be used in other European Union countries, where they are restricted to sherry. Pale Dry, Medium Dry, Pale Cream, and Cream are the styles most commonly found on labels outside Spain.)

Pale Dry Montilla matures under a film of FLOR, initially in cement or earthenware *tinajas*, then in a SOLERA, similar to those in Jerez. However, in the hot climate of Montilla-Moriles, the wines tend to have less finesse. Heavier oloroso styles are fortified and aged for longer in soleras, where they become dark and pungent. Around half the region's wines are not fortified, which puts them at an advantage in certain markets where duties are levied on alcoholic strength. These usually disappear into inexpensive commercial blends, many of which are heavily sweetened with concentrated must for export.   R.J.M.

Montlouis, overshadowed white-wine appellation in the TOURAINE district of the Loire across the river from the much larger and more famous VOUVRAY, although it has its own char-

acteristics. As in Vouvray, the CHENIN BLANC grape is grown exclusively for Montlouis, which is made in all degrees of sweetness, according to each VINTAGE's peculiarities.

The wines are generally less sharply defined than in Vouvray, tending to mature considerably earlier (which can be a great advantage). About a third of the wine produced is the usefully sturdy and characterful **Montlouis Mousseux.** Deletang is the leading producer.

Montpeyroux, the highest named CRU within the Coteaux du LANGUEDOC in southern France and, with nearby PIC-ST-LOUP, the most exciting. It produces mainly but not exclusively red wine together with some interesting VIN DE PAYS. Although Syrah, Grenache, Mourvèdre, and Cinsaut are fast taking over, Carignan has been the dominant vine variety and a small plot of 50-year-old vines is responsible for some exceptionally masterful examples from Domaine d'Aupilhac. Other fine estates busy putting the Languedoc on the world wine map include Domaines Font Caude and L'Aiguelière.

Montrachet, or Le Montrachet, the most famous GRAND CRU white burgundy, the apogee of the Chardonnay grape produced from a single vineyard in the Côte de Beaune district of the CÔTE D'OR.

Le Montrachet covers a whisker under 8 ha/20 acres straddling the borders of Puligny and Chassagne, two communes which have annexed the famous name to their own (see PULIGNY-MONTRACHET and CHASSAGNE-MONTRACHET). Part of the secret lies in the limestone, part in its perfect south-east exposition, which keeps the sun from dawn till dusk.

The principal owners and producers of Le Montrachet are the Marquis de Laguiche, Baron Thénard, DOMAINE DE LA ROMANÉE-CONTI, BOUCHARD Père et Fils, Domaines Lafon and Prieur in Meursault, and Domaines Ramonet, Colin, and Amiot-Bonfils in Chassagne. In 1991, Domaine Leflaive of Puligny purchased a small-holding. The largest slices belong to the Marquis de Laguiche, whose wine is made by Joseph DROUHIN, and Baron Thénard, whose wine is made by the NÉGOCIANT Remoissenet.

Four more grands crus are associated with Le Montrachet: Chevalier-Montrachet, Bâtard-Montrachet, Bienvenues-Bâtard-Montrachet, and Criots-Bâtard-Montrachet.

Chevalier-Montrachet is situated directly above the Puligny section of Le Montrachet, on thin, stony soil giving wines which are not quite as rich as the latter. Particularly sought after are the Chevalier-Montrachet, Les Demoiselles, from Louis LATOUR and Louis JADOT.

Bâtard-Montrachet, on the slope beneath Le Montrachet, also spans the two communes, producing rich and heady wines not quite as elegant as a Chevalier-Montrachet. In the Puligny section of Bâtard is a separate enclave, **Bienvenues-Bâtard-Montrachet**, while an extension of the Chassagne section is the rarely seen **Criots-Bâtard-Montrachet**.   J.T.C.M.

Montravel, mainly dry-white-wine appellation in the extreme west of the BERGERAC district in SOUTH WEST FRANCE, which also has a tradition of sweet-white-wine-making. The main grape variety is Sémillon and overall quality of these dry wines increased considerably in the late 1980s, with a certain amount of BARREL MATURATION having been introduced.

The appellations **Côtes de Montravel** and **Haut-Montravel** are used for small quantities of sweet wines, with the former generally denoting a MOELLEUX and the latter, a description rarely used, for an even sweeter version.

Moravia, eastern, wine-producing part of the CZECH REPUBLIC whose wine region lies just north of the Weinviertel of AUSTRIA.

Moravia is also the name of a common darkskinned grape planted in central Spain. It produces rustic wines, particularly in southeastern La MANCHA.

Morellino di Scansano. See MAREMMA.

Moreto, undistinguished red grape variety that is widely planted in Portugal, notably but not exclusively in the Alentejo.

Morey-St-Denis, important village in the Côte de Nuits district of Burgundy producing red wines from Pinot Noir grapes. Morey suffers, perhaps unfairly, in comparison with its neighbours CHAMBOLLE-MUSIGNY and GEVREY-CHAMBERTIN because its wines are usually described as being lighter versions of Gevrey or firmer than Chambolle, according to which side of the village they are located. Indeed, in the past the wines were often sold under those names.

There are four GRAND CRU vineyards, moving southwards from the border with Gevrey-Chambertin: Clos de la Roche, Clos St-Denis, Clos des Lambrays, Clos de Tart, plus a small segment of Bonnes Mares overlapping from Chambolle.

Clos de la Roche is probably the finest vineyard, giving greater depth, body, and ageing ability than most other vineyards.

Clos St-Denis, sandwiched between Clos de la Roche and the village itself, may be the quintessential wine of Morey-St-Denis—a touch lighter than Clos de la Roche, with a trace of austerity, but the pinnacle of finesse.

Excellent examples of both Clos de la Roche and Clos St-Denis have been made by Domaine Ponsot, Domaine Dujac, and the Lignier cousins.

Clos des Lambrays is all but a monopoly of the Saier brothers, who bought the run-down vineyard and winery in 1979 and won promotion from PREMIER CRU to grand cru on grounds of the vineyard's potential. As yet, despite major renovation and great attention to detail, it is not certain that wines comparable with Clos St-Denis or Clos de la Roche are being made.

Clos de Tart, which has always been a monopoly, is currently owned by Mommessin. Clos de Tart makes a fine, silky wine which does not always seem to have quite the power and concentration expected of a grand cru.

Successful premier cru vineyards in Morey-St-Denis include Les Ruchots, Clos de la Bussière (monopoly of Domaine Georges Roumier), Les Millandes, Clos des Ormes, and Les Monts Luisants. Domaine Ponsot also produces a rare and curious white wine from the latter, a proportion of which is made from Pinot Noir vines which have mutated into a type of Pinot Blanc.

See also CÔTE D'OR.   J.T.C.M.

Morgon, important BEAUJOLAIS cru around the commune of Villié-Morgon. The wines produced are considered notably denser and longer lived than most Beaujolais crus. Total ripeness is likely to be greater than in most crus, although some consider that only the wines made on the slope known as Côte de Py just south of Villié-Morgon have the real depth traditionally associated with Morgon.

Morillon is an old north-eastern French name for PINOT NOIR and is still a common name for the powerfully aromatic CHARDONNAY of STYRIA in southern Austria.

Morio-Muskat is Germany's most popular MUSCAT-like vine variety by far, although it is quite unrelated to any Muscat. Somehow Peter Morio's Silvaner × Weissburgunder (Pinot

Blanc) crossing is almost overwhelmingly endowed with sickly grapiness that recalls some of Muscat's more obvious characteristics, even though its parents are two of the more aromatically restrained varieties. It was particularly popular with the eager blenders of the PFALZ and RHEINHESSEN in the late 1970s when demand for LIEBFRAUMILCH was high: a drop of Morio-Muskat in a neutral blend of Müller-Thurgau and Silvaner can cheaply Germanize it. Total plantings are falling fast, however. If allowed to ripen fully on a good site, it can produce reasonably respectable VARIETAL wines but this is not one of Germany's finest specialities.

Moristel, light, loganberry-flavoured speciality of SOMONTANO in northern Spain. The vine is relatively frail and the light-red wine produced oxidizes easily. It may be better suited to blending than being bottled as a VARIETAL.

Mornington Peninsula, emergent wine region south east of Melbourne, in the Port Phillip zone of the Australian state of VICTORIA.

Morocco played a significant part in the world's wine trade in the 1950s and 1960s, although it never produced as much sheer quantity as neighbouring ALGERIA. Morocco's independence in 1956 signalled the start of a steady decline in the country's wine industry. Today the Moroccan wine trade is dominated by a state-owned company controlling a wide range of brand names and perhaps as much as 80 per cent of the market, and by the private, and much more innovative, Celliers de Meknès.

The uninspiring Carignan dominated the Moroccan vineyards historically although there was a later wave of planting Cinsaut, which can produce agreeable VIN GRIS, the pale pink wine which accounts for about 10 per cent of total wine production. Grenache is also important but the proportion of 'improving' grape varieties such as Cabernet Sauvignon, Syrah, Merlot, and Mourvèdre, while increasing rapidly, is still low. White grape varieties such as Clairette and Muscat tend to produce heavy, often musty, non-aromatic white wines, which in 1990 comprised barely five per cent of total production.

Morocco has its own appellation system modelled on the French APPELLATION CONTRÔLÉE and called Appellation d'Origine Garantie, or AOG, but it has yet to achieve any real significance in terms of guaranteeing quality.

Of the officially recognized zones, Meknès/Fès and Berkane have traditionally enjoyed the finest reputation.

Morocco certainly has the potential to produce reliable quantities of ripe, sometimes interesting wines, including such VINS DOUX NATURELS as its once-famous Muscat de Berkane. The local market for wine is buoyed by strong demand from the developing tourist industry.

Morocco is a relatively important producer of CORKS.
J.Ro. & D.J.G.

Morrastel is the main French synonym for Rioja's GRACIANO. It is also, confusingly, one of Spain's synonyms for MOURVÈDRE, although Monastrell is the more common Spanish name for Mourvèdre. Morrastel is the name used for the Graciano still grown in the central Asian republic of UZBEKISTAN. See also the TINTA MIÚDA of Portugal.

Moscadello, sometimes **Moscadelletto**, local variety of the MOSCATO grape in and around MONTALCINO in central Italy. Moscadello was the major wine of Montalcino for centuries, long before anyone even noted the presence of important reds. The firm Villa Banfi made an important investment in selling this sweet grapey, fizzy white wine in the 1980s, but it has not so far been able to compete successfully against better-known wines such as MOSCATO D'ASTI.

Moscatel, Spanish and Portuguese for MUSCAT. The term may be applied to both grape varieties and wines. Thus **Moscatel de Grano Menudo** is none other than MUSCAT BLANC À PETITS GRAINS, while **Moscatel de Alejandría** and **Moscatel Romano** are MUSCAT OF ALEXANDRIA. **Moscatel Rosado** on the other hand may be a South American speciality (it is certainly widely grown in both Chile and Argentina). **Moscatel de Málaga** has been identified as a local speciality of southern Spain. Most of the vines known simply as Moscatel in Spanish- and Portuguese-speaking countries are Muscat of Alexandria, although northern Spain has some of the superior small-seeded variety.

Inexpensive wines called simply Moscatel abound in Iberia and are in general simply sweet and grapey.

See also Moscatel de SETÚBAL.

Moscatel de Alejandría, Spanish name for MUSCAT OF ALEXANDRIA.

Moscatel Rosada, quantitatively important but qualitatively very unimportant pink-skinned grape grown in ARGENTINA and to a much lesser extent in Chile, for common table wine and TABLE GRAPES. It is not apparently related to any known Muscat.

Moscato, Italian for MUSCAT.

Moscato Bianco, sometimes called **Moscato di Canelli**, is the finest Muscat grape variety MUSCAT BLANC À PETITS GRAINS and is that most commonly encountered in Italy, making it the country's fourth most planted white grape variety. **Moscato Giallo** and **Moscato Rosa Trentini** (both found in the ALTO ADIGE, often called Goldmuskateller and Rosenmuskateller respectively) are distinct and different varieties with golden and pink berries respectively. **Moscato di Alexandria** is the Italian synonym for the lesser white grape variety MUSCAT OF ALEXANDRIA.

Wines called Moscato are produced all over the country and are usually made from Moscato Bianco grapes. In the south and, especially, the islands, they are typically golden and sweet.

Few of Italy's regions do not have their own Moscato-based wines. The majority of these are low in alcohol and at least lightly sweet, ideal accompaniments to fruit and fruit-based desserts. The best known and most widely popular of these wines is the Moscato planted in the Asti region in its two different forms: the sparkling ASTI version and the more lightly fizzy and less alcoholic MOSCATO D'ASTI. A drier, crisper, but still aromatic style of Moscato is produced in TRENTINO, and the better bottles can approach the quality of an average ALSACE Muscat.

Italy's south, in particular SICILY, was once renowned for its Moscato wines. Attempts to revive **Moscato di Noto** are now under way. Small quantities of Moscato-based wines are still produced in SARDINIA, in the BASILICATA, and in Apulia, but the most significant southern Moscato is **Moscato di Pantelleria**, a PASSITO wine from the Muscat of Alexandria grape, considerably more alcoholic and more lusciously sweet than the better-known Moscato d'Asti. The revived popularity of Moscato di Pantelleria in the 1980s has coincided with, and perhaps influenced, new attempts to achieve a more luscious style of Moscato in Piedmont, and a new category of passito wines, far sweeter than Moscato d'Asti

and frequently given BARREL MATURATION. Small quantities of Moscato passito have long been made in the Valle d'AOSTA, principally near the township of Chambave.

Moscato wines come in colours other than white in Italy: a pink Moscato Rosa, redolent of roses, is produced in the Alto Adige and, to a much lesser extent, in Trentino and Friuli, while red Moscato, aromatic to the point of decadence but not always particularly well made, is produced near Bergamo in the **Moscato di Scanzo** DOC zone.   D.T.

Moscato d'Asti, fragrant and lightly sweet, gently fizzy, dessert wine made in the PIEDMONT region of north-west Italy now of DOCG status. It is produced from MOSCATO BIANCO, Italy's version of the aristocratic MUSCAT BLANC À PETITS GRAINS, whose production in and around the town of Asti increased sixty-fold in the 20th century. Moscato d'Asti is something of a misnomer, however, since an important part of the production is not in the province of Asti at all but in the province of Cuneo, and a significant part is in the province of Alessandria.

As a wine, Moscato d'Asti is often lumped together with ASTI, although the two wines are, in fact, quite different. Moscato d'Asti is more personal and characterized than Asti, which is usually a blended wine of many provenances. With a maximum of one atmosphere of pressure in the bottle, a quarter that of Asti, Moscato d'Asti is only slightly frothy. Its ALCOHOLIC STRENGTH is considerably lower (5.5 per cent as opposed to Asti's 7–9.5 per cent), the less powerful aromas and flavour of Asti frequently give a sweeter sensation on the palate even if the RESIDUAL SUGAR level is normally slightly lower than that of Moscato d'Asti.

Moscato d'Asti will never be a classic dessert wine, however, its chief virtues being its delicacy and gentle sweetness that is as much suggested as forthrightly declared. It is best served with fruit and fruit-based desserts rather than with heavier desserts.

If Moscato d'Asti remains a relative drop in the overall scheme of things (3 million bottles compared with the 75 million bottles of Asti), it has by now gained a secure niche as a classic and unusually refreshing expression of one of the world's most important and popular grape varieties.   D.T.

Moscato di Sardegna, relatively new and as yet relatively unrealized DOC for light, frothy, sweet white wines made in SARDINIA in the image of ASTI.

Moscato di Strevi, fine, lightly fizzy MUSCAT made in the hills around Strevi in the east of the ASTI zone, often riper in flavour and deeper in colour than MOSCATO D'ASTI because of Strevi's warmer MESOCLIMATE. The most impressive wines by far, however, are the PASSITO versions made by Ivaldi.

Moscato Spumante, the most basic form of light, fizzy, Italian white wine made in the style of ASTI but usually with the most basic, industrial ingredients. Not to be confused with the infinitely superior MOSCATO D'ASTI.

Moscophilero, vine variety with deep-pink-skinned grapes used to make strongly perfumed white wine in GREECE, particularly on the high plateau of Mantinia in the Peloponnese. There are strong flavour similarities with fine MUSCAT. Small quantities of fruity light pink wine are also made from this spicy variety, which is also increasingly used as a blending ingredient in other parts of Greece.

Mosel and **Moselle**, the German and French names respectively for the river which rises in the Vosges mountains of France, forms the border between LUXEMBOURG (in which it plays a key part in wine production) and Germany, and joins the river Rhein or Rhine at Koblenz in Germany, 545 km/340 miles later.

France

The name Moselle is still part of today's French wine nomenclature in the VDQS **Moselle**, which, together with Côtes de TOUL, constitute what the French call their *vins de l'est* or wines of the east, the last remnants of what was once an important and flourishing Lorraine wine industry. White Auxerrois and Müller-Thurgau are the two most common vine varieties and most wines are light, crisp, white, and aromatic; a small proportion is made sparkling.

Germany

It is the Mosel's journey of 242 km/150 miles through Germany that takes it by wine villages of world class, through one of Germany's most famous quality-wine regions, the MOSEL-SAAR-RUWER. In Germany, 'Mosel' describes a sub-region for table wine (see TAFELWEIN) within the Mosel-Saar-Ruwer region. The name also forms part of an even bigger table-wine region, Rhein-Mosel. Colloquially, apart from indicating the river and the valley, Mosel describes the wine from the whole of the Mosel-Saar-

Ruwer region, regardless of quality; it is often used in this way by the world's wine trade.

As a result of its success in the English-speaking world, Moselle became a GENERIC name for any light, medium-dry, faintly aromatic wine. Some traditionally minded members of the British wine trade still divide the wines of Germany into RHINE and Moselle.

Mosel-Saar-Ruwer, the official name of GERMANY'S best-known wine region which appends to the name of the river MOSEL the names of two of its viticulturally important tributaries. The wines produced are typically white, low in alcohol, and some of the most refreshing and underrated in the world. Theirs is a wine style which no other wine region can even emulate.

Thanks partly to the world's indifference, the total area planted has been declining slowly. Many vineyards rise almost immediately from the banks of the Mosel or, less directly, from those of the SAAR and RUWER. Just downstream of Trier are the Mosel's first, steep vineyards, which continue with little interruption, on one bank or the other, all the way to Koblenz.

Downstream from Cochem, the Mosel straightens out but, for much of the way, it still flows through a gorge, deep below the surrounding countryside. Slate has been used in the region for hundreds of years as a building material, and, where it has not been present in sufficient quantity in the soil, it has been added to feed the vine with minerals and to retain warmth. Production costs in the steep Mosel vineyards remain among the highest in Germany.

The Mosel-Saar-Ruwer normally has a warm but by no means hot summer. The MESO-CLIMATE is of rather more significance and here there are considerable variations. Even in relatively gentle winters, there are usually a few very cold nights to make possible the gathering of frozen RIESLING grapes for EISWEIN.

The Mosel-Saar-Ruwer region is divided into six districts, or Bereiche, of which Bereich Bernkastel is the only one whose name appears with any frequency on bottles sold outside Germany. Nearly 40 per cent of the region's production is offered under GROSSLAGE (collective-site) names, such as Piesporter Michelsberg, Klüsserather St Michael, Zeller Schwarze Katz, or Bernkasteler Kurfürstlay. There are some 500 or more single-vineyard

(EINZELLAGE) names, of which only 60 or so have real significance in terms of the quality of wine they produce. Too often with the simple QBA quality wines, vineyard characteristics are so diluted by over-production, and hidden by added sweetness in the form of SÜSSRESERVE, that the vineyard name loses its meaning.

The ELBLING vine predominates in Bereich Obermosel, where, as in LUXEMBOURG across the Mosel, it supplies a clean, fresh, rather rustic wine. Riesling is the most widely grown vine in the region, occupying a little more than half of the planted area, and today this is the first clue in finding a good wine from the Mosel-Saar-Ruwer.

These wines, usually so light in alcohol, have to be made with particular care if their lack of BODY is not to count against them. The key to a fine Mosel-Saar-Ruwer Riesling is its backbone of fruity-tasting TARTARIC ACID, but even wines which are not dry (TROCKEN) or medium dry (HALBTROCKEN) are being sold with less RESIDUAL SUGAR than they were in the 1970s. Their structure is nowadays strengthened by more alcohol. The difference between a dry and a medium-sweet Mosel AUSLESE may well be over two per cent of actual alcohol, and so it is wrong to assume that all Mosels are light. Nevertheless, even if some Auslese Trocken is sold with over 12 per cent of natural alcohol, the quintessential Mosel remains for many non-Germans the delicate, fresh Kabinett wine, only slightly stronger in ALCOHOLIC STRENGTH, about nine per cent, than a dark, double bock beer from Munich. Mosel Kabinett at its best is unique, and one of the glories of the world of wine. Perhaps its only rival is a wine of similar quality from the NAHE.

Upstream from Koblenz

The district with the highest percentage of Riesling vines on the river Mosel starts at Koblenz and continues upstream until shortly after the narrow town of Zell, from which Bereich Zell takes its name. It has many small, steep vineyards which can be maintained only by hand. The producers' association in the district, the Erzeugergemeinschaft Deutsches Eck, is devoted exclusively to the Riesling grape and a rigid, maximum allowable yield of 80 hl/ha (4.5 tons/acre)—much less than that permitted by law. The Rieslings of Bereich Zell are generally less refined than the best of Bereich Bernkastel but their agreeable, solid, true-to-type wines in the middle price range are as

good as any that the Mosel can offer. They are steely and positive in flavour, and the wines from the vineyards near Koblenz have a not surprising affinity with those of the nearby MITTELRHEIN. The better-known villages of Bereich Zell include Winningen, Kobern, Lehmen, Pommern, Ediger, Eller, Bremm, Neef, and Bullay.

For fine Riesling from Bereich Bernkastel one should turn to the very large number of private estate bottlers who sell their wine directly to the consumer, to the wine trade, and to the restaurant business. They are a surer guide to a good Mosel than are the names of the famous villages, or of the best-known single-vineyard sites. Even that of a vineyard as prestigious as the Wehlener Sonnenuhr is not a guarantee of a high-quality wine, unless it originates from a good estate. Wines from the relatively inferior parts of a renowned vineyard, bottled by wine merchants, should still be of good quality but they will not compare with the best of estate bottlings, labelled GUTSABFÜLLUNG.

Of the approximately 60 vineyards of outstanding merit on the Mosel-Saar-Ruwer, over half are in Bereich Bernkastel. Travelling upstream, the first division individual sites start with the Prälat and Treppchen at Erden, and move on to Ürzig (Würzgarten); Zeltingen, Wehlen (Sonnenuhr); Graach (Himmelreich), Bernkastel (Doctor and Graben); Brauneberg (Juffer); Piesport (Goldtröpfchen); Dhron; and Trittenheim. Fine Mosel is a highly individual wine, which is never available in large quantities. To meet the needs of supermarkets and chain stores for large volumes of inexpensive labels, much ordinary wine, almost certainly not from Riesling, is sold under collective-site (Grosslage) names. These include the names of famous villages such as Piesport or Bernkastel.

Saar and Ruwer

The vineyards of the Saar and Ruwer rivers form two districts together making up 11 per cent of the Mosel-Saar-Ruwer region. In good vintages, the wines are a joy to taste with an abundance of flavour and wonderful acidity, but it can be difficult for the grapes to reach RIPENESS in poor years.

The main Ruwer vineyards begin near the village of the same name, and end some 10 km/6 miles upstream. Sole ownership of the Eitelsbacher Karthäuserhofberg and of the Maximin Grünhaus vineyards by two outstanding estates ensures that only top-quality wines reach the market. Leading Mosel producers also have holdings at Eitelsbach and Kasel.

The vineyards of the Saar form the Grosslage Scharzberg, whereas the most famous single vineyard is the Scharzhofberg at Wiltingen. There are a number of estates with holdings in the Scharzhofberg but, as in the Wehlener Sonnenuhr, not all of the vineyard is of the same high standard. Among other leading Saar wine villages and towns are Wawern, Ayl, Ockfen, Saarburg, and Serrig—the last two a source of uniquely steely Riesling wine.

Above Trier, the pretty rolling vineyards form Bereich Obermosel, in the state of Rheinland-Pfalz (along with the rest of the Mosel-Saar-Ruwer), and the tiny Bereich Moseltor in the Saarland. Much of the harvest is handled by the central CO-OPERATIVE cellar at Bernkastel, Moselland, which has joined forces with some two dozen estate bottlers to promote Obermosel Elbling, SEKT, and schnapps. This group was the first in Germany to be granted the right to market a dry Obermosel Elbling as a Qualitätswein garantierten URSPRUNGS, or QgU, a quality wine of guaranteed origin.

The Mosel and commerce

Moselland processes about a fifth of the average Mosel-Saar-Ruwer harvest and exports some 40 per cent of its production, of which 40 per cent was still shipped to the United Kingdom in the late 1990s. In Germany, it sells wine in bottle to the large supermarkets and in bulk to the wine trade. The large turnover of the German supermarkets and grocery chains, increased by commercial concentration in the 1980s, has given them enormous strength and buying power.

Of the region's wine sold in bottle, about 13 per cent comes from the co-operative cellars, 28 per cent from estates, and some 59 per cent is bottled by wine merchants.

As an escape from the difficulties of the cheap wine market, SPARKLING WINE can be an interesting alternative. The Saar-Mosel Winzersekt (a producers' association) concentrates on sparkling wines based on Riesling from the Mosel, Saar, and Ruwer and Elbling from the Obermosel.

While the standing of Mosel wine in Germany has been debased, there remains a small upper tier of excellent estate-bottled wine, yet no shortage of cheap and often dull wine with few of the better regional characteristics. There is also at last some exciting development in the middle price range as a new generation of innovative, talented, and quality-oriented vintners strive to achieve a following by offering excellent value. I.J. & K.B.S.

Mossel Bay, South African wine region now known as RUITERBOSCH.

Moueix, important family in the BORDEAUX TRADE, notably, but by no means exclusively, in ST-ÉMILION and POMEROL. Jean Moueix (1882–1957) bought Ch Fonroque in St-Émilion in 1930, and in 1937 his son Jean-Pierre (b. 1913) formed Établissements Jean-Pierre Moueix on the quay in Libourne, the largest town on the right bank. Increasingly successful in the postwar period, it became from 1970 the major NÉGOCIANT there. In 1956 the 70-year-old firm of Duclot in the city of Bordeaux was acquired to deal mainly with the 'left bank' districts (MÉDOC, GRAVES, and so on), as well as selling direct to private customers in France. As Bordeaux Millésimes it is prominent in the export trade. From 1968 both were headed by Jean-Pierre's elder son Jean-François (b. 1945).

In 1970, the younger son, Christian (b. 1946), became a director, with special responsibilities, along with the firm's OENOLOGIST Jean-Claude Berrouet, for the 17 estates owned or farmed by the firm. In 1982, Christian started a JOINT VENTURE in Yountville, CALIFORNIA, with two daughters of John Daniel, former owner of Inglenook, before buying them out in 1994. From a 50-ha/124-acre vineyard and an architectural landmark winery opened in 1998, a Bordeaux-style wine named Dominus is produced. He now runs the Libourne négociant.

In the 1950s, Jean-Pierre Moueix began to acquire châteaux in St-Émilion and Pomerol: Trotanoy (1953), La Fleur-Pétrus (1953), Lagrange (1959), La Grave (Trigant de Boisset) (1971) in Pomerol; and Magdelaine (1954) in St-Émilion. In the 1970s and 1980s, the firm expanded into FRONSAC, acquiring Canon, Canon de Brem, La Croix-Canon, and Canon-Moueix in the superior Canon-Fronsac appellation and La Dauphine in Fronsac.

A number of other properties are farmed on behalf of their owners, including Ch Moulin-du-Cadet in St-Émilion, and Feytit-Clinet, Lafleur-Gazin, and Latour-Pomerol in Pomerol. However, much the most important acquisition was a half-share of Ch PÉTRUS in 1964.

Christian Moueix is experimenting to a limited extent with BIODYNAMIC VITICULTURE.   E.P.-R.

mouldy, pejorative tasting term used for wine spoiled by the growth of minute fungi on grapes or winery equipment. Mouldy casks can also cause this sort of aroma. Mouldy, along with musty, is also used to describe a wine that is CORKED or otherwise tainted.   A.D.W.

Moulin-à-Vent means 'windmill' in French and is the name of one of the most famous of the BEAUJOLAIS crus, being named after a local windmill. The area includes delimited vineyards within Chénas and Romanèche-Thorins. Of all the wine produced in the Beaujolais region, Moulin-à-Vent is expected to last the longest, taste most concentrated, and therefore, in a way, to be the least typical. With time, the wines begin to taste more like old Pinot Noir than Gamay, and some 50-year-old Moulin-à-Vent can be quite a satisfying drink, even if an atypical Beaujolais. It has also generally been the most expensive. Ch des Jacques and Domaine de la Rochelle are two notable producers.

Moulis, or **Moulis-en-Médoc,** smallest of the six communal appellations of the HAUT-MÉDOC district of Bordeaux. Although it includes only about 550 ha/1,360 acres of vineyards, there is considerable diversity of TERROIR in Moulis, producing wines as varied as the occasionally brilliant Ch Chasse-Spleen, the good-value Ch Maucaillou, and a host of properties whose names include the word Poujeaux. The finest of these is usually long-lived Ch Poujeaux itself. As in Listrac, this is not CLASSED GROWTH country. Perhaps because of this, the best Moulis wines can offer good value, being as well structured as any Haut-Médoc, often with some of the perfume of Margaux to the east. Yields are more restricted in Moulis than in Listrac.

See MÉDOC and BORDEAUX.

Mount Barker, relatively cool, promising vineyard area in the Great Southern region of WESTERN AUSTRALIA.

Mount Benson, relatively new wine region in the Limestone Coast zone of SOUTH AUSTRALIA.

Mount Veeder, California wine region and AVA in the mountains between Napa and Sonoma. See NAPA Valley.

Mourvèdre, Spain's second most important black grape variety after GARNACHA (Grenache) and once Provence's most important vine. The Spaniards call it Monastrell (and occasionally Morrastel or Morastell although it has nothing to do with GRACIANO, which is known as Morrastel in France). Mourvèdre is enjoying a resurgence of popularity, especially in southern France and, to a more limited extent, in California. In the New World it is often called MATARO.

The wine produced from Monastrell's small, sweet, thick-skinned berries tends to be heady stuff, high in alcohol, tannins, and a somewhat gamey, almost animal, flavour when young and well capable of ageing provided OXIDATION is carefully avoided in the winery. It is the principal black grape variety in such DOS as ALICANTE, ALMANSA, JUMILLA, VALENCIA, and YECLA.

Mourvèdre needs France's warmest summers to ripen fully. For many decades it marked time in its French enclave BANDOL but is now regarded as an extremely modish and desirable 'improving variety' throughout the Languedoc-Roussillon.

In southern France, Mourvèdre produces wines considered useful for their structure, intense fruit, and, in good years, perfume often redolent of blackberries. The structure in particular can be a useful foil for Grenache in Provence and Cinsaut further west. In Bandol, it is typically blended with both of these, and the statutory minimum for Mourvèdre is now 50 per cent. Mourvèdre is condoned in a host of APPELLATION CONTRÔLÉE regulations all over the south of France from Coteaux du Tricastin to Collioure. Although it usually plays a useful supporting role, being fleshier than Syrah, tauter than Grenache and Cinsaut, and infinitely more charming than Carignan, varietal Mourvèdres from the Languedoc have met with commercial success.

This success has been slow to raise the reputation of Australia's Mataro (also known as Esparte), which had systematically been ripped out until the 1990s. Although encounters with unblended Australian Mataro are still relatively rare, the Barossa Valley location of most of it means that the wine tends to resemble the Spanish rather than the French version.

California's unfashionable Mataro was fast disappearing until the RHÔNE RANGERS made the connection with Mourvèdre and pushed up demand for wine from these historic stumps, notably in Contra Costa County between San Francisco and the Central Valley, where there were considerable new plantings in the early

1990s thanks to demand from the likes of Bonny Doon and Cline Cellars. By the late 1990s, the state's total plantings had risen again, to well over 300 acres.

mousseux, French for sparkling. Some Mousseux are made by the traditional method, while others may be made by the much less painstaking tank method (see SPARKLING-WINE-MAKING).

mousy. See TASTING TERMS.

mouthfeel non-specific tasting term, used particularly for red wines, to indicate those textural attributes, such as smoothness, that produce tactile sensations on the surface of the oral cavity. The sensory perception of mouthfeel involves not the senses of taste and smell but the sense of touch. ASTRINGENCY, BODY, VISCOSITY, BITTERNESS, and ACIDITY, are among the interrelated factors influencing mouthfeel. Empirical evidence indicates that wine TANNINS are critically involved with this sensation. P.J.W.

Mouton Cadet, the most successful Bordeaux BRAND, began life in 1927, a poor vintage in which Baron Philippe de Rothschild created what was effectively a SECOND WINE called Carruades de Mouton for Ch MOUTON-ROTHSCHILD. Its successor in 1930 was named Mouton-Cadet, since Philippe was the *cadet*, the youngest, of the family. Eventually, as Mouton Cadet, it developed a prosperous life of its own, and demand was so great that the flexibility of the BORDEAUX AC appellation was needed. Today Mouton Cadet is available in red, white, and rosé versions and is blended, relying heavily on the ENTRE-DEUX-MERS, from wines produced all over Bordeaux. The red version is much the most interesting one.

Mouton-Rothschild, Château, important wine estate in PAUILLAC in the BORDEAUX wine region and the only one ever to have been promoted within the 1855 CLASSIFICATION, to FIRST GROWTH. It has been in the Rothschild family since 1853.

In 1922, Baron Philippe de Rothschild took over the running of it from his father. He startled Bordeaux by employing a poster artist, Carlu, to design an art deco label, including the Rothschild arrows, for the 1924 vintage, and then proposing CHÂTEAU BOTTLING of all the first growths (and Mouton-Rothschild). He also instigated what was initially a SECOND WINE, called MOUTON CADET.

After the Second World War, Baron Philippe initiated the series of ARTIST'S LABELS, each year designed by a well-known artist, including Cocteau, Braque, Dali, Bacon, and Henry Moore.

The 72-ha/178-acre vineyard is planted with 87 per cent Cabernet Sauvignon grapes, 8 per cent Cabernet Franc, and the balance Merlot and Petit Verdot. Average production is about 20,000 cases. The wine is famously concentrated and intensely aromatic in good vintages. See also JOINT VENTURES. E.P.-R.

Mudgee, relatively isolated and well-defined wine region in AUSTRALIA, home to the country's first Chardonnay vines. See NEW SOUTH WALES.

mulled wine is wine that has been heated with sugar and spices and also, sometimes, slices of fruit and even brandy. Recipes vary and quantities are not critical. Red wine is almost invariably used, and cinnamon and cloves are common. Slow simmering retains the ALCOHOL; fast boiling dissipates it. Sugar or honey should be added to taste, and fruit peel can impart bitterness. See also GLÜHWEIN.

Müllerrebe, which translates from German as 'miller's grape', is the common, and logical, name for Germany's increasingly planted selection of Pinot MEUNIER. (Schwarzriesling is another German synonym.) It is most common in WÜRTTEMBERG, which has its own minor, low-yielding mutation called Samtrot, literally 'red velvet'.

Müller-Thurgau, white grape variety which could fairly be said to have been the bane of German wine production but which is at long last on the wane. This mediocre crossing was developed in 1882 with the aim of combining the quality of the great RIESLING grape with the viticultural reliability, particularly the early ripening, of the SILVANER. Most of the variety's synonyms (Rivaner in Luxembourg and Slovenia, Riesling-Sylvaner in New Zealand and Switzerland, Rizlingszilvani in Hungary) reflect this combination. However, recent DNA 'FINGERPRINTING' suggests that the variety is actually Riesling × CHASSELAS de Courtillier. Whatever the ingredients, the recipe resulted in a variety all too short on Riesling characteristics.

Unlike Riesling, it will ripen anywhere, producing prodigious quantities of extremely dull, flabby wine. Müller-Thurgau usually has some vaguely aromatic quality, but the aroma can often be unattractively mousy in Germany's high-yielding vineyards and is more reliably clean and pure in the variety's other spheres of influence NEW ZEALAND and the ALTO ADIGE, where growers are less demanding in terms of quantity.

Occasionally a German Müller-Thurgau could be said to express something—usually something territorial rather than anything inherent in the grape—but this bland vehicle for quantity above quality was substantially responsible for the decline in Germany's reputation as a wine producer in the 1970s and early 1980s. Typically blended with a little of a more aromatic variety such as MORIO-MUSKAT and with a great deal of SÜSSRESERVE, Müller-Thurgau was transformed into oceans of QBA sugarwater labelled either LIEBFRAUMILCH or one of the internationally recognized names such as Niersteiner, Bernkasteler, or Piesporter (see GROSSLAGE).

Outside Germany it can taste quite palatable, if rarely exciting. A handful of Italians manage it in the Alto Adige, where high altitudes keep the grapes on the vine for long enough for them to retain acidity while developing some perceptible fruit flavours. It is also increasingly planted in FRIULI and is grown as far south as EMILIA-ROMAGNA.

The variety thrives all over central and eastern Europe. It is planted in SWITZERLAND, playing an increasingly important role in the vineyards of the German-speaking area in the north and east, but is rarely responsible for wines of much intrinsic interest. Across Austria's southern border, it is also grown in SLOVENIA and is even more important to the east and north of Austria in the CZECH REPUBLIC and, particularly, HUNGARY, which is probably the world's second most important grower of this uninspiring grape. As Rizlingszilvani, it covers thousands of hectares of vineyard around Lake Balaton and produces lakesful of flabby Badacsonyi Rizlingszilvani.

Müller-Thurgau was planted enthusiastically by New Zealand grape growers in the 1950s and 1960s. Chardonnay overtook the crossing's total area in 1992, however, as it is a far more valuable crop. It would be difficult to argue that New Zealand's 'Riesling-Sylvaner' is ever a very complex wine but it does usually display a freshness lacking in German examples, despite its customary similar reliance on Süssreserve or SWEET RESERVE.

Some Oregon growers have experimented successfully with it, and fine examples have been produced in the Puget Sound vineyards of western Washington state.

Northern Europe's two smallest and coolest wine producers, ENGLAND and LUXEMBOURG, depend heavily on Müller-Thurgau, which (called Rivaner in Luxembourg) is the most planted variety in each country.

Murray river, mighty river that meanders through south-east AUSTRALIA. Thanks to a grand and historic IRRIGATION scheme, the arid riverbanks have been transformed into green arable land, also called the **Riverland** or **Riverlands**, planted with a variety of crops, including grapes. The giant wine region straddles the states of SOUTH AUSTRALIA, VICTORIA, and NEW SOUTH WALES and produces about a third of all Australian wine. See SOUTH AUSTRALIA.

Murrumbidgee Irrigation Area, or MIA, one of the irrigated wine regions of AUSTRALIA associated mainly with inexpensive wine for blending. See NEW SOUTH WALES.

Muscadel or **Muskadel**, along with Muscat of Frontignan, is the name by which MUSCAT BLANC À PETITS GRAINS, the finest Muscat vine variety, is known in South Africa. Muscadel was chiefly responsible for the famous 18th-century CONSTANTIA dessert wine, and is now used largely for fortified dessert wines and to add perfume and spice to many blends.   J.P.

Muscadelle is the famous also-ran third grape variety responsible, with Sémillon and Sauvignon Blanc, for the sweet white (and duller dry white) wines of Bordeaux and Bergerac. Like all of Bordeaux's white grape varieties except for Sauvignon, its star is waning. Four out of every five Muscadelle vines grown in Bordeaux are not in the great sweet-white-wine areas of SAUTERNES, but in the unfashionable and vast ENTRE-DEUX-MERS, including such lesser sweet-white appellations as PREMIÈRES CÔTES DE BORDEAUX, CADILLAC, LOUPIAC, and STE-CROIX-DU-MONT. Muscadelle is also being pulled up at quite a rate in the vineyards of the Dordogne *département*, including such potentially suitable appellations as MONBAZILLAC, but it is still relatively more important to Bergerac than to Bordeaux.

The variety, unrelated to any member of the MUSCAT family, shares a vaguely grapey aroma with them but has its origins in Bordeaux. Its use is almost exclusively in blends, adding the same sort of youthful fruitiness to south-western sweet whites as MEUNIER does to the north-east sparkling whites called champagne.

The variety is grown widely but not sub-stantially in eastern Europe but in only one obscure corner of the wine world does Mus-cadelle produce sensational varietal wine, the LIQUEUR TOKAY of AUSTRALIA, dark, syrupy, wood-matured concentrates for after-dinner drinking.

Muscadet, one of France's dry white com-modity wines currently undergoing revo-lution. The Muscadet region extends mainly south east of Nantes near the mouth of the Loire, on gently rolling, Atlantic-dominated countryside where hundreds of wine farmers maintain small family vine holdings devoted to one grape variety, the white MELON de Bour-gogne, a reliable but relatively neutral variety.

The most significant, and varied, appellation by far, representing more than three-quarters of production, is **Muscadet de Sèvre-et-Maine,** named after two small rivers which flow through it. Indeed, more Muscadet de Sèvre-et-Maine is produced every year than in any other Loire appellation. Particularly ambitious wines are made on the clay soils of Vallet, while those from the sandier soils of St-Fiacre are also much admired. The appellation known as **Mus-cadet des Coteaux de la Loire** is in the north and **Muscadet Côtes de Grand Lieu,** announced in 1996, is in the south west of the region. **Muscadet** is the basic appellation and tends to be much less exciting.

According to stricter regulations drawn up in the late 1990s, basic Muscadet is excluded from that substantial proportion of the wines that are matured SUR LIE, their flavour at least theoretically enriched by LEES CONTACT. This leaves the wines with rather more flavour and a small amount of CARBON DIOXIDE before bot-tling, which must be done where the wine was made and either during the spring or autumn following the harvest.

At its worst, Muscadet is an anodyne, watery, dry white with or without a little sparkle, but at its best it captures the essence of France's north Atlantic coast and provides an authentic, light, tangy, almost salty foil for its seafood. Since the mid 1980s, producers have been experimenting with such techniques as BARREL FERMENTATION and LEES STIRRING. Muscadet can no longer be dismissed as a simple, homo-geneous wine. Top producers include Guy Bossard, Jacques Guindon, Louis Metaireau, and Sauvion.

Other wines produced in the Pays Nantais are GROS PLANT, Coteaux d'ANCENIS, and FIEFS VENDÉENS. See also LOIRE.

Muscadinia, a section of the botanical genus *Vitis*.

Members of the *Muscadiniae*, the **Musca-dines,** as they are called, are found in America and Mexico. The best known is *Vitis rotundifolia* of which a number of varieties, most notably Scuppernong, are grown commercially. R.E.S.

Muscardin, light-red grape variety allowed in to CHÂTEAUNEUF-DU-PAPE.

Muscat, one of the world's great and historic names, of both grapes and wines. Indeed Muscat grapes—and there are at least four prin-cipal varieties of Muscat, in several hues of berry—are some of the very few which produce wines that actually taste of grapes. MUSCAT HAMBURG and MUSCAT OF ALEXANDRIA are raised as both wine grapes and TABLE GRAPES (although it has to be said that Hamburg is much better in the second role). MUSCAT BLANC À PETITS GRAINS is the oldest and finest, pro-ducing wines of the greatest intensity, while MUSCAT OTTONEL, paler in every way, is a rela-tive parvenu. See also various MOSCATELs and MOSCATOS.

Muscat wines, carrying many different labels, including Moscato (in Italy) and Mos-catel (in Iberia), can vary from the refreshingly low-alcohol, sweet and frothy ASTI SPUMANTE, through Muscat d'ALSACE, to sweet wines with alcohol levels between 15 and 20 per cent, usually made by adding spirit (as in the VINS DOUX NATURELS of southern France and Greece). Since a high proportion of the world's Muscat is dark-berried, and since a wide variety of wood-ageing techniques are used, such wines can vary in colour from palest gold (as in some of the more determinedly modern Muscats de FRONTIGNAN) to deepest brown (as in some of Australia's LIQUEUR MUSCATS).

There are many famous Muscats around the Mediterranean. See MOROCCO, GREECE, SICILY, and SARDINIA.

Muscat Blanc à Petits Grains is the full name of the oldest and noblest variety of Muscat with the greatest concentration of fine grape flavour, hinting at orange-flowers and spice. Its berries are not, as its principal name suggests, invariably white. In fact there are pink-, red-, and black-berried versions (although the dark berries are not so deeply pigmented that they can produce a proper red wine). Many synonyms for the variety include reference to the yellow or golden (*gallego, giallo, gelber*) colour of its berries. And Brown Muscat is one of Australia's names for a Muscat population that is more dark than light. Other names for the variety in its many different habitats include Muscat of Frontignan, Frontignac, Muscat Blanc, Muscat d'Alsace, Muskateller, Moscato Bianco, Moscato d'Asti, Moscato di Canelli, Moscatel de Grano Menudo, Moscatel de Frontignan, Muscatel Branco, White Muscat, Muscat Canelli, and Muskadel (in South Africa). Any Muscat with the words Alexandria, Gordo, Romain, Hamburg, or Ottonel in its name is *not* this superior variety.

As Moscatel de Grano Menudo it is still grown in Spain but to a limited extent. Most Spanish wines labelled Moscatel are made from Muscat of Alexandria.

Muscats of various sorts are grown widely in the CIS, particularly MUSCAT OTTONEL and the variety described as Muscat Rosé, the pink-skinned form of Muscat Blanc. Muscat Blanc is also grown in ROMANIA, where it is known as TĂMÎIOASĂ Alba, and in BULGARIA, where it may simply be called Misket. In RUSSIA it is known as Tamyanka.

In the heart of Habsburg country, Muscat Ottonel has held sway until recently. In the early 1980s, Austrians realized the greater potential inherent in their small plantings of Muskateller. Recently, dry, racy Muskatellers from Styria and occasionally the Wachau have been some of the country's most sought after and plantings are increasing.

In Hungary, too, Ottonel, simply known as Muskotaly, dominates except in the TOKAJI district, where Muscat Blanc, there called Lunel or Sargamuskotaly (Yellow Muscat), is grown. Some varietal Muscats of sweet Aszú quality are made from the few hundred hectares that supplement the Furmint and Hárslevelü that are the main ingredients in this extraordinary wine.

If anywhere could be said to be Muscat's homeland it is Greece and here, although it is today grown alongside Muscat of Alexandria (which is the prime Cypriot Muscat), Muscat Blanc à Petits Grains is accorded the honour of being the only variety allowed in Greece's most rigidly controlled Muscats such as those of Samos, Pátrai, and Kefallinía. For the moment, Greek Muscat, like its many variations on the MALVASIA theme, is almost invariably sweet, alcoholic, and redolent of history, but drier versions more suited to drinking with food are expected. See GREECE for more details.

This is the Muscat that, as MOSCATO, predominates in Italy, which grows an estimated 13,000 ha/32,000 acres of it, most profitably as underpinning for the sweet-sparkling-wine industry. The light, frothy ASTI, the subtler MOSCATO D'ASTI, and other spumante and frizzante all over north-western Italy demonstrate another facet of the variety's character. Various forms of MOSCATO can be found throughout Italy but most of its produce in the south and islands belongs to the richer, Mediterranean school of wines.

This school represents the traditional face of Muscat Blanc in France but, contrary to almost all other white grape varieties, this Muscat has been gaining ground, chiefly because of the development of less traditional forms of Muscat wine. France's total plantings of Muscat Blanc have been steadily increasing, thanks to the development of a virtually CLAIRETTE-free grapey (Tradition) version of the Rhône's fizzy CLAIRETTE DE DIE.

Muscat Blanc has also been supplanting the still more widely planted Muscat of Alexandria in Roussillon, however, where it is the superior Muscat ingredient in the many and various north Catalonian VINS DOUX NATURELS such as MUSCAT DE RIVESALTES. In the Languedoc and southern Rhône, too, its increasing area of vineyard reflects increased demand for the golden sweet Muscats of BEAUMES-DE-VENISE, FRONTIGNAN, LUNEL, MIREVAL, and ST-JEAN-DE-MINERVOIS, in which it is the exclusive ingredient.

But Muscat has been enjoying a new lease of life in the Midi vinified dry, without the addition of grape spirit to preserve its natural sweetness and add extra alcohol. Such wines with an easily recognizable aroma all too rare in southern French whites, together with their fashionably dry, light impact on the palate, have provided popular inexpensive alternatives to the dry Muscat (usually Ottonel) of Alsace.

In the New World, the variety grows, as Brown Muscat and Frontignac with all manner of colour of grape skins, in Australia, where it is capable of the great LIQUEUR MUSCATS, as well as in South Africa, where the wines it produces are known as both Frontignac and MUSCADEL. Muscat of Alexandria is very much more important than this finer Muscat in California, where most of its 1,200 acres/485 ha are in the central SAN JOAQUIN VALLEY. Once variously called Muscat Frontignan and Muscat Canelli, it is now officially called Muscat Blanc and distinguished from ORANGE MUSCAT.

Muscat d'Alsace is an Alsace synonym for the vine variety MUSCAT BLANC À PETITS GRAINS. See ALSACE.

Muscat de Beaumes-de-Venise is the often delicate VIN DOUX NATUREL from the southern Rhône village of BEAUMES-DE-VENISE, under whose name there are more details.

Muscat de Frontignan is the most common Muscat VIN DOUX NATUREL of the Languedoc. Ch de la Peyrade produces finer wine than most. It is also a French synonym for the grape variety solely responsible for it, MUSCAT BLANC À PETITS GRAINS.

Muscat de Lunel. See LUNEL for details of this southern Languedoc VIN DOUX NATUREL. It is yet another synonym for the grape variety solely responsible for it, MUSCAT BLANC À PETITS GRAINS.

Muscat de Mireval. See MIREVAL for details of this relatively unimportant southern Languedoc VIN DOUX NATUREL, although Domaine de la Capelle leads the appellation.

Muscat de Rivesaltes, the most important appellation of the Rivesaltes region in Roussillon and by far the biggest Muscat appellation in France, is made from MUSCAT OF ALEXANDRIA as well as MUSCAT BLANC À PETITS GRAINS. Much of it is of decidedly ordinary quality, although Domaine Cazes and Domaine de Chênes produce some superior bottlings. See RIVESALTES.

Muscat de St-Jean-de-Minervois is the golden VIN DOUX NATUREL speciality of St-Jean-de-Minervois in the northern Languedoc and is produced in very limited quantities. See ST-JEAN-DE-MINERVOIS.

Muscat du Cap Corse, Corsican VIN DOUX NATUREL. See CORSICA.

Muscat Hamburg is the lowest quality of the wine-producing Muscats. It comes exclusively in black-berried form and is far more common as a TABLE GRAPE than a wine grape.

Muscat of Alexandria is a Muscat almost as ancient as MUSCAT BLANC À PETITS GRAINS but its wine is distinctly inferior. In hot climates it can thrive and produce a good yield of extremely ripe grapes but their chief attribute is sweetness. Wines made from this sort of Muscat tend to be strong, sweet, and unsubtle. The aroma is vaguely grapey but can have slightly feline overtones of geranium rather than the more lingering bouquet of Muscat Blanc.

Today it is most important to wine industries in Iberia, South Africa, and Australia, where its chief respective names are Moscatel, Hanepoot, and Muscat Gordo Blanco or Lexia.

Spain has the biggest area planted with the variety, but only about half of this serves the wine industry, typically with sweet MOSCATELS of various sticky sorts. Muscat of Alexandria's various Spanish synonyms include Moscatel de España, Moscatel Gordo (Blanco), and most importantly Moscatel de MÁLAGA, which may be a close relative.

In Portugal its most famous incarnation is Moscatel de SETÚBAL but Portugal's Muscat of Alexandria grapes have also been harnessed to produce aromatic, dry, much lower alcohol Muscats whose prototype João Pires was developed, significantly, by an Australian winemaker who knew well how to transform one of Australia's most planted grape varieties into an early picked, crisp, technically perfect table wine. This is the fate of the majority of Australia's Gordo Blanco, once used mainly for fortified wines, although from cooler vineyards it can produce sound, unfortified wines that are sweet because late picked too. With SULTANA, Muscat Gordo Blanco is a mainstay of Australia's hot, irrigated vineyards. The wine produced is typically used for blending with, and often softening, more glamorous grape varieties.

Muscat of Alexandria is the dominant Muscat in South Africa and was the country's fourth most planted variety in the late 1990s, covering considerably more ground than Cabernet Sauvignon, for example. For years it provided sticky, raisiny wines for FORTIFICATION, as well as everything from GRAPE CONCENTRATE to raisins. Today some drier, lighter wines are also made from it. See SOUTH AFRICA and HANEPOOT, its traditional Afrikaans name, for more details.

As Moscatel de Alejandria it is also extremely important in Chile. It is also grown to a relatively limited extent in Argentina, Peru, Colombia, Ecuador, and even Japan.

Although Muscat Blanc is more important in GREECE, Muscat of Alexandria is grown widely there and is the Muscat that predominates in Turkey, Israel, and Tunisia, although in much of the Near East nowadays these grapes are eaten rather than drunk. The rich, dark Moscato di Pantelleria is geographically closer to Tunisia than Sicily which administers it and is made from Muscat of Alexandria, or ZIBIBBO, as it is known in much of Italy.

In France, total plantings of Muscat d'Alexandrie, or Muscat Romain, have remained at about the same level as Italy's, just over 3,000 ha almost exclusively in Roussillon, since the 1960s. Although Muscat Blanc is catching up, it is still the dominant Muscat in this most Spanish corner of France. It is most obvious in Muscat de RIVESALTES but is also blended into other varieties, chiefly GRENACHE in all hues, to produce the *département*'s other VINS DOUX NATURELS. It was the stagnation of sales of such wines in the late 1970s that provided a catalyst for today's southern French dry Muscats (see also MUSCAT BLANC À PETITS GRAINS). The important Roussillon producers Domaine Cazes of Rivesaltes began to make dry and off-dry VIN DE PAYS from Muscat grapes surplus to requirements for VIN DOUX NATUREL in the early 1980s and such wines have clearly established themselves despite a subsequent revival of interest in wines such as BANYULS, in which both Muscat of Alexandria (Muscat Romain) and Muscat Blanc are allowed. The latter Muscat predominates in both sweet and dry Muscats of the Languedoc.

Muscat of Frontignan is a common synonym for MUSCAT BLANC À PETITS GRAINS and this is the Muscat variety that is solely responsible for the VIN DOUX NATUREL of the same name. See also FRONTIGNAN.

Muscat Ottonel is the palest of all the Muscats, both in terms of the colour of wine produced and in terms of its character. Its aroma is altogether more vapid than the powerful grapey perfumes associated with MUSCAT BLANC À PETITS GRAINS and MUSCAT OF ALEXANDRIA.

Its tendency to ripen earlier than these other two Muscats has made it much easier to cultivate in cooler climates and nowadays Muscat Ottonel is the dominant Muscat cultivated in ALSACE. It is also grown in eastern Europe,

notably in AUSTRIA, where there are still substantial plantings. Until the 1980s, it was revered to the exclusion of true Muscat Blanc, or Muskateller, particularly for its rich BOTRYTIZED wines in the Neusiedlersee region, which can be very fine. It may well be that it is at its best as a late-harvest wine, for there are some fine, apparently long-living examples from both HUNGARY and ROMANIA (where the variety is often known, respectively, as Muskotaly and TĂMÎIOASĂ Ottonel. In Alsace, however, VENDANGE TARDIVE Muscat tends to remain a theoretical possibility. One of the most widely planted Muscats in the CIS is Ottonel, often known as Hungarian Muscat.

Muscat Romain, or Roman Muscat, common name for MUSCAT OF ALEXANDRIA in Roussillon.

Musigny, Le, great red GRAND CRU in Burgundy's CÔTE D'OR. See CHAMBOLLE-MUSIGNY.

Muskateller, German for MUSCAT, almost invariably the superior MUSCAT BLANC, or some mutation of it. **Gelber Muskateller,** for example, is the gold-skinned version which is increasingly recognized as superior to MUSCAT OTTONEL in Austria, where it is particularly popular in STYRIA. In Germany, Gelber Muskateller is a distinctly minority interest, and there is even less of the red-skinned **Roter Muskateller.**

Muskat-Silvaner or Muskat-Sylvaner is, tellingly, the common German-language synonym for Sauvignon Blanc and is used in Germany and Austria to a very limited but increasing extent, notably in STYRIA, where the wine is more likely to be called Sauvignon Blanc.

Muskotály, name used in HUNGARY for Muscat, usually MUSCAT OTTONEL but also occasionally a yellow-berried form of MUSCAT BLANC À PETITS GRAINS, here called Muscat Lunel.

musqué is a French term meaning both 'perfumed', as in musky, and 'muscat-like'. Many vine varieties, including Chardonnay, have a Musqué mutation which is particularly aromatic and may add to the variety's own characteristics a grapey scent reminiscent of MUSCAT.

must is the name used by wine-makers for the thick liquid that is a mixture of grape juice, stem fragments, grape skins, seeds, and pulp and that comes from the crusher-destemmer

that smashes grapes at the start of the wine-
making process.   A.D.W.

must weight, important measure of grape
RIPENESS, indicated by the concentration of dissolved compounds in grape juice or must. Since
about 90 per cent of all the dissolved solids in
grape juice are the fermentable sugars, any
measurement of these solids gives a reliable
indication of the grapes' ripeness, and therefore the POTENTIAL ALCOHOL of wine made from
them (see FERMENTATION).

Must weight may be measured approximately in the vineyard before harvest using a
refractometer, or in the winery, using a refractometer or a hydrometer, calibrated according
to one of several different scales for measuring
the concentration of dissolved solids used in
different parts of the world: BAUMÉ, BRIX, and
OECHSLE.

A typical dry wine is made from grapes
which measure between 11.1° and 13.3°
Baumé, between 20° and 24° Brix or Balling,
and between 83° and 104° Oechsle.

B.G.C. & A.D.W.

mutation, spontaneous change to genetic
material occurring during cell division in
organisms such as grapevines. Since so many
VINE VARIETIES are of ancient origin, they have
accumulated a substantial load of mutations.
Generally mutations are deleterious, but man
has had many centuries in which deliberately
to select those vines which perform best (a
process now formalized as CLONAL SELECTION),
so beneficial mutations have been maintained.

Mutation is particularly common among
certain black-berried vine varieties that degenerate easily such as PINOT NOIR, CARIGNAN,
ASPIRAN, GRENACHE, and TERRET. Most of these
have forms called variously Noir (black), Gris
(grey), Blanc (white), Rose (pink), Vert (green),
Rouge (red), and sometimes more.

Nagyburgundi is Hungarian for BLAU-FRÄNKISCH.

Nahe, wine region in GERMANY scattered over a wide area on either side of the river Nahe.

Good-quality wine is produced in many parts of the region but the greatest concentration of fine vineyards is in three main areas. First there is the pretty stretch of the river between Schloss Böckelheim and Bad Münster am Stein-Ebernburg, covering Niederhausen, Norheim, and Traisen. Here the vineyards have been modernized and reconstructed where necessary and practical, to produce world-class RIESLING wines. The DOMÄNE Niederhausen is one of the most respected producers in this part of the region, and in the Nahe valley as a whole. The second outstanding area, also famous for its Rieslings, lies on the northern outskirts of Bad Kreuznach, immediately adjacent to the town. The third is near the confluence with the Rhine at Bingen.

Only a little over a quarter of the area under vine is on flat land, and the warmer MESO-CLIMATE of sloping terrain (see HILLSIDE VINEYARDS) is as important here as it is on the MOSEL. MÜLLER-THURGAU was the most widely grown vine variety for a time, but its area decreased by 25 per cent between 1972 and 1997. Thus Müller-Thurgau has been used chiefly as part of a blend sold under a GROSS-LAGE (collective-site) name (Rüdesheimer Rosengarten, for example), although as a VAR-IETAL wine from the upper end of the region at Meddersheim, it can surprise with its firm and lively character. Some three per cent or so of LIEBFRAUMILCH originates in the Nahe, and here too Müller-Thurgau plays a role.

Among the best producers, Riesling represents about 65 to 75 per cent of their vines, and by the mid 1990s it was for the first time grown more widely in the region than any other vine variety.

In 1960, SILVANER was grown on more than half the region's vineyards but today it accounts for only 10 per cent, and its share continues to dwindle. Silvaner is a reliable vine whose wine in the Nahe is sound, solid, and usually unremarkable.

Plantings of the PINOT varieties Grauburgunder and Weissburgunder are increasing, not least because they are versatile in terms of FOOD AND WINE MATCHING. Since 1990, the area devoted to red grapes has doubled and now accounts for 10 per cent of Nahe vineyards. DORNFELDER, Spätburgunder, and PORTUGIESER are the main varieties.

For wines of finesse one must turn to the private estates, 10 of which are members of the prestigious VDP association. At its best, Nahe Riesling shows vineyard style well, and, as an increasing proportion of wine is bottled with less RESIDUAL SUGAR, other flavours also become more pronounced. In recent years, the region has seen experiments with BARRIQUES, but it is a treatment which seems better suited to wines made from Pinot than Riesling. Cool cellar fermentation has long been practised to retain freshness of flavour, and CASK AGEING in large old wooden ovals, from which all oak flavours have long dispersed, is usual for Riesling on good estates. Bottlers on the Nahe are as keen as anyone in Germany to see their wines married to food, and, probably with this in mind, well over a third of the region's quality wine is now dry (TROCKEN) or medium dry (HALBTROCKEN). Perhaps because of the region's geographical position, its wines are often likened by commentators to a cross between those of the MOSEL and those of the Rheinhessen. The comparison is fair, if a little superficial.

The two co-operative cellars worth mentioning are the Nahe-Winzer co-operative in Bretzenheim and the co-operative cellar at Meddersheim.

Good Nahe wine at all quality levels had been underpriced in Germany for years. However, by the late 1990s the leading estates improved their market position to such an extent that they obtain prices on a par with, and in 1997 higher than, those of the RHEINGAU.

I.J. & K.B.S.

Napa, small town north of San Francisco in CALIFORNIA that gives its name to **Napa County** and, California's most famous wine region and now an AVA, the **Napa Valley**.

The Napa valley proper is a long, lazy arc with its foot in San Francisco Bay and its head on the shoulder of Mount St Helena. Like most of the north–south valleys around San Francisco Bay, it has a cool end at the bay and a warm one away from it, although it is barely more than 40 miles/64 km end to end, and sometimes less than a mile wide. With more than 30,000 acres/12,000 ha of vineyard in the Napa Valley AVA, the main valley has little more land to plant, although a succession of smaller valleys in hills to the east such as Chiles and Pope valleys offer some room for expansion.

Napa's magic is derived in no small part from a magnificent diversity of exposure, climate, and soil, which has led to several sub-AVAs within the generously drawn main AVA. Both the name Napa Valley and the subappellation names appear on labels simultaneously. Distinctions among the wines makes even greater refinement of internal boundaries seem inevitable. With or without diversity, Napa has been such a congenial home to Cabernet Sauvignon that one could argue a case for Napa's having caused its popularity, not the other way around. Versatile growing conditions give Napa growers the options of Chardonnay, Sauvignon Blanc, Zinfandel, and, most notably

among recent replantings in the wake of PHYLLOXERA, Merlot.

Howell Mountain AVA

The current generation of growers and winemakers, led by Dunn Vineyards and La Jota, has turned away from Zinfandel and sharply towards Cabernet Sauvignon as the variety of choice. The district ranges upward from 1,400 ft/430 m elevation in Napa's east hills.

Mount Veeder AVA

A sub-AVA stretches out along ridgetops that separate the Napa and SONOMA valleys immediately west of the town of Napa, and is centred on the peak from which its name comes. Its oldest winery is Mayacamas, its largest the Hess Collection. Most of the plantings in it are Cabernet Sauvignon and Chardonnay.

Oakville AVA

AVA that is part of a grower plan proposed during the early 1990s to divide the Napa Valley floor into communes much as the Haut MÉDOC is divided. If the scheme ever succeeds, the sub-AVAs from south to north would be Napa, Yountville, Oakville, Rutherford, St Helena, and Calistoga. By 1994, only Oakville and Rutherford had been authorized and growers' attention was focused on other matters, such as replanting PHYLLOXERA-infested vineyards.

Rutherford AVA

With Oakville, Rutherford was part of the grower plan to divide all of the Napa Valley into community-based sub-AVAs. The west side of this middle stretch of valley, known as the Rutherford Bench, holds many of California's premier patches of Cabernet Sauvignon, including Beaulieu Vineyard Nos. 1 and 2, Inglenook, Martha's Vineyard, Bella Oaks, Bosche, Sycamore, Mondavi's To Kalon, and more.

Stags Leap District AVA

A sub-AVA well south and on the eastern side of the valley, Stags Leap District (shunning the apostrophe) celebrates Cabernet Sauvignon and Merlot, and virtually nothing else. All of its fame rests on varietals from those grapes. Other varieties grow well, but not with enough regional distinctiveness to call attention to themselves. The hallmarks of its Cabernets are a greater emphasis on berry flavours—or a lesser emphasis on herbs—than counterparts from other parts of Napa, and suppler TANNINS. Clos du Val and Stag's Leap Wine Cellars were the pioneers, since joined by Chimney Rock,

Pine Ridge, Shafer, Silverado Vineyards, Sinskey, Steltzner, and others.

Wild Horse Valley AVA

Wild Horse is an appellation east of the city of Napa. Most lies in the south-eastern corner of Napa County and within the Napa Valley AVA; a small bit spills into Solano County to the east. The Atlas Peak operation, with involvement from ANTINORI of Italy, has specialized in Sangiovese.

See also CALIFORNIA.   B.C.C.

Naracoorte Ranges, relatively new wine region in the Limestone Coast zone of SOUTH AUSTRALIA, also known as Wrattonbully.

Nardo, DOC for robust red wine made mainly from NEGROAMARO grapes in south-east Italy. See APULIA.

Navarre, known in Spanish as **Navarra,** autonomous region in north-east SPAIN which also lends its name to a denominated wine zone.

The region splits into five subzones according to climate, from the cooler slopes of the Baja Montaña close to the Pyrenean foothills and the slightly warmer Valdizarbe and Tierra Estella districts in the north of Navarre, to Ribera Alta in the centre of the region, and Ribera Baja round the city of Tudela in the south. With over 30 per cent of Navarre's vineyards, Ribera Baja has traditionally been the most important of the five subzones, although most of the new planting in the late 1980s and early 1990s took place in the cooler north.

The GARNACHA grape dominates Navarre's vineyards and accounted for over 80 per cent of total production in the late 1990s, with TEMPRANILLO accounting for some 15 per cent. Garnacha lends itself to good, dry rosé, which Navarre continues to make in large quantities. Red wines improved by leaps and bounds in the 1990s through much more careful winemaking and frequent blending of Tempranillo, Cabernet Sauvignon, Merlot, and even Syrah with Garnacha. White wines account for less than 10 per cent of the region's production and have traditionally been made from the neutral Viura, or MACABEO, grape. Chardonnay, however, has been extensively planted.

R.J.M. & V. de la S.

Nebbiolo, great black grape variety responsible for some of the finest and longest-lived wines in Italy. It is native to the PIEDMONT region in the north west, and is its most dis-

tinctive and distinguished vine. The quality of wines such as BAROLO and BARBARESCO inspires hopeful planting of the variety all over the world.

Italian Nebbiolo

Piedmont has shown its respect for Nebbiolo by restricting its planting to a few selected areas: the total production of wines from the grape rarely exceeds three per cent of the region's production. Nebbiolo is always a late ripener, and the variety is accordingly granted the most favourable HILLSIDE exposures. Perhaps as important as the vineyard site, however, are the soils in which the variety is planted: Nebbiolo has shown itself to be extremely fussy and has given best results in the DOCG zones of BARBARESCO and BAROLO. Here, Nebbiolo-based wines reach their maximum aromatic complexity, and express a fullness of flavour which balances the relatively high ACIDITY and substantial TANNINS which are invariably present.

Good Nebbiolo wines are also produced in the hills on the banks of the Sesia river in the province of Novara (see BOCA, GHEMME, SIZZANO, FARA) and in the Vercelli hills (see LESSONA, BRAMATERRA, GATTINARA). Here Nebbiolo is called SPANNA and is usually blended with softer VESPOLINA and/or BONARDA grapes.

NEBBIOLO D'ALBA, a tamer version of the grape, only suggests the heights which the variety can gain in more choice positions. The ROERO district on the left bank of the Tanaro produced better and better wine throughout the 1990s, although without the classic aromas of tar found in Barolo and Barbaresco.

Nebbiolo, often called Picutener, also plays the leading role in the postage stamp-size DOC of CAREMA on the border of the Valle d'Aosta, in the neighbouring and equally Lilliputian DOC of Donnaz in the Valle d'AOSTA itself, and in Lombardy in the VALTELLINA, where it is known as Chiavennasca—the only sizeable zone where Nebbiolo is cultivated outside Piedmont. The latter three areas produce a medium-bodied style of Nebbiolo in which the fruit must frequently struggle against the grape's tannic asperity and acidic sharpness; the added ripeness of warmer vintages is even more valuable here.

These zones apart, Nebbiolo is hardly known in Italy, although it is an ingredient in the FRANCIACORTA cocktail, and the innovative VENETO wine-maker Giuseppe Quintarelli makes a RECIOTO version of Nebbiolo.

The total area planted with Nebbiolo declined in the 1980s, to about 5,200 ha/13,000 acres in the 1990s—about half the area planted with Piedmont's Dolcetto, and about a tenth the total area of Italian vineyard planted with Barbera. D.T.

Outside Italy

Vine-growers all over the world are experimenting with Nebbiolo. The results often lack the haunting aromas that characterize the variety but isolated examples in regions as far apart as Washington state and Australia's King Valley in Victoria suggest the quest may not be fruitless. Nebbiolo has so far somewhat reluctantly accompanied Barbera to both North and South America. In California, Sangiovese has proved much more successful. High yields have tended to subsume the variety's quality in South America.

Nebbiolo d'Alba is an Italian DOC red produced from NEBBIOLO grapes grown in 32 townships surrounding the city of Alba in the PIEDMONT region and is, to all extents and purposes, a satellite appellation to BAROLO and BARBARESCO. The wines are softer, less intense, and faster maturing than a Barolo or a Barbaresco, more generically 'Nebbiolo' and less pointedly charracterful. D.T.

Nebbiolo delle Langhe, formerly a VINO DA TAVOLA of the PIEDMONT region in north-west Italy, generally producing a particularly light version of this usually intense grape. However, a few leading Barolo producers—Aldo Conterno and Elio Altare in particular—pioneered special CUVÉES for small oak BARREL MATURATION in the 1980s. These wines, which commanded a much higher price and enjoyed an entirely different prestige from the average Nebbiolo delle Langhe, carried the same classification on the label. The approval of an overall regional DOC for Piedmont in 1995 remedied this situation by creating a new DOC called Langhe Nebbiolo into which producers in Barolo, Barbaresco, Nebbiolo d'Alba, and Roero may declassify their wines. D.T.

négociant, French term for a merchant and one used particularly of wine merchants who buy in grapes, must, or wine, blend different lots of wine within an APPELLATION, and bottle the result under their own label.

The role of the négociant is particularly worthwhile in BURGUNDY, where the négociants are concentrated in Beaune, and where so many individual growers produce tiny quantities from each of a number of different appellations. The introduction of DOMAINE BOTTLING was so successful that it cast a slur on the work of the négociants by imputation, although the likes of DROUHIN and JADOT have worked hard to prove that they can be a source of more reliable wine-making skills than all but the best grower wine-makers. The Burgundy négociants have been acquiring increasingly significant vineyard holdings of their own, so that BOUCHARD PÈRE ET FILS in Beaune and Faiveley of Nuits-St-Georges, for example, are two of the CÔTE D'OR'S most subtantial vineyard owners. These large, well-established houses have been joined by a number of ambitious, smaller négociants such as Verget and Laurent, and to a lesser extent Chartron et Trebuchet and Olivier Leflaive, who now successfully present their work as high art, with concomitant prices. The term **négociant-éleveur** implies that the négociant oversees the ÉLEVAGE of the wine it sells.

Like all important French wine regions, Bordeaux also has a great concentration of négociants, many of which own CHÂTEAUX (while some of the FIRST GROWTH châteaux also now own a négociant business). See BORDEAUX TRADE.

Negoska, Greek red grape which is a softening ingredient, making very fruity, alcoholic wines, with XYNOMAVRO, in the wines of Goumenissa.

Negra Mole and **Negramoll,** Iberian dark-skinned grape variety. See TINTA NEGRA MOLE.

Négrette is the black grape variety special to the vineyards north of Toulouse in SOUTH WEST FRANCE. In Côtes du FRONTONNAIS it must dominate the blend and in Vins de LAVILLEDIEU it must constitute at least 35 per cent. Wine made from Négrette is more supple, perfumed, and flirtatious than that from the more famous south-western black grape variety TANNAT, and is best drunk young, with its fruit, sometimes described as having a slightly animal flavour, unsuppressed by heavy oak ageing.

Negroamaro, often written **Negro Amaro,** dark-skinned southern Italian grape variety whose name means 'black, bitter'. It is most common in Apulia, where it is particularly associated with Salento. Although it has traditionally been used for blending, it can produce vigorous red wines worthy of ageing as well as some lively rosé. See APULIA.

Neherleschol, extremely ancient Middle Eastern light-berried vine with enormous bunches, planted experimentally at MAS de Daumas Gassac in the Languedoc.

Nepal, tiny mountain kingdom in the Himalayas lying between India and Tibet, home to the highest vineyard in the world (2,750 m/9,000 ft).

Nerello, important Sicilian red grape variety. Nerello Mascalese is more widely planted than Nerello Cappuccio and is concentrated in the north east of the island. The wines produced tend to lack the concentration of NERO D'AVOLA although they are usually high in alcohol. Most of the wine is used for blending. See SICILY.

Nero d'Avola, red grape variety that is one of the best in Sicily and is also known as Calabrese, suggesting origins in Calabria on the mainland. Total plantings of the variety fell by a third in the 1980s, but quality-minded producers on the island value the body and ageing potential which Nero d'Avola can bring to a blend. VARIETAL Nero d'Avola has shown itself a fine candidate for BARREL MATURATION. Avola itself is in the southern part of the province of Siracusa, and nearby Pachino, on the extreme south-eastern tip of the island, is particularly reputed for the quality of its Nero d'Avola grapes. See SICILY.

Netherlands, north European country more often referred to as Holland, which has its own small, indigenous wine industry, despite the coolness of the climate. At the end of the 1990s, there were 59 active vine-growers, many of them producing only minuscule amounts. The largest producers are medal winners Apostelhoeve, Domein Backerbosch, and Hoeve Neekum. Domaine d'Heerstayen also enjoys a considerable reputation. Riesling, Müller-Thurgau, Auxerrois, Sylvaner, and Pinot Gris are grown for white wines while Pinot Noir and Gamay produce extremely light reds. Most wines are light, dry whites, however, of around 10 per cent alcohol, depending heavily on CHAPTALIZATION.   N.McG.

Neuburger, sometimes distinguished white grape variety grown almost exclusively in AUSTRIA. It is a crossing, quite possibly an accidental one, of Weissburgunder (PINOT BLANC) × SYLVANER which makes wine that tastes like an even fuller-bodied Weissburgunder. It is grown in most of Austria's wine districts, other than Styria, and in Transylvania in ROMANIA.

Neusiedlersee, shallow lake in the Burgenland region in the far east of AUSTRIA around which most of the country's best sweet white and red wines are made.

Nevers is the town that gives its name to the central French *département* of Nièvre, most famous in the wine world for the wines of POUILLY-FUMÉ and for its OAK.

New South Wales, AUSTRALIA'S most populous state, consumes far more wine than it produces, but its wine geography is developing rapidly.

The Hunter Valley, 130 km/80 miles north of Sydney, has always had a special hold on the affections (and palates) of Sydneysiders. It is also one of the internationally known regions, notwithstanding its relatively small contribution (less than three per cent) to the country's total crush, and its perverse climate. That climate is abnormally hot for a fine-wine district, although the heat is partially offset by high humidity, by afternoon cloud cover, and by substantial rainfall during the growing season.

Out of this climatic witches' brew comes exceptionally long-lived dry SEMILLON, the best peaking somewhere between 10 and 20 years of age and assuming a honeyed, buttery, nutty flavour, and texture which suggests it has been fermented or matured in oak, when (traditionally) none was used. Most remarkable is the ALCOHOLIC STRENGTH, often as low as 10 per cent. Since 1970, Chardonnay also has proved its worth: Australia's first Chardonnays of note were made in the Hunter Valley by Tyrrell's. Here the lifespan is usually much shorter, but there are exceptions. Whether young or old, Hunter Chardonnays are generous and soft, with peachy fruit and considerable VISCOSITY.

SHIRAZ was the traditional red counterpart to Semillon in the Hunter, making extremely distinctive, moderately tannic, and long-lived wines with earth and tar overtones, sometimes described as having the aroma of a sweaty saddle after a hard day's ride. At 20 to 30 years of age, the best acquire a silky sheen to their texture and move eerily close to wines of similar age from the RHÔNE valley in southeast France.

CABERNET SAUVIGNON is a relatively new arrival. By and large, Hunter Valley wines tend to be more regional than varietal in their statement, a tendency which becomes more marked with age. Small but increasing quantities of VERDELHO and MERLOT offer the most potential outside the principal four varieties.

Overall, the Hunter Valley produces better white wines than it does red, with Semillon its one unique contribution. If one is to differentiate the Upper Hunter, a separate viticultural region well to the north, from the Lower Hunter, the bias towards white wine becomes more acute in the former. Rosemount has enjoyed wide acclaim for its Chardonnay, although the Semillon in particular lacks the concentration and longevity of its lower Hunter Valley counterpart.

Nowhere in Australia is the rate of change and the pace of growth more apparent than it is in New South Wales. The development of viticulture along the entire length of the western (or inland) side of the Great Dividing Range could not have been foreseen at the start of the 1990s, but by the end of the decade was making a major contribution to the national crush.

The principal zones are the Central Ranges zone and the Southern New South Wales zone. The former takes in the regions of Mudgee, Orange, and Cowra; the latter takes in the regions of Hilltops (or Young), Canberra, and Tumbarumba.

Mudgee is first and foremost red-wine country, however well the ubiquitous Chardonnay does here. The red wines—Shiraz and Cabernet Sauvignon—are deeply coloured and intensely flavoured, and are ideal blend components for the products of the Hunter Valley's frequent wet vintages.

Elevation is as important as LATITUDE in shaping the climate (and the ensuing wine style) of the regions south down the Great Dividing Range to Orange. With most of its vineyards established on hillsides forming part of the extinct volcano Mount Canobolas, Orange is the coolest (apart from the southern outpost of Tumbarumba in the Australian Alps).

One example of the size and number of vineyard developments in Orange is a vineyard at the town of Molong, first planted in 1995 and which will be producing 6,500 tonnes a year (the equivalent of almost half a million cases of wine a year), all of which is being sold under long-term contract to SOUTHCORP. Zesty, lively Chardonnay and midweight Cabernet Sauvignon, Merlot, and Shiraz with clearly articulated varietal character are the order of the day here and in the Hilltops region.

McWilliam's has thrown its lot in with the Hilltops region, while BRL HARDY has chosen Canberra in a move which surprised most observers. Here most of the wineries have been small, clustered just outside the border of the Australian Capital Territory, but relying heavily on tourist (and local resident) trade to promote cellar-door sales.

In Cowra (and nearby Canowindra), softly fleshy Chardonnay is the mainstay, with commensurately soft Cabernet Sauvignon, Shiraz, and Merlot (roughly in that order).

The Riverina region (sometimes called the Murrumbidgee Irrigation Area, or MIA), centred around Griffith 450 km/275 miles south west of Sydney, produces around 65 per cent of the state's wine. With the notable exception of BOTRYTIZED Semillon (made in a SAUTERNES style), the wines are on a par with those produced along the irrigated RIVERLANDS of the Murray River spanning New South Wales, VICTORIA, and SOUTH AUSTRALIA. The emphasis is on white varieties and on high yields. Almost 75 per cent of the crush is of white grapes, with Semillon, TREBBIANO, and Muscat Gordo Blanco (MUSCAT OF ALEXANDRIA) together accounting for 50 per cent of the total. Shiraz utterly dominates red grape plantings (60 per cent of the total). The wines reflect the very warm climate and the quasi-hydroponic growing regimes. The technical excellence of the wineries assures clean, fault-free, mildly fruity wines well suited to the drinker of cask wine (in BOXES), and to the requirements of overseas bulk markets such as Sweden and the own brands of the British retail chains.   J.H.

New World, term much used in the wine world, initially somewhat patronizingly but with increasing admiration, to distinguish the colonies established as a result of European exploration which began with some of the longer voyages in the 15th century. As such it contrasts with the OLD WORLD of Europe and the other Mediterranean countries where the vine was widely established by the 4th century. Many of the differences between the Old and New Worlds of wine are being systematically eroded as those in the Old World increasingly adopt technical innovation and those in the New World are increasingly exposed to some of the better aspects of TRADITION.

Viticulture

The VINE VARIETIES planted in the New and Old Worlds are increasingly similar, as are the

ROOTSTOCKS onto which they are grafted, usually because the New World has slavishly concentrated on the INTERNATIONAL VARIETIES made famous in the Old World. Old World methods are more traditional, and many aspects of modern viticultural technology, especially MECHANIZATION, have been developed and first used in the New World. MECHANICAL HARVESTING and mechanical pruning, for example, were first developed in America, but by the early 1990s there was a high degree of acceptance, of the former at least, in Europe. Some vineyard sites in the Old World have been used for viticulture for hundreds of years, but there are still many potential new vineyard regions to be discovered in the New World.

Technological advance is by no means the sole prerogative of the New World, however. The development and application of new technology in Europe is the equal of anywhere in the world. R.E.S.

Wines

If New World wines can be said to have a style of their own, it is that they are much more likely to be VARIETAL both in how they are described on the label and in how they taste. Only a small, but increasing, proportion of New World wines are made with the clear intention of expressing their geographical provenance (see TERROIR), but the great majority seen on export markets at least are designed to express the fruit of the vine varieties from which they are made, together perhaps with some wood flavour. FRUIT DRIVEN is an essentially New World wine description.

New World wine-making, particularly in CALIFORNIA, has been subject to ever more rapid changes of direction and swings of FASHION than its Old World counterpart. This has been possible because both viticulturists and wine-makers in the New World are much more willing, and much freer, to experiment. (Those in the Old World are more likely to be restrained by local regulations such as the APPELLATION CONTRÔLÉE laws.)

In the Old World, with its centuries of winemaking tradition, Nature is generally regarded as the determining, guiding force. In much of the New World, however, it is regarded with suspicion, as an enemy to be subdued, controlled, and mastered in all its detail, thanks to the insights provided by science. (Most of the world's best wines are made by those who incorporate aspects of both these approaches,

although some are made almost by benevolent accident by Old World wine-makers whose grasp of scientific principles may be meagre.)

Obsession with HYGIENE is generally more marked in the New World than the Old, with the consequence that WATER use is much higher. Rubber boots are not essential for most Old World wine-makers.

In general, target TEMPERATURES throughout wine-making are lower in the New World than in the Old. This is especially true for FERMENTATION. Use of wild, natural, or ambient YEASTS is relatively rare in the New World (although it is gradually becoming rarer in the Old World just as it is becoming slightly less unusual in the New World).

The Old World red-wine-making practice of following fermentation with an extended MACERATION in the fermentation vessel is increasingly replaced in the New World by RACKING some red wines into barrel before they have completed their first fermentation, in the belief that this, particularly achieving MALOLACTIC FERMENTATION in barrel, results in a softer, fuller, earlier-maturing wine.

New World wines tend to be immediately appealing on release, whereas some Old World wines may be positively offputting to taste for their first year or two in bottle. In general, however, Old World wines are capable of more extended BOTTLE AGEING than their New World counterparts—although the proportion of exceptions to this rule is steadily increasing as New and Old Worlds move inexorably closer towards each other.

New York, north-eastern state of the UNITED STATES of America, between the Atlantic and the Great Lakes, historically an important source of wine and still second only to CALIFORNIA as a US wine-producing state. Its inland wine regions share some characteristics with those of Ontario across the border in CANADA, particularly those from south and east of Ontario. The market for wine in New York City is one of the world's most competitive and demanding.

Wine regions

New York State has four distinct wine regions, which, with some fine-tuning in the 1980s, have become six American Viticultural Areas, or AVAS. The regions are Finger Lakes (including Cayuga Lake AVA) in the central part of the state; Lake Erie at the western border; Hudson River, which begins about 40 miles/64 km north of New York City; and Long Island (including The Hamptons AVA), whose vineyards in the East End are about 90 miles east of NYC.

Finger Lakes While the picturesque Finger Lakes region is the second largest grape-growing area in the state, 90 per cent of the state's wine is produced there in 58 bonded wineries. The narrow, deep lakes were carved by Ice Age glaciers. The combination of steep slopes and deep lakes provides good AIR DRAINAGE and DRAINAGE of water, and fewer extremes of temperature in winter and summer (see LAKE EFFECT). The official Finger Lakes AVA was established in 1982, with Cayuga Lake being granted its own AVA in 1988. Riesling does exceptionally well in this cool climate, and is attracting consumer attention. Recent plantings of Pinot Noir and Cabernet Franc have also made successful wines. Lake Seneca is emerging as an important wine-producing area. Most wine is sold locally.

Lake Erie Lake Erie is one of the Great Lakes, and is the one that provides the most protection against extremes of weather to western New York.

The Lake Erie AVA was established in 1983, and includes three states: New York around Chautauqua, Pennsylvania, and Ohio, with counties that border on the lake. Lake Erie has the largest acreage in NY, but it has only eight wineries to date since most of the grapes planted in the region are for grape juice and table grapes.

Hudson River This region contains the oldest winery in the United States still in operation: Brotherhood America's Oldest Winery, Ltd. established in 1839. Among the region's wineries is Royal Kedem Wine Corporation, one of the world's largest kosher wineries. Seyval Blanc is a prominent white French HYBRID and many *viniferas* do well also.

Long Island The eastern Long Island region has been split into two AVAs: The Hamptons and the much larger North Fork. Both are peninsulas and local growers feel that the Atlantic's MARITIME influence is similar to its influence on BORDEAUX. The growing season is at least three weeks longer than other wine regions in New York state, which means that Merlot and Cabernet Franc predominate for they may be ripened fully almost every year.

Vine varieties and wines

New York has more vinous diversity than any other US state because it grows American vines, American HYBRIDS, French hybrids, and VINIFERA varieties.

American vines and hybrids The indigenous vines originally grown were *Vitis* LABRUSCA, which often hybridized by chance with other *labruscas* or even other American vine species, and produced a second generation of native grapes commonly grown today, called *labruscanas* locally, of which the blue-black-skinned CONCORD is the most planted variety. These formed the backbone of the early New York wine industry, although they are often derided today for their FOXY flavour.

The major red-pink native varieties are CATAWBA and DELAWARE. Catawba has been used in wine COOLERS and tank-method sparkling wines (see SPARKLING-WINE-MAKING). Delaware, on the other hand, is prized for use in fine sparkling wines. It has higher sugars and lower acids than Catawba. Both grow in the Finger Lakes and Lake Erie regions.

The white native varieties currently grown include NIAGARA, DUTCHESS, Elvira, and Moore's Diamond, but only Niagara has a bright future in New York state. It has a large following among those who enjoy its decidedly foxy flavour. It is grown mostly in Lake Erie and the Finger Lakes, but there is also a little in the Hudson Valley. It is finished with some RESIDUAL SUGAR to balance its intense aroma.

Of dark-skinned native varieties, Concord is widely planted, being grown in every area of New York except Long Island. It has low sugars and high acids, and the wine is invariably sweetened. Other red grapes include Fredonia, which is similar to Concord, but ripens earlier. Today it is planted mostly in Lake Erie, and used as a table grape or for juice. Ives is used similarly to Concord, and is planted mostly in the Finger Lakes. ISABELLA, which used to be very popular, has been largely replaced by other varieties.

French hybrids French hybrids represent the majority of acreage devoted to dry table wines. The most important white hybrid is SEYVAL BLANC, which grows in every New York wine region except Long Island, and which, much to the confusion of some consumers, can either be made clean and fruity in STAINLESS STEEL, or can be the much more complex result of BARREL FERMENTATION and malolactic fermentation. VIDAL BLANC and, particularly, VIGNOLES both lend themselves to making late-harvest, dessert wines, Vignoles sometimes being beneficially affected by NOBLE ROT. AURORE has been the most widely planted white hybrid grape in New York but is giving way to the prestige of Seyval Blanc. Two New York white hybrids are Cayuga GW3 and Melody. Both of these make fruity off-dry wines. Wine made from Melody is reminiscent of its Pinot Blanc parent. The red French hybrids are declining in acreage. The most famous are BACO Noir and CHAMBOURCIN, which are vinified in all styles from NOUVEAU to PORT-like; MARECHAL FOCH, which can also make a good nouveau using CARBONIC MACERATION; De Chaunac; CHANCELLOR, which needs some OAK ageing to add complexity; and Chelois, which works well in blends, especially with Baco Noir.

Vinifera In descending order of total acreage in the mid 1990s, the state's white *vinifera* varieties were Chardonnay, Riesling, Gewürztraminer, Pinot Blanc, and Sauvignon Blanc. The first four are grown successfully in all of New York's regions, but Sauvignon Blanc grows well only on Long Island. Of the red *vinifera* varieties grown in New York—Cabernet Sauvignon, Merlot, Cabernet Franc, and Pinot Noir—Merlot and Cabernet Franc show particular promise. They can make fine varietal wines on their own as well as blending well with other red Bordeaux varieties. Cabernet Sauvignon does best on Long Island. Pinot Noir performs better in the warmer areas of the Hudson Valley and Finger Lakes. *Vinifera* plantings are increasing.   H.L.

New Zealand, southern Pacific islands 1,000 miles/1,600 km away from the nearest land mass, AUSTRALIA, has an agricultural economy that is far more dependent on sheep and dairy products than it is on wine. Although production is small by world standards (one-tenth of Australia's relatively small wine output), vines are now grown on about 8,000 ha/20,000 acres in nine regions spanning 1,200 km/720 miles, almost the full length of the country's North and South Islands.

Geography and climate

New Zealand grows the world's most southerly grapes and, less significantly, the world's most easterly, thanks to an adjacent dateline. A parallel is sometimes made between the southern latitudes of New Zealand's wine regions and those of famous European regions. If New Zealand were in the northern hemisphere, the country would stretch from North Africa to Paris but the moderating influence of the Gulf Stream on European vineyards results in hotter growing conditions than in the vineyards of equivalent southern LATITUDES.

A broad climatic distinction can be made between the warmer North Island regions and those in the cooler South Island, although significant climatic differences exist within the five- to six-degree latitude span of each island. The largely MARITIME climate of New Zealand is very different from the CONTINENTAL climate of Burgundy. Bordeaux, with its proximity to the sea, is a closer match, in climate at least, to the North Island region of Hawkes Bay, which happens to produce New Zealand's finest Cabernet Sauvignon.

Chief preoccupation of New Zealand vinegrowers in the 1990s was vineyard site selection. New Zealand viticulture was for many years centred on the principal city of Auckland, an important market with one-third of the country's population. Between 1960 and 1983, wine production rose from 4.1 million l to 57.7 million l (15.2 million gal). New Zealand, it was claimed, had the fastest growing wine production in the world. In the late 1960s and early 1970s, the flat, fertile Gisborne river valley usurped Auckland's status as New Zealand's largest wine region. High yields of often relatively lowly grapes such as MÜLLER-THURGAU helped satisfy the nation's thirst for fresh, fruity, and slightly sweet table wine. Later, as PHYLLOXERA devastated Gisborne's grape crop and as demand for higher-quality wines increased, Hawkes Bay became the country's leading wine region. In 1990, Marlborough overtook Hawkes Bay and by the end of the 1990s had more than 50 per cent more productive vineyard hectares than Hawkes Bay.

Vine varieties

Although Sauvignon Blanc is the variety for which New Zealand established an international reputation, it ranks second to Chardonnay, the country's most planted variety. Pinot Noir overtook Cabernet Sauvignon in 1997 to become the country's most planted red variety, although a significant percentage of the Pinot Noir crop is destined for sparkling-wine production. Plantings of Riesling, the seventh most planted variety, continue to grow slowly as the mostly slightly sweet and frequently very good wine made from it battles to lose its unfashionable image in the local market-place. Other varieties which are planted on a total of more than 100 ha/250 acres are Muscat Dr Hogg (a bulk grape used to give extra fruitiness to basic Müller-Thurgau), Chenin Blanc, Müller-Thurgau, Merlot, and Sémillon.

Wine-making

The youthful and dynamic New Zealand wine industry has been greatly influenced by Australia. Traditional wine-making techniques from benchmark European wine regions have also been adopted, however. The country's southern hemisphere location has had a positive effect on the development of wine styles and wine-making techniques. Many young New Zealand wine-makers choose to work a second annual vintage in Europe and gain a wider perspective on the world of wine (see FLYING WINE-MAKERS). A reverse migration of mostly young French wine-makers has a similar effect.

Wine-makers in New Zealand operate relatively free from regulatory constraint. It is a remarkable tribute to the ambitions of the industry, especially abroad, that overall wine quality is as high as it is.

New Zealanders tend to worship the wine-maker rather than the vineyard. This NEW WORLD phenomenon is in direct contrast to the French view of the primacy of TERROIR. A decade or two will no doubt reveal the ephemeral nature of wine-makers and permanence of geography.

Industry organization

The industry is dominated by wine producers Montana, Corbans (who own Cooks), the Villa Maria/Vidals/Esk Valley group, and Nobilo's. Only the smaller wineries do not rely on fruit bought in from the country's grape-growers although many do supplement their own grapes with grapes grown under contract.

Every winery must belong to the Wine Institute of New Zealand, a statutory body formed in 1975 which collects a production-based fee from its members. WINZ has had an enormous influence on the development of the image and quality of local wine and has overseen New Zealand's substantial export attack on the United Kingdom, which imports more than two-thirds of all the wine exported from New Zealand.

Wine regions

Gisborne This east-coast North Island region based on the town of the same name is begin-

ning to shake off its image as a bulk-wine region and has largely recovered from phylloxera with massive replantings. Replanting also improved the mix of varieties. Müller-Thurgau, the dominant variety before replanting began in earnest, now represents only one-third of the Chardonnay acreage. Gisborne Chardonnay is certainly the country's most distinctive regional example of the variety, with soft and charming fruit flavours that often resemble ripe peach, pineapple, and melon. Gewürztraminer is Gisborne's other claim to vinous fame. Gisborne's wine-makers include the big two companies Montana and Corbans, which jointly produce about 80 per cent of the country's wine. Both companies have established large wineries in Gisborne, chiefly to process grapes for bag-in-BOX packaged blends, which accounted for nearly 60 per cent of the nation's wine sales by the late 1990s. Nestled within the large-scale, high-tech production facilities of Montana and Corbans are the small-batch presses and BARRIQUES used to make limited-edition, premium Chardonnay. At the other end of the production scale are many small LIFESTYLE WINERIES that make only premium bottled table wine or traditional-method sparkling wines. They include Millton Vineyards, New Zealand's first certified ORGANIC winery, which produces grapes and wine according to Steiner's principles of BIO-DYNAMISM. Most Gisborne grapes are grown by farmers who sell them to wineries under long-term contract, or to the highest bidder. Several Auckland wineries regularly buy Gisborne grapes which are mechanically harvested before being transported for nine hours by road in covered dump trucks. Varieties of grapes that are low in PHENOLICS, such as Müller-Thurgau, appear to suffer few ill effects and may even gain flavour from this period of compulsory SKIN CONTACT, but Sauvignon Blanc and Gewürztraminer can suffer as a result.

Hawkes Bay Hawkes Bay, around the town of Napier on the east coast of the North Island, is one of New Zealand's older wine regions and certainly one of the best. Complex soil patterns and MESOCLIMATES make it difficult to generalize about the wines of such a diverse region, particularly when they are made by such an eclectic group of wine-makers.

Chardonnay is by far the most important vine variety in Hawkes Bay, with Cabernet Sauvignon comfortably in second place, and Merlot third. Sauvignon Blanc and the rapidly declining Müller-Thurgau were fourth and fifth respectively. The best Hawkes Bay reds are Cabernet Sauvignon or a blend of Cabernet Sauvignon, Merlot, and occasionally Cabernet Franc. They have intense berry and cassis flavours, often with a gently HERBACEOUS reminder of their moderately cool-climate origin and, sometimes, strong OAK influence from up to two years' maturation in new French BARRIQUES. Syrah is rapidly finding favour with Hawkes Bay wine-makers although plantings are still relatively small and are confined to the warmer parts of the region. Hawkes Bay Chardonnay may lack the seductive charm of the Gisborne equivalent but the best have intense citrus flavours and a brooding elegance that are seldom matched by the wines of other regions. Hawkes Bay Sauvignon Blanc is a softer, fleshier wine than the better-known Marlborough Sauvignon Blanc. It often has a nectarine or stone fruit character, a useful indicator of regional identity.

Marlborough Marlborough, at the northeastern tip of the South Island, is the biggest of New Zealand's wine regions. Industry giant Montana planted the first vines in Marlborough when it established the South Island's first commercial vineyard in 1973. Other producers soon followed to establish wineries in the region or to secure a supply of grapes for the 18-hour journey north to Auckland or Gisborne. The single wine that put Marlborough Sauvignon Blanc on the international map was CLOUDY BAY, in 1985. Since 1989, the availability of contract wine-making facilities has encouraged an increasing number of vine-growers to process part or all of their crop into wine for sale under their own label.

Sauvignon Blanc is Marlborough's best-known and most planted variety. These pungent, aromatic wines that blend tropical fruit flavours with gooseberry and capsicum herbaceousness are probably the closest thing that New Zealand has to a national wine style (however much the country's wine-makers would prefer to build their international reputation on more prestigious wines, such as Chardonnay or Pinot Noir). Marlborough Chardonnay is the region's second most planted grape variety, producing a wine range of styles usually due more to wine-maker intervention than to TERROIR. A small but growing proportion of the Marlborough Chardonnay crop is used in traditional-method sparkling-wine

production. Riesling is another very successful Marlborough vine variety, which reaches its apogee as a sweet, luscious, botrytis-affected dessert wine. BOTRYTIZED wines can be produced here most years although the results vary considerably with vintage conditions.

Northland Northland, at the very northern tip of the country, was the birthplace of New Zealand wine, but the region's warm, wet, temperate climate has proved to be a barrier to good-quality wine production, particularly on the wetter west coast. Modern viticultural methods and careful site selection have allowed several producers to establish relatively rot-resistant varieties such as Cabernet Sauvignon and Syrah with promising results.

Auckland Auckland, the largest city, gives its name to the one New Zealand wine region where winery visitors can be assured of finding wines made from grapes grown as far south as Canterbury in the South Island, and are more likely to be offered wine from Marlborough and Hawkes Bay than the product of a local vineyard. New subregions, including Waiheke Island and Matakana, are now producing high-quality and highly fashionable reds which have helped raise Auckland's profile and esteem as a wine region.

Wairarapa Wairarapa, which includes the Martinborough region, is at the southern end of the North Island about one hour's drive from the nation's capital, Wellington. In 1998, Wairarapa had less than 3 per cent of the country's vines but 12 per cent of its wine-makers. They are typically small-scale, 'lifestyle' producers with a quality-at-all-costs attitude to wine-making and a passionate faith in their region's potential. Wairarapa wine-makers argue over whether the region is more suitable for Pinot Noir (Ata Rangi, Dry River, Martinborough Vineyards) or Cabernet Sauvignon (Benfield & Delamere), but there is ample evidence that both varieties perform well. In their quest to make great wine, most producers crop their vines so that YIELDS are considerably below the national average, a significant factor in the region's success.

Nelson Nelson is the South Island's most northerly wine region, nearly two hours' drive across high ranges from Marlborough. The rolling hills of Nelson rise from a scenic coastline to form a beautiful setting for the region's 15 wineries. Chardonnay is the main grape variety, with Riesling, Sauvignon Blanc, and

Pinot Noir a long way behind. The region is slightly cooler and wetter than the Marlborough average.

Canterbury Canterbury, around Christchurch on the central east coast of the South Island, has three subregions: Waipara in North Canterbury, the plains west of Christchurch, and Banks Peninsula to the east of the city. It is no surprise, given Canterbury's cool climate, that Chardonnay and Pinot Noir are the region's most planted varieties, with Riesling in third place and Sauvignon Blanc fourth.

Central Otago Central Otago grows New Zealand's, and the world's, most southerly grapevines, some of them cultivated south of the 45th parallel. It is New Zealand's only wine region with a CONTINENTAL climate providing greater diurnal and seasonal TEMPERATURE variation than any other. Most Central Otago vines are planted on HILLSIDE VINEYARDS to give better sun exposure and reduce frost risk. In 1998, Central Otago had less than three per cent of the national vineyard with 14 small but enthusiastic wine producers (twice as many as four years earlier). Yields are small but, perhaps as a result, the best Central Otago wines show impressive concentration. Pinot Noir, the region's most popular variety, has so far shown the most potential, with gentle, stylish wines. Gewürztraminer is the second most planted variety.   R.F.C.

Neyret, rare, dark-berried vine still found in the Valle d'AOSTA.

Niagara, HYBRID grown successfully in NEW YORK state. This *Vitis labrusca* variety is vigorous, productive, and withstands low temperatures well. Its wines have a strong FOXY flavour. One of its parents is CONCORD, the other Cassady, mainly *labrusca* with some VINIFERA genes.

Niederösterreich, the most important wine region in AUSTRIA, lower Austria, in the far north east of the country.

Nielluccio is CORSICA's most planted indigenous grape variety, although it was probably brought there from the Italian mainland, as it is ampelographically identical to the SANGIOVESE of Tuscany. It represented only 14 per cent of all Corsican vines in 1988, however, thanks to the domination of the coarser varieties imported by French immigrants from North Africa in the 1960s and 1970s. Often blended with the, arguably more interesting, other major indigenous red wine variety SCI-

ACARELLO, it constitutes an increasing proportion of the island's APPELLATION CONTRÔLÉE reds and, particularly, rosés, for which it is especially suitable. It is the principal ingredient in Patrimonio.

Nincusa, minor dark-berried grape grown on the coast of CROATIA.

Noah, a relatively undistinguished American HYBRID white grape variety which has been widely grown in France and eastern Europe but is of declining importance.

no-alcohol wine is a term sometimes used for wine with an ALCOHOLIC STRENGTH of less than one or two per cent. See DEALCOHOLIZED WINE.

Noble, occasional synonym for PINOT vines.

noble rot, also known as *pourriture noble* in French, *Edelfäule* in German, *muffa* in Italian, and sometimes simply as botrytis, is the benevolent form of botrytis bunch rot, in which the *Botrytis cinerea* fungus attacks ripe, undamaged white wine grapes and, given the right weather, can result in extremely sweet grapes which may look disgusting but have undergone such a complex transformation that they are capable of producing probably the world's finest, and certainly the longest-living, sweet wines. Indeed, the defining factor of a great VINTAGE for sweet white wine in areas specializing in its production is the incidence of noble rot. The malevolent form, which results if the grapes are damaged, unripe, or conditions are unfavourable, is known as grey rot.

Ideal conditions for the development of noble rot are a TEMPERATE CLIMATE in which the humidity associated with early morning mists that favour the development of the fungus is followed by warm, sunny autumn afternoons in which the grapes are dried and the progress of the fungus is restrained. In cloudy conditions in which the humidity is unchecked, the fungus may spread so rapidly that the grape skins split and the grapes succumb to grey rot. If, however, the weather is unremittingly hot and dry, then the fungus will not develop at all and the grapes will simply accumulate sugar rather than undergoing the chemical transformations associated with noble rot, so the result is less complex SWEET WINE.

It is unusual for all grapes on a vine, or even

on a single bunch, to be affected in exactly the same way, to exactly the same effect, and at exactly the same speed, which is why the HARVEST of a botrytis-affected vineyard can necessitate several passages, or TRIS, during which individual bunches, or parts of them, are picked at optimum infection level, and grapes affected by grey rot may have to be eliminated.

See SAUTERNES and BOTRYTIZED WINES.

Noir, French for black and therefore a common suffix for dark-berried vine varieties.

non-vintage, often abbreviated to NV, a blended wine, particularly champagne or sparkling wine, which may contain the produce of several different VINTAGES, although in champagne-making practice it is usually substantially based on the most recent vintage, to which some additional ingredients from older years, often called 'reserve wines', may be added.

Within the European Union, basic TABLE WINE may not be sold with a vintage year on it and is in practice often a blend made throughout the year so that the first blend of the winter season, typically, may contain a mixture of wine from both the new and last year's vintages.

North Coast, general CALIFORNIA umbrella region and AVA implying north of San Francisco but technically not including Marin County because so few grapes are grown there. It does include all vineyards in LAKE, MENDOCINO, NAPA, and SONOMA counties and has rather more homogeneous growing conditions than many suspect. The name appears on some relatively prestigious wines assembled from, especially, Napa and Sonoma and also on some pretty ordinary blends.

North East Victoria, wine zone in the Australian state of VICTORIA incorporating the wine regions of Rutherglen, King Valley, Glenrowan, and Kiewa/Ovens Valley.

North Yuba. See SIERRA FOOTHILLS.

Norton, arguably the only variety of American vine species origin making a premium-quality wine. Little known and little grown outside the eastern and midwestern UNITED STATES, Norton is undoubtedly underrated because of entrenched bias against non-VINIFERA varieties. The grapes are acidic, very dark

coloured and full flavoured, and the wine is indistinguishable by taste from European grapes.

nose, the most sensitive form of TASTING equipment so far encountered, the sense of TASTE being so inextricably linked with the sense of smell. When the nose is blocked, whether by a cold or by mechanical means, the ability to taste either food or drink is seriously impaired—so much so that cold sufferers have to resort to decongestants if the need for their tasting skills is serious.

Nose is also used as a synonym for the smell, AROMA, or BOUQUET of a wine, as in wines having 'a nose of raspberries', 'a raspberry nose', or even 'raspberries on the nose'.

This versatile word is also used as a verb by (particularly British) wine tasters who talk about 'nosing' wines when they smell them.

Nosiola, a white wine from the TRENTINO region in northern Italy made from the grape of the same name. Two DOCs share the production of the grape: Nosiola and Sorni Bianco. In this latter DOC, 70 per cent of Nosiola is blended with 30 per cent of either MÜLLER-THURGAU, PINOT BLANC, or SYLVANER. The wines have more aroma than body, and the flavours finish with a slight bitterness; they might well be fuller and more interesting if yields were lower.   D.T.

nouveau, French for new, and a specific style of wine designed to be drunk only weeks rather than months or years after the HARVEST. The most famous and successful nouveau is BEAUJOLAIS Nouveau, which, at its peak in 1988, accounted for more than 800,000 hl/21 million gal, or 60 per cent of all Beaujolais produced. The Beaujolais producers themselves are keen to point out that their Nouveaux are not simply *un phénomène 'marketing'*, but that they owe their origins to the 19th century, when the year's wine would complete its fermentation in cask while *en route* to nearby Lyons. The original term was PRIMEUR, meaning 'young produce', and from 1951 the Beaujolais producers were allowed to release their primeurs from 15 December. These young, refreshing wines enjoyed great success in the bistros of Paris in the 1950s and 1960s, and by the end of the 1960s the phrase *Le Beaujolais Nouveau est arrivé* had been coined. (One British wine merchant was already importing Beaujolais Nouveau in barrel in the early 1960s.) In the 1970s, the phenomenon spread outside France, thanks to energetic work on the part of producers such as Georges DUBŒUF and his agents around the world, and Alexis Lichine in the United States. Eventually the Nouveau was flown, with inexplicable haste and brouhaha, to markets around the world: the craze reaching Australia in 1982 and Japan and Italy in 1985. Initially the release date was fixed at 15 November, but was eventually changed to the third Thursday in November, for the convenience of the wine trade and the media, who for much of the late 1970s and 1980s were apparently fascinated by this event.

The immense commercial success of Beaujolais Nouveau inevitably spawned other Nouveaux—infant wines from other regions of France, notably Gamays made in TOURAINE and the ARDÈCHE, a range of wines made in LANGUEDOC-ROUSSILLON, and many VINS DE PAYS, particularly Côtes de Gascogne. Vin de pays Primeur or Nouveau may be released on the third Thursday of October following the harvest, a full month before Beaujolais Nouveau.

Italy produces a range of similar wines, described as **novello**, and even ENGLAND produces some nouveau.

Wine-making techniques have to be adapted to produce wines that are ready to drink so early. The majority of nouveau wines are red and many of them are produced, like Beaujolais, by CARBONIC MACERATION or semi-carbonic maceration, which yields particularly fruity, soft, aromatic red wines suitable for drinking young and slightly cool, typically involving a fermentation of only about four days, and fairly brutal STABILIZATION. White grapes, for which carbonic maceration is not suitable, are generally fermented very cool and boiled candy aromas typically result.

The great attraction of nouveau wines for producers is that they produce a financial return so quickly. As one taster remarked, their characteristic aroma is the scent of cash flow. Their appeal for the wine drinker is that they are a refreshing and stimulating reminder of the passing of the seasons. Nouveau wines do not deteriorate in bottle substantially more rapidly than non-nouveau wines, but their lifespan is inevitably shorter. A well-made nouveau from a good vintage can be opened two or even three years after the harvest without too much trepidation, although, like all nouveau wines, it should be drunk cool and without too much deliberation.

novello, Italian for new, and therefore a name applied to Italian NOUVEAU wine, sold only a few weeks after harvest.

Nuits, Côte de. The Côte de Nuits, named after the principal town of Nuits-St-Georges, is the northern half of the escarpment of the CÔTE D'OR, producing the greatest red wines of Burgundy, from the Pinot Noir grape, and very occasional white wines. The principal villages, from north to south, are GEVREY-CHAMBERTIN, MOREY-ST-DENIS, CHAMBOLLE-MUSIGNY, VOUGEOT, VOSNE-ROMANÉE, Flagey-ÉCHEZEAUX, and NUITS-ST-GEORGES. See also MARSANNAY.

Wines from FIXIN, Brochon, Prémeaux, Comblanchien, and Corgoloin may be sold as **Côte de Nuits-Villages**. These are usually but not exclusively red wines.

See also BEAUNE, CÔTE DE. J.T.C.M. & J.M.H.

Nuits-St-Georges, small market town in Burgundy giving its name to the Côte de Nuits, the northern half of the CÔTE D'OR. Nuits-St-Georges has remained fully independent of BEAUNE to the south and Dijon to the north, with numerous NÉGOCIANTS making their headquarters here. The town also boasts its own charity auction, the Hospices de Nuits, held in March, when the wines can be better judged than those of the HOSPICES DE BEAUNE in November.

The appellation Nuits-St-Georges lies both sides of the town which straddles the small river Meuzin and incorporates the vineyards of neighbouring Prémeaux-Prissey to the south. While all the wines of Nuits-St-Georges are sturdy and long lived, those abutting Vosne-Romanée to the north show the most fruit and elegance. The finest wines are normally held to come from the vineyards south of the Meuzin, where the ground is stonier and the wines are the fullest and longest lived of them all. There is more clay in the soil of the Prémeaux vineyards, making wines which are fat but a touch less fine.

Nuits boasts 27 PREMIER CRU vineyards but no GRANDS CRUS, perhaps because the town's leading vigneron, Henri Gouges, was too modest when the CLASSIFICATIONS were agreed in the 1930s. However, the eponymous Les St-Georges vineyard has always been cited as of the highest quality. Also particularly fine in the southern Nuits-St-Georges sector are Les Cailles and Les Vaucrains, both adjacent to Les St-Georges, while Les Murgers and Les Boudots on the Vosne-Romanée side and Les Argillières,

Clos l'Arlot, and Clos de la Maréchale in Premeaux have good reputations.

Some white wine is also made from the Chardonnay grape, as in the Clos l'Arlot, and from the Pinot Blanc grape in Domaine Gouges' premier cru Les Perrières.

Top producers include Henri Gouges, Robert Chevillon, Daniel Rion, and growers in neighbouring VOSNE-ROMANÉE such as Arnoux and Grivot. J.T.C.M.

numbers and wine, a combination that has assumed increasing importance as WINE-MAKING has become more scientific, and as consumers, faced with a bewildering choice of wines, seek easily appreciated assessments of wine quality.

Respected attempts have been made by experts to provide numerical measures of quality, free from the other factors that influence price. Robert PARKER in the United States, and other wine critics and publications including the influential *Wine Spectator* magazine in the USA and many more worldwide, use a scale from 50 to 100. Michael Broadbent in Britain uses one from 0 to 5, expressed in stars rather than numbers. Many tastings described in the press report numerically, sometimes just describing quality, sometimes rating value. In many countries, professional wine judges (see JUDGING) employ a 20-point system, typically with three points being given for appearance, five for aroma or bouquet, nine for flavour, and three for overall quality.

There are two reasons for wanting to apply numbers to wine. First, a number is precise: the number 17 means the same to everyone, whereas words used by tasters, such as 'earthy', although very useful, are difficult to recognize or describe. Secondly, and more importantly, numbers combine easily. For example, we can take the average of the numerical values given to a wine by several tasters to obtain an improved measure. Much criticism of numerical measures derives from the critic's inability to understand how to use the numbers, rather than from the numbers themselves; whereas words are more familiar. A similar deficiency rests with the consumer, who is misled by the precision of number to think that a wine rated 91 by Parker must be obviously better than a 90, whereas, for a reason outlined below, it need not be.

Ideally a numerical measure of a wine's quality should be reproducible. Unfortunately it is not. The evaluation of wine is too SUB-JECTIVE, and the wine itself too variable, for this to be possible. This does not rule out the usefulness of numerical measures, but it means that one has to be more careful in using them. For example, if all trained tasters gave wine A a mark in the 80s, and wine B one in the 70s, it is clear, despite the variability within the decades, that wine A is better than wine B.

Many factors may affect the variability. Wines can vary enormously at different, often quite close, stages of evolution. There is also the common phenomenon of BOTTLE VARI-ATION, common not just from case to case, but from bottle to bottle, especially but not exclusively with older wines stored in different conditions. Tasting conditions, particularly TEMPERATURE and exposure to air, influence the judgement. The tasting of one wine may be affected by the immediately previous tasting of another, with a carry-over effect from one experience to the next. There are obvious differences between judges' abilities and partialities. Judges tire easily and many cannot fairly assess more than 20 wines in a single session. A careful design of the tasting, accompanied by a rigorous analysis of the results, can produce judgements of real value. It is rare for the press report of a tasting to contain enough information for a reader to assess the value of the tasting, despite the abundance of words of doubtful precision.

Much of the joy of wine comes from its enormous variety. Numbers will not destroy this variety nor lessen the appreciation, merely help to put it on a firmer basis. To do this requires more carefully organized, comparative wine TASTINGS, and better analyses of the data obtained from them. See also wine SCORING. D.V.L.

Nuragus, white grape variety grown principally to produce the unremarkable varietal Nuragus di Cagliari on the island of SARDINIA.

NV. See NON-VINTAGE.

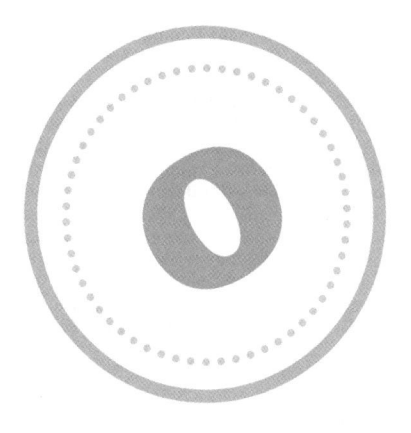

oak is a hard, supple, and watertight wood which has the simple advantage over other wood types used for casks of displaying a natural affinity with wine, imparting qualities and flavours that today's consumers appreciate as enhancing or complementing those of many wines. It can encourage clarity and stability in red wines and add new layers of complexity to many whites.

There are hundreds of species of oak, but for wine, three sorts of white oak are most important, one American and two European, all of them belonging to the botanical genus *Quercus*. American oak generally has a more obvious flavour, vanillin in character, and can be more astringent than the smoother, subtler oaks of Europe. Vital to barrel quality is not just the source of the oak, however, but its seasoning.

American oaks

There is no general agreement as to which American regions provide the best oak for wine barrels. Some people feel that oak from Minnesota and Wisconsin is best; others feel that it is too tannic. In the US alone, an estimated 150,000 to 200,000 American oak barrels are sold to producers each year, about 15 per cent more than those made of French oak, not least because they are less expensive.

American oak is also used widely by the wine industries of Spain, North and South America, and Australia. Because American oak generally has a more powerful flavour than European oak, it was for long used mainly for relatively powerful red wines such as RIOJA and other Spanish reds, Australian SHIRAZ, and warm-climate CABERNET SAUVIGNON, but cooperage techniques improved so considerably in the 1990s that it is now routinely used on a much wider range of wine styles, including Chardonnay.

European oaks

European oaks grow throughout Europe, as far east as the Urals, as far south as Sicily, as far west as Ireland, France, and Portugal, and as far north as southern Norway.

France Since the 19th century, French oak has become the standard by which all other oaks are judged. At least 200,000 French oak barrels are made and sold every year, it is estimated, of which the majority are sold to the US. The following forests all over northern France provide oak for wine barrels:

Western Loire and Sarthe: wood from forests in the western LOIRE has tight grains and is highly prized.

Limousin: wood from these oaks tends to have wide grains, is more TANNIC than the tight-grained woods and is more popular with brandy-makers than wine-makers.

Nièvre and Allier: wood from these two central *départements* just south of SANCERRE is usually tight grained and is popular for both brandy and wine.

Vosges: wood from the Vosges forests in ALSACE-Lorraine became popular with wine-makers outside the region in the early 1980s. This wood is usually tight grained and resembles the oak from Nièvre and Allier.

Jura and Bourgogne: just to the east of BUR-

GUNDY are forests which traditionally supplied Burgundy with oak. These forests are still important and supply wood mainly to Burgundian wine producers.

Argonne: located near CHAMPAGNE, this forest provides a small amount of oak for the cooperage business, principally for those few champagne producers who still ferment in barrel. Sometimes the wood is sold as Vosges.

Eastern Europe Historically, the forests of eastern Europe were extremely important sources of oak. Some coopers have conducted successful trials of wines matured in eastern European oak and, although there is still much to be learnt about making barrels with these woods, between 6,000 and 10,000 such barrels were sold, at keen prices, in the US alone in 1997—roughly 5 per cent of French oak barrel sales but growing fast.

SLOVENIA, BOSNIA HERCEGOVINA, and SERBIA have been a useful source of oak for the large casks and oval vats used by Italy's wine producers (who often called them simply Yugoslavian, or Slavonian). It is said these oaks are too tannic for French grape varieties but work well with Italy's NEBBIOLO and SANGIOVESE, but this could be a reflection of wood preparation or TERROIR.

Portugal Oak grown in the far north of Portugal can, if well seasoned, be of use to Portugal's wine-makers, being more subtle than the locally used chestnut and much cheaper than oak imported from France.

See also BARREL, BARREL FERMENTATION, BARREL MATURATION, BARREL INSERTS, OAK CHIPS and OAK ESSENCES.   M.K.

oak ageing, the process of AGEING a wine in contact with OAK. This typically involves BARREL MATURATION, ageing the wine in a relatively small oak container, although the phrase may also be used for CASK AGEING in a larger oak container, and can even be used for wines exposed to the influence of OAK CHIPS. Wines thus treated may be described as **oak aged**, **oak matured**, or **oaked**.

oak chips, useful if ersatz wine-making tool, an inexpensive alternative to top-quality BARREL MATURATION which imparts wood flavour, if none of the physical properties associated with barrel maturation.

Oak chips vary considerably both in the provenance of the OAK (from subtle Limousin to harsher American oak) and in the size of the chip (from pencil shaving to the more common cashew-nut size). Oak chips, just like BARRELS, are also subjected to different degrees of TOAST.

Oak chips are used either instead of barrel maturation or to supplement the oak flavour imparted by a used barrel. They offer considerable savings: a sufficient quantity of American oak chips to impart some degree of oak flavour could cost less than a twentieth of the cost of a new American oak barrel (and an even smaller fraction of the cost of a new French barrel). They are most effective when added during FERMENTATION. Such wines sometimes have such an overpoweringly oaky flavour that they must be blended with unoaked wine.

Oak chip use has the potential disadvantage of producing very high levels of VOLATILE ACIDS, which can make the treated wines appealing to some tasters in the short term, but can make them taste bitter in the medium term and can reduce their potential for BOTTLE AGEING.

Most wine producers are coy about admitting to using oak chips although, unlike OAK ESSENCE, oak chips may be used perfectly legally in many wine regions. A wine description which mentions 'oak maturation' or 'oak influence' without actually mentioning any form of cooperage is a good clue.

The **oak shavings** which can result from reconditioning used barrels may similarly be used, and larger **oak cubes** in a perforated bag are sometimes put into older barrels to impart wood flavour.

See also BARREL INSERTS.   G.T.

oak essences or **oak extract**, usually illegal wine-making additive (unlike OAK CHIPS) which can inexpensively substitute, at least in the short term, for some of the wood flavour imparted by BARREL MATURATION in expensive new oak. However, their ability to sustain a wine through BOTTLE AGEING is highly questionable and they should not be of interest to any serious wine producer.   G.T.

Oakville. Important centre of wine production in the NAPA Valley of California.

Oechsle, scale of measuring grape sugars, and therefore grape RIPENESS, based on the DENSITY of grape juice. This is the system used in Germany. See also MUST WEIGHT.   B.G.C.

Œil-de-Perdrix, French for partridge's eye, used as a name and tasting term for pale-pink wines, especially in the Neuchâtel canton of SWITZERLAND.

Œillade, occasional synonym for CINSAUT, especially when it is sold as a table grape.

oenologist, or, in the United States and South Africa, **enologist,** one who practises OENOLOGY. A CONSULTANT oenologist is likely to concentrate on the activities traditionally considered WINE-MAKING but increasingly concerns himself or herself with what happens in the vineyard as well as the cellar. In general usage, an oenologist is either a scientifically qualified employee or a roving consultant, as opposed to a fully employed practitioner who may or may not have scientific training, the WINE-MAKER. In California, certain winemakers are so adept and so modish that their input alone can be enough to double or treble prices and transform them into a CALIFORNIA CULT wine. Most famous of them is Helen Turley, and others include Heidi Peterson Barrett and Françoise Peschon.

oenology, or enology, the knowledge or study of wine.

Oenology has been used as synonymous with WINE-MAKING and distinct from VITICULTURE, which is concerned with vines. There is a general tendency towards including the study of viticulture as well as wine production in the term, however, as more people accept that wine is made to a great extent in the vineyard. See also OENOLOGIST.

OIV stands for Office International de la Vigne et du Vin, a Paris-based intergovernmental body.

Olasz Rizling or Olaszrizling, once Olaszriesling and still occasionally **Olasz Riesling,** is the most common name in HUNGARY for the white grape variety known in Austria as WELSCHRIESLING (under which more details appear). The variety is popular in Hungary, and only the rather ordinary DINKA is more widely planted. The Olasz Rizling produced around Lake Balaton is particularly prized. See also LASKI RIZLING and RIESLING ITALICO.

old vines are reputed to produce grapes which make better quality wine. See VINE AGE for a discussion of this common assertion.

Old World is Europe and the rest of the Mediterranean basin such as the Near East and North Africa. The term is used solely in contrast to the New World, the Old World having little sense of homogeneity. In very general terms, Old World techniques in vineyard and cellar rely more on TRADITION and less on science than in the New World. The notion of TERROIR is an important and well-established one in much of the Old World, especially France, Germany, and Italy. To most Old World producers, geography is considerably more important than technique.

For more details, see NEW WORLD.

Olifantsriver, wine region in SOUTH AFRICA.

Oltrepò Pavese, LOMBARDY'S most sizeable viticultural area, extends across the hills of a series of townships in the province of Pavia south of the Po river where the land begins to rise towards the Ligurian Apennines (the name means 'beyond the Po, in the Pavia region'). Significant quantities of grapes, PINOT NOIR in particular, are sold to the large SPUMANTE houses of PIEDMONT. Significant amounts of bulk wine have always been sold in nearby Milan, a practice which has encouraged abundant production at extremely low prices. The small size of the properties and the significant role played by CO-OPERATIVES have also tended to reward quantity over quality.

If the vast majority of the Oltrepò's production is not particularly interesting, there is no doubt that good, and occasionally very good, wine can be made in this zone. The most interesting is the blended red Oltrepò Rosso, which is based on BARBERA grapes to which CROATINA adds spice and BODY (it can sometimes have a RHÔNE-like pepperiness) and UVA RARA gives sweetness and aroma. Regrettably this blend accounts for less than five per cent of the total DOC production. Barbera (frequently sharply acidic and not helped by the generous yields permitted by the DOC rules) is more than five times as common, and Bonarda, produced from the Croatina grape and less interesting on its own than when combined with other varieties, is more than three times as common. The bland Riesling Italico (see WELSCHRIESLING) is the most significant white grape, accounting for over 15 per cent of total production. Oltrepò MOSCATO, which normally bears little resemblance to the elegant and perfumed wines produced in the bordering Piedmontese province of Alessandria, supplies another eight to nine per cent of the total. Pinot Noir is principally used for spumante, most of whose production is controlled by the CO-OPERATIVES and most of which is correct but hardly inspiring. An occasional good bottle of Oltrepò spumante and an occasional bottle of still Pinot Noir, given a Burgundian treatment and aged in OAK, indicate that the variety has real, if as yet unrealized, potential in the zone.   D.T.

Ondarrabi. See HONDARRABI.

Ondenc was once an important vine variety in GAILLAC and all over SOUTH WEST FRANCE but has fallen from favour because it yields poorly and is prone to rot.

opening the bottle is an important and potentially difficult operation for bottles closed with a cork. A wide range of corkscrews is available for opening bottles of still wine. See CORKSCREWS for details of the most efficient models and designs. See also STOPPERS for details of alternatives to CORK, most of which are much easier to open.

If the cork proves too recalcitrant for a corkscrew, the cork should simply be pushed in, if possible, and the wine poured out of the bottle, possibly into a jug, while the cork is held down with a long, thin instrument of some sort.

But before the cork can be extracted any FOIL or wax seal has to be broached. A knife blade or FOIL CUTTER is the simplest way to cut a foil neatly, just below the lip of the bottle, which should be wiped of any residue from the foil, especially if it is an old one and contains LEAD. Wax seals are more difficult to penetrate and call for a sharp knife, or foil cutter, and tolerance of a certain amount of mess.

Opening a bottle of SPARKLING WINE is potentially extremely hazardous, as the pressure inside the bottle can expel a cork so fast that it can inflict grave injury. The bottle should be held at 45 degrees (to maximize the wine's surface area) with the cork pointing in the least dangerous direction (and certainly not at anyone). The wire MUZZLE should be untwisted and discarded, while holding the cork in the bottle, usually with the top of the thumb. The bottle should then be very gently screwed off the cork with one hand while the cork is held in place with the other. The cork should be allowed to escape the bottle very slowly and the wine poured from the 45-degree angle, perhaps with a thumb in the punt (see BOTTLES). The racing driver technique of giving champagne a good shake and prising off the cork with two thumbs is about as dangerous as motor racing.

See SERVING wine for the timing of opening a bottle.

Optima is a relatively recent (1970) German *vinifera* crossing, of a Silvaner × Riesling with Müller-Thurgau. It ripens very early indeed, sometimes more than 10 days before Müller-Thurgau, and can notch up impressive ripeness readings, even if the wines themselves are flabby and undistinguished. Germany's plantings of Optima are declining.

options game, BLIND TASTING game which in practice allows novice tasters almost as great a chance of winning as professionals. Developed by Australian Len Evans, it requires an informed quiz-master who presents players with a series of increasingly precise options for the identity of the wine. A typical series of options might be: 'Australia, California, or Bordeaux?', 'left or right bank?', 'St-Estèphe, Pauillac, St-Julien, or Margaux?', 'pre-1980 or post-1979?' 'first or fifth growth?', 'Latour, Lafite, or Mouton?'. Players remain in the game only by choosing the correct successive options.

Orange, fast-growing new Australian wine region in one of the cooler parts of NEW SOUTH WALES.

Orange Muscat, white grape variety with MUSCAT characteristics apparently unrelated to MUSCAT BLANC À PETITS GRAINS. There were slightly more than 100 acres/40 ha planted in California in the late 1990s and a little in Oregon.

Orange River, wine region in SOUTH AFRICA.

order of wines to be served. This can affect how individual wines taste quite considerably. The general convention is a wise one for maximizing pleasure: dry before sweet, young before old, ordinary before fine.

A sweet wine can make dry wines taste acidic and unpleasant if they are tasted afterwards, so it makes sense to serve wines in an increasingly sweet sequence (which matches the usual sequence of foods during a meal, although serving the sweet course before cheese can upset things).

Old wines are generally more complex than callow young ones and so it generally flatters all wines if the oldest in the sequence are served last. This is not infallible, however. Sometimes young wines are so overwhelmingly robust in comparison to a delicate old wine that they may overpower it. For this reason, many tasters approach large tastings of PORT, especially vintage port, from the oldest to the youngest wine. Some wine producers, particularly but not exclusively in newer wine regions, also prefer to show their wines in chronological order of progress from old to young. And those planning particularly generous meals may find that the nuances of the oldest, finest wine they serve last may be lost on some palates already soaked in too many younger wines.

Similar considerations apply to serving wines in an upward sequence of quality.

Oregon, one of the UNITED STATES known by wine lovers for its PINOTS and part of the PACIFIC NORTHWEST. Oregon lies between CALIFORNIA and WASHINGTON state but is markedly different from both. Its propensity for ripening grapes is the most marginal of the three, significant to those who hold that grapes which struggle to ripen achieve greater complexity, and fundamental therefore to the view that it may be from the Northwest—and Oregon in particular—that the best wines of the USA will ultimately emerge. The growth of Oregon's wine industry has been a much more discreet affair than that of California and can hardly yet be considered mature. However, the lure of wine-making in the state has attracted increasingly moneyed producers (including wine guru Robert PARKER and the relatively vast King Estate).

Geography and climate

Most Oregon vines are directly exposed to the marine airflow of the Pacific Ocean, giving milder winters but cooler and wetter summers than Washington. Oregon is notoriously wet, yet in most years the majority of the rain falls between October and April, not during the crucial part of the growing season.

In any marginal ripening climate, the choice of VINE VARIETY and selection of growing site take on added importance. Oregon's best-known wine district to date is the **Willamette Valley** (pronounced with the emphasis on the *a*), which stretches 150 miles/240 km from Portland in the north to Eugene in the south. Similar, equally promising, sites can be found in the Eola Hills between McMinnville and Salem, and the area just north of the Dundee Hills known as the Chehalem ridge.

Summer temperatures show little consistency, and harvest dates can vary from early September to late November. Wine characteristics differ accordingly. Pinot Noir ripened well in most of the 1980s vintages but, as in Burgundy, individual skill, or lack of it, has often been the greater influence on final wine quality. By the 1990s, wine-making skill

had improved across the board, but a succession of rainy, difficult harvests from 1995 challenged even the most conscientious winemakers. As a result, the 1990s saw great VINTAGE variation among the wines.

There are also significant wine districts south of the Willamette Valley: the **Umpqua Valley,** the **Rogue River,** the warmer and drier **Applegate Valley,** and the **Illinois Valley** just north of the California border and cooler and wetter by virtue of its proximity to the Pacific. The potential of south-west Oregon is interesting and underdeveloped.

The economies of scale necessary for the production of cheap wine are not a feature of the Oregonian wine industry, which is therefore motivated by a need for quality rather than quantity.

Grape varieties

Pinot Noir has passed the test with many wines of commendable depth and complexity. Pinot Gris followed, achieving growing popularity in a crisp, dry style of characterful white. Chardonnay was initially widely but not wisely planted, but from the mid 1990s the produce of Dijon CLONES began a new chapter in the history of the Chardonnay in Oregon. Riesling is commercially useful, although it is not fashionable to say so, while Gewürztraminer works but is hard to grow and even harder to sell. ICE WINES made from Riesling and Gewürztraminer have been more obviously successful.

Among red wine grapes other than Pinot Noir, Gamay Noir has seen success, mostly vinified the same way as Pinot Noir to produce generally bigger wines than light, fruity Beaujolais. Merlot is rare since it usually fails to set fruit, while Cabernet Sauvignon finds most of Oregon too cool, although fine examples have started to emerge from the south of the state.

Wine-making

Oregon is a sympathetic home for any vine which does not like too much heat. Its production is best suited to quality rather than quantity. Increasingly mature vineyards and greater experience will reveal the extent to which the pioneers are justified in their hopes.

The biggest issues of the 1990s were YIELD and CLONE choices. The lower-yielding, earlier-ripening Dijon clones promise potentially more complex Pinot Noir and Chardonnay.

A typical Oregon winery both owns vineyards and buys in fruit from specialist growers. Most wineries are relatively small. Most are proud to be run personally and relatively idiosyncratically. ACIDIFICATION is rarely necessary; and although CHAPTALIZATION may be practised, wines with a natural ALCOHOLIC STRENGTH of at least 11 per cent are achieved without difficulty most years.   M.S. & L.S.H.

Orémus, Hungarian CROSSING of Furmint and Bouvier grown in the TOKAJI region to produce characterful, fiery, dry white wine.

organic viticulture, a system of grape-growing which does not employ industrially synthesized compounds as additions to the soil or vines to maintain or increase fertility, or to combat pest problems. (This definition is offered in the 1990 US Farm Bill.) It contrasts with 'conventional', sometimes even called 'industrialized', viticulture, especially in its concern for the soil and its flora and fauna as a complex, living environment.

There is considerable confusion about what exactly constitutes organic viticulture, involving a wide variety of organizations around the world with different motivations and operating principles. There are, however, several basic concepts which unite these approaches to viticulture. A primary concern is for the soil: organic viticulturists add compost and manure in preference to what they regard as injections of fast-acting chemicals. Some adherents to organic principles also believe that, because chemical fertilizers provide the same mix of nutrients to all vineyards, they can reduce the importance of site and TERROIR. A second and related basic tenet is that of protecting the natural environment, for example to avoid soil erosion and pollution.

The emphasis in organic viticulture is to transform the vineyard ecosystem from monoculture (towards which modern vineyards tend) towards polyculture. The biological diversity of the vineyard ecosystem is encouraged rather than discouraged, as is the case with conventional viticulture. This is achieved by use of cover crops, which typically consist of a mixture of grasses and legumes, the latter providing a source of nitrogen. Such cover crops also include companion plants and others which are known to have pesticidal properties.

Organic viticulture became increasingly popular during the 1980s in response to concerns about the possibility of pesticide residues in wine. Vineyard workers' health is also an issue, and pesticide poisonings were common enough until appropriate occupational health and safety guidelines were introduced in most countries.

Organic production's viability depends to a great extent on climatic conditions. While organic wines are produced in most major wine regions, it is only those areas with a warm, dry climate that can hope to produce commercial quantities of high-quality grapes on a regular basis. A number of growers in regions with a suitable warm, dry climate have adopted chemical-free growing programmes for no reasons other than economy, and that they are not seriously troubled by disease.

See also ORGANIC WINE and BIODYNAMIC VITICULTURE.   A.G.W. & J.Ro.

organic wine, imprecise term for wine made from grapes produced by ORGANIC VITICULTURE using a minimum of chemicals during wine-making.

The monitoring organizations which set and enforce standards for organic production forbid the use of most chemical additives, allowing only a minimal amount of SULPHUR DIOXIDE for use as an antioxidant, and physical treatments (such as FILTRATION) are kept to a minimum. Unfortunately, there is a lack of scientific rationale for some of the strictures applied by the monitoring organizations, at least one of which prohibits the use of TARTARIC ACID for ACIDIFICATION, but permits the addition of lemon juice, provided it comes from organically grown lemons, even though tartaric acid, and not the citric acid of lemon juice, is the predominant acid naturally present in wine.

By 1990, organic wine producers had begun to be taken seriously and by 1992 there were more than 400 producers worldwide registered with one of the monitoring organizations, while many others preferred not to belong to any association.

France remains the home of organic wine, often called *vin biologique*, with over half of the world's registered vine-growers, notably in the warm, dry climate of the south, but there are organic wine producers in all the classic French wine regions. Organic wine production in France is overseen by a plethora of monitoring organizations but some producers, such as the much-admired Ch de Beaucastel of CHÂTEAUNEUF-DU-PAPE, MAS de Daumas Gassac of the Languedoc, and Domaine de Trevallon of

Provence, prefer to follow organic principles outside any formal organization.

Germany saw the greatest increase in organic wine production in the 1980s. Ernst Loosen of the MOSEL-SAAR-RUWER is one of the more prominent growers to have adopted organic practices. In 1991, the VDP association of top German wine producers declared its intention to move towards more ecologically sound systems of production, indicating the extent to which the German consumer is concerned about pesticide sprays and high nitrate levels in water supplies.

Surprisingly, FASHION-conscious CALIFORNIA was relatively slow to embrace organic wine production, with the notable exception of Fetzer of MENDOCINO. Companies such as Wente Bros., Buena Vista, and Robert MONDAVI have incorporated elements of organic production into their vineyards and wineries.

Like Californians, with notable exceptions Australians have been slow to investigate the possibilities of organic wine production, even though the climate in most Australian wine regions is perfectly suited to organic viticulture.

Organic production methods are generally very labour intensive, and most organic wine is produced on a relatively small scale, but the interest shown by some of the wine industry's larger companies indicates that this is a subject which cannot be ignored. See also SUSTAINABLE VITICULTURE and BIODYNAMIC VITICULTURE.

A.G.W. & J.Ro.

Orion, modern vine crossing which produces crisp, aromatic wine not unlike SEYVAL BLANC, notably in England.

Orléanais, Vins de l', VDQS wines produced around the city of Orléans where the river Loire turns west, and Burgundian influence is evident in the choice of grape varieties. The pale and fragrant reds, and rosés, made from MEUNIER grapes, here called Gris Meunier, have many devotees in the French capital. Reds and rosés may also be made from Cabernet or Pinot Noir. Light white wines, which are very much in the minority, are made from Chardonnay and Pinot Gris, here called Auvernat Blanc and Gris respectively. About 10,000 cases of wine are made each year. See also LOIRE.

Ormeasco, local name for DOLCETTO on the north-western coast of Italy. See LIGURIA.

Ortega is popular as an OECHSLE booster in German wines, especially with the blenders of Rheinhessen. This crossing of Müller-Thurgau and Siegerrebe produces extremely full-flavoured wines that often lack acidity but can reach high must weights. Varietal wines are made, and QMP Ortega is a distinct possibility even in less good vintages, but a little goes a long way. Germany's total plantings have remained static since the late 1980s, half of them in Rheinhessen. The variety is also quite popular in ENGLAND, for obvious reasons.

Ortrugo, white grape grown in the hills around Piancenza in EMILIA, often blended with Malvasia.

Orvieto, dry, medium-dry, and sometimes—although increasingly rarely—sweet white wine produced near the medieval hill city of the same name, is one of Italy's historically renowned white wines and by far the most important DOC in UMBRIA. Orvieto Classico accounts for around two-thirds of the 140,000 hl/3.7 million gal produced in an average year.

Orvieto is based on 50 to 65 per cent of TREBBIANO grapes with additions of VERDELLO, GRECHETTO, DRUPEGGIO, and MALVASIA. It is overwhelmingly a dry wine, the sweet or amabile version accounting for less than five per cent of total production. Like most blends with a Trebbiano base produced in substantial quantities, dry Orvieto tends to be a bland, pedestrian product. The 1980s saw attempts to develop a richer, more luscious style of sweet Orvieto more dependent on NOBLE ROT. Some interesting wines resulted but they had to be marketed as VINO DA TAVOLA since the DOC rules for Orvieto did not foresee this development.

Commercial difficulties in the 1990s led many producers to conclude that a substantial modification of the formula for the Orvieto blend was needed, with a large increase in the overall percentage of Grechetto at the expense of Trebbiano and Drupeggio. The emergence of superior red wines from Orvieto, however, in many cases made from Sangiovese, Merlot, and Cabernet, and of lusciously sweet dessert wines based on INTERNATIONAL VARIETIES, have further complicated the picture, revealing a potential that has little relation to the wines which gave the zone its name and reputation.

D.T.

Ottavianello, Apulian name for the French red grape variety CINSAUT.

Ovens Valley, wine region in the Australian state of VICTORIA.

overcropping, a vine condition which reduces grape RIPENING and wine quality. The grapes of overcropped vines are typically lower in sugar, colour, and flavour, and have an increased PH. Wines made from such fruit are typically termed thin.

overripeness. See SURMATURITÉ.

O.W.C. stands for 'original wooden case' and is frequently used as a description in the sale of FINE WINE. See CASE.

oxidation, wine fault resulting from excessive exposure to OXYGEN (as opposed to aeration, which is deliberate, controlled exposure to oxygen). Wines spoiled by oxidation are said to be oxidized.

Oxidation is a threat as soon as the grape is crushed, which is why high-quality grapes are transported to the winery as fast as possible in shallow containers, and why field pressing stations sited as close as possible to the vineyard are increasingly common. When the grape is crushed, unless special precautions are taken to exclude oxygen, it immediately starts to react with the liberated juice compounds. The most obvious change is the browning of the juice, which is why oxidation is a much greater danger to white wines than to reds. Small amounts of SULPHUR DIOXIDE are therefore usually added at the time of crushing to counter oxidation.

Some wine-makers, however, deliberately encourage a certain amount of pre-fermentation oxidation of grape varieties such as Chardonnay in order to develop a range of flavours other than those associated with primary fruit AROMA. See WHITE-WINE-MAKING for more details.

Oxygen reacts with the PHENOLICS in both white and red wines. In whites, the COLOUR changes from light yellow to amber and ultimately brown, and at this last stage the quality of a table wine is usually seriously impaired. In reds, with their greater complement of phenolics, the colour change is much less apparent and a red wine can accommodate, and indeed benefit from, considerably greater exposure to oxygen than a white wine.

To produce table wines attractive in aroma and colour, and certainly those designed to be drunk young, the wine-maker generally restricts the exposure of must and wine to oxygen as much as is technically feasible (see PROTECTIVE WINE-MAKING).

Some wines, however, such as oloroso SHERRY, tawny PORT, and MADEIRA, owe their character to deliberate exposure to oxygen. And those who make wines of all sorts are constantly experimenting with various aspects of controlled oxidation, often motivated by the role played by oxygen in AGEING. See WHITE-WINE-MAKING and RED-WINE-MAKING.

The term MADERIZATION is sometimes used interchangeably with oxidation, although it should theoretically also involve excessive exposure to heat. A.D.W.

oxygen, colourless, odourless, tasteless gas that makes up nearly 21 per cent of the atmosphere. It is essential to all animal life forms and for many other living systems. Unlike NITROGEN, which makes up a much higher proportion of air and is inert, oxygen is highly reactive. Oxygen interacts with grape juice, must, and wine in both good ways (see BREATHING) and bad ways (see OXIDATION).

Modern wine-makers have equipment which allows most steps in making wine to exclude oxygen. One of the most effective has been the stainless-steel tank in which ULLAGE space can be filled with inert gas to exclude oxygen. Wooden vats, casks, and barrels are not sufficiently impervious for this blanketing technique. In older wineries, the oxidation of wine was minimized by frequent small additions of SULPHUR DIOXIDE, which, although it is needed less frequently as an antioxidant in modern wine-making, is still used to inhibit microbial activity. The aim of PROTECTIVE WINE-MAKING is to minimize oxidation, although see WHITE-WINE-MAKING for alternative approaches.

Oxygen plays a positive role during RED-WINE-MAKING, when the small doses of oxygen which the wine receives during the inevitable operations of filling, RACKING, and TOPPING UP deepen and stabilize COLOUR, soften and intensify flavour, and assist natural STABILIZATION and CLARIFICATION by encouraging the precipitation of the less stable phenolics.

See also OXIDATION and SERVING WINE.

A.D.W. & P.J.W.

Paarl, important wine district in SOUTH AFRICA.

Paarl Riesling. See CAPE RIESLING.

Pacherenc du Vic-Bilh, defiantly Gascon name for tangy white wines made in the MADIRAN region from a mixture of intensely local grape varieties and some imports: the local ARRUFIAC (Ruffiac), COURBU, and PETIT MANSENG, which must make up at least 60 per cent, Gros Manseng, and Sémillon and Sauvignon, which together may not represent more than 10 per cent of the blend. The deep-yellow wine can be either dry or sweet, depending on the VINTAGE, and tastes like a slightly paler version of JURANÇON, which is made further south, from a slightly different range of grape varieties. The sweet wines, made from raisined grapes, can last 10 years or so in bottle. The Plaimont co-operative has access to some excellent fruit.

Pacific Northwest, self-conscious region in the far north west of the UNITED STATES. A beautiful and unspoilt landscape and some fine regional products, including food and wine, have brought a sense of pride to the states of WASHINGTON, OREGON, and IDAHO. Comparisons with CALIFORNIA, the state to the immediate south, are habitually made.

packaging of wine most often involves bottling, but alternative packages for wine include BOXES, CANS, and CARTONS.

Padthaway, one of the cooler and more productive wine regions in SOUTH AUSTRALIA, part of the Limestone Coast zone and developed particularly by LINDEMANS.

Pagadebit, occasionally **Pagadebito,** another name for the BOMBINO BIANCO of Apulia, which is enjoying a certain revival in Romagna in north central Italy, and also grown across the Adriatic in the former Yugoslavia.

Païen, Swiss name for GEWÜRZTRAMINER.

Pais, possibly the most common grape variety in CHILE, identical to the MISSION grape of CALIFORNIA and MEXICO and a darker-skinned version of the CRIOLLA Chica of ARGENTINA. In Chile, where it is most common in the southern regions of Maule and Bío-Bío, it is also sometimes known as Negra Peruana. There were about 15,000 ha/37,000 acres in Chile in the late 1990s, about the same as total plantings of the country's most popular INTERNATIONAL VARIETY Cabernet Sauvignon. Pais may be identical to MONICA of Spain and Sardinia.

Pakistan. Vines in this Asian Islamic republic are dedicated to the production of TABLE GRAPES and DRYING GRAPES, but VINIFERA wine may occasionally be made from WILD VINES growing in the high valleys along the Silk Road.

palate, term used when describing TASTING as a process and an ability. It is generally used to describe the combined human tasting faculties in the mouth and, sometimes, NOSE. The impact of a wine on the mouth may be divided chronologically, and somewhat loosely, into its impact on the front, middle, and back palate. The word may also be used more generally as in describing a good taster as 'having a fine palate'.

Palette, miniature appellation of barely 20 ha/50 acres in PROVENCE in the hills east of Aix-en-Provence, created in 1948. A single property, Ch Simone, produces four bottles in every five, and for many years has been responsible for all the most serious wine of the appellation. FIELD BLENDS of southern vine varieties make extremely dense, long-lived reds, full-bodied rosés, and white wines which belie modern white-wine-making philosophy.

Palmela, DOC in southern Portugal. See TERRAS DO SADO.

Palombina. See PIEDIROSSO.

Palomino, white grape variety most closely associated with the making of SHERRY around JEREZ in southern Spain and generally declining in importance elsewhere. Palomino Fino has been adopted as the most suitable variety for sherry production, as distinct from the lowlier Palomino Basto or Palomino de Jerez once widely used.

The wine produced is, typically, low in both ACIDITY and fermentable sugars. This suits sherry producers but tends to make rather flabby, vapid table wines, unless substantially assisted by ACIDIFICATION.

In Spain, most Palomino Fino is grown in sherry country around Jerez but it is also being planted in CONDADO DE HUELVA. It is the main white variety in the CANARY ISLANDS.

Outside sherry country, as in France, it is often known as Listán, or Listán de Jerez. See LISTÁN for details of the declining fortunes of this variety in France.

The country with the most Palomino planted outside Spain is SOUTH AFRICA, where the variety, known as Fransdruif in Afrikaans and White French in English, has been losing ground fast but is still more widely planted than the popular PINOTAGE, for example. Much South African Palomino is distilled or used for blending into basic table wines.

California's acreage of the variety once wrongly identified as Golden Chasselas is also falling. It is found mainly in the SAN JOAQUIN VALLEY, where the wine produced is used chiefly for blending. In Australia, total plantings have fallen to fewer than 300 ha/740 acres, much of it grown in SOUTH AUSTRALIA and used for making sherry-style FORTIFIED wines. New Zealand has also grown a sur-

prising amount of Palomino considering its hardly ideal climate but these vines are being systematically replaced with more suitable varieties. Argentina has limited planting of the variety but PEDRO GIMÉNEZ predominates. CYPRUS has imported the Palomino vine because of its dependence on producing inexpensive copies of sherry.

Pamid, Bulgaria's most widely planted and least interesting indigenous grape variety producing rather thin, early-maturing red wines with few distinguishing marks other than a certain sweetness. It does not play a major role in bottles bound for export but, as Piros Szlanka, it is planted quite extensively in Hungary and to an even greater extent, as Roşioară, in Romania.

Pampanuto, also known as **Pampanino,** minor Apulian white grape which is invariably blended with more acid wine.

Pansa Blanca, synonym for the Spanish white grape variety XAREL-LO, used in ALELLA. A Pansa Rosado is also known.

Pantelleria, volcanic island at the extreme southern limit of Italy and closer in fact to Cape Bon in TUNISIA than to the southern coast of SICILY, to which it belongs administratively. Moscato di Pantelleria is one of Italy's finest dessert wines, made from the ZIBIBBO member of the MUSCAT family.

Moscato di Pantelleria comes in two different versions. The first is the regular Moscato, with a minimum alcohol level of eight per cent and 40 g/l of RESIDUAL SUGAR, although many of the better producers raisin the grapes for 10 to 12 days to achieve a higher total alcohol level and a greater quantity of residual sugar (see DRIED-GRAPE WINES); wines with a POTENTIAL ALCOHOL of 17.5 per cent can be called *vino naturalmente dolce*. The second version is lusher and richer and is true dessert style, which made the wine's reputation. This Moscato Passito di Pantelleria must have at least 14 per cent alcohol and 110 g/l residual sugar, although a current trend is to seek a more decadently sweet style, raisining the grapes for up to 30 days and arriving at close to 140 g/l of residual sugar. A PASSITO with a potential alcohol of 23.5 per cent and one year of ageing can be theoretically be called Extra, although the term is rarely encountered on labels.   D.T.

Pardina, undistinguished but widely planted white grape speciality of south-west Spain, especially in Badajoz province on the border with Portugal. It is planted on more land than any Spanish grape other than AIRÉN and produces rather ordinary, low-acid wines which oxidize easily.

Parellada, Catalan white grape variety widely used, with MACABEO and XAREL-LO, for the production of CAVA. It is the least planted of these three varieties in the PENEDÈS region most closely associated with these Spanish sparkling wines. It has been blended successfully with both Chardonnay and Sauvignon Blanc, most notably in some BARREL-AGED examples from TORRES. It is also an important variety in COSTERS DEL SEGRE.

Paris, capital of FRANCE, once the centre of a thriving wine region and still one of the few capital cities in which vineyards of any size may be found (although see also VIENNA). Today there are several suburban vineyards, and even a small vineyard in Montmartre, whose meagre produce is auctioned for charity.

Parker, Robert M., Jr. (1947–), influential American wine critic whose most obvious contribution to the literature of wine has been the concept of applying NUMBERS to wine. His SCORES, followed slavishly by some COLLECTORS and even more INVESTORS, have had a demonstrable effect on individual wine prices.

The first, complimentary issue of his bimonthly newsletter the *Wine Advocate* appeared in 1978. Although it was by no means the first American consumer wine newsletter, it was the first to use scores between 50 and 100 for individual wines quite so obviously. This system was easily and delightedly grasped by Americans familiar with high-school grades, even though Parker himself urges caution, asking readers to use the numerical ratings 'only to enhance and complement the thorough tasting notes, which are my primary means of communicating my judgments to you'. Wine salesmen have been less circumspect and use Parker's ratings mercilessly in their merchandising.

With a few notable and sometimes voluble exceptions, most agree that Parker, who has initially both under- and overrated some vintages, is a gifted taster and diligent reporter. But his success has won a degree of power over the wine market so great that it is dangerous, in that such a high proportion of producers, particularly red-wine producers, seem deliberately to be adapting the style of their wines to suit this one, compelling palate.

Paso Robles, very large California wine region and AVA on the inland side of the coastal mountains. See SAN LUIS OBISPO.

Passetoutgrains. See BOURGOGNE PASSE-TOUTGRAINS.

passing the port. One of the wine trade's most cherished traditions is the rule that PORT, particularly a decanter of vintage port, must be passed round a table from the right to the left of diners. No single satisfactory explanation has ever been advanced, although so fiercely held is the custom that a miniature railway was constructed to transport decanters across an inconvenient fireplace in the Senior Common Room of New College Oxford.

passito, Italian term for DRIED-GRAPE WINE.

pasteurization, process of heating foods, including wines, to a temperature high enough to kill all micro-organisms such as YEAST and bacteria. It is named after Louis Pasteur, the French scientist who discovered that micro-organisms were alive and the cause of much wine spoilage.

Heat sterilization techniques have improved greatly since the early versions of pasteurization, which often resulted in burnt or cooked flavours in wines treated. The techniques are relatively brutal, however, and are used only on ordinary wines which have no potential for improvement after BOTTLE AGEING.   A.D.W.

Pauillac, small port and communal appellation in the Médoc district of Bordeaux which has the unparalleled distinction of boasting three of the five first growths ranked in Bordeaux's most famous CLASSIFICATION within its boundaries—Chx LAFITE, LATOUR, and MOUTON-ROTHSCHILD—as well as a bevy of other CLASSED GROWTHS rivalling them (and each other) with increasing insistence.

This, however, is Cabernet Sauvignon country *par excellence*, and while there is considerable variation between different properties' TERROIRS and wine-making policies and capabilities, certain expressions recur in Pauillac tasting notes: cassis (blackcurrant), cedar, and cigar box (the last two sometimes a reflection of the top-quality French oak cooperage which the selling prices of Pauillac permit). A high proportion of the Médoc's most concentrated wines are produced here.

More than 1,100 ha/2,700 acres of vines qualify for the appellation in an almost continuous strip between Pauillac's boundary with ST-JULIEN to the south and ST-ESTÈPHE to the north, separated from the waters of the Gironde estuary by only a few hundred metres of *palus* too marshy for serious viticulture. This strip of vines, 3 km/2 miles wide and more than 6 km long, is dedicated to the production of the world's most famously long-lived red wine. As elsewhere in the Médoc, the layers of GRAVEL here provide the key to wine quality, offering excellent DRAINAGE, aided by the almost imperceptibly undulating topography and a series of *jalles* or streams running water off the gravelly plateau and into the Gironde.

The stars of the northern sector of Pauillac are undoubtedly the two Rothschild properties Chx Lafite and Mouton-Rothschild. Clustered around them are their satellite properties, whose wines benefit from the first-class wine-making ability of their owners. Ch Duhart-Milon-Rothschild is Lafite's fourth growth, made in the town of Pauillac. The fifth growths Ch Clerc-Milon and Ch d'Armailhac are made, to an often very high standard, close to Mouton itself. Other classed growths on this plateau just a stream away from St-Estèphe are the fifth growths Chx Pontet-Canet and the generally much less exciting Pédesclaux.

In the extreme south of the appellation, first growth Ch Latour and its near neighbours the two second growths Pichon-Lalande and Pichon-Longueville made considerable investments in their vineyards and *chais* in the late 80s and early 90s. Both Pichons have demonstrated that, just like first growth Latour, they are capable of making sublime wine at the St-Julien end of Pauillac.

In the hinterland of this southern extreme of Pauillac are neighbouring fifth growths Chx Batailley and Haut-Batailley, whose wines can challenge those of fifth growth Ch Grand-Puy-Lacoste to the immediate north, which is run impeccably by the Borie family and can offer some of Pauillac's best value. A dozen of the 18 fifth growths are in Pauillac, and none has been more successful than the Cazes family's flamboyantly styled Ch Lynch-Bages, whose standing and fame suggest a considerably higher ranking. Chx Lynch-Moussas, Croizet-Bages, and Grand-Puy-Ducasse have rarely merited the limelight, although Grand-Puy-Ducasse was extensively renovated in the 1980s. Ch Haut-Bages-Libéral, between Chx

Latour and Lynch-Bages, has produced fine vintages.

Two of Pauillac's most distinctive products do not feature in the 1855 classification. Les Forts de Latour, the SECOND WINE of Ch Latour, is regularly one of its most successful wines (and it is priced as such), while the CO-OPERATIVE at Pauillac is a particularly important one, selling some of its considerable produce under the name La Rose Pauillac.

See MÉDOC and BORDEAUX.

pays. French for country. See VIN DE PAYS.

Pécharmant, expanding red-wine appellation within the BERGERAC district in SOUTH WEST FRANCE. The wines are some of Périgord's longest-lived reds, made from Bordeaux grape varieties, especially MERLOT. Little of it escapes the region, however. Within the zone, some sweet white wine is made in the much smaller ROSETTE appellation.

Pecorino, Marches vine speciality of Italy's east coast making ever-decreasing quantities of firm, characterful white wine.

Pedernã, Vinho Verde synonym for the light-skinned ARINTO grape.

Pedro Giménez, important white grape variety in ARGENTINA, where, along with the coarse and declining CRIOLLA and CEREZA, it is one of the vines underpinning the country's substantial production of everyday wine for domestic consumption.

Pedro Luis, white grape of Andalucia called False Pedro in South Africa.

Pedro Ximénez, Pedro Jiménez, or just Pedro, white grape variety traditionally associated with ANDALUCÍA in southern Spain but now much less common than the PALOMINO Fino in the JEREZ region for sherry production. Pedro Ximénez is found all over Andalucía, VALENCIA, and EXTREMADURA. Because it is capable of producing very ripe grapes, it is particularly popular with MÁLAGA producers, some of whom depend on grapes from the MONTILLA-MORILES region, where it is by far the dominant grape variety for the sherry-like wines produced there. The other common fate of these thin-skinned grapes, which were traditionally dried in the sun to produce wines to sweeten fortified blends, is to produce somewhat flabby, neutral-flavoured dry table wines, although some rich, raisiny, sweet fortified wine called Pedro Ximénez, or simply 'PX', is bottled. The variety is also grown on Spain's CANARY ISLANDS off the Atlantic coast.

In Australia, Pedro Ximénez was once quite widely grown but its total area had fallen to just over 200 ha/500 acres by 1997. Although used mainly for inexpensive blends there, it has been known to shine, most particularly in BOTRYTIZED form to produce the rich, deep golden McWilliam's Pedro Sauterne (*sic*) made near Griffith in NEW SOUTH WALES.

Pelaverga, pale, rare, red grape of Piedmont making slightly fizzy, strawberry-flavoured wines.

Peloursin, obscure southern French red grape variety of which DURIF was a selection. There are some Peloursin vines, with Durif, in north-east Victoria in Australia. In the late 1990s, DNA 'FINGERPRINTING' identified the vines known as PETITE SIRAH in California as a FIELD BLEND of Peloursin, some true SYRAH, and mainly Durif, which turns out to be a crossing of Peloursin and Syrah.

Pemberton-Warren, wine region in the South West Australia zone of WESTERN AUSTRALIA.

Penedès, often spelt Penedés, the largest and most important denominated wine zone in CATALONIA in north-east Spain, producing an innovative range of wines. The PHYLLOXERA louse reached Penedès in 1887, by which time José Raventós had laid the foundations of CODORNÍU and the CAVA industry. Vineyards that had once produced strong, semi-fortified reds were uprooted in favour of white grapes for sparkling wine. Cava has subsequently developed a separate nationally organized DO.

Penedès underwent a second radical transformation in the 1960s and 1970s largely because of Miguel Torres Carbo and his son Miguel A. TORRES, wine producers in the heart of the region at Vilafranca del Penedès. They were among the first in Spain to install TEMPERATURE CONTROL and stainless-steel tanks. Miguel Torres, Jr., who studied OENOLOGY in France, also imported and experimented with such revolutionary vine varieties as Cabernet Sauvignon, Chardonnay, Sauvignon Blanc, Merlot, Pinot Noir, Riesling, and Gewürztraminer, which were planted alongside and blended with native varieties. Other growers followed in the Torres family footsteps and Penedès was in the 1980s one of the most dynamic and varied wine regions in Spain.

Penedès rises from the Mediterranean like a series of steps and divides into three distinct zones. Bajo, or Low, Penedès, where vineyards have been either abandoned or replanted with GARNACHA, CARIÑENA, or MONASTRELL, making sturdy reds. The second zone, Medio Penedès, is the most productive part of the region, providing much of the base wine for the sparkling-wine industry at San Sadurni de Noya (see CAVA). MACABEO, XAREL-LO, and PARELLADA are grown for Cava, together with increasing quantities of Chardonnay and red varieties such as TEMPRANILLO (often called here by its Catalan name Ull de Llebre) and Cabernet Sauvignon. Penedès Superior is the coolest part of the region where some of the best white grapes are grown. The native PARELLADA is the most important variety here, but Riesling, Muscat of Alexandria, Gewürztraminer, and Chardonnay are also successful.

By the late 1990s, however, the region was failing to confirm the high hopes placed in its red wines, which were increasingly overshadowed by those of PRIORAT.

R.J.M. & V. de la S.

Penfolds, the best-known, and largest, component part of Australia's dominant wine company SOUTHCORP responsible for a wide range of wines made from fruit grown all over South Australia and, sometimes, beyond. For more than 100 years, Penfolds, in common with most Australian wineries, concentrated on producing FORTIFIED wines and brandy, much of which was exported to the UK. In 1950, Max Schubert, then chief wine-maker, pioneered Bordeaux wine-making techniques in Australia. His ambition was to create a red that would rival the finest wines of Bordeaux for both quality and the potential to improve with age. This he achieved with **Penfolds Grange**, now widely acknowledged to be Australia's greatest wine. The intense fruit character combined with excellent use of wood gave Grange great potential as an ageing wine. Fine vintages of Grange improve for up to 30 years and beyond, and the wine has become the most decorated in Australian history.

A string of award-winning red wines from Penfolds followed. Of particular note is Bin 707 Cabernet Sauvignon. In April 1998, Penfolds released its long-awaited super-premium white wine, designed to take its place alongside Grange. Called Yattarna, it is a blend of Adelaide Hills and McLaren Vale Chardonnay, but the future regional base may well vary significantly from one vintage to the next.

S.A. & J.H.

pepper. See TASTING TERMS.

Pérignon, Dom (1639–1715), Benedictine monk who has gone down in history as 'the man who invented champagne'. The title is the stuff of fairy-tales: the transition from still to sparkling wine was an evolutionary process rather than a dramatic discovery on the part of one man. The life of Dom Pérignon was in fact devoted to improving the still wines of Champagne, and he deserves his place in the history books for that reason. Dom Pérignon introduced many practices that survive in the process of modern wine production, among them severe pruning, low yields, and careful harvesting. He also experimented to a great extent with the BLENDING process, and was one of the first to blend the produce of many different vineyards.

See also CHAMPAGNE.

S.A.

Periquita, Portuguese word meaning 'parakeet' applied to both a usefully versatile red grape variety grown all over southern Portugal (see CASTELÃO FRANCÊS) and a branded red wine from José Maria da FONSECA Successors.

Perlan, traditional name of the CHASSELAS grape in the canton of Geneva in SWITZERLAND, rarely seen on labels now that the name Chasselas de Genève is preferred.

perlant, French term for a wine that is only slightly SPARKLING. **Perlwein** is the German equivalent. See FIZZINESS.

Perle is, like WÜRZER, a GERMAN CROSSING of Gewürztraminer and Müller-Thurgau; in this case Gewürztraminer's rosy-hued grapes have been inherited but its extravagant perfume is more muted. It is declining in popularity but has been particularly useful in Franken.

Pernand-Vergelesses, village in the Côte de Beaune district of Burgundy's CÔTE D'OR producing red and white wines. The former, made from Pinot Noir, are somewhat angular in style and do not always appear fully ripe as Pernand is set back from the main sweep of the Côte and many of its vineyards have a westerly, even north-western exposition, which can retard RIPENING.

Pernand chose to suffix the name of its best red-wine vineyard, east-facing Les Vergelesses, which it shares with neighbouring Savigny-lès-Beaune, although the most sought-after wines are the whites on the Pernand side of the hill of Corton (see ALOXE-CORTON). Seventeen of the 72 ha/178 acres entitled to the GRAND CRU appellation Corton-Charlemagne lie within Pernand-Vergelesses. White Pernand wines have a hard but attractive flinty character which develops well during BOTTLE AGEING. BOURGOGNE ALIGOTÉ from this area is said to resemble white Pernand-Vergelesses as it ages; and white Pernand to approach the quality of Corton-Charlemagne.

The most successful producer based in Pernand-Vergelesses is Bonneau du Martray, one of the top names in Corton-Charlemagne.

J.T.C.M.

Perricone, SICILIAN red grape variety planted on hardly more than 1,000 ha/2,500 acres of the island. Soft varietal wines are sometimes called by its synonym Pignatello.

Perrum, Portuguese white grape variety producing rather ordinary wines in the Alentejo which is probably the same as Spain's sherry grape PALOMINO.

Peru, the first country in SOUTH AMERICA to have encouraged systematic viticulture, has about 12,000 ha/30,000 acres planted with vines, split almost equally between the wine and TABLE GRAPE industries. Almost all vines are on the central coast around Pisco and, particularly, Ica to the south, where wine-making and distillation investment is concentrated. Winter temperatures are so high that two crops a year can be harvested from the same plant (see TROPICAL VITICULTURE). Summer temperatures are also high, and rainfall is low, but IRRIGATION water is readily available from the Andes.

Vine varieties planted include ALBILLO, ALICANTE BOUSCHET, BARBERA, Cabernet Sauvignon, Grenache, MALBEC, MOSCATEL, Sauvignon Blanc, TORONTEL, as well as various table grapes.

Pessac-Léognan, important Bordeaux red- and dry-white-wine appellation created in 1987 for the most celebrated part of the GRAVES district immediately south of the city (and often still referred to as Graves). It includes all of the properties named in the 1959 CLASSIFICATION of Graves, and many other fine châteaux too. In all, about 990 ha/2,400 acres of vineyard within Pessac-Léognan produce red wine, and the total area devoted to white wine grapes had reached 280 ha by 1996.

Soils here have particularly good DRAINAGE, being made up of gravel terraces of very different eras. The ENCÉPAGEMENT for red wines is very similar to that of the MÉDOC to the immediate north, being mainly Cabernet Sauvignon grapes with some Merlot and Cabernet Franc, but the wines can be quite different. It is not fanciful to imagine that the best wines of Pessac-Léognan have a distinct aroma that reminds some tasters of minerals, some of smoke, others even of warm bricks. Ch Haut-Brion is the most obvious exponent of this genre (see HAUT-BRION for details of the red and white wines of this property and those of La Mission-Haut-Brion). Other current over-achievers include Chx Pape-Clément and Smith Haut-Lafitte, while Chx de Fieuzal, de France, and Haut-Bailly can provide some of Bordeaux's better red-wine value.

White wines made here can be some of the most characterful dry white wines in the world, made from Sauvignon (which must comprise at least a quarter of the blend) and Sémillon grapes grown generally on the lighter, sandier parts of the vineyard, and often produced with considerable recourse to BARREL FERMENTATION and BARREL MATURATION. The most admired, Domaine de Chevalier and Chx Haut-Brion and Laville-Haut-Brion, can develop in bottle over decades, and the dry white wines of Ch Malartic-Lagravière, for example, demand a decade in bottle at the very least. More recent, and more modern if still long-lasting, fine white wines are made at Ch Couhins-LURTON.

See BORDEAUX.

pétillant, French term for a lightly sparkling wine, somewhere between PERLANT and MOUS-SEUX.

petit, 'small' in French and therefore often encountered in wine and grape names.

Petit Courbu. See COURBU.

Petite Sirah, name common in both North and South America for a black grape variety which was identified in the 1970s as DURIF, sometimes spelt Duriff, a nearly extinct French vine variety. DNA 'FINGERPRINTING' techniques suggested in the late 1990s, however, that the name was applied in California vineyards to no fewer than four different vines: Durif; true SYRAH of the Rhône; Peloursin, an obscure French vine of which Durif was a selection; and a Peloursin × Durif crossing.

Petite Sirah is relatively important in a wide range of warm wine regions, especially in both California and South America, although it has been declining in California.

Although Petite Sirah has been valued as a relatively tannic, well-coloured blending partner for blowsier Zinfandels, it has been somewhat eclipsed by the fashionable true French Syrah. It has nevertheless carved out a place for itself in California, for it makes dark, well-balanced, sturdily tannic red wine of agreeable if not highly distinctive flavour. As such, it has been essential as a backbone for some everyday red blends. Sonoma and Mendocino counties seem to grow Petite Sirah best, especially the dry-farmed, elderly HILLSIDE VINEYARDS within the Russian River drainage. Louis J. Foppiano, Louis M. Martini, and Parducci Cellars have long produced polished, supple varietal examples which benefit from a few years' bottle age and which in the best vintages can be magnificent after 20 years. Ridge, Guenoc, Christopher Creek, and Stag's Leap Winery take the varietal wine to its dark, tannic limits.

In 1990, Argentina had about the same area of Petite Sirah planted as California had then, more than 1,400 ha/3,500 acres, often misleadingly calling it Sirah. It is also well known in Brazil's semi-tropical climate as Petite Sirah or Petite Syrah and has produced respectable sturdy red in Mexico.

Petit Manseng, top-quality white grape variety originally from SOUTH WEST FRANCE which is the superior form of MANSENG. Petit Manseng, which is much more suitable for sweet wines than GROS MANSENG, has particularly small, thick-skinned berries which yield very little juice but can withstand lingering on the vine until well into autumn so that the sugar is concentrated by the shrivelling process known as *passerillage*.

The variety is now being planted in the LANGUEDOC and California, already indicating that Petit Manseng is following VIOGNIER in terms of popularity with those groups who follow vine-variety FASHION.

See also JURANÇON and PACHERENC DU VIC-BILH.

Petit Pineau, synonym for the ARBOIS vine variety.

Petit Rhin, synonym for the great RIESLING grape of Germany used mainly in Switzerland.

Petit Rouge, fine red grape variety indigenous to the Valle d'AOSTA.

petits châteaux, the French term meaning literally 'small castles' has a very specific meaning in the BORDEAUX wine region. These thousands of properties are modest not so much in their extent as in their reputation and price. A CLASSED GROWTH is emphatically not a petit château, no matter how few hectares it encompasses. The greatest concentration of petits châteaux is in the appellations BORDEAUX AC, BOURG, and BLAYE, although they are found throughout the region. Some of Bordeaux's best wine value is to be found at the most conscientious petits châteaux.

See also CHÂTEAU.

Petit Verdot is one of Bordeaux's classic black grape varieties, no longer planted in any great quantity but enjoying a small revival in some quality-conscious vineyards. The vine shares Cabernet Sauvignon's thick skins and is also capable of yielding concentrated, tannic wines rich in colour. When it ripens fully, which in most Bordeaux properties happens only in riper vintages, its rich, age-worthy, sometimes rather spicy wines can make a valuable contribution to some of the best wines of the Médoc. Its inconveniently late ripening encouraged many producers to abandon it in the 1960s and 1970s so that total French plantings were just over 300 ha/740 acres in 1988. It is enjoying a limited revival in California too, mainly in Napa and Sonoma, and used mainly as an ingredient in MERITAGE blends.

The variety known as Verdot in Chile is probably Petit Verdot, but the Verdot of Argentina's Mendoza may well be the coarser, probably unrelated, Gros Verdot variety.

Pétrus, Château, in the heart of the small Pomerol plateau, is the most famous wine of POMEROL, and today the most expensive in BORDEAUX.

The 11.5 hectares are planted with 95 per cent Merlot and 5 per cent Cabernet Franc.

Although it won a gold medal at the 1878 Paris International Exhibition, and the London-based Wine Society listed the 1893, Pétrus received little international attention until the remarkable, tiny crop of 1945, and the much more widely distributed 1947. Its exceptional concentration of colour, bouquet, and richness of flavour derives from a pocket of clay in the middle of the vineyard and the subsoil which affords exceptionally good

DRAINAGE. Average production is 2,500 to 3,500 cases. However, its fame is largely due to M. Jean-Pierre MOUEIX of the Libourne merchants, who took over the sole distribution of Pétrus in 1945. The property is managed by Jean-Pierre Moueix's son Christian. The limited size of the property means that all the grapes can be harvested, at optimum ripeness, in half a day. Fermentation vessels are neither wood nor stainless steel, but mundane cement.

There is no official CLASSIFICATION of Pomerol, but Pétrus is unofficially recognized as a PREMIER CRU. It tends to fetch a much higher price than any other red bordeaux (although see Le PIN), and at AUCTION achieves even higher prices relative to the rest.   E.P.-R.

Pfalz, until 1992 known as the **Rheinpfalz,** is an important wine region in southern GERMANY in terms of both quantity and quality. In some of the villages of the district in the southern half, Bereich Südliche Weinstrasse, viticulture has expanded greatly in the last 25 years and vines occupy nearly all the available land. To the north of Neustadt in Bereich Mittelhaardt/Deutsche Weinstrasse, there are vineyards with internationally known names, thanks to wine estates with such historic reputations as Bassermann-Jordan, Bürklin-Wolf, and von Buhl, but the quality of some of the wine-making elsewhere in the Pfalz is so high that Ruppertsberg, Forst, Deidesheim, Wachenheim, Bad Dürkheim, and Kallstadt no longer have a monopoly of the best wines. The Pfalz has become one of the most exciting regions for the wine lover to visit. The Deutsche Weinstrasse, the German wine route, was set up in 1935 to link some 40 villages on a north–south axis, and to strengthen the regional identity.

Bereich Südliche Weinstrasse has a reputation for being dedicated to a high yield of indifferent-quality grapes. This still applies to producers who supply the market for cheap wine in bulk, but it is no longer true for the district as a whole. As in neighbouring RHEINHESSEN, a considerable quantity of Pfalz wines are bottled by merchants outside the region who supply basic wine to supermarkets at home and abroad, and much of this wine originates in Bereich Südliche Weinstrasse. Where there are high yields in Germany there are MÜLLER-THURGAU vines and in Bereich Südliche Weinstrasse this variety covers 25 per cent of the vineyards in production. KERNER accounts for 13 per cent and MORIO-MUSKAT, a vine with a high yield, 5 per cent. The classic RIESLING is planted on about 12 per cent of total vineyard. There is also a wide range of the GERMAN CROSSINGS introduced in the 1960s and 1970s.

On the best estates in Bereich Mittelhaardt/ Deutsche Weinstrasse, Riesling plays an important and increasing part, sometimes as the only vine. The SCHEUREBE vine reaches a peak of quality in this northern district of the Pfalz that is seldom matched elsewhere in the world, and in response to a strong demand on the home market for red wine, Spätburgunder (PINOT NOIR) is rapidly expanding.

Pfalz Riesling had a more pronounced flavour in the late 1970s, with a quite unmistakable taste of the soil. The full, slightly oxidized style (see OXIDATION) has been largely replaced by a more elegant, almost RHEINGAU-like balance. The acidity is higher than in the past, the flavour is long, and, of course, many of the best Pfalz Rieslings are dry. Across the region, over a third of all wines are now dry (TROCKEN). Pfalz wines have the advantage to a non-German palate of more BODY than most dry wines from the northern regions, and more alcohol. Because of its climate, the Pfalz is ideally placed to produce the types of wine which the market needs. On the one hand there are stylish Rieslings and Scheurebes with high ACIDITY, and on the other an increasing supply of interesting wines from the Burgunder, or PINOT, family. On some estates, Ruländer (PINOT GRIS) grapes are placed in two buckets at the harvest: those grapes showing signs of NOBLE ROT produce a full, slightly dark coloured, deep-flavoured wine, and those from the non-BOTRYTIZED grapes produce a lighter, lively, clean dry wine which is sold under the name Grauburgunder.

Good Rheinpfalz Spätburgunders resemble a cross between the soft wines of the past with low TANNINS and a red BURGUNDY. Their yields are higher than those of Burgundy but many of the vines are young and at their most productive phase. This may account for a certain lack of complexity. A natural ALCOHOLIC STRENGTH of over 13 per cent is not unusual, and if the structure of the wine often betrays the cooler climate in which the grapes are grown, perhaps this is the start of a modern Pfalz style of Spätburgunder. It is based on a clean, dry, fruity flavour without any of the farmyard smells that can come from partially rotten grapes. Extreme oaky flavours from new wood, which mask the individuality of wine, are being muted as BARREL MATURATION is mastered; in some cases it has been replaced by storage in larger casks.

The older style of light Pfalz red wine, sometimes a little sweet, is still widely represented by PORTUGIESER, which covered about 10 per cent of the region in 1997. This undemanding vine is normally allowed to produce a high yield of reddish wine, but, on the rare occasions when the crop is limited, the improvement in concentration and quality is considerable. The success of the DORNFELDER crossing is particularly remarkable. Since 1990 the number of vines has nearly doubled. Even growers who lack the technical equipment of a red-wine specialist can produce from Dornfelder a pleasant BEAUJOLAIS-style wine. However, when MALOLACTIC FERMENTATION and OAK maturation come into play, Dornfelder yields stylish wines with depth, greater length of flavour, and ageing potential, rather like a good DOLCETTO or CHINON.

There is a handful of 20 or 25 outstandingly good sites, but of the 333 individual vineyards in the Pfalz, many have no distinguishing characteristics and therefore hardly justify the use of their name on wine labels. Where some hitherto little-known villages are becoming more familiar, it is through the achievements of individual wine-makers. Amongst the up-and-coming village names, judged in this way, are Laumersheim, Grosskarlbach, Freinsheim, and Herxheim in the north of the region, and Burrweiler, Siebeldingen, Birkweiler, and Leinsweiler in the south.

An increasing amount of Pfalz wine was made into sparkling wine in the 1990s (see SEKT).

Of the roughly 10,000 vine-growers in the region, at least 60 per cent deliver their grapes to co-operative cellars, producers' associations, or merchants' cellars. Some growers own small parcels of land in the best-known sites of Bereich Mittelhaardt/Deutsche Weinstrasse, where the standards and reputation of the local CO-OPERATIVES are high. In Bereich Südliche Weinstrasse, the co-operative cellars are known for their pleasant, true-to-type, medium-price, drier wines, sold under grape names. This is the style of wine for those who wish to progress from LIEBFRAUMILCH and yet know not where to go. An indication of the success of the best co-operative cellars is the growing percentages of wine that they sell in bottle, rather than on the depressed bulk-wine market. Much wine is sold directly to the consumer.   I.J. & K.B.S.

pH, a scale of measurement of the concentration of the effective, active ACIDITY in a solution and an important statistic, of relevance to how vines grow, how grapes ripen, and how wine tastes, looks, and lasts. Low values of pH indicate high concentrations of acidity and the tart or sour taste that occurs in lemon juice, for example. Values near 7 are effectively neutral; drinking waters have pH values near 7. Values between 7 and 14 are found in basic or alkaline solutions such as caustic or washing soda. Grape must and wine are acidic, with pHs generally between 3 and 4.

The pH range of most wines is between 2.9 and 4.2. Wines with low pHs taste very tart while those with high pHs taste flat, or 'flabby'. Wines whose pH is between 3.2 and 3.5 not only tend to taste refreshingly rather than piercingly acid, they are also more resistant to harmful bacteria, age better, and have a clearer, brighter COLOUR. Wines with pH values higher than this suffer from tasting flat, looking dull, and also from being more susceptible to bacterial attack.   A.D.W., B.G.C., & P.J.W.

phenolics, sometimes called **polyphenolics** or **polyphenols**, very large group of highly reactive chemical compounds of which phenol (C_6H_5OH) is the basic building block. These include many natural colour pigments such as the ANTHOCYANINS of fruit and dark-skinned grapes, most natural vegetable TANNINS such as occur in grapes, and many FLAVOUR COMPOUNDS.

It is in its high phenolics content that red wine is distinguished from white, and it is thought that it may well be the anti-oxidative properties of phenolics which reduce the incidence of heart disease among those who consume moderate amounts of red wine. See HEALTH. See also TASTING TERMS.

Phoenix, one of the most successful disease-resistant varieties, a crossing of SEYVAL BLANC and BACCHUS which produces attractive, herbaceous, elderflower-scented wine in England.

photosynthesis, a biochemical reaction which combines water and atmospheric carbon dioxide using the energy of the sun to form sugars in plants, including vines. Important in this process are the green chlorophyll pigments in leaves which capture the sun's energy. Photosynthesis is the essential first step in the wine-making process, as the sugars formed in photosynthesis, along with other chemical products derived from sugar, are transported to grape berries, and eventually fermented into ALCOHOL to produce wine.

Photosynthesis is affected by environmental and plant factors, all of which have an effect on grape RIPENING and hence wine quality. Light, temperature, and WATER STRESS are the three most important climatic controls. A general rule is that photosynthesis is enhanced by sunny conditions and mild temperatures. These are the conditions which are known to give maximal sugar concentration in grapes and, conventionally, the best wine quality.
                                                              R.E.S.

phylloxera. This small yellow root-feeding aphid has probably had a more damaging impact on wine production than any other vine pest, or any vine disease. It attacks only grapevines, and kills vines by attacking their roots. For many years after it first invaded Europe there was no known cure.

The effects of phylloxera were first noted in France in 1863, just as the country was recovering from another great scourge of 19th-century European viticulture: oidium, or powdery mildew, which was first noted in 1847. Like powdery mildew, the phylloxera louse was an unwelcome import from America which devastated European vineyards until appropriate control measures were found. Phylloxera invasion had a major social and economic impact, involving national governments and local committees, and requiring international scientific collaboration. For a while, the very existence of the French wine industry was threatened. Eventually ROOTSTOCK use became the established method for the control of phylloxera.

Phylloxera is now widespread around the world, and few regions are free from the pest, although these include parts of Australia (on which a strict quarantine is imposed), parts of China, Chile, Argentina, India, Pakistan, and Afghanistan, and some Mediterranean islands such as Crete, Cyprus, and Rhodes. There are also small sandy vineyards in otherwise affected wine regions (see BOLLINGER and COLARES) which have never been affected by phylloxera either because of isolation or because of the soil composition.

physiological ripeness

For much of the late 20th century, phylloxera has not been regarded as a serious problem, either because it was not known in a region, or because a wide range of rootstocks are available which are suited to different varieties, soil, and climate conditions along with tolerance to other pests. About 85 per cent of all the world's vineyards were estimated in 1990 to be grafted onto rootstocks presumed to be resistant to phylloxera.

Phylloxera was noted in the 1980s, however, on ungrafted vines in parts of Greece, England, New Zealand, Australia, Oregon, and, most dramatically, on grafted vines in California. The widely used rootstock AXR1 was found to offer insufficient phylloxera tolerance, and a significant proportion of grafted vineyards in Napa and Sonoma succumbed to phylloxera and were replanted in the 1990s.   R.E.S.

physiological ripeness, or sometimes **physiological maturity,** fashionable terms loosely used by some New World wine-makers to contrast with RIPENESS measured by the normal analytical measures of MUST WEIGHT, ACIDITY, and PH. The terminology is imprecise because all grapes undergo physiological ripening irrespective of how it is assessed.

The concept includes aspects of the berry's maturation which are not measured (but could often be) and which describe changes in a ripening grape berry important to eventual quality. These include skin colour, berry texture including skin and pulp texture, seed colour and ripening, flavour, and phenolic changes. There is a notion that great wines are made when the harvest date coincides with the near optimum values of many of these parameters.

A likely important aspect of physiological ripeness which is overlooked in conventional RIPENING considerations is that of the condition of the grape skin. There is empirical evidence that wine quality can be affected, even though other aspects of fruit condition seem similar.   Z.L.

Piacentini, Colli, diverse DOC zone centred on the hills of Piacenza in Emilia in north central Italy. See EMILIA-ROMAGNA.

Piave, mainly red-wine DOC in the hinterland of Venice in north-east Italy. This is overwhelmingly Merlot territory, with some Cabernet (principally Franc); VERDUZZO and TOCAI account for the bulk of the white-wine pro-

duction. The wines, at their best, are fruity, fresh, and unpretentiously appealing. See also RABOSO, another local vine variety and varietal DOC.   D.T.

picking grapes is apparently romantic but in practice back-breaking work for humans. See also HARVEST.

Picolit, fashionable and audaciously priced sweet white VARIETAL wine made in the FRIULI region of north-east Italy, one of the more commercially successful of the DRIED-GRAPE WINES. The grape variety derives its name from the small, or *piccolo*, quantity of grapes it produces.

Some better estates still make the wine much as it was in the past, with the bunches, harvested late in mid October, left to dry and raisin on mats before pressing. Other producers have opted for a late-harvest style, with the grapes left even longer in the vineyard, picked with higher MUST WEIGHTS, but not raisined after picking. The use of small oak BARREL MATURATION is an innovation introduced in the mid 1980s. Although Picolit is generally considered a dessert wine, it is not a dessert wine of the luscious sort and is best considered a VINO DA MEDITAZIONE, a wine to be sipped alone in order to appreciate its delicate floral aromas and its light sweetness which suggests peaches and apricots.

The wine became the object of a cult enthusiasm in Italy in the late 1960s and 1970s, fetching extremely high prices that non-Italian connoisseurs find difficult to understand or justify; the Picolit boom has also resulted in frequent and illegal blending of the wine with the more neutral VERDUZZO, which has stretched the quantities available but has done no service to the wine's reputation.   D.T.

Picpoul or Piquepoul is an ancient Languedoc grape variety that is commonly encountered in Blanc, Noir, and Gris versions with the white being the most planted today, although they have frequently been mixed in the vineyard in their long history in the Midi. Piquepoul means 'lip-stinger', signifying the high acidity of its must.

Picpoul Noir produces alcoholic, richly scented, but almost colourless wine that is best drunk young. Although it is allowed as a minor ingredient in CHÂTEAUNEUF-DU-PAPE and Coteaux du LANGUEDOC, there were only 200 ha/500 acres left in all of France by the end of the 1980s.

Picpoul Blanc, on the other hand, of which 500 ha remained then, has been experiencing a small revival of interest. It can provide usefully crisp blending material in the Languedoc but it is most commonly encountered as PICPOUL DE PINET.

Picpoul de Pinet, one of the named CRUS of Coteaux du LANGUEDOC producing white wine exclusively from PICPOUL Blanc grapes. This curious speciality in the deep south of France, one of the country's few VARIETALLY named AC wines, has in the post-modern age of vinification attracted some new interest. Millions of tourists each summer see the well-signposted CO-OPERATIVE at Pinet, the most important producer of this distinctive wine and clearly visible from the main *autoroute* along the Mediterranean coast. The co-operative at Pomerols and some individual domaines such as Félines Jourdan have usually managed to coax a more interesting green-gold, lemon-flavoured wine out of the grape than this particular production centre, however.

Pic St-Loup, one of the most promising named CRUS within the Coteaux du LANGUEDOC in southern France and the least dependent on CARIGNAN grapes or CO-OPERATIVES. About 5,000 ha/12,300 acres of vineyard could in theory produce appellation wine, but only a proportion is planted with the Syrah, Grenache, and Mourvèdre vines which must comprise 90 per cent of plantings for Pic St-Loup. Much of the wine produced within the zone is VIN DE PAYS or VIN DE TABLE. Among many fine domaines producing southern-Rhône-style reds are Ch de Cazeneuve, Domaine de l'Hortus, Ermitage du Pic St-Loup, Ch de Lancyre, Ch de Lascaux, and Mas Bruguière.

Picutener, local strain of the NEBBIOLO grape in and around the Valle d'AOSTA.

Piedirosso, Italian red grape variety planted in CAMPANIA, particularly on the islands of ISCHIA and Capri. It is also known as Per'e Palummo. Plantings halved during the 1980s.

Piedmont, or Piemonte in Italian, qualitatively outstanding and highly distinctive wine region in north-west ITALY whose principal city is Turin. Piedmont's viticulture is the most stable and most evolved in Italy and has made the greatest progress both in identifying the proper areas for growing its own individual VINE VARIETIES and in the proper techniques for fermenting and ageing them. In the late 1990s, total annual wine production averaged over 3 million hl/79 million gal, with 40 per cent at DOC level, almost all of it made from a single grape variety and much of it labelled as a VARIETAL wine.

NEBBIOLO is Piedmont's noblest grape and is, with the Sangiovese of Tuscany, the grape responsible for most of Italy's greatest wines. Although there are 12 Nebbiolo-based DOCs or DOCGS, only the world-famous BAROLO and BARBARESCO supply significant amounts of wine. Piedmont's workhorse grape, supplying the region's everyday red wines (and an increasing number of smart ones), is BARBERA, grown virtually everywhere there are vineyards in the provinces of ALBA, ASTI, and Alessandria. Robust and warming, if at times rather rustic and sharply acidic, it has suffered in the past from overcropping and indifferent winemaking, but the 1980s and the 1990s saw significant improvement in quality. Luxury cuvées of Barbera, aged in new oak, now challenge the price levels of fine Barolo and Barbaresco. DOLCETTO, Piedmont's fruity red wine for young drinking, also demonstrated major improvement in the 1980s.

White grapes, with the exception of the MOSCATO used extensively for various SPUMANTE and FRIZZANTE (most notably ASTI), used to be a virtual afterthought in Piedmont, but the region's production of white wine rose from a mere 10 per cent of the regional total to 25 per cent during the 1980s. Part of this surge is due to the increasing popularity and commercial success of Asti and the emergence of MOSCATO D'ASTI as a significant wine in its own right, but wines based on CORTESE such as GAVI and those from the Colli Tortonesi and Alto Monferrato have also become increasingly popular. Native Piedmontese varieties such as ARNEIS and FAVORITA, mere curiosities in the early 1980s, were planted on 400 and 100 ha of vineyards respectively by the early 1990s. But perhaps the most surprising development of the 1980s was the arrival and rapid acceptance in Piedmont of Chardonnay. The better Langhe Chardonnays, products of BARREL FERMENTATION and BARREL MATURATION, have drawn increasing attention for their high quality relatively swiftly. Younger wine producers are also showing interest in Cabernet Sauvignon, Pinot Noir, Syrah, and Sauvignon Blanc, but these other INTERNATIONAL VARIETIES have yet to establish a real foothold in Piedmont.

In 1995, a systematic revision of the entire DOC system of Piedmont produced Italy's first overall regional DOC. The territory was divided into six broad zones: Piemonte, LANGHE, MON-FERRATO, Colline Novarese (the province of Novara), Coste della Sesia (the Colline Vercellesi), and Canavese (the CAREMA and ERBA-LUCE di Caluso zones to the north of Turin). Each of the region's cultivated varieties can be used either for a smaller, more geographically restricted DOC or DOCG or declassified into a large, more general, and hence 'lower' DOC. The Nebbiolo of Barolo, for example, can become either a Barolo DOCG or Langhe Neb-biolo DOC; the Barbera cultivated in the province of Asti can be used for either the Barbera d'Asti, Monferrato Rosso, or Barbera Piemonte DOCs.

'Lower' appellations are allowed both higher yields and lower alcoholic strength. The new system, in theory, allows all of Piedmont's wine to achieve DOC status and, by 1997, close to 80 per cent of the regional production was being declared as DOC wine.

What has not been accomplished yet has been the creation of recognized subzones or CRUS in the more renowned and important DOCs such as Barolo, Barbaresco, Barbera d'Alba, Barbera d'Asti, and Moscato d'Asti—despite a long tradition of recognizably superior wines from certain areas within these DOCs.

For more details of individual wines, see ALBA, ARNEIS, ASTI, BARBARESCO, BARBERA, BAROLO, BRACHETTO, CAREMA, CORTESE, DOL-CETTO, ERBALUCE, FAVORITA, FREISA, GATTINARA, GAVI, GRIGNOLINO, LANGHE, MOSCATO, NEBBIOLO, ROERO, RUCHÈ, SPANNA.   D.T.

Piemonte, Italian name for the PIEDMONT wine region.

Pierrevert, Coteaux de, small VDQS in the Alpine foothills of northern PROVENCE representing some of the highest vineyards in France. The area extends over a large area east of the Côtes du LUBÉRON but a declining area, 210 ha/520 acres in the late 1990s, is dedicated to making this wine. Wines of all three colours are produced and, thanks to the relative harsh-ness of the climate, they are usually marked more by acidity than body. There is no restric-tion on the proportion of Carignan which may be included in reds and rosés, although the better producers rely more heavily on Gren-ache and Syrah. Tourism in the Hautes Alpes de Provence is such that there has been little need to seek export markets.

Pigato, characterful white grape variety pro-ducing distinctively flavoured varietal wines in the north-west Italian region of LIGURIA.

Pignatello, synonym for the Sicilian red grape variety PERRICONE.

Pignerol, old Provençal white grape making a rather heavy contribution to BELLET.

Pignola is a white grape variety grown in the VALTELLINA.

Pignola Valtellinese, red grape speciality of the Valtellina zone of Lombardy in northern Italy.

Pignoletto, lively, crisp white grape grown around Bologna in northern Italy.

Pignolo, promising red grape variety native to the FRIULI region of north-east Italy. The variety, whose Italian name means 'fussy', was generally ignored by local growers who pre-ferred other, more productive, grape varieties until, like SCHIOPPETTINO, it was given a new lease of life by a European Union decree of 1978 authorizing its use in the province of Udine. Production is still on a very small scale but the results suggest encouragingly high quality. The rich, full, deep-coloured wines have shown a real affinity for BARRIQUE ageing.   D.T.

Pin, Le. The original MICROCHÂTEAU consisted of just one hectare of vines within sight of Ch PÉTRUS, the traditional holder of the crown in POMEROL. This gentle, south-facing slope of gravel and sand, with about 10 per cent clay, was bought for a million French francs in 1989 by three members of Thienpont family, Belgian NÉGOCIANTS who also own nearby Vieux-Château-Certan in Pomerol and Ch Labégorce-Zédé in Margaux as well as properties in the Côte de FRANCS. The vineyard had previously been farmed by a grower in Lalande-de-Pomerol and its produce had for years been vinified there and sold as Le Pin, but not as a CHÂTEAU BOTTLED wine. When the Thienponts bought it, a third of the vines were only a year old. The first commercial vintage was 1981, and until the mid to late 1980s the wine was quite a hard sell. Jacques Thienpont, who commuted between Belgium and Bordeaux, managed to buy out his two co-investors in 1988 and, by adding a further hectare in three contiguous plots, now owns and manages the grand total of about 5 acres. The vines are mainly Merlot, supplemented by about eight per cent Cabernet Franc. The wine was always distinctive, deep and luscious with an almost burgundian richness, absolutely in tune with the FASHION for early-maturing, sensual wines, typical of Michel ROLLAND, in fact. Le Pin was the first red bordeaux to have its MALOLACTIC FERMENTATION completed in 100 per cent new oak barrels (no great investment when the total production of the property averages 600 cases). Demand for this rarity escalated towards the end of the 1980s and the price of the fashionable 1982 vintage reached a peak of £2,500 a bottle in 1997, just before the Asian boom began to falter. It is Le Pin's success which can truly be said to have inspired the rash of new, small, luxury RIGHT BANK estates. See MICROCHÂTEAU.

Pineau, a word widely used in France as a synonym for the PINOT family of grape varieties and today associated primarily with the Loire. It is the first word of a wide range of vine synonyms, sometimes various forms of Pinot but often CHENIN, most notably as **Pineau de la Loire.**

Pineau d'Aunis, sometimes called Chenin Noir, is a variety that is neither a Pinot nor a CHENIN, but a distinct black-berried Loire vine variety. It is systematically being pulled up in favour of more fashionable or longer-living vines such as Cabernet Franc. The variety is one of the many sanctioned for the red and rosé appellations of Touraine and Anjou but is used only to a limited extent, mainly to bring peppery liveliness and fruit to rosés, although in ripe years it can yield a fine red too, notably in Coteaux du LOIR. See also Coteaux du VENDÔMOIS.

Pineau des Charentes or Pineau Charentais is the VIN DE LIQUEUR of the Cognac region and has enjoyed some *réclame* in France as a strong, sweet aperitif more likely to be the product of an artisan than of big business. The style most often encountered outside France is pale gold, decidedly sweet, and with young spirit much in evidence but there are many subtler examples, including soft, fruity rosé styles made from the same grapes as red BORDEAUX. See also FLOC DE GASCOGNE.

Pineau Menu, synonym for the ARBOIS grape.

Pinenc, local name for the FER Servadou red wine grape variety in Gascony, SOUTH WEST FRANCE.

Pinot is the first word of many a French vine variety name and is thought to refer to the shape of Pinot grape bunches, in the form of a pine (*pin*) cone. The principal true members of the Pinot family are PINOT BLANC, AUXERROIS, PINOT GRIS, MEUNIER, and PINOT NOIR, all of them related. CHARDONNAY is still occasionally called Pinot Chardonnay. DNA 'FINGERPRINTING' analysis in 1998 suggested that the following varieties may be the progeny of a member of the Pinot family and the obscure and rather ordinary variety GOUAIS BLANC: ALIGOTÉ, Aubun Vert, AUXERROIS, Bachet Noir, Beaunoir, Chardonnay, Franc Noir de la Haute-Saône, Gamay Blanc Gloriod, GAMAY Noir, Knipperlé, MELON, Peurion, Roublot, and SACY.

In German, members of the Pinot family frequently have the word Burgunder in their German names SPÄTBURGUNDER, Weisser Burgunder, and GRAUBURGUNDER, for example. There was a marked increase in the popularity of these grape varieties throughout the 1980s as tastes changed in favour of drier, fuller German wines.

Pinotage, hardy and increasingly popular red grape variety that is South Africa's curious contribution to the history of the VINIFERA vine. In 1925, Stellenbosch University Professor A. I. Perold crossed Pinot Noir and Cinsaut, then commonly and still sometimes called Hermitage in South Africa, hence the contraction Pinotage. In vineyard and bottle, this crossing disguises its parentage well. Not until 1961 did a Pinotage label appear in South Africa, on a 1959 Lanzerac. Although often scorned, even in the Cape, as a coarse red with a flamboyantly sweetish paint-like pungency, it has increasingly produced rich, long-lasting, deep-coloured wines whose wild fruitiness has been tamed by time and good oak.

Pinotage is a good vineyard performer, with intensely coloured grapes, easily attained ripeness by mid-vintage, and good fixed acidity. It is a substantial bearer, although its best wines tend to come from older, lower yielding BUSH VINE vineyards. By the 1990s, some producers began treating Pinotage more carefully, experimenting with prolonged and cooler fermentations as well as the opposite. French and more recently American oak has added an extra dimension, while more managed yields and careful handling in the cellar has shown that Pinotage can deliver dense fruit for accessibly early drinking.

Only a small percentage of what is produced will satisfy and sustain the newfound demand at the top end of the market. Most Pinotage at best produces an easy drinking, slightly aromatic red wine with some classic sweet berry flavours, TANNIN, and LENGTH. Between 1992 and 1996, South Africa's area of Pinotage increased by half to reach 3.3 per cent of the national total.

Pinotage is also grown, to a much more limited extent, in ZIMBABWE.   M.F. & J.P.

Pinot Beurot, ancient Burgundian synonym for PINOT GRIS.

Pinot Bianco is the common Italian name for the white PINOT BLANC grape of French origin. It is so widely grown in Italy that more wine may well be sold under this synonym than the total amount of wine labelled Pinot Blanc.

It is grown particularly in TRENTINO-ALTO ADIGE, VENETO, FRIULI, and LOMBARDY, although Pinot Grigio enjoys higher esteem here. Pinot Bianco is prized in the Alto Adige, however, and has produced this region's finest white wines. Italians generally vinify Pinot Blanc as a high-acid, slightly SPRITZ, non-aromatic white for early consumption, and often coax generous yields from the vine. In Lombardy, the high acid and low aroma are particularly prized by the SPUMANTE industry. Good Pinot Bianco from the Alto Adige from low-yielding vineyards, fermented and aged in oak barrels, indicates that Pinot Bianco could give much better results in Italy if it were treated with more respect.

Pinot Blanc, increasingly popular French white vine variety, is a widely planted white mutation of PINOT GRIS, which is itself a lighter-berried version of PINOT NOIR. Although its base is Burgundian, today its stronghold is in central Europe. For many years no distinction was made between Pinot Blanc and Chardonnay since the two varieties can look very similar. True Pinot Blanc is low in both vigour and productivity, while the Pinot Blanc selected for and now widely cultivated in Alsace, is much more vigorous and productive.

No Pinot Blanc is notable for its piercing aroma; its scent arrives in a cloud. Most wines based on Pinot Blanc are also relatively full bodied, which has undoubtedly helped reinforce the confusion with Chardonnay, not only in Burgundy but also in north-east Italy, where it is known as PINOT BIANCO. Although Chardonnay dominates white burgundy, Pinot Blanc is technically allowed into wines labelled BOURGOGNE Blanc and into some white MÂCON, but is no longer grown in any quantity in Burgundy.

It is Alsace that is Pinot Blanc's French stronghold, although even here it is less important in terms of total area planted than Riesling, Gewürztraminer, Silvaner, or even the white AUXERROIS with which it is customarily blended in Alsace, to be sold as 'Pinot Blanc'. In LUXEMBOURG, on the other hand, the higher acidity of Pinot Blanc makes it less highly regarded than Auxerrois.

While in Alsace it is regarded as something of a workhorse (and sometimes called Clevner or Klevner), it has been generally held in higher esteem by the Germans, who call it Weissburgunder or Weisser Burgunder. They have valued it for its apparent similarity to the world-famous Chardonnay and its ability to reach quite high MUST WEIGHTS even at relatively high yields. Planted mainly but not exclusively in eastern Germany, the PFALZ, and BADEN, it is a popular vehicle for fuller, drier wine styles designed to be drunk with food and has been keenly adopted as a suitable vehicle for BARRIQUE ageing.

As Pinot Bianco it is a popular dry white in Italy but it is in Austria that, as Weissburgunder, the variety reaches its greatest heights, and certainly its greatest must weights. Accounting for almost four per cent of the country's total vineyards, it is grown in all regions, although Riesling is more prized in the Wachau. As a dry white varietal, Weissburgunder is associated with an almond-like scent, relatively high alcohol, and an ability to age, but it has achieved its greatest glory in Austria in ultra-rich, botrytized TROCKENBEEREN-AUSLESE form, often blended, typically with WELSCHRIESLING.

Pinot Blanc is widely disseminated over eastern Europe. In Slovenia, Croatia, and Vojvodina, it is widely grown and may be called Beli (White) Pinot. It is also grown in the Czech Republic, Slovakia, and is widely used in Hungary to produce full-bodied, rather anodyne dry whites more suitable for export than indigenous vine varieties.

Vine-growers in the New World recognize that Pinot Blanc has lacked Chardonnay's glamour but there are well over 1,000 acres/400 ha of a variety called Pinot Blanc in California, mainly in Monterey, where it is sometimes treated to barrel ageing and the full range of

Chardonnay wine-making tricks, to creditable effect. Older vines bearing this name are almost certainly not Pinot Blanc but the Muscadet grape MELON. The fact that within California no great distinction has been noticed between the wines made from true Pinot Blanc and Melon adds further weight to the thesis that Melon is a Burgundian variety.

Elsewhere in the New World, Pinot Blanc is largely ignored in favour of the most famous white wine grape.

Pinot Blanco, common misnomer for CHENIN BLANC in Latin America.

Pinot Chardonnay is an old synonym for Chardonnay, the classic white grape of Burgundy.

Pinot de la Loire, misleading occasional synonym for CHENIN BLANC in the Loire.

Pinot Grigio is the common Italian name for the French vine variety PINOT GRIS and, as such, is probably the name by which the variety is best known to many wine drinkers. Most plantings are in the north east and specifically in Friuli, where it produces some of the most admired wines of COLLIO as well as a sea of reasonably undistinguished dry white with low aroma and probably the most noticeable acidity of any of the world's Pinot Gris. The Italian tendency is to pick the grapes before the variety's characteristically rapid loss of nerve at full ripening. The variety is also grown widely in LOMBARDY, although there is less fastidiousness here about distinguishing it from other hues of PINOT, especially when supplying grapes for the sparkling-wine industry. The variety can also be found as far south as EMILIA-ROMAGNA and is planted in the ALTO ADIGE—although here, as in all Germanic areas, PINOT BIANCO is favoured.

Pinot Gris is a widely disseminated, increasingly fashionable vine variety that can produce soft, gently perfumed wines with more substance and colour than most whites, which is what one might expect of a variety that is one of the best-known mutations of PINOT NOIR. If Pinot Noir berries are purplish blue and the berries of the related PINOT BLANC are greenish yellow, Pinot Gris grapes are anything between greyish blue and brownish pink—sometimes on the same bunch. At one time, Pinot Gris habitually grew in among the Pinot Noir of many Burgundian vineyards, adding softness and sometimes acidity to its red wine. Even today,

as Pinot Beurot, it is sanctioned as an ingredient in most of Burgundy's red-wine appellations and the occasional vine can still be found in some of the region's famous red-wine vineyards.

There also remain small pockets of the variety in the Loire, where it is often known as Malvoisie. It can produce perfumed, substantial wines in a wide range of different sweetness levels. It is also known as Malvoisie in the Valais in SWITZERLAND, where it can also produce full, perfumed, rich whites.

But, within France, Alsace is where Pinot Gris (here traditionally but mysteriously known as Tokay) is most revered, and with good reason. It may be less commonly planted than the other members of Alsace's noble triumvirate, Riesling and Gewürztraminer, but it is gaining ground and fulfils a unique function as provider of super-rich, usually dry, wines that can be partnered with food without the distraction of too much aroma. See ALSACE.

As with Pinot Blanc, however, much more Pinot Gris is planted in both Germany and Italy than in France. (See PINOT GRIGIO for details of Italian Pinot Gris.) In Germany, it has generally been known as RULÄNDER but, when vinified dry as it increasingly is, it is known as GRAU-BURGUNDER (or occasionally Grauer Riesling, Grauer Burgunder, or even Grauklevner).

The variety, like Pinot Blanc, is widely planted not just in Austria but in Slovenia, Moravia, and particularly ROMANIA, where it is known both as Pinot Gris and Ruländer. In Hungary, it is revered as SZÜRKEBARÁT. Within the CIS, Pinot Gris is grown in both RUSSIA and MOLDOVA.

Pinot Gris' impact on the New World has been limited but is perceptibly increasing. The variety has been one of OREGON's most successful. There has been a dramatic increase in plantings in California, mainly Monterey and Napa, in the late 1990s. And improved CLONAL SELECTION has precipitated a renewal of enthusiasm in the South Island of New Zealand and in Australia, albeit on a small scale.

The variety is also much admired for its weight and relatively low acidity in LUXEMBOURG.

Pinot Liébault, unusual and slightly more productive Burgundian selection of PINOT NOIR.

Pinot Meunier. See MEUNIER.

Pinot Nero is Italian for PINOT NOIR. The variety is quite widely planted in the north east of the country and in Lombardy, and it doubled its area in the 1980s, but few examples show great intensity of flavour. Much of the Pinot Nero planted is used by the upper reaches of the SPUMANTE industry.

Pinot Noir is the grape variety wholly responsible for red burgundy. Unlike Cabernet Sauvignon, which can be grown in all but the coolest conditions and can be economically viable as an inexpensive but recognizably Cabernet wine, Pinot Noir demands much of both vine-grower and wine-maker. It is a tribute to the unparalleled level of physical excitement generated by tasting one of Burgundy's better reds that such a high proportion of the world's most ambitious wine producers want to try their hand with this capricious vine. Although there is relatively little consistency in its performance in its homeland, Pinot Noir has been transplanted to almost every one of the world's wine regions, except the very hottest, where it can so easily turn from essence to jam.

If Cabernet produces wines to appeal to the head, Pinot's charms are decidedly more sensual and more transparent. The Burgundians themselves refute the allegation that they produce Pinot Noir; they merely use Pinot Noir as the vehicle for communicating local geography, the characteristics of the individual site, the TERROIR on which it was planted. Perhaps the only characteristics that the Pinot Noirs of the world could be said to share would be a certain sweet fruitiness and, in general, lower levels of tannins and pigments than the other 'great' French red varieties Cabernet Sauvignon and Syrah. The wines are decidedly more charming in youth and evolve more rapidly, although the decline of the very best is slow.

Part of the reason for the wide variation in Pinot Noir's performance lies in its genetic make-up. It is a particularly old vine variety and is especially prone both to mutate (as witness PINOT BLANC, PINOT GRIS, and Pinot MEUNIER) and degenerate, as witness the multiplicity of Pinot Noir CLONES available even within France.

Pinot Noir generally produces the best-quality wine on limestone soils and in relatively cool climates where this early-ripening vine will not rush towards maturity, losing aroma and acidity. There is general agreement, however, that Pinot Noir is very much more difficult to vinify than Chardonnay, needing constant monitoring and fine tuning of technique according to the demands of each particular vintage.

France

Pinot Noir is planted throughout eastern France and has been steadily gaining ground from less noble varieties so that by 1988 its total area of French vineyard was 22,000 ha/54,000 acres, twice as big as the total area planted with Pinot Meunier but less than Syrah's total—and considerably less than the total planted with Burgundy's other red vine variety GAMAY because of the vast extent of Beaujolais in comparison with the famous Côte d'Or.

The CÔTE D'OR was once the wine region with the biggest single area of Pinot Noir, but the extension of the Champagne region in the 1980s meant that, by the end of this decade, more Pinot Noir went into champagne than into red burgundy. Even in the greater Burgundy region, Pinot Noir is rarely blended with any other variety, except occasionally with Gamay in a BOURGOGNE PASSETOUTGRAINS and, increasingly, to add class to a MÂCON. The red wines of Burgundy can vary from deeply coloured, tannic, oak-aged mouthfuls that demand long bottle age to acidic dark rosés that should be drunk as young as possible. The best GRANDS CRUS are intense, fleshy, vibrant, fruity wines with structure but oak influence that is never obvious. See under individual village names specified for the CÔTE D'OR for more detail on individual wines.

Pinot Noir is also gaining ground in the Côte CHALONNAISE and, to a lesser extent, the MÂCONNAIS, typically at the expense of Gamay. Pinot Noir occupied a full quarter of all Mâconnais vineyard in 1988 and the Chalonnaise reds of MERCUREY, GIVRY, and RULLY have shown that they can often deliver a more consistent level of wine-making than more expensive appellations to the north, even if the fruit quality may be slightly more rustic.

Pinot Noir is the favoured black grape variety in northern Burgundy too, used for such wines as IRANCY and particularly northern versions of BOURGOGNE. It is cultivated even further north east for the light reds and VIN GRIS of Lorraine such as Côtes de TOUL and the wines of MOSELLE.

Although plantings of Pinot Noir increased throughout France (and indeed the world) in the 1980s, it was in CHAMPAGNE that the greatest increase was seen. It is used almost exclusively in champagne, and indeed in the production of a wide range of sparkling wines made around the world in champagne's image. In these wines, Pinot Noir is prized for its body and longevity, as well it might be for that small proportion of champagne made exclusively from Pinot Noir is usually memorably substantial. In Champagne, a small quantity of Pinot Noir is used for still red Coteaux CHAMPENOIS and ROSÉ DES RICEYS.

Pinot Noir is also planted, to a limited but increasing extent, in the most easterly vineyards of the Loire and its tributaries, most notably to make red and pink SANCERRE but also in MENETOU-SALON and ST-POURÇAIN, and is technically allowed in an array of the Loire's VDQS wines. It was taken to the vineyards of the JURA and SAVOIE from Burgundy centuries ago and is increasingly offered as a VARIETAL wine. It is rarely encountered in the south or west of France, the domains of Syrah and Cabernet Sauvignon, but there are limited plantings in the Languedoc with some intriguing, if atypical, results in cooler sites.

Pinot Noir is increasingly sought after in all areas where German is or was spoken. In Alsace, where it is effectively the only black-berried vine variety planted, it is capable of producing quite deep-coloured, perfumed, sweet reds in the ripest vintages. In cooler years, it produces deep-pink wines, often with a similar smoky perfume to a white Pinot Blanc or Pinot Gris, that can be reminiscent of old-fashioned German Spätburgunders, even down to the whiff of rot in the wettest vintages. See ALSACE.

Rest of Europe

Germany's rediscovered interest in CONNOISSEURSHIP of the 1980s and 1990s resulted in a marked increase in demand for the nation's noblest red. See SPÄTBURGUNDER.

It is fair to say, however, that, whereas Cabernet Sauvignon is often associated with the flavours of oak, Pinot Noir is often encountered with more than its fair share of sweetness, especially in inland Europe, as though over-chaptalization had been adopted as an alternative to true ripeness. Austria's Blauburgunder, for example, can taste sweet and oddly viscous unless from one of its most skilled practitioners. Total Austrian plantings are limited, however, and the native grape ST LAURENT, sometimes confusingly called Pinot St Laurent for its Pinot Noir-like soft fruitiness, is much more common.

Pinot Noir is spread widely, if not in great quantity, in the vineyards of eastern Europe, where its name is usually some variant on the local word for Burgundian. There are plantings of Burgundac Crni in parts of CROATIA, in SERBIA, where it can be quite successful, and in much paler form in KOSOVO. It is also grown to a limited extent in the CZECH REPUBLIC, SLOVAKIA, HUNGARY, BULGARIA, ROMANIA, MOLDOVA, GEORGIA, AZERBAIJAN, KAZAKHSTAN, and KYRGYZSTAN. Romania has its own subvariety known as Burgund Mare, which has been responsible for some extraordinarily soupy, yet recognizably Pinot Noir-like cheap reds.

Elsewhere in Europe, the finicky nature of the Pinot Noir vine has set a natural limit on its spread. In Iberia, there has been some successful experimentation in SOMONTANO and CATALONIA in Spain and even in the RIBATEJO in Portugal. The vine is relatively important in SWITZERLAND, particularly, as Blauburgunder, in eastern, German-speaking Switzerland. In French Switzerland, it is blended with Gamay to make the ubiquitous Dôle. There have been some noble experiments in some cooler Italian wine regions, notably LOMBARDY, where it is used for sparkling-wine production; see PINOT NERO. See also Valle d'AOSTA, BREGANZE, TRENTINO, ALTO ADIGE (where it is called Blauburgunder), COLLIO, and FRIULI, as well as OLTREPÒ PAVESE, where the rather neutral Pinot Noir is valued as an ingredient in classically made sparkling wine.

Rest of the world

It was wine producers in the New World, however, who turned the full heat of their ambitious attentions on Pinot Noir in the late 1980s and early 1990s. Some even relocated their wineries many hundreds of miles in order to be closer to sources of suitably cool-climate Pinot Noir fruit. Although for many years OREGON, with its often miserably cool, wet climate, was popularly supposed to provide America's answer to red burgundy, the number of seriously fine Pinot Noirs that emerged from CALIFORNIA in the late 1980s redefined the more southerly state's reputation for Pinot, especially but not exclusively in regions such as the Russian River district of Sonoma, Santa Barbara County, Carneros, Chalone, and the Gavilan mountains of San Benito. In Carneros, the variety is also valued as an ingredient in champagne-like sparkling wines.

The variety called **Pinot St George** in California, now in sharp decline, is unrelated to any known Pinot and is probably in fact NÉG-RETTE, while that called Gamay Beaujolais is a clone of Pinot Noir, although not one embraced by the most ambitious producers of California Pinot Noir.

Outside California and Oregon, the variety has no established American outpost of great reputation, although there were plantings in many of the UNITED STATES including NEW YORK, IDAHO, Pennsylvania, and Arizona, and the vineyards around Lake Michigan. Washington state persists with it only on its southern border with Oregon. There are pockets of Pinot Noir in CANADA, however, and they are producing increasingly successful wines.

As Pinot Negro, it is known in most Argentine provinces where vines are grown but the climate is too hot and irrigation too commonplace to produce wines of real quality, as in most of the rest of South America, although Chile had a few hundred hectares planted in cooler spots such as Chimbarongo in the early 1990s and wine quality was improving.

Across the Atlantic in SOUTH AFRICA, on the other hand, at least one producer, Hamilton-Russell, had managed to coax convincingly burgundian flavours from Pinot Noir vines grown in a particularly cool southerly spot and this has since acted as a spur to others, including neighbours Bouchard Finlayson, and Clos Cabrière—even if the quantity of true Pinot Noir planted is still minute compared with the total area of South Africa's signature black grape variety PINOTAGE.

Plantings of Pinot Noir in Australia and New Zealand, on the other hand, rose substantially in the early 1990s, with notably more success in the latter country, especially in Wairarapa Martinborough, Canterbury, and Central Otago. New Zealand has already established itself as one of the New World's most successful producers of this fickle variety. See NEW ZEALAND.

Fine Pinot Noir has been more elusive in Australia. Areas with proven success as producers of good-quality red wine (as opposed to useful ingredients for the sparkling-wine business) include Geelong, Yarra, and Mornington Peninsula, all relatively cool areas around Melbourne in Victoria, as well as Tasmania. See AUSTRALIA.

Wherever there is a wine producer with a palate, there will be experimentation with Pinot Noir.

Pinot St George, California red grape identified as NÉGRETTE and now difficult to find.

Pipers Brook, wine region in TASMANIA.

Piros Szlanka. See PAMID.

Pla del Bages, denominated wine region north west of Barcelona in Spain with just over 500 ha/1,200 acres under vine. Grape varieties are similar to those in neighbouring PENEDÈS, with foreign varieties such as Merlot and Cabernet Sauvignon planted rapidly during the 1990s.   V. de la S.

Planta Fina (de Pedralba), grown in Valencia, south-east Spain, to make sturdy, aromatic white wines.

Planta Nova, another undistinguished white Spanish grape variety planted on about 1,800 ha/4,500 acres of Valencia and Utiel-Requena.

Plantet, the Loire's most popular French HYBRID, has been more successfully eradicated from the French vinescape than some others (BACO, for example). France's total Plantet area shrank from more than 26,000 ha/63,000 acres to less than 1,000 ha between 1968 and 1988, almost all of it in the Loire, although at one point it was grown all over France's northern wine regions.

Plavac Mali, grape variety producing dense red wines all along the Dalmatian coast and on many of the Adriatic islands in CROATIA. Mali means 'small' and a white grape variety called simply **Plavac** is also known, and results in equally heady wines. Both varieties thrive on sandy soil. Plavac Mali produces wines high in tannins, alcohol, and colour which can, unusually for red wines from what was Yugoslavia, age well. Postup and Dingač are two of the better-known reds made from Plavac Mali. Some close similarities have been noted between Plavac Mali and ZINFANDEL, although the two varieties do not seem to be identical.

Plavai, late-ripening white VINIFERA grape variety native to MOLDOVA and widely planted throughout eastern Europe and the CIS. In Moldova, it is also known as Belan and Plakun; in Romania, it is called Plavana; in Austria, Plavez Gelber; in Hungary, Melvais; in the Krasnodarski region of Russia, Belan or Oliver; in Ukraine, Bila Muka or Ardanski; and in Central Asia, Bely Krugly. It is used in Russia for both table wines and brandy.

Plavina, red grape grown in northern CROATIA which may also be called Brajdica. Sometimes also used as a synonym for PLAVAC MALI.

plonk, vague and derogatory English term for wine of undistinguished quality, is a term of Australian slang that has been naturalized in Britain. During the First World War, the French *vin blanc* with its un-English nasal vowels was adapted in various fantastic ways and eventually shortened to 'plonk'. Despite its etymology, plonk need not be white.　　　L.H.-S.

podere, Italian for a farm, usually smaller than a FATTORIA and usually a subdivision of a fattoria, intended to supply enough land for the subsistence of a sharecropping family.

points out of 100, common method of SCORING wine promoted notably by American writer Robert PARKER. See NUMBERS.

Poitou, the north-west French region around Poitiers. Its name is known to wine drinkers only for **Haut-Poitou,** a VDQS zone almost due south of SAUMUR which produces a range of improving VARIETAL wines, marked by clean, fruity acidity. Almost equal quantities of reds and whites are produced from the usual middle Loire range of Bordelais, Burgundian, and Loire vine varieties. Sauvignon and Gamay can be particularly successful, as can Cabernet (a blend of both Sauvignon and Franc) in particularly ripe vintages. The co-operative at Neuville, which dominates production, has successfully experimented with OAK AGEING and traditional-method sparkling wines, including an all-Chardonnay Blanc de Blancs, called Diane de Poitiers.

Pol Roger, Champagne house founded in Épernay in 1849 and still in family hands. The wines rank high among the top champagne houses for quality, although it is one of the smaller GRANDES MARQUES. Pol Roger owns 85 ha/210 acres of vineyards on prime sites in the Vallée d'Épernay and on the Côte des Blancs. Particularly deep cellars house 6.5 million bottles, representing five years' supply. Sir Winston Churchill was a devotee of the house, even naming his racehorse Pol Roger. The compliment was repaid after his death, when all non-vintage labels exported to Britain were edged in black for 25 years. The Sir Winston Churchill Cuvée was launched in 1984 as Pol Roger's PRESTIGE CUVÉE.　　　S.A.

Pomerol, small but distinctive wine region in Bordeaux producing opulent and glamorous red wines dominated by the Merlot grape. Although they are increasingly challenged by their counterparts in its much larger neighbour ST-ÉMILION, Pomerol's most successful wines are some of the world's most sought after, but the glamour attaches to the labels rather than the countryside.

Pomerol is produced from about 784 ha/1,936 acres of vineyard on a plateau immediately north east of LIBOURNE that is as geographically unremarkable as the MÉDOC, but without even any buildings or historical landmarks of note. A confusing network of narrow lanes connects about 150 smallholdings, most of which produce only a few thousand cases of wine a year.

The most successful of the Libourne merchants is Jean-Pierre MOUEIX, whose fortunes have been interlinked with those of Pomerol. After establishing a reputation for the appellation, the firm acquired a number of properties, as well as contracts to manage other properties, including Ch Pétrus, and still sells a significant proportion of the Pomerol made in each vintage.

The success of Ch Pétrus in particular, whose wines regularly fetch prices far above those of the Médoc FIRST GROWTHS, is mirrored by worldwide demand far in excess of supply for the wines of similarly minuscule properties such as Chx Lafleur, Le PIN, L'Église-Clinet, and La Fleur de Gay.

Pomerol's finest wines are in general made on the highest parts of the plateau, which is predominantly gravel whose layers are interleaved with clay, becoming sandier in the west, where rather lighter wines are made. The subsoil here is distinguished by local iron-rich clay, of which Ch Pétrus has a stratum particularly close to the surface.

Apparently as important in fashioning wines that are plump, voluptuous, and richly fruity enough to drink at less than five years old and yet which can last for as long as many a great Médoc are VINE AGE and low yields. (At Ch Pétrus, for example, the wine produced by vines less than 12 years old is usually excluded from the ASSEMBLAGE.) Yields here are often the lowest for red bordeaux and are zealously restricted at the best properties. Pomerol is also unusual in being the only one of Bordeaux's great wine districts to have no official CLASSIFICATION. The scores of properties are in general humble farmhouses with little to distinguish one from another, and only Ch de Sales has a building of any pretensions to grandeur, and an extent of more than 40 ha. The most sought-after wines, depending on the vintage, include Chx Pétrus, Lafleur, Le Pin, La Conseillante, Trotanoy, Certan de May, La Fleur de Gay, L'Église-Clinet, Clinet, L'Évangile, Latour-à-Pomerol, and Vieux-Ch-Certan, and Ch Nenin is expected to reach new heights now that it is under the same ownership as Ch LÉO-VILLE LAS CASES.

Pommard, prosperous village in Burgundy producing the most powerful red wines of the Côte de Beaune district of the CÔTE D'OR, from the usual Pinot Noir grapes. Until the 1980s, lesser wines were often sold under this popular designation while at other times Pommard has suffered from a dearth of sufficiently conscientious producers and a perception that it offers poor value. However, a fine Pommard will be darker in colour than neighbouring VOLNAY, deeper in flavour, more tannic in structure, less charming when young but capable of developing into a rich, sturdy wine of great power after 10 years in bottle.

Pommard stretches from the border of Beaune to the edge of Volnay. On the Beaune side, the finest vineyards are Les Pézerolles and Les Épenots, including the Clos des Épeneaux MONOPOLE of Comte Armand. Towards Volnay, the most impressive PREMIER CRU vineyards include Les Chanlins, Les Jarolières, Les Fremiers, and, in particular, Les Rugiens. The lower section of the latter, Les Rugiens Bas, has the potential to make the richest wines of all in Pommard, and is frequently mentioned as being worthy of elevation to GRAND CRU status. Clos de la Commaraine, Le Clos Blanc, and Les Arvelets have also been cited in the past as good sources for Pommard. Particularly high achievers are de Courcel, Comte Armand, and many of the best growers in Volnay such as de Montille and Lafarge.   J.T.C.M.

Pontac, distinctive red-fleshed grape variety known only in SOUTH AFRICA, probably imported to the Cape from SOUTH WEST FRANCE in the late 17th century. It produces distinguished wines dark in colour, with strong though not coarse TANNINS and smoky berry flavours which emerge only after several years' BOTTLE AGEING. Low yields, virus infection, colour instability, and limited commercial prospects seemed destined to ensure its extinc-

tion. However, since the 1980s a few dedicated growers have obtained virus-treated vines and the Cape now has a direct link to its first years of VINIFERA production.   M.F.

Porongurup, coolish vineyard subregion within WESTERN AUSTRALIA's Great Southern region.

port, a FORTIFIED WINE made by adding brandy to arrest fermenting grape must which results in a wine, red and sometimes white, that is both sweet and high in alcohol. Port derives its name from Oporto (Porto), the second largest city in PORTUGAL, whence the wine has been shipped for over 300 years by English merchants.

Fortified wines are made in the image of port in places as far apart as SOUTH AFRICA, AUSTRALIA, and CALIFORNIA but, within the European Union, EU law restricts the use of the term port to wines from a closely defined area in the DOURO valley of northern Portugal.

These are the main styles of port:

Ruby—simple young fruity deep-red port.

Tawny—in theory, a wine which has been aged in wood for so much longer than a ruby that it loses colour and takes on a tawny hue. However, much of the tawny port sold today is just a blend of young ruby and white ports.

Aged tawny—tawny-coloured, delicate, nutty port aged in wood for 10, 20, 30, or 'Over 40' years.

Vintage port—the longest-lived and best wines from a single year, bottled young and left to mature for decades in bottle. Produced only in the best years, they need decanting.

Colheita—tawny ports from a single year, bottled with the date of the harvest (and, usually, bottling) on the label.

LBV—Late Bottled Vintage port is a wine from a single year, bottled between four and six years after the harvest. So-called 'traditional' LBVs need to be decanted before serving. The more common style of LBV is lighter and closer to a ruby port.

Vintage character—the port trade's great misnomer since the wines are not the product of a single year and few, if any, exhibit any of the character of vintage port. They tend to be premium rubies aged in bulk.

Single-quinta vintage—vintage ports made by a single estate or quinta.

Crusted or crusting port—similar to vintage port but not the product of a single year. Should be decanted.

White port—port made from white grapes and generally sweet.

See also DOURO.   R.J.M.

Portalegre, DOC in southern Portugal. See ALENTEJO.

Portan, a crossing of GRENACHE NOIR and Portugais Bleu (Blauer PORTUGIESER) grown to a strictly limited extent in the Midi but allowed into Vin de Pays d'Oc.

Portugais, or Portugais Bleu, is the French manifestation of the more commonly Germanic black grape variety Blauer PORTUGIESER. Its influence is only slowly declining in France, where it was once one of the most planted varieties in the Tarn *département*, in some cases at the expense of the nobler varieties responsible for red GAILLAC.

Portugal. Among European wine-producing nations, Portugal has been something of a paradox, arguably discussed in the greater world of wine more because of the CORK of which it is by far the dominant producer than for its wines. Sitting on the western flank of the Iberian peninsula, this seafaring nation which discovered so much of the NEW WORLD now clings firmly to the Old—at least in terms of its tradition of myriad indigenous vine varieties. Secluded both geographically and, for much of the 20th century until it joined the European Union in 1986, politically as well, Portugal has developed in isolation from other countries, including neighbouring SPAIN. However, the sizeable wine industry that has grown up in this small country owes much to foreign trade. Total area under vine declined from 385,000 ha/951,000 acres in the late 1980s to less than 260,000 ha in the late 1990s but in some years Portugal rather than Germany is Europe's fourth most important wine producer after Italy, France, and Spain. The Portuguese rival the French and Italians in terms of per capita wine consumption. For such a small country, Portugal produces a remarkable diversity of wines. Contrasting climatic conditions are reflected in such dissimilar wines as VINHO VERDE and PORT, which are produced in adjoining regions.

Vine varieties

Portugal's vineyards have evolved in isolation. Only a handful of varieties have crossed international frontiers, leaving Portugal like a viticultural island with a treasure trove of indigenous grape varieties. Among whites, LOU-REIRO and ALVARINHO (in Vinho Verde), BICAL (in Bairrada), ENCRUZADO (in Dão), and ARINTO (in Bucelas and throughout southern Portugal) are showing potential. Among Portugal's best and most distinctive red grapes are TOURIGA NACIONAL (in the Douro and Dão) and Tinta Roriz, Spain's TEMPRANILLO (in the Douro, known as Aragonêz in the Alentejo), BAGA (in Bairrada), CASTELÃO FRANCÊS (also known as Periquita in the south and João de Santarém in the Ribatejo), and Trincadeira (in the Alentejo). INTERNATIONAL VARIETIES such as Cabernet Sauvignon and Chardonnay have made few inroads.

Wine laws

Portugal's wine law pre-dates that of most other European countries. Since Portugal joined the European Union, the Regiões Demarcadas or RDs (demarcated regions) have been redesignated Denominação de Origem Controlada (DOC). A second tier of Indicação de Proveniencia Regulamentada (IPR) wine regions has also been introduced, now joined by a third tier of larger regions producing VINHO REGIONAL. Underpinned by the VINHO de mesa (TABLE WINE) designation, this brings Portugal's wine law roughly into line with that of other EU countries.

For more details and individual regions, see ALENTEJO, ALGARVE, BAIRRADA, BUCELAS, COLARES, DÃO, DOURO, ESTREMADURA, RIBATEJO, SETÚBAL, TERRAS DO SADO, TRÁS-OS-MONTES, VINHO VERDE, and PORT. The viticulturally important Atlantic island of MADEIRA is an autonomous part of Portugal.   R.J.M.

Portugieser or Blauer Portugieser is a black grape variety common in both senses of that word in both Austria and Germany, its name suggesting completely unsubstantiated Portuguese origins. The vine is extremely prolific, producing pale, low-acid red that, thanks to robust CHAPTALIZATION, can taste disconcertingly sweet to non-natives. Blauer Portugieser is synonymous with dull, thin red in lower AUSTRIA, and it is rarely exported.

Germany's everyday black grape variety Portugieser was overtaken in terms of total area planted by SPÄTBURGUNDER (Pinot Noir) in the 1970s, although in the early 1990s it was enjoying a renaissance of popularity with growers determined to satisfy the German thirst for red wine regardless of its quality. In the PFALZ, a high proportion of Portugieser is encouraged to produce vast quantities of pink WEISSHERBST.

Portugieser also plays an important role in the AHR region, famous for its reds, many of which depend on Portugieser as much as on the Spätburgunder for which the region is more famous.

The variety is so easy to grow, however, that it has spread throughout central Europe and beyond. It is ingeniously named KÉKOPORTO in Hungary (*kék* meaning 'blue') and ROMANIA and is grown in northern Croatia as Portugizac Crni, or Portugaljka. It may also go under the name Oporto, much to the displeasure of EU authorities.

potential alcohol, measurement of a wine or must which equates to its total ALCOHOLIC STRENGTH if all the sugar were to be fermented out to alcohol. Thus, a Sauternes might have an alcoholic strength of 13 per cent, but a potential alcohol of 20 per cent if its RESIDUAL SUGAR would ferment to a dry liquid containing 7 per cent alcohol.

Potter Valley, California wine region and AVA. See MENDOCINO.

Pouilly-Fuissé, important white-wine appellation in the MÂCONNAIS district of Burgundy which is restricted to the Chardonnay grape. The richest wines are said to come from Fuissé and Solutré, those of Vergisson being a little lighter but elegant. There is no concept of PREMIER CRU vineyards in this appellation but Pouilly-Fuissé may be followed by the name of a specific vineyard.

The wines are full bodied and ripe but do not usually attain the elegance of the finer wines from the Côte de Beaune. Normally bottled after a year's BARREL MATURATION, they are capable of ageing well thereafter, particularly Vincent's wines at the Ch de Fuissé and those of Guffens-Heynen (the family domaine associated with the NÉGOCIANT Verget). Prices can vary enormously depending on the demands of major export markets in a given year.

The small village of Pouilly also lends its name to two adjacent lesser appellations, Pouilly-Vinzelles and Pouilly-Loché. The latter is more rarely seen and may be sold as Pouilly-Vinzelles. The local CO-OPERATIVE is the prime source for both wines.   J.T.C.M.

Pouilly-Fumé, also known as Pouilly Blanc Fumé and Blanc Fumé de Pouilly, one of the Loire's most famous wines, perfumed dry whites that epitomize the Sauvignon Blanc grape (along with nearby MENETOU-SALON, QUINCY, REUILLY, and, most notably, SANCERRE). Sauvignon here is often called Blanc Fumé because the wines supposedly exhibit a 'smoky' flavour, or whiff of gunflint. The wines are certainly perfumed, sometimes almost acrid, and it takes extensive local knowledge reliably to distinguish Sancerres and Pouilly-Fumés in a blind tasting of both. Unlike that of Sancerre, the Pouilly-Fumé appellation applies only to white wines. The best Pouilly-Fumé (such as the range produced by Didier Dageneau) is perhaps a denser, more ambitiously long-lived liquid than Sancerre, for drinking at two to six years, for example, rather than one to four (although there are, as always with wine, exceptions). At the most famous estate, de Ladoucette's magnificently turreted Ch du Nozet, are bottles which prove that Pouilly-Fumé can last for decades, although whether it actually improves is a matter of taste. Some producers began experimenting with OAK for both fermentation and maturation in the mid 1980s and the wines of the region are becoming more complex with each vintage. The appellation takes its name from the small town of Pouilly-sur-Loire on the right bank of the Loire in the Nièvre *département*. The name **Pouilly-sur-Loire** is given to the zone's less distinguished VDQS wine, a usually thin and short-lived liquid made in very much smaller quantities from the CHASSELAS. In the 1970s and 1980s, Pouilly-Fumé was much favoured by FASHION, and the total area planted with Sauvignon increased considerably. Some of the finest vineyards are on the slopes above the Loire north of Pouilly between it and the village of Sancerre.

See also LOIRE.

Pouilly-Loché. See POUILLY-FUISSÉ.

Pouilly-Vinzelles. See POUILLY-FUISSÉ.

Poulsard, sometimes called **Ploussard**, is a rare dark grape speciality of the JURA, where it does particularly well in the northern vineyards. Its large, long, thin-skinned grapes give only lightly coloured wine that is distinguished by its perfume. It is so low in pigments it can make white wines. It makes particularly fine rosés, which may be left on the skins for as long as a week without tainting the wine too deeply, and can add aroma to a red blended from Poulsard, TROUSSEAU, and, increasingly, Pinot Noir.

pourriture, French for rot. *Pourriture noble* is NOBLE ROT.

Prädikat, in GERMANY a wine 'distinction', awarded on the basis of increasing grape ripeness or MUST WEIGHT: either KABINETT, SPÄT-LESE, AUSLESE, BEERENAUSLESE, EISWEIN, or TROCKENBEERENAUSLESE. According to GERMAN WINE LAW, a QMP wine is a Qualitäts-wein mit Prädikat, or 'quality wine with distinction'.

In AUSTRIA, **Prädikatswein** excludes Kabinett wine but includes, at increasing minimum must-weight levels, Spätlese, Auslese, Strohwein (or 'straw wine', see VIN DE PAILLE), Eiswein, Beerenauslese, AUSBRUCH, and Trockenbeerenauslese.

Pramaggiore. See LISON-PRAMAGGIORE.

premier cru, or premier cru classé, is one CRU judged of the first rank, usually according to some official CLASSIFICATION. The direct translation of the French term *premier cru*, much used in the context of BORDEAUX, is FIRST GROWTH. A **premier grand cru (classé)** may, as in the case of ST-ÉMILION and Ch d'YQUEM, be a rung higher even than this. In Burgundy, scores of vineyards are designated premiers crus, capable of producing wine distinctly superior to VILLAGE WINE but not quite so great as the produce of the GRANDS CRUS. See BURGUNDY in general and each of the villages on the CÔTE D'OR in particular.

Premières Côtes de Bordeaux, qualitatively important member of the BORDEAUX CÔTES group of appellations. The Premières Côtes extend for 60 km/40 miles from north of the city of Bordeaux as far as Langon in a narrow strip along the south-western edge of the ENTRE-DEUX-MERS appellation. The land dedicated to the appellation increased considerably during the first half of the 1990s, planted mainly with red grape varieties, particularly Merlot, but the region is also the only one of the Bordeaux Côtes appellations to produce significant quantities of sweet white wines, known since 1991 as **Premières Côtes de Bordeaux Cadillac,** from Sémillon, Sauvignon Blanc, and Muscadelle. (This is hardly surprising since the Premières Côtes encircle the sweet white territory of CADILLAC, CÉRONS, and STE-CROIX-DU-MONT appellations.) There is a recognizable band of seriously ambitious producers here, especially of quite concentrated

red wines which may lack the ageing potential of Bordeaux's more famous examples but can offer good value for drinking at three to five years old. Particularly successful properties include Chx Carsin, Le Doyenné, Graulet, Parenchère, and Reynon. See BORDEAUX for more detail.

The appellation Bordeaux-St-Macaire (see BORDEAUX AC) is effectively a south-eastern extension of the Premières Côtes de Bordeaux.

Pressac, Bordeaux RIGHT BANK name for the red grape variety Cot or MALBEC.

pressing, wine-making operation whereby pressure is applied, using a press, to grapes, grape clusters, or grape pomace (grape skins, stem fragments, pulp, and dead yeast) in order to squeeze the liquid out of the solid parts. See also PRESS WINE and FREE-RUN.

press wine, dark red wine squeezed from pomace (grape skins, stem fragments, pulp, and dead yeast) by means of a wine press. Press wine is generally inferior in quality to FREE-RUN wine, and generally much more astringent. A certain proportion of press wine may be incorporated into the free-run wine, especially if it lacks TANNIN. Otherwise it is used for a lesser bottling or, traditionally, given to workers at the establishment which produced it.   A.D.W.

prestige cuvée, one of several names given to a CHAMPAGNE house's highest-quality wine. Examples are ROEDERER'S Cristal bottling and MOËT & CHANDON'S Dom PÉRIGNON.

price is probably the single most important aspect of a wine to most consumers, just as the price of grapes is one of the most important variables of the viticultural year to most grape-growers.

Grape prices

Wine grapes are an important item of commerce throughout the world, and the economic fortunes of many a rural community rise and fall with wine-grape prices. Although many wine consumers have the impression that most wine grapes are grown on estates which also process them into wine, nothing could be further from the truth. The majority of the world's wine grapes are sold in the form of fresh fruit, to be vinified quite independently of the grape-grower, whether by commercial wineries or CO-OPERATIVES.

The means to determine prices for wine grapes varies from region to region. Prices are normally fixed annually, taking into account supply and demand as well as individual VINTAGE characteristics. Normally grapes are bought and sold according to VINE VARIETY and sugar content. In most regions there is some sort of representative body which oversees grape prices. However, a basic problem in buying and selling wine grapes is that their true value is not known until they are made into wine, and indeed until that wine is sold.

R.E.S.

Wine prices

The price of a wine is a function of the price of the grapes, the price of labour, the price of a winery or the debt outstanding on it, pricing policy on the part of the producer, pricing policy on the part of any merchants involved in selling it, the cost of transport, bottling, labelling, and marketing, quite apart from any DUTIES and TAXATION. The interest for the wine producer must be to maximize his or her return on capital, without acquiring a reputation for profiteering.

The interesting question for the consumer, however, is the extent to which retail wine prices, which can vary more than a thousandfold, indicate wine quality. The answer is, of course, not very closely. All sorts of factors can depress the price of a wine to make it a bargain relative to the competition. Some national economies offer particularly low production costs (such as PORTUGAL and some of South America) when translated into the currencies of many potential importers. Currency movements in general have far more (upward) impact on wine prices than most wine drinkers realize (merchants do not always pass on the benefit to consumers of downward movements). The enormous surge in demand for 1982 Bordeaux in the United States was partly the result of the strength of the American dollar relative to the French franc in 1983 when EN PRIMEUR purchases were made. Other political events can also affect wine prices. The fall of communism in eastern Europe left surplus production in countries such as BULGARIA, HUNGARY, and ROMANIA, which used to ship enormous quantities to the Soviet Union, and these emerging economies' desire for hard, western currency led them to export goods such as wine at extremely keen prices, or as part of barter deals. Specific countries may also benefit from preferential import tariffs.

Pricing policy in general may be geared to gaining a foothold in a new market, as SOUTH AFRICA needed to do after the lifting of sanctions in the early 1990s. Or it may have the result of bolstering prices in the belief that high prices automatically buy respect and prestige, a phenomenon associated with some aspirant CALIFORNIA CULT wines.

The above considerations relate to the prices of wine when it is first offered for sale. Serious wine COLLECTORS and those considering investing in wine are interested in what happens to the price of FINE WINE over time. As detailed in INVESTMENT and AUCTIONS, this depends on the precise wine and the time, and also on the rarity value of a given wine, its provenance and condition, and the general state of the market.

Although general inflation has tended to mean that wine prices inevitably rise most years, the late 1990s saw the prices of the most sought-after fine wines, the so-called TROPHY WINES, draw away from those of other wines, making such wines seem even poorer value than ever. It is ironic perhaps that at a time when the difference in quality between wines at the top and bottom ends of the market has never been narrower, the price difference has never been greater. But presumably this reflects the substantially increased number of affluent wine consumers, and the significant position that wine now holds in a number of cultures round the world.

Prieto Picudo, unusually musky grape grown in a large area mainly around the city of León in north central Spain. These white wines are light in colour but very distinctive, even if they are not officially embraced by the DO system.

Primaticcio, occasional name for Italy's MONTEPULCIANO grape.

primeur, French word for young produce which has been adapted to mean 'young wine'. French AC rules allow all of the following to be released on the third Thursday of November following the harvest: Beaujolais, Côtes du Rhône, Coteaux du Tricastin, Côtes du Ventoux, Coteaux du Languedoc, Gamays from Touraine, Anjou, and Gaillac, Coteaux du Lyonnais, Côtes du Roussillon, Mâcon Blanc, Tavel Rosé, Rosé d'Anjou, Cabernet d'Anjou, Cabernet de Saumur, Bourgogne Blanc, Bourgogne Aligoté, Bourgogne Grand Ordinaire Blanc,

Muscadet, and Gaillac Blanc. For more details of this style of wine, see NOUVEAU.

See also EN PRIMEUR for details of fine wine offered for sale before it is bottled.

Primitivo, red grape variety grown principally in APULIA in southern Italy. It might have remained relatively obscure had not its similarity to California's ZINFANDEL been noted, and DNA 'FINGERPRINTING' established that the varieties are identical. There are varietal DOCs for Primitivo di Gioia and the heady Primitivo di Manduria. Most wines labelled Primitivo are notably alcoholic and this grape was traditionally used to add weight to northern reds. The grape's potential as a VARIETAL, rather than a blending ingredient, is beginning to be recognized by the likes of the large firm Felline.

Priorat, one of Spain's most inspiring red wines made in an isolated DO zone in CATALONIA inland from Tarragona. (Its Spanish rather than native Catalan name is **Priorato**.) In the 1990s, a true revolution engulfed the region, where production methods for Priorat had barely altered since the 12th century. Priorat is one of the world's few first-class wines to be made from Garnacha (GRENACHE), together with some of the unfashionable Cariñena (CARIGNAN). The age of the vines and concomitantly extremely low yields, which average just 5 or 6 hl/ha (0.3 ton/acre), undoubtedly contribute to the intensity and strength of Priorat. Under the hot Mediterranean sun, grapes ripen to a POTENTIAL ALCOHOL of up to 18 per cent, although in the 1990s this was steadfastly reduced.

Poor, stony soils support only the most meagre of crops. MECHANIZATION is almost impossible and many steeply terraced smallholdings had been abandoned in recent years as the rural population left to find work on the coast. The success of new-wave Priorat is slowly reviving the vineyards, however.

The region is dominated by CO-OPERATIVES but there is an increasing number of well-equipped estates, traditionally led by Scala Dei, while De Müller make some good *generoso*. In the 1980s, René Barbier, recognizing Priorat's potential for top-quality red wines, located some particularly promising vineyard sites, renamed CLOS. Such French vine varieties as Cabernet Sauvignon, Merlot, Syrah, and some Pinot Noir were planted. A group of private growers took over. The wines of René Barbier (Clos Mogador), Costers del Siurana (Clos de

l'Obac), Alvaro Palacios (Finca Dofí, L'Ermita), Mas Martinet (Clos Martinet), and Clos & Terrasses (Clos Erasmus) had won worldwide acclaim by the late 1990s. Complex blends including small proportions of French varieties, careful wine-making, and ageing in new French oak barrels were the key innovations. Scala Dei, which also produces dry white and rosé wines, joined in this quality drive, with other small estates jumping on the bandwagon by the mid 1990s. The wines must reach a minimum alcoholic strength of 13.5 per cent to qualify as Priorat.   R.J.M. & V. de la S.

Procanico, Umbrian and possibly superior subvariety of TREBBIANO.

production of a particular vineyard is normally measured as YIELD. The world's production of wine totals between 250 and 300 million hl (6,600 million–7,900 million gal) annually, with wide variation according to VINTAGE. Europe is responsible for about three-quarters of the world's production, with the Americas and then Africa being the next most important continental producers. Production is falling in Europe, North Africa, and in the Americas but is tending to rise elsewhere. Some of the most marked increases in wine production have been in Australia, Japan, and China. The tables in Appendix 2 show the world's significant wine-producing countries, estimates of their total area of vineyard, as well as recent annual wine production.

Prokupac, red grape variety grown all over SERBIA, where the strong wine it produces is often blended with more international vine varieties. It is also grown in KOSOVO and MACEDONIA. Within its native land, it is often made into a dark rosé. Its stronghold is just south of Belgrade where some argue it is identical to SYRAH.

Prosecco, late-ripening white grape variety native to the VENETO region in north-east Italy. It is responsible for a popular wine of the same name, sometimes called Prosecco di Conegliano Valdobbiadene, made west of the township of Conegliano near the Piave river. Prosecco wines exist in still, but mainly fizzy and sparkling, versions, the latter two produced by the tank method of SPARKLING-WINE-MAKING. Of the 28 million bottles produced in an average year, approximately 1 million are of still wine, 7 million of FRIZZANTE or fizzy wine, and 20 million of SPUMANTE. All have the bitter finish which characterizes the grape variety. The subzone of Cartizze produces a spumante which tends towards a medium-dry style and is known as Superiore di Cartizze.

The variety is also known, to a very limited extent, in Argentina. D.T.

protective juice handling, grape- and must-processing techniques with the aim of minimizing exposure to OXYGEN and therefore the risk of OXIDATION. Grapes for red wines are much less vulnerable to damage from oxygen since they contain much greater concentrations of TANNINS and PIGMENTS.

See also SKIN CONTACT. A.D.W.

protective wine-making, wine-making philosophy founded on the need to minimize exposure to OXYGEN and concomitant risk of OXIDATION. It usually incorporates PROTECTIVE JUICE HANDLING. Red wines, because of their greater PHENOLIC content, are much less sensitive to exposure to oxygen. Indeed, if they undergo BARREL MATURATION, some exposure to oxygen during TOPPING UP contributes to the wine's maturation. See AGEING. A.D.W.

Provence, region with considerable potential in the far south east of France whose associations with tourism and hedonism have perhaps focused too much attention on its relatively expensive rosés.

As a result of its rich cultural heritage, Provence enjoys a particularly distinctive range of vine varieties, which show various historical influences from Italy, notably Sardinia. No fewer than 13 varieties are allowed in Côtes de Provence, for example, including the most important but declining CARIGNAN, CINSAUT, GRENACHE, UGNI BLANC, and CLAIRETTE, but also MOURVÈDRE, TIBOUREN, the indigenous dark-berried Calitor (known in Provençal as Pécoui Touar), Barbaroux, ROLLE (Vermentino), and SÉMILLON.

The climate here is France's most MEDITERRANEAN. The greatest climatological threat is wind, in particular the famous *mistral*, a cold wind from the north. It has the advantage of minimizing the risk of fungal diseases, and Provence is particularly suitable for ORGANIC VITICULTURE.

The magic attached to such names as the Côte d'Azur, St-Tropez, and Provence in general may have increased urban development, but it has also attracted outsiders prepared to make significant investments in vine-growing and wine-making, thereby raising standards overall.

Côtes de Provence

This is by far the most significant appellation in Provence, although the vineyard sites vary enormously. About four-fifths of production is of pale-pink dry rosé, which seems to find a growing local market almost regardless of quality. There was renewed interest in producing 'serious' rosé in the early 1990s, however, with a distinctive new style combining flavour with a fashionably pale hue, and some producers even using a limited amount of OAK maturation. The best really do seem to have a special affinity with the garlic- and oil-based cuisine of Provence, particularly *aïoli*. Much of it is sold in a special 'skittle' bottle; all of it should be consumed as young and as cool as possible. Cinsaut and Grenache are typically used particularly for rosé, but Tibouren can add real interest to a blend. Rosés must contain at least 20 per cent of SAIGNÉE wine.

The focus of attention for a new generation of serious wine producers in this appellation, however, is red wine, which accounts for just 15 per cent of production. Great efforts have been made to replace the prolific Carignan vine with the more recent 'improving varieties' Syrah and Cabernet Sauvignon with which to add structure to the suppler permitted ingredients in red and rosé Côtes de Provence: Grenache, Cinsaut, and Mourvèdre and Tibouren. The percentage of Carignan allowed in the blend is being systematically decreased.

There is considerable experimentation with different forms of ÉLEVAGE, including the use of new OAK for some of the most ambitious cuvées, typically dominated by Cabernet Sauvignon and/or Syrah, although the former may represent no more than 30 per cent of the total blend.

An increasing number of producers, especially in the coastal sector, are paying as much attention to their white-wine output as the venerable Domaines Ott at Ch de Selle has been since the beginning of the century. Rolle in particular is enjoying renewed interest.

Domaine La Bernarde, Mas Cadenet, Domaine de la Courtade, Ch Real Martin, Domaine Richeaume, Domaine du Rimauresq, Domaine St André de Figuière are some of the most successful producers. See also the individual Provence appellations of Coteaux d'AIX-EN-PROVENCE, BANDOL, LES BAUX DE PROVENCE, BELLET, CASSIS, PALETTE, and Coteaux VAROIS.

pruning of vines involves cutting off unwanted vegetative parts in the form of CANES in winter. **Summer pruning** is another term for trimming or removing shoot tips.

Winter pruning is a vineyard practice developed by man primarily to produce fewer but larger bunches of riper grapes and is particularly important in cooler climates. More than 85 per cent of each year's shoot growth may be removed. Another aim of vine pruning is to establish or maintain a shape of vine, which makes all other vineyard operations easier. Up until the 1960s, winter pruning was labour intensive, but increases in labour costs and reductions in labour supply in Australia led to experimentation with and eventual development of MECHANICAL PRUNING. Tractors equipped with circular saws or reciprocating cutter blades were able to speed the laborious process of hand pruning without serious effects on wine quality in warm regions. R.E.S.

Puglia, Italian name for the southern Italian region known by English speakers as APULIA.

Puisseguin-St-Émilion, satellite appellation of ST-ÉMILION in Bordeaux.

Puligny-Montrachet, village in the Côte de Beaune district of Burgundy's CÔTE D'OR producing very fine wines from CHARDONNAY and some less exalted reds.

Puligny contains two GRAND CRU vineyards in their entirety, Chevalier-Montrachet and Bienvenues-Bâtard-Montrachet, and two which are shared with neighbouring Chassagne: Le Montrachet itself and Bâtard-Montrachet. Below this exalted level, yet still among the finest of all white wines of Burgundy, are the PREMIER CRU vineyards. There are at least 13 of these, more if subdivisions are counted. At the same elevation as Bâtard-Montrachet lie Les Pucelles (made famous by the excellence of Domaine Leflaive's version), Le Clavoillon, Les Perrières (including the Clos de la Mouchère), Les Referts, and Les Combettes, which produces the plump wines to be expected of a vineyard adjacent to Meursault-Perrières.

A little higher up the slope, at the same ele-

vation as Le Montrachet, lie Les Demoiselles, Le Cailleret, Les Folatières (including Clos de la Garenne), and Champ Canet. Part of Les Demoiselles is classified as grand cru Chevalier-Montrachet but a very small slice remains as premier cru, being regarded, along with Le Cailleret, as the finest example.

Further up the slope, where the terrain becomes rockier and the soil almost too sparse, are Le Champ Gain, Les Truffières, Les Chalumeaux, and the vineyards attached to the hamlet of BLAGNY, which are designated as Puligny-Montrachet premier cru for white wines, and Blagny premier cru for reds.

The VILLAGE WINES of Puligny-Montrachet are less impressive. Deep cellars ideal for AGEING wine are rare in Puligny, so that few of the village's growers can prolong BARREL MATURATION for more than about a year. There are surprisingly few domaines in Puligny and a substantial proportion of its produce is contracted to the NÉGOCIANTS of Beaune. However, Leflaive, Carillon, and Sauzet are fine family producers.

See also MONTRACHET and CÔTE D'OR. J.T.C.M.

pumping over. Wine-making operation involving the circulation of fermenting red wine with the grape skins. See also MACERATION.

punching down, the manual wine-making operation of breaking up and submerging the cap of skins and other solids during red-wine fermentation. See also MACERATION.

punt, optional indentation in the bottom of wine bottles, particularly common in bottles of sparkling wine.

PX, common abbreviation for the Spanish grape variety PEDRO XIMÉNEZ, or blending wine made from it used chiefly in SHERRY production.

Pyrenees, wine region (named after the mountains separating France from Spain) centred on the town of Avoca in Australia's Central VICTORIA zone.

QbA, or Qualitätswein bestimmter Anbau-gebiete, is Germany's largest wine category, the lower ranks of so-called QUALITÄTSWEIN, or 'quality wine'. The chief requirement of a QbA wine is that all the wine in the bottle comes from only one of Germany's 13 specified wine regions (although see also LIEBFRAUMILCH). The grapes should also reach certain minimum ripeness levels in terms of MUST WEIGHT. These must weights are carefully specified for each grape variety and for each region.

The wines also have to be made from recommended grape varieties and have to earn an AP NUMBER, but this is hardly very challenging. Unlike QMP wines, QbA wines may have their alcohol content increased by CHAPTALIZATION.

This category therefore includes the great majority of wines exported from Germany, all Liebfraumilch, and the sea of anonymous medium-dry blends carrying such GROSSLAGE names as Piesporter Michelsberg and Niersteiner Gutes Domtal. Many top wine producers make one or several QbA blends depending on the vintage, and in particularly poor years some choose to declassify as QbA wines even those musts which technically qualify as a QmP in order to retain the prestige of their QmP labels.

Few QbA wines improve with age. The exceptions are several experimental styles, notably BARRIQUE-aged wines, which may not qualify as QmP wines but need several years in bottle to show at their best.

QgU or Qualitätswein garantierten Ursprungs or German quality wine of guaranteed origin. See URSPRUNGSLAGE.

QmP, or Qualitätswein mit Prädikat, is Germany's category of usually superior wines. It means literally 'quality wine with distinction' and the PRÄDIKAT can qualify as one of six distinct subcategories, determined by the grapes' MUST WEIGHT. Precise OECHSLE levels are specified by law for each combination of grape variety and region. The grapes should also be picked as specified by law (see entries under each individual Prädikat name). Unlike QBA wines, a QmP wine cannot be CHAPTALIZED. SÜSSRESERVE may be added to sweeten a QmP wine, on the other hand, but this practice is declining in response to demand for drier, more concentrated wines (see TROCKEN and HALBTROCKEN). Since the late 1980s, it has also been common for the best producers to choose to set themselves higher minimum must weights for each Prädikat than the official minima, and even to choose to declassify wine in particularly ripe vintages such as 1990 for purely marketing reasons.

The proportion of the total German harvest which qualifies as QmP wine varies enormously with the weather conditions of each year. The cool weather of 1984 yielded a harvest of which only 7 per cent qualified as QmP, while the hot 1976 summer ripened 83 per cent of the entire crop to at least Kabinett level. Most of Germany's finest wines are QmP wines, the only possible exceptions being some of the more experimental wines, notably some of those aged in BARRIQUE, which may have been refused an AP NUMBER on the ground that they lack TYPICITY, as experimental wines are wont to do.

See KABINETT, SPÄTLESE, AUSLESE, BEEREN-

AUSLESE, TROCKENBEERENAUSLESE, and EISWEIN for more details.

Qualitätswein, German for quality wine. In GERMANY, this bloated category encompasses about 95 per cent of each German vintage, including some very ordinary blends indeed, and excludes only TAFELWEIN and LANDWEIN. GERMAN WINE LAW recognizes two sorts of Qualitätswein: Qualitätswein bestimmter Anbaugebiete or QBA, often called simply Qualitätswein, and, usually recognizably superior, Qualitätswein mit Prädikat or QMP, often called PRÄDIKATSWEIN.

In AUSTRIA, Qualitätswein is the category between Landwein and Prädikatswein, and it includes not only wine officially designated Qualitätswein, but also Austria's Kabinett wine. The proportion of the total Austrian crop which qualifies as Qualitätswein varies enormously according to the character of each vintage, but can be as high as one-third.

quality wine is not only an expression widely and loosely used for any wine of good quality, it is an official wine DESIGNATION throughout the European Union, and therefore throughout most of Europe. The EU recognizes quality wine as the higher of its two general categories of wine: quality wine (which must be produced in a specified region—an indicator of European reverence for geography) and TABLE WINE. In English, it may be referred to as Quality Wine PSR, in French as VQPRD, or Vin de Qualité Produit dans les Régions Délimitées. Each member country has a different system to describe this designation, but most are based on a system of CONTROLLED APPELLATIONS (although the German system depends more on the level of natural, unaugmented sugar in grapes, or ripeness).

Country	Quality wine
France	VDQS, APPELLATION CONTRÔLÉE*
Italy	DOC*, DOCG
Spain	DO*, DOCa
Portugal	DOC
Germany	QbA*, QmP
Greece	OPE, OPAP* (see GREECE)
United Kingdom	Quality wine (see ENGLAND)
Luxembourg	Appellation contrôlée (see LUXEMBOURG)

*indicates the more important category in terms of the amount of wine likely to carry the designation

The quality of the wine in each of these categories varies widely, as does the proportion of a typical vintage which qualifies as 'quality wine' in each country. Germany is notorious in classifying more than 95 per cent of every vintage as quality wine, while in France the proportion is closer to a much more realistic 40 per cent. Like any official scheme, the above have their critics, but Italy, Spain, and Portugal have been particularly profligate in their creation of DOCS and DOS. Nevertheless, quality wine represents just 13.5, 25, and 25 per cent respectively of the total wine production of Italy, Spain, and Portugal.

quarantine of imported plant material plays an important part in international viticulture, and can put a (necessary) brake on certain aspects of its development. Like any form of agricultural quarantine, it can annoy travellers but is designed to protect farmers from the ravages which may be caused by the introduction of pests and diseases from other countries or regions.

Quarts de Chaume, extraordinary small enclave within the Coteaux du LAYON appellation producing, only in the best vintages and usually only as a result of NOBLE ROT infection, sweet white wines from BOTRYTIZED Chenin Blanc grapes. Total annual production can often be as little as a few thousand cases, from just over 40 ha/100 acres of vineyard, supposedly the finest quarter, or *quart*, of the Chaume part near Rochefort-sur-Loire of Coteaux du Layon. The naturally high acidity of the Chenin Blanc grape endows these wines, very similar to nearby BONNEZEAUX, with impressive longevity. Domaine des Baumard and Ch Pierre-Bise make particularly fine examples.

Quatourze, one of the named CRUS within the Coteaux du LANGUEDOC appellation in southern France. Production of appellation wine in this small windswept zone just west of Narbonne is small and dominated by Ch Notre-Dame du Quatourze.

Queensland, hot north-eastern state in AUSTRALIA which produces some wine despite its latitude. Queensland's viticulture was until recently restricted to the Granite Belt, situated on the inland (or western) side of the Great Dividing Range just north of the NEW SOUTH WALES border. However, the 1990s saw a significant expansion of the map north towards Toowoomba and Kingaroy and east towards the coast. Fifteen wineries produce mainly Chardonnay, Semillon, Shiraz, and Cabernet Sauvignon of relatively modest quality, relying almost entirely on the passing tourist trade. ELEVATION is the key to the otherwise sub-equatorial climate. Shiraz and Semillon are the wines with the greatest individuality.   J.H.

Quincy, rapidly expanding, historic white-wine appellation in the greater Loire region producing racy dry wines from Sauvignon Blanc vines planted on the left bank of the Cher tributary. The wines tend to be a little more rustic, less delicate, than those made in Menetou-Salon and Sancerre to the east. See also LOIRE.

quinta, Portuguese word meaning 'farm', which may also refer to a wine-producing estate or vineyard. See also PORT.

Rabo de Ovelha, white grape variety grown all over Portugal, taking its name from the 'ewe's tail' shape of its bunches. Noted more for alcohol than subtlety. Also known as **Rabigato** (cat's tail) in Vinho Verde country and the Douro.

Raboso, tough red grape variety grown in the VENETO region of north-east Italy, notably as Raboso Piave, sometimes called Friulano, on the flat valley floor of PIAVE. Raboso Veronese is grown in the provinces of Padova (Padua), Treviso, Venezia, and Rovigo. The grape has uncompromisingly high ACIDITY and rough TANNINS and its wine can taste extremely austere in youth. Stalwart defenders of the variety insist that with prolonged FERMENTATION, oxygenated by frequent PUMPING OVER, and lengthy CASK AGEING, the grape could give distinguished wines, but the reputation and price level of Raboso make it difficult to justify this kind of investment. Raboso is a permitted VARIETAL of the Piave DOC but less than 1,500 hl/39,600 gal are made each year. D.T.

racking, the wine-making operation of removing clear wine from the settled SEDIMENT or LEES in the bottom of a container. The verb to **rack** has been used thus at least since the 14th century.

Racking is usually achieved by pumping or siphoning the wine away from the sediment into an empty container but special large **racking tanks** are used by some large wineries (and breweries).

Racking forms an important part of the annual cycle of cellar work, or ÉLEVAGE, in the production of most fine wines matured in small BARRELS. Racking from barrel to barrel is very labour intensive and, with the cost of the barrels themselves, one of the chief economic arguments against BARREL MATURATION. Each racking inevitably involves a barrel that needs cleaning.

Racking is not only part of the CLARIFICATION process, it also provides aeration, which, in the case of red wines, is beneficial to the sensory properties of the wine.

Raffiac, sometimes **Raffiat**, alternative names for ARRUFIAC.

Rajinski Rizling and **Rajnai Rizling,** various eastern European names for the true RIESLING grape of Germany.

Ramandolo. See VERDUZZO.

Ramisco, red grape variety grown exclusively in the shrinking COLARES region of Portugal and therefore probably the only VINIFERA vine variety never to have been GRAFTED. It can produce wines of real character that are extremely tannic in youth but the decline of the region has made them a rarity.

rancio, imprecise tasting term used in many languages for a distinctive style of wine, often FORTIFIED WINE or VIN DOUX NATUREL, achieved by deliberately MADERIZING the wine by exposing it to OXYGEN and/or heat. The wine may be stored in barrels in hot storehouses (as for some of Australia's LIQUEUR MUSCATS and Liqueur Tokays), or immediately under the rafters in a hot climate (as for some of ROUSSILLON's vins doux naturels), or in glass BONBONNES left out of doors and subjected to the changing temperatures of night and day (as in parts of Spain). The word rancio has the same root as 'rancid' and the wines which result have an additional and powerful smell reminiscent of overripe fruit, nuts, and melted, or even rancid, butter.

Rasteau, one of the Côtes du Rhône villages in the southern RHÔNE. Its heady, slightly rustic red, white, and rosé table wines are sold as Côtes du Rhône-Villages, occasionally with the name Rasteau as a suffix.

Wines sold as Appellation Rasteau Contrôlée, on the other hand, are VINS DOUX NATURELS, sweet, fortified wines in various shades of brown and red. They are essentially alcoholic Grenache juice (90 per cent of the grapes must be GRENACHE Noir, Gris, or Blanc) treated to a range of AGEING processes.

ratafia is an old, usually domestically produced wine made in the French countryside by drying grapes to a raisin-like state and then moistening and fermenting them in the spring.

ratings, scores applied to individual wines. See NUMBERS AND WINE and SCORING.

Räuschling, white grape variety today most commonly planted in German-speaking SWITZERLAND, where it can produce fine, crisp wines.

Rebe, German for vine. **Rebsorten** are vine varieties.

Recioto, distinctive category of north-east Italian DRIED-GRAPE WINES, a historic speciality of the VENETO. The most common forms of Recioto are sweet red Recioto della VALPOLICELLA and the much rarer sweet white Recioto di SOAVE.

Recioto della Valpolicella, like its dry counterpart AMARONE, is produced from grapes which have been raisined in special drying rooms during the late autumn and winter months after the harvest; like Amarone, it is produced from the same grapes as qualify for the Valpolicella DOC, which zone has been divided into a CLASSICO subzone and a larger zone whose wines are simply called Recioto. The wine is a decisively sweet one, steps being taken to prevent the conversion of its RESIDUAL SUGARS into alcohol during the period of fermentation and ageing. A certain development of NOBLE ROT has been virtually inevitable, given the damp climate of Valpolicella during the months of raisining between November

and March, and traditionally made wines display BOTRYTIS flavours, along with a certain OXIDIZED character. A small but growing number of younger producers is now seeking to avoid the imprint of botrytis and oxidation by eliminating botrytis-affected grapes and bunches prior to fermentation (as for Amarone). Some producers are also experimenting with new barrels of 400- to 500-l/132-gal capacity in place of the traditional, considerably larger casks of old Slovenian oak.

Recioto represents a very small proportion of Valpolicella's total production, although it may well increase as a consequence of a new interest in the wine and very successful vintages in the 1990s. A Recioto of white grapes—principally GARGANEGA—which resembles a Recioto di Soave is also produced in minuscule quantities in the Valpolicella zone, but qualifies only as a VINO DA TAVOLA. D.T.

récolte, French for HARVEST. A **récoltant** is therefore a GROWER. In CHAMPAGNE, a **récoltant-manipulant** (identified by 'RM' on the label) is a grower who also makes his or her own champagne, of whom there are more than 2,000 in the region, as opposed to a **récoltant-coopérateur,** who sells champagne made by a CO-OPERATIVE, of whom there are slightly fewer.

recorking, a hazardous exercise conducted by some top wine producers and some fine-wine traders. The aim is to prolong a wine's potential longevity after extended BOTTLE AGEING may have weakened the cork.

Redondo, town in southern Portugal whose co-operative is establishing a certain reputation for its wines. See ALENTEJO for more details.

reduced. See TASTING TERMS.

reduced-alcohol wines are those with a lower than normal ALCOHOLIC STRENGTH, generally less than 5.5 per cent.

The easiest and cheapest way to produce these low-alcohol products is simply to dilute wine using water (to make a SPRITZER-type drink), natural or flavoured fruit juices, or even GRAPE JUICE to make an all-vinous product. See wine COOLERS.

Another method is to arrest fermentation before it is complete by refrigeration, resulting in a sweet, low-alcohol, often lightly sparkling drink. This is a particularly common technique in Italy and is conducted at all sorts of quality levels, from the finest MOSCATO D'ASTI to partial fermentation of LAMBRUSCO must stored throughout the year at low temperatures and transformed into relatively industrial 'Lambrusco Light' as required.

See also DEALCOHOLIZED WINE.

red-wine-making, the production of wines with reddish to purple colours. The great majority of red wines made today depend on CRUSHING and DESTEMMING of the grape clusters or bunches as a first step in their production (although see also WHOLE-BUNCH FERMENTATION and CARBONIC MACERATION).

The mixture of skins, seeds, and some stem fragments, along with the juice, then go into a fermentation vessel, where YEAST converts sugars into ALCOHOL. The natural ANTHOCYANIN pigments, which are contained in the skins of black grapes, along with FLAVOUR COMPOUNDS, FLAVOUR PRECURSORS, and large amounts of PHENOLICS (the latter originating from both the skins and seeds) are extracted into the fermenting wine by the alcohol produced by yeast during FERMENTATION and MACERATION. Without some maceration of juice and skins, wine made from dark-skinned grapes is merely pink (as described in ROSÉ-WINE-MAKING). Duration of this EXTRACTION process can be anything from a fast two- or three-day fermentation for an everyday wine to a week-long fermentation followed by a further one, two, or even three weeks' maceration for a full-bodied red wine that is designed to age.

Red-wine fermentations are almost always conducted at TEMPERATURES higher than those used for white wines. Red wines fermented at lower temperatures tend to be lighter in colour and body and to display the fruitier range of esters (compounds formed by reaction of acids with alcohols). There is usually some producer somewhere in the world deliberately fashioning light reds in this style to be consumed chilled.

Red-wine-making differs from white-wine-making not only in terms of skin–juice contact and temperature but also because some exposure to OXYGEN is more generally desirable than with white wines, and BARREL MATURATION, or at least CASK AGEING, is also more common for red wines than white.

During barrel maturation, both the substances produced in the earlier reactions between grape phenolics and oxygen and those derived from the wood interact and contribute an entirely new range of flavours. Further reactions take place during BOTTLE AGEING. The abundance and diversity of compounds in red wine explain why AGEING is so important for fine red wines.

See also WINE-MAKING.   A.D.W. & P.J.W.

red wines actually vary in colour from dark pink to almost black, with an enormous variation in the amount of blue or yellow to be seen at the rim. Their colour depends on the grape varieties used, the vintage characteristics, the health of the grapes, the wine-making methods (in particular the extent of MACERATION), the wine's PH, and the amount of time it has spent in tank, barrel, and bottle. A red wine that has suffered OXIDATION or is many decades old may be the same deep tawny colour as a very old white wine.

Red wines are produced in virtually all of the world's wine regions, although the proportion of red wines produced at the cool limit of wine production is low, since it can be difficult to develop sufficient pigmentation of most grapes' skins to produce a proper red wine.

French for red is *rouge*, Italian is *rosso*, Spanish and Portuguese more expressively *tinto*, Russian is *cherny*, and German is *rot*. Spain divides her red wines into those which really are *tinto* and lighter ones called CLARETE.

Refosco, red grape variety that makes usefully vigorous wine in the FRIULI region of north-east Italy.

The vine is cultivated both in HILLSIDE VINEYARDS and in flatter parts of Friuli and gives a deeply coloured wine with plummy flavours and a hint of almonds, a medium to full body, and a rather elevated ACIDITY which can be difficult to control or moderate.

The most promising zone for Refosco is COLLI ORIENTALI. Others include GRAVE DEL FRIULI, LISON-PRAMAGGIORE (outside Friuli), Latisana, Aquileia, and Carso. The variety is known as Teran just across the border in SLOVENIA and CROATIA, where it produces very similar wines.

D.T.

Região Demarcada, a demarcated region (RD) of PORTUGAL, although the expression is not often seen on labels. See Denominacão de Origem Controlada (DOC).

regionality, New World term for the concept, now increasingly accepted there, that the location of a vineyard plays an important part in shaping the character of the wine produced from it. It is less geographically precise and, importantly, less French, than the term TERROIR.

More and more wines in, for example, California and Australia, where this new word was coined, are labelled and marketed on a geographical as well as VARIETAL basis.

Regner is an increasingly popular German crossing of a white TABLE GRAPE Seidentraube and Gamay. This is definitely not a wine to drink as a VARIETAL (although tests in England have been successful) but is useful for blenders.

Régnié, the most recently created of the 10 BEAUJOLAIS crus (only in 1988). The wines are still establishing their identity.

Reguengos, or Reguengos de Monsaraz, town in Portugal whose co-operative is establishing a certain reputation for its wines. See ALENTEJO.

Reichensteiner is a white grape variety which is a crossing of Müller-Thurgau with a crossing of the French table grape MADELEINE ANGEVINE and the Italian Early Calabrese. Both wine and vine most closely resemble its undistinguished German parent. There are a few hundred hectares in Germany, with more than half in the Rheinhessen. The variety enjoyed considerable success in ENGLAND, where it is the third most planted variety.

Reserva, term used in both Spain and Portugal to distinguish wines from a supposedly good vintage. In Portugal, a Reserva is a wine from a good vintage with an alcohol level at least half a per cent above the regional minimum. In Spain, a red wine labelled Reserva will have had at least three years' AGEING in cask and bottle, of which a year must be in cask. The wine may not be released until the fourth year after the harvest. Spanish white wines labelled Reserva must spend a total of at least two years in cask and bottle to qualify, with at least six months of this period in OAK.

See also GRAN RESERVA and RIOJA.   R.J.M.

Reserve is a term liberally used by wine producers for various bottlings. It should be quite literally reserved itself, for superior wines, but, unlike RESERVA and RISERVA, the English term Reserve has few controls on its use.

In CHAMPAGNE, reserve wines are those held over from a given year for future blending, typically into the NON-VINTAGE cuvée.

residual sugar, occasionally RS, the total quantity of sugars remaining unfermented in the finished wine. This may include both fermentable sugars, which have for some reason remained unconverted to alcohol during FERMENTATION, and small amounts of those few sugars which are not readily fermented by typical wine YEAST. Some, but by no means all, residual sugar is tasted as SWEETNESS.

Residual sugar in wine is usually measured in grams of total sugars per litre of wine and can vary between about 1 g/l (0.1 per cent) and 25 g/l (2.5 per cent) or more. Wines with a residual sugar content of less than 2 g/l, such as the great majority of red wines and many white wines that do not taste at all sweet, are described as dry. On the other hand, many wines with a residual sugar level even as high as 25 g/l may taste dry because the sweetness is offset by high ACIDITY or possibly bitterness from TANNINS. Some ordinary wines (usually white) that are naturally high in acids may have sugars, sweet GRAPE JUICE, or sweet rectified grape must added deliberately to increase their palatability or commercial appeal.

Exceptionally sweet wines may be produced either in extraordinarily ripe years or by unusual wine-making techniques such as those involved in freeze CONCENTRATION, BOTRYTIZED, or DRIED-GRAPE WINES. The sweetest form of the unique Hungarian sweet wine TOKAJI, for example, must have a minimum residual sugar of 250 g/l.

A great sweet wine such as a fine SAUTERNES or a BEERENAUSLESE remains stable because of the action of NOBLE ROT. Both the very high residual sugar and the trace materials secreted by the BOTRYTIS into the juice inhibit fermentation. Because of this, many fine sweet wines are stable despite their high sugar levels and low alcohol levels.   A.D.W.

residues. Residues of agrochemicals, the commercial preparations used in vineyards for the control of pests, diseases, or weeds, are that portion which is found on the grapes or in wine.

resveratrol, PHENOLIC compound produced by grapevines (and other plants such as peanut and eucalyptus trees), particularly in response to microbial attack or artificial agents such as ultraviolet radiation. Wine-making procedures have a great effect on resveratrol concentration in the final product. Red wines have a much higher resveratrol content than whites, usually about 10 times as much. Resveratrol is one of a number of compounds found in wine thought to contribute to HEALTH aspects of its moderate consumption. It has been reported to reduce serum platelet aggregation, cholesterol levels, liver lipids, and act as a cancer chemo-preventative agent.   G.L.C.

retsina, resinated wine that is extremely common in GREECE, and a potent catalyst of taverna nostalgia outside it. Modern retsina is made like any other white (or rosé) wine, except that small pieces of pine resin are added to the must and left with the wine until the first RACKING separates the finished wine from all solids. Major producing areas are Attica, Euboea, and Boeotia, all in the southern part of central Greece close to Athens, but retsina is also made for local consumption all over the country. SAVATIANO is usually the principal grape, often enlivened with some RHODITIS or occasionally ASSYRTIKO, but a wide range of local grape varieties are also used, and an interesting MUSCAT retsina is made on the island of Lemnos.

Retsina is protected by the European Union as a traditional appellation. It is rarely made outside Greece and southern Cyprus, where local palates are accustomed to its distinctively pungent flavour, and visitors expect it. A South Australian version has been essayed.   M.McN.

Reuilly, expanding French appellation so far inside the bend of the Loire that it is often described as coming from central France. Its most useful manifestation is as a less expensive and sometimes purer version of the SANCERRE appellation to the east made from Sauvignon Blanc grapes in one of the riper vintages. As much red and rosé wine is made as white, however, from Pinot Noir and a little Pinot Gris (the local Gamay is sold as VIN DE PAYS). Pale-pink Reuilly has its devotees. The best wines can be finer than those of nearby QUINCY, especially from the likes of Claude Lafond. This Loire appellation is not to be confused with that of RULLY in the Côte Chalonnaise. See also LOIRE.

Rhein, German name for the river RHINE.

Rheingau, for generations the most economically successful wine region in GERMANY, the ultra-traditional area is increasingly rivalled by the more dynamic PFALZ, BADEN, and the best estates of the MOSEL-SAAR-RUWER. Over 90 per cent of the region is on the right bank of the RHINE, between Wiesbaden and the MITTELRHEIN boundary at Lorchhausen. The remainder of the Rheingau vineyards are near Hochheim (the origin of the word HOCK) on the banks of the Main, shortly before its confluence with the Rhine at Mainz.

The vineyards at Hochheim and in the central part of the region are mostly on gently rolling or flat land, but from Rüdesheim downstream to Lorchhausen the terrain is much steeper. The Rheingau soil is very varied throughout. Within the context of the whole of the German vineyard, the region has a favoured MESOCLIMATE. With its southern aspect, it is marginally warmer than much of RHEINHESSEN to the south, and its annual rainfall of a little over 600 m/23 in means that there is an adequate supply of water for the RIESLING vine to ripen its grapes long into autumn.

At Geisenheim, the Rheingau has one of the world's leading viticultural institutes, but it has not been invaded by newer GERMAN CROSSINGS to the same extent as other German regions such as Rheinhessen and the Pfalz. The Riesling vine is planted on over 80 per cent of the area under vine.

The Rheingau is principally a region for white wine. Spätburgunder (PINOT NOIR) accounts for only 10 per cent of the region's vines, but it is more important each year and the percentage doubled in the 1980s. German restaurants have encouraged the move to drier wines and have stimulated an interest in FOOD AND WINE MATCHING. This has led inevitably to a need for red wine, particularly from Spätburgunder.

In the late 1990s, over 50 per cent of all Rheingau wine which received a quality control AP NUMBER was dry or TROCKEN, and an additional third was medium dry or HALBTROCKEN. In spite of modern trends, all would probably agree that it is in rich, sweet, BOTRYTIZED wines of AUSLESE quality and upwards in a great vintage that Rheingau Riesling still reaches a peak of possible quality.

Other than in rare, very warm years such as 1976 or 1993, an increasing number of growers choose not to engage in a time-consuming and expensive gathering of grapes with noble rot for Auslese wine. Instead they leave part of the crop of healthy grapes on the vine (perhaps not in their best site), in the hope of temperatures of −8 °C/18 °F or lower and with them the chance to produce an EISWEIN.

The role of co-operatives is a relatively minor one compared with that of the private and state-owned estates. Other than at the region's two famous castles, SCHLOSS JOHANNISBERG and Schloss Vollrads, most estates of some size have vineyard holdings in a number of villages.

The *Berg* or hill at Rüdesheim, which overlooks the confluence of the Nahe and the Rhine, is famous in Germany for wines that are full in flavour and often surprisingly good in poor vintages. In the villages or towns of Geisenheim, Johannisberg, Winkel, Hattenheim, and Erbach, it is not their names alone which are likely to guarantee the quality of their wine but rather that of the bottler. All are capable of producing Riesling wines of a high order, but amongst the richest and most refined will usually be found some from Erbach and Hattenheim. In hot summers, the wines of Schloss Vollrads, Kiedrich, and Rauenthal, which lie on higher ground some distance from the Rhine, can be quite outstanding, with a flavour which seems to last for ever. Perhaps the fullest Rieslings come from the deep soil of Hochheim. With skilful wine-making, they are as fine as any in the region, and, therefore, in the world.

I.J. & K.B.S.

Rheinhessen, large, growing, and varied wine region in GERMANY. On the eastern edge of this region, the red soil of sloping vineyards such as Nierstein's Roter Hang group produces wine that is internationally recognized as of the highest quality. A third of the region's stock of RIESLING vines grows in this privileged area known as the Rheinterrasse, which stretches from Bodenheim, a little south of Mainz, to Mettenheim, north of Worms. Some parts of the Rheinterrasse face due east and, as ever in Germany, MESOCLIMATE is all important. The vineyards nearest the river RHINE are warmer throughout the year and this partly accounts for the superiority of the small collective site, or GROSSLAGE, Niersteiner Rehbach and its neighbouring single vineyard, or EINZELLAGE, in the Rheinterrasse, Nackenheimer Rothenberg.

The north of Rheinhessen has its best vineyards at Ingelheim (known in Germany over many years for its red Spätburgunder, or PINOT NOIR, wine), and at Bingen in the Scharlachberg site. In the south of Bereich Wonnegau, the wine villages of Westhofen, Bechtheim, and Osthofen are relatively well known in Germany.

There are over 400 individual vineyard sites in Rheinhessen, but over half of the region's wine is sold under the name of a Grosslage such as Niersteiner Gutes Domtal, Oppenheimer Krötenbrunnen, or Mainzer Domherr. Rheinhessen accounts for one-third of all German wine exports, and for more than 60 per cent of the country's LIEBFRAUMILCH.

More than in any other German wine region, the choice of vine variety and range of wines produced in Rheinhessen have been influenced by the peculiarities of the GERMAN WINE LAW. The official wine hierarchy is founded on the idea that a heavier MUST WEIGHT (an enhanced amount of grape sugars) relates automatically to an improvement in the quality of the future wine. Although this is normally true of RIESLING and most other long-established vine varieties growing in Germany, it does not apply to crossings such as BACCHUS, FABER, HUXELREBE, KERNER planted in the 1960s and 1970s. Their wines, often strongly scented, lacked elegance, but they met the popular German taste of the day for sweetish wine, which was reflected in the export market. The result is that, even in the late 1990s, over 70 per cent of Rheinhessen's vine varieties for white wine are either new crossings or the older crossing MÜLLER-THURGAU. However, not all Rheinhessen wine from new crossings is inferior and, where the YIELD is restricted, Müller-Thurgau (increasingly marketed under its synonym Rivaner) and, particularly, SCHEUREBE can produce wines of high quality. SILVANER is still viewed as the region's most traditional variety and is still its second most planted grape.

The area occupied by red vine varieties is increasing and in 1997 amounted to 13 per cent of the total Rheinhessen vineyard. The prolific PORTUGIESER, the successful new crossing DORNFELDER, and Spätburgunder (Pinot Noir) are the most popular varieties.

Rheinhessen is divided into three districts: Bereich Bingen, Bereich Nierstein, and Bereich Wonnegau. As Bereich Nierstein is more than three times the size of the Rheingau region, some would say that another district should be created, solely for the fine vineyards of the Rheinterrasse. The wish to be part of such a district within Rheinhessen is strong in Nierstein. Although it has many of the best individual vineyard sites in the Rheinterrasse, its reputation has been diminished by having its name linked to that of Grosslage Gutes Domtal.

The flavour from the red sandstone and slate, which is so characteristic of the northern part of the Rheinterrasse, is shown clearly and cleanly by the Rieslings from the Rothenberg site at Nackenheim and its neighbouring vineyards. They resemble a little the concentrated, firm wines grown in the Traiser Bastei site in the NAHE, but their character is more gentle. In the varied soils of Oppenheim, the Riesling wines are particularly elegant and charming, and often less full flavoured than those of Nierstein. The increasingly widespread adoption of ORGANIC VITICULTURE principles in the vineyard and cellar, lower yields, and less residual sugar in wine should all help to emphasize the regional flavour, which will be to the advantage of the embattled market for fine wines in Rheinhessen.

Almost half of the region's wine is bottled by merchants elsewhere, and a third is exported. Within Germany, Rheinhessen has become popularly associated with cheap SPÄTLESEN, sold at low prices in supermarkets, particularly to the middle-aged in the north of the country. The national swing to drier wines has reduced the Rheinhessen share of the market and, in response, a crisp, attractive, dry wine was created in 1986 called Rheinhessen Silvaner, often referred to simply as RS. Another limited edition wine, Selection Rheinhessen, was created in 1992. It may be made only from classic varieties from vines at least 15 years old and the grapes must be of Spätlese ripeness. The wines are vinified dry and are released in early October in the year after the harvest.

About 77 per cent of the wine is sold in bulk, at prices which for the last two decades have been forced down to an uneconomic level by the large supermarket buyers and their suppliers. The development in the 1980s of profitable sales of SEKT sparkling wine made from Rheinhessen base wine has therefore been welcomed in the region. The leader in this field is a producers' association founded in 1981, the Erzeugergemeinschaft Winzersekt, which offers sparkling wine bearing a vintage, the name of a vine variety, and sometimes that of a vineyard site. Extra dry and brut are the preferred styles, and the selling prices are comparable with those of the good-quality Riesling brands of the large manufacturers of German sparkling wine (see SEKT).   I.J. & K.B.S.

Rheinpfalz, German wine region. See PFALZ.

Rhein Riesling, or Rheinriesling, common synonym in German-speaking countries for the great white RIESLING grape variety of Germany.

Rheinterrasse, admired wine district in Germany. See RHEINHESSEN.

Rhine, English name for the river known in German as the **Rhein** and in French as the **Rhin**. The German 'Rhein' describes a table-wine (see TAFELWEIN) subdistrict identical to the quality-wine regions AHR, HESSISCHE BERGSTRASSE, MITTELRHEIN, NAHE, PFALZ, RHEINGAU, and RHEINHESSEN. On some wine lists in the English-speaking world, all German wines, other than those regarded as MOSEL (or often 'Moselle'), appear somewhat imprecisely under the heading 'Rhine'. A German white table wine from either Riesling or Silvaner grapes, or their derivatives, entitled to bear the name 'Rhein' may also be known as HOCK.

See also SWITZERLAND and LIECHTENSTEIN.

Rhine Riesling, common synonym for the great white RIESLING grape variety of Germany, colloquially abbreviated to 'Rhine' in Australia, where it is most common.

Rhoditis, slightly pink-skinned grape variety traditionally grown in the Peloponnese. It ripens relatively late and keeps its acidity quite well even in such hot climates as that of Ankhíalos in Thessaly in central Greece, although it can also ripen well in high-altitude vineyards. It is often blended with the softer SAVATIANO, particularly for RETSINA.

Rhône, one of the most important wine rivers, linking a range of vineyards as dissimilar as those of CHÂTEAUNEUF-DU-PAPE in southern France, sparkling SEYSSEL, and Fendant du Valais in SWITZERLAND.

In wine circles, however, the term Rhône usually means the wines made in the Rhône valley in south-east France, which themselves vary so much, north and south of an almost vine-free 50-km/30-mile stretch between approximately Valence and Montélimar, that they are divided into two very distinct zones (although the regional appellation Côtes du Rhône encompasses the less ambitious wines of the north as well as a large area of the south). The Rhône regularly produces more APPELLATION CONTRÔLÉE wine than any region other than Bordeaux, about 95 per cent of the more than 3 million hl/79 million gal produced each year being red and usually high in alcohol relative to other French wines.

The greater Rhône valley is divided into four wine districts, of which the **southern Rhône** is by far the most important in terms of quantity. The most important Rhône district in terms of the prestige of its wines is the **northern Rhône**, which includes the appellations of Hermitage and Côte Rôtie, representing serious rivals to the great names of Bordeaux and Burgundy in the quality and, especially, longevity of their best wines. The northern Rhône is quite different from the southern Rhône in terms of climate, soils, topography, and even vine varieties.

A third small but extremely ancient district about 64 km/40 miles east of Valence up the Drôme tributary comprises the Diois appellations, named after the town of Die, of CHÂTILLON-EN-DIOIS, CLAIRETTE DE DIE, CRÉMANT de Die, and Coteaux DIOIS.

And finally there are the outlying appellations that are on the eastern borders of the southern Rhône and the northern borders of PROVENCE. See Coteaux du TRICASTIN, Côtes du LUBERON, Côtes du VENTOUX, and VDQS Côtes du VIVARAIS.

It should be noted that COSTIÈRES DE NÎMES, for long considered part of the LANGUEDOC region, is effectively a western extension of the southern Rhône.

Northern Rhône

The vineyards of the northern Rhône have probably been noticed by more tourists than any others. Here, high above the *autoroute du soleil*, TERRACES have been set to work as advertising hoardings for such producers as JABOULET and CHAPOUTIER, but their produce is aimed in the main at the fine-wine connoisseur rather than at the mass market. The total production of the northern Rhône is usually less than the total production of red Châteauneuf-du-Pape, a single appellation in the southern Rhône, with Crozes-Hermitage alone representing about half of all wine produced in the north.

The northern Rhône is under the influence of a CONTINENTAL climate, with hard winters and summers, whose effect on the grapes can be exaggerated by the steep slopes to which many of the better northern Rhône vineyards cling, although soil erosion is a constant threat. The best wines are produced on inclines which are expensive to work and help to maximize the effect of the available SUNLIGHT. Since the 1980s, however, there has been considerable expansion, particularly on the flatter land in such appellations as St-Joseph and Crozes-Hermitage, but also in more restricted appellations such as Cornas and Condrieu. Most appellations are based on the right bank of the river, but the left-bank vineyards of Crozes-Hermitage, and especially Hermitage, are particularly well exposed to afternoon sunshine.

This is the prime territory of the SYRAH grape, which is the only red grape permitted in northern Rhône red wines. Fashionable VIOGNIER is the defining grape variety of the white wines Condrieu and Château-Grillet, while other white northern Rhône wines are made from the robust MARSANNE, given nerve by the more delicate ROUSSANNE grape.

Most wine-making and all vine-growing is in the hands of individuals working a family holding. About half of all wines are bottled by merchants, of which Jaboulet, Chapoutier, Delas, and GUIGAL are some of the best known. Guigal's single-vineyard bottlings and distinctive, if controversial, use of new OAK did much to raise international awareness, and prices, of the northern Rhône in the 1980s. There are very few CO-OPERATIVES, although the one at Tain l'Hermitage is well regarded.

For more details, see the specific appellations CHÂTEAU-GRILLET, CONDRIEU, CORNAS, CÔTE RÔTIE, CROZES-HERMITAGE, HERMITAGE, ST-JOSEPH, and ST-PÉRAY.

Southern Rhône

The southern Rhône has only the river in common with the northern Rhône. The countryside here in the flatter, southern part of the valley is definitively southern, almost Provençal, influenced by a MEDITERRANEAN CLIMATE.

Most wines are blends rather than made from a single vine variety. Although Syrah is increasingly widely planted to endow red wines with longevity, the main red grape variety is GRENACHE. It can in theory be supplemented or seasoned by a wide range of other local varieties, but in practice only CARIGNAN, CINSAUT, MOURVÈDRE, and Syrah are planted to any extent. Similarly, UGNI BLANC is in reality the most planted white grape variety, even though it, like Carignan, may make only a limited contribution to a blend.

CO-OPERATIVES are very important in the southern Rhône, making about 70 per cent of total production. The NÉGOCIANTS of the northern Rhône also have a long tradition of buying wine here for blending and bottling *en route* to the north. But there is also a host of individual estates, especially in Châteauneuf-du-Pape, keen to etch their own stamp on a particularly accessible appellation. Wine-making techniques here are extremely varied, including everything from full-blown CARBONIC MACERATION to fly-blown ancient, open, wooden fermenting vats of uncertain age and certain lack of HYGIENE. New oak is treated with suspicion.

The southern Rhône is the only part of France other than the LANGUEDOC-ROUSSILLON to have a tradition of making sweet VIN DOUX NATUREL: a golden Muscat version, RANCIO tawny, and ruby red.

For more details, see CHÂTEAUNEUF-DU-PAPE, GIGONDAS, LIRAC, TAVEL, and VACQUEYRAS, as well as the two vin doux naturel appellations BEAUMES-DE-VENISE and RASTEAU.

Côtes du Rhône

This expression is sometimes used for the entire Rhône valley, but the specific appellation, granted in 1937, has almost become French for red wine. The great majority of Côtes du Rhône comes from the flatter, arid, often windswept vineyards of the southern Rhône, typically a light fruity red wine made, using full or semi-CARBONIC MACERATION, by one of the many co-operatives in the region.

A significant proportion of this wine is released as a PRIMEUR, in competition with Beaujolais Nouveau. There are some notable independent estates such as Domaine Gramenon, Ch du Grand Moulas, Domaine la Réméjeanne, and Domaine St-Estève, but the two most age-worthy and exceptional red Côtes du Rhônes available are Coudelet de Beaucastel and the extraordinary Domaine de Fonsalette, produced respectively as adjuncts to two of the greatest estates in Châteauneuf-du-Pape, Chx de Beaucastel and Rayas. About two per cent of Côtes du Rhône is white, but a considerable quantity of rosé is made, specifically for summer drinking in the region.

The total area of vineyard dedicated to the appellation is about 40,000 ha/98,800 acres, a vast proportion of viticultural France matched only by the generic Bordeaux appellation. The area which qualifies for the appellation includes the fringes of smarter northern Rhône appellations as well as huge tracts of both the left and right banks of the southern

Rhône. Most of the northern Rhône NÉGOCIANTS blend and bottle their own Côtes du Rhône, and that of Guigal can show the marked Syrah character of the northern Rhône.

The great majority of grapes used for Côtes du Rhône, however, are southern, which means officially those allowed in CHÂTEAUNEUF-DU-PAPE plus the scented white Viognier, and Carignan, though Grenache tends to dominate.

Côtes du Rhône-Villages

This useful appellation represents a distinct step up in quality, and often value, from generic Côtes du Rhône. The basic maximum permitted YIELD is lower, and the appellation has adopted Châteauneuf-du-Pape's minimum alcoholic strength of 12.5 per cent for red wines. The possibility for promotion to a specific appellation exists for each named village, and first GIGONDAS then VACQUEYRAS escaped the relative anonymity of the Villages appellation. Sixteen villages are allowed to append their name to the appellation Côtes du Rhône-Villages (and very cumbersome wine names some of them make too): Rochegude, St-Maurice-sur-Eygues, Vinsobres, Rousset-les-Vignes, St-Pantaléon-les-Vignes, Cairanne, RASTEAU, Roaix, Séguret, Valréas, Visan, Sablet, BEAUMES-DE-VENISE, Chusclan, Laudun, and St-Gervais. Of these, Cairanne has long been considered ripe for promotion. Some of the most energetic and thoughtful wine producers of France are based within this appellation.

Rhône Rangers, loose affiliation of CALIFORNIA wine producers who, led by Bob Lindquist of Qupé winery and Randall Grahm of Bonny Doon, decided in the 1980s to produce wines in the image of the reds and, increasingly, whites of the RHÔNE valley in France. Such wines provided a useful outlet for the produce of old GRENACHE and Mataro (MOURVÈDRE) vines which had previously languished out of favour. It also resulted in a dramatic increase in plantings of such vine varieties as SYRAH and VIOGNIER. Joseph Phelps of NAPA was an early exponent, Bonny Doon of SANTA CRUZ a later but noisier one.

Rías Baixas, the leading DO wine zone in GALICIA, north-west Spain, producing some of the country's most sought-after dry white wines. The zone's reputation is based on the white ALBARIÑO grape, which has been accorded cult status in Spain.

Rías Baixas splits into three separate subzones, all within the province of Pontevedra. Many of the purest Albariño wines come from the Val do Salnes zone centred on the town of Cambados on the west coast. The two further subzones, O Rosal and Condado de Tea, are on the northern slopes of the river Miño facing the VINHO VERDE region in Portugal on the opposite bank. All three zones share the same granite-based subsoils and relatively cool, damp, MARITIME climate.

Eleven different vine varieties are officially permitted in Rías Baixas although Albariño accounts for 90 per cent of the vineyard area. Other white grapes which may be blended with Albariño according to local regulations include CAÍÑO BLANCO, as well as TREIXADURA and LOUREIRO (locally known as Marqués), both of which are found in the Vinho Verde region. On its own, Albariño produces a fragrant, intensely fruity, dry white wine with a natural minimum alcohol often above 12 per cent. The five permitted red grapes, including MENCÍA, ESPADEIRO, and Caíño Tinto, are relatively unimportant. R.J.M. & V. de la S.

Ribatejo, DOC region in central southern Portugal corresponding to the province of the same name on both sides of the river Tagus (Tejo) inland from the capital Lisbon. As well as being a DOC, the entire province is entitled to the VINHO REGIONAL designation of Ribatejano. The Ribatejo is second only to ESTREMADURA in the amount of wine it produces each year, although much of the Ribatejo wine is rough and astringent. Made in CO-OPERATIVES, it is bottled in 5-l flagons and sold in bars and cafés. The Ribatejo was for many years the anonymous source of some of Portugal's best red wines, the GARRAFEIRAS aged for at least three years and sold under the name of a merchant rather than that of the region. FERNÃO PIRES, ARINTO, and Talia (the Portuguese name for UGNI BLANC) are the favoured white grapes while CASTELÃO FRANCÊS (sometimes called João de Santarém or Periquita) is much the most significant red grape. INTERNATIONAL VARIETIES have been planted near Almeirim. The Ribatejo is divided into six DOCs: Almeirim, Cartaxo, Chamusca, Coruche, Santarém, and Tomar. Of these, Almeirim and Cartaxo, each dominated by a large CO-OPERATIVE winery, are the most important. R.J.M.

Ribeira Sacra, Spanish DO created in 1996. It adjoins Valdeorras to the east, and is the only GALICIAN region specializing in red wines, from the MENCÍA grape, with some whites from Godello and Albariño. V. de la S.

Ribeiro means 'riverbank' or 'riverside' in the Galician language and is the name of a red- and white-wine zone in GALICIA, north-west Spain. Ribeiro spans the valleys of the river Miño and its tributaries and Arnoia downstream from Orense. The region became a DO in 1957 but this has had little impact on exports. Over recent years, growers have been encouraged to uproot the productive but unsuitable variety PALOMINO in favour of TREIXADURA, TORRONTÉS, and LADO, white grape varieties which perform well in the damp MARITIME climate of north-west Iberia. Both varieties can be made into aromatic, crisp white wines. The deeply coloured, light-bodied red wines, mainly from red-fleshed Garnacha Tintorera grapes, are of no great interest, but some growers as Arsenio Paz have reintroduced red wines made from indigenous varieties. R.J.M. & V. de la S.

Ribera del Duero, important wine zone in CASTILE AND LEÓN in north central Spain strongly challenging RIOJA as the leading red-wine-producing region in Iberia. Ribera del Duero spans the upper valley of the river Duero (known as the DOURO in Portugal), starting some 30 km/18 miles east of the city of Valladolid. Although Bodegas VEGA SICILIA on the western margin of the denomination has been producing one of Spain's finest wines since the mid 19th century, the region was awarded DO status only in 1982. Since then more than 50 private estates have emerged.

The potential of this area was recognized by Alejandro Fernández, who played a key role in the considerable development of the region in the 1980s. Pesquera, his wine vinified from grapes growing around the village of Pesquera del Duero a short distance upstream from Vega Sicilia, was released in the early 1980s to international acclaim. Other growers (many of whom had previously sold their grapes to the CO-OPERATIVES) were thereby encouraged to make and market their own wines, soon challenging Rioja's traditional hegemony inside Spain. In the 1990s, consumption of top-quality Ribera wines soared within Spain, causing deepening concern in Rioja. Several Ribera producers attained quality levels not much below those of Vega Sicilia and Pesquera. The leading challengers included Dominio de Pingus, Ismael Arroyo, Pérez Pascuas, Félix Callejo, Teófilo Reyes, Valtravieso, Hermanos Cuadrado

CB, Pago de Carraovejas, and Dehesa de los Canónigos.

The region's principal vine variety, the Tinto Fino (also called Tinta del Pais), is a local variant of Rioja's TEMPRANILLO. It seems to have adapted to the Duero's climatic extremes and produces deep-coloured, occasionally astringent, firm-flavoured red wines without the support of any other grape variety. White wine made from the Albillo, a white variety enjoyed as a TABLE GRAPE by the locals, is not entitled to the DO but may occasionally be blended into the intense red wine to lighten the load and add glycerine content. Cabernet Sauvignon, Merlot, and Malbec, introduced by Vega Sicilia 130 years ago, are now allowed throughout the denomination. Garnacha is used in the production of rosé.   R.J.M. & V. de la S.

Ribera del Guadiana is the chosen name for a single denominated zone in Spain's EXTREMADURA region. The DO, awarded in 1998, includes such well-known areas as Tierra de Barros. The autonomous Extremadura government is actively encouraging the planting of INTERNATIONAL VARIETIES and improvements in wine quality.   V. de la S.

Ribolla, white grape variety also known as **Ribolla Gialla** to distinguish it from the less interesting **Ribolla Verde**, best known in FRIULI in north-east Italy but also grown, as Rebula, in SLOVENIA, and almost certainly the Robola of the island of Cephalonia in GREECE.

Ribolla accounts for less than one per cent of all the white DOC wines of Friuli. Rosazzo and Oslavia are generally considered the two classic areas for Ribolla Gialla. The wine is light in body, floral, not without delicacy, but high in acidity and without a particularly strong personality. Some attempts at new oak ageing have been made in recent years, particularly in Oslavia, where the wines are frankly presented as an attempt to assert a Slavic identity which has been stifled by an indiscriminate enthusiasm for INTERNATIONAL VARIETIES.

Ribolla Nera is the SCHIOPPETTINO grape.
                                                              D.T.

rich, see TASTING TERMS. The word may also be found as a label description on bottles of relatively sweet CHAMPAGNE.

Richebourg, great red GRAND CRU in Burgundy's CÔTE D'OR. See VOSNE-ROMANÉE.

riddling, an integral stage in the traditional champagne method of making SPARKLING WINES. It involves dislodging the deposit left in a bottle after a second fermentation has taken place inside it and shaking it into the neck of the inverted bottle. See SPARKLING-WINE-MAKING.

Rieslaner, increasingly rare, late-ripening Silvaner × Riesling crossing that is grown to a very limited extent in Germany's FRANKEN region, where, provided it can reach full ripeness, it can produce wines with race and curranty fruit.

Riesling, arguably the world's most undervalued, and certainly most often mispronounced grape. ('Reece-ling' is correct.) Riesling is the great vine variety of Germany and could claim to be the finest white grape variety in the world on the basis of the longevity of its wines and their ability to transmit the characteristics of a vineyard without losing Riesling's own inimitable style; in this sense it is very much more like Cabernet Sauvignon than Chardonnay. Riesling has suffered, in an era when oak and heft have been considered the height of FASHION, because it is no friend of BARRIQUES, and its wines tend to be relatively low in alcohol. In the 1960s and 1970s, the name Riesling was debased by being applied to a wide range of white grape varieties of varied and often doubtful quality, the ultimate backhanded compliment.

In the late 19th and early 20th centuries, German Riesling wines were prized, and priced, as highly as the great red wines of France. Connoisseurs knew that, thanks to their magical combination of ACIDITY and EXTRACT, these wines could develop for decades in bottle, regardless of ALCOHOLIC STRENGTH and RESIDUAL SUGAR. Riesling is made at all levels of sweetness, and it is indubitable that the high proportion of late-20th-century German wines that have been far too low in extract and, for many consumers, too high in residual sugar has damaged Riesling's reputation. The average residual sugar of Riesling made everywhere has been declining fast, but the variety will surely always be distinguished for its ability to produce great sweet wines, whether they be the cold-weather speciality EISWEIN or ICE WINE, or the late-harvest, often BOTRYTIZED, Beerenauslese and Trockenbeerenauslese and their counterparts outside Germany. Riesling's high natural level of TARTARIC ACID provides it with a much more dependable counterbalance to high residual sugar than, for example, the Sémillon grape of Sauternes.

Riesling wine, wherever produced, is also notable for its powerful, rapier-like aroma variously described as flowery, steely, honeyed, and whichever blend of mineral elements is conveyed by the individual vineyard site.

A long, slow ripening period suits Riesling best and manages to extract maximum flavour and EXTRACT, while maintaining acidity. Thus, many of Germany's (and therefore most of the world's) most admired Rieslings are grown on particularly favoured sites in cooler regions such as the MOSEL-SAAR-RUWER, whose crackling, light-bodied style of Riesling is unique.

Germany

By 1997, Riesling represented nearly 22 per cent of German plantings, and its showcase, the northerly Mosel-Saar-Ruwer, was home to about a third of the total. The finest estates here are without exception dedicated to Riesling and plant the variety on their best sites to the exclusion of all else. Some would argue that Riesling finds its finest expression on the steep banks of the Mosel and its Saar and Ruwer tributaries, ideally with a 30 per cent gradient to attract maximum ripening SUNLIGHT both directly and by reflection from the river surface. For the same reason, all the best Mosel sites face south and are sheltered from the wind. The easily warmed slate soils typical of the region can also help late-season ripening. The result is wines unique in the world for their combination of low alcohol (often only about eight per cent), striking aroma, high extract, and delicacy of texture. No other variety planted here can achieve as much subtlety.

The PFALZ region, on the other hand, the second most important for German Riesling, increased its plantings of Riesling dramatically during the 1980s and 1990s. Like neighbouring Rheinhessen, this has always been a region with a particularly varied palette of vine varieties, but the gentle climate of the Mittelhaardt provides Riesling with such shelter and favourable exposition that in many years here it can ripen naturally to produce fullbodied dry wines of really spicy, exuberant character, Spätlese Trocken in particular, yet still with a sufficiently extended growing season to keep both acidity and subtlety appetizingly high.

By 1990, the WÜRTTEMBERG region had (just)

overtaken the Rheingau as third most important grower of German Riesling, even if most of it is for local consumption and relatively dry and full bodied. The RHEINGAU is regarded as Riesling's traditional home and indeed the variety represents more than 80 per cent of all vine plantings. The best Rheingau Rieslings represent a faithful statement of their exact provenance. They are made increasingly dry and the CHARTA organization is a standardbearer for Rheingau Riesling designed to be drunk with food. The region is also famous as the original source of Germany's BOTRYTIZED sweet wines.

Riesling is also the most planted variety in Germany's smaller Mittelrhein and Hessische Bergstrasse regions and has just reasserted itself in terms of area planted over Müller-Thurgau in the NAHE, where the upper reaches of this river yield the finest, most crackling wines. In Baden, the warmer soils rarely show the variety at its best and tend to favour the various PINOT varieties. Riesling is not quantitatively important in the vine chequerboard that is RHEINHESSEN but the quality of some wines produced on the famous Rheinterrasse and around Bingen and Ingelheim defines the potential of those areas. Many of them are dry and exhibit a concentration that is truly thrilling. Riesling is relatively unknown in the redwine region of AHR and even in FRANKEN, which has generally remained faithful to Silvaner, but some distinguished, if earthy, dry wine is produced.

Elsewhere

For many wine drinkers, Riesling is acceptable only in its French form, a wine from ALSACE, the only part of France where this German vine is officially allowed. Alsace's plantings of the variety wine producers there view as their most noble increased steadily in the late 1980s. The great majority of Alsace Riesling is planted in the higher, finer vineyard of the Haut-Rhin, where GEWÜRZTRAMINER covers even more ground. What is needed to produce Alsace Riesling of real class is, as in Germany, a favoured site such as many of Alsace's famous grandscrus vineyards.

The great majority of Alsace Rieslings follow the variety's alluring perfume with a taste that is fairly alcoholic (easily 12 per cent) and bone dry. The dry climate of Alsace makes extended ripening a real possibility, however, often resulting in the prized late-harvest wines which qualify as VENDANGE TARDIVE or, even sweeter, SÉLECTION DE GRAINS NOBLES, the richest, most sumptuous ripeness category of Alsace wines.

To the north, about 10 per cent of the LUX-EMBOURG vineyard is planted with Riesling, which tends to produce dry, relatively full-bodied wines (thanks to CHAPTALIZATION) closer to Alsace in style than to the Mosel-Saar-Ruwer, which is just over the German border.

In AUSTRIA, Riesling, sometimes called **Rheinriesling** or Weisser Riesling to distinguish it from the more widely planted WELSCH-RIESLING, is quantitatively unimportant but is regarded as one of the country's finest wines when made on a favoured site. The most hallowed Austrian Rieslings are dry, concentrated, and aromatic, and a high proportion of them come from the terraced vineyards of the Wachau in lower Austria. Certain favoured sites in neighbouring Kamptal and Kremstal also enjoy a high reputation for their aristocratic, whistle-clean Rieslings. Riesling is a relatively important variety in the vineyards of Vienna, especially those of Nussberg and Bisamberg.

Not surprisingly, Riesling works well in the CONTINENTAL CLIMATE of the CZECH REPUBLIC to the immediate north of Austria's vineyards, where relatively light wines have real crackle and race. Most of SWITZERLAND is too cool to ripen Riesling properly, with the exception of some of the more schistous soils and warmest vineyards of the Valais around Sion.

Although practically unknown in Iberia (*pace* TORRES in Spain's high Penedès), Riesling has infiltrated the far north-east of Italy. It is grown with real enthusiasm in the high vineyards of the ALTO ADIGE, where it produces delicate, aromatic wines quite unlike most Italian whites. It is also grown quite successfully in FRIULI, where it is known as **Riesling Renano**, and just over the border in SLOVENIA, where it may be called **Rheinriesling**. Riesling, known as **Rizling Rajinski** and variants thereof, is also planted southwards through what was Yugoslavia in CROATIA and, less distinctively, in VOJ-VODINA.

It is planted throughout the rest of eastern Europe in Hungary and Bulgaria and to a much more limited extent in Romania but in each of these countries the climate can be too warm to coax much excitement from the variety and Welschriesling tends to reign supreme.

The country which had more Riesling planted than any other, even Germany, in the mid 1980s was what was then the USSR. It seems unlikely that the communist system encouraged the long wait for Riesling to ripen, so Soviet Riesling wines were presumably not the fullest, but it is easy to see why the variety would be popular in the cold winters of RUSSIA and the UKRAINE. Rhine Riesling is also grown in MOLDOVA and in most of the central Asian republics: KAZAKHSTAN, UZBEKISTAN, TAJIKI-STAN, KYRGYZSTAN, and TURKMENISTAN.

In the New World, true Riesling is most widely grown in AUSTRALIA, where it was the most planted white wine grape variety until Chardonnay caught up in 1990. Here, known as **Rhine Riesling**, or sometimes just **Rhine**, it has received less respect than it deserves. It is associated most intimately with the Barossa district of South Australia because of its influx of Silesian immigrants in the mid 19th century. The hot Barossa Valley floor is less suitable for this cool-climate vine, however, than the higher, cooler reaches of the Clare Valley or Eden Valley. Australian Rhine Rieslings are necessarily much higher in body and alcohol than most, but the best have carved out their own tangy, often lime-flavoured dryish style which can withstand the test of a decade in bottle admirably and can achieve a notably toasty character. Some late-harvest styles have also been made successfully. There has been talk of an Australian Riesling revival for at least a decade.

NEW ZEALAND began to produce convincing Riesling wines, notably when some producers addressed themselves to making scintillating late-harvest sweet wines (unfortunately not allowed into the EU in the late 1990s). Today, the Rieslings of Marlborough are made both dry and sweet and display excellent acidity, extract, and a delicacy unknown across the Tasman Sea in Australia. Nelson has also proved an excellent source of late-harvest bottlings.

Riesling (of some sort) is cultivated far more widely in South America, often, although not exclusively, in vineyards which ripen far too fast.

Riesling's progress in North America has been hampered simply by consumer demand for anything *but* Riesling. California's total acreage of what is known as **Johannisberg Riesling** or **White Riesling** remained static throughout the 1980s and then declined in the early 1990s. With the exception of Stony Hill's age-worthy wines, the variety is rarely made bone dry in California, and can command a decent price only if very sweet and described as Select Late Harvest (the equivalent of a German BEERENAUSLESE) or somesuch. Recognition and mastery of NOBLE ROT came only after 1973, when Jerry Luper produced one at Freemark Abbey, and in the late 1980s there were still some grape-growers willing to sell BOTRYTIZED grapes for a song, believing them beyond redemption. Such wines have trouble hanging on to their acidity and tend to brown after five years or so in bottle, although exponents such as Joseph Phelps and Ch St Jean have had more experience than most. Riesling is planted all over the state and has enjoyed particular success in the cooler patches of SANTA BARBARA, MONTEREY (Jekel), and MENDOCINO (Navarro). Certain very high vineyards such as Madroña in El Dorado County have also enjoyed success with Riesling.

WASHINGTON state claims a special affinity for Riesling, even organizing the world's first truly international conference on the subject, although total area planted declined in the late 1980s and has remained static throughout the 1990s. As in Oregon, the variety suffers from consumer passion for other varieties rather than from any inherent viticultural disadvantage.

Because of its winter hardiness, Riesling tends to be treasured in the coolest wine regions of North America. In CANADA, Riesling is cultivated with particular success in Ontario, just over the border from the Finger Lakes region of NEW YORK state, where it is also increasingly respected, not least for its ability to yield commercially interesting ICE WINE. Perhaps a Riesling revival really is just around the corner.

Riesling Italico, or Riesling Italianski, white grape variety which Germans would like to see called RIZLING Italico to distinguish it from true RIESLING, known as Riesling Renano in Italy. In Austria, it is called WELSCHRIESLING (under which more details can be found); in much of what was YUGOSLAVIA, it is called LASKI RIZLING, in the CZECH REPUBLIC, it is called Rizling Vlassky, and in HUNGARY, it is called OLASZ RIZLING. Riesling Italico was ROMANIA'S third most planted variety in the early 1990s, and was often blended with other varieties such as Muscat Ottonel. Within Italy, it is most common in the far north east, in FRIULI just over the border from SLOVENIA. Provided its tendency to overcrop is curbed, it can produce

delicate, crisp, mildly flowery wines, most in COLLIO. It is grown to a limited extent in the ALTO ADIGE and, more successfully, in LOMBARDY.

Riesling-Sylvaner is the flattering name for MÜLLER-THURGAU (which has recently been shown not to be a crossing of Riesling and Sylvaner at all but of Riesling and CHASSELAS). This name is, curiously, preferred in SWITZERLAND, where the canton of Thurgau is to be found. It has also been widely used in NEW ZEALAND, although European Union authorities disapprove.

right bank, an expression much used of that part of the BORDEAUX wine region that is on the right bank, or north, of the river DORDOGNE. It includes, travelling down river, Côtes de CASTILLON, Côtes de FRANCS, ST-ÉMILION and its satellite appellations, POMEROL and LALANDE-DE-POMEROL, FRONSAC and Canon-Fronsac, BOURG, and BLAYE. The most obvious characteristic shared by these appellations, and distinct from LEFT BANK appellations, is that the dominant grape varieties are Merlot and Cabernet Franc rather than Cabernet Sauvignon.

Rioja, the leading wine region of SPAIN, producing predominantly red wines in the north of the country. Named after the río (river) Oja, a tributary of the river Ebro, most of the Rioja wine region lies in the autonomous region of La Rioja in north-east Spain, although parts of the zone extend into the neighbouring BASQUE country to the north west and NAVARRE to the north east. Centred on the regional capital Logroño, Rioja divides into three zones along the axis of the river Ebro. **Rioja Alta** occupies the part of the Ebro valley west of Logroño and includes the wine-making town of Haro. **Rioja Alavesa** is the name given to the section of the zone north of the river Ebro which falls in the Basque province of Alava. **Rioja Baja** extends from the suburbs of Logroño south and east to include the towns of Calahorra and Alfaro.

Climate and geography

Rioja enjoys an enviable position among Spanish wine regions. Sheltered by the Sierra de Cantabria to the north and west, it is well protected from the rain-bearing Atlantic winds that drench the Basque coast immediately to the north. Yet Rioja's wine producers rarely experience the climatic extremes that burden growers in so much of central and southern Spain.

Rioja Alta and Rioja Alavesa share a similar

climate and are distinct from each other for mainly administrative reasons, although there are soil differences between the two. Many of the best grapes are grown here on the cooler slopes to the north west.

Vine varieties

Seven grape varieties (four red, three white) qualify for Rioja's Denominación de Origen (DO) and their distribution varies in different parts of the region. The most widely planted variety is the probably indigenous, black TEMPRANILLO, which ripens well on the clay and limestone slopes of Rioja Alta and Rioja Alavesa, where it forms the basis for the region's best wines.

Most Riojas are blends of more than one variety, however, and wines made from the GARNACHA vine are often used to add BODY to Tempranillo. On its own, Garnacha produces hefty, alcoholic red wines. Rioja, like neighbouring Navarre, produces rosé entirely from Garnacha grapes. Two further red varieties, Mazuelo (Cariñena or CARIGNAN) and the indigenous GRACIANO, are of relatively minor importance, although the latter has great potential, contributing to the aroma and structure of the wine.

The Cabernet Sauvignon vines which arrived with the French in the 19th century are allowed by special dispensation in vineyards belonging to the Marqués de Riscal. Several other companies have experimental plantings of this Bordeaux grape, and of white imports such as Chardonnay.

Historically, until PHYLLOXERA arrived, Rioja's chief white grape variety was the MALVASÍA. On its own, it produced rich, alcoholic, dry white wines which responded well to ageing in oak. However, Viura (known elsewhere in Spain as MACABEO) took over as the most planted light-berried variety in the region and, from the early 1970s, fresher-tasting, cool-fermented, early-bottled white wines were in FASHION all over Spain. By the 1990s, most white Riojas were made exclusively from Viura, and Malvasía vines were extremely difficult to find, although some of the traditional oak-aged whites and new barrel-fermented wines are blends of Malvasía and Viura.

Wine-making

Grapes are usually delivered to large, central wineries belonging either to one of the CO-OPERATIVES or to a merchant's bodega. Most wineries in Rioja are reasonably well equipped with a modern stainless-steel plant and facilities for TEMPERATURE CONTROL.

Rioja wine-making is characterized not by fermentation techniques but by BARREL MATURATION, however, and the shape and size of the 225-l *barrica bordelesa* introduced by the French in the mid 19th century is laid down by law. The regulations also specify the minimum ageing period for each officially recognized category of wine. In Rioja, red wines labelled CRIANZA and RESERVA must spend at least a year in oak, while a GRAN RESERVA must spend at least two years. In common with other Spanish wine regions, American OAK has been the favoured wood type for wine maturation. New American oak barrels give the soft, vanilla flavour that has become accepted as typical of Rioja, but a similar effect can also be achieved by slow, oxidative maturation in older barrels. French oak is used increasingly, however. Over 40 per cent of all Rioja falls into one of the three oak-aged categories above (the rest is either white, rosé, or sold as young, unoaked JOVEN red, much of it within Spain).

Rioja regulations also specify the length of time that an oak-aged Rioja must spend in tank or bottle before the wine can be released. Crianzas must be aged for a further year in tank or bottle, where Reservas must spend two further years. Gran Reservas, usually specially selected wines from the best vintages, must spend at least three years in bottle so that the wines are a minimum of five years old before they go on sale.

After the widespread adoption of cool fermentation techniques in the 1970s, the amount of oak-aged white Rioja progressively diminished. López de Heredia, Marqués de Murrieta, and only a few other bodegas upheld the traditional style by ageing their white wines in oak *barricas*. For whites labelled Crianza, Reserva, or Gran Reserva, the minimum wood ageing period is just six months with a further year, two years, or four years respectively before the wines may be released for sale. By the mid 1990s, a large number of producers had switched to fashionable BARREL FERMENTATION, however, in effect reviving the region's traditional white-wine vinification method.

Organization of trade

Rioja's vineyards are split among 14,000 growers, most of whom tend their plots as a sideline and have no WINE-MAKING facilities of their own. Many growers have an established contract with one of the 100 or so merchant bodegas. Others belong to one of the 30 CO-OPERATIVES that serve the region and receive around 45 per cent of the grapes. Most co-operatives sell their produce, either as must or as newly made wine, to the merchant bodegas, who blend, bottle, and market the wine under their own labels.

In the 1980s, a number of bodegas bought up large tracts of land to plant their own vine-yards, although few as yet have sufficient to supply their entire needs. A number of single ESTATES, such as Contino and Remelluri, have also emerged, with the distinction, rare for the region, of growing, vinifying, and marketing their own wines.

Like other Spanish DOs, Rioja is controlled by a CONSEJO REGULADOR. After a long debate dating from the 1970s, Rioja was granted DOCA status in 1991. The qualifications have little to do with absolute quality, the single most important being that Rioja's grape prices are at least 200 per cent above the national average.

R.J.M. & V. de la S.

Rios do Minho, VINHO REGIONAL in north-west Portugal named after the Minho province, itself named after the river (called Miño in Spanish) which forms the boundary with Spain. The boundaries of the region are the same as those for the Vinho Verde DOC but producers are allowed to make wines with higher levels of alcohol than the usual VINHO VERDE maximum of 11.5 per cent or from dif-ferent grape varieties. Wines bearing the name Rios do Minho are rarely found outside Por-tugal.   R.J.M.

ripasso, Italian term meaning literally 're-passed', for the technique of adding extra flavour, and alcohol, to VALPOLICELLA by adding the unpressed skins of AMARONE wines after these DRIED-GRAPE WINES have finished their fermentation in the spring. While this undoubtedly adds body and character to a ripasso Valpolicella, it may also impart some of the OXIDIZED and BOTRYTIS flavours of the Amarone as well, together with additional TANNINS. Some producers are therefore sub-stituting grapes that have been dried, but not to the extent required for Amarone, for the fermented Amarone skins, although this tech-nique is necessarily expensive.   D.T.

ripeness, term used to describe that stage of the continuous process of grape RIPENING or

development which is chosen by the wine-maker and/or grape processor as that desired at HARVEST. What constitutes the ideal chemical and physical composition of grapes at this point is a subjective judgement dependent on wine style, the wine-maker's current belief about optimal ripeness, FASHION, and many other factors, so ripeness is by no means an absolute term.

Ripeness is often related to MUST WEIGHT or grape-sugar concentration but sugar levels are not the only aspect of grape composition to affect what is considered ripeness. Especially in cool climates, ACIDITY levels can be closely monitored to determine the grapes' ripeness. In the search for better definitions of ripeness to improve wine quality, many other analyses are being proposed and investigated. For red wine, measurements of grape PHENOLICS, including anthocyanins and tannins, are proving useful. Individual grapes' physical con-dition, especially skin thickness and integrity, is also considered as an aspect of grape ripeness relevant to wine quality.

See also PHYSIOLOGICAL RIPENESS and GRAPE COMPOSITION AND WINE QUALITY. R.E.S. & B.G.C.

ripeness measurement. See MUST WEIGHT and RIPENESS.

riserva, Italian term usually denoting a wine given extended AGEING before release and one with a higher minimum ALCOHOLIC STRENGTH, by one or half a per cent, than the non-Riserva version. In this latter respect, there is a certain overlap with the SUPERIORE designation. Some Riserva wines, unlike Superiore wines, are obliged to undergo a certain minimum ageing period in wood in order to qualify as a Riserva; the regular bottlings of such wines are not normally aged in wood at all. The Riserva bot-tlings of the most famous Italian wines—BAR-BARESCO, BAROLO, BRUNELLO DI MONTALCINO, CHIANTI CLASSICO, VINO NOBILE DI MONTE-PULCIANO—are not necessarily aged for a longer period in wood, however, but are simply required to have been aged longer overall, either in wood or in bottle, before being released. (Chianti Classico Riserva, in fact, does not require any wood ageing whatsoever.) D.T.

Rivaner is another name for MÜLLER-THURGAU, used in LUXEMBOURG, where it is the most planted grape variety, and, increasingly, elsewhere. Rivaner sounds more appetizing.

Riverina, NEW SOUTH WALES' answer to the RIVERLAND, also known as the Murrumbidgee

Irrigation Area, or MIA. Griffith is an important wine-production centre but most wines made here are described coyly as coming from South Eastern Australia.

Riverland, the most productive wine region in AUSTRALIA, a sprawl of vineyards irrigated by the river Murray mainly in the state of SOUTH AUSTRALIA, but also part of the state of VICTORIA, which may also be called the Murray River Valley. Almost all production is high-yield, technically sound material for blending. Wine producers are generally reticent about proclaiming these provenances. South Eastern Australia is the catch-all description usually found on labels.

Rivesaltes, town north of Perpignan in southern France that gives its name to two of the biggest appellations of ROUSSILLON, Rivesaltes and **Muscat de Rivesaltes,** both of them VINS DOUX NATURELS. Muscat de Rivesaltes, which represents about 70 per cent of France's total Muscat production, can in fact be produced throughout most of Roussillon's recognized wine-producing area, together even with some sections of the Aude *département* to the north (including much of the FITOU appellation). The Rivesaltes production zone is similarly generous but specifically excludes those vineyards that produce BANYULS.

Muscat de Rivesaltes is the only Muscat vin doux naturel which may be made from MUSCAT OF ALEXANDRIA as well as the finer MUSCAT BLANC À PETITS GRAINS. Muscat de Rivesaltes should be drunk as young and cool as possible, either as an aperitif or with fruit or creamy desserts.

The even more common Rivesaltes, on the other hand, has the potential, not often realized, to be a more complex vin doux naturel, made in all conceivable colours and styles. These sweet, heady, wines can be made from any permutation of Grenache Blanc, Noir, and Gris, Maccabéo, and to a much lesser extent Torbato (here called Malvoisie du Roussillon), and the two Muscats allowed for Muscat de Rivesaltes. Varietal Rivesaltes are permitted, from a golden Maccabéo to a Grenache Noir that can be anything from crimson to deep chocolate brown, depending on its ÉLEVAGE. Rivesaltes may taste of raisins, coffee, chocolate, fruits, or nuts and the most concentrated can, like Banyuls, be some of the few wines that happily partner chocolate.

Riviera di Ponente, or Riviera Ligure di Ponente, wine from the north-western coast of Italy. See LIGURIA.

Rizling, term for the white grape variety known variously in central Europe as WELSCHRIESLING, OLASZ RIZLING, LASKI RIZLING, and RIESLING ITALICO.

Rkatsiteli, Georgian white grape variety which is probably planted much more extensively than most western wine drinkers realize. It is the most planted vine variety in the CIS, being grown in all of its wine-producing independent republics with the exception of TURKMENISTAN. In RUSSIA alone, there were nearly 60,000 ha/148,200 acres of Rkatsiteli in 1990. The variety is also widely cultivated in BULGARIA, where it has been the country's most important white grape variety, and there are more than 500 ha of it in ROMANIA. It is widely grown throughout eastern Europe and there are pockets of the variety in China and the United States as well.

Much is demanded of this variety and it achieves much, providing a base for a wide range of wine styles, including fortified wines. The wine is distinguished by a keen level of ACIDITY and good sugar levels.

In CHINA, it is known as Baiyu and has been an important source of neutral white wine for the nascent Chinese wine industry.

Roannaise, Côte, hand-crafted, lightish reds and some rosés made chiefly from locally adapted GAMAY grapes, called St-Romain à Jus Blanc here, using Beaujolais cellar techniques, usually semi-CARBONIC MACERATION. The southeast-facing slopes of the upper Loire are only one range of hills west of the BEAUJOLAIS region. APPELLATION CONTRÔLÉE status was won in 1994.

Robe, relatively new wine region in the Limestone Coast zone of SOUTH AUSTRALIA.

Robertson, important wine-producing district in SOUTH AFRICA.

Robola, wine and grape variety for which the Ionian island of Cephalonia in GREECE is most famous. The distinctively powerful, lemony dry white is made entirely from Robola grapes, which are cultivated exclusively on the island, except that the vine is almost certainly the Rebula of SLOVENIA, and the RIBOLLA of FRIULI in north-east Italy. The wine made from these early-ripening grapes is high in both acidity

Roditis

and extract and is much prized within Greece.

Roditis or Rhoditis, slightly pink-skinned Greek grape variety traditionally grown in the Peloponnese. The vine ripens relatively late and keeps its acidity quite well even in such hot climates as that of Ankialos in Thessaly in central Greece, although it can also ripen well, and makes very much more interesting wine, in high-altitude vineyards. It is often blended with the softer Savatiano, particularly for RETSINA.

Roederer, Louis, family-owned Champagne house known both for its early links with the Russian court and for its extensive vineyard ownership. The original company was founded by a M. Dubois around the year 1776; Louis Roederer joined in 1827, becoming owner in 1833.

By the mid 1990s, Roederer's own vineyards supplied 80 per cent of its requirements, thereby allowing the house to remain unusually independent. Mainly thanks to these vineyard holdings, Roederer produces far more vintages of Cristal than is usual for a PRESTIGE CUVÉE. The best cuvées of almost every harvest are blended to make a vintage Cristal.

In 1993, the house acquired 60 per cent of the capital of the holding company of Champagne Deutz. The company diversified into ST-ESTÈPHE in Bordeaux in the 1990s, acquiring Ch Beauséjour in 1992 and Ch de Pez in 1994. Outside France, the company has invested with considerable success in the Anderson Valley, near the MENDOCINO coast. Roederer Estate, one of California's finest sparkling wines, was first released in 1988.   S.A.

Roero, sandy hills on the left bank of the river Tanaro north west of Alba in the PIEDMONT region of north-west Italy producing significant quantities of red BARBERA and white ARNEIS.

Rolland, Michel (1947–), possibly the most famous CONSULTANT oenologist, responsible in several ways for the current FASHION for superripe, deep-coloured, supple red bordeaux. He and his wife Dany run a small laboratory in POMEROL on which many local growers depend for analysis. He owns Chx Le Bon Pasteur in Pomerol, Bertineau St-Vincent in Lalande de Pomerol, Rolland-Maillet in St-Émilion, and Fontenil in Fronsac, and farms Ch La Grande Clotte in Lussac-St-Émilion. The Bordeaux RIGHT BANK enterprises to which he is con-

sultant are too numerous to list (although they include L'Angélus, Beau-Séjour Bécot, Clinet, Clos l'Église, La Dominique, L'Évangile, La Gaffelière, Grand Mayne, Larmande, Pavie, Pavie-Macquin, and Troplong-Mondot). In the Médoc and Graves, they include Chx de Fieuzal, Kirwan, Léoville-Poyferré, Malescot St-Exupéry, Pape-Clément, Prieuré-Lichine, Smith-Haut-Lafitte, and La Tour Martillac. He has also made wine for Skalli of the Languedoc, the arch-promulgator of VIN DE PAYS. But it is his consultancies outside France that set him apart from all but a handful of his countrymen in the breadth of his experience: Simi, Newton, Merryvale, Cuvaison, St-Supéry, and Harlan in California; Marqués de Cáceres, Bodegas Palacio, Marqués de Griñon in Spain; Ornellaia in Italy; Trapiche in Argentina; Casa Lapostolle in Chile; Pajzos in Hungary; and many more. He took his degree at Bordeaux University during the Émile Peynaud era and has continued to declare his philosophy that wine should give maximum pleasure.

Rolle, the white grape variety traditionally most closely associated with BELLET, is now increasingly grown in the Languedoc and, especially, Roussillon, where it is frequently blended with southern French varieties such as Viognier, Roussanne, Marsanne, and Grenache Blanc. It is aromatic and usefully crisp for warm wine regions and is accepted by French authorities as identical to the VERMENTINO of Corsica, Sardinia, and southern Italy.

Romagna. Eastern part of EMILIA-ROMAGNA.

Romanée, Romanée-Conti, Romanée-St-Vivant, great red GRANDS CRUS, for more details of which see VOSNE-ROMANÉE. See also DOMAINE DE LA ROMANÉE-CONTI.

Romania, sometimes spelt **Roumania** or **Rumania,** eastern Europe's quantitatively most important wine producer with enormous unrealized potential and with almost as much vineyard as Portugal.

Although there is a coastal plain on the Black Sea coast, the country is dominated by mountains. Romania's wine regions are widely dispersed throughout the country, in a wide range of different conditions (see below). Romania lies on much the same latitudinal span as France, although its climate is much more extreme.

Wine-making
Many co-operatives still lack full TEMPERATURE

CONTROL facilities, but fully controlled stainless-steel tanks are used for some quality-wine production in wineries formerly owned by the state. If wine is aged in oak, it is usually large, old Carpathian oak. The country had a severe shortage of modern bottling facilities in the early 1990s.

Vine varieties

Romania is notable for the number and scope of its grapevine collections. It has a wide range of vine varieties, including a significant proportion of American vines and HYBRIDS and a number of purely local specialities. Romanians with an eye to export markets, however, are particularly proud of the extent of their Cabernet Sauvignon plantings, of which they have more than any single country other than France, the United States, and Chile.

The most planted varieties by far are two FETEASCAS, Fetească Albă (White) and Fetească Regală (Royal), both of which can produce perfumed white wines of varying sweetness and quality. Riesling Italico or WELSCHRIESLING is the next most planted vine variety, while there is also a significant amount of white ALIGOTÉ from Burgundy and red Merlot from Bordeaux. Other international white grape varieties include Sauvignon Blanc, Pinot Gris, RKATSITELI, MUSCAT OTTONEL, and Gewürztraminer. Contrary to popular belief, there is no more than 300 or 400 ha of either Pinot Noir or Chardonnay in the country.

Specifically Romanian varieties planted to a significant extent include the light-berried 'fat' Grasă and the aromatic 'frankincense' TĂMÎIOASĂ Românească grapes of COTNARI, and Galbenă of Odobeşvti, which makes light, crisp whites with a relatively long life. Of dark-berried varieties, Roşioară is relatively common for everyday wine, Băbească can produce light, fruity reds, and Fetească Neagră is capable of producing deep-coloured, ageworthy red wines.

Wine laws

Romania has developed a relatively sophisticated wine law based on the twin criteria of natural MUST WEIGHT (as in the GERMAN WINE LAW) and defined geographical origin (as in France's APPELLATION CONTRÔLÉE system). Still wine is divided into light table wines and quality wines. Romania has also signed letters of agreement with the European Union setting out the names of its geographical regions and recognizing those of the EU in turn. These names are used for high-quality wines of which there are the following three categories:

VS (vinuri de calitate superioara) is the equivalent of a VIN DE PAYS. The grapes must have a potential alcohol of at least 10.5 per cent and must have fermented to at least 9.5 per cent. There are 43 named regions which usually correspond to county/departmental names.

DOC (denumire de origine controlata) is a high-quality wine from a specified region, a category similar to France's AC. Minimum potential alcohol is 11.5 per cent, fermented to an actual alcohol of at least 10 per cent.

DOCC (vinuri de calitate superioara cu denumire de origine controlata si trepte de calitate) is a subdivision of DOC, from regions of the same name but with an additional expression of quality referring to the degree of ripeness/overripeness and NOBLE ROT in the wine. As in Germany's PRÄDIKAT system, each expression denotes a higher intensity of overripeness and noble rot than the last and one of these terms must appear on the label if the wine claims to be a high-quality wine. Normally only wines falling into such categories find their way to western Europe.

DOC/DOCC wines come from one of eight major regions and usually show the name of the designated district where they were made. Some of the districts have subdivisions, often called after some local geographical feature such as a small river or valley.

All three categories must come from authorized VINIFERA varieties.

Wine regions

The Romanian wine regions can be divided into the eight distinct zones listed below.

Transylvania This high central region produces almost exclusively white wines. The most important and oldest wine region is **Tîrnave**, also sometimes spelt **Tarnave**. These are some of Romania's coolest vineyards on slopes which can approach those of the MOSEL in steepness. The mainly white wines also have an appealing Mosel-like acidity. One of the most common varieties is Fetească Regală, often called Dănăşvana here. The other Fetească, Welschriesling, Muscat Ottonel, and the Austrian NEUBURGER are also grown here. Wine styles are relatively Germanic, and some sparkling wines are also made.

Vines are also grown in **Alba Iulia**, **Aiud**, **Sebeş**, **Apold de Sus**, and **Bistrita-Lechinta**.

Crişana **Miniş** in the south is one of the few

parts of Crişana known for its red wines, notably those made from Cadarcă (the Hungarian KADARKA). The traditional white variety in the Măderat region is Mustoasă, which makes light, crisp wine. Cabernet Sauvignon, Merlot, Welschriesling, Muscat Ottonel, and Feteascǎ Regalǎ are more recent imports.

In **Silvania**, Ardeleancǎ is the local vine variety, although more recent plantings have been of the two Feteascǎs and Iordanǎ.

Other wine regions are **Diosig** and **Valea lui Mihai.**

Moldavia (See MOLDOVA for details of the eastern part of the old Romanian province of Moldavia.) Possibly the oldest, and certainly the most famous wine region of what is now Romania is COTNARI. For more details of this specific sweet wine, see COTNARI. Grasǎ is the variety responsible for most of the best sweet wines, supplemented by Tǎmîioasǎ, but Muscat Ottonel is also grown, together with Feteascǎ Albǎ, Frîncuşa, and the related Tîrtǎrǎ vines are also grown and produce dry and medium-dry lesser wines.

In **Iaşi**, the traditional Moldavian Feteascǎ Albǎ is grown, mainly for light, everyday wines, together with the more recent Feteascǎ Regala, Frîncuşa, Welschriesling, Aligoté, and, unusually but successfully, Muscadelle. A SPU-MANTE style of wine is also made from Muscat Ottonel. A range of red varieties, including Merlot and Cabernet Sauvignon, is also cultivated around Iaşi, where Bǎbeascǎ shows perhaps its finest form.

In the nearby **Huşi** vineyards, sweet, scented, deep-yellow wine is made from Busuioacǎ grapes. Another local variety is Zghiharǎ.

Odobeşti vineyards are mainly dedicated to everyday table wine made from the local Galbenǎ grape. High-yield white wines are made from Feteascǎ Albǎ, Welschriesling, and Şarba, which has a grapey aroma and good acidity. In **Panciu**, some good still white and sparkling wines are made. **Coteşti** just south of Odobeşti can produce some deep-coloured red wines from Merlot, Cabernet Sauvignon, Feteascǎ Neagrǎ, and Bǎbeascǎ. **Nicoreşti** is another red-wine region, particularly well known for its Bǎbeascǎ.

Other recognized regions are **Zeletin, Tutova Hills, Bujor Hills, Iveşti**, and **Covurlui.**

Muntenia The **Dealul Mare** region is best known for its red wines from Cabernet Sauvignon, Merlot, some Pinot Noir, and Feteascǎ Neagrǎ. Some superior white wines are also produced, however, including some late-harvest wines, using the two main Cotnari varieties. Tǎmîioasǎ from Pietroasele, which may be BOTRYTIZED, has a particular reputation. Local vine specialities include Bǎşicatǎ and Gordin, known respectively as Slavita and Gordan at Drǎgǎşani in Oltenia.

Buzǎu Hills also produces some quality red wine from Merlot, Cabernet Sauvignon, and 'Burgund Mare' as well as whites from Welschriesling, Aligoté, Feteascǎ, and Muscat Ottonel. **Ştefaneşti-Argeş** is a relatively new wine area.

Oltenia The Sauvignon vine performs well in the extensive vineyards west of Bucharest, and can produce late-harvest wines, although a range of local varieties also yield a range of more basic wines. **Simbureşti** is a much smaller wine region which specializes in red-wine production, as do the **Craiova Hills, Severin,** and **Drincea.**

Banat One of the few proper names to have reached export markets on Romanian wine labels, Banat was the name of a province on the Yugoslav border. The **Teremia** vineyards produce mainly basic table wines. The slopes of **Recaş** are planted with Cabernet Sauvignon, Kadarka, and, with notable success, Burgund Mare, which also performs well in the **Tirol** region to the south. In **Buziaş-Silagiu**, white wines are a speciality, particularly those made from the local Creaţa. The **Moldova Nouǎ** region by the river Danube is planted with Burgund Mare, Cabernet Sauvignon, Merlot, and Oporto, as well as Feteascǎ Regalǎ, Welschriesling, and Muscat Ottonel.

Dobrudja **Murfatlar** is the most important wine region on the Romanian coast. Late-harvest wines are a speciality here, although noble rot is much rarer than in Cotnari. Chardonnay was introduced in an effort to create something like champagne from the chalky soils in some parts of the region. It produces low-yield, high-quality, highly concentrated fruit. There are also substantial plantings of Pinot Gris, Welschriesling, Muscat Ottonel, and Sauvignon, plus some Merlot and Cabernet Sauvignon.

In **Babadag-Istria**, red wines from Merlot, Cabernet Sauvignon, and Burgund Mare are produced in the main, while the vineyards of **Sarica Niculiţel** produce whites from Aligoté, Pinot Gris, Muscat Ottonel, and Rkatsiteli as well. **Ostrov** is largely devoted to table grape production, but some Merlot/Cabernet red wines have been exported.

Danube Terraces Most of the vines grown here are devoted to TABLE GRAPES, but some wine is produced in the regions of Dacilor, Calafat, Sadova-Corabia, and Brăila.

Roman Muscat, synonym for MUSCAT OF ALEXANDRIA.

Romorantin, a white, eastern Loire grape variety that is fast fading from the French *vignoble*. Cour CHEVERNY is an appellation especially created for Romorantin grown just west of Blois.

Ronco, north-east Italian term for a HILLSIDE VINEYARD. The widest current use is in FRIULI, where the dialect form is *ronc*. Examples can also be found in the ALTO ADIGE and in ROMAGNA. See also COLLI.   D.T.

Rondinella, Italian red grape variety grown in the VENETO, especially for Valpolicella. The vine yields profusely and is therefore extremely popular with growers but its produce is rarely sufficiently flavoursome to please consumers. Rondinella is not, fortunately, as widely planted as CORVINA.

Rondo, red-fleshed disease-resistant variety grown to a limited extent in England and treasured for its combination of early ripening and depth of colour. It makes light, fruity wines.

root, one of the three major organs of higher plants, the others being leaves and fruits/seeds. Roots' main functions are anchorage of the plant, storage of reserves of carbohydrates, absorption of water and minerals from the soil, and synthesis of specific compounds.

rootstock, the plant forming the root system of a grapevine to which a fruiting variety, or scion, is grafted. In most vineyards in the world, European wine-producing VINIFERA vines are grafted on rootstocks which are, with few exceptions, either varieties of one American vine species or more commonly HYBRIDS of several. Rootstocks are normally used to overcome soil pests or diseases, but may also be used for special soil conditions.

The use of rootstocks for grapevines became common around 1880 in France in order to combat the devastating root louse PHYLLOXERA, which attacked the roots of the European grapevine *Vitis vinifera*, and the control of phylloxera remains a major, but by no means the only, reason why rootstocks are used.

Roriz, or **Tinta Roriz**, is the most common of several Portuguese names for the Spanish red wine grape variety TEMPRANILLO, used particularly in the Douro valley, where it is one of the most planted varieties for the production of PORT. In the Alentejo it is known as Aragonêz.

rosado is Spanish and Portuguese, and **rosato** is Italian, for ROSÉ. See also CLARETE.

Rosana, Spanish name for ROUSSANNE grape.

Rosé de Loire, general, and relatively important, appellation created in 1974 for ROSÉ WINE made from a blend of Loire red grapes (Cabernet Franc, Cabernet Sauvignon, Pineau d'Aunis, Pinot Noir, Gamay, and Grolleau), of which Cabernet constitutes at least 30 per cent. The wine may be produced anywhere within the ANJOU, SAUMUR, and TOURAINE zones and usually lies, in quality terms, somewhere between Rosé d'Anjou and Cabernet d'Anjou, with the distinction that it is always dry. See also LOIRE.

Rosé des Riceys, rare, still, pink wine made in the commune of Riceys in the Aube *département*, the southern end of the CHAMPAGNE region. This dark, rose-coloured wine is made by only three producers, from Pinot Noir grapes, but can be one of France's most serious rosés. Like Champagne's still red wine Bouzy Rouge (see Coteaux CHAMPENOIS), part of its appeal may be its name.

Rosenmuskateller, German name for aromatic, pink-berried MOSCATO Rosa Trentini variety particular to the Alto Adige, northern Italy.

Rosette, very limited sweet-white-wine appellation just north of Bergerac in SOUTH WEST FRANCE. It includes some of the PÉCHARMANT zone.

rosé-wine-making, production of wines whose colour falls somewhere in the spectrum between red and white.

Two methods are in general use. The preferred technique is a short MACERATION of the juice with the skins (see SKIN CONTACT) of dark-coloured grapes just after CRUSHING for a period long enough to extract the required amount of colour or ANTHOCYANINS. The juice is then separated from the skins by draining or PRESSING and FERMENTATION proceeds as in WHITE-WINE-MAKING. See also SAIGNÉE.

Some basic rosés are made by blending a small amount of finished red wine into a finished white wine. While a pinkish colour can be achieved by this process, the hue and flavour of such a wine are quite different from those of a wine made by short-term maceration. Pink wines may also be made by using charcoal treatments to remove the colour from red wines which are for some reason not saleable as reds.

CHAMPAGNE is one of the few controlled appellations in which the blending method of rosé-wine-making is sanctioned—and in practice rosé CHAMPAGNE is more often made by blending than by maceration.

A VIN GRIS or BLUSH wine is made as above but with no maceration. Both tend to be even paler than most rosés. A.D.W.

rosé wines, wines coloured any shade of pink, from hardly perceptible to pale red. For some reason, they are rarely known as pink wines, although the English word BLUSH has been adopted for particularly pale rosés.

In France, rosés are particularly common in warmer, southern regions where there is local demand for a dry wine refreshing enough to be drunk on a hot summer's day but which still bears some relation to the red wine so revered by the French. PROVENCE is the region most famous for its rosé, often in a strange skittle-shaped bottle, although, in the greater southern RHÔNE (especially TAVEL) and the LANGUEDOC-ROUSSILLON, rosés are at least as common as white wines. Grenache and Cinsaut are two of the grapes commonly used for rosé in the south of France. The Loire valley also produces a high proportion of rosé wine of extremely varied quality and sweetness levels, particularly around ANJOU, whether lowbrow Rosé d'Anjou or highbrow Cabernet d'Anjou. See also ROSÉ DE LOIRE. VIN GRIS and SAIGNÉE are French terms for particular types of rosé.

Spain also takes pink wines seriously—so seriously that it has at least two names for them, depending on the intensity of the colour. A *rosado* is light pink, while darker-pink (light-red) wines are labelled *clarete*. Portugal's best-known pink wines are exported, as in MATEUS and LANCERS. Pink wines are not especially popular in Italy, where the term used is usually *rosato* although *chiaretto* is occasionally used for darker rosés. Official German terms for pink wines include WEISSHERBST and, in WÜRTTEMBERG, SCHILLERWEIN. See also ŒIL DE PERDRIX.

The New World is in general rather bemused by the concept of rosé, although Australia makes some swashbuckling deep pinks and South Africa has plenty of suitable Cinsaut, which is normally pressed into red-wine duty.

Roşioara. See PAMID.

Rossese, esteemed red grape variety producing distinctively flavoured varietal wines in the north-west Italian region of LIGURIA. The variety has its own DOC in the west of the region in Dolceacqua whose wines are admired, though variable.

Rossignola, optional, tart ingredient in VALPOLICELLA.

Rosso Conero, Italian red wine based on MONTEPULCIANO grapes whose full potential is yet to be realized. See MARCHES.

Rosso di signifies a red wine from the Italian zone whose name it precedes, often a declassified version of a long-lived, more serious wine such as BRUNELLO DI MONTALCINO or VINO NOBILE DI MONTEPULCIANO.

Rosso Piceno, Italian red wine based on SANGIOVESE with some MONTEPULCIANO grapes, improving in quality though not yet at the level of the better Sangiovese wines of Tuscany or Umbria. See MARCHES.

rot, loose term for the decay, with microbial interference, of any part of the vine. Rot is most commonly used as synonymous with botrytis bunch rot, which is the most important sort of rot for wine quality; it occurs sometimes in benevolent form as NOBLE ROT, but more commonly causes the loss of yield and quality in its malevolent form as grey rot.

Roter Traminer. See GEWÜRZTRAMINER.

Rotgipfler, the marginally less noble of the two white wine grape varieties traditionally associated with GUMPOLDSKIRCHEN, the dramatically full-bodied, long-lived spicy white wine of the Thermenregion district of AUSTRIA. (The other is ZIERFANDLER.) The wines are particularly high in EXTRACT, ALCOHOL, and BOUQUET.

Rouchet, Italian red grape variety. See RUCHÈ.

Roupeiro, Portuguese white grape variety grown particularly in the ALENTEJO producing basic white wine to be drunk as young as possible. It is known as Códega in the Douro and sometimes as Alva in the northern Alentejo.

Roussanne, fashionable white Rhône grape which doubtless owes its name to the russet or *roux* colour of its skin. With MARSANNE, with which it is often blended, it is one of only two vine varieties allowed into the white versions of the northern Rhône's red-wine appellations HERMITAGE, CROZES-HERMITAGE, and ST-JOSEPH and into the exclusively white but often sparkling ST-PÉRAY. In each of these appellations, Marsanne is far more widely grown because, although the wine produced is not as fine, there is more of it.

Roussanne's chief attribute is its haunting aroma, something akin to a particularly refreshing herb tea, together with acidity that allows it to age much more gracefully than Marsanne, which, in blends, can lend useful body. In the southern Rhône, Roussanne (but not Marsanne) is one of four grape varieties allowed into white CHÂTEAUNEUF-DU-PAPE, and Ch de Beaucastel here has demonstrated that carefully grown Roussanne can respond well to oak ageing. The variety is also grown in Provence (although the more common pink-berried **Roussanne du Var** is a lesser, unrelated variety used for VINS DE PAYS and ordinary table wines) and, increasingly, in the Languedoc-Roussillon, where results can be impressive. Although it is usually classified with Marsanne and Vermentino in appellation regulations, it can make a fine blending partner with the fuller-bodied Chardonnay too.

The variety is also beguilingly fine and aromatic at Chignin in SAVOIE, where it is known as Bergeron, but should not be confused with ROUSSETTE. It is grown to a limited extent in Liguria and Tuscany, where it is a permitted ingredient in Italy's Montecarlo Bianco, and can also be found in Australia. Roussanne is also increasingly popular, both for blending and as a VARIETAL, in California's Central Coast.

Roussette is the most exciting white grape variety grown in the eastern French wine region of SAVOIE, and a wine carrying its name on the label is likely to be superior.

The wine produced is relatively exotically perfumed, has good acidity, and is well worth ageing. In recognition of Roussette's superiority over the more common JACQUÈRE, **Roussette de Savoie** has its own appellation in four communes, Marestel, Monterminod, Monthoux, and most notably Frangy. If followed on the label by the name of a commune, the wine will be made exclusively of Roussette, known here as Altesse; if not, Chardonnay may constitute up to 50 per cent of the wine. **Roussette**

de Seyssel is a fine, aromatic still wine from an area most noted for its sparkling wines, in which Roussette is sometimes included to add aroma.

Roussillon, although often first encountered by outsiders as a suffix to LANGUEDOC, has a quite distinct identity, both cultural and geographical. Its inhabitants are Catalan rather than French, with a history rich in Spanish influence. Quite unlike the flat coastal plains of the Languedoc, Roussillon's topography is dominated by the eastern section of the Pyrenees, a mountain range so high that much of it remains snow covered throughout the summer. Vines and olives are two of the rare agricultural crops that can thrive in the tortured, arid valleys of the Agly, Têt, and Tech—although the lower land is today an important source of soft fruit. The climate is France's sunniest, with an average of 325 days' sunshine a year. Wine styles and techniques as well as grape varieties have much in common with neighbouring Spain, as do the relatively low yields. Despite the prevailing temperatures, Roussillon's cellars were some of France's last to install efficient TEMPERATURE CONTROL, and new OAK is still regarded as a luxury.

Awarded APPELLATION CONTRÔLÉE status as recently as 1977, **Côtes du Roussillon** has been a name in search of an image outside the region in which it is, with the exception of COLLIOURE, the sole appellation for table wines. Côtes du Roussillon can be white and rosé as well as red, but the **Côtes du Roussillon-Villages** appellation that theoretically designates the region's finest wines is only for red wines made in the northern third of the region just south of CORBIÈRES and FITOU.

The best reds tend to be like a Spanish rendering of Corbières. Côtes du Roussillon reds are typically made from Carignan (which is slowly being pulled out) fleshed out with at least 40 per cent of a blend in which Syrah and Mourvèdre must make up half, together probably with some Grenache, or its relative Lladoner Pelut. As has been the Spanish custom, white Maccabéo can constitute up to 10 per cent of the blend—although as Carignan's influence declines so should this practice. As in the Languedoc, CARBONIC MACERATION has been much employed to counter Carignan's inherent astringency but more 'traditional' vinification techniques are increasingly employed on the nobler varieties.

The reds are robust, rarely subtle, but good value. Within the northern Villages region, the small villages of CARAMANY and LATOUR-DE-FRANCE successfully lobbied to have their names allowed as suffixes to the Côtes du Roussillon-Villages appellation but it would take a skilled taster to identify either of them blind.

Whites, with their relatively low acidity, may be more difficult to make successfully, but they are also more distinctive, their full-bodied fragrance shaped by Grenache Blanc, Marsanne, Roussanne, Vermentino/Rolle, Maccabéo, and Malvoisie du Roussillon or Tourbat (Sardinia's TORBATO). The first four of these must comprise 50 per cent of the blend. Domaines de Casenove, Cazes, des Chênes, du Mas Crémat, Força-Réal, Gauby, Ch de Jau, Domaines Piquemal, and Sarda-Malet have all made some excellent wines, although CO-OPERATIVES still dominate.

Muscat and Grenache, the region's dominant vine varieties (other than Carignan) grown for VIN DOUX NATUREL, are increasingly made into less alcoholic, dry VIN DE PAYS.

A few producers, especially on the coastal plain around Rivesaltes, are trying their luck with such INTERNATIONAL VARIETIES as Chardonnay and Merlot, although it can be difficult to preserve acidity in the first and fruit concentration in the second. These wines are usually labelled as Vin de Pays des Côtes Catalanes in the northern third, Vin de Pays Catalan in the south.

Idiosyncratic but virtuoso producers such as Fernand Vaquer produce miraculous wines, also outside the appellation system and therefore some of France's most expensive VINS DE TABLE, from low-yielding traditional varieties grown on higher terraced vineyards. The vinegrowers of Roussillon are some of France's least content with the details of their appellation regulations.

RS, signature style of dry white made from the SILVANER grape produced co-operatively in the German wine region RHEINHESSEN by many of the more forward-looking producers.

RS is also a common abbreviation for RESIDUAL SUGAR.

Rubired, increasingly popular (in an age when depth of COLOUR is automatically associated with quality) red-fleshed California HYBRID, the result of crossing Alicante Ganzin with the port variety TINTO CÃO. Its productivity

and depth of colour have made the variety popular with blenders of wine, California port, and grape juice, so that acreage has been steadily increasing. It is grown, without any major viticultural problems, mainly in the hot SAN JOAQUIN VALLEY. This useful blending ingredient has also been tested in Australia.

Ruby Cabernet, once-popular red VINIFERA grape variety bred in and for CALIFORNIA in 1949 by crossing Carignan with Cabernet Sauvignon in an attempt to combine Cabernet characteristics with Carignan productivity and heat tolerance. The slightly rustic Ruby Cabernet had its heyday in California in the 1960s. Although designed to yield claret-like wines from hot regions, Ruby Cabernet has done better in California's cooler, coastal climates. Total California plantings have remained static since the 1970s, most notably in the southern SAN JOAQUIN VALLEY. It is grown by several producers in South Africa, Latin America, and also appeared increasingly on Australian wine labels during that country's red-wine shortage of the late 1990s.

Ruchè, Rouchet, or occasionally Roche, relatively obscure red grape variety of the PIEDMONT region in north-west Italy enjoying something of a revival with its own varietal DOC around Castagnole Monferrato, occasionally labelled Rouchet. Like NEBBIOLO, the wine is headily scented and its TANNINS imbue it with an almost bitter aftertaste.

Rueda, historic Spanish white-wine zone in CASTILE AND LEÓN.

For much of the 20th century, the local VERDEJO grape was Rueda's sleeping beauty. It was awoken in the 1970s, when Bodegas Marqués de Riscal of RIOJA recognized the area's potential for dry white wine and sold a fresh Rueda white alongside its Rioja reds. Rueda was awarded DO status in 1980 and the local Consejo Regulador succeeded in relaunching the native variety. Two very different forms of Rueda currently coexist: fortified and unfortified. The fortified wines (Rueda Pálido and Rueda Dorado) are declining, however, and are most often sold in bulk locally and on the northern Spanish coast. In complete contrast, modern Rueda is a light, fruity, dry white wine. It may be made from a blend of Viura (MACCABEO) and Verdejo, the latter accounting for at least 50 per cent of the blend, or it may be a Sauvignon Blanc varietal. Rueda Superior must contain at least 85 per cent Verdejo and, as more farmers convert their vineyards, there are ever more VARIETAL wines. Sauvignon Blanc was introduced by Marqués de Riscal in the early 1980s. Some fine, elegant wines have resulted, including one from one of the LURTON family of Bordeaux.

TEMPRANILLO produces some typically firm red wine in the zone but it is not permitted to bear the name Rueda. It is awaiting a new DO, Tierra de Medina.   R.J.M. & V. de la S.

Rufete, early-ripening vine variety capable of making fruity red wines and lightish port in the north of Portugal and west of Spain. It may be the same as TINTA PINHEIRA.

Ruffiac, Ruffiat. See ARRUFIAC.

Ruiterbosch, wine area in SOUTH AFRICA once known as Mossel Bay.

Ruländer is the main German name for PINOT GRIS. Since the mid 1980s, some German producers have used this synonym to differentiate sweeter styles, often made from BOTRYTIZED grapes, from a drier wine that would be labelled Grauburgunder. It is planted in most of the wine regions of Germany and is quite important in eastern Germany and the south, although it is relatively rare in the Mosel. More than half of Germany's total Ruländer plantings are in the relatively warm BADEN region, where, as Grauburgunder, it is regarded as a local speciality. Because of its inherent fatness, it can be one of Germany's more successful varieties when styled as a dry wine.

In most German-speaking wine regions—Germany, Austria, and Italy's Alto Adige—Pinot Gris is regarded as rather more ordinary than Pinot Blanc, although it can quite easily reach ripeness levels which demand a high PRÄDIKAT and therefore attention for its rich spicy character. In Austria, where its wines are typically even earthier and richer than their German counterparts, it is also commonly called Ruländer and is also much less common than Pinot Blanc, covering just one per cent of the country's vineyard, chiefly in Styria and Burgenland.

The name Ruländer is also used for some of the Pinot Gris that is widely planted in ROMANIA.

Rully, rambling village in Burgundy's CÔTE CHALONNAISE providing approximately equal quantities of red and white wines. The wines are attractive early and rarely age well. Rully is also a good source of sparkling CRÉMANT de Bourgogne. Nineteen vineyards in the village, one-sixth of the total, are designated PREMIERS CRUS, with Grésigny, Rabourcé, and Les Cloux being the most frequently seen.   J.T.C.M.

Rumania. See ROMANIA.

Rusa, occasional Romanian name for GEWÜRZTRAMINER.

Russia, the dominant state of the CIS. It is the CIS's fourth most important grape grower (after MOLDOVA, UKRAINE, and UZBEKISTAN), but is by far its major wine producer, thanks to imported grapes, must, and unfinished wine. Total Russian wine production in 1990 was 7.5 million hl/197 million gal—a considerable reduction from the 17 million hl produced in the early 1980s before President Gorbachev tried to cut alcohol consumption. By 1996, however, official statistics registered a total wine production of only 2.8 million hl.

State farms manage 90 per cent of the total vineyard area, while 6 per cent of the grape area belongs to collective farms and 4 per cent to individual households. Grapes grown in the North Caucasus, which has more than 90 per cent of Russia's vineyards, are processed mainly by state wineries; 42 secondary vinification enterprises where wine is finished and bottled are located close to Russian centres of population. Imported wine and GRAPE CONCENTRATE are processed by 50 wine enterprises. The best dry table wines of Russia are those produced in the valley of the Don, on the Black Sea coast of the Caucasus, in South Dagestan, and in the premountainous zones of the Stavropol region. Vine varieties ALIGOTÉ, RIESLING, and CABERNET predominate.

Dessert wines are produced in the Don and Kuban valleys, the Stavropol region, Dagestan, and Kabardino-Balkaria.

Sparkling wine is important to Russians. The largest production centres are in Moscow (with a capacity of 20 million bottles per year), Rostov-on-Don, St Petersburg, Nizhniy Novgorod, and Tsimlyansk. Soviet sparkling wine is produced by the Abrau-Durso winery by the traditional method (see SPARKLING-WINE-MAKING).

Vine varieties
The varietal assortment of Russia's vineyards is extremely diverse, with about 100 varieties allowed for commercial cultivation. Depending on the region, 70 to 85 per cent of vineyards are planted to wine grapes, with TABLE GRAPES accounting for the rest. Among wine grapes

cultivated in all viticultural regions of Russia, the most common is RKATSITELI, with 45 to 50 per cent. Such varieties as ALIGOTÉ, Riesling, CLAIRETTE, Cabernet Sauvignon, TRAMINER, MUSCATS, SILVANER, SAPERAVI, Merlot, Pinot Gris, and the indigenous Moldovan variety PLAVAI are also widely planted, as well as the local red Tsimlyansky.

Recently, new varieties with improved resistance to fungal diseases and frost have been introduced. Most notable are Saperavi Severny and CABERNET SEVERNY. V.R.

Russian River Valley, high-quality California wine region and AVA west of Healdsburg along that portion of the river that meanders through the hills of northern Sonoma County toward its mouth. See SONOMA.

Rust, town on the western shore of the Neusiedlersee in the Burgenland region of AUSTRIA famous for the production of sweet white AUSBRUCH wines.

Rutherford, important centre of wine production in the NAPA Valley of California.

Rutherglen, small town in north-east VICTORIA that could be said to be AUSTRALIA's answer to Oporto. It is the centre of production of Australia's most distinctive wines, both fortified, LIQUEUR MUSCAT and Liqueur Tokay.

From the late 1990s, the word 'liqueur' has been abandoned on labels. Rutherglen Muscat (sic) is categorized into the increasingly rich regular, Classic, Grand, and Rare.

Ruwer, small German river, 40 km/25 miles in length, which rises in the Hunsrück and flows into the MOSEL, downstream from Trier. In steep sites at Eitelsbach, Maximin Grünhaus, and Kasel, Rieslings from good years are among the best in Germany. They are similar in structure to those of the SAAR, but have a touch of earthiness to add individuality. See also MOSEL-SAAR-RUWER. I.J.

Ruzica, occasional alternative name for the white DINKA grape.

Saale-Unstrut, apparently expanding wine region in eastern GERMANY of terraced and sometimes isolated vineyards, starting to recover from the forlorn condition in which they were left by the former East German regime. The main producers are the cellars at Naumburg belonging to the state of Sachsen-Anhalt, and the co-operative cellar at Freyburg. All the wines from Müller-Thurgau, Silvaner, Bacchus, Gutedel (CHASSELAS), Weissburgunder (PINOT BLANC), and other vine varieties are fully fermented, and thus completely dry. The wines are naturally light in alcohol but relatively rich in extract.   I.J. & K.B.S.

Saar, river which rises in the Vosges mountains and joins the MOSEL at Konz, near Trier. Downstream from Serrig, Riesling vines grow in slate soil, resulting in steely, firm wines with a powerful aroma and long flavour. In good vintages, they are amongst the most successful in the MOSEL-SAAR-RUWER wine region of GERMANY. Only top estates or, at least, growers with vines in favoured sites can produce good wines in poor vintages. For the rest, their lesser wines can be converted into sparkling wine. Within Germany, Saar Riesling SEKT has a good reputation and a long-established position in the market. See also RUWER.   I.J.

Sachsen, or Saxony in English, the smallest wine region in GERMANY. Formerly in East Germany, it is also known colloquially as the Elbtal. Sachsen and SAALE-UNSTRUT are the most northerly wine regions in Germany and have very similar climates. The main producers are the regional CO-OPERATIVE at Meissen and the State Wine Domain at Radebeul. Müller-Thurgau, Riesling, Weissburgunder (PINOT BLANC), Grauburgunder (PINOT GRIS), and Traminer account for 70 per cent of the region's plantings. Sachsen is the only German region still growing the distinguished-sounding, but somewhat indifferent, Goldriesling (Riesling × Courtiller Musqué) vine. As in Saale-Unstrut, nearly all the wines are dry VARIETALS.

I.J. & K.B.S.

Sacramento Valley, northern part of the vast CENTRAL VALLEY of CALIFORNIA from LODI northwards. The biggest concentration of vines is in the Dunnigan Hills AVA north west of Sacramento, led by R. H. Phillips, for whom wine is but a small part of their agricultural interest. A smaller but older wine district lies near the town of Woodland north of Davis and west of Sacramento.

The CLARKSBURG AVA in particular has been a source of distinctive Chenin Blanc grapes. Other AVAs in this region include LODI, SOLANO-GREEN VALLEY, and SUISUN VALLEY.   B.C.C.

Sacy, white grape variety nowadays most closely associated with the Chablis district. Its productivity is the vine's chief attribute, its acidity the wine's most noticeable characteristic. This has been used to reasonable effect by the producers of such sparkling wines as Kriter, and the variety, called here Tresallier, is still an important ingredient in the white wines of ST-POURÇAIN. See also PINOT.

Sagrantino, lively, sometimes tannic red grape variety grown in UMBRIA in central Italy, particularly in the Montefalco area. Sagrantino di **Montefalco** was elevated to DOCG status in the mid 1990s. Sagrantino has been used as an ingredient in DRIED-GRAPE WINES but today shows promise as a carefully vinified dry red, sometimes blended with SANGIOVESE. Outstanding wines from the Arnaldo Capria winery have created much interest in the variety, but the overall level of viticultural and oenological sophistication in the production zone is not high.   D.T.

saignée, French term meaning 'bled' for a wine-making technique which results in a ROSÉ WINE made by running off, or 'bleeding', a certain amount of FREE-RUN juice from just-crushed dark-skinned grapes after a short, pre-fermentation MACERATION. The aim of this may be primarily to produce a lightly pink wine, or to increase the proportion of PHENOLICS and FLAVOUR COMPOUNDS to juice, thereby effecting a form of CONCENTRATION of the red wine which results from fermentation of the rest of the juice with the skins. The second operation has often been undertaken by ambitious producers of both red bordeaux and red burgundy.

St-Amour, the most northerly of the BEAUJOLAIS crus and an area in which a considerable amount of white Beaujolais Blanc (and ST-VÉRAN) is made. About 320 ha/790 acres of Gamay vines are planted for the production of relatively light but true red Beaujolais.

St-Aubin, village in the Côte de Beaune district of Burgundy's CÔTE D'OR tucked out of the limelight between Meursault and Puligny-Montrachet, producing two-thirds red wine from Pinot Noir and one-third white from Chardonnay. Two-thirds of the vineyard area is designated PREMIER CRU, notably Les Charmois, La Chatenière, En Remilly, and Les Murgers Dents de Chien.

White St-Aubin has some of the character of Puligny-Montrachet, especially in the warmer vintages; the reds resemble a more supple version of red Chassagne-Montrachet. Hubert Lamy is one of several fine producers based in St-Aubin.   J.T.C.M.

St-Bris, appellation for dry white wines made from Sauvignon Blanc grapes grown in the communes of St-Bris-le-Vineux, Chitry, Irancy, and parts of Vincelottes, Quennes, St-Cyr-les-Colons, and Cravant south of Auxerre and west of CHABLIS. The wine is too obscure to be made with anything other than artisan passion, but it lacks the breed and concentration of great

Loire Sauvignon made in SANCERRE, and is more of a curiosity (being technically Burgundian but made from a decidedly non-Burgundian grape) than anything else.

St-Chinian, good-value red-wine appellation in the LANGUEDOC in southern France which extends over arid, spectacular, mountainous terrain in the foothills of the Cévennes between the MINERVOIS and FAUGÈRES appellations. Some fresh, dry rosé is also made. The small town of St-Chinian itself is in the middle of the zone, which extends upwards and northwards as far as Vieussan, including Berlou and its famous CO-OPERATIVE, whose wines are sometimes labelled Berloup. The area can be divided into two very different sections. In the northern zone around Berlou and Roquebrun, vines at around 200 m/656 ft altitude grow on arid schists and yield low quantities of extremely sharply etched wines. In the southern zone closer to St-Chinian itself, the clays and limestone, typically at about 100 m, tend to result in fuller, softer wines. Carignan vines are being gradually replaced by Syrah, Grenache, Lladoner Pelut, and, in warmer sites, some Mourvèdre, the four of which must total at least 60 per cent of any blend. Cinsaut may represent no more than 30 per cent. Many producers here also grow other varieties with which to make some excellent VIN DE PAYS. Other fine producers include Domaine Borie La Vitarèle, Canet Valette, Marquise des Mûres, Ch Maurel Fonsalade, Ch Moulinier, Ch Roquebrun, and Ch Viranel.

St-Christol, the easternmost named TERROIR within the Coteaux du LANGUEDOC appellation in southern France, named after a village on the eastern boundary of the Hérault *département* with Gard. Production of appellation wine is relatively low here, and is chiefly in the hands of the village CO-OPERATIVE, although the quality of these red wines is fast improving on estates such as Domaine de la Coste.

St-Drézéry, the smallest named TERROIR within the Coteaux du LANGUEDOC appellation in southern France. Like neighbouring ST-CHRISTOL, it is named after a village on the eastern boundary of the Hérault *département* with Gard and such appellation production as there is is chiefly in the hands of the village CO-OPERATIVE, although Ch Puech-Haut makes some fine reds and whites.

Ste-Croix-du-Mont, most important of the sweet-white-wine appellations on the right bank of the GARONNE in the BORDEAUX region. At their best, these wines can resemble the wines made across the river in SAUTERNES and BARSAC, being high in alcohol, sugar, and concentration. Prices are considerably lower, however. An increasing number of producers are prepared to take the risks necessary to produce BOTRYTIZED wines, and BARREL FERMENTATION, such as introduced for the prestige cuvées of Chx Loubens, La Rame, and du Mont, is becoming increasingly common (see SAUTERNES for details). Some very ordinary, sugary MOELLEUX is also made, however.

St-Émilion, important, rapidly evolving redwine district in Bordeaux producing more wine than any other RIGHT BANK appellation, and home of most of the extravagantly priced MICROCHÂTEAUX. It takes its name from the prettiest town in the Bordeaux region by far, and one of the few to attract tourists to whom wine is of no interest.

Whereas the MÉDOC is made up of large, grand estates, St-Émilion's 400 or so smallholders are essentially farmers, albeit dedicated to a single crop. That crop is dominated by the Merlot and Cabernet Franc (here called Bouchet) vine varieties, Merlot accounting for more than 60 per cent of all vine plantings and imbuing the wines with their characteristic almost dried-fruit sweetness. A little Cabernet Sauvignon is grown, but it can be relied upon to ripen profitably only in very selected spots.

Grape varieties apart, variation is the hallmark of this extensive region. The quality of its wines can vary from light, fruity, serviceable clarets to the finest FIRST GROWTHS capable of ageing for a century or more.

Although conventionally the St-Émilion district has been divided into two general soil types—the Côtes or hillsides, and the Graves or gravelly limestone plateau—there are inevitably myriad soil types within the 5,300 ha/13,090 acres of St-Émilion. More than 3,000 ha of vineyard lie on the plain between the town and plateau and the river Dordogne. Wines made on this lower land tend to be lighter and less long lived than the wines produced on the plateau or the hillsides, and most, but not all, of them qualify for the most basic appellation, **St-Émilion.**

But the St-Émilion district also boasts a diversity of appellations and, uniquely in France, has a CLASSIFICATION of individual properties which is regularly revised, and depends on

tasting. This classification was first drawn up in 1955 and is revised every 10 years. Several hundred properties are accorded the misleadingly grand-seeming **St-Émilion Grand Cru** status. As a result of the 1996 classification, for example, almost 2,200 ha/5,400 acres qualified for the simple St-Émilion appellation while more than 3,200 ha qualified as St-Émilion Grand Cru for the 1996 harvest.

But the classification's most significant task is to identify which properties rank as **St-Émilion Grand Cru Classé** and which few qualify as **St-Émilion Premier Grand Cru Classé.** See CLASSIFICATION for details of the 1996 classification, which rated 68 properties Grands Crus Classés, of which 13 are Premiers Grands Crus Classés.

Most of the district's most highly ranked properties are either on the steep, clay-limestone hillsides immediately below the town or on a gravelly section of the plateau 5 km/3 miles west of the town and immediately adjacent to the POMEROL appellation. Of St-Émilion's two most highly ranked properties, Chx AUSONE and CHEVAL BLANC, the first is the archetypal Côtes property, with tiny, vertiginous vineyard, and cellars burrowed into the hillside, and the second is on particularly gravelly soils with clay and some of the iron-rich deposits characteristic of neighbouring Pomerol. The startling difference in the style of these wines, the second the only great wine to be made predominantly from Cabernet Franc grapes, is a telling demonstration of the variety that St-Émilion can offer.

Of traditionally famous St-Émilion properties, Ch Figeac, which pre-dated and claims to rival Ch Cheval Blanc, is (unusually for the appellation) attached to Cabernet Sauvignon. Since most other St-Émilions lack this tannic ingredient, the district's wines in general mature much faster than their left-bank counterparts.

This is particularly true of the new wave of small properties which emerged in the 1990s, whose wines are in such demand from the world's COLLECTORS and INVESTORS, in some cases selling for prices well in excess of the established FIRST GROWTHS. See MICROCHÂTEAU.

At the other extreme of value, the St-Émilion CO-OPERATIVE, l'Union des Producteurs de St-Émilion, is one of France's most ambitious, and bottles a quarter of St-Émilion's production. The whole region is characterized by a strong sense of local identity.

The satellite appellations

On the outskirts are the so-called St-Émilion satellites, Lussac-St-Émilion, Montagne-St-Émilion, Puisseguin-St-Émilion, and St-Georges-St-Émilion, encircling St-Émilion proper to the north and east. On this more rolling countryside north of the Barbanne (see LALANDE-DE-POMEROL), the vine is grown alongside other crops and viticulture accounts for about half of the total area. Co-operatives are important here and Montagne- and Lussac-St-Émilion produce significantly more wine than either Puisseguin or, especially, St-Georges, which was for many years sold exclusively as Montagne-St-Émilion. The grape varieties planted are similar to those in St-Émilion proper but the standard of wine-making is generally more rudimentary. There are, nevertheless, bargains to be sought out.

The vine variety

St-Émilion is also a synonym for the widely planted white grape variety called UGNI BLANC in France and TREBBIANO in Italy. The name is used particularly in cognac country in SOUTH WEST FRANCE, where it is widely planted, and in California, where it is not.

Ste-Foy, or Ste-Foy-Bordeaux, district in the extreme east of the BORDEAUX region on the border with, and arguably more properly part of, BERGERAC. It is named after its principal town, just 22 km/14 miles west of the town of Bergerac. Its red wines are very similar to red Bergerac and BORDEAUX AC, while its white wines are sweet and mostly undistinguished.

St-Estèphe, the northernmost of the four important communal appellations in the Haut-Médoc district of Bordeaux. St-Estèphe is separated from the vineyards of Pauillac's Ch LAFITE only by a stream—indeed Ch Lafite owns some land in the commune of St-Estèphe itself.

The soils of St-Estèphe contain their fair share of gravel, but these layers of gravel are often to be found on a clay base. These more poorly drained soils are cooler and can delay ripening, leaving St-Estèphe grapes higher in acidity than their counterparts further south in the Médoc. In Bordeaux's low-rainfall vintages, such as 1990, the water-retaining clays of St-Estèphe have their advantages, however.

A high proportion of grapes grown on St-Estèphe's 1,200 ha/2,960 acres of vines have found their way into the vats of the village's co-operative, which often uses the name Marquis de St-Estèphe. The village may boast fewer famous names and CLASSED GROWTHS than MARGAUX, PAUILLAC, and ST-JULIEN, but its wines have a distinctive style that is deep coloured, full of extract, perhaps a little austere in youth, but very long lived. This style was perceptibly softened during the 1980s as higher proportions of Merlot grapes blurred the edges of the Cabernet, and wine-making techniques, particularly CONCENTRATION, have been harnessed to make the wines seem softer and fuller.

The stars of St-Estèphe are its two second growths, Ch Montrose and Cos (formerly Ch Cos d'Estournel), whose fortunes and reputations have alternated throughout the village's relatively recent history as a fine-wine producer. Cos (pronounced 'koss') has the Médoc's most eye-catching architecture, and its wines are the commune's most ambitious, styled for many decades to come, with, recently, increasing reliance on concentration techniques. Its sister property Ch Marbuzet was in effect treated as a SECOND WINE until the emergence in the late 1990s of Les Pagodes de Cos. Ch Montrose produces much more traditionally structured, almost Ch LATOUR-like, wines, with a perceptible lightening of style in the 1980s.

St-Estèphe's other classed growths are the increasingly dramatic third growth Ch Calon-Ségur, the fourth growth Ch Lafon-Rochet, well sited between Chx Lafite and Cos, and the modest fifth growth Ch Cos-Labory. Some of the village's most conscientiously made wines, however, are such CRUS BOURGEOIS as the exotic Ch Haut-Marbuzet, Ch Meyney run by CORDIER, Chx de Pez and Beauséjour (owned by ROEDERER) and Les-Ormes-de-Pez (the latter run in tandem with Pauillac's Ch Lynch-Bages), Ch Beau-Site, and the recently reconstructed Ch Lilian-Ladouys.

See MÉDOC.

St-Georges d'Orques, named TERROIR within the Coteaux du LANGUEDOC just outside Montpellier where estates such as Ch de Fourques, Domaine de la Prose, and Domaine Henry (whose chief produce is VARIETAL vins de pays) are proving the zone's worth.

St-Georges-St-Émilion, satellite appellation of ST-ÉMILION in Bordeaux.

St-Jean-de-Minervois is the small mountain village in the far north east of the MINER-

VOIS region that gives its name to the Languedoc's most individual VIN DOUX NATUREL appellation, Muscat de St-Jean-de-Minervois. Like the other Muscats of FRONTIGNAN, LUNEL, and MIREVAL, it is made exclusively from the best Muscat variety, MUSCAT BLANC À PETITS GRAINS. The wines display more of the variety's delicate orange-flower flavours than is usually the case in Muscats other than those of BEAUMES-DE-VENISE. Domaine de Barroubio and Perna Batut are the leading producers.

St-Joseph, ambitiously expanded northern RHÔNE west-bank appellation producing mainly red wines from the SYRAH grape but also some full-bodied dry whites from the MARSANNE and, occasionally, ROUSSANNE grapes. The appellation extends from CONDRIEU in the north (where there is some overlap) to a small pocket of St-Joseph vineyards between ST-PÉRAY and the town of Valence. The heart of the region, however, is the stretch of old, terraced vineyards around the town of Tournon just across the wide river Rhône from the hill of HERMITAGE. The wines are lighter and certainly faster maturing than this northern Rhône archetype, not so much because the soils are very different but because St-Joseph's east-facing vineyards simply lose the sun up to two hours earlier in the crucial ripening season. For this reason, locals view St-Joseph as their answer to BEAUJOLAIS, a fruity wine for drinking in the first three years or so. Those less accustomed to the sheer weight of a good northern Rhône red may prefer to drink them at between two and six years old, depending on the character of the vintage, but Gripa's VIEILLES VIGNES bottling can easily repay a decade's bottle age. Red St-Joseph can be a delightfully transparent expression of Syrah fruit, and is one of the most flattering northern Rhône reds to taste young. The best should be approached in a much less reverential way than a Hermitage or a CÔTE RÔTIE, the rest (which comprise too high a proportion of the total) can be too light and insubstantial to be worth the price premium that St-Joseph can, often inexplicably, command over the other basic northern Rhône appellation CROZES-HERMITAGE. White St-Joseph represents less than 10 per cent of the appellation's total production and the best can provide lovers of white Hermitage with a good-value alternative. Other top producers include Pierre Gaillard and Jean-Louis Grippat.

St-Julien, one of the most homogeneous, reliable, and underrated village appellations in the Haut-Médoc district of Bordeaux. St-Julien may suffer in popular esteem because, unlike PAUILLAC to its immediate north and MARGAUX a few miles to the south, there is no FIRST GROWTH property within its boundaries. Instead, however, it can boast five superb second growths, two excellent third growths, four well-maintained fourth growths, and, from the 1980s at least, an unrivalled consistency in wine-making skill. St-Julien is the commune for wine connoisseurs who seek subtlety, balance, and tradition in their red bordeaux. The wines may lack the vivid, sometimes almost pastiche, concentration of a Pauillac, the austerity of a classic ST-ESTÈPHE, or the immediate charm of a stereotypical (if all too rare) Margaux, but they embody all the virtues of fine, long-lived blends of Cabernet and Merlot grapes, being deep coloured, dry, digestible, appetizing, persistent, intriguing, and rewarding.

The appellation, the smallest of the Médoc's most famous four, included about 900 ha/2,220 acres of vineyard throughout the 1990s within the communes of St-Julien and Beychevelle to its immediate south. Both gravelly soils and subsoils here are relatively homogeneous. South of St-Julien is a considerable extent of land classified merely as Haut-Médoc, but to the north the appellation is contiguous with the southern border of Pauillac, and Ch LÉOVILLE LAS CASES in the extreme north of St-Julien shares many characteristics with some fine Pauillac wines, notably Ch LATOUR, which is well within sight.

Léoville-Poyferré demonstrated something of a return to form in the 1980s. Best value, and perhaps most representative of the appellation, is Léoville-Barton, run from Ch Langoa-Barton, a fine third growth, by Anthony BARTON.

Chx Gruaud-Larose and Ducru-Beaucaillou are the other two St-Julien second growths, and produce two of the Médoc's finest wines in most vintages. Gruaud-Larose is usually the richer of the two. Ch Ducru-Beaucaillou ('beautiful pebble') is, unusually for a Médoc château, the home of its owners, the Borie family, who produce one of the most traditionally fashioned wines of the Médoc here, as

well as owning Ch Grand-Puy-Lacoste of PAU-
ILLAC.

The third growth Ch Lagrange was much
improved in the 1980s by investment from the
Japanese spirits firm Suntory, while fourth
growths Chx St Pierre, Talbot, Branaire-Ducru,
and Beychevelle are generally well run.

St-Julien's classed growths account for about
three-quarters of the appellation's total production, and even such unclassified properties
as Chx Gloria, Hortevie, and Lalande-Borie do
not believe in underpricing their admittedly
admirable produce.

See MÉDOC.

St-Laurent, as well as being one of the few
villages of any size in the MÉDOC, is the name
of a black grape variety for long thought to be
related to PINOT NOIR and today most commonly encountered in lower AUSTRIA and the
Austrian wine region Burgenland. It is capable
of producing deep-coloured, velvety reds with
sufficient concentration—provided yields are
limited—to merit ageing in oak and then bottle.
Lesser versions can be simply and soupily sweet
but the variety has been successfully blended
with such fashionable varieties as Cabernet
Sauvignon, Blauburgunder (Pinot Noir), and
also with Austria's BLAUFRÄNKISCH, notably in
Austria's Neusiedlersee-Hügelland district on
the west shore of the lake.

It has been known in eastern France and
there are a few plantings in Germany, mainly
in the Pfalz, but this is essentially an Austrian
speciality and one in which the Austrians
themselves see considerable potential.

The variety is also cultivated in the CZECH
REPUBLIC, where it is known as Vavrinecke, or
Svatovavrinecke.

St-Macaire, town in the BORDEAUX region
just across the river GARONNE from Langon in
the GRAVES district. It lends its name to Côtes
de Bordeaux-St-Macaire, a small, and declining, BORDEAUX AC regional appellation for
sweet wines.

St-Mont, Côtes de, VDQS in the Armagnac
region dominated by the dynamic Plaimont CO-
OPERATIVE. The zone is effectively a northern
extension of the MADIRAN area and much the
same grape varieties are planted, although
yields are generally higher. TANNAT must constitute at least 60 per cent of some surprisingly
juicy reds with an increasing proportion of FER
Servadou, together with the Cabernets. For
whites, local varieties ARRUFIAC (Ruffiac) and

COURBU are being encouraged, in some cases
rescued from extinction, at the expense of the
MANSENGS, thereby differentiating this wine
from JURANÇON to the south. Clairette is being
phased out. Quality is increasing with every
vintage, as is the price differential between it
and the local VIN DE PAYS des Côtes de Gascogne.

St-Péray, small and shrinking appellation for
white SPARKLING WINES that seem something
of an anomaly in the northern RHÔNE, famous
for the weight and longevity of its wines. The
Marsanne and Roussanne or Roussette grapes
grown here produce few wines of great finesse,
despite the fact that the TRADITIONAL METHOD
is employed to transform them into sparkling
wine. A considerable proportion of production
is given its first fermentation at the co-operative of Tain l'HERMITAGE before being made
sparkling in the St-Péray co-operative cellars. A
small quantity of still St-Péray is also made
which is not unlike white St-Joseph.

St-Pourçain, sometimes called St-Pourçain-
sur-Sioule, small VDQS in the centre of France.
From fewer than 500 ha/1,235 acres of vineyard
on varied soils, a wide range of wine colours
and flavours are made, being typically dry,
light in body, and relatively high in acidity.

The traditional vine variety was TRESSALLIER,
the local variant of SACY, but modern white
wines are just as likely to be made from Chardonnay and/or Sauvignon Blanc and there is a
legal limit (50 per cent in the mid 1990s) on
the amount of Tresallier which may be used
for white wines. Gamay is the most common
grape used for pink and light-red St-Pourçain,
although some Pinot Noir is also grown and
individual producers as conscientious as the
Domaine de Bellevue make increasingly
serious red wine from it. The CO-OPERATIVE in
the town of St-Pourçain-sur-Sioule itself dominates production. Promotion to APPELLATION
CONTRÔLÉE status is regularly sought.

St-Romain, exquisitely pretty village perched
on top of a cliff in the Côte de Beaune district
of Burgundy producing red wines from Pinot
Noir and white wines from Chardonnay, the
former maintaining a slight majority. There
are no PREMIERS CRUS in the appellation, which
was granted only in 1967.

The vineyards of St-Romain are situated
behind those of Auxey-Duresses and at higher
altitude than is usual in the CÔTE D'OR. In lesser
vintages the grapes do not ripen as well as

elsewhere but in warmer years the wines can be excellent value. Alain Gras makes particularly fine wines here.   J.T.C.M.

St-Saturnin, one of the most exciting of the named TERROIRS within the Coteaux du LANGUEDOC appellation in southern France named after the eponymous village but including parts of St-Guiraud, Jonquières, and Arboras. Just west of MONTPEYROUX, this zone is also in high, rugged country where little other than the vine will grow. The St-Saturnin CO-OPERATIVE is particularly dynamic, as are such individual producers as Mas Jullien, who coax maximum character out of local grape varieties grown here on the south-facing slopes of the Cévennes (although Olivier Jullien's wines are presented as straight Coteaux du Languedoc).

St-Véran, appellation created in 1971 for white wines from the Chardonnay grape in southern Burgundy, between the Mâconnais and Beaujolais, to include much of the wine that was once sold as Beaujolais Blanc. St-Véran encompasses seven communes: Davayé, Solutré-Pouilly, Prissé, Chânes, Chasselas, Leynes, and St-Vérand. The star of this appellation is arguably Domaine des Deux Roches, although most fine Pouilly-Fuissé producers also make good St-Véran.

The wines frequently have more body and ageing ability than a typical MÂCON-VILLAGES without rivalling the power and persistence of the wines of Pouilly-Fuissé, which forms an enclave within St-Véran.   J.T.C.M.

Salice Salento, DOC for robust red wine made mainly from NEGROAMARO grapes in south-east Italy. See APULIA.

Salvagnin, Vaud name for a light-red blend of Pinot Noir with a bit of Gamay in SWITZERLAND. Similar to but less common than the DÔLE of the Valais.

Salvagnin (Noir) is a Jura name for Pinot Noir, disconcertingly similar to the name of one of the Jura's own vine varieties, SAVAGNIN.

Sämling 88, common Austrian synonym for the SCHEUREBE vine variety of which several hundred hectares are planted in the southern Austrian wine regions of Burgenland and Styria. It can make some excellent BOTRYTIZED wines.

Samos. See GREECE.

Samsó, Penedès name for the CARIGNAN grape.

Samtrot. See MÜLLERREBE.

San Benito, small CALIFORNIA county inland from Monterey County. The one exception to a prevailing mediocrity in San Benito is a one-vineyard AVA named Mount Harlan after the limestone-rich slopes on which Calera winery's several celebrated blocks of Pinot Noir grow. The county has other AVAs (Cienega Valley, Lime Kiln Valley, Paicines) from which little is seen.   B.C.C.

Sancerre, dramatically situated hilltop town on the left bank of the upper Loire which lends its name to one of the Loire's most famous, and famously variable, wines: racy, pungent, dry white Sauvignon Blanc, which enjoyed enormous commercial success in the 1970s. Sancerre's dramatically simple, piercing Sauvignon flavours of gooseberries and nettles were initially introduced into the bistros of Paris in a sort of white-wine equivalent of Beaujolais but, by the late 1970s and early 1980s, Sancerre was regarded as the quintessential white wine for restaurants around the world.

The Sauvignon has adapted well to many of the varied TERROIRS around Sancerre, where, in 14 different communes, vines are cultivated, particularly on south-facing slopes. There are three distinct areas: the 'white' western vineyards are made up of clay and limestone soils that produce quite powerful wines; those between here and the town of Sancerre are high in gravel as well as limestone and produce particularly delicate wines; while those close to Sancerre itself are rich in flint and yield longer-living, particularly perfumed wines. Comparisons with POUILLY-FUMÉ, made just a few miles upstream on the opposite bank, are inevitable, although both are relatively large, heterogeneous appellations, Sancerre even more than Pouilly.

The climate here is distinctly CONTINENTAL. Wine-making in the 1970s and 1980s was a relatively simple affair of maximizing the fruit qualities by TEMPERATURE CONTROL and a fair amount of stainless steel. There have since been attempts to marry Sancerre fruit with OAK, with varying degrees of success.

Sancerre's popularity has brought with it the inevitable increase in the proportion of mediocre wine produced, sometimes over-produced, within the zone. Most Sancerre is ready for drinking almost as soon as it is bottled, and rarely improves beyond two or three years, although the best certainly keep. In years as

Sangiovese

ripe as 1989, some sweet VENDANGE TARDIVE wine was produced by the likes of Alphonse Mellot and Henri Bourgeois. Other fine producers include Lucien Crochet, Cotat, Vincent Pinard.

Sancerre also exists in light, often beguiling, red and rosé versions, made from Pinot Noir grapes. These wines enjoy a certain following, mainly in France, but need very high standards of wine-making and good weather to imbue them with a good core of fruit.

See also LOIRE.

Sangiovese, qualitatively variable red grape variety that is Italy's most planted and is particularly common in central Italy. In 1990, almost 10 per cent of all Italian vineyards were planted with some form of Sangiovese. In its various clonal variations and names (Brunello, Prugnolo Gentile, Morellino), Sangiovese is the principal vine variety for fine red wine in TUSCANY, the sole grape permitted for BRUNELLO DI MONTALCINO, and the base of the blend for CHIANTI, VINO NOBILE DI MONTEPULCIANO, and the vast majority of SUPERTUSCANS. It is, in addition, the workhorse red grape of all of central Italy, widely planted in UMBRIA (where it gives its best results in the DOCG wines Torgiano and Montefalco), in the MARCHES (where it is the base of Rosso Piceno and an important component of Rosso Conero), and in LATIUM. Sangiovese can be found as far afield as Lombardy and Valpolicella to the north and Campania to the south.

Sangiovese's principal characteristic in the vineyard is its slow and late ripening, which gives rich, alcoholic, and long-lived wine in hot years and creates problems of high ACIDITY and hard TANNINS in cool years. Over-production tends to accentuate the wine's acidity and lighten its colour, which can also OXIDIZE and start to brown at a relatively young age.

Throughout modern Tuscany, Sangiovese is now often blended with a certain proportion of the Bordeaux grape Cabernet Sauvignon, whether for Chianti (in which case the interloper should not exceed 15 per cent of the total) or a highly priced VINO DA TAVOLA. This highly successful blend, in which the intense fruit and colour of Cabernet marries well with the characteristic native variety, was first sanctioned by the DOC authorities in CARMIGNANO.

In UMBRIA, the variety dominates most of the region's best red wine, as in the Torgiano of the producer LUNGAROTTI. But in terms of quantity

rather than quality, Sangiovese is most important in Romagna (see EMILIA-ROMAGNA), where SANGIOVESE DI ROMAGNA is as common as the LAMBRUSCO vine is in Emilia. Sangiovese di Romagna wine is typically light, red, ubiquitous, and destined for early consumption. The most widely planted Sangiovese vines planted in Romagna appear to have little in common with Tuscany's most revered selections. Some Sangiovese is grown in the south of Italy, where it is usually used for blending with local grapes, and the success of Supertuscans has inevitably led to a certain amount of experimentation with the variety to the north of Tuscany too.   D.T.

Outside Italy

Like other Italian grape varieties, particularly red ones, Sangiovese was taken west, to both North and South America, by Italian emigrants. In South America, it is best known in Argentina.

In California, international recognition for the quality of Supertuscans brought a sudden increase in Sangiovese's popularity in the late 1980s and 1990s. Most substantial plantings are in the NAPA Valley, but smaller patches can be found in SONOMA County, SAN LUIS OBISPO County, and the SIERRA FOOTHILLS. Early results give real hope to Californians, showing promising balance and structure. Some had the faintly floral aromas veteran drinkers of Chiantis and Brunellos would recognize as Sangiovese, although the wines were made in Californian rather than Tuscan styles. Quality is expected to increase with VINE AGE and identification of CLONAL variations. Robert Pepi and Atlas Peak, in which the Tuscan firm of ANTINORI have an important stake, both in Napa, were some of the earliest commercial producers; Villa Ragazzi and Noceto were pioneers on a smaller scale. The grape is also grown in Washington state, although it can be difficult to match clone to site.

Sangiovese di Romagna, quantitatively important VARIETAL central Italian red made from the most widely cultivated grape variety in ROMAGNA. The reputation of the zone has been sullied by the mediocre quality of much of the wine produced, and by the efforts of a number of Tuscan producers to blame the low quality of Tuscan wines between 1965 and 1980 on the infiltration of their vineyards by high-yielding, low-quality Sangiovese di Romagna. Just like the SANGIOVESE of Tuscany, the Sangiovese of Romagna exists in many clonal variations, some of which do indeed produce abundant quantities of indifferent wine, but the better clones of Sangiovese di Romagna are by no means inferior to those of Tuscany, and the occasional bottles of fine Sangiovese produced in Romagna give tantalizing hints of possibilities yet to be exploited.

The variety is cultivated throughout the region but there can be few doubts that the best Sangiovese di Romagna comes from the hills to the south of the ancient Via Emilia, where the terrain rises towards the Apennines. The DOC reflects this widely accepted view of the most suitable terrain, confining the territory of Sangiovese di Romagna to the eastern hills of the province of Bologna and the Apennine zones of the provinces of Ravenna and Forlì. A tradition of CASK AGEING has long existed and successful experiments with small oak barrels have given results comparable to a good Tuscan VINO DA TAVOLA from Sangiovese. These superior products remain, for the moment, mere drops in the bucket: high yields and the domination of the large CO-OPERATIVES have tended to reduce Sangiovese di Romagna to its lowest common denominator.   D.T.

sangría, a mixture of red wine, lemonade, and, sometimes, spirits and fresh fruit, served typically in Spain's tourist resorts.

San Joaquin Valley, southern half of the vast Central Valley in CALIFORNIA, and that part of the state which produces the great bulk of its wine. It is California's Languedoc-Roussillon or Mezzogiorno, but so far only as a bottomless well of cheap, everyday wine. Except for the distinct AVAS of LODI and CLARKSBURG at its very northern end near the confluence of the San Joaquin and Sacramento rivers, it resists any internal dividing lines because its climate and soils are so relentlessly consistent. (Although see also MADERA, an AVA with its own specialities.)

The immense E. & J. GALLO is unquestionably the most important firm in it, making about 55 million cases of wine a year. CANANDAIGUA has a major winery at Madera producing for that firm's many labels. Bronco and the Wine Group (Franzia) are other major firms in the heart of the San Joaquin Valley.

San Luis Obispo, wine-producing county in the CENTRAL COAST AVA of CALIFORNIA midway between Los Angeles and San Francisco with a very diverse terrain and climate.

Arroyo Grande AVA

A long range of hills at the southern edge of San Luis Obispo County, Arroyo Grande was viticulturally distinguished in the 1980s only by the painstaking decision to plant 350 ha/865 acres of it for Maison Deutz, the California arm of Champagne house Deutz. This has now been sold to another French investor and renamed Laetitia. The location is one of the coolest in California and the sparkling wine made there uses the largest proportion of true Pinot Blanc (30 per cent) in the state. Hundred-year-old Zinfandel vines behind Lake Lopez do magnificently well for Saucelito Canyon winery, while Pinot Noir does quite well for Talley Vineyards in lower-lying portions of the AVA.

Edna Valley AVA

Directly south of the coastal town of San Luis Obispo, Edna Valley won quick fame for its Chardonnays beginning in the mid 1970s. Edna Valley Vineyards, part of the Chalone group, is the principal winery. Gewürztraminer has also done well, but it is not widely planted. Pinot Noir has been variable. Cool, even temperatures and fog cover result in a very long growing season.

Paso Robles AVA

An isolated inland plain, where the headwaters of the Salinas river congregate, Paso Robles earned an early reputation as a place where outlaws could hole up, no questions asked. From the 1880s onward, its role as a wine district was to produce sun-baked, high-alcohol, fiercely tannic Zinfandels. Since its confirmation as an AVA, newcomers in an expanding roster of local wineries have moved on to embrace Cabernet Sauvignon, Sauvignon Blanc, and Chardonnay. Wines from these new territories can charm early, but few have shown long staying power. The Zinfandelists have stuck with their traditional haunts in high hills to the west of town, but now even they are joining up as growers of Cabernet and Chardonnay. Meridian, J. Lohr, and Arciero represent the large players; Justin, Wild Horse, Eberle, Peachy Canyon, and Castoro the new artists; Mastantuono, Pesenti, and Tobin James the old breed. One stubborn holdout, Martin Brothers, is trying to carve out a name with Nebbiolo and other Italian varieties. Interesting recent entrants include the Perrin family (Château de Beaucastel) of CHÂTEAUNEUF-DU-PAPE, making Rhône varieties as Tablas Creek in the western sector of the appellation, and SOUTHCORP of Australia, which has planted 400 acres of Syrah and Cabernet Sauvignon in the eastern part near Creston.

York Mountain AVA

A small appellation contiguous with the western edge of the huge Paso Robles AVA. Recent efforts with Pinot Noir and Chardonnay have shown promise.

San Marino, tiny republic within Italy between the regions of EMILIA-ROMAGNA and the MARCHES. The quality of wine produced rose dramatically in the 1980s and is mostly 'exported', to tourist resorts on the Adriatic.

Santa Barbara, southern CALIFORNIA city which gives its name to the southernmost in a string of three heavily planted wine counties on California's CENTRAL COAST (see also MONTEREY and SAN LUIS OBISPO). Its southernmost vines grow hardly more than 100 miles/160 km from downtown Los Angeles. Pinot Noir and Chardonnay are prized varieties in the county because many of its vineyards hug the Pacific Ocean shore north of Cape Concepcion, where nearly eternal sea fogs create conditions cooler and cloudier than either CARNEROS or much of SONOMA County's Russian River. It was not until the wine boom of the 1970s that Santa Barbara began to assert any serious claims as a wine-producing area. Its potential seems particularly bright, in no small part because of its proximity to the trend-setting megalopolis of Los Angeles. It has only two AVAS.

Santa Maria Valley AVA

A flock of distinctive Pinot Noirs brought this AVA on the San Luis Obispo border swift identity during the 1980s. It also has proven well adapted to Chardonnay. Much more heavily planted than the Santa Ynez Valley to the south, it has only a sparse handful of wineries. Byron, Qupé, and Au Bon Climat were its most prominent wineries at the outset of the 1990s, but more recently KENDALL–JACKSON'S purchase of the Tepusquet Vineyard has made them an extremely important player. Some small artisan wineries such as Foxen have also enjoyed acclaim.

Santa Ynez Valley AVA

Although far from being the only schizophrenic AVA in California, the Santa Ynez Valley comes close to being the extreme case. It starts as a narrow, fog-beset river course between steep east–west hills that run inland from the Pacific shore at Lompoc as far as the village of Solvang. There the main valley is joined by tributary canyons from the north, which are much warmer because they are sheltered from sea fogs by elevation and higher hills. The lower end seems best suited to Pinot Noir, Chardonnay, and, perhaps, Riesling. Sanford and Babcock are prominent producers in this western section. The upper, eastern end appears to do better by Sauvignon Blanc and, mostly in blends, Cabernet Franc, Merlot, and Cabernet Sauvignon. Judgements on these varieties remain tentative however. Firestone Vineyards was the pioneer, followed by Zaca Mesa. More recent entrants to have garnered acclaim include Fess Parker (known to Americans over 40 for his television roles as Daniel Boone and Davy Crockett) and Andrew Murray.   B.C.C.

Santa Clara Valley, California wine region and AVA south of San Francisco. Its other name, Silicon Valley, explains its status in the computer industry. A few acres of Santa Clara vines persist to the west in the SANTA CRUZ MOUNTAINS and at its southern end in the Hecker Pass district, but luxury homes for computer programmers make all these vineyards more of a toy than a viable agricultural investment. San Ysidro AVA east of Gilroy is a single grower, owned by a New York winery. Sarah's Vineyard is the most charming and artistically successful among a handful of eccentric wineries operating in the Hecker Pass.   B.C.C.

Santa Cruz Mountains, diverse CALIFORNIA wine region and AVA immediately south of San Francisco. The most useful points to make about it are: it is one of California's cooler growing regions; Pinot Noir has a rich history here, although Riesling and Zinfandel had their day in the last century; Cabernet Sauvignon has won the AVA its greatest fame; and a prominent RHÔNE RANGER, Bonny Doon's Randall Grahm, started in the counterculture woods behind UC Santa Cruz. Top wineries include Ridge, David Bruce, Mt Eden, Ahlgren, Fogarty, Storrs, and Cinnabar.   B.C.C.

Santa Maddalena, known as St Magdelener by the many German speakers who make and drink it, is the most famous wine of the ALTO ADIGE in north-east Italy. It takes its name from the hill of Santa Maddalena to the east of the city of Bolzano (Bozen), long considered a particularly suitable site for the cultivation of the SCHIAVA (Vernatsch) grape from which the wine is made. Like other important Italian DOCS,

Santa Maddalena has undergone a significant enlargement of its production zone from the original nucleus (now called Santa Maddalena CLASSICO). Over 85 per cent of the current production of Santa Maddalena is Santa Maddalena Classico. The wine itself is a ruby to garnet red with aromas of berries and almonds, medium bodied with pronounced almond flavours on the finish. This bitter aftertaste is often due to the 'correction' of Santa Maddalena with more than the legally allowed 10 per cent of LAGREIN grapes to increase COLOUR, BODY, TANNINS, and potential longevity.   D.T.

Santa Maria Valley, California wine region and AVA. See SANTA BARBARA.

Santa Ynez Valley, California wine region and AVA. See SANTA BARBARA.

Santenay, somewhat forgotten village and spa in the Côte de Beaune district of Burgundy producing red wines from Pinot Noir and occasional whites. The soils in Santenay produce red wines tending to the rustic more than the elegant. They are not counted among Burgundy's finest, although they are capable of ageing well.

Most of the best vineyards, the PREMIERS CRUS La Comme, Clos de Tavannes, and Les Gravières, form an extension from Chassagne-Montrachet. Also reputed are La Maladière and Clos Rousseau. Vincent Girardin is one of the best Santenay producers.

See also CÔTE D'OR.   J.T.C.M.

Santorini, one of the southern Cyclades islands that are part of GREECE. The traditional wine of the island, which may be red, white, or rosé, is called 'brousko', from the Italian *brusco*, meaning rough. See GREECE for details of modern wines.   H.M.W.

Saperavi, Georgian red wine grape variety notable for the COLOUR and ACIDITY it can bring to a blend. As a VARIETAL wine, it is capable, not to say demanding, of long BOTTLE AGEING. Saperavi Severny, a hybrid of SEVERNY and Saperavi, has been developed in Russia.

Traditional Saperavi is planted throughout almost all of the wine regions of the CIS, although in cooler areas the acidity may be too marked for any purpose other than blending, despite its relatively high sugar levels. It has also been grown in BULGARIA for some time.

Sardinia, known as **Sardegna** in Italian, Mediterranean island 200 km/125 miles off the coast of Italy at its nearest point.

As markets for Sardinian wines have contracted and the flow of public funds to CO-OPERATIVE wineries has dwindled to a trickle, the total vineyard surface decreased in the early 1990s and the island's total production of wine has dropped from a high of 4.5 million hl to an average of around 1 million hl/26.4 million gal. The production of DOC was about 10 per cent, and viticulture dedicated to quality is developing slowly.

The powerfully alcoholic wines of Sardinia have long been prized more for beefing up wines produced in cooler climates to the north than for drinking on their own. Little has been done within the DOCs to match individual vine varieties to proper soils and climates. The production zones of the most popular varieties—VERMENTINO and CANNONAU—have been extended to include the entire surface of the island; and yields have been allowed to rise to very high levels. The result has been a general flight from DOC 'status', with several—Monica di Cagliari, Giro di Cagliari, Nasco di Cagliari—having become virtually inactive.

The existence of four different types of wine—dry, sweet, a *liquoroso*, or higher alcohol, dry wine, and a *liquoroso* sweet wine—in many of the DOCs seems programmed to create confusion, and it is far from clear that Sardinia's powerfully alcoholic wines need to reach still higher ALCOHOLIC STRENGTHS.

If the overall picture is far from encouraging, small quantities of good wines do exist and suggest that Sardinia's soil and climate have potential. Vernaccia di Oristano, although dwindling in quantities produced, can be a good approximation of a dry SHERRY with a clean and bitter finish, and the hard to find Malvasia di Bosa justly enjoys a certain reputation as a dessert wine. Refreshing bottles of Vermentino di Gallura, produced in the island's north, do exist and the wine's promotion to DOCG status in 1996, accompanied by the lowering of yields, are unquestionably a positive step for the future. An occasional good bottle of Nuragus di Cagliari only underlines the absurdity of allowing such high yields. Carignano di Sulcis has shown marked improvement in recent years, with some interesting experiments with small BARREL MATURATION.

Cannonau, thought to be a clone of GREN-

ACHE and accounting for 20 per cent of the island's total production, has produced some good wines in the province of Nuoro, particularly in the subzone of Oliena.   D.T.

Sárfehér, undistinguished, very productive white grape of Hungary traditionally grown on the sandy Great Plain for TABLE GRAPES and sparkling wines.

Sassella, subzone of the VALTELLINA in the far north of Italy.

Sassicaia, trail-blazing central Italian wine made, largely from CABERNET SAUVIGNON, originally by Mario Incisa della Rochetta at the Tenuta San Guido near BOLGHERI and one of the first Italian reds made in the image of fine red bordeaux. The first small commercial quantities were released in the mid 1970s. In the late 1990s, Sassicaia was granted its own DOC, the only wine from a single estate in Italy to enjoy this privilege. See VINO DA TAVOLA.

Saumur, town in the Loire giving its name to an extensive wine district and several appellations. Saumur is effectively a south-western extension of TOURAINE, yet is more of a centre for the wine trade of Anjou–Saumur than is Angers. The grapes grown in these latter two neighbouring regions are very similar, except that Saumur does not have Anjou's range of potentially great sweet white wines.

Saumur's most important wine (and France's most important mousseux) is **Saumur Mousseux,** a well-priced sparkling wine made from Chenin Blanc grapes with increasing amounts of Chardonnay and, usually less successful, Sauvignon Blanc. These grapes can come from an even wider area than that permitted for still Saumur, and the quality of wine-making is high among the larger houses of the town of Saumur, such as Gratien & Meyer, Langlois Chateau, and Bouvet Ladubay, and also at the important CO-OPERATIVE at St-Cyr-en-Bourg, with its extensive underground cellars hewn out of tuffeau, the local calcareous rock that predominates around Saumur. The wines have enjoyed considerable commercial success, although an increasing proportion of the base material for Saumur Mousseux is expected to be fashioned into CRÉMANT de Loire, for which the criteria are rather more rigorous.

Saumur Blanc can be remarkably difficult to distinguish from Anjou Blanc, being made substantially from Chenin Blanc and being both high in acidity and potentially long lived.

Only the most conscientious growers can coax much fruity charm out of them, however.

Saumur Rouge is a much more successful wine. It may be made from Cabernet Franc, Cabernet Sauvignon, or Pineau d'Aunis grapes, but is usually made almost exclusively from Cabernet Franc and can be a refreshing, relatively light, fruity wine. A little more Saumur Rouge is produced than Saumur Blanc, but the most significant still wine of the region is **Saumur-Champigny,** whose extraordinary expansion in the 1970s and 1980s was largely due to FASHION, and mainly Paris fashion at that. It was the St-Cyr-en-Bourg co-operative in particular that encouraged the planting of Cabernet Franc vines and developed the still-red-wine appellation with such success. Today as much as 40 per cent of all Saumur-Champigny is produced by the co-operative. Most Saumur-Champigny is too light to be worth ageing, and in many cases its substantial premium over, for example, Anjou-Villages can be difficult to justify, although it is usefully, and quintessentially, fruity and flirtatious: the BEAUJOLAIS of the Loire. Particularly reliable producers include Filliatreau, Foucault, Domaine des Roches Neuves, and Ch de Villeneuve.

A small amount of light rosé **Cabernet de Saumur** is made, usually considerably drier and less ambitious than Cabernet d'Anjou, while **Coteaux de Saumur** is Saumur's medium-sweet white, made in very small quantities from Chenin Blanc grapes.

See also LOIRE.

Saussignac, very small sweet-white-wine appellation in SOUTH WEST FRANCE. It lies within the BERGERAC district to the west of Monbazillac and produces sweet white wines, from Sémillon and some particularly successful Muscadelle grapes. Since the mid 1990s, the appellation has become an enclave of great SWEET-WINE-MAKING, led by Clos d'Yvigne and Ch Richard.

Sauterne, occasionally found on labels of GENERIC sweet white wine. Real SAUTERNES always ends in s.

Sauternes. The special distinction of this region embedded within the Graves district south of BORDEAUX is that it is dedicated, in a way unmatched by any other wine region, to the production of unfortified, sweet white wine. The appellation is reserved for wines from five communes that must adhere to regulations stipulating minimum levels of ALCO-HOLIC STRENGTH (13 per cent) and a tasting test that requires the wine to taste sweet. Three grape varieties are planted: Sémillon, Sauvignon Blanc, and Muscadelle. Sémillon is the principal grape, because it is especially susceptible to noble rot, and it accounts for about 80 per cent of a typical estate's ENCÉPAGEMENT. Sauvignon often attracts BOTRYTIS earlier than Sémillon, and its naturally high acidity can give the wine a freshness that balances the richer, broader flavours of Sémillon. Muscadelle's contribution is mostly aromatic.

Sauternes is the product of a specific MESO-CLIMATE. The communes of Sauternes, Barsac, Preignac, Bommes, and Fargues are close to two rivers, the broad GARONNE and its small tributary, the Ciron. When, in autumn, the cool, spring-fed Ciron waters flow into the warmer tidal Garonne, evening mists develop that envelop the vineyards until late morning the following day, when the sun, if it shines, burns the mist away. This moist atmosphere encourages *Botrytis cinerea*, a fungus that attacks the grapes and causes them to shrivel and rot. Mist activates the botrytis spores in the vineyards, and the alternating sunshine completes the process of desiccation.

The onset of botrytis is crucial to the evolution of the grapes. Without it, they may indeed ripen sufficiently to ensure that a sweet wine can be made, but the result will lack complexity. As outlined in more detail in NOBLE ROT, the overall effect of a benevolent botrytis infection is to increase dramatically the concentrations of TARTARIC ACID and sugar in grapes; to stimulate the production of GLY-CEROL that gives the wine its VISCOSITY; and to alter considerably the AROMA and flavour of the finished wine.

The essential difference between mediocre and great Sauternes hangs on the willingness of estate owners to wait until botrytis arrives. This act of patience is largely responsible for the cost of Sauternes. There are years, such as 1978 and 1985, when botrytis either fails to develop at all or arrives very late in the year. This introduces an economic issue unique to this region. Sauternes is exceptionally costly to make. There are a number of vintages each decade in which it is either impossible to make good sweet wine (and some grapes may be salvaged to make a dry white that qualifies only as a BORDEAUX AC) or in which, as in 1991, it can be produced only in minute quantities.

Even in excellent VINTAGES, maximum YIELDS are restricted to 25 hl/ha (1.4 tons/acre), a quantity infrequently attained. At Ch d'YQUEM, the average yield is a trifling 9 hl/ha. (In the red-wine districts of MÉDOC or ST-ÉMILION, yields of more than 45 hl/ha are routine.)

In addition, the harvest is unusually protracted. The necessity for selective harvesting, or TRIAGE, essential for Sauternes, is expensive, as teams of pickers must be kept available for a very long period. More than any other wine, Sauternes is made in the vineyard. None the less, Sauternes calls for careful vinification. Fermentation takes place in tanks or, more usually since the mid 1980s, in BARRIQUES, of which a third or more are likely to be new (see BARREL FERMENTATION). Fermentation either stops of its own accord when the wine has achieved a balance of about 14 per cent alcohol and a RESIDUAL SUGAR level that is the equivalent of a further four to seven per cent alcohol, or it is arrested with the addition of SULPHUR DIOXIDE.

In weaker vintages, CHAPTALIZATION may be permitted, although better estates avoid the practice, which merely adds sweetness rather than complexity. The wine is usually aged in oak barrels for between 18 and 36 months (see BARREL MATURATION). The necessary investment in these barriques also contributes to the high cost of production. Some estates—Chx d'Yquem, Raymond-Lafon, La Tour Blanche—use up to 100 per cent new oak, while others, such as Chx Climens or Doisy-Daëne, prefer a lesser proportion. It is a question of style rather than quality. Less distinguished lots of wine are usually sold off to NÉGOCIANTS; in 1978, Yquem bottled only 15 per cent of the crop under its own label, and in 1987, many estates marketed no wine at all.

A technological development introduced in 1985 has stirred considerable controversy. Cryoextraction can help growers to save part of a crop that might formerly have had to be rejected. Grapes are chilled for 20 hours in a cold chamber before pressing, thus eliminating water and the least ripe grapes. Cryoextraction has no effect on chemical components of the grape and its must but it is a rescue operation only, and its major drawback is cost. None the less, in damp vintages such as 1987 it came in useful for estates such as Yquem which had invested in the process.

BARSAC is the most distinctive commune, and is entitled to its own appellation, although it can also be sold as Sauternes. Its wines are often lighter and more elegant than its neighbours. The communes of Bommes and Sauternes itself tend to give the fattest wines, although exceptions are numerous.

All these factors were taken into account when in 1855 the existing estates were classified. Successful candidates were ranked as either first or second growths, with Yquem rightfully given its own super-status (see CLASSIFICATION). In the 1960s especially, standards slumped. The wines were out of FASHION and there was a string of poor vintages. Only with the excellent 1983 vintage did matters improve. Prices rose, and wise proprietors invested in long overdue improvements, which bore fruit in the superb 1986, 1988, 1989, and 1990 vintages and, more recently, the 1996 and 1997. The official 1855 classification is once again a reasonably reliable guide to quality, although a number of unclassified growths, such as Ch de Fargues (owned by Yquem), Gilette, and Raymond-Lafon, are often of first-growth quality, and price.

After a bad patch, Sauternes is again showing the quality of which it is capable. It combines power, voluptuousness, and elegance, and good bottles can evolve and improve for up to 50 years (longer in the case of Yquem). Given the risks and costs involved in its production, it remains underpriced in relation to the enormous pleasure it can bring.   S.B.

Sauvignonasse, surprisingly common white grape, also known as Sauvignon Vert, which is quite distinct from but in some places casually confused with the more famous Sauvignon Blanc. The wines produced from Sauvignonasse are much less crisp and aromatic than those of Sauvignon Blanc. Sauvignonasse is widely planted in CHILE, often called simply Sauvignon, and has been casually mixed, from vineyard to bottle, with Sauvignon Blanc.

Sauvignon Blanc is the vine variety solely responsible for some of the world's most popular, and most distinctive, dry white wines: Sancerre, Pouilly-Fumé, and a tidal wave of Sauvignon Blanc and Fumé Blanc from outside France. And in many great white wines both dry and sweet, it also adds nerve and zest to its most common blending partner SÉMILLON.

It has always shared a certain aromatic similarity with the great red wine grape Cabernet Sauvignon (something approaching HERBACEOUSNESS) and in 1997 Sauvignon Blanc's standing rose in the world of wine when DNA 'FINGERPRINTING' established that, with Cabernet Franc, Sauvignon Blanc was a parent of Cabernet Sauvignon.

Sauvignon Blanc's most recognizable characteristic is its piercing, instantly recognizable aroma. Descriptions typically include 'grassy, herbaceous, musky, green fruits' (especially gooseberries), 'nettles', and even 'tomcats'. Sauvignon cautiously cultivated in the central vineyards of the Loire, unmasked by oak, can reach the dry white apogee of Sauvignon fruit with some of the purest, most refreshingly zesty wines in the world. The best Sancerres and Pouilly-Fumés served as a model for early exponents of New World Sauvignon Blanc, although by the 1980s it was the Loire *vignerons* who copied their counterparts in New Zealand (which achieved rapid fame with this variety) in experimenting with fermentation and maturation in oak, and picking the grapes at different levels of RIPENESS to add nuance to the aroma and weight to the palate.

Oak-aged examples usually need an additional year or two to show their best, but almost all dry, unblended Sauvignon is designed to be drunk young, although there are both Loire and Bordeaux examples that can demonstrate durability, if rarely evolution, with up to 15 years in bottle (see POUILLY-FUMÉ and Pavillon Blanc de Ch MARGAUX, for example). As an ingredient in the great sweet white wines of SAUTERNES, on the other hand, Sauvignon plays a minor but important part in one of the world's longest-living wines.

France

In Bordeaux, Sauvignon is concentrated in the Entre-Deux-Mers, Graves, and the sweet-wine-producing districts in and around Sauternes. In each of these areas, it is dominated by and usually blended with Sémillon, particularly in Sauternes, where the typical blend incorporates 80 per cent Sémillon together with a little Muscadelle. BORDEAUX BLANC owes much to Entre-Deux-Mers Sauvignon although low yields and, often, expensive oak ageing, as in the best dry white PESSAC-LÉOGNAN, GRAVES, and the handful of expensive Médoc whites (sold as BORDEAUX AC), are prerequisites for a memorable performance from Sauvignon in Bordeaux.

As in red wines, the satellite areas of SOUTH WEST FRANCE reflect Bordeaux's spread of vine varieties and Sauvignon is often an easily perceptible ingredient in the dry whites of such areas as BERGERAC, Côtes du MARMANDAIS, and PACHERENC DU VIC-BILH.

It is in the Loire that Sauvignon is encountered in its purest, most unadulterated form. In the often limestone vineyards of SANCERRE, POUILLY-FUMÉ, and their eastern satellites QUINCY, REUILLY, and MENETOU-SALON, it can demonstrate one of the most eloquent arguments for marrying variety with suitable TERROIR. Most of these wines are designed to be drunk, well chilled, within two years and are none the worse for that. The variety is often called Blanc Fumé in Pouilly Fumé.

From this concentration of vineyards, which might well be considered the Sauvignon capital of the world (however much the inhabitants of Marlborough in NEW ZEALAND's South Island might dispute it), Sauvignon's influence radiates outwards: north east towards Chablis in SAUVIGNON DE ST-BRIS, south to ST-POURÇAIN-sur-Sioule, and north and west to Coteaux du GIENNOIS and CHEVERNY, as well as to a substantial quantity of eastern Loire wines, typically labelled TOURAINE. Such Sauvignons tend to be light, racy, and, of course, aromatic. With Chardonnay, it has also been allowed into the vineyards of Anjou, where it is sometimes blended with the indigenous CHENIN BLANC.

Elsewhere in France, Sauvignon Blanc has been an obvious, though not invariably successful, choice for those seeking to make internationally saleable wine in the Midi, and small plantings of Sauvignon can be found in some of the Provençal appellations.

Rest of Europe

Across the Alps, Sauvignon's most successful Italian region is the far north east in Friuli, with some ALTO ADIGE and COLLIO examples exhibiting extremely fine fruit and purity of flavour. Attempts to transfer Sauvignon to central Italy have been notably less successful. In the 1980s, Italy's plantings of Sauvignon doubled to nearly 3,000 ha/7,410 acres. There has been experimentation with BARREL MATURATION.

As wine-making skills increase in SLOVENIA, wines of similar finesse are emerging from that region, at whose north-eastern limit, in Austrian STYRIA, the variety thrives, combining fruit with aroma. As 'Muskat-Silvaner' (as the variety is known in German) it is grown but rarely in Germany, where many would argue that young Riesling can provide the same sort

of crisp, aromatic white. It is planted to a certain extent further east—even if the wines tend to be progressively heavier and sweeter. Parts of SERBIA, the Fruška Gora district of VOJVODINA, and some of the CZECH REPUBLIC clearly have potential. ROMANIA had nearly 5,000 ha of Sauvignon Blanc in the early 1990s, and neighbouring MOLDOVA also had sizeable plantings of the variety.

Sauvignon Blanc has been imported into Iberia by only the most dedicated internationalists (TORRES, for example, although see also RUEDA), and certainly Portugal and northwestern Spain have no shortage of indigenous varieties (see MINHO and GALICIA) capable of reproducing vaguely similar wine styles.

Rest of the world

There is a tendency for Sauvignon Blanc to taste oily when reared in too warm a climate, as it sometimes does in Israel and other Mediterranean vineyards where those with an eye to the export market put it through its paces.

This oiliness has been clearly perceptible in many of Australia's attempts with the variety, although by the early 1990s there was even keener appreciation of the need to reserve it for the country's cooler sites (see AUSTRALIA for more on the wines produced). Chardonnay plantings outnumber those of Sauvignon Blanc by more than four to one in Australia.

In New Zealand, on the other hand, Chardonnay has overtaken Sauvignon Blanc only fairly recently and this relatively minute wine industry can boast almost as big an area planted with Sauvignon as Australia. This is the variety that introduced New Zealand wine to the world and did it by developing its own pungent style: intensely perfumed, more obviously fruity than the Loire prototype, with just a hint of both gas and sweetness and, occasionally, gooseberries or asparagus. This style of Sauvignon can now be found in Chile and the cooler areas of North America, in the south of France, and, doubtless, even further afield before long.

'Sauvignon' is the white wine most commonly exported from CHILE, but the country's plantings tend to be of Sauvignon Blanc mixed with SAUVIGNONASSE (also known as Sauvignon Vert), a quite different variety. An increasing amount of Sauvignonasse is being replaced with true Sauvignon Blanc, however, and there is a serious attempt to distinguish the two varieties.

Thanks to Robert MONDAVI, who renamed it FUMÉ BLANC, Sauvignon Blanc enjoyed enormous success in California in the 1980s. See CALIFORNIA for more on the wines, which are occasionally sweet and even botrytized, a sort of Semillon-free Sauternes. There has also been an increase, as elsewhere in the New World, in blending in some Semillon to dry white Sauvignon to add weight and fruit to Sauvignon's aroma and acidity. Like California, WASHINGTON state makes both Sauvignon Blanc and Fumé Blanc from its declining acreage of Sauvignon. Of other American states, TEXAS has had particular success with the variety.

But perhaps Sauvignon's real success in the New World, New Zealand excepted, has been in SOUTH AFRICA, where local wine drinkers fell upon the Cape's more successful early Sauvignons as a fashionable internationally recognized wine style. By 1990, there were 3,300 ha of Sauvignon Blanc to South Africa's barely 2,400 ha of Cabernet Sauvignon, and the variety has been gaining ground steadily ever since. Sauvignon Blanc's long history on the Cape seems to be reflected in vibrant, sometimes delicate wines. Elgin seems a particularly suitable area.

Sauvignon Blanc is often simply called **Sauvignon**, especially on wine labels, but it has mutated into variants with darker-coloured berries, notably **Sauvignon Rose** and **Sauvignon Rouge**.

Sauvignon Gris, sometimes sold as a VARIETAL, is another name for Sauvignon Rose and has discernibly pink skins. It can produce more substantial wines than many a Sauvignon Blanc, and has a certain following in Bordeaux and the Loire. See also FIÉ.

Sauvignon Vert, synonym for SAUVIGNONASSE.

Savagnin is a fine but curious vine variety with small, round, pale berries. In France, it is as much a viticultural curiosity as the wine it alone produces, VIN JAUNE, is a wine-making oddity.

It is cultivated to a limited extent throughout the Jura vineyards and may be included in any of the region's white-wine appellations but is usually in practice reserved for the Jura's extraordinary, sherry-like vin jaune. Many believe it is at its finest in what remains of the vineyards of CHÂTEAU-CHALON, where it may sometimes be left to ripen as late as December.

Called Gringet, it is also a minor ingredient in the sparkling wines of Ayse in SAVOIE. It is also grown, at particularly high altitudes, in the Valais of SWITZERLAND, where it is called either Païen or Heida.

Savagnin Noir is a Jura name for PINOT NOIR.

Savatiano, Greece's most common wine grape, widely planted throughout Attica and central GREECE. This light-berried vine is the most common ingredient in RETSINA, although RHODITIS and ASSYRTIKO are often added to compensate for Savatiano's naturally low acidity. On particularly suitable sites, Savatiano can produce well-balanced dry white wines.

Savennières, distinctive and much celebrated white-wine appellation in the Anjou region of the Loire, immediately south west of the town of Angers. Total production of the appellation is less than 30,000 cases in a good vintage but these examples of dry CHENIN BLANC display such an unusual combination of nerve, concentration, and longevity that they have won devotees around the world (although mainly in northern France). In its Napoleonic heyday, Savennières was a sweet wine, but today almost all of it is dry, and unusually concentrated because maximum permitted yields are relatively low. The best wines can last for several decades, and can be unappetizingly tart at less than seven years old. Within Savennières are the two subappellations **Savennières-Coulée de Serrant**, a single estate of just 7 ha/17 acres run by the Joly family on BIODYNAMIC lines, and the 33 ha of **Savennières-La Roche-aux-Moines**, in which several different producers struggle to make a living in this frost-prone corner of the Loire valley. Domaine des Baumard makes some of the best Savennières, but this is a wine for intellectuals, not neophytes.

Across the river to the south east are the sweet-white-wine appellations of Anjou: BONNEZEAUX; Chaume; Coteaux de l'AUBANCE; Coteaux du LAYON; and QUARTS DE CHAUME. See also LOIRE.

Savigny-lès-Beaune, a small town in BURGUNDY near Beaune with its own appellation for red wine and a little white. The reds are agreeable, rivalling those of BEAUNE itself, but lack the depth and character of wines from villages such as Pommard or Volnay.

PREMIERS CRUS Les Peuillets, Les Narbantons, Les Rouvrettes, and Les Marconnets produce wines similar to those of Beaune, although lighter.

A little white wine is produced from Chardonnay. Chandon de Briailles is the leading producer based here.

See also CÔTE D'OR.   J.T.C.M.

Savoie, eastern French Alpine region on the border with Switzerland, sometimes Anglicized to **Savoy** and now strictly comprising the two *départements* Savoie and Haute-Savoie. This dramatic countryside is so popular with visitors for both winter sports and summer relaxation that only a small amount of the wine ever leaves the region.

The fact that Savoie and much of northern Italy were once part of the same kingdom may help to explain Savoie's particularly distinctive family of apparently indigenous vine varieties, and in particular suggests why the variety known as MONDEUSE in Savoie may be the REFOSCO of north-east Italy. Most Savoie wines are white and are sold under the much-ramified appellation **Vin de Savoie**, although CRÉPY, SEYSSEL, and ROUSSETTE de Savoie have their own appellations. Crépy and Seyssel are specific areas, while Roussette, also known as Altesse, is Savoie's finest white grape variety and may be produced from anywhere in the Vin de Savoie zone.

Many of the vineyards are on the banks of the river RHÔNE as it flows from Lake Geneva towards the wine region known as the Rhône valley. Seyssel is here as well as the communes of Chautagne and Jongieux, two of the 17 CRUS which can append their names to the appellation Vin de Savoie.

South of here, just south of the town of CHAMBÉRY, famous for its VERMOUTH, is a cluster of CRUS whose names may be more familiar to some wine enthusiasts than the main appellation itself: Abymes, Apremont, Arbin, Chignin, Cruet, and Montmélian.

Further north, the Chasselas grape predominates and the isolated cru of Ayze (which Michelin insists is Ayse) makes sparkling wine while a cluster of vineyards on the southeastern shores of Lake Geneva make a range of light, almost Swiss wines under the names of the crus Marignan, Marin, Ripaille, and the appellation Crépy.

The characteristics of these Vins de Savoie and the environments in which they are pro-

duced are sufficiently different to justify their being granted separate appellations. About two-thirds of production is white: crisp, delicate, lightly scented, often chaptalized in the Swiss manner, and essentially Alpine. The most widely planted variety is JACQUÈRE, which is increasingly popular with growers because of its productivity. Chardonnay is grown in some parts, and some producers are experimenting with BARREL MATURATION, but the finest varieties are Roussette, with its own appellation, and the occasional plantation of ROUSSANNE, or Bergeron.

Many of Savoie's wines are VARIETAL and, among reds, Gamay and Pinot Noir imported from Beaujolais and Burgundy respectively can be perfectly respectable, if light, examplars. Most inspiring, however, is Mondeuse, with its deep colour, peppery flavour, and slight bitterness. Mondeuse grown at Arbin has a particular reputation, and such wines go well with the local cheese-dominated cuisine. Leading producers include Domaine de l'Idylle, André et Michel Quénard, Raymond Quénard, and Philippe Viallet.

A small amount of sparkling wine may be sold as **Mousseux de Savoie** and **Pétillant de Savoie**.

See also the Vins du BUGEY.

Scheurebe is the one early-20th-century GERMAN CROSSING that deserves attention from any connoisseur. Sometimes called simply **Scheu**, it can make even better quality wines than the more widely grown KERNER, especially in the PFALZ region, where Scheurebe can make seriously exciting wine. Provided it reaches full maturity, Scheurebe wines have their own exuberant, racy flavours of blackcurrants or even rich grapefruit. It is one of the few varietal parvenus countenanced by quality-conscious German wine producers, not just because it can easily reach high PRÄDIKAT levels of ripeness, but because these are so delicately counterbalanced with the nerve of acidity—perhaps not quite so much as in an equivalent Riesling, but enough to preserve the wine for many years in bottle.

Scheurebe was decisively overtaken by Kerner in the 1980s, and is now losing ground, although there were still nearly 3,400 ha/8,400 acres of Scheurebe planted in Germany in 1997, mainly in Rheinhessen and, to a lesser extent, in the Pfalz. It also needs a relatively good site, often one which could otherwise support the great Riesling, and young Scheurebe vines are prey to frost damage. Ambitious growers can rely on good frost resistance in mature vines and on Scheurebe's useful encouragement of NOBLE ROT in good years. The variety can produce extremely fine BEERENAUSLESE and TROCKENBEERENAUSLESE which may not last quite as many decades as their Riesling counterparts but are much less rare and therefore better value.

The variety is also grown in southern Austria, where it is known as SÄMLING 88 and can make fine sweet wines.

Schiava, Italian name for the undistinguished dark-skinned grape variety known as Vernatsch by the German speakers of the Alto Adige, or Südtirol as they would call it; and as TROLLINGER in the German region of Württemberg, where it is widely grown.

It is most planted in TRENTINO-ALTO ADIGE in northern Italy, where several forms are known. Schiava Grossa (Grossvernatsch) is the most common but Schiava Gentile (Kleinvernatsch) produces better-quality, aromatic wines. The most celebrated, and least productive, subvariety is Tschaggele. Schiava-based wines in general are definitely less fashionable than a generation ago, and vineyards in Trentino-Alto Adige tend to be replanted with INTERNATIONAL VARIETIES. Schiava grapes are found in most of the non-varietal light red wines of Trentino-Alto Adige.

Schillerwein, pink-wine speciality from blending red and white wines made in the WÜRTTEMBERG region in Germany. The term is also used in German SWITZERLAND for a similar sort of wine.

Schioppettino, red grape variety native to the FRIULI region of north-east Italy. The wine is deep in colour, medium in body, but with an attractively aromatic richness hinting at violets combined with a certain peppery quality reminiscent of the RHÔNE. Although vine plantings and therefore wine production are still limited, and concentrated in the COLLI ORIENTALI, the potential seems notable.   D.T.

Schloss Johannisberg, historic RHEINGAU property associated with the development of BOTRYTIZED wines in Germany but where quality has been in decline.

Schönburger, pink-berried GERMAN CROSSING with Pinot Noir, Chasselas Rosé, and Muscat Hamburg among its antecedents which has been more useful to the wine industry of ENGLAND than to its native Germany. Its tendency to lack acidity is a positive advantage as far from the equator as Kent and Somerset. Its wines are white and relatively full bodied.

Schwarzriesling, or 'black Riesling', is a German synonym for Pinot MEUNIER.

Sciacarello (sometimes written Sciaccarello) is a speciality of the French island of CORSICA. The grape variety is capable of producing deep-flavoured if not necessarily deep-coloured reds and fine rosés that can smell of the island's herby scrubland. The vine thrives particularly on the granitic soils in the south west around Ajaccio and Sartène. The island's total plantings of this characterful variety fell in the 1980s and it is now much less important than NIELLUCCIO.

scoring individual wines, and many aspects of their production, is an increasingly popular pursuit with professionals and amateurs alike.

The increasing tendency of WINE WRITERS to award scores to individual wines is understandable. Wine drinkers are, happily, presented with more choice than ever before. Unhappily, we all seem to have less and less time to make decisions. A score which can be interpreted at a glance is one obvious way of solving those two problems. Some of the various scoring systems are discussed in NUMBERS AND WINE but the prototype is that used by the American writer Robert PARKER, who did much to promote the controversial but highly influential practice of awarding scores as points out of 100 between 50 and 100. Effectively, wines of interest to readers of his and the many other publications which now use points out of 100 are those which score more than 80. Serious COLLECTORS and INVESTORS tend to concentrate on those which score more than 90, or even 95.

These scores have had an extraordinary effect on the wine market. They enable potential investors, and even FINE-WINE TRADERS, to take a position and affect the market, without necessarily knowing anything whatever about wine. They empower new wine drinkers to make decisions independently of wine traders. And because, unlike TASTING NOTES, they can be understood universally, they can guide potential wine buyers all over the world, thus opening up the wine market in general and the fine-wine market in particular to countries without an established wine culture.

The implications of extending the market so widely for a commodity as finite as fine wine are obvious, and the effect on prices for the most restricted fine wines of all, the so-called Bordeaux MICROCHÂTEAUX, has been to lift them even above those of the traditional FIRST GROWTHS, which will doubtless continue to raise their prices as a consequence.

Quite apart from price and demand, however, scoring has affected the wines themselves. Because scores are invariably arrived at as a result of a comparative TASTING, of many different samples of the same sort of wine, it is inevitable that some of the more subtle wines are overlooked and, particularly with red wines, the deeper-coloured, more concentrated wines are likely to make a more immediate, and often favourable, impression. Of course this varies with the taster(s), but it is undeniable that, overall, wines have become more alcoholic, more concentrated, smoother-textured, and less acid—all as an indirect result of comparative tasting.

There is another, more obviously beneficial, effect of the prevalence of scoring individual wines. New, good, wine producers can make a name for themselves and their wines very much faster than has ever been the case. The downside for wine drinkers, of course, is that prices will inevitably rise steeply.

Wine scores, as those who award them try vainly to point out, can never substitute for description. But in the 1990s at least, the market seemed much more interested in numbers than words.

See NUMBERS AND WINE.

Scotland, northern British country too cold for vine-growing but with some fine-wine merchants and a long tradition of importing wine, notably from Bordeaux.

screwcap. See STOPPERS for wine.

sec is French for DRY while **secco** is Italian and **seco** is Spanish and Portuguese for dry. See SWEETNESS.

secondary fermentation, a fermentation that occurs after the completion of the normal alcoholic FERMENTATION. This may be a FERMENTATION IN BOTTLE, or the evolution of carbon dioxide that accompanies a MALOLACTIC FERMENTATION, or simply a restarting in the winery of an alcoholic fermentation of a wine that still contains fermentable sugars.

second growth. See the CLASSIFICATION of Bordeaux.

second wines are wines made from *cuves* or vines considered not good enough for the principal product, or *grand vin*, made at an estate. The phenomenon was hardly developed commercially until the 1980s, when increased competition forced ever more rigorous selection at the ASSEMBLAGE stage. Some of the more famous second wines are Ch LATOUR's Les Forts de Latour and Ch MARGAUX's Pavillon Rouge. In particularly unsuccessful VINTAGES, some properties make no *grand vin* at all so that the second wine is the only wine produced that year. In general, a second wine from a poor vintage (when a *grand vin* was also bottled) is rarely an exciting drink, but a second wine from a quality-conscious producer in a good vintage can represent good value—so long as it is not consumed alongside the *grand vin*.

sediment, the solid material which settles to the bottom of any wine container, whether it be a bottle or a vat, tank, cask, or barrel.

Sediments in bottled wines are relatively rare, and usually signal a fine wine that has already spent some years in bottle. So unaccustomed have modern wine consumers become to sediment that many (erroneously) view it as a fault. Many wine-makers therefore take great pains to ensure, through CLARIFICATION, STABILIZATION, and FILTRATION, that the great majority of wines made today, and virtually all of those designed to be drunk within their first few years, will remain free of sediment for at least a few years. Wines designed for long periods of BOTTLE AGEING, on the other hand, frequently deposit crystals of tartrates, white in white wines and dyed red or black in red wines. In red wines, compounds formed by pigments and tannins are precipitated as sediment. The heavy deposits in bottles of vintage port are a particularly dramatic example of this phenomenon. Wine-makers deliberately leave more tartrates and phenolics in wines designed for long ageing in bottle so that they are able to develop the compounds that constitute BOUQUET. A bottle of wine containing sediment needs special care before SERVING.

See also the quite different phenomenon of BOTTLE DEPOSIT.   A.D.W.

Ségalin is a recent crossing of Jurançon Noir × Portugais Bleu which has good colour, structure, and flavour and is authorized in SOUTH WEST FRANCE. (See also PORTAN.)

Seibel, common name for many of the French HYBRID vine varieties, most of them identified by number and many of them given a more colloquially appealing name. Small quantities of various Seibels are planted in some cooler wine regions around the world.

Sekt, word used in German-speaking countries to describe quality SPARKLING WINE as defined by the European Union.

Of Germany's total annual sparkling-wine production of more than 375 million bottles (a figure that steadily increases), 94 per cent can be described as Sekt, of which about 85 per cent is white. Most Sekt is inexpensive, based on Italian, French, or other non-German still wine, and sold as dry (TROCKEN) or medium-dry (HALBTROCKEN). The average Sekt consumer buys a branded wine, and is interested neither in its method of production (98 per cent acquires its sparkle by the tank method; see SPARKLING-WINE-MAKING), nor in the origin of the base wine. The most successful brands in terms of annual sales are Faber Krönung (45 million bottles), followed in order of decreasing volume by Söhnlein Brilliant, Ruttgers Club, Deinhard Cabinet, and Henkell Trocken (14 million bottles).

Deutscher Sekt, however, is made solely from German-based wine, and it is in this small part of the market where there is fine, elegant sparkling wine, mainly BRUT or extra dry. In the 1980s, there was a marked increase in the number of enterprises (including producers' associations, co-operative cellars, and private estates) making high-quality Deutscher Sekt sold under the name of a region and vineyard of origin, bearing a vintage and almost always the name of a vine variety. The acidity and finesse of RIESLING in particular make a most stylish sparkling wine, and Sekt from the PINOT family is also very successful.

Austria's Sekt producers are concentrated in the Weinviertel in lower Austria. I.J.

Sélection de Grains Nobles, the richest, most sumptuous ripeness category of ALSACE wines.

Sémillon, often written plain Semillon in non-francophone countries, a golden grape variety from south-western France, is one of the unsung heroes of white-wine production. Blended with its traditional partner SAUVIGNON BLANC, this golden-berried vine variety is the key ingredient in SAUTERNES, arguably

the world's longest-living unfortified wine, as it is in most of the great dry whites of Graves (see PESSAC-LÉOGNAN). Unblended, in Australia's HUNTER VALLEY, it is responsible for one of the most idiosyncratic and historic wine types exclusive to the New World. Thanks to its widespread establishment in Bordeaux and much of the southern hemisphere, it has been the world's most planted white grape variety capable of top-quality wine production but is not fashionable and is declining in importance.

Outside Sauternes, Sémillon seems destined to play a supplementary role. The wines it produces tend to fatness and, although capable of ageing, have little aroma in youth. Sauvignon Blanc, with its internationally recognized name, strong aroma, high acidity, but slight lack of substance, fills in all obvious gaps. But if Sémillon had traditionally been blended with Sauvignon, it attracted another blend-mate in the early 1990s, if for entirely different reasons. Sémillon does not exactly complement Chardonnay so much as provide neutral padding for it and, in a world desperate for Chardonnay, Sémillon found itself the passive ingredient in commercially motivated blends—most notably but not exclusively in Australia. And here, as elsewhere in the New World, Sémillon's weight, and high yield, make it a popular base for commercial blends.

France

Its greatest concentration is still in Bordeaux, where, although total plantings halved between 1968 and 1988, it was still the most planted white grape variety by far. On the left bank of the Garonne, in the Graves, Sauternes, and its enclave BARSAC, Sémillon still outnumbers Sauvignon in almost exactly the traditional proportions of four to one, while in the ENTRE-DEUX-MERS, where most Sémillon is planted, Sauvignon (together with varieties for financially more rewarding red-wine production) is fast replacing it.

In the great, long-lived dry whites of Graves and Pessac-Léognan, Sémillon usually predominates and inspires rich, golden, honeyed, viscous wines quite unlike any Sémillons made elsewhere. Low yields, old vines, oak ageing, and Sauvignon all play their part. In Sauternes, Sémillon's great attribute is its proneness to NOBLE ROT. This special mould, *Botrytis cinerea*, concentrates sugars and acids and shrinks yields so that the best of the resulting wines such as Ch d'YQUEM may continue to evolve for centuries. Again, oak ageing deepens Sémillon's already relatively deep gold. Similar, but usually less exciting, sweet whites are made in the nearby appellations of CADILLAC, CÉRONS, LOUPIAC, and STE-CROIX-DU-MONT.

In quantitative terms, however, Sémillon's most common expression, other than as basic white for local consumption in CHILE, is as the major ingredient in basic white bordeaux.

Like Sauvignon Blanc, Sémillon is allowed in many other appellations for dry and sweet whites of SOUTH WEST FRANCE but is perhaps most notable in qualitative terms in MONBAZILLAC.

Rest of the world

Sémillon's other great sphere of influence is South America in general and Chile in particular. Chilean Sémillon was for long somewhat fat and oily, and the tendency to overproduce has so far done little to improve this except in very isolated examples of the most ambitious producers. Argentina also has a little Sémillon.

In North America, Sémillon is generally rather scorned, lacking the image of Sauvignon Blanc, although a significant number of producers use the former to add interest to the latter. Total area planted fell in the 1990s, although some producers have experimented with producing BOTRYTIZED wines in the image of Sauternes from it. It is allowed to add weight to Sauvignon in white bordeaux MERITAGE blends. Historically LIVERMORE VALLEY has produced the best fruit for dry white VARIETALS, while it can also perform well in parts of NAPA, SONOMA, and Santa Ynez Valley in SANTA BARBARA County. Sémillon also has a relatively significant presence in Washington, where it often displays grassy, Sauvignon-like aromas, but is taken seriously by the likes of L'Ecole 41.

It is quite widespread, without being particularly important, throughout eastern Europe (see CROATIA), but it is in SOUTH AFRICA and AUSTRALIA where Sémillon had a particularly glorious past. In 1822, 93 per cent of the entire South African vineyard was planted with this variety, imported from Bordeaux. Today, however, Semillion, as it is sometimes called, accounts for less than one per cent of Cape vineyards.

Sémillon is relatively widely grown in Australia, although it was decisively overtaken by Chardonnay in the late 1980s. It is still mainly grown in NEW SOUTH WALES, making either extraordinary, age-worthy, full-bodied dry whites in the Hunter Valley or more commercial liquids, together with the odd sweet marvel, in the irrigated vineyards inland. Only the best bottles from the Hunter and Bordeaux demonstrate Sémillon's ability to age and, often, its tendency to acquire an almost orange depth of colour when it does. It was not until the 1980s, however, that Sémillon was publicly revealed as the source of the Hunter's greatest. Until then these wines, typically made from early-picked grapes given no OAK or MALOLACTIC FERMENTATION, were usually called Hunter Riesling, and occasionally Chablis and White Burgundy, depending on slight variations in style. Hunter Valley producers today are tending to make two styles of Semillon, an open, early-maturing style and another designed for BOTTLE AGEING. Semillon plantings are once again increasing in Australia.

In Australia's cooler sites such as Tasmania and the south of Western Australia, Sémillon often demonstrates the same sort of grassiness as in Washington state and in NEW ZEALAND, where plantings have steadily increased. Some interesting sweet wines have been coaxed out of Sémillon in Gisborne.

sequence of wines to be served. See ORDER.

Serbia, the largest and most central republic in what was YUGOSLAVIA. Serbia, excluding VOJVODINA, produces around one-third of all ex-Yugoslavian wine, both red and white. Broadly, the vineyard trail follows the Morava river from the Danube due south towards its source in the mountains of KOSOVO, leaving the border hills of BULGARIA to the east.

Immediately to the south of Belgrade in the Šumadija-Velika Morava region, the rather ordinary white grape variety SMEDEREVKA grows. Here too, and to the south in the Oplenac subregion, a more ambitious range of white grape varieties are now growing. Sauvignon Blanc with a potentially excellent intensity of flavour can be produced, but winemaking practices frequently leave much to be desired.

Serbia is at its best producing red wines. Its own PROKUPAC grape, used by itself or blended with more internationally known varieties, grows in all Serbian wine regions. It predominates in the small but ancient district of Zupa in the Zapadna Morava region not far south of Belgrade. The wines are well balanced, pleasantly coloured, and can demonstrate an easy, if sometimes light, fruit quality which can be used to bolster Pinot Noir and GAMAY. While Pinot Noir wines can have a very true BOUQUET, occasionally more reminiscent of German than French versions, Gamay rarely shows at all true to its Beaujolais archetype, tending rather to produce a coarse, over-extracted red if it is not well handled.

Many of the most promising red-wine vineyards lie in the region of Juzna Morava from around the towns of Niš, Leskovac, and Vranje towards the Bulgarian border. Healthy Cabernet and Merlot grapes are being grown here, often in big privately owned vineyards as well as some belonging to bottlers/brand owners who correctly identified the region as climatically suitable for these classic Bordeaux red-wine varieties in the early 1980s; their investments should bear fruit now that the vineyards are mature.

Further east, by the Bulgarian border, Timok is also being developed as a vineyard area with similar potential for classic reds, although without a modern vinification plant, potential cannot be transferred from vineyard to bottle.

A.H.M.

Sercial, Anglicized name for the Portuguese white grape variety CERCEAL. The vine ripens particularly late and grapes retain their acidity quite notably. See also MADEIRA.

service of wine. See SERVING WINE and SOMMELIERS.

serving wine involves a number of fairly obvious steps, but mastering each of them can maximize the pleasure given by any individual wine. See OPENING THE BOTTLE, BREATHING, DECANTING, GLASSES, FOOD AND WINE MATCHING, ORDER, and LEFTOVER WINE for details of these aspects of serving wine.

Perhaps the least obvious requirement of anyone serving wine is that they appear superficially mean, by filling glasses no more than two-thirds, and preferably less than half, full. This allows energetic agitation of the glass if necessary, and enables the all-important AROMA to collect in the upper part of the bowl (see TASTING).

The factor which probably has the single greatest effect on how a wine tastes, however, is temperature. Because of the well-known general rule that white (and rosé) wines should be chilled and red wines should be served at something called room temperature, and because many refrigerators are set at relatively low temperatures, in practice many white wines are served too cool and many red wines dangerously warm. See TEMPERATURE for some guidance on specific recommended serving temperatures for certain styles of wine. Few wine drinkers have wine thermometers, however, so a certain amount of experimentation with ways of changing temperature is advisable.

Cooling wine in a refrigerator is much slower than cooling wine in a container holding water and ice (two hours rather than 30 minutes to cool an average bottle from 22 to 10 °C/ 50 °F). An ice box would do the job faster but has the serious disadvantage that the bottle will be cooled right down to icebox temperature if left there. This may well freeze the wine and push the cork out. Some main refrigerator cabinets are, furthermore, set at such low temperatures that wines may emerge simply too cool. (Note that a container full of ice cubes but no water is not a very effective cooler as it provides relatively little contact between the bottle and the cooling medium.)

It is a happy coincidence that the ideal cellar temperature, around 15 °C/59 °F, is also ideal for serving a wide range of wines such as complex dry white wines and light-bodied red wines, and is not so low that it takes long to warm tannic red wines to a suitable serving temperature.

In cool climates, wine drinkers may have difficulty in warming bottles of red wine to suitably high temperatures for serving. This is one argument for decanting, into a decanter warmed with hot water. Direct heat should not be applied to a bottle, and even contact with a radiator can heat wine to such a dangerously high temperature that some of the more volatile FLAVOUR COMPOUNDS are lost and the ALCOHOL can dominate so that the wine tastes unbalanced.

One of the most effective ways of warming wine is to pour it out into glasses in a relatively warm environment. This effect is accentuated if the glasses are cupped in human hands. For this reason, it is usually wise to serve wines slightly cooler than the ideal temperature at which they are best appreciated. Warming wine in microwave ovens can be effective if the oven is big enough, and if great care is taken not to overheat.

Ambient temperature, or even the precise temperature of the taster, can affect how a wine tastes: crisp, light wines taste either delightfully refreshing or disappointingly meagre when the taster is hot or cold respectively. On the other hand, in tropical climates, where both temperature and humidity are high, it can be almost impossible to find suitable conditions in which to serve even the finest red wine as, without air conditioning, drinks heat up so rapidly that a red wine has either to be served well chilled or run the risk of being almost MULLED. Light red wines with marked ACIDITY such as BEAUJOLAIS and reds from cooler climates such as the LOIRE, NEW ZEALAND, TASMANIA, NEW YORK, and WASHINGTON can taste much more appetizing in hot climates than CLASSED GROWTH red bordeaux or fine burgundy.

One final aspect of serving wine is matching wine to guest and occasion. Part of what might generally be called CONNOISSEURSHIP, this is a pleasure associated with wine which can be almost as great as drinking it.

See also TASTING for the special conditions of serving wine for this particular purpose, a very different one from actually drinking it.

Setúbal, an overgrown fishing port on the Sado estuary south of Lisbon, the capital of PORTUGAL, is also the name of a Portuguese FORTIFIED WINE with its own DOC region. The wine is made predominantly from Moscatel (MUSCAT) grapes but local regulations allow a number of other grapes to make up 30 per cent of the blend. Wines made from at least 85 per cent Muscat may be labelled as Moscatel de Setúbal. After four or five years in large oak tanks, the wine has an amber-orange colour and a sweet spicy, raisiny character. After 20 years or more in cask, the wine is deep brown and has a rich, grapey intensity.

For details of the exciting range of table wines made on the Setúbal peninsula, see TERRAS DO SADO. R.J.M.

Severny, Russian vine variety developed from a Malengra seedling with a member of the famously cold-hardy *Vitis amurensis* vine species native to Mongolia.

See also SAPERAVI Severny and CABERNET SEVERNY.

Seyssel, wine appellation within the eastern French region of SAVOIE producing light, dry white still and sparkling wines. This is one of the few Savoie wines to escape the region itself, notably in the form of sparkling Seyssel from producers Varichon et Clerc. CHASSELAS is the dominant grape variety here, although the local MOLETTE is also grown for sparkling wines and all wines must contain at least 10 per cent of the superior local variety ROUSSETTE. The sparkling wines need to have a POTENTIAL ALCOHOL of just 8.5 per cent at harvest and must be BOTTLE FERMENTED in the region. They are light, refreshing, and the best can develop in bottle, but most are drunk locally.

Seyval Blanc, useful white grape variety that is a French HYBRID, the result of crossing two SEIBEL hybrids. It is well suited to relatively cool climates such as that of ENGLAND, where it is the most planted vine variety after MÜLLER-THURGAU. It is also popular in CANADA and, to a lesser extent, in the eastern UNITED STATES, notably in NEW YORK state. Its crisp white wines have no hint of FOXY flavour and can even benefit from BARREL MATURATION but, because it contains some non-VINIFERA genes, it is outlawed by European Union authorities for QUALITY WINE production, a bone of contention in the English wine industry.

Sforzato, Sfursat, Sfurzat, all names for a DRIED-GRAPE WINE made in the VALTELLINA zone in the far north of Italy.

Shenandoah Valley is the name of two AVA wine regions. For details of the California region, see SIERRA FOOTHILLS. There is also a Shenandoah Valley in VIRGINIA.

sherry, seriously undervalued fortified wine from the region around the city of Jerez de la Frontera in ANDALUCÍA, south-west Spain. The term sherry was used as a generic term for a wide range of FORTIFIED WINES made from white grapes, but in the mid 1990s the sherry trade successfully campaigned to have the name restricted to the produce of the Jerez DO— at least within the European Union.

The following are the main styles of sherry, most based on PALOMINO grapes:

Fino—very pale, light and bone dry.
Manzanilla—similar to Fino but matured in the seaside sherry town of Sanlúcar de Barrameda and slightly more tangy.
Amontillado—usually medium-dry commercial blends though the best are aged finos and bone dry ('seco').
Oloroso—the best are rich, dry, dark and nutty but commercial blends tend to be sweetened.
Palo-Cortado—dry, intermediate style between Amontillado and Oloroso.
Cream—usually dark and sweetened blends.

Pale cream—sweet blends with the colour bleached out.

PX—dark, sweet wines made from PEDRO XIMÉNEZ grapes.

shipping. See TRANSPORT OF WINE.

Shiraz, the Australian (and South African) name for the SYRAH grape, is a name better known by many consumers than its Rhône original. Because Australian Shiraz has been so successful in European markets, the word Shiraz has been used on wine labels for Syrah grown all over southern Europe, even the French Languedoc. Shiraz appears on possibly the majority of Australian red-wine labels, either in lone varietal splendour or in conjunction with, most often, Cabernet Sauvignon—typically labelled simply Cabernet Shiraz or Shiraz Cabernet, depending on which is the dominant variety. Viticulturally, Shiraz is identical to Syrah but the resulting wines taste very different, with Australian versions tasting much sweeter and riper, more suggestive of chocolate than the pepper and spices often associated with Syrah in the Rhône. Shiraz is now highly valued in Australia and by 1997 was challenging Chardonnay as the most widely planted wine grape of either colour. It has had particular success in the Barossa Valley in SOUTH AUSTRALIA, the Hunter Valley in NEW SOUTH WALES, and in a number of wine areas in the state of VICTORIA. See AUSTRALIA.

See also SOUTH AFRICA, which has already produced some extremely fine Shiraz.

Shiroka Melnishka. See MELNIK.

shoot positioning, spring and summertime viticultural practice of placing vine shoots in the desired position to assist in trimming, leaf removal, and harvest operations, and to facilitate the control of vine diseases and vine pests. The practice is by no means universal but is more common in wet and humid climates with high vineyard VIGOUR and a high risk of fungal diseases. R.E.S.

shoot thinning, vineyard operation normally carried out by hand in the early spring which consists of breaking off unwanted shoots arising from the vine's head. The aim of shoot thinning is to reduce the density of the CANOPY and to avoid leaf congestion later in the season. This can help improve wine quality (see CANOPY MANAGEMENT) but is common only in regions with plentiful, relatively inexpensive labour. R.E.S.

short. See TASTING TERMS.

shows, wine. See JUDGING and COMPETITIONS.

Sichel, influential wine family now made up of two very distinct branches. The family originated in Germany and was involved with wine from the early 19th century. The direct descendants of the German founders established the wine and spirits distribution company H. Sichel Söhne at Mainz in Germany in 1857 and it grew to be an important commercial force. A successful export business was developed in the 1930s, based increasingly on the branded wine BLUE NUN Liebfraumilch. It was during the 1950s that Blue Nun began to establish itself as one of the world's most successful wines. It was cleverly marketed as the wine to be drunk 'right through the meal', whatever was being eaten. The fact that the quality of Blue Nun was vastly superior to that of the average LIEBFRAUMILCH also presumably played a part in the success of the brand, of which in the mid 1980s about 2 million cases a year were sold in 81 countries. Peter M. F. Sichel directed the firm's fortunes from New York until his retirement, when the Blue Nun trademark was sold.

The Anglo-French-Scandinavian branch of the Sichel family is descended from a Dane who married a Sichel of Mainz, worked for the firm, and took his wife's name. He was sent to Bordeaux in 1883 to establish a Sichel & Company there. His grandson Allan Sichel was an influential member of the British wine trade in the mid 20th century. Allan's son Peter A. Sichel lived for many years in MARGAUX at Ch d'Angludet running the Bordeaux NÉGOCIANT Maison Sichel, developing a number of French wine BRANDS. He was a substantial shareholder in Ch Palmer and a president of the Union des Grands Crus from 1988 to 1991, being one of the most articulate voices in defence of TRADITION and subtlety in the wines of Bordeaux. He took over the business of Pierre Coste of Langon in the GRAVES in 1992, and was an early investor in CORBIÈRES in the Languedoc. The business is now run by his five sons.

Sicily, large, often hot, and viticulturally important island off the toe of ITALY which is in the throes of modernization. With over 200,000 ha/494,000 acres under vine and annual volumes of wine which average close to 10 million hl/264 million gal per year, Sicily has been rivalled only by APULIA as the most productive wine region in a country that is often the world's most productive.

The island's geography and climate—a hilly and mountainous terrain with poor soil, intense summer heat, and low rainfall—make it ideal for the classic Mediterranean agriculture of grain, olive oil, and wine, and Sicily's viticulture, in fact, enjoys a series of natural advantages which have not yet been fully exploited. The concentration on quantity over quality has done no small harm to Sicilian viticulture and has led to a chronic cycle of overproduction, declining prices, and wines which are impossible to market.

Nevertheless, a significant number of quality-orientated Sicilian wine producers emerged in the 1970s and 1980s, and their wines have had little difficulty in establishing a place for themselves in national and international markets. DOC production is still low, usually no higher than two per cent of total wine production. It should none the less be noted that a significant number of Sicily's better producers are either voluntarily or involuntarily outside the regional DOC system. The Duca di Salaparuta winery, a large NÉGOCIANT run by the regional government, Regaleali and Terre di Ginestra, two of the island's leading private estates, and Settesoli, Sicily's most important CO-OPERATIVE winery, are among the many examples of houses which market their wine as a VINO DA TAVOLA.

Sicily's wines are conventionally divided into seven zones, each corresponding to a dominant vine variety: the ZIBIBBO zone, which is the island of Pantelleria (see MOSCATO DI PANTELLERIA); the zone of white grape varieties CATARRATTO and GRILLO, which is the province of Trapani, and the DOC zones of Marsala and Alcamo in particular; the zone of PERRICONE and INZOLIA, which is the province of Agrigento; the zone of NERO D'AVOLA and Frappato, which is the provinces of Ragusa and Siracusa; the zone of NERELLO Mascalese, which is the province of Messina, both on the slopes of Mount Etna and in the north east of the province; and the zone of MALVASIA, which is the Aeolian islands, including Lipari.

Among white varieties (which are far more widely planted than red varieties), Inzolia (also known as Ansonica) and Catarratto are generally considered the best-quality grape varieties, while the somewhat neutral Grillo is best suited to the production of MARSALA. So far, Inzolia has regularly given a lighter and more fragrant wine, Catarratto a fuller and spicier wine, although much remains to be learned about the proper fermentation and ageing of each. Recent experiments with Inzolia have suggested a certain affinity with new OAK and both Inzolia and Catarratto have also shown a fruity and floral quality not unlike the wines of FRIULI and the ALTO ADIGE. In the 1990s, such grapes provided some rich pickings for FLYING WINE-MAKERS.

Nero d'Avola is undoubtedly a red variety of very high potential, capable of giving wines of great richness, texture, and longevity, in addition to aromas of some complexity; ageing in oak, which has largely replaced the traditional chestnut casks of the past, has given wines that can compete with the best southern Italian wines, such as AGLIANICO DEL VULTURE or TAURASI. Frappato in its classic zone of Vittoria can yield fruity wines with a peppery, berry character not unlike a RHÔNE wine. In combination with Nero d'Avola (the canonical blend of Cerasuolo di Vittoria), it gives a fuller wine with more ageing ability. Nerello Mascalese is also considered a red variety of some potential.

Sicily once enjoyed a great reputation for SWEET WINES, and attempts to revive the tradition are currently under way. Moscato of Pantelleria returned to the market with convincing evidence of its inherent quality, and the Malvasia delle Lipari of Carlo Hauner which emerged in the 1980s has demonstrated that the reputation of this wine was not entirely mythical either.   D.T.

Sideritis, Greek light-berried vine variety found to a limited extent near Patra and often blended with RODITIS.

Siegerrebe is a modern German vine crossing grown, like certain giant vegetables, purely by exhibitionists. In Germany it can break, indeed has broken, records for its ripeness levels, but the flabby white wine it produces is so rich and oppressively flavoured that it is usually a chore to drink. It was bred from Gewürztraminer and a red table grape. So powerful is its heady flavour that a fine Riesling is quite overpowered by even 10 per cent of Siegerrebe. German plantings, mainly in Rheinhessen and the Pfalz, are declining. The variety also can usefully bolster some blends in ENGLAND.

Sierra Foothills, wine region in gold-rush country in CALIFORNIA and an AVA. This is basically the Piedmont area on the western edge of the Sierra Nevada, the snowy mountains which separate California from the rest of the USA (from reality, in the minds of many). The Sierra Foothills AVA blankets all of the vineyards in El Dorado, Amador, and Calaveras counties, and takes in a few others in the flanking Nevada and Mariposa counties. Shenandoah Valley-California AVA and Fiddletown AVA are AVAs within Amador County; El Dorado AVA takes in the vineyards in that county. North Yuba AVA is, not surprisingly, in Yuba County.

El Dorado AVA

Where most of Amador County's vines grow at an altitude of 800 to 1,200 ft/240 to 360 m, El Dorado's start close to 1,500 ft and range up toward 3,000 ft/915 m. Predictably, conditions are cooler, and the choice of varieties leans toward Cabernet Sauvignon, Merlot, Chardonnay, and Riesling, with some Syrah and other varieties thrown in. Representative, established wineries include Sierra Vista, Boeger, Lava Cap, and Madroña.

Fiddletown AVA

Fiddletown adjoins the upper, eastern end of Shenandoah Valley-California, in the Sierra Nevada Mountain foothills east of the town of Plymouth. Amid rolling meadows and patchy pine forest it grows some of the state's oldest plantings of ZINFANDEL in a region now most famous for that grape.

Shenandoah Valley-California AVA

California is tacked onto the end of Shenandoah Valley to distinguish this one from one in VIRGINIA. It became famous for hearty Zinfandels before the turn of the century and, after a long slumber, has regained some of its old momentum since the mid or late 1970s, again with Zinfandel at the heart of the matter. Roughly a score of wineries share a modest acreage that also includes some Sauvignon Blanc, Sangiovese, and Petite Sirah. Monteviña initiated the resurgence by bottling some of the old-vine Amador Zinfandels. Leon Sobon's Shenandoah Vineyards, Domaine Terra Rouge, and Renwood-Santino carry the region's banner.

North Yuba AVA

There is just one winery, Renaissance, in the northern Sierra foothills of Yuba County. The warm, sunny site was first planted, more in hopes than expectation, to such as Riesling and Petite Sirah. Later introductions include Cabernet Sauvignon. B.C.C.

Silvaner, Grüner Silvaner, or Sylvaner, white grape variety grown mainly in Germany and central Europe. The chief characteristic of the wine produced is its high natural acid, generally lower than Riesling's in fact but emphasized by Silvaner's lack of body and frame. Provided yields are not too high, it can provide a suitable neutral canvas on which to display more geographically based flavour characteristics (see TERROIR) but Silvaner is not noted for either its longevity or its high must weights.

Most of Germany's finest Silvaners come from Franken. Here the variety, sometimes called Franken Riesling (as it may be in California), is capable of tingling concentration, and even some exciting late-harvest sweet wines. Elsewhere, Silvaner is being systematically replaced by more fashionable varieties. About half of the country's Silvaner is planted in Rheinhessen, with some particularly suitable sites in the north. See RHEINHESSEN for details of that region's special promotion of this variety, RS.

Outside Germany, Silvaner is relatively important in the CZECH REPUBLIC, is still grown in SLOVENIA and around Lake Balaton in HUNGARY, and is prized in RUSSIA for its ability to ripen early. It is also planted in the ALTO ADIGE, where it can provide light and piercing wines for youthful consumption.

In the Valais of SWITZERLAND, it is called Johannisberg and seems positively luscious in comparison with French Switzerland's ubiquitous CHASSELAS. Sylvaner is the second most planted grape variety in the Valais, where it is often called Rhin, or Gros Rhin (as opposed to Petit Rhin, the local synonym for Riesling). In villages as warm as Chamoson and Leytron, it can result in wines with more body, character, and race.

Despite its useful acidity levels, Silvaner is not widely grown in the New World, although California and Australia still grow it to a strictly limited extent.

Sirah is the name by which some PETITE SIRAH is known in South America. It should not be confused with the true Syrah of the northern Rhône.

Sizzano, red-wine DOC in the Novara hills in the sub-Alpine north of the PIEDMONT region of north-west Italy. The proportion of NEBBIOLO grapes in Sizzano is usually lower than in either GATTINARA or nearby LESSONA and BRA-

MATERRA in the Vercelli hills across the river Sesia. Sizzano is also usually plumper and earlier maturing than its northern neighbours in the Novara hills GHEMME and BOCA, although FARA may be lighter still. For more details, see SPANNA, the local name for Nebbiolo.

skin, grape. See GRAPE.

skin contact, wine-making operation with the aim of extracting FLAVOUR COMPOUNDS, FLAVOUR PRECURSORS, and ANTHOCYANINS from grape skins into grape juice or wine. In its widest sense, it is identical to MACERATION, and some form of skin contact is essential to ROSÉ-WINE-MAKING, but the term is generally used exclusively for the maceration of white grapes for about 4 to 24 hours before PRESSING and FERMENTATION with the aim of increasing flavour. Vine varieties frequently processed with skin contact are Sémillon, Sauvignon Blanc, Muscat, and Riesling.

Slovakia. When this eastern part of what was Czechoslovakia voted to split from the Czech Republic in the early 1990s, it failed to privatize its wine industry successfully. Slovakia consumes all the wine it produces except for that exported to the Czech Republic and some local Polish towns. See also CZECH REPUBLIC. A.H.M.

Slovenia, in the far north west of what was YUGOSLAVIA, was the first republic to establish its independence, in 1991. It has established by far the most successful wine industry and now has fully implemented and well-policed wine laws, a thriving private sector incorporating many excellent private estates, as well as CO-OPERATIVES and NÉGOCIANTS, such as Vinag and Slovin. The wine law permits only the very best wines to be offered for sale in 75-cl bottles and exports can seem relatively expensive as a result. They normally carry a seal of approval granted by the PSVVS (Business Association for Viticulture and Wine Production), which has so far proved to be a surprisingly disciplined assessor of its own work.

Slovenia is divided into three wine regions: the Littoral (Primorska), west of the range of hills protecting the eastern Italian border, which produces about 45 per cent of Slovenian wine; the Eastern or Drava Valley (Podravje), which is responsible for about 40 per cent; and the less important Central Southern or Sava Valley (Posavje), which produces the remainder.

The two major wine regions are heavily influenced by their neighbours. Although it produces far more red wine than white, the northern half of the Littoral is effectively a continuation of COLLIO, which was reunified with Italy only after the First World War. The southern half, which runs down to the Istrian peninsula, produces dry reds high in acidity closer in character to those of the VENETO. The Drava Valley, on the other hand, is heavily influenced by practices conducted over the border in southern Styria, or Südsteiermark (see AUSTRIA), and can even produce interesting BEERENAUSLESE and EISWEIN. It is also ideal for the production of relatively delicate, fruity white wines.

The majority of wine is produced in large, often well-equipped CO-OPERATIVES, but the number of private producers is increasing fast as land has been reprivatized. Large casks and vats of old Slovenian oak are the norm but stainless steel and new barriques are more and more in evidence.

In the north-western districts of the Drava region, Austro-Germanic styles of light, semi-sweet, floral white are the norm. In the north east, the town of Ljutomer, Anglicized to Lutomer, lent its name to a brand of Laski Rizling (WELSCHRIESLING) which was once the best-selling wine in the UK. The area also grows Gewürztraminer (known here as Traminec), Pinot Blanc, Riesling, and Sauvignon Blanc. Šipon (probably Hungary's FURMINT) makes locally prized dry white wine. Even the most basic dry whites from this region can be enormously fresh, tangy, and aromatic, like their fashionable Austrian neighbours. Sauvignon Blanc especially has international potential.

Primorski, the Littoral plateau region, is better known for its red wines, especially Italianate Teran (REFOSCO) and BARBERA, which are the kind of solid, lively, tannic wines that the Italians would recognize, and Cabernet Sauvignon and Merlot, probably this region's best products. Some very well-balanced, more internationally acceptable dry whites are also produced. PINOT BLANC and the local Rebula (see RIBOLLA) make dry wines which may yet turn out to be Slovenia's star attractions. Dessert wines are made from Malvazija (MALVASIA) and Yellow MUSCAT BLANC À PETITS GRAINS, and a little PICOLIT (yet another feature shared with FRIULI just over the border).

In the pretty rolling hills of the Sava region along with the Croatian borderland of the Drava, where there is great tourist potential, grape types are the universal Laski Rizling, Sauvignon, Pinot Beli (Blanc), and Chardonnay together with Blaufrankisch/Frankinja, Rumeni Plavec, Žametovka, Modri Pinot (Noir), Šeatlovrenka, Rizvaner/Rizvanec, Portugieser/Portugalka, Kraljevina, Žlahtnina red and white, Gamay, Kerner, and Zweigelt.

Now that wine-making techniques have improved, the wines of Slovenia are well able to compete with their immediate neighbours in Styria and Friuli, which are so respected in their native markets of Austria and Italy respectively. Dedication on the part of a new generation of wine-makers is certainly not lacking, and some of Slovenia's VARIETAL specialities, such as Šipon and Zelen, may also find favour in export markets.   A.H.M.

Smederevka, white grape variety commonly planted and admired throughout the south of what was YUGOSLAVIA and planted extensively in SERBIA and VOJVODINA. As a VARIETAL wine, it is usually dry and relatively high in both alcohol and acidity, but it is often blended with other varieties, notably LASKI RIZLING. It is also planted to a much more limited extent in HUNGARY.

smell. The smell of a wine is probably its single most important attribute, and may be called its AROMA, BOUQUET, odour or off-odour if it is positively unattractive, or even FLAVOUR.

The sense of smell is the most acute human tasting instrument but since it is so closely related to what we call the sense of taste, it is considered in detail under TASTING.

Soave, the most common, and variable, dry white wine from the VENETO region of northeast Italy. Like the neighbouring VALPOLICELLA zone, the Soave zone has expanded enormously with the creation of the Soave DOC in 1968. This is reflected in the production figures: an annual average of 130,000 hl/3.5 million gal of Soave CLASSICO is produced from the mostly HILLSIDE VINEYARDS as opposed to 370,000 hl in the expanded zone.

Soave is dominated by CO-OPERATIVES, which control 85 per cent of total production and have followed a policy of high volumes at low prices. The Soave consortium succeeded in revising the DOC rules to supplement Soave's workhorse grape GARGANEGA with up to 30 per cent Chardonnay, PINOT BLANC, or TREBBIANO di Soave. Chardonnay, the most widely planted of the new varieties, has the ability to tame and soften some of the overtly vegetal character of

overcropped Garganega, particularly by adding body to wines intended for wood ageing.

Although high-volume, mass-market Soave from areas never previously planted to vines has helped to create an image of the wine as a bland, neutral product, the wines of such small producers as Pieropan and Anselmi have demonstrated that the Garganega grape can yield wines of real character with a pungency that marries well with wood ageing. Experiments with BARRIQUES have also given positive results. These remain isolated exceptions, none the less, in a sea of mediocrity.

The 1980s saw a revival of the sweet RECIOTO di Soave, a PASSITO made from raisined Garganega grapes with a long local tradition. D.T.

Sogrape, Portugal's largest wine producer, owned by the Oporto-based Guedes family, whose success is founded on MATEUS Rosé. In the mid 1980s, Sogrape began to diversify, now producing a wide range of wines and owning enterprises throughout northern Portugal including two port shippers: FERREIRA and Forrester. It has also acquired Finca Flichman of ARGENTINA.

soil and wine quality. The SOIL has many attributes that can influence the vine grown in it, and thence the quality of both grapes and wine. Quite how influential these attributes are remains a matter of debate, with a fairly marked divergence between the OLD WORLD and NEW WORLD if not of opinion, then of interpretation.

There can be no doubt that soil characteristics do influence wine quality. However, in most situations the effects of soil are subsidiary to those of CLIMATE, VINE VARIETY, and vine management. Of the influential soil characteristics, the most important are those governing the supply of WATER to the vine, probably followed by those influencing TEMPERATURES in and above the soil. Soil chemistry and vine nutrition, within the bounds of normal vine health and growth, play little role that has yet been discerned, other than the role of nitrogen in vegetative VIGOUR and berry nitrogen content, and in some situations that of excess potassium on the PH of must and wine.

Typically, the best soils for wine quality are:
• moderately deep to deep;
• fairly light textured, often with gravel through much of the profile and at the surface;

- free draining;
- sufficiently high in organic matter to give soil friability, a healthy worm population, and adequate nutrient-holding capacity, but not, as a rule, particularly high in organic matter;
- overall, relatively infertile, supplying enough mineral elements for healthy vine growth, but only enough nitrogen early in the season to promote moderate vegetative vigour.

Solano-Green Valley, small CALIFORNIA wine region and AVA near the town of Fairfield in Solano County between San Francisco and SACRAMENTO. Most of the grapes go to modest wineries selling mostly in the neighbourhood.

solar, Portuguese term meaning a manor house which (like CHÂTEAU in France) may also be a wine-producing property.

solera, system of fractional blending used most commonly in JEREZ for maintaining the consistency of a style of SHERRY. The system is designed to smooth out the differences between vintages and is effectively a more subtle, and much more labour-intensive, version of the BLENDING of inexpensive table wines between one vintage and another, although the solera system concerns barrel-aged liquids.

The solera system is also used for blending other fortified wines such as MÁLAGA, MONTILLA, MADEIRA, LIQUEUR MUSCAT and Liqueur Tokay in Australia. If a product is labelled 'Solera 1880', for example, it should come from a solera established in 1880.

sommelier, widely used French term for a specialist wine waiter or wine steward. The sommelier's job is to ensure that any wine is served correctly and, ideally, to advise on the individual characteristics of every wine on the establishment's wine list and on FOOD AND WINE MATCHING. In some establishments, the sommelier may also be responsible for compiling the list, buying and storing the wine, and restocking whatever passes for a CELLAR.

A sommelier should present the wine or wines ordered to the host before they are opened to ensure that there has been no misunderstanding (and so that the host can especially check that the vintage corresponds to expectations). The bottle should be opened in view of the host, and, if a wine is to be DECANTED (and that is an option that any decent sommelier should be able to offer), that operation should be performed in public too.

Some sommeliers offer the cork to the host to smell, which is well meaning but is no certain guide to whether or not the wine is FAULTY. Some sublime wines come from under some rather unpleasant-smelling corks, and vice versa.

A surer guide to whether a particular bottle happens to be one of the relatively few to exhibit a fault (CORKINESS is the most common) is to examine the small tasting sample usually offered by the sommelier to the host for this very purpose. A glance will confirm that it is not cloudy or dull, or fizzing when it should not. A swift inhalation should confirm that it smells 'clean'. Few people can then resist actually tasting a mouthful, but it is generally unnecessary as the most common faults are apparent to the eye or nose. Besides, tasting a wine should reveal its all-important TEMPERATURE. This is the moment to ask for an ice bucket (for red wines if necessary) or for a bottle to be taken out of an ice bucket.

Somontano, wine zone in the foothills of the central Pyrenees, in ARAGON in north-east Spain. Somontano (meaning 'under the mountain') is one of the most impressive of Spain's recently designated DO regions. In stark contrast to much of inland Spain, Somontano looks like wine-making country.

Bodega Pirineos, once the region's CO-OPERATIVE, together with the ultra-modern, recently created wineries Viñas del Vero (vintage 1986) and Enate (1991), make virtually all Somontano's wine. The red MORISTEL grape (no relation to Monastrell) dominates, closely followed by the newly planted varieties imported into the region such as TEMPRANILLO, Cabernet Sauvignon, Merlot, and even Pinot Noir, which are preferred by the two newcomers. Pirineos has continued to develop Moristel-based wines and is recovering the almost extinct red Parraleta vine, which traditionally gave backbone to blends dominated by Moristel. Garnacha is on the wane, and is mainly used for rosés. For whites, the traditional Macabeo and almost extinct Alcañón have been joined by Chardonnay and Gewürztraminer. The modern, crisp wines now produced have nothing in common with Somontano's traditional, rustic wines.   R.J.M. & V. de la S.

Sonoma, northern CALIFORNIA town, valley, and one of the state's most important wine counties. **Sonoma County** is one of the larger of northern California's coastal counties, and one of its most historic. **Sonoma Valley** is a very small portion of Sonoma County but it rivals and occasionally beats nearby NAPA Valley for *réclame*. Vineyards are everywhere in the county. Sprawling, geologically and climatically diverse, it is the most resolutely amoebic of all the fine-wine regions, having divided and redivided itself into AVAS and sub-AVAs until they run three layers deep in several places, four in a few, and eight in one. Growing conditions are a little more homogeneous than the welter of names suggests, but Sonoma still gives would-be gurus some of their most engaging opportunities to define subtle boundaries by taste and taste alone. The full roster follows.

Alexander Valley AVA

The largest and most fully planted of Sonoma County's many vineyard valleys awakened from a long drowse of mixed black grapes for bulk red only in the late 1960s and early 1970s. Simi winery started the renaissance in 1970, when a new owner breathed life into a moribund cellar. Chateau Souverain picked up the traces in 1973 and then Jordan Vineyards added a stamp of elegance in 1976. Growth has been steady since then. KENDALL–JACKSON'S 1996 purchase of the mountain vineyards on Gauer Ranch perhaps represents another step forward for Sonoma, and GALLO'S continuous acquisition of nearly 1,500 acres/600 ha since 1988 definitely signals a new era for both Gallo and Alexander Valley.

Alexander Valley is noteworthy among other Sonoma County appellations for the fleshy voluptuousness of its wines. Accessibility is much more likely to be a general descriptor than longevity. Cabernet Sauvignon has gained a certain currency, with a signature note of chocolate warmth and agreeable MOUTHFEEL. Chardonnays also tend to bold statement and ample girth. These varieties, market driven, dominate plantings. Sauvignon Blanc and Zinfandel succeed often enough to make one wonder if they are not suited best to these particular suns and soils. RHÔNE varieties were introduced at the beginning of the 1990s and some dream of Sangiovese and other Italian varieties. Other wineries that brought Alexander Valley to wide attention in recent years were Geyser Peak, Clos du Bois, and Murphy-Goode.

Chalk Hill AVA

In essence a small sub-AVA in the foothills behind the Russian River district. Its 800 acres/320 ha are given over almost entirely to Chardonnay and Sauvignon Blanc.

Dry Creek Valley AVA

For years a sparsely settled tributary of the Russian River drainage, Dry Creek Valley has slowly emerged over the past decade as one of Sonoma County's most intriguing appellations. Among white varieties, Sauvignon Blanc stands head and shoulders above Chardonnay. Among reds, the race is more even between Zinfandel and Cabernet Sauvignon. Dry Creek's most prominent wineries in the late 1990s included Ferrari-Carano, Nalle, Pezzi-King, Michel Schlumberger, and Rafanelli.

Knights Valley AVA

A small, handsome, upland valley in Sonoma County separates the upper end of the Napa Valley from the lower end of the Alexander Valley. It was originally developed by Beringer Vineyards, but now has several growers and one winery. The most impressive grape variety to date has been Cabernet Sauvignon. However, plantings date only from the early 1970s, and much exploratory work remains to be done.

Northern Sonoma AVA

This oddity of an AVA encompasses all of Sonoma that drains into the Pacific, which is to say all but Sonoma Valley; it was proposed and is mainly used by E. & J. GALLO, but has proven useful to a few others with scattered vineyards.

Russian River Valley AVA

Most of the Russian river's course is through other AVAs in MENDOCINO and Sonoma counties. Only when the river escapes from Alexander valley at Healdsburg do the watercourse and the Russian River Valley AVA become one and the same.

Cool, often foggy, the AVA blossomed as a wine-producing region only after 1970 when new winery owners in the area began bottling locally grown grapes under Sonoma County labels. It has taken the district fewer than 20 years to prove itself eminently well adapted to still and sparkling wines from Chardonnay and Pinot Noir. In a few HILLSIDE locations such as Martinelli's Jackass Vineyard, Zinfandel does amazingly well. Joe Swan was an early pioneer. Dehlinger, De Loach, Sonoma-Cutrer, Rochioli,

Gary Farrell, and Williams & Selyem are some of the region's best-known wineries.

Sonoma-Green Valley AVA

A sub-AVA of California's Russian River Valley AVA described above, Sonoma-Green Valley lies at the western edge of the larger region, and answers to all the same descriptions. Its best-known estate is Iron Horse.

Sonoma Coast AVA

This AVA stands out as a purely artificial construction. Its sponsors (including Sonoma-Cutrer) drew boundaries to include widely scattered vineyards so they could continue to describe their wines as ESTATE BOTTLED after tightened federal regulations began requiring that both winery and vineyard be within the same AVA to qualify.

Sonoma Mountain AVA

A sub-AVA of Sonoma Valley (see below) best known for Cabernet Sauvignon, it occupies the east-facing slopes of the mountain from which it draws its name. The AVA sits above the towns of Glen Ellen and Kenwood. Its most prestigious winery is Laurel Glen.

Sonoma Valley AVA

For history, especially romantic history, no other AVA in California compares with the Sonoma Valley. In more modern times, its Hanzell Vineyard started the rush to using French oak BARRELs to age California wines and thereby revolutionized their style, most especially Chardonnay's. The valley parallels the Napa Valley to the east, and nearly touches the Russian River Valley to the north west. Its southern extremity doubles as the Sonoma portion of CARNEROS. A long, thin comma of a trough in the coast ranges, it is geologically as well as climatically complex. Some of its memorable wines portray that diversity: Zinfandel, Gewürztraminer, Pinot Noir, Chardonnay, and Cabernet Sauvignon. Sonoma Mountain (see above) is a sub-AVA. Sebastiani and Gundlach-Bundschu are the old-timers of the valley. Others of note include Kenwood, Benziger, Ravenswood, and Kunde. Carmenet is in the AVA in the eastern mountains; Matanzas Creek is in a spur called Bennett Valley to the north; Viansa and Cline are in the Carneros section to the south.

Sopron, wine region in the extreme north west of HUNGARY which is geographically part of the Neusiedlersee wine regions of AUSTRIA. Its climate is much more temperate than that of most of the rest of Hungary. Sopron produces mainly red wines, more tannic than the Hungarian norm, from grape varieties such as KÉK-FRANKOS, Cabernet, and Merlot.

sorì is a PIEDMONTESE dialect term used for vineyard sites of the highest quality, particularly for those with an exceptionally favourable southern exposure. The term was first used on a wine label by Angelo GAJA for his Sorì San Lorenzo Barbaresco 1967 and was widely imitated thereafter.   D.T.

Sousão, or Souzão, black grape variety widely planted in Portugal's Douro valley, where it is regarded as a useful, if slightly rustic, ingredient in PORT for its colour and obvious fruit character in youth. It has also been planted by aspirant makers of port-style wines in California and Australia, with a certain degree of success.

South Africa, prolific southern-hemisphere wine producer with a lustrous past (see CONSTANTIA) and now bidding for fresh recognition. From the late 1980s, the Cape began to shake off its political notoriety and vinous obscurity.

In one sense, the Cape (South Africa's vineyards are in the hinterland of the Cape of Good Hope) has been a vast distillery, draining a partly subsidized annual wine lake. The growers' body founded in 1918, the KWV (Co-operative Growers Association), was until 1998 legally empowered to determine quota limits, fix minimum prices, and predetermine production areas and limits—a system which tended to handicap the private wine producer and favour the bulk grape-grower. Under pressure, the KWV began to relinquish most of these powers in 1992, and set the stage for a much freer, livelier production scene.

Even more markedly than most wine industries, the Cape's can still be divided between the quantity-producing majority and the quality-conscious minority. More than half the annual harvest of about a million tons is destined for distillation or non-table-wine products such as grape spirit and GRAPE CONCENTRATE. Grape prices have traditionally been based principally on sugar content, not instrinsic ripeness and grape condition.

With 1.3 per cent of the world's vineyards, South Africa ranks about 20th in area under vines, but its annual output, at some 10 million hl/264 million gal makes it the world's seventh largest wine producer. Most vineyards are irrigated and there are no checks on yields. Fewer than 200 of the nearly 5,000 grape-farmers produce their own wine. The risks and discipline of cooler environments suited to classic, low-yielding varieties have been braved by those who represent the innovative side of the South African wine industry. Together with a few wholesale merchant-producers, such wine-growers began to revolutionize the Cape wine scene in the 1980s.

By the early 1990s, South Africa produced around 3,500 wines across the style spectrum, from first-rate dry whites to deep-flavoured, splendidly oaked, intense, tannic reds; feathery sparkling wines, including some made strictly in the image of champagne; and port and sherry types—all this representing a tenfold expansion of choice within a decade. It is still a chaotic renaissance on a broad scale and it flies in the face of declining domestic consumption. However, as in Europe and America, people are drinking less, but drinking better. This, coupled with a fourfold increase in exports between 1993 and 1997, means that there is now a powerful incentive to vine-growers to pursue quality rather than quantity.

This scramble for excellence has confirmed the benefits of cooler sites and matching locality to grape varieties. But Chenin Blanc, known as Steen, remains the farmers' favourite vine variety, making almost any and every style of white wine. Chenin Blanc makes up nearly one-third of all vines planted.

In the late 1990s, less than 18 per cent of Cape vineyards produced red grapes. By the early 1990s, traditional, tough, burly red blends featuring Cabernet Sauvignon, Shiraz, Cinsaut, Tinta Barroca, and the Cape's own crossing PINOTAGE were emphatically dethroned by newer styles. OAK ageing was introduced in the late 1970s and became widely used for commercial wines in the second half of the 1980s. Now most of the country's smaller cellars, and all of the producing wholesalers, use French oak for both reds and whites. Controlled MALOLACTIC FERMENTATION is widely practised while reduced dependence on flavour-stripping FILTRATION and STABILIZATION processes has also helped improve quality of the better wines.

However, poor grape quality has hindered even greater progress. While their counterparts elsewhere in the New World streaked ahead, South African government authorities were slow to release clean, virus-tested CLONES of the major classic vine varieties. The first

virus-free vineyards produced maiden wines only in the late 1980s.

If great wines are made by their markets, the Cape has another disadvantage. Its core market is distant and small: 3 million whites in the Gauteng several days' drive to the north east of the Cape. Transporting wine from Cape Town 1,600 km/1,000 miles to Johannesburg costs almost as much as container-shipping it to Europe. The black majority, the elusive dream market of Cape wine producers, remains faithful to beer, and in the Cape, the traditional wine-drinking Coloured community is consuming less.

During the 1980s, anti-apartheid sanctions excluded Cape wine from most foreign markets. South African wine paid a dear price. But as sanctions were eased in the early 1990s, the industry found itself more competitive at the bottom end of the market than the top. Denied the rigours and rewards of international competition for so long, the Cape wine industry is now sprinting to catch up with NEW WORLD excellence, innovation, and aggressive marketing. In 1993, its wine exports to the important UK market overtook those of Chile and New Zealand.

Climate and geography
The winelands are widely dispersed throughout the Western and Northern Cape, some 700 km/420 miles from north to south and 500 km across, strung between the Atlantic and Indian Oceans.

Climates and soils vary as dramatically as landscapes. The bulk of the harvest comes from hot, irrigated river valleys such as the Orange and Breede, where vineyards yield prodigiously. Around inland Robertson, there are some calcareous lime-rich outcrops akin to the chalky soil of Burgundy's CÔTE D'OR. But in the cooler coastal areas, such soils must be man made with chemical additions.

Average summer daily temperatures often exceed 23 °C/ 73 °F during the February and March harvest months, and maximum summer temperatures can scorch to nearly 40 °C. They tend to promote prolific crops, ripen grapes quickly, and can reduce flavour intensity. However, an increasing proportion of new, cooler vineyard sites are making this as questionable a generalization as the old belief that Cape vintage variations are insignificant.

Wine regions
Constantia Fabled name in the annals of Cape

wine (see CONSTANTIA), now a demarcated wine ward in Cape Town's southern suburbs, on the slim peninsula pointing into the south Atlantic, cooled by the sea on two sides for relatively slow summer ripening. Here five vineyards have, since the mid 1980s, once again been producing classic wines. Wine quality at the government-owned Groot (Large) Constantia is improving. Two neighbours, German-owned Buitenverwachting, and Klein (Little) Constantia, both with new cellars and replanted vineyards, have spearheaded the renaissance. They have been followed by Constantia Uitsig and Steenberg. Klein Constantia has demonstrated its top New World calibre with showy and powerful Sauvignon Blanc, Chardonnay, and Cabernet Sauvignon. In 1991, it became the first modern Cape estate to resuscitate the ancient Constantia style with the release of a 1986 white Muscat of Frontignan (MUSCAT BLANC À PETITS GRAINS).

Stellenbosch Charming university town 45 km east of Cape Town in the heart of the Cape winelands and traditionally home of the country's finest reds.

Although best known for Cabernet Sauvignon, Merlot, Shiraz, and Pinotage, Stellenbosch produces a host of wine types including port-style wines and some excellent Chardonnays and Sauvignon Blancs. Stellenbosch returns lower average yields than hotter, more extensively irrigated inland regions. It is the source of only about 16 per cent of the country's total wine production although it boasts the greatest concentration of leading estates, an extensive wine route network, and scores of restaurants. Estates and cellars particularly famous for their wines include Alto, Delheim, Grangehurst, Hartenberg, Jordan, Kanonkop, Lanzerac, Le Bonheur, Meerlust, Morgenhof, Mulderbosch, Neil Ellis, Rustenberg, Saxenburg, Simonsig, Stellenzicht, Thelema, Uitkyk, Vriesenhof, Vergelegen, Vergenoed, Warwick, and Zevenwacht.

Paarl Paarl means 'pearl' in Afrikaans and houses the headquarters of the South African wine industry. The Co-operative Growers' Association (KWV) handles the annual surplus, producing port-like fortified wines, brandies, and other spirits and liqueurs. Paarl's latitude, 33.4 degrees south—JEREZ in Spain is on a similar northern latitude—is cited as a reason for the quality of South Africa's SOLERA-system FLOR-sherry-style wines. A few well-known estates market a spectrum of wines, reds and whites of the classic varieties, sparkling wines, and port-style wines. The district reaches north into Tulbagh (a separate area of origin) and Wellington and east toward Franschhoek. The best-known cellars include Backsberg, Bellingham, Boschendal, Cabrière, Fairview, Glen Carlou, L'Ormarins, La Motte, Plaisir de Merle, Veenwouden, Villiera, and Welgemeend. The biggest producer is Nederburg, with a comprehensive range of 40 labels; it produced Cape's first BOTRYTIZED wine, labelled Noble Late Harvest, from Chenin Blanc in 1969.

Worcester Extensive, fertile vineyard area, delivering 20 to 25 per cent of the national crop, mainly bulk varieties for distillation or fortification. It is generally hot, heavily irrigated and served by numerous co-operatives beyond the Du Toitskloof mountains. A number of aromatic white table wines from Colombard and Chenin Blanc are popular for everyday early drinking. Worcester is the home of many a national champion fortified red and white MUSCADEL and dessert HANEPOOT.

Robertson Hot, dry district of many estates and co-operatives growing almost exclusively whites, including bold Chardonnays. Most vineyards fringe the Breede river, which provides irrigation. The many enterprising, prize-winning, close-knit growers here are typically members of the Robertson Wine Trust. Lovely Muscats, including fortified Muscadels, Gewürztraminers, off-dry Colombards, and burly Chardonnays, are produced but memorable Sauvignon Blanc is slow to emerge. An increasing number of good-quality reds is also a feature. Best-known producers include De Wetshof, Weltevrede, Van Loveren (all whites), Graham Beck (sparkling wines), Springfield, and Zandvliet (Shiraz). Robertson produces about 10 per cent of the national harvest.

Olifantsriver Chiefly bulk grape-producing region among mountains and along the Atlantic western seaboard, the majority of whose growers supply large co-operatives with wine mainly for distillation but increasingly for export.

Orange River Hottest, most northerly, and most recently established (in the 1960s) of South Africa's wine regions, producing nearly 12 per cent of the national crop. Bulk wines and huge yields are common thanks to irrigation schemes.

Little Karoo Inland, semi-desert ostrich- and sheep-farming region. A few enterprising estates here such as Boplaas and Die Krans are making hearty port-style wines and fortified Muscadels, as well as some dry table wines.

Ruiterbosch Small, new ward with promising cool vineyards. South Africa's most southerly wine region fronting the Indian Ocean, almost outside the Mediterranean climate area with its winter rainfall, producing individual white wines made from Sauvignon Blanc and Rhine Riesling. Pinot Noir is also planted.

Walker Bay Southerly, relatively cool maritime vineyards producing among South Africa's most promising wines made from the Burgundy grapes Chardonnay and Pinot Noir, from Hamilton Russell Vineyards and Bouchard-Finlayson, the first French–South African JOINT VENTURE (in this case with Paul Bouchard formerly of Bouchard Aîné et Fils of Burgundy).

Elgin Cool, high vineyards in apple-orchard country west of Cape Town. A recently designated wine ward whose early vintages of Sauvignon Blanc showed intense individuality. Hopes are also high for Pinot Noir here.

Wine-making
Although wine-making in South Africa remains in a state of flux and experimentation, at some point in the 1980s, almost in the twinkling of an eye, the small French BARRIQUE transformed the face and taste of top Cape wines. Stainless-steel, cement, and fibreglass tank vinification still styles the vast output of wine, but the boom in Chardonnays and bordeaux-style reds reflects investments in OAK by numerous cellars, from large bulk wine co-operatives to small estate operations. French oak leads the field but American and Yugoslav barrels are used too. Increasingly wine-makers are abandoning the clinical, no-risks, mass-production techniques. Chaptalization is banned. ACIDIFICATION is permitted.

Vine varieties
In South Africa, a vine variety is known as a cultivar, and South Africa is a cultivar-conscious wine country. Regional wine characteristics are still insufficiently well defined to challenge grape variety as the determining factor for quality, style, and even labelling and marketing of a wine.

White varieties constitute some 85 per cent of Cape vineyards. Chenin Blanc, known sometimes as Steen, has for long been the dominant grape variety in South Africa, and was still planted on nearly 28 per cent of all vineyard in 1996. From the 1980s, Sauvignon Blanc and Chardonnay boomed but together they made up little more than 9 per cent of the country's total vine plantings by 1996. Other major white wine grapes include, in decreasing quantity: Colombar(d), Cape Riesling (see CROUCHEN), Clairette, Sémillon, (Weisser) Riesling, Gewürztraminer, as well as various Muscats. Muscat of Alexandria, locally known as Hanepoot, doubles as a table grape. White and a mutant red MUSCADEL (Muscat Blanc à Petits Grains) remain important for fortified wines.

Highest-priced reds are Cabernet Sauvignon and the bordeaux-styled blends including Merlot and/or Cabernet Franc which proliferated from the early 1980s. Cabernet Sauvignon is South Africa's most planted INTERNATIONAL VARIETY, planted on a steady 5 per cent of the nation's vineyard. Syrah (Shiraz in South Africa) is becoming popular, on its own and blended. Pinot Noir has been generally disappointing but new clones are being tried. PINOTAGE, the Cape's own crossing of Pinot Noir and Cinsaut, is becoming increasingly popular and was the single most planted new red vine variety in 1996 (Chardonnay was the white) although it still represented only 3.3 per cent of the nation's vines.

For most of this century, high-yielding Cinsaut was the most widely planted red, but it has declined in importance and represented only 4.3 per cent of vineyard in 1996. There are yet smaller plantings of Grenache, Carignan, Zinfandel, Ruby Cabernet, and some port varieties, most commonly TINTA BARROCA, often made into a dry red. PONTAC is another South African speciality, on a minuscule scale. Gamay has made a modest impact in its Beaujolais-styled CARBONIC MACERATION mode.

Other varieties planted to a considerable extent but used principally for blending, fortified wines, distillation, or grape concentrate are all white berried. The most important are Sultana and Palomino (known curiously as White French in South Africa). They represented 11 and 4 per cent respectively of all vines in 1996.

Wine of Origin and labelling
Wine of Origin (WO) legislation introduced in 1973 ended decades of a labelling free-for-all. A wine may be 'certified' for any of the following:

estate, region, district, or ward of origin, vintage, grape variety.

Blended wines qualify for a varietal statement provided the variety makes up at least 75 per cent of the blend; and at least 75 per cent comes from one harvest. The balance may come from the preceding or subsequent year. Blends which do not claim single varietal status may state the grape composition.

Participation is voluntary and about 35 per cent of Cape-bottled wine is certified. Non-certified wine is liable to spot-check analysis for health requirements.

Wine for certification is submitted to the government-appointed Wine & Spirit Board. The wine must pass an analytical test and is blind tasted by a panel which may reject wines judged faulty or atypical, and often does.

The designation 'Estate' is the Cape's equivalent of the French Château, or Domaine. All the wine must originate from and be fermented at a registered, demarcated estate, although the definition of an estate is loose. Wine can be barrel matured and bottled at a different establishment without losing its estate status.

Wines may state a single origin but be blends of the products of several regions. The authorities have merged, on paper, various wine-growing areas.

TRADITIONAL METHOD Cape sparkling wine is not labelled Champagne but Méthode Cap Classique, even locally.

South African Wine Industry Trust

The South African Wine Industry Trust performs commercial and development services for the Cape wine industry. Included in the ambit of its responsibilities are viticultural extension services; generic wine promotion in domestic and export markets; and investment in wine education primarily to facilitate entry into the industry by members of previously disadvantaged communities. It could over time become the governing body of the Cape Wine Industry, dealing with many of the regulatory functions previously performed by the KWV.

J.P. & M.F.

South African Riesling. See CAPE RIESLING.

South America, the world's second most important wine-producing continent, after Europe, with ARGENTINA being by far the biggest producer, followed by BRAZIL and CHILE. Other, relatively minor, wine producers are, in descending order of importance, URUGUAY,

PERU, BOLIVIA, and also ECUADOR and VENEZUELA. See also the important North American wine producer MEXICO. Spain and, in some parts, Portugal were important influences in the 16th and 17th centuries, although more recently France, Italy, and the United States have helped to shape South America's wine industries. Wine quality has improved extremely rapidly in those countries—Chile, Argentina, and to a lesser extent Uruguay—which have (relatively recently) turned their attention to exporting.

South Australia, *the* wine state in AUSTRALIA. At a little under 50 per cent, South Australia's contribution to the annual CRUSH may be falling but it still dominates the country's wine output. Vine-growing is concentrated in the south-eastern corner, much of it within an hour's drive of the capital Adelaide. The two outposts are the Riverland sprawling along the Murray River (the Lower Murray zone); and Coonawarra and nearby Padthaway 325 km/200 miles south east of Adelaide, not far from the border with VICTORIA (the Limestone Coast zone).

The Barossa Valley, an hour north of Adelaide, vies with the Hunter Valley as Australia's best-known wine region. To this day, the Germanic influence of its 19th-century Silesian immigrants is everywhere to be seen.

Riesling is (and always has been) the most favoured white wine grape, even if its still-dominant plantings are increasingly moving from the valley floor to the hills of the Eden Valley district. This shift reflects two things: first, the warm climate of the valley floor, more suited to red-wine production; second, a fundamental reappraisal of the function of the Barossa Valley proper. For decades, vine plantings shrank while production soared, not because of increased YIELDS, but because the Barossa Valley wineries process a major part of the grapes grown in the Riverland, Coonawarra, Padthaway, Southern Vales, and Langhorne Creek.

Most of Australia's largest companies are based here. The presence of PENFOLDS, and the creation of its masterwork Grange, embody the glory of the Barossa Valley: substantial plantings of Shiraz dating as far back as 1860 and yielding 16 hl/ha (0.9 tons/acre) of inky, dark purple essence. There is still twice as much Shiraz grown in the Barossa as there is Cabernet Sauvignon, a situation likely to continue.

While the Barossa Valley has 50 or so wineries within its precincts, the McLaren Vale region, 45 minutes due south of Adelaide, has a greater number still and is often called the home of the small winery. The southern end of the fashionably cool and increasingly important Adelaide Hills to the east, the open plains of McLaren Vale, and the hills of the Fleurieu Peninsula offer abundant suitable land for the continuing new plantings.

This is a strongly maritime-influenced region, with considerable variation in MESO-CLIMATE. The emphasis in the 1970s and 1980s was on its melon- and citrus-tinged Chardonnay, pungent gooseberry Sauvignon Blanc, full-flavoured Riesling and Semillon. But with the resurgence of the red-wine market, attention has once again focused on its generous, gutsy red wines. Here the long-forgotten virtues of its DRYLAND Grenache have been rediscovered; whether used to make a single varietal red wine, or blended with Shiraz, many consider it Australia's best example of Rhône-style red.

The Limestone Coast zone has five regions of rapidly growing importance: Mount Benson, Robe, Naracoorte Ranges (which would like to call itself Koppamurra, but has had to plump for Wrattonbully), Coonawarra, and Padthaway. The twins of Coonawarra and Padthaway in the far south east of the state are generally recognized as producing Australia's finest Cabernet Sauvignon (Coonawarra) and some of its best Chardonnay, Sauvignon Blanc, and Riesling. Both are cool regions (Coonawarra is the cooler of the two).

While vines were first planted in Coonawarra in 1890 (by John Riddoch), for all practical purposes both regions date from the early 1960s. This explains why both areas are exclusively planted to premium grape varieties, and why the major wine companies are the dominant landholders. It is the belief of some critics that the viticultural practices adopted by the major companies have in fact prevented either region from reaching its full potential. It is a tribute to the inherent quality of each region, and to a few wine-makers and flagship brands, that the wines have such a high reputation.

The Clare Valley, just to the north west of the Barossa Valley, but joined with the Adelaide Hills in the Mount Lofty Ranges zone, is one of the unspoilt jewels of South Australia. The narrow, twisting folds of the hills provide an intimacy in total contrast to the flat, featureless plain of Coonawarra. For reasons unknown, its moderately warm climate produces Australia's finest Riesling (challenged only by that of the Eden Valley), which is a fragrant yet steely wine which ages superbly, taking on the aroma of lightly browned toast with a twist of lime as it ages.

Most of the 50 or so wineries are small; almost all produce Riesling, Shiraz, and Cabernet Sauvignon, the red wines being intensely coloured, deep flavoured, and long lived, often with a skein of eucalypt mint running through them. MALBEC also flourishes here as nowhere else, used as a blend component with Cabernet Sauvignon (sometimes with a dash of Shiraz thrown in for good measure).

Finally, there is the Riverland, stretching along the mighty Murray River from Waikerie to Renmark, producing 55 per cent of South Australia's total crush and over 30 per cent of the nation's. Most of this is of white wine destined for casks (see BOXES) or for sale in bulk to overseas markets. The Riverlands are still strongholds for Muscat Gordo Blanco (MUSCAT OF ALEXANDRIA), SULTANA, and DORADILLO, and even in Australia one cannot make silk purses out of sow's ears.   J.H.

South Coast, name loosely defining vineyards close to the CALIFORNIA coast from Los Angeles southwards to the Mexican border. TEMECULA has the only substantial vineyards within the region. San Diego County's San Pasqual also falls within it.

Southcorp. Uninspiring, and unknown to most consumers, this is the name of the dominant wine producer and vineyard owner in Australia whose output represents two in every five bottles of Australian wine. In 1990, PENFOLDS, from its headquarters in the Barossa, acquired its greatest rival, LINDEMANS, long associated with fine white wines and the Hunter Valley. In 1990, Penfolds, along with Lindemans, was acquired by South Australian Brewing Holdings, which formed the Penfolds Wine Group as its wine subsidiary. Other Australian wineries under the PWG banner were Lindemans, Leo Buring, Hungerford Hill, Killawarra, Kaiser Stuhl, Matthew Lang, Rouge Homme, Seaview, Seppelt, Tollana, Tulloch, Woodley, and Wynns Coonawarra Estate. In the early 1990s, the group began a programme of expansion outside Australia which initially included investments in California, Languedoc-Roussillon, and (briefly) MOLDOVA. In 1993,

Penfolds Wine Group was renamed Southcorp Wines Pty. Subsequent acquisitions have included Coldstream Hills in Victoria and Devil's Lair in Western Australia.

South Eastern Australia, common, catch-all geographical description for usually inexpensive much-blended wine from AUSTRALIA.

Southern Vales, important wine region in AUSTRALIA. See SOUTH AUSTRALIA.

South West France, recognized region within FRANCE which incorporates all of the wine districts in the south-western quarter of the country with the exception of BORDEAUX and Cognac. This means in effect all of the upriver wines once regarded as serious commercial rivals by the Bordelais (most notably Bergerac, Monbazillac, Côtes de Duras, Cahors, Buzet, Côtes du Frontonnais, and Gaillac travelling away from and roughly clockwise round Bordeaux), together with those made in GASCONY and BASQUE country (Côtes de St-Mont, Madiran, Pacherenc du Vic-Bilh, Jurançon, Béarn, and Irouléguy).

Few generalizations can be made about such an extensive area, except that the climate is heavily influenced by the Atlantic.

The grape varieties grown in the first group of wine districts is generally very similar to the ENCÉPAGEMENT of Bordeaux, while the southern districts can boast one of the most exciting collections of local vine varieties in Europe, including the likes of ABOURIOU, BAROQUE, DURAS, FER (Servadou), LEN DE L'EL, MANSENG, MAUZAC, NÉGRETTE, ARRUFIAC, TANNAT, JUR-ANÇON Noir and COURBU. Culturally, Gascony is one of the proudest and greediest regions of France; the region needs wines to drink with *foie gras*, duck, and goose.

For more details, see the individual entries for all the APPELLATION CONTRÔLÉE wines BÉARN, BERGERAC, BUZET, CAHORS, Côtes de DURAS, Côtes du FRONTONNAIS, Côtes du MAR-MANDAIS, GAILLAC, IROULÉGUY, JURANÇON, MADIRAN, MARCILLAC, MONBAZILLAC, PACHERENC DU VIC-BILH, PÉCHARMANT, ROSETTE, and SAUS-SIGNAC. See also the VDQS wines, some of them produced in only very small quantities, Côtes de ST-MONT, Côtes du BRULHOIS, LAVILLEDIEU, TURSAN, Vins d'ENTRAYGUES, and Vins d'ES-TAING. See also LIMOUX.

Spain, country in the grip of vinous revolution with the most land under vine in the world (about half as much again as both France

and Italy) and yet only the world's third most important producer of wine. Spain's exceptionally low average YIELDS, of about 25 hl/ha (1.4 tons/acre), reflect the extreme physical conditions in much of central Spain, where DROUGHT is a persistent problem (see below).

Spain, the third largest country in Europe, is a diverse country with distinct regional and cultural differences. This regional diversity is reflected in her wines, which range from light, dry whites in the cool Atlantic region of GALICIA to heavy, alcoholic reds in the Levante and the Mediterranean south. ANDALUCÍA in the south west is known for the production of fortified and dessert wines, the most famous of which is SHERRY.

Spain is a significant beneficiary of recent improvements in wine-making TECHNOLOGY. Modern production methods were slow to reach Spain but, when they did, typically in the early 1990s, they did so with a vengeance, with modernization sweeping one region after the other, including some (but not all) of the less glamorous ones. A programme of investment which began a decade earlier was further helped by Spain's accession to the European Union in 1986. In 1996, vineyard IRRIGATION was legalized throughout the country, radically changing prospects for the drought-stricken central and south-eastern areas.

Spanish wine law

Since joining the European Union, Spain has brought her wine law into line with that of other European countries. There is now a four-tier system.

VINO DE MESA (VdM) at the bottom of the pyramid includes all the wine made from unclassified vineyards or wine that has been declassified by blending. This is Spain's equivalent of the EU category TABLE WINE, and (as in Italy) it now includes some of the country's most expensive and prestigious wines.

VINO DE LA TIERRA (VdlT) applies to wine from a specific region provided producers conform to certain local norms. This is Spain's counterpart to France's VIN DE PAYS.

Denominación de Origen, or DO, regions are the mainstay of the system, each with its own Consejo Regulador which regulates the growing, making, and marketing of wines, ensuring that they comply with specified regional standards. However, as they proliferate, the significance of the DO has been debased (as in ITALY). At the beginning of 1998, there were 53 DO regions covering three-quarters of the total vineyard area of Spain. As if to rectify this, a new category has been introduced: Denominación de Origen Calificada (DOCA), which equates with Italy's DOCG. Rioja was the first region to be awarded DOCa status, in 1991, and was still the only one in the late 1990s.

Geography and climate

Around much of Spain, the land rises steeply from the coast. Iberia's dominant feature is the vast plateau that takes up much of central Spain. Known as the *meseta*, this undulating table land ranges in altitude from 600 to 1,000 m, tilting slightly towards the west. Four of Iberia's five major rivers (the Duero, Tajo, Guadiana, and Guadalquivir) drain westwards into the Atlantic, with the Ebro flowing south east to the Mediterranean.

Great mountain ranges known as *cordilleras* divide Spain into distinct natural regions. The north coast, from GALICIA to the Pyrenees, is relatively cool and humid with few extremes. Galicia, Asturias, and BASQUE country are intensively cultivated and densely populated. The Cantabrian Cordillera, a westerly spur of the Pyrenees, protects the main body of Spain from cool, rain-bearing north westerlies. Rioja in the upper Ebro valley is therefore shielded from the Bay of Biscay.

The Spanish climate becomes more extreme towards the centre of the central plateau. Winters are long and cold with temperatures falling well below freezing point. Summers here can be blisteringly hot with daytime temperatures sometimes rising above 40 °C. Little rain falls in the summer months and drought is a constant problem.

South and east from the central plateau the climate is increasingly influenced by proximity to the Mediterranean. The climate on the narrow coastal littoral is equable with long, warm summers giving way to mild winters. The hottest part of Spain is the broad Guadalquivir valley in Andalucía, north of the Sierra Nevada, where summer temperatures rise to 45 °C. The south-west corner of Andalucía has a climate of its own, strongly influenced by the Gulf of Cádiz and the Atlantic.

Vine varieties

The Spanish claim to have up to 600 different grape varieties, although 80 per cent of the country's vineyards are planted with just over 20 of them. The drought-resistant white AIRÉN is planted throughout central Spain, occupying about twice as much land as any other variety. Airén traditionally produced base wines for Spain's important brandy industry and OXIDIZED, alcoholic white wines for local bars and cafés, but with careful handling and improved vinification it is capable of producing some simple but refreshing dry wines. Dark-skinned GARNACHA is the second most widely planted variety, principally in the north of the country. It flourishes in windy, arid conditions, especially Navarre, Rioja Baja, Aragon, and parts of Catalonia, where Garnacha makes rather clumsy reds and some fresh, fruity rosés.

BOBAL and Monastrell (the MOURVÈDRE of France) perform Garnacha's role in the Levante. Both varieties yield dark, alcoholic reds and the occasional dry rosé.

TEMPRANILLO is Spain's most widely planted vine variety associated with quality wine, planted under such aliases as Cencibel, Ull de Llebre, and Tinto Fino in different parts of the country.

Other white varieties which are also important in Spain are the sherry grapes PALOMINO (planted in Jerez, RUEDA, and parts of Galicia) and PEDRO XIMÉNEZ (Montilla-Moriles and Málaga). The white MACABEO (also called Viura) is widely planted in Rioja and Catalonia, especially Penedès, where, along with Parellada and Xarel-lo, it is grown for CAVA sparkling wine. High-quality white varieties which are gaining ground include ALBARIÑO (Galicia) and VERDEJO (Rueda), while other promising grapes which are making a more limited come-back include the white LOUREIRA and GODELLO (both in Galicia) and the red GRACIANO (Rioja) and MENCÍA (Galicia and Castile and León).

INTERNATIONAL VARIETIES are making significant inroads in some parts of Spain. Cabernet Sauvignon, Merlot, and Chardonnay are increasingly important in Catalonia, Somontano, Navarre, and even Castile and León.

Wine-making

Spanish wine-making has changed radically since the 1960s. Stainless steel, once a rarity, is now commonplace and most bodegas have the means of TEMPERATURE CONTROL for fermentation. These improvements transformed Spanish wines, especially in La Mancha and the Levante, where temperature control is essential to preserve the primary fruit character in both red and white wine. A vogue for crisp, technically perfect, simple young whites was followed in the 1990s by a resurgence of barrel-fermented whites.

Spain continues to foster the long-established tradition of ageing red wines in OAK. The use of wooden BARRELS as vessels for fermentation and storage dates back many centuries but in the second half of the 19th century the French introduced the 225-l BARRIQUE (*barrica*) to Rioja, and its use has subsequently spread throughout the country. Unlike the French, however, most Spanish wine-makers use American oak, which is not only considerably cheaper than French oak, it can also impart a stronger flavour to the wine. The Tempranillo grape in particular seems to produce wine that responds to maturation in new oak. Spanish oak-aged reds are usually denoted by the words CRIANZA, RESERVA, or GRAN RESERVA, which are enshrined in local legislation. From the 1970s to the 1990s, the wines often showed a pungent, vanilla character but this is being superseded by more FRUIT-DRIVEN aromas and flavours, partly in response to FASHION.

Most Spanish DOs also stipulate minimum BOTTLE AGE and traditionally very few Spanish wines were released before they were ready to drink. But some growers, led by Alejandro Fernández of RIBERA DEL DUERO and the PRIORAT newcomers, started a new habit of renouncing both crianza and Reserva back labels, selling oak-aged wine as vino JOVEN, often with little bottle age.

For specific wine regions, see ANDALUCÍA, ARAGON, BASQUE, CASTILE-LA MANCHA, CASTILE AND LEÓN, CATALONIA, GALICIA, LEVANTE, NAVARRE, and RIOJA. See also SHERRY.

R.J.M. & V. de la S.

Spanna, local name for the NEBBIOLO grape in eastern PIEDMONT in north-west Italy, particularly around Gattinara in the hills of the Vercelli and Novara provinces.

Six DOC wines and one DOCG, Gattinara, are made either wholly or in part from Spanna: three in the Vercelli hills (BRAMATERRA, GATTINARA, LESSONA) and four in the province of Novara (BOCA, FARA, GHEMME, and SIZZANO). Only Gattinara and Ghemme, responsible for the longest-lived Spanna wines, have a significant production, and several of the others are virtually of postage-stamp size. The wines display strong Nebbiolo personality, although only Lessona can be 100 per cent Spanna, the other DOCs requiring blending with the less interesting VESPOLINA and BONARDA Novarese grapes. All-Spanna wines are occasionally made, however, even if they may be marketed only as a VINO DA TAVOLA. The combination of excessive CASK AGEING in old casks, and imperfectly executed or non-existent MALOLACTIC FERMENTATIONS have not been helpful to the reputation of these wines. The extreme fragmentation of vineyard property and an elderly work-force have also been handicaps, but there were significant improvements in the wines in the 1980s, and a general sense that Spanna—or at least Gattinara and Ghemme—may have turned the corner in terms of quality and recognition.   D.T.

sparkling wine, wine which bubbles when poured into a glass, an important and growing category of wine. The bubbles form because a certain amount of CARBON DIOXIDE has been held under pressure dissolved in the wine until the bottle is unstoppered.

Sparkling wine may vary in as many respects as still wine: it can be any wine COLOUR (it is usually white but pink fizz and sparkling reds such as BURGUNDY and Australian sparkling Shiraz have enjoyed a certain following); it can be any degree of SWEETNESS (although a high proportion tastes bone dry and may be labelled BRUT, while Italians specialize in medium-sweet SPUMANTE); it can vary in ALCOHOLIC STRENGTH (although in practice most dry sparkling wines are about 12 per cent, while the sweeter, lighter Spumante are between 5.5 and 8 per cent); and it can come from anywhere in the world where wine is produced.

Unlike still wines, however, sparkling wines vary in FIZZINESS, not just in the actual pressure under which the gas is dissolved in the wine, but also apparently in the character of the foam. Some sparkling wines froth aggressively in the mouth while others bubble subtly. The average size, consistency, and persistence of the bubbles also vary considerably.

To the wine-maker, however, the most obvious way in which sparkling wines differ is in how the gas came to be trapped in solution in the wine: traditional method, transversage, transfer, tank, or carbonation, in declining order of cost, complication, and likely quality of sparkling wine, together with the rarer *méthode ancestrale* and *méthode dioise*. (See SPARKLING-WINE-MAKING for details of each method.)

The most famous sparkling wine of all is CHAMPAGNE, the archetypal sparkling wine

437

made in north-eastern France, which represents about eight per cent of global sparkling-wine production. A significant proportion of all sparkling wine is made using the same basic method as is used in Champagne (known as the traditional method), much of it from the same grape varieties Pinot Noir, Chardonnay, and, to a lesser extent outside Champagne, Meunier, even though different wine regions often stamp their own style on the resulting sparkling wine. Examples of such wines were made with ever-increasing frequency in the 1980s and early 1990s in CALIFORNIA, AUSTRALIA, and ITALY particularly.

A host of fine, very individual sparkling wines is made using the traditional method but with non-champagne grapes, however. The most prodigious example of this is CAVA, the sparkling wine so popular with the Spanish. The LOIRE region of France also produces traditional-method sparkling wine in great quantity, notably in SAUMUR. All of France's new CRÉMANTS also use the traditional method. In almost every wine region in the world with aspirations to quality, some traditional-method wine has been made. Wines made by this, the most meticulous method, may be described on the label within Europe as *méthode traditionnelle*, *méthode classique*, or *méthode traditionnelle classique*. Other descriptions include 'bottle fermented' (although, strictly speaking, wines made by the transfer method may be labelled 'bottle fermented', while only those made by the traditional method can be labelled 'fermented in *this* bottle').

Similarly, in almost every wine region in the world, tank-method sparkling wine is made in considerable quantity, often for specific local BRANDS, especially for SEKT in Germany and a host of wines such as LAMBRUSCO and ASTI in Italy. The country which has been an enthusiastic market for sparkling wines is RUSSIA. Today sparkling wine is still made in enormous quantity in both Russia and the UKRAINE, much of it using the so-called continuous method. Asti and a number of other low-alcohol, sweet Italian, or Italianate, sparkling wines are made using a variation of the tank method.

The transfer method is used for some better-quality branded wines, particularly in Germany and the United States.

Some characterful sparkling wines are made eschewing DISGORGEMENT and selling the part-fermented, still-sweet wine together with the LEES of its second fermentation in bottle. These include some GAILLAC, LIMOUX, and CLAIRETTE DE DIE made by specific but similar local methods sometimes called *méthode ancestrale*.

See also specific information under OPENING THE BOTTLE, LABELLING INFORMATION, and DOSAGE.

sparkling-wine-making, making SPARKLING WINES, most obviously involves the accumulation of gas under pressure in what was initially a still 'base wine' or, ideally, blend of base wines. The most common methods of achieving this are discussed below—traditional method, transversage, transfer method, continuous method, tank method, carbonation, *méthode ancestrale*, and *méthode dioise*—but these are matters of technique rather than substance. Almost all of them depend on initiating a second FERMENTATION, which inevitably produces CARBON DIOXIDE, and most of them incorporate some way of keeping that gas dissolved under pressure in the wine, while separating it from the inconvenient by-product of fermentation, the LEES. What matters most to the quality of a sparkling wine, however, is the quality and character of the blended base wines.

Making and blending the base wine

Wines that are good raw material for the sparkling-wine-making process are not usually much fun to drink in their still state. Rather like the most suitable wines for distillation into a fine brandy, they are typically high in acidity and unobtrusively flavoured (although they should in general have more interesting fruit characters than wines destined for the still).

It is not just in Champagne, however, that sparkling-wine-makers argue that BALANCE is the key to assembling a base wine to make sparkling, and that the best sparkling wines are therefore essentially blended wines. Some fine VARIETAL sparkling wines exist (some of the best BLANC DE BLANCS champagnes, for example), but a great sparkling wine never tastes just like the still-wine version plus gas. Those who aspire to make good sparkling wine are acutely aware that any minor fault in a base wine may be amplified by the sparkling-wine-making process.

Accordingly, for better sparkling wines, grapes had invariably been hand picked up to the early 1990s since WHOLE-BUNCH PRESSING was the norm, and such MECHANICAL HARVESTERS as had been tested by then risked splitting berries and extracting harsh PHENOLICS into the grape juice which could cause astringent, coarse characteristics which would be magnified by the pressure of bubbles. It is essential to press grapes as soon as possible after picking. Press houses in the vineyards have long been *de rigueur* in Champagne and are increasingly common for other top-quality sparkling wines.

Grapes destined for sparkling wines are usually picked at lower MUST WEIGHTS than the same varieties would be if they were to be sold as a still wine.

PRESSING is an important stage in sparkling-wine-making, particularly in Champagne, where black grapes are used, as it is essential that the concentration of phenolics, both ASTRINGENCY and COLOUR, is kept to a minimum.

The wine-maker can then make the usual still-white-wine choices concerning OXIDATIVE versus PROTECTIVE methods of JUICE HANDLING; juice CLARIFICATION; choice of YEAST strain and FERMENTATION rate; protein STABILIZATION; and MALOLACTIC FERMENTATION (sparkling wines made from wines which have not undergone malolactic fermentation may be simpler and fruitier in youth).

Then comes the crucial blending stage, the true art of making sparkling wine, and one in which experience is as important as science. A large champagne house such as MOËT & CHANDON may be able to use several hundred base wines in order to achieve the house style in its basic expression, that year's NON-VINTAGE blend. A small, independent concern, especially outside Champagne, may have access to only a very limited range of base wines—a disadvantage in a poor vintage, although not necessarily in a good one. And a producer of the most basic tank-method wine may simply blend the cheapest vaguely suitable ingredients available in the market-place.

Traditional method

This method, known variously as traditional method, classic method, *méthode traditionnelle*, and *méthode classique*, is the most meticulous way of making wine sparkle; the raw ingredients vary considerably but the basic techniques do not.

Pressing and yield Pressing is the first operation defined in detail by the traditional method. Those who produce traditional-method sparkling wine acknowledge that the first juice to emerge from the press is generally the best since it is highest in sugar and acidity and lowest in phenolics, including pigments.

Base wines After the making of the base wines (described above), which usually takes place over the winter following the harvest, the final blend is made after extensive tasting, assessment, and blending. There is extreme flexibility in blending a non-dated wine and a high proportion of 'reserve wine' made in previous years may be used. (KRUG indulge in the luxury of using base wines from up to six different vintages being held in reserve.) The ingredients in a vintage-dated sparkling wine are more limited. As soon as the new blend has been made in bulk blending tanks, it usually undergoes cold STABILIZATION in order to prevent subsequent formation of TARTRATES in bottle.

Second fermentation This new blend then has a mixture of sugar and yeast added to it before bottling in particularly strong, dark bottles, usually STOPPERED with a crown cork, so that a second fermentation will occur in bottle, creating the all-important fizz. Conventionally, an addition or *tirage* of about 24 g/l of sugar is made. This creates an additional 1.2 to 1.3 per cent ALCOHOLIC STRENGTH and sufficient carbon dioxide to create a pressure inside the bottle of five to six atmospheres after disgorgement (see below), which is roughly the FIZZINESS expected of a sparkling wine, and one which can safely be contained by a wired champagne cork. During this second fermentation, the bottles are normally stored horizontally at about 12 °C/54 °F and the fermentation has produced the required pressure and bubbles after four to eight weeks.

Ageing on lees Timing of the riddling process (see below) after the second fermentation is a key element in quality and style of a traditional-method sparkling wine, the second most important factor affecting quality after blending the base wine. The longer a wine rests on the lees of the second fermentation in bottle, the more chance it has of picking up flavour from the dead yeast cells, a process known as yeast autolysis.

Most regulations for traditional-method sparkling wines specify at least nine months ageing on lees, and the minimum period for non-vintage champagne was increased to 15 months in the early 1990s (vintage champagnes are usually aged for several years).

Riddling The riddling process, known as *remuage* (shaking) in French, is one of the most cumbersome (and most publicized) parts of the traditional method, but it is undertaken for cosmetic rather than oenological reasons: to remove the deposit that would otherwise make the wine cloudy (as it does in the *méthode ancestrale* described below).

Traditionally bottles were gradually moved from the horizontal to an inverted vertical by hand, by human *remueurs* or riddlers who would shake them and the deposit every time they moved them towards the inverted vertical position in special *pupitres* or riddling racks. This was a slow and extremely labour-intensive way of moving the deposit *en masse* from the belly of the bottle to its neck. The CAVA industry based in Catalonia developed an automatic alternative in the 1970s, the *girasol* or GYRO-PALETTE, which has since been widely adopted for traditional-method sparkling-wine-making the world over.

Disgorgement and dosage The final stage in a sometimes short (but inevitably complicated) production process is to remove the deposit now in the neck of an inverted bottle. The conventional way of achieving this is to freeze the bottle neck and deposit by plunging the necks of the inverted bottles into a tray of freezing solution. The bottles are then upended, opened, and the deposit flies out as a solid pellet of ice. Bottles are then topped up with a mixture of wine and sugar syrup, the so-called DOSAGE, stoppered with a proper champagne CORK held on with a wire muzzle, and prepared for labelling. Most dry sparkling wine is sweetened so that it contains between 5 and 12 g/l RESIDUAL SUGAR, and the further from the equator the grapes are grown, the more dosage is generally required to counterbalance high natural ACIDITY, although the longer a wine is aged on lees, the less dosage it needs.

Alternative methods Disgorgement and riddling are unwieldy processes which contribute nothing to the innate quality of the sparkling wine. It is not surprising therefore that, in the 1980s, as labour costs spiralled, there was considerable research into alternative methods of expelling the sediment. One of the most successful has been the development of encapsulated yeast. Yeast can be trapped in a 'bead' made of calcium alginate. Such beads are about a few millimetres in diameter and are able to hold the yeast trapped in their interior while having big enough pores to admit sugar and nutrients into the bead so that a full second fermentation can proceed as normal.

Another possible method is to insert a membrane cartridge into the neck of the bottle. Yeast is dispensed into it and it is then plugged before the bottle is stoppered with the usual crown cap. Like the beads, the cartridge allows ingress of sugar and nutrients for fermentation to take place there, as well as allowing the carbon dioxide gas out. In this case there is no need at all for riddling, and disgorgement simply entails taking off the crown cap and allowing the pressure inside the bottle to expel the cartridge.

Transversage

Transversage is an occasional twist on the traditional method whereby, immediately after disgorgement, the contents of bottles of sparkling wine made by the traditional method are transferred into a pressure tank to which the dosage is added before the wine is bottled, typically in another (often small) size of bottle, under pressure. This is how many half-bottles, all airline 'splits' or quarter-bottles, and virtually all BOTTLE SIZES above a jeroboam of champagne are filled.

Transfer method

The transfer method, known as *méthode transfert* in French and Carstens in the United States, also depends on inducing a second fermentation by adding sugar and yeast to a blend of base wines and then bottling the result. It differs from the traditional method, however, in that riddling and disgorgement are dispensed with and, after a period of lees contact, the bottles are chilled, and their contents transferred to a bulk pressure tank where the sediment is removed by clarification, usually FILTRATION. A suitable dosage is then added and the result is once again bottled using a counterpressure filler, before being corked and wired. Such wines can demonstrate many but not all of the qualities of a traditional-method wine but the transfer method is likely to be abandoned in the long term when encapsulated-yeast and membrane-cartridge systems are adopted.

Continuous method

This process was developed in the USSR and is now used in Germany and Portugal. It involves a series of usually five reticulated tanks under

five atmospheres of pressure, the same FIZ-
ZINESS as in most sparkling wines. At one end,
base wine together with sugar and yeast is
pumped in and the second fermentation
crucial to virtually all methods of sparkling-
wine-making begins. This creates CARBON
DIOXIDE, which increases the pressure in the
tank, but the yeast cannot grow under this
pressure and so further yeast has to be added
continuously. The second and third tanks are
partly filled with some material such as wood
shavings, which offer a substantial total
surface area on which the dead yeast cells accumulate and a certain amount of autolysis, or
at least reaction between the dead yeast cells
and the wine, takes place. In the fourth and
fifth tanks there are no yeast cells and the wine
eventually emerges relatively clear, having
spent an average of perhaps three or four weeks
in the system. See also LANCERS.

Tank method or Charmat process

This very common method, also called *cuve close*
(French for sealed tank), bulk method, *granvas*
in Spanish, *autoclave* in Italian, was developed
by Eugene Charmat in the early years of the
20th century in Bordeaux. Its advantages are
that it is very much cheaper, faster, and less
labour intensive than the above processes, and
is better suited to base wines which lack much
capacity for AGEING. A second fermentation is
provoked by yeast and sugar added to base wine
held in bulk in a pressure tank and, after a
rapid fermentation, the fermentation is typically arrested by cooling the wine to −5 °C
when a pressure of about five atmospheres has
been reached. The result is clarified, a dosage
is added and the resulting sparkling wine is
bottled using a counter-pressure filler. This
style of sparkling wine is the most likely to
taste like still wine with bubbles in it, rather
than to have any of the additional attributes
which can result from fermentation in bottle.

Carbonation

Also known as the injection, or simply the
'bicycle pump', method, carbonation of wine
is achieved in much the same way as carbonation of fizzy, soft drinks: carbon dioxide
gas is pumped from cylinders into a tank of
wine which is then bottled under pressure, or
very occasionally it is pumped into bottles. The
result is a wine which has many, and large,
bubbles when the bottle is first opened, but
whose mousse rapidly fades. This is the cheapest, least critical, and least durable way of

making wine sparkle and is used for perhaps
the cheapest 10 per cent of all sparkling wines.

Méthode ancestrale or méthode rurale

This method is rarely used and results in a
lightly sparkling, medium-sweet wine, often
with some deposit, but it most closely parallels
how wines were originally made sparkling. It
involves bottling young wines before all the
RESIDUAL SUGAR has been fermented into
alcohol. Fermentation continues in bottle and
gives off carbon dioxide. Variants on this theme
are still made in Gaillac, where the method
is sometimes known as the *méthode gaillacoise*,
from the Blanquette grape in LIMOUX, and may
still occasionally be found in SAVOIE.

The wine is designed to be sweeter and less
fizzy than a traditional-method sparkling wine
and no dosage is allowed. The wine may in
some cases be decanted off the deposit and
rebottled under pressure in a form of transfer
method.

Méthode dioise

This is an unusual variation on the *méthode
ancestrale* above and the transfer method, producing wines similar to ASTI. It is used for the
sweet wine CLAIRETTE DE DIE, most of which is
made by the local CO-OPERATIVE. The base wines
are fermented in stainless steel tanks at very
low temperatures over several months. The
wine is then filtered, bottled, and fermentation
continues in bottle until an alcoholic strength
of about 7.5 per cent has been reached. The
wine is disgorged 6 to 12 months after bottling
before being filtered again and immediately
transferred to new bottles.

Spätburgunder is the chief synonym in
GERMANY for PINOT NOIR and the grape variety
that experienced the most dramatic rise in
popularity in Germany in the 1990s. Such is
German enthusiasm for red wine that Germany's total plantings almost doubled
between 1980 and 1997. Until the late 1980s,
the typical Spätburgunder was pale, sweetish
(and all too often tinged with rot-related
odours). Today it is much deeper coloured, as
alcoholic as climate will allow, fermented out
to dryness, and well structured, thanks to the
much lower yields, longer MACERATION, and
BARREL MATURATION associated with Germany's
most ambitious producers. Few of these wines
are exported since demand so much exceeds
supply within Germany, where the most significant regions for Spätburgunder are, in

Spätlese

declining order of importance, Baden, Pfalz, and Rheinhessen. Seriously sweet Spät-burgunder is occasionally made as a late-picked BEERENAUSLESE in the RHEINGAU and can command the dizzy prices associated with rarities.

Spätlese, one of the PRÄDIKATS in the QMP quality-wine category defined by the GERMAN WINE LAW. Spätlese means literally 'late harvest' and the grapes should have been picked at least a week after a preliminary picking of less-ripe grapes. Specific minimum MUST WEIGHTS are laid down for each combination of vine variety and region. These wines' additional ripeness, and therefore POTENTIAL ALCOHOL, make them excellent candidates for TROCKEN wine-making, especially in the PFALZ, RHEINHESSEN, and BADEN regions. Spätlese trocken wines can go well with all sorts of savoury foods, while sweeter Spätlesen are usually better drunk on their own, as they often lack the BODY necessary to accompany sweet foods and yet their sweetness can taste strange with many savoury dishes. See also AUSTRIA.

Spätrot, synonym for ZIERFANDLER.

spitting is an essential practice at professional TASTINGS where several dozen, often more than 100, wines are regularly offered at the same time. Members of the wine trade, and WINE WRITERS, rapidly lose any inhibitions about spitting in public. Since there are no taste receptors in the throat, spitting allows the taster to form a full impression of each wine, while minimizing the blunting effects of ALCOHOL. It does not, unfortunately, leave the taster completely unaffected by alcohol. According to the estimates of this writer, tasting 30 wines can involve ingesting almost a glass of wine.

Whatever tasters spit into is a **spittoon.** These can vary from specially designed giant metal funnels, through wooden CASES filled with sawdust, to ice buckets, jugs, or, particularly convenient at a seated tasting, personal plastic or cardboard beakers. Most professional tasting rooms are equipped with channels, or sinks with running water designed to drain away expectorated wine.

spraying, a vineyard practice of applying agrochemicals to control pests, diseases, and weeds.

spritzer, common name for a mixture of white wine and fizzy water that is usually drunk as an APERITIF.

spritzig, German term for semi-SPARKLING, applied widely to wines which are not meant to be particularly FIZZY but which have a small but attractive concentration of CARBON DIOXIDE in solution such that there is a slight prickle on the tongue when they are tasted. Spritz has become an international TASTING TERM, perhaps for onomatopoeic reasons.

spumante, Italian word for sparkling wine which is disappearing from labels. The most important of these is ASTI (once known as Asti Spumante), made from the MOSCATO BIANCO grape cultivated in the provinces of Asti, Cuneo, and Alessandria, of which over 80 million bottles may be made in an average year.

Squinzano, DOC for robust red wine made mainly from NEGROAMARO grapes in south-east Italy. See APULIA.

stabilization, group of wine-processing operations undertaken to ensure that the wine, once bottled, will not form hazes, clouds, or unwanted deposits; become gassy; or undergo rapid deterioration of flavour after bottling.

Stags Leap District, California wine region and AVA. See NAPA.

standard drinks, an attempt by health educators to quantify a normal or regular pour of alcoholic drink by the amount of pure ALCOHOL it contains. Once this has been agreed upon, the theory goes, it is easier for authorities to set safe limits for consumption. There are many stumbling blocks, however, not least the fact that by the late 1990s educators in different countries could not agree on how much alcohol a standard drink should contain. The situation is complicated for wine by the fact that its ALCOHOLIC STRENGTH is variable. Some wine labels spell out how many standard drinks each bottle contains. See also HEALTH.

Steen, South Africa's most common name for CHENIN BLANC, the Cape's most common white vine variety grown in all wine regions. Steen is also South Africa's most versatile grape, producing an astonishing spectrum of wine styles: dry, sweet, BOTRYTIZED, sparkling, brandy, and sherry types. Confusingly, wines are labelled either Chenin Blanc or Steen at the whim of the producer, while Steen is the major and often sole grape in local wines labelled **Stein,**

denoting not grape variety but an off-dry to semi-sweet white, the country's biggest-selling wine category. The wine can show lively fruity appeal for a year or two but this attraction tends to fade in dry Cape Steens.   J.P.

Steiermark, wine region in AUSTRIA known in English as STYRIA.

Stellenbosch, important wine region in South Africa, famously beautiful town within it, and the name of the only university in South Africa where both VITICULTURE and OENOLOGY may be studied.

See SOUTH AFRICA for more detail of the Stellenbosch wine region.

stemware. See GLASSES.

steward, wine. See SOMMELIER.

stoppers for wine containers are necessary to avoid harmful contact with OXYGEN and have changed remarkably little. CORKS are still the principal closures used for wine BOTTLES, although alternative stoppers are increasingly common, thanks to a perceived rise in the incidence of CORKED wine as a result of cork taint since the mid 1980s.

Modern technology offers a range of alternatives to the traditional cork. To present a viable alternative to this natural substance, they have to offer a reliable seal, present an inert substance to the wine, be easily removable, and be capable of being produced at a relatively low cost. Few have proved as successful as cork for long-term BOTTLE AGEING, however, and there is still considerable attachment on the part of many wine drinkers to the ritual of pulling a cork.

The synthetic **plastic 'cork'** (actually a polymer derivative synthetic closure) is designed to satisfy the wine drinker's need to wrestle with a CORKSCREW while using a man-made material without the fine pores which can harbour moulds and without natural cork's tendency to disintegrate. Its disadvantages are that it is not biodegradable, can be much more difficult to reinsert in a half-finished bottle, and that it is not yet proven as a suitable stopper for the long term—not least because it is thought to allow virtually no oxygen ingress.

The **screwcap** is a usefully inexpensive closure for the short and medium term. Pressure on the top seats the cap lining firmly against the bottle lip so that the seal is reasonably gas-tight. Made of non-corroding metal, usually an alloy of aluminium, the screwcap is lined with moulded cork and an inert film in contact with the wine. It also has the great advantage of requiring no equipment to remove it and being extremely easy to replace. However, unlike cork, screwcaps cannot compensate for bottle-necks whose glass finish is not completely smooth. The screwcap itself can last many years (and has kept white wines fresh for at least 10 years) but in the eyes of traditionalists has yet to prove itself the equal of cork for extended bottle ageing.

The **crown cap**, the small metal cap used on beer and soda bottles, has proved the most reliable stopper for long-term wine-bottle storage and provides an extremely cheap and efficient stopper for any sort of wine, but many wine drinkers find its association with what they regard as less sophisticated drinks unacceptable, particularly when it comes to wine SERVICE in a smart restaurant. The crown cap is also used nearly universally for closing SPARKLING WINE bottles during the TIRAGE process.

There has been experimentation with a wide range of other stoppers, but the field is still wide open to more acceptable, and more aesthetically pleasing, alternatives to a piece of bark.

See also CAPSULES.

storing wine is an important aspect of wine consumption, since wine is relatively sensitive to storage conditions and is one of the very few consumer products that can improve with age (although see AGEING for details of how few, and which, wines this applies to). Until the era of inflation, the wine trade regarded storing and ageing wine as part of their business, but since the 1960s they have steadily relinquished this role. The development of the EN PRIMEUR market and the increase in the number of wine COLLECTORS leaves many more ordinary wine drinkers with the problem of how to store wine over long periods, often a decade or two.

There are two basic choices: to consign the bottles to professional storage and/or to establish some form of domestic cellar. If wine is put in storage, it is vital that a specialist in wine storage is found, since wine is a much more fragile commodity than most things kept in warehouses, and needs specialist treatment and conditions. It is important that the wine-storage specialist is in sound financial health itself, it understands the detail of storage conditions needed, and that it provides some facility for marking individual CASES with some identification of their owner. In the case of business failure, this can make the difference between establishing possession and not.

For more details of how to identify and, if necessary, convert part of a home into a suitable place to store wine, see CELLAR.

Storage conditions

The key factors are TEMPERATURE, light, humidity, and security.

If wine is kept too hot, or exposed to strong sunlight, it rapidly deteriorates. If it is kept too cold, it can freeze, expand, and push out the stopper of whatever container it is held in.

For bottles stored for a few weeks, the primary concern is to keep them from strong direct light (white wines in colourless glass are most at risk) and to ensure that they do not reach temperatures more than about 25 °C/77 °F, at which point the wine may be spoilt and forever afterwards taste cooked.

A fairly wide range of temperatures is suitable for wine storage, although, in general, the lower the storage temperature, the slower the reactions involved in wine maturation and, the theory goes, the more complex the wine eventually. Dramatic temperature swings should be avoided and an average temperature somewhere in the range 10 to 15 °C (50–9 °F) is considered suitable (see TEMPERATURE for more details).

Some degree of humidity is beneficial, to ensure that the exposed end of the cork does not dry out and allow in oxygen. A level of 75 per cent relative humidity is usually cited, although this, like so many aspects of wine consumption rather than production, suffers from a lack of scientific research. The disadvantage of very damp cellars is that labels eventually deteriorate and make identification difficult (and some COLLECTORS, perversely, prefer pristine labels so any resale price is not prejudiced).

Bottles to be stored for more than a few weeks, however, should be stored so that any cork is kept damp and there is no possibility of its drying out and allowing in the enemy, OXYGEN. This usually entails storing the bottles horizontally, ideally in a wine rack so that individual bottles can easily be extracted, or in a BIN full of wines of the same sort. Many wine producers deliberately mark their cases in an effort to keep bottles upside down, and corks damp, during shipment.

Wine in an inverted bottle comes to no harm. Recent research has suggested that an ideal storage position for wine bottles is at a slight angle from the horizontal so that the cork is kept damp but the air bubble of ULLAGE just touches the cork rather than lying on top of the middle of the bottle. It has also been suggested that champagne ages most gracefully when stored in upright rather than horizontal bottles.

If a maturing wine is agitated, it may disturb the sediment and therefore the AGEING process (although this is an unproven hypothesis). Some cellars are specifically designed with rubber racks for bottles in order to minimize any likely vibration. The need for a secure storage space is obvious, especially since bottles of alcoholic drink seem to be widely regarded as common currency rather than private property.

It is also important that there are no strong, persistent smells in a long-term wine-storage area.

straw wines. See VIN DE PAILLE and DRIED-GRAPE WINES.

stuck fermentation, wine-maker's nightmare involving an alcoholic FERMENTATION which ceases before completion. Such fermentations are notoriously difficult to restart and the wine is at risk of spoilage from OXIDATION and bacterial disease.

Styria, small but fashionable wine region in the far south east of AUSTRIA, most famous for aromatic, lively dry whites.

subjectivity plays an unavoidable part in wine TASTING. Personal preferences inevitably play some role in wine assessment.

Südtirol, or South Tyrol. See ALTO ADIGE.

sugar concentration in grapes. See MUST WEIGHT.

Suisun Valley, small CALIFORNIA wine region and AVA flanking SOLANO-GREEN VALLEY between San Francisco and Sacramento. Suisun Valley has only a sparse scattering of vineyards and a few modest, primarily local, wineries. No particular wine type has pushed itself forward.

sulfate, sulfide, sulfite, and sulfur, the American spellings of sulphate, SULPHIDE, SULPHITE, and SULPHUR respectively.

sulphides and disulphides occur naturally during wine-making. As FERMENTATION nears completion, elemental sulphur residues on the grapes from fungicides, and even SULPHUR DIOXIDE itself, can be reduced to HYDROGEN SULPHIDE. The wine-maker can detect this problem easily because hydrogen sulphide has an intense smell of bad eggs. Fortunately, the compound is very volatile and can usually be removed by simple aeration.

In a wine-making context, any reference to 'sulphide' or 'sulphides' is invariably a criticism and usually means hydrogen sulphide. Sulphides should not be confused with SULPHITES, however. A.D.W.

sulphites and bisulphites. The analytical method usually used for the measurement of sulphites determines all of the various forms which are active in terms of smell, effect on YEAST and bacteria, and potential danger to asthmatics (see SULPHUR DIOXIDE). The term sulphites, or sulfites in the United States, is therefore used on wine labels (as in 'Contains sulphites') as an inclusive term for free sulphur dioxide, sulphurous acid (hydrated sulphur dioxide), bisulphite ion, sulphite ion, and some forms of complexed sulphites. See LABELLING INFORMATION. A.D.W.

sulphur, an element that constitutes about 0.5 per cent of the weight of the Earth's crust and one of the more important elements for mankind. Sulphur is most familiar to wine-makers as SULPHUR DIOXIDE.

Residues of elemental sulphur used in the vineyard can combine with hydrogen in new wine to produce HYDROGEN SULPHIDE, the compound responsible for the foul smell of bad eggs. See also MERCAPTANS.

Everyday wines to which high sulphur additions have been made for particular operations, or for transport, may be **desulphured**. See also SULPHITES. A.D.W.

sulphur dioxide, or SO$_2$, formed when elemental sulphur is burned in air, is the chemical compound most widely used by the wine-maker, principally as a preservative and a disinfectant.

It reacts with OXYGEN and so prevents OXIDATION, which has undesirable effects on the colour and flavour of wine. It is often added to freshly picked grapes in the form of meta-bisulphite. (The compound is therefore widely, often more liberally, used in the preparation of other foods and drinks, particularly fruit juices and dried fruits.) Sulphur dioxide has the further property, of particular value to the wine-maker, of inhibiting or killing bacteria or wild YEAST, and of encouraging a rapid and clean FERMENTATION. Other less important reasons for using sulphur dioxide in wine-making are that it helps brighten the colour of red wines and encourages the extraction of compounds from the grape skins during MACERATION.

At room temperatures and normal atmospheric pressures, the compound exists as a colourless gas with a pungent, choking aroma similar to that of a struck match.

The disadvantage of using sulphur dioxide (which all but a fraction of one per cent of wine-makers do) is that its aroma can be quite unpleasant even at fairly low concentrations, especially to some particularly sensitive tasters (who are likely to find it most noticeably on sweet Loire, sweet bordeaux, and German wines).

During the latter half of the 20th century, maximum levels of sulphur dioxide permitted by law were systematically reduced. These reductions have been made partly because the smell of sulphur dioxide is undesirable, but they are also a response to lobbyists, especially in the United States, concerned about the effect of high doses of sulphur (more than any single bottle of wine contains) on asthmatics. This latter force has resulted in compulsory LABELLING INFORMATION in various countries. In the United States, for example, all wines carry the legend 'Contains sulfites' (see SULPHITES), while Australian labels must admit that sulphur dioxide, or 'Preservative (220)', has been added. Within the European Union, sulphur dioxide is known as E220, but this need not be specified on wine labels.

There have been attempts to produce wines without any addition of sulphur dioxide. Such wines are particularly prone to oxidation and the off-flavours generated by wild yeast and bacteria and need careful handling and possibly even PASTEURIZATION. It would be impossible to produce an entirely sulphur-free wine since a small amount of sulphur dioxide is one of the by-products of the metabolic action of yeast during fermentation when the material being fermented contains sulphate salts. Since sulphate salts are natural components of such fermentable materials as dough and fruit juices, it is normal to encounter small amounts of sulphur dioxide in such fermented products as bread and wine. A.D.W. & J.Ro.

Sultana, the most important white grape variety used to produce the pale brown DRYING GRAPES sometimes called sultanas. The fruit of the Sultana vine, called THOMPSON SEEDLESS in California, is remarkable for its versatility. As well as being dried, it can be vinified into a neutral white wine and is a much sought-after crisp, green, seedless table grape. In some viticultural regions, such as Australia's RIVERLAND and California's CENTRAL VALLEY, the Sultana harvest can be diverted to whatever happens to be the most profitable end use, including wine.

In widely varying locations, it provides base material for some, usually undistinguished, wines. As Thompson Seedless it is the most widely planted grape variety in California by far, as it is in Australia. Sultana is used by both the wine and dried-fruit industries, in proportions annually dictated by market forces.

In South Africa, plantings of Sultana increased steadily throughout the 1980s, making it the country's second most planted grape variety after Chenin Blanc by the late 1990s. Much of the wine produced is distilled or made into basic FORTIFIED WINES.

summer pruning, optional vineyard operation designed to sacrifice quantity for quality. See PRUNING and CROP THINNING.

Sunbury, wine region in the Port Phillip zone of the Australian state of VICTORIA.

sunlight, the ultimate energy source of all life, and of wine itself. Through a process known as PHOTOSYNTHESIS, part of its energy is used by plants to combine CARBON DIOXIDE from the air with WATER taken up from the soil, to form sugar in grapes. This is the building block for other plant products, as well as being the immediate source of energy for all of a plant's biochemical processes, via its respiration back to carbon dioxide and water.

Supérieur, Supérieure, or Supérieures may be found suffixed to the name of an APPELLATION CONTRÔLÉE on French wine labels. The regulations for a Supérieur wine usually demand a slightly higher minimum ALCOHOLIC STRENGTH (typically by half a per cent). The term is often optional and Quelque chose Supérieure is by no means infallibly superior to plain Quelque chose.

Superiore, Italian term applied to DOC wines which are deemed superior because of their higher minimum ALCOHOLIC STRENGTH, usually by a half or one per cent, and a longer period of AGEING before commercial release. Among the more significant wines which fall into this category are the three BARBERA DOCs of PIEDMONT (Alba, Asti, Monferrato), BARDOLINO, CALDARO, GRAVE DEL FRIULI, SOAVE, VALPOLICELLA, and VALTELLINA. Both Barbera d'Alba Superiore and Barbera d'Asti Superiore must be aged in wood for at least one year. D.T.

super second, a specialist term in the FINE WINE market for CLASSED GROWTH wines from BORDEAUX to denote the best-performing wines ranked as second growths in the 1855 CLASSIFICATION of the Médoc and Graves. There is no absolute agreement about which properties qualify as super seconds but Chx Pichon-Longueville-Lalande, and more recently Pichon-Longueville (Baron), in PAUILLAC, Cos in ST-ESTÈPHE, and LÉOVILLE LAS CASES and Ducru-Beaucaillou in ST-JULIEN have all been nominated at one time or another. Other strong candidates (although not second growths) include Ch Palmer in MARGAUX, and Ch La MISSION-HAUT-BRION in PESSAC-LÉOGNAN.

super-Spanish. See MÉNTRIDA and VINO DE MESA.

Supertuscan, term sometimes used by English speakers to describe the new class of superior wines labelled VINO DA TAVOLA made in the central Italian region of Tuscany. Prototype Supertuscans were TIGNANELLO and SASSICAIA, both initially marketed by ANTINORI. See TUSCANY.

sur lie, French term meaning 'on the lees', customarily applied to white wines whose principal deviation from everyday WHITE-WINE-MAKING techniques was some form of LEES CONTACT. The term has been used most commonly for the French dry white MUSCADET to differentiate those wines which remained on their lees after fermentation, usually in tank, in an effort to increase flavour. The practice, and term, has since spread south to the LANGUEDOC and even outside France and has proved a useful way of adding flavour and value to the produce of relatively neutral grapes such as Chenin Blanc in South Africa.

surmaturité, French expression often used by Anglophones for overripeness, a usually undesirable stage in grape maturity whereby grapes start to shrivel and acid levels fall to a dangerously low level.

süss, literally 'sweet' in German. Used on labels in AUSTRIA to designate wines whose RESIDUAL SUGAR is more than 18 g/l.

Süssreserve, German term for SWEET RESERVE, the sweetening agent much used, especially in the 1970s and 1980s, for all but the finest or driest German wines. Its use is declining as GERMANY makes an increasing proportion of dry wines, however (see TROCKEN and HALBTROCKEN).

sustainable viticulture, a form of viticultural practice which aims to avoid any form of environmental degradation. The term became popular in the 1990s especially in California, and the approach is seen to be more rational than that followed in so-called ORGANIC VITICULTURE.

The system encourages ecological diversity in the vineyard and shuns the more traditional monocultural approach. An attempt is made to reduce inputs of extraneous substances, especially of agrochemicals, although there are no strict rules governing which chemicals may or may not be used. Enhancing soil fertility is fundamental, and so green cover crops are used, as is undervine ploughing rather than herbicides. See also INTEGRATED PRODUCTION.

Some producers take the notion of sustainable viticulture a stage further and use the term to embrace such economic and cultural factors as farmworker health and safety, recycling of materials, using renewable sources for their supply, as well as the environmental effects of all forms of waste and energy use.

R.E.S. & J.Ro.

Susumaiello, lively, deep-coloured red wine grape that has crossed the Adriatic to be grown on the heel of Italy.

Swan District, the hot vine heartland of the state of WESTERN AUSTRALIA, once known as Swan Valley.

sweetness. Wines taste sweet mainly because of the amount of RESIDUAL SUGAR, or RS, they contain (although the impact of this on the palate is greatly influenced by factors such as the levels of ACIDITY, TANNINS, and CARBON DIOXIDE in the wine as well as by the serving TEMPERATURE). ALCOHOL can also taste sweet, as can GLYCEROL and a high level of pectins. A dry wine with a residual sugar of less than 2 g/l that is relatively high in alcohol, such as many a Chardonnay for example, can taste quite sweet. A sweet VOUVRAY, on the other hand, made in a cool region from the naturally acidic grape variety CHENIN BLANC, may contain well over 30 g/l residual sugar, but in youth can taste dry.

A wide variety of different terms in different languages are used to describe sweetness, although they invariably relate strictly to the RESIDUAL SUGAR rather than to the taste impression. The table below gives a very approximate indication of equivalences.

Some wine drinkers have been conditioned to be suspicious of any sweetness in a wine, perhaps because neophytes generally prefer some residual sugar (which is why so many wine BRANDS contain some) and sweetness is therefore associated with a lack of sophistication. Some of the greatest wines of the world are sweet, however. So long as there is sufficient ACIDITY to balance the sweetness, a sweet wine is by no means cloying. Indeed, a comparative tasting of great young sweet wines is more likely to leave the taster with the impression of excess acidity than excess sugar.

See SWEET WINES and SWEET-WINE-MAKING.

sweet reserve, preserved GRAPE JUICE held for BLENDING purposes, usually to sweeten, or at least soften, wines high in ACIDITY. The unfermented grape sugars counterbalance the tart flavours of wines produced from grapes grown in cool regions such as much of GERMANY (where it is known as *Süssreserve*) or grapes naturally high in acidity such as UGNI BLANC and COLOMBARD.

In many wine regions, sweet reserve is being replaced by GRAPE CONCENTRATE or rectified grape must.

A.D.W.

RS g/l	English	French	German	Italian	Spanish
<5	Bone dry	Brut			
<10	Dry	Sec	Trocken	Secco	Seco
10–20	Medium dry	Demi-sec	Halbtrocken	Abboccato	Semi-seco
20–30	Medium sweet	Doux	Mild	Amabile	Dulce
30–40	Sweet	Moelleux	Lieblich	Dolce	
>40/45		Liquoreux	Süss		

sweet-wine-making, the production of wines with noticeable amounts of RESIDUAL SUGAR which may vary considerably in ALCOHOLIC STRENGTH and production techniques. Local regulations differ but, with a few exceptions, non-grape sugar may be added only (and rarely) for the purposes of CHAPTALIZATION, to increase the final alcoholic strength, and not to add sweetness after fermentation. The most common method of sweetening basic wine is the addition of some form of sweet grape juice, followed by STABILIZATION (for any wine containing sugar is theoretically susceptible to SECONDARY FERMENTATION).

The finest sweet wines are made by concentrating the sugar in grapes, however, and the combined effect of the alcohol produced and the residual sugar tends to inhibit further YEAST activity. The three common ways of doing this are by the benevolent NOBLE ROT effect of the botrytis fungus on the vine as it nears maturity in perfect conditions (see BOTRYTIZED WINES); by processing frozen grape clusters (see EISWEIN); or by drying mature grapes either on the vine or after picking (see DRIED-GRAPE WINES). Many sweet wines are made by simply leaving the grapes on the vine for as long as possible in order to concentrate the grape sugars. If rot fails to materialize, the grapes simply start to raisin or shrivel. Such wines, sweet JURANÇON, for example, described as *moelleux* in French, can be extremely rich and satisfying, but are typically less complex and less long-lived than those made from grapes transformed by the action of noble rot.

Many everyday sweet wines are made nowadays, however, simply by fermenting the wine out to dryness and subsequently adding SWEET RESERVE, GRAPE CONCENTRATE, or rectified grape must just before FILTRATION and sterile bottling. These wines owe their stability not to their composition but to the fact that all microorganisms have been filtered out. They are best drunk within a year of bottling and within a day or two of opening the bottle. Most sweet German wines of QBA level, such as LIEBFRAUMILCH, are examples of this type of wine, and the sweetening agent is called SÜSSRESERVE in German.

Another technique, commonly employed for inexpensive sweet white French wines, is to ferment a must relatively high in sugars until the alcohol level has reached about 11 or 12 per cent, and then add a substantial dose of SULPHUR DIOXIDE.

One quite different way of transforming grapes into a liquid that is both sweet and stable is to add spirit to grape juice either before fermentation (see VIN DE LIQUEUR) or during it (see VIN DOUX NATUREL). Such liquids are usually more than 15 per cent alcohol, much stronger than most table wines.

Many FORTIFIED WINES are sweet. See also WHITE-WINE-MAKING, RED-WINE-MAKING, ROSÉ-WINE-MAKING, and, particularly, BOTRYTIZED WINES, DRIED-GRAPE WINES, and EISWEIN for details of how these particularly fine sweet wines are made.

sweet wines are widely under-appreciated, especially in view of how difficult some of them are to make.

For specific modern sweet wines see AUSLESE, BANYULS, BARSAC, BEERENAUSLESE, BONNEZEAUX, BOTRYTIZED WINES, CADILLAC, CÉRONS, CLAIRETTE DE DIE, EISWEIN, JURANÇON, LATE HARVEST, LAYON, LOUPIAC, MAURY, MOELLEUX, MONBAZILLAC, MONTLOUIS, various MOSCATELS, MOSCATO, MUSCAT, PICOLIT, QUARTS DE CHAUME, RASTEAU, RECIOTO, RIVESALTES, SÉLECTION DE GRAINS NOBLES, STE-CROIX-DU-MONT, SAUTERNES, TROCKENBEERENAUSLESE, VENDANGE TARDIVE, VIN DE PAILLE, VIN SANTO, and VOUVRAY.

See SWEETNESS for details of sweet-wine descriptions in various languages and what they entail.

See also DRIED-GRAPE WINES, FORTIFIED WINES (many of which are sweet), ICE WINE, VINS DE LIQUEUR, and VINS DOUX NATURELS, most of which are sweet wines.

Switzerland, small, Alpine country in central Europe beginning to look outwards into the greater world of wine. Annual wine production is steady at more than a million hl/26.4 million gal from less than 15,000 ha/37,050 acres of often spectacular vineyards. The majority of these are in the western, French-speaking part of the country, Suisse romande. There are also extensive vineyards all over eastern, German-speaking Switzerland (or Ostschweiz), and many vineyards in Ticino, the Italian-speaking south of Switzerland (or Svizzera). The country is divided into 23 cantons, of which all produce some wine. From the early 1990s, an APPELLATION CONTRÔLÉE system was applied with increasing rigour, initially in French-speaking Switzerland. Since controls on wine imports were relaxed in the mid 1990s (and will disappear altogether for white wines in 2001), the Swiss wine industry has been forced to seek customers abroad, particularly for the most common style of wine produced in Switzerland: light, white, and relatively neutral. An increasing proportion of Swiss wine is seriously good, however. CHASSE-LAS is the principal grape variety and, when well vinified, it can express well the country's diversity of soils and climates. The Valais has a clutch of interesting indigenous grapes and some increasingly sophisticated red wines are made in all Swiss wine regions.

Climate

Although Switzerland is on a particularly suitable latitude for wine production, between 45 and 47 degrees, a high proportion of the country is simply too high. However, the country's lakes and the föhn, a local wind which warms up sizeable portions of the south of the country, particularly Graubünden in the upper Rhine Valley, enable full grape ripening to take place in many valleys and on lakesides.

Wine-making

The essential stylistic difference between Swiss wine and that of neighbouring Germany and Austria is that ACIDITY is seen as an evil rather than a virtue and MALOLACTIC FERMENTATION is routinely practised. The resulting softness in Swiss wine is emphasized by the additional alcohol provided by CHAPTALIZATION. Ordinary wines may have their alcohol content increased by up to three per cent, although Swiss consumers are increasingly favouring lighter, drier wines.

Some form of CARBONIC MACERATION is often employed for German-speaking eastern Switzerland's red wines. As elsewhere, BARREL MATURATION has become increasingly popular for Swiss reds in general.

Switzerland has several pink-wine specialities: white wines made from Pinot Noir and/or Gamay grapes such as the Valais's DÔLE Blanche. Œil-de-perdrix, 'partridge eye', is made only from Pinot Noir, originally in Neuchâtel, while Gamay provides rosé. Federweisser or WEISSHERBST is a product of German Switzerland, where SCHILLERWEIN is a local rosé.

BLENDING has played an important part in the Swiss wine industry for decades. As Switzerland remains outside the European Union, Swiss wine merchants are unencumbered by the mass of regulations which protect wines within EU countries and have long depended on imported wines, particularly deeply col-

oured red ones, to add bulk to many of their less expensive blends. (In the late 1990s, for example, Switzerland was importing about 150 times as much wine, mainly red, as it exported.) The introduction of a full APPELLATION CONTRÔLÉE system within Switzerland is focusing attention on authentic domaine-bottled all-Swiss products but small additions of imported wines were still allowed in the late 1990s.

Vine varieties

Switzerland's most planted variety, covering 45 per cent of the country's vineyard land and responsible for a remarkable 60 per cent of the country's total wine production, is CHASSELAS, or Gutedel as it is known by German speakers. In the Valais, it is called Fendant, while in the Vaud, wines are sold under their geographical appellation names rather than by its old local synonym Dorin. The same applies to Geneva, where the traditional local name is Perlan. In the Valais, the second most important variety is SYLVANER, whose wines, fuller bodied than Chasselas, are sold as Johannisberg. Gros Rhin is a Valais synonym for Sylvaner. Petit Rhin (RIESLING) is relatively rare.

The conveniently early ripening MÜLLER-THURGAU, known as Riesling–Sylvaner, is the most common white grape variety in German Switzerland, having substantially replaced the historic RÄUSCHLING vine, particularly around Zurich just south of the German border. There are signs of a revival of interest in the more distinctive variety, however. A MÜLLER-THURGAU relative, Findling, has been introduced in Geneva canton.

Other white grape varieties include PINOT GRIS, called Malvoisie in the Valais; PINOT BLANC; a little GEWÜRZTRAMINER; Chardonnay, which can be elegant in the cantons of Neuchâtel and Geneva, and richer in the Vaud and the Valais; and ALIGOTÉ, COMPLETER, Sauvignon Blanc, KERNER, and Sémillon.

Pinot Noir, called Blauburgunder in German, is Switzerland's most widely planted red grape variety by far (and the most planted vine of any sort in German Switzerland), although the productive GAMAY is more important in the Vaud and Geneva, and Merlot reigns in Ticino to such an extent that it accounts for three-quarters of production. BONDOLA is a local red grape of Ticino, and SYRAH can produce a respectably ripe wine in sheltered parts of the Valais such as Leytron and Chamoson.

A number of crossings have been developed as suitable for Switzerland's very particular growing conditions: FREISAMER, Charmont (Chasselas × Chardonnay), Gamaret and Garanoir (both Gamay × REICHENSTEINER), and, a Valais speciality, Diolinoir (Rouge de Diolly × Pinot Noir) of which some nurture great hopes.

The Valais has a rich collection of about 40 ancient indigenous varieties, each with substantial body, ageing potential, and its own whiff of history: the AMIGNE of Vétroz; the elegant Petite Arvine of Fully (now planted at MAS de Daumas Gassac in southern France); the powerfully scented HUMAGNE BLANCHE; the almost extinct Rèze; and, among dark-skinned varieties, the noble CORNALIN and the powerful HUMAGNE ROUGE. MARSANNE Blanche, also known as Ermitage, Muscat du Valais (MUSCAT BLANC À PETITS GRAINS), MUSCAT OTTONEL, and Païen or Heida (SAVAGNIN Blanc) are also grown in the Valais, the latter high up at Visperterminen.

The wine regions

The country's emerging appellation contrôlée system is applied by each canton individually.

Valais This south-western canton produces 40 per cent of every Swiss vintage. Concentrated on the south-facing slopes of the sunny upper Rhône valley, the region is known as 'the California of Switzerland'. Many of these beautiful vineyards are terraced, farmed as a part-time activity by 22,000 smallholders. Typical of what they produce is the ubiquitous FENDANT (made from the Chasselas grapes which cover one third of the *vignoble*), and medium-weight reds labelled either Pinot Noir or DÔLE, a blend in which Pinot Noir must dominate the Gamay element. (Dôle Blanche is made from a blend of Pinot Noir and Gamay grapes vinified as a white wine.)

Some of the most concentrated Sylvaners, sold here as JOHANNISBERG, come from particularly well-favoured sites at Chamoson. Petite Arvine of Fully is accorded the greatest respect, however, for its exotic intensity, while Cornalin and Humagne make some of Switzerland's most seriously age-worthy reds. Fine, sweet, late-harvest wines, made from Johannisberg (Sylvaner), Amigne, Ermitage (Marsanne), Malvoisie (Pinot Gris), and Petite Arvine picked in November and December, can easily reach 20 per cent POTENTIAL ALCOHOL. They may be described as *flétri*, or withered, a reference to partial raisining on the vine. VIN DES GLACIERS

from the Val d'Anniviers above Sierre is another local rarity with a long tradition.

Vaud Switzerland's second most important wine canton is also in French Switzerland, round the northern shore of Lake Geneva, or Lac Léman (almost everything has at least two names in Switzerland). The canton's six wine regions are La Côte, Lavaux, and Chablais on the north shore of Lake Geneva, Les Côtes de l'Orbe on the plain between Lakes Geneva and Neuchâtel, Bonvillars on Lake Neuchâtel, and Vully on Lake Morat. In all, 26 villages have their own appellation, and there are two Grands Crus: Dézaley in the commune of Puidoux and Calamin in the commune of Epesses. Chasselas accounts for 80 per cent of the production, although its character can vary from almost insultingly innocuous to an almost POUILLY-FUMÉ-like steeliness. In La Côte, the aromatic floral notes of the variety itself tend to dominate the wines. In Yvorne, Aigle, Bonvillars, and Calamin, the mineral character of individual soils can easily dominate the fruit, while Dézaley and St-Saphorin often manage to demonstrate both fruit and minerals.

A little Chardonnay and Pinot Gris are also grown here. Red wines, especially Gamay, are a speciality of La Côte. Salvagnin, a designation accorded by a special tasting panel, approximates to a Vaud version of Valais' Dôle, although it can be made from Pinot Noir or Gamay or both. Similarly, Terravin is a Chasselas whose quality has a local seal of approval. Many of Switzerland's largest NÉGOCIANTS are based here.

Geneva The vineyards around the city at the south-western end of the lake are much flatter than those of the Valais and the Vaud and benefit from good sunlight, those next to the lake often escaping spring frost danger. Chasselas dominates, Riesling–Sylvaner is on the wane, while all manner of newcomers, including Chardonnay, Aligoté, Sauvignon, Sémillon, Kerner, Freisamer, Merlot, and even Cabernet Sauvignon, are increasingly popular with growers and consumers alike. Gamay is particularly successful here, whether as a well-structured red, a PRIMEUR, or a ROSÉ.

Neuchâtel The well-situated south-facing slopes above Lake Neuchâtel produce characterful results. Chasselas as usual predominates, but Pinot Noir is also important, just as it is over the French border in the JURA.

The pale-pink Pinot Œil-de-Perdrix is a Neuchâtel invention.

Eastern cantons In the 17 German-speaking cantons of Switzerland, nearly 70 per cent of production is red wine, particularly Mariafeld and Blauburgunder (Pinot Noir) and, to a lesser extent, the crossings Gamaret and Garanoir. Räuschling is once again gaining ground in Limmatal and on the shores of the lake south of Zürich, where Blauburgunder is often labelled Clevner. Riesling–Sylvaner (Müller-Thurgau) is the dominant white grape variety of eastern Switzerland, while Completer is a local speciality of Bündner Herrschaft near the border with Austria and Liechtenstein in Graubünden, where a small quantity of sweet Freisamer and serious red wine, mainly Blauburgunder, is also produced.

Italian-speaking Switzerland Ticino is Switzerland's fourth most important wine canton, and nearly 85 per cent of its production is of the Bordeaux red variety Merlot. Higher vineyards may have to concentrate on Pinot Noir. Merlot del Ticino can be relatively light or, from well-sited vineyards and carefully vinified, often using new oak, can be a serious challenge for fine red bordeaux. Most of the best red Merlots carry the VITI seal, for which they must be tasted and assessed, while pale-pink Merlot Bianco has been popular. Sopraceneri, north of Monte Ceneri, is an important wine region of which the local red grape variety Bondola is a speciality. It tends to be included in the rustic local version of 'house wine' called Nostrano, or 'ours', as opposed to Americano, which may include the HYBRIDS and American vines still representing seven per cent of total production here.

Other cantons The German-speaking but central canton of Berne has more than 200 ha of vines, mainly on the north shore of Lake Bienne, although there are some vines on the Thunersee west of Interlaken. On the southern shores of Lake Neuchâtel are 100 ha of mainly Chasselas and Pinot Noir in the canton of Fribourg, most of them on the north shore of Lake Morat. The Swiss canton of Jura also has a few hectares of vines.

Sylvaner is the French name for the eastern European variety known in German as Silvaner (under which name details of all non-French plantings appear). In France, it is practically unknown outside ALSACE, where it is still the most planted vine in the lower, flatter, more fertile vineyards of the Bas-Rhin.

Sylvaner may be an old vine and, at one time, an extremely important one in Germany at least, but as a wine producer it can be decidedly dull. Its wines can be quite full bodied and display sufficient acidity (often more appetizing acidity levels than the PINOT BLANC, which is Alsace's other important non-noble varietal) but even the most ingenious taster can be hard pressed to find adjectives to describe the quintessential *flavour* of Sylvaner. Indeed, the Sylvaners of Alsace provide one of the most convincing arguments for the influence of TERROIR on flavour, since they do exhibit the broad, smoky perfume characteristics that are typical of Alsace wines.

Sylvaner represents one vine in every five in Alsace and has only recently fallen behind Riesling as the region's most planted vine. It provides typically bland varietal whites at the bottom of the price range, usefully crisp blending material for Alsace's widely planted but rarely vaunted AUXERROIS, but is worth ageing only when made in the sharpest of styles such as that of Trimbach.

See SILVANER for more details.

Symphony, white-berried vine crossing of Grenache Gris and Muscat of Alexandria developed in CALIFORNIA. It lives the tenuous existence of all crossings, especially ones that make powerfully aromatic wines, although in the early 1990s it enjoyed a small vogue as an off-dry table wine something like a MALVASIA Bianca, and as a sparkling wine too.

Syrah, one of the noblest black grape varieties, if nobility is bestowed by an ability to produce serious red wines capable of ageing majestically for decades. Indeed, so valued was the durability of France's HERMITAGE, arguably Syrah's finest manifestation, that many red bordeaux were in the 18th and 19th centuries *hermitagé* (see ADULTERATION AND FRAUD).

The total ANTHOCYANINS in Syrah can be up to 40 per cent higher than those in the tough, dark Carignan, which makes it, typically, a wine for the long term that responds well to OAK maturation, even new oak if the grapes are very ripe.

France

The most famous prototype Syrahs—Hermitage and more recently CÔTE RÔTIE—are distinguished by their longevity or, in the case of newer producers, ambition. Only ST-JOSEPH and that paler shadow CROZES-HERMITAGE can sensibly be broached within their first five years. Syrah that has not reached full maturation can be simply mean and astringent, with more than a whiff of burnt rubber. When planted on the fringes of the Rhône such as in the ARDÈCHE, Syrah may avoid this fate only in the ripest vintages.

Until the 1970s, French Syrah plantings were almost exclusively in and around the very limited vineyards of the northern Rhône valley and were dwarfed in area by total Syrah plantings in the vine's other major colony, Australia, where it is known as Shiraz and has been that country's major black grape variety for decades (see below).

Since then, however, Syrah has enjoyed an extraordinary surge in popularity throughout southern France so that total French plantings rose from 2,700 ha/6,670 acres in 1968 to exactly 10 times that 20 years later. The increases were noticeable throughout the southern Rhône, particularly in Châteauneuf-du-Pape country, where Syrah has been increasingly valued as endowing Grenache with life expectancy, but have been most spectacular to the west in the Languedoc, especially in the Gard and the Hérault, where Syrah has been most enthusiastically adopted as an officially approved 'improving variety' that has added structure to wines both APPELLATION CONTRÔLÉE and VIN DE PAYS. Syrah has frequently been responsible for the Midi's most successful varietal wines, usually labelled Vin de Pays d'Oc. Yields very much in excess of the low yields that characterize the arid hill of Hermitage have tended to dilute its northern Rhône characteristics in many cases, however. In the northern Rhône, it is rarely blended, except perhaps with a little Viognier, while in the south it is typically blended with Grenache and perhaps Mourvèdre and Cinsaut. In Provence, the very Australian blend of Syrah and Cabernet Sauvignon is becoming more common and Syrah is one of the most successful noble vine imports to Corsica.

Outside France

Australian Shiraz can vary from a brown, baked, dilute everyday red to the glorious, almost porty concentration of Australia's most famous wine, Penfolds Grange. See SHIRAZ.

Another unexpectedly successful site for mature, concentrated Syrah is the Valais in Switzerland, particularly around the suntrap village of Chamoson on the upper reaches of the Rhône valley. Here classic northern Rhône techniques are employed, sometimes to great effect. Italy too is flirting with Syrah, most successfully so far at Isola e Elena in Tuscany.

To ripen fully, Syrah demands a warm climate, which naturally limits its spread, but some plantings in California have been particularly successful. The most substantial Syrah plantings in the 1990s were in Mendocino and Sonoma. Effective early practitioners were McDowell Valley Vineyards, Joseph Phelps, Estrella (now Meridian), and Qupé.

Early results from the Red Willow vineyard suggest that WASHINGTON state may have considerable potential for fine, bright Syrah wines.

South Africa's Shiraz, most of it in Paarl and Stellenbosch, is producing promising results when yields are restricted. A small amount is also grown with some success in Argentina.

Syria, country in the Middle East whose vineyards have been mainly dedicated to the production of TABLE GRAPES and DRYING GRAPES rather than wine since the rise of Islamic fundamentalism in the late 1970s. Average annual Syrian wine production had fallen to 8,000 hl in the early 1980s and is still declining.

Szürkebarát, Hungarian name for PINOT GRIS, which is quite widely planted there; but its naturally low acidity can result in slightly flabby wines, particularly on the Great Plain. It is most revered within HUNGARY as Badacsonyi Szürkebarát, a rich, heavy wine from the north shore of Lake Balaton. It can yield livelier wines from the Mátra Foothills.

table grapes, the common term for those grapes specially grown to be eaten as fresh fruit. Of the grapes grown worldwide, table grapes represent the third most frequent use, following wine and dried grapes.

The varieties of grapes for fresh consumption are usually specialized and different from those for wine and drying. They should taste good, have a reasonably consistent BERRY SIZE, bright colour, firm flesh texture, not too many seeds, and skins tough enough to withstand storage and transport. Recently developed seedless varieties are increasingly popular. Some important table grape varieties are Barlinka, Calmeria, CARDINAL, CHASSELAS, Dattier, Emperor, Flame Seedless, Gros Vert, Italia, MUSCAT OF ALEXANDRIA, MUSCAT HAMBURG, Perlette, Ruby Seedless, Ribier, and SULTANA (or Thompson Seedless).   R.E.S.

table wine, term used internationally to distinguish wines of average ALCOHOLIC STRENGTH from FORTIFIED WINES, which have been strengthened by the addition of alcohol and are usually more than 15 per cent alcohol. In this context, 'table wines' rely solely on FERMENTATION for their alcoholic strength, which tends to be between 9 and 15 per cent.

Within the European Union, however, the term 'table wine' has a specific meaning and is applied to all wine produced within it that does not qualify as superior QUALITY WINE. Table wine is therefore the EU's principal, though fast-declining, wine product.

Within France, table wine is known as VIN DE TABLE. The distinct and superior category is VIN DE PAYS.

Within Italy, the situation is rather different. Although all of Italy's most basic wine (and there is a great deal of it) is designated vino da tavola, that designation has also been chosen, confusingly, by a considerable number of the best producers for some of their best wines, notably SUPERTUSCANS, whose production does not happen to conform to any rule for Italian quality wine (see VINO DA TAVOLA). Italy also has an embryonic counterpart to France's vin de pays, IGT, but by far the largest part of Italian wine is designated vino da tavola.

The reverse is the case in Germany, where less than five per cent of total production is deemed to be Deutscher TAFELWEIN or its superior category LANDWEIN. See below, however.

Spain's table wine—and some new wines made in the image of SUPERTUSCANS outside the official quality wine system—are called VINO DE MESA. Spain also has a small superior category, VINO DE LA TIERRA.

Portugal's table wine is known as VINHO de mesa and its even more nascent superior subcategory is IPR.

Greek table wine is called *epitrapezios oinos* within Greece and is rarely exported.

Most of Luxembourg's wine qualifies as quality wine, and the rest is called vin de table. See also ENGLAND.

Within the EU, table wines from different countries may be freely blended to produce **European table wine.** This is particularly common in Germany, where it may be called EWG Tafelwein, or simply Tafelwein. Within

France, however, a significant proportion of France's considerable imports from Italy and, more recently, Spain, are blended with French vin de table to produce a Vin de Table des Pays Différentes de l'EU.

Tâche, La, great red GRAND CRU in Burgundy's CÔTE D'OR. For more details, see VOSNE-ROMANÉE and DOMAINE DE LA ROMANÉE-CONTI.

Tacoronte-Acentejo, DO wine region on the west-facing slopes in the north east of the volcanic island of Tenerife in the CANARY ISLANDS. Tacoronte-Acentejo produces red wines made predominantly from the dark-berried LISTÁN Negro and Negramoll grapes. The volcanic soil imparts a peculiar character to these improving wines.   R.J.M. & V. de la S.

Taiwan, otherwise known as the Republic of China, island off, and independent of, CHINA. There is some experimentation with wine-grape growing in the south of the island, and a much bigger MADE WINE business dependent on imported GRAPE CONCENTRATE.

Tajikistan, mountainous central Asian republic of the CIS between UZBEKISTAN and China. Lowlands, plateaux, foothills, and mountain slopes suitable for viticulture occupy only seven per cent of Tajikistan's area. The climate of the country is CONTINENTAL.

Tajikistan can be divided into three viticultural zones: the Leninabad region in the north, the Ghissar valley in the centre, and the Vakhsh valley together with the Kuliab regions in the south.

In the 1990s, 25 grape varieties were in commercial cultivation, with 10 wine varieties such as RKATSITELI, SAPERAVI, Cabernet Sauvignon, Riesling, Tagobi, Bayan Shirey, and Muscat Rosé. The 20 wineries of Tajikistan in the early 1990s produced more than 50 brands of wine, most of them strong and sweet.   V.R.

Talento is the name used by a group of Italian producers of TRADITIONAL METHOD sparkling wines made principally from such noble grapes as Chardonnay and Pinot Noir to distinguish their wines from the myriad styles of sparkling wines made from all sorts of grape varieties all over Italy. Talento represents over half of the production of this type of wine in Italy and the producers who belong to the group now identify their wines as 'Talento metodo classico' (since the late 1990s the word SPUMANTE no longer appears on the label). The producers

themselves are predominantly from either TRENTINO-ALTO ADIGE or the OLTREPÒ PAVESE.
                                                    D.T.

Talia, occasionally written Thalia, Portuguese name for the ubiquitous white grape variety known in France as UGNI BLANC and in Italy as TREBBIANO.

Tamar River, wine region in TASMANIA.

Tămîioasă, name for MUSCAT grape or wine in ROMANIA. Thus Tămîioasă Alba is Romanian for MUSCAT BLANC À PETITS GRAINS, Tămîioasă Hamburg or Tămîioasă Neagrǎ is MUSCAT HAMBURG, Tămîioasă Ottonel is MUSCAT OTTONEL. Tămîioasă Românescǎ is another Romanian synonym for Muscat Blanc à Petits Grains.

Tamyanka, Russian name for MUSCAT BLANC À PETITS GRAINS.

tank method, bulk SPARKLING-WINE-MAKING process which involves provoking a second fermentation in wine stored in a pressure tank. Other names include Charmat process and *cuve close*.

Tannat is a tough, black-berried vine variety most famous as principal ingredient in MADIRAN, where its inherent astringence is mitigated by blending with Cabernet Franc, some Cabernet Sauvignon, and FER, and wood ageing for at least 20 months. Young Tannat can be so deeply coloured and tannic that it recalls NEBBIOLO. If Madiran is Tannat's noblest manifestation, slightly more approachable, if more rustic, wines are made to much the same recipe for Côtes de ST-MONT, as well as for the distinctively hard reds and rosés of IROULÉGUY and the rare reds and pinks labelled TURSAN and BÉARN.

Although it can also be found as a minor ingredient in such wines as Côtes du BRULHOIS, overall plantings in France have been declining.

There are still several thousand hectares in URUGUAY, where it is called Harriague. From here it spread to Argentina, where it is still grown to a very limited extent.

tannins, diverse and complex group of chemical compounds that occur in the bark of many trees and in fruits, including the grape.

Tannins play an important role in the AGEING of wine, particularly red wines, where pigmented tannins are crucial to the colour and sensory properties. Handling tannins during

RED-WINE-MAKING is one of the most critical steps in optimizing the quality and character of a red wine, yet the process is based almost totally on experience and intuition because our understanding of the principles involved is still rudimentary.

Tannins in wine come predominantly from the grapes and, to a much lesser extent, from the wood in which it was aged. The tannins in grapes are predominantly in the SKINS and seeds of each berry and also the stems, the amount of tannins in grape pulp being relatively insignificant. Thus, the more skins, seeds, and stems are involved in the winemaking process, the higher the possible resultant level of tannins. Tannin levels in white and rosé wines, which are made largely by excluding or minimizing these grape components, are therefore lower than in reds. The tannins present in a white wine are non-pigmented and can range from colourless through light yellow to amber. The absence of ANTHOCYANINS condensed into the tannins of white wines accounts for how different they look.

Tannins are most frequently encountered by the human palate in over-steeped tea, and by wine drinkers in young reds designed for a long life in bottle and in whites made with excessive SKIN CONTACT. They produce the taste sensation of bitterness and the physical tactile 'drying' sensation of ASTRINGENCY.

Varieties high in tannins include Cabernet Sauvignon, NEBBIOLO, Syrah, and TANNAT.

Different wood types contain different sorts of tannins, but these have most effect on wine when the wood is new. Oak tannins differ in significant ways from grape tannins, although the consequences of such differences on the stability of wine colour and on the sensory properties (including mouthfeel) of barrel-matured red wines in particular are yet to be scientifically rationalized. Wine consumers have come to expect a certain amount of wood flavour in a wide range of wines, including some relatively immature wines, both red and white, whether the result of genuine BARREL MATURATION or the use of OAK CHIPS. They are therefore often exposed to the effects of tannin on the palate, which can be considerably mitigated by the right choice of accompanying FOOD.

Wine-makers can adjust excessively high tannin levels by FINING, but given a sufficient amount of time, tannins are removed naturally during wine ageing.   A.D.W., J.Ro., & P.J.W.

Tasting tannins

Tannins cannot be smelt or tasted; they cause tactile sensations. A significant development of the 1990s was a keener appreciation of the different sorts of sensory impact of tannins on the palate (see MOUTHFEEL). Tannins may be variously described as hard, bitter (if accompanied by BITTERNESS), green, ripe (if perceptible but only after the impact of fruit that has reached PHYSIOLOGICAL RIPENESS has been felt on the palate), coarse, grainy, wood (if obviously the effect of CASK AGEING). This is clearly an area in which considerably more scientific rigour will be applied.

Tarragona, Mediterranean port in Spanish CATALONIA. Until the 1960s, wines called Tarragona were predominantly sweet, red, fortified, and drunk as a cheap alternative to PORT. Tarragona, awarded DO status in 1976, continues to ship communion wine all over the Christian world. Over 70 per cent of Tarragona's wine production today is white, however, a large proportion of which is sold to the CAVA houses in PENEDÈS. The reds are increasingly made in the fashionable style of neighbouring PRIORAT by such producers as Josep Anguera and the Capçanes CO-OPERATIVE.
                                    R.J.M. & V. de la S.

Tarrango, red wine grape variety developed in AUSTRALIA. The aim of this TOURIGA × SULTANA crossing was to provide a slow-ripening variety suitable for the production of light-bodied wines with low TANNINS and relatively high ACIDITY. As a result, some Australian wines have been fashioned in the image of BEAUJOLAIS but the variety will ripen satisfactorily only in the hot irrigated wine regions of Australia such as the RIVERLAND. Brown Brothers of Milawa have been particularly persistent with this variety.

tartaric acid, the most important of the ACIDS found in grapes and wine. Of all the natural organic acids found in plants, it is one of the rarer. The grape is the only fruit of significance that is a tartrate accumulator, and yet it is of critical importance to the wine-maker because of the major part it plays in the taste of the wine.

Grapes and the resultant wines vary considerably in their concentrations of tartaric acid. Among the thousands of cultivated VINE VARIETIES, some, PALOMINO for example, are noted for their high concentrations of tartaric acid, while others such as the Pinot Noir of Burgundy and Malbec, or Cot, are relatively low. Wines that have not undergone MAL-OLACTIC FERMENTATION generally have slightly more tartaric acid than malic acid, while those which have undergone this 'softening' process usually have many more times tartaric than malic acid; they are also more stable.

tartrates, the general term used by wine-makers to describe the harmless crystalline deposits that separate from wines during FER-MENTATION and AGEING. In English, the sub-stances are also called argols, in French *tartres* and in German *Weinstein* or 'wine stones'.

Only the most informed consumers appre-ciate the harmlessness of tartrate crystals in bottle. Although tartrates precipitated in red wines usually take on some red or brown col-ouring from adsorbed wine pigments and are commonly regarded as mere sediment, in white wines they can look alarmingly like shards of glass to the uninitiated. The modern wine industry has in the main decided that tartrate STABILIZATION is preferable to con-sumer education.

Tartrates are most commonly encountered in bottles of German wine because, coming from a relatively cool region, they have the greatest concentration of tartaric acid.

In white wines, colourless, perfectly shaped crystals of potassium acid tartrate are found. In red wines, the crystals are usually reddish brown and small and irregular in shape.

A.D.W.

Tasmania, small island state to the cool south of AUSTRALIA, with most of its vineyards clus-tered round Launceston in the north or Hobart in the south. In volume terms, the Tasmanian wine industry is as tiny as its potential is large.

Outside observers not only habitually exag-gerate the extent of Tasmania's viticulture, but are oblivious to the diversity of TERROIR and climate in the island's extremely complex geography. There are sites which are both warmer and very much drier than southern Victoria (for example the **Coal River** region in the east of Hobart, and, in terms of warmth, the **Tamar River** south of Launceston) and there are sites cooler and wetter (for example **Pipers Brook**, east of Launceston).

ZINFANDEL was once grown successfully at the Coal River; the colour and extract of the Tamar River red wines is extraordinary, hinting misleadingly at a warm to very warm climate.

The island's major producers have hitched their future to such cool-climate varieties as Riesling, Pinot Gris, Chardonnay, and Pinot Noir (the latter two for both table- and spark-ling-wine use).

Although the climate does not necessarily dictate this, whether Tasmania realizes part or all of its potential may well rest with sparkling wine—sparkling wine produced not in Tas-mania but on the mainland. BRL HARDY, Domaine Chandon, and Yalumba have all entered into long-term supply contracts with growers, but so far have not made direct invest-ments in vineyards. Should they take the next step, there would have to be an exponential increase in Tasmania's vine plantings.   J.H.

taste. What we call the sense of taste is to a very great extent the sense of smell. See TASTING. As for our own personal taste in wine, it is overall entirely SUBJECTIVE. There are no rights and wrongs in wine preferences.

tastevins, or wine tasters, as they are known by collectors of wine antiques, are shallow, often dimpled, saucers used for TASTING by pro-fessionals (and occasional self-conscious amateurs), invariably made of silver.

Some BURGUNDY producers still use tastevins in their own cellars, where they can be useful to demonstrate hue and clarity even in a dim light. For actual tasting, GLASSES are more effi-cacious, even if more fragile and less portable.

tasting, the act of consciously assessing a wine's quality, character, or identity (see BLIND TASTING). It is certainly not synonymous with, nor necessarily contemporaneous with nor accompanied by, the act of drinking it. The ideal conditions for the act of tasting, and the organization and classification of formal wine tastings, is outlined under TASTINGS. This article is concerned with the activities and mechanisms involved in consciously receiving the sensory impressions a wine can stimulate.

How we taste

Most of what is commonly called the sense of taste is in fact the sense of SMELL, whether applied to wine, or any food or drink, since by chewing we transform our food into liquid which gives off smellable vapour. To verify this it is enough to eat or drink something with the nose pinched shut, or to consider the extent to which we 'lose our appetite' when we have a head cold which blocks the nose. The human brain senses what we call flavours and aromas in the olfactory bulb, which is reached via perhaps a thousand different receptors, each sensitive to a small group of different aromas, located in the nose. These are reached mainly by the nostrils, and also by a channel at the back of the mouth called the retronasal passage (which is why most healthy people can still perceive some flavour even if they do not consciously smell what they consume). The human olfactory sense is extremely acute (although not as acute as some animals').

Concentrations of some compounds of one part per 10,000 can be sensed, recognized, and remembered by the average person. A single whiff can transport us immediately to something experienced many years before. Our high number of receptors helps us recognize all the 10,000 or so aromas that humans are capable of smelling.

The tasting capacity of the mouth is much more limited. In the mouth, our tactile sense can register FIZZINESS, TEMPERATURE, VISCOSITY, EXTRACT, the apparent heat generated on the palate by excessive ALCOHOL, and the sensation induced by TANNINS of drying out the insides of the cheeks.

The tongue also has certain taste receptors we call taste buds, which can sense the four 'primary tastes' of SWEETNESS, ACIDITY, BITTER-NESS, and saltiness. Although it can vary considerably from person to person, in very general terms these taste buds have different sensitivities so that those at the front of the tongue are usually particularly sensitive to sweetness, those on the edges of the tongue are particularly sensitive to acidity, those at the back of the tongue are particularly sensitive to bitterness, and those at the front edges are particularly sensitive to saltiness. With the exception of some wines matured near the sea such as Manzanilla SHERRY or some produced from vineyards with a serious salinity problem, very few wines taste salty. Sweetness and acidity, on the other hand, are two of the most important measurements of a wine. During tasting, therefore, the front of the tongue can usually detect the apparent sweetness of a wine (which is not necessarily the same as its RESIDUAL SUGAR). The sides of the tongue react quite markedly in many people to acidity. Some wines taste quite bitter (bitterness often accompanies, but is not the same as, ASTRINGENCY) and this bitterness is most commonly sensed on the flat rear portion of the tongue.

Some food scientists argue that our taste buds are sensitive to a fifth primary taste, that of umami, associated most commonly with monosodium glutamate (MSG), commonly used as a flavour enhancer, and with a wide range of savoury characteristics in stocks and soups.

Whether we consider umami a primary taste or not, it is clear that the mouth's tasting ability, apart from being usefully linked to the olfactory bulb by the retronasal passage, is in *measuring* the wine, assessing its dimensions of sweetness, acidity, bitterness, fizziness, viscosity, potency, and astringency. The mouth is capable of making an overall assessment of a wine's texture, while the nose senses what we call its flavour. Just as what is commonly called the sense of taste is really the sense of smell, so what is commonly called flavour is really AROMA or, in older wines, BOUQUET. (See FLAVOUR, however, for a proposal that the word be used to incorporate all the measurements sensed by the mouth.)

The essential character and most complex distinguishing marks of any wine are in its smell, which is made up of hundreds, probably thousands, of different FLAVOUR COMPOUNDS, present in widely varying permutations and concentrations in different wines.

What is commonly called tasting therefore involves persuading as many of these flavour compounds as possible to reach the olfactory bulb, while ensuring that contact is made between the wine and all of the inside of the mouth for the purposes of assessing a wine's dimensions and texture.

How to taste

The operation of tasting is generally divided into three stages involving sequentially the eye, the nose, and the mouth (although, as outlined above, this is not the same as the simple sequential application of the senses of sight, smell, and taste).

Eye The job of the eye in wine tasting is mainly to assess clarity and colour, as well as to monitor the presence of CARBON DIOXIDE and ALCOHOL (the former indicated by bubbles, the latter by any TEARS of the wine that may form on the inside of the glass when it is rotated).

The clarity of a wine is an indication, hardly surprisingly, of the extent to which CLARI-FICATION has been carried out, but also of the wine's condition. Many wine FAULTS result in a haze of some sort. In the late 1990s, anti-FILTRATION sentiment was so strong in California that some highly priced Chardonnays looked positively cloudy. A wine with particles floating in it, however, may simply be an innocent casualty of poor SERVING technique in which a wine has not been properly separated from its entirely harmless sediment. Experienced tasters can sometimes discern quality simply by looking at a wine's luminescent clarity and subtle range of hues.

The colour of a wine, both its intensity and its hue, is one of the potentially most valuable clues to any BLIND TASTER. Intensity of colour is best judged by looking straight through a glass of wine from directly above (preferably against a plain white background). Different grape varieties tend to make deeper or lighter coloured wines (Cabernet Sauvignon, Syrah, and Nebbiolo make particularly deep red wines; Gewürztraminer and Pinot Gris are examples of varieties which make particularly deep white wines, because the grape skins are deep pink). A deep colour also indicates youth, long MACERATION (possibly over-EXTRACTION), and thick-skinned grapes in a red wine; sometimes age, some OXIDATION, BARREL MATURATION, although not if preceded by BARREL FERMENTATION, in white wines.

The actual hue can also provide clues, and can be best assessed by tilting the glass away at an angle so that the different shadings of colour at the rim can be seen, again preferably against a plain white background. A bluish tinge in a red wine indicates youth, while orange/yellow indicates AGE (or OXIDATION). Very pale green in a white wine may indicate Riesling, while a pink tinge suggests that the wine was made from pink-skinned grapes such as Gewürztraminer and Pinot Gris. For more information, see COLOUR.

This stage in tasting for any purpose other than identification is usually very short and, if tasters are SCORING various aspects of a wine, many wines gain maximum points for appearance.

Nose As demonstrated above, this is the single most important stage in wine tasting. The trick is to persuade as many flavour compounds as possible to vaporize and come into contact with the olfactory bulb. It is then necessary, of course, to be in a suitable frame of mind to interpret the messages received by the olfactory bulb, which is why the act of tasting requires concentration.

The simplest way to maximize the evap-

oration of a wine's volatile elements is by the judicious use of TEMPERATURE and agitation. Higher temperatures encourage any sort of evaporation so ideal tasting temperatures tend to be slightly higher than ideal SERVING temperatures. It is unwise to taste wines so hot that the alcohol starts to evaporate at such a rate that it dominates the flavour, however, so an ideal tasting temperature for wines, red or white, is somewhere between 15 and 20 °C/59–68 °F. At these relatively elevated temperatures, faults as well as attributes should be perfectly apparent. Sparkling wines tend to be tasted slightly cooler to retain the carbon dioxide.

A further increase in the number of molecules liberated by a wine can be achieved by agitating the wine and increasing its surface area, preferably rotating it in a bowl-shaped glass with a stem (see GLASSES) so that no wine is lost.

As soon as the wine has been agitated, the aroma collects in the bowl of the partly filled glass above the wine and can be transmitted to the olfactory bulb up the nostrils with one thoughtful inhalation. (Concentration is vital to serious tasting.)

The taster monitors first whether the wine smells fresh and clean, or whether any off-odours indicate the presence of a wine FAULT. The next basic measurement might well be of the intensity of the aroma (if it is an attractive smell, then intensity is preferable). And then comes the complex part of the operation which is much more difficult to describe: the sensation and attempt at description of the individual components that make up the aroma, or 'bouquet' as it is called if it has taken on the complexities associated with AGEING. See TASTING TERMS.

Quite apart from those components which result from the grapes themselves, the aroma can provide certain overall hints about viticulture and wine-making techniques. HERBACEOUSNESS suggests that the grapes were less than fully ripe. Oak ageing may be betrayed by a certain amount of wood flavour; scents of spices and toast can be the result of the degree of TOAST which the barrels received. Tropical fruit aromas suggest that the fermentation was particularly long and cool. Diacetyl, which can smell like butter and other dairy products, is a particularly obvious sign of MALOLACTIC FERMENTATION.

As a wine undergoes gentle aeration in the glass, it may well begin to give off other compounds with time. World-famous taster Michael Broadbent, for example, keeps a series of records of how a single glass of wine tastes, marked according to how long after pouring each note was made. Most good wines seem to get better with time and then to start to deteriorate. In blind tasting, however, a taster's first impressions are usually the most accurate, and insights are rarely provided by constant repetition of the 'nosing' process.

Mouth In terms of aroma, 'flavour' in its narrow sense, the mouth, or palate as it is sometimes called, usually merely confirms the impressions already apparent to the nose when some vapour escapes the mouth and reaches the olfactory bulb via the retronasal passage. Many tasters take in a certain amount of air over their mouthful of wine to encourage this process (and are often mocked for the accompanying noise).

The main function of the mouth in the tasting process is to assess the texture and measure the dimensions rather than the character of a wine by assessing sweetness, acidity, bitterness, viscosity, and tannin level. Monitoring of the combination of sweetness, viscosity, and any sensation of 'heat' gives a good indication of the likely alcohol content of any individual wine since it tends to leave a burning sensation in the mouth. The insides of the mouth may also register the MOUTHFEEL, analysing the impact of the tannins (see Tasting TANNINS). For this reason, it is a good idea to rinse the mouth thoroughly with wine so that all possible taste receptors may come into contact with it—another reason why wine tasting looks both ridiculous and disgusting to outsiders.

After rinsing a wine around their mouths, and noting the impressions given by the vapour rising up the restronasal passage, most professional tasters then demonstrate their devotion to duty rather than alcohol by SPITTING. There are no taste receptors in the throat. The taster then notes how long the impressions given by the wine seem to persist after spitting, or swallowing.

Conclusions Perhaps the most important stage, however, is a fourth stage of analysis, in which all previous impressions are considered. This includes most particularly considering whether the measurements taken by the mouth suggest that the wine is in BALANCE, and monitoring the LENGTH of the aftertaste, these

last two factors being important indicators of quality. A fine wine should continue to make favourable sensory impressions throughout the entire tasting process.

Experience is necessary to judge balance. A significant, if decreasing, proportion of young red wines designed for long-term evolution, for example, are not by any objective criterion in balance. Their tannins may still be very marked and make the wine an unpleasantly astringent drink, even if they suggest that the wine will keep well. (Making red wines with less obvious tannins so that they can be both aged and drunk in their youth is one of the prime current preoccupations of wine-makers.) Similarly, the acidity in a young German wine may be aggressively dominant, but experience shows that it is essential to the preservation of a top-quality Riesling, for example for the 10 or 20 years' bottle ageing it may deserve. (Some would also argue that a perceptible level of SULPHUR DIOXIDE was also acceptable in such a wine.)

Professional tasting usually involves making **tasting notes**, typically under the four headings noted above. It may also involve SCORING by allotting NUMBERS to different elements according to a carefully predetermined scale, especially if wine JUDGING is involved. Tasting notes can be set out in many different ways and experienced tasters tend to devise their own abbreviations and symbols.

Tasting for pleasure, which is what most wine drinkers do every time they open a bottle, requires nothing more complicated than a moment's concentration and an open mind.

Factors affecting taste

We cannot know what other tasters experience for the tasting mechanism is far from public. Furthermore, individuals vary in their sensitivity to different compounds and dimensions of wine. But even as individuals, the way our brain processes information sent from sensory receptors changes all the time so that the same wine will have a different effect on us depending on the state of our palate. The most obvious example of this is how different something tastes before and just after we have had a mouthful of red hot chili. But even something as apparently innocent as a particularly hot drink or salty solution can affect the way we taste. An acid wine will seem less acid if tasted immediately after a very acid one, which is why the ORDER of serving and tasting is crucial, but extremely difficult to get right until every wine has been tasted.

Our overall physical well-being affects how we taste. If we are run down, we tend to produce less saliva and, because saliva contains compounds which have a buffering effect on many aspects of taste, both foods and drinks can taste quite different (this is quite apart from the fact that good HEALTH is needed to tackle a succession of alcoholic liquids).

How we taste can be quite markedly affected by our mood, and of course by the physical environment in which we taste (see TASTINGS below). Tasting in a very humid atmosphere is markedly more difficult than when the atmospheric pressure is high, flavour compounds are readily volatilized, and taste impressions seem crystal clear.

tasting notes are the usual record of professional or serious wine TASTINGS. They are conventionally divided into notes (and sometimes SCORES or NUMBERS) for what is sensed by the eye, the nose, and the mouth, together with overall conclusions (see TASTING). The thoughtful organizer of a tasting prepares a **tasting sheet** which provides as a minimum a list of complete names of all the wines served, in the relevant ORDER of serving, with sufficient space below or beside each to write full tasting notes. Tasting notes, especially of wines worth AGEING, are all the more valuable if they are dated. Most tasting notes remain of personal use only, but Michael Broadbent has produced two important books based entirely on his, and the majority of Robert PARKER's output is made up of his. Comparison of the two authors provides a reasonable guide to the different styles of British and American tasting notes respectively.

tastings, events at which wines are tasted. Informal tastings take place every time a bottle of wine is opened by a wine enthusiast. The most common sort of formal tasting is one held for the purposes of wine assessment, typically by a wine merchants keen to sell their wares, sometimes by a generic body keen to promote wines of a particular style or provenance. Formal tastings are also held by wine clubs and societies for less commercial purposes: EDUCATION or simple pleasure perhaps.

A **horizontal tasting** is one in which a number of different wines of the same VINTAGE are compared, while a **vertical tasting** is a comparison of different vintages of the same wine, most commonly the same Bordeaux CHÂTEAU.

A BLIND TASTING is one whose purpose is that the taster identifies unknown wines as closely as possible.

A **comparative tasting** is one in which various different examples of the same sort or style of wine—CLASSED GROWTHS of the same vintage, or wines from the same APPELLATION, or a single VARIETAL, for example—are tasted and compared. Such tastings increasingly form the basis of modern WINE WRITING and should be conducted blind for a true, unprejudiced assessment.

Equipment

The only essential equipment for a wine tasting, apart from the wine, is suitable GLASSES and a CORKSCREW, but it is almost impossible to hold a tasting without a substantial area of flat surface on which to put bottles and glasses safely, usually in the form of a table to which there is good access. Next most useful objects are undoubtedly spittoons (see SPITTING), and something in which to pour away LEFTOVER wine from a tasting sample (bottles plus funnels are customary although spittoons can also be used for this purpose). The thoughtful organizer ensures that there is some plain white surface against which to hold a glassful of wine (see TASTING). A truly assiduous host provides tasters with a tasting sheet on which is a full and accurate list of wines to be tasted, in the correct order, with appropriate space for tasting notes. Water for rinsing of glasses and palates and some neutral-tasting food for 'cleaning the palate' can be helpful too. Cheese is usually too strong (see FOOD AND WINE MATCHING); bread or dry, savoury crackers are generally preferred by professionals.

Conditions

Ideal conditions include a strong natural light, ambient temperature between 15 and 18 °C/ 59–64 °F, and an absence of any extraneous smells. In practice, a tasting that involves many people inevitably generates its own heat and smell, so it is wise to begin at a lower ambient temperature and not to be too exercised about a whiff of aftershave or polish, which is soon absorbed into the ambient atmosphere.

Organization

One glass per taster usually suffices, and no more than a fifteenth or even twentieth of a bottle is needed to give someone a decent tasting sample. Ensuring that tasters are served rather than serving themselves can limit wine consumption.

A suitable number of different wines to be shown at a single tasting is controversial. Some tasters claim to be able to assess up to 200 wines in a day at JUDGING sessions such as the Australian wine shows, while the most experienced professionals in CHAMPAGNE deliberately limit themselves to fewer than a dozen wines at a time. A novice taster should probably start with no more than four wines while a professional might feel a tasting which offered only 15 was hardly worth the detour.

What is clear is that it is difficult to *enjoy* more than a dozen wines at a time, and that the ORDER in which any selection is served is vital to the impression they give.

tasting terms, the myriad and oft-mocked words used by tasters in an often vain attempt to describe sensory impressions received during TASTING.

The difference between a taster and a social drinker is this need to describe, to attempt the difficult task of applying words to individual, invisible sensations, particularly the aromas sensed by the olfactory bulb.

The sense of smell is an exceptionally private one. The best we can do is describe aromas in terms of other aromas of which they remind us. Hence 'blackcurrant' or CASSIS, frequently for Cabernet Sauvignon; 'strawberry' or 'raspberry' for Pinot Noir; 'vanilla' for OAK.

There is as yet no official wine-tasting LANGUAGE, although there have been many valiant attempts at establishing one and, particularly as research on FLAVOUR COMPOUNDS and FLAVOUR PRECURSORS continues apace, this is becoming an increasingly attainable goal.

Terms used for mouth sensations

The most straightforward 'dimensional terms' describe what is sensed in the mouth as well as visual impressions—they describe what is measurable. They are useful, indisputable, and not affected by SUBJECTIVITY. Inevitably, some jargon has evolved, of which the following are the most obvious examples.

Acid—too high in ACIDITY.
Body—a noun; see BODY.
Big—high in alcohol.
Bitter—leaving the impression of BITTERNESS on the back of the tongue.
Crisp—attractively high in ACIDITY.
Fat—full bodied and viscous.

Flabby—lacking in ACIDITY.
Finish—a noun for aftertaste.
Full—of BODY.
Green—too acid, made of unripe fruit.
Hard—too much TANNIN and too little fruit.
Heavy—too alcoholic; too much EXTRACT.
Hot—too alcoholic.
Legs—see TEARS.
Light—agreeably light in BODY.
Long—impressively persistent aftertaste.
Phenolic—excessively high in astringent PHENOLICS.
Rich—full of ripe fruit without necessarily being sweet.
Short—no aftertaste or 'finish'.
Smooth—imprecise term for pleasing MOUTHFEEL.
Soft—low in TANNINS.
Well balanced—having good BALANCE.

Terms used for aroma

It is in their attempts to find 'character terms' to apply to these more subtle, more private olfactory sensations that wine tasters seem so foolish.

Some 'idioterms' are just plain fanciful, descriptions obviously applied in sheer desperation at the apparent impossibility of the task. In this category come the 'fading but well-mannered old lady'—and who can forget James Thurber's 'naive domestic burgundy but I think you'll be amused by its presumption'? A more recent example is 'sexy', an increasingly common, but delightfully imprecise, tasting term.

Other sorts of terms, 'simile terms', are applied in a serious attempt to recall palpable objects which give rise to similar aromas: the fruits, flowers, vegetable, and mineral descriptors, for example.

Particularly common terms used to describe aroma, or flavour, include:

Buttery—rich, milky smell associated with MALOLACTIC FERMENTATION.
Cassis—like blackcurrants.
Corked—tainted by TCA.
Foxy—concentrated wild strawberry smell, associated with the American vine family *Vitis* LABRUSCA.
Fruity—intense impact of fruit flavours, sometimes a euphemism for slightly sweet.
Grapey—mixture of intensely aromatic and the aromas associated with MUSCAT grapes.
Grassy—smells of grass, leaves or other green

vegetative matter, usually applied to white wines.

Herbaceous—very like grassy but usually applied to red wines.

Leafy—can do duty for either grassy or herbaceous.

Lifted—noticeably but not necessarily excessively high in VOLATILE ACIDITY.

Mouldy—smells of mould; could be as a result of TCA.

Mousy—smells of mouse; generally a telltale sign of BRETTANOMYCES.

Oaky—pejorative term for a wine excessively marked by OAK.

Pepper—either green bell pepper, particularly in unripe CABERNET SAUVIGNON, or black pepper, notably in cooler-climate SYRAH, or white pepper in some GRÜNER VELTLINER.

Reduced—a taut, almost vegetal smell that is a sign that the wine's aroma has been suppressed by a shortage of oxygen.

Toasty—see TOAST.

Volatile—excessively high in VOLATILE ACIDITY.

See also FRUIT-DRIVEN, MATURE, MOUTHFEEL, SPRITZ, TEARS.

There are also 'derivative terms', which must once have been coined by an authority and continue to be widely used even though they are literally inaccurate. So many wine tasters have been taught to describe the powerful and characteristic smell of GEWÜRZTRAMINER as 'spicy', for example (perhaps because *Gewürz* is German for 'spice'), that this is the most common tasting term for the aroma, even though it does not smell like any particular spice at all (much more like lychees, in fact).

It will be of the 'simile terms' that a common tasting vocabulary is finally composed—although there is the obstacle of many different languages and national conventions to be overcome first.

See also AROMA WHEEL and LANGUAGE OF WINE.

Taurasi, the best-known high-quality wine of the CAMPANIA region (promoted to DOCG status in 1993) and arguably of the whole of southern Italy, is produced from the AGLIANICO grape in a zone north east of the city of Avellino. Although there are 158 producers and over 220 ha/540 acres in the Taurasi zone, the firm of Mastroberardino has been until recently virtually the only label on the market and still controls over 90 per cent of the total pro-

duction of Taurasi. DOCG regulations require three years of ageing, one of which must be in wood, and RISERVA bottlings must be aged for four years. Mastroberardino's single-vineyard bottling, Radice, comes exclusively from the subzone of Lapio. D.T.

Tavel, right-bank appellation for dry rosé in the southern RHÔNE whose historic reputation is still sufficient to justify a sometimes unwarranted price premium over other rosés, although Tavel at its best manages to combine refreshment with interest and concentration of flavour. Its superiority is often more likely to be in weight than in quality; the grapes can reach such levels of RIPENESS here that the appellation enforces a maximum ALCOHOLIC STRENGTH of 13.5 per cent.

The wine is always bone dry, but the Grenache and Cinsaut grapes give the blend a certain apparent sweetness. Chilling is essential, and the wine should be drunk young, as an alternative to red wine in hot weather. Grenache is the dominant grape variety, as throughout the southern Rhône, but may not exceed 60 per cent of the blend. Ch d'Acqueria is probably the best-known estate but this appellation is no hotbed of excitement.

taxation. Wine has attracted the attention of the taxman since ancient times. Its production, sale, and distribution have been so closely regulated by the authorities for one simple reason: revenue.

TBA, understandably common abbreviation for TROCKENBEERENAUSLESE.

TCA is the musty, unpleasant-smelling compound caused by the action of chlorine on cork bark or wood and associated with CORK TAINT and CONTAMINATION. Cork is by no means its only source, however. It has been found in bulk wine and is also recognized in the food industry as a common cause of taint. See CORK TAINT for more details of how it may develop.

Tchechoslovakia. See CZECH REPUBLIC.

tears (to rhyme with 'ears'), tasting term used to describe the behaviour of the surface liquid layer that is observable in a glass of relatively strong wine. The wine wets the inside of a clean glass and climbs up a few millimetres. At the upper edge of the thin layer on the inside wall, patches of the film thicken, become more droplike, and eventually roll back down the inside wall to the liquid surface. These traces of what look like particularly viscous droplets are also sometimes called 'legs', and give some indication of a wine's ALCOHOLIC STRENGTH.

It is often thought that tears are the result of GLYCEROL but in fact entirely unrelated phenomena are responsible. The small changes in VISCOSITY and index of refraction make the drop contrast with the liquid film on the glass surface. Tears are *not* a measure of viscosity.

Temecula, CALIFORNIA high DESERT wine region and AVA inland of the coastal mountain range 35 miles north of San Diego. Temecula is the viticultural aspect of a mixed-use residential and industrial development called Rancho California, begun in the late 1960s. Within 20 years, grape-growers began to find themselves squeezed between rows of residences. However, enough vines still exist to satisfy more than a dozen small wineries and one fairly good-sized one, Callaway. White varieties have succeeded best. Sauvignon Blanc ranks foremost among them, with Chardonnay not too far behind. The odd patch of Sémillon has also done well. Some growers are still making brave tries with, especially, Cabernet Sauvignon, Petite Sirah, and Zinfandel. Callaway has been the dominant force since the outset. The other firm of substance in the late 1990s was Thornton (formerly Culbertson) while Hart and Baily are the most artistically successful among a handful of smaller outfits.

B.C.C.

temperate, a broad class of climates, usually taken to include those with an annual average temperature of less than 20 °C/68 °F, but a warmest month average temperature greater than 10 °C/50 °F.

temperature is critically important to VITICULTURE, WINE-MAKING, wine MATURATION, and SERVING WINE, each in very different ways.

Climate, viticulture, and temperature

Temperature is widely considered the most important climatological factor affecting grapevines, although others such as SUNLIGHT, rainfall, humidity, and wind are also important.

Vines in cool climates start growing in the spring at about the time when the mean air temperature reaches 10 °C/ 50 °F. The rate of vine growth and development then increases to a maximum at about 22 to 25 °C, before falling away at even higher temperatures.

The risk of killing dormant vines in winter is another basis for defining climatic suitability for viticulture, being the main limiting factor in cool climates with marked CONTINENTALITY. Most fully dormant VINIFERA vines with well-matured canes can withstand air temperatures down to about −15 °C. The winter hardiness of RIESLING, for instance, is almost certainly one of the reasons for its historical success in Germany.

Air temperature is not the only kind governing vine growth and fruiting, however. Vines and soils are warmed by sunlight, which has major effects on grape-berry temperature, leaf temperature, grape composition, and hence wine quality. Some evidence now confirms the old belief that soil temperature is also important. The composition of the soil, its colour, drainage, and the duration and angle of exposure to the sun are all important factors in this respect.

Soil and air temperatures at particular stages of vine growth or during RIPENING can have specific effects. Winter and early spring temperatures govern BUDBREAK in spring. Air-temperature variability largely determines the risk of frost damage after budbreak. Temperatures around FLOWERING contribute to differences in FRUIT SET (by influencing COULURE, most notably) and to the FRUITFULNESS of the developing new buds which form shoots and bunches the following year. Both fruit set and bud fruitfulness are favoured by moderately high temperatures. Finally, both average temperature and temperature variability during ripening can have a direct influence on fruit and wine qualities.

J.G.

Wine-making and temperature

Temperature and TEMPERATURE CONTROL are of critical importance in making good-quality wine (although great wine may have been made fortuitously, long before the theory of temperature control was understood and temperature was deliberately manipulated). Temperature has direct effects on the rates of the biochemical reactions involved in FERMENTATION, and on the slower reactions involved in CLARIFICATION and STABILIZATION of wine. REFRIGERATION slows down the reactions of harmful bacteria, as well as the reactions involved in AGEING.

White wines are in general fermented at lower temperatures than red, partly in order to conserve the primary grape AROMAS, partly because there is NO MACERATION for which heat may be useful in encouraging the extraction of phenolics and other flavour compounds from the grape skins. White-wine temperatures between 12 and 17 °C are common for fermentation in the New World to yield fruity, well-balanced, light-coloured wines quickly enough that the fermentation vessel can be used two or three times in a season (although see also BARREL FERMENTATION). Old World white-wine fermentation temperatures are likely to be closer to 18 to 20 °C. The techniques of barrel fermentation and LEES CONTACT, such as are often applied to Chardonnay grapes, often involve slightly higher fermentation temperatures too, although the small size of the barrel (in comparison with the normal stainless-steel tank) helps to control temperature.

Temperature control is also extremely important during red-wine-making. The main concern here is the extraction of sufficient TANNINS, ANTHOCYANINS, and FLAVOUR COMPOUNDS from the grape skins. Fermentation temperatures between 25 and 30 °C generally produce the best flavour and extraction in red wines, provided other conditions are optimal. Temperatures higher than this threaten the yeast activity while temperatures below it inhibit extraction.   A.D.W.

Storage temperature

In the same way that it affects the reactions involved in wine-making, temperature becomes the governing factor in the much slower reactions in bottle that constitute wine AGEING. Interactions among the thousands of natural organic chemicals in the wine during this important phase of its maturation are directly affected by temperature. A reasonable cellar temperature for ageing wines to be drunk within one's own lifetime is somewhere between 10 and 15 °C.

Even lower down the temperature scale, wine freezes at a temperature below 0 °C that is roughly half its ALCOHOLIC STRENGTH, so usually somewhere between −4 and −8 °C. For this reason, in cool climates care should be taken to insulate wine stored in places such as garden sheds or garages.

Serving temperature

The temperature at which a wine is served has a profound effect on how it smells and tastes. Different styles of wine deserve to be served at different temperatures to enhance their good points and try to mask any faults. The following are some general observations, with suggested guidelines in italics.

The higher the temperature, the more easily the volatile FLAVOUR COMPOUNDS evaporate from the surface of wine in a glass. So, to maximize the impact of a wine's AROMA or BOUQUET, it is sensible to serve it relatively warm, say between 16 and 18 °C (at temperatures over 20 °C the ALCOHOL can begin to evaporate so markedly that it unbalances the wine). *Serve complex and mature wines relatively warm.*

Conversely, the lower the temperature, the fewer volatiles will evaporate and, at a serving temperature of about 8 °C, all but the most aromatic wines appear to have no smell whatsoever. *The gustatory faults of a low-quality wine can be masked by serving it very cool.*

The higher the temperature, the more sensitive is the PALATE to sweetness, so it makes sense to serve sweet wines which may not have quite enough ACIDITY to counterbalance the sweetness quite cool, say at about 12 °C. For the same reason, medium-dry wines served with savoury food will probably taste dry if served well chilled. *In general, chill sweet wines.*

The lower the temperature, the more sensitive the palate to TANNINS and BITTERNESS. *Tannic or bitter wines such as many Italian red wines and any young red designed for ageing should be served relatively warm.*

The effect of temperature on apparent acidity is more widely disputed by scientists, but it is generally observable that flabby wines can seem more refreshing if they are served cold, say at 10 °C. (This may be related to the effect of temperature on sweetness described above.) *To increase the refreshment factor of a wine, serve it cool.*

Temperature also has an observable effect on wines containing CARBON DIOXIDE. The higher the temperature, the more gas is released, which means that fizzy wines can be unpleasantly frothy at about 18 °C. *Sparkling and lightly sparkling wines are generally best served well chilled.* Since very few wines with a complex bouquet ever have any perceptible gas, this is no great limitation (those who make Australia's extraordinary Sparkling Shiraz claim it is best served at room temperature, but these sparkling wines are not particularly fizzy).

General rules are therefore:

Serve tannic red wines relatively warm, 15–18 °C.

Serve complex dry white wines relatively warm, 12–16 °C.

Serve soft, lighter red wines for refreshment at 10–12 °C.

Cool sweet, sparkling, flabby white and rosé wines, and those with any off-odour, to 6–10 °C.

Of course, wine tends to warm up to match the ambient temperature, so initial serving temperatures at the bottom end of these brackets are no bad thing, especially in warmer environments. See SERVING WINE.

See also TASTING for its different requirements of wine temperature.

temperature control during WINE-MAKING is crucially important, as outlined in TEMPERATURE. In cool wine regions or particularly cool years, a fermentation vessel may need to be heated to encourage alcoholic FERMENTATION, most easily by circulating warm water in equipment also designed to carry cooling cold water or, in smaller cellars, simply by closing doors and installing a heater or two. Some form of heating may also be required to encourage MALOLACTIC FERMENTATION.

Tempranillo is Spain's answer to Cabernet Sauvignon, the vine variety that puts the spine into a high proportion of Spain's most respected red wines. Its grapes are thick skinned and capable of making deep-coloured, long-lasting wines that are not, unusually for Spain, notably high in alcohol.

It thrives in the often harsh climate of Rioja's higher, more Atlantic-influenced zones Rioja Alta and Rioja Alavesa, where it constitutes up to 70 per cent of all vines planted.

Wine made from Tempranillo grown in relatively cool conditions can last well but the variety does not have a particularly strong flavour identity. Some find strawberries, others spice and leather, but determining a constant aroma attributable to the grape rather than the oak in which it was aged in all-Tempranillo wines can be a fruitless task. It is easy to see why such a high proportion of Tempranillo is blended with other juicier, more perfumed varieties.

In RIOJA, these are Garnacha (GRENACHE), Mazuelo (CARIGNAN), GRACIANO, and VIURA. In Penedès, where it is known as Ull de Llebre and Ojo de Liebre in Catalan and Spanish respectively, Tempranillo stiffens and darkens the local MONASTRELL. In Valdepeñas, where, as Cencibel, Tempranillo is the dominant black grape, white grapes are commonly added to soften the wine. The variety is ideally suited to the cool conditions of RIBERA DEL DUERO, where, as Tinto Fino, it is by far the principal grape variety, but the seasoning of varieties imported from Bordeaux is an ingredient of some importance in that high plateau's most famous wine VEGA SICILIA. Indeed, throughout Spain, blends of Tempranillo with Cabernet Sauvignon and/or Merlot are becoming prevalent, notably in Navarre.

Tempranillo is now grown in practically all red-wine regions. Its synonyms also include Tinto Madrid, Tinto de la Rioja, Tinta del Pais, and Tinta de Toro.

Tempranillo is one of the very few Spanish varieties to have been adopted to any real extent in Portugal, where it is known as (Tinta) Roriz and is a valued, if not particularly emphatic, ingredient in port blends. Also in the Douro, downstream of Ribera del Duero, it has demonstrated its strength for table wines as the major ingredient in FERREIRA'S famous red Barca Velha. Tinta Roriz, also known as Aragonêz in the Alentejo, is also grown increasingly in Dão.

As **Tempranilla** and making rather light, possibly over-irrigated reds, it has been important in Argentina's wine industry but lost ground to more marketable grape varieties in the late 1980s.

There were already nearly 2,500 ha in southern France in the late 1980s, most notably in the Aude. Tempranillo is almost certainly the true identity of the unfashionable low-acid variety known in California as Valdepeñas.

As vine-growers the world over search for new, recognizably high-quality products, cuttings labelled Tempranillo are in demand internationally and particularly in Australia and California.

tenuta, Italian word for a fairly substantial agricultural holding or estate (larger than, for example, the usual PODERE).

Teran, Terrano, names for subvarieties of the red FRIULI grape variety REFOSCO used, respectively, in SLOVENIA and the CARSO DOC in the extreme east of Friuli.

Terlano, or Terlaner in German, white wines from around the town of Terlano in the ALTO ADIGE.

Termeno Aromatico. See GEWÜRZTRAMINER.

Teroldego Rotaliano, the red Teroldego grape, makes deep-coloured, seriously lively, fruity wines with relatively low tannins for early drinking. It performs this trick almost exclusively on the Rotaliano plain in TRENTINO, north-east Italy.

Terra Alta, Spanish for 'high land', is the highest of the DO wine zones in Spanish CATALONIA. Its recent development parallels that of TARRAGONA, which adjoins Terra Alta to the east. As in Tarragona, growers are following the lead of PRIORAT, notably recovering and relaunching their formerly despised GARNACHA Blanca grapes.   R.J.M. & V. de la S.

terraces make work in vineyards planted across sloping land considerably easier, and can also help combat soil erosion. The world's most famous vineyard terraces are those of the PORT wine region of the DOURO valley in northern Portugal, although they are common in much of SWITZERLAND, the northern RHÔNE, and elsewhere.

An alternative to creating terraces is to plant vines up and down the hillsides, as in Germany and other parts of northern Europe. This practice avoids the expense of forming terraces but can lead to soil erosion and worker fatigue, and some slopes are too steep for tractors. See also HILLSIDE VINEYARDS.   R.E.S.

Terrano, synonym for Teran or REFOSCO.

terra rossa, red-brown loam or clay directly over well-drained limestone found typically in regions with a MEDITERRANEAN CLIMATE. Such soils are found in southern Europe (in Spain's La MANCHA for example), North Africa, and parts of Australia. The quality of many wines made from Cabernet Sauvignon and Shiraz grapes grown at Coonawarra in SOUTH AUSTRALIA is said to owe much to the terra rossa soils there.   M.J.E.

Terras do Sado, VINHO REGIONAL in southern PORTUGAL encompassing the SETÚBAL peninsula between the Tagus and Sado estuaries and a section of the Atlantic coast. The warm, maritime climate is particularly well suited to wine-making.

Although there are many individual growers, production is largely concentrated in the hands of two firms, José Maria da FONSECA Successores in Azeitão and J. P. Vinhos (known for its João Pires brand) based at Pinhal Novo. As a result of experiments that were partly inspired by the NEW WORLD, Terras do Sado produces a wide range of different wines

including Periquita, Pasmados, Quinta de Camarate, and Quinta da Bacalhôa.

The most important red grapes are the indigenous varieties, especially CASTELÃO FRANCÊS (commonly named Periquita), which is used for red, rosé, and sparkling wines. Imported varieties such as Cabernet Sauvignon and Merlot have made inroads. MUSCAT OF ALEXANDRIA (called Moscatel de Setúbal locally) is the most significant white variety, together with ARINTO and ESGANA CÃO. Chardonnay has also been grown successfully on the limestone Arrabida hills.

Within the Terras do Sado region is the small Palmela DOC.   R.J.M.

Terras Durienses, subregion of VINHO REGIONAL Trás-os-Montes which corresponds to the Douro region. See DOURO and TRÁS-OS-MONTES.

Terret is one of the Languedoc's oldest vine varieties and, like PINOT, has had plenty of time to mutate into different shades of grape which may even be found on the same plant. **Terret Gris** was at one time by far the most planted white wine variety in the Languedoc. It can be made into a relatively full-bodied but naturally crisp varietal white, but as a name Terret lacks the magic of internationally known varieties.

Terret Blanc is declining but allowed into the white wines of Minervois, Corbières, and, to a decreasing extent, Coteaux du Languedoc.

Terret Noir is the dark-berried version, which is grown on a much more limited scale but is one of the permitted varieties in red CHÂTEAUNEUF-DU-PAPE to which it can add useful structure and interest.

terroir, much-discussed term for the total natural environment of any viticultural site. No precise English equivalent exists for this quintessentially French term and concept. Discussion of terroir is central to philosophical and commercial differences between OLD WORLD and NEW WORLD approaches to wine.

Major components of terroir are soil and local topography, together with their interactions with each other and with MACROCLIMATE to determine MESOCLIMATE and vine MICROCLIMATE. The holistic combination of all these is held to give each site its own unique terroir, which is reflected in its wines more or less consistently from year to year, to some degree regardless of variations in methods of VITICULTURE and WINE-MAKING. Thus every small plot, and in generic terms every larger area, and ultimately region, may have distinctive wine-style characteristics which cannot be precisely duplicated elsewhere. The extent to which terroir effects are unique is, however, debatable, and of course commercially important, which makes the subject controversial.

Opinions have differed greatly on the reality and, if real, the importance of terroir in determining wine qualities. Major regional classifications of European vineyards have been largely based on the concepts of terroir. NEW WORLD viticulturists and researchers, on the other hand, for long tended to dismiss it as a product of mysticism and established commercial interest.

It can certainly be argued that modern improvements in vineyard and winery technology, by raising and unifying standards of wine quality, have to some extent obscured differences in both style and quality of wines that in the past were (sometimes wrongly) attributed to terroir in its true sense. But paradoxically, the same improvements can serve to unmask genuine differences due to terroir.

An international concept?

The question remains as to how far the French concept of terroir, with its primary emphasis on soil, is relevant to other regions and viticultural systems. An overriding influence of soil and its water relations can be easily enough understood in the Bordeaux environment, with its relatively flat topography and, as a consequence, few really major differences in mesoclimate. The situation is clearly different in areas such as Germany's MOSEL-SAAR-RUWER region at the cold limit of commercial viticulture. The topographic differences between individual sites decide whether grapes, in particular the high-quality varieties such as Riesling, will ripen fully at all. Topography and mesoclimate are inescapably major components of terroir.

The New World approach to vineyard design is now much more likely to take soil differences into account. Not long ago, New World vineyards were likely to be subdivided according to existing boundaries, shape, topography, or whim. Today it is increasingly common to allow a soil survey to determine choice of variety, rootstock, even trellis system—a concession to the wisdom of Old World experience.

Vine-training techniques and IRRIGATION can to a certain extent compensate for a site's disadvantages but it seems inconceivable that such techniques will ever totally eliminate the differences in wine qualities that have traditionally been ascribed to terroir.

To the extent that terroirs remain unique, and poorly understood, one can therefore hope that they will continue to help mould the infinite variety and individuality of the best wines, giving the special nuances of character that make wine such a fascinating study for wine-maker and consumer alike. *Vivent les différences!* J.G. & R.E.S.

tête de cuvée, term occasionally used for selected top bottlings. Similar to CRÈME DE TÊTE.

Texas, south-western state in the UNITED STATES, currently the country's fifth largest wine-producing state after California, New York, Washington, and Oregon.

Cabernet Sauvignon and Chardonnay lead in total number of acres planted; Chenin Blanc (making particularly successful wines here) and Sauvignon Blanc lead in tonnage. Muscat Canelli, produced in off-dry to sweet styles, is increasingly popular and the largest winner of awards. Grapes and wine are routinely imported from California, France, and occasionally from New Mexico to augment Texas production.

Texas has six designated AVAS, listed below in chronological order of creation.

Bell Mountain, Texas's first AVA (1986), won on behalf of the unique quality and concentration of Cabernet Sauvignon grown in this small area in north-east Gillespie County 15 miles north of Fredericksburg.

Fredericksburg, within Texas Hill Country, is known for good-quality Cabernet Sauvignon and Chardonnay.

Texas Hill Country, the largest AVA in the US, included 15,000 square miles but fewer than 800 planted acres of vineyard in the late 1990s. It produces mainly pleasant whites and relatively soft reds.

Escondido Valley, an area of about 50 square miles in Pecos County in the Trans-Pecos Region near Fort Stockton. This small AVA is the home of Ste Genevieve Wines, the state's biggest winery and grower of 40 per cent of the state's grapes.

Texas High Plains, the state's most consistent AVA so far, especially for Cabernet Sauvignon and Chardonnay.

Texas Davis Mountains, one-winery AVA

granted in 1998 producing very good Cabernet Sauvignon and a small quantity of Sauvignon Blanc. D.E.T.

Thailand, south-east Asian country where viticulture began in the 1960s on the low plain around the capital Bangkok and has flourished, despite the challenges involved in TROP-ICAL VITICULTURE.

In the 1980s, grapes from vineyards in Kanchanaburi province west of Bangkok became the raw material for a popular wine cooler (called Spy) produced by the Siam Winery Company. Recently, this company has experimented with more suitable wine-grape varieties for both red and white table wines. A more conventional wine-making operation called Chateau de Loei began in 1991 in the cooler Phurua Highland district in north-east Thailand. New varieties being trialled include Cabernet Sauvignon, Ruby Cabernet, Ugni Blanc, Sauvignon Blanc, Riesling, and Muscat. With imported wines facing duties and taxes of over 300 per cent and wine drinking firmly established in Thai culture during the 1990s, thanks to the King's promulgation of the HEALTH benefits of drinking (particularly red) wine, substantial additional growth in the local industry can be expected. D.G.

third growth. See the CLASSIFICATION of Bordeaux.

Thompson Seedless is the common CALI-FORNIA name for the seedless white grape variety SULTANA. Thompson Seedless is California's most planted grape variety by far, its 267,000 acres/108,000 ha in 1997 dwarfing total plantings of California's second most planted white grape Chardonnay. Almost all of California's Thompson Seedless is planted in the hot, dry SAN JOAQUIN VALLEY, with nearly two-thirds in Fresno County, the powerhouse of California raisin production, alone. In the 1970s, Thompson Seedless was particularly useful to the California wine industry in helping to bulk out inexpensive white JUG WINE blends at a time when demand far outstripped supply of premium white wine grape varieties. Today, however, it is used either for DRYING GRAPES, as material for distillation, or for GRAPE CONCENTRATE to sweeten bottled waters or cold tea drinks.

Thouarsais, Vins du, small southern Loire VDQS just west of Haut-POITOU producing this particularly light wine, mainly from Chenin

Blanc with a little Chardonnay although a little light red is produced too.

Tibouren could almost be said to be *the* Provençal grape variety. It has a long history and the ability to produce such quintessentially Provençal wines as earthy rosés with a genuine scent of the *garrigue*. Although it is planted in strictly limited quantities, Tibouren is cultivated by a number of the more quality- and history-conscious producers of Provence and some of them bottle it as a varietal rosé.

Tierra de Barros. Spanish wine zone. See EXTREMADURA.

Tierra de Medina, proposed name for the red, Tempranillo-based wines of the RUEDA zone in Spain.

Tignanello, seminal central Italian wine first produced by the house of ANTINORI in the early 1970s. See VINO DA TAVOLA and SUPERTUSCANS.

tinta, the Spanish and Portuguese feminine adjective for red.

Tinta Amarela, productive dark-skinned Portuguese grape variety grown in the DOURO for PORT. It can yield attractively scented wines but is not widely planted. It is a much more highly regarded variety in the more arid regions of the ALENTEJO and southern Portugal, where it produces rich, powerful dry reds and is known as Trincadeira Preta.

Tinta Barroca, relatively thick-skinned port grape variety which is best suited to higher or north-facing sites in Portugal's DOURO valley, where the sweet, gentle, fruity aroma of its wines is treasured. Tinta Barroca has been the most popular variety for fortified port-like wines in South Africa's vineyards and full-throttle, unfortified VARIETAL Tinta Barroca dry(ish) red (often spelt **Tinta Barocca**) is a South African speciality.

Tinta Carvalha, productive, widely planted Portuguese grape making thin, rather ordinary red wines.

Tinta de Toro, one of many names for TEM-PRANILLO.

Tinta Francisca, lesser red grape variety used in the production of PORT in Portugal's DOURO valley, where it is not regarded as one of the finest varieties. The wine produced can be notably sweet but is not particularly concentrated.

Tinta Miúda, 'small red one', Portuguese red wine grape grown mainly in ESTREMADURA and the RIBATEJO. The vine is low-yielding but can produce seductive and powerful wines. It is thought to be the same as the GRACIANO of Rioja, and MORRASTEL of the Languedoc.

Tinta Negra Mole, by far the most commonly planted vine variety on the island of MADEIRA. It yields relatively high quantities of sweet, pale-red wine which turns amber with the madeira production process and then yellow-green with age. A variety, which may be quite distinct, is also grown under the same name on the Portuguese mainland in the Algarve and, as Negramoll, in Spain.

Tinta Pinheira, Portuguese grape variety used for making red DÃO. May be RUFETE.

Tinta Roriz, Portuguese name for TEMPRANILLO. See RORIZ.

tinto, Spanish and Portuguese for red, so that *vino* (*vinho* in Portuguese) *tinto* is red wine (as opposed to the lighter red CLARETE produced in Spain).

Like TINTA, Tinto is also the first word of many Spanish and Portuguese names and synonyms for black grape varieties. TEMPRANILLO, for example, is known as Tinto Fino in Ribero del Duero, and as Tinto Madrid, Tinto de la Rioja, Tinto del Pais, and Tinto de Toro, to name but a few synonyms, in the rest of Spain.

Tinto Cão, meaning 'red dog', top-quality black grape variety for the production of PORT. Having almost disappeared from the vineyards of the DOURO valley in northern Portugal, it is being planted with greater enthusiasm since it was identified as one of the five finest port varieties, although it is not one of the deepest coloured. It is also grown in the DÃO region and has also been planted experimentally at the University of California at Davis.

Tinto del Pais, synonym for TEMPRANILLO, as is Tinto Fino in Ribera del Duero.

tirage, French for that part of the SPARKLING-WINE-MAKING process during which sugar and yeast are added to the blended base wines in order to provoke a second fermentation, thereby creating CARBON DIOXIDE gas. It is sometimes used to include the entire period during which the sparkling wine matures on the LEES of this second fermentation.

toast, given to a barrel when forming it over a heat source, is one of the processes in barrel-making that most obviously affect eventual wine flavour. The heat source toasts the inside of the barrel to a degree that varies according to the heat of the fire and the length of time the barrel is held over it. In general, the less a barrel is toasted, the more TANNINS and other wood characteristics will be leached into the wine by the ALCOHOL. Wine matured in lightly toasted barrels therefore tends to taste 'oaky', 'woody', or even 'vegetal', while wine matured in heavily toasted barrels is more likely to taste 'toasty' or 'spicy'.

Tocai, or Tocai Friulano, the most popular and widely planted white grape variety of the FRIULI region in north-east Italy, has no connection at all with Tokay d'Alsace (an Alsace synonym for the PINOT GRIGIO which grows alongside Tocai in Friuli), and is probably completely unrelated to the great TOKAJI wine of Hungary.

In Friuli, this productive, late-budding vine variety produces the staple wine of the region's taverns and trattorie. Given its wide diffusion, it is not easy to single out particular areas of superior quality, but the Tocai of Buttrio, Manzano, and Rosazzo in the COLLI ORIENTALI, and that of the areas between Cormons and Brazzano, between Brazzano and Dolegna, and Capriva di Friuli in the COLLIO DOC, can be considered classic subzones for fine Tocai. The wine itself is light in colour and body, floral in aroma, and has pronounced almond notes on the palate and on the nose. It is designed to be drunk young.

Tocai Rosso is also used as an Italian synonym for GRENACHE Noir.

A variety called Tocai Friulano is also cultivated to a limited extent in ARGENTINA.

D.T. & J.Ro.

Tokaji, great Hungarian sweet white wine from the Tokaj-Hegyalja region in the far north east of HUNGARY of such renown it is even mentioned in the national anthem. Wines from the village of Tokaj itself may be called **Tokaj**; all others must be called Tokaji, the 'i' denoting 'from the region of'. In English-speaking countries, it was long known as **Tokay** (which has also been the name of an extraordinary Australian fortified wine, LIQUEUR TOKAY). See also TOKAY D'ALSACE, once a synonym for PINOT GRIS.

According to Hungarian wine lore, the region's ability to produce unique sweet yet fragrant wines was discovered in 1650, and the vineyards of this region were some of the first to have been subject to CLASSIFICATION, in 1700. By the 18th century, this extraordinary wine had been introduced to the French court, and was subsequently introduced to the Russian imperial court by the Habsburgs.

During most of the 20th century, Tokaji languished. Under Soviet domination, quantity rather than quality was encouraged, although a surprising number of individual growers and wine-makers continued to uphold traditions. The wine writer Hugh Johnson and other private investors set up the Royal Tokaji Wine Company in 1989 and the early 1990s saw an influx from an unusually cosmopolitan range of investors, including AXA Millésimes and another insurance giant from France and VEGA SICILIA from Spain. In 1995, they created a new vineyard classification and are dedicated to restoring the image of this noble wine, with styles of wine varying quite widely in degrees of OXIDATION.

The Tokaj-Hegyalja region includes 28 villages, including Tokaj near Hungary's northernmost boundary, which has given its name to the appellation and the region as a whole. The most famous vineyards are in Tarcal, Mád, Tállya, and Tolcsva. The quality and character of the wine differs according to the situation of individual rows in the vineyard.

The warming effect of the Carpathian mountains, which shelter the region from the east, north, and west, results in a MACROCLIMATE of humid nights and long, warm autumns, which combination, together with the confluence of the Tisza and Bodrog rivers, favours the development of NOBLE ROT (rather like SAUTERNES). Noble rot does not develop every year, but natural sugar levels of 20 g/l at picking qualify the grapes as Aszú (pronounced 'ossoo') (the Hungarian equivalent of the Austrian term AUSBRUCH). Particularly fine vintages have been 1993, 1975, 1972, and 1937. The principal grape variety grown here on about two-thirds of the vineyard is the fiery FURMINT, blended with the indigenous HÁRSLEVELÜ and occasionally perfumed by small quantities of the golden mutant of MUSCAT BLANC À PETITS GRAINS, here sometimes called Muscat Lunel, Yellow Muscat, or Muskotályos.

In sections of the vineyard where half or more of the berries have turned into shrivelled Aszú grapes, the berries are picked individually. In parts where the proportion of Aszú berries is less than 50 per cent, such a laborious process is deemed unprofitable and the

mixture of grapes is harvested and called Szamorodni, or 'as it comes'. Thus the harvest yields three different basic ingredients: the selected Aszú grapes from which Aszú wine is made; the Szamorodni mixture from which Szamorodni wine is made (dry or sweet depending on sugar content); and grapes without any Aszú content from which either base wine for Tokaji Aszú or VARIETAL wines are made. These varietal wines may be labelled Tokaji Furmint, Tokaji Hárslevelü, or Tokaji Muscat and are bottled in regular 75-cl bottles instead of the long-necked 50-cl flask special to Tokaji.

The Aszú berries are stored until the base wine, the other component for the production of Tokaji Aszú, has been fermented. They are then kneaded to a sweet paste and added, in carefully controlled proportions, to lots of base wine specially selected for their superior levels of ALCOHOLIC STRENGTH, ACIDITY, and EXTRACT.

Base wine has traditionally been measured in the special small 136-l wooden casks made in nearby Gönc, while the Aszú paste was traditionally measured in *puttonyos*, special hods with a capacity of 20 to 25 kg (44–55 lbs). The higher the number of *puttonyos* added to a Gönc cask, the sweeter the wine. Today, Tokaji Aszú may be sold as 3, 4, 5, or 6 *puttonyos* according to certain minimum levels of RESIDUAL SUGAR and extract.

The paste is now made mechanically by gentle mashing of the Aszú berries. The base wine is poured over the paste, stirred, and left to macerate and extract the special Aszú properties from the paste for between 24 and 36 hours. After gentle pressing, this new wine is racked into the special Gönc casks in which it must be matured for at least three years.

Another important ingredient in the unique style of Tokaji is the curious network of low tunnels burrowed out of the hillsides in which the wine is matured. The walls of these cool, damp cellars are lined with a fungus, *Racodium cellare*, which forms film-forming yeasts very similar to, but colder and less active than, the FLOR of Jerez on the surface of the wine in the casks. Tokaji is distinguished by the flavour of its particular grapes, high levels of acidity and extract, and varying levels of residual sugar.

The dry Tokaji Szamorodni exported by the Tokaj Kereskéd'ház usually tastes like a rather flat SHERRY, although there is every reason to suppose that quality could improve substantially. A sweeter version was also made, but it lacks the natural vitality of true Tokaji Aszú, which tastes of botrytis, quince, and raisins in youth and takes on almond, walnut, chocolate, and bread flavours with age.

Two even sweeter forms of wine are made from *aszú* berries, in tiny quantities and only in the finest years. A 7-*puttonyos* Tokaji Aszú Esszencia contains between 180 and 230 g/l residual sugar whereas Esszencia itself may contain anything from 500 to 800 g/l. Tokaji Esszencia is a lightly alcoholic syrup made from that small quantity of FREE-RUN juice that results from the storage of Aszú grapes before they are mashed to a paste. It is so high in sugar and non-fermentable components that it ferments extremely slowly, over many years. The 1997 wine law sets a minimum of five years in cask. It is intended for blending purposes only—although it is inevitably the object of much curiosity on the part of the increasing numbers of foreign visitors to the region.

As one might perhaps expect of a combination of proud Hungarians and foreign investors, Tokaji has been a hotbed of vinopolitical ferment. The most highly regarded producers include Istvá Szepsy (a descendant of Maté Szepsi), Royal Tokaji Wine Company, Oremus, Disnók, Pajzos, and Bodrog-Várhegy.

Tokay, traditional name for the great TOKAJI wine of Hungary and Australian name for the MUSCADELLE grape. See LIQUEUR TOKAY.

Tokay d'Alsace, or simply Tokay, was for long the Alsace name for PINOT GRIS. To avoid confusion with the famous Hungarian wine of the same name (although the wine-makers of Alsace would probably be horrified if anyone found the distinctive aromas of Hungarian Tokay in their Pinot Gris), Europe's vinous lawmakers proposed **Tokay Pinot Gris** as an alternative, an intermediate stage towards the eventual elimination of the word Tokay from Alsace.

tonneau, traditional Bordeaux measure of wine volume, once a large wooden cask holding 900 l, or 252 imperial wine gallons, the equivalent of four BARRIQUES. The exact equivalent of 100 CASES of wine, it is still the measure in which the Bordeaux wine trade deals.

Tonnerrois, an up-and-coming wine area near CHABLIS around the town of Tonnerre.

topping up, the operation of refilling any sort of wooden container to replace wine lost

through EVAPORATION. The container should be kept full or nearly full lest the ubiquitous acetobacter use OXYGEN from the head space to start the process of transforming wine into vinegar. See also ULLAGE.

Torbato is a white-berried grape variety today most obviously associated with SARDINIA, where varietal dry whites are produced.

Torgiano, small hillside DOC zone between Perugia and Assisi in the central Italian region of UMBRIA. It has produced small quantities of Umbria's finest red wine since the 1960s. The production of bottled wine is almost entirely in the hands of the LUNGAROTTI family, whose efforts have demonstrated that the SANGIOVESE vine can yield important results outside TUSCANY. A significant amount of CANAIOLO grapes is used in the blend, but more important yet is the wine-making philosophy which emphasized a relatively brief period of CASK AGEING in large oval casks until the mid 1970s, and some BARREL MATURATION thereafter, followed by a lengthy period of BOTTLE AGEING—up to 10 years for the RISERVA, which was awarded DOCG status in 1990. The house philosophy resulted in stellar wines in 1975 and 1979, although it is still too early to judge whether the same quality level was maintained in the 1980s.   D.T.

Toro, Spanish red-wine zone in CASTILE AND LEÓN accorded DO status in 1987. At an ALTITUDE of between 600 and 750 m/2,000–2,800 ft, growing conditions are severe. The region's principal grape variety, Tinta de Toro, is a local variant of Rioja's TEMPRANILLO which has adapted to the climatic extremes of this part of Spain. The grapes need careful handling. Left to their own devices, they will easily ripen to a POTENTIAL ALCOHOL level of 16 per cent. Local regulations permit a maximum ALCOHOLIC STRENGTH of 15 per cent but the best wines usually have a strength of around 13.5 per cent. A small number of producers have fostered a move away from the heavy, bulk reds of recent times, notably Manuel Fariña, Vega Saúco, and Frutos Villar. Other permitted varieties are Garnacha and the white Verdejo and Malvasía.   R.J.M. & V. de la S.

Torontel, Chilean name for the aromatic white grape variety TORRONTÉS Riojano.

Torres, Miguel, SA, is Spain's largest family-owned producer of wine and Spanish brandy. The Torres family owns more than 900 ha/

2,200 acres of vineyards in PENEDÈS in north-east Spain, as well as properties in Chile and California.

Perhaps the most significant development in the history of Torres, founded in 1870, came in 1959, when Miguel A. Torres went to study in Dijon. This rapidly resulted in experimental plantings of vine varieties imported from France and Germany such as Cabernet Sauvignon, Chardonnay, Riesling, Gewürztraminer, and Sauvignon Blanc. A modern laboratory was established, temperature-controlled stainless-steel fermentation vessels were installed, and red wines were bottled after just 18 months' BARREL MATURATION in cool cellars hewn out of the hillside. All of these techniques, and a host of other innovations, were then quite unknown elsewhere in Spain.

About a third of all Spanish wine produced by Torres is exported, notably to Sweden, Denmark, and the USA.

On the death of his father in 1991, Miguel A. Torres became president of the company with particular responsibilities for wine-making. He is also one of Spain's most prolific wine writers, and runs the 220-ha estate near Curicó in CHILE which he established in 1978. His sister Marimar is a food writer based in San Francisco and manages a 56-ha vineyard in SONOMA County's Green River Valley. In 1998, the Spanish company embarked on a JOINT VENTURE in China.

Torres Vedras, a DOC in western Portugal. See ESTREMADURA.

Torrontés, and Toróntes, Torontel, white grape variety or varieties gaining increasing recognition in the Spanish-speaking world.

Torrontés is the name of a distinctively flavoured indigenous variety in GALICIA in north-west Spain that is particularly common in the white wines of RIBEIRO. Within Spain, the variety is occasionally found around Cordoba.

Much more important, however, are several white grape varieties known as Torrontés in ARGENTINA, which some regard as the Argentine white wine variety with the greatest potential. Carefully vinified, Torrontés can produce wines that are light in body, high in acidity, and intriguingly aromatic in a way reminiscent of but not identical to MUSCAT, although much is also used for blending.

Torrontés Riojano is the most common Argentine subvariety and takes its name from the northern province of La Rioja, where it is by far the most planted single vine variety. This is the variety known as TORONTEL in Chile. Torrontés Sanjuanino, more commonly associated with the province of San Juan in Argentina, is rather less widely planted and less aromatic. In Chile, it is known as MOSCATEL DE AUSTRIA.

Toscana, important central Italian region known in English as TUSCANY.

Toul, Côtes de, in the far north east of France, remains, with the even more northerly French wine region on the MOSELLE, as a reminder of what was once a flourishing Lorraine wine industry. Today, Gamay is the most planted vine variety and is the usual ingredient in the local pale-pink speciality VIN GRIS and such Pinot Noir as remains is reserved for Toul's relatively light reds. AUXERROIS is the most successful variety for dry whites.

Touraine, the most important Loire region, centred on the town of Tours. This is 'the garden of France', and Loire châteaux country *par excellence*.

Touraine's most famous wines are the still red wines from the individual appellations of BOURGUEIL, CHINON, and St-Nicolas-de-Bourgueil and its still and sparkling, dry to sweet whites from VOUVRAY and MONTLOUIS.

Wines called simply Touraine come from a much larger zone that extends from SAUMUR in the west as far as the city of Blois in the east. Viticulture is concentrated on the steep banks of the Loire and its tributary the Cher east of Tours. The climate of the region also shows considerable variation, with that of the most eastern vineyards being distinctly CONTINENTAL and affected by seriously cold winters, while vineyards at the western extreme are tempered by the influence of the Atlantic.

If soil and climate vary considerably throughout Touraine, there is an enormous range of grape varieties too. White Touraine may be made from any combination of Chenin Blanc, Arbois, Sauvignon Blanc, and Chardonnay grapes, so long as Chardonnay constitutes no more than 20 per cent of the blend. A wine labelled Sauvignon de Touraine offers a very much clearer proposition to the potential buyer than one labelled simply Touraine.

Touraine Rouge, made in about the same quantity as Touraine Blanc, may be made from an even less specific blend, incorporating any or all of Cabernet Franc, Cabernet Sauvignon, Cot (Malbec), Pinot Noir, Meunier, Pinot Gris, Gamay, Pineau d'Aunis, and Grolleau.

In very general terms, Sauvignon and Gamay tend to be grown in the far east of the region, and are, respectively, the most common white and red varieties used for the Touraine appellation. From a conscientious producer, white Touraine can provide a less expensive alternative to the Loire's more famous Sauvignons produced in appellations such as SANCERRE and POUILLY-FUMÉ and these less expensive Touraine wines can be particularly successful in riper vintages such as 1996. Red Touraine is usually a distinctly leaner variant on the BEAUJOLAIS theme. Some producers label more substantial blended reds, made from Gamay, Cabernet, and Cot, Touraine Tradition, although the appellation Touraine-Villages has been proposed instead. Some white and red Touraine is, confusingly, made in quite a different style, however, most commonly but not necessarily from Chenin Blanc and Cabernet Franc grapes.

Small quantities of **Touraine Mousseux** and large quantities of **Touraine Primeur** (see PRIMEUR) are made but the region also has three subappellations in areas to add their name to that of Touraine, although they are of declining importance.

Touraine-Amboise produces mainly red wines from Gamay, Cabernet Franc, and Cot, the last of which can yield some wines with sufficient stuffing to be worth ageing. The appellation's white wines, dry to medium dry depending on the year, are made exclusively from the long-lived Chenin Blanc.

Touraine-Azay-le-Rideau produces roughly equal quantities of crisp whites from Chenin Blanc and light rosés mainly from Grolleau, which can be considerably more sprightly than the Rosé d'Anjou with which the variety is more readily associated.

In **Touraine-Mesland**, Gamay plus some Cabernet Franc and Cot is responsible for durable reds and rosés, and Chenin Blanc, together with some Chardonnay and Sauvignon, for dry whites. Touraine-Mesland's pale-pink VIN GRIS enjoys a certain reputation.

See also LOIRE.

Tourbat is the ROUSSILLON name for Sardinia's white grape variety TORBATO. It is alternatively known as Malvoisie du Roussillon and is one of the many varieties allowed into the

several VINS DOUX NATURELS of the region and Côtes du Roussillon whites.

Touriga is used as an Australian synonym for TOURIGA NACIONAL, but the Touriga of California is probably TOURIGA FRANCESA.

Touriga Francesa, robust and fine vine variety for red port that is widely grown in Portugal's DOURO valley and the TRÁS-OS-MONTES wine region. It is classified as one of the best port varieties, although the wine it produces is not as concentrated as that of TOURIGA NACIONAL. Its wines are notable for their perfume and persistent fruit. It should not be confused with the much less distinguished Portuguese variety TINTA FRANCISCA.

Touriga Nacional, the most revered vine variety for port and, increasingly, for fine dry reds. It produces small quantities of very small berries in the DOURO valley and, increasingly, the Portuguese DÃO region which result in deep-coloured, very tannic, concentrated wines. Touriga Nacional should constitute at least 20 per cent of all red Dão, although the wine's suitability as a vintage port ingredient is more obvious than as a red table wine. It has been identified as particularly suitable for the BAIRRADA region too. The variety is also planted to a limited extent in Australia, where it is used to add finesse to fortified wines.

tourism. Wine-related tourism has become increasingly important. For many centuries, not even wine merchants travelled, but today many members of the general public deliberately make forays to explore a wine region or regions. This is partly a reflection of the increased interest in both wine and foreign travel generally, but also because most wine regions and many producers' premises are attractive places. And then there is the possibility of TASTING, and buying wines direct from the source, which may involve keen prices and/or acquiring rarities.

Some tour operators and travel agents specialize in wine tourism, and the number of wine regions without their own special wine route or winery trail is decreasing rapidly.

trade, wine. Wine is better known for its sociability than its profitability. What is needed to make a small fortune in the wine business is said to be a large fortune. The wine trade is considerably more amusing, however, than many others. It routinely involves immersion in an often delicious product, travel to some of the more beautiful corners of the world (see TOURISM), and provides widely admired expertise.

One of the attractions of the wine trade is the people. It has for long attracted a wide range of individualists who, if they were not interesting and amusing before they or their visitors have tasted their wares, seem so afterwards. Producers and merchants alike tend to be generous, and to appreciate the fact that it is difficult to sell or buy wine without tasting and sharing it.

Apprenticeship is probably the easiest route into the wine trade, although some form of specialist EDUCATIONAL qualification can help too. The general areas in which full-time employment may be found include vineyard management, wine-making and quality control, sales and marketing, wholesaling, retailing, and, the job with potentially the most power and perks, buying.

tradition, an extremely important ingredient in viticulture and wine-making in many Old World regions. A significant proportion of older small-scale producers in regions such as Burgundy and the Rhône, for example, do things in the vineyard and cellar precisely because their fathers did, even if their own children are likely to have been exposed to science through some sort of formal training. These graduates may understand the reasons for some of these supposedly traditional methods better than their parents, but they do not necessarily change them.

traditional method, official European Union term for the most painstaking way of making wine sparkle. See SPARKLING-WINE-MAKING.

Trajadura, early-ripening white grape variety used to add body and a certain citrus character to Portugal's VINHO VERDE if it is picked sufficiently early. It is known as TREIXADURA across the Spanish border in GALICIA. It is often blended with LOUREIRO and sometimes with ALVARINHO.

Traminer, the less aromatic, paler-skinned progenitor of the pink-skinned white wine grape variety GEWÜRZTRAMINER. It has been grown, for example, in Moravia in what was Czechoslovakia, where it is also known as Prinç. The name derives from the town of Tramin, or Termeno, in the ALTO ADIGE. In countries as different as Germany, Italy, Austria, Romania, much of the CIS, and Australia, however, Traminer is also used as a synonym for Gewürztraminer, under which name more details can be found.

transfer method, SPARKLING-WINE-MAKING process involving provoking a second fermentation in bottle and then transferring its contents into a tank, where the wine is separated from the deposit.

transport of wine has changed considerably over the ages but a wide variety of different methods, from tanker to a bottle sent by mail, are still used. Today wine is generally transported by road and sea.

For centuries, the transport of wine meant bulk transport, and the most common container used for transporting wine was the barrel. In the latter half of the 20th century, however, container shipment in bulk tankers became the norm, although, as an increasing proportion of wine is bottled not just in its country or region of origin but actually at the winery, the most common container for transport today is probably the BOTTLE. Barrels may be an awkward shape, but bottles are breakable, and pilferage of bottled wine is considerably easier than stealing bulk wine. Wine transport across national frontiers or state lines can involve the additional problems associated with any product subject to TAXATION.

From the consumer's point of view, the most important aspect of the transport of wine is TEMPERATURE. If wine that has not been subject to considerable STABILIZATION, which includes most fine wine, is exposed to high temperatures, it may well deteriorate considerably. Conscientious producers try to avoid shipping wine in high summer, while scrupulous wholesalers insist that insulated containers are used for shipments in hot weather and/or through the Tropics.

In the late 1990s, the transport of wine, and direct shipment in particular, became even more legally restricted in the UNITED STATES.

Trás-os-Montes, VINHO REGIONAL in northeast Portugal. Meaning 'behind the mountains', Trás-os-Montes is locked in by high mountains on one side and the Spanish frontier on the other.

Wine is an important commodity in Trás-os-Montes, which includes the northern half of the PORT wine region. The high vineyards here, north of the DOURO valley, also supply wine for

MATEUS Rosé and a number of imitative brands. Table (unfortified) wines from the Douro region, not entitled to the Douro DOC because of the grape varieties used, are entitled to their own Vinho Regional: Trás-os-Montes—Terras Durienses. Three IPR regions have recently been designated in Trás-os-Montes (Chaves, Valpaços, and Planalto-Mirandes) but these wines are rarely seen outside northern Portugal.

R.J.M.

Trbljan, relatively important light-berried vine variety grown particularly on the coast of CROATIA just north of Zadar. The grape is also sometimes called Kuč.

Trebbiano, most common name for the undistinguished Ugni Blanc in Italy, where it is by far the most planted white grape variety. The word Trebbiano in a wine name almost invariably signals something light, white, crisp, and uninspiring. Ugni Blanc's most common use, as base wine for brandy, provides a clue to the character of the wine produced by Trebbiano. It is, like most copiously produced wines, low in extract and character, relatively low in alcohol, but usefully high in acidity.

In France, the variety is the country's most important white vine. See UGNI BLANC for details of Trebbiano in France.

Trebbiano is cited in more DOC regulations than any other single variety (about 80) and may well account for more than a third of Italy's entire DOC white-wine production. The variety is planted all over Italy (with the exception of the cool far north), to the extent that it is likely that the great majority of basic *vino bianco* will contain at least some of the variety, if only to add acidity and volume. Its stronghold, however, is central Italy. **Trebbiano Toscano**, covering almost 60,000 ha/148,000 acres, was Italy's third most planted vine variety in 1990, while there were more than 20,000 ha of **Trebbiano Romagnolo**, nearly 12,000 ha of **Trebbiano d'Abruzzo**, nearly 5,000 ha of **Trebbiano Giallo**, and more than 2,000 ha of **Trebbiano di Soave**.

TREBBIANO DI ROMAGNA dominates white-wine production in Emilia-Romagna, made chiefly from Trebbiano Romagnolo or the almost amber-berried Trebbiano della Fiamma. Some idea of Trebbiano's ubiquity is given by listing just some of the wines in which it is an ingredient: VERDICCHIO, ORVIETO, FRASCATI, together with, in the north, SOAVE from Trebbiano di Soave and LUGANA from Trebbiano

di Lugana. Between Tuscany and Rome, in UMBRIA, the variety can be known as Procanico. Only the fiercely varietal-conscious north-eastern corner of Italy is virtually free of this bland ballast.

Trebbiano's malign influence was most noticeable in central TUSCANY in much of the 20th century, however, where Trebbiano was so well entrenched that CHIANTI and therefore VINO NOBILE DI MONTEPULCIANO laws sanctioned its inclusion in this red wine, thereby diluting its quality as well as its colour and damaging its reputation. Trebbiano is now very much an optional ingredient, however, which is increasingly spurned by the quality-conscious red-wine producers of Tuscany.

The sea of Trebbiano still produced in Tuscany is being diverted into cool-vinified innocuous dry whites such as GALESTRO.

Perhaps Italy's most exciting Trebbiano, Valentini's Trebbiano d'Abruzzo (see ABRUZZI), is not a Trebbiano at all but is made from BOMBINO BIANCO. Nevertheless, there was a dramatic increase in plantings of a variety known as Trebbiano d'Abruzzo in the 1980s.

Trebbiano has also managed to infiltrate Portugal's fiercely nationalistic vineyards, as Thalia, and is widely planted in BULGARIA and in parts of GREECE and RUSSIA. As well as being used for MEXICO's important brandy production, Trebbiano is well entrenched in Brazil and Uruguay.

South Africa also calls its relatively limited plantings Ugni Blanc but relies more on COLOMBARD for cheap, tart blending material, as does California, whose few remaining hundred acres of the vine called 'St-Emilion' there are exclusively in the Central Valley, although interesting VARIETAL versions are not entirely unknown. Australia, where Colombard is also more important, has about 800 ha of Trebbiano, used as a usefully tart ingredient in basic blended whites.

The influence of Trebbiano/Ugni Blanc will surely decline as wine drinkers seek flavour with increasing determination.

Trebbiano di Romagna, abundant VARIETAL central Italian dry white made from a grape variety which differs little from the TREBBIANO of Tuscany. Most Trebbiano di Romagna is, at best, suitable for a picnic. D.T.

Treixadura, Galician name for Portugal's scented, delicate white TRAJADURA and treated in much the same way. This is the main grape of Ribeiro and may be blended with Galician Torrontés and Lado. It is also grown in the Rías Baixas region, where it is often blended with Albariño and possibly LOUREIRA.

Trentino, the southern and principally Italian-speaking half of Italy's central Alpine region of TRENTINO-ALTO ADIGE. Trento is the regional capital. Viticulture is centred on the valley of the Adige and the hills immediately to the east and west of the river. Although the region is far to Italy's north, the climate is not necessarily cool, as heat rapidly builds up at lower altitudes during the summer months. More than 70 per cent of the vineyards are registered for DOC wine production, a proportion second only to the ALTO ADIGE in Italy.

The DOC structure consists of one large regional DOC, supplemented by the various VARIETAL wines, together with five more or less geographically specific supplementary DOC zones. The Sorni DOC is minuscule. Teroldego Rotaliano suggests that the Teroldego grape seems to have found its ideal home on the Rotaliano plain, where the Foradori winery has demonstrated Teroldego's potential for serious, concentrated wines. The DOC zone of Caldaro, on both sides of Lake Caldaro, is shared with the Alto Adige and SCHIAVA is the dominant grape. Valdadige, a long stretch of the Adige river, is the DOC for predominantly a red blend of Schiava and LAMBRUSCO and a white blend of various INTERNATIONAL VARIETIES (Pinot Blanc, Pinot Gris, Müller-Thurgau, Chardonnay, and Welschriesling). Casteller is a DOC zone on both sides of the border with the province of Verona for a red blend of Schiava, Merlot, and Lambrusco.

Trentino's most important wines, however (with the exception of the 5 million bottles of Chardonnay-based SPARKLING WINES produced every year), are unquestionably the 17 varietal wines of the Trentino DOC. Chardonnay is the most important white, followed by Müller-Thurgau, Pinot Gris, and Pinot Blanc; Cabernet, Merlot, MARZEMINO, LAGREIN, and Pinot Noir are the leading reds. Yields are too generous to give wines of superior quality, but Trentino's greatest handicap is the market-driven spirit of wine production, which has planted and vinified according to consumer tastes of the moment without much regard for specific characteristics of soil and MESOCLIMATE.

Significant historical traditions matching individual varieties and individual subzones do exist none the less: Müller-Thurgau in Faedo and the Val di Cembra; Cabernet in the Vallagarina and between Pressano and Lavis; Lagrein in the Campo Rotaliano and in Rovereto della Luna; NOSIOLA in Lavis, Faedo, and the Valle dei Laghi; Pinot Noir in Civezzano and in the hills to the north of Trento; Chardonnay in vineyards over 400 m/1,300 ft in altitude. High-level Chardonnay, Müller-Thurgau, Cabernet and Merlot, and Pinot Noir, frequently treated to BARREL MATURATION, began to emerge from these specific subzones in the 1980s, indicating an important potential for high-quality wines which has yet to be tapped. CO-OPERATIVES market nearly three-quarters of the total production.   D.T.

Trentino-Alto Adige, northern Italian region through which flows the Adige river (called Etsch by the region's many German speakers). It is made up of the ALTO ADIGE, or the South Tyrol, in the north and TRENTINO in the south.

Trepat, indigenous red wine grape of northeast Spain, particularly in Conca de Barberá and Costers del Segre, used mainly for light rosés.

Tressallier is a white grape variety grown in the Allier *département* notably for ST-POURÇAIN. It is certainly traditional there, but not unanimously acclaimed nowadays.

Tressot, Burgundian name for the Jura's TROUSSEAU vine.

tri, French for a sorting process, notably postal but, in a wine-making context, it means the selection of suitable grapes. This usually takes the form of a TRIAGE on reception of the grapes at the winery or cellar but in the production of BOTRYTIZED wines a *tri*, or several *tris*, is made in the vineyard whereby the pickers proceed along the rows selecting only those clusters, and occasionally only those berries, that have been successfully attacked by NOBLE ROT. In a difficult year such as 1972, as many as 11 *tris* might be made at Ch d'YQUEM, and in the end no SAUTERNES carrying that illustrious name was produced.

triage is the French and common winemaking term for the sorting of grapes according to quality prior to wine-making. Freshly picked bunches of grapes are typically spread on a sorting table or slowly moving belt so that substandard examples can be plucked off and thrown away. In the production of BOTRYTIZED sweet white wines, all but the grapes uniformly infected with NOBLE ROT are rejected. Such sorting is a labour-intensive process that requires training. Its expense can be justified only for relatively fine wines.   A.D.W.

Tricastin, Coteaux du, extensive appellation on the eastern fringes of the southern RHÔNE for mainly red and rosé wines with a very small amount of white. Although the climate here is definitively MEDITERRANEAN, the higher ALTITUDES and more exposed terrain produce rather lighter wines than those of Côtes du Rhône which they resemble. The best wine comes from sheltered, south-facing slopes, but acidity levels are usually noticeable beneath the superficial warmth of the southern vine variety perfume. The appellation has benefited from standard-bearers such as Domaine Tour d'Élyssas and Domaine de Grangeneuve.

Grenache, Cinsaut, and Syrah are the principal vine varieties grown, although up to 20 per cent of Carignan, and of the permitted white varieties Grenache Blanc, Clairette, Picpoul, Bourboulenc, Ugni Blanc, Marsanne, Roussanne, and Viognier, may also be included.

The wines are similar to those of the much larger Côtes du VENTOUX appellation to the immediate south, which was also promoted to full APPELLATION CONTRÔLÉE status in 1973.

trichloroanisole. See TCA.

Trimbach, family-run wine producer based at Ribeauvillé in ALSACE. The company was established in 1626. Today it is particularly successful in the United States and its wines are characterized by very fine fruit and high acidity. Even its Sylvaner can stand many years' BOTTLE AGEING. Two of its most famous bottlings are Rieslings: the rare and long-lived Clos Ste-Hune (in fact from the Alsace Grand Cru Rosacker) and Cuvée Frédéric Émile.

trimming, the vineyard operation of removing unwanted shoot growth which can cause SHADING and can hinder SPRAYING.

Trincadeira das Pratas, traditional Portuguese white grape grown mainly in Estremadura, the Ribatejo, and Terras do Sado. It can, but does not always, produce delicate, perfumed dry white wines.

Trincadeira Preta, name for the fine red wine grape TINTA AMARELA in the southern Portuguese region of Alentejo, where it shows great potential.

Triomphe (d'Alsace), HYBRID bred in Alsace from Knipperlé and a *riparia-rupestris* American vine. The wine produced, however deep coloured, tastes FOXY. The vine is responsible for some English reds.

trocken, German for 'dry', and an emotive term when applied to the wines of GERMANY. Wine drinkers within Germany fell for this style in the early 1980s, years ahead of foreigners, who are slowly being won over by the products of particularly ripe vintages.

The term can be applied to a still wine with a maximum of 4 g/l RESIDUAL SUGAR, or up to 9 g/l if the total ACIDITY is less than the residual sugar by no more than 2 g/l (9 g/l residual sugar and total acidity not less than 7 g/l). The proportion of German still wine that is described as trocken varies considerably between regions (with a higher proportion in southern regions) but it averages about 28 per cent (from just 16 per cent in the mid 1990s).

In Austria, trocken signifies a maximum residual sugar level of under 9 g/l.

See also HALBTROCKEN and SWEETNESS.

Trockenbeerenauslese, sometimes known as TBA, the ripest and rarest of the Prädikats in the QMP quality-wine category defined by the GERMAN WINE LAW. *Trockenbeeren* refers to grapes *(Beeren)* shrivelled by NOBLE ROT. Many VINTAGES yield no Trockenbeerenauslese wine at all in Germany (although it is more frequent in Austria). Even riper grapes and higher MUST WEIGHTS are needed for this ultra-rich, usually deep-golden-orange, usually heavily BOTRYTIZED wine than for BEERENAUSLESE. An even higher minimum POTENTIAL ALCOHOL is required than for SAUTERNES, generally produced in a much warmer climate. It is inevitable therefore that these rarities command exceptionally high PRICES, which go some way to compensating the producer for the many passages (see TRI) through the vineyard, the risk of losing all the grapes to grey rot or rain, and the difficulty of vinifying such sticky juice. There has been a tendency to produce slightly less sweet Trockenbeerenauslesen than was the norm in the 1970s, while EISWEIN production has become more common. See also AUSTRIA.

Trollinger, or Blauer Trollinger, is the most common German name for the distinctly ordinary black grape variety known as SCHIAVA in Italy, VERNATSCH in the Tyrol, and Black Hamburg by many who grow and buy TABLE GRAPES. In Germany, it is grown almost exclusively in WÜRTTEMBERG. To suit local tastes (and most Trollinger is consumed within Württemberg and within the year), the wines are often relatively sweet and are rarely worth serious study.

trophy wines, small group of wines more expensive than any others and becoming more so under sustained attack from the world's best-heeled COLLECTORS, INVESTORS, and drinkers. A Bordeaux FIRST GROWTH from a fine VINTAGE is a trophy wine, as is virtually every bottle produced by one of the MICROCHÂTEAUX, Chx d'YQUEM and PÉTRUS. Most wines from DOMAINE DE LA ROMANÉE-CONTI and Domaine LEROY count, as do the single-vineyard bottlings of GUIGAL, most PRESTIGE CUVÉES from Champagne, TROCKENBEERENAUSLESEN from top German growers and Austrians such as Kracher, VEGA SICILIA, L'Ermita of PRIORAT, Dominio de Pingus, and the most lauded SUPERTUSCANS and GAJA bottlings. New World trophy wines include PENFOLDS Grange, Clarendon Hills Astralis, and all the CALIFORNIA CULT wines. The key to identifying trophy wines is their international fame and, especially, PRICE. Their prices rose markedly in the late 1990s because of the dramatic increase in the number of potential buyers of these wines, all made in strictly limited quantities, prepared to acquire them at any price.

tropical viticulture. Although the grapevine is regarded by many as a strictly temperate plant, it is now increasingly grown in the tropics, defined approximately as the region bordered by the tropics of Cancer and Capricorn. Countries in which some grapes are cultivated in tropical conditions include AUSTRALIA, Colombia, BOLIVIA, BRAZIL, ECUADOR, INDIA, INDONESIA, KENYA, Laos, MEXICO, Nigeria, the Philippines, Sri Lanka, THAILAND, VENEZUELA, and VIETNAM.

The majority of tropical grapes are consumed as TABLE GRAPES. However, increasing amounts are used as DRYING GRAPES, especially in India, or fermented into wine.   J.V.P.

Trousseau is the name of one of the two principal dark grape varieties indigenous to the JURA, and is more robust and deeply coloured than POULSARD although it is in serious decline as Pinot Noir, and Chardonnay, become ever

more popular. Trousseau is said to be the same as Portugal's BASTARDO, and a variety for long called Cabernet Gros and occasionally, erroneously, Touriga in Australia. In both of these countries it is commonly used for sweet, dessert wines.

The lighter-berried mutation **Trousseau Gris** may well be the variety called Gray Riesling in CALIFORNIA.

Tsaoussi, white grape speciality of the Greek island of Cephalonia, where it may be blended with the more distinctive ROBOLA.

Tsolikauri, relatively important white wine grape of GEORGIA, although only about a tenth as widely planted there as the popular RKATSITELI.

Tumbarumba, relatively new Australian wine region. See NEW SOUTH WALES.

Tunisia, North African country which in some years produces more wine than MOROCCO and almost as much as ALGERIA. Total vineyard area has fallen, and just over half is dedicated to wine production as opposed to TABLE GRAPES.

Main grape varieties planted are Carignan, Grenache, Clairette, Beldi, and Cinsaut and, in more limited quantity, Cabernet Sauvignon, Mourvèdre, and Syrah. Most of the wines produced are either full-bodied reds or light rosés, although some dry Muscat of Alexandria is also produced.

Turkey, eastern Mediterranean country that is the world's fourth most important grower of grapes, only a very small proportion of which is made into wine.

The grape-growing regions include considerable climatic variation. The Thrace region in the hinterland of Istanbul is very much part of Europe and shares the warm coastal climate of its neighbours the far south west of BULGARIA and the extreme north east of GREECE. Responsible for 40 per cent of Turkish wine production, the region grows such European grape varieties as Gamay, Sémillon, Clairette, Pinot Noir, and Riesling as well as such Turkish varieties as Yapincak and Papazkarasi. European varieties such as Sémillon, Grenache, and Carignan are also grown on the Aegean coast, which accounts for about 20 per cent of Turkey's wine production.

Anatolia, which produces the remainder of Turkish wine, has the most demanding climate, with severe winters and very hot and sunny summers. Wine production is dominated by the state-owned Tekel, together with two big private companies Kavaklidere and Doluca.

Wine production is divided fairly equally between often-oxidized whites and relatively alcoholic reds with a few rosés.

Turkmenistan, central Asian republic of the CIS that sprawls between the Caspian Sea, UZBEKISTAN, Afghanistan, and Iran. A minor wine producer, it specializes in TABLE GRAPES and raisins. The vast Karakumy desert occupies a large part of this hot, dry country.

The vineyards are in the Ashkhabad region (70 per cent of the total grape area), the Mary region (15 per cent), and the Chardzhou region. Only 21 grape varieties were cultivated on a commercial scale in the early 1990s, with eight wine varieties such as Terbash, Tara Uzüm Ashkhabadski, RIESLING, SAPERAVI, Kizil Sapak, and Bayan Shirey. V.R.

Tursan, small VDQS in the Landes in SOUTH WEST FRANCE producing wine made from mainly red, mainly TANNAT grapes, mostly from the CO-OPERATIVE and sold locally. The white version is of more interest and is virtually a one-producer wine, but what a producer: three-star chef Michel Guérard of Eugénie-lès-Bains, who lavishes such care as BARREL MATURATION on the local white grape variety, the BAROQUE, under which are more details.

Tuscany, or Toscana in Italian, the most important region in central ITALY. Today Tuscany is at the centre neither of Italy's economic life nor of its political life, but it is the region which formed Italy's language, its literature, and its art, and has thus assumed a central place in the country's culture and self-image.

Geography and vine varieties
The Tuscan countryside is famously undulating. A full 68 per cent of the region is officially classified as hilly and HILLSIDE VINEYARDS supply the vast majority of the better-quality wines.

SANGIOVESE has been, until recently, virtually synonymous with fine wine in Tuscany and, although the variety is widely planted throughout central Italy, the Tuscan climate and soils have thus far given incomparable results for this variety. The Arno river marks the northern border for cultivation of Sangiovese in Tuscany, with only the small DOC zones of CARMIGNANO and MONTECARLO near Lucca giving interesting wines at a more northerly latitude. Southwards through the CHIANTI CLASSICO area to the zones of VINO NOBILE DI MONTEPULCIANO and BRUNELLO DI MONTALCINO, the wines become richer, fuller, more intense, and more alcoholic. Montalcino is, in fact, the only viticultural area of Tuscany where Sangiovese has always been fermented on its own; both CHIANTI and Vino Nobile were blended wines in the past, with CANAIOLO, MALVASIA, and TREBBIANO being used to soften Sangiovese's youthful asperity. This practice is gradually dying out except for wines deliberately shaped and marketed for early consumption. Chianti Classico, Vino Nobile di Montepulciano, and Brunello di Montalcino are all DOCG wines and have all shown a gradual but notable increase in overall quality since the late 1970s. The finest wines of each area are regularly included in lists of the world's outstanding wines.

Tuscan viticulture was dominated until recently by large estates owned by wealthy local families, the majority of them of noble origin, and tilled by a work-force of sharecroppers. Tuscan ownership of Tuscan viticulture is now part of history, but the new wave of vintners from Milan, Rome, and Genoa—joined in the 1980s by a sizeable contingent of foreigners—has shown both a commendable commitment to quality and an equally commendable openness to new and more cosmopolitan ideas. See also ANTINORI, FRESCOBALDI, and RICASOLI, local noble families with considerable wine interests.

White wines
Trebbiano has been the basis of the regional production, and more than a dozen Trebbiano-based DOC wines currently exist in Tuscany. The wines have little character and have gradually gone out of FASHION in the market-place; their future, if any, appears to be confined to a quaffing public in search of low prices. Scattered patches of VERMENTINO exist but the variety has yet to establish a clear identification with Tuscany. Interest in white wines was strong in the 1980s, however, and pioneering producers in Chianti experimented with white INTERNATIONAL VARIETIES—principally Chardonnay and Sauvignon. Results have been mixed thus far. Some striking white wines were made, however, if only in small quantities. In the 1990s, interest shifted to early-ripening reds,

particularly Merlot, as the most suitable alternative to Sangiovese in cooler sites.

Supertuscans

Far less marginal are the new breed of Tuscan red wines, the so-called Supertuscans, often made with the assistance of French VINE VARIETIES and in an international style. Their development dates from the late 1960s and early 1970s, first as experiments or even for mere *divertissement*, but the startling results obtained in such all-CABERNET wines as Sassicaia and such Sangiovese/Cabernet blends as Tignanello from ANTINORI have established these products as a fundamental category in the overall Tuscan picture. Few estates in Chianti have not joined in the scramble to produce a wine of this prestigious type, and small BARREL MATURATION, now extended to Sangiovese, has yielded a new style of Tuscan wine greatly appreciated by consumers who once disdained Chianti. Merlot is increasingly planted as an alternative to Cabernet, with impressive results, and in the 1990s significant amounts of Syrah vines began to bear fruit, with uneven results.

Chianti still towers over these new wines, none the less. It is Italy's largest single group of DOCs, supplying 80 per cent of the region's annual total of 1.2 million hl of DOC wine and close to a third of the total Tuscan wine production of 3 million hl in an average year.

For more details of specific Tuscan wines, see BOLGHERI, BRUNELLO DI MONTALCINO, CARMIGNANO, CHIANTI, CHIANTI CLASSICO, CHIANTI RUFINA, ELBA, GALESTRO, MONTECARLO, VERNACCIA, VINO DA TAVOLA, VINO NOBILE DI MONTEPULCIANO, VIN SANTO.   D.T.

Txakoli, Basque for CHACOLÍ.

typicity, a wine-tasting term adapted from the French *typicité* or Italian *tipicità* (the English word is **typicality**) for a wine's quality of being typical of its type, geographical provenance, and even its VINTAGE year—a wine characteristic much discussed by professionals. And it is perhaps because typicity is a subjective notion, rather than a physical attribute that can be measured by analysis, that it is so much discussed. Individual tasters are likely to differ as to what they consider typical of a particular wine description, just as they are likely to differ in their impressions of the wine under consideration.

Typicity need not and may not concern the average wine drinker, who is right to demand merely that the wine tastes good, but it becomes important in wine JUDGING if the wine has been entered into a particular class. It is also important to professional wine buyers, particularly when choosing wines to represent a GENERIC range.

Each wine type demands a different set of characteristics. For example, a very young red wine smelling strongly of CARBONIC MACERATION would be accorded high marks for typicity if a young BEAUJOLAIS, but none as a young BORDEAUX.

It should be added, however, that, as winemakers increasingly travel between wine regions, absorbing and applying different techniques, some distinctions between what were regarded as wine archetypes are being eroded, and there is more disagreement than ever as to what constitutes typicity.

Ugni Blanc (which is in fact Italy's ubiquitous TREBBIANO) is France's most planted white grape variety by far, and yet is rarely seen on a wine label. Just as AIRÉN, Spain's most planted white variety, supplies that country's voracious brandy stills, so the copious, thin, acid wine of Ugni Blanc washes through the stills of the Cognac and Armagnac regions.

Often called Clairette Ronde (although not related to CLAIRETTE), it is still among the five most planted varieties in the southern Rhône and Provence, in most of whose appellations it is allowed to play a subsidiary role. There are still small plantings of it in Corsica and it was only in the late 1980s that Sauvignon Blanc overtook Ugni Blanc as Bordeaux's second most planted white grape variety. It is still widely planted in the north west of the Gironde, where, like COLOMBARD, it is allowed in Bordeaux Blanc up to 30 per cent and is sometimes tellingly called Muscadet Aigre, or 'sour Muscadet'.

For more details of this variety, which probably produces more wine than any other, see TREBBIANO (although the variety is usually known throughout South America, where it is widely planted, as Ugni Blanc).

Ukraine, independent republic in the south west of the CIS, its second most important grape grower after MOLDOVA and its fifth most important wine producer. The climate is mild, mostly CONTINENTAL.

Commercial viticulture is concentrated in the Crimea, in the Odessa region, the Kherson region, the Nikolayev region, the Trans-

carpathian region, and the Zaporozh'ye region, these vineyards accounting for 88 per cent of the total vineyard area. About 700 state and collective farms grow grapes, and the largest of them are located in the Crimea. State farms in the Ukraine may export to Russia, KAZAKHSTAN, MOLDOVA, and other CIS members.

Vineyards are planted mostly to VINIFERA varieties grafted on phylloxera-resistant ROOTSTOCKS, although some MUSCADINES are also grown. The largest areas are planted to wine grapes such as RKATSITELI, ALIGOTÉ, Cabernet Sauvignon, SAPERAVI, Riesling, SAUVIGNON VERT, GEWÜRZTRAMINER, Pinot Gris, SERCIAL, BASTARDO, Fetiaska (see FETEASCA), Bastardo Magarachski, and white Sukhomlinski. Newly bred varieties are also being introduced.

The Crimea produces high-quality white and red table wines and 'yellow' FORTIFIED wines such as Sercial Magarach, Massandra, and Oreanda, as well as SHERRY- and MADEIRA-like wines. Wines produced by the MASSANDRA winery are the pride of the republic.

SPARKLING WINE production is important in Ukraine and wineries produce 50 million bottles of this popular drink each year. Most common grape varieties used for base wines are Pinot Blanc, Aligoté, Riesling, and Fetiaska.

Of all CIS members, Ukraine has made most notable progress towards establishing its own wine law.   V.R.

ullage has had a variety of meanings and uses in the English-speaking wine trade. It can mean the process of EVAPORATION of wine held in wooden containers such as a BARREL. The head space left in the container is also called the ullage, or 'ullage space', and the wine in that state is said to be 'on ullage'. The word ullage is also used for any space in a stoppered wine bottle not occupied by wine (see FILL LEVEL). And ullage is also used as a verb so that a bottle or barrel not entirely full is said to be 'ullaged'.

Ull de Llebre, meaning 'hare's eye', is the Catalan name for TEMPRANILLO.

Umbria may be the fourth smallest of ITALY'S 20 regions in terms of both physical size and population but it is undergoing some exciting vinous developments.

ORVIETO is still the region's biggest DOC, accounting for 80 per cent of Umbria's total DOC production. Other DOC white wines based on TREBBIANO grapes, simple products at best, are made in the zones of Colli del Trasimeno, Colli Perugini, TORGIANO, Colli Altotiberini, Colli Martani, and Colli Amerini. Trebbiano is often referred to as Procanico in Umbria, although some claim that Procanico is actually a superior CLONE of Trebbiano. SANGIOVESE is the region's principal red grape variety, giving pleasant, if not memorable, wines in the Colli Altotiberini, Colli Amerini, Colli Martani, Colli Perugini, and Colli del Trasimeno DOCs; the wines produced near Lake Trasimeno are allowed up to 40 per cent of the GAMAY grape in the blend, and to the west of the lake some all-Gamay wines are produced, although they are more an oddity than a serious imitation of BEAUJOLAIS.

Sangiovese has reached its heights in Umbria in the wines produced by LUNGAROTTI in the Torgiano DOCG, and, as Rosso di Montefalco, also gives good results in the HILLSIDE VINE-YARDS of the small MONTEFALCO DOC zone between Assisi and Terni, where it is blended with a small percentage of the local SAG-RANTINO. This last variety, which in the past yielded notably rustic wines high in TANNINS, demonstrated in the 1990s that it can respond well to more careful vinification and ageing techniques. The elevation of Sagrantino di Montefalco to DOCG status, however, is perhaps more of a vote of confidence in the future than an accurate reflection of the prevailing quality level of all producers.

More surprising yet perhaps was the number of high-quality wines to emerge from Umbria in the 1990s, the result in many cases of input from Tuscan investors and OENOLOGISTS. San-giovese continued to improve, but many of these new wines were from Merlot, Cabernet Sauvignon, Pinot Noir, and Chardonnay, the latter at times blended with GRECHETTO to provide a distinctively Umbrian style of BARREL-FERMENTED white wine. In the late 1990s, inter-est in these new wines was high, both in Italian and international markets, not least because many were priced well below similar products from nearby Tuscany. D.T.

United Kingdom. See Great BRITAIN.

United States of America, very important producer of wine and DRYING GRAPES, and a significant consumer of fine wine. The USA is the world's fourth biggest producer of wine, having overtaken Argentina in the early 1990s.

Wine is made in at least 46 of the 50 states of the United States. Much is sold locally, but the wines of CALIFORNIA, NEW YORK, WASH-INGTON, OREGON, and TEXAS have become important commercially and have inter-national distribution. They are treated sep-arately in this book, as are MISSOURI, VIRGINIA, and IDAHO.

In the following survey, several wine-pro-ducing states are grouped, sometimes across political boundaries, into regions of similar climate and geography. Vine varieties grown tend to be either VINIFERA varieties, American HYBRIDS, or more usually French hybrids. A large proportion of American wines are FRUIT WINES, including berry wines, made from fruits other than grapes.

The USA's relatively recent and tentative answer to CONTROLLED APPELLATIONS is the AVA, an officially recognized American Viticultural Area. See AVA.

New England North-east US region that includes, from north to south, the states of Maine, New Hampshire, Vermont, Mas-sachusetts, Connecticut, and Rhode Island, containing 38 wineries. The two AVAs are Western Connecticut Highlands and South-eastern New England. Within the coastal win-eries (Massachusetts, Connecticut, and Rhode Island), Westport Rivers, in Massachusetts, is the most easterly US vineyard, and the largest vineyard in New England. Its reputation is based on TRADITIONAL METHOD sparkling wines. Both HAIGHT Vineyard in Connecticut and Sakonnet Vineyard in Rhode Island were estab-lished in the mid 1970s, and are in full pro-duction today. Coastal wineries enjoy a climate moderated by Long Island Sound and the Atlantic Ocean. The climate for northern and western regions in these states is more severe. Grapes grown are *viniferas*, especially Chardonnay, and red and white hybrids. Fruit wines, mead, and cider are also made.

Lake Erie One of the Great Lakes, it borders CANADA to the north, while its eastern and southern shores border north-western Pennsylvania, northern Ohio, and western NEW YORK. Lake Erie is an AVA, the first US tri-state appellation, established in 1983. In Pennsylvania, wines are produced from *vinifera*, hybrids, native American grapes, and other fruits, planted in a wide range of MESOCLIMATES that vary with the proximity to the lake (see LAKE EFFECT). Presque Isle Wine Cellars has been in production there since 1964.

Ohio, west of Pennsylvania, had 53 wineries in 1998, mostly BOUTIQUES, up from 24 in 1979. The Lake Erie region, an AVA in the most northerly part of the state, has 22 wineries. Markko Vineyard is part of a group of wineries on the south shore of Lake Erie, from Buffalo in New York state to Toledo, Ohio. Located in Lake Erie, North Bass Island is a subappellation of Isle St George AVA, which is, in turn, a subappellation of the Lake Erie AVA. Riesling is promising statewide, and Pinot Gris is gaining new interest. A great deal of sparkling wine is made, and Meier's Wine Cellars, established in 1856, is noted for its FORTIFIED WINES. Meier's new facility, Firelands, is a major CO-OPERATIVE, consisting of five wineries, producing still and sparkling wines. Grand River Valley, a recent AVA, is 10 miles south of Lake Erie. South of Lake Erie there are 16 wineries in the central Ohio heartland and 15 in the Ohio River Valley, an AVA at the south-west border of the state. The Ohio River Valley is another tri-state appellation, and includes some wineries in southern Indiana and Kentucky.

Lake Michigan This Great Lake is bordered by Michigan, Indiana, Illinois, and Wisconsin, with most favourable vineyard sites being in the northern and southern parts of Michigan, bordering on Lake Michigan's eastern shoreline. Half of the state's 20 commercial wineries are in the northern region around Traverse City, which has two AVAs: Leelanau Peninsula and Old Mission Peninsula. The *viniferas* and French hybrids produced have the acidity to make crisp table wines and sparkling wines that can benefit from BOTTLE AGEING. The southern part of the state also has two AVAs: Lake Michigan Shore and a smaller subappellation, Fennville. The oldest and largest winery in the state, in the southern region, is St Julian Wine Co., in Paw Paw, which makes table wines, DEALCOHOLIZED WINES, and juices. French hybrids are in the majority. Of the red *vinifera* varieties, Cabernet Franc is the most widely planted, followed by Merlot and Pinot Noir. Whites include Chardonnay, Pinot Gris, and Riesling, which has become increasingly popular now that it is vinified dry. Every few years, ICE WINE is made in both the northern and southern regions. Cherries and apples are used widely for fruit wines.

Indiana has 18 wineries making table and sparkling wines, which comprise 85 per cent of production, as well as fruit and berry wines and mead. Most wineries are small and family-owned. The best sites can grow *vinifera* successfully. Major varieties include Cabernet Franc, Cabernet Sauvignon, Chardonnay, and Riesling. North-west and north-central areas are planted with cold-hardy varieties including *labruscanas* such as Concord, Catawba, and Delaware, and French hybrids such as Seyval Blanc, Vidal Blanc, Vignoles, and Chambourcin.

Illinois has 10 wineries. The French hybrids Chambourcin, Vidal Blanc, and Vignoles are most important.

Wisconsin has 12 wineries, but Wollersheim Winery, along with its new acquisition Cedar Creek Winery, accounts for half of the state's production. The AVA is Lake Wisconsin. Fruit wines are very important, but hot summers enable even red grapes to ripen fully. The French hybrid (MARÉCHAL) FOCH is the most important red grape, and is vinified in all styles from BLANC DE NOIRS to full-bodied, barrel-aged wines.

Middle Atlantic states These include New Jersey, south-eastern Pennsylvania, Maryland, VIRGINIA, and West Virginia. New Jersey's small wine industry consists of at least 15 wineries, divided between Warren Hills AVA in the north west and Egg Harbor in the south west. Several vineyards have been established recently growing *vinifera* vines exclusively, but two-thirds of the vines grown are French hybrids. Unionville Vineyards is most famous. Besides the more usual *viniferas*, the cold-hardy RKATSITELI is grown in the southern portion of the state.

The majority of Pennsylvania's 54 wineries are now in the south east of the state. The largest and best-known winery is Chaddsford, on the Brandywine river. Grapes, as well as other fruits, are grown on the high plateau around the Susquehanna river in a historic area known as York Highlands, and up into the Lehigh valley. The most popular *viniferas* are Cabernet Sauvignon, Cabernet Franc, Pinot Noir, Chardonnay, and Riesling. French hybrids include Vidal Blanc and Seyval Blanc, and the red Chambourcin. Naylor Wine Cellars makes exceptional Chambourcin in many styles. Six wineries, three in Pennsylvania and three in Maryland, straddling the Mason-Dixon Line, have formed the Mason-Dixon Wine Trail. There are three AVAs located in the area: Lancaster Valley, Cumberland Valley, and Central Delaware Valley, besides Lake Erie (see above).

Maryland, with 10 wineries, is best known among wine lovers for being the home of Robert PARKER, and for Boordy Vineyard and Nursery, which produces table wines and sparkling wines from both *vinifera* and hybrids.

Perhaps the greatest growth in eastern viticulture has been in VIRGINIA, however. See separate entry.

Midwestern states The midwestern wine-producing states are MISSOURI, Arkansas, and Iowa. See separate entry for Missouri. Arkansas' wineries are in the western part of the state near Altus, a mountain plateau above the Arkansas river, which is an AVA within the Arkansas Mountain AVA, south of the Ouchita Mountains. Ozark Mountain Region, a tri-state AVA, includes portions of Altus and Ozark Mountain in Arkansas, plus a portion of Oklahoma and Missouri. Wiederkehr Wine Cellars, established in 1880, is the largest and most important winery. The most important *vinifera* varieties, in descending order of acreage, are Chardonnay, Cabernet Sauvignon, Merlot, (French) Colombard, (White) Riesling, Sauvignon Blanc, Pinot Gris, and Pinot Noir. The most important VITIS *aestivalis* is Cynthiana-NORTON. Hybrids include Vignoles, Seyval Blanc, Vidal Blanc, and Chambourcin. *Labruscana* grapes, especially Concord, are also grown commercially, and some MUSCADINES are also grown.

Iowa's wineries, in the Amana area, enjoy a local following.

South-western states These include TEXAS, discussed elsewhere, and New Mexico, Arizona, and Colorado. New Mexico has 19 wineries and two AVAs, Mesilla Valley and Mimbres Valley, and has made some impact commercially, particularly with traditional-method sparkling wines. *Vinifera* varieties do best in the warmer, southern part of the state, while hybrids can withstand the cold of the northern, high desert plateaux.

Arizona, just west of New Mexico, has similar growing conditions, but there is a strong focus on growing *vinifera* grapes. The TERRA ROSSA, or red soil, in the south east appears promising for Pinot Noir and Cabernet Sauvignon vines. Colorado, north of New Mexico, also favours *vinifera* production. The main vineyard areas are west of the Continental Divide, and the plains east of Denver.

South-eastern states In Georgia, North and South Carolina, Florida, Tennessee, Louisiana, and Mississippi, overall climatic conditions are predominantly hot and humid. Georgia, whose main winery is Chateau Elan, however, and North Carolina, with its famous Biltmore Estate, and about 10 other wineries, are able to grow *vinifera* grapes in the cooler highlands. While Scuppernong is the most historic of the MUSCADINES associated with this area, commercial growing is based on varieties such as Blanc du Bois and Magnolia.

Hawaii This chain of islands in the Pacific Ocean, outside the continental USA, but one of the 50 states, produces mainly FRUIT WINES, notably still and sparkling pineapple wines, as well as some grape wines, the westernmost source of such, on the island of Maui.

See also specific entries on CALIFORNIA, WASHINGTON, OREGON, IDAHO, TEXAS, VIRGINIA, MISSOURI, and NEW YORK.   H.L.

Ursprungslage, German term for a 'site of origin' and the proposed replacement for the GROSSLAGE collective site. The word Ursprungslage should appear on labels of wines from them, and, unlike Grosslage, each Ursprungslage may produce wines only of a particular style, according to officially registered grape variety, acidity, alcoholic strength, and residual sugar. The consumer should therefore have some idea what sort of wine to expect from a bottle carrying the name of a particular Ursprungslage. A quality wine of guaranteed origin, or **Ursprung**, may be described as QgU, or a Qualitätswein garantierten Ursprungs. See MOSEL-SAAR-RUWER, for example.

Uruguay is South America's fourth most important wine-producing country. Uruguayans drink more wine per head than any South Americans apart from the Argentines (see Appendix 2), and all vineyards are dedicated to wine. Some efforts are now being made to export their sometimes excellent wines. Until the mid 1990s, Uruguayan wine was, typically, an internationally unfashionable deep rosé, not unlike a Spanish CLARETE, made from an unusually sweet and stern blend of TANNAT and MUSCAT HAMBURG. HYBRIDS are rapidly being replaced by more internationally acceptable grape varieties, however, such as Pinot Blanc (which may actually be Chenin), Sauvignon Blanc, Chardonnay, Cabernet Sauvignon, Cabernet Franc, and Merlot, together with some Riesling, Gewürztraminer, and even Viognier. Vidiella, a form of FOLLE NOIRE, is a national speciality.

Vine-growing is widely spread over the country but nearly 90 per cent of all vineyards are still in the south. Perhaps the country's most distinctive wine region is the central vineyards of Carpinteria and El Carmen, where good day–night TEMPERATURE variation and poor, shallow soils have been cited by visiting French experts as evidence of greatest potential.

Greater wine-making sophistication should increase Uruguayan presence in the international market-place. A national body dedicated to promoting Uruguayan wine quality, INAVI (Instituto Nacional de Vitivinicultura), was created as recently as 1988.

USA. See UNITED STATES of America.

Utiel-Requena, Spanish wine region producing some sturdy reds, and mostly rosés, in the hills inland from VALENCIA in south-east Spain. Utiel-Requena is the coolest of the five wine regions of the LEVANTE and was once famous for its heavy DOBLE PASTA reds. Consequently the region is dominated by the sweet, dark BOBAL grape variety, although TEMPRANILLO is rapidly gaining in importance.

R.J.M.

Uva Abruzzi, occasional name for the red MONTEPULCIANO grape.

Uva di Troia, good-quality southern Italian red grape variety named after a village near Foggia and fast declining in popularity with growers. See APULIA.

Uva Rara, red wine grape variety too widely grown in the OLTREPÒ PAVESE in Lombardy in northern Italy to justify its Italian name, whose literal translation is 'rare grape'. Often called, misleadingly, BONARDA Novarese, it is grown in the Novara hills and used in a range of scented red wines to soften the SPANNA grapes grown here.

Uzbekistan, independent central Asian republic that is part of the CIS. It is a major supplier of TABLE GRAPES but apparently also produces nearly one million hl of wine a year, more than any other member of the CIS other than Moldova and Ukraine.

Uzbekistan is in the very heart of central Asia, on the same latitude as Italy. Commercial grape culture is centred on the 10 zones of Uzbekistan with the most suitable soil and climate conditions. The leading viticultural zones are the Samarkand, Tashkent, and Bukhara regions.

The country's assortment of vines still has features typical of the viticulture of central Asia. In the 1990s, 36 varieties were officially allowed for commercial viticulture, of which 20 were table and dried-fruit varieties. Wine grape varieties included ALEATICO, RIESLING, Kuljinkski, Hungarian Muscat, MUSCAT Rosé, Soiaki, Bayan Shirey, SAPERAVI, RKATSITELI, MORRASTEL, and Khindogny.

Uzbekistan produces dry, strong, and dessert wines as well as sparkling wines and brandies.

Vaccarèse, rare, relatively light-red grape variety permitted in CHÂTEAUNEUF-DU-PAPE producing wines similar to CINSAUT.

Vacqueyras, after GIGONDAS, the second one of the Côtes du Rhône villages to be awarded its own appellation, in 1990. Vacqueyras may be red, white, or rosé, although only a minuscule proportion of its vines are white grape varieties. Most of the wine is like a super-concentrated Côtes du Rhône-Villages, made in the communes of Vacqueyras and Sarrians between Gigondas and BEAUMES-DE-VENISE. The appellation rules are very similar to those of Gigondas, and thus to those of Châteauneuf-du-Pape, although only half the grapes in a red Vacqueyras have to be Grenache. The rest are usually Syrah, Mourvèdre, and Cinsaut. Vacqueyras tends to be distinctly more rustic than good Gigondas, but producers such as Ch des Tours, now operated in conjunction with Ch Rayas of CHÂTEAUNEUF-DU-PAPE, at least back up that rusticity with power and concentration.

Valdadige, or Etschtaler in German, basic appellation of the Adige (Etsch) valley used principally by producers in TRENTINO and also by some in eastern VENETO. Vineyards in the ALTO ADIGE theoretically qualify but the Alto Adige appellation is usually used instead.

Valdeorras, easternmost wine zone in GALICIA in north-west Spain. Steeply terraced vineyards are planted predominantly with inappropriate but productive vine varieties such as GARNACHA and the white PALOMINO. The indigenous white GODELLO is being aggressively replanted. If carefully vinified, it can produce an aromatic wine with an ALCOHOLIC STRENGTH of 12 to 13 per cent. In the late 1990s, some of Spain's most acclaimed BARREL-FERMENTED whites were Godello wines from Valdeorras made by the Guitián family, who pioneered this style. The MENCÍA grape, which makes light, fruity reds for early drinking, is similarly respected by a new wave of producers in Valdeorras.   R.J.M. & V. de la S.

Valdepeñas, wine region in CASTILE-LA MANCHA in south central Spain producing soft, ripe red wines. The sea of rolling vineyards that is Valdepeñas is really an extension of La MANCHA, but Valdepeñas has developed a reputation for quality over and above its larger neighbour and has consequently earned a separate denomination, or DO. Valdepeñas shares the arid, CONTINENTAL conditions that prevail through much of central Spain.

As in La Mancha, the white AIRÉN is the dominant grape variety. But Valdepeñas is traditionally known for red wine rather than white. The red Cencibel, as the TEMPRANILLO of Rioja is known here, has been gaining ground. Much of the 'red' wine made in the region is a blend of red and white grapes somewhat lacking in colour and BODY. The best red wines, however, are made exclusively from Cencibel, which has the capacity to age well in OAK. Most of the wines exported from Valdepeñas are either RESERVAS or GRAN RESERVAS matured in American oak casks. Some of the wines can taste unappetizingly baked from the heat, but the best have the soft, smooth, vanilla character (although not the price tag) of a well-aged RIOJA.   R.J.M.

Valdepenas is also the name of a relatively unusual red grape variety grown in California which is thought to be TEMPRANILLO.

Valdiguié, sometimes called Gros Auxerrois, has been all but eradicated from France but is still to be found in California. It occasionally turns up on the label of a fruity VARIETAL wine.

Valençay, shrinking VDQS region on the south bank of the Cher tributary of the Loire in northern France at the far south-eastern end of the TOURAINE district. The most successful of the LOIRE varieties grown here is Sauvignon Blanc (Valençay is only about 20 miles/30 km from the appellations QUINCY and REUILLY) but crisp wines of all three colours are made for drinking young from Cabernets, Cot (Malbec), Gamay, Pinot Noir, Chardonnay, and Arbois.

Valencia, Spain's biggest port and third largest city, also lends its name to an autonomous region and one of five wine denominations (see DO) in the Levante. The vineyards are well away from the city, inland from the fertile market gardens and paddy fields bordering the Mediterranean. Production of white wine exceeds red. Neutral dry whites are made from the MERSEGUERA grape, although the local Moscatel Romano (MUSCAT OF ALEXANDRIA) produces some good, pungent dessert MISTELAS. MONASTRELL and the pink-fleshed GARNACHA Tintorera together produce rather coarse red wines, although the latter can produce some fresh, dry rosé. See LEVANTE.   R.J.M.

Valgella, subzone of the VALTELLINA in the far north of Italy.

Valle d'Aosta. See AOSTA.

Valle de la Orotava, denominated wine region covering the lush northern flanks of the Teide mountain on Tenerife in the Spanish CANARY ISLANDS. Much improved reds, whites, and rosés from the typical Canary Islands grape varieties are rarely seen outside Tenerife.

V. de la S.

Valle Isarco, or Eisacktaler in German, pure, dry white wines from the ALTO ADIGE.

Valpolicella, red wine of extremely varied quality from the VENETO region in north-east Italy. The Valpolicella, like a number of other historic areas of Italy, saw its production zone greatly enlarged when it achieved DOC status in 1968. The original Valpolicella zone, whose wines alone may be labelled Valpolicella CLASSICO, now accounts for less than half the total production of about 340,000 hl/9 million gal. Valpolicella SUPERIORE, with an ALCOHOLIC STRENGTH of at least 12 per cent and an obligatory ageing period of one year, is a more ambitious product than the regular bottling, which may have only 11 per cent alcohol and no ageing requirement. The subzone of the Valpantena, where the Bertani family has important vineyard holdings, is a legally permitted subdenomination on labels.

The DOC regulations, which imposed a maximum limit of 70 per cent of CORVINA grapes in the wine, have not been helpful to Valpolicella; Corvina is generally considered the grape with the most personality in the blend. The high acidity of the Molinara and the neutral character of the Rondinella contribute little to the overall quality level. Wines made exclusively from Corvina began to appear in the late 1980s, but they qualify only as a VINO DA TAVOLA. By 1990, Corvina plantings outnumbered those of Rondinella 3 : 2. The widespread use of the best grapes either for the production of such DRIED-GRAPE WINES as local specialities RECIOTO and AMARONE, or for Valpolicella Superiore, has doubtlessly weakened the regular Valpolicella bottlings. A general increase in the quality level of Amarone in the 1990s and renewed market interest in this wine have not yet been translated to Valpolicella, despite the fact that such leading houses as Quintarelli, Allegrini, and Dal Forno have demonstrated that good Amarone and Recioto need not come at the expense of the base wine of the zone.

There is no question, however, that the Valpolicella's single greatest handicap has been the socio-economic structure of the zone's production: over 50 per cent of the grapes are handled by the CO-OPERATIVES and 20 per cent by large industrial wineries, many of which have no vineyard holdings; both have been dedicated to a policy of high-volume production at low prices.

RIPASSO is a common technique employed by better producers for reinforcing the standard Valpolicella wines, and converts them, thanks to the increased ALCOHOLIC STRENGTH, into a Valpolicella SUPERIORE. This technique requires, ideally, unpressed skins used for

Amarone, or at least some partially dried grape skins. The fact remains, however, that there are not enough dried grapes or Amarone skins for the vast bulk of Valpolicella production, and the wine, which once had the reputation of a fruity, eminently drinkable, medium-weight product, has become, for the most part, rather thin and acidic.

See also AMARONE and RECIOTO. D.T.

Valréas, one of the Côtes du Rhône villages. See RHÔNE.

Valtellina, the northernmost zone in Italy where the NEBBIOLO grape (here called Chiavennasca) is cultivated, is a narrow valley formed by the river Adda as it flows from east to west before emptying its waters into Lake Como. Despite its 46-degree latitude, the valley—protected to the north by the Rhaetian and Lepontine Alps—has a relatively privileged climate (not unlike the warmer wine regions across the border in SWITZERLAND) with a high percentage of sunny days during the year. None the less, the wines themselves, while unmistakably Nebbiolo, do tend to have less body and roundness, and more perceptible TANNINS and ACIDITY, than the classic wines of the LANGHE or those made from SPANNA in the Novara-Vercelli hills, and can be sold only at considerably lower prices.

The production zone is divided into nearly 500 ha/1,250 acres of Valtellina SUPERIORE, elevated to DOCG status in 1998, and the nearly 700 ha of regular Valtellina. Wines of the Superiore zone have a minimum ALCOHOLIC STRENGTH of 12 per cent. Regular Valtellina is generally a simpler and less age-worthy wine which need reach only 11 per cent of alcohol.

NÉGOCIANT houses market 88 per cent of the Valtellina's production. Another substantial portion, 10 per cent, is marketed by CO-OPERATIVE wineries, leaving the zone with a virtual absence of the small producers whose work has been so fundamental in improving the quality and image of the famous Langhe wines BAROLO and BARBARESCO.

The Valtellina also produces a wine called Sforzato (also seen with dialect names of Sfursat or Sfurzat) from raisined grapes; unlike a RECIOTO, the wine is dry and must have a minimum of 14.5 per cent of alcohol. D.T.

varietal, descriptive term for a wine named after the dominant grape variety from which it is made. The word is increasingly misused in place of VINE VARIETY. A varietal wine is distinct

from a wine named after its own geographical provenance (as the great majority of European wines are), and a GENERIC wine, one named after a supposed style, often haphazardly borrowed from European geography, such as 'Chablis' and 'Burgundy'. Varietal wines are most closely associated with the NEW WORLD, where they constitute the great majority of wines produced.

Originally, when the United States' acreage of classic vine varieties was relatively limited, a varietal needed only 51 per cent of that variety in the blend to be so labelled. In 1973, this requirement was increased to 75 per cent. Despite the emergence of the MERITAGE category of superior blends, varietal wines continue to be viewed by many as California's premier statement of quality.

The French INAO authorities are hostile towards varietal labelling, understanding that they have nothing to gain and much to lose by entering into this commonwealth of nomenclature. Within France, varietal wines (typically VIN DE PAYS) are widely regarded as of lower rank than APPELLATION CONTRÔLÉE wines. The INAO stated in the early 1990s that its eventual aim was to eradicate grape varieties from the names and labels of all appellation contrôlée wines, possibly even those of ALSACE and certainly such familiar combinations of grape and geography as Sauvignon de TOURAINE. This has not prevented even quite eminent producers in BURGUNDY from printing 'Pinot Noir' and 'Chardonnay' on their export labels in addition to the geographical name of the appellation.

In their 1990s attempts to reformulate the DOC system and wine-quality categories, the Italian authorities have been equally keen to emphasize their uniqueness, place, over grape variety. Such attitudes are understandable and, in the long term, may pay dividends, but there is little doubt that an important factor in the success of many New World wines has been the ease with which consumers can grasp the concept of varietal labelling. In the 1980s, Chardonnay and Cabernet Sauvignon became the most recognizable names in the world of wine.

Most varietal wines are based on a single vine variety but examples made up of a blend of two or even three different varieties have become increasingly common, especially when there is a shortage of certain popular varieties. Common varietal blends are Semillon/

Chardonnay (possibly stretched with some Colombard or Chenin Blanc) and Sauvignon/Semillon among white wines and Cabernet/Merlot, Cabernet/Shiraz, Syrah/Merlot, and Grenache/Shiraz/Mourvèdre. It is usual to list the varieties on the label in declining order of importance in the blend.

See VINE VARIETIES.

variety of vine or grape. See VINE VARIETIES.

Varois, Coteaux, enclave within the Côtes de PROVENCE appellation which takes its name from the Var *département*. The wine achieved AC status in 1993 and by the late 1990s the area was producing vast quantities of rosé, while one-third of production was red wine, some of it potentially exciting, and there was a little extremely varied white.

Reds and rosés may incorporate an almost dazzling array of varieties: Grenache, Syrah, Cinsaut, Mourvèdre (which will ripen only in the warmest sites), Cabernet Sauvignon, Carignan (limited to half of any one parcel of vines), and the ancient Provençal variety Tibouren. This gives the better producers an exciting palette from which to work; some of them produce several different blends which vary in style by virtue of both varietal mix and ÉLEVAGE. For white wines, Grenache Blanc is added to those varieties permitted for Côtes de Provence Blanc (see PROVENCE), although Rolle is increasingly appreciated. Ch Routas and Domaine du Deffends are dependable exporters.

VDN is sometimes used as an abbreviation for VIN DOUX NATUREL.

VDP, or the Verband Deutscher Prädikats- und Qualitätsweingüter, important association of about 190 of the finest wine estates in GERMANY. Although its collective holdings account for a mere 3.5 per cent of Germany's total vineyard area, this group produces a remarkable proportion of its finest wines.

The VDP's contribution to the image of fine and rare German wines is based on its members' uncompromising dedication to high quality, starting with stringent, self-imposed regulations. These stipulate that members must have holdings in the top vineyard sites; produce lower YIELDS and higher MUST WEIGHTS than required by the GERMAN WINE LAW; plant at least 80 per cent of their vineyards with vine varieties traditionally associated with their

regions; practise environmentally sound methods; be established as full-time growers of sound reputation; and submit to regular (at least every five years) VDP compliance inspections. Members' labels and capsules carry the VDP logo and name.

VDQS stands for **Vin Délimité de Qualité Supérieure,** France's minuscule interim wine-quality designation between VIN DE PAYS and APPELLATION CONTRÔLÉE, which in 1997 accounted for less than one per cent of the nation's wine production. The VDQS category is very much a testing ground for smaller wine regions, many of which are eventually promoted to full AC status. There is a relatively high concentration of VDQS designations on the fringes of the LOIRE, or of SOUTH WEST FRANCE. The regulations governing the more recently granted VDQS wines are every bit as strict as AC rules.

Vega Sicilia, concentrated and long-lived red wine that is Spain's undisputed equivalent of a FIRST GROWTH, made on a single property now incorporated into the RIBERA DEL DUERO denomination. This farm has been making wine in its present form since 1864 but the current style was defined around 1900, when the winery was the property of Cosme Palacio, a Rioja grower. A succession of different owners have since managed to maintain the quality and reputation of Vega Sicilia as Spain's finest red wine. However, Vega Sicilia fell on lean times at several junctures, and was able to make a substantial leap in quality and, more importantly, in consistency after being bought by the Alvarez family in 1982.

The vineyards overlooking the river Duero (DOURO in Portugal) are planted mainly with Tinto Fino but Cabernet Sauvignon, Merlot, and Malbec together make up about 20 per cent of the total production. A tiny quantity of old-vine white Albillo remains.

Bodegas Vega Sicilia once produced three wines, all red. Two styles of Valbuena were released after maturing for three and five years respectively in French and American oak; only a five-year-old VINTAGE-dated version is now made. But it is the Vega Sicilia Unico that attracts the most attention. Restricted to the best VINTAGES, it is often released after spending about 10 years in a combination of wooden tanks; small, new BARRIQUES; large, old barrels; and bottles. Vega Sicilia can hardly be described as an exuberant wine and, perhaps because of its high price, the Unico occasionally attracts criticism. It is, however, an extraordinarily compact yet powerful, persistent wine with a restrained yet complex character that is uncommon in most of Spain. The best vintages of Vega Sicilia Unico and the rare multi-vintage Reserva Especial last for decades.

In 1991, Bodegas Vega Sicilia acquired the nearby Liceo winery and created the immediately acclaimed Bodegas Alión, which make much more modern reds from 100 per cent Tempranillo grapes, aged in new French oak.

R.J.M. & V. de la S.

Veltliner, Valtlin Zelene, Veltlinske Zelené, Veltlini, common synonyms for the Austrian white grape variety GRÜNER VELTLINER, also known in darker-skinned mutations as **Roter Veltliner**, which can produce characterful wines in ripe years, and occasionally **Brauner Veltliner**. Another important white grape variety, chiefly encountered in Austria, is FRÜHROTER VELTLINER, sometimes known as Veltliner in the far north east of Italy.

vendange French word for HARVEST.

Vendange Tardive means literally 'late harvest' and is used increasingly throughout France but most commonly, and most specifically, in ALSACE, where strict regulations cover its production, even if too many producers are meeting only the bare minima. Although all Vendange Tardive wines are made from ripe grapes, and without the aid of CHAPTALIZATION, the wines themselves vary considerably in how sweet they are, with some of them tasting rich but almost bone dry. Labels give no clue as to how sweet these wines taste, making FOOD AND WINE MATCHING particularly difficult. SÉLECTION DE GRAINS NOBLES is Alsace's even riper category. See also AUSLESE and BEERENAUSLESE, their counterparts in Germany.

vendemmia, Italian for VINTAGE year or HARVEST. Vendimia is Spanish for harvest.

Vendômois, Coteaux du, a VDQS producing a wide range of wines between the Coteaux du LOIR and the city of Vendôme. The wines are necessarily light and crisp, this far from the equator, but a pale-pink VIN GRIS from the PINEAU D'AUNIS grape can be an attractive local speciality. Slightly more solid reds may be made from Pinot Noir, Gamay, or either Cabernet, and Chenin Blanc is the principal grape,

nowadays often aided and abetted by Chardonnay, for some particularly tart white wines which represent about one bottle in six.

See also LOIRE.

Veneto, historically and currently important wine region in north-east ITALY. It stretches westward to Lake Garda and northward to the Alps and the Austrian border from the terra firma behind the lagoons and city of Venice. The region usually produces more wine than any other in Italy apart from APULIA and SICILY, with an average annual production of more than 7.5 million hl/187.5 million gal.

In theory, a significant proportion of Veneto wine is of good quality, with DOC wine representing well over a quarter of the total. The reality is somewhat different. This proportion has been artificially inflated both by drastic enlargements of the DOC zones and/or by sanctioning extremely generous YIELDS (in the case of Valpolicella, Soave, Bardolino, and Prosecco). The resulting wines, though nominally of DOC level, are too frequently characterless. Good bottles of Bardolino, Valpolicella, and Soave are not difficult to find, however, and the CORVINA vine variety which forms the basis of Valpolicella, and GARGANEGA, the base of Soave, are capable of making interesting wines if grown in the proper area. Although native varieties, in particular Tocai, Garganega, and Verduzzo, are cultivated in these zones, the most interesting wines and the greatest potential are undoubtedly represented by light, fruity styled Merlot and Cabernet, although the relatively high yields and cool climate can often give a distractingly HERBACEOUS quality. The Garganega-based Bianco di Custoza and Gambellara, two country cousins of Soave, the lightly sparkling Prosecco of Conegliano with a bitter finish, and the Moscato of the Colli Euganei (no rival to MOSCATO D'ASTI but with the true, grapey character) round out the regional picture, a picture characterized by large quantities of pleasant and easy-drinking wines which seem to suffer from a lack of ambition and competitive spirit.

For details of notable specific wines, see AMARONE, BARDOLINO, BIANCO DI CUSTOZA, BREGANZE, GAMBELLARA, LISON-PRAMAGGIORE, PIAVE, PROSECCO, RABOSO, RECIOTO, SOAVE, and VALPOLICELLA. D.T.

Venezuela is a minor South American wine producer, and consumer, but TROPICAL VITI-

CULTURE has been practised, mainly for TABLE GRAPES, since the arrival of European immigrants at the end of the 19th century. In the late 20th century, wine producers used GRAPE CONCENTRATE as their raw material for products that range from LAMBRUSCO-like blends to base wines for SANGRÍA. One of the most viticulturally suitable regions is Mérida in Lagunillas, where at altitudes of about 1,100 m the climate is cooler than elsewhere and annual total rainfall (unevenly spread) is between 300 and 400 mm. Vines are also grown in Barquistimeto and in even drier areas to the north. Most of the vine varieties grown are table grapes, HYBRIDS such as Jacquez and Isabella, and a relative of CRIOLLA. A little GRILLO, BARBERA, and MALVASIA are also grown, however.

Ventoux, Côtes du, large and growing appellation on the south-eastern fringes of the southern RHÔNE between the Coteaux du TRICASTIN (also promoted to full AC status in 1973) and the Côtes du LUBÉRON.

The predominantly red and rosé wines are made mainly from a blend of Grenache, Syrah, Cinsaut, and Carignan—very similar to those of Tricastin, except that the proportion of Carignan can be 30 per cent in Ventoux whereas it is 20 per cent in Tricastin. Ventoux is even more dominated by the CO-OPERATIVES than Tricastin, and the wines generally taste even lighter than those of Tricastin. The red wines in particular can taste refreshing when drunk chilled in the region's high summer, but they too often lack substance and real interest, although Domaine des Anges and the highly successful BRAND La Vieille Ferme, which has been based on Ventoux wines, provide honourable exceptions to this. More ambition and closer co-operation with possible markets could have dramatic and exciting consequences on the wine styles of this under-performing appellation.

Clairette and Bourboulenc are the principal varieties for the small quantities of white produced. The Bourboulenc in particular could produce some wine of real interest here.

veraison, word used by English speakers for that intermediate stage of grape-berry development which marks the beginning of RIPENING, when the grapes change from the hard, green state to their softened and coloured form. It is derived from the French term *véraison*.

Vérargues, or Coteaux de Vérargues, one of the named CRUS within the Coteaux du LANGUEDOC appellation in southern France. The zone overlaps substantially with that of MUSCAT DE LUNEL east of Montpellier and is immediately south of ST-CHRISTOL. In the late 1990s, the most interesting wines made in the zone were Muscats from Domaine La Croix St-Roch rather than any Coteaux du Languedoc.

Verdea, light-berried vine speciality of the Colli Piacentini in north-central Italy.

Verdeca, Apulia's most popular light-berried vine producing neutral wine suitable for the VERMOUTH industry and declining in popularity.

Verdejo, characterful grape with distinctive blue-green bloom that is the Spanish RUEDA region's pride and joy (and has staved off a challenge for primacy from imported SAUVIGNON BLANC, with which it is often blended). Wines produced are aromatic, herbaceous (with a scent somewhat reminiscent of laurel), but with great substance and extract, capable of ageing well into an almost nutty character. Also grown in CIGALES and TORO.

Verdelho, Portuguese white grape varieties.

The name is most closely associated with the island of Madeira, where the Verdelho vine became increasingly rare in the post-PHYLLOXERA era. The relatively few Verdelho vines on the island produce small, hard grapes and musts high in acidity. A dark-skinned **Verdelho Tinto** is also grown there. See MADEIRA.

Verdelho is also grown in the DOURO valley in northern Portugal, where it is also known as Gouveio. Gouveio is almost certainly identical to Galicia's Godello, which is also known as Verdello.

A vine known as Verdelho has had notable success in vibrant, tangy, full-bodied table wines in Australia, particularly in the Hunter Valley of New South Wales and some of the hotter regions of Western Australia, although it is regarded by some as the classic white grape of McLaren Vale in South Australia. Some of these wines can develop well in bottle.

Verdello, white grape variety known both in UMBRIA, where it was once prized for its ACIDITY but is now rapidly losing ground, and SICILY. A connection with Portugal's VERDELHO, and

Verdicchio

therefore Spain's Godello, seems likely but is unproven.

Verdicchio, one of central Italy's classic white wines, is produced from the Verdicchio grape in two DOC zones of its home territory of the MARCHES: Verdicchio dei Castelli di Jesi, to the west of Ancona and a mere 30 km/20 miles from the Adriatic Sea, and Verdicchio di Matelica, considerably further inland and at higher altitudes, close to the regional border with UMBRIA. The wines share common characteristics, although the Verdicchio di Matelica, with lower yields and better exposed HILLSIDE VINEYARDS, can be a fuller, more characterful wine. Matelica's 225-odd ha (560 acres) are dwarfed, however, by the more than 2,300 ha of the Castelli di Jesi. This latter DOC is divided into a CLASSICO zone, with over 85 per cent of the total vineyard area, and a zone of regular Verdicchio dei Castelli di Jesi. Close to 60 per cent of the production of the Castelli di Jesi DOC is controlled by CO-OPERATIVES, and NÉGOCIANT houses control three-quarters of the remaining 40 per cent.

Like many central Italian white wines, Verdicchio was once fermented on its skins, giving it a certain fullness and authority albeit often at the expense of any delicacy. It is now a more 'correct', if perhaps less distinctive, wine, although the lemony acidity and the bitter almonds of the aftertaste are still identifiably present in the better bottles of the DOC. A notable improvement in quality in the two DOC zones in the 1990s modified opinions of the grape's potential. Verdicchio is expected to become one of central Italy's most interesting wines.

Perhaps partly because of its high natural acidity, Verdicchio was one of the first Italian SPARKLING WINES, and pleasant bottles of bubbly Verdicchio remain an integral part of the DOC production. D.T.

Verdiso, lively light-skinned grape speciality of Treviso in north-east Italy.

Verdot. The variety known as Verdot in Chile is probably Bordeaux's PETIT VERDOT, but the Verdot in Argentina's Mendoza may well be the coarser, probably unrelated, Gros Verdot, an undistinguished old Bordeaux variety.

Verduzzo, white grape variety grown in north-east Italy. It is cultivated principally in FRIULI in six different DOC zones: AQUILEIA, COLLI ORIENTALI, GRAVE, ISONZO, LATISANA, and LISON-PRAMAGGIORE. Only the Grave and the Colli Orientali produce significant quantities and the Verduzzo of the Colli Orientali is qualitatively far superior. The wine exists both in a dry and a sweet version, although the latter, obtained either by late harvesting or by raisining the grapes (see DRIED-GRAPE WINES), can frequently be more medium dry than lusciously sweet. Sweet Verduzzo, although less common than dry Verduzzo, is the more interesting wine, golden in colour and often with a delightful density and honeyed aromas, even if it lacks the complexity of an outstanding dessert wine. Dry Verduzzo is less characterful, and the grapes' TANNINS often impart an odd astringency which is more noticeable when it has been fermented dry.

Ramandolo, to the north of Udine, is considered the classic zone for fine sweet Verduzzo, and has its own DOC. D.T.

Vermentino, attractive, aromatic white grape variety widely grown in Sardinia, Liguria, to a limited extent in Corsica, and to an increasing extent in Languedoc-Roussillon, where it is a recently permitted variety in many appellations, including white Côtes du Roussillon. It is thought by most authorities to be identical to the variety long grown in eastern Provence as ROLLE and sometimes known in north-western Italy as Rollo. In CORSICA, it is sometimes called Malvoisie de Corse, and some believe that the variety is related to the MALVASIA family. Vermentino is Corsica's most planted white grape variety and dominates the island's white APPELLATION CONTRÔLÉE wines. In Sardinia, it is picked deliberately early to retain acid levels but still manages to produce lively wines of character, although attempts at a richer, fuller style have also emerged, notably from Capichera in the **Vermentino di Gallura** DOCG, created in 1996.

vermouth, herb-flavoured FORTIFIED wine available in many different styles and qualities but usually a much more industrial product than wine.

Vernaccia, name used for several, unrelated Italian grape varieties, mainly white but sometimes red, from the extreme north of the peninsula (VERNATSCH being merely a Germanic version of Vernaccia) to the fizzy red **Vernaccia di Serrapetrona** of the MARCHES and the **Vernaccia di Oristano,** which is an almost SHERRY-like wine made on the island of SARDINIA. The most highly regarded form is VERNACCIA DI SAN

GIMIGNANO, which is said to have no relationship to the Sardinian **Vernaccia di Cagliari** vine.

The name is so common because it comes from the same root as the word 'vernacular', or indigenous.

Vernaccia di San Gimignano, distinctive dry white wine made from the local VERNACCIA vine variety, probably unrelated to any other Vernaccia, cultivated around the famous towers of San Gimignano in the province of Siena in TUSCANY in central Italy. The wine was elevated to DOCG status in 1993. DOC recognition had been awarded in March of 1966, making Vernaccia di San Gimignano the first ever DOC, which saved the wine from what seemed a fatal decline.

At its best, the wine has a crisp, refreshing quality and an attractively bitter finish. Despite its renewed popularity and attempts to give it further complexity with small BARREL MATURATION, the wine has only attained modest quality and price levels. In the long run, it may well have a lesser significance in its own place of origin, as leading producers in San Gimignano have begun to achieve striking success with serious red wines based on SANGIOVESE grapes (which have always been grown here), and with more international varieties such as Cabernet Sauvignon and Chardonnay.   D.T.

Vernatsch, German name for the undistinguished light-red grape variety SCHIAVA.

Veronelli, Luigi (1926–), Italy's most influential food and wine critic since 1956, when he founded the magazine *Il Gastronomo* and began to collaborate with Italy's major daily newspapers, news weeklies, and RAI-TV, the national television network. Veronelli was an unabashed Francophile from his first writings and a frank admirer of the French APPELLATION CONTRÔLÉE system, in particular of its designated CRUS, a CLASSIFICATION which he has attempted to apply to Italian vineyards and their products in his many books on his country's wines.

For many years Veronelli represented the only possible means of obtaining commercial recognition and visibility for Italy's small producers and he can be credited with the discovery and identification of the large majority of the country's better producers. If the career has been a controversial one, it is safe to say that the current Italian wine scene would be virtually unrecognizable without his work,

and the emergence of Italian VITICULTURE and OENOLOGY dedicated to quality would have been considerably slower and more uncertain.
      D.T.

Vespaiola, white grape variety grown in the VENETO region of north-east Italy, said to take its name from the wasps (*vespe*) attracted by the sugar levels of its ripe grapes. Its most famous product is the Torcolato sweet wine of BREGANZE, although in this Vespaiola is blended with Tocai and Garganega, and the DRIED-GRAPE WINE-making technique may well be the most important ingredient.

Vespolina, low-yielding red grape variety known almost exclusively in, and therefore probably native to, the area around GATTINARA in the PIEDMONT region of north-west Italy. Commonly blended with NEBBIOLO, occasionally in the company of BONARDA Piemontese, it is also grown in the OLTREPÒ PAVESE zone across the border in LOMBARDY, where it is known as Ughetta.

Veuve Clicquot, Champagne house as famous for its eponymous founder, the first great champagne widow (*veuve* in French), as for its wines. Nicole Barbe Ponsardin (1777–1866) married François Clicquot, an owner of Champagne vineyards, in 1798. François Clicquot died in 1805, leaving Mme Clicquot in charge of the company, which she renamed Veuve Clicquot-Ponsardin. 'La Grande Dame' is credited with inventing the RIDDLING process called *remuage*, and adapting a piece of her own furniture into the first riddling table for that purpose. She devised the famous yellow label, still used for the NON-VINTAGE wine. On her death, the company passed to her former chief partner, another shrewd businessman, Édouard Werlé, and the house remained in the hands of the Werlé family until in 1987 it became part of the Moët Hennessy-Louis Vuitton group (see LVMH). The house style is based on Pinot Noir grapes and, in particular, those grown at Bouzy, where the house has large holdings. La Grande Dame is Clicquot's PRESTIGE CUVÉE, named, of course, after the widow. In 1990, the Champagne house purchased a majority stake in the WESTERN AUSTRALIAN winery Cape Mentelle and its New Zealand subsidiary CLOUDY BAY.   S.A.

Victoria, third most important wine state in AUSTRALIA, with over 250 wineries.

What is now the North East Victoria zone,

with Rutherglen as its epicentre, became the focus of wine-making after the First World War, producing a range of FORTIFIED and red table wines, the latter almost indistinguishable from some of the former. Foremost among the fortified wines were, and are, the unctuous LIQUEUR MUSCAT and Liqueur Tokay, wines of unique style and extraordinary concentration of flavour deriving in part from the shrivelled grapes and in part from long BARREL MATURATION in tin sheds which unconsciously mimic the *estufas* of MADEIRA. These unique wine styles are increasingly called simply Muscat and Tokay. The North East Victoria zone is divided into four regions: Rutherglen, Glenrowan, the King Valley, and the Ovens Valley. The latter two regions produce wines (or provide the grapes for other makers) of radically different styles, mainly sparkling wine, but also light- to medium-bodied table wines.

The Port Phillip zone has six regions clustered around Melbourne: the Yarra Valley, the Mornington Peninsula, Geelong, South Gippsland, Sunbury, and the Macedon Ranges. Over 130 wineries here enjoy a range of climatic conditions all cooler than those of Bordeaux. Pinot Noir and Chardonnay are the dominant varieties, capable of producing wines of world class. Cabernet Sauvignon, Cabernet Franc, and Merlot also flourish, particularly in the Yarra Valley.

The Central Victoria zone encompasses the Goulburn Valley, Central Victorian High Country, and Bendigo. The Goulburn Valley and Bendigo are noted for their full-bodied red wines, while the High Country (notably including Mount Helen in the Strathbogie Ranges) produces more delicate styles and sparkling-wine base material.

The Pyrenees, Grampians (formerly known as Great Western), and Far South West (Drumborg) regions fall in the Western Victoria zone. The first two are predominantly red-wine producers, of Shiraz in particular. Intriguingly, this variety can produce wines redolent of pepper and spice (harking back to France's RHÔNE valley) or eucalypt mint (challenging the famous Martha's Vineyard of California's NAPA Valley), but always with masses of dark berry fruit and ample TANNINS. The Far South West boasts a substantial vineyard owned by Seppelt at Drumborg, and a handful of small wineries. But it has a climate, and—more importantly, perhaps—TERRA ROSSA soil similar

to that of Coonawarra. It seems only a question of time before major plantings materialize, effectively representing an extension of SOUTH AUSTRALIA's Limestone Coast zone.

The Murray river meanders east for over 500 km/305 miles as it marks the border between Victoria and NEW SOUTH WALES with major areas of RIVERLAND viticulture around Echuca, Swan Hill, Robinvale, and, most significantly, Mildura. Karadoc, just to the east of Mildura, is home to LINDEMANS and Australia's largest winery, crushing up to 50,000 tonnes a year, rather more than any single French winery. Merbein is home to Mildara, while Deakin Estate, Alambie, and BRL-HARDYS' Buronga wineries (the latter just across the Murray river in New South Wales) are major producers. Lindemans tells it all with its Bin 65 Chardonnay, blended in 15,000-hl/396,000-gal tanks, and one of the largest Chardonnay BRANDS in the world.   J.H.

Vidal, white grape variety and a French HYBRID more properly known as **Vidal Blanc** or **Vidal 256** and widely grown in CANADA, where it is particularly valued for its winter hardiness. Grown to a limited extent in the eastern UNITED STATES, particularly NEW YORK state, it is a hybrid of Ugni Blanc and one of the Seibel parents of SEYVAL BLANC. The wine produced, like Seyval's, has no obviously FOXY character and can smell attractively of currant bushes or leaves. Its slow, steady ripening and thick skins make it particularly suitable for sweet, late-harvest (non-botrytized) wines and ICE WINE, for which it, with RIESLING, is famous in Canada. Vidal-based wines do not have the longevity of fine Rieslings, however.

Vidigueira, DOC in southern Portugal. See ALENTEJO for more details.

vieilles vignes is French for 'old vines'. The term is used widely on wine labels in the hope that potential buyers are aware that wine quality is often associated with senior VINE AGE, at least in the Old World. There are few effective controls on the use of the term, however, and little agreement about exactly how many years it is before a vine can be deemed old. BOLLINGER was one of the first producers to use the term, for the produce of vines which were never grafted post-PHYLLOXERA.

Vienna, capital city of AUSTRIA and, unusually, a wine region in its own right.

Vietnam, small, south-east Asian country with a history of viticulture dating from French colonial times. Recent attempts to revive viticultural traditions and make wine have met with modest success. The most suitable locations for conventional viticulture in this hot and wet country are in the highlands. Contrarily, however, Vietnam's first commercial wine-making venture, the Ninh Thuan Winery, was established on the steamy southern coastal plain at Phan Rang, 350 km/210 miles north east of Ho Chi Minh City (formerly Saigon). The winery, with an initial one-million-bottle capacity, is a JOINT VENTURE between the British firm Allied Domecq and a local company targeting the domestic market. First wines, both still and sparkling, were released in 1995. INTERNATIONAL VARIETIES are being trialled under Australian technical supervision. CHAMBOURCIN produces prolifically and copes best with the humidity.

vigne is French for a VINE. **Vigneron** is French for a vine-grower, some say derived from *vigne ronde*, implying that a vigneron actually prunes the vines himself whereas a VITICULTEUR merely grows them.

The term *vigneron* is now used widely outside France for a wide range of people engaged in wine production. A **vignoble** is French for a VINEYARD, although the term *vignoble* can be used more broadly as in 'the entire French *vignoble*'.

vigour in a viticultural sense is the vine's vegetative growth, an important aspect of any vine. This may seem of unlikely interest to wine drinkers, but the level of vineyard vigour is a vital factor in wine quality. Low-vigour vines do not always have sufficient leaf area to ripen grapes properly, while high-vigour vines typically produce thin, pale, acidic wines often wrongly thought to result from OVERCROPPING.

High vigour is a common problem of modern vineyards, for many and varied reasons. The vines may be planted in a region with a benign climate on too deep a soil, which is well supplied with water (from rainfall and/or irrigation) and nutrients (from natural fertility or fertilizers or added compost). Modern control methods can also keep vines free of stress associated with weeds, pests, and diseases. CANOPY MANAGEMENT techniques are used to maintain yield and wine quality in such situations.   R.E.S.

Vilana, white grape variety that is native to and the most widely grown on the island of Crete (see GREECE). It is responsible for the most delicate examples of dry white Peza made there.

Villages, common suffix of an APPELLATION CONTRÔLÉE name for a French wine. Generally speaking, an X-Villages wine must be made from one or several of a selection of communes whose produce is known to be superior to that of the rest of the X zone. See, for example, BEAUJOLAIS, MÂCON, and Côtes du RHÔNE.

village wine is a term used particularly in Burgundy for a wine which qualifies for an APPELLATION that coincides with the name of the village or commune in which the wine is made. It contrasts with a lesser GENERIC wine, which takes the name of a region, and wines from PREMIER CRU and GRAND CRU vineyards.

vin, French for wine and therefore a much-used term (see below). **Vin blanc** is white wine, **vin rosé** is pink, **vin rouge** is red wine, **vin mousseux** is sparkling wine, and so on. For **vin ordinaire**, see VIN DE TABLE. For **vin biologique**, see ORGANIC WINE. For **vin blanc cassis**, see KIR.

viña, viñedo Spanish word for VINEYARD.

Vin Délimité de Qualité Supérieure. See VDQS.

vin de liqueur, strong, sweet drink made by adding grape spirit to grape juice for a golden vin de liqueur, or to whole, dark-skinned grapes for a red vin de liqueur. The term has also been adopted by European Union authorities (although not by this book) to encompass all FORTIFIED wines.

The principal members of this special category of French specialities are PINEAU DES CHARENTES and FLOC DE GASCOGNE.

vin de paille is French for 'straw wine' (Strohwein in German), a small group of necessarily expensive but often quite delicious, long-lived, sweet white wines. These are essentially a subgroup of DRIED-GRAPE WINES made from grapes dried on straw mats.

Today, production of this rarity is virtually confined to particularly ripe vintages and the most conscientious producers of Hermitage, ARBOIS, occasionally L'ÉTOILE, and Côtes du JURA.

Average yields are minuscule once the grapes have been raisined, but the results are luscious in the extreme, and are invariably bottled in a half-bottle.

The Jura producers often suspend their SAV-AGNIN, POULSARD, or Chardonnay grapes to raisin them rather than laying them out on straw. The minimum POTENTIAL ALCOHOL allowed is 18 per cent (as opposed to 14 per cent in Hermitage). The grapes are generally pressed at Christmas time, and 100 kg/220 lbs of grapes may yield fewer than 20 l/5 gal of juice. Jura producers also customarily age their vins de paille in cask for several years. The wines often have a natural alcoholic strength of about 15 per cent and are capable of long BOTTLE AGEING.

There is renewed, if limited, experimentation with making vin de paille in Alsace and, unlike BOTRYTIZED wine, this is one wine style with which any curious and dedicated wine-maker can experiment.

vin de pays, French expression meaning 'country wine' which was adopted for an intermediate category of wines created in FRANCE in 1973, and formalized in 1979, to recognize and encourage the production of wines that are distinctly superior to basic VIN DE TABLE, and which, in theory at least, offer some stamp of regional identity. Hence the creation of more than 140 different vins de pays, all of them carrying some geographical designation mirroring the principles of the APPELLATION CONTRÔLÉE (AC) system. To qualify as a vin de pays, a wine must not be blended, must be produced in limited quantities, must be made of certain specified grape varieties, must reach a certain minimum ALCOHOLIC STRENGTH, and must be submitted to a tasting panel, as well as coming from a specified area. By 1993, more than a fifth of all wine produced in France was sold as a vin de pays of some sort and the proportion had risen to 27 per cent by 1997.

In many regions, the vine-grower has a clear choice between making an appellation wine or producing a vin de pays, either because yields are too high to qualify for an AC, or because he or she grows (as is often the case with new or imported INTERNATIONAL VARIETIES) grape varieties permitted by the local vin de pays regulations but prohibited by those of the local AC.

There are three levels of vin de pays:

Four are regional: Vin de Pays d'Oc from the LANGUEDOC; Vin de Pays du Jardin de la France from the LOIRE; Vin de Pays du Comté Tolosan, most of SOUTH WEST FRANCE; and Vin de Pays des Comtés Rhodaniens, incorporating ARDÈCHE, BEAUJOLAIS, JURA, SAVOIE, and the northern RHÔNE.

About 50 are departmental. These are named after one of France's *départements*, or counties, such as Vin de Pays de l'Hérault, Vin de Pays de Loire-Atlantique, Vin de Pays de Tarn-et-Garonne, or Vin de Pays de l'Ardèche (these are, respectively, specific *départements* within each of the regions above).

Even more are locally specific. These may be named after some historical or geographical phenomenon such as Vin de Pays des Coteaux de Murviel, Vin de Pays des Marches de Bretagne, Vin de Pays des Coteaux du Quercy, or Vin de Pays des Coteaux de l'Ardèche (each a local denomination within the four departmental vins de pays specified above).

Some of these locally specific vins de pays names are virtually unused, some of the smaller ones have been developed as commercially useful exclusivities by individual merchants, and many of them are unknown outside their district of origin. Some of the local names are simply too difficult for export markets, often unsure of the exact spelling of even vin de pays, to grasp.

Other exercises in nomenclature have represented strokes of genius. The image of Corsica is transformed in the name Vin de Pays de l'Île de Beauté, just as the Loire sounds even prettier as the Jardin de la France, while Roussillon's vins de pays quite rightly emphasize the region's ethnic origins in Vin de Pays Catalans and Vin de Pays des Côtes Catalanes.

A certain amount of red, and some white, vin de pays PRIMEUR is produced each year, and may be released on the third Thursday of October (thereby beating Beaujolais NOUVEAU by a full month).

The vins de pays which have enjoyed enormous success outside France are those labelled as VARIETALS, a concept viewed with such distaste by the INAO, which oversees AC labelling, that vins de pays present the modern consumer with virtually the only means of acquiring a wine that is both French and labelled with a familiar grape variety such as Chardonnay, Sauvignon Blanc, Merlot, or Cabernet Sauvignon (or, increasingly, with a less familiar variety such as Marsanne, Terret, or Viognier). Some non-French customers could be much more attracted by a Chardonnay, Vin de Pays d'Oc, than, for example, a full AC counterpart carrying a less familiar name such as St-Romain or a Bugey. Reverence for the words 'appellation contrôlée' is a French phenomenon. Vins de pays have been particularly successful in Germany and Great Britain.

The most important single vin de pays is Vin de Pays d'Oc, which is France's prime source of varietal wine. About 85 per cent of all vins de pays come from the Languedoc-Roussillon, Provence, or the southern Rhône. A further 6 per cent come from the Loire.

In every 10 bottles of vin de pays, about 7 are red, 2 are rosé, and 1 is white. In general in the 1980s, they sold at lower prices than most AC wines, often quite rightly as many of these wines can be thin on flavour. Some producers, however, are becoming increasingly ambitious in their wine-making techniques and a number of vins de pays may be the products of low yields and expensive BARREL FERMENTATION or BARREL MATURATION, and may be offered, and sold, at relatively robust prices. The pioneer was MAS de Daumas Gassac, an internationally famous wine which is sold merely as a departmental Vin de Pays de l'Hérault, but there are now scores, if not hundreds of equally ambitious producers of vins de pays, especially in the Languedoc-Roussillon, making some of the best-value wines in the world.

Vin de Savoie. See SAVOIE.

Vin des Glaciers, also known as Vin du Glacier, 'glacier wine', is a local speciality in the Val d'Anniviers near Sierre in the Valais of SWITZERLAND. The white wine, traditionally made of the now obscure Rèze vine, comes from communally cultivated vines and is stored at high altitudes in casks refilled just once a year on a SOLERA system. The resultant product is deliberately MADERIZED and valued for its rarity.

vin de table, the French form of TABLE WINE and France's most basic level of wine, which is now dwindling to a relative trickle. By 1997, this, the lowliest of French wine categories, accounted for just 12 per cent of the nation's output, well under half the amount that qualified as VIN DE PAYS.

Vin de table is, typically, light red wine made in areas of the LANGUEDOC-ROUSSILLON not delimited as APPELLATION CONTRÔLÉE territory. There are no limits on YIELDS in table-wine production and typical grape varieties are likely to be high-yielding CARIGNAN together with ARAMON and ALICANTE BOUSCHET. Some white vin de table is also made, and some vin de table is produced in virtually every part of France where vines are grown.

France's vin de table has been light and thin ever since the plains of the LANGUEDOC were planted at the end of the 19th century. Red vin de table has traditionally needed BLENDING with darker, more alcoholic wine which was originally imported from ALGERIA and subsequently from southern Italy, Sicily, and Spain.

There is still a serious surplus of vin de table, however, and a significant proportion of it has been subject to compulsory distillation as part of the European Union's efforts to remedy this. The area of vineyard dedicated to vin de table production has also contracted markedly as the vin de pays designation has been developed, and as poorer-quality vineyard sites have been targeted by VINE PULL SCHEMES.

Much of it is sold locally, in bulk, for blending with other table wines or to producers of VERMOUTHS or other FORTIFIED wines and wine-based products.

vin doux naturel is a sweet fortified wine made by artificially arresting the conversion of grape sugar to alcohol by adding spirit halfway through, resulting in a particularly strong, sweet half-wine in which grape flavours dominate wine flavours. They are normally made of the grape varieties MUSCAT and GRENACHE, and should have an alcoholic strength of at least 14 per cent.

A young vin doux naturel, like port, tastes relatively simply of grapes, sugar, and alcohol and is usually served chilled as an aperitif. Non-vintage-dated vins doux naturels are common, particularly among the Languedoc Muscats. See MUSCAT DE FRONTIGNAN, MUSCAT DE LUNEL, MUSCAT DE MIREVAL, and MUSCAT DE ST-JEAN-DE-MINERVOIS.

For details of France's other vins doux naturels, see Muscat de BEAUMES-DE-VENISE, RASTEAU, BANYULS, MAURY, RIVESALTES, and MUSCAT DE RIVESALTES.

Vin du Bugey. See BUGEY.

vine, the plant, often known as the grapevine, whose fruit is transformed into WINE.

A vine in its broadest sense is any plant with a weak stem which supports itself by climbing on neighbouring plants, walls, or other supports. Of this group of plants, the grapevine is the most famous, and the most commercially important. (In this work the word vine is used to mean the grapevine.)

Because the vine is unable to support itself, it is generally grown on trellis systems, on some combination of wood posts and wire. Vines can be trained so that they are free standing but this requires special pruning and training to keep the trunk short, otherwise the vine will fall over.

Most of the world's wine is made from the VINIFERA species of the *Vitis* genus.

Grapevines are the world's most important fruit crop, with about 7.7 million ha/19 million acres of vineyards producing almost 60 million tonnes of fruit in the late 1990s. Grapes are used for wine-making in all of its forms, for brandy, for consumption as TABLE GRAPES and DRYING GRAPES, for fresh GRAPE JUICE, for GRAPE CONCENTRATE, rectified grape must, and for limited industrial products. However, wine production is the major use and accounts for 80 per cent of all vineyard output.

The grapevine is grown on all continents except Antarctica, but most of the world's vineyards are in Europe. *Vitis vinifera* cannot tolerate extreme winter cold. Requiring warm summers for fruit maturation, the vine is grown approximately between the 10 and 20 °C isotherm in both hemispheres, or about between latitudes 30 degrees north and 50 degrees north, and 30 degrees south and 40 degrees south. Principally in order to minimize the damage associated with fungal diseases, the grapevine has traditionally been grown in MEDITERRANEAN CLIMATES with warm, dry summers and mild, wet winters. The ready availability of agrochemicals, and to a lesser extent disease-tolerant varieties, has allowed this range to be extended, especially since the Second World War. Winter dormancy is essential for vine longevity, and the hot and humid climates nearer the equator are not conducive to either grape production or wine quality (although see TROPICAL VITICULTURE).   R.E.S.

vine age, easily observable by the width of the vine's trunk, is widely considered a factor affecting wine quality, with widespread consensus that, in general, older vines make better wine. Indeed, this idea is enshrined in APPELLATION CONTRÔLÉE legislation which, in many cases, specifically excludes the produce of vines less than three or sometimes more years old.

vine density is a measure of how closely spaced vines are in the vineyard, both within the row and between rows. The choice of vine spacing is one of the most fundamental decisions in planting a vineyard, and between, even within, the world's wine regions there is enormous variation in spacing. The traditional vineyards of France's Bordeaux, Burgundy, and Champagne regions have about 10,000 plants per ha (4,050 per acre) (and sometimes more). In many NEW WORLD vineyards, on the other hand, 1,080 vines per ha is quite common. Probably the most widely spaced vineyards of the world are those of the Vinho Verde region in Portugal, La Mancha in Spain, and some parts of Chile, Japan, and Italy.

It is widely held that high vine densities lead to improved wine quality. It is true that many of the world's most famous vineyards, especially in the Old World, have very narrow spacings, and therefore high densities, but it is difficult to argue that this is a prerequisite for quality production.

OLD WORLD vineyards are generally planted more densely than those of the NEW WORLD. Many New World vineyards were planted after the introduction of tractors, necessitating row spacings of about 3 m or more. By contrast, most European vine-growers have chosen to persist with narrow rows and to develop either narrow tractors, or over-row tractors.

Vineyard density is a major consideration affecting the vineyard's yield, quality, cost of establishment and maintenance, and therefore profitability. Planting costs are proportional to the number of plants used; costs for trellis systems and DRIP IRRIGATION are higher with narrower row spacings. The time taken to plough and spray is also greater when rows are closer together.

Under most circumstances, the YIELD of densely planted vineyards is higher, especially in the first years of the vineyard's life and with vines planted on low soil potential.   R.E.S.

vine pull schemes, schemes whereby growers receive some sort of incentive to pull out vines. The most comprehensive of these schemes to combat various wine surpluses is that embarked upon by the European Union in 1988, which in the first five years encouraged growers, mainly in southern France and southern Italy, to pull out a total of 320,000 ha/790,400 acres, the equivalent of the entire vineyard area of the United States.

Other national vine pull schemes may be directed at particular types of vine in an effort to reduce production of certain wine types— usually in recent history wine of the most basic sort. Such schemes were applied in ARGENTINA and NEW ZEALAND in the late 1980s, for example.

vine spacing. See VINE DENSITY.

vine varieties, distinct types of vine within one species of the vine genus *Vitis*. Different vine varieties produce different varieties of grape, so that the terms vine variety and grape variety are used almost interchangeably. Each variety of vine, or grape, may produce distinct and identifiable styles and flavours of wine. Vine variety is *cépage* in French, *cepa* in Spanish, *Rebsorte* in German, and *uva* in Italian.

Most of the vine varieties we know today (CABERNET SAUVIGNON and CHARDONNAY, for example) were selections from WILD VINES. These varieties have been supplemented by some which have developed naturally by MUTATION, and by HYBRIDS and CROSSES which initially occurred in nature.

Most important vine varieties used to produce wine are of the European vine species *Vitis* VINIFERA. A number of varieties of American vine species and their American HYBRIDS have also been used to make wine, however, although many suffer a bad reputation because of the resultant wines' FOXY character (the dark-skinned NORTON is a notable exception). American species are also used as ROOTSTOCKS. Wine has also been made from a range of Asian vine species and from the French hybrids.

There are approximately 10,000 known varieties of *vinifera* but modern French authorities list fewer than 220 varieties of commercial significance in modern France. Italy and Portugal have a particularly rich heritage of vine varieties, however, and Galicia in north-west Spain is reputed to boast as many as 1,000 indigenous vine varieties.

Vine varieties are often named for the colour of their berries, with many French varieties, for example, coming in *noir* (black), *rouge* (red), *violet*, *rose* (pink), *gris* (grey-pink), *jaune* (yellow), *vert* (green), and *blanc* (white) hues. This book uses the convention of adopting a capital letter for each word in a vine variety's name, even though Pinot noir may be strictly more correct than Pinot Noir. Examples of mutants are Pinot Blanc and Pinot Gris, while Sauvignon Vert is a quite different variety from Sauvignon Blanc. See individual variety names for more details.

Most widely planted varieties

Of all vine varieties, remarkably few have achieved an international reputation, and most of these are French. Obvious examples of these INTERNATIONAL VARIETIES include Cabernet Sauvignon, Pinot Noir, Syrah (Shiraz), Merlot, Chardonnay, Sauvignon Blanc, and Sémillon. There is little correlation between these most famous varieties and the vine varieties which cover the greatest total area of vineyard land: such varieties as AIRÉN, GRENACHE (Garnacha), RKATSITELI, TREBBIANO (Ugni Blanc), and CARIGNAN are more widely planted even than Cabernet Sauvignon, some of these varieties being used substantially for brandy production and, in the case of the first two, being planted to Spain's relatively low VINE DENSITY.

Choice of variety

Vine-growers are rarely free to choose which vine variety to plant in a given vineyard. They may have acquired a planted vineyard in full production and cannot afford the crop loss involved in changing variety. Different varieties need different conditions of soil and climate. Cabernet Sauvignon simply will not ripen regularly in cool regions, for example.

In France, and much of the European Union, the varieties permitted may be regulated by the APPELLATION CONTRÔLÉE (AC) laws, which authorize only specified varieties for each appellation, distinguishing between principal and secondary varieties (see Appendix 1 for full details), or by the regulations which control the production of more basic VIN DE TABLE. These laws have subsequently been overtaken by European Union laws with the similar intent of allowing only specified varieties. For discussion of these restrictions, see VINE VARIETIES, EFFECT ON WINE.

In the New World, the choice of vine variety or varieties is often in practice determined by the style of wine that is eventually desired, many of them involving just one vine variety (often sold as a VARIETAL wine). Examples of mono-varietal AC wines within France are Muscat de Frontignan, Muscadet, and Sancerre. Blends of two varieties often include those which are complementary, such as the productive and full-bodied Marsanne mixed with the lighter, rarer Roussanne for white Hermitage, or the lightly coloured Aramon with Alicante-Bouschet. Celebrated blends of three varieties include Sémillon, Sauvignon Blanc, and Muscadelle in Sauternes, and Pinot Noir, Chardonnay, and Meunier in champagne. Even more complex blends of varieties are common in red bordeaux and in Châteauneuf-du-Pape, both styles which are emulated in the New World. The mix of vine varieties that go into a single wine, or are planted on a single property, is called its *encépagement* in French and *uvaggio* in Italian.

Varieties themselves are often subdivided into various CLONES. While particular clones of many varieties have been selected through performance evaluation by CLONAL SELECTION, typically they cannot be separated by appearance.   R.E.S. & J.Ro.

vine varieties, effect on wine. Of all the factors such as SOIL, CLIMATE, VITICULTURE, and detailed WINE-MAKING techniques which have an effect on wine quality, vine variety is probably the easiest to detect in a BLIND TASTING. The colour of the grapes' skin determines what COLOUR of wine can be produced: red wine only from dark-skinned grapes. Only grape varieties which ripen readily and/or are prone to NOBLE ROT are likely to produce good SWEET WINES, while only those with high levels of natural acidity are likely to produce good brandy or SPARKLING WINES. But, even more important in identification, individual grape varieties tend to produce wines with identifiably different flavours. Indeed, in very general terms, it is a mark of quality in a vine variety that it is capable of producing wines with distinguished flavours, even if those flavours are heavily influenced by weather, TERROIR, and vineyard practice. Lesser vine varieties tend to produce wines that are neutral and undistinguished, however promising the vineyard site.

When more than one vine variety is used to produce a single wine, it is important that the wines produced by those varieties are complementary. Cabernet Sauvignon tends to blend well with wines that have more obvious fruit such as Merlot or warm-climate Syrah/Shiraz, for example, while the weight of Sémillon is a good foil for the aroma and acidity of Sauvignon Blanc.

Wine quality is maximized if the vine variety or vine varieties are well suited to the site. Although to an increasing extent varieties are selected for new vineyards on the basis of climatic similarity with a classic wine region, matching vine variety to site is considered in its infancy in most of the NEW WORLD (even if certain combinations such as Coonawarra for Cabernet Sauvignon vines, or Central Coast and Oregon for Pinot Noir, established themselves earlier than most). In parts of the Old World, on the other hand, the matching of vine variety to site, or even whole regions, is so entrenched (see VINE VARIETIES) that some would argue it amounts to restriction. The varieties Cabernet Sauvignon and Merlot undoubtedly perform extremely well in Bordeaux, but it is perhaps an unnecessary constraint to forbid Bordeaux vine-growers from planting, say, Syrah.

Varieties vary in the range of environments they can tolerate. Chardonnay and to a slightly lesser extent Syrah, for example, are extremely versatile. Chardonnay can produce good wine in climates which vary from the coolness of Chablis to the hot interior valleys of California. Varieties such as Pinot Noir and Nebbiolo, on the other hand, appear to be extremely fastidious. See also CLIMATE AND WINE QUALITY.

The French APPELLATION CONTRÔLÉE system, which officially disapproves of citing vine varieties on the label, even as interpretation of a geographical appellation, is predicated on the belief that for every appellation there is an ideal vine variety, or that the character of the appellation is stronger than that of any vine variety. While this is an attractive proposition (and it is certainly true that, for example, the appellation of a red bordeaux or a white Alsace wine is often more strongly identifiable than any single vine variety), it seems questionable for most wine regions, even within France. Regulations in other European Union wine-producing countries tend to emulate those of France.   R.E.S. & J.Ro.

vineyard, name given to the field where grapevines are grown.

The contrast in connotations between the very words vineyard and field illustrates something of the special nature of vines as a crop. This may be partly connected with the symbolism of and pleasures associated with wine, but is also a function of the aesthetic appeal of vineyards in all seasons. The beauty of vineyards and vines plays an important part in wine TOURISM; it is difficult to imagine substantial numbers of people making a pilgrimage to a region famous for any other agricultural crop.

In most parts of the world, the vineyard is a well-defined entity, generally well demarcated by the borders of the straight rows. *Vignoble* is a common French term for a vineyard at all quality levels. In Bordeaux, and elsewhere, CRU may be used synonymously with a top-quality vineyard, while in Burgundy the terms CLIMAT or, in the case of a walled vineyard, CLOS are more common. In Italy the terms cru, *vigna*, SORI, and RONCO are all used. Recognition of single vineyards is less developed in Spain although innovator Miguel TORRES uses the term *pago*.

Even relatively small vineyards are rarely homogeneous in terms of soil, topography, and MESOCLIMATE. Soils in particular may vary considerably within one single vineyard. Sometimes, when the soil, topography, and climate are uniform over an area much larger than a single vineyard, as in COONAWARRA in South Australia (although the soils are much, much more varied than the climate or topography), then the region as a whole may earn a reputation for good quality rather than certain vineyards within it.

Vineyards vary in size, depending on many factors. Owing to fragmentation of vineyards by inheritance, some vineyard owners in BURGUNDY may lay claim to only a few rows often indistinguishable to outsiders from the adjacent vines. At the other end of the scale, in the New World there are often large corporate vineyards. One of the world's largest vineyards is the 2,800-ha/6,920-acre San Bernabe ranch in the Salinas Valley of MONTEREY in California.

Some vineyards are particularly famous for their wine because of their particular combination of VINE VARIETY, CLONE, ROOTSTOCK, and climate conditions. Of particular importance are the soil conditions, which, together with mesoclimate, constitute what the French (and others) call TERROIR. A feature, for example, of the famous Bordeaux PREMIERS CRUS is that as well as producing great wine in good years they are also able to do well in acknowledged low-quality years. This is a function not just of appropriate vineyard management, but also of the terroir which allows the vine to ripen the fruit adequately when other, less exalted vineyards cannot.

See also HILLSIDE VINEYARDS.   R.E.S. & J.Ro.

vin gris is not, happily, a grey wine but a pink wine that is usually decidedly paler than most ROSÉ, made exactly as a white wine from dark-skinned grapes, and therefore without any MACERATION. No rules govern the term *vin gris*, but a wine labelled **gris de gris** must be made from lightly tinted grape varieties described as *gris* such as CINSAUT or GRENACHE GRIS.

In France, where it is a speciality of the Côtes de TOUL and certain parts of the Loire, *vin gris* is usually made from pressing, but not macerating, dark-skinned grapes, often Gamay, which rarely ripen sufficiently to produce a deeply coloured red. It is also made in the Midi, notably beside the saltpans of the Camargue by Listel. The term is also occasionally encountered in the New World—although BLUSH wines are extremely similar to, if almost invariably sweeter than, *gris* wines. See also SCHILLERWEIN and other German light pinks.

vinho, Portuguese for wine, and **vinho de mesa** is Portugal's basic TABLE WINE. A **vinho maduro** is one that has been matured, for at least a year. A **vinho verde**, on the other hand, is a 'green' or young wine, designed to be drunk early.

vinho regional, third tier of designated wine regions in Portugal roughly equivalent in status to the French VIN DE PAYS (see also DOC and IPR). These large regions covering entire provinces permit greater flexibility in terms of permitted grape varieties and ageing requirements. The vinho regional designation is therefore popular with innovative wine-makers wishing to bottle relatively young wines or blend Portuguese and foreign grape varieties. In the centre and south of the country (Estremadura, Ribatejo, Terras do Sado, and Alentejo), producers are largely ignoring the DOCs and IPRs in favour of vinho regional. See also TRÁS-OS-MONTES, RIOS DO MINHO, and BEIRAS.   R.J.M.

Vinho Verde, light, acidic, often slightly sparkling, and highly distinctive wine produced in north-west PORTUGAL whose name means 'green wine', a reference to the youthful state in which it is customarily sold. It is produced in verdant countryside inland from the coast north of the city of OPORTO which is known as the Costa Verde or Green Coast. The Vinho Verde DOC region is Portugal's largest demarcated wine region, extending from Vale da Cambra south of the river Douro to the river Minho that forms the frontier with Spain over 130 km/80 miles to the north.

The Vinho Verde DOC officially divides into six subregions, distinguished by climatic differences and the white grape varieties grown there. The area around the town of Monção on the Spanish border produces one of the best but least typical Vinhos Verdes from the ALVARINHO grape. Alcohol levels of up to 13 per cent set these wines apart, and, thanks to a combination of consumer demand and low yields, they are relatively expensive. Further south around the towns of Braga, Barcelos, and Guimarães, the dominant grape varieties are LOUREIRO, TRAJADURA (both known, with slightly different spellings of their names, in GALICIA in Spain), and Pedernã (see ARINTO). These high-yielding vines produce wines that are light and acidic with an alcoholic strength typically between 8 and 10 per cent. Inland towards the river Douro around the town of Baião, AVESSO is the most important variety, producing a slightly fuller style of wine in a warmer, drier climate. With the exception of Alvarinho wines from Monção, under the local legislation Vinhos Verdes may not exceed 11.5 per cent and wines more alcoholic than this fall into the vinho regional designation of RIOS DO MINHO.

Nearly half of all Vinho Verde produced, however, is not the widely exported white wine but a fizzy, acidic, light, dry red with only about 10 per cent alcohol made from grapes such as Azal, Vinhão, and Espadeiro and a large number of high-yielding HYBRIDS. Foreign palates struggle with these deep-coloured, rasping reds and little red Vinho Verde leaves the north of Portugal.

In the 1980s and 1990s, a number of single estates or QUINTAS have emerged, making high-quality VARIETAL wines from grapes such as Alvarinho, Loureiro, and Avesso. Although Vinho Verde is traditionally bone dry, most commercial BRANDS are sweetened to appeal to overseas markets. Unfortunately, few bottles carry a VINTAGE, but both red and white Vinho Verde should be drunk within a year after the harvest while the wine retains its characteristic fruit and freshness.   R.J.M.

vinifera, the European species of *Vitis* that is the vine most used for wine production, to which all the most familiar VINE VARIETIES belong.

Vinifera is one of about 60 species of the *Vitis* genus, the majority of which originate in the Americas or Asia. *Vinifera* grapes are used principally for wine-making, TABLE GRAPES, and DRYING GRAPES.

vinification, the practical art of transforming grapes into wine. In its widest sense, it is synonymous with WINE-MAKING, but strictly encompasses only those processes which take place in the winery up to the point at which

the ÉLEVAGE of the new wine begins. See also OENOLOGY.

vin jaune, meaning literally 'yellow wine' in French, extraordinary style of wine made in France, mainly in the JURA region, using a technique similar to that used for making SHERRY. The most famous *vin jaune* appellation is CHÂTEAU-CHALON. A similar wine, called *vin de voile*, is made by at least one producer in GAILLAC.

vino, Italian for wine and, colloquially and unfairly, English for basic quaffing wine, or PLONK.

vino da meditazione, unofficial but useful Italian category of wines too complex (and often too alcoholic and/or sweet) to drink with food. Such wines should be sipped meditatively after a meal.

Although they do not employ the same terminology, and produce wines much lighter in alcohol, some Germans effectively treat fine wine as a *vino da meditazione*.

vino da tavola, Italian for TABLE WINE, the official European Union category denoting the lowest of the vinous low, but much wider in scope in a country with such little regard for law as ITALY. While the great majority of each Italian wine harvest qualifies as basic vino da tavola, typically red from Apulia and white from Sicily, sold at rock-bottom prices (or drained off into the European wine lake), vino da tavola may also designate some of the finest, and most expensive, wines Italy produces, made outside the constraining rules of the official DOC and DOCG quality-wine systems.

These new **vini da tavola** were born in 1974 with the appearance of TIGNANELLO and SASSICAIA, both marketed by the Florentine house of ANTINORI. Although the wines were produced in entirely different geographical zones (CHIANTI CLASSICO and BOLGHERI respectively) and from entirely different grape varieties (a predominance of Sangiovese and Cabernet Sauvignon respectively), they shared four significant characteristics that were to mark the evolution of this category of wines. They both represented an attempt to give more body, intensity, and longevity to Tuscan red wines, which had become rather fruity and light-hearted in the preceding 15 years. Unlike the prevailing Tuscan red-wine norm, these blends excluded white grapes. Non-traditional, non-Italian varieties were used in both blends (the 1975 Tignanello substituted Cabernet Sauvignon for the native CANAIOLO). And, in a move that was to delight French coopers, small oak barrels, principally of French origin, were used for the BARREL MATURATION of both wines. This latter innovation was a radical break with the local practice of using large casks of Yugoslav oak, and marked a movement towards a more international style. The move was not welcomed by all in the domestic market and forced Antinori to seek a wider international public for the wines; it also forced them to seek more flavour intensity and concentration in the wines to avoid an overwhelming oakiness.

The blend of the 1975 Tignanello (80 per cent Sangiovese, 20 per cent Cabernet Sauvignon—the first vintage had included three per cent Malvasia) rapidly became canonical and was to prove extremely influential over the following 15 years. Although Cabernet Sauvignon has remained principally a blending grape in Tuscany, a certain number of Cabernet Sauvignon-based wines began to appear, particularly after the middle of the 1980s. The native Sangiovese grape was hardly neglected, however, and a substantial number of BARRIQUE-aged, 100 per cent Sangiovese wines began to appear in the 1980s, the pioneering effort being Montevertine's Le Pergole Torte in 1977.

Experiments with earlier maturing varieties Syrah and, with notable success, Merlot became increasingly common in the late 1980s, both for blending with Sangiovese and for VARIETAL wines. The first Pinot Noirs appeared at the same time, although the suitability of this Burgundian variety to the Tuscan climate has yet to be demonstrated. Some non-traditional white varieties were also planted, notably Chardonnay and Sauvignon Blanc, and various OAK treatments essayed.

Sassicaia was a pioneering wine, not only in its use of Cabernet but also in its revaluation of a zone never known for producing fine or even commercial wine. Its example has been followed by other peripheral areas of Tuscany. At the time, these could not qualify as DOC wines, just as non-traditional varietal wines in an area such as Chianti Classico cannot be given DOC status.

If high-priced vini da tavola were initially confined to Tuscany, the mid 1980s saw a significant expansion of the phenomenon. Ambitious producers saddled with poorly conceived DOCs and/or a poor image for the wines of their zone were quick to profit by the example of Tuscany. Superior Sangiovese from Romagna and superior versions of INTERNATIONAL VARIETIES from Friuli and the Trentino, frequently barrique aged, followed suit. Some of these wines returned to the DOC fold in the 1990s, partly as a result of the greater prestige and credibility now accorded to the wines of their zones and regions, but many important wines were still deliberately sold as vini da tavola in the late 1990s.

Piedmont, with a more consolidated viticultural tradition and with a certain number of prestigious DOCG wines, was slower to accept the idea that the term vino da tavola could be a viable alternative, but Barbera, the region's most widely planted variety, existed in a bewildering variety of styles. It was therefore almost inevitable that the first important small barrel-aged Barberas in Piedmont were vini da tavola and, as the number of these wines increased, many producers—not only in Asti or the Monferrato, but also in the LANGHE—began to release their basic Barbera as a DOC wine and their superior Barbera as a vino da tavola. As a region with a significant amount of experimentation with newly introduced international varieties, Piedmont eventually followed the Tuscan example. Younger producers' experiments with Nebbiolo/Barbera blends, or even more baroque blends such as Barbera/Cabernet Sauvignon, combinations obviously neither imagined nor covered by existing DOCs, had no alternative to vino da tavola status until the creation of an overall regional DOC in 1995. They are now being marketed as either Langhe Rosso or Monferrato Rosso, though several important stragglers evidently prefer to continue as vini da tavola.

Italian wine thus does not follow the example of French or German viticultural classification, whose finest and most expensive products are almost inevitably the appellation wines and whose respective VIN DE TABLE and TAFELWEIN enjoy a generally low status.

Vino da tavola as an indication on labels for better-quality wines is gradually being phased out in favour of the recently developed IGTS, with the exception of PIEDMONT, whose overall regional DOC provides a suitable alternative. This remains a lower category than DOC and reflects the difficulties which are still encountered in placing many of the country's best wines into established traditional categories.

See also CAPITOLARE and SUPERTUSCAN. D.T.

vino de la tierra, category of wines from specially designated zones in SPAIN which have not qualified for DO status. The category is the equivalent of the French VIN DE PAYS.

vino de mesa, Spanish term for TABLE WINE, the most basic category for wine coming from vineyards that do not qualify for either VINO DE LA TIERRA or DO status. An increasing number of quality estates placed outside DO limits now use this appellation, as Italy's SUPERTUSCANS did before them. They include Dominio de Valdepusa; Dehesa del Carrizal and Manuel Manzaneque in Castile-La Mancha; Bodega Las Monjas in Andalucía; and Mauro and Abadía Retuerta in Castile and León.

Vino Nobile di Montepulciano, potentially majestic and certainly noble red wine made exclusively in the township of Montepulciano 120 km/75 miles south east of Florence in the hills of TUSCANY in central Italy. It was one of the first four DOCGs conferred in 1980. Officially the wine is the classic Tuscan blend of SANGIOVESE, here called Prugnolo Gentile, with small amounts of CANAIOLO, TREBBIANO, and MALVASIA grapes. The DOCG regulations were modified in 1989, however, to permit the elimination of white grapes, and the better producers freely admit to making their wines entirely of Prugnolo Gentile even though the theoretical maximum is 80 per cent.

The wine is rather fuller in body and more alcoholic than Chianti. It has so far not shown the aromatic finesse and elegance of the best Chianti or Brunello. Poor practices in both vineyard and cellar led to a notable decline in the wine's quality between the late 1960s and the mid 1980s. Some progress has been made subsequently, but the wines have not been able to gain the prestige or fetch the prices in the market-place of the better Chianti Classico Riservas and are undoubtedly the poor relation of Brunello di Montalcino and the more glamorous wines labelled VINO DA TAVOLA, although the price and quality gap continues to narrow in the 1990s. Some experimentation with small oak barrels and with alternative vine varieties is taking place, though such developments remain marginal. Avignonesi is the most innovative producer, with a wide range of red and white vini di tavola.

Earlier-maturing, lighter local wine is declassified as Rosso di Montepulciano, a DOC created in 1989. D.T.

Vin Santo, 'holy wine', TUSCANY's classic amber-coloured dessert wine, is produced throughout this central Italian region. It is made traditionally from the local white grapes TREBBIANO and MALVASIA which have been dried on straw mats under the rafters, in the hottest and best-ventilated part of the house (see DRIED-GRAPE WINES). The grapes were normally crushed between the end of November and the end of March, and then aged in small barrels. These barrels were frequently made of chestnut, but the 1980s saw a decisive turn towards OAK. The barrels themselves are sealed and never topped up, resulting inevitably in ULLAGE and OXIDATION, which gives the wine its characteristic amber colour.

The wine comes in a bewildering range of styles from the ultra-sweet to a bone-dry version which more closely resembles a dry fino SHERRY than a dessert wine.

Attempts to ratify production techniques and anchor the wine to specific areas began with three partially overlapping DOCs, although a large proportion of Vin Santo remains non-DOC. Many other Tuscan zones followed suit by creating their own DOCS in the mid 1990s. All the zones impose a substantial percentage of Trebbiano in the blend, despite the conviction of most of the better producers that it is the Malvasia grape that makes the better wine.

The quality of the wine itself varies wildly, not only as a result of variation in grape composition, RESIDUAL SUGAR and wine-making competence, but because the land is divided between so many smallholders, all of whom seem to feel obliged to produce Vin Santo as an obeisance to the tradition of offering this wine to guests as a gesture of esteem. Although some delicious Vin Santo is made, there is also a considerable proportion with serious wine FAULTS. DOC rules insist the wine is matured for at least three years, and the better producers rarely release their Vin Santo before five years. Cask maturation, without RACKING, lasts from 4 to more than 10 years for the most traditionally made Vin Santo.

Trentino also produces its own version of Vin Santo called **Vino Santo,** a decisively sweet DRIED-GRAPE WINE. These wines are quite different from Tuscan Vin Santo since they are aged in barrels subject to regular TOPPING UP, although they too are decidedly artisanal and very variable in quality.   D.T.

Vins de Moselle. See MOSELLE.

vintage can either mean the physical process of grape-picking and wine-making, for which see HARVEST, or it can mean the year or growing season which produced a particular wine, for which see VINTAGE YEAR. A vintage wine is one made from the produce of a single year.

vintage assessment is notoriously difficult because quality and character can vary so much between producers and properties. A vintage is often assessed at the most difficult stage in its life, its infancy, for reasons of commerce and curiosity. Wine merchants and WINE WRITERS habitually taste wines from the most recent vintage in a wine region important for INVESTMENT when they are just a few months old and are still in cask. Quite apart from the fact that the wines are at this stage still being made (see ÉLEVAGE), samples may give a misleading impression either because too long has elapsed since they were drawn from cask (OXIDATION is a common problem), or, if they are tasted directly from cask, because they are undergoing a distorting treatment such as FINING. Furthermore, this sort of vintage assessment is long before the ASSEMBLAGE process and can only provide a snapshot of embryonic wine from a small proportion of the total number of barrels produced.

This sort of comparative tasting can usually give some indication as to which are the most and least successful wines of a given vintage, but it can be difficult to stand back from the individual samples, accurately remember exactly how the same wines from previous vintages tasted at the same stage, and make any reliable assessment of the likely characteristics and potential of the young vintage as a whole.

The assessment of a mature vintage is a much less hazardous process that is usually undertaken in the form of a horizontal TASTING, although of course SUBJECTIVITY plays its part as it does in all tasting.

See Appendix 4 for this writer's VINTAGE CHART.

vintage charts are both useful and notoriously fallible, partly because young VINTAGE ASSESSMENT is so fraught with difficulty. Most vintage charts take the form of a grid mapping ratings for each combination of wine region and year. The least sophisticated vintage charts content themselves with a NUMBER for each major wine region: Bordeaux 1990 '9' (out of 10), for instance. More sophisticated charts divide Bordeaux into its main districts, and add a letter indicating maturity: Margaux 1990 '90E' (90 out of 100, E for early maturing), for instance. The fact that this same vintage chart suggests that Graves 1990 is '90R' (R for ready to drink) already demonstrates how difficult it is to generalize about a district in which there may be hundreds of different producers, each with a different wine-making policy and style of wine.

The most useful vintage charts are the most detailed, but also those that are regularly updated on the basis of continuous and relevant tasting.

See Appendix 4 for this writer's vintage chart.

vintage year, the year in which a wine was produced and the characteristics of that year. Most, but not all, of its characteristics result from particular WEATHER conditions experienced. In the southern hemisphere, a **vintage-dated** wine invariably carries the year in which the grapes were picked, even though much of the vine growth cycle was actually in the previous year. In the northern hemisphere, vintage-dated wines carry the year in which both the vine growth occurred and the grapes were picked (with the exception of those rare examples of EISWEIN picked in early January, which are dated with the year whose vine growth produced the wine). The expression 'vintage year' is also sometimes used of a year producing particularly high quality wines.

In a literal sense, all young wine is vintage wine, being from a single year. Only at the BLENDING stage may wine of a recent year, or vintage, be mixed with older wines into an undated blend. Most everyday wines—such as the TABLE WINE category designated by the European Union, the JUG WINES of the USA, and CASK WINE in Australia—are not vintage dated. Some top-quality CHAMPAGNE is NON-VINTAGE too. In most circumstances, however, a non-vintage wine is inferior to a vintage-dated one.

The vintage year printed on a wine label can help the consumer decide when to open a particular bottle, being particularly relevant to

Viognier

wine meant for AGEING (others, the great majority of wines, should simply be drunk as young as possible).

Vintages are seldom uniformly good, medium, or bad, even within a small area. A generally recognized 'vintage' year can have its failures, often for reasons totally beyond the competence of vignerons and wine-makers. Equally, 'poor' vintages can usually still produce good wines from particular locations and grape varieties.

See Appendix 4 for details of individual vintages. See also LABELLING INFORMATION.

Viognier became one of the world's most fashionable white grape varieties in the early 1990s, mainly because its most famous wine CONDRIEU is distinctive, associated with the modish RHÔNE, and, most importantly, relatively scarce. CHÂTEAU-GRILLET is the only other all-Viognier French appellation.

The grapes are a deep yellow and the resulting wine is high in colour, alcohol, and a very particular perfume redolent of apricots, peaches, and blossom. Condrieu is one of the few highly priced white wines that should probably be drunk young, while this perfume is at its most heady and before the wine's slightly low acidity fades.

The variety declined to an official total of just 14 ha/35 acres in the French agricultural census of 1968—mostly in the three northern Rhône appellations in which it is allowed, Condrieu, Château-Grillet, and, to an even lesser extent, CÔTE-RÔTIE, in which it may be included as a perfuming agent up to 20 per cent of the Syrah-dominated total. But by 1997, more than 100 ha/250 acres of Viognier qualified for the Condrieu appellation and Viognier plantings in the LANGUEDOC and California rose rapidly. Australian producers were experimenting with it by the mid 1990s and some particularly fine examples had been made in central Italy. The relative scarcity of such a fashionable grape has led to blends, both with other white Rhône varieties such as Roussanne, Marsanne, and Rolle or Vermentino and, surprisingly successfully, with Chardonnay.

Today the consumer can choose from a range of recognizably perfumed, if slightly light, southern French varietal Viogniers. The California way with Viognier is a notably alcoholic one, but when it works, these monsters can be magnificent. As well as being grown in the Ardèche, throughout the Languedoc, and to a

certain extent in Roussillon, Viognier is planted increasingly in the southern Rhône, especially for white Côtes du Rhône, and also in Provence.

Varietal Viognier has been exported from both Argentina and Uruguay.

Viosinho, useful, crisp, northern Portuguese white grape grown in the Douro and Trás-os-Montes.

Viré-Clessé, white-wine appellation created in 1998 for two of the better villages within the MÂCON appellation in southern Burgundy.

Virginia, middle Atlantic state in the eastern UNITED STATES in which wine production has recently increased substantially. VINIFERA grapes now outnumber HYBRIDS and native grapes by almost 4 : 1. Chardonnay and the red Bordeaux varieties do exceptionally well. The climate is warm, but growers have to guard against fungal diseases. The total number of wineries had by 1998 increased to more than 50. Six AVAs are Montecillo (home of Thomas Jefferson); Virginia Eastern Shore, influenced by the Chesapeake Bay; Northern Neck—George Washington's Birthplace in northern Virginia close to the ready market of Washington, DC; Shenandoah Valley (an AVA not to be confused with the California AVA of the same name) nestled in the Blue Ridge Mountains; North Fork of Roanoke; and Rocky Knob in southwest Virginia. Horton Cellars in Gordonsville is producing a popular Viognier.   H.L.

Visan, one of the Côtes du Rhône villages. See RHÔNE.

viscosity, the quality of being viscous, the extent to which a solution resists flow or movement. Honey is more viscous than sugar syrup, for example, which is considerably more viscous than water. Viscosity, which approximates to what wine tasters call BODY, can be sensed by the human palate in the form of resistance as the solution is rinsed around the mouth.

A very sweet wine is more viscous than a dry one, even if they have the same ALCOHOLIC STRENGTH. Alcohol itself is more viscous than water, and higher-strength wines are therefore more viscous than lower-strength wines. The most viscous wines of all therefore are those that are both sweet and strong. The dissolved solids in wine, the wine's EXTRACT, also add marginally to its viscosity, so the less a wine has been subjected to FILTRATION and FINING, the more viscous it is.

It has been thought that the viscosity and the (quite unrelated) GLYCEROL content of a wine were the main factors in the formation of 'tears' on the inside of a wine glass. In fact, while they may be minor factors, the explanation is very different; see TEARS. A.D.W.

Vital, white grape grown in Estremadura in western Portugal which is known as MALVASIA Fina in the Douro.

viticulture, the science and practice of grape culture. Viticulture is practised consciously by VITICULTURISTS, often instinctively by grape-growers or vine-growers. Viticultural practices vary enormously around the world; some of these differences are highlighted under NEW WORLD.

For still wines, it is arguable that the VITI-CULTURIST can have a greater impact on wine quality than the WINE-MAKER since so many of the factors affecting quality are viticultural. The belief that 'wine is made in the vineyard not the cellar' became increasingly widespread during the 1990s.

viticulturist, someone who practises VITI-CULTURE.

Viura is a common Spanish synonym for MACABEO and is therefore what Riojanos call their dominant white grape variety.

Vivarais, Côtes du, VDQS on the right bank of the RHÔNE immediately opposite Coteaux du TRICASTIN in the wild and beguiling Ardèche. Widely dispersed vineyards produce mainly light reds and rosés from Grenache and Syrah grapes, with no more than 10 per cent of Carignan and Cinsaut combined (more Cinsaut is allowed in the rosés). A small amount of white is made from Clairette, Grenache Blanc, and Marsanne. Production is dominated by CO-OPERATIVES, whose more profitable business may be producing varietal VINS DE PAYS de l'Ardèche from non-appellation varieties.

Vlassky Rizling, Czech name for WELSCH-RIESLING.

Vojvodina, autonomous region within SERBIA in the far north east of what was YUGOSLAVIA. The best of the vineyards adjoin the vineyards of CROATIA to the west and sweep south beyond the town of Novi Sad nearly to Belgrade itself. Viticulturally they are an extension of the inland Croatian region

with much the same mix of white grape varieties for the most part. There are also some good red wines made from Cabernet Sauvignon and Merlot. The SMEDEREVKA vine, called after the town of Smederevo south of Belgrade, makes large amounts of very ordinary white wine usually drunk with mineral water as a SPRITZER. Some of the wines from this area are potentially the best-balanced whites in what was Yugoslavia.

Close to the Hungarian border lies a region which owes its roots much more to HUNGARY than to Yugoslavia. Even the grapes reflect the Hungarian viticultural tradition. Laski Rizling (WELSCHRIESLING) still predominates but red wine grapes include KADARKA and Frankovka (BLAUFRÄNKISCH) while EZERJÓ and Kövedinka (the DINKA of Hungary) are among white wine grapes. Even MUSCAT OTTONEL tends to be more prevalent here and in Hungary than in the rest of Yugoslavia.

A further, rather unexciting part of the Vojvodina vineyard sits on the northern bank of the Danube just where it crosses the Romanian border. More Smederevka and more Laski Rizling grow here. BANAT RIZLING grows here and in Romania and is reputed to have a better, more solid style than Laski Rizling.

See YUGOSLAVIA. A.H.M.

volatile. All wines are volatile in that they contain volatile FLAVOUR COMPOUNDS and some level of VOLATILE ACIDS, but volatile is used as a pejorative tasting term for a wine in which the level of acetic acid has risen unacceptably high.

volatile acidity of a wine is its total concentration of volatile acids, those naturally occurring organic ACIDS of wines that happen to be separable by distillation. Wine's most common volatile acid by far is acetic acid.

Very low concentrations of acetic acid do not affect the taste of wine adversely. Increasing concentrations change the taste, however, from added complexity and fruitiness to a frankly vinegary flavour. Most everyday wines are very low in acetic acid but some red wines may be excessively acetic. A few fine wines, usually mature reds in bottle, are rich enough in BODY, TANNINS, and ALCOHOL to bear concentrations of acetic acid that do not impair flavour but are sometimes said to lift it (see TASTING TERMS). A.D.W.

volatility, property of having excessive VOLA-TILE ACIDS.

Volnay, attractive small village in the Côte de Beaune district of Burgundy's CÔTE D'OR producing elegant red wines from Pinot Noir.

More than half Volnay's vineyards are of PREMIER CRU status, stretching in a broad swathe from Pommard to Meursault, continuing into the latter village. Because Meursault is renowned for its white wines, its single really fine red-wine vineyard of Les Santenots is sold as Volnay Santenots. The best part of this vineyard is Les Santenots-du-Milieu, although it is not as typical of Volnay as Le Cailleret, which it abuts, or Champans. These two vineyards express the astonishing, velvety finesse of Volnay. Clos des Chênes, just above Le Cailleret, is also very fine but a little lighter.

Excellent vineyards close to the village include Taillepieds, the Clos de la Bousse d'Or, monopoly of Domaine de la Pousse d'Or, which also owns an excellent enclave within Le Cailleret known as the Clos des 60 Ouvrées, and the Clos des Ducs of the Marquis d'Angerville. Volnay's finest producers include Michel Lafarge, Pousse d'Or, de Montille, d'Angerville, and most of the best producers in MEURSAULT who also have vineyards in Volnay.   J.T.C.M.

Vöslau, wine centre in lower AUSTRIA in the Thermenregion district.

Vosne-Romanée, village in the Côte de Nuits district of Burgundy producing arguably the finest red wines made anywhere from Pinot Noir grapes. As well as excellent wines at VILLAGE and PREMIER CRU level, there are six GRAND CRU vineyards.

The grands crus are Romanée-Conti, La Romanée, La Tâche, Richebourg, Romanée-St-Vivant, and La Grande Rue. Between them they produce, with Musigny and Chambertin, the greatest wines of the Côte de Nuits. They have more finesse than any other but to this is allied as much power and stuffing as their nearest rivals.

Romanée-Conti, a sublime vineyard whose wines can be the most expensive in the world, is the monopoly of the DOMAINE DE LA ROMANÉE-CONTI (DRC). La Romanée is the monopoly of the Liger Belair family, whose wine is distributed by BOUCHARD Père et Fils. About 300 cases are made each year from the tiny 0.84 ha/2 acres of La Romanée; double that amount is produced from the 1.80 ha of Romanée-Conti.

Another monopoly of the Domaine de la Romanée-Conti, and regarded as nearly as fine as the vineyard from which it takes its name, is La Tâche, whose 6 ha (including the vineyard of Les Gaudichots) produce a wine which is explosively seductive even when young, whereas Romanée-Conti takes longer to show its astonishing completeness. La Tâche seems to thrive even in lesser years.

The next most sought-after Vosne-Romanée wine is Richebourg, whose 8 ha are shared between 10 growers, notably Domaine de la Romanée-Conti, Domaine LEROY, branches of the Gros family, and Domaine Méo-Camuzet. As the name suggests, this is one of the most voluptuous wines of Burgundy and can equal La Tâche in some years.

Romanée-St-Vivant can also make very fine wine but it is usually lighter and less powerful than its neighbours. There are half a dozen owners, of which the largest is Domaine de la Romanée-Conti (5.3 ha out of 9.43). Domaine Leroy and Louis LATOUR's Domaine de Corton Grancey are the next largest owners.

Between La Tâche to the south and La Romanée-Conti to the north lie the 1.4 ha of La Grande Rue, originally classified as premier cru but promoted, as its location suggests is only right, to grand cru. The vineyard is a monopoly of Domaine Lamarche, whose wines have not so far stood comparison with those of their illustrious neighbours.

Amongst the best of Vosne-Romanée's premier-cru vineyards are Clos des Réas, Les Malconsorts, and Les Chaumes on the Nuits-St-Georges side, Cros Parantoux made famous by Henry Jayer, above the grands crus, and Les Beauxmonts and Les Suchots abutting Flagey-Échézeaux. Part of Les Beauxmonts is actually in the latter commune, although it is sold as Vosne-Romanée, as is the village wine of Flagey.

While the renown of the Domaine de la Romanée-Conti dominates Vosne-Romanée, it should not overshadow other significant influences such as Henri Jayer, for his unparalleled wine-making skills; René Engel for his patriarchal influence and local historical research and publications during a long life; and now Lalou Bize-LEROY, who has bought and transformed the former Domaine Nöellat. Other particularly fine domaines are those owned by the various members of the Gros family and Grivot.

See also CÔTE D'OR.   J.T.C.M.

Vougeot, small village in the Côte de Nuits district of Burgundy producing red wines from the Pinot Noir grape. There are only 4.8 ha/11.8 acres of vineyards producing VILLAGE WINE and 11.7 ha designated PREMIER CRU; the village's fame rests squarely with the 50.6 ha GRAND CRU, Clos de Vougeot, the largest grand-cru vineyard of the CÔTE D'OR.

When the wines could be blended by the Cistercian monks to produce a complete wine from differing constituent parts, Clos de Vougeot doubtless deserved its reputation. Now that the vineyard is fragmented between 80 or more owners, far too many of the wines are below standard through the inadequacies of some of the raw material and many of the production techniques of the less conscientious producers.

Classic Clos de Vougeot is likely to be dense and ungiving when young, robust rather than elegant. However, after a decade it opens out into one of the most complete wines of the Côte d'Or with deep, rich flavours reminiscent of truffles and undergrowth.

Of the premier-cru vineyards, Le Clos Blanc, producing an unusual white wine from Chardonnay, is the monopoly of producers Héritier-Guyot, and Clos de la Perrière is in the sole possession of Domaine Bertagna. The other premiers crus are Les Cras, rarely seen, and Les Petits Vougeots.

Reliable producers of Clos de Vougeot include Méo-Camuzet, Anne Gros, and René Engel.

See also CLOS DE VOUGEOT and CÔTE D'OR.

J.T.C.M.

Vouvray, the most important individual white-wine appellation in the TOURAINE district of the Loire. The wines of Vouvray vary enormously in quality, thereby offering a true representation of the grape variety from which Vouvray is exclusively made. Vouvray is CHENIN BLANC and, to a certain extent, Chenin Blanc is Vouvray (although ARBOIS grapes are theoretically allowed into Vouvray too). No other wine made only from this long-lived middle Loire grape, often called Pineau de la Loire, is made in such quantity: a total of more than 100,000 hl/2.6 million gal apiece of still and sparkling wine. (The proportion of sparkling wine produced increased during the 1990s.) Only COTEAUX DU LAYON can begin to rival Vouvray for the total area of Chenin Blanc planted.

Vouvray itself is a particularly pretty small town on the northern bank of the Loire just east of Tours. It was not until the creation of the Vouvray appellation in 1936 that Vouvray established an identity of its own.

Making top-quality Vouvray is as hazardous as making any top-quality sweet white wine which owes its sweetness to NOBLE ROT or extreme RIPENESS. The vine-grower is entirely at the mercy of the weather, and the harvest in Vouvray is one of France's last, usually lasting until well into November, often involving a number of TRIS through the vineyard.

Wine-making here is distinguished by the need to bottle pure fruit and its naturally high acidity as early and as unadorned as possible. Neutral fermentation vessels such as large old oak casks or stainless steel tanks are used, MALOLACTIC FERMENTATION is rigidly suppressed, and the AGEING process is expected to occur, extremely slowly, in bottle.

The style of wine made by the best producers such as Huet, Poniatowski, Champalou, Domaine des Aubuisières, and Clos Naudin is determined completely by the weather. In the least generous VINTAGES, only dry and possibly sparkling wines are made. The best years yield very sweet, golden nectars that are naturally MOELLEUX, or even LIQUOREUX, but are so high in acidity that most are almost unpleasant to drink in their middle age between about three years old and two to three decades. Some of the finest Vouvrays can still taste lively, and richly fruity, at nearly a century. A relatively high proportion of medium-dry demi-sec is also produced in many years, and it too demands a considerable amount of BOTTLE AGEING before the acidity has muted and the wine can be served as a fine accompaniment to many savoury dishes, including those that are richly sauced.

Commercial Vouvray also exists, on the other hand, as simply a medium-sweet, reasonably acid, white wine that has little capacity for development.

Vouvray Mousseux can often offer more interest than other Loire sparkling wines, to those who appreciate the honeyed aromas of Chenin Blanc, at least. The wines have weight and flavour, and are suitable for drinking with meals as well as before them.

See also LOIRE.

VQPRD, abbreviation for the European Union term **Vin de Qualité Produit dans une Région Déterminée**, meaning QUALITY WINE. Although it is essentially a French expression, the initials are sometimes seen on labels of superior bottlings from any European country.

Vranac, red grape variety that is a speciality of MONTENEGRO in what was YUGOSLAVIA. The wines produced are deep in colour and can be rich in EXTRACT, responding unusually well to oak AGEING. There is an element of refreshing bitterness on the finish of these wines that suggests some relationship to an Italian variety just across the Adriatic. Vranac is one of the few indigenous grape variety names to appear on the label of wines exported from what was Yugoslavia. It is also grown, less successfully, in MACEDONIA.

waiter, wine. See SOMMELIER.

Wales. Several small vineyards in sheltered corners of southern Wales produce either Welsh Vineyards QUALITY WINE or United Kingdom TABLE WINE. See ENGLAND.

Walker Bay, coastal ward of the Overberg wine district in SOUTH AFRICA.

Wälscher, occasional Austrian synonym for CHASSELAS.

Wälschriesling. See WELSCHRIESLING.

Washington, dynamic fruit-growing state in the PACIFIC NORTHWEST of the United States which has, with little fuss or fanfare, crept into second position behind California as an American VINIFERA wine producer. Producing just five per cent of the national wine total, it is a very distant second behind California, but its reputation for quality is not so very far behind.

Geography and climate

Washington is the USA's leading apple and hop state, both crops being good viticultural markers, but there is a sharp difference between the climates of western and viticulturally much more important eastern Washington.

Western Washington is mild and damp the year round because of the proximity of the Pacific Ocean and the inland sea called the Puget Sound, overlooked by Seattle. Population, limited space, and marginal growing conditions combine to limit plantings in western Washington to less than one per cent of the state's total. The state's newest appellation of Puget Sound covers the islands and land adjoining the waters of the Puget Sound, into the Cascade foothills.

Eastern Washington, a vast area of rolling farmland screened from marine air by the towering barrier of the Cascade Mountains, has hot, desert-dry summers and cold to arctic winters. Virtually all of the vineyards in eastern Washington fall within the Columbia Valley AVA. Inside it, in turn, are the important Yakima Valley appellation, which encompasses about 40 per cent of the state's vineyards, and the nascent Walla Walla Valley one.

Vine varieties and wine styles

Washington grows more American vines than VINIFERA but most of their produce is used for juice, jam, jelly, and flavourings. Almost all wines are *vinifera*, VARIETAL, and are generally distinguished from those of California by bright fruit and relatively crisp acidity. Although the state is arguably best known for its Merlot, the second most planted grape variety, white grapes have predominated. Fast declining acreage hides the fact, but Riesling remains a variety that the state grows particularly well, for both drier wines and sweeter late-harvest ones, some of the latter being BOTRYTIZED. By the early 1990s, Semillon was delivering more exciting wines than Riesling, however, and with greater consistency. One after another of these wines has demonstrated the kind of structure and balance that promise well for longevity. The best performances of Riesling and Semillon notwithstanding, Chardonnay dominated vineyard and cellar alike in Washington throughout the 1990s. While typical Chardonnays range from merely good to quite good, the variety's fortunes were sustained more by consumer demand than inherent superiority. Other white varieties with good track records from more limited plantings are Sauvignon Blanc and Chenin Blanc. Gewürztraminer has been steady, though workaday. Müller-Thurgau has shown occasional brightness in a scattering of vineyards in the Puget Sound basin, an isolated patch of vines west of the Cascade Mountains.

Reds blossomed later than whites in Washington. The first great hope, Cabernet Sauvignon, remains important but was overtaken by Merlot in 1991. By nature, Washington Cabernet Sauvignons lean towards ripe flavours and noticeable alcohol levels. The prevailing style has called for ample tannins and hearty oak flavours. The net effect has been wines dramatic in youth but without great staying power. Merlot arrived in the vineyards several years behind Cabernet Sauvignon and quickly demonstrated richer flavours in wines of more restrained structure. Durability is still an unanswered question, although several examples hint at the possibility of reasonably long life in bottle. Blends of these two Bordeaux grape varieties, with or without Cabernet Franc, the state's third most planted red grape, are increasingly common and show promise. Syrah clearly has a serious long-term future in Washington. Among other red grape varieties, Washington has an American monopoly on the obscure but usefully low acid variety they call Lemberger (see LIMBERGER and BLAUFRÄNKISCH), which several wineries produce as a quite rewarding fresh, fruit-rich wine meant to be drunk in its youth. One or two producers have even essayed large-scale, oak-aged wines with it, as in AUSTRIA. There has been some not-entirely-unsuccessful experimentation with SANGIOVESE and NEBBIOLO.

The producers

The dominant force in Washington wine is Stimson Lane Company, the owner of a range of labels which includes Ch Ste Michelle, Domaine Ste Michelle, Columbia Crest, Snoqualmie, Farron Ridge, and Saddle Mountain. In the late 1990s, the firm owned nearly a third of the state's vineyards and distinguished some of its best fruit with single-vineyard bottlings. Some of the most sought-after wines are made in Walla Walla by Leonetti and in Puget Sound

by Quilceda Creek and Andrew Will. Other important labels by volume and reputation include the Seattle-based Columbia Winery, which produces fine wines from Red Willow vineyards, Hogue Cellars, and Woodward Canyon. L.S.H.

water is the most important constituent of wine (see WINE COMPOSITION) and is as essential to those who produce it as to those who consume it.

Soil water, the product of rainfall and/or IRRIGATION, is a prerequisite for vine growth and survival. PHOTOSYNTHESIS, without which grapes would never ripen, depends on water being available.

Water is also vital in the winery: HYGIENE'S best friend is the hosepipe, and many systems of TEMPERATURE CONTROL depend on copious supplies of water. In a small and decreasing number of wine regions, wine may be diluted to reduce ACIDITY. In warmer regions, however, the trend towards picking grapes riper and riper has resulted in higher and higher levels of alcohol, sometimes so high that the operation known euphemistically as 'humidification' has been employed either to improve the wine's BALANCE or to ensure its final ALCOHOLIC STRENGTH is not too high for legal or labelling purposes.

For centuries wine was always diluted with water but the modern wine drinker rarely chooses to dilute his or her wine (other than to make the occasional SPRITZER). However, for HEALTH reasons he or she is well advised to drink at least as much water alongside every glass of wine. Despite its incontrovertible appeal, wine is a poor quencher of thirst.

water stress is the physiological state of plants, including vines, suffering from a shortage of water. Water stress during the later stages of the viticultural growing season is common, since a considerable proportion of the world's vines are grown in MEDITERRANEAN CLIMATES, where rain falls principally in the winter months. It is commonly held that some water stress is desirable for optimum wine quality, especially for red wines, but there is little agreement about exactly how much. IRRIGATION can be used to overcome water stress, although it is outlawed in some countries.

There is no doubt that severe water stress interrupts grape RIPENING and reduces wine quality, as for example may be observed in Algeria. It is by no means clear whether water stress leads to higher sugars and better wine in dry viticultural areas such as the LANGUEDOC-ROUSSILLON in southern France. In humid maritime climates, such as that of BORDEAUX, however, there has been ample demonstration that mild water stress during ripening is favourable to wine quality. For example, the Bordeaux growing seasons of 1996, 1995, 1989, and 1990, all superior VINTAGES, were all relatively dry.   R.E.S.

weather, probably the single most exasperatingly unpredictable variable in the viticultural equation, as in most other farming activities. The weather in a specific growing season is the most important influence on the characteristics of a particular VINTAGE YEAR. See also CLIMATE, MACROCLIMATE, DROUGHT, SUNLIGHT, and TEMPERATURE.

Wein (pronounced 'vine') means 'wine' in German. It is therefore the first syllable of a host of important German wine names such as **Weinbau**, which means 'vine-growing', and **Weingut**, meaning 'wine estate' as distinct from a **Weinkellerei**, which buys in grapes, must, or wine but probably owns vineyards only if it describes itself as the all-purpose Weingut-Weinkellerei. A **Weinprobe** is a wine tasting.

weisser, meaning 'white', is a common prefix in German for pale-skinned grape varieties. **Weissburgunder** or **Weisser Burgunder** is PINOT BLANC, for example, while Blauer Burgunder is PINOT NOIR.

Weisser Riesling, common synonym for the great white RIESLING grape variety of Germany.

Weissherbst, special sort of pink wine made from a single grape variety in the AHR, RHEINGAU, RHEINHESSEN, PFALZ, WÜRTTEMBERG, and BADEN wine regions of GERMANY. It may be either a QBA or QMP wine, and in Baden, Weissherbst made from Spätburgunder (PINOT NOIR) has enjoyed local popularity. See also SCHILLERWEIN. The term is also used in German SWITZERLAND for very much the same style of wine.

Welschriesling, or Wälschriesling, white grape variety which, as Germans are keen to point out, is completely unrelated to the great RIESLING grape of Germany. Indeed it rankles with many Germans that the noble word is even allowed as a suffix in the name of this inferior variety; they would prefer that the word Rizling were used, as in **Welsch Rizling** or **Welschrizling,** which it is in many of its many synonyms.

Welschriesling may be the variety's most common name in AUSTRIA, but Welschrizling is obediently used in BULGARIA, its most common name in HUNGARY is OLASZ RIZLING, in SLOVENIA and VOJVODINA it is LASKI RIZLING, and in the CZECH REPUBLIC it is the very similar Rizling Vlassky. Only in CROATIA does it acquire a name of any distinction, Graševina. The Italians call it RIESLING ITALICO (as opposed to Riesling Renano, which is the Riesling of Germany) and variants of this are used all over eastern Europe, notably in ROMANIA (although most of the 'Riesling' planted in the CIS is true German Riesling). The variety is one of the few common white wine grapes in ALBANIA, as it is in what was for long its close political ally CHINA.

Although Welschriesling has little in common with Riesling, it too is a late-ripening vine whose grapes keep their acidity well and produce light-bodied, relatively aromatic wines. Welschriesling can easily be persuaded to yield even more productively than Riesling, however, and indeed this and its useful acidity probably explain why it is so widely planted throughout eastern Europe and, partly, why so much of the wine it produces is undistinguished (although low technological standards in many wineries in what was YUGOSLAVIA, for example, have also played a part).

As a wine, Welschriesling reaches its apogee in AUSTRIA, specifically in some particularly finely balanced, rich late-harvest wines made on the shores of the Neusiedlersee in Burgenland. In particularly favoured vintages, the NOBLE ROT forms to ripen grapes up to TROCKENBEERENAUSLESE level, while retaining the acidity that is Welschriesling's hallmark, although Austrian TBAs rarely have the longevity of their German counterparts. The bulk of Austria's Welschriesling, however, goes into light dryish wines for early drinking, notably in Burgenland and Styria. It has also been known as Riesler in Austria.

See also OLASZ RIZLING and LASKI RIZLING.

Western Australia, or WA. AUSTRALIA'S biggest state has the country's most isolated wine regions in its south-west corner.

Nowhere have the winds of change blown harder since 1970 than in Western Australia. In that year more than 90 per cent of the state's wine was made from grapes grown in the Swan

Valley; by 1996 it was 15 per cent and still falling. The other side of the coin has been the emergence of the Margaret River and Great Southern regions spanning the far south-western corner of the state.

In a manner reminiscent of the Barossa Valley in SOUTH AUSTRALIA, the hot Swan Valley remains the source of much of Western Australia's wine, largely through a single company, Houghton (part of BRL HARDY). As well as producing Houghton White Burgundy (or HWB, as it is called in Europe) from VERDELHO, CHENIN BLANC, and CHARDONNAY grown in the Swan Valley and at Gingin (just to the north), Houghton has large vineyards at Frankland in the Great Southern, and is a major purchaser of grapes throughout that region and the Margaret River. The Swan Valley has the dubious distinction of being the hottest region in Australia, with harvest typically beginning in January.

The Margaret River, 240 km/146 miles to the south, is still at a latitude of 34 degrees south, and therefore completely reliant upon the cooling influence of the Indian Ocean to provide its TEMPERATE climate. Here Cabernet Sauvignon produces a wine which consistently combines elegance with strength, redcurrant fruit with a seasoning of gravelly GOÛT *de terroir*. Merlot is frequently blended with it. Pungently grassy and intense Semillon and Sauvignon Blanc also perform with distinction. These two are more often than not blended with each other (and sometimes with Chenin Blanc as a third partner). Chardonnay is the other grape of importance, making wine which is often complex and sometimes long lived.

Riesling has never succeeded in the Margaret River, but comes emphatically into its own in the far-flung, colder, and usually more CONTINENTAL sites of the Lower Great Southern area (including Mount Barker and Frankland). Here it produces crisp, tightly structured wines which evolve slowly but with grace, mirroring the slow development of the equally taut yet fragrant Cabernet Sauvignon, while Pinot Noir has proved its liking for Albany on the extreme southern coastline. This is a huge and diverse region. Chardonnay and Shiraz also do well, Sauvignon Blanc a little less so.

The Pemberton-Warren region is important although still a relative newcomer, filling part of the gap between the eastern boundary of the Margaret River and the western boundary of the Great Southern region. Its pioneers (including the late Gérard Potel of Domaine de la Pousse d'Or in VOLNAY) saw exciting possibilities for Pinot Noir and Chardonnay, but events to date suggest that Merlot may be an even better bet.

Geographe, a more-or-less coastal region running north from the Margaret River region, has cannibalized part of what was the South West Coastal Plain region, making the latter's hold on life tenuous.   J.H.

white has a special meaning when applied both to grapes and wine. Any light-skinned grape may be called a white grape, even though the grape skin is not white but anything from pale green through gold to pink. In a similar fashion, white wines are not white, but vary in colour from almost colourless to deep gold. See COLOUR.

White French, inappropriate South African name for the PALOMINO grape, an adaptation of Fransdruif.

White Riesling, common synonym for the great white RIESLING grape variety of Germany.

white-wine-making, the production of wines with almost imperceptible to golden COLOUR. If the juice is separated from the grape skins gently and soon enough (as in the production of CHAMPAGNE), white wines can be made from black-skinned grapes, but the great majority of white wines are made from grapes with yellow or green skins. As with any WINE-MAKING operation, the production of white wines usually entails CRUSHING and DESTEMMING the grape clusters or bunches on arrival at the winery, although occasionally white grapes may be crushed beforehand at a field pressing station (and see also WHOLE-BUNCH PRESSING). After crushing and destemming, the liquid is separated from the solids by draining and PRESSING. The timing of the separation of juice from solids constitutes the major difference between red- and white-wine-making: before FERMENTATION for whites and afterwards for reds.

Prolonged contact between juice and grape skins (see SKIN CONTACT and MACERATION) encourages the transfer of soluble materials, including PHENOLICS, FLAVOUR COMPOUNDS, and FLAVOUR PRECURSORS, from the skins to the juice. The extracted phenolics are generally undesirable in a white wine, for they lead to excessive astringent and bitter tastes. The skin phenolics also lead to the development of amber to brown colours deemed inappropriate for white wines. The challenge for the white wine-maker is therefore to find the balance between appropriate transfer of the flavour compounds and minimal phenolic extraction. Because of their light colour and delicate flavours, white wines show the unappetizing effects of OXIDATION much faster than red wines and so white-wine-making is in general a more delicate operation than RED-WINE-MAKING.

White wines are usually fermented and processed cooler than normal room TEMPERATURE. Only a small, but much-vaunted, proportion of white wine comes into contact with wood but BARREL FERMENTATION followed by BARREL MATURATION is an increasingly common phenomenon, particularly for wines made from the Chardonnay grape. Among these barrel-fermented white wines, LEES STIRRING is also increasingly popular, as is MALOLACTIC FERMENTATION, once associated predominantly with red wines. A.D.W. & P.J.W.

white wines, made with much less SKIN CONTACT, are much lower in PHENOLICS than red wines. This does not necessarily mean, however, that they are inherently less interesting, or shorter lived (see AGEING). They vary enormously in colour from virtually colourless to deep gold and even, in extreme age, deep tawny (the same colour as some very old red wines). They are made in virtually all wine regions, although in hot regions ACIDIFICATION and some form of refrigeration are usually needed to produce white wines suitable for modern tastes.

French for white is *blanc*, Italian is *bianco*, Spanish is *blanco*, Portuguese is *branco*, German is *weiss*, while in most eastern European languages, including Russian, the word for white is some variant of *byeli*.

White Zinfandel, undeterred by the fact that it is neither white nor crucially Zinfandel, was California's great commercial success story of the 1980s. Although he was not the first to vinify California's ubiquitous ZINFANDEL grapes as a white, and therefore BLUSH, wine, Bob Trinchero of Sutter Home launched 'White' Zinfandel down the commercial slipway in 1972 and was to see his own sales rocket from 25,000 cases in 1980 to 1.5 million cases six years later. The wine evolved as a way of making California's vast acreage of Zinfandel acceptable to the predominantly white-wine-drinking American public. So successful was it that it stimulated an outbreak of new plantings of the variety expressly to keep pace with demand for this decidedly ersatz version. The wine is usually pale pink, decidedly sweet, often enlivened with a touch of gas, and scented with more than a dash of other, more obviously aromatic, grape varieties such as Muscat or Riesling. So successful was the wine that it begat styles such as **White Grenache**, designed to glamorize vineyard Cinderellas.

whole-bunch fermentation, ultra-traditional method of red-wine FERMENTATION in which grape berries are not subjected to DESTEMMING. The possible disadvantages are that the stems may impart harsh TANNINS to the wine. The advantages are that the stems can ease the drainage of the juice through the cap, and encourage healthy oxygenation by increasing the cap's interface with the atmosphere during MACERATION. This practice is most common in BURGUNDY.

whole-bunch pressing, special WHITE-WINE-MAKING technique whereby the grapes are not subjected to DESTEMMING and bunches of ripe grapes are pressed whole. This technique is almost universal in the production of top-quality SPARKLING WINES and most other white wines from dark-skinned grapes and in the direct pressing of BOTRYTIS-affected clusters of super-ripe grapes as in SAUTERNES. It is also increasingly popular with some quality-conscious producers of white wines in some wine regions since the juice that results tends to be low in PHENOLICS and high in quality.

Wien. VIENNA as its natives know it.

Wildbacher, or **Blauer Wildbacher,** dark-skinned grape variety that is a speciality of western STYRIA in AUSTRIA. The variety has been increasingly popular with growers and almost all of it is made into the local pink speciality, Schilcher wine, enlivened by Wildbacher's high acidity and distinctive perfume.

wild vines, plants of the genus *Vitis* growing in their natural state without any cultivation by man. Such vines are often found climbing trees but may also grow as shrubs. They are widespread in the Americas, especially in the east and south east, and in Asia. Wild vines are important to modern viticulture as they are the source of many of the present-day varieties.

wine, alcoholic drink made by fermenting the juice of fruits or berries (see FRUIT WINES).

The definition relevant to this book, and accepted throughout Europe, is that wine is 'the alcoholic beverage obtained from the fermentation of the juice of freshly gathered grapes, the fermentation taking place in the district of origin according to local tradition and practice'. This is to distinguish 'proper' wine from alcoholic drinks made from imported grape concentrate, which are known in Europe as MADE WINE. These include BRITISH WINE and a significant proportion of the liquid produced by HOME WINE-MAKING. New World definitions of wine are very similar except that the last phrase is omitted and wine may be made from a mixture of grapes grown many hundreds of miles apart.

Editorial note:

See WINE COMPOSITION, WINE-MAKING, WINE TYPES and the other entries which immediately follow. The word 'wine' appears only in their titles. Otherwise, for wine trade see TRADE, etc. For details of specific wines, see under their names or their provenance.

wine composition differs quite considerably from GRAPE COMPOSITION, partly because parts of the grape are discarded during WINE-MAKING, and partly because the processes involved effect a complicated series of transformations. Alcoholic FERMENTATION, for example, transforms sugars into alcohol, while MALOLACTIC FERMENTATION reduces the level of malic acid in favour of lactic acid. The precise composition of a wine varies with WINE TYPE, HARVEST conditions and date, VINTAGE characteristics, and the age of the wine (see AGEING for details of how wine composition may change with age).

wine-maker, one who makes WINE. In its broadest sense, the term includes those who engage in HOME WINE-MAKING as a hobby, although in a professional sense a wine-maker is someone employed (sometimes by themselves) to produce wine. An increasing proportion of such people recognize that wine production includes every aspect of vineyard management, and there are wine producers all over the world whose production is so small that they personally conduct, or at least oversee, every stage from planting to marketing (usually with markedly different degrees of success in each area). A wine production unit of any size, however, will employ both a VITICULTURIST, or vineyard manager, and

a wine-maker. Larger wine producers may even employ a team of wine-makers, each with different responsibilities.

While most (though not all) modern wine-makers have studied OENOLOGY, and will certainly consider themselves oenologists, the term OENOLOGIST is more usually applied to an outside CONSULTANT rather than to a full-time employee in Europe. The most temporary wine-makers of all are a new breed known colloquially as FLYING WINE-MAKERS.

Like the chef, the wine-maker enjoyed a brief period of near cult status during the early 1980s, when for a time certain men (and a few women) were treated as though capable of fashioning superior wine out of almost any quality of grapes, a FASHION that was most notable in the New World but by no means confined to it. VITICULTURISTS have been lobbying against this view, however, to become the wine gurus of the 1990s.

Most successful wine-makers understand that making fine wine depends not only on a respectful understanding of the complicated biochemistry involved but also, perhaps more importantly, on an appreciation of the greatest potential within each lot of grapes and then the skill and patience to reveal that potential in the finished wine.

wine-making, the practical art of producing WINE. In its most general sense, it encompasses all operations in both vineyard and cellar but for the purposes of this article, wine-making excludes vine-growing, or VITICULTURE.

Wine-making in brief is a series of simple operations, the first of which is CRUSHING or smashing the fruit to liberate the sugar in the juice for FERMENTATION, which is the second step and occurs naturally when YEAST cells come into contact with sugar solutions. The new wine must then be subjected to various treatments to ensure CLARIFICATION and STABILIZATION and various other cellar operations which are collectively called ÉLEVAGE before the final step, bottling.

Details in this sequence of operations vary considerably with WINE TYPE and its origin. General (as opposed to local) differences of technique dictated by different sorts of wine are outlined in WHITE-WINE-MAKING, RED-WINE-MAKING, ROSÉ-WINE-MAKING, SWEET-WINE-MAKING, and SPARKLING-WINE-MAKING. One of the most obvious is the stage at which the juice is separated from the skins by PRESSING (before fermentation for white wines, after fermentation for red wines).

Before fermentation, some amelioration of the grape juice may be needed. In many cooler wine regions, fermentable sugars may be added to the basic fruit juice to increase the eventual alcoholic strength (see CHAPTALIZATION). In warmer regions, on the other hand, ACIDIFICATION may be permitted at some point during wine-making. Some SULPHUR DIOXIDE is almost invariably added at this stage as a disinfectant.

The application of yeast is another crucial step in wine-making. Yeasts utilize sugar to build new yeast cells. If the yeast's access to oxygen is restricted, as in a large container, after an initial multiplication phase, the yeast switches to a second metabolic process of which the end products are mainly potable ALCOHOL and carbon dioxide. The alcohol produced dissolves additional substances such as plant ACIDS, TANNINS, colouring and flavouring materials from the grape pulp—and skins in the case of red wines. In a very real sense, wine is a by-product of the yeasts' metabolic activity operating under less than optimum conditions. Heat is another product generated by the yeasts' metabolism, and refrigeration may well be needed in order to control TEMPERATURE below the level at which yeasts are fatally damaged.

The new wine is usually separated from its LEES once fermentation is complete (except in the case of some white wines deliberately matured with LEES CONTACT). The normal technique is to let all the debris settle on the bottom of the container for a few days before RACKING, drawing off the wine from the top. This wine, opaque with its load of suspended yeast cells and fine debris, is further clarified, usually by FILTRATION or centrifugation. This clarification process is often encouraged by adding a FINING agent which attracts suspended particles towards it and then helps them fall to the bottom of the container.

A second, softening fermentation, MALOLACTIC FERMENTATION, may take place in wines high in MALIC ACID, naturally or encouraged, during or after the primary alcoholic fermentation.

Other optional steps include MACERATION of skins and pulp or wine which may take place before, during, and/or after fermentation. Alternative methods of vinification include CARBONIC MACERATION.

It is important to minimize the new wine's exposure to OXYGEN, whatever its colour. In older wineries, this was accomplished by keeping the wine in wooden containers and TOPPING UP at frequent intervals to replace losses by evaporation. Modern inert containers such as stainless-steel tanks, once filled, lose no wine by evaporation. They have the additional advantage that, when there is insufficient wine to fill a tank completely, the empty head space can be filled with nitrogen or carbon dioxide, thus eliminating the problem of exposure of the wine to oxygen.

A common step immediately after red-wine fermentation is to rack the wine off the skins into wooden BARRELS as this aids both clarification and the MATURATION process. For the highest-quality red wines, some time in new OAK barrels is common, the shape and size of barrel, duration of stay, and proportion of total production put into new oak varying according to wine type, vintage, and the producer's aspirations. Other red wines, or these wines after a year in new oak, may be aged in used oak or larger wooden casks, or red wines may proceed directly to inert storage tanks and omit a wood-ageing stage altogether.

Only a small proportion of white wines are aged in wood, stainless steel being the preferred material for both fermentation and storage. An increasing proportion of top-quality white wines (especially those made from the Chardonnay grape), however, are fermented in small oak barrels (see BARREL FERMENTATION). They may then be allowed to rest on the lees from which certain flavour characteristics may be encouraged to develop by LEES STIRRING. Most white wine is clarified, stabilized, and bottled early to avoid exposure to oxygen and minimize any risk of OXIDATION.

The great majority of wines, whatever their colour, are bottled before the next vintage (so that storage capacity for only one year's production is needed). Wood-matured table wines will normally be bottled within two years of the vintage, however, while many FORTIFIED and some other wines treated to exceptionally long wood maturation (such as some Italian, Spanish, and Portuguese reds) may be matured in cask for much longer than this.

Before the wine can be bottled, it may be necessary to make a selection from different lots, and to assemble these ingredients into a final blend, although the BLENDING may well have been carried out at a much earlier point in the wine's evolution. (See also ASSEMBLAGE.)

The final step in the wine-making process before bottling is to subject the wine to analysis in order to check that it is stable and meets legal requirements.

Ideally wines should be given several months' BOTTLE AGEING before dispatch to ensure stability and to allow the wine to recover from the shock of bottling and, more specifically, possible BOTTLE SICKNESS.   A.D.W.

Wine of Origin. Superior-quality designation scheme in SOUTH AFRICA.

winery, modern, essentially NEW WORLD term for the premises on which wine is made. It may mean either the entire enterprise, or it may mean specifically the building or buildings used for wine-making. The nearest French equivalent is CAVE. Winery design is a specialist art currently being most obviously perfected in northern CALIFORNIA, where, neatly, the FASHION is for caves: wine-making facilities burrowed into hillsides, the cost of maintaining suitable temperatures and humidity in such subterranean tunnels being minimal.

wine tasters. The animate sort are humans, often of widely varying abilities, experiences, preferences, and prejudices, engaged in the pursuit of wine TASTING. The inanimate sort are shallow, usually silver, saucers for tasting young wines, known in French, and often in English, as TASTEVINS.

wine types may be classified in several ways, the most usual being by alcohol level. Those whose ALCOHOLIC STRENGTH is entirely due to FERMENTATION, and usually in the range of 9 to 15 per cent, are what we tend to call simply 'wine' or sometimes 'table wine' (although TABLE WINE has a specific meaning within the European Union). Such wines may be further classified by COLOUR into RED WINES, WHITE WINES, and ROSÉ WINES. Or they may be classified according to their concentration of dissolved carbon dioxide as SPARKLING WINES, still wines, and a host of terms in between such as PERLANT and FRIZZANTE. Wines may also be classified according to SWEETNESS.

Wines with higher concentrations of alcohol, between 15 and just over 20 per cent, are called FORTIFIED WINES in this book since (with the exception of some DRIED-GRAPE WINES) they owe some of their alcoholic strength to the process of FORTIFICATION, or the addition of spirit. PORT and SHERRY are the best

known of these wines, officially called 'vins de liqueur' in EU terminology. This higher-strength category also includes sweet alcoholic drinks made by adding grape spirit to fermenting grape juice at various points, such as VIN DOUX NATURELS and VIN DE LIQUEUR.

Wines which have been deliberately manipulated so that their alcohol levels are particularly low, say below 5.5 per cent, are sometimes called LOW-ALCOHOL wines. (Some regular wines, such as MOSCATO D'ASTI and lighter SAAR wines, may have a natural alcoholic strength of between 5 and 9 per cent.)

Wine types may also be loosely, and somewhat subjectively, classified according to when they are drunk into APERITIF wines (sometimes called 'appetizer wines'), 'food wines' or 'dinner wines', and SWEET WINES or dessert wines.

Although geographical classifications are of wines not wine types, once-popular GENERIC wines represent an attempt at a geographical classification of wine types.

wine writers, imprecise term to include all those who communicate through the various media on the subject of wine. Some of them style themselves wine critics (notably the consumerist Robert PARKER), while such literary stylists as Hugh Johnson and Gerald Asher are undoubtedly wine writers. An increasing proportion of commentators hardly ever write at all but occupy regular slots on radio or television, often reaching a much wider audience than any author could hope to.

Wine writing is a parasitical activity enabled by vine-growing and wine-making but more usually associated with wine TASTING, and even wine drinking, than with either of the former. See also LANGUAGE OF WINE.

Winzer, which is the German equivalent of the French vigneron, is a common prefix in Germany for a CO-OPERATIVE wine cellar, as in **Winzergenossenschaft**, **Winzerverein**, and **Winzervereinigung**.

wood has been the most popular material for wine CONTAINERS both for transport and storage for centuries and even today trees are almost as important to some wines as vines.

For fine wines, wood is still valued as the prime material for maturing (see BARREL MATURATION and CASK AGEING) and for fermenting certain types of white wine (see BARREL FERMENTATION).

The chemistry of wine's maturation in wood

is still not fully understood but experience shows that wood inevitably exposes the wine to a certain amount of OXYGEN, and actively aids CLARIFICATION and STABILIZATION of the wine matured in it—quite apart from the wide range of flavours and characteristics which may be added and transformed as a result of exposure to that particular wood, either directly as wood flavour or indirectly as wood influence.

Worcester, hot inland wine district in SOUTH AFRICA.

world production of wine is concentrated in two bands of generally TEMPERATE to MEDITERRANEAN climate in each hemisphere, very roughly between latitudes 35 and 50, although local conditions affect this considerably. (Parts of the Far East are being developed for viticulture, despite high rainfall in some of these areas, but most of these industries are too young to feature in official statistics.)

Total production of wine is affected by each year's weather, by the effects of VINE PULL SCHEMES, offset by those of new plantings. The underlying trend is downwards, largely because of determined efforts by the European Union to reduce its wine surplus, mirrored by a similar initiative in Argentina, another major producing country.

See also Appendix 2B.

Wrattonbully, alternative name for Naracoorte Ranges, a relatively new wine region in the Limestone Coast zone of SOUTH AUSTRALIA.

Württemberg, relatively large and growing wine region in southern GERMANY with 11,196 ha/27,665 acres of vineyard which loosely follow the river Neckar and its tributaries. The

main part of the region lies between Stuttgart and Heilbronn, with the vineyards to the north mingling with those of BADEN. Steep and expensive-to-maintain terraced slopes look down on the Neckar.

A quarter of the region is planted in RIESLING, with that produced at Flein, a few kilometres south of Heilbronn, enjoying much local esteem. Of the remaining white wine varieties, all of which are declining, KERNER and MÜLLER-THURGAU both occupy about 7 per cent of the area under vine. Of the red wine varieties, which became increasingly important during the 1990s, TROLLINGER is planted on almost 25 per cent of the region's vineyard, followed by the 16 per cent devoted to Müllerrebe (MEUNIER), known locally as Schwarzriesling, and LIMBERGER (Blaufränkisch) with 9 per cent. Spätburgunder (PINOT NOIR) is less important here than in neighbouring BADEN and accounts for only 4.5 per cent of the region's vines.

Judged by international standards, much of the red wine produced here is pale, light, and soft, but that is how the locals like it. Per capita wine consumption here, 35 l a year, is the highest in Germany, and considerable quantities of red wine are imported to satisfy local demand. In 1997, 90 per cent of all new plantings were of dark-skinned varieties.

Most registered growers own less than 1 ha/2.47 acres, so CO-OPERATIVE cellars are necessary. They handle over 80 per cent of the grape harvest. There is a small number of ancient and highly regarded state- and privately owned estates, of which 12 are members of the prestigious VDP association. The best of their wines are serious and comparable in quality with those from good wine-makers in Baden.

K.B.S. & I.J.

Xarel-lo, white grape variety producing powerful still and sparkling wines in its native CATALONIA. It is particularly important in ALELLA, where it is known as Pansa Blanca. It is most commonly found in PENEDÈS, however, where, with Parellada and Macabeo, it makes up most CAVA blends. The wine it produces can be very strongly flavoured. It is the smell of Xarel-lo that typically distinguishes so many Cavas from other TRADITIONAL METHOD sparkling wines.

Xeres, is the name of a red grape variety available in California and exported to Australia thought to be the same as Rioja's GRACIANO.

Xynisteri, the most common white grape variety grown on CYPRUS. It is preferred to the dark-skinned MAVRO for the rich fortified wine COMMANDARIA, the island's most distinctive wine.

Xynomavro, black grape variety grown all over northern GREECE as far south as the foothills of Mount Olympus, where Rapsani is produced. Its name means 'acid black' and the wines can indeed seem harsh in youth but they age well, as mature examples of Naoussa can demonstrate. It is blended with a small proportion of the local Negoska to produce Goumenissa and is also used as a base for sparkling wine on the exceptionally cool, high vineyards of Amindeo. The wines tend to be relatively soft but to have good acid and attractive bite.

Yarra Valley, wine region that is cool in both senses just north east of Melbourne, in the Port Phillip zone of the Australian state of VICTORIA.

Ycoden-Daute-Isora, the most ancient, but recently denominated, wine region in the Spanish CANARY ISLANDS, centred on the town of Icod de los Vinos. It produces the best dry whites in the islands, from the LISTÁN Blanco grape. V. de la S.

yeast, single-celled agent vital to the FERMENTATION process, which, starved of oxygen, transforms grape juice to wine. Sugars are used as an energy source by yeast, with ALCOHOL and CARBON DIOXIDE as by-products of the reactions.

The nomenclature of various yeasts is far from straightforward but *Saccharomyces cerevisiae* is the name now most frequently used for the yeast involved in making wine and beer and in leavening bread. Within this yeast species are several hundred different strains or selections, each with real or fancied minor differences.

Studies have shown that in long-established wine regions, a number of other yeast genera are naturally present in significant populations and frequently participate in the winemaking process. Contrary to popular belief, such yeasts are found not on grape skins but are airborne. Spread around wineries and vineyards by insects, these are collectively known as **wild yeast.** More sensitive to SULPHUR DIOXIDE, and intolerant of an ALCOHOLIC STRENGTH much above five per cent, these wild yeasts are generally active during the early stages of 'spontaneous fermentations', those occurring when no sulphur dioxide and no specially cultivated cultured yeast (see below) is added to the grape juice. Fortunately, there are usually enough *Saccharomyces cerevisiae* cells present with the wild yeast with the grapes as they come into the winery from the vineyard so that these latter yeasts continue the fermentation above the unstable alcoholic strength of five per cent, depleting the supply of sugar and producing a stable wine. Once a winery begins to use wild yeast consistently, the wild-yeast population tends to stabilize with a particular mixture of yeasts suitable for wine fermentation so that **ambient yeast** may be a more appropriate term. Such mixtures of yeast genera and species, often called **'natural yeast'**, have been much more commonly used in the traditional wine regions of Europe than cultured yeast.

Increasing numbers of Old World producers, the majority of New World wine-makers, and certainly all of those worried about minimizing risk, use **cultured yeast**, however, sometimes called **pure culture** or **inoculated yeast.** The advantage of cultured yeasts, of which only one strain is usually added, is that the strain has been specially selected (from ambient yeasts) so that its behaviour is predictable and the fermentation will proceed smoothly and, of most importance, to completion without the risk of a STUCK FERMENTATION. Individual wine-makers often favour certain strains of cultured yeast, often for practical WINE-MAKING reasons. The differences in the wines produced may often be

521

too small to be detected by the average consumer.

The advantage of a well-adapted population of ambient or natural yeast is that there are many different strains and, because of their different abilities and aptitudes, they may be capable of producing a wine with a wider range of flavours and characteristics, a phenomenon that some wine-makers believe is even more marked when, as is increasingly the case, LEES CONTACT is encouraged. Such a view had not been confirmed by science in the late 1990s, however, partly because of the difficulty of working with mixed-culture fermentations and the difficulties of identification of the yeasts involved.   A.D.W. & J.Ro.

Yecla, denominated wine zone in the LEVANTE, south-east Spain, producing mainly rather coarse red wines. Sandwiched between JUMILLA, ALICANTE, and ALMANSA, Yecla is dominated by La Purísima, the largest CO-OPERATIVE in Spain. The red MONASTRELL represents 80 per cent of all grapes grown in the region. The private Bodegas Castaño is pioneering more ambitious wines by adding Cabernet Sauvignon, Tempranillo, and Merlot to Monastrell.
R.J.M. & V. de la S.

yield, an important statistic in wine production, which measures how much a vineyard produces.

Factors affecting yield

Vineyard yield depends on many factors, which will be briefly described here. For a more complete discussion see the individual factors listed.

Yield may be measured as either a weight of grapes or a volume of wine (see below), and is usually considered per unit area of vineyard, since this is what matters in farming economics. Those who believe that increasing VINE DENSITY is associated with improved wine quality argue that yield per vine is a more important consideration. Disciples of CANOPY MANAGEMENT, on the other hand, argue that the amount of sunlit leaf area per unit of land is more important than yield per vine.

Yield per vine depends on the number of bunches per vine, and the average bunch weight. The number of bunches per vine depends on the winter PRUNING policy, the BUD-BREAK, and the number of bunches per shoot. Bunch weight depends on the number of FLOWERS per bunch, and the success of FRUIT SET in forming berries, then on the weight of individual berries.

Yield per vine depends on VINE AGE (very old vines often produce very little), the way the vines have been managed, and on the WEATHER over at least the last two years, together with other factors such as vine pests and vine diseases.

After pruning, the weather is one of the most important factors affecting vineyard yield. Cold winters, for example, promote a high degree of budbreak, but frosts in spring can kill young shoots and bunches. Warm, sunny weather promotes FLOWERING and pollination, but cold, wet, and unsuitable weather can cause poor FRUIT SET. Some varieties are more prone than others to poor set. Drought conditions can also reduce fruit set, but the more common DROUGHT effect is to reduce berry size, often to less than half that of vines well supplied with water. Rain will generally increase yield as it causes berries to swell, but too much rain near harvest causes bunch rot and potentially a considerable, possibly total, loss in yield.

How yield is measured

Conventional units of yield are the weight of fresh grapes per unit land area, such as tonnes/ha, or tons/acre. (One ton/acre is about 2.5 tonnes/ha.) This is the standard measurement in most NEW WORLD wine regions.

Although many Italians and Swiss measure yield in weight of grapes, in most European countries production is measured in volumes of wine per unit area, normally expressed as hectolitres per hectare, or hl/ha. In many cases, this measurement is an extremely important one, often limited to a maximum (depending on the VINTAGE) specified by local regulation (see APPELLATION CONTRÔLÉE, DOC, etc.).

Yields and wine quality

A necessary connection between low yields and high-quality wine has been assumed at least since Roman times when *Bacchus amat colles* encapsulated the prevailing belief that low-yielding HILLSIDE VINEYARDS produced the best wine. Wine law in many European countries is predicated on the same belief and the much-imitated APPELLATION CONTRÔLÉE laws of France specify maximum permitted yields for each appellation.

There is little doubt that heavily cropped vines with a low LEAF TO FRUIT RATIO ripen more slowly, so that in cooler climates the fruit may not reach full RIPENESS and wine quality suffers. It is less widely understood, however, that undercropping can also adversely affect wine quality. A high leaf to fruit ratio will certainly ripen grapes, but the shaded CANOPY MICROCLIMATE will produce grapes high in potassium and PH and low in PHENOLICS and flavour.

It should also be noted that, within a given wine region (Bordeaux is a notable example), there is no correlation between size of the crop and quality of the wine. Some of the finest red bordeaux VINTAGE YEARS of the 1980s, for example, were also those in which yields were relatively high; while the lowest crop levels of the decade were recorded in lesser vintages such as 1984 and 1980.

There are countless commercial examples of high vineyard yields associated with low quality, however. Such vineyards are commonly planted with so-called 'bulk wine' varieties which also contribute to lower quality.

The yield which a vineyard can ripen properly will depend on the VINE VARIETY, the region, vine management practices, and climate as well as weather. For example, a yield of 8 tonnes/ha, or 56 hl/ha, might be considered excessive in a very cool climate, but a yield five times this figure might be easily ripened to a similar or higher sugar level in a warmer climate. Some varieties seem more prone than others to crop-level effects on wine quality, and in general red wine varieties are more affected than white. PINOT NOIR is an outstanding example, as the obvious inverse relationship between yield and quality in red burgundy demonstrates. MERLOT is another example.

Some specific examples

Vineyard yields vary enormously around the world and, in some regions with less dependable climates, from year to year. Among the highest reported yields are about 100 tonnes/ha for TABLE GRAPES grown in Israel (if their juice were made into wine, this would convert into about 1,750 hl/ha!). Commercial, well-managed vineyards in irrigated DESERT regions in California, Australia, and Argentina can routinely produce 15 tons/acre (260 hl/ha). At the other end of the spectrum, pests, disease, drought, or bunch rot can all reduce yields to less than 1 tonne/ha, or 7 hl/ha. See Ch d'YQUEM as well as Domaine LEROY and CHAPOUTIER for some examples of particularly low yields, encouraged for the sake of wine quality.

Certain wine types, most red wines, for example, are more sensitive to yield. Vineyards dedicated to sparkling wines are in general allowed to yield rather more than those dedicated to still-wine production.

The fact that yields are officially limited by regulation in the two most important wine-producing countries of France and Italy has undoubtedly encouraged worldwide respect for low yields, and perhaps some inertia in researching ways of increasing both quality and quantity. It should be noted, however, that the official maxima cited in wine regulations are now almost routinely increased in France by a device called the *plafond limite de classement*, or PLC, which allows a certain increase (often 20 per cent) on the base yield according to the conditions of the year. Average yields for the top appellations of the MÉDOC in 1989, 1990, and 1996, for example, were between 55 and 60 hl/ha when the theoretical maximum yield is 45 hl/ha.   R.E.S. & J.Ro.

York Mountain, California wine region and AVA. See SAN LUIS OBISPO.

Yquem, Château d', the greatest wine of SAUTERNES and, according to the famous 1855 CLASSIFICATION, of the entire BORDEAUX region. It is sweet, golden, and apparently almost immortal.

Probably the first vineyard-owning family were the de Sauvages, who bought the estate in 1711. It was acquired by the Lur Saluces family, who still run the property, in 1785. From before the First World War until 1968 the estate was run by the Marquis Bernard de Lur Saluces but since then it has been managed by Comte Alexandre, who also owns Ch de Fargues in Sauternes (although in 1999 LVMH acquired majority ownership after a bitter family struggle).

The vineyard extends to 90 ha/220 acres in production out of a total of 102 ha. The vines planted are 80 per cent Sémillon and 20 per cent of the usually more productive Sauvignon Blanc. Production averages 5,500 cases, a fraction of the typical output of a top red-wine property in the MÉDOC. The secret of Yquem's renown is its suceptibility to noble rot, and its ability to run risks and sacrifice quantity for painstakingly upheld quality. An average of six passages, or TRIS, are made through the vineyard each year so that only the BOTRYTIS-affected grapes are picked. The maximum yield is 9 hl/ha (0.5 tons/acre), compared with the normal 25 in Sauternes. The juice is pressed

Yugoslavia

three times, and then treated to three years' BARREL MATURATION in new OAK casks. Unlike nearly all other Sauternes, it is not sold until in bottle. The cost of the whole operation makes Yquem a very expensive wine. In 1987, facilities for cryoextraction, or freeze CONCENTRATION, were controversially installed for use in poor vintages.

Since 1959, a dry white wine, Y, or Ygrec, has been produced but intermittently. Notably alcoholic, it has more than a hint of a Sauternes.   E.P.-R.

Yugoslavia, eastern European union of peoples that existed for barely 60 years before breaking up amid bloodshed, privation, and extreme ethnic tension at the beginning of the post-communist era in the early 1990s.

Viticulture in this war-torn collection of tribes and states is as rich and varied in potential as the people themselves. That potential was just beginning to be realized as civil war intervened. For ease of reference, the name Yugoslavia is still used here, although no political implication is intended. Although Yugoslavia is now sometimes used to refer to the Serbian rump excluding Slovenia, Croatia, Bosnia Hercegovina, and Macedonia, wine-making techniques and styles described below still apply to all of ex-Yugoslavia except SLO-VENIA, which owes a far more direct debt to Italy and Austria. Slovenia does, however, share its viticultural practices with the other countries of the group.

Yugoslavia ran from north west to south east parallel to, and on a latitude with, ITALY. The area of major white-wine production runs inland along the north-east border from eastern Slovenia through eastern CROATIA and into the northern half of SERBIA.

The best of the reds come from the south-eastern third of what was Yugoslavia along the coasts of MONTENEGRO and KOSOVO and inland in MACEDONIA and eastern Serbia.

Considerable quantities of wine of both colours is produced along the rest of the coast and islands, the vast majority of which is consumed locally.

Considering the geographical proximity and similarity to Italy, Yugoslavian wines are remarkably dissimilar to those produced across the Adriatic Sea, mainly because of the differences in vine-variety mix between the two countries.

Wine-making practices also frequently differ from Italy's. White-wine-making especially is often more rustic, using riper grapes which show more EXTRACTION, and sometimes more AROMA. According to market demand and available resources, reds may be made light, sweet, with a very short time spent on skins for the German market or strong and heavily coloured for the local and more eastern markets. INTERNATIONAL VARIETIES such as Cabernet Sauvignon tend to be more classically handled. Both white and red grapes can show very true, fully ripened varietal characteristics.

Exports, once higher than a million hl a year, fell sharply in the late 1980s and early 1990s. Relatively little remains of the once enormous trade in light, sweetish red wines shipped to Germany from Kosovo and medium-dry Laski Rizling shipped to the UK from Slovenia.

By 1993, Yugoslavia was splitting into political components which correspond reasonably well to the boundaries of wine regions previously defined by state law. For more details, therefore, see (roughly from north to south) under SLOVENIA, CROATIA, VOJVODINA, SERBIA, KOSOVO, MONTENEGRO, BOSNIA HERCEGOVINA, and MACEDONIA.   A.H.M.

Zalema, Spanish white grape variety grown particularly in the southern CONDADO DE HUELVA zone, where its musts and wine can oxidize easily. It is being replaced by higher-quality varieties such as PALOMINO.

Zefir, Hungarian crossing of LEÁNYKA and HÁRSLEVELŰ producing soft, spicy wine.

Zenit, Hungarian crossing of BOUVIER and EZERJÓ which ripens usefully early to produce crisp, fruity but not particularly aromatic wines.

Zentralkellerei, a vast central co-operative wine cellar peculiar to GERMANY, where there are three, including the vast Badische Winzerkeller at Breisach in BADEN. These *Zentralkellereien* draw in wine from smaller CO-OPERATIVES, or *Winzergenossenschaften*. Other *Zentralkellereien* are at Kitzingen in FRANKEN and Möglingen in WÜRTTEMBERG.

Zibibbo, Sicilian name for the MUSCAT OF ALEXANDRIA white grape variety, sometimes made into wine, notably Moscato di PANTELLERIA, although more usually sold as TABLE GRAPES.

Zierfandler, the more noble of the two white wine grape varieties traditionally associated with GUMPOLDSKIRCHEN, the dramatically full-bodied, long-lived spicy white wine of the Thermenregion district of AUSTRIA. (The other is ROTGIPFLER.) It ripens very late, as its synonym Spätrot suggests, but keeps its acidity better than Rotgipfler. Unblended, Zierfandler has sufficient nerve to make late-harvest wines

with the ability to evolve over years in bottle, but most Zierfandler grapes are blended, and sometimes vinified, with Rotgipfler. The variety, as Cirfandli, is also known in Hungary.

Zilavka, relatively successful white grape variety planted in Hercegovina (see BOSNIA HERCEGOVINA) in what was Yugoslavia. The variety manages to combine high alcohol with high acidity and a certain nuttiness of flavour. The Zilavka made around the inland town of Mostar is particularly prized. It is not, however, necessarily made exclusively from Zilavka grapes. Zilavka is also increasingly planted in MACEDONIA.

Zimbabwe, southern African country with small-scale commercial wine industry. The most promising vineyards are 40 km/25 miles east of the capital Harare at Marandera. Chenin Blanc, Colombard, and CAPE RIESLING vines produce passable dry and off-dry whites with South African PINOTAGE making reds. The Monis Group (whose best range is the Mukuyu Collection) and African Distillers own the biggest wineries, drawing from widely scattered vineyards at Bulawayo and Mutare. Zimbabwe uses South African, German, Australian, and New Zealand wine-making expertise and its wines improved enormously in the late 1990s, thanks to input from FLYING WINE-MAKERS. J.P. & Mo.F.

Zinfandel is an exotic black grape variety of European origin cultivated predominantly in California that has tended to mirror the giddily changing fashions of the American wine business.

Zinfandel's European origins rested on local hypothesis rather than internationally accredited fact until the application of DNA 'FINGERPRINTING' to vines in the early 1990s. Only then was it irrefutably demonstrated that, as had been suspected, Zinfandel is one and the same as the PRIMITIVO of southern Italy, whose presence in Apulia was first chronicled at the end of the 18th century.

In 20th-century California, Zinfandel has occupied much the same place as SHIRAZ (Syrah) in Australia and suffered the same lack of respect simply because it is the most planted black grape variety, often planted in unsuitably hot sites and expected to yield more than is good for it. Zinfandel may not be quite such a potentially noble grape variety as Syrah but it is certainly capable of producing fine wine if yields are restricted and the weather cool enough to allow a reasonably long growing season.

Although Zinfandel has been required to transform itself into virtually every style and colour of wine that exists, it is best suited to dry, sturdy, unsubtle, but vigorous reds with an optimum lifespan of four to eight years. Such wines are rarely blends, although Ridge Vineyards are exponents of FIELD BLENDS which include PETITE SIRAH. Since the early 1990s, however, other premium producers such as Ravenswood, Rosenblum, and Storybook Mountain have commanded prices which justify more expensive handling of this ascendant variety, including several picking passes (TRIS) through the vineyard and more luxurious OAK treatments. See CALIFORNIA for more details of Zinfandel the wine, both red and white. Dry Creek Valley in SONOMA has demonstrated a particular aptitude for this underestimated variety.

Thanks to the enormous popularity of WHITE ZINFANDEL, Zinfandel plantings, which had been declining, increased during the late 1980s, mostly in the Central Valley, so that they totalled 34,000 acres in 1992, just ahead of California's total acreage of its second most important black grape variety Cabernet Sauvignon. This trend continued in the late 1990s as red Zinfandel enjoyed a resurgence, driving total plantings to 43,500 acres/17,400 ha in 1996, more than any other red wine grape.

It is also grown to a much more limited extent in warmer sites in other western states in the USA, and some South African growers have also taken advantage of their climate's suitability for Zinfandel. Australia is another obvious location for this unusual variety and Cape Mentelle in Western Australia has been particularly successful with it. There is even an experimental, if discreet, plot in HERMITAGE in south-east France.

Zweigelt, Zweigeltrebe, or Blauer Zweigelt is Austria's most popular dark-berried grape variety even though this BLAUFRÄNKISCH × ST-LAURENT crossing was bred only in 1922. At its best, it combines some of the bite of the first with the body of the second, although it is sometimes encouraged to produce too much dilute wine. It is widely grown throughout all Austrian wine regions and can occasionally make a serious, age-worthy wine, even though most examples are best drunk young. So successful has it been in Austria that the variety has also been planted on an experimental basis in Germany and England. The export fortunes of the variety may, oddly enough, be hampered by its originator's uncompromisingly Germanic surname. If only he had been called Dr Pinot Noir.

Complete list of controlled appellations and their permitted grape varieties

It is still impossible to tell from the labels of most geographically named wines which grapes were used to make them. The following is a unique guide to the varieties officially allowed into the world's *controlled* wine appellations (therefore by no means all known wine names), listed by local name alphabetically by country, grouped where appropriate into alphabetically listed regions within that country, and listed alphabetically by appellation name within that region. Italics denote minor grapes. R, W, P, and S denote red, white, pink, and sparkling wines respectively.

Austria

Gumpoldskirchner (W) Rotgipfler, Zierfandler

Steiermark Schilcher (P) Blauer Wildbacher

Croatia

Hvar (W) Trbljan

Pelješac, Postup, Dingač, Prošek, Faros, Potomje (R) Plavac Mali

Cyprus

Commandaria (R) Mavro, Xynisteri

France

ALSACE AND NORTH EAST

Crémant d'Alsace (S) Riesling, Pinot Blanc, Pinot Noir, Pinot Gris, Auxerrois, Chardonnay

Vin d'Alsace Edelzwicker (W) Gewürztraminer, Riesling, Pinot Gris, Muscat Blanc à Petits Grains, Muscat Ottonel, Pinot Blanc, Pinot Noir, Sylvaner, Chasselas

Other Alsace wines are varietally labelled.

Côtes de Toul (R) Pinot Meunier, Pinot Noir (P) Gamay, Pinot Meunier, Pinot Noir, *Aligoté, Aubin, Auxerrois* (W) Aligoté, Aubin, Auxerrois

Vins de Moselle Auxerrois, Gewürztraminer, Pinot Meunier, Müller-Thurgau, Pinot Noir, Pinot Blanc, Pinot Gris, Riesling, *Gamay*

BORDEAUX

Blaye (R) Cabernet Sauvignon, Cabernet Franc, Merlot, Malbec, *Prolongeau (Bouchalès), Béquignol, Petit Verdot* (W) Merlot Blanc, Folle Blanche, Colombard, *Pineau de la Loire (Chenin Blanc), Frontignan, Sémillon, Sauvignon Blanc, Muscadelle*

Bordeaux, Bordeaux Clairet, Bordeaux Supérieur (R, P) Cabernet Sauvignon, Cabernet Franc, Merlot, Carmenère, *Malbec, Petit Verdot*

Bordeaux Sec (W) Sémillon, Sauvignon Blanc, Muscadelle, *Merlot Blanc, Colombard, Mauzac, Ondenc, Ugni Blanc*

Bordeaux Côtes de Francs (R) Cabernet Sauvignon, Cabernet Franc, Merlot, *Malbec* (W) Sémillon, Sauvignon Blanc, *Muscadelle*

Bordeaux Haut-Benauge (W) Sémillon, Sauvignon Blanc, *Muscadelle*

Bordeaux Mousseux (R, S) Cabernet Sauvignon, Cabernet Franc, Merlot, *Carmenère, Malbec, Petit Verdot* (W, S) Sémillon, Sauvignon Blanc, Muscadelle, *Ugni Blanc, Merlot Blanc, Colombard, Mauzac, Ondenc*

Bourg, Côtes de Bourg, Bourgeais (R) Cabernet Sauvignon, Cabernet Franc, Merlot, Malbec, *Gros Verdot, Prolongeau (Bouchalès)* (W) Sauvignon Blanc, Sémillon, *Muscadelle, Merlot Blanc, Colombard*

Côtes de Blaye (W) Sémillon, Sauvignon Blanc, Muscadelle, *Merlot Blanc, Folle Blanche, Colombard, Pineau de la Loire (Chenin Blanc)*

Côtes de Castillon (R) Cabernet Sauvignon, Cabernet Franc, Merlot, *Malbec (Cot)*

Crémant de Bordeaux (R, S) Cabernet Sauvignon, Cabernet Franc, Merlot, *Carmenère, Malbec, Petit Verdot, Ugni Blanc, Colombard* (W, S) Sémillon, Sauvignon Blanc, Muscadelle, *Ugni Blanc, Colombard* (P, S) Cabernet Sauvignon, Cabernet Franc, Merlot, *Carmenère, Malbec, Petit Verdot*

Entre-Deux-Mers, Entre-Deux-Mers Haut-Benauge (W) Sémillon, Sauvignon Blanc, Muscadelle, *Merlot Blanc, Colombard, Mauzac, Ugni Blanc*

Fronsac, Canon Fronsac, Côtes Canon Fronsac (R) Cabernet Sauvignon, Cabernet Franc (Bouchet), Merlot, *Malbec (Pressac)*

Graves (R) Cabernet Sauvignon, Cabernet Franc, Merlot, *Malbec, Petit Verdot*

Graves Supérieures (W) Sémillon, Sauvignon Blanc, Muscadelle

Graves de Vayres (R) Cabernet Sauvignon, Cabernet Franc, Merlot, *Petit Verdot* (W) Sémillon, Sauvignon Blanc, Muscadelle, *Merlot Blanc*

Margaux, Listrac-Médoc, Pessac-Léognan, Premières Côtes de Bordeaux (R) Cabernet Sauvignon, Cabernet Franc, Merlot, *Carmenère, Malbec (Cot), Petit Verdot*

Pauillac, St-Estèphe, St-Julien, Médoc, Haut-Médoc, Moulis (R) Cabernet Sauvignon, Cabernet Franc, Merlot, *Carmenère, Malbec, Petit Verdot, Gros Verdot*

Pomerol, Lalande-de-Pomerol, Néac, Lussac-St-Émilion, Montagne-St-Émilion, Parsac-St-Émilion, Puisseguin-St-Émilion, St-Georges-St-Émilion (R) Cabernet Sauvignon, Cabernet Franc (Bouchet), Merlot, *Malbec (Pressac)*

Premières Côtes de Blaye (R) Cabernet Sauvignon, Cabernet Franc, Merlot, *Cot* (W) Sémillon, Sauvignon Blanc, Muscadelle, *Merlot Blanc, Colombard, Ugni Blanc*

St-Émilion (R) Merlot, Cabernet Sauvignon, Cabernet Franc, *Carmenère, Malbec (Cot)*

Ste-Foy-Bordeaux (R) Cabernet Sauvignon, Cabernet Franc, Malbec, *Petit Verdot* (W) Sémillon, Sauvignon Blanc, Muscadelle, *Merlot Blanc, Colombard, Mauzac, Ugni Blanc*

Sauternes, Barsac, Ste-Croix-du-Mont, Loupiac, Cadillac, Cérons, Premières Côtes de Bordeaux, Pessac-Léognan, Côtes de Bordeaux, St-Macaire (W) Sémillon, Sauvignon Blanc, *Muscadelle*

BURGUNDY

REGIONAL APPELLATIONS

Bourgogne Grand Ordinaire (R) Pinot Noir, Gamay, *César, Tressot* (P) *Pinot Gris, Pinot Blanc, Chardonnay* (W) Chardonnay, Aligoté, Pinot Blanc, Melon de Bourgogne, *Sacy*

Bourgogne Passetoutgrains (R) Gamay, *Pinot Noir, Pinot Blanc, Pinot Gris, Chardonnay*

Bourgogne Mousseux (S) Chardonnay, Pinot Blanc, Pinot Noir, Pinot Beurot, Pinot Liébault, *César, Tressot*

Bourgogne, Bourgogne Clairet, Bourgogne Rosé, Bourgogne Hautes Côtes de Beaune, Bourgogne Rosé Hautes Côtes de Beaune, Bourgogne Clairet Hautes Côtes de Beaune, Bourgogne Hautes Côtes de Nuits, Bourgogne Rosé Hautes Côtes de Nuits, Bourgogne Clairet Hautes Côtes de Nuits, Bourgogne Côte Chalonnaise, Bourgogne Rosé Côte Chalonnaise, Bourgogne Clairet Côte Chalonnaise (R, P) Pinot Noir, Pinot Liébault, *César, Tressot, Pinot Blanc, Pinot Gris, Chardonnay* (W) Chardonnay, *Pinot Blanc*

Bourgogne Aligoté, Bourgogne Aligoté Bouzeron (W) Aligoté, *Chardonnay*

Crémant de Bourgogne (S) Pinot Noir, Chardonnay, Pinot Gris, Pinot Blanc, *Gamay, Aligoté, Melon de Bourgogne, Sacy*

BEAUJOLAIS

Beaujolais, Beaujolais Supérieur, Beaujolais-Villages (R, P) Gamay, *Pinot Noir, Pinot Gris, Chardonnay, Aligoté, Melon de Bourgogne* (W) Chardonnay, Aligoté

Brouilly, Chénas, Chiroubles, Fleurie, Juliénas, Morgon, Moulin-à-Vent, St-Amour (R) Gamay, *Chardonnay, Aligoté, Melon de Bourgogne*

Côte de Brouilly (R) Gamay, *Pinot Noir, Pinot Gris, Pinot Blanc, Chardonnay*

Régnié (R) Gamay

CHABLIS REGION

Irancy (R) Pinot Noir, César, Tressot, *Pinot Liébault, Pinot Beurot*

Petit Chablis, Chablis, Chablis Premier Cru, Chablis Grand Cru (W) Chardonnay

St-Bris (W) Sauvignon Blanc

CÔTE CHALONNAISE

Note: The communes indicated with an asterisk contain premier cru vineyards.

Givry (R) Pinot Noir, *Pinot Beurot, Pinot Liébault, Chardonnay* (W) Chardonnay, *Pinot Blanc*

Mercurey*, Rully* (R) Pinot Noir, *Pinot Beurot, Pinot Liébault, Chardonnay* (W) Chardonnay

Montagny* (W) Chardonnay

CÔTE D'OR

Note: The communes indicated with an asterisk contain premier-cru vineyards.

Côte de Beaune, Côte de Beaune-Villages, Côte de Nuits-Villages, Auxey-Duresses*, Beaune*, Blagny, Chassagne-Montrachet*, Chorey-lès-Beaune, Fixin*, Ladoix, Meursault*, Monthelie, Nuits-St-Georges*, Pernand-Vergelesses*, Puligny-Montrachet*, St-Aubin*, St-Romain, Sante- nay*, Savigny-lès-Beaune*, Vins Fins de la Côte de Nuits, Vougeot* (R) Pinot Noir, *Pinot Liébault, Chardonnay, Pinot Blanc, Pinot Gris* (W) Chardonnay, *Pinot Blanc*

Aloxe-Corton*, Maranges*, Morey-St-Denis* (R) Pinot Noir, *Pinot Liébault, Chardonnay, Pinot Blanc, Pinot Gris* (W) Chardonnay

Chambolle-Musigny*, Gevrey-Chambertin*, Pommard*, Volnay*, Volnay Santenots*, Vosne-Romanée* (R) Pinot Noir, *Pinot Liébault, Chardonnay, Pinot Blanc, Pinot Gris*

Marsannay (R) Pinot Noir, *Pinot Gris, Chardonnay* (W) Chardonnay, *Pinot Gris*

Marsannay Rosé (P) Pinot Noir, Pinot Gris

CÔTE D'OR—GRANDS CRUS

Bonnes-Mares, Chambertin, Chambertin-Clos de Bèze, Chapelle-Chambertin, Charmes-Chambertin, Griotte-Chambertin, Latricières-Chambertin, Mazis-Chambertin, Mazoyères-Chambertin, Ruchottes-Chambertin, Clos des Lambrays, Clos de la Roche, Clos St-Denis, Clos de Tart, Clos de Vougeot, Echézeaux, Grands Echézeaux, La Grande Rue, Richebourg, Romanée-Conti, Romanée-St-Vivant, La Romanée, La Tâche, (R) Pinot Noir, *Pinot Liébault, Pinot Blanc, Pinot Gris, Chardonnay*

Musigny, Corton (R) Pinot Noir, *Pinot Liébault, Pinot Blanc, Pinot Gris, Chardonnay* (W) Chardonnay

Corton-Charlemagne, Montrachet, Bâtard-Montrachet, Bienvenues-Bâtard-Montrachet, Chevalier-Montrachet, Criots-Bâtard-Montrachet (W) Chardonnay

Charlemagne (W) Chardonnay, *Aligoté*

MÂCONNAIS

Mâcon, Mâcon Supérieur, Mâcon-Villages, or Mâcon followed by a commune name (e.g. Mâcon Chardonnay, Mâcon Viré, Mâcon Lugny) (W) Chardonnay, *Pinot Blanc*

Mâcon, Mâcon Supérieur, or Mâcon

followed by a commune name (e.g. Mâcon Chardonnay, Mâcon Viré, Mâcon Lugny) (R, P) Gamay, Pinot Noir, Pinot Gris

Pouilly-Fuissé, Pouilly-Vinzelles, Pouilly-Loché, St-Véran (W) Chardonnay

CHAMPAGNE

Champagne, Coteaux Champenois (S) Pinot Noir, Pinot Meunier, Chardonnay

Rosé de Riceys (P) Pinot Noir

CORSICA, see PROVENCE

LANGUEDOC-ROUSSILLON

Cabardès, Côtes du Cabardès (R, P) Grenache, Syrah, Cinsaut, *Cabernet Sauvignon, Merlot, Cabernet Franc, Cot, Fer, Carignan, Aubun Noir*

Clairette de Bellegarde, Clairette du Languedoc (W) Clairette

Collioure (R) Grenache, Mourvèdre, *Carignan, Cinsaut, Syrah* (P) Grenache, Mourvèdre, *Carignan, Cinsaut, Syrah, Grenache Gris*

Corbières (R, P) Carignan, Grenache, Cinsaut, *Lladoner Pelut, Mourvèdre, Piquepoul Noir, Terret Noir, Syrah, Maccabeu, Bourboulenc, Grenache Gris* (W) Bourboulenc, Clairette Blanche, Grenache Blanc, Maccabeu, Muscat Blanc à Petits Grains, Piquepoul Blanc, Terret Blanc, Marsanne, Roussanne, Vermentino Blanc

Costières de Nîmes (R, P) Carignan, Grenache, Mourvèdre, Syrah, Cinsaut (W) Clairette Blanc, Grenache Blanc, Bourboulenc Blanc, Ugni Blanc

Coteaux du Languedoc (R) Carignan, Grenache, Lladoner Pelut, *Counoise Noir (Aubun), Grenache Rosé, Terret Noir, Picpoul Noir* (P) Carignan, Grenache, Lladoner Pelut, *Counoise Noir (Aubun), Grenache Rosé, Terret Noir, Picpoul Noir, Bourboulenc, Carignan Blanc, Clairette, Maccabéo, Picpoul, Terret, Ugni Blanc*

Côtes de la Malepère, VDQS (R) Merlot, Cot, Cinsaut, *Cabernet Sauvignon, Cabernet Franc, Grenache, Lladoner Pelut Noir, Syrah* (P) Cinsaut, Grenache, Lladoner Pelut Noir, *Merlot, Cot, Cabernet Sauvignon, Cabernet Franc, Syrah*

Côtes de Millau, VDQS (R) Gamay, Syrah, *Cabernet Sauvignon, Fer Servadou, Duras* (P) Gamay, *Syrah, Cabernet Sauvignon, Fer Servadou, Duras* (W) Chenin Blanc, Mauzac.

Côtes du Roussillon (R, P) Carignan, Cinsaut, Grenache, Lladoner Pelut Noir, Syrah, Mourvèdre, Maccabeu Blanc (W) Grenache Blanc, Maccabeu Blanc, Tourbat Blanc/Malvoisie du Roussillon, Marsanne, Roussanne, Vermentino

Côtes du Roussillon-Villages (R) Carignan, Cinsaut, Grenache, Lladoner Pelut Noir, Syrah, Mourvèdre, Maccabéo

Faugères (R, P) Carignan, Cinsaut, Grenache, Mourvèdre, Syrah, Lladoner Pelut Noir

Fitou (R) Carignan, Grenache, Mourvèdre, Syrah, Lladoner Pelut Noir, *Cinsaut, Maccabéo Blanc, Terret Noir*

Minervois (inc La Livinière) (R, P) Grenache, Syrah, Mourvèdre, Lladoner Pelut Noir, Carignan, *Cinsaut, Picpoul Noir, Terret Noir, Aspiran Noir* (W) Grenache Blanc, Bourboulenc Blanc (Malvoisie), Maccabeu Blanc, Marsanne Blanche, Roussanne Blanche, Vermentino Blanc (Rolle), *Picpoul Blanc, Clairette Blanche, Terret Blanc, Muscat Blanc à Petits Grains*

St-Chinian (R, P) Carignan, Cinsaut, Grenache, Lladoner Pelut Noir, Mourvèdre, Syrah

LOIRE AND CENTRAL FRANCE

Anjou, Anjou Gamay, Anjou Pétillant, Rosé d'Anjou, Rosé d'Anjou Pétillant, Saumur, Saumur Champigny, Saumur Pétillant (R) Cabernet Franc, Cabernet Sauvignon, Pineau d'Aunis (P) Cabernet Franc, Cabernet Sauvignon, Pineau d'Aunis, Gamay, Cot, Groslot (W) Chenin Blanc, *Chardonnay, Sauvignon Blanc*

Anjou Coteaux de la Loire (W) Chenin Blanc

Anjou Mousseux (W, S) Chenin Blanc, *Cabernet Sauvignon, Cabernet Franc, Cot, Gamay, Groslot, Pineau d'Aunis* (P, S) Cabernet Sauvignon, Cabernet Franc, Cot, Gamay, Groslot, Pineau d'Aunis

Anjou-Villages (R) Cabernet Sauvignon, Cabernet Franc

Bourgueil, St-Nicolas-de-Bourgueil
(R) Cabernet Franc, *Cabernet Sauvignon*

Bonnezeaux (W) Chenin Blanc

Cabernet d'Anjou, Cabernet de Saumur (P) Cabernet Sauvignon, Cabernet Franc

Châteaumeillant (R, W, P) Gamay, Pinot Gris, Pinot Noir

Cheverny (R) Gamay, Pinot Noir, *Cabernet Franc, Cabernet Sauvignon, Cot* (P) Gamay, Pinot Noir, *Cabernet Franc, Cabernet Sauvignon, Cot, Pineau d'Aunis* (W) Sauvignon Blanc, *Chardonnay, Arbois (Menu Pineau), Chenin Blanc*

Chinon (W) Chenin Blanc (Pineau de la Loire) (R, P) Cabernet Franc (Breton), *Cabernet Sauvignon*

Coteaux d'Ancenis (W) Chenin Blanc, Pinot Gris (Malvoisie) (R, P) Cabernet Sauvignon, Cabernet Franc, Gamay, *Gamay de Chaudenay, Gamay de Bouze*

Coteaux de l'Aubance (W) Chenin Blanc (Pineau de la Loire)

Coteaux du Layon, Coteaux du Layon Chaume (W) Chenin Blanc (Pineau de la Loire)

Coteaux du Loir (W) Chenin Blanc (Pineau de la Loire) (R) Pineau d'Aunis, Cabernet Franc, Cabernet Sauvignon, Gamay, Cot (P) Pineau d'Aunis, Cabernet Franc, Cabernet Sauvignon, Gamay, Cot, Groslot

Coteaux de Saumur (W) Chenin Blanc (Pineau de la Loire)

Coteaux du Vendômois (W) Chenin Blanc, *Chardonnay* (R) Pineau d'Aunis, *Gamay, Pinot Noir, Cabernet Franc, Cabernet Sauvignon* (P) Pineau d'Aunis, *Gamay*

Côtes d'Auvergne (R, P) Gamay, Pinot Noir (W) Chardonnay

Côtes de Gien, Coteaux du Giennois (R, P) Gamay, Pinot Noir (W) Sauvignon Blanc

Cour-Cheverny (W) Romorantin Blanc

Crémant de Loire (W, P, S) Chenin Blanc, Cabernet Franc, Cabernet Sauvignon, Pineau d'Aunis, Pinot Noir, Chardonnay, Menu Pineau, *Grolleau Noir, Grolleau Gris*

Fiefs Vendéens (R, P) Gamay, Pinot Noir, *Cabernet Franc, Cabernet Sauvignon, Négrette, Gamay Chaudenay* (W) Chenin Blanc, *Sauvignon Blanc, Chardonnay*

Gros Plant du Pays Nantais (W) Gros Plant (Folle Blanche)

Haut Poitou (W) Sauvignon Blanc, Chardonnay, Chenin Blanc, *Pinot Blanc* (R, P) Pinot Noir, Gamay, Merlot, Cot, Cabernet Franc, Cabernet Sauvignon, *Gamay de Chaudenay, Grolleau*

Jasnières (W) Chenin Blanc (Pineau de la Loire)

Menetou-Salon (W) Sauvignon Blanc (R, P) Pinot Noir

Montlouis (W) Chenin Blanc (Pineau de la Loire)

Muscadet, Musacadet Côtes de Grand Lieu, Muscadet des Coteaux de la Loire, Muscadet de Sevre-et-Maine (W) Melon

Pouilly-Fumé, Blanc Fumé de Pouilly (W) Blanc Fumé (Sauvignon Blanc)

Pouilly-sur-Loire (W) Chasselas, Blanc Fumé (Sauvignon Blanc)

Quart de Chaume (W) Chenin Blanc (Pineau de la Loire)

Quincy (W) Sauvignon Blanc

Reuilly (W) Sauvignon Blanc (R, P) Pinot Noir, Pinot Gris

Rosé de Loire (P) Cabernet Franc, Cabernet Sauvignon, Pineau d'Aunis, Pinot Noir, Gamay, Grolleau

St-Pourçain (R) Gamay, Pinot Noir, *Gamay Teinturiers* (W) Tressallier, St-Pierre-Doré, Aligoté, Chardonnay, Sauvignon Blanc

Sancerre (W) Sauvignon Blanc (R, P) Pinot Noir

Saumur Mousseux (W, S) Chenin Blanc, Chardonnay, Sauvignon Blanc, Cabernet Franc, Cabernet Sauvignon, Cot, Gamay, Grolleau, Pineau d'Aunis, Pinot Noir (P, S) Cabernet Franc, Cabernet Sauvignon, Cot, Gamay, Grolleau, Pineau d'Aunis, Pinot Noir

Savennières (W) Chenin Blanc (Pineau de la Loire)

Touraine, Touraine Azay-le-Rideau, Touraine Amboise, Touraine Mesland, Touraine Pétillant (W) Chenin Blanc (Pineau de la Loire), Arbois (Menu Pineau), Sauvignon Blanc, *Chardonnay* (R) Cabernet Franc (Breton), Cabernet Sauvignon, Cot, Pinot Noir, Pinot Meunier, Pinot Gris, Gamay Noir à Jus Blanc, Pineau d'Aunis (P) Cabernet Franc (Breton), Cabernet Sauvignon, Cot, Pinot Noir, Pinot Meunier, Pinot Gris, Gamay Noir à Jus Blanc, Pineau d'Aunis, Grolleau, *Gamay de Chaudenay, Gamay de Bouze, Gamay à Jus Coloré*

Touraine Mousseux (W, S) Chenin Blanc (Pineau de la Loire), Arbois (Menu Pineau), *Chardonnay, Cabernet Franc (Breton), Cabernet Sauvignon, Pinot Noir, Pinot Meunier, Pinot Gris, Pineau d'Aunis, Cot, Grolleau* (R, S) Cabernet Franc (Breton) (P, S) Breton, Cot, Noble, Gamay, Grolleau

Valençay (R, P) Cabernet Franc, Cabernet Sauvignon, Cot, Gamay, Pinot Noir, *Gascon, Pineau d'Aunis, Gamay de Chaudenay, Grolleau* (W) Arbois, Chardonnay, Sauvignon Blanc, *Chenin Blanc, Romorantin*

Vouvray (W) Gros Pinot (Pineau de la Loire, Chenin Blanc), Petit Pinot (Menu Pinot)

Vins de l'Orléanais (R, P) Pinot Noir, Pinot Meunier, Cabernet (W) Auvernat Blanc (Chardonnay), Auvernat Gris (Pinot Meunier)

Vins du Thouarsais (W) Chenin Blanc, *Chardonnay* (R, P) Cabernet Franc, Cabernet Sauvignon, Gamay

Note: Gamay means Gamay Noir à Jus Blanc unless otherwise stated.

LOIRE FRINGES

Côte Roannaise (R, P) Gamay
Côtes du Forez (R, P) Gamay

JURA

Arbois (R) Poulsard Noir, Trousseau, Pinot Noir (W) Savagnin Blanc, Chardonnay, Pinot Blanc

Note: Pinot Noir and Pinot Blanc are not permitted for the production of vin de paille; other grapes are as above.
Arbois Rosé is made from a blend of black and white grapes.

Château-Chalon (W) Savagnin Blanc

Côte de Jura vins jaunes (W) Savagnin Blanc

Côtes du Jura (R) Poulsard Noir, Trousseau, Pinot Noir (W) Savagnin Blanc, Chardonnay, Pinot Blanc

Côtes du Jura Mousseux (S) Grapes as above

Côtes du Jura Rosé is made from a blend of black and white grapes.

L'Étoile (W) Chardonnay, Poulsard, Savagnin Blanc

L'Étoile Mousseux (S) As above

L'Étoile vin jaune (W) Savagnin Blanc

Note: Pinot Noir and Pinot Blanc are not permitted for the production of vin de paille; other grapes are as above.

PROVENCE AND CORSICA

Ajaccio (P) Barbarossa, Nielluccio, Sciacarello, Vermentino Blanc, *Carignan, Cinsaut, Grenache* (W) Ugni Blanc, Vermentino Blanc

Bandol (R) Mourvèdre, Grenache, Cinsaut, *Syrah, Carignan, Tibouren, Calitor (Pécoui Touar)* (P) Mourvèdre, Grenache, Cinsaut, *Syrah, Carignan, Tibouren, Calitor (Pécoui Touar), Bourboulenc, Clairette, Ugni Blanc, Sauvignon Blanc* (W) Bourboulenc, Clairette, Ugni Blanc, *Sauvignon Blanc*

Bellet, Vin de Bellet (R) Braquet, Folle Noir (Fuella), Cinsaut, *Grenache, Rolle, Roussanne, Spagnol (Mayorquin), Clairette, Bourboulenc, Chardonnay, Pignerol, Muscat Blanc à Petits Grains* (P) Braquet, Folle Noir (Fuella), Cinsaut, *Grenache, Roussanne, Rolle, Spagnol (Mayorquin), Clairette, Bourboulenc, Pignerol* (W) Rolle, Roussanne, Spagnol (Mayorquin), *Clairette, Bourboulenc, Chardonnay, Pignerol, Muscat Blanc à Petit Grains*

Cassis (R, P) Grenache, Carignan, Mourvèdre, Cinsaut, Barberoux, *Terret, Aramon* (W) Ugni Blanc, Sauvignon Blanc, Doucillon (Bourboulenc), Clairette, Marsanne, Pascal Blanc

Coteaux d'Aix-en-Provence, Les Baux de Provence (R, P) Cabernet Sauvignon, Carignan, Cinsaut, Counoise,

Grenache, Mourvèdre, Syrah (W) Bourboulenc, Clairette, Grenache Blanc, Sauvignon Blanc, Sémillon, Ugni Blanc, Vermentino Blanc

Coteaux de Pierrevert, VDQS (R, P) Carignan, Cinsaut, Grenache, Mourvèdre, Oeillade (Petit), Syrah, Terret Noir (W) Clairette, Marsanne, Picpoul, Roussanne, Ugni Blanc

Coteaux Varois (R) Grenache, Syrah, Mourvèdre, *Carignan, Cinsaut, Cabernet Sauvignon* (P) Grenache, Cinsaut, *Syrah, Mourvèdre, Carignan, Tibouren* (W) Clairette, Grenache Blanc, Rolle, Sémillon, Ugni Blanc

Muscat du Cap Corse (W) Muscat Blanc à Petits Grains

Palette (R, P) Mourvèdre, Grenache, Cinsaut (Plant d'Arles), *Téoulier (Manosquin), Durif, Muscat Noir de Provence, Muscat de Marseille/d'Aubagne, Muscat Hamburg, Carignan, Syrah, Castets, Brun Fourca, Terret Gris, Petit-Brun, Tibouren, Cabernet Sauvignon* (W) Clairette à Gros Grains/Clairette à Petits Grains/Clairette de Trans/Picardan/Clairette Rosé, *Ugni Blanc, Ugni Rosé, Grenache Blanc, Muscat de Frontignan, Pascal, Terret-Bourret, Piquepoul, Aragnan, Colombard, Tokay*

Patrimonio (R, P) Nielluccio, *Grenache, Sciacarello, Vermentino Blanc* (W) Vermentino Blanc, *Ugni Blanc*

Côtes de Provence (R, P) Carignan, Cinsaut, Grenache, Mourvèdre, Tibouren, *Barberoux, Cabernet Sauvignon, Calitor (Pécoui Touar), Clairette, Roussanne du Var, Sémillon, Ugni Blanc, Vermentino Blanc (Rolle)* (W) Clairette, Sémillon, Ugni Blanc, Vermentino Blanc/Rolle

Vin de Corse (R, P) Nielluccio, Sciacarello, Grenache, *Cinsaut, Mourvèdre, Barbarossa, Syrah, Carignan, Vermentino (Malvoisie de Corse)* (W) Vermentino (Malvoisie de Corse), *Ugni Blanc (Rossola)*

RHÔNE

Châteauneuf-du-Pape (R) Grenache Noir, Cinsaut, Syrah, Mourvèdre, *Picpoul, Terret Noir, Counoise, Muscardin, Picardan, Vaccarèse, Clairette, Roussanne, Bourboulenc* (W) Grenache Blanc, Bourboulenc, Roussanne, *Clairette, Picpoul*

Châtillon-en-Diois (R, P) Gamay, *Syrah, Pinot Noir* (W) Aligoté, Chardonnay

Clairette de Die (S) Muscat Blanc à Petits Grains, *Clairette Blanche*

Condrieu, Château-Grillet (W) Viognier

Cornas (R) Syrah

Coteaux de Die (W) Clairette Blanche

Coteaux de Pierrevert, VDQS (R, P) Carignan, Cinsaut, Grenache Noir, Mourvèdre (Petit) Syrah, *Oeillade, Terret Noir* (W) Clairette Blanche, Marsanne, Picpoul Blanc, Roussanne, Ugni Blanc

Côte Rôtie (R) Syrah, *Viognier*

Coteaux du Tricastin (R, P) Grenache Noir, Cinsaut, Mourvèdre, Syrah, Picpoul, *Carignan, Grenache Blanc, Picpoul Blanc, Clairette Blanche, Bourboulenc, Ugni Blanc, Marsanne, Roussanne, Viognier* (W) Grenache Blanc, Picpoul Blanc, Clairette Blanche, Bourboulenc, Ugni Blanc, Marsanne, Roussanne, Viognier

Côtes du Lubéron (R, P) Grenache Noir, Syrah, Mourvèdre, Cinsaut, Carignan, *Counoise Noir, Picpoul Noir, Gamay, Pinot Noir* (W) Grenache Blanc, Clairette Blanche, Bourboulenc, Ugni Blanc, Rolle, *Roussanne, Marsanne*

Côtes du Rhône, Côtes du Rhône-Villages (R) Grenache Noir, Cinsaut, Syrah, Mourvèdre, *Terret Noir, Carignan, Counoise, Muscardin, Vaccarèse, Pinot Noir, Calitor, Gamay, Camarèse* (P) Grenache Noir, Camarèse, Cinsaut, Carignan comprising 90% of the blend, the remaining 10% could be any of these other varieties: (W) Clairette, Roussanne/Roussette, Bourboulenc, *Viognier, Picpoul, Marsanne, Grenache Blanc, Picardan, Mauzac, Pascal Blanc*

Côtes du Ventoux (R, P) Grenache Noir, Syrah, Cinsaut, Mourvèdre, Carignan, *Picpoul Noir, Counoise, Clairette, Bourboulenc, Grenache Blanc, Roussanne* (W) Clairette, Bourboulenc, Grenache Blanc, *Roussanne*

Côtes du Vivarais (R) Grenache Noir, Syrah, *Cinsaut, Carignan* (P) Grenache Noir, Cinsaut, *Syrah* (W) Clairette Blanche, Grenache Blanc, Marsanne

Crémant de Die (S) Clairette Blanche

Gigondas (R) Grenache Noir, *Syrah, Mourvèdre* (P) Grenache Noir 80%, the remainder can consist of any of the varieties under Côtes du Rhône

Haut-Comtat, VDQS (R, P) Grenache, *Carignan, Cinsaut, Mourvèdre, Syrah*

Hermitage, Crozes-Hermitage, St-Joseph (R) Syrah, *Marsanne, Roussanne* (W) Marsanne, Roussanne

Lirac (R, P) Grenache Noir, Cinsaut, Mourvèdre, Syrah, *Carignan* (W) Clairette Blanc, Grenache Blanc, Bourboulenc, *Ugni Blanc, Picpoul, Marsanne, Roussanne, Viognier*

St-Péray (W) Roussanne (Roussette), Marsanne (S) Roussanne (Roussette), Marsanne

Tavel (P) Grenache Noir, Cinsaut, Clairette Blanche, Clairette, Picpoul, Calitor, Bourboulenc, Mourvèdre, Syrah, Carignan

Vacqueyras (R) Grenache Noir, Syrah, Mourvèdre (P) Grenache Noir, *Mourvèdre, Cinsaut.* With the exclusion of Carignan, all the other grapes that go into Côtes du Rhône are also allowed (W) Grenache Blanc, Clairette Blanc, Bourboulenc, *Marsanne Blanc, Roussanne Blanc, Viognier*

RHÔNE FRINGES

Coteaux du Lyonnais (R) Gamay (P) Gamay (W) Chardonnay, Aligoté

SAVOIE AND BUGEY

Crépy (W) Chasselas

Vin de Bugey, Vin de Bugey Mousseux, Vin de Bugey Pétillant, Vin de Bugey followed by a commune name (R, P) Gamay, Pinot Noir, Poulsard, Mondeuse plus up to 20% of the white grapes listed here (W) Chardonnay, Roussette, Aligoté, Mondeuse Blanche, Jacquère, Pinot Gris, Molette

Roussette de Bugey (W) Roussette, Chardonnay

Vins de Bugey-Cerdon (W, R) Gamay, Poulsard, Pinot Noir, Pinot Gris

Note: Varietal labelling is used for all the Bugey appellations where a wine is exclusively from one variety.

For the commune of:
Chignin-Bergeron (W) Roussanne

For the communes of:
Marignan and Ripaille (W) Chasselas

For the commune of:
Ste-Marie d'Alloix (P, R) Gamay, Persan, Étraire de la Dui, Servanin, Joubertin (W) Verdesse, Jacquère, Aligoté, Chardonnay

Note: Red wines may be made with the addition of up to 20% white grapes.

Roussette de Savoie (W) Roussette, *Chardonnay*

Note: Where the designation Roussette de Savoie is followed by the name of a commune, the wine must be 100% from Roussette.

Seyssel (W) Roussette

Seyssel Mousseux (S) Chasselas, *Roussette*

Vin de Savoie (P, R) Gamay, Mondeuse, Pinot Noir, *Persan, Cabernet Sauvignon, Cabernet Franc, Étraire de la Dui, Servanin, Joubertin* (W) Aligoté, Roussette, Jacquère, Chardonnay, Malvoisie, Mondeuse Blanche, *Chasselas, Gringet, Roussette d'Ayze, Marsanne, Verdesse*

Note: An addition of up to 20% of the white grapes listed above is permitted in the production of red Vin de Savoie.

Vin de Savoie Pétillant (W) the above white grapes plus Molette

Vin de Savoie Mousseux (S) Molette

Where the designation Vin de Savoie is followed by the name of a commune, the following grape varieties may be used:
For the communes of: Abymes, Apremont, Arbin, Ayze, Charpignat, Chautagne, Chignin, Cruet, Montmélian, St-Jean-de-la-Porte, St-Jeoire-Prieuré: R, W, & P as Vin de Savoie

Vin de Savoie Ayze (Pétillant & S) (W) Gringet, Roussette, Mondeuse Blanche, *Roussette d'Ayze*

SOUTH WEST FRANCE

Béarn (R, P) Tannat, *Cabernet Franc (Bouchy), Cabernet Sauvignon, Fer (Pinenc), Manseng Noir, Courbu Noir* (W) Petit Manseng, Gros Manseng, *Courbu, Lauzet, Camaralet, RaYat, Sauvignon Blanc*

Bergerac, Bergerac Sec (W) Sémillon, Sauvignon Blanc, Muscadelle, Ondenc, Chenin Blanc, *Ugni Blanc*

Bergerac, Côtes de Bergerac (R, P)
Cabernet Sauvignon, Cabernet Franc,
Merlot, *Malbec (Cot), Fer Servadou, Merille*
(Périgord)

Blanquette de Limoux Mousseux,
Crémant de Limoux (W, S) Mauzac,
Chardonnay, Chenin Blanc

Blanquette Méthode Ancestrale
Mousseux (W, S) Mauzac

Buzet (R, P) Merlot, Cabernet Sauvignon,
Cabernet Franc, Malbec (Cot) (W) Sémillon, Sauvignon Blanc, Muscadelle

Cahors (R) Malbec (Cot), Merlot, Tannat,
Jurançon Noir

Côtes du Brulhois (R, P) Cabernet
Sauvignon, Cabernet Franc, Merlot, Fer,
Cot, Tannat

Côtes de Duras (W) Sauvignon Blanc,
Sémillon, Muscadelle, Mauzac, *Rouchelin,*
Pineau de la Loire (Chenin Blanc), Ondenc, Ugni
Blanc (R, P) Cabernet Sauvignon, Caber-
net Franc, Merlot, Malbec (Cot)

Côtes du Frontonnais/Fronton/Villau-
dric (R, P) Négrette, *Cot, Mérille, Fer, Syrah,*
Cabernet Franc, Cabernet Sauvignon, Gamay,
Cinsaut, Mauzac

Côtes du Marmandais (R, P) Cabernet
Franc, Cabernet Sauvignon, Merlot, *Abour-*
iou, Merlot (Cot), Fer, Gamay, Syrah (W) Sauvignon Blanc, *Muscadelle, Ugni Blanc, Sémillon*

Côtes de Montravel, Haut-Montravel
(W) Sémillon, Sauvignon Blanc,
Muscadelle

Côtes de St-Mont, VDQS (R, P) Tannat,
Cabernet Sauvignon, Cabernet Franc, Merlot,
Fer (W) Arrufiac, Clairette, Courbu, *Gros*
Manseng, Petit Manseng

Gaillac (R, P) Duras, Fer Servadou, Gamay,
Syrah, *Cabernet Sauvignon, Cabernet Franc,*
Merlot (W) Len de L'el, Mauzac Rosé,
Muscadelle, Ondenc, Sauvignon Blanc,
Sémillon

Gaillac Premières Côtes (W) Len de L'el,
Mauzac, Mauzac Rosé, Muscadelle,
Ondenc, Sauvignon Blanc, Sémillon

Gaillac Mousseux (doux) (W) Len de L'el,
Mauzac, Mauzac Rosé, Muscadelle,
Ondenc, Sauvignon Blanc, Sémillon

(P) Duras, Fer Servadou, Gamay, Syrah,
Cabernet Sauvignon, Cabernet Franc, Merlot

Irouléguy (R, P) Cabernet Sauvignon,
Cabernet Franc, Tannat (W) Courbu,
Manseng

Jurançon, Jurançon Sec (W) Petit
Manseng, Gros Manseng, *Courbu,*
Camaralet, Lauzet

Limoux (W) Chardonnay

Madiran (R) Tannat, *Cabernet Sauvignon,*
Cabernet Franc/Bouchy, Fer (Pinenc)

Marcillac (R, P) Fer Servadou, *Cabernet*
Sauvignon, Cabernet Franc, Merlot

Monbazillac, Rosette (W) Sémillon,
Sauvignon Blanc, Muscadelle

Montravel (W) Sémillon, Sauvignon
Blanc, Muscadelle, Ondenc, Chenin Blanc,
Ugni Blanc

Pacherenc du Vic-Bilh (W) Arrufiac,
Courbu, Gros Manseng, Petit Manseng,
Sauvignon Blanc, Sémillon

Pécharmant (R) Cabernet Sauvignon,
Cabernet Franc, Merlot, Malbec (Cot)

Saussignac (W) Sémillon, Sauvignon
Blanc, Muscadelle, Chenin Blanc

Tursan, VDQS (R, P) Tannat, Cabernet
Sauvignon, Cabernet Franc (Bouchy), Fer
Servadou (Pinenc) (W) Baroque, *Sauvi-*
gnon Blanc, Petit Manseng, Gros Manseng,
Claverie, Cruchinet, Raffiat, Claret de Gers,
Clairette

Vins d'Entraygues et du Fel, VDQS (R, P)
Cabernet Franc, Cabernet Sauvignon, Fer,
Gamay Noir à Jus Blanc, Jurançon Noir,
Mouyssaguès, Négrette, Pinot Noir
(W) Chenin Blanc, Mauzac

Vins d'Estaing, VDQS (R, P) Fer
Servadou, Gamay Noir à Jus Blanc,
Jurançon Noir, Abouriou, Merlot, Cabernet
Franc, Cabernet Sauvignon, Mouyssaguès,
Négrette, Pinot Noir, Duras, Castets (W)
Chenin Blanc, Roussellou (St-Pierre Doré),
Mauzac

Vins de Lavilledieu, VDQS (R) Négrette,
Mauzac, Bordelais, Morterille (Cinsaut),
Chalosse (Béquignol), *Syrah, Gamay,*
Jurançon Noir, Picpoul, Milgranet, Fer (W)
Mauzac, Sauvignon Blanc, Sémillon,

Muscadelle, Blanquette, Ondenc, Chalosse Blanche (Claverie)

Tokaji Aszú Muscat (W) Furmint, Hárslevelű, Muscat Blanc à Petits Grains

Germany

Liebfraumilch (W) Müller-Thurgau, Silvaner, Kerner, and/or (most unusually) Riesling must constitute 70%

Greece

Amindeo (R) Xynomavro

Anhialos (W) Roditis, *Savatiano*

Archanes (R) Kotsifali, Mandelaria

Dafnes (R) Liatiko

Goumenissa (R) Xynomavro, *Negoska*

Limnos (W) Muscat of Alexandria

Mantinia (W) Moscophilero

Côtes de Meliton (R) Limnio, Cabernet Sauvignon, Cabernet Franc (W) Athiri, Roditis, Assyrtiko, *Sauvignon Blanc, Ugni Blanc*

Naoussa (R) Xynomavro

Nemea (R) Aghiorghitiko

Paros (R) Monemvassia (Malvasia), *Mandelaria*

Patras (W) Roditis

Peza (R) Kotsifali, Mandelaria (W) Vilana

Rapsani (R) Xynomavro, Krassato, Stavroto

Rhodes (R) Mandelaria (W) Athiri

Samos (W) Muscat Blanc à Petits Grains

Santorini, Santorini Vissanto (W) Assyrtiko, *Athiri, Aidini*

Sitia (R) Liatiko

Zitsa (W) Debina

Hungary

Bulls Blood of Eger (Egri Bikavér) (R) Kékfrankos, Cabernet Sauvignon, Merlot, *Kékoporto*

Tokaji (W) Furmint, Hárslevelű, Muscat Blanc, *Orémus*

Italy

ABRUZZI

All DOC wines are varietal

APULIA

Alezio (R, P) Negroamaro, *Malvasia Nera, Sangiovese, Montepulciano*

Brindisi (R, P) Negroamaro, *Susumaniello, Malvasia Nera, Sangiovese, Montepulciano*

Cacc'e Mmitte di Lucera (R) Montepulciano, Uva di Troia, Sangiovese, Malvasia Nera, Trebbiano Toscano, Bombino Bianco, Malvasia del Chianti

Castel del Monte (W) Pampanuto (Pampanino), Chardonnay (R) Uva di Troia, Aglianico (P) Bombino Nero, Aglianico

Copertino (R, P) Negroamaro, *Malvasia Nera di Brindisi, Malvasia Nera di Lecce, Sangiovese, Montepulciano*

Gioia del Colle (R, P) Primitivo, Montepulciano, Sangiovese, Negroamaro, Malvasia Nera (W) Trebbiano Toscano

Gravina (W) Malvasia del Chianti, Greco di Tufo, Bianco d'Alessano, *Bombino Bianco, Trebbiano Toscano, Verdeca*

Leverano (P, R) Negroamaro, *Malvasia Nera di Lecce, Sangiovese, Montepulciano, Malvasia Nera* (W) Malvasia Bianca, *Bombino Bianco, Trebbiano Toscano*

Lizzano (P, R) Negroamaro, *Bombino Nero, Pinot Nero, Malvasia Nera di Lecce, Sangiovese, Montepulciano, Malvasia Nera* (W) Trebbiano Toscano, Chardonnay, Pinot Bianco, *Malvasia, Lunga Bianca (Malvasia), Sauvignon Blanc, Bianco d'Alessano*

Locorotondo (W) Verdeca, Bianco d'Alessano, *Fiano, Bombino, Malvasia Toscano*

Martina (W) Verdeca, Bianco d'Alessano, *Fiano, Bombino, Malvasia Toscano*

Matino (P, R) Negroamaro, *Malvasia Nera, Sangiovese*

Nardò (P, R) Negroamaro, *Malvasia Nera di Lecce, Montepulciano*

Orta Nova (P, R) Sangiovese, *Uva di Troia, Montepulciano, Lambrusco Maestri, Trebbiano Toscano*

Ostuni (W) Francavilla, *Bianco d'Alessano,* Verdeca

Rosso Barletta (R) Montepulciano, Sangiovese, *Malbec*

Rosso Canosa (R) Uva di Troia, *Montepulciano, Sangiovese*

Rosso di Cerognola (R) Uva di Troia, Negroamaro, *Sangiovese, Barbera, Montepulciano, Malbec, Trebbiano*

Salice Salentino (P, R) Negroamaro, *Malvasia Nera di Lecce, Malvasia Nera di Brindisi*

San Severo (W) Bombino Bianco, Trebbiano Toscano, *Malvasia Bianca* (P, R) Montepulciano, Sangiovese

Squinzano (P, R) Malvasia Nera di Brindisi, Malvasia Nera di Lecce, Sangiovese

BASILICATA

Varietal DOCs only

CALABRIA

Cirò (P, R) Gaglioppo, *Trebbiano Toscano*

Donnici (P, R) Gaglioppo, Mantonico Nero, Greco Nero, Malvasia Bianco, Mantonico Bianco, *Pecorello*

Lamezia (W) Greco, Trebbiano, Malvasia (P, R) Nerello, Mascalese, Nerello Cappuccio, Gaglioppo, Magliocco, Greco Nero, Marsigliana (Greco Nero)

Melissa (W) Greco Bianco, Trebbiano Toscano, Malvasia Bianca (R) Gaglioppo, Greco Nero, Greco Bianco, Trebbiano Toscano, Malvasia

Pollino (R) Gaglioppo, Greco Nero, Malvasia Bianca, Montonico Bianco, Guarnaccia Bianca

Sant'Anna di Isola Capo Rizzuto (R, P) Gaglioppo, Nerello Mascalese, Nerello Cappuccio, Malvasia Nera, *Nocera*

San Vito di Luzzi (W) Malvasia Bianca, Greco, Trebbiano Toscano (R, P) Gaglioppo, *Malvasia, Greco Nero, Sangiovese*

Savuto (R, P) Gaglioppo, Greco Nero, Nerello Cappuccio, Magliocco Canino, Sangiovese, Malvasia Bianca, Pecorino

Scavigna (W) Trebbiano Toscano, Chardonnay, Greco Bianco, Malvasia (P, R) Gaglioppo, Nerello Cappuccio, Aglianico

CAMPANIA

Campi Flegrei (W) Falanghina, Biancolella, Coda di Volpe (R) Piedirosso, Aglianico, *Sciascinoso*

Capri (W) Falanghina, Greco, *Biancolella* (R) Piedirosso

Castel san Lorenzo (R) Barbera, Sangiovese (W) Trebbiano, Malvasia

Cilento (R) Aglianico, Piedirosso, Barbera (P) Sangiovese, Aglianico, Primitivo, Piedirosso (W) Fiano, Trebbiano Toscano, Greco Bianco, Malvasia

Falerno del Massico (W) Falanghina (R) Aglianico, Piedirosso, *Primitivo, Barbera*

Guardia Sanframondi/Guardiolo (W) Malvasia Candia Bianco, Falanghina (R) Sangiovese

Ischia (W) Forastera Bianco, Biancolella (R) Guarnaccia, Piedirosso

Penisola Sorrentina (W) Falanghina, Biancolella, Greco (R) Piedirosso, Sciascinoso, Aglianico

Solopaca (W) Trebbiano Toscano, Falanghina, Malvasia, Coda di Volpe (R) Sangiovese, Aglianico, *Piedirosso, Sciascinoso*

Taburno Bianco (W) Trebbiano Toscano, Falanghina (R) Sangiovese, Aglianico (S) Coda di Volpe, Falanghina

Taurasi (R) Aglianico

Vesuvio (W) Coda di Volpe, Verdeca, Falanghina, Greco (R) Piedirosso, Sciascinoso, *Aglianico*

EMILIA-ROMAGNA

Bianco di Scandiano (W) Sauvignon Blanc (Spergola)

Bosco Eliceo (W) Trebbiano Romagnolo, Sauvignon Blanc, Malvasia Bianca di Candia

Bosco Eliceo Sauvignon (W) Sauvignon Blanc, *Trebbiano Romagnolo*

Cagnina di Romagna (R) Refosco (Terrano)

Colli Bolognesi (W) Albana, Trebbiano Romagnolo

Colli di Parma (R) Barbera, Bonarda Piemontese, Croatina

Colli di Parma Malvasia (W) Malvasia Candia Aromatico, *Moscato Bianco*

Colli Piacentini Gutturnio (R) Barbera, Croatina (Bonarda)

Colli Piacentini Monterosso Val d'Arda (W) Malvasia di Candida Aromatica, Moscato Bianco, Trebbiano Romagnolo, Ortrugo, *Beverdino, Sauvignon Blanc*

Colli Piacentini Trebbianino Val Trebbia (W) Ortrugo, Malvasia di Candida Aromatica, Moscato Bianco, Trebbiano Romagnolo

Colli Piacentini Val Nure (W) Malvasia di Candida Aromatica, Trebbiano Romagnolo, Ortrugo

Lambrusco di Sorbara (R, P) Lambrusco di Sorbara, Lambrusco Salamino

Lambrusco Grasparossa (R, P) Lambrusco Grasparossa, *Fortana (Uva d'Oro)*

Aquileia (P) Merlot, Cabernet Franc, Cabernet Sauvignon, Refosco Nostrano, Refosco dal Peduncolo Rosso

Carso Terrano (R) Terrano, *Piccola Nera, Pinot Noir*

Collio Goriziano/Collio (W) Ribolla Gialla, Malvasia Istriana, Tocai Friulano, *Chardonnay, Pinot Bianco, Pinot Grigio, Riesling Italico, Riesling Renano, Sauvignon Blanc, Müller-Thurgau, Traminer Aromatico* (R) Merlot, Cabernet Franc, Cabernet Sauvignon, *Pinot Nero*

Grave del Friuli (W) Chardonnay, Pinot Bianco (P, R) Cabernet Franc, Cabernet Sauvignon (W, S) Chardonnay, Pinot Bianco, Pinot Nero

Isonzo (W) Tocai Friulano, Malvasia Istriana, Pinot Bianco, Chardonnay (R) Merlot, Cabernet Franc, Cabernet Sauvignon, *Refosco dal Peduncolo Rosso, Pinot Nero* (S)

Pinot Bianco, *Chardonnay, Pinot Nero*

Latisana (P) Merlot, Cabernet Franc, Cabernet Sauvignon, Refosco Nostrano, Refosco dal Peduncolo Rosso (W, S) Chardonnay, Pinot Bianco, Pinot Nero

Bianco Capena (W) Trebbiano, Malvasia, *Bellone, Bombino*

Cerveteri (W) Trebbiano, Malvasia, *Verdicchio, Tocai, Bellone, Bombino* (R) Sangiovese, Montepulciano, Cesanese, *Canaiolo Nero, Carignano, Barbera*

Colli Albani (W) Malvasia, Trebbiano

Colli Lanuvini (W) Malvasia, Trebbiano

Cori (W) Malvasia, Trebbiano, Bellone (R) Montepulciano, *Nero Buono di Cori, Cesanese*

Est! Est!! Est!!! di Montefiascone (W) Malvasia, Trebbiano

Frascati (W) Malvasia, Trebbiano, *Greco*

Genazzano (W) Malvasia, Bellone, Bombino, Trebbiano, Pinot Bianco (R) Sangiovese, Cesanese

Marino (W) Malvasia, Trebbiano

Montecompatri Colonna (W) Malvasia, Trebbiano, *Bellone, Bonvino*

Velletri (W) Malvasia, Trebbiano (R) Sangiovese, Montepulciano, Cesanese, *Bombino Nero*

Vignanello (W) Malvasia, Trebbiano (R) Sangiovese, Ciliegiolo

Zagarolo (W) Malvasia, Trebbiano

Cinqueterre (W) Bosco, Albarola, Vermentino

Colli di Luni (R) Sangiovese, Canaiolo, Pollera Nera, Ciliegiolo Nero (W) Vermentino, Trebbiano Toscano

Riviera Ligure di Ponente Ormeasco (R) Dolcetto

LOMBARDY

Botticino (R) Barbera, Schiava Gentile, Marzemino, Sangiovese

Capriano del Colle (R) Sangiovese, Marzemino, Barbera, *Incrocio Terzi No. 1* (W) Trebbiano di Soave, *Trebbiano Toscano*

Cellatica (R) Schiava Gentile, Barbera, Marzemino, Incrocio Terzi No. 1

Colli Morenici Mantovani del Garda (R) Merlot, Rossanella (Molinara), *Negrara, Sangiovese* (W) Trebbiano Giallo, Trebbiano Toscano, Trebbiano di Soave, Pinot Bianco, *Riesling Italico, Malvasia di Candida*

Franciacorta (R) Cabernet Franc, Barbera, Nebbiolo, Merlot (W) Pinot Bianco, Chardonnay (S) Pinot Bianco, Chardonnay, Pinot Grigio, Pinot Nero

Lambrusco Mantovano (R) Lambrusco Viadanese, Lambrusco Maestri, Lambrusco Marani, Lambrusco Salamino, *Ancellotta, Fortana, Uva d'Oro*

Lugana (W) Trebbiano di Lugana

Oltrepò Pavese (non-varietal) (R, P) Barbera, Croatina, Uva Rara, Ughetta (Vespolina), Pinot Nero

Riviera del Garda Bresciano/Garda Bresciano (W) Riesling Italico, Riesling Renano (R, P) Groppello, Sangiovese, Marzemino, Barbera

San Colombano al Lambro (R) Croatina, Barbera, Uva Rara

San Martino della Battaglia (W) Tocai Friulano

Valcalepio (R) Merlot, Cabernet Sauvignon (W) Pinot Bianco, Chardonnay, Pinot Grigio

Valtellina (R) Chiavennasca, *Pinot Nero, Merlot, Rossola, Pignola Valtellinese*

MARCHES

Colli Maceratesi (W) Maceratino, *Trebbiano Toscano, Verdicchio, Malvasia Toscana, Chardonnay*

Colli Pesaresi (R) Sangiovese (W) Trebbiano

Falerio dei Colli Ascolani (W) Trebbiano, Passerina, Verdicchio, Malvasia Toscana

Focara Rosso (R) Sangiovese, *Pinot Nero*

Roncaglia Bianco (W) Trebbiano, Pinot Nero

Rosso Conero (R) Montepulciano, *Sangiovese*

Rosso Piceno (R) Montepulciano, Sangiovese, *Trebbiano, Passerina*

MOLISE

Biferno (R, P) Montepulciano, Trebbiano, Aglianico (W) Trebbiano Toscano, Bombino Bianco, Malvasia

Pentro di Isernia (W) Trebbiano Bianco, Bombino Bianco

PIEDMONT

Asti (W, S) Moscato

Barbaresco (R) Nebbiolo Michet, Nebbiolo Lampia, Nebbiolo Rosé

Barbera d'Asti, Barbera del Monferrato (R) Barbera, *Freisa, Grignolino, Dolcetto*

Barolo (R) Nebbiolo Michet, Nebbiolo Lampia, Nebbiolo Rosé

Boca (R) Nebbiolo (Spanna), Vespolina, Bonarda Novarese

Brachetto d'Acqui (R) Brachetto, *Aleatico, Moscato Nero*

Bramaterra (R) Nebbiolo (Spanna), Croatina, Vespolina

Carema (R) Nebbiolo

Casalese (W) Cortese

Colli Tortonesi (R) Barbera, *Freisa, Bonarda Piemontese, Dolcetto* (W) Cortese

Fara (R) Nebbiolo (Spanna), *Vespolina, Bonarda*

Gabiano (R) Barbera, Freisa, Grignolino

Gattinara (R) Nebbiolo (Spanna), Vespolina, Bonarda di Gattinara

Gavi (W) Cortese

Ghemme (R) Nebbiolo (Spanna), *Vespolina, Bonarda*

Grignolino d'Asti (R) Grignolino, *Freisa*

Grignolino del Monferrato Casalese (R) Grignolino, *Freisa*

Lessona (R) Nebbiolo (Spanna), *Vespolina, Bonarda*

Loazzolo (W) Moscato

Monferrato Ciaret (R) Barbera, Bonarda, Cabernet Franc, Cabernet Sauvignon, Dolcetto, Freisa, Grignolino, Pinot Nero, Nebbiolo

Piemonte Spumante (S) Chardonnay, Pinot Bianco, Pinot Grigio, Pinot Nero

Roero (R) Nebbiolo, *Arneis*   (W) Arneis

Rubino di Cantavenna (R) Barbera, *Grignolino, Freisa*

Ruchè di Castagnole Monferrato (R) Ruchè, *Barbera, Brachetto*

Sizzano (R) Nebbiolo, *Vespolina, Bonarda*

SARDINIA

Campidano di Terralba (R) Bovale Sardo, Bovale di Spagna, *Pascal di Cagliari, Greco Nero, Monica*

Mandrolisai (P, R) Bovale Sardo, Cannonau, Monica

SICILY

Alcamo (W) Catarratto Bianco Commune, Catarratto Bianco Lucido, *Damaschino, Grecanico, Trebbiano Toscano*

Cerasuolo di Vittoria (R) Frappato, Calabrese, *Grosso Nero, Nerello Mascalese*

Contessa Entellina (W) Ansonica, *Catarratto Bianco Lucido, Grecanico, Chardonnay, Sauvignon Blanc, Müller-Thurgau*

Eloro (P, R) Nero d'Avola, Frappato, Pignatello

Etna (W) Carricante, Catarratto Bianco Commune, *Trebbiano, Minnella Bianca* (P, R) Nerello Mascalese, Nerello Mantellato (Nerello Cappuccio)

Faro (R) Nerello Mascalese, Nerello Cappuccio, *Calabrese, Gaglioppo, Sangiovese, Nocera*

Marsala (W) Grillo, Catarratto, Pignatello, Calabrese, Nerello Mascalese, Inzolia, Nero d'Avola, *Damaschino*

TRENTINO-ALTO ADIGE

Caldaro/Lago di Caldaro (R) Schiava, Pinot Nero, Lagrein

Casteller (R) Schiava, Merlot, Lambrusco

Klausner Leitacher (R) Schiava, *Portoghese, Lagrein*

Sorni (R) Schiava, Teroldego, Lagrein (W) Nosiola, Müller-Thurgau, Sylvaner, Pinot Bianco

Trentino (W) Chardonnay, Pinot Bianco (R) Cabernet Franc, Cabernet Sauvignon, Merlot (Vin Santo), Nosiola

Trento (W or P, S) Chardonnay, Pinot Bianco, Pinot Nero, Pinot Meunier

Valdadige (W) Pinot Bianco, Pinot Grigio, Riesling Italico, Müller-Thurgau, Chardonnay, Bianchetta Trevigiana, Trebbiano Toscano, Nosiola Veraccia, Garganega (R) Schiava, Lambrusco, Merlot, Pinot Nero, Lagrein, Teroldego, Negrara

TUSCANY

Bianco della Valdinievole (W) Trebbiano Toscano, Malvasia del Chianti, Canaiolo Bianco, Vermentino

Bianco dell'Empolese (W) Trebbiano Toscano

Bianco di Pitigliano (W) Trebbiano Toscano, Greco, Malvasia Toscana, Verdello, Grechetto, *Chardonnay, Sauvignon Blanc, Pinot Bianco, Riesling Italico*

Bianco Pisano di San Torpe (W) Trebbiano

Bianco Vergine Valdichiana (W) Trebbiano

Bolgheri (W) Trebbiano, Vermentino, Sauvignon Blanc   (R, P) Cabernet Sauvignon, Merlot, Sangiovese

Candia dei Colli Apuani (W) Vermentino, Albarola

Carmignano (R) Sangiovese, Canaiolo Nero, Cabernet Franc, Cabernet Sauvignon, Trebbiano Toscano, Canaiolo Bianco, Malvasia del Chianti

Carmignano/Barco Reale di Carmignano (R) Sangiovese, Canaiolo

Nero, *Cabernet Franc, Cabernet Sauvignon, Trebbiano Toscano, Canaiolo Bianco, Malvasia*

Chianti (R) Sangiovese, Canaiolo Nero, Trebbiano, Malvasia del Chianti

Colli dell'Etruria Centrale (R) Sangiovese, *Canaiolo Nero, Trebbiano, Malvasia, Cabernet Franc, Cabernet Sauvignon, Merlot* (W) Trebbiano Toscano, *Malvasia del Chianti, Pinot Bianco, Pinot Grigio, Chardonnay, Sauvignon Blanc*

Colline Lucchese (R) Sangiovese, Canaiolo, Ciliegiolo, Colorino, Trebbiano, Vermentino (W) Trebbiano Toscano, Greco, Grechetto, Vermentino Bianco, Malvasia

Elba (W) Trebbiano (Procanico) (R) Sangiovese (Sangioveto)

Montecarlo (W) Trebbiano, Sémillon, Pinot Grigio, Pinot Bianco, Vermentino, Sauvignon Blanc, Roussanne (R) Sangiovese, Canaiolo Nero, Ciliegiolo, Colorino, Malvasia Nera, Syrah, Cabernet Franc, Cabernet Sauvignon, Merlot

Monteregio di Massa Marittima (R) Sangiovese (W) Trebbiano, Vermentino, Malvasia, Ansonica

Montescudaio (W) Trebbiano, Vermentino, Malvasia (R) Sangiovese, Trebbiano Toscano, Malvasia

Parrina (R, P) Sangiovese (W) Trebbiano, Ansonica, Chardonnay

Pomino (R) Sangiovese, Canaiolo, Cabernet Sauvignon, Cabernet Franc, Merlot (W) Pinot Bianco, Chardonnay, Trebbiano

Rosso di Montalcino (R) Sangiovese

Rosso di Montepulciano (R) Sangiovese, Canaiolo Nero

Sassicaia (R) Cabernet Sauvignon

Val d'Arbia (W) Trebbiano, Malvasia, Chardonnay

Val di Cornia (W) Trebbiano, Vermentino, *Malvasia, Ansonica, Biancame, Clairette, Pinot Bianco, Pinot Grigio* (R) Sangiovese, *Canaiolo, Ciliegiolo, Cabernet Sauvignon, Merlot*

Vino Nobile di Montepulciano (R) Sangiovese, Canaiolo Nero

Vino Santo Occhio di Pernice (P) Sangiovese, Merlot

Colli Altotiberini (W) Trebbiano Toscano, Malvasia del Chianti (R) Sangiovese, Merlot, Trebbiano Toscano, Malvasia del Chianti Nero

Colli Amerini (W) Trebbiano Toscano, Grechetto, Verdello, Garganega, Malvasia Toscana (R) Sangiovese

Colli del Trasimeno (R) Sangiovese, Ciliegiolo, Gamay, Malvasia del Chianti, Trebbiano Toscana (W) Trebbiano Toscana, Malvasia del Chianti, Verdicchio Bianco, Verdello, Grechetto

Colli Perugini (R) Sangiovese, Montepulciano, Ciliegiolo, Barbera, Merlot (W) Trebbiano Toscano, Verdicchio, Grechetto, Garganega, Malvasia del Chianti

Montefalco (W) Grechetto, Trebbiano Toscano (R) Sangiovese, Sagrantino

Orvieto (W) Trebbiano Toscano (Procanico), Verdello, Grechetto, Canaiolo Bianco (Drupeggio), Malvasia Toscana

Torgiano (W) Trebbiano Toscano, Grechetto (R) Sangiovese, Canaiolo, *Trebbiano Toscano, Ciliegiolo, Montepulciano* (S) Chardonnay, Pinot Nero

Torgiano Riserva (R) Sangiovese, Canaiolo, *Trebbiano Toscano, Ciliegiolo, Montepulciano*

Arnad-Montjovet (R) Nebbiolo, *Dolcetto, Vien de Nus, Pinot Nero, Neyret, Freisa*

Chambave (R) Petit Rouge, *Dolcetto, Gamay, Pinot Nero* (W) Moscato

Donnaz (R) Nebbiolo (Picutener), Freisa, Neyret

Enfer d'Arvier (R) Petit Rouge, Vien de Nus, Neyret, Dolcetto, Pinot Nero, Gamay

Nus (R) Vien de Nus, Petit Rouge, Pinot Nero (W) Malvoisie

Torrette (R) Petit Rouge, *Gamay, Pinot Nero, Fumin, Vien de Nus, Dolcetto, Mayolet, Premetta*

Valle d'Aosta (W) Müller-Thurgau, Pinot Grigio, Petite Arvine, Chardonnay, Blanc de Morgex (R) Petit Rouge, Chambave, Dolcetto, Gamay, Pinot Nero, *Premetta*, Fumin

VENETO

Bardolino (R) Corvina, Rondinella, Molinara, Negrara, *Rossignola, Barbera, Sangiovese, Garganega*

Bianco di Custoza (W) Trebbiano Toscano, Garganega, Tocai Friulano, Cortese, Malvasia, Pinot Bianco, Chardonnay, Riesling Italico

Breganze (W) Tocai, *Pinot Bianco, Pinot Grigio, Riesling Italico, Sauvignon Blanc, Vespaiolo* (R) Merlot, *Groppello Gentile, Cabernet Franc, Cabernet Sauvignon, Pinot Nero, Freisa*

Colli Berici Chardonnay (W) Chardonnay, *Pinot Bianco*

Colli Berici Garganega (W) Garganega, *Trebbiano di Soave (Trebbiano Nostrano)*

Colli Berici Pinot Bianco (W) Pinot Bianco, *Pinot Grigio*

Colli Berici Sauvignon (W) Sauvignon Blanc, *Garganega*

Colli Berici Spumante (S) Garganega, *Pinot Bianco, Pinot Grigio*

Colli Berici Tocai Italico (W) Tocai Italico, *Garganega*

Colli Berici Tocai Rosso (R) Tocai Rosso, *Garganega*

Colli di Conegliano (W) Incrocio Manzoni 6.0.13., Pinot Bianco, Chardonnay, *Sauvignon Blanc, Riesling Renano* (R) Cabernet Franc, Cabernet Sauvignon, Marzemino, Merlot, *Incrocio Manzoni 2.15*

Colli Euganei (W) Garganega, Prosecco (Serprina), Tocai Friulano, Sauvignon Blanc, *Pinella, Pinot Bianco, Riesling Italico, Chardonnay* (R) Merlot, Cabernet Franc, Cabernet Sauvignon, Barbera, Raboso Veronese

Gambellara (W) Garganega

Lessini Durello (W) Durella, *Garganega, Trebbiano di Soave, Pinot Bianco, Pinot Nero, Chardonnay*

Fior d'Arancio (W) Moscato Giallo

Montello e Colli Asolani (R) Merlot, Cabernet Franc, Cabernet Sauvignon

Montello e Colli Asolani Cabernet (R) Cabernet Franc, Cabernet Sauvignon, *Malbec*

Montello e Colli Asolani Chardonnay (W) Chardonnay, *Pinot Bianco, Pinot Grigio*

Montello e Colli Asolani Merlot (R) Merlot, *Cabernet Sauvignon, Cabernet Franc*

Montello e Colli Asolani Pinot Bianco (W) Pinot Bianco, *Chardonnay, Pinot Grigio*

Montello e Colli Asolani Pinot Grigio (W) Pinot Grigio, *Chardonnay, Pinot Bianco*

Montello e Colli Asolani Prosecco (W) Prosecco, *Chardonnay, Pinot Bianco, Pinot Grigio, Riesling Italico, Bianchetta Trevigiana*

Prosecco di Conegliano-Valdobbiadene/Prosecco di Conegliano/Prosecco di Valdobbiadene (W) Prosecco, *Verdiso, Pinot Bianco, Pinot Grigio, Chardonnay*

Refrontolo Passito (R) Marzemino

Soave (W) Garganega, Pinot Bianco, Chardonnay, Trebbiano

Torchiato di Fregona (W) Prosecco, Verdiso, *Boschera*

Valpolicella (R) Corvina Veronese, Rondinella, Molinara

Portugal

Alcobaça (IPR) (R) Periquita, Baga, Trincadeira (W) Vital, Tamarez, Fernão Pires, Malvasia, Arinto

Alenquer (R) Camarate, Mortágua, Periquita, Preto Martinho, Tinta Miúda (W) Vital, Jampal, Arinto, Fernão Pires

Almeirim (R) Castelão Nacional, Poeirinha (Baga), Periquita, Trincadeira Preta (W) Fernão Pires, Arinto, Rabo de Ovelha, Talia, Trincadeira das Pratas, Vital

Arruda (R) Camarate, Trincadeira, Tinta Miúda (W) Vital, Jampal, Fernão Pires

Bairrada (R) Baga, Castelão Francês, Tinta Pinheira (W) Maria Gomes, Bical, Rabo de Ovelha

Biscoitos (IPR) (W) Arinto, Terrantez, Verdelho

Borba (R) Aragonêz, Periquita, Trincadeira

(W) Perrum, Rabo de Ovelha, Roupeiro, Tamarez

Bucelas (W) Arinto, Esgana Cão

Carcavelos (R, W) Galego Dourado, Boal, Arinto, Trincadeira Torneiro, Negra Mole

Cartaxo (R) Castelão Nacional, Periquita, Preto Martinho, Trincadeira Preta (W) Fernão Pires, Talia, Trincadeira das Pratas, Vital, Arinto

Castelo Rodrigo (IPR) (R) Aragonêz Bastardo, Marufo, Rufete, Touriga Nacional (W) Malvasia Fina, Siria, Tamarez

Chamusca (R) Castelão Nacional, Periquita, Trincadeira Preta (W) Fernão Pires, Talia, Arinto, Trincadeira das Pratas, Vital

Chaves (IPR) (R) Tinta Amarela, Bastardo, Tinta Carvalha (W) Gouveio, Malvasia Fina, Códega, Boal

Colares (R) Ramisco (W) Arinto, Jampal, Galego Dourado, Malvasia

Coruche (R) Periquita, Preto Martinho, Trincadeira Preta (W) Fernão Pires, Talia, Trincadeira das Pratas, Vital

Cova da Beira (IPR) (R) Aragonêz, Baga, Bastardo, Jaén, Marufo, Moreto, Periquita, Rufete, Tinta Carvola, Touriga Nacional, Trincadeira (W) Alicante Branco, Arinto, Bical, Fonte Cal, Malvasia, Rabo de Ovelha, Siria

Dão (R) Alfrocheiro Preto, Bastardo, Jaén, Tinta Pinheira, Tinta Roriz, Touriga Nacional (W) Encruzado, Assario Branco, Barcelo, Borrado das Moscas, Cerceal, Verdelho

Douro (R) Touriga Nacional, Touriga Francesa, Tinta Roriz, Tinta Barroca, Tinto Cão, Tinta Amarela, Mourisco Tinto, Bastardo (W) Gouveio, Viosinho, Rabigato, Malvasia Fina, Donzelinho

Encostas d'Aire (IPR) (R) Periquita, Baga, Trincadeira Preta (W) Fernão Pires, Arinto, Tamarez, Vital

Encostas de Nave (IPR) (R) Touriga Nacional, Touriga Francesa, Tinta Barroca, Mourisco Tinto (W) Malvasia Fina, Folgosão, Gouveio

Évora (R) Periquita, Trincadeira, Aragonêz, Tinta Caida (W) Arinto, Rabo de Ovelha, Roupeiro, Tamarez

Graciosa (IPR) (W) Arinto, Boal, Fernão Pires, Terrantez, Verdelho

Granja-Amareleja (R) Moreto, Periquita, Trincadeira (W) Mantuedo, Rabo de Ovelha, Roupeiro

Lafões (IPR) (R) Amaral, Jaén (W) Arinto, Cerceal

Lagoa (R) Negra Mole, Periquita (W) Crato Branco

Lagos (R) Negra Mole, Periquita (W) Boal Branco

Madeira (R) Tinta Negra Mole, Bastardo, Malvasia Roxa, Verdelho Tinto (W) Sercial, Verdelho, Boal, Malvasia, Terrantez

Moura (R) Alfrocheiro, Moreto, Periquita, Trincadeira (W) Antão Vaz, Fernão Pires, Rabo de Ovelha, Roupeiro

Óbidos (IPR) (R) Periquita, Bastardo, Camarate, Tinta Miúda (W) Vital, Arinto, Fernão Pires, Rabo de Ovelha

Palmela (R) Periquita, Alfrocheiro, Bastardo, Cabernet Sauvignon, Trincadeira (W) Fernão Pires, Arinto, Rabo de Ovelha, Moscatel de Setúbal, Tamarez, Vital

Pico (IPR) (W) Arinto, Terrantez, Verdelho

Pinhel (IPR) (R) Bastardo, Marufo, Rufete, Touriga Nacional (W) Bical, Cerceal, Fonte Cal, Malvasia, Rabo de Ovelha, Siria, Tamarez

Planalto-Mirandês (IPR) (R) Touriga Nacional, Touriga Francesa, Tinta Amarela, Mourisco Tinto, Bastardo (W) Gouveio, Malvasia Fina, Rabigato, Viosinho

Portalegre (R) Aragonêz, Grand Noir, Periquita, Trincadeira (W) Arinto, Galego, Roupeiro, Assário, Manteudo, Fernão Pires

Portimão (R) Negra Mole, Periquita (W) Crato Branco

Port (R) Touriga Francesa, Touriga Nacional, Bastardo, Mourisco, Tinto Cão, Tinta Roriz, Tinta Amarela, Tinta Barroca (W) Gouveio (Verdelho), Malvasia Fina,

Rabigato (Rabo di Ovelha), Viosinho, Donzelinho, *Códega*

Redondo (R) Aragonêz, Moreto, Periquita, Trincadeira (W) Fernão Pires, Rabo de Ovelha, Mantendo, Roupeiro, Tamarez

Reguengos (R) Aragonêz, Moreto, Periquita, Trincadeira (W) Manteudo, Perrum, Rabo de Ovelha, Roupeiro

Santarém (R) Castelão Nacional, Periquita, Preto Martinho, Trincadeira Preta (W) Fernão Pires, Arinto, Rabo de Ovelha, Talia, Trincadeira das Pratas, Vital

Setúbal (W) Moscatel de Setúbal (Muscat of Alexandria), Moscatel Roxo, Tamarez, Arinto, Fernão Pires

Tavira (R) Negra Mole, Periquita (W) Crato Branco

Tomar (R) Castelão Nacional, Baga, Periquita (W) Fernão Pires, Arinto, Malvasia, Rabo de Ovelha, Talia

Torres Vedras (R) Camarate, Mortágua, Periquita, Tinta Miúda (W) Vital, Jampal, Rabo de Ovelha, Arinto, Fernão Pires, *Seara Nova*

Valpaços (IPR) (R) Touriga Nacional, Touriga Francesa, Tinta Roriz, Tinta Amarela, Tinta Carvalha, Mourisco Tinto, Cornifesto, Bastardo (W) Códega, Fernão Pires, Gouveio, Malvasia Fina, Boal, Rabigato

Varosa (R) Alvarelhão, Tinta Barroca, Tinta Roriz, Touriga Francesa, Touriga Nacional (W) Malvasia Fina, Arinto, Borrado das Moscas, Cerceal, Gouveio, Fernão Pires, Folgosão

Vidigueira (R) Alfrocheiro, Moreto, Periquita, Trincadeira (W) Antão Vaz, Mantuedo, Perrum, Rabo de Ovelha, Roupeiro

Vinho Verde (R) Vinhão (Sousão), Espadeiro, Azal Tinto, Borraçal, Brancelho, Pedral (W) Loureiro, Trajadura, Padernã, Azal, Avesso, Alvarinho

---

Romania

Cotnari (W) Grasă, Tămîioasă, Francusa, Fetească Albă

Spain

Alella (W) Pansá Blanca (Xarel-lo), Garnacha Blanca, Macabeo, *Chardonnay, Pansá Rosado, Chenin Blanc* (R) Ull de Llebre (Tempranillo), Garnacha Tinta, Garnacha Peluda

Alicante (R) Monastrell, Garnacha Tinta, Bobal (W) Merseguera, Moscatel Romano, Verdil

Almansa (R) Monastrell, Cencibel, Garnacha Tintorera (W) Merseguera

Ampurdán-Costa Brava (R) Garnacha Tinta, Cariñena, Cabernet Sauvignon, Merlot, Tempranillo, Garnacha, Syrah (W) Macabeo, Garnacha Blanca, Chenin Blanc, Riesling, Muscat, Gewürztraminer, Macabeo, Chardonnay, Parellada, Xarel-lo

Bierzo (R) Mencía, Garnacha Tintorera (W) Godello, Doña Blanca, Malvasía, Palomino

Binissalem (R) Manto Negro, Callet, Tempranillo, Monastrell (W) Moll, Parellada, Macabeo

Bizkaiko Txakolina/Chacoli de Vizcaya (W) Hondarrabi Zuri, Folle Blanche (Gros Plant) (R) Hondarrabi Beltza

Bullas (R) Monastrell, Tempranillo (W) Macabeo, Airén

Calatayud (R) Garnacha Tinta, Tempranillo, Cariñena, Juan Ibáñez, Monastrell (W) Viura, Garnacha Blanca, Moscatel Romano, Malvasía

Campo de Borja (R) Garnacha, Tempranillo (W) Macabeo

Cariñena (R) Garnacha, Tempranillo, Cariñena, Juan Ibáñez, Monastrell, Cabernet Sauvignon (W) Viura, Garnacha Blanca, Parellada, Moscatel Romano

Cava (S) Xarel-lo, Parellada, Macabeo, Chardonnay

Chacoli de Guetaria (W) Hondarrabi Zuri (R) Hondarrabi Beltza

Cigales (R) Tempranillo, Garnacha (W) Verdejo, Viura, Palomino, Albillo

Note: All white grapes may be used for rosé wines.

Conca de Barbera (W) Macabeo, Parellada (R) Trepat, Garnacha, Ull de Llebre (Tempranillo), Cabernet Sauvignon

Condado de Huelva (W) Zalema, Palomino, Garrido Fino, Moscatel

Costers del Segre (W) Chardonnay, *Macabeo, Parellada, Xarel-lo, Garnacha Blanca* (R) Tempranillo, Cabernet Sauvignon, Merlot, *Monastrell, Trepat, Mazuelo (Cariñena), Garnacha Tinta*

Jumilla (R) Monastrell, Garnacha Tintorera, Cencibel (W) Merseguera, Airén, Pedro Ximénez

Lanzarote (W) Burrablanca, Breval, Diego, Listán Blanca, Malvasía, Moscatel, Pedro Ximénez (R) Listán Negra, Negramoll

Malaga (W) Moscatel, Pedro Ximénez

La Mancha (R) Cencibel, *Garnacha, Moravia* (W) Airén, *Pardillo, Verdoncho, Macabeo*

Méntrida (R) Garnacha, Tinto Madrid, Cencibel

Monterrei (W) Verdello, Doña Blanca, Palomino, Godello, Treixadura (R) Mencía, *Tinto Fino (Tempranillo)*

Montilla-Moriles (W) Pedro Ximénez, Lairén (Airén), *Baladi, Torrontés, Moscatel*

Navarra (R) Tempranillo, Garnacha Tinta, Cabernet Sauvignon, Merlot, *Mazuelo, Graciano* (W) Viura, *Moscatel de Grano Menudo (Muscat de Frontignan), Malvasia Riojana, Chardonnay, Garnacha Blanca*

La Palma (W) Albillo, Bastardo Blanco, Bermejuela, Bujariego, Burrablanca, Forastera Blanca, Bual, Listán Blanco, Malvasía, Moscatel, Pedro Ximénez, Sabro, Torrontés, Verdello (R) Almuñeco (Listán Negro), Bastardo Negro, Malvasía Rosada, Moscatel Negro, Negramoll, Tintilla

Penedès (R) Tempranillo, Garnacha Tinta, Cabernet Franc, Merlot, Pinot Noir, Cabernet Sauvignon, Monastrell, Cariñena, Samsó (W) Parellada, Xarel-lo, Macabeo, Subirat Parent, Gewürztraminer, Muscat d'Alsace, Chardonnay, Sauvignon, *Chenin Blanc, Riesling*

Priorato (R) Garnacha Tinta, *Garnacha Peluda, Cariñena, Cabernet Sauvignon* (W) Garnacha Blanca, *Macabeo, Pedro Ximénez, Chenin Blanc*

Rias Baixas (W) Albariño, *Treixadura, Loureira Blanca, Caiño Blanco Torrontés* (R) Brancellao, Caiño Tinto, Espadeiro, Loureira Tinta, Mencía, Sousón

Ribeira Sacra (W) Albariño, Loureira, Godello, Doña Blanca, Torrontés, *Palomino* (R) Mencía, Brancellao, Sousón, Merenzao

Ribeiro (W) Treixadura, Loureira, Albariño, *Jerez (Palomino), Torrontés, Godello, Macabeo, Albillo* (R) Caiño, Garnacha (Alicante), Ferrón, Sousón, Mencía, Tempranillo, Brancellao

Ribera del Duero (R) Tinto Fino/Tinta del País (Tempranillo), *Garnacha Tinta (Tinto Aragonés), Cabernet Sauvignon, Merlot, Malbec, Albillo*

Rioja (R) Tempranillo, Garnacha, *Graciano, Mazuelo, and Cabernet Sauvignon (experimental)* (W) Viura, *Malvasia Riojana, Garnacha Blanca*

Rueda (W) Verdejo, Viura, *Sauvignon Blanc, Palomino Fino*

Somontano (R) Moristel, Tempranillo, Cabernet Sauvignon, Merlot (W) Viura, Alcañón, Chardonnay, Pinot Noir, Chenin Blanc, Gewürztraminer

Tacoronte-Acentejo (R) Listán Negro, Negramoll (W) Malvasía, Moscatel Blanco, Listán (Palomino)

Tarragona (R) Garnacha Tinta, Cariñena, Ull de Llebre (Tempranillo), *Cabernet Sauvignon, Merlot* (W) Macabeo, Xarel-lo, Parellada, Garnacha Blanca, *Chardonnay, Muscat*

Terra Alta (W) Garnacha Blanca, Macabeo, *Chardonnay, Colombard* (R) Cariñena, Garnacha Tinta, Garnacha Peluda, *Pinot Noir, Pinot Meunier, Cabernet Sauvignon, Merlot*

Toro (R) Tinto de Toro (Tempranillo), *Garnacha Tinta, Cabernet Sauvignon* (W) Malvasia, Verdejo Blanco

Utiel-Requena (R) Tempranillo, Bobal, Garnacha Tinta, *Cabernet Sauvignon* (W) Macabeo, Merseguera, *Planta Nova, Chardonnay*

Valdeorras (R) Mencía, Garnacha, Gran Negro, Maria Ordoña (Merenzao) (W) Godello, Palomino, Valenciana (Doña Blanca), Lado

Valdepeñas (R) Cencibel (W) Airén

Valencia (W) Merseguera, Malvasia Riojana, Planta Fina, Pedro Ximénez, Moscatel Romano, Macabeo, Tortosí (Bobal Blanco) (R) Monastrell, Garnacha Tintorera, Garnacha Tinta, Tempranillo, Forcayat

Vinos de Madrid (R) Tinto Fino, Garnacha (W) Malvar, Airén, Albillo

Ycoden-Daute-Isora (W) Bastardo Blanco, Bermejuela, Forastera Blanca, Bual, Listán Blanco, Malvasía, Moscatel, Pedro Ximénez, Sabró, Torrontés, Verdello, Vijariego (R) Bastardo Negro, Listán Negra, Malvasía Rosada, Moscatel Negra, Negramoll, Tintilla, Vijariego Negro

Yecla (R) Monastrell, Garnacha, Cabernet Sauvignon, Tempranillo   (W) Merseguera, Verdil

Switzerland

Dôle (R) Pinot Noir, *Gamay*

Goron (Valais), Salvagnin (Vaud) (R) Pinot Noir, Gamay

L'Œil-de-Perdrix de Neuchâtel (P) Pinot Noir

Total vineyard area by country

Europe	'000s hectares	'000s acres
Spain	1,180	2,914
France	914	2,257
Italy	899	2,220
Portugal	260	642
Romania	253	627
Moldova	159	393
Uzbekistan	132	326
Hungary	131	324
Greece	129	319
Ukraine	125	309
Bulgaria	109	269
Germany	106	261
Georgia	100	247
Russia	85	210
Serbia/Montenegro	82	202
Azerbaijan	66	163
Croatia	59	146
Austria	49	121
Macedonia	31	77
Turkmenistan	28	69
Armenia	22	54
Slovakia	20	49
Slovenia	20	49
Switzerland	15	37
Czech Republic	13	32
Kazakhstan	12	30
Kyrgyzstan	12	30
Albania	5	12
Bosnia Hercegovina	4	10
Luxembourg	1	2
UK	1	2
Malta	1	2
Total	**5,023**	**12,405**

Asia	'000s hectares	'000s acres
Turkey	602	1,486
Iran	270	666
China	194	479
Syria	86	212
Iraq	53	131
Afghanistan	52	128
India	43	106
Korea	30	74
Lebanon	26	64
Yemen	24	59
Japan	22	54
Cyprus	20	49
Pakistan	9	22
Israel	8	19
Taiwan	3	7
Jordan	2	5
Other countries	12	30
Total	**1,456**	**3,591**

Americas	'000s hectares	'000s acres
United States	364	899
Argentina	210	519
Chile	144	356
Brazil	60	148
Mexico	41	101
Peru	11	27
Uruguay	11	27
Canada	7	17
Bolivia	4	10
Venezuela	1	2
Other countries	5	12
Total	**858**	**2,118**

Total vineyard area by country

Africa	'000s hectares	'000s acres
South Africa	111	274
Algeria	56	138
Egypt	56	138
Morocco	50	123
Tunisia	27	66
Libya	7	17
Tanzania	3	7
Madagascar	2	5
Other countries	1	2
Total	**313**	**770**

Oceania	'000s hectares	'000s acres
Australia	98	242
New Zealand	9	22
Total	**107**	**264**

WORLD TOTAL 7,757   19,148

Note: These 1998 OIV figures include vineyards dedicated to table grapes and drying grapes.

	1986-90		1991-5	
	'000s hectolitres	'000s US gals	'000s hectolitres	'000s US gals
Italy	60,226	1,591,171	61,225	1,617,565
France	65,344	1,726,388	54,325	1,435,267
Spain	33,656	889,192	26,750	706,735
United States	17,121	452,337	16,790	443,592
Argentina	18,836	497,647	15,587	411,809
Germany	10,915	288,374	10,939	289,008
South Africa	8,572	226,472	9,529	251,756
Portugal	8,455	223,381	7,153	188,982
Romania	7,502	198,203	5,508	145,521
Australia	4,463	117,912	4,810	127,080
Moldova	n.a.	n.a.	4,358	115,138
Hungary	4,062	107,318	3,822	100,977
Greece	4,337	114,584	3,668	96,909
China	2,734	72,232	3,480	91,942
Chile	4,103	108,401	3,326	87,873
Russia	n.a.	n.a.	3,110	82,166
Brazil	2,918	77,094	3,095	81,770
Serbia/Montenegro	n.a.	n.a.	2,615	69,088
Austria	2,854	75,403	2,484	65,627
Mexico	1,183	31,255	2,234	59,022
Bulgaria	3,261	86,156	1,885	49,802
Croatia	n.a.	n.a.	1,869	49,379
Ukraine	n.a.	n.a.	1,793	47,371
Uzbekistan	n.a.	n.a.	1,343	35,482
Switzerland	1,280	33,818	1,202	31,757
Georgia	n.a.	n.a.	1,056	27,900
Azerbaijan	n.a.	n.a.	1,030	27,213
Macedonia	n.a.	n.a.	1,004	26,526
Uruguay	795	21,004	846	22,351
Slovenia	n.a.	n.a.	822	21,717
Slovakia	n.a.	n.a.	763	20,158
Cyprus	667	17,622	590	15,588
Japan	542	14,320	552	14,584

	1986–90		1991–5	
	'000s hectolitres	'000s US gals	'000s hectolitres	'000s US gals
Algeria	687	18,151	536	14,161
Czech Republic	n.a.	n.a.	506	13,369
Belorussia	n.a.	n.a.	505	13,342
New Zealand	464	12,259	443	11,704
Kazakhstan	n.a.	n.a.	379	10,013
Tunisia	299	7,900	349	9,221
Morocco	431	11,387	335	8,851
Tajikistan	n.a.	n.a.	325	8,587
Canada	386	10,198	319	8,428
Armenia	n.a.	n.a.	258	6,816
Turkey	290	7,662	257	6,790
Lebanon	82	2,166	229	6,050
Luxembourg	165	4,359	173	4,571
Israel	156	4,122	122	3,223
Albania	239	6,314	117	3,091
Bosnia Hercegovina	n.a.	n.a.	101	2,668
Peru	98	2,589	93	2,457
Madagascar	77	2,034	87	2,299
Paraguay	75	1,982	76	2,008
Malta	20	528	28	740
Egypt	20	528	24	634
Bolivia	19	502	20	528
England & Wales	11	291	18	476
Turkmenistan	n.a.	n.a.	15	396
Belgium	2	53	1	26
Other countries	221	5,839	188	4,967
World total	**267,568**	**7,069,148**	**265,067**	**7,003,071**

Note: These figures are based on official OIV statistics.

	1996		1998	
	'000s hectolitres	'000s US gals	'000s hectolitres	'000s US gals
Italy	58,773	1,552,783	54,188	1,431,593
France	59,650	1,575,953	52,671	1,391,515
Spain	32,675	863,274	30,320	801,024
United States	18,643	492,548	20,450	540,269
Argentina	12,681	335,032	12,673	334,808
Germany	8,300	219,286	10,834	286,223
South Africa	8,739	230,884	8,156	215,473
Australia	6,784	179,233	7,415	195,897
Chile	3,824	101,030	5,475	144,644
Romania	7,663	202,456	5,002	132,148
Hungary	4,188	110,647	4,180	110,431
Serbia/Montenegro	3,489	92,179	4,025	106,341
Greece	4,109	108,560	3,826	101,179
Portugal	9,529	251,756	3,621	95,663
China	4,300	113,606	3,550	93,787
Bulgaria	2,000	52,840	3,308	87,394
Brazil	2,320	61,294	2,782	73,498
Austria	2,110	55,746	2,703	71,411
Croatia	1,958	51,730	2,277	60,156
Moldova	3,598	95,059	2,194	57,963
Russia	2,550	6,737	2,100	55,480
Macedonia	1,010	26,684	1,803	47,633
Uzbekistan	1,740	45,971	1,470	38,836
Japan	675	17,834	1,301	34,371
Switzerland	1,304	34,452	1,172	30,963
Uruguay	954	25,205	1,132	29,906
Mexico	1,130	29,855	1,112	29,378
Slovenia	932	24,623	894	23,619
Ukraine	763	20,158	728	19,233
Cyprus	559	14,769	710	18,757
Azerbaijan	350	9,247	650	17,172
Georgia	730	19,287	650	17,172
New Zealand	573	15,139	606	16,010
Slovakia	376	9,934	490	12,945
Czech Republic	628	16,592	450	11,889
Algeria	392	10,357	360	9,511
Tunisia	221	5,839	352	9,299
Canada	300	7,926	343	9,062
Morocco	284	7,503	298	7,873
Turkey	265	7,001	278	7,344

Wine production by country

	1996		1998	
	'000s hectolitres	'000s US gals	'000s hectolitres	'000s US gals
Belorussia	190	5,020	232	6,129
Tajikistan	195	5,152	195	5,152
Kazakhstan	114	3,012	191	5,046
Lebanon	307	8,111	186	4,914
Turkmenistan	16	423	168	4,438
Luxembourg	149	3,937	160	4,227
Peru	111	2,933	120	3,170
Albania	170	4,491	105	2,774
Paraguay	77	2,034	92	2,431
Israel	90	2,378	90	2,378
Madagascar	86	2,272	89	2,351
Armenia	78	2,061	80	2,114
Bosnia Hercegovina	54	1,427	54	1,427
Malta	31	819	32	845
Egypt	25	661	26	687
Bolivia	20	528	20	528
England & Wales	24	634	12	317
Belgium	1	26	1	26
Other countries	138	3,646	121	3,197
World total	**272,945**	**7,150,574**	**258,523**	**6,829,924**

Note: These figures are based on official OIV statistics.

Per capita wine consumption by country

	1991		1996		1998	
	litres	US gals	litres	US gals	litres	US gals
Luxembourg	60.30	15.93	50.40	13.32	70.36	18.59
France	67.00	17.70	60.00	15.85	61.09	16.14
Italy	60.28	15.93	59.37	15.69	54.92	14.51
Slovenia	40.00	10.57	40.00	10.57	48.74	12.88
Portugal	62.00	16.38	58.46	15.45	47.34	12.51
Switzerland	47.20	12.47	41.17	10.88	40.93	10.81
Argentina	55.01	14.53	41.47	10.96	39.52	10.44
Spain	39.77	10.51	37.71	9.96	38.07	10.06
Uruguay	25.40	6.71	*30.30	*8.01	35.13	9.28
Austria	33.70	8.90	32.00	8.45	34.42	9.10
Denmark	23.60	6.24	26.80	7.08	30.08	7.95
Hungary	30.00	7.93	30.00	7.93	28.54	7.54
Greece	32.40	8.56	30.93	8.17	28.25	7.46
Germany	26.10	6.90	22.90	6.05	23.32	6.16
Serbia/Montenegro	22.10	5.84	19.90	5.26	20.06	5.29
Australia	17.70	4.68	18.10	4.78	19.98	5.25
Romania	19.30	5.10	31.50	8.32	18.95	5.01
Chile	29.50	7.79	15.80	4.17	16.24	4.29
Netherlands	16.50	4.36	13.30	3.51	16.18	4.27
UK	10.29	2.72	12.50	3.30	14.22	3.76
Sweden	12.78	3.38	12.60	3.33	12.48	3.30
Cyprus	13.20	3.49	13.10	3.46	11.81	3.12
New Zealand	12.10	3.20	9.90	2.62	11.21	2.96
Norway	6.90	1.82	7.58	2.00	9.93	2.62
South Africa	9.06	2.39	9.30	2.46	8.58	2.27
Canada	8.28	2.19	7.08	1.87	8.28	2.19
USA	7.12	1.88	7.70	2.03	7.88	2.08
Finland	4.49	1.19	5.19	1.37	6.14	1.62
Czech Republic	*11.80	*3.12	11.80	3.12	6.13	1.62
Ireland	4.50	1.19	7.00	1.85	5.98	1.58
Slovakia	*11.80	*3.12	13.10	3.46	5.25	1.39
Japan	0.91	0.24	1.39	0.37	2.55	0.67
Tunisia	2.20	0.58	3.09	0.82	2.07	0.55

Per capita wine consumption by country

	1991		1996		1998	
	litres	US gals	litres	US gals	litres	US gals
Brazil	1.83	0.48	1.58	0.42	1.59	0.42
Israel	3.50	0.92	4.20	1.11	1.29	0.34
Peru	0.47	0.12	0.61	0.16	0.70	0.18
Morocco	0.99	0.26	1.40	0.37	0.63	0.17
Turkey	0.47	0.12	*0.40	*0.11	0.36	0.10
Mexico	0.22	0.06	0.28	0.07	0.16	0.04

Note: These figures are based on statistics collated by the OIV. An asterisk indicates an estimated figure.

Up-and-coming wine regions and producers

This is necessarily an arbitrary list. Happily for us all, new, quality-conscious wine producers are establishing themselves almost weekly, and new wine regions are developing at an almost equally hectic pace. This, however, is a snapshot of the many promising regions and producers whose success seems most obvious to me at the beginning of the 21st century. Many of them have a glorious history which is currently being revived; others are complete newcomers. Some hover, potentially deliciously, in between.

Jancis Robinson

Regions

ALENTEJO, Portugal
CANARY ISLANDS, Spain
GEORGIA, CIS
GREECE
Valle del Uco, Argentina
MUSCADET, France
Niagara Peninsula, CANADA
NEW SOUTH WALES, Australia
Otago, NEW ZEALAND
PRIORAT, Spain
RHEINHESSEN, Germany
ROUSSILLON, France
TERRA ALTA, Spain
TORO, Spain
MAREMMA, Italy
MALTA
MOROCCO
ST-ÉMILION, France
SICILY, Italy
TUNISIA
URUGUAY
WASHINGTON, USA

Producers

Abadia Retuerta, RIBERA DEL DUERO (just outside)
Abbazia S. Anastasia, SICILY
Hervé Arlaud, MOREY-ST-DENIS
Boekenhoutskloof, Franschhoek, SOUTH AFRICA
Antonio Caggiano, TAURASI
Cantina del Notaio, AGLIANICO DEL VULTURE
Celler de Capçanes, TARRAGONA
Cims de Porrera, PRIORAT
Clos d'Yvigne, SAUSSIGNAC
Finca Allende, RIOJA
Frankland Estate, WESTERN AUSTRALIA
Freycinet, TASMANIA
Yves et Mathide Gangloff, CÔTE RÔTIE and CONDRIEU
Ch Grande Cassagne, COSTIÈRES DE NÎMES
Greenock Creek, BAROSSA VALLEY
Guitián, VALDEORRAS
Peter Jakob Kühn, RHEINHAU
Josef Leitz, RHEINGAU
Long Meadow, NAPA VALLEY
Nepenthe, ADELAIDE HILLS
Bruno Paillard, CHAMPAGNE
Rudi Pichler, Wachau, AUSTRIA
Nicolas Potel, VOLNAY
Rebholz, PFALZ
Schlossgut Diel, NAHE
Tardieu Laurent, RHÔNE
Unison, Hawkes Bay, NEW ZEALAND
François Villard, CONDRIEU

Generalizations about vintages are hazardous, extremely approximate, but keenly sought, even by wine professionals. A wine made in a great vintage by a poor wine-maker is likely to give less pleasure than one made in a less successful vintage by a good one. Localized weather conditions (hail or freak downpours, for example) can result in quality variation even within a square mile. The ideal vintage chart could have hundreds of very-slightly-different ratings for tiny individual regions and subregions. The chart overleaf provides only a thumbnail sketch of likely quality variation by year and should certainly not be followed slavishly. In Bordeaux in 1998, for example, properties in the Graves region (notably those in Pessac-Léognan) fared very much better than the average for the Médoc region, definitely rating a 4, whereas some of the lesser Médocs would rate only 3. Similarly, in Australia, many would argue that Barossa Shiraz was a perceptible notch better in 1998 than in 1996, but this chart's aim is simplicity and half scores have therefore been eschewed.

Overleaf is a symbolic representation of the editor's personal assessment of the most relevant combinations of vintage year and wine type, supplemented by inside information by regional contributors to the *Concise Wine Companion*. The number indicates average quality (5 denoting the finest vintages, 0 the least successful), and the direction of the arrow denotes the vintage's average state of maturity (an arrow pointing upwards denotes a vintage which can be kept for many years, a horizontal arrow denotes a vintage which is ready to drink, while an arrow pointing downwards denotes a vintage which is generally past its best).

Each wine type encompasses a wide range of quality levels. The vintage rating applies to a serious example of the quality level specified. Lesser quality levels generally mature faster; the less expensive the example, the less ageing potential it has. Grander, more expensive examples than the quality level specified here generally mature more slowly so, for example, some grand-cru 1985 red burgundy may not yet be ready to drink, even though the chart suggests that, for premier-cru red burgundy, this vintage has reached its peak.

Personal taste also affects quality ratings. Those who rate ripeness and alcohol above all else may be better served by other vintage charts. This applies particularly to white and to a lesser extent red burgundy, for example. For many tasters, the ideal white burgundy is one that is big, weighty, verging on fat. The ratings in this vintage chart tend to celebrate a higher level of acidity in a young white burgundy than palates reared on California or Australian Chardonnay might enjoy. The 1993 vintage, for example, divides wine drinkers into two camps. (And for a snapshot of the relative longevity of Chardonnay and Riesling, it is instructive to compare the overall direction of arrows against white burgundy and the wines of Germany/Alsace.)

Wine drinking and assessment is a thoroughly enjoyable but, above all, subjective activity.

	1998	1997	1996	1995	1994	1993	1992	1991	1990
Red bordeaux									
Médoc second growth/Graves counterpart	4 ↗	3 ↗	5 ↑	5 ↗	3 ↗	1 →	0 ↘	0 ↘	5 ↗
St-Émilion Grand Cru Classé/Pomerol counterpart	5 ↗	4 ↗	4 ↑	5 ↗	4 ↗	2 →	0 →	1 ↘	5 ↗
White bordeaux									
Classed-growth Sauternes/Barsac	4 ↑	5 ↑	5 ↗	3 ↗	2 ↗	n.a.	n.a	n.a.	5 ↗
Red burgundy									
Premier-cru Côte de Nuits	3 ↑	3 ↗	5 ↑	5 ↗	2 ↗	4 ↗	2 →	4 →	5 ↗
White burgundy									
Premier-cru Côte de Beaune	1 ↗	4 ↗	5 ↑	5 ↗	3 →	4 ↗	5 ↗	3 ↘	4 →
Rhône									
Hermitage/ Côte Rôtie	3 ↑	4 ↗	4 ↗	4 ↗	3 ↗	0 →	2 →	4 ↗	5 ↗
Châteauneuf-du-Pape	5 ↑	3 →	3 →	4 ↗	3 ↗	3 ↗	1 →	0 ↘	5 →
Italy									
Barolo/Barbaresco	5 ↑	5 ↑	5 ↑	4 ↑	2 ↗	3 ↗	1 →	3 →	5 ↗
Chianti Classico/ Supertuscan/Brunello di Montalcino	4 ↑	5 ↑	3 ↗	5 ↑	3 ↗	4 ↗	1 →	3 →	5 ↗
Spain									
Rioja Reserva (red)	4 ↑	3 ↑	4 ↗	5 ↗	5 ↗	2 →	3 →	4 →	3 →
Ribera del Duero	3 ↑	3 ↑	5 ↗	4 ↗	5 ↗	1 →	3 →	4 →	4 →
Germany/Alsace									
Rhine Spätlese/ Alsace Riesling	4 ↑	5 ↑	5 ↗	4 ↗	5 ↗	4 ↗	4 ↗	3 ↗	5 ↗
California									
North Coast Cabernet Sauvignon	3 ↑	4 ↑	3 ↑	5 ↗	5 ↗	3 ↗	3 ↗	3 ↗	5 ↗
Australia									
South Australian Barossa Shiraz	5 ↑	4 ↗	5 ↗	3 ↗	4 ↗	3 ↗	3 →	5 ↗	5 →

KEY: *Quality rating* (0–5, 5 is best)
Maturity: ↑ Wine with many years ahead of it; ↗ Maturing wine that could be drunk but would benefit from cellaring; → Ready to drink; ↘ Fading fast; fruit typically in retreat; ↓ Over the top; for necrophiliacs?

1989	1988	1987	1986	1985	1984	1983	1982	1981	1980	1979
5 ↗	3 ↗	0 ↘	4 ↗	4 →	0 ↘	3 ↗	5 →	2 →	1 ↘	2 ↘
5 →	3 ↗	1 ↘	3 ↗	4 →	0 ↘	3 →	5 →	2 →	1 ↘	2 →
5 ↗	5 ↗	n.a.	4 ↗	3 ↗	n.a.	4 ↗	1 →	3 →	3 →	2 →
4 →	3 ↗	2 →	1 ↘	4 →	0 ↘	2 →	2 ↘	1 ↘	2 ↘	2 ↓
5 →	3 ↘	0 ↘	5 ↘	5 →	0 ↓	4 ↘	2 ↓	1 ↓	0 ↓	3 ↓
5 →	5 ↗	1 ↘	1 →	5 ↗	1 ↘	5 ↗	3 →	0 ↘	1 ↘	4 ↘
5 ↗	4 →	0 ↓	1 ↘	4 →	1 ↘	4 →	1 ↘	4 →	3 ↘	4 →
5 ↗	4 ↗	2 →	3 →	5 →	1 ↘	3 ↘	5 ↗	3 →	3 ↘	4 ↘
2 ↘	4 ↗	2 →	3 →	5 →	1 ↘	4 →	4 →	3 →	3 ↘	4 ↘
4 →	2 ↘	4 →	3 ↘	3 →	2 ↘	3 →	4 →	5 →	3 ↘	3 ↘
4 →	3 ↘	3 ↘	5 →	4 →	2 ↘	4 →	4 →	5 →	3 ↘	3 ↘
5 ↗	4 ↗	3 ↗	3 →	4 →	3 →	5 →	3 ↘	3 →	3 →	4 ↘
2 →	1 ↘	4 →	4 ↘	5 ↗	4 →	1 ↘	2 →	3 →	3 →	2 →
3 ↘	4 →	4 ↘	5 →	3 ↘	2 ↓	3 ↘	3 ↘	3 ↘	4 →	3 ↓